Roger Ebert's
Movie Yearbook
2002

Roger Ebert's Movie Yearbook 2002

**Andrews McMeel
Publishing**

Kansas City

This book is dedicated
to Robert Zonka, 1928–1985.
God love ya.

Contents

Introduction

At the Cannes Film Festival in May 2001, much talk centered around Todd McCarthy's angry column in *Variety*, where the showbiz bible's chief film critic wondered if Hollywood studio bosses even see the films they release. McCarthy's *j'accuse* came after a particularly nasty stretch of mass-marketed releases in which the stars were buried in excrement, stuck their arms into the anal orifices of unhappy animals, or, in the notorious *Freddy Got Fingered*, swung a newborn baby by its umbilical cord. The stars of movies aimed at teenage boys do things on-screen that the geeks in sideshows would have turned down.

It was in that melancholy context that I flew up to London a week later for a conference on American Classic Films at the London University Institute of United States Studies. Speakers discussed *On the Waterfront, Dr. Strangelove, Chinatown,* and *Raging Bull,* four films that could not find financing today. American mass-market releases are currently dominated by gross and stupid movies aimed at teenage boys who attend early and often, helping those movies "win the weekend." They're forgotten two weeks later, but not before driving good movies out of the marketplace.

For every silver lining, there is a cloud. *Crouching Tiger, Hidden Dragon* grossed more than $100 million in the United States—a record for a subtitled film—but the year before, all subtitled films together grossed less than $50 million, $20 million less than the first weekend's take of *The Mummy Returns*. It used to be said that imported films didn't play many cities; today they don't play many states. The American independent movement, aka the Sundance Generation, produces interesting films every year, which sink untended in the marketplace. Home video and cable are the lifelines that allow good movies to break even.

And yet, always there is hope. If you look at the movies themselves and not simply at the box office, American movies are in an emerging golden age. It is possible to see inventive and even important new work every week of the year if you live in a city with good theaters or have a cable system that offers Bravo, Sundance, or the Independent Film Channel. Directors such as Quentin Tarantino, Paul Thomas Anderson, Spike Jonze, Curtis Hanson, Julie Taymor, Kenneth Lonergan, Alison MacLean, Steven Soderbergh, Todd Solondz, David Gordon Green, and Darren Aronofsky are doing work as interesting as circa 1970 golden-agers such as Scorsese, Coppola, Altman, and Malick. The movies are there. It is just that they have to fight so hard for distribution.

At Sundance every January, there are 120 new American movies and sections for world cinema and documentaries. The festival has been haunted for three years by the Blair Witch—the prospect that a movie shot on cheap cameras, with a budget the price of a midsize car, can gross $200 million. The fact that it happened once is almost proof that it can never happen again. More likely is a moderate hit like Lonergan's wonderful Sundance winner *You Can Count on Me,* which got an Oscar nomination for Laura Linney and paid a nice return on investment.

Most Sundance "hits" don't do that well. *You Can Count on Me* shared the grand prize with *Girlfight,* Karyn Kusama's powerful story of a young Puerto Rican girl who wants to be a boxer. It sank at the box office. (Curious: It was thematically identical with *Billy Elliott,* telling the flip side of the same gender-in-rebellion story. *Girlfight* was about a girl who wanted to be a boxer, *Billy Elliott* was about a boy who wanted to be a dancer, both kids faced stubborn working-class fathers, etc. *Girlfight* was a tougher and less sentimental film, which may have counted against it.)

At Sundance and again at Cannes, North American film critics gathered in gloom, because we know there are good new films, we can *name* them, we do all we can to spread the word, and the audience sleepwalks into *Joe Dirt* or *Tomcats.* All the same, I've arrived at the melancholy conclusion that the American indie movement is able to put together a more interesting week of premieres at Sundance than the rest of the world is able to do in the official selection at Cannes.

Also at Cannes, I went to a luncheon given by the Montreal Film Festival, where we debated if there would be an audience in "middle America" for the film that opened Cannes, Baz Luhrmann's *Moulin Rouge.* We wondered (1) Will middle Americans think *Moulin Rouge* must be a French film with subtitles? (2) Will they hear it is a musical and stay away? (3) Will the story (which has all the subtlety of *La Bohème*) be too complex? (4) Will they understand how a woman could be a romantic heroine and a whore at the same time?

In any event, the movie got many enthusiastic reviews but grossed about $54 million at the U.S. box office—not what was expected for a film with a $52 million budget. Since it was as much fun as the other summer weekend warriors, why did fewer people go? Could it be that teenage boys know all about mummies, dinosaurs, tomb raiders, and apes, but that a movie set in Paris sounds like homework to them?

Prof. Edwin Jahiel, who teaches cinema at the University of Illinois, told me that when he showed Godard's *My Life to Live* to his students, many of them had never heard of a "pimp." The general level of information possessed by the average American moviegoer has been eroding year by year. Young Americans are better educated than before, but in narrow, career-oriented specialties. They have less background in the arts and humanities. They read less. They visit only those Web pages that already interest them. They want movies that, in Hitchcock's phrase, "play the audience like a piano." The slightest challenge, difficulty, or complexity causes them to shy. I noticed this tendency years ago, when my phone rang at the *Sun-Times* and a reader asked what I knew about *Cries and Whispers.* I said I thought it was the best film of the year. Reader: "That doesn't sound like anything we'd like to see."

Where is there room for hope? The problem is not with making the films, but with finding distribution and audiences. The most hopeful recent innovation was the Shooting Gallery Film Series, which twice a year took a package of six films out for two-week runs in Loews theaters in twenty-two cities. This sidestepped the formidable cost of opening and advertising each movie separately. A few Shooting Gallery titles like Mike Hodges's *Croupier* launched in this way, generated spontaneous enthusiasm, and went on to successful commercial runs. But in the summer of 2001, Shooting Gallery went out of business, a visionary idea defeated by public indifference.

Another idea is to integrate the production of indie films with the cable channels that will eventually show them. Jonathan Sehring heads the production arm of the Independent Film Channel, which financed two of the most interesting films at Sundance this year, both by Richard Linklater *(Slackers; Dazed and Confused)*. His *Waking Life* starts with digital footage and then brings in thirty artists, each with a distinctive style, to rotoscope and animate each character. His *Tape* is a digitally filmed three-hander shot entirely in a motel room with Ethan Hawke, Uma Thurman, and Robert Sean Leonard. The business plan is to combine outside distribution with eventual airing on IFC or Bravo.

Cable is the answer for some films. There was not a better female performance in 2001 than Emma Thompson's work in *Wit*, the Mike Nichols film about an English professor dying of cancer. It would have been an Oscar contender—but it didn't even open in theaters; it played on HBO. Major indie director Allison Anders bypassed theaters for her *Things Behind the Sun*, figuring she could attract 400,000 moviegoers but four million cable watchers. In smaller towns, cable is the alternative to the deadening sameness of the multiplexes. (And yet consider the case of the Vickers Theater in Three Oaks, Michigan, a town of 3,000, which shows first-run art movies every weekend and always sells out; there is an audience, but it has to be identified and respected.)

The key word "digital" brings up another possibility. Digital projection has been discussed in recent years as a cheaper alternative to celluloid. If American theaters ever did go digital, I would be intensely unhappy, since even the best digital projection doesn't approach light through celluloid, and those who say it does are deceiving themselves. That particular step in the digital revolution seems to be on hold, however, after the Winter 2001 ShoWest convention in Las Vegas, where the studios refused to subsidize the $150,000-per-booth cost of digital projection, and the exhibitors said they wouldn't pay for it themselves. One supplier has offered to install the projectors in return for a 7.5 percent cut of the box office, a figure exhibitors have shown no enthusiasm for.

If digital projection is not good enough for big-screen mainstream movies such as *Titanic* or *Gladiator*, it may be right for a more modest task. What if cheaper, mid-market digital projectors (like the Runco image quadruplers) were used in smaller indie/art boutique theaters, which could change their programs frequently? What about a national chain of digital art houses with frequent program changes? If the movies were supplied on cheap high-definition discs, the same title could play simultaneously in fifty cities with a national campaign; these days, many indie films can afford to have only a dozen prints working, which means the original publicity is months in the past. Even as an opponent of mainstream digital projection, I can see how this distribution model would help the indies sneak around the multiplex gridlock.

If experiments like this aren't tried, the North American indie generation will continue to be locked out of national distribution. It's important to understand that the national chains are booked without the slightest thought about the quality of the movies or the nature of various local markets. College towns and factory towns get the same block-booked dreck. A thinly stretched network of independent houses, museum programs, film societies, and the rare art multiplex, all operating on small margins, stand between American independent films and oblivion.

ROGER EBERT

Acknowledgments

My editor is Dorothy O'Brien, tireless, cheerful, all-noticing. She is assisted by the equally invaluable Julie Roberts. My friend and longtime editor Donna Martin suggested this new approach to the annual volume. The design is by Cameron Poulter, the typographical genius of Hyde Park. My thanks to production editor Christi Clemons-Hoffman, who renders Cameron's design into reality. I have been blessed with the expert and discriminating editing of John Barron, Laura Emerick, Miriam DiNunzio, Jeff Wisser, Darel Jevins, Avis Weathersbee, Jeff Johnson, and Teresa Budasi at the *Chicago Sun-Times;* Sue Roush at Universal Press Syndicate; and Michelle Daniel at Andrews McMeel Publishing. Many thanks are also due to the production staff at *Ebert & Roeper,* and to Marsha Jordan at WLS-TV. My gratitude goes to Carol Iwata, my expert personal assistant, and to Marlene Gelfond, at the *Sun-Times.* And special thanks and love to my wife, Chaz, for whom I can only say: If more film critics had a spouse just like her, the level of cheer in the field would rise dramatically.

ROGER EBERT

Key to Symbols

★★★★ A great film
★★★   A good film
★★   Fair
★   Poor

G, PG, PG-13, R, NC-17:
Ratings of the Motion Picture
Association of America

G   Indicates that the movie is suitable for general audiences

PG   Suitable for general audiences but parental guidance is suggested

PG-13 Recommended for viewers 13 years or above; may contain material inappropriate for younger children

R   Recommended for viewers 17 or older

NC-17 Intended for adults only

141 m. Running time

1999   Year of theatrical release

☞   Refers to "Questions for the Movie Answer Man"

Reviews

A

The Adventures of
Rocky & Bullwinkle ★ ★ ★
PG, 90 m., 2000

Rene Russo (Natasha), Jason Alexander (Boris), Piper Perabo (Karen Sympathy), Randy Quaid (Cappy Von Trapment), Robert De Niro (Fearless Leader), June Foray (Rocky [voice]), Keith Scott (Bullwinkle [voice]), Keith Scott (Narrator), Janeane Garofalo (Minnie Mogul). Directed by Des McAnuff and produced by Jane Rosenthal and Robert De Niro. Screenplay by Kenneth Lonegran, based on characters developed by Jay Ward.

The original *Rocky & Bullwinkle* TV show was smarter than it needed to be, and a lot of adults sneaked a look now and then. It helped point the way to today's crossover animated shows like *The Simpsons*. Now comes the movie version of the TV show (which was canceled in 1964), and it has the same mixture of dumb puns, corny sight gags and sly, even sophisticated in-jokes. It's a lot of fun.

The movie combines the animated moose and squirrel with live action—and even yanks three of the characters (Natasha, Boris, and Fearless Leader) out of the TV set and into the real world (where they're played by Rene Russo, Jason Alexander, and Robert De Niro, explaining, "We're attached to the project").

The breathless narrator portentously explains: "Expensive animation characters are converted to even more expensive movie stars!" The narrator (Keith Scott), of course, always seemed to stand outside the action and know that *R&B* was only a cartoon (at one point he complains he has been reduced to narrating the events of his own life). And the movie is also self-aware; when someone (I think maybe Fearless L) breathlessly announces, "There has never been a way to destroy a cartoon character until now!" he's asked, "What about Roger Rabbit?"

The plot involves a scheme by Fearless Leader to win world domination by hypnotizing everyone with RBTV (Really Bad TV). Only Rocky and Bullwinkle have long years of experience at foiling the evil schemes of Fearless, Natasha, and Boris, and as they fumble their way to a final confrontation we also get a coast-to-coast road movie (cheerfully acknowledged as a cliché by the narrator).

The movie has a lot of funny moments, which I could destroy by quoting, but will not. (Oh, all right: At one point Rocky cries, "We have to get out of here!" and Bullwinkle bellows: "Quick! Cut to a commercial!") As much fun as the wit is the film's overall sense of well-being; this is a *happy* movie and not the desperate sort of scratching for laughs we got in a cartoon retread like *The Flintstones in Viva Rock Vegas*. It's the sort of movie where De Niro parodies his famous "Are you talking to me?" speech with such good-natured fun that instead of groaning, we reflect—well, everyone else has ripped it off, so why shouldn't he get his own turn?

The movie is wall-to-wall with familiar faces, including Janeane Garofalo as a studio executive, Randy Quaid as the FBI chief, Whoopi Goldberg as a judge, John Goodman as a cop, Billy Crystal as a mattress salesman, James Rebhorn as the president, and Jonathan Winters in three roles. Rene Russo makes a persuasive Natasha, all red lipstick, seductive accent, and power high heels, and De Niro's patent leather hair and little round glasses will remind movie buffs of Donald Pleasance.

But the real discovery of the movie is its (human) lead, a twenty-three-year-old newcomer named Piper Perabo, who plays an FBI agent. She has fine comic timing, and is so fetching she sort of stops the clock. Like Renee Zellweger in *Jerry Maguire*, she comes more or less out of nowhere (well, a couple of obscure made-for-videos) and becomes a star right there before our eyes.

Comedy is such a fragile art form. *The Adventures of Rocky & Bullwinkle* isn't necessarily any more brilliant or witty or inventive than all the other recent retreads of classic cartoons and old sitcoms. But it feels like more fun. From time to time I'm reminded of George C. Scott's Rule No. 3 for judging movie acting: "Is there a joy of performance? Can you tell that

1

the actors are having fun?" This time, you can. There's a word for this movie, and that word is jolly.

The Adventures of Sebastian Cole ★ ★ ★

R, 99 m., 1999

Adrian Grenier (Sebastian Cole), Clark Gregg (Hank/Henrietta), Aleksa Palladino (Mary), Margaret Colin (Joan), Marni Lustig (Jessica), John Shea (Hartley). Directed by Tod Williams and produced by Karen Barber and Jasmine Kosovic. Screenplay by Williams.

The Adventures of Sebastian Cole is a coming-of-age movie that puts a new spin on some of the challenges faced by sensitive teenagers. It's not unusual to have problems with a stepfather—but it's fairly rare for the stepfather to announce he's decided to become a woman. It's also rare for a movie to show a teenager who needs guidance, and a parent willing to provide it. The fathers of most movie teenagers are absent, stupid, or cruel; Sebastian's is wise and loving, first as Hank, then as Henrietta.

Sebastian (Adrian Grenier) is an introverted, screwed-up member of a dysfunctional upper-class family. He wants to be a writer. He's good-looking, but with so little self-confidence that when a girl seriously likes him, he dumps her. We can guess from an early scene what a confusion his life has been. At a family holiday dinner, we meet his divorced parents, who are both with their new spouses, in one of those uneasy exercises designed to provide continuity for the children, who in fact only want to flee the table.

His mother, Joan (Margaret Colin), is bright, pretty, British, and usually drunk. She's married to a floppy-haired hulk named Hank (Clark Gregg). Sebastian's father, Hartley (John Shea), is an architect with a new Asian-American wife who hardly even seems to be there, so little does she ever say. Then there is Sebastian's sister, Jessica (Marni Lustig), who has a boyfriend on a motorcycle and yearns to climb on behind him and ride far, far away.

Soon after this tortured family event, Hank calls together his wife and stepchildren and calmly announces that he has decided to become a woman. This doesn't go over well. Jessica leaves on the boyfriend's motorcycle and enrolls at Stanford, which is more or less as far as you can get from Dutchess County in New York. Sebastian listens to Hank's news in stunned silence. Hank wants to remain married to Joan, but she pulls out and moves back to England. At first Sebastian lives with her, but as she recedes into heavier drinking he moves back in with Hank, who is the only parent who really cares for him. Hank is firm, with traditional values, and sets rules for Sebastian.

The Adventures of Sebastian Cole might have developed along predictable lines as a sitcom about coming of age with a transsexual as your parent. But the movie avoids easy and cheap shots, and actually grows more perceptive and thoughtful, until at last we're drawn in on the simple human level: These are people worth knowing.

Clark Gregg's performance as Hank and Henrietta is the most remarkable element of the movie. No matter what he does with clothing and hair, he looks like a large man in a dress. But there is no simpering, no coquetry, no going for laughs; in his heart he knows he is a woman, and he is true to that inner conviction with a courage that the movie doesn't need to underline because it permeates the performance. At one point, he has to hit someone to defend his honor; when Sebastian asks him, "Where'd you learn to fight like that?" his answer approaches perfection.

Sebastian is not thrilled by the emergence of Henrietta, and blames everything on his stepfather: "If you hadn't been so selfish and thought only of yourself, we'd all still be together and happy. Things were perfectly fine before." But they were not. Joan, the mother, was drifting into drunken passivity. And the biological father, Hartley, a famous architect, has a revealing talk with his son: "If you're serious about being a writer, you've got to sacrifice the people you love to your work." It's pretty clear that's what Hartley did.

Adrian Grenier, an actor previously unknown to me, at first appears to be just another movie hunk, but he reveals depths and quiet notes and by the end of the film has created a complex character. His Sebastian is uncertain about himself, without goals, afraid of emotional involvement, and yet with a certain cocky daring; faced with spending another year in school because of a missing P.E. requirement, he fakes proficiency at karate.

His relationship with a girl his age, Mary (Aleksa Palladino), seems truer to life than the simplified soap opera romances we often get in teenage movies. They're both uncertain about their emerging sexuality; she likes him, finds a charming way to let him know that, and has to wait a year for the lesson to take. And because he likes her so much, he breaks off communication. Why do guys do that? Girls have been asking that question for centuries.

The film, written and directed by Tod Williams, reminded me of *A Soldier's Daughter Never Cries* (1998), another movie about children emerging from an unconventional family. That one, based on a memoir by the daughter of the novelist James Jones, showed a happy family. Sebastian Cole comes from an unhappy one—but Hank/Henrietta makes it all right by being willing to invest time and trouble in caring about him. This movie, which must sound odd, is reassuring: A good kid can survive a lot and turn out all right, despite the pain along the way.

An Affair of Love ★ ★ ★ ½
R, 80 m., 2000

Nathalie Baye (Elle), Sergi Lopez (Lui). Directed by Frederic Fonteyne and produced by Patrick Quinet, Rolf Schmid, and Claude Waringo. Screenplay by Philippe Blasband.

She takes an ad in a sex paper. There is something she has always wanted to do with a man, and now, in her forties, she has decided it will never happen unless she acts boldly. He answers the ad. They meet in a café. They are presentable and ordinary—nice people, we sense. They agree to go to a hotel, and the room door closes. We never find out what happens between them in the room. It is what they were both looking for. When they are asked, after the affair is over, if it was "good," we can see from their faces that it was.

An Affair of Love is a story about "He" and "She," two adults who have a strong desire and act on it. It is about the desiring itself, not about what they desire. That makes it more intriguing than if we knew their secret—and sexier. We are reminded of the great scene in *Belle de Jour* where Catherine Deneuve plays a housewife who works afternoons in a brothel. A client opens a little box and shows her what is inside. Whatever it is, she refuses his request—she wants nothing to do with it. What is in the box is the same thing that is behind the room door in this movie, and in the briefcase in *Pulp Fiction*—a void to tantalize our imaginations.

But the movie is not simply about sex. If it were, it would have to play fair and reveal the secret. It is about these people. Gradually, shyly, they get to know each other. We see right away that Lui likes Elle. Eventually she grows very fond of him too. Because they have a deal (they will meet as strangers, they will be anonymous, they will rendezvous only to fulfill their mutual desire), it takes a long while before the personal feels free to replace the impersonal. Once a week they do something (literally) beyond our wildest imaginations, but eventually they gather the courage to consider the ultimate next step: having ordinary sex.

The affair is over when the movie begins. That much is made clear immediately. Elle and Lui speak to an unseen interviewer about their memories of the experience. Their memories do not always agree. That is the way, sometimes. They recall events that violated their privacy—the collapse of an old man in the hotel, for example. When they tried to help him, they fell into their everyday roles, and that added too much information, endangering the fantasy.

The actors are Nathalie Baye and Sergi Lopez. She is about ten years older than he is, but age is not relevant: From the looks on their faces they are lucky to have found someone alive at the same time who wants to do what they do. There are times, during the affair, when they seem tired, not physically, but mentally, the way you get when all your desires are answered at once. Their minds are accustomed to wishing for their fantasy, but not to dealing with it. They must hardly be able to sleep.

Will they live happily ever after? Since the movie opens by telling us they did not, we wonder—why not? In answering this question, the writer-director, Frederic Fonteyne, makes a movie about love and sex that is wiser and more useful than the adolescent fantasies enacted by adults in Hollywood pictures. How

3

does the old saying go? "Be careful what you wish for, because you might get it."

Their relationship is not about liking each other, this movie observes, and it is not about sex or orgasm. It is about having a part of you that has been your precious secret since you can first remember, a part you thought you could never share, and finding someone whose own secret part is a match for your own. The discovery of this other person forces you to catch your breath as the two of you, together, regard what stands for truth and beauty in your lives. You are not in love with the other person, so much as the two of you share a tenderness because each knows how hard the other has looked, and how hopeless the search seemed at times.

That's why it is so essential that the movie never reveal their secret. Any answer at all to our curiosity would be a disappointment—except for one. And that is the one answer we already have, and no movie can know.

Affliction ★ ★ ★ ★
R, 114 m., 1999

Nick Nolte (Wade Whitehouse), Sissy Spacek (Margie Fogg), James Coburn (Glen Whitehouse), Willem Dafoe (Rolfe Whitehouse), Mary Beth Hurt (Lillian), Jim True (Jack Hewitt), Marian Seldes (Alma Pittman), Holmes Osborne (Gordon LaRiviere). Directed by Paul Schrader and produced by Linda Reisman. Screenplay by Schrader, based on the novel by Russell Banks.

Nick Nolte is a big, shambling, confident male presence in the movies, and it is startling to see his cocksure presence change into fear in Paul Schrader's *Affliction.* Nolte plays Wade Whitehouse, the sheriff of a small New Hampshire town, whose uniform, gun, and stature do not make up for a deep feeling of worthlessness. He drinks, he smokes pot on the job, he walks with a sad weariness, he is hated by his ex-wife, and his young daughter looks at him as if he's crazy.

When we meet Glen, his father, we understand the source of his defeat. The older man (James Coburn) is a cauldron of alcoholic venom, a man whose consolation in life has been to dominate and terrorize his family. There are scenes where both men are on the screen to-gether, and you can sense the sheriff shrinking, as if afraid of a sudden blow. The women in their lives have been an audience for cruelty; of the older man's wife, it is said, "Women like this, it's like they lived their lives with the sound turned off. And then they're gone."

Affliction is based on a novel by Russell Banks, whose work also inspired *The Sweet Hereafter.* Both films are set in bleak winter landscapes, and both involve a deep resentment of parental abuse—this one more obviously, since Sheriff Whitehouse's entire unhappy life has been, and still is, controlled by fear of his father. We're reminded of other films Schrader wrote (*Taxi Driver, Raging Bull, The Mosquito Coast*) or directed (*Mishima, Hardcore*), in which men's violence is churned up by feelings of inadequacy. (He also wrote *The Last Temptation of Christ,* in which at least one line applies: "Father, why hast thou forsaken me?")

Wade Whitehouse is a bad husband, a bad father, and a bad sheriff. He retains enough qualities to inspire the loyalty, or maybe the sympathy, of a girlfriend named Margie (Sissy Spacek), but his ex-wife (Mary Beth Hurt) looks at him in deep contempt, and his brother Rolfe (Willem Dafoe), the film's narrator, has been wise to clear out of the town and its poisons.

Early in the film, Wade decides to show a little enterprise on the job. A friend of his has gone out as a hunting guide for a rich man and returned with the man's expensive gun, some bloodstains, and a story of an accident. Wade doesn't believe it was an accident, and like a sleepwalker talking himself back to wakefulness, he begins an investigation that stirs up the stagnant town—and even rouses him into a state where he can be reached, for the first time in years, by fresh thoughts about how his life has gone wrong.

Because there are elements of a crime mystery in *Affliction,* it would be unwise to reveal too much about this side of the plot. It is interrupted, in any event, by another death: Wade and Margie go to the old man's house to find that Wade's mother, Glen's wife, lies dead upstairs and Glen is unable to acknowledge the situation. It is even possible that the sick woman crawled upstairs and was forgotten by a man whose inner eye has long been focused only on his own self-diagnosis: not drunk enough, drunk just right, or too drunk?

Rolfe returns to town for the funeral and to supply missing elements from the story of their childhood, and the film ends in an explosion that seems prepared even in the first frame. Its meaning is very clear: Cruelty to a child is not over in a moment or a day, but is like those medical capsules embedded in the flesh, which release their contents for years.

Nolte and Coburn are magnificent in this film, which is like an expiation for abusive men. It is revealing to watch them in their scenes together—to see how they're able to use physical presence to sketch the history of a relationship. Schrader says he cast Coburn because he needed an actor who was big enough, and had a "great iconic weight," to convincingly dominate Nolte. He found one. Coburn has spent a career largely in shallow entertainments, and here he rises to the occasion with a performance of power.

There is a story about that. "I met with Coburn before the picture began," Schrader told me, "and told him how carefully Nolte prepares for a role. I told Coburn that if he walked through the movie, Nolte might let him get away with it for a day, but on the second day all hell would break loose. Coburn said, 'Oh, you mean you want me to really act? I can do that. I haven't often been asked to, but I can.'" He can.

After Life ★ ★ ★ ★
NO MPAA RATING, 118 m., 1999

Arata (Takashi Mochizuki), Taketoshi Naito (Ichiro Watanabe), Erika Oda (Shiori Satonaka), Susumu Terajima (Satoru Kawashima), Takashi Naito (Takuro Sugie), Hisako Hara (Kiyo Nishimura). Directed by Hirokazu Kore-eda and produced by Sato Shiho and Akieda Masayuki. Screenplay by Kore-eda.

The people materialize from out of clear white light as a bell tolls. Where are they? An ordinary building is surrounded by greenery and an indistinct space. They are greeted by staff members who explain, courteously, that they have died and are now at a way station before the next stage of their experience.

They will be here a week. Their assignment is to choose one memory, one only, from their lifetimes: one memory they want to save for eternity. Then a film will be made to reenact that memory, and they will move along, taking only that memory with them, forgetting everything else. They will spend eternity within their happiest memory.

That is the premise of Hirokazu Kore-eda's *After Life,* a film that reaches out gently to the audience and challenges us: What is the single moment in our own lives we treasure the most? One of the new arrivals says that he has only bad memories. The staff members urge him to think more deeply. Surely spending eternity within a bad memory would be—well, literally, hell. And spending forever within our best memory would be, I suppose, as close as we should dare to come to heaven.

The film is completely matter-of-fact. No special effects, no celestial choirs, no angelic flimflam. The staff is hardworking; they have a lot of memories to process in a week, and a lot of production work to do on the individual films. There are pragmatic details to be worked out: Scripts have to be written, sets constructed, special effects improvised. This isn't all metaphysical work; a member of an earlier group, we learn, chose Disney World, singling out the Splash Mountain ride.

Kore-eda, with this film and the 1997 masterpiece *Maborosi,* has earned the right to be considered with Kurosawa, Bergman, and other great humanists of the cinema. His films embrace the mystery of life, and encourage us to think about why we are here and what makes us truly happy. At a time when so many movies feed on irony and cynicism, here is a man who hopes we will feel better and wiser when we leave his film.

The method of the film contributes to the impact. Some of these people, and some of their memories, are real (we are not told which). Kore-eda filmed hundreds of interviews with ordinary people in Japan. The faces on the screen are so alive, the characters seem to be recalling events they really lived through in a world of simplicity and wonder. Although there are a lot of characters in the movie, we have no trouble telling them apart because each is unique and irreplaceable.

The staff members offer a mystery of their own. Who are they, and why were they chosen to work here at the way station instead of moving on to the next stage like everybody else?

The solution to that question is contained in revelations I will not discuss, because they emerge so naturally from the film.

One of the most emotional moments in *After Life* is when a young staff member discovers a connection between himself and an elderly new arrival. The new arrival is able to tell him something that changes his entire perception of his life. This revelation, of a young love long ago, has the same kind of deep, bittersweet resonance as the ending of *The Dead*, the James Joyce short story (and John Huston film) about a man who feels a sudden burst of identification with his wife's first lover, a young man now long dead.

After Life considers the kind of delicate material that could be destroyed by schmaltz. It's the kind of film that Hollywood likes to remake with vulgar, paint-by-the-numbers sentimentality. It is like a transcendent version of *Ghost*, evoking the same emotions, but deserving them. Knowing that his premise is supernatural and fantastical, Kore-eda makes everything else in the film quietly pragmatic. The staff labors against deadlines. The arrivals set to work on their memories. There will be a screening of the films on Saturday—and then Saturday, and everything else, will cease to exist. Except for the memories.

Which memory would I choose? I sit looking out the window as images play through my mind. There are so many moments to choose from. Just thinking about them makes me feel fortunate. I remember a line from Ingmar Bergman's film *Cries and Whispers*. After the older sister dies painfully of cancer, her diary is discovered. In it she remembers a day during her illness when she was feeling better. Her two sisters and her nurse join her in the garden, in the sunlight, and for a moment pain is forgotten and they are simply happy to be together. This woman who we have seen die a terrible death has written: "I feel a great gratitude to my life, which gives me so much."

Agnes Browne ★ ★ ½
R, 92 m., 2000

Anjelica Huston (Agnes Browne), Marion O'Dwyer (Marion Monks), Ray Winstone (Mr. Billy), Arno Chevrier (Pierre), Niall O'Shea (Mark Browne), Ciaran Owens (Frankie Browne), Roxanna Williams (Cathy Browne), Carl Power (Simon Browne), Mark Power (Dermot Browne), Gareth O'Connor (Rory Browne). Directed by Anjelica Huston and produced by Jim Sheridan, Arthur Lappin, Huston, and Greg Smith. Screenplay by John Goldsmith and Brendan O'Carroll, based on the novel *The Mammy* by O'Carroll.

Agnes Browne is an Irish housewife with six sons and a daughter and her husband dead since ten minutes past four this afternoon, giving a piece of her mind to the government clerk who wants to see a certificate before paying out the poor man's death benefits. She doesn't make much money with her fruit and vegetable cart in a street market, but she's got her pride and her friends, and her children all wear matching sweaters to the funeral—even if they match because they all came from the same charity agency.

Agnes (Anjelica Huston) is like the lucky twin of Angela McCourt, the heroine of *Angela's Ashes*. Things are grim but not bleak, and at least there's no drunken husband in the picture (one of her youngest is so overcome at the funeral he holds two oranges up to block his eyes). She's best friends with Marion (Marion O'Dwyer), who runs the next cart in the market, and if she's not overly smart at least she's observant and thoughtful.

Anjelica Huston might seem like an unlikely actress to play her, and to direct *Agnes Browne*, but reflect that her father, the director John Huston, maintained a country home (almost a castle, really) in Ireland during her childhood, and that she grew up feeling as Irish as American. Her accent can't be faulted, and neither can her touch for detail: not the realistic details of *Angela's Ashes*, but the pop fiction details of what's essentially a warmhearted soap opera.

The supporting characters come on-screen all but wearing descriptive labels on cords around their necks. Consider Mister Billy, played by Ray Winstone, an actor so good at being mean that two of England's best actors (Tim Roth and Gary Oldman) both cast him as an abusive father in their first movies. Mister Billy is the neighborhood loan shark, a man who hands you the cash and expects you to pay interest on it for the rest of your life.

Agnes has to borrow from him to finance her husband's funeral, and when she's able to pay him back in a lump sum, his eyes narrow with disappointment. When her son Frankie finds a trade and needs to buy tools, Mister Billy is there with another loan, and sinister intentions.

Some days are sunny, some cloudy in Agnes's life. She is flattered to be asked out on a date by the French baker Pierre (Arno Chevrier), and saddened when Marion gets bad news about a medical exam. And always in the back of her head is a dream, which, her aim being modest, is to meet Tom Jones. Whether she marries Pierre or meets Jones, as well as the state of Marion's health and the outcome of Frankie's loan, I will leave you to discover.

This is a modest but likable film, and Anjelica Huston plays a heroine who makes us smile. But it's skimpy material, and I'm not sure why Huston was attracted to it; her first film as a director, *Bastard Out of Carolina* (1996), a story about child abuse, was fiercer and more passionate. *Agnes Browne* is not consequential enough to inspire a visit to a theater, but as a video rental it's not a bad idea.

A.I. Artificial Intelligence ★ ★ ★
PG-13, 145 m., 2001

Haley Joel Osment (David), Jude Law (Gigolo Joe), Frances O'Connor (Monica Swinton), Brendan Gleeson (Lord Johnson-Johnson), Sam Robards (Henry Swinton), William Hurt (Professor Hobby), Jake Thomas (Martin Swinton). Directed by Steven Spielberg and produced by Kathleen Kennedy, Spielberg, and Bonnie Curtis. Screenplay by Spielberg and Ian Watson, based on the short story "Supertoys Last All Summer Long" by Brian Aldiss.

Greatness and miscalculation fight for screen space in Steven Spielberg's *A.I. Artificial Intelligence,* a movie both wonderful and maddening. Here is one of the most ambitious films of recent years, filled with wondrous sights and provocative ideas, but it miscalculates in asking us to invest our emotions in a character that is, after all, a machine.

"What responsibility does a human have to a robot that genuinely loves?" the film asks, and the answer is: None. Because the robot does not genuinely love. It only genuinely seems to love. We are expert at projecting human emotions into nonhuman subjects, from animals to clouds to computer games, but the emotions reside only in our minds. *A.I.* evades its responsibility to deal rigorously with this trait, and goes for an ending that wants us to cry but had me asking questions just when I should have been finding answers.

At the center of the movie is an idea from Brian Aldiss's 1969 short story, "Supertoys Last All Summer Long," about an advanced cybernetic pet that is abandoned in the woods. When real household animals are abandoned, there is the sense that humans have broken their compact with them. But when a manufactured pet is thrown away, is that really any different from junking a computer? (I hope Buzz Lightyear is not reading these words.) From a coldly logical point of view, should we think of David, the cute young hero of *A.I.,* as more than a very advanced gigapet? Do our human feelings for him make him human?

Stanley Kubrick worked on this material for fifteen years, before passing it on to Spielberg, who has not solved it either. It involves man's relationship to those tools that so closely mirror our own desires that we confuse them with flesh and blood; consider that Charles Lindbergh's autobiography, *We,* is about himself and an airplane. When we lose a toy, the pain is ours, not the toy's, and by following an abandoned robot boy rather than the parents who threw him away, Spielberg misses the real story.

The film opens with cerebral creepiness, as Professor Hobby (William Hurt) presides at a meeting of a company that makes humanoid robots (or "mechas"). We are in the future; global warming has drowned the world's coastlines, but the American economy has survived thanks to its exploitation of mechas. "I propose that we build a robot that can love," Hobby says. Twenty months later, we meet Monica and Henry (Frances O'Connor and Sam Robards), a married couple whose own child has been frozen until a cure can be devised for his disease. The husband brings home David (Haley Joel Osment), a mecha who looks as lifelike and lovable as—well, Haley Joel Osment.

"There's no substitute for your own child!" sobs Monica, and Henry tries to placate her: "I'll take him back." Cold, but realistic; David is only a product. Yet he has an advanced chip that allows him to learn, adapt, and "love," when Monica permanently "imprints" him. In some of the most intriguing passages in the film, Spielberg explores the paradoxes that result, as David wins their love and yet is never—quite—a real boy. He doesn't sleep, but he observes bedtime. He doesn't eat, but so fervent is his desire to belong that he damages his wiring by ingesting spinach (wouldn't a mecha be programmed not to put things into its mouth?). David is treated with cruelty by other kids; humans are frequently violent and resentful against mechas. Why? Maybe for the same reason we swear at computers.

Events take place that cause David's "mother" to abandon him in the woods, opening the second and most extraordinary section of the movie, as the little mecha, and Teddy, his mecha pet bear, wander lost through the world, and he dreams of becoming a real boy and earning Monica's love. He knows *Pinocchio* from his bedtime reading, and believes that the Blue Fairy might be able to make him real. David and Teddy are befriended by Gigolo Joe (Jude Law), a love mecha living the life of a hustler. There is a sequence at a Flesh Fair, not unlike a WWF event, at which humans cheer as damaged mechas are destroyed grotesquely. Eventually, after a harrowing escape, they arrive at Rouge City, where a wizard tells David where to look for the Blue Fairy.

It's here that *A.I.* moves into its most visionary and problematical material, in spectacular scenes set in a drowned New York. There are secrets I won't reveal, but at one point David settles down to wait a very long time for the Blue Fairy, and the movie intends his wait to be poignant, but for me it was a case of a looping computer program—not a cause for tears, but a cause for rebooting. In the final scenes, David is studied in a way I will not reveal; it is up to us to determine who, or what, his examiners are.

The movie is enormously provocative, but the story seems to skew against its natural grain. It bets its emotional capital on David and his desire to be a real boy, but it's the old wood-carver Geppetto, not the blockhead puppet, who is the poignant figure in *Pinocchio*. The movie toys with David's nature in the edgy party scenes, but then buys into his lovability instead of balancing on the divide between man and machine. Both of the closing sequences—the long wait and an investigation—are unsuccessful. The first goes over the top. The second raises questions it isn't prepared to answer. There are a couple of possible earlier endings that would have resulted in a tougher movie.

Haley Joel Osment and Jude Law take the acting honors (and, of course, Hurt is perfect at evoking the professor). Osment, who is on-screen in almost every scene, is one of the best actors now working. His David is not a cute little boy but a cute little boy *mecha;* we get not the lovable kid from *The Sixth Sense* but something subtly different. The movie's special effects are awesome. The photography by Janusz Kaminski reflects Spielberg's interest in backlighting, bright whites, and the curiously evocative visible beams of flashlights. The effects seamlessly marry the real with the imaginary.

A.I. is audacious, technically masterful, challenging, sometimes moving, ceaselessly watchable. What holds it back from greatness is a failure to really engage the ideas it introduces. The movie's conclusion is too facile and sentimental, given what has gone before. It has mastered the artificial, but not the intelligence. ☞

Aimee & Jaguar ★ ★ ★
NO MPAA RATING, 125 m., 2000

Maria Schrader (Felice Schragenheim [Jaguar]), Juliane Kohler (Lilly Wust [Aimee]), Johanna Wokalek (Ilse), Heike Makatsch (Klarchen), Elisabeth Degen (Lotte), Detlev Buck (Gunther Wust), Inge Keller (Lilly [today]), Kyra Mladeck (Ilse [today]), Margit Bendokat (Mrs. Jager). Directed by Max Farberbock and produced by Gunter Rohrback and Hanno Huth. Screenplay by Farberbock and Rona Munro, based on the book by Erica Fischer.

Felice is Jewish and a lesbian, in Berlin in 1943—which means she is walking around with a suspended sentence of death. She takes incredible chances. She works for an underground resistance group, and her daytime job is as the assistant to the editor of a Nazi newspaper ("What would I do without you?" he asks). Her strategy is to hide in plain view; her boldness is a weapon. Then she falls in love with Lilly.

Lilly (Juliane Kohler) is the mother of four. Her husband is away at the front. The first time we see her, she is at a Beethoven concert with a German officer—not her husband. She cheats. He cheats, even with their nanny. It is wartime. One night at a club Lilly is swept up by Felice (Maria Schrader) and her friends; she's too naive at first to know they are lesbians, and doesn't figure out Felice is Jewish until she is finally told. Why would you suspect that of an employee of the Nazis?

Aimee & Jaguar (those were Lilly and Felice's pet names for each other) is based on a true story. Lilly Wust is alive even today, at eighty-five, and is the subject of a book that inspired the film. Felice almost certainly died in the concentration camps; her death was hastened because Lilly heedlessly tried to visit her there, calling the wrong kind of attention. War is a time for desperate and risky love affairs, but theirs was so dangerous it was like an act of defiance against the laws, the state, the world, all set against them.

It is pretty clear that Germany is losing the war, that the end is not far away; the bombs rain on Berlin, and through her underground sources Felice knows even better than her editor of the German defeats. The movie suggests that a few Jews who did escape identification were able to survive in a sort of shadowland. Early in the film, a German woman in a rest room sells food stamps to women she knows (or assumes) are Jewish, and later other Germans know Felice's secret but do not reveal it. They support a genocidal state, but are unwilling to take personal action. There is even a subtle and delicately written scene suggesting that the editor of the Nazi paper realizes Felice is not what she seems, and chooses not to know.

For Lilly, love with Felice is a revelation. At first she doesn't even realize her new friend is a lesbian, and when Felice kisses her she reacts with horror. On reflection, she is not so horrified at all, and soon they are lovers. There is a sex scene in the movie, not graphic in its visual details but startling in its intensity, that is one of the most truthful I have seen. Most lovers in the movies are too in command; the actors fear the embarrassment of lost control. A person having an orgasm can look funny, even ridiculous, to an outsider, which is why you won't find many movie stars who really

want to fake it all that well. When Lilly and Felice make love, there is a trembling, a fear, a loss of control that colors all the scenes that follow.

Maria Schrader plays Felice with a kind of doomed and reckless bravery. She must know her days are numbered. She cannot get away with her deception forever, and when she is caught, she will not be just any Jew, but one who penetrated to the center of the Nazi establishment—who partied with those who had condemned her to death. She is initially attracted to Lilly as sort of a lark; it might be fun to take this officer's wife, this mother of four little Aryans, and conquer her. Then they are both surprised by love.

There is a moment in the film when it appears that the nightmare is ending. A report spreads of Hitler's death after the failed assassination plot by some of his officers. No one knows quite how to respond; Felice is too cautious to reveal her feelings, but among Berliners in general there is the unstated feeling that the war was lost anyway, and might as well end. Then Hitler goes on the radio to declare himself untouched, and for Felice his voice is a death sentence: She will not get another pass, she senses. "I'm Jewish, Lilly," she tells her lover. Lilly looks at her in surprise, and then asks, "How can you love me?" It is the crucial moment of the movie.

Aimee & Jaguar has some holes in its storytelling that raise questions. How can Lilly's husband return from the fighting seemingly at will? Was Felice hired by the newspaper without any personal documentation? These questions do not matter. What matters is that at a turning point in her life, Felice is given a chance to escape Germany, and stays. Maybe she didn't have a choice. This is the kind of story that has to be true; as fiction, it would not be believable.

All About My Mother ★ ★ ★ ½
R, 101 m., 1999

Cecilia Roth (Manuela), Eloy Azorin (Esteban), Marisa Paredes (Huma Rojo), Candela Pena (Nina), Antonia San Juan (Agrado), Penelope Cruz (Sister Rosa), Rose Maria Sarda (Rosa's Mother), Fernando Fernan Gomez (Rosa's Father), Toni Canto (Lola). Directed by

Pedro Almodovar and produced by Agustin Almodovar. Screenplay by Pedro Almodovar.

Pedro Almodovar's films are a struggle between real and fake heartbreak—between tragedy and soap opera. They're usually funny, too, which increases the tension. You don't know where to position yourself while you're watching a film like *All About My Mother,* and that's part of the appeal: Do you take it seriously, like the characters do, or do you notice the bright colors and flashy art decoration, the cheerful homages to Tennessee Williams and *All About Eve,* and see it as a parody? Even Almodovar's camera sometimes doesn't know where to stand: When the heroine's son writes in his journal, the camera looks at his pen from the point of view of the paper.

All About My Mother is one of the best films of the Spanish director, whose films present a Tennessee Williams sensibility in the visual style of a 1950s Universal-International tearjerker. Rock Hudson and Dorothy Malone never seem very far offscreen. Bette Davis isn't offscreen at all: Almodovar's heroines seem to be playing her. Self-parody is part of Almodovar's approach, but *All About My Mother* is also sincere and heartfelt; though two of its characters are transvestite hookers, one is a pregnant nun, and two more are battling lesbians, this is a film that paradoxically expresses family values.

The movie opens in Madrid with a medical worker named Manuela (Cecilia Roth) and her teenage son, Esteban (Eloy Azorin). They've gone to see a performance of *A Streetcar Named Desire,* and now wait across the street from the stage door so Esteban can get an autograph from the famous actress Huma Rojo (Marisa Paredes). She jumps into a taxi (intercut with shots from *All About Eve* of Bette Davis eluding an autograph hound), and Esteban runs after her and is struck dead in the street. That sets up the story, as Manuela journeys to Barcelona to inform Esteban's father of the son's death.

There is irony as the film folds back on itself, because its opening scenes show Manuela, now a hospital coordinator but once an actress, performing in a video intended to promote organ transplants. In the film grieving relatives are asked to allow the organs of their loved ones to be used; later Manuela plays the same scene for real, as she's asked to donate her own son's heart.

The Barcelona scenes reflect Almodovar's long-standing interest in characters who cross the gender divide. Esteban's father is now a transvestite prostitute. In a scene worthy of Fellini, we visit a field in Barcelona where cars circle a lineup of flamboyant hookers of all sexes, and where Manuela, seeking her former lover, finds an old friend named Agrado (Antonia San Juan). The name means "agreeable," we're told, and Agrado is a person with endless troubles of her own who nevertheless enters every scene looking for the laugh. In one scene she dresses in a Chanel knockoff and is asked if it's real. As a street hooker she couldn't afford Chanel, but her answer is unexpected: "How could I buy a real Chanel with all the hunger in the world?"

There are unexpected connections between the characters, even between Esteban's father and Sister Rosa (Penelope Cruz), a nun who works in a shelter for battered prostitutes. And new connections are forged. We meet the actress Huma once again, and her girlfriend and costar Nina (Candela Pena): "She's hooked on junk and I'm hooked on her." When Nina flakes out, Manuela is actually able to understudy her role, having played it years ago. And Agrado finds a job as Huma's personal assistant. Meanwhile, the search goes on for the missing lover.

Manuela is the heroine of the film and its center, but Agrado is the source of life. There's an extraordinary scene in which she takes an empty stage against a hostile audience, and tries to improvise a one-woman show around the story of her life. Finally she starts an inventory of the plastic surgeries that assisted her in the journey from male to female, describing the pain, procedure, and cost of each, as if saying, "I've paid my dues to be who I am today. Have you?"

Almodovar's earlier films sometimes seemed to be manipulating the characters as an exercise. Here the plot does handstands in its eagerness to use coincidence, surprise, and melodrama. But the characters have a weight and reality, as if Almodovar has finally taken pity on them—has seen that although their plights may seem ludicrous, they're real enough to hurt. These are people that stand outside conventional life and its rules, and yet affirm them. Families are where you find them and how you make them, and home, it's said, is the place where, if you have to go there, they have to take you in.

All the Little Animals ★ ★ ★
R, 112 m., 1999

John Hurt (Mr. Summers), Christian Bale (Bobby), Daniel Benzali (De Winter), James Faulkner (Mr. Whiteside), John O'Toole (Lorry Driver), Amanda Boyle (Des), Amy Robbins (Bobby's Mother), John Higgins (Dean). Directed and produced by Jeremy Thomas. Screenplay by Eski Thomas, based on the novel by Walker Hamilton.

All the Little Animals is a particularly odd film that, despite its title, is not a children's movie, a cute animal movie, or the story of a veterinarian, but a dark and insinuating fable. Because it falls so far outside our ordinary story expectations it may frustrate some viewers, but it has a fearsome single-mindedness that suggests deep Jungian origins. Like the 1989 fantasy *Paperhouse*, it seems to be about more than we can see.

Its hero is a twenty-four-year-old named Bobby (Christian Bale), who sustained some brain damage in a childhood accident and is now slightly impaired and often fearful. Much of his fear is justified; his stepfather, De Winter (Daniel Benzali), killed Bobby's mother by "shouting her to death," and now threatens him with imprisonment in a mental home unless he signs over control of the family's London department store.

Bobby flees. He hitches a ride with a truck driver who gleefully aims to kill a fox on the road. Bobby wrestles for the wheel, the truck overturns, the driver is killed, and everything is witnessed by a man standing beside the road. This is Mr. Summers (John Hurt), a gentle and intelligent recluse who lives in a cottage in the woods and devotes his life to burying dead animals. "The car is a killing machine, pure and simple," Mr. Summers snaps; he is even offended by the insects that die on windshields.

Who is this man really? What's his story? Why does he seem to have plenty of money?

The movie is all the more intriguing because it roots Mr. Summers in reality, instead of making him into some kind of fairy-tale creature. He heats Campbell's soup for Bobby, gives him a blanket, tells him he can stay the night. There is no suggestion of sexual motivation; Mr. Summers is matter-of-fact, reasonable, and motivated entirely by his feelings about dead animals.

Bobby follows the man on his rounds, and then asks to stay and share his work. Mr. Summers agrees. Sometimes they go on raids. One is a guerrilla attack on a lepidopterist, who has built a trap for moths in his backyard, and sips wine and listens to classical music while the helpless creatures flutter toward nets around a bright light. "Smash his light!" Mr. Summers spits, and Bobby runs awkwardly forward with a rock to startle the smug bug collector.

All goes well until De Winter comes back into the picture, and then Bobby and Mr. Summers tell each other their stories, and we learn that the movie is not a simple tale of good and evil, and that Mr. Summers is a great deal more complicated than we might have anticipated. When he's heard Bobby's story, he suggests they visit De Winter and simply sign over the store to gain Bobby's freedom—but De Winter doesn't see it that way, especially not after Summers (who looks a little shabby) sneezes and gets snot on De Winter's exquisite suit.

The performances are minutely observed, which enhances the movie's dreamlike quality. Hurt builds Mr. Summers out of realistic detail, and Benzali makes De Winter into a cold, hard-edged control freak; he's a villain that would distinguish any thriller and redeem not a few. What drives him? Why is he so hateful? Perhaps he's simply pure evil, and entertains himself by putting on a daily performance of malevolence. Of course, anyone so rigidly controlled is trembling with fear on the inside.

Here's an intriguing question: What is this movie about? It's not really about loving animals, and indeed it's creepy that Mr. Summers (and Bobby) focus more on dead ones than living specimens. Is it about death? About fear, and overcoming it? About revenge? The appeal of archetypal stories is that they seem like reflections of the real subject matter: Buried issues are being played out here at one remove.

Most movies are one-dimensional and gladly declare themselves. This movie, treated that way, would be about an insecure kid, a vicious stepfather, and a strange coot who lives in the woods. But *All the Little Animals* refuses to reduce its story to simple terms, and the visible story seems like a manifestation of dark and secret undercurrents. Even the ending, which some will no doubt consider routine revenge, has a certain subterranean irony.

The film is by a first-time director, Jeremy Thomas, a leading British producer who has worked with such directors as Bertolucci, Roeg, and Cronenberg. He says he was so struck (indeed, obsessed) by the original novel by Walker Hamilton that he felt compelled to film it. He has wisely not simplified his obsession or made it more accessible, but has allowed the film to linger in the shadow world of unconscious fears.

All the Pretty Horses ★ ★ ★ ½
PG-13, 117 m., 2000

Matt Damon (John Grady Cole), Henry Thomas (Lacey Rawlins), Lucas Black (Jimmy Blevins), Rubén Blades (Don Hector Rocha y Villarel), Penelope Cruz (Alejandra), Robert Patrick (John Grady's Father), Bruce Dern (Judge), Sam Shepard (Banker), Miriam Colon (Alfonsa). Directed and produced by Billy Bob Thornton. Screenplay by Ted Tally, based on the novel by Cormac McCarthy.

Billy Bob Thornton's *All the Pretty Horses* is an elegiac Western about two young cowboys, and then a third, who ride from Texas into Mexico in search of what may be left of the Old West. The movie is really as simple as that. It touches on adventure and romance, but isn't really about them. It's about the mythic idea of heading south on a good horse, with a change of clothes, some camp gear, and a gun, and seeing what happens. It takes place in 1949. A few years later, its heroes would have headed down Route 66 in a Chevy convertible.

The movie stars Matt Damon and Henry Thomas as John Grady Cole and Lacey Rawlins, and they're followed on the trail by a kid named Jimmy Blevins (Lucas Black), who is riding more horse than the other two can convince themselves he paid for. He wants to come along and they let him, although one observes he is going to get them into trouble and is right.

In Mexico they get involved in a misunderstanding, or maybe it isn't, about stealing horses that requires them to leave in a hurry. The kid knows it's his fault and does the right thing, keeping to the trail in front of the pursuers, while John and Lacey lose themselves in the sagebrush.

Following no particular plan, they end up on a ranch owned by Don Hector Rocha y Villarel (Rubén Blades), who values his private airplane but not nearly as much as he values his daughter, Alejandra (Penelope Cruz). John breaks some wild mustangs for Don Hector, and discusses fine points of horse breeding, on which the two men find themselves in agreement. Don Hector gives them a job, and John and Alejandra are attracted to each other like those two little Scotty dogs with the magnets in them.

Thornton cares about the story, I think, but he's not distracted by it. The real subject of his movie is the *feeling* of being young, on horseback, in a foreign country, in trouble, and in love. *All the Pretty Horses* reminds me, in a strange way, of *George Washington,* another new movie. The two films have nothing in common except for how much they want to fix in the memory the way it was to be at that place, at that time: They use dialogue as if it were music, to establish a mood.

Listen carefully to the opening scenes of *All the Pretty Horses.* Something interesting is going on. The dialogue, by Ted Tally, is put in the foreground of the sound track instead of being surrounded by the ambience. It remains at the same volume from scene to scene. It overlaps a little strangely—anticipating or tarrying—so that we understand the words are not being illustrated by the pictures, but are evoking them. Indoors, outdoors, the presence of the dialogue dominates the track, and natural noises and music are in the background. Thornton goes to a more naturalistic sound style later in the film, but at the beginning he seems to be reminding us that this is a memory being told.

It is a tribute to Damon's performance that even in love scenes or when he fights for his life in prison, he never seems to be the "hero," but is more like a guy this stuff is happening to. Henry Thomas and Lucas Black (from Thornton's earlier film *Sling Blade*) also do a good job of not being "characters" and just being there. Tally's dialogue never gives them too much to say. They figure it out and we figure it out without a lot of words.

That same economy of language works in two lovely supporting performances, by Miriam Colon as Alfonsa, the eagle-eyed aunt of Alejandra, and Bruce Dern, as a judge on the Texas side. "I won't have her unhappy or gossiped about," the aunt warns John. She warns him away from her niece—and later warns him off again, when the stakes are higher. She's not made into a standard old shrew, but is wise, self-possessed, and knows very well what trouble she is trying to avert. The Dern character has a key scene in a courtroom, but the next scene is in a sense the most important in the movie, because what John really wants is to confess and have his sins forgiven, and the judge knows that.

You can see how this movie could have been jacked up into a one-level action picture, but what makes it special is how Thornton modulates the material. Even the prison knife-fight scenes aren't staged as action confrontations, but as quick, desperate, and strangely intimate. This is the kind of movie it's best to see on a big screen, where the size of the sky and the colors of the land can do their work. It's as if the events are bigger than the people—as if John Grady Cole will never again be such a reckless damn fool kid as he was during this year, and will always sort of regret that.

Almost Famous ★ ★ ★ ★
R, 124 m., 2000

Patrick Fugit (William Miller), Billy Crudup (Russell Hammond), Frances McDormand (Elaine Miller), Kate Hudson (Penny Lane), Jason Lee (Jeff Bebe), Philip Seymour Hoffman (Lester Bangs), Zooey Deschanel (Anita Miller), Michael Angarano (Young William), Noah Taylor (Dick Roswell). Directed by Cameron Crowe and produced by Crowe and Ian Bryce. Screenplay by Crowe.

Oh, what a lovely film. I was almost hugging myself while I watched it. *Almost Famous* is funny and touching in so many different ways. It's the story of a fifteen-year-old kid, smart and terrifyingly earnest, who through luck and pluck gets assigned by *Rolling Stone* magazine to do a profile of a rising rock band. The magazine has no idea he's fifteen. Clutching his pencil and his notebook like talismans, phoning a veteran critic for advice, he plunges into the experience that will make and shape him. It's as if Huckleberry Finn came back to life in the 1970s and instead of taking a raft down the Mississippi got on the bus with the band.

The kid is named William Miller in the movie; he's played by Patrick Fugit as a boy shaped by the fierce values of his mother, who drives him to the concert that will change his life, and drops him off with the mantra, "Don't do drugs!" The character and the story are based on the life of Cameron Crowe, the film's writer-director, who indeed was a teenage *Rolling Stone* writer, and who knows how lucky he was. Crowe grew up to write and direct *Say Anything* (1989), one of the best movies ever made about teenagers; in this movie, he surpasses himself.

The movie is not just about William Miller. It's about the band and the early 1970s, when idealism collided with commerce. The band he hooks up with is named Stillwater. He talks his way backstage in San Diego by knowing their names and hurling accurate compliments at them as they hurry into the arena. William wins the sympathy of Russell Hammond (Billy Crudup), the guitarist, who lets him in. Backstage, he meets his guide to this new world, a girl who says her name is Penny Lane (Kate Hudson). She is not a groupie, she explains indignantly, but a Band Aide. She is, of course, a groupie, but she has so much theory about her role it's almost like sex for her is a philosophical exercise.

William's mom, Elaine (Frances McDormand), is a college professor who believes in vegetarianism, progressive politics, and the corrupting influence of rock music. Banning the rock albums of her older daughter Anita (Zooey Deschanel), she holds up an album cover and asks Anita to look at the telltale signs in Simon and Garfunkel's eyes: "Pot!" Anita, who had played the lyrics "I Walked Out to Look for America," leaves to become a stewardess.

William walks out too, in a way. He intends to be away from school for only a few days. But as Russell and the rest of Stillwater grow accustomed to his presence, he finds himself on the bus and driving far into the Southwest. Along the way, he observes the tension between Russell and Jeff Bebe (Jason Lee), the lead singer, who thinks Russell is getting more attention than his role definition deserves: "I'm the lead singer and you're the guitarist with mystique."

William has two guardian angels to watch over him. One is Penny Lane, who is almost as young as he is, but lies about her age. William loves her, or thinks he does, but she loves Russell, or says she does, and William admires Russell, too, and Russell maintains a reserve that makes it hard to know what he thinks. He has the scowl and the facial hair of a rock star, but is still only in his early twenties, and one of the best moments in the movie comes when William's mom lectures him over the phone about the dangers to her son: "Do I make myself clear?" "Yes, ma'am," he says, reverting to childhood.

William's other angel is the legendary rock critic Lester Bangs (Philip Seymour Hoffman), then the editor of *Creem:* "So you're the kid who's been sending me those articles from your school paper." He ignores the kid's age, trusts his talent, and shares his credo: "Be honest, and unmerciful." During moments of crisis on the road, William calls Lester for advice.

Lester Bangs was a real person, and so are Ben Fong Torres and Jann Wenner of *Rolling Stone,* played by look-alike actors. The movie's sense of time and place is so acute it's possible to believe Stillwater was a real band. As William watches, the band gets a hit record, a hotshot producer tries to take over from the guy who's always managed them, they switch from a bus to an airplane, and there are ego wars, not least when a T-shirt photo places Russell in the foreground and has the other band members out of focus (there's a little *Spinal Tap* here).

Almost Famous is about the world of rock, but it's not a rock film; it's a coming-of-age film about an idealistic kid who sees the real world, witnesses its cruelties and heartbreaks, and yet finds much room for hope. The Penny Lane character is written with particular delicacy, as she tries to justify her existence and explain her values (in a milieu that seems to have none). It breaks William's heart to see how the married Russell mistreats her. But Penny denies being hurt. Kate Hudson has one scene so well acted it takes her character to another level. William tells her, "He sold you to Humble Pie for 50 bucks and a case of beer." Watch the silence, the brave smile, the tear, and the precise spin she puts on the words, "What *kind* of beer?" It's not an easy laugh. It's a whole world of insight.

What thrums beneath *Almost Famous* is Cameron Crowe's gratitude. His William Miller is not an alienated bore, but a kid who had the good fortune to have a wonderful mother and great sister, to meet the right rock star in Russell (there would have been wrong ones), and to have the kind of love for Penny Lane that will arm him for the future and give him a deeper understanding of the mysteries of women. Looking at William—earnestly grasping his tape recorder, trying to get an interview, desperately going to Lester for advice, terrified as Ben Fong Torres rails about deadlines, crushed when it looks like his story will be rejected—we know we're looking at a kid who has the right stuff and will go far. Someday he might even direct a movie like *Almost Famous.*

Note: Why did they give an R rating to a movie perfect for teenagers? ☞

Along Came a Spider ★ ★
R, 105 m., 2001

Morgan Freeman (Detective Alex Cross), Monica Potter (Agent Jezzie Flannigan), Michael Wincott (Gary Soneji), Jay O. Sanders (Detective Kyle Craig), Dylan Baker (Mayor Carl Monroe), Raoul Ganeev (Agent Charles Chakley), Billy Burke (Agent Michael Devine), Penelope Ann Miller (Katherine Rose Dunne). Directed by Lee Tamahori and produced by David Brown and Joe Wizan. Screenplay by Marc Moss, based on a novel by James Patterson.

A few loopholes I can forgive. But when a plot is riddled with them, crippled by them, made implausible by them, as in *Along Came a Spider,* I get distracted. I'm wondering, since Dr. Alex

Cross is so brilliant, how come he doesn't notice yawning logical holes in the very fabric of the story he's occupying?

Dr. Cross (Morgan Freeman) is a District of Columbia police detective, a famous forensic psychologist whose textbook is quoted by other cops. As the movie opens, he loses his partner in one of those scenes where you're thinking, gee, I didn't know the police had *that* kind of technology. A woman cop has a small camera concealed on her being, which takes a TV signal of the killer, who is driving a car, and relays it to Cross in a helicopter, causing us to wonder if there is a way to arrest this guy at less taxpayer expense.

After this chase, Cross goes into a depression and passes the time building model boats—until his phone rings and it's another diabolical killer, who once again has devised an elaborate cat-and-mouse game for the detective to play. No killers in Washington ever just want to murder somebody; they're all motivated by the desire to construct elaborate puzzles for Cross.

No one is better than Morgan Freeman at being calm and serious and saying things like, "He's really after somebody else." Freeman was brilliant at unraveling the diabolical pattern in *Seven* (1995), and the success of that movie inspired the splendid *Kiss the Girls* (1997), where he first played Cross, the hero of six novels by James Patterson. In *Girls,* he intuited that the madman wasn't killing his victims but collecting them. Now comes another criminal who has read way too many James Patterson novels.

I will tread carefully to avoid revealing surprises, since the movie socks us with one every five minutes, counting on our astonishment to distract us from implausibilities. The film opens with a strangling and a kidnapping at an exclusive private school. The kids have parents so important that the Secret Service has agents permanently assigned. Because the hostage is the daughter of a senator, Cross finds himself working with Agent Jezzie Flannigan (Monica Potter), who found time for a career despite a lifetime of explaining to people how her name is spelled.

The school's students have computer monitors at every desk, and are challenged by their teacher to see who can find Charles Lind-

bergh's home page in the fewest possible clicks. (Answer: Go to Google, type in "Lindbergh," get 103,000 results, discover he doesn't have a home page.) Most kids their age are already busy creating viruses to bring the economy to its knees. Why such a lamebrained exercise? Dr. Cross figures it out.

The correct Lindbergh page, which he finds immediately out of 103,000 possibilities, has been put up by the kidnapper (or come to think of it, has it?), and includes a live cam shot with resolution so high Cross can read the name on a bottle of pills. This clue, plus the kidnapper's insistence on communicating through Cross, gets him on the case, partnered with Agent Flannigan.

Kiss the Girls, directed by Gary Fleder, had a palpable sense of time and place; deep, moist, shadowy, ominous woodlands figured heavily. *Along Came a Spider,* directed by Lee Tamahori (of the great *Once Were Warriors*), is also thick with atmosphere, and evokes the damp, wet gloom of a chilly season. As Cross and Flannigan follow leads, we also see the kidnapper and his victim, and are filled with admiration for her imagination; she is able to escape, set fires, swim toward shore, and perform other feats far more difficult than a Google search.

But then . . . well, there's not much more I can say without giving away astonishing surprises. The film contains two kinds of loopholes: (1) those that emerge when you think back on the plot, and (2) those that seem like loopholes at the time, and then are explained by later developments which may contain loopholes of their own.

Of Morgan Freeman as a movie actor, no praise is too high. Maybe actors should be given Oscars not for the good films they triumph in, but for the weak films they survive. The focus of his gaze, the quiet authority of his voice, make Dr. Cross an interesting character even in scenes where all common sense has fled. And the look and texture of the film are fine; Tamahori and cinematographer Matthew F. Leonetti have created a convincing sense of place (to be sure, they shot their Virginia exteriors in British Columbia, but, hey, that's a place too). Michael Wincott makes a satisfactory bad guy, especially when his mastermind schemes start blowing up in his face.

But, man, are you gonna be talking when you

come out of this movie! Saying things like "but why . . ." and "if she . . ." and "wouldn't he . . ." and "how come . . ." as you try to trace your way back through the twisted logic of the plot. Here's a sample question: Dr. Cross mentions a $12 million ransom and later explains that the person he was talking to should have known it was $10 million but never said anything. And I'm thinking, should that person have even known about the ransom at all? Well, maybe, if . . . but I dunno. There are places in this movie you just can't get to from other places in this movie.

The Amati Girls ★

PG, 91 m., 2001

Cloris Leachman (Dolly), Mercedes Ruehl (Grace), Dinah Manoff (Denise), Sean Young (Christine), Lily Knight (Dolores), Paul Sorvino (Joe), Lee Grant (Aunt Spendora), Edith Field (Aunt Loretta), Cassie Cole (Carla), Marissa Leigh (Laura), Doug Spinuzza (Armand), Mark Harmon (Lawrence). Directed by Anne De Salvo and produced by James Alex, Melanie Backer, Steven Johnson, Michael I. Levy, and Henry M. Shea Jr. Screenplay by De Salvo.

A lot of saints are mentioned in *The Amati Girls*, including Christopher, Lucy, Cecelia, Theresa (the Little Flower), and the BVM herself, but the movie should be praying to St. Jude, patron saint of lost causes. Maybe he could perform a miracle and turn this into a cable offering, so no one has to pay to see it.

The movie's a tour of timeworn clichés about family life, performed with desperation by a talented cast. Alone among them, Mercedes Ruehl somehow salvages her dignity while all about her are losing theirs. She even manages to avoid appearing in the shameless last shot, where the ladies dance around the kitchen singing *Doo-wah-diddy, diddy-dum, diddy-dum.*

The movie is about a large Italian-American family in Philadelphia. Too large, considering that every character has a crisis, and the story races from one to another like the guy on TV who kept all the plates spinning on top of the poles. This family not only has a matriarch (Cloris Leachman) but her superfluous sister (Lee Grant) and their even more superfluous

sister (Edith Field). There are also four grown daughters, two husbands, two hopeful fiancées, at least three kids, and probably some dogs, although we never see them because they are no doubt hiding under the table to avoid being stepped on.

The adult sisters are Grace (Ruehl), who is married to macho-man Paul Sorvino ("No Padrone male will ever step foot on a ballet stage except as a teamster"); Denise (Dinah Manoff), who is engaged to Lawrence (Mark Harmon) but dreams of show biz (she sings "Kiss of Fire" to demonstrate her own need for St. Jude); Christine (Sean Young), whose husband, Paul (Jamey Sheridan), is a workaholic; and poor Dolores (Lily Knight), who is retarded. Denise and Christine think Grace is ruining her life with guilt because when she was a little girl she ran away and her mother chased her and fell, which of course caused Dolores to be retarded.

Sample subplot. Dolores decides she wants a boyfriend. At the church bingo night, she sits opposite Armand (Doug Spinuzza), who, we are told "has a head full of steel" after the Gulf War. This has not resulted in Armand being a once-normal person with brain damage, but, miraculously, in his being exactly like Dolores. At the movies, after they kiss, he shyly puts his hand on her breast, and she shyly puts her hand on his.

You know the obligatory scene where the reluctant parent turns up at the last moment for the child's big moment onstage? No less than two fathers do it in this movie. Both Joe (Sorvino) and Paul have daughters in a ballet recital, and not only does Joe overcome his loathing for ballet and even attend rehearsals, but Paul overcomes his workaholism and arrives backstage in time to appear with his daughter.

The movie has one unexpected death, of course. That inspires a crisis of faith, and Dolores breaks loose from the funeral home, enters the church, and uses a candlestick to demolish several saints, although she is stopped before she gets to the BVM. There are also many meals in which everyone sits around long tables and talks at once. There is the obligatory debate, recycled from *Return to Me*, about who is better, Frank Sinatra or Tony Bennett. And an irritating editing twitch: We are shown the outside of every location before we cut inside. There is also one priceless conversation, in which Lee Grant explains to Cloris Leachman that her hair is tinted "copper bamboo bronze." For Cloris, she suggests "toasted desert sunrise." The Little Flower had the right idea. She cut off her hair and became a Carmelite.

American Beauty ★ ★ ★ ★

R, 120 m., 1999

Kevin Spacey (Lester Burnham), Annette Bening (Carolyn Burnham), Thora Birch (Jane Burnham), Wes Bentley (Ricky Fitts), Mena Suvari (Angela Hayes), Chris Cooper (Colonel Fitts), Peter Gallagher (Buddy Kane), Allison Janney (Barbara Fitts). Directed by Sam Mendes and produced by Bruce Cohen and Dan Jinks. Screenplay by Alan Ball.

American Beauty is a comedy because we laugh at the absurdity of the hero's problems. And a tragedy because we can identify with his failure—not the specific details, but the general outline. The movie is about a man who fears growing older, losing the hope of true love, and not being respected by those who know him best. If you never experience those feelings, take out a classified ad. People want to take lessons from you.

Lester Burnham, the hero of *American Beauty,* is played by Kevin Spacey as a man who is unloved by his daughter, ignored by his wife, and unnecessary at work. "I'll be dead in a year," he tells us in almost the first words of the movie. "In a way, I'm dead already." The movie is the story of his rebellion.

We meet his wife, Carolyn (Annette Bening), so perfect her garden shears are coordinated with her clothing. We meet his daughter, Jane (Thora Birch), who is saving up for breast implants even though augmentation is clearly unnecessary; perhaps her motivation is not to become more desirable to men, but to make them miserable about what they can't have.

"Both my wife and daughter think I'm this chronic loser," Lester complains. He is right. But they are not without their reasons. At an agonizing family dinner, Carolyn plays Mantovanian music that mocks every mouthful; the music is lush and reassuring, and the family

is angry and silent. When Lester criticizes his daughter's attitude, she points out correctly that he has hardly spoken to her in months.

Everything changes for Lester the night he is dragged along by his wife to see their daughter perform as a cheerleader. There on the floor, engrossed in a sub-Fosse pom-pom routine, he sees his angel: Angela (Mena Suvari), his daughter's sixteen-year-old classmate. Is it wrong for a man in his forties to lust after a teenage girl? Any honest man understands what a complicated question this is. Wrong morally, certainly, and legally. But as every woman knows, men are born with wiring that goes directly from their eyes to their genitals, bypassing the higher centers of thought. They can disapprove of their thoughts, but they cannot stop themselves from having them.

American Beauty is not about a Lolita relationship, anyway. It's about yearning after youth, respect, power, and, of course, beauty. The moment a man stops dreaming is the moment he petrifies inside, and starts writing snarfy letters disapproving of paragraphs like the one above. Lester's thoughts about Angela are impure, but not perverted; he wants to do what men are programmed to do, with the most beautiful woman he has ever seen.

Angela is not Lester's highway to bliss, but she is at least a catalyst for his freedom. His thoughts, and the discontent they engender, blast him free from years of emotional paralysis, and soon he makes a cheerful announcement at the funereal dinner table: "I quit my job, told my boss to go fuck himself, and blackmailed him for $60,000." Has he lost his mind? Not at all. The first thing he spends money on is perfectly reasonable: a bright red 1970 Pontiac Firebird.

Carolyn and Jane are going through their own romantic troubles. Lester finds out Carolyn is cheating when he sees her with her lover in the drive-thru lane of a fast-food restaurant (where he has a job he likes). Jane is being videotaped by Ricky (Wes Bentley), the boy next door, who has a strange light in his eyes. Ricky's dad (Chris Cooper) is an ex-Marine who tests him for drugs, taking a urine sample every six months; Ricky plays along to keep the peace until he can leave home.

All of these emotional threads come together during one dark and stormy night when there is a series of misunderstandings so bizarre they belong in a screwball comedy. And at the end, somehow, improbably, the film snatches victory from the jaws of defeat for Lester, its hero. Not the kind of victory you'd get in a feel-good movie, but the kind where you prove something important, if only to yourself.

American Beauty is not as dark or twisted as *Happiness*, 1998's attempt to shine a light under the rock of American society. It's more about sadness and loneliness than about cruelty or inhumanity. Nobody is really bad in this movie, just shaped by society in such a way that they can't be themselves, or feel joy. The performances all walk the line between parody and simple realism; Thora Birch and Wes Bentley are the most grounded, talking in the tense, flat voices of kids who can't wait to escape their homes. Bening's character, a Realtor who chants self-help mantras, confuses happiness with success—bad enough if you're successful, depressing if you're not.

And Spacey, an actor who embodies intelligence in his eyes and voice, is the right choice for Lester Burnham. He does reckless and foolish things in this movie, but he doesn't deceive himself; he knows he's running wild—and chooses to, burning up the future years of an empty lifetime for a few flashes of freedom. He may have lost everything by the end of the film, but he's no longer a loser.

American Movie ★ ★ ★ ★
R, 104 m., 2000

Mark Borchardt (Filmmaker), Mike Schank (Friend/Musician), Uncle Bill (Mark's Uncle), Monica Borchardt (Mark's Mom), Cliff Borchardt (Mark's Dad), Chris Borchardt (Mark's Brother), Alex Borchardt (Mark's Brother), Ken Keen (Friend), Joan Petrie (Mark's Girlfriend).
A documentary directed by Chris Smith and produced by Sarah Price.

If you've ever wanted to make a movie, see *American Movie*, which is about someone who wants to make a movie more than you do. Mark Borchardt may want to make a movie more than anyone else in the world. He is a thirty-year-old odd-job man from Menomonee Falls, Wisconsin, who has been making movies since he was a teenager, and dreams of an epic

about his life, which will be titled *Northwestern*, and be about "rust and decay."

Mark Borchardt is a real person. I have met him. I admire his spirit, and I even admire certain shots in the only Borchardt film I have seen, *Coven*. I saw it at the 1999 Sundance Film Festival—not because it was invited there, but because after the midnight premiere of *American Movie* there wasn't a person in the theater who didn't want to stay and see Mark's thirty-five-minute horror film, which we see him making during the course of the documentary.

American Movie is a very funny, sometimes very sad, documentary directed by Chris Smith and produced by Sarah Price, about Mark's life, his friends, his family, his films, and his dreams. From one point of view, Mark is a loser, a man who has spent his adult life making unreleased and sometimes unfinished movies with titles like *The More the Scarier III*. He plunders the bank account of his elderly Uncle Bill for funds to continue, he uses his friends and hapless local amateur actors as his cast, he enlists his mother as his cinematographer, and his composer and best friend is a guy named Mike Schank who after one drug trip too many seems like the twin of Kevin Smith's Silent Bob.

Borchardt's life is a daily cliff-hanger involving poverty, desperation, discouragement, and die-hard ambition. He's behind on his child support payments, he drinks too much, he can't even convince his ancient Uncle Bill that he has a future as a moviemaker. Bill lives in a trailer surrounded by piles of magazines that he possibly subscribed to under the impression he would win the Publishers' Clearing House sweepstakes. He brightens slightly when Mark shows him the portrait of an actress. "She wants to be in your movie, Bill!" Bill studies the photo: "Oh, my gorsh!" But when Mark tells him about great cinema, what he hears is "cinnamon." And when Bill fumbles countless takes while trying to perform the ominous last line of *Coven* and Mark encourages him to say it like he believes it, Bill answers frankly, "I *don't* believe it."

Smith's camera follows Borchardt as he discusses his theories of cinema (his favorite films: *Night of the Living Dead* and *The Seventh Seal*). We watch as Mark and Bill go to the bank so Bill can grudgingly sign over some of his savings. He is at cast meetings, where one local actor (Robert Jorge) explains in a peeved British accent that *Coven* is correctly pronounced "CO-ven." Not according to Mark, who says *his* film is pronounced "COVE-n." "I don't want it to rhyme with 'oven'!"

Some of the scenes could work in a screwball comedy. One involves an actor being thrown headfirst through a kitchen cabinet. To capture the moment, Mark recruits his long-suffering Swedish-American mother, Monica, to operate the camera, even though she complains she has shopping to do. He gets on the floor behind his actor, who finds out belatedly that Mark's special-effects strategy is simply to ram the actor's head through the door. The first time, the actor's head bounces off. Mark prepares for take two. One reason to see *Coven* is to appreciate that shot knowing what we know now. For another shot, Mark lies flat on the frozen ground to get low-angle shots of his friends, dressed in black cloaks. "Look menacing!" he shouts. That's hard for them to do, since their faces are invisible.

If Mark's mother is supportive, his father stays out of sight, sticking his head around a doorway occasionally to warn against bad language. Mark has two brothers, who are fed up with him; one says he would be "well suited to factory work," and the other observes, "His main asset is his mouth."

And yet Mark Borchardt is the embodiment of a lonely, rejected, dedicated artist. No poet in a Paris garret has ever been more determined to succeed. To find privacy while writing his screenplays, he drives his old beater to the parking lot of the local commuter airport, and composes on a yellow legal pad. To support himself, he delivers the *Wall Street Journal* before dawn and vacuums the carpets in a mausoleum. He has inspired the loyalty of his friends and crew members, and his girlfriend observes that if he accomplishes 25 percent of what he hopes to do, "that'll be more than most people do."

Every year at Sundance young filmmakers emerge from the woodwork, bearing the masterpieces they have somehow made for peanuts, enlisting volunteer cast and crew. Last year's discovery was not *Coven* but *The Blair Witch Project*. It cost $25,000 and so far has grossed $150 million. One day Mark Borchardt hopes for that kind of success. If it never comes, it won't be for lack of trying.

American Pie ★ ★ ★
R, 110 m., 1999

Jason Biggs (Jim), Jennifer Coolidge (Stifler's Mom), Shannon Elizabeth (Nadia), Alyson Hannigan (Michelle), Chris Klein (Oz), Clyde Kusatsu (English Teacher), Eugene Levy (Jim's Dad), Natasha Lyonne (Jessica). Directed by Paul Weitz and produced by Warren Zide, Craig Perry, Chris Moore, and Chris Weitz. Screenplay by Adam Herz.

American Pie is a comedy about four high school senior boys who make a pact to lose their virginity before the end of the school year. This alone makes it almost touchingly old-fashioned; I did not know Hollywood still permitted high school seniors to be virgins.

Real teenagers are no doubt approximately as inexperienced and unsure as they have always been, and many wisely avoid the emotional and physical dangers of early sex, but in the movies the kids make the adults look backward. Teenagers used to go to the movies to see adults making love. Now adults go to the movies to see teenagers making love. I get letters from readers complaining that Clint Eastwood or Sean Connery are too old for steamy scenes, but never a word from anyone who thinks the kids played by Christina Ricci or Reese Witherspoon are too young.

American Pie was released in the middle of a summer when moviegoers were reeling at the level of sexuality, vulgarity, obscenity, and gross depravity in movies aimed at teenagers (and despite their R ratings, these movies obviously have kids under seventeen in their crosshairs). Consider that until a few years ago semen and other secretions and extrusions dare not speak their names in the movies. Then *There's Something About Mary* came along with its hair-gel joke. Very funny. Then came *Austin Powers* with its extra ingredient in the coffee. Then *South Park,* an anthology of cheerful scatology. Now *American Pie,* where semen has moved right onto the menu, not only as a drink additive but also as filling for a pie that is baked by the hero's mom. How long will it be before the money shot moves from porn to PG-13?

19

I say this not because I am shocked, but because I am a sociological observer and want to record that the summer of 1999 was the season when Hollywood's last standards of taste fell. Nothing is too gross for the new comedies. Grossness is the point. While newspapers and broadcast television continue to enforce certain standards of language and decorum, kids are going to movies that would make longshoremen blush. These movies don't merely contain terms I can't print in the paper—they contain terms I can't even describe in other words.

I rise to the challenge. I seek an underlying comic principle to apply. I find one. I discover that gross-out gags are not funny when their only purpose is to gross us out, but they can be funny when they emerge unwittingly from the action. It is not funny, for example, for a character to drink a beer that has something in it that is not beer. But it is funny in *There's Something About Mary* when the Ben Stiller character discovers he has the same substance dangling from his ear and Cameron Diaz mistakes it for hair gel.

It is funny because the characters aren't in on the joke. They are embarrassed. We share their embarrassment and, being human, find it funny. If Stiller were to greet Diaz *knowing* what was on his ear, that would not be funny. Humor happens when characters are victims, not when they are perpetrators. Humor is generated not by content but by context, which is why *Big Daddy* isn't funny. It's not funny because the Adam Sandler character knows what he is doing and wants to be doing it.

But back to *American Pie*. It involves a great deal of sexual content which in my opinion is too advanced for high school, and a lot of characters who are more casual about it than real teenagers might be. But it observes the rules of comedy. When the lucky hero gets the foreign exchange student into his bedroom and she turns out to be ready for a romp, it is funny that he has forgotten and left his CU-See Me software running, so that the entire Internet community can watch him be embarrassed. It would not be funny if he left it on deliberately.

The film is in the tradition of *Fast Times at Ridgemont High, National Lampoon's Animal House,* and all the more recent teen sex comedies. It is not inspired, but it's cheerful and hardworking and sometimes funny, and—here's the important thing—it's not mean. Its characters are sort of sweet and lovable. As I swim through the summer tide of vulgarity, I find that's what I'm looking for: Movies that at least feel affection for their characters. Raunchy is okay. Cruel is not.

American Psycho ★ ★ ★

R, 100 m., 2000

Christian Bale (Patrick Bateman), Willem Dafoe (Donald Kimball), Jared Leto (Paul Allen), Reese Witherspoon (Evelyn Williams), Samantha Mathis (Courtney Rawlinson), Chloe Sevigny (Jean), Justin Theroux (Timothy Price), Matt Ross (Luis Carruthers). Directed by Mary Harron and produced by Edward R. Pressman, Chris Hanley, and Christian Halsey Solomon. Screenplay by Guinevere Turner and Harron, based on the novel by Bret Easton Ellis.

It's just as well a woman directed *American Psycho.* She's transformed a novel about bloodlust into a movie about men's vanity. A male director might have thought Patrick Bateman, the hero of *American Psycho,* was a serial killer because of psychological twists, but Mary Harron sees him as a guy who's prey to the usual male drives and compulsions. He just acts out a little more.

Most men are not chain-saw killers; they only act that way while doing business. Look at the traders clawing each other on the floor of the stock exchange. Listen to used-car dealers trying to dump excess stock on one another. Consider the joy with which one megacorp raids another, and dumps its leaders. Study such films as *In the Company of Men, Glengarry Glen Ross, Boiler Room,* or *The Big Kahuna.* It's a dog-eat-dog world, and to survive you'd better be White Fang.

As a novel, Bret Easton Ellis's 1991 best-seller was passed from one publisher to another like a hot potato. As a film project, it has gone through screenplays, directors, and stars for years. It was snatched up for Oliver Stone, who planned to star Leonardo Di Caprio, before ending up back in Harron's arms with Christian Bale in the lead. (To imagine this material in Stone's hands, recall the scene in Ken Russell's *The Music Lovers* where Tchaikovsky's head explodes during the 1812 Overture, then spin it out to feature length.)

Harron is less impressed by the vile Patrick Bateman than a man might have been, perhaps because as a woman who directs movies she deals every day with guys who resemble Bateman in all but his body count. She senses the linkage between the time Bateman spends in the morning lovingly applying male facial products, and the way he blasts away people who annoy him, anger him, or simply have the misfortune to be within his field of view. He is a narcissist driven by ego and fueled by greed. Most of his victims are women, but in a pinch a man will do.

The film regards the male executive lifestyle with the devotion of a fetishist. There is a scene where a group of businessmen compare their business cards, discussing the wording, paper thickness, finish, embossing, engraving, and typefaces, and they might as well be discussing their phalli. Their sexual insecurity is manifested as card envy. They carry on grim rivalries expressed in clothes, offices, salaries, and being able to get good tables in important restaurants. It is their uneasy secret that they make enough money to afford to look important, but are not very important. One of the film's running jokes is that Patrick Bateman looks so much like one of his colleagues (Jared Leto) that they are mistaken for each other. (Their faces aren't really identical, but they occupy empty space in much the same way.)

The film and the book are notorious because Bateman murders a lot of people in nasty ways. I have overheard debates about whether some of the murders are fantasies ("Can a man really aim a chain saw that well?"). All of the murders are equally real or unreal, and that isn't the point: The function of the murders is to make visible the frenzy of the territorial male when his will is frustrated. The movie gives shape and form to road rage, golf course rage, family abuse, and some of the scarier behavior patterns of sports fans.

You see why Harron has called the film "feminist." So it is—and a libel against the many sane, calm, and civilized men it does not describe. But it's true to a type, all right. It sees

Bateman in a clear, sharp, satiric light, and it despises him. Christian Bale is heroic in the way he allows the character to leap joyfully into despicableness; there is no instinct for self-preservation here, and that is one mark of a good actor. When Bateman kills, it is *not* with the zeal of a villain from a slasher movie. It is with the thoroughness of a hobbyist. Lives could have been saved if instead of living in a high-rise, Bateman had been supplied with a basement, a workbench, and a lot of nails to pound.

Among Giants ★ ★ ★
R, 94 m., 1999

Pete Postlethwaite (Ray), Rachel Griffiths (Gerry), James Thornton (Steve), Lennie James (Shovel), Andy Serkis (Bob), Rob Jarvis (Weasel), Alan Williams (Frank), Emma Cunniffe (Barmaid). Directed by Sam Miller and produced by Stephen Garrett. Screenplay by Simon Beaufoy.

Sometimes movies are simply about actors. There is a story, but only to give them something to talk about while being themselves. With the right actors, a film can essentially be about the way they talk, the look in their eye, their personal style and grace. *Among Giants* is a movie like that. It stars Pete Postlethwaite and Rachel Griffiths as an unlikely couple who fall in love, but mostly it just stars them being interesting.

Postlethwaite you may recall from *In the Name of the Father,* the 1994 Irish film where he won an Oscar nomination for playing the father of a man unjustly accused of being an IRA bomber. Griffiths was an Oscar nominee, playing the sister of a doomed musician in *Hilary and Jackie* (1998). I've seen them both several times; when you look at them you always know how their characters are feeling.

Among Giants was written by Simon Beaufoy, who also wrote *The Full Monty,* and once again combines working-class camaraderie and sex, this time in the same couple. Postlethwaite is Ray, the foreman of a freelance work gang that signs on to paint a long row of electrical power pylons that march across the British landscape. He's in his forties, wiry, ruddy, balding. Griffiths plays Gerry, a backpacker from Australia, making her way around the world and climbing peaks that interest her.

"How long you been out on the road?" he asks her when they meet.

"How long is a piece of string?"

"You get lonely?"

"Yeah, I do."

Something intangible passes between them, and soon she's back, asking for a job. Ray's gang is leery of a woman, but Gerry points out that she's a climber, not afraid of heights—or work. Ray hires her. It's the beginning of a long summer in which the men build campfires to brew their tea, and sleep in vans or tents, and spend their days high in the air with paint buckets (singing "Stand By Me" at one point).

Ray lives in a nearby town, and we learn that he has an estranged wife and kids. He considers himself divorced, but the formalities haven't taken place. Gerry lives in her tent. She is a strange, winsome loner: "All I've got is a whole bunch of people I'm never gonna see again, and a whole lot of places I'm never gonna go back to." One night Ray kisses her. They fall in love.

The complications of their romance provide the main line of the story. The counterpoint comes from details about the other characters in the work gang, especially a young man who relates to Ray as a surrogate father. The film is thick with atmosphere, and knows its way around blue-collar pubs where everybody wears jeans and cowboy shirts on Friday nights, the band plays C&W, and (in a scene that will seem realistic to British viewers and unlikely to Americans) the customers are skillful line dancers.

We are aware at some level that the whole story is a contrivance. The logistics are murky: Who is the man who hires the work gang, and why does he treat them like illegals, and why exactly is the power off now but scheduled to be turned on at the end of the summer? (No prizes for guessing that the uncertainty about power is the setup for his dramatic scene.) Those are questions that can be asked, but the answer is that the whole reality of the film is simply a backdrop to the relationship of these two characters.

They make an odd match. They're probably twenty years apart in age. They're prideful loners. Yet they have a certainty about their physical styles that makes them a good match. They both like to climb, they both work hard, and there is a scene where they frolic, not under a waterfall, but under a falling sheet of water inside the cooling tower of a power plant. Haven't seen that before.

One of the gifts of the movies is to allow us to guess what it might be like to be somebody else. As actors, Postlethwaite and Griffiths have the ability to evoke people it might be interesting to be, or know. The director, Sam Miller, uses this gift in unexpected ways. There is a scene where Gerry uses her climbing skills to traverse entirely around the four walls of a pub without ever touching the floor. Haven't seen that before, either.

Amores Perros ★ ★ ★ ½
R, 153 m., 2001

Emilio Echevarria (El Chivo), Gael Garcia Bernal (Octavio), Goya Toledo (Valeria), Alvaro Guerrero (Daniel), Vanessa Bauche (Susana), Jorge Salinas (Luis), Laura Almela (Julieta), Marco Perez (Ramiro). Directed and produced by Alejandro Gonzalez Inarritu. Screenplay by Guillermo Arriaga.

Amores Perros arrives from Mexico trailing clouds of glory—it was one of this year's Oscar nominees—and generating excitement on the Internet, where the fanboys don't usually flip for foreign films. It tells three interlinked stories that span the social classes in Mexico City, from rich TV people to the working class to the homeless, and it circles through those stories with a nod to Quentin Tarantino, whose *Pulp Fiction* had a magnetic influence on young filmmakers. Many are influenced but few are chosen: Alejandro Gonzalez Inarritu, making his feature debut, borrows what he can use but is an original, dynamic director.

His title translates as *Love's a Bitch,* and all three of his stories involve dogs who become as important as the human characters. The film opens with a disclaimer promising that no animals were harmed in the making of the film. That notice usually appears at the ends of films, but putting it first in *Amores Perros* is wise, since the first sequence involves dog fights and all three will be painful for soft-hearted animal lovers to sit through. Be warned.

"Octavio and Susana," the first segment, begins with cars hurtling through city streets in a chase and gunfight. The images are so quick and confused, at first we don't realize the bleeding body in the backseat belongs to a dog. This is Cofi, the beloved fighting animal of Octavio (Gael Garcia Bernal), a poor young man who is helplessly in love with Susana (Vanessa Bauche), the teenage bride of his ominous brother, Ramiro (Marco Perez). Flashbacks show how Cofi was shot after killing a champion dog; now the chase ends in a spectacular crash in an intersection—a crash that will involve all three of the movie's stories.

In the second segment, "Daniel and Valeria," we meet a television producer (Alvaro Guerrero) who has abandoned his family to live with a beautiful young model and actress (Goya Toledo). He's rented a big new apartment for her; Valeria's image smiles in through a window from a billboard. But then their happiness is marred when Valeria's little dog chases a ball into a hole in the floor, disappears under the floorboards, and won't return. Is it lost, trapped, or frightened? "There are thousands of rats down there," they warn each other.

Then Valeria is involved in the same crash; we see it this time from a different angle, and indeed it comes as a shock every time it occurs. Her leg is severely injured, and one complication leads to another—while the dog still snuffles under the floor, sometimes whining piteously, sometimes ominously silent. This sequence surely owes something to the great Spanish director Luis Buñuel, who made some of his best films in Mexico, and whose *Tristana* starred Catherine Deneuve as a beauty who loses her leg. The segment is sort of dark slapstick—morbid and ironic, as the romance is tested by the beauty's mutilation and by the frustration (known to every pet owner) of a dog that *will not* come when it is called.

From time to time during the first two segments, we've seen a street person, bearded and weathered, accompanied by his own pack of dogs. The third segment, "El Chivo and Maru," stars the famous Mexican actor Emilio Echevarria, who, we learn, is a revolutionary turned squatter, and supports himself by killing for hire. He is approached by a man who wants to get rid of his partner, and is inspired to add his own brutal twist to this murder scheme. The three stories have many links, the most interesting perhaps that El Chivo has rescued the wounded dog Cofi and now cares for it.

Amores Perros at 153 minutes is heavy on story—too heavy, some will say—and rich with character and atmosphere. It is the work of a born filmmaker, and you can sense Inarritu's passion as he plunges into melodrama, coincidence, sensation, and violence. His characters are not the bland, amoral totems of so much modern Hollywood violence, but people with feelings and motives. They want love, money, and revenge. They not only love their dogs but also desperately depend on them. And it is clear that the lower classes are better at survival than the wealthy, whose confidence comes from their possessions, not their mettle.

The movie reminded me not only of Buñuel but also of two other filmmakers identified with Mexico: Arturo Ripstein and Alejandro Jodorowsky. Their works are also comfortable with the scruffy underbelly of society, and involve the dangers when jealousy is not given room to breathe. Consider Jodorowsky's great *Santa Sangre*, in which a cult of women cut off their own arms to honor a martyr. *Amores Perros* will be too much for some filmgoers, just as *Pulp Fiction* was and *Santa Sangre* certainly was, but it contains the spark of inspiration. ☞

Analyze This ★ ★ ★
R, 106 m., 1999

Robert De Niro (Paul Vitti), Billy Crystal (Ben Sobol), Lisa Kudrow (Laura MacNamara), Chazz Palminteri (Primo Sindone), Joe Viterelli (Jelly), Richard Castellano (Jimmy), Molly Shannon (Caroline), Max Casella (Nicky Shivers). Directed by Harold Ramis and produced by Paula Weinstein and Jane Rosenthal. Screenplay by Peter Tolan, Ramis, and Kenneth Lonergan.

"Do you know who I am?" the mobster asks the shrink.
"Yes, I do."
"No, you don't."
"No, I don't."

The psychiatrist is only too happy to please Paul Vitti, the boss of the New York mob. But Vitti is in a vulnerable position: He's lost his nerve, he has panic attacks, he breaks out crying during sentimental TV commercials. If his rivals find out, he's dead.

A comic situation like this depends on casting to elevate it from the environs of sitcom, and *Analyze This* has Robert De Niro and Billy Crystal to bring richness to the characters. Also a large, phlegmatic man named Joe Viterelli, as a bodyguard named Jelly who tries dimly to understand why the most feared criminal in America needs help from this little head doctor.

Analyze This is funny partly because De Niro and Crystal do what we expect them to do, and partly because they don't. De Niro kids his screen image from all those mob movies by Scorsese and others, making the psychiatrist compliments he cannot refuse.

"You're good."

"Well, I . . ."

"No! You're good!"

"I'm good."

Crystal's character, named Ben Sobol, is the kind of guy who figures if he can just keep talking, sooner or later he'll say the right thing. What we don't expect is that the characters take on a certain human dimension, and we care for them a little. This isn't a deeply involving human drama, you understand, but attention is paid to personalities, and the movie isn't all gag lines.

Of course there has to be a Meet Cute to explain how Ben Sobol meets the mob, and it's handled in a funny setup scene where the shrink's car rams the back of a car with an extra passenger in the trunk. The gangsters are only too happy to forget the incident, even though Crystal wants to call the cops; eventually Jelly accepts the psychiatrist's card, and still has it in his pocket when Vitti needs help.

Vitti's archenemy is a mobster named Primo Sindone (Chazz Palminteri), who would strike if he had any suspicion of his rival's weaknesses. That's why utter secrecy is important, and why Sobol is horrified when he discovers his son eavesdropping on their sessions. "You cannot tell a single person!" he shouts at the kid. "You mean," says the kid, "take it off the Internet?" Sobol is a divorced man about to remarry (to Lisa Kudrow), but Jelly comes for him even in the middle of a wedding, and it begins to look to his fiancée's parents as if he's a mobster himself.

Crystal can go over the top when he needs to, but here he wisely restrains his manic side, and gets into a nice rhythm with De Niro's fearful gangster. The movie surrounds them with fairly lively violence (the shrink himself ends up in a shark tank at one point), but a lot of the mob scenes are satires of *The Godfather* and its clones. There's even a dream sequence where the psychiatrist imagines himself being shot in the street in exactly the same way Don Vito Corleone was in the movie, with Vitti too slow to save him. He describes the dream to Vitti. "I was Fredo?" Vitti says. "I don't think so."

The director and cowriter is Harold Ramis, whose work ranges from broad comedy like *Caddyshack* to the fine-tuned observation of *Groundhog Day*. Here he's presented with all sorts of temptations, I suppose, to overplay the De Niro character and turn the movie into an *Airplane!*-type satire of gangster movies. I think he finds the right path—allowing satire, referring to De Niro's screen past, and yet keeping the focus on the strange friendship between two men who speak entirely different languages. (When Sobol explains Freud's theory that some men subconsciously want to kill their fathers and marry their mothers, Vitti's response is to the point: "You ever seen my mother?")

A movie like this will be thought of almost entirely in terms of De Niro and Crystal, with a nod to Palminteri and Kudrow, and yet I think what holds the parts together is the unexpectedly likable character of Jelly. Joe Viterelli makes the bodyguard not just a mobster, not just a tough guy, but an older man who is weary after many years in service, but loyal and patient with his weirdo boss. As Jelly patiently pads about trying to deal with the disturbing news that his boss is cracking up and seeing a shrink, he lends a subtle dimension to the movie; he gives Vitti a context, and someone who understands him. The comedy here isn't all on the surface, and Viterelli is one reason why.

Angela's Ashes ★ ★ ½
R, 145 m., 2000

Emily Watson (Angela), Robert Carlyle (Malachy [Dad]), Michael Legge (Older Frank), Ciaran Owens (Middle Frank), Joe Breen (Young Frank), Ronnie Masterson (Grandma Sheehan), Pauline McLynn (Aunt Aggie), Liam Carney (Uncle Pa Keating), Eanna MacLiam (Uncle Pat), Andrew Bennett (Narrator). Directed by Alan Parker and produced by Parker, Scott Rudin, and David Brown. Screenplay by Parker and Laura Jones, based on the book by Frank McCourt.

Frank McCourt's book *Angela's Ashes* is, like so much of Irish verbal history, suffering recollected in hilarity. I call it verbal history because I know from a friend of his that the stories so unforgettably told in his autobiography were honed over years and decades, at bars and around dinner tables and in the ears of his friends. I could have guessed that anyway, from the easy familiarity you hear in his voice on the audiobook he recorded, the quickening rhythm of humor welling up from the description of grim memories. Some say audiobooks are not "real" books, but in the case of *Angela's Ashes* the sound of the author's voice transforms the material with fondness and nostalgia. McCourt may have had a miserable childhood, but he would not trade it in for another—or at least would not have missed the parts he retells in his memories.

That whole sense of humor is mostly missing from Alan Parker's film version of *Angela's Ashes,* which reminded me of Mark Twain's description of a woman trying to swear: "She knows the words, but not the music." The film is so faithful to the content of the book that it reproduces scenes that have already formed in my imagination. The flooded downstairs in the Limerick home, the wretched family waiting for a father who will never come home with money for eggs and bacon, the joy of flying down the street on a post office bicycle—all of these are just as I pictured them. What is missing is the tone. The movie is narrated by Andrew Bennett, who is no doubt a good actor and blameless here, but what can he do but reproduce the words from the page without Mc-

Court's seasoning of nostalgia? McCourt's voice tells us things he has seen. Bennett's voice tells of things he has heard about.

The result is a movie of great craft and wonderful images, lacking a heart. There must have been thousands of childhoods more or less like Frank McCourt's, and thousands of families with too many children, many of them dying young, while the father drank up dinner down at the pub and the mother threw herself on the mercy of the sniffy local charities. What made McCourt's autobiography special was expressed somehow beneath the very words as he used them: These experiences, wretched as they were, were not wasted on a mere victim, but somehow shaped him into the man capable of writing a fine book about them. There is in *Angela's Ashes* a certain lack of complaint, a sense in which even misery is treasured, as a soldier will describe his worst day of battle with the unspoken subtext: "But I survived, and I love to tell the story, because it is the most interesting thing that has ever happened to me."

The movie stars Emily Watson and Robert Carlyle as Angela and Malachy McCourt, Frank's parents. It is impossible to conceive of better casting of Angela, and although other actors (Tim Roth, Gary Oldman) might have done about as good a job as Carlyle, how much can be done with that poor man who has been made shifty-eyed, lying, and guilty by the drink? We do not even blame him as he leaves his family to starve while he pours their money into the pockets of the manufacturers of Guinness Stout: Clearly, he would not drink if it were at all within his control. But he is powerless over alcoholism, and it has rendered him not a man but simply the focus of the family's bad luck.

What is touching is the way Frank, and soon his younger brother Malachy, treasure those few moments when Dad was too abashed or impoverished to drink, and lavished some attention on them. Consider my favorite sequence, in which the boys' shoes are letting in the rain, and Dad nails tire rubber to the soles. At school, flopping along on their little Michelin snowshoes, they're laughed at by the other kids, until the Christian brother who teaches the class reprimands them all, and points up dramatically to the crucifix on the schoolroom wall: "You don't see our Blessed Savior sportin' shoes!"

It is the "sportin'" that does it, that makes it work, that reveals McCourt's touch. The possibility that the dying Christ would, could, or even desired to "sport" shoes turns the whole sentence and the whole anecdote around, and it becomes not the story of schoolroom humiliation, but a rebuke to those classmates so foolish as to be sportin' shoes themselves. In the mechanics of that episode is the secret of the whole book, and although it comes across well in the film, so many of the similar twists, ironies, and verbal revenges are missed. The film lacks the dark humor with which the Irish like to combine victory with misfortune (as in the story of the man who cleverly fed his horse less and less every day, until "just when he finally had the horse trained to eat nothing—the horse died!").

Frank is played at various ages by Joe Breen (young), Ciaran Owens (middle), and Michael Legge (older). He comes across as determined to make his own way and get out of Limerick and back to New York where he was born, and there are scenes of him picking up spilled coal from the road as a little boy, impressing the brothers with his essay "Jesus and the Weather," getting his first job, falling in love, and coming home drunk the first time ("Jesus!" cries his mother. "It's your father you've become!").

The grim poverty of the lane in Limerick where the family lived for much of the time is convincingly re-created by Parker and production designer Geoffrey Kirkland, although Parker is much too fond of a shot in which Frank and Malachy splash deliberately through every puddle they can find, indoors and out, season after season and year after year. Surely they would eventually learn to keep their feet dry? And although we know from the book that the flooded downstairs was "Ireland" and the dry upstairs was "Italy," was the family so entirely without resources that a plank could not be found to make a bridge from the door to the stairs?

What is wonderful about *Angela's Ashes* is Emily Watson's performance, and the other roles are convincingly cast. She has the kind of bitterness mixed with resignation that was forced on a woman in a country where marriage to a drunk was a life sentence, and it was a greater sin to desert him than to let him starve her children. At one point, Dad leaves to seek work in England, complaining that she has "refused her wifely duties." His husbandly duties, of course, consisted of fathering more children to starve and die, and buying rounds like a big shot down at the pub.

Angel Eyes ★ ★ ★
R, 104 m., 2001

Jennifer Lopez (Sharon), Jim Caviezel (Catch), Terrence Howard (Robby), Sonia Braga (Mrs. Pogue), Jeremy Sisto (Larry), Victor Argo (Mr. Pogue), Shirley Knight (Elanora Davis). Directed by Luis Mandoki and produced by Mark Canton and Elie Samaha. Screenplay by Gerald DiPego.

Jennifer Lopez is the real thing, one of those rare actresses who can win our instinctive sympathy. She demonstrates that in *Angel Eyes*, playing a tough cop who does everything she can to wall out the world, and yet always seems worthy of trust and care. The film's story involves the cop's skittish, arm's-length relationship with a man named Catch (Jim Caviezel), whose walls are higher than her own.

Who is this Catch, anyway? He walks the streets in a long overcoat, head down, lonely, depressed, looking like one of the angels in *Wings of Desire*. Once a week he brings groceries to a shut-in named Nora (Shirley Knight). The first time he sees Sharon, the Lopez character, he stops and stares at her through a restaurant window—not with lust or curiosity, but as if he's trying to repair some lost connection.

Lopez constructs Sharon, not out of spare parts from old cop movies, but in specific terms. She is a good cop from a technical point of view—firm, confident, brave. She wants to do well and punish evil, and only gradually do we learn that her orientation toward this career may have been formed early, when she called the cops on her abusive father (Victor Argo) as he beat up her mother (Sonia Braga). Her father has disowned her for that, her brother is still mad about it, and even her mother defends the man. He never did it again, after all, she argues, to which Sharon replies that perhaps he would have if she hadn't acted. Fighting other lawbreakers may be her way of proving she was right in the first place.

The movie, directed by Luis Mandoki, has intriguing opening scenes. Is this a thriller? A supernatural movie? Who do the angel eyes belong to? An angel? Or does Catch only come on like a guardian angel, while reserving secrets of his own? We are still asking these questions during a stretch of the film where Sharon is staring at a gun in her face, and her life is saved by . . . Catch.

They talk. It is like a verbal chess game. Catch doesn't simply answer questions, he parries them; his responses redefine the conversation, as an unexpected move changes the logic on the board. She invites him home. He pokes through drawers. She likes him. She begins to kiss him. He doesn't want to be kissed. They settle into a cat-and-mouse rhythm in which one and then the other flees, and one and then the other pursues. She follows him to his apartment. It is empty except for a futon. "This is it," he says. "I live here. I walk around town. That's it, except for how I feel about you."

But how does he feel about her? *Angel Eyes* is a complex, evasive romance, involving two people who both want to be inaccessible. It's intriguing to see their dance of attraction and retreat. Meanwhile, secrets about both their family situations emerge; credit the screenwriter, Gerald DiPego, for not resolving the standoff with the father with an easy payoff.

There are lots of movies about cops because their lives lend themselves to excitement in a movie plot. They get involved with bad guys. They see action. They spend a lot of time drinking coffee in diners because a booth in a diner provides an ideal rationale for a face-to-face two-shot that doesn't look awkward or violate body language. For these and other reasons *Angel Eyes* is a cop movie, but its real story doesn't involve the police; it involves damaged lives and the possibility that love can heal.

Jim Caviezel, who has been in movies for ten years, emerged in *The Thin Red Line* (1998) and then played Dennis Quaid's son in *Frequency*—the one who contacts his father with a radio signal that travels back in time. Here he has an elusive, dreamy quality, using passivity as a mask for sharp, deep emotions. Since he ap-

parently has no desire to meet anyone, why is he so attracted to Sharon? The answer has been waiting for us since the opening scene.

Lopez has a hard assignment here, remaining plausible in action scenes and touchy, slippery dialogue scenes. She and Caviezel play tricky notes, and so do the other actors, especially Victor Argo as a stubborn, hard man and Sonia Braga as his conflicted wife. The screenplay doesn't let them off the hook. And notice what simplicity and conviction the veteran Shirley Knight brings to her role, never straining for an effect, never punching up false emotions, embodying acceptance. This is a surprisingly effective film.

Note: Because Angel Eyes *steps so surely for so long, I suspect the movie's very last seconds were dictated over the director's dead body. The movie arrives at exactly the right note at the end, and then the sound track bursts prematurely into David Gray singing "Sail Away With Me Honey" and shatters the mood. I know Hollywood believes every audience must be patronized with an upbeat ending, but this movie has earned its final silence, and deserves it. Couldn't the screen have at least decently faded to black before the jarring music crashes in?*

Anna and the King ★ ★
PG-13, 149 m., 1999

Jodie Foster (Anna), Chow Yun-Fat (King Mongkut), Bai Ling (Tuptim), Tom Felton (Louis), Syed Alwi (The Kralahome), Randall Duk Kim (General Alak), Lim Kay Siu (Prince Chowfa), Melissa Campbell (Princess Fa-Ying). Directed by Andy Tennant and produced by Lawrence Bender and Ed Elbert. Screenplay by Steve Meerson and Peter Krikes, based on the diaries of Anna Leonowens.

King Mongkut of Siam and Anna Leonowens, the English schoolmarm who tries to civilize him, make up one of the most dubious odd couples in pop culture. Here is a man with twenty-three wives and forty-two concubines, who allows one of his women and her lover to be put to death for exchanging a letter, and yet is seen as basically a good-hearted chap. And here is Anna, who spends her days in flirtation with the king, but won't sleep with him because—well, because he isn't white, I guess.

Certainly not because he has countless other wives and is a murderer.

Why is she so attracted to the king in the first place? Henry Kissinger has helpfully explained that power is the ultimate aphrodisiac, and Mongkut has it—in Siam, anyway. Why is he attracted to her? Because she stands up to him and even tells him off. Inside every sadist is a masochist, cringing to taste his own medicine.

The unwholesome undercurrents of the story of Anna and the King of Siam have nagged at me for years, through many ordeals of sitting through the stage and screen versions of *The King and I*, which is surely the most cheerless of Rodgers and Hammerstein's musicals. The story is not intended to be thought about. It is an exotic, escapist entertainment for matinee ladies, who can fantasize about sex with that intriguing bald monster, and indulge their harem fantasies. There is no reason for any man to ever see the play.

Now here is a straight dramatic version of the material, named *Anna and the King,* and starring Jodie Foster opposite the Hong Kong action star Chow Yun-Fat. It is long and mostly told in the same flat monotone, but has one enormous advantage over the musical: It does not contain "I Whistle a Happy Tune." The screenplay has other wise improvements on the source material. The king, for example, says "and so on and so on" only once, and "et cetera" not at all. And there is only one occasion when he tells Anna her head cannot be higher than his. Productions of the musical belabor this last point so painfully they should be staged in front of one of those police line-ups with feet and inches marked on it.

Jodie Foster's performance projects a strange aura. Here is an actress meant to play a woman who is in love, and she seems subtly uncomfortable with that fate. I think I know why. Foster is not only a wonderful actor but an intelligent one—one of our smartest. There are few things harder for actors to do than play beneath their intelligence. Oh, they can play dumb people who are supposed to be dumb. But it is almost impossible to play a dumb person who is supposed to be smart, and that's what she has to do as Anna.

She arrives in Siam, a widow with a young boy, and finds herself in the realm of this egotistical sexual monster with a palace full of women. Yes, he is charming; Hitler is said to have been charming, and so, of course, was Hannibal Lecter. She must try to educate the king's children (sixty-eight, I think I heard) and at the same time civilize him by the British standards of the time, which were racist, imperialist, and jingoistic, but frowned on such Siamese practices as chaining women for weeks outside the palace gates.

By the end of the movie, she has danced with the king a couple of times, come tantalizingly close to kissing him, and civilized him a little, although he has not sold off his concubines. She now has memories that she can write in her journal for Rodgers and Hammerstein to plunder on Broadway, which never tires of romance novels set to music.

Foster, I believe, sees right through this material and out the other side, and doesn't believe in a bit of it. At times we aren't looking at a nineteenth-century schoolmarm, but a modern woman biting her tongue. Chow Yun-Fat is good enough as the king, and certainly less self-satisfied than Yul Brynner. There is a touching role for Bai Ling, as Tuptim, the beautiful girl who is given to the king as a bribe by her venal father, a tea merchant. She loves another, and that is fatal for them both. There is also the usual nonsense about the plot against the throne, which here causes Anna, the king, and the court to make an elaborate journey by elephant so that the king can pull off a military trick I doubt would be convincing even in a Looney Tune.

Credits at the end tell us Mongkut and his son, educated by Anna, led their country into the twentieth century, established democracy (up to a point), and so on. No mention is made of Bangkok's role as a world center of sex tourism, which also, of course, carries on traditions established by the good king.

The Anniversary Party ★ ★ ★
R, 115 m., 2001

Alan Cumming (Joe Therrian), Jennifer Jason Leigh (Sally Therrian), Gwyneth Paltrow (Skye Davidson), John Benjamin Hickey (Jerry Adams), Parker Posey (Judy Adams), Kevin Kline (Cal Gold), Jennifer Beals (Gina Taylor), Phoebe Cates (Sophia Gold), Jane Adams (Clair Forsyth), John C. Reilly (Mac Forsyth), Mina

Badie (Monica Rose), Denis O'Hare (Ryan Rose), Michael Panes (Levi Panes). Directed by Alan Cumming and Jennifer Jason Leigh and produced by Cumming, Leigh, and Joanne Sellar. Screenplay by Cumming and Leigh.

The Anniversary Party is a long night's journey into day with a group of Hollywood types— actors, directors, photographers, agents—and a couple of neighbors who are invited over. The occasion is a get-back-together party for Joe and Sally Therrian (Alan Cumming and Jennifer Jason Leigh), he a writer-director, she an actress who hears time's winged chariot drawing near. It's their sixth anniversary, although they've lived apart for most of the past year; the issues between them involve his infidelity, sometime bisexuality and drug use, and his decision not to cast his wife in a role obviously inspired by her. He believes that, in her late thirties, she's too old to play herself. (I am reminded of Margaret Cho's documentary *I'm the One That I Want,* where she describes the CBS sitcom producer who told her she was too fat to play herself, and should be a little less Chinese-y.)

This is not an original idea for a movie. I can think of a dozen movies about all-night parties at which painful truths are revealed. What makes *The Anniversary Party* intriguing is how close it cuts to the bone of reality—how we're teased to draw parallels between some of the characters and the actors who play them. Cumming is not a stranger to sexual ambiguity, Leigh is indeed in her thirties (although, unlike her character, at the top of her form), and look at some of the others.

Kevin Kline plays an actor who is no longer the first choice to play romantic leading men. Phoebe Cates, his real-life wife, plays an actress who has retired from acting to be a mother and wife. Gwyneth Paltrow plays the rising young star who gets multimillion-dollar paychecks, and has been cast in Joe's new movie. Other stars play recognizable types. Jennifer Beals is a savvy photographer who once slept with Joe. John Benjamin Hickey is the couple's business manager, and Parker Posey is his motormouth wife. Michael Panes plays Levi Panes (no coincidence, I assume), Sally's best pal and court jester. John C. Reilly is the director who desperately needs a hit, and is troubled because Sally is sleepwalking through her role in his new movie. Jane Adams is his neurotic, anorexic wife, in the throes of postpartum depression; she looks typecast, until you see her as a robust country schoolteacher in *Songcatcher,* and realize it's just acting. The next-door neighbors, happy to be invited to a party with so many stars, are played by Denis O'Hare and Mina Badie.

In the earlier days of this genre, the characters got drunk in order to blurt out what they were really thinking (see such examples as *Long Day's Journey Into Night* and *The Boys in the Band*). The truth serum this time is the drug ecstasy, brought along by the Paltrow character and inspiring an orgy of truth-telling, sexual cheating, and other reasons they're going to hate themselves in the morning. The movie doesn't use the drug simply as a story element, but knows it is dangerous and weaves it into a subtle thread of material about addiction and recovery; unless you watch carefully, you may miss the alcoholic who chooses this night to have a relapse.

The appeal of the film is largely voyeuristic. We learn nothing we don't already more or less know, but the material is covered with such authenticity and unforced, natural conviction that it plays like a privileged glimpse into the sad lives of the rich and famous. We're like the neighbors who are invited. Jennifer Jason Leigh and Alan Cumming cowrote and codirected, and are confident professionals who don't indulge their material or themselves. This isn't a confessional home movie, but a cool and intelligent look at a lifestyle where smart people are required to lead their lives according to dumb rules.

The movie was shot with a digital camera. Yes, you can tell. (Critics who say it looks as good as film are like friends who claim you don't look a day older.) It doesn't have the richness and saturation of film, but on the other hand, it does capture a spontaneity that might have been lost during long setups for lighting and camera (the shooting schedule was only four weeks). There are perfect uses for digital, and a movie like this is one of them. Leigh and Cumming and their cinematographer, the veteran John Bailey, wisely prefer the discipline of classic cinematography to the dizziness of handheld, and treat their little camera as if it were a big one. (Every digital camera should come with a warning label: "Just because you can move this around a lot doesn't mean you have to.")

I mentioned that some of the actors seem to be playing themselves. It might be more correct to say they are playing characters who we think of as being like themselves. Paltrow, for example, is not a mock-humble diva, but a smart pro who grew up in the industry and probably eavesdropped on parties like this from the top of the stairs. The tone we get from the whole movie reflects that knowingness: Being invited to a party like this (and leading these lives) is not the gold at the end of the rainbow, but what you get instead of the rainbow.

Another Day in Paradise ★ ★ ★
R, 101 m., 1999

James Woods (Mel), Melanie Griffith (Sid), Vincent Kartheiser (Bobbie), Natasha Gregson Wagner (Rosie), James Otis (Reverend), Branden Williams (Danny), Brent Briscoe (Clem), Peter Sarsgaard (Ty), Lou Diamond Phillips (Gangster). Directed by Larry Clark and produced by Stephen Chin, Clark, and James Woods. Screenplay by Christopher Landon and Chin, based on the book by Eddie Little.

Another Day in Paradise is a lowlife, sleazeball, drugs-and-blood road movie, which means its basic materials will be familiar to audiences of the post–*Easy Rider* decades. There's not much new here, but then there's so rarely something new at the movies that we're sometimes grateful to see the familiar done well.

What brings the movie its special quality is the work of James Woods and Melanie Griffith and their mirror images, played by Vincent Kartheiser and Natasha Gregson Wagner. Woods and Griffith play types they've played before, but with a zest and style that brings the movie alive—especially in the earlier scenes, before everything gets clouded by doom. Woods plays Uncle Mel, who describes himself: "I'm just a junkie and a real good thief. Kind of go together." Griffith is his woman, Sid. They met because he was her drug dealer.

The movie opens with the younger couple, Bobbie and Rosie (Kartheiser and Wagner). He breaks into a junior college to burgle a vending machine, gets in a struggle with a security guard, is badly wounded, and stabs the guard to death. Soon he's being treated by Uncle Mel. "Are you a doctor?" he asks. "Yeah, sure. I'm a doctor shooting you up with heroin," says Mel sarcastically.

As Bobbie recovers, Mel spins visions of the four of them as a family, setting out on a glorious adventure on the road. He's a spieler, a fast-talking spinner of visions, and Sid backs him up with warmth and encouragement. As a sample of the paradise ahead, she takes them on a shopping spree and then to a nightclub (where the kids get drunk and have to be hauled home by the grown-ups).

We know the good times can't last. Mel needs money too badly because he needs drugs— and because he needs drugs, he's willing to get money in dangerous ways. Soon Bobbie has learned about concealing himself in crawl spaces, and Mel is masterminding a particularly inept crime. The arc of the story is preordained: Early glorious scenes of freedom on the road, followed by lowering clouds, gathering omens, and the closing net of fate.

They do a lot of drugs in the movie. There are five scenes of shooting up and one of snorting, according to the invaluable "Screen It" Website (which helpfully adds that the f-word is used "at least" 291 times). The writer-director is Larry Clark, whose *Kids* (1995) told the harrowing story of young street teenagers in Manhattan, playing with sex and drugs as if they were harmless toys. Clark is drawn to decadence and marginal lifestyles, and he finds special interest in the tension generated by kids in danger.

In Kartheiser and Wagner, he finds performers in the tradition of Juliette Lewis and Brad Pitt in *Kalifornia* (1993) or, indeed, Martin Sheen and Sissy Spacek all those years ago in *Badlands* (1973). The underlying story structure is from *Bonnie and Clyde*, which itself was inspired by earlier road movies. The road and crime and doom seem to fit together easily in the movies.

If there are no new insights in *Another Day in Paradise*, at least there are old arias powerfully sung. James Woods and Melanie Griffith enjoy the possibilities of their characters—they enjoy the supercharged scenes of speed, fear, fantasy, and crime. Woods has played variations on this character many times (how many times have we seen him driving a car, smoking, and talking like a demented con man?). Griffith is like the last rose of summer: still fragrant, but you can see her energy running out, until finally it is more important for her to escape Uncle Mel than to have access to his drugs.

A movie like this reminds me of what movie stars are for. We see them many times in many movies over a period of years, and grow used to their cadences and their range. We invest in them. Those that we like, we follow. James Woods is almost always interesting and often much more than that. Melanie Griffith has qualities that are right for the role she plays here. The kids, Kartheiser and Wagner, are talented but new. It's a sign that you're a movie lover and not just a fan when you start preferring the fine older vintages to the flavors of the month.

AntiTrust ★ ★
PG-13, 108 m., 2001

Ryan Phillippe (Milo Hoffman), Tim Robbins (Gary Winston), Rachael Leigh Cook (Lisa Calighan), Claire Forlani (Alice Poulson), Yee Jee Tso (Teddy Chin), Tygh Runyan (Larry Banks), Ned Bellamy (Phil Grimes), Douglas McFerran (Bob Shrot), Zahf Hajee (Desi). Directed by Peter Howitt and produced by Keith Addis, David Nicksay, and Nick Wechsler. Screenplay by Howard Franklin.

They might have been able to make a nice little thriller out of *AntiTrust*, if they'd kept one eye on the Goofy Meter. Just when the movie is cooking, the needle tilts over into Too Goofy and breaks the spell. What are we to make of a brainy nerd hero who fears his girlfriend is trying to kill him by adding sesame seeds to the Chinese food, and administers himself a quick allergy test at a romantic dinner by scratching himself with a fork and rubbing on some of the brown sauce? Too goofy.

The movie uses a thinly disguised fictional version of Bill Gates as its hero—so thinly, I'm surprised they didn't protect against libel by having the villain wear a name tag saying, "Hi! I'm not Bill!" This billionaire software mogul, named Gary Winston, is played by Tim Robbins as a man of charm, power, and paranoia.

"Anybody working in a garage can put us out of business," he frets, and he's right. Cut to a garage occupied by Milo Hoffman (Ryan Phillippe) and his best buddy, Teddy Chin (Yee Jee Tso), who are on the edge of a revolutionary communications breakthrough.

Winston's company, which seems a *whole* lot like Microsoft, is working toward the same goal. In fact, Winston claims his new Synapse global communications system will, and I quote, "link every communications device on the planet." Too goofy. In order to discourage his competitors, Winston has announced a release date for his new software while it is still being written (details like this are why the company seems a whole lot like Microsoft).

He needs a software breakthrough, and he thinks Milo and Teddy can provide it. He invites them up for a tour of his company's campus in the Pacific Northwest. Teddy declines: He hates the megacorp and believes code should be freely distributed. Milo accepts, and before he goes is visited by an agent from the (pre-Bush) Department of Justice (Richard Roundtree), who is preparing an antitrust case against Winston. "If you see something up there that hits you the wrong way, do the right thing," the agent says, offering Milo, who stands on the brink of untold millions, a salary much higher than you can earn at McDonald's.

Milo takes the junket to the software campus, and is shown around by cool young software dudes and a sexy software babe named Lisa (Rachel Leigh Cook), whose vibes suggest she likes him. Then he gets a tour of Winston's palatial high-tech lakeside home, which even includes computers that sense when you're in a room and play your favorite music while displaying your favorite art on the digital wall screens. "Bill Gates has a system like this," says Milo, just as we were thinking the exact same words. "Bill who?" says Winston. "His is primitive."

Milo decides to go to work for the megacorp, and is flattered by all the personal attention he gets from Winston, a friendly charmer who has a habit of dropping around even in the middle of the night. At one point when Milo is stuck, Winston hands him a disk with some code on it that "might help," just as a TV set in the background is reporting a news story about the death of a gifted software programmer. Hmmm.

Milo's girlfriend from his garage days was the loyal and steadfast Alice Poulson (Claire Forlani), who comes to visit and smells a rat in Lisa. And sure enough the little software vixen gets her talons in Milo and begins to seduce him away from Alice, although if Milo were not such a nerd and had seen a few thrillers in between programming worldwide communications, he would be able to predict her secret agenda as easily as we can.

There's a moment in the movie you should savor, if you see it. Teddy continues to work back in the garage, and has a breakthrough he summarizes as, "It's not in the box. It's in the band." Soon after, Teddy is beaten senseless in what is disguised as a racist attack. Soon after that, Winston tells Milo: "It's not in the box. It's in the band." Milo's delusions collapse as he realizes Winston will kill for code, and to eliminate the competition. This is a realization we have long since arrived at, but for Winston it is earth-shattering, as we can see because the movie's editing goes into hyperdrive. There's a berserk montage of remembered dialogue, jagged images, tiling cameras, echo chamber effects, everything but a woo-woo-woo alarm horn. Too goofy. In Ingmar Bergman's *Persona,* when one character realizes the other one isn't nice, the film itself seems to break. In *AntiTrust* it's like the projector explodes.

The movie then degenerates into fairly conventional thriller material, like chases, deadly stalkings through dark interior spaces, desperate sesame-seed allergy tests, and so on. At the end we are left with an argument that software code should not be copyrighted because "human knowledge belongs to the world." Stirring sentiments, although it is unlikely that a free digital version of this movie will be posted on the Net anytime soon.

Any Given Sunday ★ ★ ★

R, 170 m., 1999

Al Pacino (Tony D'Amato), Cameron Diaz (Christina Pagniacci), Dennis Quaid (Jack "Cap" Rooney), James Woods (Dr. Harvey Mandrake), Jamie Foxx (Willie Beamen), LL Cool J (Julian Washington), Matthew Modine (Dr. Oliver Powers), Charlton Heston (The Commissioner), Ann-Margret (Margaret Pagniacci), Lawrence Taylor (Shark), Lauren Holly (Cindy Rooney). Directed by Oliver Stone and produced by Lauren Shuler Donner, Clayton Townsend, and Dan Halsted. Screenplay by Stone, John Logan, and Daniel Pyne.

Oliver Stone's *Any Given Sunday* is a smart sports movie almost swamped by production overkill. The movie alternates sharp and observant dramatic scenes with MTV-style montages and incomprehensible sports footage. It's a miracle the underlying story survives, but it does.

The story's expose of pro football will not come as news to anyone who follows the game. We learn that veteran quarterbacks sometimes doubt themselves, that injured players take risks to keep playing, that team doctors let them, that overnight stardom can turn a green kid into a jerk, that ESPN personalities are self-promoters, that owners' wives drink, that their daughters think they know all about football, and that coaches practice quiet wisdom in the midst of despair. We are also reminded that all big games are settled with a crucial play in the closing seconds.

These insights are not startling, but Stone and his actors give them a human face, and the film's dialogue scenes are effective. Al Pacino, comfortable and convincing as Tony D'Amato, a raspy-voiced curmudgeon, tries to coach the Miami Sharks past a losing streak and into the play-offs, and the movie surrounds him with first-rate performances. We're reminded that very little movie material is original until actors transform it from clichés into particulars.

Jamie Foxx joins Pacino in most of the heavy lifting as Willie Beamen, a third-string quarterback in a game where the two guys above him have been carried off on stretchers. He's so nervous he throws up in the huddle ("That's a first," D'Amato observes), but then catches fire and becomes an overnight sensation. In a broken-field role that requires him to be unsure and vulnerable, then cocky and insufferable, then political, then repentant, Foxx doesn't step wrong.

The team's original owner was a sports legend who had a handshake deal with D'Amato, but with the owner's death, control has passed to his daughter (Cameron Diaz), whose mother (Ann-Margret) is never far from a martini.

These two characters are written as women who will never really be accepted in a man's game. The mother knows it, but her daughter still doesn't. Diaz hopes to get rich by moving the franchise; her mother has kept the world of pro football under close observation for many years, and not found much to inspire her.

Dennis Quaid plays the veteran quarterback whose injury sets the plot into motion—and he, too, is seen in an unexpected light, as an on-field leader privately haunted by insecurity. There's a stunning moment when he considers retirement and is slapped by his wife (Lauren Holly), who won't hear of it; he complains, "Ever since college people have been telling me what to do."

Even at 170 minutes, *Any Given Sunday* barely manages to find room for some of its large cast. James Woods and Matthew Modine clash as team doctors with different attitudes toward life-threatening conditions, and pro veteran Lawrence Taylor has a strong supporting role as a player who wants to keep playing long enough to earn his bonus, even at the risk of his life. And there are lots of other familiar faces: Charlton Heston, Aaron Ekhardt, Edward Burns, Bill Bellamy, Jim Brown, LL Cool J, John C. McGinley, Lela Rochon, even Johnny Unitas as an opposing coach.

The reason they aren't better developed is that so much of the film's running time is lost to smoke and mirrors. There isn't really a single sequence of sports action in which the strategy of a play can be observed and understood from beginning to end. Instead, Stone uses fancy editing on montage close-ups of colorful uniforms and violent action, with lots of crunching sound effects. Or he tilts his camera up to a football pass, spinning against the sky. This is razzle-dazzle in the editing; we don't get the feeling we're seeing a real game involving these characters.

There's a lot of music, though, and even a fairly unconvincing MTV music video for Jamie Foxx to star in. It's as if Stone wanted to pump up the volume to conceal the lack of on-field substance. In his films like *JFK* and *Nixon,* there was a feeling of urgent need to get everything in; we felt he had lots more to tell us, and would if he could. *Any Given Sunday* feels stretched out, as if the story needed window dressing. It's like the second unit came back with lots of full-frame shots of anonymous football players plowing into each other in close-up, and Stone and his editors thought they could use that to mask their lack of substantial, strategic, comprehensible sports action footage. Adding to the distraction is the fact that the outcome of every single play matches the dramatic needs of the script.

It's a close call here. I guess I recommend the movie because the dramatic scenes are worth it. Pacino, Quaid, and Foxx have some nice moments together, and the psychology of the veteran coach is nicely captured in the screenplay by Stone, John Logan, and Daniel Pyne. But if some studio executive came along and made Stone cut his movie down to two hours, I have the strangest feeling it wouldn't lose much of substance, and might even play better.

Anywhere But Here ★ ★ ★
PG-13, 114 m., 1999

Susan Sarandon (Adele August), Natalie Portman (Ann August), Shawn Hatosy (Cousin Benny), Eileen Ryan (Lillian), Corbin Allred (Peter), Caroline Aaron (Realtor), Ray Baker (Ted [Stepfather]), Hart Bochner (Josh Spritzer), Michael Milhoan (Cop). Directed by Wayne Wang and produced by Laurence Mark. Screenplay by Alvin Sargent, based on the novel by Mona Simpson.

Wayne Wang's *Anywhere But Here* is about a frustrated mother who believes she is rotting away in a small Wisconsin town. She buys a used Mercedes, shoves her teenage daughter inside, and drives them cross-country to Beverly Hills, where she will put her M.A. in early education to work, and her daughter will go to auditions and be discovered by the movies.

That is the plan, anyway. Her daughter, who has not been consulted, is angry and resentful at being yanked away from the family she loves, and doesn't share her mother's social-climbing obsessions (their first apartment isn't in "the posh part of Beverly Hills, but it's in the school district").

The affordable streets they live on reminded me of *The Slums of Beverly Hills,* the 1998 movie where jobless Alan Arkin steers his kids into the same school system, but *Anywhere But Here* isn't a rip-off of the earlier movie—it's more as if the mom saw it, and made up her mind to try the same thing. (For that matter, it's based on Mona Simpson's 1987 novel, so the inspiration may have traveled the other way.)

The mother is Adele August (Susan Sarandon), sexy, wildly optimistic, consumed by her visions. Her daughter Ann (Natalie Portman) is a serious kid, smart and observant, who is tired of her mom's sudden inspirations. I think there's a possibility that Adele is manic, but the movie doesn't go that route, preferring to see her as a dreamer who needs to grow up.

Adele is right and wrong about the small town. Wrong to leave the way she does, because going away to college might have provided a saner transition for her daughter. Right that her second husband, Ted, Ann's stepfather, "will always be an ice-skating instructor," and Ann's fate is not to be "a nothing girl in a nothing factory in a nothing town." Adele waited too long to make her own move, and doesn't want Ann to make the same mistake. Well, parents have been living through their children since the dawn of time.

Beverly Hills is a challenge to the two of them. Ann gets along fairly well at school, but her mother is insecure behind her brassy facade, and afraid to go to the posh holiday party she moved to California so they could be invited to. She deceives herself about one-night stands, like a pickup by Dr. Josh Spritzer (Hart Bochner), who is "more than just a dentist. He's writing a screenplay." Ann has seen enough of romance to be wary of it, even though she attracts the attention of a nice kid named Peter (Corbin Allred), who quotes T. S. Eliot's *Four Quartets* while jogging—always a good sign.

The movie's interest is not in the plot, which is episodic and "colorful," but in the performances. Sarandon bravely makes Adele into a person who is borderline insufferable. This isn't Auntie Mame, but someone with deep conflicts and inappropriate ways of addressing them. And Ann is complex too. The movie is narrated in her voice ("Mother made an amazing amount of noise when she ate, like she was trying to take on the whole world"), and her drift seems to be that her mother did the right thing in the wrong way for the wrong reason. (When a family tragedy brings them back to Wisconsin, "the streets weren't as wide, the trees seemed lower, the houses smaller.")

Sarandon's role is trickier and more difficult, but Portman gets your attention. Her big career break was in *The Phantom Menace,* where she played young Queen Amidala, but her talent first glowed in *Beautiful Girls* (1996), where she was just on the other side of the puberty line, and vibrated with . . . well, kindness and beauty, I'd say. In *Anywhere But Here,* she gets yanked along by her out-of-control mother, and her best scenes are when she fights back, not emotionally, but with incisive observations.

The screenplay is by Alvin Sargent, who is gifted with stories of troubled kids *(The Sterile Cuckoo, Ordinary People).* Here he has two good supporting characters: not only the poetry-quoting Peter, but also a cousin named Benny (Shawn Hatosy) back home, who is Ann's best friend and soul mate. These kids, and a richer high school classmate who is not, in fact, a snob, give the movie a reality; we sense teenagers trying to construct rational lives from the wreckage strewn by their parents.

Arlington Road ★ ★
R, 117 m., 1999

Jeff Bridges (Michael Faraday), Tim Robbins (Oliver Lang), Joan Cusack (Cheryl Lang), Hope Davis (Brooke Wolfe), Robert Gossett (FBI Agent Carver), Mason Gamble (Brady Lang), Spencer Treat Clark (Grant Faraday), Stanley Anderson (Dr. Archer Scobee). Directed by Mark Pellington and produced by Peter Samuelson, Tom Gorai, and Marc Samuelson. Screenplay by Ehren Kruger.

Arlington Road is a conspiracy thriller that begins well and makes good points, but it flies off the rails in the last thirty minutes. The climax is so implausible we stop caring and start scratching our heads. Later, thinking back through the film, we realize it's not just the ending that's cuckoo. Given the logic of the ending, the entire film has to be rethought; this is one of those movies where the characters only seem to be living their own lives, when in fact they're strapped to the wheels of a labyrinthine hidden plot.

In the days when movies were made more carefully and were reluctant to insult the intelligence of their viewers, hard questions would have been asked at the screenplay level and rewrites might have made this story more believable. But no. Watching *Arlington Road*, I got the uneasy feeling that the movie was made for (and by) people who live entirely in the moment—who gape at the energy of a scene without ever asking how it connects to what went before or comes after. It's a movie that could play in *Groundhog Day*; it exists in the eternal present.

Jeff Bridges stars as Faraday, a professor of terrorism (no smiles, please), whose late wife was an FBI agent shot dead in a botched raid. Hitchcock would have made him an ordinary guy and exploited the contrast with the weird plot he's trapped in, but making him a professor lets the movie shoehorn in lots of info as he lectures, narrates slide shows, and takes his students on field trips.

Faraday's key academic belief is that big terrorist events are not the work of isolated loners. We see photos of a federal building blown up in St. Louis and hear his doubts about the official theory that it was the work of one man, who acted alone and died in the blast. "We don't want others," he tells his students. "We want one man, and we want him fast—it gives us our security back."

As the film opens, Faraday sees an injured kid wandering down the street. He races him to an emergency room, and later finds he is the son of some folks who have moved in across the street—Oliver and Cheryl Lang (Tim Robbins and Joan Cusack). Faraday and his girlfriend, a graduate student with the wonderful movie name of Brooke Wolfe (Hope Davis), grow friendly with the Langs. But then Faraday, who like all terrorism professors, no doubt, has a streak of paranoia, begins to pick up little signals that the Langs are hiding something.

His investigation into Lang's background is hard to accept, depending as it does on vast coincidences. (After he finds an old newspaper article about Lang on the Internet, he journeys to a library and looks up the same material on old-fashioned microfilm, just so Lang can come up behind him and see what he's looking at.) To be fair, some of the implausibities in this stage of the movie can be explained once the movie is over and we rethink the entire plot.

But leave the plot details aside for a second.

What about the major physical details of the final thriller scenes? How can anyone, even skilled conspirators, predict with perfect accuracy the outcome of a car crash? How can they know in advance that a man will go to a certain pay phone at a certain time so that he can see a particular truck he needs to see? How can the actions of security guards be accurately anticipated? Isn't it risky to hinge an entire plan of action on the hope that the police won't stop a car speeding recklessly through a downtown area?

It's here that the movie completely breaks down. Yes, there's an ironic payoff, and yes, the underlying insights of the movie will make you think. But wasn't there a way to incorporate those insights and these well-drawn, well-acted characters into a movie that didn't force the audience to squirm in disbelief? *Arlington Road* is a thriller that contains ideas. Any movie with ideas is likely to attract audiences who have ideas of their own, but to think for a second about the logic of this plot is fatal.

The Astronaut's Wife ★ ★ ½
R, 110 m., 1999

Johnny Depp (Spencer Armacost), Charlize Theron (Jillian Armacost), Joe Morton (Sherman Reese), Clea Duvall (Nan), Nick Cassavetes (Alex), Tom Noonan (Jackson McLaren). Directed by Rand Ravich and produced by Andrew Lazar. Screenplay by Ravich.

The Astronaut's Wife is a movie so effectively made that it's a shame the story finally isn't worthy of it. It builds suspense with exquisite care, only to release it with more or less exactly what we've been anticipating; it's one of those Peggy Lee movies where we leave the theater humming, "Is that all there is?" And yet the setup is an effective one, and there's a point about halfway through where you're still thinking it's really a pretty good film.

Johnny Depp stars as Spencer Armacost, a U.S. astronaut who's trapped in space outside the space shuttle, along with another crew member, for two agonizing minutes after an explosion. Charlize Theron is his wife, Jillian, who waits with dread on Earth for news: Is he dead or alive? He's alive, it turns out, and after a comatose stay in the hospital, he's released along with Alex, the other crew member (Nick Cassavetes).

But . . . something is wrong. Jillian finds him strangely changed. They've been happy living in Florida, where she teaches the second grade, but suddenly he announces he's taken a high-level executive position with a New York aerospace firm. "You always said you were a flyer," she says. "I'm done up there," he announces, while the score by George S. Clinton coils uneasily beneath the dialogue.

What happened in space to make him so odd? There's a NASA official (Joe Morton) who has a good idea, but the movie is more entertaining while it keeps us in suspense. There are lots of those scenes much beloved of movies set in the world of high finance, where the guests at black-tie charity benefits move easily through vast spaces, holding their champagne glasses, while wives look in concern across the room at their troubled husbands. There's even one of those moments where the husband is seen in distant conversation with the ominous head of the big corporation (Tom Noonan), who of course has a shaved head and looks like a very rich sadist.

Not all of those corporate-suspense scenes end, however, with the husband making urgent love to his wife while they're just out of sight on the balcony—but we somehow know it's not just a sex scene; there's more to it than that, and soon memories of *Rosemary's Baby* begin to coil down there with the music. More of the plot I must not reveal. I will say that the filmmakers do a good job of building us up for a movie with the weight of, say, *Contact*, only to finally give us a payoff more appropriate for one of those Michael Douglas thrillers about selfish adulterers.

Johnny Depp has a thankless role, as a man who must spend most of the movie withholding information and projecting ominous mystery. As the title character, Charlize Theron has more water to carry, and she's . . . well, okay, but remember Kathleen Quinlan as an astronaut's wife in *Apollo 13* and you'll see how the role could have more depth and dimension. Whenever a movie lingers on the details of a gynecological exam ("This will feel cold"), you know the heroine can't trust her husband.

There are a couple of shots in the movie

that are simply wonderful. One comes after Jillian is taken into a large room at NASA headquarters and stands in front of a wall-size TV monitor that shows the pilot's-eye view of the shuttle landing. With gradually tighter framing, cinematographer Allen Daviau makes it look as if Jillian herself is racing toward Earth. I liked that, and I also liked the way a retirement party is given an edge of menace through the manipulation of points of view. But it's rarely effective when a movie resorts to a montage of earlier alarming events just when it should be showing us new ones.

The Astronaut's Wife didn't have good buzz. New Line Cinema, indeed, declined to hold advance critics' screenings—sometimes an ominous sign. In fact the movie is better than its rep; the setup is tantalizing, and if the payoff is a disappointment, it's not a disgrace. Many a worse movie has been previewed for the press. Maybe I felt let down because the earlier scenes led me to expect more. This is the kind of movie you wouldn't want to stop watching halfway through. Three-quarters, maybe.

At First Sight ★ ★
PG-13, 124 m., 1999

Val Kilmer (Virgil Adamson), Mira Sorvino (Amy Benic), Kelly McGillis (Jennie Adamson), Steven Weber (Duncan Allanbrook), Bruce Davison (Dr. Charles Aaron), Nathan Lane (Phil Webster), Ken Howard (Virgil's Father), Laura Kirk (Betsy Ernst). Directed by Irwin Winkler and produced by Winkler and Rob Cowan. Screenplay by Steve Levitt, based on the story "To See and Not See" by Oliver Sacks, M.D.

The Oliver Sacks case study that inspired *At First Sight* tells the story of a man who has grown accustomed to blindness, and then is offered an operation that will restore sight. The moment when the bandages are removed all but cries out to be filmed. But to have sight suddenly thrust upon you can be a dismaying experience. Babies take months or years to develop mind-eye-hand coordination; here is an adult blind person expected to unlearn everything he knows and learn it again, differently.

The most striking moment in *At First Sight* is when the hero is able to see for the first time since he was three. "This isn't right," he says, frightened by the rush of images. "There's something wrong. This can't be seeing!" And then, desperately, "Give me something in my hands," so that he can associate a familiar touch with an unfamiliar sight.

If the movie had trusted the fascination of this scene, it might have really gone somewhere. Unfortunately, its moments of fascination and its good performances are mired in the morass of romance and melodrama that surrounds it. A blind man can see, and *still* he's trapped in a formulaic studio plot.

The buried inspiration for this film, I suspect, is not so much the article by Oliver Sacks as *Awakenings* (1990), another, much better movie based on another report by Sacks. Both films have similar arcs: A handicapped person is freed of the condition that traps him, is able to live a more normal life for a time, and then faces the possibility that the bars will slam shut again. *Charly* (1968), about a retarded man who gains and then loses normal intelligence, is the classic prototype.

In *Awakenings,* Robert De Niro played a man locked inside a rare form of Parkinson's disease. Under treatment by a brilliant doctor (Robin Williams), the disease goes into remission, and the man, who had not been able to speak or move for years, regains normal abilities. He even falls a little in love. Then the regression begins. In *At First Sight,* Val Kilmer plays a blind man who meets and falls in love with a woman (Mira Sorvino). She steers him to a doctor (Bruce Davison) whose surgical techniques may be able to restore his sight.

The woman, Amy, is a New York architect. She's left an unhappy relationship: "For the last five years I have lived with a man with the emotional content of a soap dish." She goes to a small resort town on vacation and sees a man skating all by himself on a forest pond. Later, she hires a massage therapist, who turns out to be the same person, a blind man named Virgil (Kilmer). The moment he touches her, she knows he is not a soap dish. She begins to cry as the tension drains from her.

Virgil knows his way everywhere in town, knows how many steps to take, is friendly with everybody. He is protected by a possessive older sister named Jennie (Kelly McGillis), who sees Amy as a threat: "We're very happy here, Amy. Virgil has everything he needs." But Amy and Virgil take walks, and talk, and make love, and soon Virgil wants to move to New York City, where Amy knows a doctor who may be able to reverse his condition.

The movie is best when it pays close attention to the details of blindness and the realities of the relationship. When the two of them take shelter from the rain in an old building, for example, he is able to sense the space around him by the sound of the rain outside. Some of his dialogue is sweetly ironic; when they meet for a second time, he says, "I was describing you to my dog, and how well you smelled."

All of this is just right, and Kilmer and Sorvino establish a convincing, intimate rapport—a private world in which they communicate easily. But the conventions of studio movies require false melodrama to be injected at every possible juncture, and so the movie manufactures a phony and unconvincing breakup, and throws in Virgil's long-lost father, whose presence is profoundly unnecessary for any reason other than to motivate scenes of soap-opera psychology.

The closing credits tell us the movie is based on the true story of "Shirl and Barbara Jennings, now living in Atlanta." My guess is that their story inspired the scenes that feel authentic, and that countless other movies inspired the rest. Certainly the material would speak for itself, if the screenplay would let it: Every single plot point is carefully recited and explained in the dialogue, lest we miss the significance. Seeing a movie like this, you wonder why the director, Irwin Winkler, didn't have more faith in the intelligence of his audience. The material deserves more than a disease-of-the-week docudrama simplicity.

Note: For a contrast to the simplified melodrama of At First Sight, *see* Hilary and Jackie, *which examines relationships and handicaps in a more challenging and adult way.*

Atlantis: The Lost Empire ★ ★ ★ ½
PG, 95 m., 2001

With the voices of: Michael J. Fox (Milo), James Garner (Rourke), Cree Summer (Princess Kida), Don Novello (Vinny), Phil Morris (Dr. Sweet), Claudia Christian (Helga), Jacqueline Obradors (Audrey), John Mahoney (Preston Whitmore), Corey Burton (Moliere), Jim Varney (Cookie),

Florence Stanley (Mrs. Packard), Leonard Nimoy (King of Atlantis). Directed by Gary Trousdale and Kirk Wise and produced by Don Hahn. Screenplay by Tab Murphy, based on a story by Wise, Trousdale, Joss Whedon, Bryce Zabel, Jackie Zabel, and Murphy.

Disney's *Atlantis: The Lost Empire* is an animated adventure movie with a lot of gusto and a wowser of a climax. It's an experiment for the studio. Leaving behind the song-and-dance numbers and the cute sidekicks, Disney seems to be testing the visual and story style of anime—those action-jammed animated Japanese movies that occupy shelves in every video store, meaning someone must be renting them.

The movie is set in 1914, a favorite period for stories like this, because technology was fairly advanced while people could still believe that a sunken continent or lost world or two might have gone overlooked. Just as the *Jurassic Park* movies owe something (actually, a lot) to Arthur Conan Doyle's *The Lost World*, so does *Atlantis* spring from the old Edgar Rice Burroughs novels about a world in the center of Earth. (There is also discussion on the Web about how it springs even more directly from a 1989 Japanese anime named *Nadia: The Secret of Blue Water*.)

All stories like this require a rich, reclusive billionaire to finance an expedition to the lost corners of Earth, and *Atlantis* has Preston Whitmore (voice by John Mahoney), who lives Citizen Kane–style behind vast iron gates in a mysterious citadel, and puts together a team to go to the bottom of the sea.

Whitmore summons the linguist Milo Thatch (voice by Michael J. Fox) to join the expedition; he knew Milo's grandfather, and trusts an ancient notebook in which the old man perhaps recorded the secret of Atlantis. Milo himself has spent much time trying to convince Smithsonian scientists of the possibility of a sunken continent; he works at the institute—as a janitor.

The diving team, which uses a sub Captain Nemo would have envied, is led by the rough-and-ready Rourke (James Garner) and includes a mixed bag of adventurers, including Vinny the explosives man (Don Novello), who has voluptuous ambitions for blowing up stuff real good; Moliere the Mole (Corey Burton), the digging expert; Rourke's first mate Helga (Claudia Christian), a scheming vamp; Audrey the mechanic (Jacqueline Obradors); Doctor Sweet (Phil Morris); Cookie the cook (the late Jim Varney); and Mrs. Packard (Florence Stanley), who chain-smokes while handling communications.

You will note among this crew no dancing teacups, even though the movie was directed by Gary Trousdale and Kirk Wise, who made the wonderful *Beauty and the Beast* for Disney. Perhaps that's because of the influence of a comic-book artist named Mike Mignola, previously unknown to me but described by my colleague Elvis Mitchell as the creator of an underground comic character named Hellboy; his drawing style may have something to do with the movie's clean, bright, visual look, which doesn't yearn for the 3-D roundness of *Toy Story* or *Shrek*, but embraces the classic energy of the comic-book style. You especially see that in the movie's spectacular closing sequence—but I'm getting ahead of the story.

Atlantis is protected by fearsome robotic sea leviathans, which all but destroy the expedition before Rourke, Milo, and the crew succeed in penetrating a volcano and reaching the ocean floor in their sub, where Milo is befriended by Princess Kida (Cree Summer). The submerged land is ruled by her father the king (Leonard Nimoy), who wants to banish the outsiders, but Kida has eyes for Milo in a subplot owing more than a little to *The Little Mermaid*.

Atlantis itself seems desperately in need of fresh blood—not for population (since the residents are 1,000 years old and going strong) but for new ideas, since the land has fallen into apathy and disrepair. Princess Kida is kind of a reformist, nudging her father to get off his throne and organize some public works projects.

Now about that closing sequence. If you recall the ballroom scene in *Beauty and the Beast*, you will remember the exhilarating way directors Trousdale and Wise liberated their characters not only from gravity but from the usual rules of animation, so that they careered thrillingly through the air. Multiply that several times, and you get the excitement of a final battle that brings to animated life the kind of explosive energy we sense imprisoned in the printed KA-BOOM!s, KERRR-ASSHHHH!es, and THUNK!s of those full-page drawings in action comic books, where superheroes battle for control of the universe.

The story of *Atlantis* is rousing in an old pulp science fiction sort of way, but the climactic scene transcends the rest, and stands by itself as one of the great animated action sequences. Will the movie signal a new direction for Disney animation? I doubt it. The synergy of animated musical comedies is too attractive, not only for entertainment value but also for the way they spin off hit songs and stage shows. What *Atlantis* does show is a willingness to experiment with the anime tradition—maybe to appeal to teenage action fans who might otherwise avoid an animated film. It's like *20,000 Leagues Under the Sea* set free by animation to look the way it dreamed of looking.

Austin Powers: The Spy Who Shagged Me ★ ★ ½
PG-13, 95 m., 1999

Mike Myers (Austin Powers/Dr. Evil), Heather Graham (Felicity Shagwell), Elizabeth Hurley (Vanessa Kensington), Rob Lowe (Young Number Two), Michael York (Basil Exposition), Robert Wagner (Number Two 1999), Seth Green (Scott Evil), Gia Carides (Robin Swallows), Verne Troyer (Mini-Me). Directed by Jay Roach and produced by Suzanne Todd, Jennifer Todd, Demi Moore, and Eric McLeod. Screenplay by Mike Myers and Michael McCullers.

There are some big laughs in *Austin Powers: The Spy Who Shagged Me,* but they're separated by uncertain passages of noodling. You can sense it when comedians know they have dead aim and are zeroing in for the kill. You can also sense it when they don't trust their material. The first *Austin Powers* movie burst with confidence: Mike Myers knew he was onto something. This time, too many scenes end on a flat note, like those *Saturday Night Live* sketches that run out of steam before they end. *SNL* cuts to music or commercials; *Austin Powers* cuts to song-and-dance interludes.

The key to a lot of the humor in the first film was that Austin Powers had been transported lock, stock, and barrel from the sixties to the nineties, where he was a sexist anachro-nism. The other satirical target was the James Bond series. This second film doesn't want to be a satire so much as just zany, raunchy slapstick.

The Spy Who Shagged Me seems to forget that Austin is a man out of his time; there are few laughs based on the fact that he's thirty years past his sell-by date, and there's so much time travel in this movie that half of the time he's back in the sixties again. Even when he's in the nineties, however, the women seem to take him on his own terms. Myers and his collaborators, flush with the victory of the first film, have forgotten that Austin is a misfit and not a hero.

The plot again involves Austin and his arch-enemy, Dr. Evil (both played by Myers). Thirsting for revenge after being exiled into Earth orbit, Evil wants to travel through time to when Powers was cryogenically frozen, and steal his mojo. (In case you were wondering, a beaker of mojo looks like Kool-Aid with licorice ropes floating in it.)

I didn't use a stopwatch, but my guess is that Evil has more screen time than Austin this time. There are several revelations. Early in the movie, in a funny sequence set on *The Jerry Springer Show,* Dr. Evil's son, Scott (Seth Green), appears, complaining that he hates his dad. Later a secret of parentage is revealed, *Star Wars*–style. And Evil acquires a midget double named Mini-Me, played by Verne Troyer and inspired, Myers has said, by the miniature Marlon Brando in *The Island of Dr. Moreau.*

In a film with a lot of babes, Heather Graham plays the lead babe, Felicity Shagwell, a spy dedicated to her craft. In one scene that had the audience cringing when they should have been laughing, she goes to bed with a villain from Scotland named Fat Bastard, who wears a kilt, "weighs a metric ton," and is covered with greasy chicken bits. (Study the end credits for a surprise about the actor playing the F.B.)

There were some laughs (but more groans) during a scene where Austin mistakes a fecal brew for coffee; the movie is going for the kind of gross-out humor that distinguished *There's Something About Mary,* but what this sequence proves is that the grosser a scene is, the funnier it has to be to get away with it. I saw the movie with an audience recruited from the radio audience of Mancow Muller, Chicago's most cheerful vulgarian, and if *they* had a mixed reaction, middle America is likely to flee from the theater.

The movie succeeds, however, in topping one of the best elements in the first film, which was when Austin's private parts were obscured by a series of perfectly timed foreground objects. After Dr. Evil blasts off in a phallic spaceship, characters look up in the sky, see what the ship looks like, and begin sentences that are completed by quick cuts to other dialogue. (If I told you the names of some of the people you'd get the idea, but that wouldn't be fair to the movie.)

There is an underlying likability to Austin Powers that sort of carries us through the movie. He's such a feckless, joyful swinger that we enjoy his delight. Myers brings a kind of bliss to the Bond lifestyle. I also liked Seth Green as Evil's son, not least because he has obviously studied *Ebert's Bigger Little Movie Glossary* and knows all about the Fallacy of the Talking Killer (when Evil gets Powers in his grasp, Evil's son complains, "You never kill him when you have the chance to"). And the movie has fun by addressing the audience directly, as when Austin introduces Burt Bacharach and Elvis Costello, or later observes, during a scene set in the British countryside but shot in the Los Angeles hills, "Funny how England looks in no way like Southern California." Oh, and the tradition of homage to *Beyond the Valley of the Dolls* continues with a bit part for the Russ Meyer superstar Charles Napier.

Note: This film obtained a PG-13 rating—depressing evidence of how comfortable with vulgarity American teenagers are presumed to be. Apparently you can drink shit, just as long as you don't say it.

Autumn Tale ★ ★ ★
PG, 112 m., 1999

Marie Riviere (Isabelle), Beatrice Romand (Magali), Alain Libolt (Gerald), Didier Sandre (Etienne), Alexia Portal (Rosine), Stephane Darmon (Leo), Aurelia Alcais (Emilia), Matthieu Davette (Gregoire), Yves Alcais (Jean-Jacques). Directed by Eric Rohmer and produced by Francoise Etchegaray, Margaret Menegoz, and Rohmer. Screenplay by Rohmer.

It is hard not to fall a little in love with Magali. A woman in her late forties, heedless of makeup, dressed in jeans and a cotton shirt, forever pushing her unruly hair out of her eyes, she runs a vineyard in the Rhone district of southern France. She is a widow with a son and daughter, both grown. She loves her life and the wines she makes, but yes, sometimes she feels lonely. And how will the right man, or any man, find her while she lives in such splendid isolation?

Her friend Isabelle, happily married, takes Magali's plight to heart. One day, in an opening scene that effortlessly establishes the characters and their lives, they walk around Magali's land, talking of the similarities between weeds and flowers, and the aging of wines and women. Isabelle (Marie Riviere) asks Magali (Beatrice Romand) why she doesn't seek a man by placing a personal ad. Magali would rather die. So Isabelle places the ad herself. She will audition the candidates and arrange a meeting between Magali and the chosen man.

There are other characters, in particular young Rosine (Alexia Portal), who is currently the girlfriend of Magali's son, Leo, but used to date an older philosophy professor named Etienne (Didier Sandre). Rosine doesn't take Leo seriously ("He's just a filler"), but adores Magali, and decides to fix her up with Etienne. Without suspecting it, Magali is headed for two possible romantic adventures.

Eric Rohmer's *Autumn Tale*, which tells this story, is the latest in a long, rich series of films by the perceptive French director, who tells stories about people we'd like to know, or be. His movies are about love, chance, life, and coincidence; he creates plots that unfold in a series of delights, surprises, and reversals. When there is a happy ending, it arrives as a relief, even a deliverance, for characters who spend much of the movie on the very edge of missing out on their chances for happiness.

Rohmer, now seventy-nine, was the editor of the famous French film magazine *Cahiers du Cinema* from 1956 to 1963. He was a founding member of the French New Wave, which includes Godard, Truffaut, Resnais, Malle, and Chabrol. He makes his movies in groups. *Six Moral Tales*, which he said was not so much about what people did as what they thought about while they were doing it, included three that made him famous: *My Night at Maud's* (1969), *Claire's Knee* (1971), and *Chloe in the Afternoon* (1972). Then came his *Comedies and Proverbs,* and now his current series, *Tales of the Four Seasons.*

His films are heavily, craftily plotted, and yet wear their plots so easily that we feel we're watching everyday life as it unfolds. Consider the complexities of *Autumn Tale,* as both Isabelle and Rosine maneuver to arrange meetings between Magali and the men they've chosen for her. There are complications and misunderstandings, and Isabelle is almost accused of being unfaithful to her own husband (whom she adores, she says, although we never see him because Rohmer wisely knows he's not needed).

Everything comes together at a virtuoso scene that Rohmer stages at a wedding party. Magali is present, reluctantly, and so are the men, and of course all three misunderstand almost everything that happens. Since we like Gerald (Alain Libolt), the guy who answered the personal ad, and think Etienne is a twerp, we know who we're cheering for, but Rohmer creates quiet suspense by elegantly choreographing the movements at the party—who is seen, and when, and why, and in what context—until finally a smile and a nod of approval are exchanged over a glass of wine, and we feel like cheering. (The approval is of the wine, not the characters, but from it all else will follow.)

Even though I enjoy Hollywood romantic comedies like *Notting Hill,* it's like they wear galoshes compared to the sly wit of a movie like *Autumn Tale.* They stomp squishy-footed through their clockwork plots, while Rohmer elegantly seduces us with people who have all of the alarming unpredictability of life. There's never a doubt that Julia Roberts will live happily ever after. But Magali, now: One wrong step, and she's alone with her vines forever.

B

Baby Boy ★ ★ ★ ½
R, 129 m., 2001

Tyrese Gibson (Jody), Omar Gooding (Sweetpea),
A. J. Johnson (Juanita), Taraji P. Henson (Yvette),
Snoop Dogg (Rodney), Tamara LaSeon Bass
(Peanut), Ving Rhames (Melvin). Directed
and produced by John Singleton. Screenplay
by Singleton.

John Singleton's *Baby Boy* is a bold criticism of young black men who carelessly father babies, live off their mothers, and don't even think of looking for work. It is also a criticism of the society that pushes them into that niche. There has never been a movie with this angle on the African-American experience. The movie's message to men like its hero is: Yes, racism has contributed to your situation— but do you have to give it so much help with your own attitude?

In the opening sequence, we meet Jody (Tyrese Gibson), a twenty-year-old who has children by two women and still lives in his room in his mother's house. He drives his girlfriend Yvette (Taraji P. Henson) home from a clinic where she has just had an abortion. She is understandably sad and in pain, a little dopey from pills. She doesn't want to talk. In that case, says Jody, she won't mind if he borrows her car. He does, and uses it to visit his other girlfriend.

That scene will not come as a shock to Mary A. Mitchell, the *Chicago Sun-Times* columnist who has written a series of sad, angry articles about absentee fathers and "man-sharing" in the black community, where drugs, crime, and prison have created a shortage of eligible men. Her columns are courageous; the African-American community prefers to present a positive front and keep its self-criticism behind closed doors. She takes heat for what she writes. Now Singleton, too, dares to take a hard look at his community. Ten years ago, in *Boyz N the Hood*, he told a brilliant story about young men in a movie made by a young man. Now he returns to the same neighborhood, South Central in Los Angeles. His characters are a little older, and he is older, too, and less forgiving.

Baby Boy doesn't fall back on easy liberal finger-pointing. There are no white people in this movie, no simplistic blaming of others; the adults in Jody's life blame him for his own troubles, and they should. At some point, as Jody's mother, Juanita (A. J. Johnson), tells him again and again, he has to grow up, move out, get a job, and take care of his family.

Jody doesn't even bother to answer, except to accuse her of not loving him. He likes the life he leads, and doesn't consider employment as an option. He sponges off of two women: his mother, and Yvette, who has a job. Also in the picture is Peanut (Tamara Laseon Bass), the mother of his other child. But it's Yvette he loves. Still, he plays around, and she knows it and in a certain way accepts it, although she gets mad when she can never drive her own car, which she's making payments on. She screams that he lies to her, and his answer is a logical masterpiece: "I'm out in these streets telling these ho's the truth. I lie to you because I care about you."

All would be well if Jody could keep on sleeping in his childhood bedroom (where he still builds model cars), eat his mother's cooking, drive Yvette's car, sleep with his women, and hang with his boys—especially his best friend, Sweetpea (Omar Gooding). But Yvette is fed up. Sweetpea is getting involved with dangerous gang types. Yvette's old boyfriend (Snoop Dogg) is out of prison and hanging around. And at home, most disturbingly, his mother has a new boyfriend named Melvin (Ving Rhames), who has no patience with him. Melvin has spent ten years in the slammer, is determined to go straight, has a landscaping business, and moves in and marks his territory. Jody knows things are different when he finds Melvin stark naked in the kitchen, scrambling eggs for Juanita. "I was like you, Jody," he says. "Young, dumb, and out of control."

Juanita herself is a piece of work, a still-youthful woman who loves her backyard garden and tries patiently, over and over, to cut through Jody's martyrdom and evasion. When he complains to her that Yvette has locked him out, she levels: "What would *you* do if Yvette f——— around on you, took your car, and left you in a hot house all day with a baby?" An excellent question. Yvette answers it, in a way, by stealing back her own car, so the "baby boy" is reduced to riding his childhood bicycle around the neighborhood.

When John Singleton burst on the scene with *Boyz N the Hood*, he brought the freshness of direct, everyday experience to movies about black Americans. He was still in his mid-twenties, fresh out of South Central, already a legend for the way, at sixteen, he started hanging around the USC film school—volunteering as a gofer until the dean concluded, "We might as well make him a student, since he acts like he is one anyway." Singleton comes from the same background as his characters, knows them, sees aspects of himself and his friends in them. Like many self-made men, he is impatient with those, like Jody, who do not even try.

He has a gift for finding good actors. *Boyz* was Cuba Gooding Jr.'s first movie. Here we meet Cuba's brother Omar, also gifted. Tyrese Gibson, already known as a singer, model, and music video DJ, is a natural, unaffected actor who adds a spin of spoiled self-pity to Jody. Taraji P. Henson has some of the most difficult scenes as Yvette, who does love her man, but despairs of him, and is tired to the bone of working, child care, and caring, too, for Jody, the twenty-year-old "baby boy." And there is a wonderful rapport between A. J. Johnson and Ving Rhames as the mother and her ex-con boyfriend; they have an exuberant sex life, feel they deserve a second chance at happiness, and have lived long enough and paid enough dues to be impatient with Jody's knack for living off the land.

Baby Boy has a trailer that makes it look like a lot of fun—like a celebration of the lifestyle it attacks. I was reminded of the trailer for *Boyz N the Hood*, which seemed to glorify guns and violence, although the movie deplored them. I asked Singleton about it at the time, and he said, "Maybe some kids will see the trailer and come to see the movie, and leave with a lot of ideas they didn't have before." Maybe so. I have a notion the Yvettes of the world are going to love this movie, and march their Jodys in to see it.

Baby Geniuses ½★
PG, 94 m., 1999

Kathleen Turner (Elena) Christopher Lloyd (Heap), Miko Hughes (voice) (Sly), Kim Cattrall (Robin), Peter MacNicol (Dan), Dom DeLuise (Lenny), Ruby Dee (Margo). Directed by Bob Clark and produced by Steven Paul. Screenplay by Clark and Greg Michael, based on a story by Paul, Francisca Matos, and Robert Grasmere.

Bad films are easy to make, but a film as unpleasant as *Baby Geniuses* achieves a kind of grandeur. And it proves something I've long suspected: Babies are cute only when they're being babies. When they're presented as miniature adults (on greeting cards, in TV commercials, or especially in this movie), there is something so fundamentally *wrong* that our human instincts cry out in protest.

Oh, you can have fun with a baby as a movie character. *Look Who's Talking* (1989) was an entertaining movie in which we heard what the baby was thinking. *Baby's Day Out* (1994), with its fearless baby setting Joe Mantegna's pants on fire, had its defenders. But those at least were allegedly real babies. *Baby Geniuses* is about toddlers who speak, plot, scheme, disco dance, and beat up adults with karate kicks. This is not right.

The plot: Kathleen Turner plays a woman with a theory that babies can talk to each other. She funds a secret underground lab run by Christopher Lloyd to crack the code. Her theory is based on the Tibetan belief that children have Universal Knowledge until they begin to speak—when their memories fade away.

This is an old idea, beautifully expressed by Wordsworth, who said that "heaven lies about us in our infancy." If I could quote the whole poem instead of completing this review, believe me, we'd all be happier. But I press on. The movie involves a genius baby named Sly, who escapes from the lab and tries to organize fellow babies in revolt. The nauseous sight of little Sly on a disco floor, dressed in the white suit from *Saturday Night Fever* and dancing to "Stayin' Alive" had me pawing under my seat for the bag my Subway Gardenburger came in, in case I felt the sudden need to recycle it.

Every time the babies talk to one another, something weird happens to make it look like their lips are in synch (think of talking frogs in TV commercials). And when the babies do things that babies don't do (hurl adults into the air, for example), we lose all track of the story while trying to spot the visual trick.

There's only one way the movie might have worked: If the babies had been really, really smart. After all, according to the theory, they come into this world "trailing clouds of glory" (Wordsworth again: the man can write). They possess Universal Knowledge. Wouldn't you expect them to sound a little like Jesus or Aristotle? Or at least Wayne Dyer? But no. They arrive to this mortal coil (Shakespeare) from that level "higher than the sphery chime" (Milton), and we expect their speech to flow in "heavenly eloquence" (Dryden). But when they open their little mouths, what do they say? "Diaper gravy"—a term used four times in the movie, according to a friend who counted (Cleland).

Yes, they talk like little wise guys, using insipid potty-mouth dialogue based on insult humor. This is still more evidence for my theory that the greatest single influence on modern American culture has been Don Rickles.

Bait ★ ★ ★
R, 110 m., 2000

Jamie Foxx (Alvin Sanders), David Morse (Edgar Clenteen), Doug Hutchison (Bristol), Kimberly Elise (Lisa Hill), David Paymer (Agent Wooly), Mike Epps (Stevie Sanders), Nestor Serrano (Agent Boyle), Jamie Kennedy (Agent Blum). Directed by Antoine Fuqua and produced by Sean Ryerson. Screenplay by Tony Gilroy, Andrew Scheinman, and Adam Scheinman.

Bait is a deadpan action comedy with a little Hitchcock, a little Bond, and a lot of attitude. It's funny and clever, and it grows on you, especially with the tension between Jamie Foxx's trash-talking thief and David Morse's monomaniac federal agent. It's one of those movies where you start out thinking you've seen it all before, and the longer it runs, the less you've seen before. There's even an effective use of the exhausted old Red Digital Readout gambit.

The movie opens with the high-tech robbery of $42 million in bullion from the Federal Gold Reserve in New York. Two guards are executed. The mastermind is Bristol (Doug Hutchison), a genius computer hacker but a poor judge of men, who unwisely entrusts the getaway truck to a slob partner who drives off without him. The feds nab the partner, and he's interrogated by the hard-boiled U.S. agent Clenteen (David Morse). The guy keeps asking for a doctor, but Clenteen doesn't get the message until another agent (David Paymer) comments, "I don't think he's kidding."

The getaway driver is dead. That leaves both the feds and the hacker desperate to find out where the gold is hidden. One man may know: Alvin Sanders (Jamie Foxx) shared the same prison cell with the dead man, and may have learned something. Clenteen devises a diabolical scheme. He will implant Alvin with a miniature audio and tracking chip, allowing agents to eavesdrop on every word and follow every move. He'll be bait to lure Bristol—and then the feds will pounce.

This is all setup for a movie that is funny in an oblique, underplayed sort of way. It's kidding itself but doesn't always admit it. It doesn't go for obvious laughs, like a Martin Lawrence movie might have, but uses Foxx's wisecracking, ad-lib style to create Alvin as a character who gets more complicated the more time we spend with him. In his opening scenes, as Alvin bungles the theft of a shipment of prawns, I was writing "condescending" in my notes: He was coming across as a broad, urban stereotype, not too smart. Then it became clear than Alvin uses his persona as a shield, a weapon of humor to protect and deflect. By the end of the movie, when he sets up his own sting to find out who's following him, we're not surprised.

A lot of the best scenes involve federal agents in a monitoring post, eavesdropping on Alvin's life, his conversations, his problems with his girlfriend (Kimberly Elise), and the trouble his brother (Mike Epps) gets him in. This isn't reality TV but reality radio; the agents start to like Alvin—all except for the hard-edged Clenteen, who was born without a sense of humor. Alvin's brother involves him in a stolen car scam, and the feds panic that their bait will be back in jail before he can catch the fish. They try to control his life without letting him know they exist, arranging for him to come into money—in scenes that Foxx milks for all they're worth.

Hutchison, as Bristol, the computer genius and killer thief, does an effective John Malkovich number. He's calm, until he shrieks; calculated, until he cracks; all business, until he gets involved in a bizarre scheme involving kidnapping, bombs, torture, and a racetrack sequence that owes more than a little to Hitchcock (and something to the Marx Brothers' *A Day at the Races*).

In my review of *The Watcher*, I was complaining about killers who spend more time devising elaborate booby traps for the cops than in committing their crimes. Now I forgive Bristol for the same practice. It's all in how you do it—in the style. And while Keanu Reeves's killer in *The Watcher* seemed interested only in playing mind games with James Spader's FBI man, Bristol, here, has a more realistic motivation—he wants his $42 million.

Some will argue that the climax at the racetrack is preposterous. They will be right. The secret hiding place for the gold also raises a lot of questions—like, how easy would it actually be to put it there? Those are not the kinds of questions that are relevant to a film like this. It's over the top, an exercise in action comedy that cuts loose from logic and enjoys itself. And it's intriguing the way the Foxx character conceals his thinking even from the audience at times—how he is more than he seems, and finds it prudent to keep that fact to himself.

The Ballad of Ramblin' Jack ★ ★ ★
NO MPAA RATING, 112 m., 2000

A documentary directed by Aiyana Elliott and produced by Elliott, Paul Mezey, and Dan Partland. Screenplay by Elliott and Dick Dahl.

Ramblin' Jack Elliott is beloved by those who know him and his work, but because of disputes with record companies, breakups with managers, and his ramblin' ways, not many people do. His importance to the larger music world is as the link between Woody Guthrie and Bob Dylan. He was Guthrie's protégé, was at his bedside during his illness, sang his songs in the Village during the early folk revival, and was imitated by Dylan right down to the harmonica in the neck brace. Arlo Guthrie, who may have a bone to pick, says: "There wouldn't be no Bob Dylan without Ramblin' Jack Elliott."

The Ballad of Ramblin' Jack is a documentary made by his daughter, Aiyana, who is thirtyish and observes, "I can't remember ever having had an actual conversation with my dad." Making the film was perhaps a way to get to know him better, but it doesn't work that way; Elliott has a knack for ramblin' right off topic, and when he takes his daughter on a drive in Mendicino to visit "the house where we came closest to being a family," he can't find it. At another point he explains that a birthday call was six days late because "I couldn't find a phone."

If he was not a good dad, he was at least an excellent rambler, often booking himself from gig to gig. I saw him first at the University of Illinois YMCA in the early 1960s, playing to a small roomful of folkies, and then again in Chicago's Old Town during the folk revival. He was more a personality than a great singer; it wasn't so much what he did as what he stood for, and even his own sister, noting that he learned to play the guitar while a rodeo cowboy, adds, "He should have taken singing lessons." Yet Elliott won a Grammy in 1995, and was given the National Medal of Arts in 1998 by President Clinton.

Elliott was born Elliott Charles Adnopoz, son of a Brooklyn doctor, in 1931. He ran away from home to join the rodeo, and has been rambling ever since. Elliott arguably provided Dylan with more than an insight into the music of Woody Guthrie: "What Dylan really took from Ramblin' Jack were lessons on how to configure a complete persona out of a mundane middle-class Jewish upbringing," writes Henry Cabot Beck of Film.com.

As Dylan turned into one of the biggest stars of the early 1960s, Elliott "didn't even notice at first" that his act had been copied (and, in all fairness, improved upon—not to mention the additional dimension of Dylan's songwriting). Real hurt came later, at a 1967 Guthrie tribute concert; Dylan was the headliner, Elliott at first was not even invited. By then Elliott's career was ramblin' out of control, and the film quotes an early manager, Harold Leventhal, who says: "I respected his talent but he was too disorganized. [With Jack], if there's a plan, it comes from whatever wife he happens to be with."

For Aiyana Elliott, daughter by the fourth

wife, all of this is just the historical backdrop to a life during which her father was briefly glimpsed between rambles. He was on the road, or had signed on to crew a sailboat, or had turned up with a new girlfriend, and it was no fun "having the world's greatest rambler as your dad." Her documentary is an effort to pin down Elliott, but he is unpinnable, and her specific questions get answers that drift off into free association. His concerts, we gather, were much the same way: "He never knew what the program would be, and there wasn't even a song list taped to the guitar. Sometimes he'd start a song without even deciding on the key." Old footage from a Johnny Cash TV show shows Cash looking on quizzically as Elliott tunes, and tunes, and tunes.

The movie reminded me of another recent documentary, *Pop and Me*, about a father and son who embark on a round-the-world trip during which they plan to get to know each other better, and find that wherever they go, their relationship has preceded them. Some parents are elusive, and some children are never going to get closure, and *The Ballad of Ramblin' Jack* hovers intriguingly between homage and revenge.

Bamboozled ★ ★
R, 135 m., 2000

Damon Wayans (Pierre Delacroix), Savion Glover (Manray/Mantan), Jada Pinkett-Smith (Sloan Hopkins), Tommy Davidson (Womack/Sleep 'n' Eat), Michael Rapaport (Dunwitty), Mos Def (Big Black Africa). Directed by Spike Lee and produced by Lee and Jon Kilik. Screenplay by Lee.

"You've been hoodwinked. You've been had. You've been took. You've been led astray, led amok. You've been bamboozled."

So said Malcolm X, as quoted by Spike Lee in the production notes to *Bamboozled*, his perplexing new film. To Malcolm, the bamboozlers were white people in general, but in Lee's films they're the television executives, black and white, who bamboozle themselves in the mindless quest for ratings. The film is a satirical attack on the way TV uses and misuses African-American images, but many viewers will leave the theater thinking Lee has misused them himself.

That's the danger with satire: To ridicule something, you have to show it, and if what you're attacking is a potent enough image, the image retains its negative power no matter what you want to say about it. *Bamboozled* shows black actors in boldly exaggerated blackface for a cable production named "Mantan—The New Millennium Minstrel Show." Can we see beyond the blackface to its purpose? I had a struggle.

The movie stars Damon Wayans as Pierre Delacroix, a Harvard graduate who is a program executive at a cable TV network. He works under a boss who is, in his own eyes, admirably unprejudiced: Dunwitty (Michael Rapaport) says Delacroix's black shows are "too white," and adds: "I have a black wife and two biracial kids. Brother man—I'm blacker than you."

Well, Delacroix isn't very black; his accent makes him sound like Franklin Pangborn as a floorwalker. But he's black enough to resent how Dunwitty and the network treat him (when he's late to a meeting, his boss says he's "pulling a Rodman"). In front of his office, he often passes two homeless street dancers, Manray (Savion Glover) and Womack (Tommy Davidson). Fed up with the news that he's not black enough, Delacroix decides to star them in a blackface variety show set in a watermelon patch on an Alabama plantation.

The new show shocks and offends many viewers, but turns into an enormous hit, sending the plot into twists and terrorist turns that are beside the issue. The central questions any viewer of *Bamboozled* has to answer are How do I feel about the racist images I'm seeing? and Is Spike Lee making his point?

I think he makes his point intellectually; it's quite possible to see the film and understand his feelings. In conversation Lee wonders why black-themed shows on TV are nearly always comedies; why are episodic dramas about blacks so rare? Are whites so threatened by blacks on TV that they'll only watch them being funny? An excellent question. And when Lee says the modern equivalent of a blackface minstrel show is the gangsta-rap music video, we see what he means: These videos are enormously popular with white kids, just as minstrel shows were beloved by white audiences, and for a similar reason: They package entertainment within demeaning and negative black images.

Lee's comments are on target, but is his film? I don't think so. Lee's spin on a gangsta-rap video or an African-American domestic comedy might be radically revealing. And what about execs rewriting scenes and dialogue according to their narrow ideas? (Margaret Cho's concert doc *I'm the One that I Want* tells of executives at CBS asking for rewrites to make the Korean-American comedian "less ethnic.")

To satirize black shows on TV, Lee should have stayed closer to what really offends him; I think his fundamental miscalculation was to use blackface itself. He overshoots the mark. Blackface is so blatant, so wounding, so highly charged, that it obscures any point being made by the person wearing it. The makeup is the message.

Consider the most infamous public use of blackface in recent years. Ted Danson appeared in blackface at a Friar's Club roast for his then-girlfriend Whoopi Goldberg. The audience sat in stunned silence. I could feel the tension and discomfort in the room. In his defense, Danson said the skit had been dreamed up and written by Whoopi. One of his lines was about how he'd invited Whoopi home to dinner and his parents had asked her to clean up the kitchen after the meal. Not funny when Danson said it. If Whoopi had said it about herself, it would have been funny, with an edge. But if Whoopi had said it while wearing blackface? Not funny. After Danson's flop, comedian Bobcat Goldthwait summed up the mood: "Jesus Christ, Ted, what were you thinking of? Do you think black people think blackface is funny in nineteen ninety and [bleeping] three?"

No, and white people don't, either. Blacks in blackface eating watermelon and playing characters named Sleep 'n' Eat, Rufus, and Aunt Jemima fail as satire and simply become—well, what they seem to be: crude racist caricatures.

I think Spike Lee misjudged his material and audience in the same way Whoopi Goldberg did, and for the same reason: He doesn't find a successful way to express his feelings,

angers, and satirical points. When Mel Brooks satirizes Nazis in the famous "Springtime for Hitler" number in *The Producers,* he makes Hitler look like a ridiculous buffoon. But what if the musical number had centered on Jews being marched into gas chambers? Not funny. Blackface is over-the-top in the same way—people's feelings run too strongly and deeply for such exaggerated satire to be effective. The power of the racist image tramples over the material and asserts only itself.

Barenaked in America ★ ★ ★
NO MPAA RATING, 90 m., 2000

Featuring the band members of Barenaked Ladies: Ed Robertson, Steven Page, Jim Creeggan, Kevin Hearn, and Tyler Stewart. Directed by Jason Priestley and produced by Cheryl Teetzel and Susanne Tabata.

If you knew a lot about movies but nothing about a band named Barenaked Ladies, you might reasonably assume that *Barenaked in America* was a spoof—a *Spinal Tap*-style mockumentary aimed at the popular image of Canadians as people who are awfully nice. While most band documentaries wade through sex, drugs, and rock 'n' roll, this one has no sex, no drugs, and the kind of rock 'n' roll that reminds one of their fans of "something I'd hear at a dorm party."

It's groundbreaking when the lead singer comes out in chinos and a dress shirt with the buttons stretching over his tummy. But the movie becomes even stranger when the camera goes aboard the tour bus. What do the band members do on the bus? Play euchre. Yes, euchre. "Euchre is a Canadian thing," one of the sidemen says. "I don't know if Americans have ever heard of it." Oh, and I almost forgot: There is sex on the bus, but it doesn't involve groupies and orgies. A couple of the guys giggle about sneaking out in the morning to dispose of used Kleenex.

Barenaked Ladies is a real band, and a popular one. It has a lot of fans, and one reason for its appeal is that they're the Slim Whitman of rock bands: When they sing a song it sounds like you could do it too, about as well as they can. You couldn't; there's a lot of musicianship buried in their deceptively square stage act, but it sounds like you could.

The Ladies started as street buskers in Toronto, selling cassettes of their work. They came to the attention of MuchMusic, that cable channel that looks like a multicultural and countercultural MTV. They haven't done a single thing to glitz up their act or to appear as anything other than what they are: nice Canadian boys having fun. When Jim Creegan, the bass player, gets a vocal solo, what song does he choose? "Itsy Bitsy Spider." Another one of their songs is about a farmer who loves Anne Murray. Then there's tape of an Anne Murray Christmas special on which the Barenaked Ladies sing "God Rest Ye, Merry Gentlemen."

Steve Page, the chubby one, is the lead singer. Ed Robertson, with the dyed blond goatee and cropped hair, is the other front man. Just before the tour started, they lost their longtime lead singer and keyboardist Kevin Hearn, who was diagnosed with leukemia. Midway through the tour Kevin is feeling good enough to join them onstage, but it is somehow typical of the Barenaked Ladies that management supplies him with an electronic keyboard that's "covered with cigarette welts, with a lot of keys that have turned yellow and don't work." Also onstage, in addition to bass, drums, and backup guitar, are occasional French horn and accordion players.

The documentary, directed by Jason Priestley, arrives in Boston, where the Ladies fill an enormous arena with their fans. We get the usual sound bites outside the hall, but not the usual opinions: "They look like guys you'd see working at the Gap," one fan says.

The Rolling Stones once figured in a documentary where someone was literally murdered by Hells Angels in front of the stage. There are dangers in being a Barenaked Lady too. When the band plays its hit "If I Had a Million Dollars," fans throw Kraft dinners onto the stage. Those boxes have sharp edges, Steve observes, and it can hurt if one hits you.

Battlefield Earth ½★
PG-13, 117 m., 2000

John Travolta (Terl), Barry Pepper (Jonnie Goodboy Tyler), Forest Whitaker (Ker), Kim Coates (Carlo), Richard Tyson (Robert the Fox), Michael MacRae (District Manager Zete), Michael Byrne (Parson Staffer), Sean Hewitt (Heywood). Directed by Roger Christian and produced by Elie Samaha, Jonathan D. Krane, and John Travolta. Screenplay by Corey Mandell and J. D. Shapiro, based on the novel by L. Ron Hubbard.

Battlefield Earth is like taking a bus trip with someone who has needed a bath for a long time. It's not merely bad; it's unpleasant in a hostile way. The visuals are grubby and drab. The characters are unkempt and have rotten teeth. Breathing tubes hang from their noses like ropes of snot. The sound track sounds like the boom mike is being slammed against the inside of a fifty-five-gallon drum. The plot . . .

But let me catch my breath. This movie is awful in so many different ways. Even the opening titles are cheesy. Sci-fi epics usually begin with a stab at impressive titles, but this one just displays green letters on the screen in a type font that came with my Macintosh. Then the movie's subtitle unscrolls from left to right in the kind of "effect" you see in home movies.

It is the year 3000. The race of Psychlos have conquered Earth. Humans survive in scattered bands, living like actors auditioning for the sequel to *Quest for Fire.* Soon a few leave the wilderness and prowl through the ruins of theme parks and the city of Denver. The ruins have held up well after 1,000 years. (The books in the library are dusty but readable, and a flight simulator still works, although where it gets the electricity is a mystery.)

The hero, named Jonnie Goodboy Tyler, is played by Barry Pepper as a smart human who gets smarter thanks to a Psychlo gizmo that zaps his eyeballs with knowledge. He learns Euclidean geometry and how to fly a jet, and otherwise proves to be a quick learner for a caveman. The villains are two Psychlos named Terl (John Travolta) and Ker (Forest Whitaker).

Terl is head of security for the Psychlos, and has a secret scheme to use the humans as slaves to mine gold for him. He can't be reported to his superiors because (I am not making this up), he can blackmail his enemies with secret recordings that, in the event of his death, "would go straight to the home office!" Letterman fans laugh at that line; did the filmmakers know it was funny?

Jonnie Goodboy figures out a way to avoid slave labor in the gold mines. He and his men simply go to Fort Knox, break in, and steal it. Of course it's been waiting there for 1,000 years. What Terl says when his slaves hand him smelted bars of gold is beyond explanation. For stunning displays of stupidity, Terl takes the cake; as chief of security for the conquering aliens, he doesn't even know what humans eat, and devises an experiment: "Let it think it has escaped! We can sit back and watch it choose its food." Bad luck for the starving humans that they capture a rat. An experiment like that, you pray for a chicken.

Hiring Travolta and Whitaker was a waste of money, since we can't recognize them behind pounds of matted hair and gnarly makeup. Their costumes look purchased from the Goodwill store on Tatoine. Travolta can be charming, funny, touching, and brave in his best roles; why disguise him as a smelly alien creep? The Psychlos can fly between galaxies, but look at their nails: Their civilization has mastered the hyperdrive but not the manicure.

I am not against unclean characters—at least now that the threat of Smell-O-Vision no longer hangs over our heads. Lots of great movies have squalid heroes. But when the characters seem noxious on principle, we wonder if the art and costume departments were allowed to run wild.

Battlefield Earth was written in 1980 by L. Ron Hubbard, the founder of Scientology. The film contains no evidence of Scientology or any other system of thought; it is shapeless and senseless, without a compelling plot or characters we care for in the slightest. The director, Roger Christian, has learned from better films that directors sometimes tilt their cameras, but he has not learned why.

Some movies run off the rails. This one is like the train crash in *The Fugitive*. I watched it in mounting gloom, realizing I was witnessing something historic, a film that for decades to come will be the punch line of jokes about bad movies. There is a moment here when the Psychlos' entire planet (home office and all) is blown to smithereens, without the slightest impact on any member of the audience (or, for that matter, the cast). If the film had been destroyed in a similar cataclysm, there might have been a standing ovation.

The Beach ★ ★
R, 119 m., 2000

Leonardo DiCaprio (Richard), Tilda Swinton (Sal), Virginie Ledoyen (Francoise), Guillaume Canet (Etienne), Robert Carlyle (Daffy), Paterson Joseph (Keaty), Lars Arentz Hansen (Bugs). Directed by Danny Boyle and produced by Andrew MacDonald. Screenplay by John Hodge, based on the book by Alex Garland.

The Beach is a seriously confused film that makes three or four passes at being a better one, and doesn't complete any of them. Since Leonardo DiCaprio is required to embody all of its shifting moods and aims, it provides him with more of a test than a better film might have; it's like a triathlon where every time he sights the finish line, they put him on a bicycle and send him out for another fifty miles.

The early scenes deliberately evoke the opening of *Apocalypse Now*, with its sweaty close-ups, its revolving ceiling fans, and its voice-overs by DiCaprio trying to sound like Martin Sheen. In a fleabag hotel in Bangkok, a fellow traveler (Robert Carlyle) tells him of an island paradise, hard to find but worth the trip. Will his journey borrow from a Joseph Conrad novel (*Victory*, say) as *Apocalypse Now* borrowed from *Heart of Darkness*?

No such luck, DiCaprio's character, named Richard, recruits a French couple in the next room, and as they set out for the legendary island, the movie abandons Conrad and *Apocalypse* and borrows instead from *The Blue Lagoon* on its way to a pothead version of *Lord of the Flies*. This is the kind of movie where the heroes are threatened by heavily armed guards in a marijuana field, and that's less alarming than when they jump off a ledge into a deep pool. Later they'll go swimming in glowing clouds of plankton, and Richard will face a shark in one-on-one combat.

Many of the scenes look, frankly, like time-fillers. Richard and his new French friends Francoise (Virginie Ledoyen) and Etienne (Guillaume Canet) arrive safely at a sort of retro hippie commune, where the pot is free, the bongos beat every night, and all is blissful on the beach, watched over by the stern eye of Sal (Tilda Swinton), the community's leader. It's paradise, Richard tells us—except for his lust for Francoise. So will this become a love triangle? No, because Francoise, once enjoyed, is forgotten, and besides, Etienne only wants her to be happy. Those French. A later encounter with Sal is more like plumbing than passion, and both sex scenes are arbitrary—they aren't important to the characters or the movie.

But then many of the sequences fall under the heading of good ideas at the time. Consider, for example, a strange interlude in which Richard becomes the hero of a video game, stomping through the landscape in computerized graphics. There is an echo here from *Trainspotting*, a better film by the same director, Danny Boyle, in which special effects are used to send the hero on a plunge into the depths of the world's filthiest toilet. There the effects worked as comic exaggeration; here they're just goofy.

What is important, I guess, is Richard's evolution from an American drifter in the Orient into a kind of self-appointed Tarzan, who takes to the jungle and trains himself, well aware that a movie so pointless and meandering will need contrived violence to justify the obligatory ending. In a paroxysm of indecision, the film's conclusion mixes action, existential resignation, the paradise-lost syndrome, and memories of happier days, the last possibly put in for studio executives who are convinced that no matter how grim a movie's outcome, it must end on a final upbeat. Watching *The Beach* is like experiencing a script conference where only sequences are discussed—never the whole film.

What is it about, anyway? There are the elements here for a romantic triangle, for a man-against-the-jungle drama, for a microcosm-of-civilization parable, or for a cautionary lesson about trying to be innocent in a cruel world. The little society ruled over by Sal is a benevolent dictatorship—you can be happy as long as you follow the rules—and that's

material for satire or insight, I guess, although the movie offers none.

There is one extraordinary development. One of the commune guys is bitten by a shark, and when his anguished screams disturb the island idyll of the others, Sal simply has him moved out of earshot. This event suggests the makings of another, darker movie, but it's not allowed to pay off or lead to anything big.

Maybe that's because the whole film is seen so resolutely through Richard's eyes, and the movie doesn't want to insult its target demographic group or dilute DiCaprio's stardom by showing the character as the twit that he is. In a smarter film Richard would have been revealed as a narcissistic kid out of his depth, and maybe he would have ended up out in the woods where his screams couldn't be heard.

Beautiful ★
PG-13, 113 m., 2000

Minnie Driver (Mona Hibbard), Joey Lauren Adams (Ruby), Hallie Kate Eisenberg (Vanessa), Kathleen Turner (Verna Chickle), Leslie Stefanson (Joyce Parkins), Bridgette Wilson (Miss Texas), Kathleen Robertson (Miss Tenessee), Ali Landry (Belindy [Miss American Miss]). Directed by Sally Field and produced by John Bertolli and B. J. Rack. Screenplay by Jon Berstein.

Beautiful should have gone through lots and lots more rewrites before it was imposed on audiences. It's a movie with so many inconsistencies, improbabilities, unanswered questions, and unfinished characters that we have to suspend not only disbelief but intelligence.

The movie tells the story of Mona, a girl who dreams of becoming a beauty queen, and grows up to become obsessed with her dream. Her life is not without difficulties. As a child from Naperville, Illinois, she is graceless, wears braces, chooses costumes Miss Clarabell would not be seen in, cheats, and is insufferably self-centered. As an adult, played by Minnie Driver, she gets rid of the braces, but keeps right on cheating, until by the time she becomes Miss Illinois she has survived her fourth scandal.

Sample scandal. A competitor in a pageant plans to twirl a fire baton. Mona paints the baton with glue so the girl's hand gets stuck to it, and then dramatically races onstage to save the girl with a fire extinguisher. Don't they press criminal charges when you do things like that?

As a girl, Mona is best pals with Ruby, a girl who for no good reason adores her. As an adult, Ruby (now played by Joey Lauren Adams) works as a nurse but inexplicably devotes her life to Mona's career. Mona has had a child out of wedlock, but because beauty contestants aren't supposed to have kids, Ruby even agrees to pose as the little girl's mom.

Why? Why does Ruby devote her entire life to Mona and become a surrogate mother? Search me. Because the plot makes her, I guess. Mona has parents of her own, a mother and a stepfather who are sullen, unhelpful, drink too much, and spend most of their time being seen in unhelpful reaction shots. The screenplay is no help in explaining their personalities or histories. They're props.

Mona's daughter, Vanessa (Hallie Kate Eisenberg), is at least a life source within the dead film, screaming defiantly in frustration because Mona keeps forgetting to take her to her soccer games. She suspects Mona is her real mom, and seems fed up being used as a pawn (at one point she gets on the phone to order some foster parents).

And what about Joyce Parkins (Leslie Stefanson), a TV reporter who hates Mona? She knows Mona has a child and is planning to break the story, but no one who has watched television for as long as a day could conceivably believe her character or what she does. Consider the big Miss American Miss pageant, where Joyce keeps telling her viewers she's about to break a big scandal. She is obviously not on the same channel as the pageant, so she must be on another channel. What are that channel's viewers watching when Joyce is not talking? Joyce, I guess, since she addresses them in real time whenever she feels like it. The staging is so inept she is actually seen *eavesdropping* on the pageant by placing her ear near to a wall. No press gallery? Not even a portable TV for her to watch?

As for Mona herself, Minnie Driver finds herself in an acting triathlon. Mona changes personalities, strategies, and IQ levels from scene to scene. There is no way that the Mona of the heartrending conclusion could develop from the Mona of the beginning and middle of the film, but never mind: Those Monas aren't possible, either. They're made of disconnected pieces, held together with labored plot furniture. (I was amazed at one point when people told Mona what the matter with her was, and then she went home and lay down on the sofa and we got flashback voice-overs as memories of the accusing voices echoed in her head. That device was dated in 1950.)

Driver would have been miscast even if the screenplay had been competent. She doesn't come across like the kind of person who could take beauty pageants seriously. Oddly enough, Joey Lauren Adams (the husky-voiced would-be girlfriend from *Chasing Amy*) could have played the beauty queen—and Driver could have played the pal.

And what about Ruby, the nurse played by Adams? She can't be at the big pageant because she's in jail accused of deliberately killing an elderly patient at a nursing home by giving her an overdose of pills. This would be too gruesome for a comedy if anything were done with it, but the death exists only as a plot gimmick—to explain why Ruby can't be there. The filmmakers have no sense of proportion; Ruby could just as easily have been stuck in a gas station with a flat tire and provided the same reaction shots (watching TV) in the climax. Why kill the sweet old lady?

Now consider. Mona has been involved in four scandals. She scarred one of her competitors for life. Her roommate and manager is in jail charged as an Angel of Death. A TV newswoman knows she has a secret child. What are the odds *any* beauty pageant would let that contestant onstage? With this movie, you can't ask questions like that. In fact, you can't ask any questions. This is Sally Field's first film as a director. The executives who greenlighted it did her no favors. You can't send a kid up in a crate like this.

Beautiful Creatures ★ ½
R, 88 m., 2001

Rachel Weisz (Petula), Susan Lynch (Dorothy), Iain Glen (Tony), Maurice Roeves (Ronnie McMinn), Alex Norton (Hepburn), Pauline Lynch (Sheena), Tom Mannion (Brian McMinn). Directed by Bill Eagles and produced by Simon

Donald and Alan Wands. Screenplay by Donald.

I spent last week at the Conference on World Affairs at the University of Colorado, Boulder, where one of my fellow panelists created a stir by standing up and shouting that the women on his panel were "man-haters," and he was fed up and wasn't going to take it anymore.

He would have had apoplexy if he'd seen *Beautiful Creatures*, from Scotland. Here is a movie about two of the most loathsome women in recent cinema, and the movie thinks the male characters are the villains. It gets away with this only because we have been taught that women are to be presumed good and men are to be presumed evil. Flip the genders in this screenplay, and there would not be the slightest doubt that the characters named Petula and Dorothy are monsters.

Consider, for example, the setup. Dorothy (Susan Lynch) has been unwise enough to shack up with a boyfriend who is not only a junkie but also a golfer. This makes her a two-time loser. She pawns his golf clubs. He gets revenge by throwing her brassiere in boiling water, dyeing her dog pink, and stealing her money, which is from the pawned golf clubs. Any golfer (or junkie) will tell you that at this point, they are approximately morally even.

Dorothy leaves the house and comes upon a disturbance in the street. Petula (Rachel Weisz) is being beaten by Brian (Tom Mannion). Why is he doing this? Because the movie requires this demonstration of typical male behavior. Dorothy is already mad, and now she loses it. She slams Brian with a pipe to the back of the head, and the two women, instantly bonding, carry his unconscious body to Dorothy's flat, where they share a joint while Brian dies in the bathtub. "You just get sick listening to all that gonna (bleeping) kill you stuff," Dorothy explains.

Imagine a scene where a man slams a woman with a pipe, and then joins her boyfriend in dragging the body into the bathtub and sharing a joint while she dies. Difficult. Even more difficult in a comedy, which, I neglected to mention, *Beautiful Creatures* intends to be. But I don't want to get mired in male outrage. Men are more violent than women, yes, and guilty of abuse, yes, although the percentage of male monsters is incalculably higher in the movies than in life. Like Thelma and Louise, Dorothy and Petula commit crimes that are morally justifiable because of their gender. We even like them for it. They have to conceal the death, for example, because "no one would believe" they had not committed murder. My own theory is that any jury in Scotland would believe their story that the man was violent and Dorothy had come to the defense of a sister.

The movie, set in Glasgow and one of the many offspring of *Trainspotting*, uses local color for a lot of its gags. Instead of picketing *The Sopranos*, Italian-Americans should protest the new wave of films from Scotland, which indicate Scots make funnier, more violent, more eccentric, and more verbal gangsters than they do. Films and TV shows that portray ethnic groups as interesting and colorful are generally a plus, since those viewers dumb enough to think every story is an "accurate portrait" are beyond our help anyway.

The plot. The dead man has a brother who is a rich bad guy. The women cut off the corpse's finger and send it with a ransom demand. A detective (Alex Norton) comes to investigate, gets in on the scheme, and alters it with designs of his own. Meanwhile, the junkie boyfriend turns up again, and one thing leads to another. You know how it is.

There is some dark humor in the movie, of the kind where you laugh that you may not gag. And the kind of convoluted plotting that seems obligatory in crime films from Scotland (consider *Shallow Grave*). I am not really offended by the movie's gender politics, since I am accustomed to the universal assumption in pop (and academic) culture that women are in possession of truth and goodness and men can only benefit from learning from them. In fact, if the movie had been able to make me laugh, I might have forgiven it almost anything.

Beautiful People ★ ★ ★
R, 107 m., 2000

Charlotte Coleman (Portia Thornton), Charles Kay (George Thornton), Rosalind Ayres (Nora Thornton), Roger Sloman (Roger Midge), Heather Tobias (Felicity Midge), Danny Nussbaum (Griffin Midge), Siobhan Redmond

(Kate Higgins), Gilbert Martin (Jerry Higgins). Directed by Jasmin Dizdar and produced by Ben Woolford. Screenplay by Dizdar.

A man boards a London bus, locks eyes with another man, and immediately starts to fight with him. Thrown off the bus, they chase each other through the streets and eventually end up in adjacent hospital beds, still ready to fight. One is a Croat, one is a Serb, and so they hate each other.

Ah, but hate is not limited to Bosnians. In the next bed is the Welsh firebomber, a man who torched the holiday cottages of twenty English weekenders before burning himself on the face. Elsewhere in *Beautiful People* we see three skinheads attacking a black kid, and a foreigner who is mistaken for a thief while trying to return a wallet, and the beat goes on even at the breakfast tables of the ruling class: "God!" says the wife of a government official, "Antonia Fraser is so bloody Catholic."

Beautiful People, written and directed in London by the Bosnian filmmaker Jasmin Dizdar, is about people who hate because of tribal affiliation, which is a different thing than hating somebody you know personally and have good reasons to despise. One of its interlocking stories involves a pregnant Bosnian woman who wants an abortion because her baby, the product of a rape, "is my enemy."

The movie loops and doubles back among several stories and characters, like Robert Altman's *Short Cuts* or Paul Thomas Anderson's *Magnolia.* The insights in one story cast light on the problems of another, and sometimes the characters meet—as when a young woman doctor falls in love with a patient, and brings him home to meet her stuffy family. Nor are the moral judgments uncomplicated. Although she explodes when her family condescends to the man, the fact remains that he speaks only about six words of English, and so her own affection for him is condescending too.

The most involving story involves a young heroin addict named Griffin (Danny Nussbaum), who has always been a trial for his parents ("Remember sixth form," his father asks, "when all of the teachers went on strike because no one wanted to teach him?"). As part of an involved attempt to attend a football match, Griffin stumbles onto an airfield, falls asleep on an air freight pallet, and is dropped by parachute into Bosnia as part of an airlift of UN aid supplies.

This has the aroma of an urban legend to it, like the scuba diver who was scooped up by a fire-fighting airplane and dumped onto a forest fire. In *Beautiful People,* it works like one of those fairy tales where a naughty child gets his comeuppance by trading places with one less fortunate. Here what happens is that Griffin, dazed and withdrawing, stumbles around the war zone and ends up behaving rather well.

There is another character stumbling there, too: a BBC war correspondent who loses his mind in the chaos of blood and suffering. Shipped home, he tries to check himself into a hospital to have his leg amputated; he has "Bosnian Syndrome," a doctor whispers, and perhaps he feels guilty to have two legs when so many do not.

I have made the film sound grim. Actually it is fairly lighthearted, under the circumstances; like *Catch-22,* it enjoys the paradoxes that occur when you try to apply logic to war. Consider the sequence where the foreigner walks into a café, annoys a British woman with his friendliness, and then, after she stalks out, he sees she has forgotten her billfold. He runs after her, is mistaken for a madman, and is injured in traffic. Another urban legend? Not if you saw the story only last week about a black taxi passenger in Chicago whose innocent presence so terrified his immigrant driver that the cabbie careened at top speed down one-way streets looking for a cop.

Why are we so suspicious of one another? It may be a trait hard-wired by evolution: If you're not in my tribe, you may want to eat my dinner or steal my mate. The irony about those two Bosnian patients, fighting each other in the London hospital, is that they're the only two people in the building who speak the same language. So to speak.

Bedazzled ★ ★
PG-13, 93 m., 2000

Brendan Fraser (Elliot Richards), Elizabeth Hurley (The Devil), Frances O'Connor (Alison Gardner), Orlando Jones (Dan), Miriam Shor (Carol), Paul Adelstein (Bob), Toby Huss (Jerry). Directed by Harold Ramis and produced by

Ramis and Trevor Albert. Screenplay by Ramis, Peter Tolan, and Larry Gelbart.

Watching *Bedazzled*, I was reminded of the ancient newspaper legend about the reporter sent to cover the Johnstown Flood. "God stood on a mountaintop," he wrote, "and saw what his flood waters had wrought." His editor cabled back: "Forget flood. Interview God." Why was I remembering this old story? Because, in the new comedy *Bedazzled*, Brendan Fraser falls in love with Frances O'Connor and, to win her, sells his soul to the devil, who is played by Elizabeth Hurley. Forget girl, I'm thinking. Seduce Satan.

Not that Hurley is that good a Satan—just that she's the ranking babe in this movie. As Satan, she seems too composed and collected. A certain zaniness is required; Satan must have been quite a madcap to leave heaven in order to spend eternity as a troublemaker. In the original *Bedazzled* (1967), Peter Cook played Satan and Raquel Welch played Lust, one of the seven deadly sins. That seven-to-one ratio between Satan's evil genius and its sinful building blocks is, I think, about right.

The new movie has been directed by Harold Ramis from a screenplay that uses the 1967 film more as inspiration than source. It is lacking in wickedness. It doesn't smack its lips when it's naughty. When its hero sells his soul to the devil, what results isn't diabolical effrontery, but a series of contract negotiations and consumer complaints.

The movie stars Brendan Fraser as Elliot, an office nerd whose goofy grin and effusive banalities send his coworkers into hiding. For three years he has dreamed of the lovely Alison (Frances O'Connor, splendid in *Mansfield Park*), who barely notices him. Then he meets the devil with a red dress on: This is Hurley, who offers him the standard contract, seven wishes for his soul. What always goes wrong with these deals is that the human words his request in the wrong way, and the sneaky devil tricks him. This is bad business. Since Satan wants to win souls, he (or she) should deliver magnificently on every promise, so that by number four or five the satisfied customers are telling their friends, and Satan is getting pass-along business.

Fraser is a wonderful comic actor—better than he gets the credit for, because he creates funny characters instead of exploding in what is intended as funny behavior. Here he finds himself reincarnated (or remodulated, or whatever the process is called) as a Colombian drug lord, a bucktoothed New Age nice guy, an NBA star, Abraham Lincoln, and so on. He's often very funny; I liked the courtside interview after an NBA game where he drips buckets of sweat.

The problem with his seven wishes and their associated interludes is that they're not funny enough, consistently enough. The double-cross after every wish works like a punch line that comes before the joke. He requests, we see what went wrong, and then the movie lingers too long while developing the situation.

Why not some twists and U-turns? What if Elliot figured out how to word the perfect wish? ("You, as Satan, already know what would really make me happy. I want you to grant it unconditionally, without loopholes.") There's a hint of that in the scene where he asks to be made the world's most sensitive man, and finds himself in an alternative universe where Alison loves him, but is bored by how sensitive he is: "I want a life with a man who will ignore me and take me for granted and only pretend to be interested in me to get in my pants."

Funny, but the movie never reaches escape velocity, and Elizabeth Hurley is too calm to be the devil. She lacks abandon, risk, and maniacal self-amusement. She doesn't crank it up enough. I was reminded of another old story, about the time Jack L. Warner heard that Ronald Reagan was thinking of running for president. "That can't be right," he said. "Ronald Reagan for best friend. Jimmy Stewart for president." Walking out of the screening, I was thinking: Elizabeth Hurley for girlfriend, Courtney Love for Satan.

Before Night Falls ★ ★ ★ ½
R, 143 m., 2001

Javier Bardem (Reinaldo Arenas), Olivier Martinez (Lazaro Gomez Carilles), Andrea Di Stefano (Pepe Malas), Johnny Depp ("Bon Bon"/Lieutenant Victor), Sean Penn (Cuco Sanchez), Michael Wincott (Herberto Zorilla Ochoa), Najwa Nimri (Fina Correa), Vito Maria Schnabel (Teenage Reinaldo). Directed by

Julian Schnabel and produced by Jon Kilik. Screenplay by Cunningham O'Keefe, Lazaro Gomez Carilles, and Schnabel, based on the memoirs of Reinaldo Arenas.

Born into crushing poverty in pre-Castro Cuba, young Reinaldo Arenas was told by a teacher than he had a gift for poetry. When his father heard this news, he slammed his fist down on the table and beat the boy. That more or less sets the pattern for Arenas's life: He tries to exercise his gifts as a poet and a novelist, and society slaps him down. It doesn't help that he's a homosexual.

Arenas believed the great betrayal in his life was by Fidel Castro. As a teenager, Reinaldo hitchhiked to the hills and joined the revolution, but once Castro came to power he showed little sympathy for artists and none for homosexuals. Arenas was an outcast and for seven years a prisoner in Cuba—until 1980, when he took advantage of the boat exodus for criminals, gays, the mentally ill, and others considered unfit to be Cubans. Ten years later, in Manhattan, dying of AIDS, he committed suicide, using pills and (just to be sure) a plastic "I Love NY" bag over his head.

Before Night Falls tells the story of Arenas's life through the words of his work and the images of Julian Schnabel's imagination. Schnabel, the painter, makes his screen a rich canvas of dream sequences, fragmented childhood memories, and the wild Cuban demimonde inhabited by Arenas and others who do not conform. There is no sequence more startling than one where Arenas stumbles onto a ragtag commune of refuseniks and finds that in the roofless ruin of an old cathedral they are building a hot-air balloon with which they hope to float to Florida. The balloon actually makes one brief flight. Did this episode actually happen? I would like to think that it did.

This is Schnabel's second film, and his second about an artist who is also a moody, difficult outcast. The first film was *Basquiat* (1996), about Jean Michel Basquiat, the Manhattan graffiti artist who rose briefly from homelessness to fame before sinking into madness. Arenas describes a similar trajectory. For both men, joy seems to come primarily at those moments when they are actually creating. Sex (for Arenas) and drugs (for Basquiat) are a way to avoid work, loneliness, and pain, but they lead to trouble, not release. Arenas claimed to have slept with 5,000 men by the age of twenty-five. That is not the record of a man who finds sex satisfying, but of one who does not.

Arenas is played by Javier Bardem, a Spanish actor with a specialty in macho heterosexuality (if you doubt me, see *Jamon, Jamon*). He doesn't play Arenas as a gay man so much as a man whose body fits like the wrong suit of clothes. We accept Arenas as gay in the movie because the story says he is, and because there are after all no rules about how a homosexual should look or behave—but there is somehow the feeling that the movie's Arenas is not gay from the inside out, but has chosen the lifestyle as part of a compulsion to defy Castro in every way possible. The film contains two more-convincing homosexual characters, both played by Johnny Depp: Lieutenant Victor, a sleek, tight-trousered military officer, and "Bon Bon," a flamboyant transvestite who struts through Castro's prisons and proves incredibly useful by smuggling out one of Arenas's manuscripts, concealing it in that place where most of us would be most inconvenienced by a novel, however brilliant.

What is most heroic about Arenas is his stubbornness. He could make his life easier with a little discretion, a little cunning, a little tact, and even a small ability to tell the authorities what they want to hear. There must have been a lot of gay men in Cuba who didn't make their lives as impossible as Arenas did. Consider the character of Diego, in *Strawberry and Chocolate*, the 1993 movie by the great Cuban director Tomas Gutierrez Alea. The movie is set in 1979, Diego is clearly gay, and yet he lives more or less as he wants to, because he is clever and discreet.

There is a little something of the spoiled masochist about Arenas. One would not say he seeks misery, but he wears it like a badge of honor, and we can see his mistakes approaching before he does. This is not a weakness in the film but one of its intriguing strengths: Arenas is not presented as a cliché, as the heroic gay artist crushed by totalitarian straightness, but as a man who might have been approximately as unhappy no matter where he was born. That angle between Arenas and his society is perhaps what inspired his work. Trapped on the margin, he wrote in spite of everything, and the anguish of creation was a source of energy. One is reminded a little of the Marquis de Sade, as portrayed in *Quills*. It was never simply what they wrote, but that, standing outside convention, taunting the authorities, inhabiting impossible lives, they wrote at all.

Being John Malkovich ★ ★ ★ ★
R, 112 m., 1999

John Cusack (Craig Schwartz), Cameron Diaz (Lotte Schwartz), Catherine Keener (Maxine), John Malkovich (John Horatio Malkovich), Mary Kay Place (Floris), Orson Bean (Dr. Lester), Byrne Piven (Captain Mertin). Directed by Spike Jonze and produced by Michael Stipe, Sandy Stern, Steve Golin, and Vincent Landay. Screenplay by Charlie Kaufman.

What an endlessly inventive movie this is! Charlie Kaufman, the writer of *Being John Malkovich*, supplies a stream of dazzling inventions, twists, and wicked paradoxes. And the director, Spike Jonze, doesn't pounce on each one like fresh prey, but unveils it slyly, as if there's more where that came from. Rare is the movie where the last half-hour surprises you just as much as the first, and in ways you're not expecting. The movie has ideas enough for half a dozen films, but Jonze and his cast handle them so surely that we never feel hard-pressed; we're enchanted by one development after the next.

John Cusack stars as Craig, a street puppeteer. His puppets are dark and neurotic creatures, and the public doesn't much like them. Craig's wife, Lotte, runs a pet store, and their home is overrun with animal boarders, most of them deeply disturbed. Lotte is played by Cameron Diaz, one of the best-looking women in movies, who here looks so dowdy we hardly recognize her; Diaz has fun with her talent by taking it incognito to strange places and making it work for a living.

The puppeteer can't make ends meet in "today's wintry job climate." He answers a help-wanted ad and finds himself on floor 7½ of a building. This floor, and how it looks, and

why it was built, would be inspiration enough for an entire film or a Monty Python sketch. It makes everything that happens on it funny in an additional way, on top of why it's funny in the first place.

The film is so rich, however, that the floor is merely the backdrop for more astonishments. Craig meets a coworker named Maxine (Catherine Keener) and lusts for her. She asks, "Are you married?" He says, "Yeah, but enough about me." They go out for a drink. He says, "I'm a puppeteer." She says, "Waiter? Check, please." Keener has this way of listening with her lips slightly parted, as if eager to interrupt by deconstructing what you just said and exposing you for the fool that you are.

Behind a filing cabinet on the 7½th floor, Craig finds a small doorway. He crawls through it, and is whisked through some kind of temporal-spatial portal, ending up inside the brain of the actor John Malkovich. Here he stays for exactly fifteen minutes, before falling from the sky next to the New Jersey Turnpike.

Whoa! What an experience. Maxine pressures him to turn it into a business, charging people to spend their fifteen minutes inside Malkovich. The movie handles this not as a gimmick but as the opportunity for material that is somehow funny and serious, sad and satirical, weird and touching, all at once. Malkovich himself is part of the magic. He is not playing himself here, but a version of his public image—distant, quiet, droll, as if musing about things that happened long ago and were only mildly interesting at the time. It took some courage for him to take this role, but it would have taken more courage to turn it down. It's a plum.

Why are people so eager to enter his brain? For the novelty, above all. Spend a lifetime being yourself and it would be worth money to spend fifteen minutes being almost anybody else. At one point, there's a bit of a traffic jam. Lotte finds herself inside his mind while Maxine is seducing him. Lotte enjoys this experience, and decides she wants to become a lesbian, or a man. Whatever it takes. This is hard to explain, but trust me.

The movie just keeps getting better. I don't want to steal the surprises and punch lines. Even the Charlie Sheen cameo is inspired. At one point Malkovich enters himself through his own portal, which is kind of like being pulled down into the black hole of your own personality, and that trip results in one of the most peculiar single scenes I've ever seen in the movies. Orchestrating all this, Cusack's character stays cool; to enter another man's mind is, of course, the ultimate puppeteering experience.

Every once in a long, long while a movie comes along that is like no other. A movie that creates a new world for us, and uses it to produce wonderful things. *Forrest Gump* was a movie like that, and so in their different ways were *M*A*S*H, This Is Spinal Tap, After Hours, Babe,* and *There's Something About Mary.* What do such films have in common? Nothing. That's the point. Each one stakes out a completely new place and colonizes it with limitless imagination.

Besieged ★

R, 92 m., 1999

Thandie Newton (Shandurai), David Thewlis (Mr. Kinsky), Claudio Santamaria (Agostino). Directed by Bernardo Bertolucci and produced by Massimo Cortesi. Screenplay by Bertolucci and Clare Peploe, based on a story by James Lasdun.

Note: I've found it impossible to discuss this film without mentioning important plot points. Otherwise, as you will see, the review would be maddeningly vague.

Bernardo Bertolucci's *Besieged* is a movie about whether two people with nothing in common, who have no meaningful conversations, will have sex—even if that means dismissing everything we have learned about the woman. It is also about whether we will see her breasts. How can a director of such sophistication, in a film of such stylistic grace, tell such a shallow and evasive story?

But wait. The film also involves race, politics, and culture, and reduces them all to convenient plot points. The social values in this movie would not have been surprising in a film made forty years ago, but to see them seriously proposed today is astonishing. In a hasty moment I described the film as "racist," but it is not that so much as thoughtless and lacking in all empathy for its African characters, whose real feelings are at the mercy of the plot's sexual desires.

The film opens in Africa, with an old singer chanting a dirge under a tree. We see crippled children. A teacher in a schoolroom tries to lead his students, but troops burst in and drag him away. The young African woman Shandurai (Thandie Newton) sees this. The teacher is her husband. She wets herself. So much for the setup. The husband will never be given any weight or dimension.

Cut to Rome, where Shandurai is a medical student, employed as a maid in the house of Mr. Kinsky (David Thewlis). He will always remain "Mr. Kinsky" to her, even in a love note. He is a sardonic genius who plays beautifully upon the piano and occupies a vast apartment given him by his aunt and hung with rich tapestries and works of art. Given the size and location of the apartment, she was a very rich aunt indeed. The maid's quarters are spacious enough for a boutique, and Mr. Kinsky's rooms are reached by a spiral staircase to three or four levels.

Thandie Newton is a beautiful woman. She is photographed by Bertolucci in ways that make her beauty the subject of the shots. There's a soft-core undertone here: She does housework, the upper curves of her breasts swelling above her blouse. Little wisps of sweaty hair fall down in front of those wonderful eyes. There is a montage where she vacuums and Mr. Kinsky plays—a duet for piano and Hoover.

It is a big house for two people, very silent, and they move around it like stalkers. One day she drops a cleaning rag down the spiral staircase and it lands on Mr. Kinsky's head. He looks up. She looks down. Mr. Kinsky decides he loves her. There is a struggle. "Marry me! I'll do anything to make you love me!" She throws him a curve: "You get my husband out of jail!"

He didn't know she was married. Other things divide them, including their different tastes in music. He performs the classics, but one day plays rhythmic African rhythms for her. She smiles gratefully, in a reaction shot of such startling falseness that the editor should never have permitted it. Later Shandurai has a speech where she says how brave, how courageous, her husband is. Eventually we gather that Mr. Kinsky is selling his possessions to finance the legal defense of the husband. Even the piano goes.

All of this time the film has been performing a subtle striptease involving Shandurai, who has been seen in various stages of partial or suggested nudity. Now, at the end, we see her breasts as she lies alone in bed. I mention this because it is so transparently a payoff; Godard said the history of cinema is the history of boys photographing girls, and Bertolucci's recent films (like *Stealing Beauty*) underline that insight.

I am human. I am pleased to see Thandie Newton nude. In a film of no pretension, nudity would not even require any justification; beauty is beauty, as Keats did not quite say. But in *Besieged* we have troublesome buried issues. This woman is married to a brave freedom fighter. She says she loves and admires him. Now, because Mr. Kinsky has sold his piano to free her husband, she gets drunk and writes several drafts of a note before settling on one ("Mr. Kinsky, I love you"). She caresses herself and then steals upstairs and slips into his bed. Do they have sex? We don't know. In the morning, her freed husband stands outside the door of Mr. Kinsky's flat, ringing the bell again and again—ignored.

If a moral scale is at work here, who has done the better thing: A man who went to prison to protest an evil government, or a man who freed him by selling his piano? How can a woman betray the husband she loves and admires, and choose a man with whom she has had no meaningful communication?

To be fair, some feel the ending is open. I felt the husband's ring has gone unanswered. Some believe the ending leaves him in uncertain limbo. If this story had been by a writer with greater irony or insight, I can imagine a more shattering ending, in which Mr. Kinsky makes all of his sacrifices, and Shandurai leaves exactly the same note on his pillow—but is not there in the morning.

The film's need to have Shandurai choose Mr. Kinsky over her husband, which is what I think she does, is rotten at its heart. It turns the African man into a plot pawn, it robs him

of his weight in the mind of his wife, and then leaves him standing in the street. *Besieged* is about an attractive young black woman choosing a white oddball over the brave husband she says she loves. What can her motive possibly be? I suggest the character is motivated primarily by the fact that the filmmakers are white.

Best in Show ★ ★ ★ ½
PG-13, 90 m., 2000

Jennifer Coolidge (Sherri Ann Ward Cabot), John Michael Higgins (Scott Donlan), Michael Hitchcock (Hamilton Swan), Eugene Levy (Gerry Fleck), Jane Lynch (Christy Cummings), Michael McKean (Stefan Vanderhoof), Catherine O'Hara (Cookie Fleck), Parker Posey (Meg Swan), Fred Willard (Buck Laughlin), Christopher Guest (Harlan Pepper). Directed by Christopher Guest and produced by Karen Murphy. Screenplay by Guest and Eugene Levy.

I am a dog lover, but I am not a dog fancier. I can understand people who dote on their dogs, but I cannot understand dog shows, which make dogs miserable while bringing out the worst traits of their owners. Dogs were not put on Earth to pose, prance, sit, point, and have their coats shampooed. They were created to chew shoes, bark at cars, have accidents on the rug, and get their tummies scratched.

That's why I approve of *Best in Show*, a wickedly funny mocumentary by Christopher Guest that makes fun of a Philadelphia dog show with every instrument in the satirist's arsenal, from the skewer to the mallet. Built around the improvisational techniques of Second City, the movie is consistently just plain funny and sometimes ascends to a kind of crazed genius. Consider Parker Posey's rage and loathing, for example, as she assaults a store clerk who cannot supply a Busy Bee dog toy. Her dog has lost its toy and is fretting, and the way she screams, "Busy Bee! Busy Bee!" you'd think she was looking for emergency snakebite remedy.

The movie introduces several dogs and their owners, who are seen in their homes and then followed to the Mayflower Kennel Club's dog show, where a telecast of the event includes color commentary by Buck Laughlin (Fred Willard). Bearing certain points of similarity to Joe Garagiola, Buck is genial, chatty, weirdly misinformed, and easily lost in the overgrown byways of his mind. He wonders aloud if a bribe would help to sway the judges, confuses Columbus with the Pilgrims, comments knowingly on a dog's attempt to hump the leg of its owner, and speculates that the bloodhound's chances might improve if he wore a little Sherlock Holmes hat and had a pipe in his mouth.

Harlan Pepper, the bloodhound's owner (played by Guest) is single, and that seems appropriate: Don't ask me why, but bloodhounds, even female bloodhounds, have always seemed like bachelors to me. The other dogs belong to couples (and a threesome) who seem in some cases to be more inbred than their animals.

Consider Gerry and Cookie Fleck, from Florida, and their Norwich terrier, Winky. Eugene Levy and Catherine O'Hara, who play the Flecks, obviously have need of a dog to deflect their attentions from each other. Gerry, for example, was born with two left feet. Literally. And Cookie's mating habits are infamous among her fellow dog owners; one of the running jokes is Gerry's perplexed look as one man after another seems to know his wife far better than he should.

Parker Posey's character met her mate (Michael Hitchcock) when their eyes locked as they visited Starbucks shops across the street from each other. Their conversations seem to be conducted largely by using the names of retail products: "We are so lucky," she observes, "to have been raised among catalogs."

The bountifully siliconed Sherri Ann Ward Cabot (Jennifer Coolidge), not light-years in difference from Anna Nicole Smith, cuddles with her geriatric millionaire husband ("We could not talk or talk forever and still find things to not talk about"), but seems to have a complex and perhaps rewarding relationship with Christy Cummings (Jane Lynch), the lesbian dominatrix they've hired to train their poodle. Stefan Vanderhoof (Michael McKean) and Scott Donlan (John Michael Higgins) are a gay couple whose twin shih tzus are the apples of their eyes.

With this film Christopher Guest nails down his command of the comedy mocumentary, a genre he helped to invent by cowriting and starring in *This Is Spinal Tap* (about a rock band coming apart at the seams) and by writing, directing, and starring in *Waiting for Guffman* (about a small town hiring an allegedly hotshot Broadway director for its 150th anniversary pageant). *Guffman* starred many of the same actors (Guest, Levy, Willard, O'Hara, Hitchcock, and Posey), and in both films some of their dialogue seems based on improvisations, especially as conversations veer into revealing detours.

Just as *Guffman* ended with the ill-fated pageant, *Best in Show* ends with the dog show itself, depending on the built-in structure of the competition to bring all of the owners and their stories together at the same time. Satires have a way of running out of steam, but the suspense of the judging process keeps the energy high, even apart from an assist by the dog who attacks a judge, inspiring Buck's most appreciative play-by-play commentary.

Best Laid Plans ★
R, 90 m., 1999

Alessandro Nivola (Nick), Reese Witherspoon (Lissa), Josh Brolin (Bryce), Rocky Carroll (Bad Ass Dude), Michael G. Hagerty (Charlie), Terrence Howard (Jimmy), Jamie Marsh (Barry), Sean Nepita (Freddie). Directed by Mike Barker and produced by Alan Greenspan, Betsy Beers, Chris Moore, and Sean Bailey. Screenplay by Ted Griffin.

X-rays can pass through the human body in much the same way that certain movies can pass through my mind. Hold up a photographic plate on the other side, and all you'd see would be some kidneys and a paper clip. I went to see *The Usual Suspects* twice and could not persuade my mind to engage with it; *Best Laid Plans* is the same kind of experience.

I am prepared to concede that I missed the boat on *The Usual Suspects*. So many people like it so much that they must have their reasons. I will see it yet again one of these days. I vividly remember Kevin Spacey's performance, which I enjoyed for its energy and texture, but I remember him sort of floating through the movie without hitting anything. I do not feel the need to see *Best Laid Plans* again. It's not that I don't remember it. It's that I don't care.

There is a moment in a certain kind of movie when I realize I am being toyed with. That everything is Not As It Seems. That we're trapped in a labyrinth of betrayals, double-reverses, surprises, and astonishing revelations, and that whatever is being established in this scene will be destroyed in the next. It's not just that I don't care—it's that the movie doesn't either. Its characters are pawns in a chess game, and all the action is designed to reveal hidden traps and buried strategies.

There are some double-reverse movies that work. *Body Heat* comes to mind. But *Body Heat* was not an exercise. It was a conspiracy with a purpose, a motivation, and an outcome. At every moment I *cared* about the characters—I believed in them, and it made a difference what they'd do next. I was being toyed with, but not *merely* being toyed with.

Best Laid Plans is a movie with several surprises too many. It opens in a bar with two old friends, Nick and Bryce (Allesandro Nivola and Josh Brolin), having a drink after several years. A girl named Lissa (Reese Witherspoon) walks in. Flash cut to later that evening. It's Nick's place. There's a panic call from Bryce. He picked up Lissa, brought her home, thought things were proceeding on schedule, and then was accused of rape and assault. Bad news. There's worse. Currently he has Lissa chained to a pool table of the place where he's house-sitting, so now it's also kidnapping, endangerment, who knows? What's next? Murder?

Nick hurries over to help bail out his old friend, and at this point I must not reveal any more of the plot because reality begins to shift beneath our feet and there are fundamental surprises, and then surprises about them. Give us a break, I'm thinking. Either cut through the funny stuff, or make it worth watching. But *Best Laid Plans*, directed by Mike Barker from a screenplay by Ted Griffin (who wrote *Ravenous*, much better), is so concerned with being a film that it forgets to be a movie.

This is cutting edge, film school, Sundance, indie flash. Wow, this guy can manhandle a camera. And we can picture the screenplay

meetings—three-by-five cards manipulated like jigsaw pieces to make sure all the elements join up again at the end. By the conclusion of this movie, the characters have been put through so many changes they need name tags and cue cards just to know who they still are and what they still need to say.

Here's my question: Would the same story, told in a linear form, without the gimmicks and with more attention to the personalities and behavior of the characters, have been more entertaining than this funhouse mirror version? I say it's worth a try.

Beyond the Mat ★ ★ ★
R, 92 m., 2000

With Mick "Mankind" Foley, Terry Funk, "Jake the Snake" Roberts, "Stone Cold" Steve Austin, Coco BWare, The Rock, Chyna, Vince McMahon, and others. A documentary directed by Barry Blaustein and produced by Brian Grazer, Ron Howard, Michael Rosenberg, Barry Bloom, and Blaustein. Screenplay by Blaustein.

Beyond the Mat is the wrestling documentary that Vince McMahon had barred from advertising on his World Wrestling Federation programs. Why? Because it shows an old pro maintaining on crack cocaine, and children weeping at ringside while their daddy is beaten bloody? Not at all. Because he doesn't have a cut of the profits.

Even if you've never watched a professional wrestling match on television, you've probably heard the words "Mr. McMahon" just while surfing past the channel. Here he explains why the WWF is like the Muppets: "They're both family owned, and they both have real human beings playing characters."

Uh-huh. We see him interviewing Darren Drozdov, a former pro football player who wants to wrestle and has a unique skill: He can vomit "on command." McMahon gives him a ring name, "Puke," and envisions a scenario: "After you've regurgitated on your opponent or the referee . . ." Drozdov is sent to the minor leagues for seasoning, and calls his mother with the good news.

Other subjects of the documentary have been around a long time. Terry Funk is over fifty, has been wrestling forever, and hears the doctor forecast a lifetime of pain from his wrecked knees. Then he climbs into the ring again. He can hardly walk, but during the match he seems to come to life, giving audiences the show they expect.

It is a show, yes. *Beyond the Mat* makes no secret of the fact that every match is scripted, and that the outcomes are not in doubt. But we knew that. What I didn't fully realize, until I saw this film, is how real the show is. Just because you script a guy being thrown out of the ring doesn't mean it's painless when he bounces off a table and onto the floor. You can't bleed unless you're cut. And sometimes things go wrong; a wire cage mesh breaks and a wrestler falls maybe twenty feet to the mat. That hurts. Last year a wrestler named Owen Hart fell seventy feet and was killed when his harness failed while he was being lowered into a ring.

Mick "Mankind" Foley comes across as one of the nicest guys in the film, a family man with small children who's a gentle teddy bear when he's not in the ring. He explains to his kids how it's all carefully planned, how his opponent doesn't really hate him, and then the two preschoolers sit at ringside as their daddy is handcuffed and beaten with a chair. He starts to bleed. They start to cry. "Close your eyes," their mother says, before finally taking them out of the room. They watch in the dressing room as a medic applies first aid to Foley's cuts and checks for a concussion.

Later, the filmmakers show Foley their footage of his kids crying, and he is sobered. He vows never to let them watch a fight again. We sense the care in his voice, but we also wonder: What were they doing ringside in the first place? What do kids know about scripts?

Beyond the Mat was written and directed by Barry Blaustein, a onetime *Saturday Night Live* writer and successful film producer, mostly of Eddie Murphy projects *(Coming to America, Boomerang, The Nutty Professor)*. He confesses to being a TV wrestling fan all his life. There's real pain when he meets one of his old heroes, "Jake the Snake" Roberts, once a superstar, now reduced to barnstorming the back roads for small change.

Roberts opens up in an extraordinary way to the camera. He talks about an unhappy childhood, a mother who was thirteen when she married. He has shaky relationships with his own family, and when Blaustein arranges a meeting with his estranged daughter at the Ramada, she's so nervous she wants to bring along two friends. A fight promoter says Jake demands crack before doing a show, and Jake agrees he's had drug problems.

What we wonder is, how can you be a pro wrestler and not use drugs? A working wrestler performs twenty-six to twenty-seven days in a month—twice on weekends. It's not all on TV. There are bus and plane trips to far-flung arenas, where even on a good day (no serious injuries) their bodies are slammed around in a way that might alarm a pro football player. Have you ever heard of a pro wrestler being suspended for drug use? Do they even check for drugs? Only asking.

Beyond the Mat isn't a slick documentary; some of it feels like Blaustein's home movie about being a wrestling fan. But it has a hypnotic quality. Those who oppose boxing because of its violence acknowledge that it is at least a supervised sport, with rules and safeguards. Wrestling is not a sport but a spectacle, in which weary and wounded men, some obviously not in the best of shape, injure each other for money.

At one point we see two wrestlers set each other on fire and then throw each other on barbed wire. There are ways to do this in which you do not get burned severely or lacerated—much. But it's not simple trickery, and what goes on in the ring clearly really does hurt, sometimes a lot. After a bloody match, two wrestlers slap each other on the back, and explain, "The more you hurt each other, the more money you make, so the more you like each other." Not capitalism's finest hour. ☞

Bicentennial Man ★ ★
PG, 132 m., 1999

Robin Williams (Andrew), Embeth Davidtz (Little Miss/Portia), Sam Neill (Sir), Oliver Platt (Rupert Burns), Kiersten Warren (Galatea Robotic/Human), Wendy Crewson (Ma'am), Hallie Kate Eisenberg (Little Miss, seven years old), Lindze Letherman (Little Miss, nine years old). Directed by Chris Columbus and produced by Wolfgang Petersen, Gail Katz, Neal Miller, Laurence Mark, Chris Columbus, Mark Radcliffe, and Michael Barnathan. Screenplay by Nicholas

Bicentennial Man begins with promise, proceeds in fits and starts, and finally sinks into a cornball drone of greeting-card sentiment. Robin Williams spends the first half of the film encased in a metallic robot suit, and when he emerges, the script turns robotic instead. What a letdown.

Williams plays a robobutler named Andrew, who arrives in a packing crate one day outside the home of a family that is destined to share him for four generations, each and every moment of which seems mercilessly chronicled. His first owner is Sir (Sam Neill), who introduces Andrew to a dubious wife (Wendy Crewson) and a daughter named Little Miss, who grows up to be played by Embeth Davidtz (she also plays her own granddaughter).

At first the robot is treated unkindly. "It is a household appliance, yet you treat it like it is a man," an associate frets to Sir. But he comes around. It's clear from the first that Andrew is some kind of variant, smarter and more "human" than your average robot, although just as literal. In the early scenes, which have a life of their own, Andrew jumps out a window when told to, and has a lot of trouble mastering the principle of the "knock knock" joke. He also demonstrates various consequences of the Three Laws of Robotics, which were obviously devised by Isaac Asimov so that men of the future will be able to shout "gotcha!" at their robots.

From the first moment we see Andrew, we're asking ourselves, is that really Robin Williams inside the polished aluminum shell? *USA Today* claims it is, although at times we may be looking at a model or a computer-generated graphic. The robot's body language is persuasive; it has that same subtle courtliness that Williams himself often uses. Andrew also has good timing, which is crucial, since many of the movie's payoffs depend on the robot expressing its feelings through body language. ("One would like to have more expression," Andrew complains at one point. "One has thoughts and feelings that presently do not show.")

Peter Weller, who starred in *RoboCop*, told me it was the most excruciating physical or-

deal of his lifetime, spending weeks inside a heavy costume under movie lights that raised the temperature over 100 degrees. Williams must have undergone a similar ordeal. His performance depends on the comic principle that it's funny when a man is subjected to the rules of a machine; everything we see here has its mirror image in the assembly-line sequence at the beginning of Chaplin's *Modern Times*. Unfortunately for this movie, it's funnier when a man becomes a machine than when a machine becomes a man, because man's free will is being subverted, while the machine has none.

The plot is based on a story by Asimov and a novel by Asimov and Robert Silverberg. It deals with the poignancy of an android that has humanlike feelings, and must live indefinitely, whereas all the humans must die. There are consolations. Andrew is allowed to bank his own income, and compound interest can work wonders for an immortal being; eventually he is rich, and goes on an odyssey to find a soul mate.

His search leads to the shabby laboratory of Rupert Burns (Oliver Platt), who tinkers with used robots, and the two of them fashion a new body for Andrew that looks much like Robin Williams. There is also the problem of finding Andrew a soul mate; will it be an advanced robot, or will his own progress make it plausible for him to consider a relationship with a human? Andrew can't reproduce, of course, but logic suggests he might make a versatile and tireless lover.

The movie's buried themes have to do with self-determination and the rights of the individual. Like many of Asimov's robot stories, it deals with the enigma of having the intelligence of a man, without the rights or the feelings. *Bicentennial Man* could have been an intelligent, challenging science-fiction movie, but it's too timid, too eager to please. It wants us to like Andrew, but it is difficult at a human deathbed to identify with the aluminum mourner.

Strange, how definitely the film goes wrong. At the sixty-minute mark, I was really enjoying it. Then it slowly abandons its most promising themes and paradoxes and turns into a series of slow, soppy scenes involving love and death. And since the beloved woman is essentially always the same person (played by Davidtz), the movie begins to seem very long and very slow, and by the end, when Andrew hopefully says, "See you soon," we hope he is destined for Home Appliance Heaven.

Big Daddy ★ ½
PG-13, 95 m., 1999

Adam Sandler (Sonny Koufax), Joey Lauren Adams (Layla), Jon Stewart (Kevin Gerrity), Rob Schneider (Delivery Guy), Cole and Dylan Sprouse (Julian), Leslie Mann (Corinne), Allen Covert (Phil), Kristy Swanson (Vanessa), Josh Mostel (Arthur), Steve Buscemi (Homeless Guy). Directed by Dennis Dugan and produced by Sid Ganis and Jack Giarraputo. Screenplay by Steve Franks, Tim Herlihy, and Adam Sandler, based on a story by Franks.

Big Daddy is a film about a seriously disturbed slacker who adopts a five-year-old and tutors him in cynicism, cruel practical jokes, and antisocial behavior. It's not every film where an adult role model throws himself in front of a moving car just to cheer the kid up. "Man, this Yoo Hoo is good!" the adult tells the tyke. "You know what else is good? Smoking dope!"

On the way down in the elevator after the *Big Daddy* screening, a fellow critic speculated that the line about weed was intended not as a suggestion, but as a feeler: The hero was subtly trying to find out if the kid and his friends were into drugs. I submit that so few five-year-olds are into drugs that it's not a problem, and that some older kids in the audience will not interpret the line as a subtle feeler.

Big Daddy stars Adam Sandler as Sonny Koufax, a layabout who won $200,000 in a lawsuit after a cab ran over his foot, and now hangs around the Manhattan loft that he shares with his roommate, a lawyer played by Jon Stewart—who must be doing well, since the space they occupy would sell or rent for serious money. Sonny's girlfriend, Vanessa (Kristy Swanson), tells him to get a real job, but he says he has one: He's a toll-booth attendant, I guess, although the movie gives him nothing but days off.

Just after the roommate heads out of town, little Julian (played by twins Cole and Dylan Sprouse) is dropped at the door. He is allegedly the roommate's love child. Sonny tries to turn the kid over to Social Services, but they're closed for Columbus Day, and so he ends up taking Julian to Central Park for his favorite pastime, which is throwing tree branches in the paths of speeding in-line skaters. One middle-aged blader hits a branch, takes a nasty fall, and ends up in the lagoon. What fun.

The predictable story arc has Sonny and Julian bonding. This is not as easy as it sounds, since any Adam Sandler character is self-obsessed to such a degree that his conversations sound like interior monologues. It is supposed to be funny that Sonny has a pathological hostility against society; when Mc-Donald's won't serve them breakfast, he throws another customer's fries on the floor, and when a restaurant won't let the kid use the rest room, he and the kid pee on the restaurant's side door.

The movie is filled to the limit with all the raunchy words allowed by the PG-13 rating, and you may be surprised how many and varied they are. There's a crisis when a social worker (Josh Mostel) turns up, and Sonny impersonates his roommate and claims to be the kid's dad. We're supposed to think it would be nice if Sonny could win custody of little Julian. I think it would be a tragedy. If the kid turns out like Sonny, he's probably looking at prison time or heavy-duty community service. Sonny is the first couch potato I've seen with road rage.

The film is chock-full of supporting characters. The most entertaining is Layla (Joey Lauren Adams), whose sister is engaged to Sonny's roommate. (The sister is an ex-Hooters girl, leading to more talk about hooters than a non-drug-using five-year-old is likely to require.) Adams, who was so good in *Chasing Amy,* is good here, too, bringing a certain sanity to the plot, although I don't know what a smart girl like Layla would see in this closed-off, angry creep. Even when Sonny tries to be nice, you can see the passive aggression peeking around his smile.

The final courtroom scene is one of those movie fantasies where the judge bangs her gavel while everyone in the movie grandstands—yes, even the homeless person (Steve Buscemi) who has tagged along for the ride, an old drunk from Sonny's local bar, and the gay lawyers Sonny knows from law school. (Like many gay characters in comedies, they kiss and hug at every opportunity; why don't they just wear signboards?)

There have been many, many movies using the story that *Big Daddy* recycles. Chaplin's *The Kid* used Jackie Coogan as the urchin; *Little Miss Marker* (versions by Shirley Temple and Walter Matthau) was about an innocent tyke and a bookie; James Belushi's *Curly Sue* has some of the same elements. What they had in common were adults who might have made good parents. *Big Daddy* should be reported to the child welfare office.

Big Eden ★ ★
PG-13, 118 m., 2001

Arye Gross (Henry Hart), Eric Schweig (Pike Dexter), Tim DeKay (Dean Stewart), George Coe (Sam Hart), Louise Fletcher (Grace Cornwell), Nan Martin (Widow Thayer), Veanne Cox (Mary Margaret). Directed by Thomas Bezucha and produced by Jennifer Chaiken. Screenplay by Bezucha.

Big Eden tells a story of gay love in a small Montana town whose citizens are so accepting of homosexuality that the old coots around the cracker barrel at the general store rush to the window to monitor the progress of a triangle involving the local hunk, the artist feller from New York, and a tall, silent Indian. Earlier, the Widow Thayer, who failed to fix up the New Yorker with the local girls, discovers her error and throws a party so he can meet the local boys.

This is the same Montana that's next door to Wyoming, where a gay man named Matthew Shepard was murdered not long ago. Or rather, it is not the same Montana, but some kind of movie fantasy world in which all the local folk know and approve of the fact that Henry Hart (Arye Gross) is gay; by the end of the film, they're ready to use crowbars on the door to Henry's closet. This is the kind of movie small town with no ordinary citizens; everyone has a speaking role, and they all live in each other's pockets, know each other's business, and have jobs that allow them to drop into the general store and each other's kitchens with the frequency of neighbors on a sitcom.

That's not to say the movie doesn't have a lot of sweetness and warmth. Until the plot becomes intolerably cornball, there's charm in the story of how the withdrawn Henry returns to Big Eden after his granddad (George Coe) has a stroke. He's welcomed by Grace (Louise Fletcher), the local teacher, and learns immediately that "Dean is back in town." That would be Dean Stewart (Tim DeKay), Henry's hunky best friend in high school, and the object of an unrequited crush that spans the decades. Now Dean is divorced, and smiling at Henry during Sunday church services.

Grandpa starts to mend, Henry helps Grace in the local school, and the Widow Thayer is hired to cook meals for the two men. But Widow Thayer is a fearsomely bad cook, and soon the wonderfully named Pike Dexter (Eric Schweig) is secretly preparing gourmet meals from recipes on the Internet, and feeding the widow's swill to his dog. Pike is an Indian who runs the general store, despite painful shyness and a deep reluctance to say more than three words at a time.

We think the plot may involve local homophobia. But no: Everybody in this town is pro-gay. Then we think perhaps Henry and Dean will fall in love. They seem headed in that direction until a scene so awkwardly written and acted that it seems to have been pounded into the plot with sledgehammers (you'll know the scene I mean; ask yourself exactly how and why it justifies Henry's later anger, in another awkward scene). Finally it turns out that Henry's future lies in the arms of Pike, whose life changes the day he checks *The Joy of Cooking* out of his own lending library. (The movie misses a golden opportunity; Pike should have selected *The Settlement Cook Book*, with its cover motto, "The way to a man's heart is through his stomach.")

There are things in the movie that are very good. I admired George Coe's work in a difficult role (listen to his reading of the line, "God has done a good job here"). I liked Louise Fletcher's unforced intelligence and goodwill. Ayre Gross plays a character who at times is willfully obtuse, but it would be fatal to be more open—since the moment he acknowledges his gayness, the plot, which depends on him being the least liberated person in town, would collapse.

I had real troubles, I must admit, with the coots who gather at the general store. I doubt that in the real world all six of these bewhiskered, pipe-puffing, jeans-wearing, cowboy-hatted old cowboys would be cheerleaders for a gay romance. I also found Pike's character a puzzle. In the opening scenes he seems either retarded or mentally ill, but by the end love has conquered all and repaired it. The last scene is painfully overdone; a shy "like to dance?" and a fade-out would have worked a lot better than the current ending. When you lay it on too thick, the audience is distracted by implausibility rather than identifying with the characters.

Whether Henry will find happiness in Big Eden we can only wonder. Some may think him courageous to abandon his art career in Manhattan to join the circle of Pike's admirers around the cracker barrel. I think it is a prudent decision. Based on the one example of Henry's painting that we see, his artistic talents are best suited to designing gift-wrap paper.

The Big Kahuna ★ ★ ★ ½
R, 90 m., 2000

Kevin Spacey (Larry), Danny DeVito (Phil), Peter Facinelli (Bob). Directed by John Swanbeck and produced by Elie Samaha, Kevin Spacey, and Andrew Stevens. Screenplay by Roger Rueff.

There are two religions in America, one spiritual, one secular. The first worships in churches, the second at business conventions. Clergy of both religions wear dark suits and ties (or roman collars). They exchange a lot of business cards. *The Big Kahuna* is about an uneasy confrontation between these two systems of faith.

True believers are similar whatever their religion. Their theology teaches: We know the right way. We are saved. We support one another and strive to convert the heathen. Those who come with us will know the kingdom of heaven—or will be using the best industrial lubricant. Adherents of both religions often meet in hotels, attend "mixers," and participate in "workshops" at which the buried message is: The truth is in this room.

The Big Kahuna is about a tool and die industry convention in a Wichita hotel. In a "hospitality suite" on an upper floor, three men wait uneasily. Their company sells industrial lubricants. Their entire convention depends on landing the account of a man named Dick Fuller, referred to as the Big Kahuna. The men are Larry (Kevin Spacey), Phil (Danny DeVito), and Bob (Peter Facinelli). Larry and Phil have been comrades for a long time—road warriors who do battle at conventions. Bob is a young man, new to the firm, at his first convention. Larry is edgy, sardonic, competitive. Phil is more easygoing. Phil is the backslapper; Larry is the closer. "I feel like I've been shaking somebody's hand one way or another all of my life," Phil says.

The film mostly takes place within that one hotel room. Yes, it is based on a play. I like that. I like the fact that it is mostly dialogue among three people on one set. That is the way to tell this story. Why does every filmed play trigger movie critics into a ritual discussion of whether (or how, or if) the play has been "opened up"? Who cares? What difference would it make if the movie set some scenes in the coffee shop and others in the park across the street? The story is about these three guys and what they say to one another. Keeping it in one room underlines their isolation: They are in the inner sanctum of their religion.

The movie, directed by John Swanbeck and written by Roger Rueff, is sharp-edged, perfectly timed, funny, and thoughtful. Spacey and DeVito are two of the smartest actors in the movies, filled with the joy of performance, and they exchange their dialogue with the precision of racquetball players, every volley redefining the game. They talk about business strategy, sales goals, the cutthroat world of industrial lubricants, the mystical power of the Big Kahuna to transform their lives. There is not one word about the technical side of lubricants; they couldn't care less. Lubricants are the Maguffin. They could be selling auto parts, ladies' ready-to-wear, or kitchen gizmos.

Bob, the kid, is softer and more unformed. He hasn't been broken in (or down) by life on the road. It appears that the Big Kahuna did not visit their suite. But in the small hours of the morning, during a postmortem, Larry and Phil discover that the great man was indeed in the room, wearing someone else's name tag—and that Bob talked to him for hours. What did they talk about? The Big Kahuna was depressed by the death of his dog.

That leads to a larger discussion, about a topic close to Bob's heart—his personal savior, Jesus Christ. Bob believes in Jesus like Larry and Phil believe in sales. "We talked about Christ," he says, quietly and simply, filled with enormous self-satisfaction. "About *Christ?*" screams Larry. "Did you mention what line of industrial lubricant Jesus uses?"

Those who are not true believers may be left cold by this film. For those who link their lives to a cause, it may have a real resonance. The tricky thing may be realizing that the two systems are interchangeable. If Larry and Phil believed in Jesus, and Bob wanted to land the big contract, the dialogue could stay about the same, because the story is about their personalities, not their products.

Now here's a funny thing. This movie premiered last January at Sundance. A lot has been written about it since then. You can read about the actors, the dialogue, the convention, the Kahuna, the industrial lubricants. But you can search the reviews in vain for any mention of Jesus Christ. Most of the reviewers seem to have forgotten that Bob is born-again. Maybe it never registered. From their secular viewpoint, what they remember is that Bob had the Kahuna in the palm of his hand and blew the deal, but they don't remember why.

That underlines how, once you sign onto a belief system, you see everything through that prism, and anything outside of it becomes invisible. *The Big Kahuna* is remarkable in the way it shows the two big systems in conflict. Of course, there is such a species as the Christian businessman, who has his roots in a strain of the Protestant ethic. He believes that prospering and being saved go hand in hand. Maybe Bob was onto something. Maybe he had the right approach to Dick Fuller. Maybe that's why Fuller is the Big Kahuna.

Big Momma's House ★ ★
PG-13, 99 m., 2000

Martin Lawrence (Malcolm), Nia Long (Sherry), Paul Giamatti (John), Jascha Washington (Trent), Terrence Howard (Lester), Anthony Anderson (Nolan), Ella Mitchell (Big Momma). Directed by Raja Gosnell and produced by David T. Friendly and Michael Green. Screenplay by Darryl Quarles and Don Rhymer.

Any movie that employs an oven mitt and a plumber's friend in a childbirth scene cannot be all bad, and I laughed a lot during *Big Momma's House.* I also spent a certain amount of time staring at the screen in disbelief. While it's true that comedy can redeem bad taste, it can be appalling when bad taste thinks it is being redeemed by comedy and is wrong. The movie's opening toilet scene, featuring the biggest evacuation since we pulled out of Vietnam, is a grisly example.

Martin Lawrence stars in the movie as Malcolm, an FBI agent who is a master of disguise. A vicious bank robber named Lester (Terrence Howard) escapes from prison, and Malcolm and his partner John (Paul Giamatti) conduct a surveillance on Lester's girlfriend Sherry (Nia Long), who may know where $2 million in loot has been concealed. Sherry, afraid of Lester, flees with her child to the Georgia home of her grandmother, Big Momma (Ella Mitchell). And when Big Momma is called out of town, Malcolm disguises himself as the 350-pound juggernaut, deceives Sherry, and infiltrates the case from within, while his partner keeps watch from the house across the street.

This is all essentially an attempt by Lawrence to follow Eddie Murphy's disguise as a fat guy in *The Nutty Professor,* and credit should also go to Robin Williams in *Mrs. Doubtfire.* The whole enterprise has been ratcheted down several degrees in taste, however; while Murphy's funniest scene involves vast explosions of intestinal gas, Big Momma's noisy visit to the bathroom is scary, not funny.

Martin Lawrence is a gifted actor, and with clever makeup, padding, and sass he creates a fake Big Momma who doesn't look completely like a drag queen, although she comes close. It's doubtful her granddaughter, neighbors, and would-be boyfriend would be fooled. But we go along with the gag, since the plot is no more than a flimsy excuse for Big Momma to behave in a way that most 350-pound grandmothers in their sixties would find impossible. We see Big Momma playing a pickup basketball game, including a reverse dunk that ends with her hanging from the hoop. Big Momma in karate class, throwing the instructor around the room. Big Momma in church, letting some four-letter words slip into her testimony and covering up with a quick segue to "Oh, Happy Day!"

The funniest scene involves a pregnant neighbor in the throes of childbirth—which is how Malcolm the FBI agent finds out Big Momma is a midwife. The zany editing of the childbirth scene makes it work, and the appearance of the oven mitt is the high point of the film. Other scenes are not handled so well; when Big Momma's sexy granddaughter climbs into bed with her, for example, Malcolm has a physiological reaction not entirely explained by his flashlight. This is a recycling of the classic bed scene between Steve Martin and John Candy in *Planes, Trains and Automobiles* ("Those aren't pillows!"), not handled nearly as well.

The movie's one of those ideas that seems increasingly labored as the plot drags on. A little of Big Momma is funny enough, but eventually we realize Martin Lawrence is going to spend virtually the entire movie in drag (he appears as Malcolm only long enough to stir up a sweet romance with Sherry). The problem is that Lawrence's gifts come packaged with his face and voice: Present him as Big Momma all the time, and you lose his star power. It's the same problem John Travolta presents in *Battlefield Earth*. We don't go to a big star's movie to see him as an unrecognizable character. The movie has some big laughs, yes, but never reaches takeoff velocity.

The Big Tease ★ ★
R, 86 m., 2000

Craig Ferguson (Crawford Mackenzie), Frances Fisher (Candy Harper), Mary McCormack (Monique Geingold), David Rasche (Stig Ludwiggssen), Chris Langham (Martin), Donal Logue (Eamonn), Isabella Aitken (Mrs. Beasie Mackenzie), Kevin Allen (Gareth Trundle). Directed by Kevin Allen and produced by Philip Rose. Screenplay by Sacha Gervasi and Craig Ferguson.

In the theory of comedy, more attention should be paid to the time between the laughs. It's easy enough to get a laugh in a movie, but tricky and difficult to build comic momentum, so that underlying hilarity rolls over from one laugh to the next and the audience senses it's looking at a funny movie instead of a movie with funny moments.

The Big Tease is a movie with a lot of laughs, but they come one at a time. It doesn't build, and by the time we get to the big payoff it's kind of dragging. I could describe moments and lines to you and you'd probably laugh, but sitting there in the audience, you want it to roll, and it meanders.

The film stars Craig Ferguson, a gifted comic actor from Glasgow (and *The Drew Carey Show*), as a gay hairdresser named Crawford Mackenzie—by his own admission the finest hairdresser, indeed, in Scotland. When an invitation arrives from the World Freestyle Hairdressing Championship in Los Angeles, he vibrates with excitement: Here at last is his chance to compete against the big names in hairdressing. Accompanied by a documentary film crew, he flies off to L.A., only to discover belatedly that he has been invited, not to compete, but to sit in the audience (between Daniel Day-Lewis and Carrot Top), and is expected to pay all his own bills.

He's crushed, but not defeated. With the now-desperate doc crew following him around and lending him that air of vague importance bestowed by any camera, he invades the sanctum of the legendary Stig Ludwiggssen (David Rasche), defending hairdressing champion, a Norwegian twit with an accent that casts doubt on his Norwegian or any other origins. Rasche is wonderful in the role, conveying that towering self-importance so often displayed by the giants of inconsequential fields; having once overheard Jose Eber when he was mad at a rental car agent, I can even speculate that Rasche's portrait is not particularly exaggerated.

To be considered for the competition, Crawford needs a union card. His quest for one occupies the middle passages of the movie. At one point he is reduced to grooming the animal costumes at a theme park. He thinks his fellow Scotsman Sean Connery might come to the rescue (perhaps he will remember the time Crawford groomed his hairpiece), and confronts Connery's publicist, played by Frances Fisher with dead-on accuracy.

Whether he gets his card, and what happens at the bizarre hairdressing finals, I leave it to you to discover. I found Ferguson likable as the hairdresser out of water, and enjoyed Fisher, Rasche, and Mary McCormack as the head of the competition. But somehow *The Big Tease* never quite attains takeoff velocity. Maybe it needed to position itself a little closer to the ground and go for the comedy of observation rather than exaggeration. I trust, anyway, that the final competition is an exaggeration. If it is anywhere at all close to real life, just the telecast of the real thing would have been funny enough.

Billy Elliot ★ ★ ★
R, 110 m., 2000

Jamie Bell (Billy), Julie Walters (Mrs. Wilkinson), Gary Lewis (Dad), Jamie Draven (Tony), Nicola Blackwell (Debbie), Stuart Wells (Michael), Adam Cooper (Billy [aged 25]), Jean Heywood (Grandmother). Directed by Stephen Daldry and produced by Greg Brenman and John Finn. Screenplay by Lee Hall.

Billy Elliot is the flip side of *Girlfight*. While the recent American film is about a girl who wants to be a boxer and is opposed by her macho father but supported by her brother, this new British film is about a boy who wants to be a ballet dancer but is opposed by his macho father and brother. Both films feature supportive adults who encourage the dreams, both oppose rigid gender definitions, both end in a big fight/dance. *Girlfight* is tougher, *Billy Elliot* sweeter. I suppose that's appropriate.

The movie takes place in 1984 in a British coal mining town, where Billy (Jamie Bell) trudges off to boxing lessons for which he is ill equipped. Life at home is tense because his father (Gary Lewis) and brother Tony (Jamie Draven) are striking miners. One day, at the other end of the village hall, he sees ballet lessons being taught by a chain-smoking disciplinarian (Julie Walters), and his eyes grow large. Soon he is shyly joining her class, the only boy in a crowd of tutus.

Billy's father equates male ballet dancers with homosexuality, but Billy doesn't seem to be gay, a fact he discovers to his sudden embarrassment during a pillow fight with his friend Debbie (Nicola Blackwell). Billy's best friend, Michael (Stuart Wells), is gay, however— a cross-dresser who reaches the high point of his young life by putting on one of the tutus. Michael is attracted to Billy, who doesn't reciprocate, but seems unusually sophisticated about the implications for a boy his age.

The movie is sort of awkwardly cobbled together, and there are big shifts in character without much explanation. Billy's dad, a supporter of the strike, not only begins to understand his son's dream, but actually becomes a strike breaker to get money for Billy to attend an important audition. I can believe a coal miner supporting his son's dancing dreams, but anyone who believes he would become a scab to raise the money doesn't know much about union miners.

Still, the movie is as much parable and fantasy as it is realistic. The character of the transvestite Michael in particular seems based more on wishful thinking than on plausible reality; would a gay boy of his age in this neighborhood of this town in 1984 be quite so sure of himself? Julie Walters, a 1984 Academy nominee for *Educating Rita*, is spirited and colorful as the ballet teacher, and Gary Lewis is somehow convincing as the dad even when the screenplay requires him to make big offscreen swings of position. Jamie Bell is an engaging Billy, earnest and high-spirited, and a pretty good dancer too.

The movie was directed by Stephen Daldry, a well-known stage director, and photographed by Brian Tufano, who has one shot that perfectly illustrates the difference between how children and adults see the world. Billy's friend Debbie is walking along a fence, clicking a stick against the boards. She doesn't notice that she is suddenly walking in front of a line of cops, called up against the striking miners and carrying plastic shields; she clicks on those too.

Note: Once again, we are confronted by a movie that might be ideal for teenagers about Billy Elliot's age, but it has been slapped with the R rating. While kids will gladly sneak into R-rated movies they hope will be violent or scary, the R barrier only discourages them from films that could be helpful or educational. In the case of Billy Elliot, the movie contains only mild violence and essentially no sex, and the R is explained entirely by the language, particularly the f-word. The filmmakers believe that is a word much used by British coal miners, and I am sure they are correct

There are two solutions to the linkage of the f-word and the R rating: (1) The MPAA should concede the melancholy fact that every teenager has heard this and most other nasty words thousands of times, or (2) filmmakers should sacrifice the f-word in order to make their films more available to those under seventeen.

Black and White ★ ★ ★

R, 100 m., 2000

Bijou Phillips (Charlie), Power (Rich Bower), Scott Caan (Scotty), Ben Stiller (Mark Clear), Allan Houston (Dean), Claudia Schiffer (Greta), Mike Tyson (Himself), Brooke Shields (Sam), Robert Downey Jr. (Terry), Stacy Edwards (Sheila), Gaby Hoffmann (Raven), Jared Leto (Casey), Marla Maples (Muffy), Kim Matulova (Kim), Joe Pantoliano (Bill King). Directed by James Toback and produced by Michael Mailer, Daniel Bigel, and Ron Rotholz. Screenplay by Toback.

Like James Toback himself, his new film is in your face, overflowing with ideas, outrageous in its connections, maddening, illogical, and fascinating. Also like its author, it is never boring. Toback is the brilliant wild child of indie cinema, now a wild man in his fifties, whose films sometimes seem half-baked, but you like them that way: The agony of invention is there on the screen.

Black and White is one of those Manhattan stories where everyone knows each other: rich kids, ghetto kids, rappers, Brooke Shields, the district attorney, a rogue cop, a gambler, a basketball star, Mike Tyson, recording executives. They're all mixed up in a story about race, sex, music, bribery, fathers, sons, murder, and lifestyles. What's amazing is how it's been marketed as a film about white kids who identify with black lifestyles and want to be black themselves. There's a little of that, and a lot more other stuff. It's a crime movie as much as anything.

The sex has gotten the most attention; the opening scene, of a threesome in Central Park, had to be recut three times to avoid an NC-17 rating (you can see the original version, murk-

ily, on the Web). We meet Charlie (Bijou Phillips), the rich girl who "wants to be black" and also adds, later: "I'm a little kid. Kids go through phases. When I grow up, I'll be over it. I'm a kid from America."

True, the racial divide of years ago is blurred and disappearing among the younger siblings of Generation X. The characters in this movie slide easily in and out of various roles, with sex as the lubricant. Toback's camera follows one character into a situation and another out of it, gradually building a mosaic in which we meet a black gangster named Rich (hip-hop producer Power), a rap group (Wu-Tang Clan), a basketball guard named Dean (real-life Knick Allan Houston), his faithless Ph.D. candidate girlfriend (Claudia Schiffer), a crooked cop (Ben Stiller), a documentary filmmaker (Brooke Shields), the husband everyone but she knows is gay (Robert Downey Jr.), and heavyweight champ Mike Tyson, playing himself, and improvising some of the best scenes.

The story, which involves bribery, murder, and blackmail, I will leave for you to discover. Consider the style. Toback has observed that for musicians like Wu-Tang Clan, their language is their art form, so he didn't write a lot of the dialogue in the movie. Instead, he plugged actors into situations, told them where they had to go, and let them improvise. This leads to an electrifying scene where Downey makes a sexual advance on Mike Tyson ("In the dream, you were holding me . . ."), and Tyson's reaction is quick and spontaneous.

But now compare that with another scene where Brooke Shields makes a pass at Tyson. Downey is one kind of an actor, Shields another. Downey is in character, Shields is to some degree playing herself, and Tyson is completely himself. What we are watching in the second scene is Brooke Shields the celebrity playing a character who is essentially herself, acting in an improvised scene. So the scene isn't drama; it's documentary: cinema verité of Shields and Tyson working at improvisation. It's too easy to say the scene doesn't work because Shields is not quite convincing: It *does* work because she's not quite convincing. Toback's films have that way of remaining alive and edgy, and letting their rough edges show.

The plot is sometimes maddening. Without revealing too much, I will say that a great deal

69

hinges on the policeman (Stiller) being able to count on a chain of events he could not possibly have anticipated. He needs to know that the basketball player will tell his girlfriend something, that she will tell another person, and that the other person will eventually try to hire as a killer the very person who suits the cop's needs. Unlikely.

Against untidiness like that, Toback balances passages of wonderful invention. Downey has a scene where he tries to tell Shields he is gay. Tyson ("I'm a man who has made too many mistakes to be known for his wisdom") has a scene where he gives advice to a friend who wants to know if he should have someone killed. Toback plays the manager of a recording studio who brushes off a rap group that wants to hire space, but the next day is happy to talk to their white manager (wary of the shootings associated with some rap artists, he explains, "What I cannot afford is a corpse in my lobby"). And to balance Charlie's rich white girl play-acting ("I want to be black") is a more sensible black girl ("I'm from the 'hood and I don't want to live there. I go back and see my friends and they wanna get out").

Black and White is not smooth and well-oiled, not fish, not fowl, not documentary, not quite fiction, and not about any single theme you can pin down. Those points are all to its credit.

The Blair Witch Project ★ ★ ★

R, 88 m., 1999

Heather Donahue (Heather), Joshua Leonard (Josh), Michael Williams (Mike). Directed and edited by Eduardo Sanchez and Daniel Myrick. Screenplay by Sanchez and Myrick. Produced by Gregg Hale and Robin Cowie.

We're instinctively afraid of natural things (snakes, barking dogs, the dark), but have to be taught to fear walking into traffic or touching an electrical wire. Horror films that tap into our hard-wired instinctive fears probe a deeper place than movies with more sophisticated threats. A villain is only an actor, but a shark is more than a shark.

The Blair Witch Project, an extraordinarily effective horror film, knows this and uses it. It has no fancy special effects or digital monsters, but its characters get lost in the woods, hear noises in the night, and find disturbing stick figures hanging from trees. One of them discovers slime on his backpack. Because their imaginations have been inflamed by talk of witches, hermits, and child-murderers in the forest, because their food is running out and their smokes are gone, they (and we) are a lot more scared than if they were merely being chased by some guy in a ski mask.

The movie is like a celebration of rock-bottom production values—of how it doesn't take bells and whistles to scare us. It's presented in the form of a documentary. We learn from the opening titles that in 1994 three young filmmakers went into a wooded area in search of a legendary witch: "A year later, their footage was found." The film's style and even its production strategy enhance the illusion that it's a real documentary. The characters have the same names as the actors. All of the footage in the film was shot by two cameras—a color video camcorder operated by the director, Heather (Heather Donahue), and a 16mm black-and-white camera operated by the cameraman, Josh (Joshua Leonard). Mike (Michael Williams) does the sound. All three carry backpacks and are prepared for two or three nights of sleeping in tents in the woods. It doesn't work out that way.

The buried structure of the film, which was written and directed by Eduardo Sanchez and Daniel Myrick, is insidious in the way it introduces information without seeming to. Heather and her crew arrive in the small town of Burkittsville ("formerly Blair") and interview locals. Many have vaguely heard of the Blair witch and other ominous legends; one says, "I think I saw a documentary on the Discovery Channel or something."

We hear that children have been killed in the woods, that bodies have disappeared, that strange things happened at Coffin Rock. But the movie wisely doesn't present this information as if it can be trusted; it's gossip, legend and lore, passed along half-jokingly by local people, and Heather, Josh, and Mike view it as good footage, not a warning.

Once they get into the woods, the situation gradually turns ominous. They walk in circles. Something happens to their map. Nature itself begins to seem oppressive and dead. They find ominous signs. Bundles of twigs. Unsettling stick figures. These crude objects are scarier than more elaborate effects; they look like they were created by a being who haunts the woods, not by someone playing a practical joke. Much has been said about the realistic cinematography—how every shot looks like it was taken by a hand-held camera in the woods (as it was). But the visuals are not just a technique. By shooting in a chill season, by dampening the color palette, the movie makes the woods look unfriendly and desolate; nature is seen as a hiding place for dread secrets.

As fear and desperation grow, the personalities of the characters emerge. "We agreed to a scouted-out project!" one guy complains, and the other says, "Heather, this is *so* not cool!" Heather keeps up an optimistic front; the woods are not large enough to get lost in, she argues, because "this is America. We've destroyed most of our natural resources." Eventually her brave attitude disintegrates into a remarkable shot in which she films her own apology (I was reminded of Scott's notebook entries as he froze to death in Antarctica).

At a time when digital techniques can show us almost anything, *The Blair Witch Project* is a reminder that what really scares us is the stuff we can't see. The noise in the dark is almost always scarier than what makes the noise in the dark. Any kid can tell you that. Not that he believes it at the time.

Blast From the Past ★ ★ ★
PG-13, 106 m., 1999

Brendan Fraser (Adam), Alicia Silverstone (Eve), Christopher Walken (Calvin), Sissy Spacek (Helen), Dave Foley (Troy), Joey Slotnick (Soda Jerk), Dale Raoul (Mom). Directed by Hugh Wilson and produced by Renny Harlin and Wilson. Screenplay by Bill Kelly and Wilson.

Blast From the Past opens with a cocktail party in 1962 at the home of Calvin and Helen Webber, where some of the guests whisper about how brilliant, but weird, Calvin is. Their host meanwhile mixes cocktails, tells bad jokes, and hints darkly that "I could take a simple yacht battery and rig it to last a year, easily."

Suddenly President Kennedy appears on TV to announce that Russian missiles in Cuba are aimed at targets in America. Calvin (Christopher Walken) hustles the guests out the door and hurries his pregnant wife (Sissy Spacek) into an elevator to take them down to his amazingly well-stocked bomb shelter, where fish grow in breeding tanks, and the decor of their surface home has been exactly reproduced—right down to the lawn furniture on the patio.

Calvin is a brain from Cal Tech who has been waiting for years for the big one to drop. His prudence is admirable but his luck is bad: There's no nuclear war, but a plane crashes on his house and sends a fireball down the elevator shaft, convincing him there is one. So he closes the heavy steel doors and informs Helen that the time locks won't open for thirty-five years—"to keep us from trying to leave."

That's the setup for Hugh Wilson's quirky comedy that turns the tables on *Pleasantville*. That was a movie about modern characters visiting the 1950s; this is about people emerging into the present from a thirty-five-year time warp. In the sealed atmosphere far below Los Angeles, nothing changes. Calvin and Helen watch kinescopes of old Jackie Gleason programs ("People will never get tired of watching these," Calvin smiles, while Helen's eyes roll up into her head). Tuna casserole is still on the menu. And unto them a son is born, named, of course, Adam, and played as an adult by Brendan Fraser.

Adam is trained by Calvin to speak several languages, and he masters science, math, and history, while his mother teaches him good manners and gives him a dance lesson every day. His dad even tries to explain the principles of baseball to him. Try it sometime. Calvin is pleased as punch with how well his shelter is functioning, but Helen grows quietly stir-crazy and starts to hit the cooking sherry. Her wish for her son: "I want you to marry a nice girl from Pasadena." His birthday wish for himself: "A girl. One who doesn't glow in the dark."

Eventually the locks open, and Adam is sent to the surface, where his family's pleasant neighborhood has been replaced by a ruined strip mall made of boarded-up storefronts and porno shops, and populated by drunks and transvestite hookers. "Subspecies mutants," he decides. Then he meets a real girl who doesn't glow in the dark, the inevitably named Eve

(Alicia Silverstone). She can't believe his perfect manners, his strange clothes, his lapses of current knowledge, or his taste in music. But eventually, as is the custom in such movies, they fall in love.

Brendan Fraser has a way of suggesting he's only passing through our zone of time and space. He was the "Encino Man" and "George of the Jungle," and even in *Gods and Monsters* his haircut made him look a little like Frankenstein's creature. Here he fits easily into the role of a nice man who has a good education but is, to borrow the title of Silverstone's best movie, clueless.

Blast From the Past is the first screen credit for writer Bill Kelly, who coscripted with the director, Wilson *(The First Wives Club* and the overlooked *Guarding Tess)*. It's a sophisticated and observant film that wears its social commentary lightly but never forgets it, as Adam wanders through a strange new world of burgeoning technology and decaying manners. His innocence has an infectious charm, although the worldly-wise Eve can hardly believe he doesn't know the value of his dad's baseball card collection (wait until she hears about his dad's stock portfolio).

The movie is funny and entertaining in all the usual ways, yes, but I was grateful that it tried for more: that it was actually about something, that it had an original premise, that it used satire and irony and had sly undercurrents. Even the set decoration is funny. I congratulate whoever had the idea of putting Reader's Digest Condensed Books on the shelves of the bomb shelter—the last place on Earth where you'd want to hurry through a book.

Blood Guts Bullets and Octane ★ ★ ½
NO MPAA RATING, 87 m., 1999

Joe Carnahan (Sid French), Dan Leis (Bob Melba), Ken Rudulph (FBI Agent Jared), Dan Harlan (Danny Woo), Kurt Johnson (Hillbilly Sniper), Mark S. Allen (FBI Agent Franks), Kellee Benedict (FBI Agent Little). Directed by Joe Carnahan and produced by Dan Leis, Leon Corcos, and Patrick M. Lynn. Screenplay by Carnahan.

I've had a busy day on the Tarantino beat. First I reviewed a movie named *Go* that seemed inspired by *Pulp Fiction,* then I had a cup of coffee, and here I am back at the keyboard reviewing *Blood Guts Bullets and Octane,* which is so indebted to QT's kinetic style that it doesn't even pause to put commas in its title. One thing you have to say about the long shadow of *Pulp Fiction:* In a season dominated by movies that end at the senior prom, at least the QT retreads are generally more energetic and inventive, and involve characters over seventeen.

The story behind *BGB&O* is an inspiring fable for would-be filmmakers. Its writer-director-editor-star, Joe Carnahan of Sacramento, shot it in three weeks for less than $8,000, and cheerfully let it be known at Sundance that his cast and crew were paid "partly in Doritos." Like Robert Rodriguez's *El Mariachi,* the bargain price was enough to make a video version for showing to distributors; Lions Gate ponied up a reported $100,000 in postproduction sound and transfer work to get the movie into theaters in 35mm.

What Carnahan made for his money is a fabulous calling card: This movie shows that he can direct, can generate momentum even in the face of a problematic story, and knows how to find and cast natural actors, including himself. There is real talent here. The most engaging aspect of the film is its spoken dialogue, which largely involves used car salesmen and seems inspired by David Mamet's real estate agents in *Glengarry Glen Ross.* (Consider this line: "The best in this business are, by virtue, fabulous salesmen." Using "by virtue" without explaining by virtue of *what* is prime Mamet.)

The movie opens in a torrent of words, as two desperate used car salesmen named Sid and Bob (Carnahan and Dan Leis) try to close a sale while screaming into the phone to a supplier who hasn't delivered the cars he promised. They're going under fast, swamped by the TV ads of their powerful competitor, Mr. Woo (Dan Harlan). Then they're offered $250,000 to simply hang onto a vintage Pontiac Le Mans for two days—to just park it on their lot.

This is a car with a lot of history. An FBI agent has traced it from South America to California, and reckons thirty-four dead bodies are associated with it. There's something in its trunk, but the trunk, Sid and Bob discover, is wired to a bomb and can't be opened. The locked trunk functions for much of the movie like the trunk in *Repo Man* and the briefcases in *Pulp Fiction* and *Ronin;* it contains the MacGuffin.

Carnahan is nothing if not stylistically open-minded. He uses color, black-and-white, flash frames, tilt shots, weird points of view, whatever. True to the QT tradition, he also fractures his time line and moves back and forth between elements of his story. He ends up with a lot of icing and very little cake, and his ending is an exercise in narrative desperation, but for most of the way he holds our attention, if not our interest: If he can do this with smoke and mirrors, think what he might be able to accomplish with a real budget.

Blood Simple: 2000 Director's Cut ★ ★ ★ ★
R, 97 m., 2000

John Getz (Ray), Frances McDormand (Abby), Dan Hedaya (Julian Marty), M. Emmet Walsh (Loren Visser), Samm-Art Williams (Meurice), Deborah Neumann (Debra), Raquel Gavia (Landlady), Van Brooks (Man from Lubbock). Directed by Joel Coen and produced by Ethan Coen. Screenplay by Joel Coen and Ethan Coen.

The genius of *Blood Simple* is that everything that happens seems necessary. The movie's a blood-soaked nightmare in which greed and lust trap the characters in escalating horror. The plot twists in upon itself. Characters are found in situations of diabolical complexity. And yet it doesn't feel like the film is just piling it on. Step by inexorable step, logically, one damned thing leads to another.

Consider the famous sequence in which a man is in one room and his hand is nailed to the windowsill in another room. How he got into that predicament, and how he tries to get out of it, all makes perfect sense when you see the film. But if you got an assignment in a film class that began with a close-up of that hand snaking in through the window and being nailed down, how easy would it be to write the setup scenes?

This was the first film directed by Joel Coen, produced by Ethan Coen, and cowritten by the brothers. Their joint credits have since be-

come famous, with titles like *Miller's Crossing, Raising Arizona, Barton Fink,* and the incomparable *Fargo.* Sometimes they succeed and sometimes they fail, but they always swing for the fences, and they are masters of plot. As I wrote in my original review of *Blood Simple:* "Every individual detail seems to make sense, and every individual choice seems logical, but the choices and details form a bewildering labyrinth." They build crazy walls with sensible bricks.

What we have here is the fifteenth anniversary "director's cut" of *Blood Simple,* restored and rereleased. Its power remains undiminished: It is one of the best of the modern *film noirs,* a grimy story of sleazy people trapped in a net of betrayal and double cross. When it uses clichés like The Corpse that Will Not Die, it raises them to a whole new level of usefulness. The Coens are usually original, but when they borrow a movie convention, they rotate it so that the light shines through in an unexpected way.

How exactly is this a "director's cut"? It runs ninety-seven minutes. The original film had the same running time. The term "director's cut" often means the director has at last been able to restore scenes that the studio or the MPAA made him take out. The Coens have kept all the original scenes in *Blood Simple,* and performed a little nip and tuck operation, tightening shots of dialogue they think outstayed their usefulness. It is a subtle operation; you will not notice much different from the earlier cut. The two running times are the same, I deduce, because the brothers have added a tongue-in-cheek preface in which a film restoration expert introduces the new version and claims that it takes advantage of technological breakthroughs made possible since the original came out in 1985.

Blood Simple was made on a limited budget, but like most good films seems to have had all the money it really needed. It is particularly blessed in its central performances. Dan Hedaya plays the unshaven owner of a scummy saloon who hires a private eye to kill his wife and her lover. The wife (Frances McDormand) is having an affair with one of the bartenders (John Getz). The detective is played by that poet of sleaze, M. Emmet Walsh. He takes the bar owner's money and then kills the bar owner.

Neat. If he killed the wife, he reasons, he'd still have to kill the bar owner to eliminate a witness against him. This way, he gets the same amount of money for one killing, not two.

Oh, but it gets much more complicated than that. At any given moment in the movie there seems to be one more corpse than necessary, one person who is alive and should be dead, and one person who is completely clueless about both the living and the dead. There is no psychology in the film. Every act is inspired more or less directly by the act that went before, and the motive is always the same: self-preservation, based on guilt and paranoia.

Blood Simple is comic in its dark way, and obviously wants to go over the top. But it doesn't call attention to its contrivance. It is easy to do a parody of *film noir*, but hard to do good *film noir*, and almost impossible to make a film that works as suspense and exaggeration at the same time. *Blood Simple* is clever in the way it makes its incredulities seem necessary.

In my 1985 review, I tried to explain that: "It keys into three common nightmares: (1) You clean and clean but there's still blood all over the place; (2) you know you have committed a murder, but you're not sure how or why; (3) you know you've forgotten a small detail that will eventually get you into a lot of trouble." Those feelings are so elemental that the movie involves us even though we know the Coens are laughing as they devise their fiendish complications. In a strange way, the contrivances also help excuse the blood and gore. If you are squeamish, here is the film to make you squeam.

Blow ★ ★ ½
R, 119 m., 2001

Johnny Depp (George Jung), Penelope Cruz (Mirtha), Franka Potente (Barbara), Paul Reubens (Derek Foreal), Ray Liotta (Fred Jung), Jacque Lawson (Biker), Cliff Curtis (Pablo Escobar), Ethan Suplee (Tuna), Rachel Griffiths (Ermine Jung). Directed by Ted Demme and produced by Demme, Denis Leary, and Joel Stillerman. Screenplay by David McKenna and Nick Cassavetes, based on the book by Bruce Porter.

Blow stars Johnny Depp in a biopic about George Jung, a man who claims that in the late 1970s he imported about 85 percent of all the cocaine in America. That made him the greatest success story in drugs, an industry that has inspired more movies than any other. So why is he such a sad sack? Why is his life so monotonous and disappointing? That's what he'd like to know. The last shot in the film shows the real George Jung staring out at us from the screen like a man buried alive in his own regrets.

The story begins in a haze of California dreamin' for George, who escapes West from an uninspiring Massachusetts childhood, a relentless mother (Rachel Griffiths), and a father (Ray Liotta) who doesn't want to deal with bad news about his son. In the Los Angeles environs of Manhattan Beach, George smokes pot, throws Frisbees, meets stewardesses, and engages in boozy plans with his friend Tuna (Ethan Suplee), who asks him, "You know how we were wondering how we were gonna get money being that we don't want to get jobs?"

The brainstorm: Import marijuana from Mexico in the customs-free luggage of their stewardess pals and sell it to eager students at eastern colleges. This is a business plan waiting to be born, and soon George is wealthy, although not beyond his wildest imaginings. His first love is a stewardess named Barbara (Franka Potente, from *Run, Lola, Run*) and it's fun, fun, fun, and her daddy never takes her T-Bird away.

These opening chapters in the life of George Jung tell a story of small risk and great joy, especially if your idea of a good time is having all the money you can possibly spend and hopelessly conventional ideas about how to spend it. How big a house can you live in? How many drugs can you consume? George never actually planned to become a drug dealer and is a little bemused at his good luck. Even a 1972 bust in Chicago seems like a minor bump in the road (speaking in his own defense, he tells the judge, "It ain't me, babe").

Back on the streets, George finds clouds obscuring the California sun. Barbara dies unexpectedly (i.e., not because of drugs), and his success attracts the interest of a better class of narcotics cop. He becomes a fugitive, and it is his own mother who rats on him with the cops, even while his father is beaming at what might seem to be his success.

In Danbury Prison, he tells us, "I went in with a bachelor's of marijuana and came out with a doctorate in cocaine." As the 1970s roll on, the innocence of pot has been replaced by the urgency of cocaine. Soon George is making real money as a key distributor for his new friend Pablo Escobar (Cliff Curtis) and the Medellin drug cartel of Colombia. It's with their cocaine that he racks up his record market share. And there is a new woman, Mirtha (Penelope Cruz), sexy as hell, but a real piece of work in the deportment department. At one point she gets him arrested by throwing a tantrum in their car.

The Colombians, of course, are heavy-hitters, and George tries to protect his position by concealing the identity of his key California middleman, a onetime hairdresser named Derek Foreal (Paul Reubens). But the Colombians want to know that name really bad, and meanwhile George might be asking, is a rich man under the shadow of sudden death measurably happier than a man with a more mundane but serene existence?

This is not, alas, a question that occurs to George Jung. Indeed, not many questions occur to him that are not directly related to getting, spending, and sleeping with. The later chapters of his life grow increasingly depressing. He was never an interesting person, never had thoughts worth sharing or words worth remembering, but at least he represented a colorful type in his early years: the kid who smokes a little weed, finds a source, starts to sell, and finds himself with a brand-new pair of roller skates. By his middle years, George is essentially just the guy the Colombians want to replace and the feds want to arrest. No fun.

The dreary story of his final defeats is a record of backstabbing and broken trusts, and although there is a certain poignancy in his final destiny, it is tempered by our knowledge that millions of lives had to be destroyed by addiction so that George and his onetime friends could arrive at their crossroads.

That's the thing about George. He thinks it's all about him. His life, his story, his success, his fortune, his lost fortune, his good luck, his bad luck. Actually, all he did was operate a tollgate between suppliers and addicts. You wonder, but you never find out, if the reality of those destroyed lives ever occurred to him.

The movie, directed by Ted Demme and written by David McKenna and Nick Cassavetes (from an as-told-to book by Bruce Porter), is well made and well acted. As a story of the rise and fall of this man, it serves. Johnny Depp is a versatile and reliable actor who almost always chooses interesting projects. The failure is George Jung's. For all the glory of his success and the pathos of his failure, he never became a person interesting enough to make a movie about. The appearance of Ray Liotta here reminds us of Scorsese's *GoodFellas,* which took a much less important criminal and made him an immeasurably more interesting character. And of course Al Pacino's *Scarface* has so much style he makes George Jung look like a dry-goods clerk. Which essentially he was. Take away the drugs, and this is the story of a boring life in wholesale. ☞

Blue Streak ★ ★ ★
PG-13, 93 m., 1999

Martin Lawrence (Miles Logan), Luke Wilson (Detective Carlson), Peter Greene (Deacon), William Forsythe (Hardcastle), Dave Chappelle (Tulley), Tamala Jones (Janiece), Nicole Ari Parker (Melissa Green). Directed by Les Mayfield and produced by Toby Jaffe and Neal H. Moritz. Screenplay by Michael Berry, John Blumenthal, and Steve Carpenter.

Blue Streak ranks in the upper reaches of the cop buddy genre, up there in *Lethal Weapon* territory. It has the usual ingredients for a cop comedy, including the obligatory Dunkin' Donuts product placement, but it's assembled with style—and it's built around a Martin Lawrence performance that deserves comparison with Richard Pryor and Eddie Murphy, with a touch of Mel Gibson's zaniness in the midst of action.

The movie opens with a high-tech caper scene; jewel thief Miles Logan (Lawrence) and his team put together a complicated plan involving illegal entry, alarm system workarounds, and steel getaway cables. Everything goes wrong, alas, and Lawrence is cornered on a construction site with a $17 million diamond. He tapes it inside an air duct, is arrested, and goes to prison.

Two years pass. On the street again, he finds his old girlfriend isn't happy to see him ("I didn't come to visit you for two years. Isn't that a sign?"). There is worse news. The building under construction turns out to be a police station, and the diamond is hidden deep inside. How to get it? He tries to get to the burglary department on the third floor by impersonating a crazy pizza-delivery guy. That's not a great idea, but he keeps improvising, and is somehow mistaken for a real cop. Soon he's out on the street with a partner (Luke Wilson), who is from the traffic division and thrilled to be working with an ace like Miles.

It's pretty clear that Miles isn't a standard cop. It doesn't take long for his partners to discover his name and badge number don't check out. But he's so confident, and so ruthless in roughing up suspects, they assume he's a genuine law enforcement officer of some description, who has infiltrated the department. His superior (William Forsythe) admires everything about him, and engages in debates about his true identity. FBI? Internal Affairs? CIA?

The movie, directed by Les Mayfield *(Encino Man)*, doesn't settle for the gag that Miles is a thief impersonating a cop. It takes that as a starting point and wrings laughs out of it— for example, in a funny scene where Miles walks in on a convenience store holdup that's being pulled by an old criminal buddy of his. While the other cop covers them from a distance, Miles engages in a desperate and unorthodox form of plea bargaining. If the old buddy doesn't blow his cover, Miles will promise him $10,000 and only one night in jail. Okay, $20,000?

I've seen enough car chases to last several lifetimes, but I like a good one when it's handled well, and the action in the last act of this movie is not only high-style, but makes sense in terms of the plot. Good casting of villains is essential in action comedies (remember Joe Pesci in *Lethal Weapon 2*?), and here the sinister Peter Greene is a convincing counterpoint. The villain always has to be the thankless straight man in a plot like this; he's never in on the joke, which is the joke.

Martin Lawrence is a comic actor with real talent not always shown to best advantage. *Bad Boys,* his 1995 cop buddy movie with Will Smith, was not a career high point, and it took a certain nerve to make another one. But *Blue Streak* works. Lawrence himself was in shaky condition at the time of its release, recovering from a nearly fatal case of heat exhaustion. A movie like this is evidence that in the right material, he has a real gift. But he should dial down on the jogging.

Body Shots ★ ★
R, 99 m., 1999

Sean Patrick Flanery (Rick Hamilton), Jerry O'Connell (Michael Penorisi), Amanda Peet (Jane Bannister), Tara Reid (Sara Olswang), Ron Livingston (Trent Barber), Emily Procter (Whitney Bryant), Brad Rowe (Shawn Denigan), Sybil Temchen (Emma Cooper). Directed by Michael Cristofer and produced by Harry Colomby and Jennifer Keohane. Screenplay by David McKenna.

Body Shots suffers from a fatal misapprehension. It thinks it is about date rape, when actually it is about alcoholism. That's why the ending is inconclusive and unsatisfactory; not only does it fail to find answers—but they would be to the wrong questions.

The movie is about dating values and practices among affluent thirty-something professionals in Los Angeles. Some scenes are played straight to the camera, as if the characters are in a documentary. The girls as well as the guys are mostly looking for sex, and a "meaningful relationship" would be an unexpected bonus. The facile dialogue can't disguise the shallowness, but why should these characters have original thoughts about sex when nothing else in their lives is carefully examined?

Separate groups of men and women end up at the same bar, go on to another club, and split up. A pro football hero named Michael (Jerry O'Connell) ends up with a cute blonde named Sara (Tara Reid). They are both drunk. She pays for the $25 cab ride to her place on the beach in Santa Monica. They make out on the beach, go inside, and have sex. He says it was consensual, that she hit her head on the bed and got mad at him when he forgot her name. She says it was rape.

Each character is talked to urgently and privately by friends. Rick (Sean Patrick Flanery) quizzes the defiant and angry Michael, who is sure Sara was coming on to him and wanted sex, but cannot remember exactly what happened in her apartment. Jane (Amanda Peet) questions Sara, who also does not remember, although she has given the police a complete account of the rape. "Do you ever have blackouts?" another friend, Whitney (Emily Procter), asks her. Sara says no. Whitney reminds Sara of a couple of dramatic blackouts all her friends witnessed. Of course, by definition you cannot remember a blackout (this is the Heineken Uncertainty Principle).

As the movie dribbles to its inconclusive conclusion, we are left with the notion that in this case date rape may be in the mind of the beholder. Men see things one way, women another. Both Sara and Michael make persuasive arguments for their versions of events, while the film, which takes no sides, carefully presents both versions of the sexual encounter. This is like soft porn with a choice of point of view: First we see Sara's bra taken off, then we see it ripped off.

None of the characters (and perhaps none of the filmmakers) are enlightened about alcoholism. One danger sign of alcoholism is when a guy uses a Magic Marker to write DO ME on your forehead during a party, and you don't notice, as Sara doesn't. And what about her friend Whitney, whose part-time job consists of passing out free shots for a brand promotion at a club and setting a good example by tossing them back herself. I'm not saying that the job brands Whitney as an alcoholic (everyone has to earn a living), but that moderate drinkers somehow rarely find themselves employed as the free-shot girl.

It isn't surprising that Rick and Jane, the best friends, don't notice their friends are drunks. The movie's opening shot shows Rick and Jane in bed, still dressed, and the first line of dialogue is more realistic than most waking-up lines in the movies: "Do you have any Tylenol, honey?"

Body Shots means well and has some pointed dialogue about legal pitfalls, but it's clueless about its real subject. My own theory of date rape is that if you think you had sex and you didn't want to, but you're not sure why or how

(or if) it happened, it's probably a good idea to call AA before you call the cops.

Boiler Room ★ ★ ★ ½
R, 119 m., 2000

Giovanni Ribisi (Seth), Vin Diesel (Chris), Nia Long (Abby), Nicky Katt (Greg), Scott Caan (Richie), Ron Rifkin (Seth's Father [Marty]), Jamie Kennedy (Adam), Taylor Nichols (Harry Reynard), Ben Affleck (Jim). Directed by Ben Younger and produced by Suzanne Todd and Jennifer Todd. Screenplay by Younger.

Boiler Room tells the story of a nineteen-year-old named Seth who makes a nice income running an illegal casino in his apartment. His dad, a judge, finds out about it and raises holy hell. So the kid gets a daytime job as a broker with a Long Island bucket shop that sells worthless or dubious stock with high-pressure telephone tactics. When he was running his casino, Seth muses, at least he was providing a product that his customers wanted.

The movie is the writing and directing debut of Ben Younger, a twenty-nine-year-old who says he interviewed a lot of brokers while writing the screenplay. I believe him. The movie hums with authenticity, and knows a lot about the cultlike power of a company that promises to turn its trainees into millionaires, and certainly turns them into efficient phone salesmen.

No experience is necessary at J. P. Marlin: "We don't hire brokers here—we train new ones," snarls Jim (Ben Affleck), already a millionaire, who gives new recruits a hard-edged introductory lecture, crammed with obscenities and challenges to their manhood. "Did you see *Glengarry Glen Ross*?" he asks them. He certainly has. Mamet's portrait of high-pressure real-estate salesmen is like a bible in this culture, and a guy like Jim doesn't see the message, only the style. (Younger himself observes that Jim, giving his savage pep talks, not only learned his style from Alec Baldwin's scenes in *Glengarry* but also wants to *be* Baldwin.)

The film's narrator is Seth Davis (Giovanni Ribisi), an unprepossessing young man with a bad suit who learns in a short time to separate suckers from their money with telephone fantasies about hot stocks and IPOs. Everybody wants to be a millionaire *right now*, he observes. Ironically, the dream of wealth he's selling with his cold calls is the same one J. P. Marlin is selling him.

In the phone war room with Seth are several other brokers, including the successful Chris (Vin Diesel) and Greg (Nicky Katt), who exchange anti-Jewish and Italian slurs almost as if it's expected of them. At night the guys go out, get drunk, and sometimes get in fights with brokers from other houses. The kids gambling in Seth's apartment were better behaved. We observe that both gamblers and stockbrokers bet their money on a future outcome, but as a gambler you pay the house nut, while as a broker you collect the house nut. Professional gamblers claim they do not depend on luck but on an understanding of the odds and prudent money management. Investors believe much the same thing. Of course, nobody ever claims luck has nothing to do with it unless luck has something to do with it.

The movie has the high-octane feel of real life, closely observed. It's made more interesting because Seth isn't a slickster like Michael Douglas or Charlie Sheen in *Wall Street* (a movie these guys know by heart), but an uncertain, untested young man who stands in the shadow of his father the judge (Ron Rifkin) who, he thinks, is always judging him. The tension between Seth and the judge is one of the best things in the film—especially in Rifkin's quiet, clear power in scenes where he lays down the law. When Seth refers to their relationship, his dad says: "Relationship? What relationship? I'm not your girlfriend. Relationships are your mother's shtick. I'm your father."

A relationship does grow in the film, however, between Seth and Abby (Nia Long), the receptionist, and although it eventually has a lot to do with the plot, what I admired was the way Younger writes their scenes so that they actually share hopes, dreams, backgrounds, and insecurities instead of falling into automatic movie passion. When she touches his hand, it is at the end of a scene during which she empathizes with him.

Because of the routine racism at the firm, Seth observes it must not be a comfortable place for a black woman to work. Abby points out she makes $80,000 a year and is supporting a sick mother. Case closed, with no long, anguished dramaturgy over interracial dating;

they like each other, and have evolved beyond racial walls. Younger's handling of their scenes shames movies where the woman exists only to be the other person in the sex scene.

The acting is good all around. A few days ago I saw Vin Diesel as a vicious prisoner in the space opera *Pitch Black,* and now here he is, still tough, still with the shaved head, but now the only guy at the brokerage that Seth really likes and trusts enough to appeal to. Diesel is interesting. Something will come of him.

Boiler Room isn't perfect. The film's ending is a little too busy; it's too contrived the way Abby doesn't tell Seth something he needs to know; there's a scene where a man calls her by name and Seth leaps to a conclusion when in fact that man would have every reason to know her name; and I am still not sure exactly what kind of a deal Seth was trying to talk his father into in their crucial evening meeting. But those are all thoughts I had afterward. During the movie I was wound up with tension and involvement, all the more so because the characters are all complex and guilty, the good as well as the bad, and we can understand why everyone in the movie does what they do. Would we? Depends.

The Bone Collector ★ ★
R, 118 m., 1999

Denzel Washington (Lincoln Rhyme), Angelina Jolie (Amelia Donaghy), Queen Latifah (Thelma), Michael Rooker (Captain Howard Cheney), Mike McGlone (Detective Kenny Solomon), Luis Guzman (Eddie Ortiz), Ed O'Neill (Lieutenant Paulie Sellitto), Leland Orser (Richard Thompson), John Benjamin Hickey (Dr. Barry Lehman). Directed by Phillip Noyce and produced by Martin Bregman, Louis A. Stroller, and Michael Bregman. Screenplay by Jeremy Iacone, based on the book by Jeffery Deaver.

The Bone Collector is assembled from off-the-shelf thriller contrivances, likable characters, and utter absurdity, with one of those scores that's the musical equivalent of trying to scrape the burnt meat off the bottom of the pot: *Unnngh! Unnngh! Unnngh!* Its big romantic scene has the girl cop caressing the index finger of the boy cop, which is the only part of him below the neck that still has any feeling. Freud has a lot to atone for.

The movie is a peculiar experience to sit through, because the quality of the acting is so much better than the material deserves. Denzel Washington and Angelina Jolie create characters we really like; there's chemistry when they're together, and they're surrounded by the good energy of supporting players like Queen Latifah, Luis Guzman, and Ed O'Neill. It's sad watching them wade through one of those plots where a depraved serial killer leads everyone in a find-the-corpse version of "Where's Waldo?"

Washington plays Lincoln Rhyme, a hero cop who has written twelve books on crime-scene forensics. He is paralyzed by a falling beam on the job: "I have one finger, two shoulders, and a brain." He occupies a bed in his Manhattan loft, which is one of those rent-controlled movie apartments large enough to house an entire task force for a serial killer manhunt (which it does—his buddies move in with their desks and computers). Rhyme is tended by a nurse named Thelma (Queen Latifah), who slaps an oxygen mask on him and chants "now breathe with me" when he goes into spasms. He manipulates his bed, his TV, his computer, and various analytical devices with a remote-control breathing tube and an extremely versatile one-button mouse.

We meet a beat cop named Amelia Donaghy (Angelina Jolie). She is the first on the scene of a gruesome murder: A man buried in gravel, with only his hand showing. One finger is amputated; on its stump is his wife's wedding ring. We know right away the killer is a contestant in the ever-escalating Hollywood Serial Killer sweepstakes, in which villains don't simply kill, but spend the time and patience of a set decorator on arranging the crime scene. No six Agatha Christie mysteries contain as many clues, each one lovingly placed by hand, as this guy leaves.

Some of them are very, very easy to miss, consisting of microscopic bits of paper about the size of *this* word, which, when pieced together by the two cops, lead to a used-book store where, wouldn't you know, a lot of books tumble from a top shelf and Amelia is able to turn to the very page where the next murder is illustrated. Just think. If she hadn't stumbled

over that rare volume, we might have been denied a scene where a father drowns but his young daughter is resuscitated—for no dramatic purpose, mind you, since she says nothing and is never seen again, but simply so sentimentalists in the audience can think, "Whew! At least she didn't drown!" In a movie where a man gets his face eaten off by rats, these humanitarian interludes are touching.

Most of the plot consists of a series of laboriously contrived setups requiring the young woman to enter dark, dangerous places all by herself, her flashlight penetrating a Spielbergian haze that makes its beam visible. She walks into subterranean rat holes and abandoned factories where the homicidal maniac is, hopefully, lurking. She goes in alone so as not to disturb the forensics of the crime scene. If she gets killed, I guess the next cop goes in alone, too, to preserve her scene.

These Women in Danger thriller units alternate with the obligatory Superior Officer Who Is Always Angry, Wrong, and a Pig. This thankless role is played by Michael Rooker, who is required to be mistaken about everything, and who keeps trying to put Amelia under arrest, apparently on charges of brilliant police work. He's the obvious suspect, which means—well, you know what it means. Most movies with a zillion clues have the good manners to supply a couple that are helpful. This movie's villain appears so arbitrarily he must have been a temp worker, in for the day.

Book of Shadows: Blair Witch 2 ★ ★
R, 90 m., 2000

Kim Director (Kim Director), Jeffrey Donovan (Jeffrey Donovan), Erica Leerhsen (Erica Leerhsen), Tristen Skyler (Tristen Skyler), Stephen Turner (Stephen Turner). Directed by Joe Berlinger and produced by Bill Carraro, Daniel Myrick, and Eduardo Sanchez. Screenplay by Berlinger and Dick Beebe.

To direct a sequel to their phenomenal *Blair Witch Project*, Daniel Myrick and Eduardo Sanchez made an unexpected choice: Joe Berlinger, codirector of the documentaries *Paradise Lost: The Child Murders at Robin Hood Hills* and *Paradise Lost 2: Revelations*. Those two films make a persuasive case that three innocent young men from Arkansas are in prison, one on death row, because of local hysteria over teenagers who wear black and listen to heavy metal music. Meanwhile, a person who seems to be the real killer all but confesses on camera.

The movies are deadly serious because they make the case that injustice is being done. Lives are at stake. I wondered earlier why Berlinger would want to make a fiction film on witchcraft and black magic, but suspended judgment: He is one of the best documentarians around. But now that I've seen *Book of Shadows: Blair Witch 2*, I'm disturbed.

The movie shows no special insight that made it necessary for Berlinger to direct it. It's a muddled, sometimes atmospheric, effort that could have come from many filmmakers. At the same time, because of loaded characters and dialogue, *BW2* supplies ammunition to those who think the Arkansas prisoners are guilty. I can imagine a preacher thundering from his pulpit: "This Berlinger comes down here and makes a couple of propaganda films making us look bad, and then what does he do? Make a film glorifying black magic and witches."

If the film had argued against the mind-set that essentially framed the West Memphis Three, that would be one thing. But it doesn't. This is not one of Joe Berlinger's proudest days.

But what about the movie itself—apart from Berlinger's involvement? It opens promisingly as a documentary about the effect that the first movie had on the (fictional) town of Burkittsville, Maryland, where the Blair Witch was rumored to haunt the nearby woods. Tourists have descended on the town, locals are on eBay selling twig sculptures like those in the movie, and the exasperated local sheriff patrols the woods with a bullhorn, shouting, "Get out of these woods and go home! There is no goddamned Blair Witch!"

We meet a group of witch fanciers who have signed up for an overnight tour in the woods. The Blair Witch Hunt, as it is called, is led by a tour guide (Jeff Donovan) who, we will learn, is a former mental patient, now cured, apparently. Others include Erica, a witch who practices wicca, which is the white-magic form of witchcraft; Stephen and his girlfriend, the pregnant Tristen, who are writing a book on

the hysteria caused by the film; and Kim, who dresses in black and says, in an oblique reference to the *Paradise Lost* movies, "Where I come from, people believe because I dress in black I'm some kind of killer." (In keeping with the *BW* pseudorealistic approach, all of the actors play characters who have their names.)

The group plunges into the woods, where they begin to argue about their different approaches to the experience. I liked Erica's cautionary wiccan lore: "The first rule of wicca is, do no harm, because whatever you do will come back to you threefold." This sounds like *Pay It Forward* in reverse. Soon they have a confrontation with another tour group, which leads to an unconvincing shoving match. The other group is advised to seek out Coffin Rock, with fatal results, and eventually the sheriff gets involved and the movie intercuts interrogation scenes as the Witch Hunt group are quizzed by the law.

Like the first movie, this one has two visual styles (but not nearly as much of that hand-held photography that forced some patrons to recycle their popcorn bags). Most of it is in 35mm. The rest is video footage shot by the protagonists. The 35mm footage may or may not accurately reflect how the characters remember what happened; the video footage may or may not be an objective record of some of the same events. And . . . is there really a Blair Witch? The answer, if any, may come in *BW3*, now being prepared by Myrick and Sanchez.

Book of Shadows: Blair Witch 2 is not a very lucid piece of filmmaking (and contains no Book of Shadows). I suppose it seems clear enough to Berlinger, who cowrote it and helped edit it, but one viewing is not enough to make the material clear, and the material is not intriguing enough, alas, to inspire a second viewing. The characters are not strongly and colorfully established, there is no persuasive story line, and what planet does that hey-rube sheriff come from? He breaks the reality with every appearance.

The Blair Witch Project was perhaps one of a kind. Its success made a sequel inevitable, but this is not the sequel, I suspect, anyone much wanted. The opening scenes—the documentary showing the townspeople affected by the first film—is a more promising approach, because instead of trying to cover similar ground, it goes outside the first film and makes its own stand.

Bootmen ★ ½
R, 95 m., 2000

Adam Garcia (Sean Ikden), Sam Worthington (Mitchell Ikden), Sophie Lee (Linda), William Zappa (Walter), Richard Carter (Gary), Susie Porter (Sara), Dein Perry (Anthony). Directed by Dein Perry and produced by Hilary Linstead. Screenplay by Steve Worland.

Bootmen is the story of a young dancer and his friends who revisit the clichés of countless other dance movies in order to bring forth a dance performance of clanging unloveliness. Screwing metal plates to the soles of their work boots, they stomp in unison on flat steel surfaces while banging on things. Imagine Fred Astaire as a punch-press operator.

The movie has been adapted by director Dein Perry from his own performance piece, which he might have been better advised to make into a concert film. It takes place in Australia, where Sean (Adam Garcia) dreams of becoming a dancer. His salt-of-the-earth father, a steelworker, opposes the plan. Sean cannot face life without dance in Newcastle, a steel town, despite the charms of the fragrant Linda (Sophie Lee), a hairdresser who has given him to understand that he might someday, but not yet, enjoy her favors. He flees to Sydney to pursue his career, leaving behind his brother Mitchell, who basks in the old man's favor by adopting a reasonable occupation and stealing cars for their parts.

In Sydney, Sean encounters a hard-nosed choreographer (William Zappa), a staple of dance movies, who is not easy to impress. Sean is too talented to be dismissed, but at rehearsals he angers the star (Dein Perry himself) because the star's girlfriend likes his looks, and Sean gets fired. It is one of the oddities of this movie about dance that almost everyone in it is not merely straight but ferociously macho; it's as if the Village People really did work eight hours a day as linemen, Indian chiefs, etc. I am not suggesting that all, or most, or many dancers are gay, but surely one has heard that some are?

Sean returns disillusioned but undefeated to Newcastle, where Mitchell meanwhile has gotten the lonely Linda drunk, plied her with morose theories about Sean's long absence, and bedded her during an alcoholic lapse of judgment on her part (Mitchell has no judgment). Sean arrives in the morning, discovers that Mitchell and Linda have sailed into waters that Linda had assured him would remain uncharted pending their own maiden voyage, and becomes so depressed that we realize we have reached the Preliminary Crisis as defined in elementary screenwriting outlines.

Now what? It remains only for the steel mills to close so that Sean can realize that the millworkers should be retrained as computer experts. But there are no computers. Why not have a benefit? Sean gathers his friends and says, in other words, "Say, gang! Let's rent the old steel mill, and put on a show!" He trains his buddies in the art of synchronized stomping so that the town can turn out to watch them clang and bang. Judging by the crowd they attract, and estimating $10 a ticket, they raise enough money for approximately two computers, but never mind; cruel fate will quickly turn these recycled steelworkers into unemployed dot-com workers, so the fewer, the better.

Is there a scene near the end of the performance where the once-bitter dad enters, sees that his son is indeed talented, and forgives all? Is Linda pardoned for her lapse of faithfulness? Do Mitchell and Sean realize that even though Mitchell may have slept with the woman Sean loves it was because Mitchell had too much to drink, something that could happen in any family? Do the townspeople of Newcastle give a lusty ovation to the performance? Is there an encore? Veteran moviegoers will walk into the theater already possessing the answers to these and many other questions.

Bounce ★ ★ ★
PG-13, 102 m., 2000

Ben Affleck (Buddy Amaral), Gwyneth Paltrow (Abby), Natasha Henstridge (Mimi), Johnny Galeckie (Buddy's Secretary), Jennifer Grey (Mrs. Guererro), Tony Goldwyn (Greg), Joe Morton (Jim), David Paymer (Lawyer), Alex D. Linz (Scott). Directed by Don Roos and produced by Michael Besman and Steve Golin. Screenplay by Roos.

Bounce begins with flights delayed at Chicago's O'Hare airport. One guy gives another guy his boarding pass, the plane crashes, the other guy dies. The survivor is Buddy (Ben Affleck), an alcoholic ad executive from Los Angeles, whose boozing now spirals out of control, until he joins AA and finds that one of the twelve steps involves making amends to those he harmed with his drinking. So he pays a call on Abby (Gwyneth Paltrow), the widow of the man who died in the crash.

Strictly speaking, Buddy has no amends to make. He was doing the other guy a favor. It wasn't his fault that the flight crashed. But he tracks down Abby, discovers she's a real-estate agent, and arranges for her to get a commission on a building his agency was going to buy anyway. Then she asks him to a Dodgers game, and before you know it they're in love and he's bonding with her kids.

The problem, of course, is that he hasn't told her he's responsible in some cosmic, fateful way for her husband's death. He means to, but he puts it off. Lovers with untold secrets are a familiar movie situation, seen earlier this year in *Return to Me* when Minnie Driver can't tell David Duchovny his late wife's heart was transplanted into her chest.

Bounce builds toward a big revelation scene, of course, and when it comes, it has to be perfectly aimed and well acted because both actors are on thin ice. The moment of truth in *Bounce* is not quite right. The revelation is delayed a few scenes beyond its natural place in the film, and we grow restless; we enjoy the suspense only up to a point. Buddy moistens his lips, clears his throat, and coughs nervously and *still* doesn't tell Abby, and it begins to feel like the movie's playing with us.

There have been hints that the secret may not be revealed verbally. A videotape was made at the airport, and because all props are brought onstage for a reason, we know sooner or later that the tape, showing Buddy with the dead guy, will be seen again. Thinking ahead, I began to wonder how director Don Roos would use the tape. I guessed that maybe before Abby had a chance to look at the tape, the two would share a moment of tenderness and then

one of the kids would pop the tape into the VCR and the truth would start playing, unnoticed at first, in the background. Stage this correctly and you might have one of those scenes an audience remembers for a long time.

Incredibly, Roos keeps Abby offstage for the moment of revelation. We don't see her when she learns the truth, and she's not there when he sees the tape. What a missed opportunity. *Bounce* has a strong setup, good characters, intelligent dialogue, and attractive characters, but it loses its way in technique. In movies with this story structure, all depends on the precise timing of the delay and the revelation, and *Bounce* misses. Not by a lot, but by enough.

I liked the movie anyway. I liked it because of the convincing way the relationship got started. And because Buddy's gay secretary (Johnny Galeckie) isn't afraid to talk back to him—about alcoholism and Abby. And because of the way Buddy got closer to the kids. And because Paltrow dials down her beauty and becomes a convincing widow. And because I *wanted* them to become lovers, which means they sold me on themselves.

Bowfinger ★ ★ ★ ½
PG-13, 97 m., 1999

Steve Martin (Bowfinger), Eddie Murphy (Kit Ramsey), Eddie Murphy (Jiff), Heather Graham (Daisy), Christine Baranski (Carol), Jamie Kennedy (Dave), Barry Newman (Kit's Agent), Adam Alexi-Malle (Afrim). Directed by Frank Oz and produced by Brian Grazer. Screenplay by Steve Martin.

It is a plan of audacity and madness: Bowfinger, a low-rent movie producer, will make a film with a top Hollywood action star, and the star won't even know he's making the picture. "He doesn't like to see the camera, and he never talks to his fellow actors," Bowfinger (Steve Martin) tells his trusting crew. "We'll use a hidden camera." The movie, to be titled *Chubby Rain*, will be about aliens in raindrops.

The big star, named Kit Ramsey (Eddie Murphy), is an ideal choice for this strategy, because he's crazy enough to believe in strange encounters. He's a member of Mind Head, a cult that recruits insecure Hollywood types, gives them little white pyramid hats to wear, and pumps them full of New Age babble. And Bowfinger's actors and crew want to believe him, because this is as close as they'll ever get to being in a movie.

Bowfinger, written by Martin and directed by Frank Oz *(Little Shop of Horrors),* understands how deeply people yearn to be in the movies, and how fame can make you peculiar. Like Mel Brooks's *The Producers,* it's about fringe players who strike out boldly for the big time. The shabby frame house on a dead-end street has a sign outside promoting glorious enterprises ("Bowfinger International Pictures"), but inside everything is debt, desperation, and dreams.

Bowfinger is a bottom-feeder with a coterie even more hapless than he is. His screenplay is by his Iranian accountant, Afrim (Adam Alexi-Malle). His flunky is Dave (Jaime Kennedy), who specializes in being deceived because otherwise he would have nothing at all to believe in. His leading actress, Carol (Christine Baranski), has been kept on hold for years. "We'll hire the best crew we can afford!" Bowfinger declares, backing his vehicle up to the Mexican border and loading four illegal immigrants. And straight off the bus, swinging her suitcase, her lips parted with desire, comes Daisy (Heather Graham), an Ohio girl who's prepared to sleep her way to the top but didn't realize she'd start so close to the bottom.

All these characters are like an accident waiting to happen to Kit Ramsey, hilariously played by Eddie Murphy in his third best comic performance of recent years. The second best was in *The Nutty Professor.* The best is a second role in this film: As Jiff, a hapless loser hired to be Kit's double, Murphy creates a character of such endearing cluelessness that even in a comedy he generates real affection from the audience.

Murphy makes Kit into a loudmouthed image-monger with a racial chip on his shoulder; complaining about Arnold's "I'll be back" and Clint's "Make my day," he says, "The white man gets all the best catchphrases." Terrified by the smallest detail of daily living, he has frequent sessions with his Mind Head guru (Terence Stamp), who leads him patiently through reminders of good and bad behavior (one of his problems is too funny for me to spoil with even a hint).

But it's as Jiff that Murphy gets his biggest laughs. Here is a man so grateful to be in a film, so disbelieving that he has been singled out for stardom, that he dutifully risks his life to walk across a busy expressway. Murphy shows here, as he did in *The Nutty Professor* and on *Saturday Night Live,* a gift for creating new characters out of familiar materials. Yes, Jiff looks like Kit (that's why he got the job as a double), but the person inside is completely fresh and new, and has his own personality and appeal. Although Murphy is not usually referred to as a great actor (and comedians are never taken as seriously as they should be), how many other actors, however distinguished, could create Jiff out of whole cloth and make him such a convincing and funny original?

Martin is also at the top of his form, especially in an early scene where he pitches his project to a powerful producer (Robert Downey Jr.). Martin steals a suit and a car to make an impressive entrance at the restaurant where Downey is having a power lunch, but undercuts the effect a little by ripping out the car phone and trying to use it like a cell phone—staging a fake call for Downey to overhear. Downey handles this scene perfectly, right down to his subdued doubletake when he sees the cord dangling from the end of the phone. His performance is based on the truth that strange and desperate pitches are lobbed at producers every day, some of them no less bizarre than this one. Instead of overreacting to Martin's craziness, Downey plays the scene to humor this guy.

Bowfinger is one of those comedies where everything works, where the premise is not just a hook but the starting point for a story that keeps developing and revealing new surprises. Like a lot of Steve Martin's other writing, it is also gentle and good-natured: He isn't a savage ironist or a vulgarian, and when he makes us laugh, it's usually about things that are really funny. Shell-shocked by gross and grosser comedies, we can turn to *Bowfinger* with merciful relief.

Boys and Girls ★ ★
PG-13, 100 m., 2000

Freddie Prinze Jr. (Ryan), Claire Forlani (Jennifer), Jason Biggs (Hunter), Heather

Donahue (Megan), Amanda Detmer (Amy). Directed by Robert Iscove and produced by Sue Baden-Powell, Harvey Weinstein, and Bob Weinstein. Screenplay by the Drews (Andrew Lowery and Andrew Miller).

Boys and Girls is about a boy and a girl who meet when they are both about twelve and carry on a love-hate relationship for the next ten years, until they finally sleep with each other, with disastrous results. It is clear they're in love, but after that night of bliss a great chill forms between them, and she doesn't understand why.

I thought I did understand why. The other day on the radio, Terry Gross was interviewing Jeffrey Eugenides, the author of *The Virgin Suicides.* In that novel, now made into a movie by Sofia Coppola, a boy and a girl have sex in the middle of the football field on prom night—and the next morning, when she awakes, she is alone. Trip, the boy, is the narrator, and tells us: "I liked her a lot. But out there on the football field, it was different."

Terry Gross gently grilled Eugenides about that passage. She was interested, she said, because Trip's behavior was—well, not atypical of boys after sexual conquests, and a lot of women, courted and then dumped, were curious about that cruel male pattern. Eugenides declined to analyze Trip's behavior. He'd known people like Trip, he said, and he thought it was just the sort of thing Trip would do.

I have a theory to explain such postcoital disillusionment: Boys cannot deal with their dreams made flesh. He has idealized a woman who now turns out to be real, who engages in the same behavior as ordinary women, who allows herself to be despoiled (so he thinks) by his lust, which he has been taught to feel guilty about. He flees in shame and self-disgust. Boys get over this, which is the good news, but by losing their idealism about women, which is the bad news.

This is an excellent theory, but *Boys and Girls* does not use it. Instead, confusing the sexes, it supplies the boy with a motive for his behavior that in the real world would more likely come from a girl. He cut off contact between them, he says, because it was the greatest moment of his life, and he knew then that she was his true love, and when she said it had perhaps been "a mistake," and that they should move on and go back to being "best friends," nothing had ever hurt him more. Of course, she was just trying to say what she thought he wanted to hear, because she really loved him, but . . .

Their dilemma is fueled by the movie convention in which the characters say the wrong things and do not say the right things, and remain baffled by a situation long after it has become clear to us. But then Ryan and Jennifer (for those are their names) are not quick studies anyway. It takes them ten years and countless Meet Cutes before they finally break down and have their first kiss. They specialize in that form of sex most maddening for the audience, "coitus postponus."

They're both awfully nice people. They're played by Freddie Prinze Jr. and Claire Forlani as good and sweet and honest and sensitive, and we like them a lot. We also like his best friend (Jason Biggs) and hers (Amanda Detmer). Perky Heather Donahue, survivor of the *Blair Witch,* gets good screen time as his interim girlfriend. They are so lovable that we earnestly wish they'd grow up and develop more interesting and complex personalities. We are reminded of the theory that American society prolongs adolescence far beyond its natural life span. If these characters were French and engaging in the same dialogue and behavior, we would guess their age at about thirteen.

I was amused by their college majors. He is a structural engineer, as we can see in scenes that invariably show him studying balsa-wood models of bridges with a perplexed expression. After his junior year, the models do not collapse any more, so he must be learning something. She studies Latin. Why? "Because I plan to do postgraduate work in Italy." In the Vatican City, I hope.

Boys and Girls is soothing and harmless, gentle and interminable. It is about two people who might as well fall in love, since fate and the plot have given them nothing else to do and no one else to do it with. Compared to the wisdom and wickedness of *High Fidelity,* this is such a slight movie. It's not that I don't like it. It's that I don't care.

Boys Don't Cry ★ ★ ★ ★
R, 114 m., 1999

Hilary Swank (Brandon Teena), Chloe Sevigny
(Lana), Alicia Goranson (Candace), Alison
Folland (Kate), Peter Sarsgaard (John), Brendan
Sexton III (Tom). Directed by Kimberly Peirce
and produced by Eva Kolodner, Jeff Sharp,
and John Hart. Screenplay by Peirce and
Andy Bienen.

Sex was more interesting when we knew less
about it, when we proceeded from murky impulses rather than easy familiarity. Consider
the Victorians, slipping off to secret vices, and
how much more fun they had than today's
Jerry Springer guests ("My girlfriend is a dominatrix"). The intriguing border between the
genders must have been more inviting to cross
when that was seen as an opportunity rather
than a pathology. One of the many virtues of
Boys Don't Cry, one of the best films of 1999, is
that never once does it supply the tiresome
phrase, "I am a man trapped in a woman's body."
Its motto instead could be, "Girls just wanna
have fun."

Teena Brandon doesn't think of herself as a
sexual case study; nothing in her background
has given her that vocabulary. She is a lonely
girl who would rather be a boy, and one day
she gets a short haircut, sticks a sock down the
front of her jeans, and goes into a bar to try
her luck. She is not a transsexual, a lesbian, a
cross-dresser, or a member of any other category on the laundry list of sexual identities;
she is a girl who thinks of herself as a boy, and
when she leaves Lincoln, Nebraska, and moves
to the small town of Falls City in 1993, that is
how she presents herself. By then she has become Brandon Teena, and we must use the
male pronoun in describing him.

All of this is true. There is a documentary,
The Brandon Teena Story, that came out earlier in 1999 and shows us photographs of
Brandon, looking eerily like Hilary Swank,
who plays the role in *Boys Don't Cry.* In that
film we meet some of the women he dated
("Brandon knew how to treat a woman") and
we see the two men later charged with Brandon's rape and, after the local law authorities
didn't act seriously on that charge, murder a

few days later. Like Matthew Shepard in Wyoming, Brandon died because some violent men
are threatened by any challenge to their shaky
self-confidence.

Boys Don't Cry is not sociology, however,
but a romantic tragedy—a *Romeo and Juliet*
set in a Nebraska trailer park. Brandon is not
the smartest person on Earth, especially at
judging which kinds of risks to take, but he is
one of the nicest, and soon he has fallen in
love with a Falls City girl named Lana (Chloe
Sevigny). For Lana, Brandon is arguably the
first nice boy she has ever dated. We meet two
of the other local studs, John (Peter Sarsgaard)
and Tom (Brendan Sexton III), neither gifted
with intelligence, both violent products of brutal backgrounds. They have the same attitude
toward women that the gun nut has about
prying his dying fingers off the revolver.

The film is about hanging out in gas stations and roller rinks, and lying sprawled on a
couch looking with dulled eyes at television,
and working at soul-crushing jobs, and about
six-packs and country bars and Marlboros.
There is a reason country music is sad. Into
this wasteland, which is all Lana knows, comes
Brandon, who brings her a flower.

The Lana character is crucial to the movie,
and although Hilary Swank deserves all praise
for her performance as Brandon, it is Chloe
Sevigny who provides our entrance into the
story. Representing the several women the real
Brandon dated, she sees him as a warm, gentle,
romantic lover. Does Lana know Brandon is a
girl? At some point, certainly. But at what point
exactly? There is a stretch when she knows,
and yet she doesn't know, because she doesn't
want to know; romance is built on illusion, and
when we love someone, we love the illusion
they have created for us.

Kimberly Peirce, who directed this movie
and cowrote it with Andy Bienen, was faced
with a project that could have gone wrong in
countless ways. She finds the right note. She
never cranks the story up above the level it's
comfortable with; she doesn't underline the
stupidity of the local law-enforcement officials
because that's not necessary; she sees Tom and
John not as simple killers but as the instruments of deep ignorance and inherited antisocial pathology. (Tom knows he's trouble; he

holds his hand in a flame and then cuts himself, explaining, "This helps control the thing inside of me so I don't snap out at people.")

The whole story can be explained this way: Most everybody in it behaves exactly according to their natures. The first time I saw the movie, I was completely absorbed in the characters—the deception, the romance, the betrayal. Only later did I fully realize what a great film it is, a worthy companion to those other masterpieces of death on the prairie, *Badlands* and *In Cold Blood*. This could have been a clinical Movie of the Week, but instead it's a sad song about a free spirit who tried to fly a little too close to the flame.

The Brandon Teena Story ★ ★ ★

NO MPAA RATING, 90 m., 1999

A documentary directed and produced by Susan Muska and Greta Olafsdottir.

Brandon Teena was a "good kisser" and "knew how to treat a woman," we are told, and even after Brandon's secret was revealed—"he" was a biological female born Teena Brandon—there is a certain wistfulness in the memories of her girlfriends. None of the women who dated Brandon seem particularly angry about the deception, and after we've spent some time in the world where they all lived, we begin to understand why: Most of the biological men in *The Brandon Teena Story* are crippled by a vast, stultifying ignorance. No wonder a girl liked a date who sent her flowers and little love notes.

Consider, for example, the sheriff in the rural area where Brandon Teena and two bystanders were shot dead. We hear his words on tape as he interviews Brandon, who was raped by those who would commit the murders a few days later. To hear the interrogation is to hear words shaped by prejudice, hatred, deep sexual incomprehension, and ignorance. I cannot quote most of what the sheriff says—his words are too cruel and graphic—but consider that he is interviewing, not a rapist, but a victim, and you will get some notion of the atmosphere in some corners of the remote Nebraska district where the murders occurred.

The sheriff did not like it one bit that a woman was pretending to be a man. There is the hint that a woman who behaves like this deserves whatever she gets; that it is natural for a red-blooded man to resent any poaching on his phallic preserve. The tapes also preserve the voice of Brandon, who was twenty or twenty-one at the time and sounds very young, insecure, and confused. "I have a sexual identity crisis," we hear at one point.

The documentary includes photos of Brandon, or Teena, at various ages, and although the clothing gradually becomes masculine and the haircut gets shorter, I must say that I never really felt I was looking at a man. Perhaps the deception would have worked only in a rural and small-town world far removed from the idea of gender transitions. The two men who were convicted of the murders were apparently deceived; they considered Brandon a friend, before growing suspicious and brutally stripping their victim of her clothes and, apparently, virginity.

But what about the women Brandon dated? Their testimony remains vague and affectionate. They were not lesbians (and neither was Brandon—who firmly identified with a male identity), but they were responsive to tenderness and caring and "good kissing." One woman in the film dated both one of the murderers and Brandon; given a choice between the narrow-minded dimness of the man and the imagination of someone prepared to cross gender lines, the more attractive choice was obviously Brandon.

The film itself is not slick and accomplished. It plays at times like home video footage, edited together on someone's computer. There are awkward passages of inappropriate music, and repeated shots of the barren winter landscape. Oddly enough, this is an effective style for this material; it captures the banality of the world in which individuality is seen as a threat. The testimony in the film is often flat and colorless (the killers are maddeningly passive and detached). Even the hero, Brandon Teena, was only slowly coming to an understanding of identity and sexuality.

Watching the film, I realized something. It is fashionable to deride TV shows like *Jerry Springer* for their sensational guests ("My boyfriend is really a girl!"). But as I watched *The Brandon Teena Story*, I realized that Brandon lived in a world of extremely limited sexual information, among people who assumed that men are men and women are women, and any violation of that rule calls for the death penalty. To the degree that they have absorbed anything at all from church or society, it is that homosexuals are to be hated. If tabloid TV contains the message that everyone has to make his or her own accommodation with life, sex, and self-image, then it's performing a service. It helps people get used to the idea that some people are different. With a little luck, Jerry Springer might have saved Brandon Teena's life.

Bread and Roses ★ ★ ★ ½
R, 106 m., 2001

Pilar Padilla (Maya), Adrien Brody (Sam), Elpidia Carrillo (Rosa), Jack McGee (Bert), George Lopez (Perez), Alonso Chavez (Ruben), Monica Rivas (Simona). Directed by Ken Loach and produced by Rebecca O'Brien. Screenplay by Paul Laverty.

If you work in a building with janitors, how much do they get paid? Is it enough to decently support a family? Have you given any thought to the question? I haven't. Ken Loach's *Bread and Roses*, a drama about a janitorial strike in Los Angeles, made me think. It suggests that the people who manage your building pay the janitors as little as they possibly can, and pass the savings on to your employers. Here is a statistic: In 1982, union janitors in Los Angeles were paid $8.50 an hour. In 1999, nonunion janitors were paid $5.75. Do they have a health plan? Don't make me laugh.

Under the trickle-down theory, if the boss makes millions and the janitor makes $5.75, in the long run we all benefit. How does this work in practice? A simple illustration will suffice. When both parents have to moonlight in underpaid jobs, that gives their children an opportunity to get in trouble on the streets, leading to arrests, convictions, and millions of dollars pumped into the economy through the construction of new prisons and salaries for their guards. Right now America has a larger percentage of its population in prison than

any other Western nation, but that is not good enough.

Bread and Roses tells its story through the eyes of Maya (Pilar Padilla), an illegal immigrant newly arrived in Los Angeles. Her sister Rosa (Elpidia Carrillo) gets her a job in a sleazy bar, but Rosa is a good girl and doesn't like it: "I want to work with you cleaning the offices." Rosa gets Maya hired in a high-rise, where she has to kick back her first month's salary. Maya meets Sam (Adrien Brody), an organizer for the janitor's union, who is trying to sign up the workers in the building.

For some of my readers, the key words in the previous paragraph were "illegal immigrant." Why, they are thinking, should such a person have a job in America at all, let alone complain about the low wages? This attitude is admirable in its idealism, but overlooks the fact that the economy depends on workers who will accept substandard wages. The man who hires Maya certainly knows she is illegal. That man's boss, as they say, "knows but doesn't know." The man above him doesn't know and doesn't care—he's only interested in delivering janitorial services to the building management at the lowest possible price.

If the janitors were paid a decent wage plus health benefits, there would be no shortage of American citizens to take the jobs, so it is better this way, especially since the illegal workers have no rights and are easily intimidated. If the Mexican border were sealed, Los Angeles would be a city without janitors, gardeners, car washes, and maids. And in Michigan, who would pick the fruit?

Sam the organizer encourages Maya and her friends to organize for the union within the building—secretly, of course. Rosa, the sister, is not so enthusiastic: "We could all lose our jobs, and then who would pay the bills?" There is a juicy scene where the striking janitors invade a housewarming by a big Hollywood agency which has just taken offices in the building. Do the star clients know their agents are exploiting the workers? (Credit here to Ron Perlman and other actors who play recognizable extras.)

Sam is played by Brody as a complex character, filled with anger but also with a streak of zany street comedian. He's trapped in the middle, since the union's bosses, like all bosses, are basically establishment. When his boss argues that a strike might cost the union too much money, Sam snaps back: "No more $40 million to give the Democrats." Sam and Maya are drawn to one another, and there is a shy little love scene, but Ken Loach is not the kind of director to confuse his real story with the love story; he knows that no matter what happens between Sam and Maya, the janitors are still underpaid and the strike is still dangerous. That same stubborn integrity prevents him from giving the movie a conventional happy ending. Just think. If he had directed *Pearl Harbor,* it would have ended sadly.

Loach is left-wing but realistic. The best scene in *Bread and Roses* argues against Sam, Maya, and the union. It is a searing speech by Rosa, delivered by Elpidia Carrillo with such force and shaming truth that it could not have been denied the Oscar—if the Academy voters in their well-cleaned buildings ever saw movies like this. Rosa slices through Maya's idealism with hard truths, telling her sister that she worked as a prostitute to pay for Maya's education, and indeed slept with the supervisor to get Rosa her job. "I've been whoring all my life, and I'm tired," she says. Now she has a sick husband and kids to feed and they take priority over the union and the college-boy organizer.

The more you think about it, the more this movie's ending has a kind of nobility to it. Loach, who has always made films about the working class *(Riff-Raff, My Name Is Joe, Ladybird, Ladybird),* is too honest to believe in easy solutions. Will the union get its contract? Will Maya and Sam live happily ever after? Will the national minimum wage ever be a living wage? Will this movie change anything, or this review make you want to see it? No, probably not. But when you come in tomorrow morning someone will have emptied your wastebasket.

Bride of the Wind ½★
R, 99 m., 2001

Sarah Wynter (Alma Mahler), Jonathan Pryce (Gustav Mahler), Vincent Perez (Oskar Kokoschka), Simon Verhoeven (Walter Gropius), Gregor Seberg (Franz Werfel), Dagmar Schwarz (Anna Moll), Wolfgang Hubsch (Karl Moll), August Schmolzer (Gustav Klimt), Francesca Becker (Maria). Directed by Bruce Beresford and produced by Lawrence Levy and Evzen Kolar. Screenplay by Marilyn Levy.

"I'm not just any widow! I'm Mahler's widow!"
—Alma Mahler

She must have been a monster. The Alma Mahler depicted in *Bride of the Wind* is a woman who prowls restlessly through the beds of the famous, making them miserable while displaying no charm of her own. Whether this was the case with the real woman I do not know. But if she was anything like the woman in this movie, then Gustav Mahler, Gustav Klimt, Oskar Kokoschka, Walter Gropius, and Frank Werfel should have fled from her on sight.

Bride of the Wind, which tells her story, is one of the worst biopics I have ever seen, a leaden march through a chronology of Alma's affairs, clicking them off with the passion of an encyclopedia entry. The movie has three tones: overwrought, boring, laughable. Sarah Wynter, who plays Alma, does not perform the dialogue but recites it. She lacks any conviction as a seductress, seems stiff and awkward, and should have been told that great women in turn-of-the-century Vienna didn't slouch.

We first meet her going to a ball her father has forbidden her to attend. He is stern with her when she returns. So much for her adolescence. We move on to a dinner party where she flirts with the artist Klimt (August Schmolzer), who labors over one-liners like, "Mahler's music is much better than it sounds." She insults Mahler (Jonathan Pryce) at dinner, offending and fascinating him, and soon the older man marries her.

She has affairs throughout their marriage. She cheats with the architect Gropius (Simon Verhoeven), who unwisely writes a love letter to Alma but absentmindedly addresses it to Gustav—or so he says. "You drove me to him," she pouts to her husband. Mahler is always going on about his music, you see, and thinks himself a genius. Well, so does Gropius. The screenplay shows the egos of the men by putting big, clanging chunks of information in the dialogue. Sample:

"You've been very kind, Herr Gropius."
"Dancing is one of the two things I do well."
"And what is the other?"
"I am an architect."

Since Alma already knows this, the movie misses a bet by not having her ask, winsomely, "Is there a ... third ... thing you at least do not do badly?"

There is. Another affair is with the sculptor and painter Oskar Kokoschka (Vincent Perez), who goes off to fight the war, is shot through the head, and bayoneted after falling wounded. In what the movie presents as a dying vision, he imagines Alma walking toward him. Since his head is flat on the ground, she walks toward him sideways, rotated ninety degrees from upright. But, of course, a vision stands upright no matter what position one's head is in, or dreams would take place on the ceiling.

Oskar's mother posts herself outside Alma's house with a pistol, seeking revenge for her son's death. "I was never popular with mothers," Alma sighs. She becomes involved with the writer Werfel. Just when we are wondering if Oskar's mother is still lying in ambush outside the gates, Kokoschka himself returns a year later—alive!—and surprises her in her drawing room. "It's not every man who is shot in the head, bayoneted, and lives to tell about it," he observes. Then he sees she is pregnant and rejoices that she decided to have his baby after all, instead of an abortion. "But it has been a year," Alma tells him. "Think, Oskar! A year."

The penny falls. He stalks away, disgusted either at the fact that she is bearing another man's child, or that he cannot count. I meanwhile am thinking that when one is reported dead in action, it is only common good manners to wire ahead before turning up unexpectedly at a lover's house. Ben Affleck makes the same mistake in *Pearl Harbor*.

Bride of the Wind was directed by Bruce Beresford, who has made wonderful films (*Tender Mercies, Crimes of the Heart, The Fringe Dwellers, Driving Miss Daisy*). At a loss to explain this lapse, I can only observe that another of his filmed biographies, *King David* (1985), was also

very bad. Maybe there is something about a real-life subject that paralyzes him.

If Sarah Wynter is not good as Alma Mahler, the other actors seem equally uneasy—even the usually assured Pryce and Perez. Something must have been going wrong on this production. Even that doesn't explain the lack of Bad Laugh Control. Filmmakers need a sixth sense for lines that might play the wrong way. For example: After Alma has slept with as many Viennese artists as she can manage without actually double-booking, she quarrels with the latest. Her winsome little daughter, Maria (Francesca Becker), whines, "Is he going to leave us? Are you going to send him away?" Alma replies, "What made you think that?" Wrong answer. At the end of the movie there are titles telling us what happened to everyone; Gropius moved to America and went on to become a famous architect, etc. We are not surprised to learn that little Maria went on to be married five times.

Bridget Jones's Diary ★ ★ ★ ½
R, 95 m., 2001

Renée Zellweger (Bridget Jones), Colin Firth (Mark Darcy), Hugh Grant (Daniel Cleaver), Honor Blackman (Penny), Crispin Bonham-Carter (Greg), Gemma Jones (Bridget's Mum), Jim Broadbent (Bridget's Dad), James Callis (Tom), Embeth Davidtz (Natasha). Directed by Sharon Maguire and produced by Tim Bevan, Jonathan Cavendish, and Eric Fellner. Screenplay by Richard Curtis, Andrew Davies, and Helen Fielding, based on the novel by Fielding.

Glory be, they didn't muck it up. *Bridget Jones's Diary*, a beloved book about a heroine both lovable and human, has been made against all odds into a funny and charming movie that understands the charm of the original, and preserves it. The book, a fictional diary by a plump, thirty-something London office worker, was about a specific person in a specific place. When the role was cast with Renée Zellweger, who is not plump and is from Texas, there was gnashing and wailing. Obviously the Miramax boys would turn London's pride into a Manhattanite, or worse.

Nothing doing. Zellweger put on twenty-something pounds and developed the cutest little would-be double chin, as well as a British accent that sounds reasonable enough to me. (*Sight & Sound,* the British film magazine, has an ear for nuances and says the accent is "just a little too studiedly posh," which from them is praise.)

As in the book, Bridget arrives at her thirty-second birthday determined to take control of her life, which until now has consisted of smoking too much, drinking too much, eating too much, and not finding the right man, or indeed much of any man. In her nightmares, she dies fat, drunk, and lonely, and is eaten by Alsatian dogs. She determines to monitor her daily intake of tobacco and alcohol units, and her weight, which she measures in stones. (A stone is fourteen pounds; the British not only have pounds instead of kilos but stones on top of pounds, although the other day a London street vendor was arrested for selling bananas by the pound in defiance of the new European marching orders; the next step is obviously for Brussels to impound Bridget's diary.)

Bridget's campaign proceeds unhappily when her mother (who "comes from the time when pickles on toothpicks were still the height of sophistication") introduces her to handsome Mark Darcy (Colin Firth), who is at a holiday party against his will and in a bad mood and is overheard (by Bridget) describing her as a "verbally incontinent spinster." Things go better at work, where she exchanges saucy e-mails with her boss, Daniel Cleaver (Hugh Grant). His opener: "You appear to have forgotten your skirt." They begin an affair, while Darcy circles the outskirts of her consciousness, still looking luscious but acting emotionally constipated.

Zellweger's Bridget is a reminder of the first time we became really aware of her in a movie, in *Jerry Maguire* (1996), where she was so cute and vulnerable we wanted to tickle and console her at the same time. Her work in *Nurse Betty* (2000) was widely but not sufficiently praised, and now here she is, fully herself and fully Bridget Jones, both at once. A story like this can't work unless we feel unconditional affection for the heroine, and casting Zellweger achieves that; the only alternate I can think of is Kate Winslet, who comes close but lacks the self-destructive puppy aspects.

The movie has otherwise been cast with de-

pendable (perhaps infallible) British comic actors. The first time Hugh Grant appeared on-screen, I chuckled for no good reason at all, just as I always do when I see Christopher Walken, Steve Buscemi, Tim Roth, or Jack Nicholson—because I know that whatever the role, they will infuse it with more than the doctor ordered. Grant can play a male Bridget Jones (as he did in *Notting Hill*), but he's better as a cad, and here he surpasses himself by lying to Bridget about Darcy and then cheating on her with a girl from the New York office. (An "American stick insect," is what Bridget tells her diary.)

Colin Firth on the other hand must unbend to become lovable, and when we do finally love him, it's largely because we know what an effort it took on his part. *Bridget Jones's Diary* is famously, if vaguely, patterned after Jane Austen's *Pride and Prejudice;* Firth played Mr. Darcy in the BBC's 1995 adaptation of the novel, and now plays another Darcy here. I didn't see the TV version but learn from the critic James Berardinelli that Firth "plays this part exactly as he played the earlier role, making it evident that the two Darcys are essentially the same."

It is a universal rule of romantic fiction that all great love stories must be mirrored by their low-comedy counterpoints. Just as Hal woos Katharine, Falstaff trifles with Doll Tearsheet. If Bridget must choose between Mark and Daniel, then her mother (Gemma Jones) must choose between her kindly but easy-chair-loving husband (Jim Broadbent) and a dashing huckster for a TV shopping channel.

The movie strings together one funny setpiece after another, as when Bridget goes in costume to a party where she *thought* the theme was "Tarts & Vicars." Or when she stumbles into a job on a TV news show and makes her famous premature entrance down the fire pole. Or when she has to decide at the beginning of an evening whether sexy underwear or tummy-crunching underwear will do her more good in the long run. Bridget charts her own progress along the way, from "tragic spinster" to "wanton sex goddess," and the movie gives almost unreasonable pleasure as it celebrates her bumpy transition.

Bringing Out the Dead ★ ★ ★ ★
R, 118 m., 1999

Nicolas Cage (Frank), Patricia Arquette (Mary), John Goodman (Larry), Ving Rhames (Marcus), Tom Sizemore (Walls), Marc Anthony (Noel), Cliff Curtis (Cy Coates), Mary Beth Hurt (Nurse Constance). Directed by Martin Scorsese and produced by Scott Rudin and Barbara De Fina. Screenplay by Paul Schrader, based on the novel by Joe Connelly.

"I came to realize that my work was less about saving lives than about bearing witness. I was a grief mop."

The speaker is Frank, a paramedic whose journeys into the abyss of human misery provide the canvas for Martin Scorsese's *Bringing Out the Dead*. There may be happiness somewhere in the city, but the barking voice on Frank's radio doesn't dispatch him there. His job is to arrive at a scene of violence or collapse, and try to bring not only help but encouragement.

"Do you have any music?" he asks the family of a man who seems dead of a heart attack. "I think it helps if you play something he liked." As the old man's Sinatra album plays in the background, he applies the defibrillator to his chest and shouts, "Clear!" The corpse jumps into life like a movie monster. The psychology is sound: Sinatra may not bring the dead to life, but he will give the family something to do, and the song will remind them of their dad's happier times.

Frank is played by Nicolas Cage, seen in the movie's close-up with his eyes narrowed in pain. He cruises the streets of Hell's Kitchen with a series of three copilots, in a three-day stretch during which he drifts in and out of sanity; he has hallucinations of an eighteen-year-old homeless girl named Rose, whose life he failed to save, whose death he wants to redeem. Like Travis Bickle, the hero of Scorsese's *Taxi Driver* (1976), Frank travels the night streets like a boatman on the River Styx, while steam rises from manholes as if from the fires below. Travis wanted to save those who did not want saving. Frank finds those who desperately want help, but usually he is powerless.

The movie is based on a novel by Joe Connelly, himself once a New York paramedic. The screenplay by Paul Schrader is another chapter in the most fruitful writer-director collaboration of the quarter-century *(Taxi Driver, Raging Bull, The Last Temptation of Christ)*. The film wisely has no real plot, because the ambulance driver's days have no beginning or goal, but are a limbo of extended horror. At one point he hallucinates that he is helping pull people's bodies up out of the pavement, freeing them.

To look at *Bringing Out the Dead*—to look, indeed, at almost any Scorsese film—is to be reminded that film can touch us urgently and deeply. Scorsese is never on autopilot, never panders, never sells out, always goes for broke; to watch his films is to see a man risking his talent, not simply exercising it. He makes movies as well as they can be made, and I agree with an observation on the Harry Knowles Web site: You can enjoy a Scorsese film with the sound off, or with the sound on and the picture off.

Now look at *Bringing Out the Dead*. Three days in Frank's life. The first day his copilot is Larry (John Goodman), who deals with the grief by focusing on where his next meal is coming from. To Larry, it's a job, and you can't let it get to you. Day two, Larry works with Marcus (Ving Rhames), who is a gospel Christian and uses emergencies as an opportunity to demonstrate the power of Jesus; bringing one man back to life, he presents it as a miracle. On the third day, the day Christ rose from the dead, Frank's partner is Walls (Tom Sizemore), who is coming apart at the seams and wreaks havoc on hapless patients.

Haunting Frank's thoughts as he cruises with these guys are two women. One is Rose, whose face peers up at him from every street corner. The other is Mary (Patricia Arquette), the daughter of the man who liked Sinatra. After her dad is transferred to an intensive care unit, his life, such as it is, consists of dying and being shocked back to life, fourteen times one day, until Frank asks, "If he gets out, are you gonna follow him around with a defibrillator?" Mary is a former druggie, now clean and straight, and Frank—well, I was going to say he loves her, but this isn't one of those autopilot movies where the action hero has a romance in between the bloodshed. No, it's not love; it's need. He thinks they can save each other.

Scorsese assembles the film as levels in an

inferno. It contains some of his most brilliant sequences, particularly two visits to a high-rise drug house named the Oasis, where a dealer named Cy (Cliff Curtis) offers relief and sur-cease. Mary goes there one night when she cannot stand any more pain, and Frank follows to save her; that sets up a later sequence in which Frank treats Cy while he is dangling near death.

All suffering ends at the same place, the emergency room of the hospital nicknamed Our Lady of Perpetual Misery, where the receiving nurse (Mary Beth Hurt) knows most of the regulars by name. She dispenses the same advice in many forms: Stop what you're doing. But they don't listen, and will be back again. Noel (Marc Anthony) stands for many street people, tied to a gurney, screaming for a glass of water, hour after hour, while the ER team labors to plug the leaks, gaps, and wounds of a night in the city. They make long stories short: "This guy's plant food."

Nicolas Cage is an actor of great style and heedless emotional availability: He will go anywhere for a role, and this film is his best since *Leaving Las Vegas*. I like the subtle way he and Scorsese embody what Frank has learned on the job, the little verbal formulas and quiet asides that help the bystanders at suffering. He embodies the tragedy of a man who has necessary work and is good at it, but in a job that is never, ever over.

Bringing Out the Dead is an antidote to the immature intoxication with violence in a film like *Fight Club*. It is not fun to get hit, it is not redeeming to cause pain, it does not make you a man when you fight, because fights are an admission that you are not smart enough to survive by your wits. *Fight Club* makes a cartoon of the mean streets that Scorsese sees unblinkingly.

Bring It On ★ ★
PG-13, 95 m., 2000

Kirsten Dunst (Torrance Shipman), Eliza Dushku (Missy Pantone), Gabrielle Union (Isis), Jesse Bradford (Cliff), Nicole Bilderback (Whitney), Clare Kramer (Courtney), Ian Roberts (Choreographer). Directed by Peyton Reed and produced by Marc Abraham and Thomas A. Bliss. Screenplay by Jessica Bendinger.

I jump! You can look but don't you hump.
I'm major. I roar. I swear I'm not a
whore.
We cheer as we lead. We act like we're on
speed.
Hate us 'cause we're beautiful—but we
don't like you either.
We're cheerleaders! We are cheerleaders!

Those are lyrics from the opening musical number of *Bring It On*—yet another example of the most depressing trend of the summer of 2000, the cynical attempt by Hollywood to cram R-rated material into PG-13–rated movies. This is done not to corrupt our children, but (even worse) with complete indifference to their developing values. The real reason is more cynical: Younger teenagers buy a lot of tickets and are crucial if a movie hopes to "win the weekend." The R rating is a penalty at the box office. So movies that were born to be R, like *Gone in 60 Seconds, Coyote Ugly,* and *Bring It On,* are trimmed to within a millimeter of the dividing line and released as PG-13, so that any child tall enough to push its dollars through the ticket window is cheerfully admitted, with or without an adult.

Bring It On shows every evidence of beginning life as a potentially funny, hard-edged R-rated comedy. There's raunchy language, a half-nude locker-room scene, jokes about sex, and those startling cheerleader songs. I smiled at the songs; I might have enjoyed the movie if it had developed along the lines of *Animal House* or *American Pie*. Instead, we get a strange mutant beast, half Nickelodeon movie, half R-rated comedy. It's like kids with potty-mouth playing grown-up.

The movie stars Kirsten Dunst *(The Virgin Suicides)* and Gabrielle Union *(She's All That)* as the captains of two opposing cheerleader squads, one from an affluent San Diego suburb (which apparently contains no parents) and the other from a mostly black high school in East Compton. Dunst is the new captain of her team, which is the defending national champion cheerleading squad even though it supports a team barely able to stumble into the field. Union visits their practice one day to reveal that their previous captain had stolen all of their winning routines from East Compton. This year that will make a difference, she says, because East Compton is going to the nationals.

In desperation, Dunst breaks the rules and hires a professional choreographer (Ian Roberts), who shouts at them like a drill sergeant but has the moves of a Chippendale's dancer. As he puts them through new routines, we get subplots involving the standard characters in all teenage movies, including the cool guy who is somebody's brother, the snotty teacher, and the bitchy girl who gets her comeuppance. There's the usual suspense about whether the heroine will end up with the guy she likes, despite massive attacks of Idiot Plot misunderstandings.

This movie wants it all. In addition to the sex comedy, the romance, the cheerleading intrigue, and the condescending treatment of the black school, there's also the big climax at the cheerleading competition, so that a movie that has exhausted every possible high school cliché can now recycle all the obligatory plot gimmicks involving the Big Game. Will our team, which used the illegal choreographer, win or lose? In a movie with a memory, it might lose, but short-term memory loss is a symptom of movies like this, and the choreographer, who was illegal to make a quick plot point, is long forgotten by the time the movie gets to the finals.

Bring It On contains within it the seeds of a sharp and observant high school satire, maybe something in the same league (although not as high in the standings) as *Election* or *Rushmore*. I'll bet anything Jessica Bendinger's original screenplay was a lot smarter than the dumbed-down PG-13 version we get here. The movie as it now stands is too juvenile and insipid for older teenagers and has way too much language and sex for kids thirteen and below.

As an entry in the PG-13 category, it's not as appalling as *Coyote Ugly*, which basically instructs young girls that there's money to be made in the bimbo business. But it illustrates the same point: The MPAA's rating system, having first denied American moviegoers any possibility of a workable adult category, is now busily corrupting the PG-13 rating. The principle seems to be: As long as we act sanctimonious by creating a climate in which legitimate adult films cannot be made, we can get away with maximizing the box office by opening up the PG-13. The MPAA in the summer of 2000 reveals itself as more willing to peddle smut to children than to allow adults to make their own choices.

Brokedown Palace ★ ★ ★
PG-13, 100 m., 1999

Claire Danes (Alice), Kate Beckinsale (Darlene), Bill Pullman (Yankee Hank), Daniel Lapaine (Nick Parks), Lou Diamond Phillips (U.S. Official), Jacqui Kim (Yon Green). Directed by Jonathan Kaplan and produced by Adam Fields and A. Kitman Ho. Screenplay by Fields and David Arata.

Brokedown Palace tells the story of two American teenage girls who are sentenced to spend most of their lives in a Thai prison. Their crimes are apparently harmless: being silly and naive. Yet it is a fact that they had drugs in their possession when they passed through Thai customs on their way to Hong Kong, and that is a practice the Thai authorities do not find amusing.

The girls are Alice (Claire Danes) and Darlene (Kate Beckinsale). They're high school buddies who plan a graduation trip to Hawaii, and then secretly change their designation to the more exotic Thailand without telling their parents. Once there, they find a $6 guest house and sneak into a luxury hotel to sip expensive drinks at poolside. They get caught trying to charge the bill to the wrong room, but they are saved from trouble by a friendly Australian, Nick (Daniel Lapaine), who takes care of the bill and makes smooth romantic moves, first toward Alice, then toward Darlene.

By now alarm bells are going off among moviegoers who have seen *Return to Paradise* (1998), not to mention *Midnight Express* (1978). A lot of foreign countries sentence drug traffickers to life, or death, and trusting Americans are sitting ducks for smooth-talking smugglers who take advantage of them.

Return to Paradise posed a fascinating moral dilemma, since three friends went to Malaysia but two were already safe back in the United States when the third was busted for possession of hashish. The deal: He'll get death, because of the amount in his possession. But if both friends return to share the blame, they'll all get three years. If one returns, he and the prisoner will get six years. If you're selfish but don't want your friend to die, obviously the best deal for you is if the other guy goes back while you stay at home.

Brokedown Palace doesn't offer a simple moral equation like that—at least not at first, although the ending sets a challenge for the audience. The two girls are sentenced to thirty-three years, and in desperation find a local American lawyer named Yankee Hank (Bill Pullman) who agrees to take their case. (As he's on the phone with one of their fathers, he doodles how much money he can ask for. $40,000? $30,000?) He's greedy but honest, and doubtful about a lot of things, including the story the girls tell about the friendly Australian.

The heart of the film is in the performances of Danes and Beckinsale after they're sent to prison. Consider. One moment your entire life is ahead of you: college, marriage, kids, a career, a home, middle age, fulfillment. The next moment all of that has been taken away. Your future has been locked in a foreign prison. One poignant scene shows the girls shouting across an open space to visitors—friends and relatives from home, whose lives continue while theirs are on hold.

The movie, directed by Jonathan Kaplan *(Over the Edge, The Accused)* plays the material straight, to great effect. There are no sneaky plot tricks or grandstand plays, and the reasoning of a Thai judge, during an appeal hearing, is devastating in its logic. There is, however, an interesting development at the end, which I will not even hint at, which requires the audience to decide whether or not something can be believed, and what exactly are the motives behind it.

Claire Danes, clear-eyed and straightforward, plays Alice as just a little more complex than her friend. She comes from a poorer background, has a reputation for getting into trouble, and doesn't seem trustworthy to Darlene's dad. Pullman, weighing the pros and cons, dealing with a cynical and unhelpful U.S. embassy official (Lou Diamond Phillips), has seen cases like this before. The girls should have known not to trust strangers, to be suspicious of a free trip to Hong Kong, to never let their luggage out of the sight of both of

them. Should have. Now they have a lot of time to think about that.

The Broken Hearts Club ★ ★ ★
R, 91 m., 2000

Zach Braff (Benji), Dean Cain (Cole), Andrew Keegan (Kevin), Nia Long (Leslie), John Mahoney (Jack), Mary McCormack (Anne), Matt McGrath (Howie), Timothy Olyphant (Dennis), Ben Weber (Patrick), Billy Porter (Taylor), Justin Theroux (Marshall). Directed by Greg Berlanti and produced by Mickey Liddell and Joseph Middleton. Screenplay by Berlanti.

"I'm twenty-eight years old and all I'm good at is being gay," complains Marshall (Justin Theroux), one of the gay friends who hang out together in *The Broken Hearts Club*. To cheer himself up, he should rent *The Boys in the Band* (1970), and find out how much better gay men are at being gay than they used to be. The new movie acts like a progress report; instead of angst, Freudian analysis, despair, and self-hate, the new generation sounds like the cast of a sitcom, trading laugh lines and fuzzy truisms. The earlier movie half-suggested it was impossible to be gay and happy. That possibility would not occur to the *Broken Hearts* characters.

The movie takes place in the predominately gay area of West Hollywood, where its heroes hang out in coffee shops, restaurants, clubs, and each other's homes. Most of the principals are not sleeping with one another, although some are, and others are not sleeping with anyone. Mostly, they talk, and the movie listens. What it discovers is that gay men, like straight men, spend an extraordinary amount of time thinking about sex. And that they can be insecure, unfaithful, lonely, and deceptive (when an actor recycles lines from an audition to make a touching breakup speech, his ex asks, "Are you reading that off of your hand?").

Life centers around the Broken Hearts, a restaurant run by the fatherly Jack (John Mahoney), who also sponsors a softball team. Many of the characters are members of the team, and there's a funny scene where the handsome Cole (Dean Cain, from *Lois & Clark: The New Adventures of Superman*) steps up to the plate and gets the phone number of the opposing catcher between strikes. Mostly, though, dates don't come that easily, and Patrick (Ben Weber) complains, "Gay men in L.A. are 10s looking for an 11. On a good night, and if the other guy's drunk enough, I'm a 6."

What's striking about the movie is the ordinariness of its characters and what they talk about. This is a rare gay-themed movie that relaxes. Historically, many movies about gays have had a buried level of—I dunno, call it muted hysteria, anxiety, impending doom. It's the *Kiss of the Spider Woman* syndrome, with characters dramatizing what they see as their own current or impending tragedies. *The Broken Hearts Club* is not about neurosis, resentment, AIDS, or secrecy, and the humor can be described as sarcastic rather than bitchy. The big difference between this picture and your regular guy movie is that there aren't any girls (except for a lesbian sister and her lover). There are no complaints about parents. One guy says his mother was a sixties love child: "In high school, she caught me smoking pot and all she said was, 'I hope you didn't pay market.'"

The lighthearted tone is set right at the beginning, as a group of friends play a game to see who can act the straightest the longest before one reveals an OGT (Obviously Gay Trait). We are introduced to the definition of "meanwhile," which is a word introduced into any conversation when an interesting sex object walks by. One of the characters lands a date with a handsome J. Crew model, then drops him because he doesn't like the Carpenters. There's a debate: "Who would you kick out of bed? Morley Safer or Mike Wallace?" This is exactly the way straight guys talk, except they substitute Cameron Diaz and Jennifer Lopez. (Answer: "I'd kick them both out of bed for Ed Bradley, circa 1980.")

All, of course, is not banter. There's tension between Patrick and Leslie (Nia Long), the girlfriend of his sister (Mary McCormack). There's bitterness about "gym bunnies" and their obsessions with "sex and protein shakes." There are moments of truth, involving a romance threatened by roving-eye syndrome, and the movie is so eager to get to an obligatory funeral scene that we can diagnose the doomed character almost from his entrance. The writer-director, Greg Berlanti, one of the creators of *Dawson's Creek,* has mastered his

screenplay workshops and knows just when to introduce the false crisis, the false dawn, the real crisis, and the real dawn.

But the movie is so likable we go with it on its chosen level. It's almost the *point* of *The Broken Hearts Club* that it doesn't crank up the emotion. It insists on the ordinariness of its characters, on their everyday problems, on the relaxed and chatty ways they pass their time. The movie's buried message celebrates the arrival of gays into the mainstream. That key line ("I'm twenty-eight years old and all I'm good at is being gay") is like an announcement liberating gay movies from an exclusive preoccupation with sexuality. *The Broken Hearts Club* is good at things other than being a gay movie. There you are.

Broken Vessels ★ ★ ★
R, 90 m., 1999

Todd Field (Jimmy), Jason London (Tom), Susan Traylor (Susy), James Hong (Mr. Chen), Patrick Cranshaw (Gramps), Roxana Zal (Elizabeth). Directed by Scott Ziehl and produced by Ziehl and Roxana Zal. Screenplay by Ziehl, David Baer, and John McMahon.

"I could have gotten off the train before it left the station," Tom muses early in *Broken Vessels.* "There were plenty of warnings." He has moved from Altoona to Los Angeles and taken a job as a rescue squad member, touring the city in an ambulance with his new partner, Jimmy—who, it is said, is a gifted paramedic but has gone through a lot of partners.

The two men are like freelance pirates, sailing the city streets, grabbing bodies instead of plunder. Jimmy "has his own system," Tom learns. It includes rest stops in topless bars, sex in the back of the ambulance, buys from street-corner cocaine dealers, and direct methods with unruly clients (one injured man who goes berserk in the back of the ambulance gets a jolt to the head from a fibrillator).

Tom is played by Jason London as a man who wants to do right but lacks the will or the knack. He's swept into the world of Jimmy (Todd Field), who is smart, competent, and has the tunnel vision of the addict. Everything he does falls into two categories: pre-using and post-using. Working on the rescue squad gives him a free pass to roam the city streets, and a certain invulnerability. And he knows the places to hide the ambulance, like culverts and cemeteries. Work is the price he has to pay for the use of the job.

The film, tightly wound and convincing, was directed, coproduced, and cowritten by Scott Ziehl. It has passages of dark humor, but life in the ambulance is not zany; even when Tom and Jimmy do funny or crazy things, it's because of a desperation that begins as a sort of thrumming beneath the action, and ends as raw desperation. Jimmy has a twisted view of drugs and honor, as if it's his duty to use. The symbol of his addiction is Gramps (Patrick Cranshaw), an old man who has needed his daily fix of heroin since long before Jimmy was born. For Gramps, the ambulance makes house calls. And it is perhaps no accident that the heroin intended for Gramps's last fix becomes Jimmy's first.

If cocaine makes life unmanageable, heroin is no improvement, and soon Jimmy and Tom need more money than they have. Their daily lives are disintegrating around them. Tom's gay roommate throws him out after he throws up in the goldfish tank. He moves in with Jimmy. His next-door neighbor is a speed freak named Susy (Susan Traylor, in a performance beautifully edged with hysteria). Soon she has an occupant for the shed behind her house: a weird little guy and his drug factory. The job meanwhile comes down to futile threats from their boss (James Hong) and police questioning about property stolen from patients. The police don't seem very curious.

Susy has a roommate named Elizabeth (Roxana Zal) for about five minutes, before Elizabeth sizes up the situation and moves out. Tom likes Elizabeth, dates her a little, forgets her in the confusion of drugs, calls her in need and desperation. He feels so abandoned and lonely in the middle of the night, alone and with the sick feeling of needing drugs. Elizabeth sensibly tells him he needs help. He does, but the only help he can imagine is to find more drugs. This is like treating a cold with virus injections.

The story arc of *Broken Vessels* is familiar from a lot of other movies about drug users who crash and burn. They don't use to feel good. They use to stop feeling awful. Relief is a window that opens briefly after using, and then slams shut again. What makes the movie special is the way both lead actors find the right quiet notes for their performances. No prizes here for chewing the wallpaper; they're ordinary, quiet, smart guys whose best thinking can't get them out of the trap they've laid for themselves.

The Brothers ★ ★ ★
R, 103 m., 2001

Morris Chestnut (Jackson Smith), D. L. Hughley (Derrick West), Bill Bellamy (Brian Palmer), Shemar Moore (Terry White), Tamala Jones (Sheila West), Gabrielle Union (Denise Johnson), Julie Benz (Jesse Caldwell), Jenifer Lewis (Louise Smith), Clifton Powell (Fred Smith). Directed by Gary Hardwick and produced by Darin Scott and Paddy Cullen. Screenplay by Hardwick.

The Brothers is another movie about black guys who have been friends since childhood and how wedding bells are breaking up that old gang of theirs. This is getting to be a genre; I was reminded of *The Wood* (1999). What makes this one interesting is the way one couple actually deals with the crisis that threatens to keep them apart, instead of saying all the wrong things at the wrong times in traditional Idiot Plot fashion.

An early scene, of course, shows the friends playing basketball together. This is obligatory, showing how they cling to the innocence of those earlier days before romance and responsibility cluttered their lives. We meet Jackson the pediatrician (Morris Chestnut), Brian the lawyer (Bill Bellamy), Terry the executive (Shemar Moore), and Derrick the teacher (D. L. Hughley), who married young and regrets it. Now there's a crisis: Terry announces that he's going to get married.

The others, of course, oppose this decision, especially the married Derrick, whose marriage is approaching a crisis stage because of his wife's refusal to engage in oral sex. Derrick takes this as a personal affront—as proof she doesn't love him—and the arguments they have on this subject are among the movie's more tedious.

Jackson is a fervent opponent of premature

marriage; they are, after all, young urban professionals, the cream of the crop, and deserve to play the field for a few more years. Then he meets a freelance photographer named Denise (Gabrielle Union), and is thunderstruck by love. Their relationship redeems the movie, because it involves real issues, and not simply plot points that are manipulated to keep them apart until it's time to push them together.

At first, Jackson and Denise seem too good to be true. They were made for each other. They're happy not simply in romantic montages, but even in dialogue sequences where we sense a meeting of the minds. Then Jackson finds out something from Denise's past, which I will not reveal, except to say that Denise is blameless, and that Jackson has all the information he needs to realize this. (In an Idiot Plot, she would be blameless, but Jackson would be kept in the dark by contortions of the screenplay.)

No, it's not information Jackson needs, but a better understanding of himself, and of his troubled relationship with his divorced parents. And as he works on that, there is a strong scene where Denise tries to reason with him. She is persuasive and logical and emotional; she's arguing for her own happiness as well as his. This is precisely the kind of scene I yearn for in Idiot Plots, where the characters should say something but never do. She gives it her best shot, and so when Jackson stubbornly sticks to his wrongheaded position, it's about the characters, not the screenplay mechanics.

Gabrielle Union you may recall from *Bring It On* (2000), the dueling cheerleader comedy. This movie demonstrates how teenager comedies can obscure real talent. The cast is generally good, but writer-director Gary Hardwick doesn't give them the scenes that Chestnut and Union get. There is, for example, an awkward scene in a restaurant; the lawyer (Bellamy) brings in a white date (Julie Benz) who is a karate expert, and they run into a black woman judge who is one of his former girlfriends. There is a fight, which is stagy, artificial, and leads to race-based dialogue from the lawyer that seems out of character.

Even the divorced parents of the Morris Chestnut character get good scenes (his whole family seems to be in a better movie than the others). His mother, Louise (Jenifer Lewis), and his father, Fred (Clifton Powell), have had their good and bad times; their son resents the father and sides with the mother, and doesn't see their marriage with an adult's sense of complexity. It's interesting how he has to deal with his parents in order to learn how to deal with the woman he loves, and both parents have well-written scenes.

As for the others, well, the less said about the marriage in crisis over oral sex, the better. There might be useful or entertaining things to say about such a dilemma, but this movie doesn't find them. The subplot about Terry's approaching marriage is pretty standard sitcom stuff. And so on. The movie's a mixed bag, but worth seeing for the good stuff, which is a lesson in how productive it can be to allow characters to say what they might actually say.

Buena Vista Social Club ★ ★
NO MPAA RATING, 101 m., 1999

A documentary featuring Ibrahim Ferrer, Compay Segundo, Ruben Gonzalez, Omara Portuondo, Luis Barzaga, Joachim Cooder, Ry Cooder, Pio Leyva, Manuel "Puntillita" Licea, Eliades Ochoa, and others. Directed by Wim Wenders and produced by Ulrich Felsberg and Deepak Nayar.

There's an overwhelming temptation to praise *Buena Vista Social Club* simply because it is about legendary performers and wonderful music. But that praise should really go to the Grammy-winning 1997 album of the same name, produced by Ry Cooder, who rediscovered an almost vanished generation of Cuban musicians in Havana and assembled them for a last hurrah. It is a touching story, and the musicians (some more than ninety years old) still have fire and grace onstage, but, man, does the style of this documentary get in the way.

Wim Wenders, who directed it, seems to have given his cameramen a few basic instructions that they follow over and over again for the entire movie. One shot of a camera circling a musician on a chair in a big room would have been splendid—especially since the interiors in the movie are of beautiful, decaying Havana locations. But the camera circles obsessively. In big empty rooms, in bars, on verandahs, in rehearsal halls, in a recording studio, it circles and circles annoyingly.

When it isn't circling, there's another problem. The credits say the film was made on two digital cameras; one seems to have been handheld by a cameraman with the shakes. One camera is level, smooth, and confident. The other has the jitters so badly that you can sense the editor cutting away from it as much as he can. The unstable handheld look can be an interesting choice in certain situations. As a style, it becomes a problem.

Then there is the question of how to show Ry Cooder in the film. Yes, he is the godfather of this project, and there would be no film and no Buena Vista Social Club without him. But the filmmakers seem too much in awe of him. When the musicians give concerts in Amsterdam and at Carnegie Hall, the onstage footage keeps returning to a single repetitive camera move: focus on musician, then pan up to Ry Cooder smiling benevolently. He is positioned in the top row of the onstage musicians, on the strong visual axis just to the right of center, and the camera keeps glancing up at him as if for approval from the teacher.

Then there's the problem of presenting the music. I didn't expect a concert film, but I did expect that I might be allowed to hear one song all the way through, with the cutting dictated by the music. No luck. The songs are intercut with biographical testaments from the veteran musicians. These in themselves are splendid: The stories of how these performers grew up, learned their music, flourished, were forgotten, and then rediscovered are sometimes amazing, always moving (as when we reflect that the singer Ibrahim Ferrer, "the Cuban Nat King Cole," dominating the orchestra and the audience at Carnegie Hall, was shining shoes when Cooder found him). But the movie's strategy is to show them in performance, then cut away to their story, leaving the songs stranded.

When the Social Club gets to New York, the Carnegie Hall concert should have been the climax. (Consider the emotional payoff of the not dissimilar *The Weavers: Wasn't That a Time!* Consider, too, Terry Zwigoff's magical documentary *Louie Bluie*, about Martin, Bogan, and the Armstrongs—also elderly musicians who were belatedly rediscovered.) Instead of

pausing sometimes to simply listen to the music, Wenders intercuts Carnegie Hall with shots of the musicians visiting the Empire State Building and Times Square, looking in souvenir shop windows, talking about how wonderful it all is, as if they were on a school trip. This is condescending. The movie reminded me of a concert where somebody behind me is talking and moving around all the time. Let them play.

When they do, it is magical. We meet not only Ferrer, who has all of the ease and charisma of a born star, but a pianist named Ruben Gonzalez, who is eighty years old and complains of arthritis but has a strong and unmistakable piano style; Compay Segundo, a guitarist and singer, over ninety; and Omara Portuondo, "the Cuban Edith Piaf," luxuriating in the joy of the music. And many more; the faces become familiar, the music becomes seductive.

Wenders's visual texture for the film is interesting. He overexposes slightly with moderately high contrasts and then washes the picture out a little; it's like the watercolor technique where you finish the painting, let it dry, and then let it soak briefly in a pan of water so that the strong colors remain and others become more faded. It's a nice surface for the film, and appropriate.

But there's that constant humming undercurrent of adulation for Ry Cooder—who I am sure is a good man and a gifted musician and does not need to be shown so constantly that his presence becomes like product placement. I was reminded uncannily of those old *Amateur Hour* programs on TV, where the emcee beamed benevolently on one act after another. The musicians of the Buena Vista Social Club needed to be rediscovered, but that's all they needed: They came ready to play. I bought the album. You should, too. If this movie comes out on DVD, I hope the other side contains bonus concert footage.

But I'm a Cheerleader ★ ★ ★
R, 81 m., 2000

Natasha Lyonne (Megan), Clea DuVall (Graham), Cathy Moriarty (Mary Brown), RuPaul Charles (Mike), Bud Cort (Peter), Mink Stole (Nancy), Michelle Williams (Kimberly). Directed by Jamie Babbit and produced by Andrea Sperling and

Leanna Creel. Screenplay by Brian Wayne Peterson.

The danger signals are clear. Megan eats tofu, listens to Melissa Etheridge songs, and has pillowcases decorated with Georgia O'Keeffe's gynecological flowers. She is obviously a lesbian. Another clue: When she kisses her boyfriend, she fantasizes about her fellow cheerleaders. Since kissing her boyfriend is something like having her tonsils cleaned by Roto-Rooter, her fantasies can be explained, but not excused.

Her friends and parents stage an intervention. Yes, it is not too late for Megan (Natasha Lyonne) to be reprogrammed. An organization named True Directions is called in. And one afternoon an astonished Megan is confronted by the evidence of her orientation, and encouraged by Mike (RuPaul Charles), the reprogrammer, to seek the path back to the straight life.

Megan is thunderstruck. It has never occurred to her that she is a lesbian, although indeed she may be. *But I'm a Cheerleader* is about her sudden transition from pom-poms to indoctrination, from high school silliness to a desert camp ruled by the fierce and unsmiling Mary Brown (Cathy Moriarty). The movie seeks the general tone of a John Waters film, although Waters might have been ruder and more polished. Director Jamie Babbit goes more for the raucous and the slapstick, and succeeds, mostly; some of the jokes don't work, but satire is always chancy, and best when it's closest to life.

There are, I am informed, actually camps like this, where gay teenagers are slammed back into the closet. The people who run them may not be as deeply into denial as Mary Brown (whose son, Rock, has moves with a weed whacker that would only be envied at Chippendale's). I don't know what luck such outfits have; people are inclined to be who they think they are and to change, if at all, only voluntarily.

Life at True Directions is draconian. Long lists of regulations are issued. Inmates attend compulsory meetings based on twelve-step programs where they analyze their "addiction." And there are classes devoted to implanting gender behavior, as when the girls practice at diapering baby dolls and the boys chop logs.

Mary's lessons in vacuuming look oddly rhythmic, and Mike's car-repair classes are ripe with double entendres ("add a little more oil and shove it in and out"). The staff of True Directions is more sex-obsessed than the patients.

Megan's best friend at True Directions becomes a girl named Graham (Clea DuVall) who's going through the motions to please the staff and helps Megan figure out if she is or isn't homosexual. Other key characters include the residents of a gay "free house" not far away, where True Directions prisoners can find shelter. And there's a nearby gay bar, good for illicit midnight excursions. Everyone in the neighborhood seems preoccupied with homosexuality in one way or another.

But I'm a Cheerleader is not a great, breakout comedy, but more the kind of movie that might eventually become a regular on the midnight cult circuit. It feels like an amateurnight version of itself, awkward, heartfelt, and sweet. Natasha Lyonne, with her lower lip in a perpetual pout, is a likable heroine—not too smart, not too rebellious, more confused than troubled. And Cathy Moriarty brings great comic resolve to her role: She'd be a good drill instructor in the lesbian marines.

Butterfly ★ ★ ★
R, 97 m., 2000

Fernando Fernan Gomez (Don Gregorio), Manuel Lozano (Moncho), Uxia Blanco (Rosa), Gonzalo Uriarte (Ramon), Alexis De Los Santos (Andres), Jesus Castejon (D. Avelino), Guillermo Toledo (Otis), Elena Fernandez (Carmina), Tamar Novas (Roque). Directed by Jose Luis Cuerda. Screenplay by Rafael Azcona, based on the collection of short stories *Que Me Quieres, Amor* by Manuel Rivas.

Butterfly takes place during that brief moment in Spain between the formation of the Republic and the civil war. A history lesson will be necessary for most viewers, and the movie provides it, explaining that the old order of church, military, and monarchy was overthrown by a new leftist government, legally elected, which was then challenged by the right.

The war that followed was like a rehearsal for World War II, with Hitler testing his Luftwaffe and Russia supplying the communist side. The story was more complicated, because the Russians also fought for control of the left against the democratic socialists and the anarchists; Orwell's *Homage to Catalonia* tells the whole story from the point of view of an observer who was left-wing but anticommunist.

The point is that freedom flickered briefly before being crushed by big players on the world stage, who ushered in Franco and decades of dictatorship. People dared to admit their real religious beliefs (or lack of them), and to prefer democracy to the king. And in a village in Galicia, a seven-year-old boy is preparing for his first day of school.

His name is Moncho (Manuel Lozano), and he is frightened because his older brother sometimes comes home after being beaten. In class, when the teacher calls him to the front of the room, Moncho pees his pants and flees. But then the teacher comes calling. He is a kindly old man named Don Gregorio (Fernando Fernan Gomez), who explains he would never beat anyone. He coaxes the boy back into class, and gently introduces him to the world and its wonders. He gives him two presents in particular: *Treasure Island,* by Stevenson, and a butterfly net. Together, the old man and the boy study nature.

The boy's father is a tailor. Moncho's home life is happy, and enlivened by his older brother's enthusiastic interest in the opposite sex. There are, however, scandalous secrets in the village, which lend an ironic twist to one of the subplots. But in general, life is good—until the fascist uprising changes their lives forever.

Butterfly is based on the short stories of Manuel Rivas, and indeed ends like a short story, with a single word that colors everything that went before. Because the film marches so inexorably toward its conclusion, it would be unfair to hint at what happens, except to say that it provides a heartbreaking insight into the way that fear creates cowards.

Fernando Fernan Gomez, who plays the teacher, had the title role in *The Grandfather,* a 1998 Spanish film that got an Oscar nomination and won Gomez the Goya Award as Spain's best actor of the year. I found it a little too sentimental; *Butterfly,* while not lacking in sentiment, excuses it by being seen through the eyes of a naive child, and dilutes it with nostalgia and regret. The film's ending poses a hard question for the viewer: Would we behave more bravely than the characters on the screen do? We are fortunate to live in easy times.

C

Cabaret Balkan ★ ★ ★ ★
NO MPAA RATING, 100 m., 1999

Nikola Ristanovski (Boris), Nebojsa Glogovac (Taxi Driver), Miki Manojlovic (Michael), Marko Urosevic (Alex), Bogdan Diklic (John), Dragan Nikolic (John's Boxer Friend), Mira Banjac (Bosnian Serb Mother), Danil Bata Stojkovic (Viktor). Directed by Goran Paskaljevic and produced by Antoine de Clermont-Tonnerre and Paskaljevic. Screenplay by Dejan Dukovski and Paskaljevic, based on Dukovski's play *Bure Baruta*.

Cabaret Balkan is a scream of agony over the madness in Kosovo and the neighboring lands where blood feuds run deep and the macho virus is a killer epidemic. It's a film about violence, sadism, brutality, and the hatred of women, which seems to go hand in hand with those pastimes. The director, Goran Paskaljevic, opens his film with a taxi driver telling a returning citizen: "This is a goddamned lousy country; why would anyone want to come back?" The film shows us nothing to contradict his statement.

Yes, I know, the "former Yugoslavia," as we now wistfully refer to it, contains beauty and greatness. But what is going on there now, the film argues, is ugliness. The dark side has taken over and decent citizens on both sides flee for their lives, or choose the lesser of evils. It's hard at times to tell which side the characters are on, a New York critic complains. Yes, this film might reply, but what difference does it make? They're all doomed.

The movie's device is a series of interlocking, self-contained stories. Some of the same characters turn up from time to time, like haunting reminders. After a while many of the dominant males seem to blur together into one composite: an alcoholic middle-aged man with an absurd mustache, lurching through the world killing, vomiting, urinating, bleeding, belching, swearing, and entertaining himself by terrorizing women.

Some of the episodes end with surprises—not because we don't see them coming, but because we can't believe that the characters are complete monsters. We are inevitably dis-appointed: None of the men in this movie are nice, except for a few bewildered older men (one of whom crushes a lout's skull and then cradles him, sobbing, "My boy, my boy"). Small events escalate into exercises in terror, and the men in the film seem to be consumed by violence. None of the killings in the film are overtly political; *Cabaret Balkan* seems to argue that monstrous behavior is so ingrained in a sick culture that ethnic cleansing is just an organized form of everyday behavior.

Example: Bus passengers are terrorized by a cretin who hijacks the bus. The elderly driver eventually kills him. A woman passenger, the target of the hijacker's sexual rage, stumbles out of the bus and into the car of her boyfriend, who instantly flies into a jealous rage and accuses her of encouraging the other man. As the two argue, two other men approach, hold them both at gunpoint, and start the next act. Or consider an ordinary traffic accident that escalates: The wronged driver finds the apartment of the other driver's parents and breaks everything in sight. (The other driver got into the crash in the first place because he was cruising the streets harassing single women.)

The most harrowing episode, which starts quietly and escalates, involves a war widow traveling on a train. A large menacing man comes in, sits down, wants her to smoke and drink with him, forces his conversation on her, orders another passenger out of the compartment, and begins the preliminaries to rape. She breaks free and desperately grabs a grenade from her bag. He wrenches the grenade away from her and contemptuously pulls the pin, holding the grenade with one hand as he holds her with the other.

The buried argument of *Cabaret Balkan* seems to be that violence and macho sexual insecurity are closely linked. I was reminded of *Savior* (1998), the film where Dennis Quaid plays a mercenary fighting for the Serbs; he finds himself protecting a woman who has been raped, and whose father and brother want to kill her—because, you see, she has therefore brought dishonor on her family. It is not a crime to rape, but to be raped. Such diseased values, *Cabaret Balkan* seems to suggest, almost inevitably lead to savagery, and indeed the intimidation of women is the primary way the men in this movie express their manhood.

Amazingly, *Cabaret Balkan* is an enormous hit in its homeland, no doubt among the many good citizens who are fed up. Societies can rip themselves to pieces only so long before they are forced to wonder how their values could possibly survive the cost of fighting for them. When war leaves no ideals worth defending, there is only the consolation of depriving the other side of any shreds of remaining standards. Of all the movies about all the tragic places where old hatreds fester over ethnic, racial, and religious animosity, this is the angriest, and therefore possibly the bravest.

Note: The film was released "unrated." Of course, no film that considers violence this unblinkingly and bravely can qualify for an R; that rating is more hospitable toward films that make it look like fun.

Cast Away ★ ★ ★
PG-13, 140 m., 2000

Tom Hanks (Chuck Noland), Helen Hunt (Kelly Frears), Christopher Noth (Jerry Lovett), Nick Searcy (Stan), Lari White (Bettina Peterson), Viveka Davis (Pilot Gwen), Lauren Birkell (Lauren Madden). Directed by Robert Zemeckis and produced by Tom Hanks, Jack Rapke, Steve Starkey, and Zemeckis. Screenplay by William Broyles Jr.

Tom Hanks does a superb job of carrying *Cast Away* all by himself for about two-thirds of its running time, but isn't much helped by additional characters in the opening and closing sequences. Here is a strong and simple story surrounded by needless complications, and flawed by a last act that first disappoints us and then ends on a note of forced whimsy.

Hanks plays Chuck Noland, a time-obsessed Federal Express executive who troubleshoots all over the world, arranging hurry-up package transfers in Moscow before flying off to solve problems in Asia. Helen Hunt plays his fiancée, Kelly Frears, who tries her best to accept a man ruled by a beeper. She comes from clock-watching stock, and for Christmas gives Chuck her grandfather's railroad watch.

Noland hitches a ride on a FedEx flight across the Pacific, which is blown off course before crashing after an onboard explosion. That seems like two catastrophes when one would have done, but director Bob Zemeckis uses the storm for scenes of in-flight fear, wisely following Hitchcock's observation that from a suspense point of view, an explosion is over before you get your money's worth.

Noland survives the crash and floats in a life raft to a deserted island. And . . . am I telling too much of the story? I doubt it, since the trailers and commercials for this movie single-mindedly reveal as much of the plot as they can, spoiling any possible suspense. Not only do they tell you he gets off the island, they tell you *what happens then.* What am I to do? Pretend you haven't seen the ad, or discuss what we all know happens?

The early scenes are essentially busywork. Exotic locales like Moscow add a little interest to details about Noland's job. An airport farewell to the fiancée is obligatory, including the inevitable reassurances about how Chuck will be right back and they'll have a wonderful New Year's Eve. Then the crash.

The movie's power and effect center on the island. Chuck the time-and-motion man finds himself in a world without clocks, schedules, or much of a future. There's something wonderfully pathetic about the way he shouts "Hello? Anybody?" at the sand and trees. Those are his last words for a time, as he tries to remember childhood lessons about firemaking and shelter construction. Then there's a four-year flash-forward and we see the formerly plump Chuck as a gaunt, skinny survivor. (Zemeckis shut down the movie while Hanks lost weight.)

I find it fascinating when a movie just watches somebody doing something. Actual work is more interesting than most plots. Chuck splits coconuts, traps fish, builds fires, and makes use of the contents of several FedEx boxes that washed up with him (too bad nobody was mailing K rations). And he paints a face on a volleyball and names it Wilson—a device which, not incidentally, gives him an excuse for talking out loud. Hanks proves here again what an effective actor he is, never straining for an effect, always persuasive even in this unlikely situation, winning our sympathy with his eyes and his body language when there's no one else on the screen.

I liked every scene on the island and wanted more of them. There's a lovely moment when he squats on the ground, contemplating a crate that has washed up, and the shot is composed as an homage to *2001*, Hanks's favorite film. I also liked the details of his escape. A shot of the giant bow of an ocean tanker, looming over his raft, could have been the setup for the movie to end. But no. As the trailers incredibly reveal, he returns home, where . . .

Well, I can't bring myself to say, just on the chance you're still reading and don't know. Let's say that the resolution of an earlier story strand is meant to be poignant and touching, but comes across flat and anticlimactic. And that the smile at the end of the film seems a little forced.

I would have preferred knowing much less about *Cast Away* on my way into the theater. Noland's survival should be an open question as far as the audience is concerned. You might assume that the 20th Century–Fox marketing department gave away the secrets over the dead body of director Zemeckis, but no: Zemeckis apparently *prefers* to reveal his surprises in the trailers. He got a lot of flak earlier this year when the ads for his previous film, *What Lies Beneath,* let you know Harrison Ford was the bad guy, there was a ghost, etc. At that time he was quoted by David Poland's Web column:

> We know from studying the marketing of movies, people really want to know exactly everything that they are going to see before they go see the movie. It's just one of those things. To me, being a movie lover and film student and a film scholar and a director, I don't. What I relate it to is McDonald's. The reason McDonald's is a tremendous success is that you don't have any surprises. You know exactly what it is going to taste like. Everybody knows the menu.

A strange statement, implying as it does that Zemeckis is a movie lover, student, and scholar but that he doesn't market his movies for people like himself. This is all the more depressing since he usually makes good ones. ☞

The Castle ★ ★ ★

R, 85 m., 1999

Michael Caton (Darryl Kerrigan), Anne Tenney (Sal Kerrigan), Stephen Curry (Dale Kerrigan), Anthony Simcoe (Steve Kerrigan), Sophie Lee (Tracey Kerrigan), Wayne Hope (Wayne Kerrigan), Tiriel Mora (Dennis Denuto), Eric Bana (Con Petropoulous), Charles "Bud" Tingwell (Lawrence Hammill). Directed by Rob Sitch and produced by Debra Choate. Screenplay by Santo Cilauro, Tom Gleisner, Jane Kennedy, and Sitch.

Early in *The Castle*, the happy Kerrigan family is served a chicken dinner by Sal, wife of proud Darryl and mother of daughter Tracey and three sons Dale, Steve, and Wayne; Wayne, currently in prison, is the only one missing from the table. Dad (Michael Caton) observes something on the chicken and asks his wife (Anne Tenney) what it is. "Seasoning," she says proudly. Dad beams: "Seasoning! Looks like everybody's kicked a goal."

And so life spins along at 3 Highview Crescent in Melbourne, where the Kerrigan home sits surrounded by its built-on rooms, screened-in porch, greyhound kennel, big-dish satellite, and carport. For Darryl, it is not so much a house as a shrine to one of the best darn families in the universe, and he proudly points out the plastic Victorian gingerbread trim and the fake chimney to an inspector—who is there, as it turns out, to condemn the property under the laws of public domain.

The Kerrigans don't want to move. They've been told that the three most important words in real estate are "location, location, location"— and how could they improve on their home's convenient location, so close to the airport? So close, indeed, that jumbo jets pass within inches of the property line and the house trembles when they take off.

The Castle, directed by Rob Sitch, is one of those comic treasures like *The Full Monty* and *Waking Ned Devine* that shows its characters in the full bloom of glorious eccentricity. The Kerrigans may be the proudest and happiest family you've ever met, what with Dad's prosperous tow-truck business, and the inventions of Steve (Anthony Simcoe), the "idea man," who specializes in fitting tools together so they can do two jobs equally badly. Tracey (Sophie Lee) is the only college graduate (from beauty school), and Dale (Stephen Curry) is the narrator, frequently quoting his dad, who observes, as he gazes up at pylons towering over the home, that "power lines are a reminder of man's ability to generate electricity."

Dad is a bit of an idea man himself, taking advantage of a narrow room by building an even narrower pool table for it. Meanwhile, Steve searches the *Trader* ad paper for bargains, making sudden discoveries: "Jousting sticks! Make us an offer!" So tightly knit is the family that Dale proudly reports that during mealtimes, "the television is definitely turned down." So it is with a real sense of loss that the Kerrigans discover they may be evicted from their castle, a fate they share with their neighbors Jack and Farouk.

The movie's comic foundation is the cozy if spectacularly insular family life of the Kerrigans. They think almost as one: When Darryl rises to offer the toast at his daughter's wedding, he begins expansively with, "Speaking as the bride's parents . . ." Australia seems to abound with peculiar households, and the Kerrigans are wholesome, positive-thinking versions of such strange samples of Aussie family life as the dysfunctional weirdos in *Muriel's Wedding* and the sisters in *Love Serenade,* who date a disk jockey who is a fish. I can picture them in the audience to view the finals in *Strictly Ballroom.*

The film develops suspense with a big (or, actually, a very small) courtroom finale. The Kerrigans determine to mount a legal battle against eviction and hire an attorney named Dennis Denuto (Tiriel Mora) to represent them, against his own advice (he specializes in repossessions). When he approaches the bench, it is to ask the judge, "How am I doing?" or to whisper urgently, "Can you give me an angle?" He gives the case his best shot (Dale informs us he "even learned Roman numerals" for the appeal), but it isn't until a kindly old expert in constitutional law (Charles "Bud" Tingwell) comes on board that they have a prayer.

This is the sort of movie the British used to make in black-and-white, starring Peter Sellers, Alec Guinness, Terry-Thomas, and Ian Carmichael. It's about characters who have a rock-solid view of the universe and their place

in it, and gaze out upon the world from the high vantage point of the home that is their castle. The movie is not shocking or daring or vulgar, but sublimely content—as content as the Kerrigans when Mom not only serves pound cake for dessert but is so creative she actually tops it with icing sugar. At a time like that, she doesn't need to be told she's kicked a goal.

Catfish in Black Bean Sauce ★ ½
PG-13, 111 m., 2000

Paul Winfield (Harold Williams), Mary Alice (Dolores Williams), Chi Muoi Lo (Dwayne), Lauren Tom (Mai), Kieu Chinh (Thanh), Sanaa Lathan (Nina), Tyler Christopher (Michael), Tzi Ma (Vinh), Wing Chen (Samantha). Directed and produced by Chi Muoi Lo. Screenplay by Lo.

Here's a first draft for a movie that could have been extraordinary. The story materials are rich and promising, but the film is a study in clumsy construction, dead-end scenes, murky motivation, and unneeded complications. Still, at its heart, *Catfish in Black Bean Sauce* has a compelling story to tell, and there are scenes that come to life enough to show us what we're missing.

The movie is about two Vietnamese war waifs being raised by an African-American couple. Harold Williams (Paul Winfield) encountered them while working in an adoption center, and he and his wife, Dolores (Mary Alice), raised them and love them. Dwayne (played by the writer-director, Chi Muoi Lo) fully accepts them as his parents, but his older sister, Mai (Lauren Tom), still searches for their birth mother.

Dwayne's life is further complicated. His girlfriend Nina (Sanaa Lathan, from *Love and Basketball*) seems to like him more than he likes her. His roommate Michael (Tyler Christopher) is dating a Chinese girl named Samantha (Wing Chen) who may be a Chinese boy named Sam. Does Dwayne like Michael more than Nina?

The screenplay is constructed like a sitcom, with dramatic entrances and exits, lots of punch lines, and quiet moments interrupted by bombshells. At one point Dwayne blurts out, "Will you marry me?" to Nina, whose answer is interrupted by Mai's sudden entrance: "I've found Ma!"

The imminent arrival of their long-lost mother, Thanh (Kieu Chinh), puts the family in an uproar; Dolores and Harold didn't even know Mai was still looking for her. But note how filmmaker Lo is too clever by half: Instead of a carefully written airport scene showing the tensions involved, he throws in an irrelevant fantasy sequence involving a cowboy oil man.

Mai is married to a Vietnamese-American infomercial ham—an excuse for unnecessary comic infomercials, of course. She has prepared a guest bedroom for Thanh, who prefers instead to stay with Dwayne and Michael, who hardly have room for her. Meanwhile, Dolores prepares a Chinese-African dinner, which offers countless cross-cultural possibilities, most of them blown in an awkward sequence where Thanh pulls out a bottle of Vietnamese sauce, they all try it, and their reaction shots are so impenetrable we can't tell if it's too hot, too nasty, or simply an insult to Dolores's cooking.

Lo obviously has a lot of material he wants to consider, but the subplot of the transsexual Samantha is a blind alley. Given the drama at the heart of this story, who cares about Dwayne's roommate's girlfriend? There is a well-written and acted conversation between Dwayne and Michael (who argues that his love for Samantha does not make him gay), but this really works only if Dwayne is jealous, and the movie doesn't seem to know if he is or not. Certainly he is sullen and uncommunicative around Nina, the woman he allegedly loves; the movie lacks a single scene to suggest why Nina puts up with this slug.

Paul Winfield, Mary Alice, and Kieu Chinh provide the anchors for the picture—three adults whose feelings and identities are clearly established. But even here Lo bypasses perceptive dramatic scenes for concocted sitcom payoffs, including a false health crisis and a hair-pulling wrestling match on the floor between the two mothers that is wrong in every atom.

All of the material is here for another, better picture. *Catfish in Black Bean Sauce* was obviously shot quickly on a low budget, and lacked anyone willing to tell Lo his screenplay was simply not ready to be filmed. It stands as a missed opportunity. A wiser course might have been to show it to potential investors as a sketch for a more evolved production, with a better screenplay, more insights into the characters, and less deadwood.

The Caveman's Valentine ★ ★ ★
R, 105 m., 2001

Samuel L. Jackson (Romulus), Colm Feore (Leppenraub), Ann Magnuson (Moira), Damir Andrei (Arnold), Aunjanue Ellis (Lulu), Tamara Tunie (Sheila), Peter MacNeill (Cork), Jay Rodan (Joey/No Face). Directed by Kasi Lemmons and produced by Danny DeVito, Michael Shamberg, Stacey Sher, Elie Samaha, and Andrew Stevens. Screenplay by George Dawes Green, based on his novel.

The detective in *The Caveman's Valentine* is a raving lunatic on his bad days, and a homeless man on a harmless errand on his good ones. Once he was a brilliant pianist, a student at Julliard. Now he lives in a cave in a park. His dreadlocks reach down to his waist, and his eyes peer out at a fearsome world. You'd be fearful, too, if your enemy lived at the top of the Chrysler Building and attacked you with deadly rays.

Romulus Ledbetter is one of Samuel L. Jackson's most intriguing creations, a schizophrenic with sudden sharp stabs of lucid thought and logical behavior, whose life is changed one day when the frozen body of a young man is found outside his cave in a city park. The police believe the man, a transient, froze to death. Romulus thinks he knows better. And his desire to unmask the real killer draws him out of his cave and into a daring foray into the New York art world.

Romulus is not without connections. His daughter, Lulu (Aunjanue Ellis), is a policewoman. But she is hardly convinced by his first suspect: his enemy in the Chrysler Building. By the time he discards that hypothesis and zeroes in on a fashionable photographer named Leppenraub (Colm Feore), it's too late for anyone to take him seriously—if they ever could have in the first place.

The challenge for Jackson and his director, Kasi Lemmons, is to make Romulus believable both as the caveman and as a man capable of solving a murder. Too much ranting and raving, and Romulus would repel the audience. Too much logic, and we don't buy him as mentally ill. Even the clothes and the remarkable hair have to be considered; this is not a man you would want to sit next to during a three-day bus trip, but, on the other hand, he doesn't tilt over into repellent grunge (like the aliens in *Battlefield Earth*). It's remarkable the way Jackson begins with the kind of character we'd avert our eyes from, and makes him fascinating and even likable.

This is Lemmons's second film; after her remarkable debut *Eve's Bayou* (1997), she repeats her accomplishment in fleshing out a story with intriguing supporting characters. Chief among these is Leppenraub, a gay photographer who savors S and M imagery, and his employee/lover Joey (Jay Rodan), who makes digital videos. If Leppenraub killed the dead young man, did Joey film it? Romulus is able to enter the photographer's world through an unlikely route, involving a bankruptcy lawyer who befriends him, cleans him up, and enlists him as a pianist at a party. At one of Leppenraub's openings, the dreadlocked caveman looks at the photographs with the clear eye of the mad but logical, and says exactly what he thinks.

Is this a reach, suggesting that the caveman and the photographer could find themselves in the same circles? Not in the art world, where unlikely alliances are forged every day; the movie *Basquiat* is about an artist who made the round trip from the streets to the galleries. It's also plausible, if unlikely, that the cleaned-up Romulus, an exciting man with an electric presence, could attract the sexual attention of Leppenraub's sister, Moira (Ann Magnuson), who seduces him because she likes to shock, she likes to try new things, and she likes the guy (of course, she doesn't know his whole story).

The actual solution to the murder mystery was, for me, the least interesting part of the movie. *The Caveman's Valentine* is based on a crime novel by George Dawes Green, who also wrote the screenplay, and like many procedurals it has great respect for clues, sudden insights, logical reasoning, holes in stories, and all the beloved devices of the detection genre. Although the detective in this case may be completely original, his method (under the madness) is traditional. At the end all is settled and solved, but I agree with Edmund Wilson in his famous essay on detective novels when he concluded, essentially, "so what?"

The solution simply allows the story to end. The engine that makes the story live is in the life of Romulus: in how he survives, how he thinks, how people see in him what they are looking for. To watch Samuel L. Jackson in the role is to realize again what a gifted actor he is, how skilled at finding the right way to play a character who, in other hands, might be unplayable. I think the key to the whole performance is in his walk. It's busy and bustling, as if he's late for an appointment that he's rather looking forward to. He seems absorbed in his thoughts and plans, a busy man, with the jam-packed calendar of the mad.

Cecil B. Demented ★ ½
R, 88 m., 2000

Melanie Griffith (Honey Whitlock), Stephen Dorff (Cecil B. Demented), Alicia Witt (Cherish), Adrian Grenier (Lyle), Larry Gilliard Jr. (Lewis), Maggie Gyllenhaal (Raven), Jack Noseworthy (Rodney), Mike Shannon (Petie), Harriet Dodge (Dinah), Ricki Lake (Libby). Directed by John Waters and produced by John Fiedler, Joe Caracciolo Jr., and Mark Tarlov. Screenplay by Waters.

My best guess is that John Waters produced the talent shows in his high school. There's always been something cheerfully amateurish about his more personal films—a feeling that he and his friends have dreamed up a series of "skits" while hanging out together. *Cecil B. Demented* takes this tendency to an almost unwatchable extreme, in a home movie that's like a bunch of kids goofing off.

To be sure, he has real stars in the picture; Melanie Griffith stars *as* a Hollywood star, and Stephen Dorff plays the cult leader who kidnaps her as part of his guerrilla assault on mainstream cinema. But they're used more as exhibits than performers (Look! It's Melanie Griffith!). The movie has a radical premise, as Weathermen-type movie lovers try to destroy dumb commercial films, but it is pitched at the level of a very bad sketch on *Saturday Night Live*.

Cinema guerrilla Cecil B. Demented (Dorff)

and his cult group kidnap Griffith, who will be forced to star in their own film. Their targets include the Maryland Film Commission, the big shots who produced Griffith's own new film, and *Gump Two,* a sequel to *Forrest Gump,* which is being shot in Baltimore. Some of this stuff is funny in concept (when they attack the director's cut of *Patch Adams,* that's good for a laugh, although the scene itself isn't).

And Griffith, as a spoiled star named Honey Whitlock, gets into the spirit. She makes the life of her assistant (Ricki Lake) miserable, she makes impossible demands, she sends back a limousine that's the wrong color (not fiction; I once actually saw Ginger Rogers do this), and she is not a good sport when it comes to eating Maryland seafood ("I'm not interested in some kind of meal you have to beat with a mallet while wearing some stupid little bib, while families of mutants gawk in your face").

But the story and dialogue are genuinely amateur night, and there are times when you can almost catch the actors giggling, like kids in a senior class sketch. It's been like that in a lot of Waters's movies, from the raunchy early sleazoids like *Pink Flamingos,* through his transitional phase *(Polyester)* to his studio productions *(Hairspray, Cry-Baby, Serial Mom).* Now he seems to have returned to his middle period again, if such a thing is possible.

Cecil B. Demented got its title, Waters says, because that's what he was called in an early review. Like Ed Wood (but inevitably at a higher level of artistry), he seems to enjoy the actual process of making films: He likes to go to the set, have actors say "Action!" and see everyone have a good time. Sometimes, in this film, that geniality works against him; the actors are having a better time than we are.

Too much of the movie feels like the kind of film where you're supposed to say, "Look! There's . . ." and fill in the name of a faded TV personality. Patricia Hearst, who appeared in Waters's funny *Cry-Baby,* is back, for example, to add ironic weight to a story about a kidnap victim who identifies with her captors. How entertaining is that really supposed to be?

Waters has always embraced a tacky design look in his films, and here a lot of the sets seem decorated by stuff everybody brought from home. Old movie posters are plastered on the walls, the cult hangs around in what looks like a rec room, and there are movie in-jokes everywhere. (Cult members have the names of their favorite directors tattooed on their arms.)

Cecil also tells us, "I don't believe in phony life-affirming endings." He sure doesn't. The ending of *Cecil B. Demented* may be phony, but it's not life-affirming. One wonders if the script simply says, "Everyone runs around like crazy."

There will, however, always be a (small) corner of my heart filled with admiration for John Waters. He is an anarchist in an age of the cautious, an independent in an age of studio creatures, a man whose films are homemade and contain no chemicals or preservatives. Even with *Cecil B. Demented,* which fails on just about every level, you've got to hand it to him: The idea for the film is kind of inspired. When this kid gets out of high school he's going to amount to something. You wait and see.

The Cell ★ ★ ★

R, 108 m., 2000

Jennifer Lopez (Catherine Deane), Vince Vaughn (Agent Novak), Vincent D'Onofrio (Carl Stargher), Marianne Jean-Baptiste (Dr. Miriam Kent), Jake Weber (Agent Ramsey), Dylan Baker (Henry West), Patrick Bauchau (Lucien Baines), Gerry Becker (Dr. Cooperman), James Gammon (Teddy Lee), Catherine Sutherland (Anne Marie Vicksey), Jake Thomas (Young Stargher), Pruitt Taylor Vince (Dr. Reid). Directed by Tarsem and produced by Julio Caro and Eric McLeod. Screenplay by Mark Protosevich.

The Cell is a bizarre mixture of science fiction and serial murders, mind games and pop psychology, wild images and haunting special effects. It's a thriller and a fantasy, a police movie and a venture into the mind of a killer so perverse he could see Hannibal Lecter and raise him. For all of its visual pyrotechnics, it's also a story where we care about the characters; there's a lot at stake at the end, and we're involved. I know people who hate it, finding it pretentious or unrestrained; I think it's one of the best films of the year.

Jennifer Lopez stars, as Catherine Deane, a social worker who has a knack for establishing rapport with troubled clients. She is recruited for a project in which experimental technology is used to establish a link between her mind and that of a little boy locked inside a coma. Can she coax him out? The opening images, of black stallions and desert vistas, show her riding across the sands in a flowing white dress, and then finding the little boy in a landscape filled with stark Dali trees, and almost making contact, before . . .

The director, named Tarsem, uses this story to establish the mind-sharing methodology. The mind-trips take place in a sci-fi laboratory, with earnest scientists peering through plate-glass windows at their eerie subjects, who are suspended in midair wearing virtual reality gear. We meet the millionaire parents of the little boy, learn about his problems, and get to know Catherine, who is played by Lopez as quiet, grave, and confident.

In a parallel story, the FBI finds the body of the latest victim of a serial killer who drowns his captives and then makes them up to look like dolls. Vince Vaughn plays an agent named Novak, who believes the killer has a ritual he goes through—a ritual that means his latest victim has only hours to live before a clockwork mechanism brings about her death. Using slim clues and brilliant lab work, the FBI is able to capture the killer, a vile man named Carl Stargher (Vincent D'Onofrio). But how to get him to reveal where his latest captive is hidden? The FBI turns to Catherine Deane and the scientists in charge (Marianne Jean-Baptiste, Dylan Baker, and Pruitt Taylor Vince), who warn that she risks psychic harm by venturing into Stargher's unwholesome subconscious.

The screenplay, by Mark Protosevich, is ingenious in the way it intercuts three kinds of stories. On one level The Cell is science fiction about virtual reality, complete with the ominous observation that if your mind thinks it's real, then it is real, and it could kill you. On another level the movie is a wildly visionary fantasy in which the mind-spaces of Stargher and Deane are landscapes by Jung out of Dali, with a touch of the Tarot deck, plus light-and-sound trips reminiscent of 2001. On the third level, the movie is a race against time, in which a victim struggles for her life while the FBI desperately pieces together clues; these scenes

reminded me of The Silence of the Lambs. The intercutting is so well done that at the end there is tension from all three directions, and what's at stake is not simply the life of the next victim, but also the soul of Carl Stargher, who lets Catherine get glimpses of his unhappy childhood.

Stargher's sexual practices are also suggested, somewhat obliquely. Like the predators in Seven, The Silence of the Lambs, and Hannibal, Stargher is a creature of neo-S&M, a seriously twisted man whose libido needs such complicated tending it hardly seems worth the trouble. We are left with a few technical questions (how did he embed the hooks in his own back?), but a movie like this is more concerned with suggesting weirdness than explaining it.

The Cell is one of those movies where you have a lot of doubts at the beginning, and then one by one they're answered, and you find yourself seduced by the style and story. It plays fair all the way through—it develops its themes and delivers on them, instead of copping out like Hollow Man by making a U-turn into a slasher film. It's not often the imagination and the emotions are equally touched by a film, but here I was exhilarated by the boldness of the conception while still involved at a thriller level.

I don't seek out advance information about movies because I like to go in with an open mind. Walking into the screening of The Cell, I knew absolutely nothing about the plot or premise, but a TV producer in New York made a point of telling me how much she hated it, and various on-line correspondents helpfully told me how bad they thought it was. Did we see the same movie?

We live in a time when Hollywood shyly ejects weekly remakes of dependable plots, terrified to include anything that might confuse the dullest audience member. The new studio guidelines prefer PG-13 cuts from directors, so we get movies like Coyote Ugly that start out with no brains and now don't have any sex, either. Into this wilderness comes a movie like The Cell, which is challenging, wildly ambitious, and technically superb, and I dunno: I guess it just overloads the circuits for some people.

Tarsem (he dropped his surname, Duamdwar) is a first-time director who comes to movies via music videos and commercials (indeed his title sequence in the desert looks like it could lead into a beer ad as easily as a psychological fantasy). He must have seized this project with eager ambition. Like other emerging directors (Spike Jonze, David O. Russell, Paul Thomas Anderson) he likes to take big chances; he reminds me of how Spike Lee and Oliver Stone came lunging out of the starting gate.

Tarsem is an Indian, like M. Night Shyamalan of *The Sixth Sense,* and comes from a culture where ancient imagery and modern technology live side by side. In the 1970s, Pauline Kael wrote, the most interesting directors were Altman, Scorsese, and Coppola, because they were Catholics whose imaginations were enriched by the church of pre-Vatican II, while most other Americans were growing up on Eisenhower's bland platitudes. Now our whole culture has been tamed by marketing and branding, and mass entertainment has been dumbed down. It is possible the next infusion of creativity will come from cultures like India, still rich in imagination, not yet locked into malls.   ☞

The Center of the World ★ ★ ★ ½
NO MPAA RATING, 86 m., 2001

Peter Sarsgaard (Richard Longman), Molly Parker (Florence), Carla Gugino (Jerri), Balthazar Getty (Brian Pivano). Directed by Wayne Wang and produced by Peter Newman and Wang. Screenplay by Ellen Benjamin Wong (pseudonym for Wang, Paul Auster, and Siri Hustvedt).

Sex isn't the subject of *The Center of the World.* It's the arena. The subject is making money, and the movie is about two people who hate their jobs. Richard (Peter Sarsgaard) is a computer whiz whose company is about to go public and make him a millionaire. Florence (Molly Parker) is a lap dancer in a strip club, but technically not a prostitute. You can be aroused by her, but you can't touch her. Richard is the same way. He skips a meeting with investors, and disappears as his company floats its IPO. You can profit from his skills, but you can't have him.

Here are two people who want to succeed only on their own terms. The big difference between them, as she points out, is "money. You have it and I don't." As a sex worker, her strategy is to get the client's money without giving herself. She meets Richard in a coffee shop. He finds out where she works, turns up, and buys a lap dance. He's fascinated. He asks her to go to Las Vegas for a weekend. She says she's not that kind of person. "I can compensate you," he says. "Compensate" is a revealing word in this context. He offers her $10,000. She says he'll have to observe her rules. He agrees.

He may actually be happy to agree. She's spared him from performance anxiety. He gets the intrigue, the excitement, the mystique, and her full attention, and avoids physical and psychological risk. Nice deal. Good for her, too, because she needs money but doesn't think of herself as a prostitute (she's "really" a drummer in a rock band). Wayne Wang says his film was inspired by the strip clubs of the Silicon Valley. They bring together men who have too much money and no interest in relationships with women who have too little money and no interest in relationships.

Sex supplies the stakes. It's the currency of the microeconomy created for a weekend by Richard and Flo. She manufactures sex, he consumes it, and cash flow is generated. When she goes a little further than her guidelines permit, that's like Alan Greenspan lowering interest rates. The casual observer may think the weekend is all about sex; more evolved viewers will notice that the sex is not very fulfilling, very original, or very good; what is fascinating are the mind games. They're like negotiations. Flo is the better negotiator, but then of course she's the market-maker.

In theory, a prostitute and her client form a closed system, in which everything in their private lives, even their real names, may be kept secret. Because Richard and Flo met socially before entering into their agreement, information leaked out. She knows he's about to make millions of dollars, although all she wants is $10,000. The commitment involved in getting the millions would interfere with her idea of herself. We in the audience get more information because we eavesdrop during their private moments; he deals by e-mail with partners who are enraged that he stiffed the investors and (they hear) is in Vegas with a hooker on the company's biggest day. She calls a Vegas friend named Jerri (Carla Gugino), who gives her technical advice; she tells Jerri she "kinda likes" the guy.

Now look at their sex. Her rules permit action only between 10 P.M. and 2 A.M. The rest of the time, they sightsee, visit restaurants, play video games. The sex in theory will not involve intercourse. They have connecting rooms. At 10 P.M. she throws open the doors, dressed dramatically in "erotic" clothes that are pretty routine. She does advanced versions of a lap dance. He wants to go further. "You want real?" she asks. "I'll show you real." What she shows him is real, all right, but scant consolation for an onlooker.

At one point they practice something called "fire and ice," which involves ice cubes and hot sauce, and has been compared by credulous reviewers with the most famous scene in *Last Tango in Paris*. The difference is, in *Last Tango* something was really happening between two unpaid and involved participants; in *The Center of the World*, it's erotic showbiz. (Show me a sexual practice that involves ice cubes and hot sauce, and I will show you a sexual practice that would be improved without them.) The movie has also been compared to *Leaving Las Vegas*, but couldn't be more different. That was about agony and redemption, and the hooker was a healing angel. This movie is about two entrepreneurs.

The suspense in *The Center of the World* is not about whether Flo and Richard will have real sex. The suspense involves whether they'll start to like each other. He tells her he's in love, but guys always say that. She kinda likes him, but having started off in this way, can she ever have sex with him that will not seem, in some way, like a subtle extension of prostitution? To this intrigue is added another level when Jerri, the friend, visits their suite with a story of being beaten up. Is Richard being scammed by the two women?

In a scenario like this, it's impossible to figure out what's real. Does Richard love Flo, or the erotic illusion she creates, or the freedom from responsibility she makes possible? Does Flo like Richard, or his money, or the gamesmanship of dancing closer to the flame? When they spontaneously find themselves turned on out-side the four-hour time zone, is that real, or does it feed off the excitement of breaking the rules? The situation is complicated because all of their interruptus brinksmanship has been a turn-on. They're only human.

If you understand who the characters are and what they're supposed to represent, the performances are right on the money. Flo is not supposed to be a sexy tart, and Richard is not supposed to be a lustful client. They're sides of the same coin, and very much alike. You want real? This movie shows you real. For Richard and Flo, real is a weekend in Vegas trying to figure out what they really want, and how much they're willing to sell off in order to buy it.

Center Stage ★ ★ ★
PG-13, 113 m., 2000

Amanda Schull (Jody), Ethan Stiefel (Cooper Neilson), Peter Gallagher (Jonathan Reeves), Sascha Radetsky (Charlie), Shakiem Evans (Erik), Zoe Saldana (Eva Rodriguez), Donna Murphy (Juliette [Teacher]), Susan Mary Pratt (Maureen), Ilia Kulik (Sergei). Directed by Nicholas Hytner and produced by Laurence Mark. Screenplay by Carol Heikkinen.

Center Stage follows a group of young ballet students through their first year of advanced training at the fictional American Ballet Academy in New York. They had to be very good to get in. Only three will be chosen at the end of the year to join the company. They work hard, but when they are not actually dancing, they are a lot like freshmen in any college; they survive romances, they party, they gossip, they despair and dream, and they smoke too much.

Dancers do tend to smoke a lot. It's bad for their wind, but they think it helps them to lose weight. The movie knows that and a lot of other things about the world of ballet; it feels like an inside job. It isn't so perceptive about its characters, who tend to fall into recognizable types (the ingenue, the rebel, the girl who's too fat, the girl who is pushed by her mother). Here it's similar to *Fame*, but not as electrifying. But if you look at *Center Stage* as another example of the school movie of the week, with auditions taking the place of the senior prom, you realize it's a lot smarter and more perceptive—and it's about something.

It is about the union of hard work and artistic success. To be a world-class ballet dancer is to be an athlete of the highest order, and if you look at ballet as a sport, it has many Michael Jordans and the NBA had only one. The movie casts real dancers in many of the roles, and that provides an obvious standard of excellence that gives the movie an underlying authenticity.

Ethan Stiefel, considered by many to be the best male dancer in the world, plays Cooper, the lead—the star of the company, who has just lost his girlfriend to Jonathan (Peter Gallagher), the company's head. He becomes attracted to Jody (Amanda Schull), one of the new students, and in a predictable progression invites her into his bed and into the new ballet he is creating.

Predictable, yes, but not with all the soap-opera payoffs we might fear. The movie uses the materials of melodrama, but is gentle with them; it's oriented more in the real world, and doesn't jack up every conflict and love story into an overwrought crisis. That restraint is especially useful in creating the character Eva Rodriguez (Zoe Saldana), the class rebel, who talks back to the teacher (Donna Murphy), comes late to rehearsals, has a bad attitude—and yet actually has the best attitude of all, because she dances out of her love for dance, not because of ambition or duty.

Some of the other students are not so lucky. One has been pushed into dancing by her mother. One has a body-image problem. And so on. But a lot of these kids are pretty normal, apart from their demanding profession. In a dance club, Sergei (Ilia Kulik), from Russia, tries to pick up two women. They both want to know what he does. He says he's a ballet dancer, and they turn away. With the next woman, he has more luck. "Mafia," he explains.

The movie doesn't force it, but it has the pleasures of a musical. It ends with two big ballet numbers, wonderfully staged and danced, and along the way there are rehearsals and scenes in a Broadway popular dance studio that have a joy and freedom. Film is a wonderful way to look at dance, because it gets you closer and varies the point of view, but since the death of the Hollywood musical there hasn't

been enough of it. *Center Stage* has moments of joy and moments of insight, and is about both human nature and the inhuman demands of ballet.

Chalk ★ ★ ★
NO MPAA RATING, 135 m., 2000

Edwin Johnson (Watson), Johnnie Reese (Jones), Kelvin Han Yee (T.C.), Don Bajema (Dorian James), Denise Concetta Cavaliere (Lois), John Tidwell (Johnnie), Destiny Costa (Wanda). Directed by Rob Nilsson and produced by Rand Crook and Ethan Sing. Screenplay by Don Bajema and Nilsson.

Rob Nilsson's *Chalk* opens with half an hour of murky, grungy scene-setting in a San Francisco pool hall. Out of this miasma, the story gradually wells up; without quite realizing when it happens, we pass from passive witnesses to active watchers. What purpose does the shapeless opening serve? Perhaps to immerse us in the movie's world, to provide a passage from one reality to another.

The story, once its outlines have become clear, involves a black man in his sixties named Watson (Edwin Johnson), who runs a pool hall with his two sons. He spent time in Japan, we learn, where he perhaps fathered Jones (Johnnie Reese), who is half-Asian. His other son is the adopted Korean-American T.C. (Kelvin Han Yee), who walked into the pool hall one day.

Jones wants to set up a high-stakes pool game between T.C. and a man named Dorian James (Don Bajema), who is a ranking professional. T.C. hesitates. He has choked before, and there are hints that Jones hopes T.C. will fail again. Then T.C. discovers that Watson is dying, and decides to take the $10,000 match and prove himself to his adoptive father. Filling out the canvas is Lois (Denise Concetta Cavaliere), T.C.'s girlfriend, who works as the bartender in the pool hall.

As I describe this plot you are perhaps thinking of *The Hustler* or *The Color of Money*, but *Chalk* feels nothing like those films. It is more like a movie extruded from the world in which it is set. Information about its making is essential to understanding its feeling. It was directed by Nilsson, a fiercely independent filmmaker whose earlier titles include *Northern Lights* (1979), about a farmer-labor strike in Minnesota, and *On the Edge* (1986), with Bruce Dern's great performance as an outlaw runner who makes one last great effort.

Around 1990, Nilsson moved to San Francisco and started a filmmaking workshop in the Tenderloin area, recruiting street people and marginal survivors as his actors and technicians. Only two of the actors in *Chalk* are professionals (Johnson and Bajema). The others do not play themselves, precisely, but their characters are informed by people they know and where they live.

The visual style, with Mickey Freeman as cinematographer, is deliberately stylized; *Chalk* looks like *film noir* seen through a glass darkly, with backlit highlights. Although Nilsson's hero is Cassavetes, the film does not feel improvised, but more as if the video camera waited patiently for the right moments.

Much of the dialogue is half-heard, elliptical, allusive. A few conversations play out at length. One of the best has T.C. talking with a pool hustler who lives in his van and remembers when he had, and lost, a mobile home: "Pool players don't make as much as volleyball players—even dart players. If you're not in the top 10, forget about it." He gives T.C. advice on how to beat Dorian James, if indeed Dorian can be beaten.

The other conversation is between Dorian and his girlfriend Wanda (Destiny Costa), and it involves his request that she do something particularly painful to him as part of his preparation for the match. Their talk is desultory; he asks, she refuses, they fight, embrace, rest, talk quietly, and he brings up the subject again. We sense depths of loneliness and insecurity.

The $10,000 match, which occupies perhaps the last forty-five minutes of the film, is for the first player to win seven games. The movie makes the progress of the games clear, and yet doesn't dwell on them, because the real contest is between the players. During two of the games, Freeman's camera adopts the fast-moving, tabletop "ball eye view" approach used by Scorsese in *The Color of Money,* maybe just to show that he can. After the match is settled, there is another payoff, quick, painful, and brutal, which we didn't see coming.

Chalk is not the kind of movie many people will appreciate at first viewing. You have to understand who Nilsson and his actors are, and give some thought to the style to appreciate it. It is not just one more *Hustler* clone, that's for sure, but a plunge into the hermetic world these characters have created and inhabit. There may be a world outside the pool hall, but when T.C. goes to the beach one day, he's like a fish out of water. And inside the hall, old errors, ancient drug habits, and deep psychic wounds make happiness, we realize, impossible.

Charlie's Angels ½★
PG-13, 92 m., 2000

Cameron Diaz (Natalie), Drew Barrymore (Dylan), Lucy Liu (Alex), Bill Murray (Bosley), Sam Rockwell (Eric Knox), Kelly Lynch (Vivian Wood), Tim Curry (Roger Corwin), John Forsythe (Voice of Charlie). Directed by McG and produced by Leonard Goldberg, Drew Barrymore, and Nancy Juvonen. Screenplay by Ryan Rowe, Ed Solomon, and John August.

Charlie's Angels is eye candy for the blind. It's a movie without a brain in its three pretty little heads, which belong to Cameron Diaz, Drew Barrymore, and Lucy Liu. This movie is a dead zone in their lives, and mine.

What is it? A satire? Of what? Of satires, I guess. It makes fun of movies that want to make fun of movies like this. It's an all-girl series of mindless action scenes. Its basic shot consists of Natalie, Dylan, and Alex, the angels, running desperately toward the camera before a huge explosion lifts them off their feet and hurls them through the air and smashes them against windshields and things—but they survive with injuries only to their makeup.

Why, I am asking, is this funny? I am thinking hard. So much money and effort was spent on these explosions that somebody must have been convinced they had a purpose, but I, try as I might, cannot see them as anything other than action without mind, purpose, humor, excitement, or entertainment.

The movie's premise will be familiar to anyone who ever watched the original TV show. I never watched the show, and the plot was familiar even to me. A disembodied voice (John Forsythe) issues commands to the three babes who work for his detective agency, and they perform his missions while wearing clothes possibly found at the thrift shop across the street from Coyote Ugly.

Barrymore, Diaz, and Liu represent redhead, blonde, and brunette respectively (or, as my colleague David Poland has pointed out, T, A, and Hair). Sad, isn't it, that three such intelligent, charming, and talented actresses could be reduced to their most prominent component parts? And voluntarily too. At the tops of their careers, they *chose* to make this movie (Barrymore even produced it). They volunteered for what lesser talents are reduced to doing.

The cast also contains Bill Murray, who likes to appear unbilled in a lot of his movies, and picked the wrong one to shelve that policy. He is winsome, cherubic, and loopy, as usual, but the movie gives him nothing to push against. There's the curious feeling he's playing to himself. Sam Rockwell plays a kidnapped millionaire, Tim Curry plays a villain, and ... why go on?

In the months to come there will be several movies based on popular video games, including one about "Tomb Raiders" and its digital babe, Lara Croft. *Charlie's Angels* is like the trailer for a video game movie, lacking only the video game and the movie.

Chicken Run ★ ★ ★ ½
G, 85 m., 2000

Mel Gibson (Rocky), Miranda Richardson (Mrs. Tweedy), Tony Haygarth (Mr. Tweedy), Julia Sawalha (Ginger), Jane Horrocks (Babs), Lynn Ferguson (Mac), Imelda Staunton (Bunty), Benjamin Whitrow (Fowler), Timothy Spall (Nick), Phil Daniels (Fetcher). Directed by Peter Lord and Nick Park and produced by Lord, Park, and David Sproxton. Screenplay by Karey Kirkpatrick.

Mrs. Tweedy isn't fooling. Despite her twee British name, she's not a nice little old lady chicken farmer. She means business. Early in *Chicken Run*, she singles out a chicken who hasn't been laying its daily egg, and condemns it to the chopping block. Since this is an animated film, we expect a joke and a close escape. Not a chance. The chicken gets its head

chopped off, the other chickens hear the sickening thud of the ax—and later, in case there's the slightest shred of doubt about what happened, we see chicken bones.

So it truly is a matter of life and death for the chickens to escape from the Tweedy Chicken Farm in *Chicken Run,* a magical new animated film that looks and sounds like no other. Like the otherwise completely different *Babe,* this is a movie that uses animals as surrogates for our hopes and fears, and as their chickens run through one failed escape attempt after another, the charm of the movie wins us over.

The film opens as a spoof on the World War II prison pictures like *The Great Escape* and *Stalag 17* (the most important location in the movie is Hut 17). Most of the chickens are happy with captivity and free meals ("Chicken feed! My favorite!"), but one named Ginger has pluck, and tries one escape attempt after another, always being hurled into the coalhole for a week as her punishment. Her cause grows more urgent when Mrs. Tweedy (voice by Miranda Richardson) decides to phase out the egg operation and turn all of her chickens into chicken pies.

Ginger (voice by Julia Sawalha) has tried everything: tunnels, catapults, disguises, deceptions. Mr. Tweedy (Tony Haygarth) is sure the chickens are mapping intelligent escape plans, but can't convince his wife, who is sure they are too stupid. Then a godsend arrives: Rocky the Flying Rooster (Mel Gibson), an American bird who is on the run from a circus. Surely he can teach the chickens to fly and they can escape that way?

Maybe, maybe not. There are many adventures before we discover the answer, and the most thrilling follows Ginger and Rocky through the bowels of the chicken pie machine, in an action sequence that owes a little something to the runaway mine train in *Indiana Jones and the Temple of Doom.* There are tests of daring and skill in the escape plan, but also tests of character, as the birds look into their souls and discover hidden convictions.

In a more conventional movie, the plot would proceed on autopilot. Not in *Chicken Run,* which has a whimsical and sometimes darker view of the possibilities. One of the movie's charms is the way it lets many of the characters be true eccentrics (it's set in England in the 1950s and sometimes offers a taste of those sly old Alec Guinness comedies). Characters like the Royal Air Force veteran rooster with a sneaky secret exist not to nudge the plot along but to add color and texture: This movie about chickens is more human than many formula comedies.

The movie is the first feature-length work by the team of Peter Lord and Nick Park, who've won three Oscars (Park) and two Oscar nominations (Lord) for the work in Claymation, a stop-action technique in which Plasticine is minutely changed from shot to shot to give the illusion of 3-D movement. Park is the creator of the immortal Wallace and Gromit, the man and his dog who star in *The Wrong Trousers* and *A Close Shave*.

Here, they bring a startling new smoothness and fluid quality to their art. Traditional Claymation tweaks and prods the clay between every shot; you can almost see the thumbprints. Their more sophisticated approach here is to start with Plasticine modeled on articulated skeletons, and clothe the models with a "skin" that gives them smoothness and consistency from shot to shot. The final effect is more like *Toy Story* than traditional Claymation.

What I like best about the movie is that it's not simply a plot puzzle to be solved with a clever escape at the end. It is observant about human (or chicken) nature. A recent movie like *Gone in 60 Seconds* is the complete slave of its dim-witted plot and fears to pause for character development, lest the audience find the dialogue slows down the action. *Chicken Run,* on the other hand, is not only funny and wicked, clever and visually inventive, but . . . kind and sweet. Tender and touching. It's a movie made by men, not machines, and at the end you don't feel wrung out or manipulated, but cheerful and (I know this sounds strange) more hopeful.

Children of Heaven ★ ★ ★

PG, 87 m., 1999

Amir Naji (Ali's Father), Amir Farrokh Hashemian (Ali), Bahare Seddiqi (Zahra), Nafise Jafar-Mohammadi (Roya), Fereshte Sarabandi (Ali's Mother), Kamal Mir Karimi (Assistant), Behzad Rafiee (Trainer), Dariush Mokhtari (Ali's Teacher). Directed by Majid Majidi and produced by the Institute for the Intellectual Development of Children and Young Adults. Screenplay by Majidi.

Children of Heaven is very nearly a perfect movie for children, and of course that means adults will like it too. It lacks the cynicism and smart-mouth attitudes of so much American entertainment for kids, and glows with a kind of good-hearted purity. To see this movie is to be reminded of a time when the children in movies were children, and not miniature stand-up comics.

The movie is from Iran. Immediately you think kids would not be interested in such a movie. It has subtitles. Good lord!—kids will have to read them! But its subtitles are easy for eight- or nine-year-olds, who can whisper them to their siblings, and maybe this is their perfect introduction to subtitles. As for Iran: The theme of this movie is so universal there is not a child who will not be wide-eyed with interest and suspense.

The film is about a boy who loses his sister's shoes. He takes them to the cobbler for repairs, and on the way home, when he stops to pick up vegetables for his mother, a blind trash-collector accidentally carries them away. Of course the boy, named Ali, is afraid to tell his parents. Of course his sister, named Zahra, wants to know how she is supposed to go to school without shoes. The children feverishly write notes to each other, right under their parents' noses.

The answer is simple: Zahra will wear Ali's sneakers to school every morning, and then run home so that Ali can put them on for his school in the afternoon. But Zahra cannot always run fast enough, and Ali, who is a good student, gets in trouble for being late to class. And there is a heartbreaking scene where Zahra solemnly regards her own precious lost shoes, now on the feet of the ragpicker's daughter.

I submit that this situation is scarier and more absorbing for children than a movie about Godzilla or other manufactured entertainments. When you're a kid, you know you're not likely to be squished by a giant lizard, but losing something that has been entrusted to you? And getting in trouble at school? That's big time.

Majid Majidi's film has a wonderful scene

where Ali and his father bicycle from the almost medieval streets and alleys of the old town to the high-rises and luxury homes where the rich people live. The father hopes for work as a gardener, but he is intimidated by the challenge of speaking into the intercoms on the gates of the wealthy. His son jumps in with offers of pruning, weeding, spraying, and trimming. It is a great triumph.

And then there is a footrace for the poor children of the quarter. The winner gets two weeks in a summer camp and other prizes. Ali doesn't care. He wants to place third, because the prize is a new pair of sneakers, which he can give to his sister. My guess is that the race and its outcome will be as exciting for many kids as anything they've seen at the movies.

Children of Heaven is about a home without unhappiness. About a brother and sister who love one another, instead of fighting. About situations any child can identify with. In this film from Iran, I found a sweetness and innocence that shames the land of Mutant Turtles, Power Rangers, and violent video games. Why do we teach our kids to see through things before they even learn to see them?

Chill Factor ★ ★
R, 105 m., 1999

Cuba Gooding Jr. (Arlo), Skeet Ulrich (Tim Mason), Peter Firth (Captain Andrew Brynner), David Paymer (Dr. Richard Long), Hudson Leick (Vaughn), Daniel Hugh Kelly (Colonel Leo Vitelli), Kevin J. O'Connor (Telstar), Judson Mills (Dennis). Directed by Hugh Johnson and produced by James G. Robinson. Screenplay by Drew Gitlin and Mike Cheda.

In April 1999 at the University of Colorado, wounded by students who jeered at my affectionate review of *Speed 2*, I recklessly announced a contest to make a film named *Speed 3*. Entries couldn't be more than five minutes long and had to be about something that couldn't go slower than fifty miles an hour.

Chill Factor looks exactly like the first entry in my contest, but I have reluctantly had to disqualify it because it exceeds the time limit by 100 minutes, and it's not about speed but temperature. With just a tweak here and there, however, it could qualify as a parody of *Speed*—

one of those *Airplane!*-type spoofs by Zucker-Abrahams-Zucker. Where are the ZAZ boys when we need them?

I promise you the movie is played straight. It is really supposed to be a thriller and we are really supposed to be thrilled. I explain that to prepare the ground for the information that the story involves a chemical weapon that cannot be allowed to grow warmer than fifty degrees, and about two brave citizens who try to keep it away from evil terrorists by keeping it in the back of a speeding ice-cream truck. Yes. There is also a sequence where they use an aluminum rowboat as a toboggan, sliding down a steep hill into a river, where the dangerous substance can be dragged behind the boat because the stream is "fed by glaciers."

The heroes are played by Skeet Ulrich, who thinks he is in a Jerry Bruckheimer production, and Cuba Gooding Jr., who has been in *Jerry Maguire* for the last four years, including Oscar appearances. The biological weapon has been developed by Dr. Richard Long (David Paymer), whose dialogue seems to have been phoned in by the team of Carl Sagan and Mephistopheles. Early on he announces an "epiphany" about a "new molecular configuration," in which, as I murkily recall, he plans to remove atoms from one side of his molecules and stick them on the other side instead. He discovers that his plan is flawed when a test goes wrong, defoliating not 200 yards of a remote island, but five miles. Eighteen soldiers die, their flesh erupting like cheese on a burnt pizza. "Oh, my God!" he cries. "I am become Death—the destroyer of worlds."

Usually a line like that sets up a mournful aria, but in *Chill Factor* it simply results in a ten-year prison sentence for Brynner (Peter Firth), the U.S. military man in charge of the operation. Embittered, and who wouldn't be, he gets out of prison and comes looking for Dr. Long and his magic formula. Follow this closely: Because Brynner believes the United States does things it condemns other nations for doing, he therefore plans to sell the deadly poison to the terrorists with the most money.

Nobody questions this logic, but then there are a lot of logical gaps in this movie. How, for example, does a short-order clerk on the run in a stolen ice-cream truck find a hardware store with the precise materials necessary to contrive a fake version of the poison vials in the refrigerated cannister? How can you blow up both ends of a tunnel and not cut off the electricity inside? How can you be shot in the leg with a high-powered rifle and then run with only sort of a limp?

The movie is abundantly stocked with items borrowed from *Ebert's Bigger Little Movie Glossary*. The red digital readout is handy, of course, distracting from the question of what kind of chemical compound explodes at fifty degrees. The Talking Killer Syndrome sinks two scenes. So eager is *Chill Factor* to include every possible cliché, indeed, that it even keeps one as a spare: An amusement park turns up complete with Ferris wheel and merry-go-round, and then is completely forgotten, leaving us longing for the missing scenes of screaming children tumbling off their wooden horses and running through the funhouse.

Chocolat ★ ★ ★
PG-13, 121 m., 2000

Juliette Binoche (Vianne Rocher), Victoire Thivisol (Anouk Rocher), Johnny Depp (Roux), Alfred Molina (Comte de Reynaud), Hugh O'Conor (Pere Henri), Lena Olin (Josephine Muscat), Peter Stormare (Serge Muscat), Judi Dench (Amande Voizin), John Wood (Guillaume Blerot), Leslie Caron (Madame Audel), Carrie-Anne Moss (Caroline Claimont). Directed by Lasse Hallstrom and produced by David Brown, Kit Golden, and Leslie Holleran. Screenplay by Robert Nelson Jacobs, based on the novel by Joanne Harris.

Chocolat is about a war between the forces of paganism and Christianity, and because the pagan heroine has chocolate on her side, she wins. Her victory is delayed only because, during Lent, a lot of the locals aren't eating chocolate. The movie takes place "once upon a time" in a small French village where utter tranquillity, by which is meant stagnancy, has reigned since time immemorial, until "a sly wind blew in from the north," bringing with it Vianne (Juliette Binoche), who opens the chocolate shop, after which nothing is ever again the same.

The movie is charming and whimsical, and

Binoche reigns as a serene and wise goddess. Like Catherine Deneuve's, her beauty is not only that of youth but will carry her through life, and here she looks so ripe and wholesome that her very presence is an argument against the local prudes. Whether her character has deeper agendas, whether she is indeed a witch, as some believe, or a pagan priestess as she seems to hint, is left unresolved by the movie—but anyone who schedules a Fertility Celebration up against Easter Sunday is clearly picking a fight.

The town is ruled by Count de Reynaud (Alfred Molina), whose wealth and books do not console him for the absence of his countess, who is allegedly visiting Venice but may just have packed up and moved out. The count styles himself as the local arbiter of morals, even writing the sermons that Father Henri (Hugh O'Conor) delivers from the pulpit while the complacent aristocrat's lips move contentedly in unison.

There are troubles in the town, quickly confided to Vianne, who consoles Josephine (Lena Olin) after she is beaten by her husband, Serge (Peter Stormare). It is a convention in such stories that husbands tend toward wifebeating, and a quiet argument is made for the superior state of Vianne, who is the unmarried mother of Anouk (Victoire Thivisol) and thus harbors no potential brute beneath her roof. She does, however, have an interest in the opposite sex, represented by Roux (Johnny Depp), who anchors his houseboat in the nearby river and shocks the bourgeoisie with its communal lifestyle.

Vianne's chocolates contain magic ingredients, like the foods in *Like Water for Chocolate*, and soon her shop is a local healing center. One confection seems to work like Viagra, while others inspire love, not lust, and inspire an old man (John Wood) to screw up his courage and confess to a local widow (Leslie Caron) that he has adored her forever. Even Amande (Judi Dench), Vianne's opinionated old landlady, melts under the influence and ends her long hostility to her daughter (Carrie-Anne Moss).

Chocolat was directed by Lasse Hallstrom (*Cider House Rules, My Life as a Dog, What's Eating Gilbert Grape*). It's the sort of movie you can enjoy as a superior fable, in which the values come from children's fairy tales but adult themes have been introduced. It goes without saying in such stories that organized religion is the province of prudes and hypocrites, but actually *Chocolat* is fairly easy on the local establishment—they're not evil people, although they resent outsiders like the Depp character; they're more like tranquil sleepwalkers who wake up and smell the coffee, or in this case the chocolate. Even the count is converted, and is shocked when he finds that his reckless language has inspired a local dimwit to set a dangerous fire.

I enjoyed the movie on its own sweet level, while musing idly on the box-office prospects of a film in which the glowing, life-affirming local Christians would prevail over glowering, prejudiced, puritan, and bitter druidworshipers. That'll be, as John Wayne once said, the day. ☞

Chopper ★ ★ ★
NO MPAA RATING, 90 m., 2001

Eric Bana (Chopper), Simon Lyndon (Jimmy Loughnan), Kenny Graham (Keith Read), Dan Wyllie (Bluey), David Field (Keithy George), Vince Colosimo (Neville Bartos), Kate Beahan (Tanya). Directed by Andrew Dominik and produced by Michele Bennett. Screenplay by Dominik, based on books by Mark Brandon Read.

It is not agreed how "Chopper" Read got his nickname. Some say it was because he chopped off the toes of his enemies. Others believe it was because he had his own ears chopped off, or because he had his teeth capped in metal. He is Australia's most infamous prisoner, a best-selling author, a vicious killer, a seething mass of contradictions. *Chopper* tells his story with a kind of fascinated horror.

Is everyone in Australia a few degrees off from true north? You can search in vain through the national cinema for characters who are ordinary or even boring; everyone is more colorful than life. If England is a nation of eccentrics, Australia leaves it at the starting line. Chopper Read is the latest in a distinguished line that includes Ned Kelly, Mad Max, and Russell Crowe's Hando in *Romper Stomper*. The fact that Chopper is real only underlines the point.

Since the real Chopper is again behind bars, the film depends entirely on its casting, and in a comedian named Eric Bana the filmmakers have found, I think, a future star. He creates a character so fearsome and yet so clueless and wounded that we can't tell if the movie comes to praise or bury him. There is a scene in the movie where Chopper is stabbed by his best friend, and keeps right on talking as if nothing has happened; his nonchalance is terrifying. And another where he shoots a drug dealer and then thoughtfully drives him to the emergency room. Bana's performance makes the character believable—in fact, unforgettable. We feel we're looking at a hard man, not at an actor playing one.

As the film opens, Chopper is in prison watching himself on television. He seems curiously conflicted about what he sees—as if the Chopper on TV has been somehow constructed by others and then installed inside his skin. The writer-director Andrew Dominik and producer Michele Bennett, who met Chopper Read while preparing the film, sensed the same thing. "After we'd passed some time with him," says Bennett, "we could see that he was waiting to gauge our reaction before he proceeded. We did offer to show him the script, but he declined, remarking, 'Anything I say would be fiddling. I want to know what you think of me,' so we didn't pursue it. He pretends that he doesn't care how he's perceived by others, but I suspect he really does."

That's how he comes across as a film—as a man who seems to stand outside himself and watch what Chopper does. He's as fascinated by himself as we are, and isolated from his actions. Even pain doesn't seem to penetrate. He looks down at blood pouring from his body as if someone else has been wounded, and then up at his attacker as if expressing regret that it should have come to this.

The movie wisely declines to offer a psychological explanation for Chopper's violent amorality. But it provides a clue in the way he stands outside criminal gangs and has no associates; he is not a "criminal," if that word implies a profession, but a violent psychopath who is seized by sudden rages. There is a startling

117

moment in the film, during a brief stretch on the streets between prison sentences, when he revisits old haunts and old friends and seems genial and conciliatory—until his mad-dog side leaps out in uncontrolled fury. The earlier niceness was not an act to throw people off their guard, we sense; he really was feeling friendly, and did not necessarily anticipate the sudden rush of rage.

Eric Bana's performance suggests he will soon be leaving the comedy clubs of Australia and turning up as a Bond villain or a madman in a special-effects picture. He has a quality no acting school can teach and few actors can match: You cannot look away from him. The performance is so . . . strange. The parts you remember best are the times when he seems disappointed in others, or in himself, as if filled with sadness that the world must contain so much pain caused to or by him. Of course in creating this Chopper, he may simply be going along with the original Chopper's act, and the real Chopper Read with his TV interviews and best-sellers may be a performance too. Whatever the reality, Chopper is a real piece of work, and so is Bana.

Note: Chopper Read speaks in an unalloyed Australian accent that may be difficult for some North American audiences; he's no toned-down mid-Pacific Crocodile Dundee. I understood most of what he was saying. And when you don't catch the words, you get the drift.

Chuck & Buck ★ ★ ★
R, 95 m., 2000

Mike White (Buck), Chris Weitz (Chuck), Lupe Ontiveros (Beverly), Beth Colt (Carlyn), Paul Weitz (Sam), Maya Rudolph (Jamila), Mary Wigmore (Diane), Paul Sand (Barry), Gino Buccola (Tommy), Directed by Miguel Arteta and produced by Matthew Greenfield. Screenplay by Mike White.

Buck's mother coughs, and dies. That releases him from his childhood, which has lasted well into his twenties. He invites his boyhood friend Chuck to come to the funeral. Chuck, a music executive from L.A., arrives with his fiancée, Carlyn. Buck grins at Chuck confidingly. "You . . . wanna go see my room?" he asks. This line, early in *Chuck & Buck,* sets up the tone of

the movie. Buck is stuck at the age of twelve or thirteen; Chuck has grown up, and now finds himself stalked by a weirdo who still wants to be his junior high school buddy.

This surface story would be enough for most movies, but *Chuck & Buck* has subterranean depths, and is a study in how we handle embarrassing situations—or don't handle them. Buck (Mike White, the film's author) is a gawky case of arrested development, who stands too close and doesn't know when to stop talking and never realizes when he's not welcome. He's had only one valued relationship in his life, with Chuck (Chris Weitz), and assumes it has been the same with Chuck. "I noticed there aren't any pictures of me around," he says on his first visit to Chuck's house.

How did he get invited to visit Chuck and Carlyn (Beth Colt)? At his mother's funeral, she unwisely asked him to visit them if he was ever in L.A., and a few days later, he was in L.A. Buck visits Chuck at his office, tails him to lunch, turns up everywhere, sucking on his little Tootsie Pops down to the fudge surprise. Chuck tells him bluntly to get lost. But it's not that simple. Chuck bears some of the responsibility for Buck's feelings, and he knows it.

Freed of his long captivity in his mother's house, Buck finds more than Chuck to interest him in Los Angeles. He discovers a little fringe theater, writes an autobiographical play named *Frank & Hank,* and convinces Beverly, the stage manager (Lupe Ontiveros), to direct it. In the theater scenes, White and his director, Miguel Arteta, avoid obvious traps and take the movie to another level. It would be easy to turn Buck into a comic figure and surround him with caricatures, but the movie allows all of the people at the theater to be as real as they might actually be, and to deal with Buck as the case study he so manifestly is.

Ontiveros, as Beverly, takes one look at Buck and clocks him as one of the countless odd jobs who circle show business like flies. She agrees to direct his play for $25 an hour, firm, cash, and guarantees it one performance. One of the actresses finishes a rehearsal and flatly declares, "I'm not inviting my agent." An actor named Sam (Paul Weitz, Chris's brother), clueless and not very swift, takes his role with utter seriousness. He asks Buck up to his apartment, complains about a neighbor "who won't let me hold parties in the hall," smoothly rebuffs Buck's advance without batting an eye, and thinks Buck would make a great neighbor since he wouldn't object to the parties.

All of these supporting characters give *Chuck & Buck* the texture that makes it more than just a psychological stalker movie. By treating Buck as real people might plausibly treat him, they prevent us from seeing him as a comic figure. He really is this sad, strange person, and that realization sets up the final events in the movie, which wouldn't work otherwise.

What is the movie about? It seems to be about buried sexuality or arrested development, but it's also a fascinating study of behavior that violates the rules. Most of us operate within a set of conventions and instincts that lead us through conversations and relationships. We know precisely how close we are to one another, and our behavior reflects that. Some people, through ignorance or hostility, don't observe the rules. How should we handle them? Chuck may have grown up normally while Buck got stuck behind, but in their own personal war, Buck has all the best moves.

The Cider House Rules ★ ★
PG-13, 129 m., 1999

Tobey Maguire (Homer Wells), Charlize Theron (Candy Kendall), Delroy Lindo (Mr. Rose), Erykah Badu (Rose Rose), Paul Rudd (Wally Worthington), Michael Caine (Dr. Wilbur Larch), Jane Alexander (Nurse Edna), Kathy Baker (Nurse Angela). Directed by Lasse Hallstrom and produced by Richard N. Gladstein. Screenplay by John Irving, based on his novel.

The Cider House Rules tells the story of an orphan who is adopted by his own orphanage and raised by the doctor in charge—who sees him as a successor. At one point he runs away to pick apples and fall in love, but his fate awaits him and has been sealed at his birth.

At least, I think that's what the story is about. Other critics have zeroed in on the movie's treatment of abortion. Dr. Larch (Michael Caine), in charge of the orphanage, will provide abortions without question because, in the 1930s and 1940s, he wants to save young

women from the coat hook artists of the back alleys. He has taught Homer (Tobey Maguire), his protégé, everything he knows about medicine, but Homer is opposed to abortion.

This results in a "controversial pro-choice stance on abortion" (David Rooney, *Variety*), or "it makes men the arbiters of what happens to a woman's body" (Amy Taubin, *Village Voice*). James Berardinelli, a leading Web critic, thinks it provides a "reasonably balanced perspective" on the debate, but Peter Brunette, another leading Web critic, doesn't even mention Homer's doubts. Nor does the *New York Times*.

If I had to choose, I'd vote with Taubin, who notes that Dr. Larch will perform an abortion on request, but Homer believes it is justified only in cases of rape or incest (not unknown in this movie). A larger question remains: Why is there such a muddle about the movie's subject? I left the theater wondering what the movie thought it was about, and was unable to say. It's almost deliberately unfocused; it shows us many events without guiding them to add up to anything definite.

The story begins at an orphanage in St. Cloud's, Maine, where you go to "add a child to your life, or leave one behind." Dr. Larch, who rules benevolently, is beloved by his staff and orphans. At lights-out he salutes them: "Good night, you princes of Maine—you kings of New England!" Larch is an old-fashioned progressive who would be a secular saint were it not for a few flaws, such as snuggling with his nurses and addicting himself to ether.

He names the baby Homer Wells, and essentially adopts the kid himself, teaching him everything he knows about medicine and grooming him to take over the institution. (If forged papers are necessary, no problem.) Homer, meanwhile, wonders if he might not be allowed to choose his own path in life.

Candy (Charlize Theron) and her boyfriend Wally (Paul Rudd) arrive at the orphanage for an abortion. Homer becomes their friend and follows them to Wally's family farm, where he joins an apple-picking crew headed by Mr. Rose (Delroy Lindo) and including his daughter, Rose Rose (Erykah Badu). Manual labor clears Homer's head and fresh air delights him; he embraces this world, and after Wally goes off to fight in World War II, Homer and Candy fall in love. Eventually it becomes clear that

Rose is an incest victim, and Homer must decide whether to offer her an abortion.

All of this somehow sounds more dramatic than it plays. The *Cider House Rules* has been adapted by John Irving from his own novel, and we learn from his book *My Movie Business: A Memoir,* that he wrote the first draft thirteen years ago, and has seen the project through four directors, finally settling on Lasse Hallstrom *(My Life as a Dog, What's Eating Gilbert Grape).* An author, of course, treasures all the episodes in his stories, and perhaps there was a tendency to keep in as much as possible without marshaling it toward a payoff. The result is a film that plays like a Victorian serial—*David Copperfield,* for example, which is read to the orphans—in which the ending must not come before the contracted number of installments have been delivered.

The Cider House Rules is often absorbing or enchanting in its parts. Michael Caine's performance is one of his best, and Charlize Theron is sweet and direct as the girl. But Tobey Maguire is almost maddeningly monotone as Homer (is his performance inspired by Benjamin in *The Graduate*?) and the movie never does resolve its ambiguity toward Mr. Rose, who is guilty of incest and yet—somehow, murkily—not entirely a monster. The story touches many themes, lingers with some of them, moves on, and arrives at nowhere in particular. It's not a story so much as a reverie about possible stories.

The Circle ★ ★ ★ ½
NO MPAA RATING, 91 m., 2001

Mariam Palvin Almani (Arezou), Nargess Mamizadeh (Nargess), Fereshteh Sadr Orfani (Pari), Monir Arab (Ticket Seller), Elham Saboktakin (Nurse), Fatemeh Naghavi (Mother), Mojhan Faramarzi (Prostitute). Directed and produced by Jafar Panahi. Screenplay by Kambozia Partovi.

Few things reveal a nation better than what it censors. In America, the MPAA has essentially eliminated adult sexuality from our movies, but smiles on violence and films tailored for the teenage toilet-humor market. Now consider *The Circle,* a film banned in Iran. There is not a single shot here that would seem of-

fensive to a mainstream American audience— not even to the smut-hunting preacher Donald Wildmon. Why is it considered dangerous in Iran? Because it argues that under current Iranian law, unattached women are made to feel like hunted animals.

There is no nudity here. No violence. No drugs or alcohol, for sure. No profanity. There is a running joke that the heroines can't even have a cigarette (women cannot smoke in public). Yet the film is profoundly dangerous to the status quo in Iran because it asks us to identify with the plight of women who have done nothing wrong except to be female. *The Circle* is all the more depressing when we consider that Iran is relatively liberal compared to, say, Afghanistan under the Taliban.

Jafar Panahi's film begins and ends with the same image, of a woman talking to someone in authority through a sliding panel in a closed door. In the opening shot, a woman learns that her daughter has given birth to a girl when the ultrasound promised a boy; she fears angry reprisals from the in-laws. In the closing shot, a woman is in prison, talking to a guard. In closing the circle, the second shot suggests that women in strict Muslim societies are always in prison in one way or another.

The film follows a series of women through the streets of a city. We follow first one and then another. We begin with two who have just been released from prison—for what crime, we are not told. They want to take a bus to a city where one of them hopes to find a safe harbor. But they have no money and lack the correct identification. They run through the streets and down back alleys at the sight of policemen, they crouch behind parked cars, they ask a ticket-seller to give them a break and sell them a ticket though they have no ID. At one point it's fairly clear that one of the women prostitutes herself (offscreen) to raise money to help the other. Men all over the world are open-minded about exempting themselves from the laws prohibiting other men from frequenting prostitutes.

If you have no ID, you cannot leave town. If you have no ID, you cannot live in a town. Your crime, obviously, is to be a woman living outside the system of male control of women; with a husband or a brother to vouch for you, you can go anywhere, sort of like baggage. The argument is that this system shows respect for women, just as Bantustans in South Africa gave Africans their own land, and American blacks in Jim Crow days did not have to stand in line to use white rest rooms. There is a universal double-speak in which subjugation is described as freedom.

We meet another woman, who has left her little daughter to be found by strangers. She hides behind a car, her eyes filled with tears; as a single mother she cannot care for the girl, and so dresses her up to look nice, and abandons her. We meet another woman, a prostitute, who is found in the car of a man and cannot prove she is related to him. She is arrested; the man seems to go free. Has there ever been a society where the man in this situation is arrested and the woman goes free? The prostitute at least gets to smoke on the prison bus (not when she wants to, but after the men light up, so the smoke will not be noticed).

The movie is not structured tautly like an American street thriller. There are handheld shots that meander for a minute or two, just following women as they walk here or there. The women seem aimless. They are. In this society, under their circumstances, there is nowhere they can go and nothing they can do, and almost all of the time they have to stay out of doors. They track down rumors: A news vendor, for example, is said to be "friendly" and might help them. From time to time, a passing man will say something oblique, like "Can I help you?" but that is either casual harassment or a test of availability.

The Iranian censors may ban films like *The Circle,* but it got made, and so did the recent *The Day I Became a Woman,* about the three ages of women in such a society. One suspects that videotapes give these films wide private circulation; one even suspects the censors know that. I know a director from a communist country where the censor had been his film school classmate. He submitted a script. The censor read it and told his old friend, "You know what you're really saying, and I know what you're really saying. Now rewrite it so only the audience knows what you're really saying."

A Civil Action ★ ★ ★ ½
PG-13, 118 m., 1999

John Travolta (Jan Schlichtmann), Robert Duvall (Jerome Facher), Tony Shalhoub (Kevin Conway), William H. Macy (James Gordon), Zeljko Ivanek (Bill Crowley), Bruce Norris (William Cheeseman), John Lithgow (Judge Skinner), Kathleen Quinlan (Anne Anderson), David Thornton (Richard Aufiero). Directed by Steven Zaillian and produced by Scott Rudin, Robert Redford, and Rachel Pfeffer. Screenplay by Zaillian based on the book by Jonathan Harr.

A Civil Action is like John Grisham for grown-ups. Watching it, we realize that Grisham's lawyers are romanticized hotshots living in a cowboy universe with John Wayne values. The real world of the law, this movie argues, has less to do with justice than with strategy, and doesn't necessarily arrive at truth. The law is about who wins, not about who should win.

The movie costars John Travolta and Robert Duvall as the leaders of two opposing legal teams. At issue are the deaths by leukemia of twelve children. Travolta's argument is that the deaths were the result of pollution by two large corporations, W. R. Grace and Beatrice. Duvall, working for Beatrice, argues that neither the pollution nor its results can be proven. He also angles to separate Beatrice from its bedmate, Grace, correctly perceiving that the Grace legal strategy is unpromising.

Beatrice and Grace are real companies, and *A Civil Action* is based on a nonfiction best-seller by Jonathan Harr, which won the National Book Award. But the movie takes fictional liberties, which have been much discussed in the financial press. In particular, the Grace lawyer, William Cheeseman (Bruce Norris), is said not to be a doofus in real life. For the facts, read the book or study the case; the movie is more concerned with how the law works, and how perhaps the last thing you want is a lawyer who is committed heart and soul to your cause. What you want is a superb technician.

Duvall plays Jerome Facher, brilliant and experienced, who hides his knowledge behind a facade of eccentricity. He knows more or less what is going to happen at every stage of the case. He reads the facts, the witnesses, the court, and his opposition. There is a moment at which he offers the plaintiffs a $20 million settlement, and an argument can be made, I think, that in the deepest recesses of his mind he knows it will not be necessary. He makes the offer in the same spirit that Vegas blackjack tables offer "insurance"—he thinks he'll win, but is guarding the downside. His style is indirection; his carefully nurtured idiosyncrasies conceal his hand.

Travolta plays Jan Schlichtmann, the head of a small firm of personal injury attorneys who take on cases they believe they can win. Often their clients are too poor to pay legal fees, but Schlichtmann's firm eats the legal costs itself, hoping for a rich slice of an eventual settlement. Essentially, he's gambling with the firm's money every time he accepts a case. That's why he turns down the delegation of parents who tell about the deaths of their children: He doesn't see enough money in it to justify the risk. (The movie has a hard-boiled discussion of how much various victims are "worth." A white male professional struck down in his prime gives the biggest payoff; a dead child is worth the least of all.)

From the point of view of his financial well-being, Schlichtmann makes two mistakes. First, he decides the parents have a moral case. Second, he begins to care too much about justice for them and loses his strategic bearings. (Of course, all follows from his discovery that the polluters, whom he thought were small, shabby local firms, are actually owned by rich corporations.)

The movie, written and directed by Steven Zaillian, doesn't simplify the issues and make Schlichtmann into a romantic hero. He's more the kind of guy you refer to affectionately as "that poor sap." We hear what he hears: the emotion in the voice of one of the mothers (Kathleen Quinlan) who asks him to take the case because "all we want is somebody to apologize to us." And the heartrending story of how one of the boys died, told by his father (David Thornton) in details so sad that Schlichtmann is very deeply moved—which is, perhaps, not the best thing for his clients.

Zaillian is clear about his movie's approach. This is not a film in which a hero attorney beats up the bad guys in a climactic court-

room scene. The movie doesn't even end with its courtroom scene, but has a wry aftermath. No major characters are painted in black-and-white terms, least of all Duvall's; he is not a man without emotions and sympathies, we sense, but simply a man whose long and wise experience of the law has positioned him above the fray. He's fascinated by the law, by its opportunities and maneuverings, by its realities. Like a chess player, he knows that to win a tournament it is sometimes wise to offer a draw even when you think you can win it.

Some of the film's tension comes not from the battle between good and evil, but from the struggle between Schlichtmann's firm and its creditors. The small firm eventually sinks $1.4 million into the case, the homes of all the partners are mortgaged, and in the background during some scenes their furniture is being removed. William H. Macy plays their accountant, whose function is to announce steady progress toward professional and personal bankruptcy.

This is Zaillian's second film. His first was *Searching for Bobby Fischer* (1993), one of the most absorbing films of recent years, about a child chess prodigy whose great gift might take him to the top of the game—but at what personal price? *A Civil Action* is also about the gulf between skill and justice. In the law as in chess, the better player usually wins. It has nothing to do with which is the better person. The theme of Zaillian's first film, I wrote, was: "What makes us men is that we can think logically. What makes us human is that we sometimes choose not to." That's the message this time too. There's a subtext: When hiring an attorney, go for the logician.

The Claim ★ ★ ★ ½
R, 120 m., 2001

Peter Mullan (Daniel Dillon), Sarah Polley (Hope Dillon), Wes Bentley (Donald Dalglish), Milla Jovovich (Lucia), Nastassja Kinski (Elena Dillon), Julian Richings (Bellanger), David Lereaney (Saloon Actor), Sean McGinley (Sweetley). Directed by Michael Winterbottom and produced by Andrew Eaton. Screenplay by Frank Cottrell Boyce, based on the novel *The Mayor of Casterbridge* by Thomas Hardy.

In the town of Kingdom Come, winter is more of a punishment than a season. High in a pass of the Sierra Nevada, its buildings of raw lumber stand like scars on the snow. The promise of gold has drawn men here, but in the winter there is little to do but wait, drink, and visit the brothel. The town is owned and run by Mr. Dillon, a trim Scotsman in his forties who is judge, jury, and (if necessary) executioner.

I dwell on the town because the physical setting of Michael Winterbottom's *The Claim* is central to its effect. Summer is a season for work, but winter is a time for memory and regret. Mr. Dillon (Peter Mullan) did something years ago that was wrong in a way a man cannot forgive himself for. He lives in an ornate Victorian house, submits to the caresses of his mistress, settles the affairs of his subjects, and is haunted by his memories.

Two women arrive in Kingdom Come. One is a fading beauty named Elena (Nastassja Kinski), dying of tuberculosis. The other is her daughter, about twenty, named Hope (Sarah Polley). They have not journeyed to Kingdom Come to forgive Mr. Dillon his trespasses. It becomes clear who they are, but the movie is not about that secret. It is about what happened twenty years ago, and what, as a result, will happen now.

To the town that winter also comes Donald Dalglish (Wes Bentley), a surveyor for the railroad. Where the tracks run, wealth follows. What they bypass will die. Dalglish is young, ambitious, and good at business. He attracts the attention of Lucia (Milla Jovovich), who is not only Mr. Dillon's comfort but the owner of the brothel. She kisses him boldly on the lips in full view of a saloon-full of witnesses, sending a message to Mr. Dillon: If he doesn't want to keep her, others will. Dalglish is not indifferent, but he is more intrigued by the strange young blonde woman, Hope, who stands out in this grimness like the first bud of spring.

The past comes crashing down around them all—and then the future arrives to finish them off. Mr. Dillon's fate, which he fashions for himself, is all the more complex because he has done great evil but is in some ways a good man. Nor is Dalglish morally uncomplicated. In the hard world they inhabit, no one can afford to act only on a theoretical basis.

The Claim is parsimonious with its plot, which is revealed on a need-to-know basis. At first, we're not even sure who is who; dialogue is half-heard, references are unclear, the townspeople know things we discover only gradually. The method is like Robert Altman's in *McCabe and Mrs. Miller,* and Antonia Bird's in the underrated 1999 Western *Ravenous* (a movie that takes place in about the same place and time as this one). Like strangers in town, we put the pieces together for ourselves.

The movie is so rooted in the mountains of the American West that it's a little startling to learn *The Claim* is based on Thomas Hardy's 1886 British novel *The Mayor of Casterbridge.* Winterbottom filmed *Jude,* a version of Hardy's *Jude the Obscure,* in 1996. By transmuting Hardy into a Western here, he has not made a commercial decision (Westerns are not as successful these days as British period pictures), but an artistic one, perhaps involving his vision of Kingdom Come, a town which is like a stage waiting for this play.

Winterbottom is a director of great gifts and glooms. His *Butterfly Kiss* (also 1996) starred Amanda Plummer in a great performance as a kind of homeless flagellant saint. Here he tells the story of another kind of self-punishing character, and Peter Mullan's performance is private and painful, as a man whose first mistake is to give away all he has, and whose second mistake is to try to redeem himself by giving it all away again. Mullan (*My Name Is Joe*) is like a harder, leaner, younger (but not young) Paul Newman, coiled up inside, handsome but not depending on it, willing to go to any lengths to do what he must. Intriguing, how he makes a villain sympathetic, in a movie where the relatively blameless Dalglish seems corrupt.

A movie like this rides on its cinematography, and Alwin H. Kuchler evokes the cold darkness so convincingly that Kingdom Come seems built on an abyss. Like the town of Presbyterian Church in *McCabe and Mrs. Miller,* it is a folly built by greed where common sense would have steered clear. There are two great visual scenes, the arrival of the railroad and the moving of a house, one exercising public will, the other private will. And an ending uncannily like *McCabe and Mrs. Miller*'s, although for an entirely different reason.

Winterbottom is a director comfortable with ambiguity. In movies like *Wonderland* (1999), *Welcome to Saravejo* (1997), and others, he's reluctant to corner his characters into heroism or villainy. In the original Hardy novel, the Dillon character, named Henchard, is a drunk who pays so well for his sins that he seems more like Job than a sinner being punished. Dillon, who was also a drunk, tells the woman he has wronged, "I don't drink anymore. I want you to know that." For his time and place, he has grown into a hard but not bad man, and when he has a citizen horsewhipped, the man explains that the town would have lynched him—the whipping saved his life. The strength of *The Claim* is that Dillon and Dalglish are on intersecting paths; Dillon is getting better, while Dalglish started out good and is headed down.

Claire Dolan ★ ★ ★ ½
NO MPAA RATING, 95 m., 2000

Katrin Cartlidge (Claire), Colm Meaney (Roland), Vincent D'Onofrio (Elton). Directed by Lodge Kerrigan and produced by Ann Ruark. Screenplay by Kerrigan.

"I'm here for you," Claire Dolan tells one of her clients. "I can't get you out of my head," she whispers to another over the telephone. "You're not like other men," she tells a third. He is exactly like other men. All men are like other men when they visit a prostitute. "What do you want?" she says. "You can tell me."

Lodge Kerrigan's *Claire Dolan* is a film about a woman whose knowledge about men encompasses everything except how to trust them and find happiness with them. She is a Manhattan prostitute, mid-priced, who presents herself as a quiet, almost shy woman dressed in understated good taste. She has none of the flamboyance of the typical movie hooker, is not voluptuous, looks her clients straight in the eye while lying to them about how much she's missed them. Some guys like that. Makes them think they're doing the poor deprived girl a favor.

Claire is played by Katrin Cartlidge (the sister-in-law in *Breaking the Waves*) as a woman whose profession has given her an instinctive knowledge about how to deal with some men.

There is a scene in the movie where she is seated in a bar, bothering no one, not looking for attention. Two men walk up. "I'm not looking for company," she says. "That's not your decision," says the first man, who is aggressive and menacing. She seems in danger. She looks up at the man who is looming over her, his aggression pulsing in his face. Then she looks at his sidekick, who hangs back. "I prefer him," she says. "He's better-looking than you. Would you let him go first?"

The scene is no longer than my description of it. It is just about perfect. She has changed the subject. She understands the tension that must exist between two men who have agreed to harass a woman. Beneath their relationship is a fear of women, which links to sexual insecurity; she has castrated the first by preferring the second, and called the bluff of the second by depriving him of his leader. The men are stopped cold, and skulk away.

Much of the movie consists of Claire Dolan's business dealings. Her clients are white-collar guys in offices and hotel rooms. They believe her praise. Maybe it's what they're really paying her for. She isn't very enthusiastic during sex— sometimes she seems repelled or indifferent— but the men don't notice or care. When she doesn't follow the script, though, they have a way of turning vicious.

Her pimp, who has known her since she was a child in Dublin, is Roland (Colm Meaney, his neat little lips swimming in a face so broad he looks like Humpty-Dumpty). He addresses her with formal politeness. We see he is strong and vicious, but with Claire he has an enigmatic relationship based on buried mutual history, which perhaps involves her dying mother, and perhaps involves money he has loaned her for the mother's care (the movie is wisely vague). They work well together, Roland tells a taxi driver who thinks he loves her, because she was born to be a prostitute, likes it, and will always be one.

Whether that statement is true is the movie's central question. The taxi driver is named Elton (Vincent D'Onofrio). They spend some monosyllabic time together, make love successfully and then unsuccessfully, and agree to have a child. "We can make this work," she says. "All right," he says. They cannot make it work, because he cannot understand her profession or her pimp; he shadows her, and even goes to the extreme of hiring a new girl in the pimp's stable in order to vicariously understand how it might be between Claire and a client.

If a movie like this had a neat ending, the ending would be a lie. We do not want answers, but questions and observations. The film is bleak about sex. It avoids the common Hollywood assumption that hookers love sex (many producers apparently believe the same lies Claire tells her clients). It is the second film by writer-director Lodge Kerrigan, whose *Clean, Shaven* was a portrait of a schizophrenic. In both films he accepts the challenge of central characters who do not let us know what they're thinking. We have to look and listen and decide for ourselves. I think Claire Dolan will make a good mother. I think she can make it work. Not with Elton, but by herself, which is the only way she can live and not have to lie.

The Closer You Get ★ ★
PG-13, 92 m., 2000

Niamh Cusack (Kate), Sean McGinley (Ian), Ian Hart (Kieran), Ewan Stewart (Pat), Sean McDonagh (Sean), Cathleen Bradley (Siobhan), Pat Shortt (Ollie), Deborah Barnett (Ella). Directed by Aileen Ritchie and produced by Uberto Pasolini. Screenplay by William Ivory, based on a story by Herbie Wave.

See enough of its movies and a nation's cinema can tell you something about the nation involved. It may be right, it may be wrong, but there it is. I now assume, for example, that everyone in Australia is a little strange, and half of them are bizarre eccentrics. The French, they are worried all the time. Americans live trapped inside the clichés of genre fiction, and so do the Canadians, only they are nicer, unless they are in David Cronenberg films.

And the Irish are sweet, cheerful folk who live in each other's pockets, settle things by communitywide debate, gang up men against women, and visit home briefly between pubs. They are also blessed with great verbal alacrity, and there would be a great many more of them if the women were not so opinionated and the men so baffled by women with opinions.

This picture has nothing to do with the Irish I have met during half a dozen visits to the Emerald Isle, who are likely to be successful professionals benefiting from a booming economy and a standard of living higher than England's. But the Irish have no one but themselves to blame for their screen image, except in the case of *The Closer You Get*, which was produced by an Italian.

Umberto Pasolini earlier made *The Full Monty*, which made millions of dollars with its heartfelt and bawdy comedy about six unemployed Englishmen who became male strippers. Now he has moved to the west of Ireland, to county Donegal, upon whose sainted strands late one night I once kissed a publican's redhaired daughter.

She was, I must admit, a good deal like Siobhan (Cathleen Bradley), the heroine of *The Closer You Get*, who will stand for no nonsense from Kieran (Ian Hart), the local butcher—who is both her employer and her obvious mate, if he were not so daft he doesn't realize it. "Siobhan is a hard case," Kieran laments, by which he means that she is disinclined to conduct both sides of their courtship while he slips out for a few pints with his mates.

This is a town starved for entertainment. The priest livens things up by mounting loudspeakers on the bell tower and playing tapes of the bells from St. Peter's in Rome. (Then he starts a film society and books *The Ten Commandments,* but is sent *10* instead.) The local lads, despairing of the standoffish women in town, chip in to buy an ad in the *Miami Herald* to invite American women to their annual dance. The local women retaliate by inviting a band of alarmingly swarthy and hirsute Spaniards, who make the pale Donegal locals look like they've spent too much time in the cellar counting the root vegetables.

Everyone in *The Closer You Get* is nice, and Ian Hart's butcher is especially likable, with his brown hair dyed platinum in a failed attempt to look hip. But the movie is too thin and low-key to generate much comic energy. Compared to *Waking Ned Devine,* it's dilute and transparent. And I doubt many contemporary Irish young people are this naive and shy. It's a sweet film, mildly pleasant to watch, but it's not worth the trip or even a detour.

The Color of Paradise ★ ★ ★ ½
PG, 90 m., 2000

Mohsen Ramezani (Mohammad), Hossein Mahjub (Hashem), Salime Feizi (Granny). Directed by Majid Majidi and produced by Mehdi Karimi. Screenplay by Majidi.

Words appear on a black screen: "To the glory of God." I was reminded of Catholic grade school, where every page of homework began at the top with our childish handwriting: "JMJ"—for Jesus, Mary, and Joseph. Was I dedicating my arithmetic to heaven, or requesting a miracle?

There is no doubt in the mind of Majid Majidi, the Iranian writer and director of *The Color of Paradise*. His work feels truly intended for God's glory, unlike so much "religious art" that is intended merely to propagandize for one view of God over another. His film looks up, not sideways. In this and his previous film, the luminous Oscar nominee *Children of Heaven*, he provides a quiet rebuke to the materialist consumerism in Western films about children. (Both films have subtitles, but they're not too difficult for any child who can read.)

The Color of Paradise is about a blind boy. Quick and gentle, in love with knowledge, acutely attuned to the world around him, Mohammad loves his lessons at a school for the blind. He is loved at home by his grandmother and his two sisters. But his father, Hashem, does not love him. Hashem is a widower, ambitious to marry into a prosperous family, and he fears the possession of a blind son will devalue him in the marriage market.

As the film opens, the school term is over, and the other boys have been picked up by their parents. Mohammad waits alone outside his school, for a father who does not come. There is a remarkable sequence in which he hears the peep of a chick that has fallen from its nest. The boy finds the chick, gently takes it in his hand, and then climbs a tree, listening for the cries of the lost one's nest-mates. He replaces the bird in its nest. God, who knows when a sparrow falls, has had help this time from a little blind boy.

The father finally arrives, and asks the head-master if Mohammad can stay at the school over the vacation term. The answer is no. Hashem reluctantly brings the boy home with him, where his grandmother and sisters welcome him. Mohammad is under no illusions about his father's love. Local children attend a school. Mohammad has all the same books, in Braille, and begs to be allowed to attend. In class, he knows the answers—but his father forbids him to continue at the school, possibly hoping to keep his existence a secret. Eventually the boy is apprenticed to a blind carpenter, who will teach him how to build cabinets by touch. This might be a good job for some, but not for Mohammad, who is eager to compete in the world of the seeing.

For all of its apparent melodrama, *The Color of Paradise* is not an obvious or manipulative film. It is too deliberately simple. And it is made with delicacy and beauty. The sound track is alive with natural sounds of woodpeckers, songbirds, insects and nature, voices and footfalls. A blind person would get a good idea of the locations and what is happening—as Mohammad does. The performance by young Mohsen Ramezani, as the boy, is without guile; when he cries once in frustration, we do not see acting, but raw grief.

The ending, after a sequence in which the boy is in great danger, will strike some as contrived. Certainly it is not subtle by our cynical Western standards. If Hollywood told this story, the father would have a change of heart. In Iran, heaven intervenes more directly—as if God, having tested Mohammad as much as he dares, has the change of heart Himself.

The Color of Paradise is a family film that shames the facile commercialism of a product like *Pokemon* and its value system based on power and greed. Because they do not condescend to young audiences, Majidi's films, of course, are absorbing for adults as well, and there is a lesson here: Any family film not good enough for grown-ups is certainly not good enough for children.

Company Man ½ ★
PG-13, 81 m., 2001

Douglas McGrath (Allen Quimp), Sigourney Weaver (Daisy Quimp), John Turturro (Crocker

Johnson), Anthony LaPaglia (Fidel Castro), Ryan Phillippe (Rudolph Petrov), Denis Leary (Fry), Woody Allen (Lowther), Alan Cumming (General Batista). Directed by Peter Askin and Douglas McGrath and produced by Guy East, Rick Leed, John Penotti, and James W. Skotchdopole. Screenplay by Askin and McGrath.

Company Man is the kind of movie that seems to be wearing a strained smile, as if it's not sure we're getting the jokes. If it could, it would laugh for us. It's an arch, awkward, ill-timed, forced political comedy set in 1959 and seemingly stranded there.

Astonishing, that a movie could be this bad and star Sigourney Weaver, John Turturro, Anthony LaPaglia, Denis Leary, Woody Allen, Alan Cumming, and Ryan Phillippe. I am reminded of Gene Siskel's classic question, "Is this movie better than a documentary of the same actors having lunch?" In this case, it is not even better than a documentary of the same actors ordering room service while fighting the stomach flu.

In addition to the cast members listed above, the movie stars Douglas McGrath, its author and codirector, who is a low-rent cross between Jack Lemmon and Wally Cox and comes across without any apparent comic effect. He plays Allen Quimp, rhymes with wimp, a grammar teacher from Connecticut whose wife (Weaver) frets that he needs a better job. To get her and his own family off his back, he claims to be a CIA agent, and that leads, through a series of events as improbable as they are uninteresting, to his involvement in the defection of a Russia ballet star (Phillippe) and his assignment to Cuba on the eve of Castro's revolution.

His contact agent there is Fry, played by Denis Leary, who looks appalled at some of the scenes he's in. Example: As Fry denies that a revolutionary fever is sweeping the island, a man with a bottle full of gasoline approaches them and borrows a light from Quimp. Soon after, the man runs past in the opposite direction and they pass (without noticing—ho, ho) a burning auto. And not any burning auto, but an ancient, rusty, abandoned hulk filled with phony gas flames obviously rigged and turned

on for the movie. How does it help the revolution to restage ancient auto fires?

But never mind. Fry introduces Quimp to Lowther (Woody Allen), the CIA's man in charge, who also denies a revolution is under way, while turning aside to light his cigarette from a burning effigy of Batista (ho, ho). The mystery of what Woody Allen is doing in this movie is solved in a two-name search on the Internet Movie Database, which reveals that McGrath cowrote the screenplay for Allen's *Bullets Over Broadway.* Now Allen is returning the favor, I guess.

Well, that was a funny movie, and the same search identifies McGrath as the writer-director of *Emma* (1996), a nice little comedy with Gwyneth Paltrow. So he is obviously not without talent—except in this movie. Maybe the mistake was to star himself. He doesn't have the presence to anchor a comedy; all those jokes about Quimp the nonentity ring true, instead of funny.

As bad movies go, *Company Man* falls less in the category of Affront to the Audience and more in the category of Nonevent. It didn't work me up into a frenzy of dislike, but dialed me down into sullen indifference. It was screened twice for the Chicago press, and I sat through the first thirty minutes of the second screening, thinking to check it against a different crowd. I heard no laughter. Just an occasional cough, or the shuffling of feet, or a yawn, or a sigh, like in a waiting room.

The Contender ★ ★ ★ ★
R, 126 m., 2000

Joan Allen (Laine Hanson), Gary Oldman (Shelly Runyon), Jeff Bridges (President Jackson Evans), Christian Slater (Reginald Webster), Sam Elliott (Kermit Newman), William Petersen (Jack Hathaway), Saul Rubinek (Jerry Toliver), Philip Baker Hall (Oscar Billings), Mike Binder (Lewis Hollis). Directed by Rod Lurie and produced by Marc Frydman, Douglas Urbanski, Willi Baer, and James Spies. Screenplay by Lurie.

The Contender, a thriller about the first woman nominated to be vice president, hinges on a question from her past: Did she more or less willingly participate in group sex while she was in college? "That's Hanson getting gang-banged," an investigator says, smacking his lips over an old photo from a sorority party. If it really is, she's going to have trouble getting congressional confirmation.

The movie is frankly partisan. Its sentiments are liberal and Democratic, its villains conservative and Republican. When I asked its star, Jeff Bridges, if the plot was a veiled reference to Monicagate, he smiled. "Veiled?" he said. "I don't think it's so veiled." The difference between Senator Laine Hanson (Joan Allen) and President Bill Clinton is that when zealots start sniffing her laundry, she simply refuses to answer their questions. "It's none of your business," she tells GOP Representative Shelly Runyon (Gary Oldman), whose inquiring mind wants to know.

As the movie opens, an incumbent vice president has died in office. It is universally assumed that a man will be named to replace him, and a leading candidate is Senator Jack Hathaway (William Petersen), who has recently made headlines as a hero. While he was on a fishing trip, a car plunged off a bridge near his boat and he dove into icy waters in an unsuccessful attempt to save the woman trapped inside. It is an adventure like this, not a lifetime of service, that the image-mongers like, but the senator's misfortune is that his rescue attempt failed. "A girl died and you let it happen," he's told sorrowfully by presidential advisers, and President Jackson Evans (Jeff Bridges) consoles him cryptically: "You're the future of the Democratic Party, and you always will be."

The president wants to make history by appointing a woman, and Senator Hanson looks like the best choice. She is happily married, has a young child, and when we first see her is having robust sex (on a desktop) with her husband. Runyon, the Oldman character, doubts any woman should be trusted with the nuclear trigger: What if she has her period or something? He is delighted with evidence she may have been the life of the party on campus.

The movie's story of confirmation hearings, backstage politics, and rival investigations unfolds as a political thriller based on suspense and issues. Senator Hanson flatly refuses to answer any questions about her sexual past, and for a time it looks as if the president may have to dump her as a nominee. Is she really taking an ethical stand, or covering up something? There is a remarkable scene between Hanson and Runyon, who have lunch together in a private club, the Republican shoveling down his meal and talking with his mouth full as if he would like to chew on her too.

The movie was written and directed by Rod Lurie, a former Los Angeles film critic who is the son of the political cartoonist Ranan Lurie. He grew up with politics discussed at every meal, he says; his first movie, *Deterrence,* starred Kevin Pollack as a president faced with a nuclear crisis. I liked the way that film dealt with issues and ideas, but *The Contender* is a leap forward, more assured, more exciting, more biting.

Most American movies pretend there are no parties; even in political movies, characters rarely reveal their affiliations. *The Contender* does take sides, most obviously in the character of the GOP congressman Runyon, who is played by Oldman as an unprincipled power broker with an unwholesome curiosity about other people's sex lives. Whether you are in sympathy with the movie may depend on which you found more disturbing: the questions of the Starr commission or Clinton's attempts to avoid answering them. Full disclosure: I could imagine myself reacting as Clinton did, but to ask Starr's questions would have filled me with self-disgust.

Joan Allen is at the center of the movie, in one of the strongest performances of the year. Some actresses would have played the role as too sensual, others as too cold; she is able to suggest a woman with a healthy physical life who nevertheless has ethical standards that will not bend. She would rather lose the vice presidency than satisfy Runyon's smutty curiosity, and through her the movie argues that we have gone too far in our curiosity about private behavior.

Jeff Bridges plays the president as a man who got elected by seeming a great deal more affable and down-home than he really is. He's forever ordering food and pressing it upon his guests, in gestures that are not so much hospitality as decoys. His top aides, played by Sam Elliott and Saul Rubinek, have a terse shorthand that shows they understand the folksy act but aren't deceived by it. And Christian Slater has a slippery role as a freshman Democratic congressman who is prepared to barter his vote for a seat on Runyon's committee.

And what about Runyon, in Gary Oldman's performance? Oldman is one of the great actors, able to play high, low, crass, noble. Here he disappears into the character, with owly glasses, a feral mouth, and curly locks teased over baldness. He plays the kind of man who, in high school, would rather know who was sleeping with the cheerleaders than sleep with one himself. There are two revealing scenes involving his wife, who knows him better than anyone should have to.

Of course, if he is right about Hanson, then he is not a bad man—merely an unpleasant one. But even if he is right he is wrong, because he opposed the nominee because she is a woman; her shady past is only a means of attacking her. This is one of those rare movies where you leave the theater having been surprised and entertained, and then start arguing. *The Contender* takes sides and is bold about it. Most movies are like puppies that want everyone to pet them.   ☞

Cookie's Fortune ★ ★ ★ ★
PG-13, 118 m., 1999

Glenn Close (Camille Dixon), Julianne Moore (Cora Duvall), Liv Tyler (Emma Duvall), Chris O'Donnell (Jason Brown), Charles S. Dutton (Willis Richland), Patricia Neal (Cookie Orcutt), Ned Beatty (Lester Boyle), Niecy Nash (Deputy Wanda), Lyle Lovett (Manny Hood), Donald Moffat (Jack Palmer), Courtney B. Vance (Otis Tucker), Ruby Wilson (Josie Martin). Directed by Robert Altman and produced by Altman and Etchie Stroh. Screenplay by Anne Rapp.

Cookie's Fortune is Robert Altman's sunniest film, a warmhearted comedy that somehow manages to deal with death and murder charges without even containing a real villain. True, the Glenn Close character comes close to villainy by falsifying a death scene, but since she's in the middle of directing the Easter play at her church, maybe it's partly a case of runaway theatrical zeal.

The movie takes place in the small town of Holly Springs, Mississippi, where Altman assembles a large cast of lovable characters. He's a master of stories that interconnect a lot of people (*M*A*S*H, Nashville, The Player, Short Cuts)*, and here one of the pleasures is discovering the hidden connections.

The film begins with a false alarm. A black man named Willis (Charles S. Dutton) wanders out of a bar, seems to break into a home, and studies the guns displayed in a cabinet. An elderly white woman (Patricia Neal) comes downstairs and finds him, and then we discover they're best friends. Neal plays Cookie, a rich widow who misses her husband fiercely. Glenn Close is Camille Dixon, her niece, who before long discovers Cookie's dead body and rearranges the death scene to make it look like a break-in and a murder.

Meanwhile, Altman's camera strolls comfortably around town, introducing us to Cora (Julianne Moore), Camille's dim sister; Emma (Liv Tyler), Cora's daughter, who takes a pass on genteel society and works at the catfish house; and the forces down at the police station, including the veteran officer Lester (Ned Beatty), Jason the doofus rookie (Chris O'Donnell), and Wanda the deputy (Niecy Nash). Some of these people have roles in the Easter play, which is *Salome* (the letterboard in front of the church says it's "by Oscar Wilde and Camille Dixon").

The key dramatic event in the film is the arrest of Willis on suspicion of murder, even though everyone in the town is convinced he could not have committed such a crime. His fingerprints are indeed on the guns in Cookie's house, but no wonder, since he just finished cleaning them.

"He's innocent. You can trust me on that," declares Lester the cop.

"What makes you so sure of that?"

"Because—I fish with him."

Emma also believes he's innocent, and demonstrates her confidence by moving into his jail cell. The cell door is kept open, which is convenient for Emma and Jason the doofus deputy, since they are desperately in love and sneak off behind the Coke machine for rumpy-pumpy whenever possible.

"They read you your rights?" the lawyer (Donald Moffat) asks Willis. "Yeah, and gave me a cup of coffee and an issue of *Field and Stream.*" Also a Scrabble board. Meanwhile, Camille and Cora (who has been sworn to secrecy about the falsified death scene) are beside themselves: They like Willis and are horrified he's under arrest, but to free him would involve incriminating themselves.

Altman and his writer, Anne Rapp, use the crime story as a way to reveal connections of one sort or another between almost everyone in the movie. They also show a small southern town that is not seething with racism, classism, and ignorance, but is in fact a sort of heavenly place where most people know and like one another, and are long accustomed to each other's peculiarities. (There's a lovely scene where the bar owner tries to explain to the cops, without really saying so, that it is Willis's custom to steal a half-pint of Southern Comfort when he's broke, and return it when he's in funds.)

Altman has always been good with sly humor at the edges of his frame. He doesn't only focus on the foreground action, but allows supporting characters to lead their own lives on the edges. Notice in particular the delightful character of Wanda (Niecy Nash), the African-American deputy, who wields a tape recorder with great drama. There's a scene where a state investigator arrives from Jackson to look into the case, and is a handsome black man (Courtney B. Vance). He interviews the blues singer at the bar (Ruby Wilson), while Wanda mans the tape recorder, and both women subtly but shamelessly flirt with him.

Cookie's Fortune is the kind of comedy with a lot of laughs, and even more smiles. The cast blends so smoothly you can believe they all live in the same town. There is a great warmth at the center of the story, in the performance by Charles S. Dutton, who is one of the most likable characters in any Altman film (his scenes with Liv Tyler include some very tricky revelations, which they both handle with perfect simplicity). Glenn Close has the richest comedy in the film, as the meddling, stage-struck director ("The two of you keep forgetting this is ancient Galilee!"). Patricia Neal's role is brief, but crucial and touching. Ned Beatty's sheriff uses fishing as his metaphor for life.

Altman's films are sometimes criticized for being needlessly enigmatic and elliptical, for ending at quixotic moments, for getting too cute with the asides. He does sometimes commit those sins, if sins they are, but in the service of creating movies that are fresh and original. *Cookie's Fortune* has no ragged edges or bother-

some detours, and flows from surprise to delight. At the end, when just deserts are handed out, it arrives at a kind of perfection.

The Corruptor ★ ½
R, 111 m., 1999

Chow Yun-Fat (Nick Chen), Mark Wahlberg (Danny Wallace), Ric Young (Henry Lee), Elizabeth Lindsey (Louise Deng), Paul Ben-Victor (Schabacker), Jon Kit Lee (Jack), Andrew Pang (Willy Ung), Brian Cox (Sean Wallace), Kim Chan (Uncle Benny). Directed by James Foley and produced by Dan Halsted. Screenplay by Robert Pucci.

Even when it's transplanted to the streets of New York's Chinatown, as *The Corruptor* is, the Hong Kong action genre has certain obligatory requirements. Low-angle shots of bad guys looming over the camera, for example. And the sound of a metallic whoosh when there's a quick cut from one scene to the next. And what seems like more dialogue during action scenes than before and after them.

The Corruptor touches these bases, and has an icon as its lead: Chow Yun-Fat, who has made almost seventy films and has recently followed Jackie Chan into the American market (*Replacement Killers,* with Mira Sorvino, in 1998). His *Hard Boiled* (1992), directed by the master of the genre, John Woo, is a cult favorite. *The Corruptor* isn't in that league.

Chow Yun-Fat plays Nick Chen, a tough cop in an all-Asian station house in Chinatown. A white cop named Danny (Mark Wahlberg) is assigned to the precinct, and greeted with much suspicion: He will stand out, he won't be trusted, he doesn't understand the Chinese, etc. This is a setup for one of the weariest of all cop formulas, the cop-buddy movie, in which opposites first repel and then attract. Will Nick and Danny be friends by the end of the movie? What do you think?

But there are a couple of fundamental twists I dare not reveal, involving secrets held by both men—a secret, in Danny's case, that makes you wonder how his superiors could possibly have hoped for him to operate effectively in an Asian environment. No matter; the plot chugs along as the cops get involved in a scheme involving the boss of Chinatown,

Uncle Benny (Kim Chan, who according to the Internet Movie Database played a character with exactly the same name in *Lethal Weapon 4*—is this trivia, or homage?).

Everybody in Chinatown is more or less on the take, but there are degrees of immorality, and Nick is the kind of cop who tries to be realistic and principled at the same time. As for Danny: Well, I just never believed he was a cop at all. Mark Wahlberg was effective in a much more difficult role in *Boogie Nights*, but he's not an action star and he never feels at home in the role.

There's an opportunity for some kind of love or human interest with another cop in the precinct, played by Elizabeth Lindsey; she's set up as a major character, but given a role so underwritten (or badly edited) that she spends a lot of time just standing in the backgrounds of other people's shots. The problem with relationships is that they involve personalities and dialogue, and there's not much time for those in an action picture.

The director is James Foley, who is obviously not right for this material. It's a shame, actually, that he's even working in the genre, since his gift is with the intense study of human behavior, and his best films include *Glengarry Glen Ross, At Close Range*, and *After Dark, My Sweet*. John Woo, who might have brought crackling energy to this material (especially if he nixed the casting of Wahlberg), wouldn't be right for *Glengarry*. So there you are.

Cotton Mary ★ ★
R, 125 m., 2000

Greta Scacchi (Lily MacIntosh), Madhur Jaffrey (Cotton Mary), Sakina Jaffrey (Rosie), James Wilby (John MacIntosh), Prayag Raaj (Abraham), Laura Lumley (Theresa), Sarah Badel (Mrs. Evans), Joanna David (Mrs. Smythe), Gemma Jones (Mrs. Davids), Neena Gupta (Blossom). Directed by Ismail Merchant and produced by Nayeem Hafizka and Richard Hawley. Screenplay by Alexandra Viets.

Ismail Merchant's *Cotton Mary* centers on the stories of two women: an Anglo-Indian who wants to be white, and a white British woman who wants to brood and sulk and be left alone. We don't like either character, but what we can't understand is the British woman's sullen passivity and indifference to her household; a faithful servant is fired, her husband has an affair, a crazy woman takes charge of her new baby, and she hardly seems to notice. The film wants to make larger points, but succeeds only in being a story of derangement.

The British Raj shut down in 1947, and Indians took over their own country for the first time in centuries. But many people of British descent, born there, considered it home and stayed after independence. The best portrait of that time I've read is Paul Scott's *Staying On*, the novel that followed his masterful *Raj Quartet*. *Cotton Mary* is like a lurid reduction of material set in a similar time and place, without the human insights—either in the story or between the characters.

As the story opens, a British woman named Lily (Greta Scacchi) has given birth, but has no milk. Mary (Madhur Jaffrey), a nurse at the hospital, takes the sickly child to her sister Blossom (Neena Gupta), who lives in a poorhouse and serves as a wet nurse. Lily hardly seems to notice. When she finally asks, "Mary, how do you feed the baby?" and is told, "Mother's milk, madam," that seems to satisfy her. She is maddeningly incurious.

Mary insinuates herself into the household, which is run by the aged family servant Abraham (Prayag Raaj). Soon she plots to convince Lily to fire Abraham (who can clearly see Cotton Mary is mad) and replace him with her own candidate, the cousin of a cousin. Abraham is the most convincing and touching character in the movie; when Lily tells him to go home, he protests, "But madam, this is my home." The newly hired cousin is a drunk; Lily sees him staggering around the garden, pulling up plants, and does nothing.

Lily's husband, John (James Wilby), a reporter for the BBC World Service, is absent much of the time covering alarming portents, and when he returns it is to have an affair with Mary's shapely friend Rosie (Sakina Jaffrey). But this affair is more obligatory than necessary, and supplies little more than a perfunctory sex interest. Meanwhile, the household goes to pieces while Cotton Mary dreams ominously of having white babies.

What is the point of this movie? To show that some Anglo-Indians identified with the departing British? Of course they did. When British men first arrived in India as soldiers and traders, they engaged in widespread liaisons and marriages with Indian women, and that custom ended only with the arrival of large numbers of British women, who introduced racism into the mix; similar feelings were mirrored on the Indian side. The Raj provided a privileged place for Anglo-Indians, but when the British departed, mixed-race people like Cotton Mary were left without a safety net. This story could be told more poignantly if Mary were not so clearly bonkers that her race is beside the point.

As for Lily, is she suffering from postpartum depression, or is she so clueless because the story requires her to notice almost nothing around her? A competent person would have treasured Abraham and left instructions for Mary to be barred from the house, and then there would have been no story. I think of the old couple in *Staying On,* and their lifelong loyalty to one another—their friendship with the manager of the nearby hotel, and their clockwork firing of their faithful servant (who refuses to be fired), and the loneliness of the local Anglican church, surrounded by the gravestones of ghosts whose descendants have all gone back to England. That is a story. *Cotton Mary* is a soap opera.

Coyote Ugly ★ ★
PG-13, 101 m., 2000

Piper Perabo (Violet Sanford), Adam Garcia (Kevin O'Donnell), Maria Bello (Lil), Melanie Lynskey (Gloria), Izabella Miko (Cammie), Bridget Moynahan (Rachel), Tyra Banks (Zoe), John Goodman (Dad). Directed by David McNally and produced by Jerry Bruckheimer and Chad Oman. Screenplay by Gina Wendkos.

Coyote Ugly is a cliff-hanger in which Piper Perabo ventures into a Jerry Bruckheimer production and escapes more or less untouched. The film stars her as one of a group of heedless wenches who dance on a bar and pour straight shots down the throats of the seething multitude. In a movie of this sort, it is inevitable that the song "I Will Survive" will sooner or later be performed by drunken pals. Next week's opening, "The Replacements,"

makes us wait an hour to hear it. *Coyote Ugly* takes no chances and puts it under the opening titles. Do you get the feeling these movies are assembled from off-the-shelf parts?

There is a story beloved in movie lore about the time Howard Hawks asked John Wayne to appear in *Rio Lobo.* Wayne had already starred in Hawks's *Rio Bravo* and *El Dorado,* which were essentially the same picture. So was *Rio Lobo.* "Shall I send over the script?" asked Hawks. "Why bother?" asked the Duke. "I've already been in it twice."

Does Jerry Bruckheimer have the same nagging feeling of déjà vu as he compares each new screenplay to those that have gone before? I wonder if he suspects his movie may not be original, as he contemplates a story about a girl from New Jersey who dreams of being a songwriter, moves to Manhattan, meets a guy, gets a job, and has a heartrending reconciliation with her dad, all in a movie that ends (yes, it really does) with the final line, "What do you do when you realize all your dreams have come true?"

Bruckheimer and his director bring superb technical credits to this wheezy old story, and they add wall-to-wall music to make it sound like fun. But you can only pump up the volume so far before it becomes noise. I don't ask for startling originality in a movie like *Coyote Ugly.* I don't object to the scene in which the heroine and her guy neck in a convertible and regard the lights on a Manhattan bridge. I am not even surprised that the hero drives a classic car (no characters in Bruckheimer movies drive cars less than twenty-five years old unless they are parents or gangsters). I don't even mind the obligatory dialogue, "It's payback time!" All I ask is that I be surprised a couple of times. Give me something I can't see coming, and make it more unexpected than a beloved character getting hit by a car instead of having a heart attack.

In the movie, Piper Perabo, who has big-time star power, plays Violet, a working-class girl from South Amboy, New Jersey, who packs up and moves to a cheap apartment in Chinatown (where she meets not a single Chinese person), and gets a job in Coyote Ugly, a bar that would be the result if you took the bar in *Cocktail* and performed reckless experiments on its DNA.

It's the kind of bar you would fight to get out of—and you'd have to. Customers are jammed so tightly together the fire marshal can barely wedge his way into the room. They are offered no mixed drinks, no wine, just "Jim, Jack, Johnny Red, Johnny Black, and Jose—all my favorite friends," according to Lil (Maria Bello), the sexy blonde who owns the club. "You can have it any way you want it as long as it's in a shot glass."

Violet auditions for her job, which consists of dancing on top of the bar, pouring drinks, dumping ice on customers who get into fights, and spraying the others every so often with the soda gun. These are skilled dancers. They can do Broadway routines on a slippery bar top, while drunks grab at their ankles. Every once in a while, just for variety, they pour booze on the bar and set it on fire. Many of the movie's shots are high-angle, looking down at the customers, their mouths upturned and gulping like gasping fish. Illuminated by garish neon, they bear an uncanny resemblance to Hieronymus Bosch's paintings of the damned roasting in hell.

After a shaky start Violet becomes a hit at the bar, while trying to place tapes of her songs around town. She has stage fright, you see, and can't sing her own songs because she's afraid to sing in front of an audience, although she will obviously do almost anything else.

She meets Kevin (Adam Garcia), an awfully nice Australian short-order cook, who encourages her, and even bribes a guy to give her an audition by trading his precious Spiderman comic. They would no doubt have steamy sex except that Bruckheimer, a student of straws in the wind, knows this is the summer when PG-13, not his old favorite R, is the coveted rating. (His *Gone in 60 Seconds* was also PG-13, which may explain why Angelina Jolie was missing from most of the picture.) *Coyote Ugly* finally leads up to the questions: (1) Does she find the courage to sing? (2) Do they stay together after their Idiot Plot misunderstanding? and (3) Do all of her dreams come true?

There is a reason to see the movie, and that reason is Piper Perabo, whom I first noticed in *The Adventures of Rocky and Bullwinkle*, writing that she was "so fetching she sort of stops the clock." She has one of those friendly Julia Roberts smiles, good comic timing, ease and confidence on the screen, and a career ahead of her in movies better than this one. Lots better.

Cradle Will Rock ★ ★ ★
R, 132 m., 1999

Hank Azaria (Marc Blitzstein), Emily Watson (Olive Stanton), Rubén Blades (Diego Rivera), Joan Cusack (Hazel Huffman), John Cusack (Nelson Rockefeller), Angus MacFadyen (Orson Welles), Cary Elwes (John Houseman), Philip Baker Hall (Gray Mathers), Cherry Jones (Hallie Flanagan), Bill Murray (Tommy Crickshaw), John Carpenter (William Randolph Hearst), Vanessa Redgrave (Comtesse LaGrange), Susan Sarandon (Margherita Sarfatti), John Turturro (Aldo Silvano). Directed by Tim Robbins and produced by Robbins, Jon Kilik, and Lydia Dean Pilcher. Screenplay by Robbins.

It was a time when the rich flirted with communists and fascists, when the poor stood in breadlines, when the class divide in America came closer to the boil than ever before or since. The 1930s were a decade when the depression put millions out of work and government programs were started to create jobs. One of them was the Federal Theater Project, which funded "free theater for the people" all over the country, but was suspected by Congressman Martin Dies of harboring left-wing influences. Since the last right-wing theater was in ancient Greece, his was a reasonable suspicion.

Tim Robbins's sweeping, ambitious film, *Cradle Will Rock,* is a chronicle of that time, knitting together stories and characters both real and fictional, in a way similar to John Dos Passos's novel *USA*. It tells the story of the production of Marc Blitzstein's class-conscious musical *The Cradle Will Rock;* its opening has been called the most extraordinary night in the history of American theater.

Intercut with that production are stories about Nelson Rockefeller (John Cusack), the millionaire's son who partied with the Mexican communist painter Diego Riviera (Rubén Blades) and commissioned his mural for Rockefeller Center; and the newspaper publisher William Randolph Hearst (John Carpenter) and fictional steel tycoon Gray Mathers (Philip Baker Hall), who bought Renaissance masterpieces secretly from Mussolini, helping to finance Italian fascism. We meet theatrical giants such as Orson Welles (Angus MacFadyen) and John Houseman (Cary Elwes). And little people like the homeless Olive Stanton (Emily Watson), who eventually sang the opening song in *Cradle*, and Tommy Crickshaw (Bill Murray), a ventriloquist so conflicted that he helps a young clerk (Joan Cusack) rehearse her red-baiting testimony, while his dummy sings "The Internationale," apparently on its own.

There is a lot of material to cover here, and Robbins covers it in a way that will be fascinating to people who know the period—to whom names like Welles, Rockefeller, Hearst, and Rivera mean something. For those who don't have some notion of the background, the film may be confusing and some of its characters murky. It needs a study guide, and viewing *Citizen Kane* might be a good place to start.

The film's anger is founded in the way Dies and his congressional red-hunters brought the full wrath of the government down on poverty-stricken theater people whose new musical might be a little pink, while ignoring fat cats like Hearst, who not only bought paintings from Mussolini for bags full of cash, but whose newspapers published flattering stories about the dictator from his former mistress Margherita Sarfatti (played by Susan Sarandon).

Nelson Rockefeller's flip-flops provide in some ways the best material in the film. Swept up in the heady art currents of the time, Rockefeller commissioned Rivera to paint a mural—and then, while the painter and his assistant were busy covering a huge wall of Rockefeller Center, was unhappy to learn the amorphous blobs hovering above portraits of the rich were molecules of syphilis and bubonic plague. The last straw was Rivera's addition of a portrait of Lenin. Rocky ordered the mural sledgehammered to dust, and its destruction is intercut with the crisis in the *Cradle Will Rock* production (one syphilis molecule escapes the hammers and clings to the wall in defiance).

Cradle Will Rock was produced under the aegis of Welles and Houseman, whose Mercury Theater then dominated radio drama, and whose *Citizen Kane* was only a few years in the future. Welles was a golden boy, only twenty-one, flamboyant and cocky. When union actors declare a rest break during a rehearsal, he thunders, "You're not actors! You're smokers!" Then he limousines off to "21" for oysters and champagne. Welles comes across as an obnoxious and often drunken genius in a performance by MacFadyen that doesn't look or sound much like the familiar original (ironically, Tim Robbins would make an ideal Welles).

Houseman is more admirable, especially after Federal Theater funds are cut off and the army padlocks the theater where *Cradle Will Rock* is set to open. He and Welles lead a defiant march uptown to another theater, and when Actors' Equity forbids its members to step foot on stage, composer Blitzstein (Hank Azaria) plays his score on a piano, and the cast members stand up in the audience to perform their roles.

The power of the Bliztstein play itself never really comes across in the film. It's too fragmented, and its meaning seems less political than theatrical. It's not what the play says that matters, so much as the fact that it was performed despite attempts to silence it. Its opening night was, in a way, an end of an era. Welles and Houseman soon went off to Hollywood and America went off to war, and it was thirty years before young Americans felt revolutionary again. Nelson Rockefeller went on to portray a "moderate" Republican, Hearst retired to San Simeon, and Rockefeller Center lost a tourist draw. Think how amusing the Lenin portrait would seem today, and imagine the tour guides pointing out the molecules of bubonic plague.

Crazy/Beautiful ★ ★ ★
PG-13, 95 m., 2001

Kirsten Dunst (Nicole Oakley), Jay Hernandez (Carlos Nunez), Joshua Feinman (Football Player), Bruce Davison (Tom Oakley), Lucinda Jenney (Courtney Oakley), Taryn Manning (Maddy), Keram Malicki-Sanchez (Foster). Directed by John Stockwell and produced by Rachel Pfeffer, Harry J. Ufland, and Mary Jane Ufland. Screenplay by Phil Hay and Matt Manfredi.

She's a wild child, a drinker, a truant, sexually bold, deliberately reckless. He's a model student, serious, responsible, who wants to attend Annapolis. She's the daughter of a liberal white congressman. He's the son of a hardworking Mexican-American woman. She goes after him because he's a hunk. He likes her but is frightened by her wildness, which is against his nature. Will she lead him into trouble, or will he help her grow up and quiet her demons? *Crazy/Beautiful*, which is about these questions, is an unusually observant film about adolescence.

The movie stars Kirsten Dunst and Jay Hernandez as Nicole and Carlos. Both actors are natural and unaffected—they level with their characters, instead of trying to impress us. They're students at a magnet high school in Pacific Palisades; she lives in Malibu, he lives in the barrio, and when she gets him into trouble and he's assigned to detention, he's angry: "I'm bussed two hours both ways. If I wanted to screw up, I'd do it in my own school, and get a lot more sleep." Nicole is self-destructive and parties with the wrong crowd; perhaps because Carlos uses his intelligence and has goals, he represents not just a cute guy but a self that she lost along the way.

Of course they are in love. Hormones take over when you're seventeen. But even during sex he's worried by her behavior. She brings him home, they get into bed, he insists on a condom, and then he sees her father wandering by the pool outside her window. He's alarmed, but she laughs: "That's my dad. He doesn't care. I can do anything. We're using a condom—he'd be so proud. And a person of color in his daughter's bed!"

Actually, it isn't quite that simple, and her father, Tom (Bruce Davison), is a good man who is written without resorting to the usual stereotypes about well-meaning but clueless adults. At one point he forbids Carlos to see his daughter—for the boy's own good, since he considers his daughter irredeemable, a lost cause. There are times when we agree.

Both characters find elements in the other they envy. "You don't care about what people think, and when I'm with you I don't care about what people think," says Carlos, who actually cares a great deal. Nicole works hard on her reputation for trouble, but there's a part of her that mourns, "I wish I wasn't the child that everybody learned what not to do from."

One of Nicole's problems is that her mother is dead, and her father's second wife has given him a perfect little child that they both dote on. The mother is obsessed by the tiniest rash on her child, but indifferent to the entire scope of Nicole's life. Carlos has problems at home, too, but of a different nature: His father is absent, and he carries the burden of his family's hopes. His mother and older brother are fiercely protective of him and hostile to Nicole, partly because she is white, even more because she is obviously trouble.

Crazy/Beautiful, directed by John Stockwell, written by Phil Hay and Matt Manfredi, is like a tougher, less-sentimental mirror version of *Save the Last Dance*. In that one, a white girl attends a black boy's inner-city high school, but in both films there are cultural differences, resentment because of color, a feeling of star-crossed loves, and the sense that each can help the other.

Crazy/Beautiful is tougher, and would have been tougher still, I understand, if the studio hadn't toned it down to get the PG-13 rating. It was originally intended to include drug use and irresponsible sex, and play as a cautionary message—but the R rating would have limited it to those over seventeen, and these days, alas, the warnings need to come a little sooner. As it stands, the movie sets up real tension between Nicole's self-destructive behavior and Carlos's responsible nature. And because of the real conviction that Dunst and Hernandez bring to the roles, we care about them as people, not case studies.

Crazy in Alabama ★ ★
PG-13, 104 m., 1999

Melanie Griffith (Lucille), David Morse (Dove), Lucas Black (Peejoe), Cathy Moriarty (Earlene), Meat Loaf Aday (Sheriff John Doggett), Louis Miller (Taylor Jackson), Rod Steiger (Judge Mead), Richard Schiff (Norman), John Beasley (Nehemiah), Robert Wagner (Harry Hall). Directed by Antonio Banderas and produced by Debra Hill. Screenplay by Mark Childress.

Crazy in Alabama is an ungainly fit of three stories that have no business being shoehorned into the same movie. The first one is familiar: events seen through the eyes of a young boy in a small town, who recalls, "And after that day nothing was ever the same again." This point of view could have worked with either of the other two stories, but not both at once: (1) ditzy dame snaps after years of cruel husband, leaves for Hollywood to find fame and fortune; and (2) local black boy becomes the focus of a civil rights crusade.

It is a symptom of the movie's confused agenda that although the outcome produces two trials, it is the ditzy dame whose fate is settled on-screen, and not the man charged with the death of a black boy. One wonders whether the eccentric local judge, who has such sympathy for a sexy brunette who chops off her husband's head, will be such a humanitarian when it comes to judging a racist white sheriff in a town with no black voters.

The head-chopping is announced almost in the first scene. Melanie Griffith plays Lucille, a woman who is clearly insane, and who kills her husband, decapitates him to be sure he is dead, and leaves for Hollywood to be discovered. She takes his head along, and frequently hears his voice, in scenes that are like a comic reprise of Peckinpah's *Bring Me the Head of Alfredo Garcia*. Her journey takes her through New Orleans and the Southwest, where she slinks and flirts her way out of arrests, and finally to Hollywood, where her career takes an unexpected turn.

Meanwhile, through the eyes of young Peejoe (Lucas Black), we see not only his loony Aunt Lucille but also the story of Taylor Jackson (Louis Miller), a black boy about his same age, who wants to swim in the segregated local pool and is warned off by the sheriff (Meat Loaf Aday) with the thought-provoking line, "You are trespassing on public property!" His determination leads to a local civil rights struggle, a death, and a visit from Martin Luther King Jr., and for young Peejoe, yes, after that summer nothing would ever be the same again.

The film is the directorial debut of the actor Antonio Banderas, Melanie Griffith's husband, who does a competent, professional job, although at the outset they should have realized that each of their main stories would curdle the other one. When a boy is dead in a civil rights case, that kind of takes the comedy out of the sexy nutcase defending herself in court. Nor is her self-justification very persuasive: "You spend all day making a beautiful meal

for your husband, and he comes home and gobbles it down, and a little piece of you dies." Yeah, and a big piece of him.

The Crew ★ ½
PG-13, 88 m., 2000

Richard Dreyfuss (Bobby Bartellemeo), Burt Reynolds (Joey "Bats" Pistella), Dan Hedaya (Mike "The Brick" Donatelli), Seymour Cassel (Tony "Mouth" Donato), Carrie-Anne Moss (Detective Olivia Neal), Jennifer Tilly (Ferris), Lainie Kazan (Pepper Lowenstein), Jeremy Piven (Detective Steve Menteer). Directed by Michael Dinner and produced by Barry Sonnenfeld and Barry Josephson. Screenplay by Barry Fanaro.

Hot on the heels of *Space Cowboys*, which was about four astro-codgers, here comes *The Crew*, about four mobster-codgers. Go with the cowboys. One difference between the two movies is that *Space Cowboys* develops quirky characters and tells a story that makes it necessary for the old friends to have a reunion, while *The Crew* is all contrivance and we don't believe a minute of it.

Of course, *The Crew* wants only to be a comedy, not a bittersweet coda to *Wise Guys*. But even at that it fails, because we don't buy the opening premise, which is that four onetime heavy-duty mobsters would all retire to the same seedy residential hotel on South Beach in Miami, there to tick down their days lined up in wicker chairs on the porch, watching the dollies go by. This is a situation that shouts out Plot, not Life, and everything that happens to them seems generated from overconfident chuckles in the screenwriting process.

The retired mobsters are Bobby Bartellemeo, Joey "Bats" Pistella, Mike "The Brick" Donatelli, and Tony "Mouth" Donato (Bobby violently rejected a nickname in his youth and never got another). In the same order, they're played by Richard Dreyfuss, Burt Reynolds, Dan Hedaya, and Seymour Cassel. After this movie and *Mad Dog Time* (1996), which reached a kind of grandeur as one of the worst films of all time, Dreyfuss and Reynolds should instruct their agents to reject all further mob "comedies" on sight. The later stages of their careers cannot withstand another one.

The plot has to do with plans to upgrade their fleabag hotel into yet another art-retro South Beach yuppie playpen. The old guys like where they live and want to preserve it, so they dream up a cockamamie scheme in which they steal a corpse from the morgue (Hedaya has a part-time job among the stiffs) and bring it back to the hotel, where they plan to shoot it and make it look like a murder, except that, as "Bats" complains, the old guy "looks like the pope." And so he does—Pope Pius XII, who was several popes ago, back when young "Bats" was no doubt taking a livelier interest in the church.

One thing leads to another. Turns out the corpse is in fact the ancient father of a current Miami crime lord. The old guy had Alzheimer's, wandered away from the nursing home, died anonymously, and it was just their bad luck to make the wrong choice at the morgue. Their pseudo-whack of the old dead guy is imprudently revealed by "Mouth" to a nightclub stripper named Ferris (Jennifer Tilly), whose stepmother turns out to be Pepper Lowenstein (Lainie Kazan), known to the mafiacodgers from the deli she used to run in New York, back in their carefree youth when they were blowing up trucks. Into the mix come two local detectives (Carrie-Anne Moss and Jeremy Piven), and one of them has an unexpected link to the past too.

And so on. Somehow it all needs to be more desperate, or more slapstick, or have more edge, or turn up the heat in some other way. Lainie Kazan's presence suggests one obvious idea: Why not a comedy about four Mafia widows in Miami Beach? The Crew unfolds as a construction, not a series of surprises and delights. Occasionally a line of dialogue or two will float into view, providing a hint of the edge the whole movie might have had. (My favorite: A gun dealer, happily selling them a shotgun with no background check, adds, "Don't thank me—thank the Republicans.")

Comparing this to Space Cowboys, I realize how much more heft and dimension the cowboys had. Attention was paid to making them individuals, instead of just rattling off attributes and body types. And Clint Eastwood, who directed that movie, is a better filmmaker than Michael Dinner, who seems too content and not hungry enough—too complacent that his material will sell itself. There is also the fact that Eastwood, James Garner, Tommy Lee Jones, and Donald Sutherland have built up goodwill and screen authority by avoiding movies like The Crew instead of making them.

Crime and Punishment in Suburbia ★ ★ ★
R, 98 m., 2000

Monica Keena (Roseanne Skolnik), Ellen Barkin (Maggie Skolnik), Michael Ironside (Fred Skolnik), Vincent Kartheiser (Vincent), James DeBello (Jimmy), Jeffrey Wright (Chris), Blake C. Shields (Moznick), Conchata Ferrell (Bella). Directed by Rob Schmidt and produced by Pamela Koffler, Larry Gross, and Christine Vachon. Screenplay by Larry Gross.

Crime and Punishment in Suburbia is no doubt "flawed"—that favorite moviecrit word—and it suffers from being released a year after the similar American Beauty, even though it was made earlier. But it is the kind of movie that lives and breathes; I forgive its shortcomings because it strives, and because it contains excellent things. To lean back and dismiss this movie, as most critics have done, is to show ingratitude. A messy but hungry film like this is more interesting than cool technical perfection.

The story is a dark, juicy melodrama involving the kinds of things that happen only in soap operas and in real life. Imagine American Beauty told from the point of view of the cheerleader. Her name is Roseanne (Monica Keena), and she is popular in school, where she dates the quarterback of the football team. But there is a cloud in her eyes, an inner failure to believe in herself. At home, where the dinner table creates an eerie echo of American Beauty, we see that her stepfather (Michael Ironside) is a pathetic drunk and her mother (Ellen Barkin) is fed up—not that her mother is a saint, either.

All of this is observed by a classmate named Vincent (Vincent Kartheiser) who silently sits behind her in the movies, who lurks across the street from her house, who takes her picture with a telephoto lens, and fits the profile of a stalker. But there is more to Vincent. He is a complicated boy with an angelic face, and a mom

137

who looks at him and says, "It's gonna be so interesting to see what you're like after you get out of this stage." Taking a clue from the movie's title, we wonder if he represents Raskolnikov, the hero of Dostoyevsky's novel. But director Rob Schmidt and writer Larry Gross have borrowed little other than the title and the workings of guilty emotions from *Crime and Punishment*. Vincent seems inspired more by the angels in *Wings of Desire*, who keep secret watch over their humans, want to help them, and finally descend to the physical level so they can touch and heal them.

Roseanne needs healing. She needs somebody who *sees* her—not the popular blonde cheerleader but the girl whose home life is hell and whose boyfriend is painfully limited. She needs a boy she can sing with, but she's never heard the song. Monica Keena does a great deal with Roseanne, a character who is herself an actress—pretending to be a daughter, a girlfriend, a cheerleader, all the time screaming inside.

Save the rest of the review for later if you plan to see the movie. One night the defiant mother goes out drinking with her girlfriend and picks up a bartender (Jeffrey Wright) who is probably nicer than she deserves. Her husband suspects an affair, finds them at the yogurt stand, and starts a fight. The scandals sink Roseanne at school, where the rumor machine whispers that her mother has left home to live with a black pimp. Black, yes; pimp, no. One drunken night the self-pitying stepfather (it is one of Ironside's best performances) forces himself on Roseanne. She convinces her quarterback (James DeBello) that they must murder him.

The attack echoes Raskolnikov's experience with the messiness of murder. The wrong person ends up charged with the crime because of circumstantial evidence. And the movie arrives at last at its Dostoyevskian component, as guilt eats away at the true killers. Some people are just not made to get away with murder; their freedom seems wrong to them. Now it is time for Vincent to come forward in his essential goodness, like Sonia (who was an inspiration and affront to Raskolnikov), and offer redemption, which is what Sonia did.

The movie is rated R. It's a funny thing.

Many of the PG-13 movies aimed at teenagers (*Coyote Ugly*, for example) seem corrupt and without value. Many of the R-rated movies about teenagers (like this film, *Welcome to the Dollhouse*, and *Almost Famous*) seem ideal for thoughtful teenagers. The MPAA counts the beans but never tastes the soup. Make a worthless movie but limit the nudity and language, and get a PG-13. Make a movie where the characters live with real problems and try to figure out what to do, and god forbid our children should be exposed to such an experience.

Crocodile Dundee in Los Angeles ★ ★
PG, 95 m., 2001

Paul Hogan (Mick Dundee), Linda Kozlowski (Sue Charlton), Jere Burns (Arnan Rothman), Jonathan Banks (Milos Drubnik), Aida Turturro (Jean Ferraro), Paul Rodriguez (Diego), Alec Wilson (Jacko), Serge Cockburn (Mikey Dundee). Directed by Simon Wincer and produced by Paul Hogan and Lance Hool. Screenplay by Matthew Berry and Eric Abrams.

I don't want to see a movie about Crocodile Dundee; I just want to hang out with him. Anyone who can rassle crocodiles and be that nice must know the secret of life. If he knew the secret of making movies, there'd be no stopping the bloke.

Crocodile Dundee in Los Angeles is a movie about a genial man and his sweet wife and nice son, and how they leave the Outback and fly to L.A. and foil an international smuggling ring. I've seen audits that were more thrilling.

The movie recycles the formula of the original *Crocodile Dundee* movie from 1986, and the 1988 sequel. Together those two titles rang up a worldwide gross in the neighborhood of $610 million for Paul Hogan. Good on ya, mate! The only mystery about the third movie, more intriguing than anything in its plot, is why there was a thirteen-year delay before the next title in such a lucrative series.

Paul Hogan is just plain a nice guy. He's low-key and folksy, and hardly ever gets mad, and has such a studied naïveté regarding life in the big city that he not only comes from the Outback but must live in a soundproof hole out there. Like the hero of *Memento* he seems to suffer from short-term memory loss, which is why in movie after movie he can expose himself to would-be muggers, or walk into gay bars without realizing it.

In *Crocodile Dundee in Los Angeles,* he lives in a town with a population of twenty with his partner, Sue (Linda Kozlowski), who met him in the first movie when she was a New York TV reporter. He runs Outback safaris, traps crocodiles, and picks his son, Mikey, up after school. Sue, whose father is an international press baron, is happy to live so far from town, as indeed she might be, considering that Croc does the dishes and only occasionally puts an animal trap in to soak with the china. Now her father asks her to fill in for a deceased reporter in his Los Angeles bureau, and that leads Sue and Croc to stumble over a scheme in which money-losing movies are made in order to cover up a scam.

The movie is pokey and the jokes amble on-screen, squat down on their haunches, and draw diagrams of themselves in the dust. But enough Croc-bashing. Truth in journalism compels me to report that *Crocodile Dundee* is at least genial family entertainment, quite possibly of interest to younger audiences, and entirely lacking in the vomitous content of such other current films as *See Spot Run, Joe Dirt,* and *Freddy Got Fingered.*

Since the studios are advertising those excremental exercises in places where kids develop a desire to see them, it is good, after they see *Spy Kids,* to have an innocent and harmless entertainment like *Crocodile Dundee in Los Angeles* as another choice. It may not be brilliant, but who would you rather your kids took as role models: Crocodile Dundee, David Spade, or Tom Green? It is a melancholy milestone in our society when parents pray, "Please, God, let my child grow up to admire a crocodile rassler," but there you have it.

Crouching Tiger, Hidden Dragon ★ ★ ★ ★
PG-13, 119 m., 2000

Chow Yun Fat (Li Mu Bai), Michelle Yeoh (Yu Shu Lien), Zhang Ziyi (Jen Yu), Chang Chen (Lo), Lung Sihung (Sir Te), Cheng Pei Pei (Jade Fox), Li Fa Zeng (Governor Yu), Gao Xian (Bo).

Directed by Ang Lee and produced by Bill Kong, Hsu Li Kong, and Lee. Screenplay by James Schamus, Wang Hui Ling, and Tsai Kuo Jung, based on the novel by Wang Du Lu.

The best martial arts movies have nothing to do with fighting and everything to do with personal excellence. Their heroes transcend space, gravity, the limitations of the body, and the fears of the mind. In a fight scene in a Western movie, it is assumed the fighters hate each other. In a martial arts movie, it's more as if the fighters are joining in a celebration of their powers.

To be sure, people get killed, but they are either characters who have misused their powers, or anonymous lackeys of the villain. When the hero stands in the center of a ring of interchangeable opponents and destroys them one after another, it's like a victory for the individual over collectivism—a message not lost in the Asian nations where these movies are most loved. The popularity of strong heroines is also interesting in those patriarchal societies.

Ang Lee's *Crouching Tiger, Hidden Dragon* is the most exhilarating martial arts movie I have seen. It stirred even the hardened audience at the 8:30 A.M. press screening at Cannes. There is a sequence near the beginning of the film involving a chase over rooftops, and as the characters run up the sides of walls and leap impossibly from one house to another, the critics applauded, something they rarely do during a film, and I think they were relating to the sheer physical grace of the scene. It is done so lightly, quickly, easily.

Fight scenes in a martial arts movie are like song-and-dance numbers in a musical: After a certain amount of dialogue, you're ready for one. The choreography of the action scenes in *Crouching Tiger* was designed by Yuen Wo-Ping, whose credits include *The Matrix,* and who understands that form is more important than function. It's not who wins that matters (except to the plot, of course); it's who looks most masterful.

There's also a competition to find unlikely settings for martial arts scenes. In *Legend of Drunken Master,* the recently rereleased Jackie Chan movie, a bed of glowing coals is suspended in the air next to an elevated factory railway. Why? So Chan can fall into them. In *Crouching Tiger, Hidden Dragon,* Ang Lee and Yuen Wo-Ping give us a scene of startling daring and beauty when two protagonists cling to the tops of tall, swaying trees and swing back and forth during a swordfight.

Watching this scene, I assumed it was being done with some kind of computer trickery. I "knew" this because I "knew" the actors were not really forty feet in the air holding onto those trees. I was wrong. Everything we see is real, Lee told me. Computers were used only to remove the safety wires that held the actors. "So those were stunt people up there?" I asked, trying to hold onto some reserve of skepticism. "Not for the most part," he said. "Maybe a little stunt work, but most of the time you can see their faces. That's really them in the trees." And on the rooftops too, he told me.

The film stars Chow Yun Fat and Michelle Yeoh—she a veteran martial arts star who has extraordinary athletic abilities (as Jackie Chan and many of the other stars of the genre also do). Two other key characters are played by Zhang Ziyi (as Jen Yu) and Cheng Pei Pei (as Jade Fox). Long rehearsal and training went into their scenes, but what's unusual about *Crouching Tiger, Hidden Dragon* is the depth and poetry of the connecting story, which is not just a clothesline for action scenes, but has a moody, romantic, and even spiritual nature.

The story involves Li Mu Bai (Chow Yun Fat), a warrior who has vowed to avenge the death of his master. He has for many years been in love with Yu Shu Lien (Michelle Yeoh), and she with him, but their personal feelings wait upon vengeance and upon their attempts to recapture Green Destiny, a sword that once belonged to Li Mu Bai's master. That brings Yu Shu Lien into contact with the governor's daughter, Jen Yu (Zhang Ziyi), who has a secret I will leave you to discover. The other major character, Jade Fox (Cheng Pei Pei), stands between the heroes and their dreams.

This story, like all martial arts stories, is at some level just plain silly, but Ang Lee *(The Ice Storm, Sense and Sensibility)* and his longtime collaborator James Shamus (who wrote the screenplay with Wang Hui Ling and Tsai Kuo Jung) are unusually successful in bringing out the human elements, especially the unrealized

love between the Chou Yun Fat and Michelle Yeoh characters. There are times when they're together that you forget about the swords and are just watching a man and a woman, tenderly cherishing the unspoken bond between them. Zhang Ziyi's character, the governor's daughter, is also intriguing because she chafes at the rules that limit her and realizes a secret fantasy life.

There are those, I know, who will never go to a martial arts movie, just as some people hate Westerns and Jack Warner once told his producers, "Don't make me any more movies where the people write with feathers." But like all ambitious movies, *Crouching Tiger, Hidden Dragon* transcends its origins and becomes one of a kind. It's glorious, unashamed escapism, and surprisingly touching at the same time. And they're really up there in those trees. ☞

Croupier ★ ★ ★
NO MPAA RATING, 91 m., 2000

Clive Owen (Jack Manfred), Kate Hardie (Bella), Alex Kingston (Jani de Villiers), Gina McKee (Marion), Nicholas Ball (Jack's Father). Directed by Mike Hodges and produced by Jonathan Cavendish. Screenplay by Paul Mayersberg.

You have to make a choice in life: Be a gambler or a croupier.

So believes Jack Manfred, the hero of *Croupier,* whose casino job places him halfway between the bosses and the bettors, so he can keep an eye on both. He is a cold, controlled man, at pains to tell us, "I do not gamble." True enough, he does not gamble at casino games of chance, but in his personal life he places appalling bets, and by the end of the film is involved with three women and a scheme to defraud the casino.

Manfred (Clive Owen) wants to be a writer, and narrates his own story in the third person, as if he's writing it. With his slicked-back black hair, symmetrical good looks, and cold detachment, he's a reminder of Alain Delon's professional killer in *Le Samourai*—a man who wants to stay aloof and calculate the odds, but finds himself up to the neck in trouble anyway. There's the hint that this is a pattern, and that at one time he did gamble, obsessively.

The key figure in Jack's life is his father (Nicholas Ball), who was indeed a gambler, a Jack-the-lad who womanized, drank, gambled, and ran roughshod over Jack's early years. Jack's secret is that his hard, calculating facade has been hammered together as a shield over the little boy inside.

Jack's father, now in South Africa, lines up a job for him at the roulette wheels of a London casino. Jack never gambles, but he does deal, and is a skilled card manipulator (we imagine his dad teaching the boy to shuffle). The movie knows its way around casinos, and particularly observes how the dealers, with their strange hours and surreal jobs, tend to date each other instead of outsiders ("incest," the screenplay calls it). He observes dispassionately as punters line up to try their luck, and the movie notices what complete indifference the dealers have for their clients: Whether they win or lose, the work shift is exactly as long.

Jack has a girlfriend named Marion (Gina McKee), who is a store detective. "I want to marry a writer, not a (bleeping) croupier," she tells him. During the course of the story he also has liaisons with a dealer named Bella (Kate Hardie) who works on his shift. And he meets the glamorous Jani de Villiers (Alex Kingston), a casino client from South Africa—wild, reckless, in debt, a sexual predator who wants to hook him on a scheme to cheat the casino. Jack is just detached enough from his job, just enough of a mechanic intrigued by the intricacies of the plot, to be interested.

The movie was directed by Mike Hodges, whose *Get Carter* (1971) is one of the best of the hard-boiled British crime movies. It was written by Paul Mayersburg *(The Man Who Fell to Earth, Eureka)*, who must have done his research, since the casino scenes feel real: This isn't an unconvincing movie casino (even though it was built on a set in Germany), but a convincing portrayal of one of those smaller London operations where the plush and the gilt and the tuxedos on the gorillas at the door don't quite cover the tarnish.

The plot is more than we bargained for. I will not hint at the details, which lead to an unexpected and satisfactory but not entirely convincing ending. The point of the movie is not the plot but the character and the atmosphere; Hodges is bemused by Jack Manfred, who thinks he can stand outside his own life, control it, figure the odds, and turn it into a novel.

The choice of Clive Owen as the star is a good one. He's got the same sort of physical reserve as Sean Connery in the *Bond* pictures; he doesn't give himself wholly to the action, but seems to be keeping a part of his mind outside of it, measuring and calculating. This is not just a strategy but essential to his personality. We sense that his father had a way of catching him off balance, and that he vowed that when he grew up he would never be fooled again. If he ever did grow up.

Cruel Intentions ★ ★ ★
R, 97 m., 1999

Sarah Michelle Gellar (Kathryn Merteuil), Ryan Phillippe (Sebastian Valmont), Reese Witherspoon (Annette Hargrove), Selma Blair (Cecile Caldwell), Louise Fletcher (Helen Rosemond), Joshua Jackson (Blaine Tuttle), Eric Mabius (Greg McConnell), Sean Patrick Thomas (Ronald Clifford). Directed by Roger Kumble and produced by Neal H. Moritz. Screenplay by Kumble.

Teenagers once went to the movies to see adults making love. Now adults go to the movies to see teenagers making love. *Cruel Intentions* is a modern-day version of *Dangerous Liaisons,* with rich kids in a prep school playing roles that were written for jaded French aristocrats in the wicked 1782 novel by Choderlos De Laclos. He created a world of depraved amorality, in which the only goal was to indulge one's selfishness. It's refreshing, after the spongebrained teenage romances of recent months, to see this movie reflecting that cynicism—up to a point. It crash-lands with an ending of soppy moralizing, but until the end, it's smart and merciless in the tradition of the original story.

The film stars Ryan Phillippe, a slinky schemer in the tradition of James Spader, as Sabastian Valmont, a rich kid who lives in a Manhattan mansion with his stepsister Kathryn Merteuil (Sarah Michelle Gellar). He's known as an unprincipled seducer who "has never uttered a single word without dishonorable intentions." She's a minx who's angered when her current boyfriend dumps her for the sweeter Cecile (Selma Blair), and in revenge she urges Sebastian to conquer Cecile and destroy her reputation.

Agreed, says Sebastian, but soon he finds a greater challenge—the virginal Annette (Reese Witherspoon), daughter of the new headmaster at their expensive school. She's written an article for *Seventeen* magazine praising premarital virginity, and Sebastian bets Kathryn he can deflower her. The wager: If he loses, his stepsister gets his classic sports car. If he wins, he gets his stepsister.

Sebastian pulls heartstrings, tells lies, and employs devious seductive strategies, and the movie is startling in its frank language and forthright approach to sex; it's like a throwback to the 1970s. The plot's Machiavellian emotional strategies remind us of the same story as it was told in Stephen Frears's *Dangerous Liaisons* (1988) and Milos Forman's *Valmont* (1989), but the much younger actors create the uncanny illusion of a high school production of a grown-up play. Are teenagers capable of sexual strategies this devious and sophisticated? I doubt it; few adults are, and even those who qualify may simply lack the energy.

The movie's at its best in the scenes between Gellar and Phillippe, who develop a convincing emotional charge, and whose wickedness seems to work as a sexual stimulant. There's one scene where she persuades him, emotionally and physically, to do what she wants, and we are reminded that slow, subtle eroticism is, after all, possible in the movies—even though recently it has been replaced by calisthenics. Gellar is effective as a bright girl who knows exactly how to use her act as a tramp, and Phillippe seems cold and detached enough to make it interesting when he finally gets skewered by the arrow of true love.

The best parts of the movie allow us to see how good it might all have been, with a little more care. It steps wrong in three ways. The first is with the ending, which lacks the courage to take the story to its logical conclusion, and instead contrives a series of moralistic payoffs that are false and boring. The second is with the treatment of some gay characters; surely kids as sophisticated as those in this story would be

less homophobic. The third is with the use of a black character (Sean Patrick Thomas), Cecile's cello instructor, whose race is uneasily employed in awkwardly written scenes.

Still, overall, the film at least has style and wit, and a lot of devious fun with its plot. Compared to the sluggish *Jawbreaker*, it's a wake-up call. I almost hesitate to repeat my usual complaint about movies where twentysomethings play teenagers. Yes, the characters in this movie look too old to be sixteen or seventeen, but on the other hand, if actors are too young to attend R-rated movies, should they be making them? Only kidding.

The Cup ★ ★ ★
G, 94 m., 2000

Orgyen Tobgyal (Geko), Neten Chokling (Lodo), Jamyang Lodro (Orgyen), Lama Chonjor (Abbot), Godu Lama (Old Lama), Thinley Nudi (Tibetan Layman), Kunsang (Cook Monk), Kunsang Nyima (Palden), Pema Tshundup (Nyima), Dzigar Kongtrul (Vajra Master). Directed by Khyentse Norbu and produced by Malcolm Watson and Raymond Steiner. Screenplay by Norbu.

In the courtyard of their monastery, dressed in traditional robes, their heads shaven, young monks play a game of soccer, kicking around a Coke can. This image, near the beginning of *The Cup*, symbolizes its cheerful truce between the sacred and the mundane. The movie is a lighthearted comedy with serious undertones about the Chinese campaign against the traditions of Tibet.

The film takes place at a Tibetan monastery in exile in India, which from time to time receives Tibetan children whose parents have smuggled them past the border guards so that they can be raised in the ancient Buddhist teachings. And so they are, in a monastery which seems a little like any boarding school for irrepressible kids. "We shave our heads so that girls will not find us attractive," one explains to another, sighing that it doesn't work in the opposite direction.

The monastery is overseen by an abbot (Lama Chonjor), who is old and holy and deep and revered, and human, with a twinkle in his eye. He knows that the ancient ways in which he was raised are now in collision with the modern world, and so he is not altogether astonished when a fourteen-year-old student named Orgyen (Jamyang Lodro) stirs up desire among his fellow students to watch the World Cup finals on TV.

Why is this match so important? Because the World Cup itself is an obsession for most males in most of the world, of course, but especially because the final is between France and Brazil, "and France supports the cause of Tibet."

The abbot's assistant (Orgyen Tobgyal) is not an unreasonable man, and agrees to take the request to the holy man, who after due thought agrees. But official permission is only the first of many hurdles for the young monks, who now must raise the money to rent a television set and a satellite dish, and transport both to the monastery. Their attempts are told against a backdrop of daily life and human (and sacred) comedy in the monastery.

In addition to the Coke can, we see a lot of soccer magazines, studied by the students at least as intently as their sacred texts. And we get a real sense for these monks as human beings whose calling does not set them aside from contemporary society so much as give them a distinctive position in it. Often Tibetan monks are portrayed in the movies as distant and almost inhuman: automatons of worship. These are men and boys for whom Buddhism is a religion, a calling, a profession, and a reasonable way to live. Perhaps Westerners are too much in awe of the spirituality they encounter, and it took an insider to see the humanity involved.

The Cup, which is the first feature film ever made in Bhutan, was directed by Khyentse Norbu, a lama who must have learned a lot about filmmaking while serving as Bernardo Bertolucci's assistant during the filming of *Little Buddha*. The film has a distinctly Western feel in its timing and character development; it's not an inaccessible exercise in impenetrable mysteries, but a delightful demonstration of how spirituality can coexist quite happily with an intense desire for France to defeat Brazil.

The movie was a runner-up for the Audience Award at the Toronto Film Festival in 1999, and was also a hit at Sundance in 2000, where I met Khyentse Norbu, and was struck

by his poise and a certain distance he kept from those around him; his body language seemed to suggest he was interested in more evolved questions than what films Miramax was picking up. Then I learned that in addition to being a lama and a director, he is also considered to be the incarnation of the nineteenth-century saint Jamyang Khyentse Wangpo. And I thought: Of course. So many sinners have directed films that it is only fair for a saint to have a chance.

CyberWorld 3D ★ ★ ★
NO MPAA RATING, 48 m., 2000

With the voices of: Jenna Elfman (Phig), Matt Frewer (Frazzled), Robert Smith (Buzzed, Wired), Dave Foley (Hank the Technician). An animated film with material from several sources. Linking sequences directed by Colin Davies and Elaine Despins. Produced by Steve Hoban and Hugh Murray. Screenplay by Charlie Rubin, Hoban, and Murray.

CyberWorld 3D, shown in the giant-screen IMAX format, is remarkable not only for what it shows us, but for the wider world of 3-D animation it predicts. It looks better than most other 3-D films I've seen—clearer, brighter, more convincing. And it uses new software and technology to take existing flat animation, from such sources as the movie *Antz* and *The Simpsons* TV show, and process it into convincing 3-D.

This is not a makeshift transfer, but a fundamental reuse of the original material; everything in this movie looks made from scratch for 3-D, even though only about half of it really was. What the movie is telling us is that many animated films can be reconfigured into 3-D while retaining the elements of drawing and visual style that made them distinctive in the first place (indeed, *Shrek*, a 2001 animated feature from DreamWorks, will be retrofitted for the IMAX 3-D screen after its conventional theatrical run).

Like the recent retread of Disney's *Fantasia 2000* and earlier IMAX 3-D efforts, *CyberWorld 3D* takes advantage of the squarish six-story screen to envelop us in the images; the edges of the frame don't have the same kind of distracting cutoff power they possess in the smaller rectangles of conventional theaters. Then IMAX adds its custom-made headsets, which flicker imperceptibly so we see first out of one eye, then the other, while tiny speakers next to our ears enhance the reality of the surround sound. I have been watching 3-D since *Bwana Devil* (1952), and not until I saw it in IMAX did I consider it anything other than a shabby gimmick.

How does *CyberWorld 3D* take a 2-D source like *The Simpsons* TV show and convert it into 3-D? With animation, it's more direct than it seems. Begin with the fundamental method of 3-D, which is to shoot each image twice, with cameras spaced slightly apart, just as our eyes are. Project both images on the screen, and view them through glasses that create the illusion they are one 3-D image instead of (take the glasses off) two slightly out-of-register 2-D images. Our eye-mind system is tricked by the stereoscopic illusion into reading the two flat images as one image with depth.

Now move on to the building blocks of animation. While live action's POV resides in the camera, animation has a virtual camera— the point of view supplied by the animator. Using new software developed by Intel and IMAX, filmmakers are able to break the animation materials down into separate elements and reshoot them, in a sense, from two points of view, allowing the separation necessary for 3-D. It's more complicated than that, but the effect is astonishing.

More than one kind of animation is used in *CyberWorld 3D*. The separate self-contained segments are animated with the new system,

which takes existing film and gives it three dimensions. They float within a linking story that has been done with conventional computer-generated 3-D. This story stars a sprightly young girl named Phig (voice by Jenna Elfman), who takes us on a tour of a vast, high-tech virtual space where the individual segments seem to reside inside self-contained modules. Open one portal and find the Simpsons; open another, and find a thrilling futuristic city with sky trains, and so on.

Phig, meanwhile, is harassed by three cyber nuisances named Frazzled (voice by Matt Frewer), Buzzed (Robert Smith), and Hank the Technician (Dave Foley). This linking story is as inane as IMAX can make it; there's an unwritten rule that the hosts or other narrative devices of IMAX films condescend to the audience. Phig is shallow and silly, but she does at least figure in some wondrous animation, as when she glides through the interior space, has a vertiginous fall, and eventually journeys down a black hole.

CyberWorld 3D gathers several impressive stand-alone works of animation; to describe every one would be beside the point. It's more of a demo than a stand-alone work, and lacks even the unifying concept of *Fantasia 2000*. No matter; the point is to show us what can be done with recycled traditional animation in the IMAX 3-D process, and the demonstration is impressive. I'm looking forward to the IMAX version of *Shrek* and, eventually, classics like *Snow White and the Seven Dwarfs*. The only animation that's probably IMAX-proof is *South Park*, which is 2-D and proud of it.

D

Dancer in the Dark ★ ★ ★ ½
R, 160 m., 2000

Bjork (Selma), Catherine Deneuve (Kathy),
David Morse (Bill), Peter Stormare (Jeff),
Joel Grey (Oldrich Novy), Vincent Paterson
(Samuel), Cara Seymour (Linda), Jean-Marc
Barr (Norman). Directed by Lars von Trier
and produced by Vibeke Windelov.
Screenplay by von Trier.

Some reasonable people will admire Lars von Trier's *Dancer in the Dark,* and others will despise it. An excellent case can be made for both positions.

The film stars Bjork, the Icelandic pop star, as Selma, a Czech who has immigrated to America, has a small son, works as a punch-press operator, is going blind, and is saving her money for an operation to prevent her son from going blind too. To supplement her income she fastens straight pins to cards for a fraction of a penny per card. She keeps her money in a candy box. If I told you the movie was set in 1912 and starred Lillian Gish, you might not have the slightest difficulty in accepting this plot; whether you would like it, of course, would depend on whether you could make the leap of sympathy into the world of silent melodrama.

But the movie is set not in 1912 but in 1964. People still went blind, but plots had grown more sophisticated by then—and even more so by 2000, when this film won the Cannes Film Festival. Since it is impossible to take the plot seriously on any literal level, it must be approached, I think, as a deliberate exercise in soap opera. It is valid to dislike it, but not fair to criticize it on the grounds of plausibility, because the movie has made a deliberate decision to be implausible: The plot is not a mistake but a choice.

Bjork and her son live in a house trailer behind the home of Bill, a local cop (David Morse), who is in thrall to his materialistic wife. He earns, she spends. She thinks he has a big inheritance, and "it makes her proud," he confides in Bjork, to see him visiting his safety deposit box. In fact, the box is empty. The cop likes or loves Bjork or something (he is too gormless to be sure), but betrays her trust. This leads to a deadly confrontation between them, which is stretched out like one of those silent scenes where a victim staggers, speaks, staggers, speaks some more, falls down, curses the fates, tries to climb up, laments, falls over again, etc. Either you see this for what it is, von Trier deliberately going for effect, or it seems silly. Maybe it seems silly anyway, but you can admire his nerve.

Selma is followed everywhere by Jeff (Peter Stormare, from the chipper scene in *Fargo*). He wants to be her boyfriend. She's not looking for a boyfriend right now. It is important to note that both Selma and Jeff are simple-minded. Today we would call them retarded; in 1912 they would have been about as smart as many characters in melodrama. Selma also has a good friend named Kathy (Catherine Deneuve—yes, Catherine Deneuve), who figures out Selma is going blind and wants to help her but is defeated by her stubbornness.

The movie begins with Selma rehearsing for a leading role in a local production of *The Sound of Music.* It is interrupted by several song-and-dance numbers. Most of the film is shot in fairly drab digital video, but the musical numbers have brighter colors. They're set in locales like the factory floor and a railroad bridge. Against their jolly notes must be set the remarkably graphic death that closes the movie.

The first press screening at Cannes was at 8:30 A.M. That's the screening where all the real movie people attend—the critics, festival heads, distributors, exhibitors, film teachers, other directors, etc. (the evening black-tie audience is far more philistine). After the screening, the auditorium filled with booing and cheering—so equal in measure that people started booing or cheering *at* one another.

I sat in my seat, ready to cheer or boo when I made up my mind. I let the movie marinate, and saw it again, and was able to see what von Trier is trying to do. Having made a "vow of chastity" with his famous Dogma 95 statement, which calls for films to be made more simply with handheld cameras and available light, he is now divesting himself of modern fashions in plotting. *Dancer in the Dark* is a brave throwback to the fundamentals of the cinema—to heroines and villains, noble sacrifices and dastardly betrayals. The relatively crude visual look underlines the movie's abandonment of slick modernism.

Dancer in the Dark is not like any other movie at the multiplex this week, or this year. It is not a "well-made film," is not in "good taste," is not "plausible" or, for many people, "entertaining." But it smashes down the walls of habit which surround so many movies. It returns to the wellsprings. It is a bold, reckless gesture. And since Bjork has announced she will never make another movie, it is a good thing she sings.
☞

Dark Days ★ ★ ★ ½
NO MPAA RATING, 84 m., 2000

A documentary directed and produced by Marc Singer.

"Nobody in his right mind would come down here," says one of the cave dwellers of *Dark Days*. That is the advantage of living in the railroad tunnels below New York City. You don't get attacked by kids, hassled by cops, or ripped off in homeless shelters. You're on your own.

Marc Singer's film shows an extraordinary world that exists below the streets of Manhattan. In the perpetual darkness of the tunnels, people make their homes. They build shacks out of cardboard and lumber, and fill them with furniture dragged down from above. Tapping into city lines, they have light and water, and many have stoves, refrigerators, and TV sets.

One thinks of documentaries about life at the bottom of the sea, where giant worms live in the warmth of sulfur vents. Life is opportunist and finds its way everywhere, and there is something Darwinian about these tunnel dwellers, who have found a niche where they can survive. They are not, they emphasize, "homeless."

Singer heard about the tunnel people on a news broadcast. He went looking for them, and then came back to film them. Eventually, making *Dark Days* became his obsession; he spent all of his money on it, until he was homeless. It is a film about people who have fallen

through the cracks, but still share most of the same ambitions and hopes as the rest of us.

Many of the tunnel people keep cats to fight the rats. Others bait traps with lye. Rats and cold are the big problems, and having your stuff stolen. On the plus side, people look out for each other, and there is a guy named Tito who has become something of a cook: "Until I was in rehab, I never liked eggplant. Now it's the chef's special."

Some show Singer photos of their pets, but more rarely of their families. Old memories still hurt. One recalls his first hit of cocaine, and how much he liked it. "But I never got back to that first high. I made a mess of myself." His wife issued an ultimatum: the drugs, or me. He took the drugs.

Dee is a woman who also has a crack problem. She was in jail when she saw on TV that her two kids were burned in a fire. Now she lives in the tunnels. One of her neighbors has a chain-link enclosure for his dogs: "It's hard to keep a place clean with dogs," he observes.

The dwellers journey to the surface for food and treasure. "Kosher restaurants are the best," one says, "because the food isn't all mixed up with coffee grounds." They look for cans and bottles that can be redeemed. Sometimes they find things they can sell: "Gay porno is the best."

Watching this movie, I was reminded of George Orwell's *Down and Out in Paris and London,* his memoir of eighteen months spent living in abject poverty. What he learned, he said, was that tramps were not tramps out of choice, but necessity. Hard luck and bad decisions had led to worse luck and fewer choices, until they were stuck at the bottom. To call a homeless person lazy, he said, was ignorant, because the homeless must work ceaselessly just to stay alive. To tell them to get a job is a cruel joke, given their opportunities. *Dark Days* is the portrait of men and a few women who stubbornly try to maintain some dignity in the face of personal disaster. You could call them homemakers.

The Day I Became a Woman ★ ★ ★ ½
NO MPAA RATING, 78 m., 2001

Fatemeh Cheragh Akhtar (Hava [Young Girl]), Hassan Nabehan (Boy [Her Friend]),

Shahrbanou Sisizadeh (Mother), Ameneh Pasand (Grandmother), Shabnam Toloui (Ahoo [Bicyclist]), Cyrus Kahouri Nejad (Ahoo's Husband), Mahram Zeinal Zadeh (Osman), Nourieh Mahiguirian (Rival Cyclist), Azizeh Seddighi (Hourfa [Old Woman]), Badr Irouni Nejad (Young Boy). Directed by Marziyeh Meshkini and produced by Makhmalbaf Film House. Screenplay by Mohsen Makhmalbaf. In Farsi with English subtitles.

The Day I Became a Woman links together three stories from Iran—the three ages of women—involving a girl on the edge of adolescence, a wife determined not to be ruled by her husband, and a wealthy widow who declares "whatever I never had, I will buy for myself now."

All three of the stories are told in direct and simple terms. They're so lacking in the psychological clutter of Western movies that at first we think they must be fables or allegories. And so they may be, but they are also perfectly plausible. Few things on the screen could not occur in everyday life. It is just that we're not used to seeing so much of the *rest* of everyday life left out.

The first story is about Hava, a girl on her ninth birthday. As a child she has played freely with her best friend, a boy. But on this day she must begin to wear the chador, the garment which protects her head and body from the sight of men. And she can no longer play with boys. Her transition to womanhood is scheduled for dawn, but her mother and grandmother give her a reprieve, until noon. They put an upright stick in the ground, and tell her that when its shadow disappears, her girlhood is over. She measures the shadow with her fingers, and shares a lollypop with her playmate.

The second episode begins with an image that first seems surrealistic, but has a pragmatic explanation. A group of women, all cloaked from head to toe in black, furiously pedal their bicycles down a road next to the sea. A ferocious man on horseback pursues one of the women, Ahoo, who is in the lead. This is a women's bicycle race, and Ahoo's husband does not want her to participate. He shouts at her, at first with solicitude (she should not pedal with her bad leg) and then with threats (a bike is "the devil's mount," and he will divorce her). She pedals on as the hus-

band is joined by other family members, who finally stop her forcibly.

The third story begins like an episode from a silent comedy, as a young boy pushes a wheelchair containing an old woman, who is alert as a bird. She directs him into stores where she buys things—a refrigerator, a TV, tables and chairs—and soon she is at the head of a parade of boys pushing carts filled with consumer goods. We learn she inherited a lot of money and plans to spend it while she can, on all the things she couldn't buy while she was married. The scene concludes with a Felliniesque image I will not spoil for you; it is the film's one excursion out of the plausible and into the fantastic, but the story earns it.

The Day I Became a Woman is still more evidence of how healthy and alive the Iranian cinema is, even in a society we think of as closed. It was directed by Marziyeh Meshkini, and written by her husband, Mohsen Makhmalbaf (whose own *Gabbeh,* from 1996, found a story in the tapestry of a rug). It is a filmmaking family. Their daughter, Samira, directed *The Apple* in 1998, and last year her *Blackboards* was an official selection at Cannes (not bad for a twenty-year-old). Unlike the heroines of this film, the women of the Makhmalbaf family can think about the day they became directors. In fact, Iranian women have a good deal more personal freedom than the women of many other Islamic countries; the most dramatic contrast is with Afghanistan.

One of the strengths of this film is that it never pauses to explain, and the characters never have speeches to defend or justify themselves (the wife in the middle story just pedals harder). The little girl will miss her playmate, but trusts her mother and grandmother that she must, as they have, modestly shield herself from men who are not family members. Only the old grandmother, triumphantly heading her procession, seems free of the system—although she, too, has a habit of pulling her shawl forward over her head, long after any man could be seduced by her beauty; the gesture is like a reminder to herself that she is a woman and must play by the rules.

Deep Blue Sea ★ ★ ★
R, 106 m., 1999

Saffron Burrows (Dr. Susan McAlester), Samuel L. Jackson (Russell Franklin), Thomas Jane (Carter Blake), LL Cool J/James Todd Smith ("Preacher" Dudley), Jacqueline McKenzie (Janice Higgins), Michael Rapaport (Tom Scoggins), Stellan Skarsgard (Jim Whitlock). Directed by Renny Harlin and produced by Akiva Goldsman, Tony Ludwig, and Alan Riche. Screenplay by Duncan Kennedy, Donna Powers, and Wayne Powers.

Sharks, it is said, are all teeth and muscle, and have been doing two things very efficiently for millions of years: moving and eating. *Deep Blue Sea* resembles a shark. It moves ceaselessly, and someone gets eaten from time to time.

The movie is a skillful thriller by Renny Harlin, who made *Die Hard 2* and *Cutthroat Island,* and here assembles a neat package of terror, sharks, and special effects. That isn't as easy as it sounds. After slogging through the predictability of countless would-be action thrillers, I admired the sheer professionalism of this one, which doesn't transcend its genre, but at least honors it.

The premise: A scientist (Saffron Burrows) has devised a way to use the brain tissue of sharks to cultivate a substance that might be useful in fighting Alzheimer's. A big corporation underwrites the research and maintains a deep-sea station with shark corrals and underwater living and research areas. One of the sharks escapes and tries to eat a boat. The head of the corporation (Samuel L. Jackson) pays a visit to the station and meets the other key characters, including a shark wrangler (Thomas Jane), a Bible-quoting cook (LL Cool J), and crew members including Jacqueline McKenzie, Michael Rapaport, Stellan Skarsgard, and Aida Turturro.

Some of these characters turn up on the shark menu, although the timing and manner of their ingestion is often so unexpected that I'll say nothing more. The shark attacks are intercut with a desperate escape plot, after storms and explosions incapacitate the station and the characters are trapped below the waterline in areas threatened by water pressure and sharks.

Common sense, of course, has nothing to do with the screenplay, ingeniously devised by Duncan Kennedy, Donna Powers, and Wayne Powers. Its premise is that the sharks' brains have been increased fivefold, with a corresponding increase in intelligence, so that the sharks can figure out the layout of the station and work together to batter down watertight doors, swim down corridors, etc. The most obvious problem with this premise is that just because a shark is smarter doesn't mean it has more information; the smartest shark in the world would only know how to be a smart shark if it had a way to learn.

But never mind. The sharks exist in *Deep Blue Sea* as the McGuffins, creating situations that require the characters to think fast, fight bravely, improvise their way out of tight spots, dangle between flames and teeth, etc. There's a little perfunctory scientist-bashing, but not much (the Burrows character violates ethical guidelines, but, hey, it's for a good cause—fighting Alzheimer's).

Jackson is more or less the straight man in the cast. Jane handles most of the action duties, convincingly if, of course, not plausibly (in other words, he looks like he can hold his breath underwater indefinitely even though we know it's impossible). The surprise in the cast is LL Cool J, who has a kind of Cuba Gooding Jr. quality as a cook whose best friend is a parrot, and who hides from the shark in an oven, which the shark cleverly sets to five hundred degrees.

The movie is essentially one well-done action sequence after another. It involves all the usual situations in movies where fierce creatures chase victims through the bowels of a ship/space craft/building (the *Alien* movies, *Deep Rising,* etc). It's just that it does them well. It doesn't linger on the special effects (some of the sharks look like cartoons), but it knows how to use timing, suspense, quick movement, and surprise.

Especially surprise. There is a moment in this movie when something happens that is completely unexpected, and it's over in a flash—a done deal—and the audience laughs in delight because it was so successfully surprised. In a genre where a lot of movies are retreads of the predictable, *Deep Blue Sea* keeps you guessing.

The Deep End of the Ocean ★ ½
PG-13, 108 m., 1999

Michelle Pfeiffer (Beth), Treat Williams (Pat), Whoopi Goldberg (Candy), Jonathan Jackson (Vincent [sixteen]), John Kapelos (George Karras), Cory Buck (Vincent [seven]), Ryan Merriman (Sam). Directed by Ulu Grosbard and produced by Kate Guinzberg and Steve Nicolaides. Screenplay by Stephen Schiff, based on the novel by Jacquelyn Mitchard.

Ulu Grosbard's *The Deep End of the Ocean* is a painfully stolid movie that lumbers past emotional issues like a wrestler in a cafeteria line, putting a little of everything on its plate. It provides big roles for Michelle Pfeiffer and Treat Williams, but doesn't provide them with the screenplay support they need; the result is awkwardness when characters express emotions the audience doesn't share.

(There's no way I can discuss the failure of the movie without revealing details, so if you plan to see it, I'd suggest reading this review later to preserve the surprises.)

Pfeiffer and Williams play the parents of a three-year-old boy who is kidnapped from a hotel lobby during a class reunion. They are befriended by a detective (Whoopi Goldberg), who reveals she is gay, for no other reason than to provide a politically correct line, since her sexuality is utterly irrelevant to the story. Nine years pass, they move to Chicago, and then the boy is found again—mowing their lawn. He was kidnapped by a neurotic classmate of Pfeiffer's, who later married and then committed suicide. So the child has been raised by an adoptive father who of course had no idea he was kidnapped.

The film's most crippling failure is in the treatment of the father, who is played with gentleness and great strength by John Kapelos. The audience knows, but the movie apparently doesn't, that the real drama in the later stages is in the father's story. We suffer with Pfeiffer and Williams as they grieve their lost child and fight over the blame, but after nine years their life has fallen into a rhythm, and it is the other family that is ripped apart when the boy's true identity is revealed.

Consider. You raise a son from infancy in a happy household, only to have him snatched away from you, just like that. (The movie doesn't even supply the usual hearings, social workers, etc.) There is a scene at the other home, with Kapelos protesting his innocence to dozens of cops, and then an awkward scene in which the story of the kidnapping is explained in snappy dialogue. (This scene feels suspiciously as if it were slapped in as a replacement for cuts.)

And then . . . well, the boy is back with his birth family eating pizza. And then there is a scene at night, with an older brother curling up on the floor next to his bed. And then the family goes to church, where the priest welcomes him back to his birth family—with no mention of or reference to the adoptive father, who is sitting in another pew. And then a scene in the Italian restaurant that Williams owns; the kid is recruited for an Italian dance, but prefers a Greek dance he learned from his father.

All of this time, all of these scenes are undermined by our concern for the father. How does he feel? The film eventually allots him one brief but telling speech ("This was my wife and my son. This wasn't some lunatic and the boy she kidnapped. Not to me.") The weight it is given is suggested by Treat Williams's question to his wife after the man's visit: "So, what happened?"

The boy misses his adoptive father and the only home he has ever known, but he's almost too articulate about it ("[My mom] didn't mean to be sick. So why am I being punished?"). Oh, there's a scene where the boy and his new family fight over where he's going to spend Thanksgiving. But we never see the outcome. Where *did* he spend Thanksgiving and how did it go? And the film's ending, when it comes, feels unconvincingly neat. King Solomon could not have divided the child with more skill.

The movie's background details feel shoveled in for effect, instead of growing organically from the story. Consider that Treat Williams is said to run an Italian restaurant.

The character talks, acts, and moves like no Italian-American restaurant owner I have ever encountered. He projects the aura of a Kinko's franchisee. There is a scene on a Saturday morning where the guy is in his workshop building *birdhouses*, for cripe's sake. (These are Screenplay Birdhouses—provided by the prop department to give him something to hold in his hands.) Eventually he says, "I've got to go to work." At noon on a Saturday? Any Italian restaurant owner worth his oregano would have been up before dawn, visiting the produce market and supervising the marinara.

Such lapses wouldn't be fatal in a better movie, but *The Deep End of the Ocean* is unconvincing from start to finish. One can see that Pfeiffer's performance would have adorned a better screenplay, and that Jonathan Jackson, as the family's older son, has a convincing screen presence. But the film curiously seems to be long and slow, and yet missing large chunks of the story (it runs 108 minutes, but early press material clocks it at 148). My best guess: It was filmed before it was adequately written.

Desert Blue ★ ★ ★
R, 93 m., 1999

Brendan Sexton III (Blue), Kate Hudson (Skye), Christina Ricci (Ely), Casey Affleck (Pete), Sara Gilbert (Sandy), Ethan Suplee (Cale), John Heard (Lance), Isidra Vega (Haley), Lucinda Jenney (Caroline). Directed by Morgan J. Freeman and produced by Andrea Sperling, Nadia Leonelli, and Michael Burns. Screenplay by Freeman.

Imagine the town in *The Last Picture Show* after thirty more years of shrinking and loneliness, and you'd have the town in *Desert Blue*. Both movies are about teenage friends with not much to do, but the kids in *Desert Blue* are more resigned; there's a kind of sweet sadness to their exile—all except for Ely (Christina Ricci), who entertains herself by blowing things up.

Baxter, California ("pop. 89," according to the shot-up sign outside town), is known for one thing: the world's largest ice-cream cone, a forlorn structure that sits in the desert like a god on Easter Island. The cone was built by the late father of Blue (Brendan Sexton III). At the time of his suicide, the father was working on a water park, but then the Empire Cola company grabbed all the water, and now the park is just a shabby relic of water slides, picnic tables, and rowboats with no place to float.

Into this town one day comes a professor of roadside culture (John Heard), who wants to research the ice-cream cone. He's traveling with his daughter, Skye (Kate Hudson), a TV starlet who has an audition tomorrow in L.A. A truck overturns outside town, spilling the secret ingredient of Empire Cola (or whatever it is they really manufacture in that sinister plant outside town), and the authorities throw up roadblocks. Skye and her dad are trapped in the town. He welcomes the chance to research rural culture. She's a snob and thinks the local kids are hayseeds.

They're not. Most of them plan to leave Baxter (Ricci plans to do it by blowing herself up), but in the meantime they enjoy each other's company. They're gentle with one another, as if they deserve a certain pity just because they live here, and *Desert Blue*, in its sweet and unaffected way, succeeds in making a convincing movie about eccentrics without their performances obstructing the view.

The movie was written and directed by Morgan J. Freeman (not the actor), whose *Hurricane Streets* (1997) was a Sundance winner about young teenagers who are petty thieves on the Lower East Side of New York. I like *Desert Blue* more, but in both films I like the way Freeman doesn't pump up the volume. The overturned trailer, the arrival of the FBI, the mystery of a motel fire, and even Ricci's enthusiastic dynamitings are all played in a kind of bemused detachment. This is the herbal tea version of Oliver Stone's *U Turn*. Even when the FBI shoots at someone, it's handled as a terrible mistake, not an action scene.

Skye can't believe it at first when they're trapped in the town. She's an ambitious little number, worried about her audition, but soon the understated acceptance of the local kids begins to get to her, and she pairs off with Blue and begins to hear about his father's dreams of a water park and a better life. Perhaps they have a future together: Skye and Blue, get it?

A movie like this depends on tone more

than anything else. Moviegoers who don't like the rhythm may grow impatient. It's not a romance, a drama, or an adventure, but the evocation of a time and place. The characters are odd because they grew up that way. Even Ricci's love of dynamite is inspired not by hostility but by skill and boredom: One of her early targets is chosen because it was "just sitting there." We are no doubt expected to reflect that the same words could describe the whole town.

Destiny ★ ★ ½
NO MPAA RATING, 135 m., 1999

Nour el-Cherif (Averroes), Laila Eloui (Gypsy Woman), Mahmoud Hemeida (Al Mansour [Caliph]), Safia el-Emary (Averroes's Wife), Mohamed Mounir (The Bard), Khaled el-Nabaoui (Nasser [Crown Prince]), Abdallah Mahmoud (Borhan), Ahmed Fouad Selim (Cheikh Riad). Directed by Youssef Chahine and produced by Humbert Balsan and Gabriel Khoury. Screenplay by Chahine and Khaled Youssef.

Destiny takes place in twelfth-century Spain, but could take place today. It is an odd, brave film, part impassioned melodrama, part musical, taking a broad popular approach to questions of religious belief. It was directed by an Egyptian, financed from France, set in the Spanish province of Andalusia, and photographed in Lebanon and Syria. It's completely off the map for most American moviegoers, which is one of its charms.

The story involves an Arabic philosopher named Averroes, who believed that the Koran was open to interpretation. Yes, he taught, the book is the word of God, but God gave us intelligence so that we might reason about his words and not blindly follow their literal meanings. After all, to assume that the mind of God can be reduced to ordinary human language and contained in mere words is itself a kind of heresy. And those who oppose the interpretation of the Koran are of course imposing their own interpretation upon it.

As the film opens, one of Averroes's followers is being burned at the stake, the bonfire fed by his writings. The burning man calls out to his son to seek out the philosopher, and the main story takes place in Andalusia, where Averroes has gathered a group of disciples who study his books and copy them out by hand. Ah, but that gives a wrong idea of the film, which is not about scholars in their cells, but about politics, sexual passion, jealousy, and romance, and contains several song and dance numbers. Imagine *My Dinner with André* as a musical.

Andalusia is ruled by a caliph who has two sons, one a follower of Averroes, the other a party animal who is lured into the camp of fundamentalists. One feels of these fundamentalists, as one often does about the type in general, that they're driven not so much by what they believe, as by their fear or envy of those who do not agree. The movie argues that a belief that cannot stand up to free debate is not a belief worth holding.

Political intrigue is rife in the area. The caliph supports Averroes, but is opposed by a cult that hopes to overthrow him. Meanwhile, his oldest son is concealing a forbidden love with a gypsy woman, and his trusted adviser is working both sides of the street. A secret project is set in motion, to copy out the writings of Averroes and spirit them far away, in case the tide turns and his books are burned again (a good possibility).

Much of the film's interest comes from historical details. We hear of the great Arabic contributions to mathematics, and we see a fascinating invention, a telescope that uses the magnifying power of water in order to work. We see a society that is part European, part Arabic, in which Islam is as much a political movement as a religious one. And then there is the uncanny way the characters have of looking toward the camera and simply breaking out into song. (I was reminded of Woody Allen's *Everyone Says I Love You,* which was equally direct in the way ordinary people moved from speech to singing.)

There are places in the world where *Destiny,* directed by the veteran Egyptian filmmaker Youssef Chahine, would be controversial—even dangerous. In those places, the music and romance will help find a wider audience for a charged message. The interest in this country is more indirect. The film is naive and simple at times, even clumsy in its musical sequences, and yet lurking beneath its story is a conflict between rationalism and fundamentalism that is as fraught today as it ever was.

As I write these words, Serbs are slaughtering ethnic Albanians and we are bombing Serbs, all because of religious and ethnic differences that date back almost to the period of this film. At the end of *Destiny,* Chahine quotes Averroes: "Ideas have wings. No one can stop their flight." Heartening words. But are they flying or fleeing?

Deterrence ★ ★ ★
R, 101 m., 2000

Kevin Pollak (Walter Emerson), Timothy Hutton (Marshall Thompson), Sheryl Lee Ralph (Gayle Redford), Sean Astin (Ralph), Bajda Djola (Harvey), Mark Thompson (Gerald Irving), Michael Mantell (Taylor Woods), Kathryn Morris (Lizzie Woods), Clotilde Courau (Katie). Directed by Rod Lurie and produced by Marc Frydman and James Spies. Screenplay by Lurie.

Not long before election day 2008, the president of the United States is making a campaign tour through Colorado when a sudden snowstorm traps him in a roadside diner. Alarming news arrives: Saddam Hussein's son has sent Iraqi troops into Kuwait, and 80 percent of America's troops are far away, committed in the Sea of Japan. What to do? Drop the bomb, obviously.

Or at least threaten to. That's the strategic tactic tried by President Walter Emerson, played by Kevin Pollak as a man who wasn't elected to the highest office but got there through a combination of unforeseen events. He doesn't look very presidential, and he's not terrifically popular with the voters, but the office makes the man, they say, and Emerson rises to the occasion with terrifying certitude: Yes, he is quite prepared to drop the first nuclear weapon since Nagasaki.

This story unfolds in a classic closed-room scenario. The storm rages outside, no one can come or go, and the customers and staff who were already in the diner get a front-row seat for the most momentous decision in modern times. Although the president cannot move because of the weather, he can communicate, and he negotiates by telephone and speaks to the nation via a camera from the cable news crew that's following him around.

Watching the film, I found a curious thing happening. My awareness of the artifice dropped away, and the film began working on me. The situation, it is true, has been contrived out of the clichés of doomsday fiction. The human relationships inside the diner are telegraphed with broad strokes (and besides, wouldn't the Secret Service clear the room of onlookers while the president was conducting secret negotiations with heads of state?). There is a ludicrous moment when the president steps outside into the storm with his advisers to tell them something we're not allowed to hear. And the ending is more or less inexcusable.

And yet the film works. It really does. I got caught up in the global chess game, in the bluffing and the dares, the dangerous strategy of using nuclear blackmail against a fanatic who might call the bluff. With one set and low-rent props (is that an ordinary laptop inside the nuclear briefcase "football"?), *Deterrence* manufactures real suspense and considers real issues.

The movie was written and directed by Rod Lurie, the sometime film critic of *Los Angeles* magazine. On the basis of this debut, he can give up the day job. He knows how to direct, although he could learn more about rewriting. What saves him from the screenplay's implausibilities and dubious manipulation is the strength of the performances.

Kevin Pollak makes a curiously convincing third-string president—a man not elected to the office, but determined to fill it. He is a Jew, which complicates his Middle East negotiations and produced a priceless theological discussion with the waitress (Clotilde Courau). He is advised by a chief of staff (Timothy Hutton) and his national security adviser (Sheryl Lee Ralph), who are appalled by his nuclear brinkmanship, and who are both completely convincing in their roles. The screenplay gives them dialogue of substance; the situation may be contrived, but we're absorbed in the urgent debate that it inspires.

I mentioned the ending. I will offer no hints, except to say that it raises more questions than it answers—questions not just about the president's decisions, but about the screenwriter's sanity. *Deterrence* is the kind of movie that leaves you with fundamental objections. But that's after it's over. While it's playing, it's surprisingly good.

Deuce Bigalow: Male Gigolo ★ ½
R, 84 m., 1999

Rob Schneider (Deuce Bigalow), William Forsythe (Detective Chuck Fowler), Eddie Griffin (T. J. Hicks), Arija Bareikis (Kate), Oded Fehr (Antoine Laconte), Gail O'Grady (Claire), Richard Riehle (Bob Bigalow), Jacqueline Obrador (Elaine Fowler). Directed by Mike Mitchell and produced by Sid Ganis and Barry Bernardi. Screenplay by Haris Goldberg and Rob Schneider.

I laughed, yes, I did, several times during *Deuce Bigalow: Male Gigolo*. That's proof, if any is required, that I still possess streaks of immaturity and vulgarity. May I never lose them. There is a scene where Deuce the gigolo dates a woman so gigantic that her feet are almost too large for him to massage. I mean these are seriously large feet. Very funny.

There is a scene, too, where a pimp lectures Deuce on his place in the gigolo food chain. It is an illustrated lecture, with three varieties of tropical fish as the visual aids. Deuce is not like the rare imported fish, or even the beautiful domestic fish, but the bottom-feeder, down there with the plastic scuba diver. Very funny, especially the way the actor Eddie Griffin handles the explanation.

I laughed enough toward the beginning of *Deuce Bigalow*, indeed, that my hopes began to rise: Would this be that hardest of all films to pull off, a really funny comedy? I hoped, and then my hopes began to flag, and by the end I was hunkered down in my seat, depressed, waiting for the misery to end. It's like someone let all the air out after about the twenty-five-minute mark.

The movie stars Rob Schneider, from *Saturday Night Live*, as a tropical fish tank cleaner. He's so luckless in love that he has to buy sea snails just in the hopes that the girl behind the counter at the fish store will dip her T-shirt into the tank. When he sees a handsome stud (Oded Fehr from *The Mummy*) with a pretty babe, he is filled with envy—especially when he finds out the babe is paying the stud, who is a gigolo.

Many plot complications result. The fearsome gigolo hires the innocuous tank cleaner to baby-sit his valuable fish while he goes to Switzerland. And then, when Deuce desperately needs to raise money and the phone starts to ring, he finds himself backing into the gigolo racket, so to speak. He is well advised by the pimp, who is an expert on what the movie calls (about a million times) man-whores.

So of course we get a series of dates that Deuce goes out on, and a romantic plot about Kate (Arija Bareikis), the one girl he really likes. (What would you guess the chances are that she finds out he was paid for their first date and gets mad at him?) Deuce works his way through a series of dates with problems: Tina with the big feet, who is about eight feet tall; the Jabba Lady, who is very large; Ruth, who has Tourette's syndrome; and other women who are missing a limb or suffer from narcolepsy or blindness. (His date with the Tourette's victim is creative; he takes her to a baseball game, where everything she shouts sounds appropriate.)

The movie also has a police detective (William Forsythe) who is a compulsive exhibitionist, and in general alternates vulgarity, obscenity, scatology, and cruelty. Not for nothing is Deuce's dad a washroom attendant (and don't get me started on his mother, Bangkok Betty). After the early flashes of humor, the material settles down into a long, dull slog. The plot demonstrates what people will do for money, and so does the movie. It's the kind of picture those View 'n' Brew theaters were made for, as long as you don't View.

Diamonds ★
PG-13, 89 m., 2000

Kirk Douglas (Harry), Dan Aykroyd (Lance), Corbin Allred (Michael), Lauren Bacall (Sin-Dee), Kurt Fuller (Moses), Jenny McCarthy (Sugar), Mariah O'Brien (Tiffany), June Chadwick (Roseanne). Directed by John Asher and produced by Patricia T. Green. Screenplay by Allan Aaron Katz.

Diamonds is a very bad movie and a genuinely moving experience. As the story of three generations of menfolk who go looking for long-lost diamonds and find hookers with hearts of gold, it is unbearable dreck. As a demonstration of Kirk Douglas's heart and determination, it is inspiring.

Douglas suffered a stroke years ago, which left his speech impaired, a problem which the film addresses directly by showing him, in his first scene, doing speech therapy with a videotape. This therapy (or other therapy and a lot of determination) must have worked, because Douglas's speech is easily understandable (as clear, indeed, as Robert De Niro's stroke victim in *Flawless*). And the Kirk Douglas personal style is unaffected: He was always one of the cocky, high-energy stars, the life force made lithe and springy.

Diamonds feels like it was conceived as a showcase for Douglas at eighty-three, and so it is, but what a dreary story and unconvincing characters he has been surrounded with. Dan Aykroyd plays his son, and Corbin Allred plays his fifteen-year-old grandson. We get phoned-in scenes involving a lack of communication between them and learn that Aykroyd believes it's time for his old man to give up his independence and move into a retirement home.

Nothing doing! says Douglas, playing a former boxing champion named Harry who still likes to duke it out (there are flashbacks of him in the ring, lifted from his 1949 film *Champion*). He wants to live independently, and tells his son and grandson about some diamonds that he was given decades ago to throw a fight in Reno. The diamonds are still hidden inside the walls of the house of a man named Duff the Muff, he says, and they should all three go to Nevada and recover them. As a plot premise, this would look thin in an Adam Sandler movie.

The men travel south from Canada in the obligatory vintage convertible, its top down to make it easier to shoot all three passengers. Harry might get pneumonia in the winter weather, but nobody thinks of that—and besides, the old guy is feisty enough to get smart with the border guards. In Nevada, when their diamond search experiences a setback, they all end up at a brothel, where the young grandson draws Jenny McCarthy and Kirk Douglas gets the warmhearted madam, played by Lauren Bacall, who seems right at home as the nurturing angel, as indeed she should, having nursed the ailing John Wayne character back

to life, so to speak, in *The Shootist* twenty-five years ago.

The scenes in the brothel are mostly unforgivable, especially the byplay between Allred and McCarthy, who is reminded of the high school sweetheart she left behind. The climax involving the diamonds is so wheezy that we could meet during our lunch hours and pep it up. Characters so simple in plots so tired with dialogue so banal are not easily found; it is painful to watch actors speaking dialogue that is clearly inferior to the thoughts that must be running through their minds at the very same time.

But tribute must be paid to Kirk Douglas. I remember meeting him over several days in 1969, while writing a profile for *Esquire* magazine. I was almost bowled over by his energy, his zest for life, his superb physical condition. He could hardly sit still. He bounded from his chair to the side of a desk to a yoga position on the floor, talking rapid-fire about his career and hopes, and I have never forgotten what determination and joy he seemed to gather into every day of living. You can see that same quality in *Diamonds*, and seeing it is a way to enjoy the film—alas, the only way.

Dick ★ ★ ★ ½
PG-13, 90 m., 1999

Kirsten Dunst (Betsy Jobs), Michelle Williams (Arlene Lorenzo), Dan Hedaya (Dick), Will Ferrell (Bob Woodward), Bruce McCulloch (Carl Bernstein), Saul Rubinek (Henry Kissinger), Teri Garr (Helen Lorenzo), Dave Foley (Bob Haldeman), Jim Breuer (John Dean), Harry Shearer (G. Gordon Liddy). Directed by Andrew Fleming. Produced by Gale Anne Hurd. Screenplay by Fleming and Sheryl Longin.

Dick is the flip side of *All the President's Men*, explaining at last all of the loose ends of the Watergate scandal—how the duct tape got on the Watergate lock, who Deep Throat really was, and why the 18½-minute gap appeared on the White House tapes. We also learn that Richard M. Nixon resented the fact that his dog didn't follow him around adoringly, like the Kennedy and Johnson dogs; at one point, he snarls, "Checkers—shut up! I'll feed you to the Chinese!"

The movie is a bright and sassy comedy, seeing Watergate entirely through the eyes of its prime movers, who are revealed to be two fifteen-year-old girls. Betsy Jobs (Kirsten Dunst) and Arlene Lorenzo (Michelle Williams) are best friends who live in the Watergate complex, and one night they sneak downstairs to mail a letter to the Bobby Sherman Fan Club; they slap the tape on the door lock, it's discovered by a security guard, and the White House burglars are busted inside Democratic National Headquarters.

Ah, but it doesn't end there. The girls are on a class trip to the White House when they spot a man they'd seen in the Watergate. He's G. Gordon Liddy (Harry Shearer), but they don't know that; they get separated from their group and wander the White House corridors, stumbling upon shredding operations and cash rooms, and overhearing crucial conversations in the Oval Office itself.

President Nixon (Dan Hedaya, very funny) grows concerned over how much they may have heard and puts on a show of false good cheer: "How would you young ladies like to be the White House dog walkers?" Calling every day to walk Checkers, they dimly perceive that all is not as it should be in the Oval Office, and the plot reveals how they became Deep Throat, why John Dean had an attack of conscience, and why their rendition of Olivia Newton-John's "I Love You" appeared on a tape in the desk drawer of Rosemary Woods.

Yes, Arlene, the apple-cheeked one with the merry smile, gets a crush on Nixon. There's a funny dream sequence in which he appears to her riding a white charger on the beach, but even funnier is the classroom scene where, like millions of teenage girls before her, she tries out a married name by writing it in her notebook: "Mrs. Arlene Nixon."

Dick, directed by Andrew Fleming and written by Fleming and Sheryl Longin, finds just the right tone for its merciless satire: not strident, not wacky, but kind of earnest and intent, as the girls, who are not geniuses, blunder onto one incriminating secret after another. Their motivation seems to stem from ordinary teenage attributes, like curiosity, idealism, and romance.

The crusading reporters Woodward and Bernstein (Will Ferrell and Bruce McCulloch),

on the other hand, are played more broadly—Woodward as a self-important totem pole, Bernstein as an insecure runt. They're always trying to grab the phone away from each other, and their Watergate coverage, so majestic when seen from the outside, is portrayed as the work of a couple of ambitious reporters on a power trip, believing everything the teenage ditzos tell them. (Of course, everything the girls tell them turns out to be correct.)

Comedy like this depends on timing, invention, and a cheerful cynicism about human nature. It's wiser and more wicked than the gross-out insult humor of many of the summer's other comedies. Consider the scene where the girls accidentally bake cookies with a secret herbal ingredient from their brother's stash and take them to Nixon, who offers one to Leonid Brezhnev. His mood is so altered that Nixon tells them, "You know, girls, I think your cookies just saved the world from nuclear catastrophe."

Dan Hedaya's president looks a little like the real Nixon, and the match of the public persona is uncanny, as he complains to Henry Kissinger (Saul Rubinek) about his enemies, his insecurities, and his dog. He grows bitter as his administration collapses around him, eventually retreating to bourbon and recrimination, while even the faithful Arlene grows disenchanted ("You're prejudiced and you have a potty mouth").

Will the movie play for audiences who don't remember Watergate—for teenage Kirsten Dunst fans? I think so, because it contains all the information the audience really needs to know, although older viewers will enjoy the wealth of cross-references, as when the Plumbers offer Nixon menus of dirty tricks. *Dick* is a sly little comic treasure.

Dinosaur ★ ★ ★
PG, 84 m., 2000

Voices of: Alfre Woodard (Plio), Ossie Davis (Yar), Max Casella (Zini), Hayden Panettiere (Suri), D. B. Sweeney (Aladar), Samuel E. Wright (Kron), Peter Siragusa (Bruton), Julianna Margulies (Neera), Joan Plowright (Baylene), Della Reese (Eema). Directed by Ralph Zondag and Eric Leighton and produced by Pam Marsden. Screenplay by John Harrison and

Robert Nelson Jacobs, based on an original screenplay by Walon Green.

If a film had been made in the Jurassic age, it might have looked a lot like *Dinosaur*. The movie is startling in its impact. Against a backdrop of nature that is clearly real, we see dinosaurs that are scarcely less real. We feel the same sense of wonder that was stirred by *Jurassic Park*. These great beasts ruled the earth much longer than we have, their unlikely bodies sketched out in exaggerated Darwinian strokes.

The visual look of *Dinosaur* is a glimpse of wonders to come. The movie sends the message that computer animation is now sophisticated enough to mimic life itself in full motion, with such detail that the texture of reptilian skin seems as real as a photograph in *National Geographic*. The problem, as always, is to match the artistry with the technique.

The film opens with a little short story about an egg. The egg is first glimpsed in the nest of an iguanodon, which is fairly friendly looking, as dinosaurs go. Predators attack the parents and disturb the nest, and then the egg is snatched by a scampering little critter that runs away with it. There's a fight for possession, the egg drops into a stream, is swallowed and then disgorged by a river monster, is snatched up by a flying creature, and finally dropped from the sky to land in the habitat of lemurs.

Lemurs are, of course, about as cute as mammals can get. There were not any lemurs looking like this at the time of the dinosaurs, but never mind: The movie does a little overlapping of its eras to expand the cast, and to give the mammals in the audience a point of identification. The egg hatches, a mother lemur takes the baby iguanodon into its arms, and then . . . she speaks.

I can't tell you how disappointed I was to hear that voice. I guess I had forgotten that this movie wasn't going to be a reckless leap into the distant past, but a fairy tale in which the dinosaurs are human in all but outer form. They not only talk, they also have personalities, and they argue, plan, scheme, and philosophize, just like humans. They even have human values; when one of the leaders says it's going to be "survival of the fittest" on a long desert trek, he comes across as cold and

heartless. If there is one thing I think I know about dinosaurs, it's that sentimentality for the underdog played no part in their decision making.

I wonder why I was disturbed by the sound of dinosaurs with human voices. I know that cartoons can speak. I expect them to. When the dinosaurs spoke in *The Land Before Time*, that was fine with me. But *Dinosaur* looked so real that it didn't play like an animated film for me—it felt more like a nature documentary. There is a continuum reaching from Mickey Mouse to *Jurassic Park*, and at some point on that continuum the animals stop wisecracking and start eating one another. *Dinosaur* feels too evolved for cute dialogue.

Why are we as a species so determined to impose our behavior on creatures that are manifestly not human, and all the more wondrous for not being so? Why must we make the past more "accessible" by translating it into the terms of the present? At one point during the desert trek, simians climb aboard a dinosaur for a free ride, and it complains, "Just what I need—a monkey on my back." A dinosaur, even one that spoke English, would be unlikely to know what that line implied—and so will the kids in today's audience.

I don't know if Disney has a house rule about which animals can speak and which cannot, but guidelines seem to be emerging. The rule is, if you are a predatory carnivore, you don't talk, but if you are a pacifist, a vegetarian, or cute, you do. In *Tarzan* the apes spoke, but the leopards didn't. In *Dinosaur*, all of the creatures speak except for the vicious carnotaurs. A Faustian bargain seems to be at work: If you are an animal in a Disney picture, you can speak, but only if you are willing to sacrifice your essential nature.

All of this is of limited interest, I know, to the hordes clamoring to see this movie. Most younger kids probably assume that dinosaurs *can* speak, because they hear them speaking on TV every day. Even adults will probably not wonder if dinosaurs really roared. I enjoyed the movie as sheer visual spectacle, and I felt a certain awe at sequences like the meteor shower or the discovery of water beneath a parched lake bed. I was entertained, and yet I felt a little empty-handed at the end, as if an enormous effort had been spent on making these dinosaurs seem real, and then an even greater effort was spent on undermining the illusion.

The Dish ★ ★ ★ ½
PG-13, 101 m., 2001

Sam Neill (Cliff Buxton),Kevin Harrington (Ross "Mitch" Mitchell), Tom Long (Glenn Latham), Patrick Warburton (Al Burnett), Genevieve Mooy (May McIntyre), Tayler Kane (Rudi Kellerman), Bille Brown (Prime Minister), Roy Billing (Mayor Bob McIntyre), Eliza Szonert (Janine Kellerman), Lenka Kripac (Marie McIntyre). Directed by Rob Sitch and produced by Michael Hirsh, Santo Cilauro, Tom Gleisner, Jane Kennedy, and Sitch. Screenplay by Cilauro, Gleisner, Kennedy, and Sitch.

In a sheep pasture outside the little town of Parkes in New South Wales stands the pride and joy of Australian astronomy, a radio telescope the size of a football field. Most days it eavesdrops on the stars. In 1969, it gets a momentous assignment: Relaying the television signals from the Moon that will show Neil Armstrong's one small step for man, one giant leap for mankind.

Parkes is agog. This is the town's shining hour. *The Dish,* a smiling human comedy, treats the Moon walk not as an event 240,000 miles away, but as a small step taken by every single member of mankind, particularly those in Parkes. Resigned to thinking of themselves as provincials in a backwater, they're thrilled and a little humbled by their role on the world stage. True, NASA is relying on its primary telescope in Goldstone, California, and Parkes is only the backup—but still!

Mayor Bob McIntyre and his wife, Maisie (Roy Billing and Genevieve Mooy), nervously prepare for visits from the prime minister and the U.S. ambassador. Out at the telescope, Cliff Buxton (Sam Neill), the imperturbable, pipe-smoking scientist in charge of the telescope, steadies his team. There's Glenn (Tom Long), the soft-spoken mathematician, Mitch (Kevin Harrington), in charge of keeping the equipment humming, and Al (Patrick Warburton), the American observer from NASA, whose black horn-rims and foursquare demeanor make him seem like Clark Kent. Patrolling the

parameters of the site, prepared to repel foreign invaders and curious sheep, is Rudi the security guard (Tayler Kane), whose sister, Janine (Eliza Szonert), is in love with Mitch and effortlessly penetrates Rudi's defenses.

Since we all know Neil Armstrong and his shipmates returned safely from the Moon, *The Dish* can't develop suspense over the outcome of the mission. But it's a cliffhanger anyway, through the ingenious device of making the movie more about Parkes than about the Moon. The movie is "inspired by fact" (very loosely, I suspect), but who can remember if the historic TV signals were relayed by Parkes or Goldstone? Since we've met the locals in Parkes, we're as eager as they are to have it be them.

But it won't be simple. Director and cowriter Rob Sitch (whose *The Castle* is one of the funniest comedies of recent years) intercuts the drama of the approaching Moon walk with the drama of the momentous visit to Parkes by the prime minister and the ambassador. At the observatory, embarrassing technical problems pop up when the town blows a fuse. And at a crucial moment, high gusts of wind threaten to topple the telescope right over onto the sheep.

Sitch laces the Moon walk and the local plots together so effortlessly that it would be unfair to describe his plot developments. I will be vague, then, in mentioning the visit by the U.S. ambassador, who arrives at the telescope at a particularly delicate moment, but leaves satisfied that he has at least heard Neil Armstrong speaking from the Moon. There is also the inspired solution to another crisis, when Parkes "loses" the spacecraft after a power outage, and Glenn tries to find it with frantic mathematical calculations before the team hits upon a solution of stunning simplicity.

The Dish is rich in its supporting characters. I like the mayor's daughter Marie (Lenka Kripac), who has moved on from the sunny, idealistic 1960s and already embodies the sullen, resentful 1970s. I like the way Mayor Bob and his wife so cheerfully and totally dote on each other—and the way she tries to get him to use the upscale name "May" for her, when he's been calling her "Maisie" as long as he can remember. And the way Rudi the security guard is in fact the town's greatest security threat.

With *The Dish* and *The Castle,* Sitch and his producing partner Michael Hirsh have made enormously entertaining movies. Perhaps just as important, they've made good-hearted movies. Recent Hollywood comedy has tilted toward vulgarity, humiliation, and bathroom humor. Sometimes I laugh at them, even a lot; but I don't feel this good afterward. *The Dish* has affection for every one of its characters, forgives them their trespasses, understands their ambitions, doesn't mock them, and is very funny. It placed second for the People's Choice Award at the 2000 Toronto Film Festival—after *Crouching Tiger, Hidden Dragon.* That's about right.

Disney's The Kid ★ ★ ★
PG, 101 m., 2000

Bruce Willis (Russ Duritz), Spencer Breslin (Rusty Duritz), Emily Mortimer (Amy), Lily Tomlin (Janet), Jean Smart (Deirdre Lafever), Chi McBride (Kenny), Daniel Von Bargen (Sam Duritz), Dana Ivey (Dr. Alexander), Susan Dalian (Giselle). Directed by Jon Turteltaub and produced by Turteltaub, Christina Steinberg, and Hunt Lowry. Screenplay by Audrey Wells.

Bruce Willis is developing a nice little sideline, costarring with children in films with supernatural elements. After *The Sixth Sense* in the summer of 1999, here is *Disney's The Kid,* which (despite the Disney trademark in the title) is not really a kid's picture but aimed more or less at the *Sixth Sense* audience. It's a sweet film, unexpectedly involving, and shows again that Willis, so easily identified with action movies, is gifted in the areas of comedy and pathos: This is a cornball plot, and he lends it credibility just by being in it.

He plays Russ Duritz, a Los Angeles "image consultant" who needs a lot of consulting on his own image. He's rude, abrasive, dismissive, angry. Trapped next to a TV anchorwoman on a plane, he first tries to ignore her, then delivers a devastating critique of her hair, eyebrows, makeup, clothes, voice, and the horse she rode in on. In the office, he tyrannizes his assistant (Lily Tomlin), who survives only because of a tough, humorous shell.

Strange things begin to happen. If *The Sixth Sense* was about a kid who keeps seeing dead people, this one is about a guy who is dead in-side and keeps seeing a kid. A pudgy little kid, who leads him into a diner that later seems to have disappeared. The kid eventually allows himself to be cornered. They compare distinguishing characteristics, and Russ is forced to the amazing conclusion that this kid is *himself,* a few days before his own eighth birthday.

I don't know about you, but I would be able to recognize myself at eight without looking for scars and markings. Still, maybe Russ, so sleek and groomed, doesn't want to remember that he was once a pudgy little pushover. The kid, called Rusty (Spencer Breslin), is lovable and direct, and seems to know what's going on in a way old Russ doesn't. (Clue: The movie could have been called *Ebenezer Willis and the Ghost of Childhood Past.*) Together, the boy and the man share memories and revisit the scenes of childhood defeats, and the adult begins to understand why he is so cold to his father, to the world, and to himself.

The movie was directed by Jon Turteltaub *(While You Were Sleeping)* and written by Audrey Wells *(The Truth About Cats and Dogs),* and has that nice mixture of sentiment and comedy that both of those movies found. I like Rusty's attitude as he confronts the full horror of growing up. At one point, quizzing Russ about his life, he discovers that Russ doesn't even have a dog.

"No dog? I grow up to be a guy with no dog?"

Russ admits that he does.

"What do I do?" the kid asks.

"You're an image consultant," says the adult.

The kid takes inventory. "So . . . I'm forty, I'm not married, I don't fly jets, and I don't have a dog? I grow up to be a loser!"

The movie reveals more supernatural dimensions as it goes along. At first it appears to simply be about a visit from Russ's childhood self. Then, through shadowy mechanisms, the boy and man are able to revisit and even revise scenes from the past, and particularly a crucial playground fight involving a bully and a scheme to tie firecrackers around the neck of a three-legged dog named Tripod.

The movie's quick-fix psychology argues that Rusty grew up to be sour old Russ because he didn't stand up for his rights on the playground. This time, after Russ takes Rusty to train under a client who is a professional boxer, Rusty does a better job of defending himself, which does *not* simply change the future (as in *Back to the Future*), but more obscurely allows Russ to learn the same lesson at forty that Rusty now learns at eight.

The problem here is that this lesson is the same old macho John Wayne BS in which the secret of being a happy man is to learn to fight. That's the same lesson preached in *The Patriot*. Both movies dismiss the possibility that men can think and reason their way out of difficulty, and they teach that the answer lies in revenge, assisted by fighting skills. Both movies, otherwise so dissimilar, have plots that absolutely depend on these values. (*The Patriot*, to be fair, provides powerful motivation after a British monster kills one of the hero's sons and prepares to hang another, which is even worse than mistreating poor Tripod, although PETA might not think so.) When will a mainstream, big-budget, mass-market movie argue that one can use intelligence instead of violence to settle a dilemma? To quote John Wayne, "That'll be the day."

These observations aside, *Disney's The Kid* is warmhearted and effective, a sweet little parable that involves a man and a boy who help each other become a better boy and a better man (there are parallels, of course, with *Frequency*). I smiled a lot, laughed a few times, left feeling good about the movie. I am still mystified by the title. If Disney added the studio name to *The Kid* to avoid confusion with the 1921 Charlie Chaplin classic starring Jackie Coogan—well, I'm surprised they believe that many people remember it, and a little touched. ☞

Dogma ★ ★ ★ ½
R, 125 m., 1999

Ben Affleck (Bartleby), Matt Damon (Loki), Linda Fiorentino (Bethany), Salma Hayek (Serendipity), Jason Lee (Azrael), Alan Rickman (Metatron), Chris Rock (Rufus), Janeane Garofalo (Clinic Girl), George Carlin (Cardinal Glick), Jason Mewes (Jay), Kevin Smith (Silent Bob). Directed by Kevin Smith and produced by Scott Mosier. Screenplay by Smith.

Kevin Smith's *Dogma* grows out of an irreverent modern Catholic sensibility, a by-product of parochial schools, where the underlying faith is taken seriously but the visible church is fair game for kidding. For those raised in such traditions, it's no reach at all to imagine two fallen angels finding a loophole to get back into heaven. I can remember passionate debates during religion class about whether, if you missed your Easter duty, you could double back across the International Date Line and cover yourself.

Of course, the faith itself does not depend on temporal rules, and *Dogma* knows it. Catholicism, like all religions, is founded on deeper mysteries than whether you will go to hell if you eat meat on Friday. I am reminded of the wonderful play *Sister Mary Ignatius Explains It All for You*, in which a pre–Vatican II nun tries to cope with changes in church law; as I recall, her advice was to eat meat *once* on a Friday, to show you know the pope is right—and then never eat it again.

As someone who values his parochial school education and still gets into interminable debates about church teachings, I enjoyed *Dogma*'s approach, which takes church teaching jokingly and very seriously indeed—both at the same time. It reflects a mentality I'm familiar with. (For example, it's a sin to harbor an impure thought, but how many seconds counts as harboring?) I am also familiar with the types at William Donohue's small but loud Catholic League, which protested this film as blasphemous.

Every church has that crowd—the holier-than-thous who want to be your moral traffic cop; when they run meetings, they drive you crazy with Robert's Rules of Order. It's interesting that no official church spokesman has seconded them. You'd think the church might tell the league to stop embarrassing it, but no, that would be no better than the league attacking Smith. We are actually free in this country to disagree about religion, and blasphemy is not a crime.

What's more, I think a Catholic God might plausibly enjoy a movie like *Dogma*, or at least understand the human impulses that made it, as he made them. ("He's lonely—but he's funny," an angel says in the movie.) After all, it takes Catholic theology absolutely literally, and in such detail that non-Catholics may need to be issued catechisms on their way into the theater (not everybody knows what a plenary indulgence is). Sure, it contains a lot of four-letter words, because it has characters who use them as punctuation. But, hey, they're vulgarities, not blasphemies. Venial, not mortal. Sure, it has a flawed prophet who never gives up trying to get into the heroine's pants, but even Saint Augustine has been there, done that.

The story: Matt Damon and Ben Affleck play Loki and Bartleby, two angels cast out of heaven and exiled for all eternity in Wisconsin. They hear about a trendy bishop (George Carlin) who wants to give the church an upbeat new image. He's rededicating a cathedral in New Jersey in the image of Buddy Jesus, a Christ who blesses his followers with the A-OK sign. Anyone entering the cathedral will get a plenary indulgence (which means that if you are in a state of grace, all temporal punishment for sin is remitted, and you can enter directly into heaven). Bartleby and Loki see the loophole: Walk through the church doors, and they qualify again for heaven.

There is a problem with this plan (apart from the obvious one, which is that church rules govern men, not angels). The problem is explained by Metatron (Alan Rickman), an angel who appears inside a pillar of fire in the bedroom of Bethany (Linda Fiorentino). After she douses him with a fire extinguisher, he explains that if the angels reenter heaven, God will be proven fallible—and all existence will therefore end. He tells Bethany that she is the last surviving relative of Jesus on Earth, that two prophets will appear to her, and that she must follow them in order to stop the angels and save the universe.

Fiorentino is a laconic, edgy actress with an attitude. That makes her perfect for this role. In an earlier draft of Smith's screenplay, the character was a bimbo, but she's much better like this, grown-up and sardonic. It's fun to watch her handle the prophets, who turn out to be a couple of slacker mall rats (Jason Mewes and Smith himself). Later she meets Rufus, the thirteenth apostle (Chris Rock), who has a grievance about why he was left out of the New Testament.

If the film is less than perfect, it is because Smith is too much in love with his dialogue. Like George Bernard Shaw, he loves to involve his characters in long, witty conversations about matters of religion, sexuality, and politics. *Dogma* is one of those rare screenplays, like a Shaw playscript, that might actually read better than it plays; Smith is a gifted comic writer who loves paradox, rhetoric, and unexpected zingers from the blind side.

There is a long tradition that commercial American movies challenge conventional piety at great risk. For a long time, any movie dealing with religion had to be run past Hollywood's resident monsignors, ministers, and rabbis for approval (the habits of actual orders of nuns could not even be portrayed, which led to great ingenuity in the costume department). On the other hand, nobody has any problem with a movie that treats spiritual matters on the level of the supernatural. This has led to an emerging antireligion based on magic, ghosts, mediums, and other New Age voodoo. Talk shows allow "psychics" to answer your questions over the phone, but God forbid they would put on a clergyman to supply thoughtful spiritual advice. And if a movie dares to deal with what people actually believe, all hell, so to speak, breaks loose.

Kevin Smith has made a movie that reflects the spirit in which many Catholics regard their church. He has positioned his comedy on the balance line between theological rigidity and secular reality, which is where so many Catholics find themselves. He deals with eternal questions in terms of flawed characters who live now, today, in an imperfect world. Those whose approach to religion is spiritual will have little trouble with *Dogma,* because they will understand the characters as imperfect, sincere, clumsy seekers trying to do the right thing. Those who see religion more as a team, a club, a hobby, or a pressure group are upset. This movie takes theological matters out of the hands of "spokesmen" and entrusts it to—well, the unwashed. And goes so far as to suggest that God loves them. And is a Canadian. ☞

Double Jeopardy ★ ★ ½
R, 105 m., 1999

Tommy Lee Jones (Travis Lehman), Ashley Judd (Libby Parsons), Bruce Greenwood (Nick Parsons), Annabeth Gish (Angie), Roma Maffia (Margaret Skolowski), Davenia McFadden (Evelyn Lake). Directed by Bruce Beresford and produced by Leonard Goldberg. Screenplay by David Weisberg and Douglas S. Cook.

Some jerk sent me an e-mail revealing the secret of *Double Jeopardy.* It's a secret the movie's publicity is also at pains to reveal. I know it's an academic question, but I'll ask it anyway: Why go to the trouble of constructing a screenplay that conceals information if you reveal it in the ads? Once tipped off, are we expected to enjoy how the film tells us what we already know?

If through some miracle you have managed to avoid learning anything about *Double Jeopardy,* you might want to stop reading after my next sentence. This is the sentence, and it advises you: not a successful thriller but with some nice dramatic scenes along with the dumb mystery and contrived conclusion.

Now that the idealists have bailed out, the rest of us can consider *Double Jeopardy,* which stars Ashley Judd as a woman named Libby, who thinks she is happily married until, and I quote from the *first* sentence of the Paramount press release, she is "framed for the murder of her husband." This is, come to think of it, not such a surprise anyway, considering that Judd is pure-faced and clear-eyed, and her husband is played as a weasel. When they go sailing and the Coast Guard finds her in a blood-soaked nightgown on a blood-smeared deck with a knife in her hand, we make an intuitive leap that she isn't a slasher. (The movie's trailer provides a helpful hint: "Libby Parsons is in prison for a crime she didn't commit!")

The whole business of how she was framed, and how she tries to find her husband and regain custody of her child, is basically just red meat the director throws to the carnivores in the audience. You know and I know and anyone over the age of ten knows that the movie is not going to end without that kid back in Libby's arms, probably with some heartrending music.

What makes the film interesting isn't the story, but a prison sequence and a relationship.

Libby in prison is befriended by a couple of women prisoners who killed their husbands but are otherwise the salt of the earth. They create a nice dynamic. Not as realistic and evolved as Sigourney Weaver's startling jail scenes in *A Map of the World,* but not bad for a genre picture. One of the prisoners gives her an interesting piece of legal advice: Since she has already been tried and convicted for the murder of her husband, she cannot be tried for the same crime twice. Therefore, "You can walk right up to him in Times Square and pull the (I must have missed a word here) trigger and there's nothing anybody can do about it."

Caution, convicted killers: I am not sure this is sound legal advice. I believe the constitutional protection against double jeopardy has a couple of footnotes, and I urge you to seek legal advice before reopening fire. It's good enough for Libby, however, and when she gets out of prison she determines to find her betraying louse of an ex-husband and their child.

She's assigned to a halfway house, where her parole officer is a hard-bitten man of few and succinct words played by Tommy Lee Jones. And their scenes together are good ones. When she feeds him the same heartfelt lines that worked with the parole board, he barks, as only Tommy Lee Jones can bark, "I'm not interested in your contrition. I'm interested in your behavior. Get out of here and behave yourself."

How Jones and Judd find themselves underwater is a little unlikely, but so what. As you know from the ads, at one point she's handcuffed to a sinking car. At another point, a terrifying thing happens to her in a New Orleans cemetery. And there is a charity auction of society bachelors at which she makes some Hitchcockian moves. You may have to play the video at slo-mo to figure out how everything happens in the big climax, but by then the movie is basically just housekeeping anyway.

Double Jeopardy was directed by Bruce Beresford. He and Ashley Judd and Tommy Lee Jones have all been involved in wonderful films in the past—films that expand and inspire, like *Tender Mercies* and *Driving Miss Daisy* (Beresford), *Ruby in Paradise* and *Normal Life*

(Judd), and *The Executioner's Song* and *JFK* (Jones). This movie was made primarily in the hopes that it would gross millions and millions of dollars, which probably explains most of the things that are wrong with it.

Double Take ★
PG-13, 88 m., 2001

Orlando Jones (Daryl Chase), Eddie Griffin (Freddy Tiffany), Gary Grubbs (T. J. McCready), Daniel Roebuck (Agent Norville), Sterling Macer Jr. (Agent Gradney), Benny Nieves (Martinez), Garcelle Beauvais (Chloe Kent), Vivica A. Fox (Shari). Directed by George Gallo and produced by David Permut and Brett Ratner. Screenplay by Gallo, based on *Across the Bridge* by Graham Greene.

Double Take is the kind of double-triple-reverse movie that can drive you nuts because you can't count on *anything* in the plot. Characters, motivations, and true identities change from scene to scene at the whim of the screenplay. Finally, you weary of trying to follow the story. You can get the rug jerked out from under you only so many times before you realize the movie has the attention span of a gnat, and thinks you do too.

Orlando Jones stars as Daryl Chase, a businessman who becomes the dupe of a street hustler named Freddy Tiffany (Eddie Griffin). The movie opens with Daryl as the victim of a complicated briefcase-theft scam, which turns out not to be what it seems, and to involve more people than it appears to involve. Freddy is at the center of it, and Daryl soon learns that Freddy will be at the center of everything in his life for the rest of the movie.

Who is this guy? He seems to have an almost supernatural ability to materialize anywhere, to know Daryl's secret plans, to pop up like a genie, and to embarrass him with a jive-talking routine that seems recycled out of the black exploitation pictures of the 1970s. The movie's attitudes seem so dated, indeed, that when I saw a computer screen, it came as a shock: The movie's period feels as much pre-desktop as it does pretaste.

Freddy embarrasses Daryl a few more times, including during a fashion show, where he appears on the runway and shoulders aside the models. Meanwhile, Daryl discovers he is under attack by mysterious forces, for reasons he cannot understand, and to his surprise Freddy turns out to be an ally. The obnoxious little sprite even helps him out of a dangerous spot in a train station by changing clothes with him, after which the two men find themselves in the dining car of a train headed for Mexico. The switch in wardrobe of course inspires a switch in personalities: Freddy orders from the menu in a gourmet-snob accent, while Daryl is magically transformed into a ghetto caricature who embarrasses the waiter by demanding Schlitz Malt Liquor.

And so on. Wardrobes, identities, motivations, and rationales are exchanged in a dizzying series of laboriously devised "surprises," until we find out that nothing is as it seems, and that isn't as it seems, either. It's not that we expect a movie like this to be consistent or make sense. It's that when the double-reverse plotting kicks in, we want it to be funny, or entertaining, or anything but dreary and arbitrary and frustrating.

The movie was directed by George Gallo, who wrote the much better *Midnight Run* and here again has latched onto the idea of a nice guy and an obnoxious one involved in a road trip together. One of his problems is with Eddie Griffin. Here is a fast-thinking, fast-talking, nimble actor who no doubt has good performances in him, but his Freddy Tiffany is unbearable—so obnoxious he approaches the fingernails-on-a-blackboard category. You know you're in trouble when your heart sinks every time a movie's live wire appears on the screen. I realized there was no hope for the movie, because the plot and characters had alienated me beyond repair. If an audience is going to be entertained by a film, first they have to be able to stand it.

Doug's 1st Movie ★ ½
G, 77 m., 1999

Directed by Maurice Joyce and produced by Jim Jinkins, David Campbell, Melanie Grisanti, and Jack Spillum. Screenplay by Ken Scarborough. With the voices of: Thomas McHugh (Doug Funnie, Lincoln), Fred Newman (Skeeter Valentine, Mr. Dink, Porkchop, Ned), Constance Shulman (Patti Mayonnaise), Chris Phillips

(Roger Koltz, Boomer, Larry, Mr. Chiminy), Gay Hadley (Guy Graham), Doug Preis (Bill Bluff, Doug's Dad, Secret Agent).

Doug's 1st Movie is a thin and less-than-thrilling feature-length version of a Saturday morning animated series, unseen by me. Chatter on the Web suggests it was originally intended to go straight to video, but was rechanneled into theaters after the startling success of *The Rugrats Movie*. Since Doug originally started on Nickelodeon, where *Rugrats* resides, the decision made sense—or would have if this had been a better movie.

The plot: Skeeter, the best pal of twelve-year-old Doug, finds a polluted pond and is about to take a photo when a nasty trick is played on him by some schoolmates who pretend to be a monster. Then a real monster emerges from the waters behind him.

This creature, which serves as proof that the lake is polluted, is actually such a nice monster that it argues for, not against, pollution. It borrows the name Herman Melville from the cover of the book it's reading *(Moby-Dick)*, and becomes a secret friend of Doug and Skeeter's, in *E.T.* fashion.

The plot thickens: The lake is being polluted by the evil Bill Bluff, a local industrialist. Bluff's spy at the school is Guy Graham, editor of the school paper. Guy is also Doug's rival for the love of Patti Mayonnaise, whom Doug wants to take to the prom. Patti grows convinced that Doug is cheating on her with an exchange student, who is actually the monster in drag.

Meanwhile . . . but is the plot of any importance? I think not. It is the vehicle for some fairly routine animation, and characters who may inspire Saturday morning TV watchers but left me indifferent. They have a kind of joy in stupidity. I did like one sequence in the film, involving the ultimate in virtual reality: a VR experience in which everything is exactly as it is in real life, except more expensive.

Will kids like this movie? Who can say? *Rugrats* it ain't.

Down to Earth ★

PG-13, 87 m., 2001

Chris Rock (Lance Barton), Regina King (Suntee), Mark Addy (Cisco), Eugene Levy (Keyes), Frankie Faison (Whitney), Jennifer Coolidge (Mrs. Wellington), Greg Germann (Sklar), Chazz Palminteri (Mr. King). Directed by Chris Weitz and Paul Weitz and produced by Sean Daniel, James Jacks, and Michael Rotenberg. Screenplay by Elaine May, Warren Beatty, Chris Rock, Lance Crouther, Ali LeRoi, and Louis C.K.

Down to Earth is an astonishingly bad movie, and the most astonishing thing about it comes in the credits: "Written by Elaine May, Warren Beatty, Chris Rock, Lance Crouther, Ali LeRoi, and Louis C.K." These are credits that deserve a place in the Writer's Hall of Fame, right next to the 1929 version of *The Taming of the Shrew* ("screenplay by William Shakespeare, with additional dialogue by Sam Taylor").

Yes, Chris Rock and his writing partners have adapted Elaine May's Oscar-nominated 1978 screenplay for *Heaven Can Wait* (Warren Beatty falls more in the Sam Taylor category). It wasn't broke, but boy, do they fix it.

The premise: Lance Barton (Rock) is a lousy stand-up comic, booed off the stage during an amateur night at the Apollo Theater. Even his faithful manager, Whitney (Frankie Faison), despairs for him. Disaster strikes. Lance is flattened by a truck, goes to heaven, and discovers from his attending angel (Eugene Levy) that an error has been made. He was taken before his time. There is a meeting with God, a.k.a. "Mr. King" (Chazz Palminteri), who agrees to send him back to Earth for the unexpired portion of his stay.

The catch is, only one body is available: Mr. Wellington, an old white millionaire. Lance takes what he can get and returns to Earth, where he finds a sticky situation: His sexpot wife (Jennifer Coolidge) is having an affair with his assistant, who is stealing his money. Meanwhile, Lance, from his vantage point inside Mr. Wellington, falls in love with a young African-American beauty named Suntee (Regina King).

Let's draw to a halt and consider the situation as it now stands. The world sees an old white millionaire. So does Suntee, who has disliked him up until the point where Lance occupies the body. But we in the audience see Chris Rock. Of course, Rock and Regina King make an agreeable couple, but we have to keep reminding ourselves he's a geezer, and so does she, I guess, since soon they are holding hands and other parts.

The essential comic element here, I think, is the disparity between the two lovers, and the underlying truth that they are actually a good match. Wouldn't that be funnier if Mr. Wellington looked like . . . Mr. Wellington? He could be played by Martin Landau, although, come to think of it, Martin Landau played an old white millionaire who got involved with Halle Berry and Troy Beyer in *B.A.P.S.* (1997), and don't run out to Blockbuster for *that* one.

The real problem with Mr. Wellington being played by an old white guy, even though he is an old white guy, is that the movie stars Chris Rock, who is getting the big bucks, and Chris Rock fans do not want to watch Martin Landau oscillating with Regina King no matter *who* is inside him. That means that in the world of the movie everyone sees an old white guy, but we have, like, these magic glasses, I guess, that allow us to see Chris Rock. Well, once or twice we sort of catch a glimpse of the millionaire, in reflections and things, but nothing is done with this promising possibility.

The story then involves plots against and by Mr. Wellington, plus Lance's scheming to get a better replacement body, plus Suntee being required to fly in the face of emotional logic and then fly back again, having been issued an emotional round-trip ticket. If I were an actor, I would make a resolution to turn down all parts in which I fall in and out of love at a moment's notice, without logical reason, purely for the convenience of the plot.

Chris Rock is funny and talented, and so I have said several times. I even proposed him as emcee for the Academy Awards (they went for an old white millionaire). This project must have looked promising, since the directors are the Weitz brothers, Chris and Paul Weitz, fresh from *American Pie*. But the movie is dead in the water.

Dr. Akagi ★ ★ ★
NO MPAA RATING, 128 m., 1999

Akira Emoto (Dr. Akagi), Kumiko Aso (Sonoko), Jyuro Kara (Umemoto), Jacques Gamblin (Piet), Masanori Sera (Toriumi). Directed by Shohei Imamura and produced by Hisa Ino and Koji Matsuda. Screenplay by Imamura and Daisuke Tengan.

Dr. Akagi is the kind of family doctor that Spencer Tracy might have played in a 1940s Hollywood film—if Hollywood doctors in those days had lived with prostitutes, befriended morphine addicts, sheltered escaped prisoners of war, and dug up bodies to remove their livers. But I make him sound like a wild man, and in fact he is a gentle, driven soul—more an absentminded professor than a mad scientist.

The doctor (Akira Emoto) is the subject of the new film by Shohei Imamura, the Japanese director who makes films along the fault line between everyday life and outlaw human behavior. "I am interested in the relationship between the lower part of the human body and the lower part of the social structure," he has said. His previous film, *The Eel*, which won the Palme d'Or at the 1997 Cannes festival, was about a wife-murderer who is released from prison and sets up a barbershop in a remote area. Now here is *Dr. Akagi*, set during the last days of World War II.

Because of the war, its hero is the only family doctor for miles around, and in the first shot we see him running to a bedside. "Being a family doctor is all legs," he says. He is known locally as "Dr. Liver," because his diagnosis is invariably the same: hepatitis, treated with an injection of glucose. Sometimes he doubles as a social worker, as when a mother moans to him that her son, a respectable clerk at city hall, has taken up with a prostitute. He is not much shocked, not even when he finds the clerk has embezzled funds to pay the woman. Her name is Sonoko (Kumiko Aso) and she eventually falls in love with Dr. Akagi. How much in love? She was raised in a red-light district, where her mother lectured her, "No freebies!" But for Akagi, it's free—or would be, if he didn't reject her enthusiastic assaults.

He's too busy. He has a theory about why

hepatitis cases are spreading so quickly, and experiments with new kinds of microscopes, borrowing an arc lamp from a movie projector to see the little microbes more clearly. Sonoko, peering over his shoulder, asks if there are male and female bacteria, and is shocked to learn there are not: "You mean there is no prostitution in nature?" She moves in and becomes the doctor's housekeeper. His laboratory assistant is another doctor, addicted to drugs. An oddly secular monk joins the household. When a Dutch POW escapes from a torture chamber, Akagi takes him in, too, treating his wounds and letting him help with the research.

Imamura's work reflects on Japanese life as it has changed in his lifetime (he is seventy-two). His best film is *Vengeance Is Mine* (1979), based on the true story of a serial killer who travels the countryside, hunted and hunting. In 1989, he made *Black Rain,* about the aftermath of radioactive fallout in a village near Hiroshima. I will never forget his famous *Ballad of Narayama,* the 1983 Cannes grand prize winner, based on a Japanese legend about a village that takes its old people up onto the mountain to die when they outlive their usefulness.

Dr. Akagi is more matter-of-fact. It is about a busy middle-aged man who treats all manner of illness, physical and mental, while obsessing over hepatitis. At one point he literally does dig up a corpse to dissect a fresh liver (the mourners find it curious that the doctor specifies the abdomen be kept iced after death). There is a war going on all during the movie, and indeed Akagi's son dies, but daily life in the village bumbles along, punctuated only by air raids and announcements of smaller rice rations.

Imamura allows himself poetic touches, sparingly. When the telegram arrives telling Akagi that his son is dead, he shreds it into tiny pieces and throws it into the air; countless more little paper scraps float down like snow, a reminder of how many telegrams the war has inspired. And at the end, Akagi and the former prostitute are out in a boat when an atomic bomb falls. He looks at the mushroom cloud and observes that it resembles a hypertrophied liver.

Dr. Dolittle 2 ★ ★ ★
PG, 88 m., 2001

Eddie Murphy (Dr. John Dolittle), Jeffrey Jones (Joseph Potter), Kevin Pollak (Jack Riley), Steve Irwin (Himself), Kyla Pratt (Maya Dolittle), Raven-Symone (Charisse Dolittle), Kristen Wilson (Lisa Dolittle). With the voices of: Norm Macdonald (Lucky), Lisa Kudrow (Ava), Steve Zahn (Archie), and Molly Shannon. Directed by Steve Carr and produced by John Davis and Joseph Singer. Screenplay by Larry Levin, based on the stories of Hugh Lofting.

Dr. Dolittle 2 is a cute, crude, and good-hearted movie about a doctor who can talk to the animals—and listen, too, often to them loudly passing gas. It combines the charm of the 1998 movie with the current Hollywood obsession with intestinal tracts, resulting in a movie that kids, with their intense interest in digestive details, may find fascinating.

Eddie Murphy stars as a famous veterinarian who now runs his own animal clinic (complete with twelve-step therapy groups for ownerless dogs). His home life is almost more demanding than his work: His daughter Charisse (Raven-Symone) is sixteen and starting to date, and his wife (Kristen Wilson) is remarkably patient with a house full of pets and a yard full of animals, including a raccoon who comes to summon the doctor to an emergency.

The crisis: A forest is about to be leveled by a plump, sneering enemy of the ecology (Jeffrey Jones), and the animals, led by a Godfather-style beaver, hope Dolittle can help. The forester is represented by a slick attorney (Kevin Pollack), and Dolittle recruits his lawyer wife to defend his case in court.

Much depends on the fact that the land is the habitat of a female bear, member of a protected species. But since she can't reproduce all by herself, the villain's lawyer argues, what's the use of preserving her habitat? Dolittle, thinking fast, recruits a male performing bear from a circus. Can the bear be persuaded to perform those functions that a male bear in the wild does naturally? When the bear proves shy, Dolittle turns into an animal sex counselor.

All of this is helped immeasurably by the doctor's ability to speak to the animals (who all speak the same language—English, curiously enough). There are no nasty animals in the movie, except for a crocodile who does his dirty work just offscreen, and the bear is so accommodating he actually visits Dolittle in a rustic restaurant, enters the toilet, and seems familiar with the function, if not the limitations, of a toilet seat. The bear, in fact, is one of the funniest elements in the movie; it is about as happy to be in the forest as Woody Allen would be.

There's also a sequence, perhaps inspired by a scene in *The Edge,* where the bear creeps out onto a precariously balanced log to try to grab some honey and prove himself a man, or bear. Will the bear master the intricacies of the reproductive process? Will Dr. and Mrs. Dolittle accept a measly compromise offer of ten acres? The story takes an unexpected twist when the animals of the world go on strike and shut down Sea World.

Dr. Dolittle 2 is not the kind of movie that rewards deep study, and it's an easy assignment for Murphy, whose work in the *Nutty Professor* movies is much more versatile (and funnier). As the PG rating suggests, this is a movie aimed at younger audiences, who are likely to enjoy the cute animals, the simple plot, the broad humor, and Dolittle's amazingly detailed explanation (to the bear) of how a bear's elimination system shuts itself down during hibernation.

The Dreamlife of Angels ★ ★ ★ ½
R, 113 m., 1999

Elodie Bouchez (Isa), Natacha Regnier (Marie), Gregoire Colin (Chris), Jo Prestia (Fredo), Patrick Mercado (Charly). Directed by Erick Zonca and produced by Francois Marquis. Screenplay by Zonca and Roger Bohbot.

The French believe that most of the characters in American movies, no matter what their ages, act like teenagers. I believe that the teenagers in most French movies seem old, wise, and sad. There is a lesson here, perhaps that most American movies are about plots, and most French movies are about people.

The Dreamlife of Angels serves as an example. It is about two twenty-year-olds who are already marked by the hard edges of life. They meet, they become friends, and then they find themselves pulled apart by sexuality, which one of them sees as a way to escape a lifetime of hourly wages. This is a movie about a world where young people have to work for a living. Most twenty-year-old Americans in the movies receive invisible monthly support payments from God.

We meet Isa (Elodie Bouchez), a tough little nut with a scar over one eye and a gift of gab. She's a backpacker who cuts photos out of magazines, pastes them to cardboard squares, and peddles them in bars as "tourist views." She doesn't really expect to support herself that way, but it's a device to strike up conversations, and sure enough she meets a guy who offers her a job—as a seamstress in a sweatshop.

At work, she meets Marie (Natacha Regnier). The two women become friends, and Isa moves in with Marie. They hang out in malls and on the streets, smoking, kidding, playing at picking up guys. They aren't hookers; that would take a degree of calculation and planning ability that they lack—and, besides, they still dream of true romance. Isa tells Marie about one guy she met when she was part of a remodeling crew working on his house. They slept together, but when the job was over, she left, and he let her leave. She wonders if maybe she missed a good chance. Unlikely, Marie advises.

Marie steals a jacket and is seen by Chris (Gregoire Colin). He owns a club, and asks them to drop in one night. They already know the bouncers, and Marie has slept with one of them. Soon it comes down to this: Chris has money, Marie has none, and although her friendship with Isa is the most important relationship in her life, she is willing to abandon it in order to share Chris's bed and wealth. Isa, who in the beginning looked like a mental lightweight, has the wisdom and insight to see how this choice will eventually hurt Marie. But Marie will not listen.

The movie understands what few American movies admit: Not everyone can afford the luxury of following their hearts. Marie has already lost the idealism that would let her choose the bouncer (whom she likes) rather than the owner (whom she likes too, but not for the same reasons). The story is played out against the backdrop of Lille, not the first

French city you think of when you think of romance. In this movie it is a city of gray streets and tired people, and there is some kind of symbolism in the fact that Marie is house-sitting her apartment for a girl in a coma.

The movie was directed and cowritten by Erick Zonca, a forty-three-year-old Parisian who lived in New York from the age of twenty, worked at odd jobs for ten years, then became the director of TV commercials. He returned to France to make his features; this is his third. He creates an easy familiarity with Isa and Marie. The story is about their conversation, their haphazard progress from day to day; it doesn't have contrived plot points.

I can't easily imagine Isa and Marie in Los Angeles, nor can I imagine an American indie director making this film, which contains no guy-talk in diners, no topless clubs, no drug dealers in bathrobes, no cigars. This year's Critics Week at Cannes has just announced that it was unable to find a single American film it admired enough to program. *The Dreamlife of Angels* shared the Best Actress Award between Bouchez and Regnier last year in the Cannes main competition. There you have it.

Drive Me Crazy ★ ★ ½
PG-13, 94 m., 1999

Melissa Joan Hart (Nicole Maris), Adrian Grenier (Chase Hammond), Stephen Collins (Mr. Maris), Susan May Pratt (Alicia), Mark Webber (Dave), Kris Park (Ray Neeley), Gabriel Carpenter (Brad), Lourdes Benedicto (Chloe Frost). Directed by John Schultz and produced by Amy Robinson. Screenplay by Rob Thomas.

Drive Me Crazy is maybe the eighth movie of 1999 to hinge on a date to the big high school dance. The basic plot has three variations: (1) Will the heroine go with the guy she really likes? (2) Will the guy have sex for the first time? and (3) Will anyone be killed by a mad slasher? Like the Sammy Sosa of movie critics, I will clear the bases by giving away all three endings at once: The answer is always "yes."

What distinguishes *Drive Me Crazy* from your average prom movie is that the characters are more intelligent, and have dialogue written with a certain wit and insight. They're not the victims of the plot but its controllers, consciously taking charge of events. And here's a switch: None of them believes the world will end if they go to the dance with the wrong person. The movie is about kids who are as smart as real high school students, while most prom movies have characters who are no smarter than their parents.

The movie stars Melissa Joan Hart, who is "Sabrina, the Teenage Witch" on TV but here comes across perky and wholesome, a Doris Day for our time. She's Nicole, the chairman not of the prom but of the big high school Centennial Dance. She wants to go to the dance with a basketball star, but he strays out of her grasp. Then her thoughtful eye falls on her next-door neighbor, Chase (Adrian Grenier), who has just been dumped by a brunette vixen. He's a member of the outsider crowd at high school, given to commenting on the "fascist nature of pep rallies," but she takes him to the Gap, gets him a haircut, and he cleans up well. By pretending to be dating, they can both save face. Nicole and Chase are obviously right for one another, but have to make that discovery slowly, through many difficulties, including heartrending misunderstandings when she sees him kissing the bad girl. You know the drill.

There are some serious notes. His mom died a few years ago, and that led to tension between Chase and Nicole when they were in junior high—tension she analyzes in a scene not only touching but, for some audience members, probably helpful. Her parents are divorced, and her dad is the kind of guy who turns up unpredictably and stages father-daughter moments in which he takes her up in a hot-air balloon and hands her *Zen and the Art of Motorcycle Maintenance,* suggesting it might help her understand him. She throws it overboard. I felt like cheering.

Drive Me Crazy is slight and sweet, not a great high school movie but kinda nice, with appealing performances by Hart and Grenier. I remember him with respect from *The Adventures of Sebastian Cole,* in which his stepfather wanted to have a sex change. That was a much better movie, which suffered because audiences are shy about stories that take more than a sentence to summarize.

Despite my affection, I can't quite recommend *Drive Me Crazy*. The good stuff needs more energy behind it. John Schultz's direction is lackadaisical. Scenes arrive without feeling necessary. Plot points are belabored. These characters deserve a quicker pace; sometimes they feel ahead of the movie. Still, there's this: Although *Drive Me Crazy* is indeed based on one of the three basic prom plots, it isn't based on the other two.

Driven ★ ★ ½
PG-13, 109 m., 2001

Sylvester Stallone (Joe Tanto), Til Schweiger (Beau Brandenburg), Kip Pardue (Jimmy Bly), Burt Reynolds (Carl Henry), Estella Warren (Sophia Simone), Cristian de la Fuente (Memo Moreno), Gina Gershon (Cathy Moreno), Robert Sean Leonard (DeMille Bly), Stacy Edwards (Lucretia "Luc" Jones). Directed by Renny Harlin and produced by Elie Samaha, Sylvester Stallone, and Harlin. Screenplay by Stallone, based on a story by Stallone and Harlin.

Whether they admit it or not, many fans go to auto races to see crashes, and they'll see a lot of them in *Driven*. Cars slam into walls, tumble upside down, come apart in midair, land in water, explode in flames, fall on top of other cars and disintegrate. So serious are these crashes that one of the movie's heroes injures his ankle. No one is killed, I guess. There is a horrible multicar pileup in the final race, but it serves only to clear the field for the movie's stars and is never referred to again.

Most of the crashes are apparently done with special effects, and there are subtle moments when you can tell that: A car in midair will jerk into split-second freeze-frames, or pieces of sheet metal will fly toward us more slowly than in real life. But we get our money's worth; the races consist of quick cutting between long shots of real races, close-ups of narrowed eyes behind face masks, close-ups of feet pushing the pedal to the metal, POV shots of the track (sometimes in a blur or haze), the crashes, and the finish lines.

Director Renny Harlin, an expert at action, has made better pictures (*Die Hard 2*, *Cutthroat Island*), but delivers the goods here and adds a wall-to-wall music track that pumps up the volume. He cuts almost as quickly in the dialogue scenes; his camera, often handheld, circles the actors and sometimes he cuts after every line of dialogue. The music continues. *Driven* is a movie by, for, and about the attention deficit disordered.

Sylvester Stallone stars and wrote the screenplay, which was originally inspired by his desire to make a biopic about the Brazilian racing great Ayrtan Senna, who was killed in 1994. The first drafts may have contained bio, but the final draft is all pic, and the characters are off the shelf. Stallone plays a hotshot retired driver whose comeback problems are quickly dealt with ("What about the fear?" "The fear is gone"). Burt Reynolds is the wheelchair-bound owner of a racing team. Til Schweiger plays the defending champion from Germany. Kip Pardue plays a rookie phenom, in a role once penciled in for Leonardo DiCaprio. And Robert Sean Leonard is the phenom's brother, required to utter the thankless dialogue: "I saw this eight-year-old goofy-looking kid on a go-kart come from three laps behind to beat kids twice his age." Think about that. Three laps on a go-kart track. At Captain Mike's Go-Kart Track in Sawyer, Michigan, where I practice the sport, you don't even get enough time to *fall* that far behind.

The movie is rated PG-13, and so the women, like the drivers, have to act with their eyes, lips, and shoulders. The gorgeous Canadian supermodel Estella Warren plays Sophia, who is dumped by the champ, dates the rookie, and is taken back by the champ. She has lips that could cushion a nasty fall and swimmer's shoulders that look great except in that off-the-shoulder dress that makes them look wider than Stallone's. Gina Gershon plays the mean girl who used to date Stallone and dumped him for another driver ("He's a younger, better you," she explains). Gershon has sexy lips too, but goes for sneers, pouts, and curls—she's doing a self-satire. Then there's a journalist played by Stacy Edwards who will follow the team for the season. "She's doing an exposé on male dominance in sports," explains Reynolds, only smiling a little, as if to himself, at this line.

It's tough to fit all these relationships in between the races, but Harlin uses an interesting device. Not only does Reynolds communicate with his team members by headset, but so do the girls; there are times when three people are shouting advice at a guy doing 195 miles per hour. The Edwards character nevertheless disappears so inexplicably from the story (apart from reaction shots) that when she's there at the end, Stallone (who has been holding hands with her) says, "Glad you stuck around."

The movie is so filled with action that dramatic conflict would be more than we could handle, so all of the characters are nice. There are no villains. There is a shoving match over the girl, but no real fights, and afterward a character actually apologizes.

One of the action sequences is noteworthy. The phenom, mad at the girl, steals a race car from an auto show in Chicago and hits 195 miles per hour through the Chicago Loop with Stallone chasing him in another race car. Although this high-speed chase is tracked by helicopters, so inefficient are the Chicago police that after the kid pulls over, Stallone has time to give him the first trophy he ever won *and* deliver a lecture about faith and will—and *still* we don't even hear any sirens in the background from the Chicago police—perhaps because, as students of geography will observe, the two characters are now in Toronto.

I mentioned that all of the characters are nice (except for Gershon, who sticks to bitchiness in a stubborn show of integrity). The feel-good ending is a masterpiece even in a season where no audience can be allowed to exit without reassurance. There's an endless happy-happy closing montage at a victory celebration, with hugs and champagne, and all the characters smile at all the other characters, and outstanding disagreements are resolved with significant little nods. ☞

Drop Dead Gorgeous ★ ★
PG-13, 97 m., 1999

Kirstie Alley (Gladys Leeman), Ellen Barkin (Annette), Kirsten Dunst (Amber), Denise Richards (Becky), Brittany Murphy (Lisa Swenson), Allison Janney (Loretta), Will Sasso (Hank Vilmes), Amy Adams (Leslie Miller). Directed by Michael Patrick Jann and produced by Gavin Polone and Judy Hofflund. Screenplay by Lona Williams.

Sometimes I wonder how anyone could have thought a screenplay was funny enough to film. The script for *Drop Dead Gorgeous*, on the other hand, must have been a funny read. It's the movie that somehow never achieves takeoff speed. Subtle miscalculations of production and performance are probably responsible; comedy is a fragile rose, eager to wilt.

The movie takes place in Mount Rose, Minnesota, a setting created after long study of *Fargo*. The fiftieth anniversary of the Miss Teen Princess America contest is approaching, and the local chairwoman is former winner Gladys Leeman (Kirstie Alley), whose daughter Becky (Denise Richards) is a leading contender. Her big competition: trailer-park cutie Amber (Kirsten Dunst), whose alcoholic mother, Annette (Ellen Barkin), is burned in a fire and spends much of the movie with a beer can permanently fused to the flesh of her hand.

Now there's an example of how a mental image can be funnier than a real one—how a screenplay can fail to translate. You possibly smiled as you read about Annette's hand being fused to a beer can. I did as I wrote the words. But the image of the charred can embedded in scarred flesh is not funny, and every time it turns up it casts its little pall.

Another example. One of the contestants has put herself on a four-hundred-calorie-a-day diet and is a patient at a recovery center for anorexics. Nevertheless, she's determined to compete in the pageant, and arrives onstage in a wheelchair. Funny as a satirical concept? Yes. Funny as a sight? No, because the concept, not the image, contains the joke.

The movie was written by Lona Williams, who is herself a beauty pageant survivor. She understands the backstage politics of such events, especially at the local level, where almost everyone has a buried agenda. Some of the mothers are using their daughters as surrogate reminders of their own faded beauty. Some of the daughters are compensating for insecurity;

they think a crown will affirm their worth. Other daughters are resentful puppets. Some of the older men enjoy the proximity to nubile contestants. Some of the women may too.

I sometimes wonder if anybody involved in beauty pageants at the administrative level is completely without motivations they would rather not discuss. The idea of devoting your life to running an event at which young women are judged on the basis of their beauty and personality—as evaluated in a game show format—gets creepier the more you think about it.

As the title of *Drop Dead Gorgeous* suggests, some of the characters turn up dead or injured. The ferocious intensity of the parents is a reminder of *The Positively True Adventures of the Alleged Texas Cheerleader-Murdering Mom,* a made-for-cable movie that's one of the great buried comic treasures of recent years, with a Holly Hunter performance that would have been Oscar material if the movie had opened in theaters. Both films are savage, but *Cheerleader-Murdering Mom* was rich in human nature, while *Drop Dead Gorgeous* simply manipulates the ideas of satire without connecting to the underlying truth. I believed the Holly Hunter character would do what she did for the reasons she had; I felt the Kirstie Alley character was generated by a screenplay.

There is, however, a lot of funny stuff in *Drop Dead Gorgeous,* and Lona Williams has a future as a comedy writer—maybe in the Dave Barry/Molly Ivins tradition, since her ideas seem more literary than cinematic. I liked the idea of a contestant's dramatic reading being from *Soylent Green.* And the way another contestant kills two birds with one stone in the talent section of the contest by singing "I Love You, Baby" to Jesus. The notion that Mount Rose is famous as the "home of the oldest living Lutheran" (recently deceased) is worthy of Garrison Keillor's Lake Wobegon.

The attempt to link Lutherans with gun nuts is less successful; Becky belongs to the Lutheran Sisterhood Gun Club, but this doesn't ring true because, well, it doesn't fit with the general notion of Lutherans as pretty peaceable folks. For satire to work, it has to contain a kernel of truth. What made *Fargo* brilliant was the way it combined satire with affection and accuracy.

The climax of *Drop Dead Gorgeous* contains a few cheerfully disgusting scenes that qualify it to open in this Summer of Raunch. But once again, the ideas are funnier than the images. Contestants get food poisoning during their trip to the finals, and vomit into the atrium lobby of the host hotel. Funny to read about? You bet. To see? Judge for yourself.

Drowning Mona ★ ★
PG-13, 91 m., 2000

Danny DeVito (Chief Rash), Bette Midler (Mona Dearly), Neve Campbell (Ellen), Jamie Lee Curtis (Rona), Casey Affleck (Bobby), William Fichtner (Phil Dearly), Marcus Thomas (Jeff Dearly), Kathleen Wilhoite (Lucinda), Peter Dobson (Feege). Directed by Nick Gomez and produced by Al Corley, Bart Rosenblatt, and Eugene Musso. Screenplay by Peter Steinfeld.

Everyone in Verplanck, New York, drives a Yugo. An older Yugo, since the car hasn't been manufactured since its country went out of business. We learn that Verplanck was selected as a test market when the Yugo was being introduced to the United States. That explains why everyone was driving them then. After we meet the local residents, we understand why they're driving them now: They can't afford to replace them.

As the movie opens, a local woman named Mona Dearly (Bette Midler) speeds down a country road and directly into the Hudson River when her brakes fail. It is a measure of the local intelligence that when the car and driver are dragged to shore some hours later, the doctor checks her pulse. "She's dead," he confirms to Chief Rash (Danny DeVito), who nods grimly and begins a murder investigation.

Lucinda (Kathleen Wilhoite), the local garage mechanic, checks out the death vehicle and confirms his suspicions: The car was rigged. All four brake drums were tampered with, the brake fluid was drained, and the perp also drained some other fluids just to be on the safe side. Now Rash has to decide who killed Mona Dearly.

Almost everyone in town is a suspect. As played in flashbacks by Midler, Mona is a ferocious harridan who may have hacked off her own son's hand just because he was trying to snatch her beer. There are, to be fair, other theories about how Jeff (Marcus Thomas) lost his hand, although in every scenario he was reaching for a beer. Jeff might have wanted to kill her. Or perhaps the murderer was her husband, Phil (William Fichtner), who is having an affair with Rona (Jamie Lee Curtis), a waitress at the local diner (who is also having an affair with Jeff, so maybe she killed Mona just because she was tired of hearing about her from both men).

Or maybe Bobby (Casey Affleck), Jeff's landscaping partner, killed her to save the embarrassment of having her create a scene at his wedding to Ellen (Neve Campbell), Chief Rash's daughter. The possibility upsets Ellen, who explains, in some of the movie's best dialogue: "I can't marry a murderer. That's not who I am. That's not what I'm about."

It helps to understand that everyone in Verplanck is dim to one degree or another, except for the Rash family. The chief is not rash, but fairly levelheaded as he patiently sorts his way through a case that seems to reduce itself to a series of bar fights dimly remembered by drunks. No one in the movie is particularly vicious (well, Jeff's no prize), and the urgency of the case is undermined by the general agreement that Verplanck is calmer and happier now that Mona's gone.

The movie was directed by Nick Gomez, who in *Laws of Gravity* and *New Jersey Drive* brought a Cassavetes touch to working-class crime and confusion. The characters this time could be lightened up and dumbed-down versions of the confused drunks in *Laws of Gravity*, their social lives centered on bars, their center of gravity the bartender. These are the kind of people who don't like to be thrown out of bars because it's a loss of valuable drinking time.

My problem was that I didn't care who killed Mona Dearly, or why, and didn't want to know anyone in town except for Chief Rash and his daughter. The Jamie Lee Curtis character looks like she has some colorful insights to share, but isn't given the dialogue to do it—she's more of a plot marker than a person.

She does figure, however, in a quiet little in-joke. Ever notice how a lot of movie smokers seem to have just lighted their cigarettes? Hers are always burned down precisely half an inch, and then we see her lighting a new one from the old one, and realize, yeah, she only smokes them for the first two puffs. A very quiet little in-joke indeed, but I mention it anyway, so the filmmakers will know their work was not in vain.

Dr. Seuss' How the Grinch Stole Christmas ★ ★
PG, 102 m., 2000

Jim Carrey (The Grinch), Jeffrey Tambor (Mayor of Whoville), Taylor Momsen (Cindy Lou Who), Christine Baranski (Martha May Who-Vier), Molly Shannon (Betty Lou Who), Anthony Hopkins (Narrator), Josh Ryan Evans (Eight-Year-Old Grinch), Jeremy Howard (Dru Lou Who), Frankie Ray (Who). Directed by Ron Howard and produced by Brian Grazer and Howard. Screenplay by Jeffrey Price and Peter S. Seaman, based on the book by Dr. Seuss.

The Grinch who stole Christmas has a reason for growing up to be so bitter. As a child, he was picked on for being green and having hair all over his body and having a beard. Show me the child who would not pick on such a classmate and I will show you Baby Jesus. But if *Dr. Seuss' How the Grinch Stole Christmas* had only worked on that angle some more, had drummed up a little more sympathy for the Grinch, maybe we wouldn't want to pick on him too.

This is a movie that devotes enormous resources to the mistaken belief that children and their parents want to see a dank, eerie, weird movie about a sour creature who lives on top of a mountain of garbage, scares children, is mean to his dog, and steals everyone's Christmas presents. Yes, there's a happy ending, and even a saintly little girl who believes the Grinch may not be all bad, but there's not much happiness before the ending, and the little girl is more of a plot device than a character.

The Grinch is played by Jim Carrey, who works as hard as an actor has ever worked in a movie, to small avail. He leaps, he tumbles, he contorts, he sneers, he grimaces, he taunts, he flies through the air and tunnels through the garbage mountain, he gets stuck in chimneys and blown up in explosions, and all the time . . .

Well, he's not Jim Carrey. After John Travolta

171

and Robin Williams were paid many millions to appear inside unrecognizable makeup in *Battlefield Earth* and *Bicentennial Man*, did it occur to anyone that when audiences go to a movie with a big star, they buy their tickets in the hopes of being able to *see* that star? Carrey has hidden behind invented faces before, in *The Mask*, for example, but his Grinch, with his pig-snout nose and Mr. Hyde hairdo, looks more like a perverse wolf man than the hero of a comedy.

The movie uses gigantic sets and lots of special effects and trick photography to create Whoville, which is inside a snowflake, and where all the Whos live in merry jollity, preparing for Christmas. The Grinch lives in a cave on the garbage mountain that towers over the town, brooding and gnashing and remembering old wounds and childhood hurts. Eventually the happiness below is so unbearable to him that he descends on the town and steals all the Christmas presents, and only the touching faith of little Cindy Lou Who (Taylor Momsen) redeems him.

But the general outlines of the story, expanded here, will be familiar from Dr. Seuss. What is strange is how the inspiration of his drawings has been expanded almost grotesquely into a world so unattractive and menacing. Red is the dominant color in the palate—not Santa red, but a kind of grungy, brownish red, so much of it we yearn to slake our eyes on green or blue. The film seems shot through a subtle filter that just slightly blurs everything, and the result is not cheerful. All of the characters, as I have mentioned, have noses that look like atrophied upturned pig snouts, which is nice if you like atrophied upturned pig snouts, but not if you don't.

The balance is off. There should be more scenes establishing sympathy for the Grinch, fewer scenes establishing his meanness, more scenes to make the townspeople seem interesting, a jollier production design, and a brighter look overall. I am not a mind reader and cannot be sure, but I think a lot of children are going to look at this movie with perplexity and distaste. It's just not much fun. Adults may appreciate Carrey's remarkable performance in an intellectual sort of way and give him points for what was obviously a supreme effort, but the screenplay doesn't give

the Grinch any help. Of course, I may be wrong. As the Grinch himself observes, "One man's toxic sludge is another man's potpourri." Or vice versa, I'm afraid.

Dr. T and the Women ★ ★ ★
R, 122 m., 2000

Richard Gere (Dr. T), Helen Hunt (Bree), Farrah Fawcett (Kate), Laura Dern (Peggy), Shelley Long (Carolyn), Tara Reid (Connie), Kate Hudson (Dee Dee), Liv Tyler (Marilyn). Directed by Robert Altman and produced by Altman and James McLindon. Screenplay by Anne Rapp.

Robert Altman would never admit this, but I believe Doctor T, the gynecologist in his latest film, is an autobiographical character. Played by Richard Gere with tact, sweetness, and a certain weary bemusement in the face of female complexity, Dr. T works for and with women, and sometimes dares to love them. So with Altman, who is more interested in women than any other great director, with the exception of Ingmar Bergman.

In a time when almost all movies revolve around men, Altman alone gives more than equal time to his female characters. He has built whole films *(Brewster McCloud, Three Women)* around a woman like Shelley Duvall, whose face and presence fascinated him when he discovered her as a waitress in a Texas coffee shop. Many of his best films, like *Nashville; Come Back to the Five and Dime, Jimmy Dean, Jimmy Dean;* and *Cookie's Fortune,* are dominated by female characters. And in *Dr. T and the Women,* he creates a galaxy of Dallas women— old, young, wonderful, crabby, infatuated, independent—and surrounds his hero with them. When you hear that Dr. T is a gynecologist played by Richard Gere, you assume he is a love machine mowing down his patients. Nothing could be further from the truth.

The Altman character Dr. T most resembles is the hapless frontier businessman played by Warren Beatty (like Gere a Hollywood sex symbol) in *McCabe and Mrs. Miller.* Desperately wanting to do the right thing, not sure he knows what that is, baffled by a woman who does not seem to need him, McCabe, like Dr. T, is that rare creature, a male hero who does not represent the director's need to dominate. Altman in his personal life is inseparable from his wife, Katherine, and surrounds himself with women as writers, producers, and colleagues. At a time when most movies have no interesting roles for women, actresses seek his sets like the promised land.

Yet *Dr. T* has been accused of misogynism—the hatred of women. How can this be? It is a comedy with sneaky, dark undertones about the shopping classes of Dallas—rich women who (Altman explains) live in a city with no river, shore, or mountains, and are forced to seek solace in upscale malls. They dress expensively, they are perfectly groomed and made up, they drive luxury cars, they buy, they lunch. "Work" is their word for plastic surgery, not labor. To make a film about them is not the impulse of a misogynist, but of a documentarian. They exist. Altman rather loves some of them. So does Dr. T.

This is Richard Gere's nicest role. He works hard as a gynecologist. He cares about his patients. Listen as he counsels one who is upset about the approach of menopause. See how he lets one smoke on the examination table, because she must. He trusts his nursing staff, which is a bulwark against the unceasing parade of women in his waiting room; he loves and is faithful to his wife, Kate (Farrah Fawcett), and he cares for his daughters. One, Dee Dee (Kate Hudson), is something like a Dallas Cowgirl, and is engaged to be married. The other, Connie (Tara Reid), is a guide at the Conspiracy Museum, pointing out the X on the pavement where JFK was shot.

One day Kate goes shopping with her chic friends, and something cracks. She wanders through the mall, shedding clothes (in front of the Godiva store), ending up nude in a fountain. She is institutionalized. A psychiatrist explains she suffers from the "Hestia Complex," a complaint affecting "affluent upper-class women who have pretty much all they need." She is too fortunate and too loved, and has cracked up because she cannot understand why she deserves her good fortune.

This diagnosis has enraged certain feminist critics of the film, who see it reflecting hostility toward women. But why? We have had countless films about men abusing women (Fawcett starred in one of them), but let there

be one film in which women suffer from affluence, idleness, and too much love, and it is an attack on the sex. I find the movie's purpose ironic and satirical, not hateful, and certainly Dr. T continues to love his wife and to visit her, although his visits seem to make her worse, not better.

It is only after Kate seems likely to be institutionalized indefinitely that Dr. T begins to see another woman, at first without really meaning to cheat. She is Bree (Helen Hunt), the new golf pro at his country club, and she has a tactful frankness about what she wants. She invites him over for dinner, and there is a tables-turned quality about the way Dr. T is the "date," given a drink, and left to stand around and smile, while Bree shows off by slapping the steaks on the grill.

Because this is an Altman film, there are a lot of other major roles; he is too expansive to be limited by the tunnel vision of most screenplays, and with his writer, Anne Rapp, he juggles several story lines. Sometimes characters in the backgrounds of shots are involved in entirely other plots than those in the foreground. One of these is Carolyn (Shelley Long), the nurse who runs Dr. T's office and imagines herself as his wife. There is also screen time for Dr. T's two daughters, so different in the ways they turned out—there is something revealing about her materialist culture that Dee Dee is clearly prepared, even at her tender age, to make a marriage of convenience.

What holds the stories and the characters together is the decency of Dr. T, and Gere seems wholly comfortable with the role. He plays a good man of modest requirements and dutiful conscience, plugging away, trying to get his job done, trying not to be driven mad by Freud's unanswerable question, "What do women want?" Because this is a comedy, he even finds the answer, sort of.

Dudley Do-Right ★ ★ ½
PG, 75 m., 1999

Brendan Fraser (Dudley Do-Right), Sarah Jessica Parker (Nell Fenwick), Alfred Molina (Snidley Whiplash), Eric Idle (The Prospector), Robert Prosky (Inspector Fenwick), Alex Rocco (The Chief), Corey Burton (Announcer's Voice), Jack Kehler (Howard). Directed by Hugh Wilson and produced by John Davis, Joseph M. Singer, and J. Todd Harris. Screenplay by Wilson, based on characters developed by Jay Ward.

Dudley Do-Right is a genial live-action version of the old cartoon, with a lot of broad slapstick humor that kids like and adults wince at. I did a little wincing the ninth or tenth time Dudley stepped on a loose plank and it slammed him in the head, but I enjoyed the film more than I expected to. It's harmless, simpleminded, and has a couple of sequences that are better than Dudley really deserves.

The hero is a square-jawed Canadian Mountie who lives in Semi-Happy Valley and combats wrongdoing in his own dim way. He's played by Brendan Fraser, who, after great success in making a live-action character out of a cartoon figure in *George of the Jungle*, has less to work with this time. But work with it he does, dreaming sadly of his lost horse (named Horse) and pining for Nell Fenwick (Sarah Jessica Parker), his childhood sweetheart. He's joyous when Nell returns to the little town, having capped a brilliant academic career with the U.S. ambassadorship to Guam.

His other childhood playmate was Snidley K. Whiplash (Alfred Molina), who dressed in black even as a tot, and has grown up into a mustache-twirling villain who likes his role because "the bad guy has more fun." (Whiplash ties a banker to the railroad tracks, in a nod to the cartoon's tradition, but spares Nell, which will offend traditionalists.)

The plot: Snidley devises a scheme to frighten away all the residents of Semi-Happy Valley with rumors of vampires and replace them with the 999 members of his gang. Then he salts the local streams with gold nuggets, to inspire a Gold Rush (we see Canadian border posts flattened by a stampede of what the TV news calls "Yuppie wetbacks"). He'll fleece the newcomers and get rich.

Dudley is the only lawman standing in his way (until, that is, Nell's father, a veteran inspector, strips him of his authority). His closest ally is the chief (Alex Rocco), head of the local Kumquat tribe, which stages a Corn Festival that looks a lot like a Vegas dance revue. The festival is the funniest thing in the movie (except perhaps for the use of the "Indian Love Song"), although the chief makes little pre-

tense of ethnic authenticity: "Indians? This is basically a dinner theater we're running here."

The Corn Festival sets up one of those moments that, even in a so-so comedy, can blindside us with surprise laughter. As Dudley and Nell leave the festival, rowing across a lake in a canoe, Nell sighs, "I wish we could have stayed for the fireworks." I'd spoil the joke by explaining why this line is so funny, but you'll see. There are also some nice quasi-*Star Wars* scenes involving the prospector (Eric Idle), who tutors Dudley in a Semi-Happy version of the Force.

Fraser is stalwart and credulous as Dudley, Parker is wide-eyed and easily astonished as Nell, and Molina plays Whiplash so broadly he almost needs to stand sideways. Viewers below a certain age (nine?) will probably find the movie enormously entertaining, and truth to tell, I kinda sorta liked it myself. Not enough to recommend it to those in the upper grades, but enough to remember parts with a smile.

Duets ★ ★ ½
R, 113 m., 2000

Maria Bello (Suzi Loomis), Andre Braugher (Reggie Kane), Paul Giamatti (Todd Woods), Huey Lewis (Ricky Dean), Gwyneth Paltrow (Liv), Scott Speedman (Billy), Angie Dickinson (Blair). Directed by Bruce Paltrow and produced by Kevin Jones, Paltrow, and John Byrum. Screenplay by Byrum.

Duets has little islands of humor and even perfection, floating in a sea of missed marks and murky intentions. There must have been a lot of scenes that everybody was happy with on the set that day, but they don't add up—the movie is all over the map. Its fundamental error is to try to squeeze bittersweet heartbreak and goofy social satire into the same story. Just when the movie gets the rhythm, it steps on its own feet.

The screenplay by John Byrum weaves together the stories of three couples, all destined to meet at a $5,000 karaoke contest in Omaha. All three stories involve ancient movie formulas: (1) the daughter who wants to bond with her long-lost father, (2) the black guy and white guy from different worlds who become best friends, and (3) the slut with a good heart who redeems the aimless guy who lacks faith in himself. Combine these three relationships with the payoff of a big contest that only one couple can win, and you have an exercise in recycling.

Still, if the movie had found one tone and stayed with it, the material might have worked better—there's a lot of isolated stuff to like in this movie. The fatal miscalculation is to make one of the stories (the black guy and white guy) deeper and more somber than the others, so the film is forever plunging into gloom and then trying to get the grin back on its face.

Paul Giamatti is touching and, at first, funny as a sales executive who gets fed up with his brutal workload, walks out on his family, and hits the road. He meets Andre Braugher, an ex-con with a violent past, and in some weird way they bond during a karaoke night in a bar on the highway to nowhere. I liked the way that both of these characters were literally transformed once they stepped into the karaoke spotlight.

We also meet Huey Lewis as a professional karaoke hustler (he bets he can out-sing anyone in the house, and can), and Gwyneth Paltrow, as the daughter he never knew. He's a rolling stone, but she wants him to stay put long enough for her to get to know him. The third couple is another karaoke pro (Maria Bello) who hands out sexual favors like she's presenting her credit card, and a taxi driver (Scott Speedman) who dropped out of studies for the priesthood and now has no focus in his life.

The surprise among these actors is Huey Lewis, who has worked in other movies (notably Robert Altman's *Short Cuts*) but here generates an immediate interest in his first scene—we watch him conning a karaoke champ, and savor the timbre of his voice and the planes of his face. The camera likes him. At the end of the movie, a high point will be his karaoke duet with Paltrow (who can sing amazingly well). Watch his taunting grin as he gets a rise out of his target with insults about karaoke.

But about that world of karaoke: I believe the film when it tells me there are regulars on the karaoke circuit who travel from town to town, going for the prize money. Yes, and hustlers like the Lewis character, who is like a pool shark of an earlier age, getting the bartender to hold the money and then blowing away the competition. I believe it, and yet the songs sung by the characters seem to belong in a different kind of a movie. In a musical, it's expected that characters sing the songs all the way through, but in a drama they should be only an element in a larger idea of a scene; when the drama stops cold so a song can be performed, the song is fun, but the movie's pacing suffers.

There's another curious thing that happens. The karaoke finals upstage the dramatic payoffs. The real karaoke world doesn't want to stay in the background, but edges into the spotlight with its intrinsic interest. In the big $5,000 contest, there's a fat kid in a Hawaiian shirt who comes onstage. We never see him again and he has no spoken dialogue, but he stops the show because he is, in a touching way, so fascinating. I'm sure Bruce Paltrow, the film's director, left him in for the same reason I'm writing about him—because he had a haunting quality. But a movie is in trouble when you start thinking that a documentary about that kid and the other karaoke regulars would be more interesting than the resolution of the three pairs of formula stories.

Dungeons & Dragons ★ ½
PG-13, 105 m., 2000

Justin Whalin (Ridley), Marlon Wayans (Snails), Thora Birch (Empress Savina), Zoe McLellan (Marina), Kristen Wilson (Norda), Lee Arenberg (Elwood), Bruce Payne (Damodar), Jeremy Irons (Profion). Directed by Courtney Solomon and produced by Thomas M. Hammel, Kia Jam, and Solomon. Screenplay by Topper Lilien and Carroll Cartwright.

Dungeons & Dragons looks like they threw away the game and photographed the box it came in. It's an amusing movie to look at, in its own odd way, but close your eyes and the dialogue sounds like an overwrought junior high school play. The movie tells the story of a power struggle in the mythical kingdom of Izmer, where a populist empress wants power for the common man but an elitist member of the ruling caste plans a coup. High marks for anyone who can explain the role that dragons play in the Izmerian ecology.

The plot does not defy description, but it discourages it. Imagine a kingdom that looks half the time like a towering fantasy world of spires and turrets, castles and drawbridges—and the other half like everyone is standing around in the wooded area behind Sam's Club on the interstate. Imagine some characters who seem ripped from the pages of action comics and other characters who look like their readers. Imagine arch, elevated medievalese alternating with contemporary slang. The disconnects are so strange that with a little more effort they could have become a style.

Empress Savina (Thora Birch) rules in a land where the Mages run everything and the commoners do all the work. She fights for equality, but a scheming Mage named Profion (Jeremy Irons—yes, Jeremy Irons) wants to wrest power from her. This will involve obtaining a magic scepter, which I think (this is a little obscure) is powered by a gem known as the Dragon's Eye. Plugging the eye into the scepter will allow Profion to command the kingdom's dragons, overthrow the empress, and retain power for himself and his fellow Mages.

Meanwhile (there are a lot of meanwhiles in this film), enter two thieves, Ridley (Justin Whalin) and Snails (Marlon Wayans). Ridley is a cross between action hero and mall rat; Snails tilts more toward Stepin Fetchit ("Be careful!" Ridley is always telling Snails, and then he'll turn and bang his head on a beam). Soon they accumulate three sidekicks: Marina (Zoe McLellan), who knows a lot of magic, El-wood the dwarf (Lee Arenberg), and Norda (Kristen Wilson), whose breastplate is a metallic salute to the guns of Navarone.

These five bumble about in undistinguished settings and then occasionally venture into sets so hallucinatory in their medieval Gothery that they look stolen from another movie. Their archenemy is Damodar (Bruce Payne), the sadistic shaven-headed enforcer for Profion, whose ears contain long snaky Roto Rooter–type things that spring out on flexible arms and suck out people's brains and stuff.

And then there are the dragons. What, I asked myself, is their nature? Are they intelligent? Loyal? Obedient? Do they wait for eons in dungeons until they are needed? Do they eat? Reproduce? At one point Profion releases one from its lair, but he hasn't fitted his scepter with the correct missing part, and so the dragon attacks and breathes fire and has to be skewered by a falling gate. (Its blood flows into a river that begins to burn, just like the Cuyahoga before the cleanup.)

The dragons apparently exist in order to materialize in the sky and flap ominously above Izmer until they are vaporized by magic. What use they are in war is hard to figure. How would the Mages enjoy life if the dragons burned down Izmer? These and other questions percolate during a great deal of swordplay, interrupted by shouted dire imprecations from Jeremy Irons, who has not had so much fun since Juliette Binoche decided she had to ravish him right then and there in *Damage*.

E

Earth ★ ★ ★
NO MPAA RATING, 104 m., 1999

Aamir Khan (Dil Navaz, Ice Candy Man),
Nandita Das (Shanta, the Ayah), Rahul Khanna
(Hasan, the Masseur), Kitu Gidwani (Bunty
Sethna), Maia Sethna (Lenny Sethna),
Kulbushan Kharbanda (Imam Din), Gulshan
Grover (Mr. Singh). Directed by Deepa Mehta
and produced by Mehta and Anne Masson.
Screenplay by Mehta, based on the novel
Cracking India by Bapsi Sidhwa.

England, having colonized India at its leisure,
granted it independence with unseemly haste.
Even its most outspoken nationalists were taken
aback when Lord Mountbatten, the British
viceroy, unexpectedly announced that the date
for independence was a few months, not a few
years, in the future. The British decision to
pull out by August 15, 1947, left a country with
no orderly way to deal with the rivalries between Hindus and Muslims, and the partition
of India and Pakistan along religious lines led
to bloodshed, massacres, and, as this film calls
it, "the largest and most terrible exchange of
population in history."

Earth is a film that sees that tragedy through
the eyes of a group of friends in Lahore, then
in India, now in Pakistan. There are Muslims,
Hindus, Sikhs, Parsis, even a Christian or two.
They have lived side by side since time
immemorial, and the more idealistic think that
situation can continue. But as India has
proven, along with Northern Ireland, the
Middle East, and Yugoslavia, many members
of all faiths consider it no sin to murder a
nonbeliever.

The film is told as a melodrama and romance, not docudrama, and that makes it all
the more effective. It sees much of the action
through the eyes of a little brace-legged Parsi
girl named Lenny, whose beautiful Hindu
nanny, or "ayah," is admired by all the men in
a circle of friends. The ayah is Shanta (Nandita
Das), with glowing eyes and a warm smile. She
slowly comes to love Hasan, a masseur (Rahul
Khanna), who is Muslim. She likes, but does
not love, Dil, known as "Ice Candy Man" and
played by the Indian star Aamir Khan. Her life

is pleasant in a wealthy Parsi household ruled
by Lenny's kind mother and officious father.

The friends meet in a nearby park for talk
that sometimes grows political. They all agree
they are above hatreds based on religion. The
little girl looks and listens. Often she is present
when Hasan courts the shy Shanta, and even
watches as they share their first bashful kiss—
just before the screen turns black and ominous music introduces shots of Hindu refugees
treking from the new Pakistan to India, and
Muslims making the opposite journey.

It is hard for us to imagine the upheaval and
suffering unleashed when the British washed
their hands of the jewel in their crown. Imagine a United States in which those with a last
name beginning with a vowel had to leave their
homes and belongings and trek north, while
those with a consonant had to leave everything behind and trek south. Now add bloodthirsty mobs of zealots on all sides, with rumors
of atrocities spreading like wildfire.

The film is based on the novel *Cracking India*
by Bapsi Sidhwa. It is said to be partly autobiographical. She remembers the last moments of
harmony between the groups, in particular a
day spent on rooftops flying brightly colored
kites. A few weeks later, from the same rooftops, some of the same people watch Hindu
tenements in flames (the "firemen" spray gasoline on them) and a Muslim man torn in two
by a mob that ties his arms to two automobiles. At home, little Lenny and her brother
tear her favorite doll in two, and the ayah tearfully tries to stitch it back together.

The closing scenes must have been repeated
a thousand times over, as a mob tries to find a
hidden person of the wrong religion, and good-
hearted people try to offer protection. There is
a kind of inevitable logic involved in the way a
child would view such a situation and cause
harm while trying to help. This is the kind of
film that makes you question any religion that
does not have as a basic tenet the tolerance of
other religions. If God allows men to worship
him in many forms, who are we to kill them in
his name?

Earth was written and directed by Deepa
Mehta, a Canadian whose previous film, *Fire*
(1997), was the first serious Indian film to deal

with lesbianism. After sex and Partition, she plans to move on to *Water,* about "what happens when Hinduism comes in direct conflict with conscience." In a society still touchy about these subjects, she is nothing if not courageous. (Although the Sidhwa novel won the top literary award in Pakistan, *Earth* has been banned there; in India, censors cut out the gentle, sweet sex scene and made five other cuts.)

The fact is, many Americans do not know India and Pakistan were once one country, and few could provide an explanation of Partition. *Earth* is effective because it doesn't require much history from its viewers, explains what needs to be known, and has a universal message, which is that when a mob forms in the name of a religion, its first casualty is usually the teachings of that religion.

East Is East ★ ★ ★
R, 96 m., 2000

Om Puri (George Khan), Linda Bassett (Ella Khan), Jordan Routledge (Sajid Khan), Archie Panjabi (Meenah Khan), Emil Marwa (Maneer Khan), Chris Bisson (Saleem Khan), Jimi Mistry (Tariq Khan), Raji James (Abdul Khan). Directed by Damien O'Donnell and produced by Leslee Udwin. Screenplay by Ayub Khan-Din, based on his play.

George Khan is like that performer on the old Ed Sullivan show, who tried to keep plates spinning simultaneously on top of a dozen poles. He runs from one crisis to another, desperately trying to defend his Muslim worldview in a world that has other views. George is a Pakistani immigrant to England, living in Manchester in 1971 with his British wife and their unruly herd of seven children, and his plates keep falling off the poles.

As the movie opens, George glows proudly as his oldest son goes through the opening stages of an arranged marriage ceremony. The bride enters, veiled, and as she reveals herself to her future husband we see that she is quite pretty—and that the would-be husband is terrified. "I can't do this, Dad!" he shouts, bolting from the hall. George is humiliated.

George is played by Om Puri, as a mixture of paternal bombast and hidebound conservatism. His wife, Ella (Linda Bassett), has worked

by his side for years in the fish-and-chips shop at the corner of their street of brick working-class row houses. After their oldest son flees, they are left with a houseful, including a neighborhood ladies' man, a shy son, a would-be artistic type, a jolly daughter, and little Sajid, the youngest, who never, ever takes off his jacket with its fur-trimmed parka. There is even a son who agrees with his father's values.

Puri plays George Kahn as the Ralph Cramden of Manchester. He is bluff, tough, big, loud, and issues ultimatums and pronouncements, while his long-suffering wife holds the family together and practices the art of compromise. His own moral high ground is questionable: He upholds the values of the old country, yet has moved to a new one, taken a British wife although he left a Muslim wife behind in Pakistan, and is trying to raise multiracial children through monoracial eyes.

There's rich humor in his juggling act. His family is so large, so rambunctious, and so clearly beyond his control that it has entirely escaped his attention that little Sajid has never been circumcised. When this lapse is discovered, he determines it is never too late to right a wrong, and schedules the operation despite the doubts of his wife and the screams of Sajid. And then there is the matter of the marriages he is trying to arrange for his No. 2 and No. 3 sons—oblivious of the fact that one of the boys is deeply in love with the blond daughter of a racist neighbor who is an admirer of Enoch ("Rivers of blood") Powell, the anti-immigration figurehead (who has been confused in some reviews, perhaps understandably, with the 1930s fascist leader Oswald Mosley).

Of course the neighbor would have apoplexy if he discovered his daughter was dating a brown boy. And George would have similar feelings, although more for religious reasons. One purpose of the rules and regulations of religions is to create in their followers a sense of isolation from nonbelievers, and what George is fighting, in 1971 Britain, is the seduction of his children by the secular religion of pop music and fashion.

East Is East is related in some ways to *My Son, the Fanatic,* another recent film starring Om Puri as an immigrant from Pakistan. In that one, the tables are turned: Puri plays a taxi driver who has drifted away from his religion and falls in love with a prostitute, while his son becomes the follower of a cult leader and invites the man into their home.

In both films, the tilt is against religion and in favor of romance on its own terms, but then all movie love stories argue for the lovers. Two Oscar winners, *Titanic* and *Shakespeare in Love*, were both stories of romance across class lines, and *American Beauty* and *Boys Don't Cry* were about violating taboos; it could be that movie love stories are the most consistently subversive genre in the cinema, arguing always for personal choice over the disapproval of parents, church, ethnic groups, or society itself.

If there is a weakness in *East Is East*, it's that Om Puri's character is a little too serious for the comedy surrounding him. He is a figure of deep contradictions, trying to hold his children to a standard he has eluded his entire life. Perhaps the real love story in the movie is the one we overlook, between George and his wife, Ella, who has stood by him through good times and bad, running the fish shop and putting up with his nonsense. When he blusters that he will bring over his first wife, who understands his thinking, Ella tells him, "I'm off if she steps foot in this country!" But he's bluffing. His own life has pointed the way for his children. It's just that he can't admit it, to them or himself.

Note: This is a provocative film for useful discussions between parents and children. The R rating is inexplicable.

East-West ★ ★ ½
PG-13, 121 m., 2000

Sandrine Bonnaire (Marie), Oleg Menchikov (Alexei), Catherine Deneuve (Gabrielle), Sergei Bodrov Jr. (Sacha), Ruben Tapiero (Serioja [Seven]), Erwan Baynaud (Serioja [Fourteen]). Directed by Regis Wargnier and produced by Yves Marmion. Screenplay by Rustam Ibragimbekov, Sergei Bodrov, Louis Gardel, and Wargnier.

If the Soviet Union had made honorable use of the idealism it inspired in the West, it might have survived and been a happier place today. Marxism seduced and betrayed some of the best minds of its time. The executioner was Stalin. One of his cruel tricks, after the end of World War II, was to invite Russians in exile to return to the motherland—and then execute many of them, keeping the rest as virtual prisoners of the state.

East-West tells the fictional story of one couple who returned. Marie (Sandrine Bonnaire) is French; she married Alexei (Oleg Menchikov), a doctor, in Paris. He is eager to return and help in the rebuilding of Russia, and she loves him and comes along. Their disillusionment is swift and brutal. They see arriving passengers treated like criminals, sorted into groups, and shipped away into a void where many disappeared.

Alexei is spared because the state needs doctors, but the couple is lodged in a boardinghouse where the walls are thin and many of their neighbors seem to be, in one way or another, informers. Marie is suspect because she speaks French and therefore, given the logic of the times, could be a spy. The old woman who once owned the house also speaks French, comforts Marie, is informed on, and dies—possibly not of natural causes.

The film, directed by Regis Wargnier (*Indochine*), tells its story not in stark, simple images, but with the kind of production values we associate with historical epics. The music by Patrick Doyle is big and sweeping, as if both the score and the visuals are trying to elevate a small story to the stature of, say, *Dr. Zhivago*. But Marie is not Lara Zhivago. She is a materialist Parisian who isn't a good sport about sharing spartan facilities, who complains to a husband who is doing his best, who unilaterally does things that endanger them both.

Not that she is a bad woman. She has the kind of strong-willed independence that would be safe enough, and effective, in the West. She is simply slow or reluctant to see that such behavior in Russia is suicidal. Her husband, born and raised in Russia, preaches patience and stealth, not techniques she is familiar with.

East-West shows physical deprivation, but makes it clear that its characters are starving mostly for the clear air of freedom. It shows a system that is unjust and brutal, but made barely livable because the ordinary humans who enforce it are prey to universal human feelings. Good people tend to want to do good things no matter what their duty commands them. Both Marie and Alexei find friends in the bureaucracy, and both find romantic friends,

179

too; Marie's is a swimmer whose ability may be the key to their freedom.

Toward the end of the film there is a set piece worthy of a vintage thriller. A famous left-wing French actress named Gabrielle (Catherine Deneuve) arrives on tour, is made aware of the plight of the couple, and tries to help them. Her plan depends on an intuitive knowledge of how Soviet guards will react to foreign visitors; the payoff is suspenseful.

And yet the movie as a whole lacks the conviction of a real story. It is more like a lush morality play, too leisurely in its storytelling, too sure of its morality. I remember *The Inner Circle* (1992), by Andrei Konchalovsky, which starred Tom Hulce as Stalin's movie projectionist, a nonentity who through his job was able to see the dark side of the great man. It is told matter-of-factly, more in everyday detail and less in grand gestures. *East-West* has too large a canvas for its figures.

Edge of 17 ★ ★
NO MPAA RATING, 100 m., 1999

Chris Stafford (Eric), Tina Holmes (Maggie), Andersen Gabrych (Rod), Stephanie McVay (Mom), Lea DeLaria (Angie), John Eby (Dad), Antonio Carriero (Andy), Jason Sheingross (Steve). Directed by David Moreton and produced by Moreton and Todd Stephens. Screenplay by Stephens.

Edge of 17 is more about sex and less about love than most coming-out movies; its young hero, Eric, seems to aim directly for gay bars and empty promiscuity without going through intermediate stages of self-discovery, idealism, or the qualities encompassed in the code word *pride*. He cheerfully wants to become a slut. This doesn't make him unusual; the libido is stronger than the intelligence in many teenagers. He'll grow up eventually.

The movie is set in Sandusky, Ohio, in 1984, and said to be based in part on the memories of its writer, Todd Stephens. It was an era when flamboyantly gay pop acts were highly visible, and the film cites Boy George and the Bronski Beat. It's about a summer of sexual initiation for Eric (Chris Stafford), a spacy teenager who seems a little dazed a lot of the time; later he'll learn to mask his cluelessness with cool detachment.

Eric gets a summer job in the restaurant of an amusement park. Also on the staff: his best friend Maggie (Tina Holmes), a lesbian manager named Angie (Lea DeLaria), and a blond guy named, inevitably, Rod (Andersen Gabrych), who wants to seduce him. Eric doesn't have the usual tumultuous struggle against his emerging gay identity; Rod smiles at him, Eric gets the idea, and in a relatively short while they're sharing quality time in the meat locker. It's obvious to Angie, and even in an unacknowledged way to Maggie, that they're an item.

We see a little of Eric's home life. His dad (John Eby) is a salt-of-the-earth type, and his mom (Stephanie McVay), a much more fully developed character, is a former musician who put her career on hold for marriage and motherhood, but takes pride in the New Age compositions Eric pieces together on his electronic keyboard. As Eric's hairstyle morphs from moptop to David Bowie and his eyeliner consumption goes up, she begins to worry—especially when he starts staying out all night and (although not enough is made of this) coming home drunk.

Rod turns out to be a disappointment as a first love; he quickly disappears back into "the gay dorm at OSU." He makes a poor role model. "Don't call me again," he tells the lonely Eric on the phone one night. Depressed, Eric heads for the Universal Fruit and Nut Co., Sandusky's only gay bar, where the manager is, inevitably, Angie from the summer restaurant job. Angie welcomes him joyfully, reassures him there is life after coming out, and introduces him to three aging queens, one in drag, who become his buddies.

It is enormously helpful of Angie not to card Eric, who she knows is four years underage, since the gay bar will play such a central role in the plot. Soon Eric has his second sexual experience, a quickie in the parking lot with another guy who likes him only for his body. "Uh, wouldn't you like my phone number?" Eric offers. Depressed by his experiences as a mindless sex object, he turns for consolation to Maggie, who helps him find out if he likes straight sex (he doesn't). Maggie, Eric's mother, and Angie the manager are the most fully realized characters in the movie, which doesn't offer a single positively drawn male homosexual.

Watching the movie, I thought, yes, for a lot of people straight and gay, the initiation to sexuality is like this: awkward physical couplings, loneliness, misunderstanding, angst, and then finally you grow interested in the person attached to the sexual organs and not the other way around. *Edge of 17* may be more realistic, if less encouraging, than a more sensitive gay coming-out story like the British film *Get Real*. It deals with physical details with almost startling frankness, and doesn't sentimentalize.

If it seems to introduce Eric directly into the world of gay clichés (drag queens and strangers in the night), perhaps in Sandusky in 1984 that was the only visible gay culture, and more substantial relationships were low-profile. My hope for Eric is not merely that he grows comfortable with his sexuality, but that he becomes a more interesting conversationalist, hopefully before I see him in another movie.

The Edge of the World ★ ★ ★
NO MPAA RATING, 81 m., 1937 (rereleased 2000)

John Laurie (Peter Manson), Belle Chrystall (Ruth Manson), Eric Berry (Robbie Manson), Kitty Kirwan (Jean Manson), Finlay Currie (James Gray), Niall MacGinnis (Andrew Gray), Grant Sutherland (The Catechist), Campbell Robson (The Laird). Directed by Michael Powell and produced by Joe Rock. Screenplay by Powell.

Michael Powell was one of the greatest British directors—the best in the land after Alfred Hitchcock decamped to Hollywood—and his major films stand like bedrock in film history: *The Red Shoes, The Life and Death of Colonel Blimp, Black Narcissus, The Thief of Bagdad, A Matter of Life and Death, Peeping Tom*.

Powell was a quixotic individualist whose works also include films far from the mainstream, strange works like *A Canterbury Tale*, about a pervert who takes advantage of wartime blackouts to pour glue into women's hair. When I taught a class on Powell at the University of Chicago, the students applauded all of his films but one, *Tales of Hoffmann*, a mannered operatic production they found unbearable, walking out to discuss it mournfully in the hallway.

His two-volume autobiography is the best ever written by a director: *A Life in Movies* and *Million Dollar Movie*. His life paralleled the development of the cinema. Born in 1905, he died in 1990 still deeply involved in the cinema as a consultant to Scorsese, Coppola, and other successors. He began in silent films, made talkie thrillers he was indifferent to, and reached "the turning point of my life in art" with *The Edge of the World* (1937), the first of his films that he "wanted to make." It has long been unavailable, but has now returned in a restored 35mm print which made its way through art theaters on its way to video.

It is a strange, haunting, beautiful film, shot on location on the spare Scottish island of Foula, in the cold North Sea. Like Robert Flaherty's documentary of Irish islanders, *Man of Aran*, made three years earlier, it tells the story of a dying way of life. But it was risky to mention Flaherty's film to Powell, who rejected comparisons: "He hasn't got a story," he tells a friend in his autobiography, "just a lot of waves and seaweed and pretty pictures. This is a *drama!* An *epic!* About people!"

The inhabitants of Foula have supported themselves since time immemorial by fishing, and by the wool from their prized sheep herds. Now modern trawlers are grabbing the fishing market, and it is time for these rugged islanders to weigh their future—should they move to the mainland? The story involves two young men, Andrew and Robbie, and Robbie's twin sister, Ruth. Ruth and Andrew are engaged to be wed. The two men and their fathers stand on opposite sides of the question of evacuating the island, and there is a "parliament" at which all the island men sit in a circle and discuss the issue. Andrew and Robbie decide to settle it more simply: They will have a race to the top of a 1,300-foot sea cliff.

One is killed, which leads to the estrangement of the two families and more complications when it becomes evident that Ruth is pregnant. But the story is not told as hamhanded melodrama; all of the characters respect one another, and the daily struggle to win a living from the hard land has made them stalwart and brave.

Watching the movie, I made a note about Powell's extraordinary close-ups of faces. Then in his book I found he went to extraordinary lengths, when money and time were running out, to get those close-ups, many shot from small boats in rising seas: "Why didn't I trick these shots in the studio? It was the faces. Islanders have an inner strength and repose that other men and women do not have, and it shows in their faces."

The film's location shooting creates a palpable sense of the time and place. No set designer would dare build a church as small as the one on Foula, where the congregation crams in shoulder-to-shoulder, and inches separate the first pew from the pulpit (one parishioner tells the dour preacher about his sermon, "One hour and fifteen minutes. Let them beat that in Edinburgh if they can!"). Small touches, like a kitten in an old lady's lap, and chickens foraging for their dinner in farmyards, seem unplanned.

The reception of this film allowed Powell to sign a contract with Alexander Korda, then the most powerful British producer, and soon he would begin his long association with the screenwriter Emeric Pressburger (they signed their productions "The Archers," and their trademark was an arrow striking a bull's-eye). Their films together made glorious use of Technicolor and theatricality, so striking that the opening credits of Kenneth Branagh's new *Love's Labour's Lost* pay obvious homage to them.

This first "serious" film by Powell doesn't seem to predict his career. You can't imagine the maker of this film going on to make *The Red Shoes*. What it does show, though, is a voluptuous regard for visual images. The cliff-climbing scenes are especially dramatic, and, watching them, I realized that in most climbing scenes the climbers seem heroic. Here they seem tiny and endangered. It is the cliff that seems heroic, and that is probably the right way around.

EDtv ★ ★ ½
PG-13, 122 m., 1999

Matthew McConaughey (Ed Pekurny), Jenna Elfman (Shari), Woody Harrelson (Ray Pekurny), Sally Kirkland (Jeanette), Martin Landau (Al), Ellen DeGeneres (Cynthia Topping), Rob Reiner (Whitaker), Dennis Hopper (Hank), Elizabeth Hurley (Jill), Adam Goldberg (John), Viveka Davis (Marcia), Clint Howard (Ken). Directed by Ron Howard and produced by Brian Grazer and Howard. Screenplay by Lowell Ganz and Babaloo Mandel, based on the film *Louis XIX: Le Roi des Ondes*.

Now that two movies have been made about a man living twenty-four hours a day on television, how long until TV actually tries this as a programming idea? *EDtv* arrives less than a year after *The Truman Show*, and although the two films have different approaches (*Truman* is a parable; *EDtv* is an ambitious sitcom), they're both convinced that enormous audiences would watch intently as a man brushes his teeth, clips his nails, and is deceived by a wicked woman.

Is this true? Would they? Much would depend on the nature of the experiment, of course. *The Truman Show* gathered its poignancy from the fact that its hero didn't know he was on TV. *EDtv* is about a man who auditions for the job; as his brother points out, "How many chances do guys like us get?" The two movies offer us a choice: Would you rather be a hidden voyeur, or watch an exhibitionist?

I'd rather be a voyeur. The star of a TV show like this is likely to show me more about human nature if he doesn't know I'm watching. The kind of guy who would agree to having his whole life televised, on the other hand, is essentially just a long-form Jerry Springer guest. Anyone who would agree to such a deal is a loser, painfully needy, or nuts. And since the hero of Ron Howard's *EDtv* isn't really any of those things, the film never quite feels convincing.

The film stars Matthew McConaughey as Ed Pekurny, a Texas charmer who is discovered during auditions by a desperate cable channel. He can talk "regular" or he can talk Texan, he says, demonstrating accents as a TV executive (Ellen DeGeneres) watches, enraptured. Televising Ed's life is her idea; her boss (Rob Reiner) has his doubts at first, until she points out their current ratings are lower than the Gardening Channel ("People would rather watch soil").

Ed is signed by the channel, which also gets releases from the people in his world, including his brother Ray (Woody Harrelson), Ray's girlfriend, Shari (Jenna Elfman), his mother (Sally Kirkland), and his stepfather (Martin Landau). The first hours of the new show are slow-going (including the toenail-clipping demonstration), but things pick up after it's revealed that Ed and Shari are poised to start cheating on Ray ("I just kissed my boyfriend's brother on television!").

The movie strikes an uneasy bargain between being about television, and just being a straightforward romantic comedy. After a few setup scenes, we never have the notion that Ed's *whole* life is being shown on TV; the alleged *cinema verité* approach has an uncanny way of always being there for the right moments, with the right camera angles. And when they're needed for story conflict, new characters arrive; Ed's birth father (Dennis Hopper) appears for some touching confessions, and when a *USA Today* poll shows that viewers are bored with Shari, the producers arrange for a British sex bomb (Elizabeth Hurley) to appear on Ed's viewfinder.

The juiciest character is Ray, played by Woody Harrelson as a man always on the edge of someone else's success. After it's announced on TV that he's a lousy lover, he actually produces a defense witness—a former girlfriend who testifies, "I've had worse." The character I never quite understood was Shari, who becomes totally disillusioned with the idea of having her romance telecast, even though she's so oblivious to the cameras that she dumps Ray and embraces Ed in full view of millions during the first few days.

The movie has a lot of TV lore, including programming meetings presided over by Reiner, whose enthusiasm for EDtv grows as DeGeneres loses hers. The story arc is obvious: TV is bad for invading the privacy of these lives, and we're bad for watching. Still, Ray was right: The brothers had nothing going for them before, and now Ed is rich and famous. If he doesn't have the girl he loves, at least he has Elizabeth Hurley as a consolation prize. The story keeps undercutting its own conviction that TV is evil.

I enjoyed a lot of the movie in a relaxed sort of way; it's not essential or original in the way

The Truman Show was, and it hasn't done any really hard thinking about the ways we interact with TV. It's a businesslike job, made to seem special at times because of the skill of the actors—especially Martin Landau, who gets a laugh with almost every line as a man who is wryly reconciled to very shaky health ("I'd yell for her, but I'd die"). After it's over, we've laughed some, smiled a little, and cared not really very much.

8½ Women ★ ★ ★
R, 120 m., 2000

John Standing (Philip Emmenthal), Matthew Delamere (Storey Emmenthal), Vivian Wu (Kito), Shizuka Inoh (Simato), Barbara Sarafian (Clothilde), Kirina Mano (Mio), Toni Collette (Griselda), Amanda Plummer (Beryl). Directed by Peter Greenaway and produced by Kees Kasander. Screenplay by Greenaway.

Having met Peter Greenaway, I find it easier to understand the tone of his films. Not a lighthearted man, he is cerebral, controlled, so precise in his speech he seems to be dictating. "He talks like a university lecturer," I wrote after meeting him in 1991, "and gives the impression he would rather dine alone than suffer bores at his table." Yet there is an aggressive, almost violent, streak of comedy in his makeup; one can imagine him, like Hitchcock, springing practical jokes.

Consider a scene in *8½ Women*, his new film. It takes place in a staid Swiss cemetery. His hero, Philip Emmenthal (John Standing), is a billionaire who has just lost his beloved wife. He arrives at the services dressed in a white summer suit, because his wife disliked dark clothing. He is informed that a black suit is absolutely required by the bylaws.

Enraged, defiant, stubborn, Philip grimly strips down until he is standing naked on the gravel; observing the letter of the law, he demands even black underwear. He is surrounded by minions who lend him their own clothing— a black shirt, black tie, pants, coat, even underwear ("it looks like a swimming suit," its wearer explains, "and I was hoping to go swimming later"). His decision has forced his employees to strip as well, and now, dressed in black, he walks a few feet to one side and we see what we could not see before—that the preacher and all of the mourners were waiting nearby, in full view of everything.

Now how is this funny? Trying to imagine other kinds of comedies handling the material, I ran it through Monty Python, Steve Martin, and Woody Allen before realizing it has its roots in Buster Keaton—whose favorite comic ploy was to overcome obstacles by applying pure logic and ignoring social conventions or taboos. Keaton would have tilted it more toward laughs, to be sure; Greenaway's humor always seems dour, and masks (not very well) a lot of hostility. But, yes, Keaton.

One possible approach to 8½ Women, I think, is to view it as a slowed-down, mannered, tongue-in-cheek silent comedy, skewed by Greenaway's anger and desire to manipulate. The movie's title evokes memories of the ways Greenaway numbers, categorizes, sorts, and orders the characters in his other films. His titles Drowning by Numbers and A Zed and Two Noughts show the same sensibility; he distances himself from the humanity of his characters by treating them like inventory.

Here, however, real emotion is allowed to fight its way onto the screen. Philip is in genuine mourning for his dead wife ("Who will hold and comfort me now she's gone?"), and his hopelessness moves his son, Storey (Matthew Delamere). There is a scene, offscreen but unmistakably implied, in which they have incestuous sex, perhaps as a form of mutual comfort, and many scenes in which Greenaway, so interested in male nudity, has them naked in front of mirrors and each other. This is not the nudity of sexuality, but of disclosure; a billionaire stripped of his clothes (and his Rolls-Royces and chateaus and servants) is just, after all, a naked man with flat feet and a belly.

Father and son have been involved in a scheme to take over a series of pachinko parlors in Kyoto, Japan. Pachinko is an addictive form of pinball, much prized by the Japanese. They meet a woman who has gambled away most of her family's money on pachinko, and are surprised to discover that her father and her fiancé both suggest she sleep with Storey (or Philip) to work off the debt. (This does not represent a loss of honor, the translator ex-

plains, because the Emmenthals are not Japanese, thus do not count.)

This woman becomes one of the first of eight and a half women the father and son move into their Geneva mansion, in an attempt to slake their grief with the pleasures of the flesh. All of the women are willing participants, for reasons of their own—the one in the bizarre body brace, the one unhappy unless she is pregnant, an amputee who only counts as a half, and so on. Greenaway deliberately does not build or shoot any of the movie's many sex scenes in a revealing or erotic way; they are always about power, manipulation, control.

Apart from the father's real scenes of grief, the film is cold and distant. It shows its bones as well as its skin; some of its shots are superimposed on pages from the screenplay that describes them. It is not possible to "like" this film, although one admires it, and is intrigued. Greenaway does not much require to be liked (is my guess), and what he is doing here has links to deep feelings he reveals only indirectly. At two times in the film, father and son watch Fellini's 8½, particularly the scene where the hero gathers all of the women in his life into the same room and tries to tame and placate them. After the second viewing, the father asks the son, "How many film directors make films to satisfy their sexual fantasies?" "Most of them," his son replies. This one for sure.

8MM ★ ★ ★
R, 123 m., 1999

Nicolas Cage (Tom Welles), Joaquin Phoenix (Max California), James Gandolfini (Eddie Poole), Peter Stormare (Dino Velvet), Anthony Heald (Longdale), Chris Bauer (Machine), Catherine Keener (Amy Welles), Amy Morton (Mrs. Mathews). Directed by Joel Schumacher and produced by Gavin Polone, Judy Hofflund, and Schumacher. Screenplay by Andrew Kevin Walker.

Joel Schumacher's 8MM is a dark, dank journey into the underworld of snuff films undertaken by a private investigator who is appalled and changed by what he finds. It deals with the materials of violent exploitation films, but in a nonpornographic way; it would rather horrify than thrill. The writer is Andrew Kevin Walker, who wrote *Seven,* and once again creates a character who looks at evil and asks (indeed, screams) "Why?"

The answer comes almost at the end of the film, from its most vicious character: "The things I do—I do them because I like them. Because I want to." There is no comfort there, and the final shots, of an exchange of smiles, are ironic; Walker accepts that pure evil can exist, and that there are people who are simply bad; one of his killers even taunts the hero: "I wasn't beaten as a child. I didn't hate my parents."

The movie stars Nicolas Cage as an enigmatic family man named Tom Welles, who works as a private investigator and comes home to a good marriage with his wife (Catherine Keener) and baby. He specializes in top-level clients and total discretion. He's hired by the lawyer for a rich widow who has found what appears to be a snuff film in the safe of her late husband; she wants reassurance that the girl in the film didn't really die, and Welles tells her snuff films are "basically an urban legend—makeup, special effects, you know."

The film follows Welles as he identifies the young woman in the film, meets her mother, follows her movements, and eventually descends into the world of vicious pornographers for hire, who create films to order for a twisted clientele. Joel Schumacher has an affinity for dark atmosphere (he made *The Lost Boys, Flatliners,* and two of the Batman pictures). Here, with Mychael Danna's mournful music and Robert Elswit's squinting camera, he creates a sense of foreboding even in an opening shot of passengers walking through an airport.

The purpose of the film is to take a fairly ordinary character and bring him into such a disturbing confrontation with evil that he is driven to kill someone. Tom Welles, we learn, went to a good school on an academic scholarship, but although his peers "went into law and finance," the rich widow's attorney muses, "you chose surveillance." Yes, says Welles: "I thought it was the future." Mostly his work consists of tailing adulterers, but this case is different. He meets and talks with the mother of the girl in the film, traces her journey to Hollywood, and then enlists a guide to help him explore the hidden world of the sex business.

This is Max California (Joaquin Phoenix), who once aimed high but now works in porno retail; the film suggests that the Los Angeles economy takes hopeful young job-seekers and channels them directly into the sex trades. Through Max, Welles meets Eddie Poole (James Gandolfini), the kind of guy who means it when he says he can get you whatever you're looking for. And through Eddie, they meet Dino Velvet, a vicious porn director played by Peter Stormare—who was the killer who said almost nothing in *Fargo,* and here creates a frightening set of weirdo verbal affectations. The star of some of his films is Machine (Chris Bauer), who doesn't like to remove his mask.

We expect Welles to get into danger with these men, and he does, but *8MM* doesn't treat the trouble simply as an occasion for action scenes. There is a moment here when Welles has the opportunity to get revenge, but lacks the will (he is not a killer), and he actually telephones a victim and asks to be talked into it. I haven't seen that before in a movie, and it raises moral questions that the audience has to deal with, one way or another.

I know some audience members will be appalled by this film, as many were by *Seven.* It is a very hard R that would doubtless have been NC-17 if it had come from an indie instead of a big studio with clout. But it is a real film. Not a slick exploitation exercise with all the trappings of depravity but none of the consequences. Not a film where moral issues are forgotten in the excitement of an action climax. Yes, the hero is an ordinary man who finds himself able to handle violent situations, but that's not the movie's point. The last two words of the screenplay are "save me," and by the time they're said, we know what they mean.

Election ★ ★ ★ ½
R, 104 m., 1999

Matthew Broderick (Jim McAllister), Reese Witherspoon (Tracy Flick), Chris Klein (Paul Metzler), Phil Reeves (Walt Hendricks), Mark Harelik (Dave Novotny), Delaney Driscoll (Linda

Novotny), Jessica Campbell (Tammy), Molly Hagan (Diane McAllister), Colleen Camp (Judith R. Flick). Directed by Alexander Payne and produced by Albert Berger, Ron Yerxa, David Gale, and Keith Samples. Screenplay by Payne and Jim Taylor, based on the novel by Tom Perrotta.

I remember students like Tracy Flick, the know-it-all who always has her hand in the air while the teacher desperately looks for someone else to call on. In fact, I *was* a student like Tracy Flick. "A legend in his own mind," they wrote under my photo in the Urbana High School yearbook. I remember informing an English teacher that I didn't know why we were wasting time on the short stories of Eudora Welty when I could write better ones myself.

Tracy is smarter than that, and would never occupy such an exposed position. She's the subject of Alexander Payne's *Election,* a wicked satire about an election, for student government president, a post Tracy wants to win to go along with her collection of every other prize in school. What sets this film aside from all the other recent high school movies is that it doesn't limit itself to the worldview of teenagers, but sees Tracy mostly through the eyes of a teacher who has had more than enough of her.

Tracy is embodied by Reese Witherspoon, an actress I've admired since she had her first kiss in *The Man in the Moon* (1991), and who moved up to adult roles in *Freeway* (1997), a harrowing retelling of "Little Red Riding Hood" with Kiefer Sutherland as the wolf. She was a virginal headmaster's daughter in *Cruel Intentions,* which opened last month, but she hits her full stride in *Election* as an aggressive, manipulative vixen who informs a teacher she hopes they can work together "harmoniously" in the coming school year.

The teacher is Jim McAllister (Matthew Broderick), the kind of man who turns up for an adulterous liaison and succeeds only in getting a bee sting on his eyelid. He thinks he knows what she means about "harmoniously," since last year she seduced a faculty member who was one of his best friends. Much as McAllister detests her, he also lusts after her; talking another student into running against

her is his version of a cold shower. His recruit is a slow-witted jock named Paul (Chris Klein), and the race gets complicated when Paul's lesbian sister, Tammy (Jessica Campbell), jumps into the race on a platform of dismantling the student government "so we'll never have to sit through one of these stupid elections again."

Election is not really about high school, but about personality types. If the John Travolta character in *Primary Colors* reminded me of Bill Clinton, Tracy Flick puts me in mind of Elizabeth Dole: a person who always seems to be setting you a logical puzzle for which she is the answer. What is Tracy Flick's platform? That she should win simply because she is the school's (self-)designated winner. When a candidate turns up on election day having baked 480 customized cupcakes for the voters, doesn't she seem kind of inevitable?

For Jim McAllister, the Tracy Flicks have to be stopped before they do damage to themselves and others. She is always perfectly dressed and groomed, and is usually able to conceal her hot temper behind a facade of maddening cheerfulness. But she is ruthless. She reminds me of a saying attributed to David Merrick: "It is not enough for me to win. My enemies must lose."

The story, based on a novel by Tom Perrotta, shows McAllister as a dedicated teacher who is simply steamrollered by Tracy Flick. He narrates the film in a tone balanced between wonder and horror, and Broderick's performance does a good job of keeping that balance. Whatever else, he is fascinated by the phenomenon of Tracy Flick. We're inevitably reminded of Sammy Glick, the hero of Budd Schulberg's Hollywood classic *What Makes Sammy Run?* who had his eye on the prize and his feet on the shoulders of the little people he climbed over on his way to the top. *Election* makes the useful observation that although troublemakers cause problems for teachers, it's the compulsive overachievers who can drive them mad.

Alexander Payne is a director whose satire is omnidirectional. He doesn't choose an easy target and march on it. He stands in the middle of his story and attacks in all directions. His first film was *Citizen Ruth* (1996), starring

Laura Dern as a pregnant, glue-sniffing young woman who was a moronic loser, but inspired a focus for a court battle between pro-choice and antiabortion forces. What was astonishing about his film (and probably damaged it at the box office) was that he didn't choose sides, but satirized both sides with cheerful open-mindedness.

Now here is a movie that is not simply about an obnoxious student, but also about an imperfect teacher, a lockstep administration, and a student body that is mostly just marking time until it can go out into the world and occupy valuable space. The movie is not mean-spirited about any of its characters; I kind of liked Tracy Flick some of the time, and even felt a little sorry for her. Payne doesn't enjoy easy targets and cheap shots. What he's aiming for, I think, is a parable for elections in general—in which the voters have to choose from among the kinds of people who have been running for office ever since high school.

The Emperor's New Groove ★ ★ ★
G, 78 m., 2000

With the voices of: David Spade (Emperor Kuzco), John Goodman (Pacha), Eartha Kitt (Yzma), Patrick Warburton (Kronk), Wendie Malick (Pacha's Wife, Chicha). Directed by Mark Dindal and produced by Randy Fullmer. Screenplay by David Reynolds, based on the story by Chris Williams and Dindal.

In animation circles the word "cartoon" is frowned upon because it makes people think of a film that is 6 minutes long and stars Bugs Bunny, rather than a film that is 100 minutes long and grosses $200 million. I've trained myself to refer to "animated features," but now here comes Disney's *The Emperor's New Groove*, and the only word for it is "cartoon."

I mean that as a compliment. *Groove* is not an animated musical telling an archetypal fable about mermaids, lions, or brave young Chinese girls. It's a goofy slapstick cartoon, with the attention span of Donald Duck. The plot is a transparent excuse to string together the sight gags, and the characters are slapped together, too, although they wisely look like the actors who voice them, so in a way we know them already.

Consider the Emperor Kuzco, who rules over a mythical kingdom somewhere in South America. He's voiced by David Spade, and he's a lot like the characters Spade often plays, a laconic, cynical wiseguy fascinated by himself. A little of Spade goes a long way, but here the animation provides enough distance so that I actually found myself enjoying Kuzco, even if his name does sound like a discount store.

Kuzco makes the mistake, early in the film, of firing an aged crone named Yzma (Eartha Kitt), who vows revenge. Her sidekick is Kronk (Patrick Warburton, from *Seinfeld*), a cook who would truly like to be an evil accomplice but simply cannot focus his mind on the task; he's distracted by his first love, cooking. One of the running gags is Yzma's attempt to whip Kronk into a frenzy of villainy, and his own genial disinterest in her plots.

Kuzco spends his days in ill will. He has recently displaced a village, and now has his eye on a nice hilltop site for his summer palace "Kuzcotopia"—a hill currently occupied by the jolly peasant Pacha (John Goodman), his pregnant wife, Chicha (Wendie Malick), and their children. Kuzco orders them banished, not long before Yzma slips him a potion that is intended to kill him but, through a miscalculation, merely turns him into a llama.

The life of a llama does not by its nature lend itself to being lived by a smart-ass emperor, something Kuzco quickly discovers. He slinks away into the jungle, which is fearsome and frightening, especially at night, and although he has always been into self-pity he now finds real-life inspiration for his tears. Enter Pacha, who is a really nice guy and helps the llama even after he finds out the animal is occupied by the emperor who wanted to displace his family. Their relationship, which continues Spade's long-running tradition of picking fat guys as movie costars, is unusual among Disney pictures because the lead is the jerk and the sidekick is the hero.

That's the plot, more or less. It would be thin if this were the typical uplifting Disney fable, but it isn't. *The Emperor's New Groove* seems to have been made over in a corner of the Disney lot by animators who just wanted to laugh a lot and wear funny hats. The film's director is Mark Dindal, who worked on the visuals of *The Little Mermaid* and *Aladdin,* but whose most relevant credit is a 1997 Warner Bros. animated feature named *Cats Don't Dance.* It didn't do much business, perhaps because audiences look for the Disney trademark on most animation, but I liked its visual aliveness and its cheeky storytelling quality.

He brings the same quality to *The Emperor's New Groove*—he wants to be silly in the moment and trust the movie to take care of itself. His style here has been compared to the classic Chuck Jones and Tex Avery cartoons at Warner Bros., where sentimentality is avoided, wisecracks are valued, and the animators sneak social and media satire in between the gags.

The Emperor's New Groove began life, I understand, as quite a different kind of movie—a portentous, ambitious Disney feature along the lines of *Mulan* or *Pocohantas.* Apparently that vein didn't yield gold, and some of the original footage was junked while other scenes were retracked and the original musical score was largely shelved. I don't know what the earlier version would have been like, but this version is a zany tonic, more upbeat and funnier than the lugubrious *Grinch.*

The movie doesn't have the technical polish of a film like *Tarzan,* but is a reminder that the classic cartoon look is a beloved style of its own. When the Looney Tunes trademark came on the screen at the kiddie matinee of long ago, the kiddies would cheer in unison because they knew they were going to have unmitigated fun. *The Emperor's New Groove* evokes the same kind of spirit.

The Emperor's Shadow ★ ★ ★
NO MPAA RATING, 116 m., 1999

Ge You (Composer Gao Jianli), Jiang Wen (Emperor Ying Sheng), Xu Qing (His Daughter, Yueyang). Directed by Zhou Xiaowen and produced by Tong Gang, Hu Yuesheng, and Cai Huansong. Screenplay by Lu Wei. In Mandarin with English subtitles.

The Emperor's Shadow tells the story of two boys raised at the same breast as foster brothers. One becomes emperor—the founder of China's Qin dynasty, circa 200 B.C. The other becomes his court composer, more or less over his own dead body. The film, which has caused some alarm in China because it may be read as an argument against government interference in the arts, is filmed as a large-scale costume epic, with countless extras, rivers running with blood, and dramatic readings of lines like, "You are the only man with the right to call me brother."

Once you accept the likelihood that no subtle emotional nuances are going to be examined in the course of the film, it's absorbing. The same story told today might seem a tad melodramatic, but the magnificent settings and the exotic world of the Chinese court inspire a certain awe. The director, Zhou Xiaowen, has possibly studied such Japanese epics as *Ran* and *Kagemusha,* and uses the Kurosawa-style telephoto lens to compress armies of men into faceless patterns moving on a plain; our first sight of imperial style comes when horses draw up with the emperor's carriage, which is about the same size and design as the location office on a construction site.

The emperor is named Ying Sheng (Jiang Wen). Although his predecessor ordered, "After my death, execute anyone who supports musicians," Ying is a music lover, and that causes a lifetime of agony for the composer Gao Jianli (Ge You), who lives in a neighboring province and wants to be left alone to pluck his gin (an instrument that looks like the ancestor of Chet Atkins's flatbed steel guitar).

Ying conquers Gao's province, has the composer hauled before him, and orders him to compose an anthem. His first effort ("10,000 men must suffer so that one may reach heaven") strikes the emperor as just possibly a veiled criticism of his reign. When Gao demurs at his request for a rewrite, Ying starts beheading slaves, which seems to confirm the accuracy of the first version, but eventually persuades Gao.

Meanwhile, Gao has fallen in love with Yueyang (Ying Zheng), the emperor's daughter, whose legs are paralyzed. Her form of locomotion is to be passed from arm to arm by the (remaining) slaves, her head above the crowd like a Super Bowl hero. Yueyang has been betrothed to a famous general, but likes Gao, and they make love, after which she discovers she can walk. Gao asks Ying if he can marry Yueyang, but Ying refuses. Still, moved by the miracle, he tries to be reasonable: "Look, her general will certainly die in battle within the next five years, and after a year of mourning, she can marry you. Can't you wait?"

The interesting dynamic in the film is that Ying, an absolute ruler who can enforce his will on anyone, is utterly baffled by Gao's independent spirit. Their arguments sometimes sound more like sibling quarrels than master and servant. Ying is forever ordering fearsome punishments against Gao and then repenting, sometimes too late (he doesn't mind having the musician blinded by the fumes of horse urine thrown into a coal fire, but is outraged to discover that it hurts).

The movie is not subtle or especially insightful, but it is intrinsically interesting (when have you seen these characters or situations before?), and sumptuously mounted and photographed. One of its closing images, of Ying mounting a pyramid, provides the closest thing to a message: It's lonely at the top. (On the other hand, as Mel Brooks reminds us, "It's *good* to be the king.") The end titles provide information about the Qin dynasty that adds a nice wry zinger.

Encounter in the Third Dimension ★ ★
NO MPAA RATING, 45 m., 1999

Stuart Pankin (Professor), Stuart Pankin (Voice of M.A.X.), Cassandra Peterson (Elvira, Mistress of the Dark), Harry Shearer (Narrator), Andrea Thompson (Ruth in the Booth). Directed by Ben Stassen and produced by Charlotte Clay Huggins. Screenplay by Kurt Frey and Stassen.

Encounter in the Third Dimension resembles several other giant-screen IMAX releases in being interesting primarily because of the size of the screen. The movie packages a lot of information about 3-D movies into a goofy story about a scientist who wants to demonstrate his latest 3-D invention.

The story is pretty lame, and the info is familiar. Is there likely to be anyone in the audience who isn't familiar with the 3-D effect of the Stereopticon? (Children know it as the familiar ViewMaster.)

Still, no doubt about it, the 3-D effect in IMAX and its cousin, Omnimax, is the best I've seen. That's because of the huge screen, which covers peripheral vision, and the oversize projectors that pump out a lot of brightness. The glasses, which resemble science-fiction headsets, contain shutters that separate the images for each eye. The result is truly three-dimensional, all right. There was an undersea IMAX film shot in 3-D that I really enjoyed.

But the underlying problem with 3-D remains exactly the same as when *Bwana Devil* and *House of Wax* first hit the screen in the 1950s: It's unnecessary most of the time, and distracting the rest of the time. The ordinary 2-D illusion of movies has long been accepted all over the world as an acceptable illusion of reality. The 3-D illusion seems used mostly to throw things at the audience. That gets old after a while. If the purpose of a movie's story is to absorb us, every exaggerated 3-D effect breaks our reverie and calls attention to the technique itself.

In *Encounter in the Third Dimension*, we meet a professor (Stuart Pankin) who hopes to unveil his new gimmick, Real-O-Vision. He has enlisted Elvira ("Mistress of the Dark," the credits remind us) to sing a song in this new process, but she keeps getting interrupted as the machinery breaks down, and so the professor dispatches a flying robot named M.A.X. (voice also by Pankin) to entertain us while he works on his invention.

The primary function of M.A.X., it goes without saying, is to zoom toward the audience and hang in midair, seemingly inches from our faces. Dr. Johnson once said of a dog standing on its hind legs: "It is not done well, but one is surprised to find it done at all." Watching M.A.X. whizzing about, I reflected that it was done well, but, alas, I did not want it done at all.

End of Days ★ ★
R, 118 m., 1999

Arnold Schwarzenegger (Jericho Cane), Gabriel Byrne (The Man), Kevin Pollack (Chicago), Robin Tunney (Christine York), Rod Steiger (Father Kovak). Directed by Peter Hyams and produced by Armyan Bernstein and Bill Borden. Screenplay by Andrew W. Marlowe.

"There are forces here you couldn't possibly comprehend."

—dialogue

You can say that again. *End of Days* opens with a priest gazing out his window at the Vatican City and seeing a comet arching above the moon like an eyebrow. He races to an old wooden box, snatches up a silver canister, pulls out an ancient scroll, unrolls it and sees—yes! A drawing of a comet arching above the moon like an eyebrow! For verily this is the dreaded celestial display known as the "Eye of God."

The priest bursts into an inner chamber of the Vatican where the pope sits surrounded by advisers. "The child will be born today!" he gasps. Then we cut to "New York City, 1979" and a live childbirth scene, including, of course, the obligatory dialogue, "Push!" A baby girl is born, and a nurse takes the infant in its swaddling clothes and races to a basement room of the hospital, where the child is anointed with the blood of a freshly killed rattlesnake before being returned to the arms of its mother.

Already I am asking myself, where is William Donohue when we need him? Why does his Catholic League attack a sweet comedy like *Dogma* but give a pass to *End of Days,* in which we learn that once every 1,000 years a woman is born who, if she is impregnated twenty years later by the Prince of Darkness during the hour from 11 to 12 P.M. on the last day of the millennium, will give birth to the anti-Christ, who will bring about, yes, the end of days? Meanwhile an internal Vatican battle rages between those who want to murder the woman, and the pope, who says we must put our faith in God.

The murder of the woman would, of course, be a sin, but perhaps justifiable under the circumstances, especially since the humble instrument chosen by God to save the universe is an alcoholic bodyguard named Jericho Cane, played by Arnold Schwarzenegger. Jericho and his partner (Kevin Pollack) find themselves investigating a puzzling series of events, including a man with his tongue cut out who nevertheless screams a warning and is later nailed to the ceiling of his hospital room.

Movies like this are particularly vulnerable to logic, and *End of Days* even has a little fun trying to sort out the reasoning behind the satanic timetable. When Jericho has the Millennium Eve timetable explained to him, including the requirement that the Prince of Darkness do his dirty deed precisely between 11 P.M. and midnight, he asks the very question I was asking myself: "Eastern Standard Time?"

The answer, Jericho is told, is that the exact timing was meticulously worked out centuries ago by the Gregorian monks, and indeed their work on this project included, as a bonus spin-off, the invention of the Gregorian calendar. Let's see. Rome is six hours ahead of New York. In other words, those clever monks said, "The baby will be conceived between 5 and 6 A.M. on January 1, Rome time, but that will be between 11 P.M. and 12 A.M. in a city that does not yet exist, on a continent we have no knowledge of, assuming the world is round and there are different times in different places as it revolves around the Sun, which of course it would be a heresy to suggest." With headaches like this, no wonder they invented Gregorian chant to take the load off.

End of Days involves a head-on collision between the ludicrous and the absurd, in which a supernatural being with the outward appearance of Gabriel Byrne pursues a twenty-year-old woman named Christine (Robin Tunney) around Manhattan, while Jericho tries to protect her. This being a theological struggle Schwarzenegger style, the battle to save Christine involves a scene where a man dangles from a helicopter while chasing another man across a rooftop, and a scene in which a character clings by his fingertips to a high window ledge, and a scene in which a runaway subway train explodes, and a scene in which fireballs consume square blocks of Manhattan, and a scene in which someone is stabbed with a crucifix, and . . .

But the violence raises another question. How exactly do the laws of physics apply to the Byrne character? Called "The Man" in the credits, he is Satan himself, for my money, yet seems to have variable powers. Jericho shoots him, but he pulls up his shirt so we can see the bullet holes healing. Then Jericho switches to a machine gun, and the bullets hurl The Man backward and put him out of commission for a time, before he attacks again. What are the rules here? Is he issued only so much anti-injury mojo per millennium?

The movie's final confrontation is a counterpoint to the Times Square countdown toward the year 2000. Only a churl would point out that the new millennium actually begins a year later, on the last day of 2000. Even then, *End of Days* would find a loophole. This is the first movie to seriously argue that "666," the numerical sign of Satan, is actually "999" upside down, so that all you have to do is add a "1" and, whoa! You get "1999."

The End of the Affair ★ ★ ½

R, 105 m., 1999

Ralph Fiennes (Maurice Bendrix), Stephen Rea (Henry Miles), Julianne Moore (Sarah Miles), Heather Jay Jones (Henry's Maid), James Bolam (Mr. Savage), Ian Hart (Mr. Parkis), Samuel Bould (Lance Parkis), Cyril Shaps (Waiter), Penny Morrell (Bendrix's Landlady). Directed by Neil Jordan and produced by Stephen Woolley and Jordan. Screenplay by Jordan, based on the novel by Graham Greene.

It is raining much of the time in *The End of the Affair*, and that is as it should be. The film is about love and adultery in cold, dark, wartime London—when sex was a moment of stolen warmth, an interlude between the air raids and the daily grind of rationing and restrictions. In the opening scene, two men meet on Clapham Common in the rain, and we can almost smell their damp, fungoid woolen suits, cut with the smoke of their cigarettes.

One is a government official named Henry Miles (Stephen Rea). The other is a novelist named Maurice Bendrix (Ralph Fiennes). Henry is married to Sarah (Julianne Moore). Maurice was her lover. Now both men are out in the rain and Sarah is apparently meeting secretly with a new friend. That's what Henry wants to talk to Maurice about. He doesn't suspect Maurice of adultery: He simply wants his help, as a friend, in hiring a private detective to follow Sarah.

This story and milieu are from a 1951 novel by Graham Greene, said to be based on his own wartime love affair and drenched with the Catholicism that was central to his work at that time. The engine of the story could come from melodrama or a thriller: A man unwittingly asks his wife's former lover for help in identifying her present lover. But in Greene, and in this adaptation by Neil Jordan, it is all so much more worldly, weary, and bittersweet than that, because Maurice feels he is being cheated on too. The new lover, if there is one, has made two cuckolds.

Maurice and Sarah met at a party just before the war, we learn. Henry was even then a sad sack with his attention always on his work. The two fell instantly in love and carried on a passionate affair until one day during their lovemaking the earth literally shook, and it appeared that Maurice had been killed in a German raid. We see all of this in flashback, and how when the dust cleared and Maurice crept slowly back to consciousness, Sarah was on her knees in prayer. Afterward things were never the same. Sarah withdrew from Maurice, turned cold and unavailable, and eventually he retreated into a long bitterness. Now we are back up to the meeting of the two men in the rain.

All of this makes an intriguing novel, and *The End of the Affair* is Greene dancing on the divide between the rules of religion and the lusts of the flesh. His adulterous husbands and sinning priests have to deal not only with built-in guilt but with the rules of the Church, which they never believe in more than while breaking them. The novel is a largely interior affair, existing inside Maurice's mind as he ponders again and again how a woman could seem so close and then suddenly be so far away.

The film, on the other hand, is as hangdog as Stephen Rea's face in the first scene. It is the story of characters who desperately require more lightness and folly; one can be grim in the confessional and yet be permitted a skip in the step on leaving the church. The characters seem too glum. We see release but miss joy. Sarah and Maurice meet for energetic sex, but their conversation doesn't suggest the kind of idealism required by great love. For a novelist, Maurice is surprisingly pedestrian in his speech, and we have to hear him telling Sarah he is jealous of her shoes, "because they will take you away from me." Not impossible dialogue (we are reminded of Prince Charles's fantasies involving feminine hygiene products), but we expect better from a novelist.

Greene has a good feel for muted low comedy in his supporting characters, and the best turn in *The End of the Affair* is by Ian Hart, as Mr. Parkis, the detective hired by Maurice to follow Sarah. Parkis brings along his boy, Lance (Samuel Bould), an earnest little fellow with a bold birthmark on his cheek and hair brilliantined flat like his dad's. Lance can hardly understand adultery, but joins in the game of following, snooping, and spying, as Parkis beams with pride. Nothing belittles a man more than suspicion of the woman he loves, and somehow a private detective is always able to choose just those words to make the man feel even shabbier and sneakier.

If the movie were not so downbeat and its literary pedigree so distinguished, the resolution would be soap opera. The outcome, indeed, would be right at home on a religious cable station (although the sex would have to be handled more disapprovingly). Without revealing the outcome I cannot express my doubts about it, but if I could have drawn Sarah aside before her fateful turning point, I would have told her the following parable. A woman tumbles out of the choir loft of a church and her dress catches in the chandelier. She swings above the congregation with her bloomers exposed. The priest in the pulpit thunders, "He who looks shall be stricken blind!" One altar boy claps a hand to his face and whispers to the other: "I'm going to risk one eye."

Endurance ★ ★ ★
G, 83 m., 1999

Himself (Haile Gebrselassie), Bekele Gebrselassie (Haile's Father), Shawananness Gebrselassie (Haile's Mother), Yonas Zergaw (Young Haile), Assefa Gebrselassie (Haile's Brother), Alem Tellahun (Haile's Wife), Tizazu Mashresha (Haile's Police Trainer). Directed by Leslie Woodhead and produced by Edward R. Pressman, Terrence Malick, and Max Palevsky. Screenplay by Woodhead.

The sound of the runner's breathing is like a percussion instrument made of wind. Each exhalation is a thrum of effort. He runs as if he has been running since time immemorial. His name is Haile Gebrselassie, and after he set a new record at the Atlanta Olympics in 1996, *Runner's World* magazine described him as "the greatest distance runner of all time."

Endurance is a film about Gebrselassie, his early life on an Ethiopian farm, his training, his shy courtship, and his Olympic triumph. It is not a documentary, exactly; scenes are written and staged, and actors play him at younger ages. But it is drawn from his life. His father, brother, and wife play themselves, and the footage of his triumph at Atlanta is real. So, I think, is the sound of his breathing.

The runner was raised in a rural area, where his father wanted him to stay and work on the farm. But in 1980, when the Ethiopian runner Miruts Yifter won the 10,000-meter race at the Moscow Olympics running barefoot, young Haile, like all of his countrymen, was stirred to hear the Ethiopian national anthem played after his victory. He determined to become a runner, and we see him as a boy (played by his nephew, Yonas Zergaw), running everywhere on the farm where his family of twelve lived in a mud hut.

Gebrselassie himself takes over the role as a teenager, and there is a scene where he and his father stand on a hilltop, the landscape unfolding below them, as he explains his plans to go to Addis Ababa to go into serious training for the Olympics. His father prefers him to stay on the farm. There is a stilted, formal quality to their conversation that oddly enough gives it more force: We are not seeing actors, but the real people somewhat self-consciously re-creating a conversation they actually had.

The British director, Leslie Woodhead, uses title cards to separate the sections of his film and provide information about Gebrselassie. "Finished 99th in first marathon," we read, and then a little later, "Two years of hard training." As we see marathon runners winding their way through the city streets: "A thousand others with the same dream." Gebrselassie doesn't fit the stereotype of the long-distance runner, tall and long-limbed. He is compact, wiry, muscular. The secret of his greatness, we gather, is that he ran and ran, longer and harder than anyone else, until in his big race he was simply the best prepared.

There are glimpses of his personal life. A shy date with a girl named Alem (who plays herself, and became his wife). One has coffee, the other a Fanta orange drink. Later, he has a heart-to-heart talk with her about his father's disappointment. The father's feelings are understandable: He has lost a strong son to help on the farm, so that the boy can move to the city and . . . run?

The footage of the race itself is never less than thrilling, as such races always are; the close-up lens lets us see the pain of the runners, who by the end are relying mostly on will and endurance. John Powell's music is not exhilarating boilerplate, as scores often are during films about athletics. Instead, it is brooding, introspective, almost sad, suggesting how the runners must look within themselves and endure their burning lungs in a race of such length and difficulty. There is a lot of time to be by yourself in a 10,000-meter race.

I learn from the *Variety* review of the film that the filmmakers had the eight leading contenders under contract, so that they were almost assured of being able to tell the story of the winner. Fair enough, but in Haile Gebrselassie they surely got the most interesting of subjects, a runner whose triumph must be explained almost entirely from within his own determination. He didn't come from a background of training, coaching, and determination, but from the rural hills, where we see him running to school, running to the water well, running to the fields, always with that stoic thrumming of his breath.

Enemy at the Gates ★ ★ ★
R, 131 m., 2001

Jude Law (Vassili), Joseph Fiennes (Danilov), Ed Harris (Konig), Rachel Weisz (Tania), Bob Hoskins (Khrushchev), Ron Perlman (Koulikov), Gabriel Marshall-Thomson (Sacha), Eva Mattes (Mother Filipov), Matthias Habich (General von Paulus). Directed by Jean-Jacques Annaud and produced by Annaud and John D. Schofield. Screenplay by Annaud and Alain Godard.

Enemy at the Gates opens with a battle sequence that deserves comparison with *Saving Private Ryan,* and then narrows its focus until it is about two men playing a cat-and-mouse game in the ruins of Stalingrad. The Nazi is sure he is the cat. The Russian fears he may be the mouse.

The movie is inspired by true events, we're told, although I doubt real life involved a love

triangle; the film might have been better and leaner if it had told the story of the two soldiers and left out the soppy stuff. Even so, it's remarkable, a war story told as a chess game where the loser not only dies, but goes by necessity to an unmarked grave.

This is a rare World War II movie that does not involve Americans. It takes place in the autumn of 1942 in Stalingrad, during Hitler's insane attack on the Soviet Union. At first it appeared the Germans would roll over the ragged Russian resistance, but eventually the stubbornness of the Soviets combined with the brutal weather and problems with supply lines deliver Hitler a crushing defeat and, many believe, turn the tide of the war.

We see the early hopelessness of the Soviet cause in shots showing terrified Russian soldiers trying to cross a river and make a landing in the face of withering fire. They are ordered to charge the Germans across an exposed no-man's-land, and when half are killed and the others turned back, they are fired on by their own officers, as cowards. This is a sustained sequence as harrowing, in its way, as Spielberg's work.

One of the Russians stands out. His name is Vassili (Jude Law), and we know from the title sequence that he is a shepherd from the Urals, whose marksmanship was learned by killing wolves that preyed on his flock. In the heat of battle, he kills five Germans, and is noticed by Danilov (Joseph Fiennes), the political officer assigned to his unit. As Russian morale sinks lower, Danilov prints a leaflet praising the heroic shepherd boy.

We learn that Vassili is indeed a good shot, but has little confidence in his own abilities (in the opening sequence, he has one bullet to use against a wolf, and misses). Danilov encourages him, and as the battle lines solidify and both sides dig into their positions, Vassili continues to pick off Germans and star in Danilov's propaganda. Even Nikita Khrushchev (Bob Hoskins, looking uncannily like the real thing), the leader of the Soviet defense of Stalingrad, praises the boy and the publicity strategy.

As German resolve falters, they bring in their own best sniper, a sharpshooter named Konig (Ed Harris), a Bavarian aristocrat who in peacetime shoots deer. He is older, hawk-faced, clear-eyed, a professional. His assignment is to kill Vassili and end the propaganda. "How will you find him?" he's asked. "I'll have him find me."

The heart of the movie is the duel between the two men, played out in a blasted cityscape of bombed factories and rubble. The war recedes into the background as the two men, who have never had a clear glimpse of each other, tacitly agree on their ground of battle. The director, Jean-Jacques Annaud, makes the geography clear—the open spaces, the shadows, the hollow pipes that are a way to creep from one point to another.

The duel is made more complicated when Vassili meets Sacha (Gabriel Marshall-Thomson), a boy of seven or eight who moves like a wraith between the opposing lines and is known to both snipers. Through Sacha, Vassili meets his neighbor Tania (Rachel Weisz), a Jewish woman whose parents were killed by the Nazis. Vassili falls in love with Tania—and so does Danilov, and this triangle seems like a plot device to separate the scenes that really interest us.

Sacha is a useful character, however. As a child of war he is old beyond his years, but not old enough to know how truly ruthless and deadly a game he is involved in. His final appearance in the film brings a gasp from the audience, but fits into the implacable logic of the situation.

Annaud (Quest for Fire, In the Name of the Rose, Seven Years in Tibet) makes big-scale films where men test themselves against their ideas. Here he shows the Nazi sniper as a cool professional, almost without emotion, taking a cerebral approach to the challenge. The Russian is quite different; his confidence falters when he learns who he's up against, and he says, simply, "He's better than me." The strategy of the final confrontation between the two men has a kind of poetry to it, and I like the physical choices that Harris makes in the closing scene.

Is the film also about a duel between two opposing ideologies, Marxism and Nazism? Danilov, the propagandist, paints it that way, but actually it is about two men placed in a situation where they have to try to use their intelligence and skills to kill each other. When Annaud focuses on that, the movie works with rare concentration. The additional plot stuff and the romance are kind of a shame.

Entrapment ★ ★ ★
PG-13, 113 m., 1999

Sean Connery (Mac), Catherine Zeta-Jones (Gin), Ving Rhames (Thibadeaux), Will Patton (Cruz), Maury Chaykin (Conrad Greene), Kevin McNally (Haas), Terry O'Neill (Quinn), Madhav Sharma (Security Chief). Directed by Jon Amiel and produced by Sean Connery, Michael Hertzberg, and Rhonda Tollefson. Screenplay by Ron Bass and William Broyles.

Entrapment is the very embodiment of a star vehicle: a movie with a preposterous plot, exotic locations, absurd action sequences, and so much chemistry between attractive actors that we don't care. It stars Sean Connery and Catherine Zeta-Jones in a caper that reminded me of *To Catch a Thief, Charade, Topkapi,* and the stunt sequences in Bond pictures. I didn't believe a second of it, and I didn't care that I didn't.

The film is about thieves. Connery plays a man named Mac, who is getting along in years but is still respected as the most resourceful master thief in the world. Jones plays Gin, who in the early scenes is established as an insurance investigator who sets an elaborate trap for Mac. I will be revealing little about the plot if I say that neither of these people is precisely as they seem.

Watching the film, I imagined the trailer. Not the movie's real trailer, which I haven't seen, but one of those great 1950s trailers where big words in fancy typefaces come spinning out of the screen, asking us to Thrill! to risks atop the world's tallest building, and Gasp! at a daring bank robbery, and Cheer! as towering adventure takes us from New York to Scotland to Malaysia.

A trailer like that would only be telling the simple truth. It would also perhaps include a few tantalizing shots of Zeta-Jones lifting her leather-clad legs in an athletic ballet designed to avoid the invisible beams of security systems. And shots of a thief hanging upside down from a seventy-story building. And an audacious raid through an underwater tunnel.

And a priceless Rembrandt. And a way to steal $8 billion because of the Y2K bug. And so on.

It works because it is made stylishly, because Connery and Zeta-Jones are enormously attractive actors, and because of the romantic tension between them. I got a letter the other day complaining about the age differences between the male and female leads in several recent pictures—and, to be sure, Connery at sixty-nine and Zeta-Jones at twenty-nine remember different wars. But the movie cannily establishes ground rules (Mac lectures that thievery is a business that permits no personal relationships), and so instead of questioning why they're erotically involved, we wish they would be.

The plot, by Ron Bass and William Broyles, is put together like a Swiss watch that keeps changing time zones: It is accurate and misleading at once. The film consists of one elaborate caper sequence after another, and it rivals the Bond films in its climactic action sequence, which has Mac and Gin hanging from a string of holiday bulbs beneath the walkway linking the two towers of the Petronas Twin Towers in Kuala Lumpur. The stunt and f/x work here do a good job of convincing us that human beings are actually dangling precariously seventy stories in the air, and I for one am convinced that Zeta-Jones personally performs an earlier stunt, in which she treats an old wooden beam in Mac's Scottish castle as if it were a parallel bar at the Olympics. Most of the movie's action is just that—action—and not extreme violence.

Watching Connery negotiate the nonsense of the plot is an education in acting: He treats every situation as if it is plausible but not that big of a deal, and that sets the right tone. He avoids the smile in the voice that would give away the silliness of the plot. When he says, "I'm never late. If I'm late, it's because I'm dead," we reflect that some actors can get away with lines like that and others can't, and Connery is the leader of the first group.

As for Catherine Zeta-Jones, I can only reflect, as I did while watching her in *The Mask of Zorro,* that while beautiful women are a dime a dozen in the movies, those with fire, flash, and humor are a good deal more scarce. Taking her cue perhaps from Connery, she

also plays a preposterous role absolutely straight. The costars and Jon Amiel, the director, respect the movie tradition they're working in, instead of condescending to it. There are scenes in this film when astounding revelations are made, and although I didn't believe them, I accepted them, which is more difficult and enjoyable.

Erin Brockovich ★ ★
R, 126 m., 2000

Julia Roberts (Erin Brockovich), Albert Finney (Ed Masry), Aaron Eckhart (George), Marg Helgenberger (Donna Jensen), Cherry Jones (Pamela Duncan), Peter Coyote (Kurt Potter), Scotty Leavenworth (Matthew), Gemmenne De La Pena (Katie). Directed by Steven Soderbergh and produced by Danny DeVito, Michael Shamberg, and Stacey Sher. Screenplay by Susannah Grant.

Erin Brockovich is *Silkwood* (Meryl Streep fighting nuclear wastes) crossed with *A Civil Action* (John Travolta against pollution), plus Julia Roberts in a plunging neckline. Roberts plays a real-life heroine who helped uncover one of the biggest environmental crimes in history. But her performance upstages the story; this is always Roberts, not Brockovich, and unwise wardrobe decisions position her character somewhere between a caricature and a distraction.

I know all about the real Erin Brockovich because I saw her on *Oprah,* where she cried at just the right moment in a filmed recap of her life. She was a divorced mom of three with few employment prospects, who talked her way into a job at a law firm, began an investigation on her own initiative, and played a key role in a pollution suit that cost Pacific Gas and Electric a $333 million settlement.

There is obviously a story here, but *Erin Brockovich* doesn't make it compelling. The film lacks focus and energy, the character development is facile and thin, and what about those necklines? I know that the real Brockovich liked to dress provocatively; that's her personal style and she's welcome to it. But the Hollywood version makes her look like a miniskirted hooker, with her bras that peek cheerfully above her necklines.

Oh, the movie tries to deal with the clothes. "You might want to rethink your wardrobe a little," her boss (Albert Finney) tells her. She inelegantly replies, "I think I look nice, and as long as I have one ass instead of two, I'll wear what I like." Yeah, fine, after she's already lost her own personal injury suit by flashing cleavage on the witness stand and firing off four-letter words. When she dresses the same way to go door-to-door in a working-class neighborhood where industrial chemicals have caused illness, we have to wonder whether, in real life, she was hassled or mistrusted.

Whether she was or wasn't, the costume design sinks this movie. Julia Roberts is a sensational-looking woman, and dressed so provocatively, in every single scene, she upstages the material. If the medium is the message, the message in this movie is sex.

That's all the more true because the supporting characters are not vivid or convincing. Albert Finney is one of the most robust and powerful actors in the movies, but here, as a personal injury lawyer named Ed Masry, he comes across like an office manager at H & R Block. He's dampened; there's no fire in his performance, and when he complains that the cost of the lawsuit may bankrupt him, all we can think about is the infinitely greater impact of John Travolta's similar dialogue in *A Civil Action*.

Erin has a kind of relationship with her next-door neighbor, George, a Harley fan who becomes a baby-sitter for her children. George is played by Aaron Eckhart, who was so dominant in *In the Company of Men,* but here, wearing a twirpy John Ritter beard that he doesn't seem comfortable with, he's a shallow cipher. The couple can't even have convincing arguments because there's not enough between them in the first place.

Seeing the details of Brockovich's home life, her relationship with her kids and friends, the way she talks, the way she postures, we're always aware that there's a performance going on. Streep was so much more convincing in the somewhat similar role of Karen Silkwood. We understand that Pacific Gas and Electric has polluted groundwater and is apparently responsible for death and disease, but it never emerges as much of a villain, and in the pallid confrontations with their attorneys there's

none of the juice that Robert Duvall's company attorney brought to *A Civil Action*.

Steven Soderbergh, who directed, has blown a great opportunity to make the movie that the real Erin Brockovich calls for. Susannah Grant's by-the-numbers screenplay sees the characters as markers on a storyboard rather than flesh-and-blood humans. Scenes with members of the suffering families genuflect in the direction of pathos, but are cut and dried. It doesn't feel like we're seeing Erin Brockovich share the pain, but like we're seeing Julia Roberts paying a house call (again, we remember the power of *A Civil Action*).

Erin Brockovich has a screenplay with the depth and insight of a cable-TV docudrama, and that won't do for a 126-minute "major production." Maybe it's not that the necklines are distracting. Maybe it's just that the movie gives us so little to focus on that they win by default.

An Everlasting Piece ★ ★ ★
R, 109 m., 2000

Barry McEvoy (Colm), Brian F. O'Byrne (George), Anna Friel (Bronagh), Billy Connolly (The Scalper). Directed by Barry Levinson and produced by Louis DiGiaimo, Mark Johnson, Levinson, Jerome O'Connor, and Paula Weinstein. Screenplay by Barry McEvoy.

Anecdotes are polished in Ireland until they haven't a word to spare, with the listeners nodding at the familiar lines they've heard a hundred times. Some of the scenes in *An Everlasting Piece* have the feel of tales rehearsed in pubs for years. The scene, for example, where the hero's mother and his sister open the door and find his brother passed out drunk on the lawn. They haul him in, strip him of his wet clothes, and drop him facedown on the sofa. But when his face is revealed, of course it isn't the brother at all.

My guess is that Barry McEvoy, who wrote the movie and stars in it, didn't dream that up. I have a feeling it actually happened to somebody. The whole movie feels like that, even the dramatic parts—not in the details but in the tone. It's about two barbers in a prison for the insane, one Catholic, one Protestant, who go into the hairpiece business in Northern Ireland and find that hairpieces, like everything else in that unhappy land, have a way of getting mixed up with sectarian politics.

The lads are Colm (McEvoy) and George (Brian F. O'Byrne), and Colm got his job because his girlfriend, Bronagh (Anna Friel), works in the prison. The work is steady, although the conditions leave something to be desired, as when one prisoner tries to bite off Colm's ear. Then they hear of a prisoner named the Scalper (Billy Connolly), so called because he tried too hard to create a market for his wares, who before his imprisonment was the only retailer of hairpieces in Northern Ireland.

There is now obviously a market that needs to be served, and Colm and George call their new company the Piece People, with George selling to Protestants, Colm selling to Catholics, and either one willing to be less than frank about his religion if it means making a sale. They hope to have the market to themselves, but a rival firm, Toupee or Not Toupee, sets up in business, and they get involved in a desperate sales competition to sell thirty pieces by the end of the year.

The movie is light on plot and heavy on incident, including several sales calls on peculiar or difficult clients, and a run-in with the IRA, whose leader doesn't know whether to shoot them or buy a piece from them. When the piece is later found at the scene of an IRA crime, the police come calling, and the Piece People seem to face a choice between jail and kneecapping.

The movie, wicked and cheeky, was directed by Barry Levinson (*Diner, Rain Man, Wag the Dog*), who has set four pictures in his hometown of Baltimore and now seeks the same kind of local color in Belfast, even if the details are different. He apparently decided to make the movie after coming across the original screenplay by McEvoy, a journeyman actor who based his own character, he says, on his father.

The movie has the ring of old, beloved, and partially but not entirely true stories. One detail is unexpectedly from life. Colm's home is shown in the middle of a vacant lot in Belfast, a wasteland bisected by a "peace wall" between the Protestant and Catholic sections, with a wire mesh fence to protect the home from firebombs. This house actually exists, I understand, and so of course do the conditions in Northern Ireland, where people try to go about their daily business while troops patrol the streets and a bitter struggle continues.

The key scene in *An Everlasting Piece* is a conversation between Colm and George as they contemplate selling hairpieces to a roomful of British soldiers who have lost their hair through stress. Colm, the Catholic, explains to his friend that he welcomes this sale to the enemy as a "gesture," which he can make although his friend cannot. Why not? "Because we're right and you're wrong," Colm explains, undercutting somewhat the benevolence of the gesture and leaving George trying to puzzle out the logic.

Evolution ★ ★ ½
PG-13, 103 m., 2001

David Duchovny (Ira Kane), Orlando Jones (Harry Block), Ted Levine (Dr. Woodman), Julianne Moore (Allison Reed), Seann William Scott (Wayne Green), Dan Aykroyd (Governor Lewis), Wayne Duvall (Dr. Paulson), Michael Bower (Danny Donald), Wendy Braun (Nurse Tate). Directed by Ivan Reitman and produced by Daniel Goldberg, Joe Medjuck, and Reitman. Screenplay by David Diamond, David Weissman, and Don Jakoby.

I can't quite recommend *Evolution*, but I have a sneaky affection for it. It's not good, but it's nowhere near as bad as most recent comedies; it has real laughs, but it misses real opportunities. For example, by giving us aliens who are sort of harmless, it sets up a situation where the heroes should be trying to protect them. But no. Everybody wants to kill them, apparently because the national psyche has reverted to the 1950s, when all flying saucers were automatically fired on by the army.

Ivan Reitman, who directed the film, also made *Ghostbusters*, and there are times when you can see that he remembers his earlier success all too well. Both movies have vast gaseous monsters, although only this one, keenly alert to the bodily orifice du jour, gives us "Help! I'm Trapped Up the Alien's Sphincter!" jokes. I have days on the movie beat when I don't know if I'm a critic or a proctologist.

As the film opens, a would-be fireman (Seann William Scott) is practicing by rescuing an inflatable doll from a burning shack, when a flaming meteor crashes nearby. Harry Block (Orlando Jones), a scientist from nearby Glen Canyon Community College, is called to investigate and brings along his friend, science instructor Ira Kane (David Duchovny). They discover the meteor has "punched through" to an underground cavern, where it is oozing strange sluglike little creatures.

Kane and Bloch have a nice double-act together; like the characters in *Ghostbusters* they talk intelligently and possess wit and irony, and are not locked into one-liners. Jones even gets a laugh out of a significant nod, which is not easy in a movie with this decibel level. I also liked the way they came up with a popular drugstore item as a weapon against the invaders.

The alien creatures have the amazing ability to evolve in brief generations into whatever the screenplay requires: flying dinosaurs, creepy-crawlies, savage reptiles, even a sad-eyed ET clone that has an *Alien* tooth-monster hiding down its throat. The army is called in, led by Dr. Woodman (Ted Levine), a soldier-scientist who worked with Ira Kane once before ("he's a dangerous disgrace"). Turns out Ira inoculated platoons of soldiers with a substance with such side effects as diarrhea, blindness, facial paralysis, and hair loss. The army named this tragic syndrome after Kane; I found myself thinking of funnier names for it, starting with the Bald Runs.

Dr. Woodman's assistant is Allison Reed (Julianne Moore), whose character trait is that she falls over everything. She is, however, funny in other ways, and sides with the two community college guys when her boss tries to freeze them out of the investigation. Meanwhile, the evolving creatures take on weird manifestations while the Mother of All Creatures is expanding down there in that cavern, generating all manner of strange offspring, while preparing to make an appearance in the grand finale.

The aliens are clever and bizarre movie creatures, designed by special-effects wizard Phil Tippett, who applied "the basic theory of panspermia," according to the press notes, which I always study after movies like this. It will come as news to panspermists that pan-

sperm can evolve into amphibians, reptiles, birds, and mammals within a week; *Evolution* parts company with the basic theory almost before the publicist can get it into the notes, but never mind: One does not attend this movie for scientific facts. That is what the *Star Trek* movies are for.

Would it surprise you if I said that after ninety minutes of preparation, we discover that the entire movie has been leading up to a moment when the Orlando Jones character finds himself occupying the business end of a giant alien's digestive tract? Not if you have a sense of fair play. Earlier in the movie, a little alien crawls under Jones's skin and lodges in *his* intestines, inspiring emergency measures by a doctor who cries, "There's no time for lubricant!"—inspiring Jones to utter the best line in the movie, "There's *always* time for lubricant!"

eXistenZ ★ ★ ★
R, 97 m., 1999

Jennifer Jason Leigh (Allegra Geller), Jude Law (Ted Pikul), Willem Dafoe (Gas), Ian Holm (Kiri Vinokur), Don McKellar (Yevgeny Nourish), Callum Keith Rennie (Hugo Carlaw), Sarah Polley (Merle), Christopher Eccleston (Levi). Directed by David Cronenberg and produced by Robert Lantos, Andras Hamori, and Cronenberg. Screenplay by Cronenberg.

Guys are always using the same lame excuses. First Ted licks Allegra's bio-port. Then he says, "That wasn't me—it was my game character!" Allegra is the world's leading designer of virtual reality games. Her newest game is named eXistenZ, and the bio-port plugs directly into the lower spine and connects to the game's control pod via an "umbrycord." When you're hooked up, you can't tell the game from reality. Not even if you designed the game.

eXistenZ is the new film from David Cronenberg, the Canadian director who must be a thorn in the side of the MPAA ratings board. He's always filming activities that look like sex, but don't employ any of the appurtenances associated with that pastime. In his previous film, *Crash*, the characters exhibited an unhealthy interest in wounds. This time it's bio-ports. And what about those "MetaFlesh

Game Pods," input devices that combine the attributes of a joystick, a touch pad, and a kidney? They pulse with a life of their own, and Allegra holds hers as if it's a baby, or a battery-powered shiatsu machine.

eXistenZ arrived a few weeks after *The Matrix,* another science-fiction movie about characters who find themselves inside a universe created by virtual reality. *The Matrix* is mainstream sci-fi, but *eXistenZ,* written by Cronenberg, is much stranger; it creates a world where organic and inorganic are not separate states, but kind of chummy. Consider the scene where an oil-stained grease monkey implants a bio-port in the hero, using a piece of equipment that seems designed to give a lube job to a PeterBilt.

Jennifer Jason Leigh, that fearless adventurer in extreme roles, plays Allegra, whose new game is being marketed by Antenna Research. Jude Law is Ted, the company's marketing trainee. She barely misses being killed during a demonstration of eXistenZ, when an assassin slips past the metal detectors at the door with a gun made of flesh and blood. Ted helps her escape, and later, when he cuts the bullet out of her shoulder, he discovers it's not a bullet but a . . . hmmm, this is interesting . . . a human tooth. She decides Ted needs his own bio-port, and looks for a "country gas station." When she finds one (with a sign that says Country Gas Station) we assume they're inside the game, which is why she knows the station's name: She wrote it, and maybe also created its owner, named Gas (Willem Dafoe).

She knows her way around this world, and isn't surprised when they're told, "Look for a Chinese restaurant in the forest—and order the special." The owner rattles off the chef's daily selection, explaining that "mutant reptiles and amphibians produce previously unknown taste sensations." But Ted insists on *the* daily special and gets a dish that's really bony. No wonder. The bones click together into a gun. And soon they visit the Trout Farm, where organic game pods are grown, and come up against Kiri Vinokur (Ian Holm), owner of Cortical Systematics, a rival game firm.

Cronenberg's film is as loaded with special effects as *The Matrix,* but they're on a different scale. Many of his best effects are gooey, indescribable organic things, and some of the most memorable scenes involve characters eating things that surgeons handle with gloves on. He places his characters in a backwoods world that looks like it was ordered over the phone from L.L. Bean. Then he frames them with visuals where half the screen is a flat foreground that seems to push them toward us, while the other half is a diagonal sliding off alarmingly into the background.

eXistenZ is likely to appeal especially to computer game players, since it's familiar with that world and speculates on its future development. Allegra explains to Ted such phenomena as "genuine game urges"—"something your game character was born to do." She regards her programming handiwork with musings like, "I've devoted five of my most passionate years to this strange little creature." At one point she's alarmed to discover, "I'm locked outside my own $38 million game!" And without the password, it looks like neither she nor anyone else can get back inside. What? You mean she didn't back up her disk?

The Exorcist (2000 Version) ★ ★ ★ ½ (1973 Version) ★ ★ ★ ★
R, 132 m., 2000

Linda Blair (Regan), Ellen Burstyn (Chris MacNeil), Jason Miller (Father Karras), Max von Sydow (Father Merrin), Lee J. Cobb (Detective Kinderman), Kitty Winn (Sharon), Jack MacGowran (Burke), Rev. William O'Malley (Father Joe Dyer). Directed by William Friedkin and produced by William Peter Blatty. Screenplay by Blatty, based on his novel.

I want to write about William Friedkin's *The Exorcist,* and instead find myself faced with the film's "director's cut." Here is one of the great horror films, and it has been subjected to editorial tinkering—no doubt to justify the advertising line, "The version you've never seen." No, and you don't need to, either

I've revisited *The Exorcist* over the years and found it effective every time. Because it's founded on characters, details, and a realistic milieu, the shocks don't date; they still seem to grow from the material. In the early 1990s, I joined Owen Roizman, the film's cinematographer, in a shot-by-shot analysis of the film over four days at the Hawaii Film Festival. As we dissected it I gained an appreciation of the craft of the film—how it embeds the sensational material in an everyday world of misty nights, boozy parties, and housekeeping details, chats in a laundry room, and the personal lives of the priests. The movie is more horrifying because it does not seem to want to be. The horror creeps into the lives of characters preoccupied with their lives: Father Karras with his mother and his faith, Father Merrin with his work and health, Chris MacNeil with her career and marriage.

The movie also gains power because it takes its theology seriously—for a movie, anyway. *The Exorcist* was able to create a convincing portrait of priests at work, of their private lives, their fears and temptations. Instead of hurrying to exorcism as a cinematic stunt, it pauses for Father Karras (Jason Miller) to tell Regan's mother, Chris (Ellen Burstyn), that the best way to obtain an exorcism would be to take a time machine back to the sixteenth century. Exorcism has been replaced by modern discoveries about mental illness, he says, and we note he is a psychiatrist.

Above all, the movie's power came from the shocking nature of the victim—a sweet-faced young girl, who is poked and prodded by medical science, examined by fearsome machines, and gruesomely possessed by her evil visitor. There has been much discussion over the years about whether Linda Blair, the actress, was exploited by the film; she has said she was not, and the most fearsome scenes were accomplished with special effects and doubles, while the foul dialogue was dubbed by Mercedes McCambridge.

The Exorcist was and is a brilliant horror film, one with an archetypal ability to reach and disturb us. It will survive as long as people care about well-made movies. But now we are faced with this new version, some twelve minutes longer than the original. The restored material doesn't come as a surprise; some of it has been seen as outtakes on earlier video releases, and all of it has been much discussed by Friedkin and William Peter Blatty, the film's author and producer. Blatty has often said that Friedkin's original cut of about 140 minutes was "perfect." But the studio forced him to trim it to two hours. Friedkin defended the shorter version, saying his trims helped the pacing. This new version seems more like a "producer's cut" than a "director's cut." Although Friedkin endorses it, it reflects Blatty's long-standing preferences.

Having seen the new version and reviewed my laser disc of the original version, I noticed four areas of difference between the 1973 and 2000 versions. One change is probably useful, the second neutral, the third pointless, the fourth catastrophic. There may be other changes I missed, including some flash-frames of satanic faces, but here's what stood out:

1. Early in the film, Regan, the possessed girl, is subjected to invasive testing and a spinal tap, with lots of queasy close-ups of needles and fluids. This scene provides a preliminary medical explanation for Regan's behavior and sets up the later bedtime dialogue between mother and daughter about "what the doctor said"—dialogue that is unsupported in the 1973 version. It's useful.

2. The priests Karras and Merrin (Max von Sydow) have a talk on the stairs after the first round of exorcism, and Merrin suggests the true satanic target may not be the girl but those around her—the devil wants them to despair. The scene is interesting from a theological point of view, but interrupts the momentum.

3. We see the "spider walk," an infamous scene much discussed by *Exorcist* buffs where Regan is seen walking downstairs upside down, crab-style. This shot strikes me as a distracting stunt, and since it exists in isolation from the scenes around it, feels gratuitous.

4. The original ending of *The Exorcist* shows Regan and her mother leaving their house for the last time. "She doesn't remember any of it," her mother tells Father Dyer (Reverend William O'Malley). Regan greets him politely, focuses on his Roman collar, and suddenly hugs him. They get in the car, which begins to pull away, and then stops so that Chris can give the priest Father Merrin's medal, found in Regan's room. His hand closes over it. The car drives away. The priest looks down the fatal stairs below Regan's bedroom window. He turns away. Music and fade-out.

In the new version, after Chris gives Dyer the medal, he gives it back to her, and her hand closes over it. This is an unnecessary extra beat, but nothing compared to what follows. As the car drives away, Dyer looks down the stairs, walks toward the house, and encounters Kinderman (Lee J. Cobb), the police detective. They have a conversation about movies—some nonsense about a version of *Wuthering Heights* starring Jackie Gleason and Lucille Ball. Hello? An ending that struck the perfect closing note has been replaced by one that jars and clangs and thumbs its nose at the film.

While these scenes may have various rationales in the minds of Friedkin and Blatty, they have one obvious rationale in the thinking at the studio: They provide an excuse for the theatrical rerelease and will help sell the video, even to those who already own the earlier version. That is not good enough. If the changes don't make the film better, they should not have been made. If I were showing *The Exorcist* to a friend, I would show the 1973 version without the slightest hesitation. I hope Warner Bros. doesn't suppress it in favor of this marketing ploy.

Note: Friedkin took strong exception to my remarks about marketing opportunities as one of the reasons for this version. See the Answer Man exchange. ☞

The Eyes of Tammy Faye ★ ★ ★
PG-13, 79 m., 2000

A documentary produced and directed by Randy Barbato and Fenton Bailey.

"When she was born," her aunt recalls, "she had perfectly manicured fingernails." She still does. She also has eyelashes so firmly attached that she never removes them: "They have to sort of wear out. When one falls off, I replace it." Tammy Faye, once the evangelizing queen of a global satellite network, now "living in virtual exile in a gated community in Palm Springs," is the subject of *The Eyes of Tammy Faye,* a new documentary by Fenton Bailey and Randy Barbato.

Her saga is well known. How she and first husband, Jim Bakker, began as traveling evangelists, parlayed a puppet show into TV stardom, created three TV networks, were the first Christian broadcasters with their own satellite, and built the theme park Heritage USA near Charlotte, North Carolina—while Jim, according to the courts, was defrauding his viewers of millions. He went to prison, is now on parole and remarried. After their divorce ("we're still friends"), Tammy married Roe Messner, who oversaw construction on Heritage USA. Alas, he was convicted of bankruptcy fraud, and spent two years in prison, being released in early 1999.

All movies about women like this are required by law to contain the words, "She's a survivor." But John J. Bullock, the gay cohost of her most recent talk show, *John J. and Tammy Faye,* puts a new spin on it: "She's a survivor. After the Holocaust, there will be roaches, Tammy Faye, and Cher."

When Jim and Tammy were on the air in the 1980s, I confess to watching them, not because I was saved, but because I was fascinated. They were like two little puppets—Howdy Doody and Betty Boop made flesh. Tammy Faye cried on nearly every show, and sang with the force of a Brenda Lee, and when she'd do her famous version of "We're Blest," yes, dear reader, I would sing along with her.

The documentary reveals that she was a bundle of nerves in those days, as Jim withdrew into an obsession with Heritage USA empire-building (and brooded, no doubt, over his infamous one-night stand with Jessica Hahn). Tammy became addicted to pills, and her attention sometimes seemed to drift; directors Bailey and Barbato plundered the video archives to find moments like the one where Jim says, "Now Tammy's going to sing for us," and Tammy is discovered wandering at the back of the set, gazing at a prop and saying, "I'm looking at this boat."

But she did have chemistry and a natural TV presence, and narrator RuPaul Charles points out that she'd do two or three shows in a row, entirely ad-lib, completely comfortable without a script.

RuPaul? Yes, the famous drag queen is the film's narrator, and a subtext of *The Eyes of Tammy Faye* is that unlike most Christian televangelists (especially her nemesis Jerry Falwell) she has always been friendly with gays. Old videotape shows her commiserating with an HIV-positive preacher at a time when mainstream shows still shunned the topic of AIDS, and she chose the gay Bullock as the cohost on her comeback attempt. (One segment shows him pulling a brassiere out of her purse and waving it over his head, claiming it's his.)

Codirectors Bailey and Barbato are also openly gay, and there was a hint in some of their remarks after the Sundance premiere of the film that they got into this project because they saw Tammy Faye as a camp icon. So she is, as in a sequence where she explains the amazing contents of her makeup kit ("I don't know what this is," she confesses about one product). But she is also, we sense, a woman of great generosity of spirit, and a TV natural: The star she most reminds me of is Lucille Ball.

Was she in on the scams? She was never charged, never brought to trial. In the doc she walks through the ruins of Heritage USA, which has been padlocked for ten years ("I'd love to give this place a good coat of paint"), and the Palm Springs home she and Jim shared at the end. She lived in comfort, and still does. But the movie tacitly implies she didn't do anything criminal, that what you saw on TV was the real Tammy Faye, all of her, with no hidden edges or secrets. In terms of broadcast hours, she lived more of her life on live TV than perhaps anyone else in history. She was like Jim Carrey in *The Truman Show*—only in on the secret.

Eyes Wide Shut ★ ★ ★ ½
R, 159 m., 1999

Tom Cruise (Dr. William Harford), Nicole Kidman (Alice Harford), Sydney Pollack (Victor Ziegler), Marie Richardson (Marion), Rade Sherbedgia (Milich), Thomas Gibson (Carl), Vinessa Shaw (Domino), Todd Field (Nick Nightingale), Alan Cumming (Desk Clerk), Leelee Sobieski (Milich's daugher), Carmela Marner (Waitress). Produced and directed by Stanley Kubrick. Screenplay by Kubrick and Frederic Raphael. Inspired by *Traumnovelle*, a novel by Arthur Schnitzler.

Stanley Kubrick's *Eyes Wide Shut* is like an erotic daydream about chances missed and opportunities avoided. For its hero, who spends two nights wandering in the sexual underworld, it's all foreplay. He never actually

has sex, but he dances close and holds his hand in the flame. Why does he do this? The easy answer is that his wife has made him jealous. Another possibility is that the story she tells inflames his rather torpid imagination.

The film has the structure of a thriller, with the possibility that conspiracies and murders have taken place. It also resembles a nightmare; a series of strange characters drift in and out of focus, puzzling the hero with unexplained details of their lives. The reconciliation at the end of the film is the one scene that doesn't work; a film that intrigues us because of its loose ends shouldn't try to tidy up.

Tom Cruise and Nicole Kidman star as Dr. Bill and Alice Harford, a married couple who move in rich Manhattan society. In a long, languorous opening sequence, they attend a society ball where a tall Hungarian, a parody of a suave seducer, tries to honey-talk Alice ("Did you ever read the Latin poet Ovid on the art of love?"). Meanwhile, Bill gets a come-on from two aggressive women, before being called to the upstairs bathroom, where Victor, the millionaire who is giving the party (Sydney Pollack), has an overdosed hooker who needs a doctor's help.

At the party, Bill meets an old friend from medical school, now a pianist. The next night, at home, Alice and Bill get stoned on pot (apparently very good pot, considering how zonked they seem) and she describes a fantasy she had about a young naval officer she saw last summer on Cape Cod: "At no time was he ever out of my mind. And I thought if he wanted me, only for one night, I was ready to give up everything."

There is a fight. Bill leaves the house and wanders the streets, his mind inflamed by images of Alice making love with the officer. And now begins his long adventure, which has parallels with Joyce's "Nighttown" section of *Ulysses* and Scorsese's *After Hours*, as one sexual situation after another swims into view. The film has two running jokes, both quiet ones: Almost everyone who sees Bill, both male and female, reacts to him sexually. And he is forever identifying himself as a doctor, as if to reassure himself that he exists at all.

Kubrick's great achievement in the film is to find and hold an odd, unsettling, sometimes erotic tone for the doctor's strange encounters. Shooting in a grainy high-contrast style, using lots of backlighting, underlighting, and strong primary colors, setting the film at Christmas to take advantage of the holiday lights, he makes it all a little garish, like an urban sideshow. Dr. Bill is not really the protagonist but the acted-upon, careening from one situation to another, out of his depth.

Kubrick pays special attention to each individual scene. He makes a deliberate choice, I think, not to roll them together into an ongoing story, but to make each one a destination—to give each encounter the intensity of a dream in which *this* moment is clear but it's hard to remember where we've come from or guess what comes next.

The film pays extraordinary attention to the supporting actors, even cheating camera angles to give them the emphasis on two-shots; in several scenes, Cruise is like the straight man. Sydney Pollack is the key supporting player, as a confident, sinister man of the world, living in old-style luxury, deep-voiced, experienced, decadent. Todd Field plays Nick, the society piano player who sets up Bill's visit to a secret orgy. And there is also a wonderful role for Vinessa Shaw as a hooker who picks up Dr. Bill and shares some surprisingly sweet time with him.

The movie's funniest scene takes place in a hotel where Bill questions a desk clerk, played by Alan Cumming as a cheerful queen who makes it pretty clear he's interested. Rade Sherbedgia, a gravel-voiced, bearded patriarch, plays a costume dealer who may also be retailing the favors of his young daughter. Carmela Marner is a waitress who seems to have learned her trade by watching sitcoms. And Marie Richardson is the daughter of a dead man, who wants to seduce Dr. Bill almost literally on her father's deathbed.

All of these scenes have their own focus and intensity; each sequence has its own dramatic arc. They all lead up to and away from the extraordinary orgy sequence in a country estate, where Dr. Bill gate-crashes and wanders among scenes of Sadeian sexual ritual and writhings worthy of Bosch. The masked figure who rules over the proceedings has ominous presence, as does the masked woman who warns Dr. Bill he is in danger. This sequence has hypnotic intensity.

The orgy, alas, has famously undergone digital alterations to obscure some of the more energetic rumpy-pumpy. A shame. The events in question are seen at a certain distance, without visible genitalia, and are more atmosphere than action, but to get the R rating the studio has had to block them with digitally generated figures (two nude women arm in arm, and some cloaked men).

In rough draft form, this masking evoked Austin Powers's famous genital hide-and-seek sequence. Later I saw the polished version of the technique and will say it is done well, even though it should not have been done at all. The joke is that *Eyes Wide Shut* is an adult film in every atom of its being. With or without those digital effects, it is inappropriate for younger viewers. It's symbolic of the moral hypocrisy of the rating system that it would force a great director to compromise his vision, while by the same process making his adult film more accessible to young viewers.

Kubrick died in March. It is hard to believe he would have accepted the digital hocus-pocus. *Eyes Wide Shut* should have been released as he made it, either "unrated" or NC-17. For adult audiences, it creates a mesmerizing daydream of sexual fantasy. The final scene, in the toy store, strikes me as conventional moralizing—an obligatory happy resolution of all problems—but the deep mystery of the film remains. To begin with, can Dr. Bill believe Victor's version of the events of the past few days? I would have enjoyed a final shot in a hospital corridor, with Dr. Bill doing a double take as a gurney wheels past carrying the corpse of the piano player.

F

Faithless ★ ★ ★ ½
R, 142 m., 2001

Lena Endre (Marianne), Erland Josephson
(Bergman), Krister Henriksson (David), Thomas
Hanzon (Markus), Michelle Gylemo (Isabelle),
Juni Dahr (Margareta), Philip Zanden (Martin
Goldman), Therese Brunnander (Petra Holst).
Directed by Liv Ullmann and produced by Kaj
Larsen. Screenplay by Ingmar Bergman.

The island is Faro, where Ingmar Bergman
lives, and the house is Bergman's house, and
the beach is where he walks, and the office is
where he works, and we can see a shadowy
16mm film projector in the background, and
remember hearing that the Swedish Film Institute sends him weekly shipments of films to
watch. And the old man in the film is named
"Bergman," although we don't learn that essential piece of the jigsaw until the final credits.

Or perhaps the house and its office are a set.
And perhaps "Bergman" is partly Ingmar Bergman and partly the director's fictional creation. And surely, we think, he has a DVD
player by now. *Faithless*, a film made from his
screenplay and directed by Liv Ullmann, is
intriguing in the way it dances in and out of
the shadow of Bergman's autobiography. We
learn in his book *The Magic Lantern*, for example, that in 1949 he was involved in an affair
something like the one in this film—but we
sense immediately that *Faithless* is not a memoir of that affair, but a meditation on the guilt
it inspired.

Bergman, the son of a Lutheran bishop, has
in his eighties forsaken the consolations of
religion but not the psychic payments that it
exacts. His film feels like an examination of
conscience, and he's hard on himself. It's with
a start we realize that Ullmann is also one of
his former lovers, that they have a child together, and that in her vision he has clearly
been forgiven his trespasses.

The movie is about a messy affair from
"Bergman's" past, and it is about the creative
process. As it begins, the old man (Erland
Josephson) has writing paper on the desk before him, and is talking with an actress (Lena
Endre). It becomes clear that this actress is not
physically present. The dialogue suggests the
director has enlisted this woman, or her memory, to help him think through a story he is
writing. But she is also the woman the story is
about. And she sometimes seems to be reading her story from his notes—as if he created
her and she exists only in his words.

The woman is named Marianne. She is married to Markus (Thomas Hanzon), a symphony
conductor, often away on tours. They have a
daughter of eight or nine, Isabelle (Michelle
Gylemo). David (Krister Henriksson) is Markus's best friend. One night while Markus is
away David asks Marianne if he may sleep
with her. She laughs him off, but then agrees
they can share the same bed as brother and
sister. Soon they have hurtled into a passionate affair, unforeseen and heedless.

It is clear that David is "Bergman" at an earlier age. He is a film director with vague projects in mind, he has long been attracted to
Marianne, and he is, let us say, a louse. What
becomes clear during the course of the film is
that Markus is no saint either, and that he uses
his daughter as a hostage in the unpleasant-
ness that results.

Ullmann has a sure sense for the ways people
behave in emotional extremity. *Faithless* is not
made of soap opera sincerity, but from the
messiness of people who might later wish they
had behaved differently. When Markus surprises the naked David in bed with Marianne,
he projects not jealous anger, but a kind of
smarmy "gotcha!" triumph (for their part, they
giggle nervously).

It is David who feels sexual jealousy; when
Marianne returns from Markus with the news
she has regained custody of her child, David
thinks "something doesn't sound right," and
cross-examines her until he forces out a description of how Markus raped her as the cost
of custody. (This rape, described but not seen,
has the same kind of reality in the mind's eye
as the monologue about the boys on the beach
in *Persona*.)

At one point in the film, "Bergman" reaches
out and tenderly touches the cheek of David,
and Ullmann has said this is the old man forgiving the young man, even though the old
man can never forgive himself.

Ingmar Bergman has had his name on films for nearly sixty years. Some are among the best ever made. In old age he has grown more inward and personal, writing versions of his autobiography, usually to be directed by close friends. The films shot on Faro are in a category by themselves: chamber films, spare, chilly, with grateful interiors warmed by fires or candles. In *Faithless,* scenes in Stockholm and Paris show cozy interiors, boudoirs, restaurants, theaters, cafés. And then all is reduced to the spare, stark office—almost a monk's cell—where "Bergman" sits and remembers, summons his muses, and writes.

The Family Man ★ ★ ½
PG-13, 124 m., 2000

Nicolas Cage (Jack Campbell), Tea Leoni (Kate Reynolds), Jeremy Piven (Arnie), Don Cheadle (Cash), Makenzie Vega (Annie), Josef Sommer (Lassiter). Directed by Brett Ratner and produced by Marc Abraham, Tony Ludwig, Alan Riche, and Howard Rosenman. Screenplay by David Diamond and David Weissman.

It's a funny thing about supernatural movies. The black characters are always the ones with all the insights into the occult, but they rarely get to be the occulted. Consider Whoopi Goldberg in *Ghost,* Will Smith in *The Legend of Bagger Vance,* and now Don Cheadle in *The Family Man.* They're all on good terms with the paranormal, but act only as guides for Demi Moore, Matt Damon, Nicolas Cage, et al. They're always the medium but never the message.

In *The Family Man,* Cage plays Jack Campbell, a businessman who is ruled by his career. He has no personal life to speak of, works on Christmas Eve, and doesn't even bother to return a phone message from Kate Reynolds (Tea Leoni), his girlfriend from college. In 1987, we learn, Jack flew off for a year in London even though Kate tearfully begged him to stay. She feared if he left they'd never get married, and she was right.

Now, through the paranormal intervention of a taxi driver (Cheadle) who acts as his guide, or portal, or something, Jack goes to sleep as a wealthy bachelor and awakens in a parallel time-track where apparently he did fly back

from London, marry Kate, and father a six-year-old and a baby. He also now has a dog, which is slobbering all over him.

The heart of the movie is his gradual realization that his other life has somehow disappeared, that he's now a family man, that he has been granted the opportunity to experience all that he missed by putting his career ahead of personal goals. I always wonder, in movies like this, why the hero has been transferred into the alternate life but has retained the original memories—but, of course, if he had the alternate memories he wouldn't know anything had happened.

Tea Leoni *(Deep Impact, Flirting with Disaster)* is lovable as the wife, and does a good job of covering the inevitable moments when she *must,* we think, realize that a stranger is inhabiting her husband's body. The story takes a sitcom turn as Jack finds out he works for his father-in-law as a tire salesman, and tries to talk his way back into the big money in Manhattan.

I liked the movie, liked Cage, liked Leoni, smiled a lot, and yet somehow remained at arm's length, because I was having a parallel-life experience of my own. I kept remembering a movie named *Me Myself I,* which came out in spring 1999 and did a more persuasive and thoughtful job of considering more or less the same plot. In that one, Rachel Griffiths is a workaholic writer who through supernatural intervention is transported into married life with the guy she loved fifteen years ago. She suddenly has three children, etc. The two movies even share a plot point: One of the kids is observant and knows this is not their real parent. "When's Mommy gonna be home?" asks her son; "You're not really daddy, are you?" asks his daughter.

Why similar movies get made at the same time is a good question. Demi Moore's *Passion of Mind* was about a character shuttling nightly between two lives. And of course another wellspring of *The Family Man* is *It's a Wonderful Life,* except that this time the dark version is reality and the warm family world is the fantasy—or whatever it is.

One problem with the underlying plot is, how do you dispose of the family in the alternative world after the supernatural visitor learns his lesson? *Me Myself I* handled that

205

neatly with actual contact between the two versions of the heroine. *The Family Man* doesn't find a satisfactory resolution: Not that it's crucial, but it would have been nice. The movie is sweet, light entertainment, but could have been more.

Fantasia 2000 ★ ★ ★
G, 75 m., 1999

Featuring Steve Martin, Bette Midler, James Levine, Itzhak Perlman, James Earl Jones, Angela Lansbury, Quincy Jones, and Penn and Teller. Directed by Pixote Hunt, Hendel Butoy, Eric Goldberg, James Algar, Francis Glebas, Gaetan Brizzi, and Paul Brizzi and produced by Donald W. Ernst.

After the worldwide acclaim that greeted his *Snow White and the Seven Dwarfs*, the first full-length color animated feature, Walt Disney's imagination soared. He had been assured by no less than the great Soviet director Sergei Eisenstein that *Snow White* was the greatest film ever made, and he saw no boundaries for the infant art of feature animation. In 1940, he produced *Fantasia,* a marriage of animation and classical music, and insisted it be shown only in his new process, Fantasound, which used an assembly of sixty-four speakers that gave audiences their first experience of what is now familiar as "surround sound."

The experiment was a disaster. Most exhibitors refused to install the speakers. Audiences, distracted by the gathering clouds of World War II, were not in a fanciful mood. And critics who praised Disney's earlier effort as art, now slapped him down to earth again, accusing him of being too pretentious. The critic Ernest Rister writes that Disney was personally embittered by the reception given his brainchild, and determined to stick to more commercial projects in the future. He remained fascinated by technical innovations (Rister points out that he shot the TV show *Davy Crockett* in color even when TV was all black-and-white, because he knew color was inevitable). But after *Fantasia* he never again crawled out so far on an artistic limb.

His original plan for *Fantasia* was to constantly renew the film, adding fresh segments, warehousing old ones, showing it in Fanta-

sound as a sort of classical repertory for moviegoers. Now comes *Fantasia 2000,* produced by his nephew Roy, to continue that vision more than thirty years after Walt's death. Walt the tinkerer, who designed sound systems and movie cameras and got personally involved in designing the sights and sounds of the attractions at Disneyland, would have appreciated his nephew's boldness in shooting the film in the IMAX high-resolution, giant-screen process.

IMAX has even more than Walt's sixty-four speakers, and a five-story screen that literally envelops the audience in the experience. Mind-expanding audiences in 1968 went to the revival of *Fantasia* and sat in the front row (or even stretched out on the floor in front of the screen). Now the whole audience gets the same total immersion, in the images and the music by the Chicago Symphony Orchestra conducted by James Levine. Movies like this renew my faith that the future of the cinema lies not in the compromises of digital projection, but by leaping over the limitations of digital into the next generation of film technology.

Fantasia 2000 as a film is not the equal of the original *Fantasia,* maybe because it aims a little lower, for broader appeal. Some of the animation is powerful, including a closing segment with a theme of ecological healing. Other sections, including the opening abstraction of triangles dancing to Beethoven's "Fifth Symphony," seem a little pedestrian. Computer-animated experiments such as those shown on *The Mind's Eye* videos are more daring than anything in *Fantasia 2000.*

Still, as exactly what it is, *Fantasia 2000* is splendid entertainment, and the IMAX system is an impressive costar. My favorite sequence is the closing one, in which Stravinsky's Firebird Suite is illustrated by a blasted landscape that slowly renews itself. I also admired animator Eric Goldberg's interlocking New York stories, which accompanied Gershwin's "Rhapsody in Blue." The artistic inspiration for this section is said to be the great caricaturist Al Hirschfeld, but, curiously, I thought the style owed more to Ludwig Bemelmans and his "Madeleine" drawings. Certainly it has a different look than anything previously signed by the Disney studios, which has always specialized in the "clear line" style.

One section suited to the towering IMAX screen is Ottorino Respighi's music "Pines of Rome," illustrated by Hendel Butoy as a fantasy involving whales who gambol in the sea, in the sky, and eventually even in space. One effective sequence shows them moving through vast underwater ice caverns; I was reminded of the IMAX film *Antarctica,* with its footage of scuba divers inside glacial caverns.

Hendel Butoy's animation in the segment devoted to Shostakovich's Piano Concerto No. 2 plays wonderfully as a self-contained film. Based on Hans Christian Andersen's fable *The Steadfast Tin Soldier,* it's a three-way struggle in which a broken toy soldier, with only one leg, falls in love with a toy ballerina and protects her from a Jack-in-the-Box with evil designs.

Mickey Mouse's famous "Sorcerer's Apprentice" section, everyone's favorite from the 1940 film, is the only segment repeated here. Even though it's been carefully restored and subjected to a "degraining" process to help it play better in IMAX, it's not as visually sharp as the rest of the film. That's not a criticism of the source material but a demonstration of how breathtakingly detailed the IMAX picture is. The older film offers a retro look appropriate to a sequence nearly sixty years old, and then Mickey's stable mate Donald Duck leaps onscreen in the next section, helping Noah on his ark to Elgar's "Pomp and Circumstance." One animal missed by Noah turns up in Goldberg's animation for Saint-Saens's "Carnival of the Animals." It's a yo-yoing flamingo.

The segments are separated by guest hosts whose contributions seem rather labored; we see Steve Martin, Bette Midler, Itzhak Perlman, James Earl Jones, Angela Lansbury, Quincy Jones, and Penn and Teller. The original film used Deems Taylor, a famed radio commentator, to add an elevated and slightly wry tone; the new approach assumes an audience that needs a laugh break after each exhausting foray into the highbrow.

IMAX films are usually limited to forty-five minutes because of the huge size of the film reels (the projection booth looks like the *Starship Enterprise*). Only *Fantasia 2000* and the Rolling Stones documentary *At the Max* have exceeded that length. *Fantasia 2000* will eventually of course immigrate to home video. But IMAX is the way to see it—not just as a film, but as an event.

The Fast and the Furious ★ ★ ★
PG-13, 101 m., 2001

Vin Diesel (Dominic Toretto), Paul Walker (Brian), Jordana Brewster (Mia Toretto), Michelle Rodriguez (Letty), Rick Yune (Johnny Tran), Beau Holden (Ted Gessner). Directed by Rob Cohen and produced by Neal H. Moritz. Screenplay by Ken Li, Gary Scott Thompson, Erik Bergquist, and David Ayer.

The Fast and the Furious remembers summer movies from the days when they were produced by American-International and played in drive-ins on double features. It's slicker than films like *Grand Theft Auto,* but it has the same kind of pirate spirit—it wants to raid its betters and carry off the loot. It doesn't have a brain in its head, but it has some great chase scenes, and includes the most incompetent cop who ever went undercover.

According to the "In a World" Guy, who narrates the trailer, the movie takes place "In a world . . . beyond the law." It stars Vin Diesel, the bald-headed, mug-faced action actor who looks like a muscular Otto Preminger. He plays Toretto, a star of the forbidden sport of street racing who rockets his custom machine through Los Angeles at more than 100 mph before pushing a button on the dashboard and *really* accelerating, thanks to a nitrous oxide booster. He also runs a bar where his sister Mia (Jordana Brewster) serves "tuna salad on white bread, no crusts" every day to Brian (Paul Walker), who looks a little like white bread, no crusts himself.

Brian hangs out there because he wants to break into street racing, and because he likes Mia. Toretto's gang is hostile to him, beats him up, disses him, and he comes back for more. He ends up winning Toretto's friendship by saving him from the cops. The races involve cars four abreast at speedway speeds down city streets. This would be difficult in Chicago, but is easy in Los Angeles, because, as everybody knows, L.A. has no traffic and no cops.

Actually, Brian is a cop, assigned to investigate a string of multimillion-dollar truck hijackings. The hijackers surround an eighteen-wheeler with three Honda Civics, shoot out

207

the window on the passenger side, fire a cable into the cab, and climb into the truck at high speeds. This makes for thrilling action sequences when it works, and an even more thrilling action sequence when it doesn't, in a chase scene that approaches but does not surpass the climax of *The Road Warrior*.

During the chases, we observe that there is *no* other traffic on the highway—just the trucks and the Hondas. Anyone who has ever driven a Honda next to an eighteen-wheeler will know that a Humvee is the wiser choice, but never mind. And only a hopeless realist would observe that leaping through the windshield of a speeding truck is a dangerous and inefficient way of stealing VCRs. In Chicago, the crooks are more prudent, and steal from parked trucks, warehouses, and other unmoving targets. Toretto should try it.

Anyway, Brian at first seems just like a guy who wants to race, but is revealed as a cop in an early scene, although not so early the audience has not guessed it. He works for a unit that has its undercover headquarters in a Hollywood house, and as he enters it his boss says, "Eddie Fisher built this house for Elizabeth Taylor in the 1950s." I am thinking: (1) This is almost certainly true or it would not be said in a movie so stingy with dialogue, and (2) Is this the first time Brian has seen his unit's office?

One of the nice things about the movie is the way it tells a story and explains its characters. It's a refreshing change from such no-plot, all-action movies as *Gone in 60 Seconds*. We learn a little about Toretto's father and his childhood, and we see Brian and Mia falling in love—although I think in theory you are not supposed to date the sister of a guy you are undercover to investigate. Michelle Rodriguez, the star of the underappreciated boxing movie *Girlfight*, costars as a member of the hijack gang, and gets to land one solid right on a guy's jaw, just to keep her credentials.

The Fast and the Furious is not a great movie, but it delivers what it promises to deliver, and knows that a chase scene is supposed to be about something more than special effects. It has some of that grandiose, self-pitying dialogue we've treasured in movies like this ever since *Rebel Without a Cause*. "I live my life a quarter-mile at a time," Toretto tells Brian. "For those

ten seconds, I'm free." And, hey, even for the next thirty seconds, he's decelerating. ☞

Fast Food, Fast Women ★ ½
R, 95 m., 2001

Anna Thomson (Bella), Jamie Harris (Bruno), Louise Lasser (Emily), Robert Modica (Paul), Lonette McKee (Sherry-Lynn), Victor Argo (Seymour), Angelica Torn (Vitka), Austin Pendleton (George). Directed by Amos Kollek and produced by Hengameh Panahi. Screenplay by Kollek.

There's nothing wrong with *Fast Food, Fast Women* that a casting director and a rewrite couldn't have fixed. The rewrite would have realized that the movie's real story involves a sweet, touching romance between two supporting characters. The casting director would have questioned the sanity of using Anna Thomson in the lead role.

The sweet love story stars Louise Lasser in her best performance, as Emily, a widow who finds Paul (Robert Modica) through a personals ad. Their courtship is complicated by pride and misunderstanding, and by way too many plot contrivances. The lead role involves Thomson as Bella, a waitress who is said to be thirty-five.

A gentleman does not question a lady about her age, but Thomson was playing adult roles twenty years ago, has obviously had plastic surgery, and always dresses to emphasize her extreme thinness and prominent chest, so that we can't help thinking she's had a boob job.

Faithful readers will know I rarely criticize the physical appearance of actors. I would have given Thomson a pass, but the movie seems to be inviting my thoughts about her character, since Lasser's character has one big scene where she confesses she's not really as young as she claims, and another where she wonders if she should have her breasts enlarged—and then Thomson's character asks the taxi driver, "Aren't I voluptuous enough?" It's unwise to have one character being honest about issues when we're supposed to overlook the same questions raised by another character.

The movie takes place in one of those movie diners where everybody hangs out all day long and gets involved in each other's business. Bella rules the roost, pouring coffee for Paul and his pal Seymour (Victor Argo). The diner has so many regulars, it even has a regular hooker, Vitka (Angelica Torn), who stutters, so that guys can't tell she's asking them if they feel like having a good time. We learn that for years Bella has been having an affair with the married George (Austin Pendleton), who claims to be a Broadway producer, but whose shows sound like hallucinations. He spends most of their time together looking away from her and grinning at a private joke.

Bella meets a cab driver named Bruno (Jamie Harris), who has become the custodian of two children, leading to more misunderstandings that threaten to derail their future together. And then Bruno meets Emily, Seymour falls for Wanda, a stripper in a peep show, and there comes a point when you want to ask Amos Kollek, the writer-director, why the zany plot overkill when your real story is staring you in the face? (You want to ask him that even before the zebras and the camels turn up, and long before the unforgivable "happy ending.")

Lasser and Modica, as Emily and Paul, are two nice, good, lovable people who deserve each other, and whenever the movie involves their story, we care (even despite some desperate plot contrivances). Lasser's vulnerability, her courage, and the light in her eyes all bring those scenes to life, as does Paul's instinctive courtesy and the way he responds to her warmth. There's the movie. If it has to pretend to be about Bella, Kollek as the director should at least have been able to see the character more clearly—clearly enough to know the audience cannot believe she is thirty-five, and thinks of her whenever anyone else mentions plastic surgery.

Felicia's Journey ★ ★ ★ ½
PG-13, 114 m., 1999

Bob Hoskins (Hilditch), Elaine Cassidy (Felicia), Arsinee Khanjian (Gala), Peter McDonald (Johnny Lysaght), Gerard McSorley (Felicia's Father), Brid Brennan (Mrs. Lysaght), Claire Benedict (Miss Calligary), Danny Turner (Young Hilditch). Directed by Atom Egoyan

and produced by Bruce Davey. Screenplay by Egoyan, based on the novel by William Trevor.

Atom Egoyan's *Felicia's Journey* tells the story of two children escaping from their parents. One of the children is middle-aged now, an executive chef for a factory lunchroom. The other is a young Irish girl, in England to seek the boy who said he would write her every day, and then never wrote at all. It is their misfortune that the paths of these two children cross.

The man is named Hilditch. He is played by Bob Hoskins, that sturdy, redoubtable fireplug. At work his staff is in thrall to his verdict. He sips a soup and disapproves: "It starts with the stock!" He lives alone in a huge house where nothing seems to have changed since the 1950s. He spends his evenings cooking ambitious dinners like a saddle of lamb, and eating them all by himself, listening to Mantovani on a record player. His drives a Morris Mini-Minor, a bulbous little car designed along the same lines as its driver.

The girl is named Felicia (Elaine Cassidy). She is sweet and bewildered. She gave her love to Johnny (Peter McDonald), who left for England—to work in a lawn-mower factory, he said. She is pregnant. Johnny has not written. Her father (Gerard McSorley) is a rabid Irish nationalist who is convinced Johnny has gone to join the British Army. He is offended by his daughter's pregnancy not on moral but political grounds: "You are carrying the enemy within you!"

Felicia takes the ferry to England and goes looking for Johnny's lawn-mower factory. Kindly Mr. Hilditch sees her wandering the streets and offers her guidance, and even a ride to a nearby town where Johnny might be working. Hilditch explains that his wife is a patient in the hospital there. We slowly gather that Mr. Hilditch is not a nice man, that he has no wife, that Felicia is in some kind of danger. The look of the film, wet, green, brown, cool, dark, underlines the danger.

The key to *Felicia's Journey* is that it has understanding for both characters—for Felicia, who is innocent, and for Hilditch, who is the product of a childhood that turned him out very wrong. Atom Egoyan is drawn to stories like this, stories about the lasting injuries of childhood, and in one way or another both his *The Sweet Hereafter* and *Exotica* are about damaged girls and predatory men. *Felicia's Journey* is based on a novel by William Trevor, and when he read it, Egoyan must have felt an instant sympathy with the material.

Trevor is one of the greatest living writers, and one who approaches his characters with the belief that to understand all is to forgive all. There are no villains in his work, only deserving and undeserving victims. The story of Felicia is not uncommon: Johnny loved her and left her. If there were more about Johnny in Trevor's story, we would know why. The glimpses we have of Johnny make him seem thoughtless and heartless, but then we see his mother, and get a hint of what he is escaping from.

What we gather about Hilditch, on the other hand, is that as a child he was not mistreated, so much as smothered. Anything is toxic in large enough quantities, even love. We eventually understand his connection to the old videotapes of a French cookery program, which he watches while he prepares food, and we find out why one room of his house is filled with cooking appliances. Hilditch is a real piece of work. We see him mostly as an adult, and then in flashbacks as a child. In both manifestations he reminded me of Alfred Hitchcock, who wanted his tombstone to read: "You see what can happen if you are not a good boy." Hilditch has grown into a bad boy who knows how to seem like a good one, seeking out young and helpless girls and offering them his aid. Naming some of his "lost girls" to Felicia, he says, "I was the world to them. In their time of need, they counted on me."

Some will find the ending of the film, with its door-to-door evangelist (Claire Benedict) unlikely. True, Miss Calligary is a *deus ex machina,* but I prefer her intervention to a more conventional thriller ending. Irony is usually more satisfying than action. And as Hilditch kneels on the wet grass next to a grave, there is pathos and at the same time that cold Hitchcockian humor.

Egoyan is such a devious director, achieving his effects at a level below the surface. He never settles for just telling a story. He shows people trapped in a matrix of their past and their

needs. He embraces coincidences and weird lurches in his plots, because he doesn't want us to grow too confident that we know how things must turn out. He almost never provides a tear-jerking scene, an emotional climax, a catharsis. It's as if his films inject materials into our subconscious, and hours later, like a slow reaction in a laboratory retort, they heat up and bubble over. You leave *Felicia's Journey* appreciating it. A week later, you're astounded by it.

15 Minutes ★ ★ ★
R, 120 m., 2001

Robert De Niro (Eddie Flemming), Edward Burns (Jordy Warsaw), Kelsey Grammer (Robert Hawkins), Karel Roden (Emil Slovak), Oleg Taktarov (Oleg Razgul), Melina Kanakaredes (Nicolette Karas), Vera Farmiga (Daphne Handlova). Directed by John Herzfeld and produced by Keith Addis, David Blocker, Herzfeld, and Nick Wechsler. Screenplay by Herzfeld.

I want to know if you think this is possible. Two creeps videotape themselves committing murder, and then attempt to sell the video to a reality news show for $1 million. They plan to beat the murder charges with an insanity plea, adding that they were abused as children.

I think it is possible. I heard about a documentary at Sundance this year where a fraternity boy videotaped his friend in a sex act that the woman claimed was rape. The video, later sold to the press by law enforcement officials, is included in the documentary, so you can decide for yourself.

What kind of person would do something like that? (I refer both to the fictional murder plot and to the rape footage.) The kind of person, I imagine, who appears on the Jerry Springer show, a program I study for signposts on our society's descent into barbarism. When you say these people have no shame, you have to realize that "shame" is a concept and perhaps even a word with which they are not familiar. They will eagerly degrade themselves for the fifteen minutes of fame so famously promised them by Andy Warhol.

15 Minutes is a cynical, savage satire about violence, the media, and depravity. It doesn't have the polish of *Natural Born Killers* or the wit of *Wag the Dog*, but it's a real movie, rough edges and all, and not another link from the sausage factory. A couple of the early reviews have called it implausible. They doubt that real killers would sell their footage to TV and then watch it in a Planet Hollywood, hoping to be spotted and arrested. See, that's the funny thing. I think there are people who would.

The movie stars Robert De Niro as a Manhattan detective who has become a celebrity, Edward Burns as a fire inspector, and Kelsey Grammer as a cross between Springer and Geraldo Rivera. Working the other side of the street are Karel Roden and Oleg Taktarov as Emil and Oleg, one Czech, one Russian, who fly into Kennedy airport and are robbing an electronics store within hours of getting off the plane. Emil dreams of becoming rich and famous through violence, and Oleg videotapes his efforts—at first just for fun, later as part of a scheme. Emil loves America because "no one is responsible for what they do!" and Oleg idolizes Frank Capra, the poet of the little man who shoves it to the system.

The movie, written and directed by John Herzfeld, is the work of a man intoxicated by characters and locations. His previous film, *2 Days in the Valley* (1997), was the same way, filled with characters who spinned into each other and bounced apart like pinballs. His movie may overachieve, may weary sometimes as it hurries between plotlines, but I prefer this kind of energy and ambition to a plodding exercise in action clichés. Herzfeld has something he wants to say.

His premise depends on Emil and Oleg being perfectly amoral idiots, shaped in their homelands by overdoses of American TV and movies. Since their countries are saturated with U.S. entertainment, and since the most popular exports are low-dialogue action shows, this is not a stretch. Is their view of America hopelessly brutal and unrealistic? Yes, but it is the view we export for study abroad.

They shoot, slash, burn, and pillage their way through Manhattan, attacking former friends, call girls, and bystanders. Meanwhile, Burns, as the fire inspector, finds evidence that a fire was set to conceal a murder, and De Niro engages in a little jockeying for position in the media spotlight because he wants credit for the investigation. His publicity efforts are helped by his friendship with Grammer, a star of reality TV, and by his affair with a TV reporter (Melina Kanakaredes).

Emil and Oleg are really the center of the movie. They reminded me of Dick Smith and Perry Hickock from *In Cold Blood*, except the vicious amorality of the 1968 movie no longer seems so totally alien to the society surrounding it; programs like Grammer's *Top Story* are based on, feed on, depend on there being people like these.

The movie is far from unflawed. I have a private theory that half the time you see a character tied to a chair, the screenwriter ran out of ideas. Some of the getaways are unlikely. The ending is on autopilot. But there's an absolutely sensational scene where Burns tries to help a woman escape from a burning apartment; it's the best work along these lines since *Backdraft*. And poignant personal moments for De Niro that keep his character from simply being a publicity hound. And performances by Karel Roden and Oleg Taktarov that project the kind of flat, empty-headed, blank-faced evil that is so much scarier than evil by people who think about what they're doing.

Some movies, however good, seem to be simply technical exercises. Others, even if flawed, contain the seed of inspiration. John Herzfeld has not made a great movie yet, but on the basis of his first two, he might. He cares, he strives, he's not content. While you're watching the movie, you question details and excesses. Afterward, you admire it for the passion of its attack, and the worthiness of its targets.

Fight Club ★ ★
R, 139 m., 1999

Brad Pitt (Tyler Durden), Edward Norton (Narrator), Helena Bonham Carter (Marla Singer), Meat Loaf Aday (Robert Paulsen), Jared Leto (Angel Face). Directed by David Fincher and produced by Art Linson, Cean Chaffin, and Ross Grayson Bell. Screenplay by Jim Uhls, based on the novel by Chuck Palahniuk.

Fight Club is the most frankly and cheerfully fascist big-star movie since *Death Wish*, a celebration of violence in which the heroes write themselves a license to drink, smoke, screw, and beat each other up. Sometimes, for variety, they beat themselves up. It's macho porn— the sex movie Hollywood has been moving toward for years, in which eroticism between the sexes is replaced by all-guy locker-room fights. Women, who have had a lifetime of practice at dealing with little-boy posturing, will instinctively see through it; men may get off on the testosterone rush. The fact that it is very well made and has a great first act certainly clouds the issue.

Ed Norton stars as a depressed urban loner filled up to here with angst. He describes his world in dialogue of sardonic social satire. His life and job are driving him crazy. As a means of dealing with his pain, he seeks out twelve-step meetings, where he can hug those less fortunate than himself and find catharsis in their suffering. It is not without irony that the first meeting he attends is for postsurgical victims of testicular cancer, since the whole movie is about guys afraid of losing their balls.

These early scenes have a nice sly tone; they're narrated by the Norton character in the kind of voice Nathanael West used in *Miss Lonelyhearts*. He's known only as the Narrator, for reasons later clear. The meetings are working as sedative and his life is marginally manageable when tragedy strikes: He begins to notice Marla (Helena Bonham Carter) at meetings. She's a "tourist" like himself—someone not addicted to anything but meetings. She spoils it for him. He knows he's a faker, but wants to believe everyone else's pain is real.

On an airplane, he has another key encounter, with Tyler Durden (Brad Pitt), a man whose manner cuts through the fog. He seems able to see right into the Narrator's soul, and shortly after, when the Narrator's high-rise apartment turns into a fireball, he turns to Tyler for shelter. He gets more than that. He gets in on the ground floor of Fight Club, a secret society of men who meet in order to find freedom and self-realization through beating each other into pulp.

It's at about this point that the movie stops being smart and savage and witty, and turns to some of the most brutal, unremitting, nonstop violence ever filmed. Although sensible people know that if you hit someone with an ungloved hand hard enough, you're going to end up with broken bones, the guys in *Fight Club* have fists of steel, and hammer one another while the sound-effects guys beat the hell out of Naugahyde sofas with Ping-Pong paddles. Later, the movie takes still another turn. A lot of recent films seem unsatisfied unless they can add final scenes that redefine the reality of everything that has gone before; call it the Keyser Soze syndrome.

What is all this about? According to Durden, it is about freeing yourself from the shackles of modern life, which imprisons and emasculates men. By being willing to give and receive pain and risk death, Fight Club members find freedom. Movies like *Crash* must play like cartoons for Durden. He's a shadowy, charismatic figure, able to inspire a legion of (white) men in big cities to descend into the secret cellars of Fight Club and beat each other up. Only gradually are the final outlines of his master plan revealed. Is Tyler Durden in fact a leader of men with a useful philosophy? "It's only after we've lost everything that we're free to do anything," he says, sounding like a man who tripped over the Nietzsche display on his way to the coffee bar in Borders. In my opinion, he has no useful truths. He's a bully—Werner Erhard plus S&M, a leather club operator without the decor. None of the Fight Club members grow stronger or freer because of their membership; they're reduced to pathetic cult members. Issue them black shirts and sign them up as skinheads. Whether Durden represents hidden aspects of the male psyche is a question the movie uses as a loophole—but is not able to escape through, because *Fight Club* is not about its ending but about its action.

Of course, *Fight Club* itself does not advocate Durden's philosophy. It is a warning against it, I guess; one critic I like says it makes "a telling point about the bestial nature of man and what can happen when the numbing effects of day-to-day drudgery cause people to go a little crazy." I think it's the numbing effects of movies like this that cause people to go a little crazy. Although sophisticates will be able to rationalize the movie as an argument against the behavior it shows, my guess is that audiences will like the behavior but not the argument. Certainly they'll buy tickets because they can see Pitt and Norton pounding on each other;

a lot more people will leave this movie and get in fights than will leave it discussing Tyler Durden's moral philosophy. The images in movies like this argue for themselves, and it takes a lot of narration (or Narration) to argue against them.

Lord knows the actors work hard enough. Norton and Pitt go through almost as much physical suffering in this movie as Demi Moore endured in *G.I. Jane,* and Helena Bonham Carter creates a feisty chain-smoking hellcat who is probably so angry because none of the guys think having sex with her is as much fun as a broken nose. When you see good actors in a project like this, you wonder if they signed up as an alternative to canyoneering.

The movie was directed by David Fincher, and written by Jim Uhls, who adapted the novel by Chuck Palahniuk. In many ways it's like Fincher's movie *The Game* (1997), with the violence cranked up for teenage boys of all ages. That film was also about a testing process in which a man drowning in capitalism (Michael Douglas) has the rug of his life pulled out from under him, and has to learn to fight for survival. I admired *The Game* much more than *Fight Club* because it was really about its theme, while the message in *Fight Club* is like bleeding scraps of Socially Redeeming Content thrown to the howling mob.

Fincher is a good director (his work includes *Alien 3,* one of the best-looking bad movies I have ever seen, and *Seven,* the grisly and intelligent thriller). With *Fight Club* he seems to be setting himself some kind of a test—how far over the top can he go? The movie is visceral and hard-edged, with levels of irony and commentary above and below the action. If it had all continued in the vein explored in the first act, it might have become a great film. But the second act is pandering and the third is trickery, and whatever Fincher thinks the message is, that's not what most audiences members will get. *Fight Club* is a thrill ride masquerading as philosophy—the kind of ride where some people puke and others can't wait to get on again.

The Filth and the Fury ★ ★ ★ ½
R, 105 m., 2000

A documentary directed by Julien Temple and produced by Anita Camarata and Amanda Temple.

At the height of their fame, the Sex Pistols inspired a London city councilor to observe, "Most of these guys would be much improved by sudden death." In a decade when England was racked by unemployment, strikes, and unrest, its season of discontent had a sound track by the Pistols. They sang of "Anarchy in the U.K.," and their song "God Save the Queen (She Ain't No Human Being)" rose to No. 1 on the hit charts—but the record industry refused to name it. In *The Filth and the Fury,* a hard-edged new documentary about the Pistols, we see a Top 10 chart with a blank space for No. 1. Better than being listed, Johnny Rotten grinned.

The saga of the Sex Pistols is told for the third time in *The Filth and the Fury.* Not bad for a band that symbolized punk rock but lasted less than two years, fought constantly, insulted the press, spit on their fans, were banned from TV, were fired by one record company twenty-four hours after being signed, released only one album, pushed safety pins through noses and earlobes to more or less invent body piercing, broke up during a tour of the United States, and saw front man Sid Vicious accused of murdering his girlfriend and dying of a drug overdose.

Director Julien Temple based his *Great Rock and Roll Swindle* (1980) on a version of the Pistols story supplied by Malcolm McLaren, their infamously self-promoting manager, and now, twenty years later, Temple tells the story through the eyes and in the words of the band members themselves. In between came Alex Cox's *Sid & Nancy* (1986), with Gary Oldman's shattering performance as the self-destructive Sid Vicious.

It wasn't what the band stood for. It was what they stood against. "Attack, attack, attack," says lead singer Johnny Rotten in the film. Now once again John Lydon, he appears along with guitarist Steve Jones, drummer Paul Cook, McLaren, original band member Glen Matlock (deposed by Vicious), and even Vicious himself, in an interview filmed a year before his death. The surviving members are backlit so we cannot see their faces, which would have provided a middle-aged contrast to the savage young men on the screen; McLaren talks from behind a rubber bondage mask like those he and girlfriend Vivienne Westwood sold in their boutique Sex, on Kings' Road.

McLaren claimed the Sex Pistols were entirely his invention, and painted himself as a puppet master. Lydon, who calls him "the manager" throughout the film, says, "There was never a relationship between the manager and me except he stole my ideas and used them as his own." The truth probably resides in between.

I had a glimpse of the Sex Pistols in 1977, when McLaren hired Russ Meyer to direct them in a movie, and Meyer hired me to write it (McLaren and Rotten were fans of our *Beyond the Valley of the Dolls*). I wrote a screenplay in Los Angeles with McLaren feeding me background and ideas. Then Meyer and I flew to London to meet with Rotten, Vicious, Cook, and Jones. (Meyer, wary of McLaren's trademark bondage pants, insisted on sitting on the aisle: "If we have to evacuate, he'll get those goddamned straps tangled up in the seats.")

I remember a surrealistic dinner involving Rotten, Meyer, and myself ("We won the Battle of Britain for you," Meyer sternly lectured Rotten, while I mused that America was not involved in the Battle of Britain and Rotten was Irish). Rotten seemed amused by the fact that Meyer was unintimidated by his fearsomely safety-pinned facade. As we drove him home, he complained bitterly that McLaren had the band on a salary of £8 a week, borrowed £5 from Meyer, and had us stop at an all-night store so he could buy a six-pack of lager and cans of pork and beans.

The truth is, no one made much money off the Pistols, although McLaren made the most. The plug was pulled on our film, *Who Killed Bambi?* after a day and a half of shooting, when the electricians walked off the set after McLaren couldn't pay them. Meyer had presciently demanded his own weekly pay in advance every Monday morning.

The catch-22 with punk rock, and indeed with all forms of entertainment designed to

shock and offend the bourgeoisie, is that if your act is *too* convincing, you put yourself out of business, a fact carefully noted by today's rappers as they go as far as they can without going too far.

The Sex Pistols went too far. They never had a period that could be described as actual success. Even touring England at the height of their fame, they were booked into clubs under false names. They were hated by the establishment, shut down by the police, and pilloried by the press ("The Filth and the Fury" was a banner headline occupying a full front page of the *Daily Mirror*). That was bad enough. Worse was that their own fans sometimes attacked them, lashed into a frenzy by the front line of Rotten and Vicious, who were sometimes performers, sometimes bearbaiters.

Rotten was the victim of a razor attack while walking the streets of London; McLaren not only failed to provide security, he wouldn't pay taxi fares. Vicious was his own worst enemy, and if there was one thing that united the other three band members and McLaren, it was hatred for Sid's girlfriend, Nancy Spungen, who they felt was instrumental in his drug addiction. "Poor sod," today's John Lydon says of his dead bandmate.

To see this film's footage from the '70s is to see the beginning of much of pop and fashion iconography for the next two decades. After the premiere of *The Filth and the Fury* at Sundance, I ran into Temple, who observed: "In the scenes where they're being interviewed on television, they look normal. It's the interviewers who look like freaks." Normal, no. But in torn black T-shirts and punk haircuts, they look contemporary, unlike the dated polyestered, wide-lapeled, and blow-dried creatures interviewing them.

England survived the Sex Pistols, and they mostly survived England, although Lydon still feels it is unsafe for him to return there. He now has an interview program on VH-1 and the Web. Cook and Jones lead settled lives. McLaren still has bright ideas. Vivienne Westwood has emerged as one of Britain's most successful designers, and poses for photographs in which she has a perfect resemblance to Mrs. Thatcher. And as for Sid, my notes from the movie say that while the Pistols were signing a record deal in front of Buckingham Palace and insulting the queen, Sid's father was a Grenadier Guard on duty in front of the palace. Surely I heard that wrong?

Final Destination ★ ★ ★
R, 90 m., 2000

Devon Sawa (Alex Browning), Ali Larter (Clear Rivers), Kerr Smith (Carter Horton), Kristen Cloke (Valerie Lewton), Daniel Roebuck (Agent Weine), Chad E. Donella (Tod Waggner), Seann William Scott (Billy Hitchcock). Directed by James Wong and produced by Glen Morgan, Warren Zide, and Craig Perry. Screenplay by Jeffrey Reddick, Morgan, and Wong.

Final Destination observes the time-honored formula of the Dead Teenager Movie: It begins with a lot of living teenagers, and dooms them. But the movie, made by two veterans of *The X Files* TV series, is smarter and more original than most DTMs. It has mordant humor, Rube Goldberg death traps, and sophomoric but earnest discussions of fate. Also an opening sequence that assures this film will never, ever, be shown on an airplane.

The movie begins with a high school class boarding a plane for a class trip to Paris. Alex (Devon Sawa), one of the students, has a vision, vivid and terrifying, of the plane exploding in flight. He jumps up to get off, has a fight with another student, and ends up being ejected along with five other students and a teacher. Then the airplane takes off and, you guessed it, explodes in midair.

This scenario is, of course, in the worst possible taste in view of the real-life fate of TWA flight 800, also bound for Paris with students aboard. I will observe that and not belabor it. The explosion is a setup for the rest of the movie, in which it appears that the survivors may also be marked for death—and that Alex is psychic and can foresee their deaths.

Can he really? That's where the movie gets interesting, since instead of using his eerie precognitions as a gimmick, the movie allows the characters to talk urgently about their feelings of doom and helplessness. The film in its own way is biblical in its dilemma, although the students use the code word "fate" when what they are really talking about is God. In their own terms, in their own way, using teenage vernacular, the students have existential discussions.

Final Destination isn't all dialogue, however, and there's a weird disconnection between the words and the action. One after another, the characters die, almost always because of a bizarre chain of connected events. To describe them would be to spoil the fun—if that's what it is—as lightning, natural gas, knives, trains, laundry cords, power lines, and flying metal shards are choreographed by fate (or You Know Who).

Why must these students die? Well, everybody does. Why should they be the exception? As the movie opens, they're filled like most teenagers with a sense of their own immortality, and gradually their dilemma wears them down.

The movie is neither quite serious nor quite ironic; sometimes it's funny, but in a creepy way rather than in the breezier style of the *Scream* movies. The very last shot, set in Paris but filmed in Canada (during a last-minute reshoot in January), is a shaggy dog trick. I laughed, I guess, but the movie really deserves better. My guess is the original ending was more considered, but New Line was afraid of it.

The director is James Wong. He and cowriter Glen Morgan worked on *The X-Files, 21 Jump Street,* and *Millennium.* They haven't made a great or distinguished film, but, working within a tired genre with a talented cast, they've brought unusual substance and impact to the DTM. The vision of the airplane crash is remarkably scary, and other scenes, like a car stopped on railroad tracks, work even though they're clichés—because of the dialogue and the motivations of the characters.

Final Destination will no doubt be a hit and inspire the obligatory sequels. Like the original *Scream,* this movie is too good to be the end of the road. I have visions of my own. I foresee poor Alex making new friends and then envisioning *their* deaths as they embark on ocean liners, trains, buses, and dirigibles. It's a funny thing about Hollywood: It can't seem to get enough of dead teenagers. Talk about biting the hand that feeds you.

Final Fantasy: The Spirits Within
★ ★ ★ ½
PG-13, 105 m., 2001

Voices of: Ming-Na (Dr. Aki Ross), Alec Baldwin (Gray Edwards), Steve Buscemi (Neil), Peri Gilpin (Jane Proudfoot), Ving Rhames (Ryan), Donald Sutherland (Dr. Sid), James Woods (General Hein). Directed by Hironobu Sakaguchi and produced by Jun Aida, Chris Lee, and Akio Sakai. Screenplay by Al Reinert, Sakaguchi, and Jeff Vintar.

Other movies have been made entirely on computers, but *Final Fantasy: The Spirits Within* is the first to attempt realistic human characters. Not Shrek with his trumpet ears, but the space soldier Gray Edwards, who looks so much like Ben Affleck that I wonder if royalties were involved. The movie, named after a famous series of video games, creates Planet Earth, circa 2065, where humans huddle beneath energy shields and wraithlike aliens prowl the globe.

The film tells a story that would have seemed traditional in the golden age of Asimov, van Vogt, and Heinlein. But science-fiction fans of that era would have wept with joy at the visuals, and they grabbed me too. I have a love of astonishing sights, of films that show me landscapes and cityscapes that exist only in the imagination, and *Final Fantasy* creates a world that is neither live-action nor animation, but some parallel cyber universe.

The characters live in that cyberspace too. Not for an instant do we believe that Dr. Aki Ross, the heroine, is a real human. But we concede she is *lifelike,* which is the whole point. She has an eerie presence that is at once subtly unreal and yet convincing; her movements (which mirror the actions of real actors) feel about right, her hair blows convincingly in the wind, and the first close-up of her face and eyes is startling because the filmmakers are not afraid to give us a good, long look—they dare us not to admire their craft. If Aki is not as real as a human actress, she is about as real as a Playmate who has been retouched to a glossy perfection.

The story involves a struggle by Aki and a band of Deep Eyes (futuristic human warriors) to defend the survivors of an alien invasion of Earth. Humans live inside energy shields that protect some of the largest cities, and they venture out cautiously, armored and armed, to do battle with the aliens, who look like free-form transparent monster nightmares; I was reminded of the water creature in *The Abyss.* The aliens can infect humans with their virus, or essence, and Aki (Ming-Na) thinks she can defeat them by channeling the eight "spirit waves" of Earth—or Gaia, the planetary soul.

Her allies include Gray (Alec Baldwin), the leader of the Deep Eyes troop, and Dr. Sid (Donald Sutherland), her wise old teacher. Her other teammates include the pilot Neil (Steve Buscemi) and the fighters Ryan (Ving Rhames) and Jane Proudfoot (Peri Gilpin). Leading the forces of evil is General Hein (James Woods), who wants to blast the aliens with his high-tech orbiting space cannon.

Those who find a parallel between Hein's cannon and George W. Bush's missile shield will find it easy to assign Aki and her friends to the environmentalists; they believe Earth's mantle sits above a Gaia-sphere containing the planet's life force, and that if the cannon destroys it, not only the aliens but all human life will die. One of Aki's early expeditions is to find, rescue, and tend a tiny green growing thing that has survived in the wasteland caused (I think) when a giant meteorite crashed into Earth and released the aliens it contained.

The aliens are strange creatures, made stranger still by the film's inconsistency in handling them. Without revealing one major secret about their essence, I can ask how they seem to be physical and conceptual both at once. They defeat a human not by physically attacking him, but by absorbing his life essence. Yet they can be blasted to smithereens by the weapons of the Deep Eyes. Maybe the human weapons are not conventional, but operate on the aliens' wavelength; either I got confused on that point, or the movie did.

Enough about the plot, which is merely the carrier for the movie's vision. The reason to see this movie is simply, gloriously, to look at it. Aki has dream scenes on another planet, where a vast, celestial sphere half fills the sky. We see New York City in 2065, ruined, ghost-like, except for the portions under the protective dome. There are action sequences that only vaguely obey the laws of gravity, and yet seem convincing because we have become familiar with the characters who occupy them: shots like the one where we look straight up at Aki standing on the surface of a shimmering lake. The corridors and machines composing the infrastructure of the protective dome surpass any possible real-world sets.

Final Fantasy took four years to create. A computer animation team, half-Japanese, half-American, worked in Hawaii with director Hironobu Sakaguchi; they shot many of the physical movements and then rotoscoped them, and artists were assigned to specialize in particular characters. The most realistic are probably Dr. Sid and Ryan. It all comes together into a kind of amazing experience; it's as if you're witnessing a heavy-metal story come to life.

Is there a future for this kind of expensive filmmaking ($140 million, I've heard)? I hope so, because I want to see more movies like this, and see how much further they can push the technology. Maybe someday I'll actually be fooled by a computer-generated actor (but I doubt it). The point anyway is not to replace actors and the real world, but to transcend them—to penetrate into a new creative space based primarily on images and ideas. I wouldn't be surprised if the Star Wars series mutated in this direction; George Lucas's actors, who complain that they spend all of their time standing in front of blue screens that will later be filled with locations and effects, would be replaced by computerized avatars scarcely less realistic.

In reviewing a movie like this, I am torn between its craft elements and its story. The story is nuts-and-bolts space opera, without the intelligence and daring of, say, Spielberg's *A.I.* But the look of the film is revolutionary. *Final Fantasy* is a technical milestone, like the first talkies or 3-D movies. You want to see it whether or not you care about aliens or space cannons. It exists in a category of its own, the first citizen of the new world of cyberfilm.

Finding Forrester ★ ★ ★
PG-13, 133 m., 2000

Sean Connery (William Forrester), Rob Brown (Jamal Wallace), F. Murray Abraham (Professor Crawford), Michael Nouri (Dr. Spence), Anna Paquin (Claire), Busta Rhymes (Terrell), Joey Buttafuoco (Security Guard), Michael Pitt (Coleridge), Stephanie Berry (Janice).

Directed by Gus Van Sant and produced by Sean Connery, Laurence Mark, and Rhonda Tollefson. Screenplay by Mike Rich.

Movies about writers are notoriously hard to do, since writing by its nature is not cinematic. *Finding Forrester* evades that problem by giving us a man who wrote one good novel a long time ago, and now writes no more: He has turned into a recluse afraid to leave his own apartment. This is William Forrester (Sean Connery), who keeps an eye on his Bronx neighborhood by using binoculars from his upper-floor window. "The man in the window" attracts the attention of black teenagers playing basketball on a court below, and that leads to the turning point in the life of Jamal Wallace (Rob Brown).

Jamal is a brilliant student who has no one to share his brilliance with. At school he conceals his learning because, as an adult observes, "Basketball is where he gets his acceptance." He gets C's when his SAT scores show him to be an A student, and he stars on the high school team. One night on a dare he sneaks into Forrester's apartment, is startled by the old writer, and begins a strange friendship. Jamal gets someone to read his writings. Forrester gets someone to lure him out of his hibernation.

Finding Forrester was directed by Gus Van Sant, written by Mike Rich, and bears some similarity to Van Sant's *Good Will Hunting* (1997), also about a working-class boy with genius. The stories are really quite different, however, not least because Connery's character is at least as important as Brown's, and because the movie has some insights into the dilemma of a smart black kid afraid his friends will consider him a suck-up.

The movie contains at least two insights into writing that are right on target. The first is William's advice to Jamal that he give up waiting for inspiration and just start writing. My own way of phrasing this rule is: The Muse visits during composition, not before. The other accurate insight is a subtle one. An early shot pans across the books next to Jamal's bed, and we see that his reading tastes are wide, good, and various. All of the books are battered except one, the paperback of Joyce's *Finnegans Wake*, which looks brand-new and has no creases on its spine. That's the book everyone buys but nobody reads.

The scenes between the old man and the teenager are at the heart of the movie, and it's a pleasure to watch the rapport between Connery, in his fiftieth year of acting, and Brown, in his first role. Forrester gives the kid all kinds of useful advice about being a writer, including the insight, "Women will sleep with you if you write a book." That's something Jamal might have figured out for himself, but Forrester is even more encouraging: "Women will sleep with you if you write a *bad* book."

Jamal gets a scholarship to a private academy (his SAT is high enough that it's not an athletic scholarship, although the board certainly hopes he'll play). On its faculty is the embittered Crawford (F. Murray Abraham), coincidentally an old enemy of Forrester's, who simply doesn't believe an African-American basketball player from the Bronx can write at Jamal's level. That sets up the crisis and the payoff, which will remind some viewers of *Scent of a Woman*.

I was reminded of another movie, a great one, named *The Loneliness of the Long Distance Runner* (1962). In both that movie and this one, a disadvantaged young man simply refuses to perform like a trained seal because he knows that will be a lethal blow against his adult tormentors. In a movie where sports supplies an important theme, Jamal's crucial decision supplies the best insight in the story about his journey between two worlds.

The Five Senses ★ ★ ★

R, 105 m., 2000

Molly Parker (Anna Miller), Mary-Louise Parker (Rona), Gabrielle Rose (Ruth), Elize Frances Stolk (Amy Lee Miller), Nadia Litz (Rachel), Daniel MacIvor (Robert), Philippe Volter (Richard), Clinton Walker (Carl), Marco Leonardi (Roberto), Brendan Fletcher (Rupert). Directed by Jeremy Podeswa and produced by Podeswa and Camelia Frieberg. Screenplay by Podeswa.

"You can smell love," says Robert. "If anyone I used to be in love with still loves me, I can tell." He makes dates with former lovers to sniff them across a café table, and meanwhile

Richard, an eye doctor who is going deaf, hires a hooker to listen to music with him. Ruth the massage therapist still has her touch with her clients, but is out of touch with her daughter Rachel. Rachel allows a little girl to wander out of her sight and get lost. Rona is great at decorating cakes, but they don't taste good.

The Five Senses tells interlocking stories about people who are losing their senses, and fear they are losing themselves in the process. But to state the film's subject that directly is to miss the way the writer-director, Jeremy Podeswa, intercuts the stories. He doesn't insist on the senses and the danger of their loss, but allows the fears of his characters to emerge in stories that have weight of their own. Like *Magnolia* and *Short Cuts*, the real subject of the movie is loneliness.

The lost child provides the central story. While Ruth (Gabrielle Rose) massages Anna (Molly Parker), Ruth's young teenage daughter Rachel (Nadia Litz) is assigned to take Anna's young daughter to the park. There Rachel meets Rupert (Brendan Fletcher), a boy about her age, who invites her to follow a couple into the woods. Fascinated by indistinct views of the couple making love, Rachel forgets the little girl, who wanders away and is lost. The search for the girl occupies much of the film, although Podeswa gives the audience a clue that the girl may be safe. In its labyrinthine way, the story curls back to Rachel and Rupert, who play a game with makeup and wigs that may, ironically, help them get better in touch with themselves ("It's like looking at you inside out," Rachel tells him).

There is bittersweet humor in some of the other stories. The bad cake baker, Rona (Mary-Louise Parker), has fallen in love with a chef during a trip to Italy. Roberto (Marco Leonardi) follows her back to Toronto, moves in, cooks delicious dishes, makes love, is happy. But Rona cannot believe her good luck and fears Roberto is simply after money or a passport. Against this lighter comedy stands the sadness of Richard (Philippe Volter), the eye doctor, who is consciously collecting a library of remembered sounds against the day when he goes deaf.

Love has its way of finding paths around problems, and that is the discovery of Robert (Daniel MacIvor), a bisexual housecleaner who works for a couple whose house he cannot quite figure out. She is a perfume designer, and one day when she lets him sniff a new perfume, everything suddenly becomes clear.

A story like *The Five Senses* sounds like a gimmick, but Podeswa has a light touch when dealing with the senses and a sure one when telling his stories. The evolution of Rachel, the angry young girl, is especially touching; as we find out more about her problems and the reasons she can't communicate with her mother, we begin to care. She's a lot more than just the girl who lost the child in the park. And the missing child's mother, Anna, is more than simply a cliché of a grief-stricken parent. She deals with the loss with her mind as well as her feelings, does not necessarily blame Ruth's daughter, finds herself depending on Ruth, and prays in a way that is particularly touching.

Interwoven stories like this can have a particular effect on me. Most movies tell linear plots in which the hero moves from A to B, accompanied by human plot devices. They can be very involving, but I also like the messiness of movies that cut from one story to another, showing how lives can intersect and separate. Some people find these kinds of movies contrived. I think it is just the opposite. A to B stories are obviously plots. Stories like this one show that life goes on all around, and over and beneath, and inside, the artifice of plot.

Flawless ★ ★ ★
R, 111 m., 1999

Robert De Niro (Walt Koontz), Philip Seymour Hoffman (Rusty), Barry Miller (Leonard Wilcox), Wanda De Jesus (Karen), Chris Bauer (Jacko), Daphne Rubin-Vega (Tia), Skipp Sudduth (Tommy), Wilson Jermaine Heredia (Cha-Cha), Nashom Benjamin (Amazing Grace), Scott Allen Cooper (Ivana), Rory Cochrane (Pogo). Directed by Joel Schumacher and produced by Schumacher and Jane Rosenthal. Screenplay by Schumacher.

I don't know if worlds really exist like the one in *Flawless*. I don't know if there are still dance halls in New York where you pay by the dance, although I see them from time to time in the movies. Or rooming houses where everyone is

a character out of Tennessee Williams. Or stories that can involve, at the same time, hero cops, drag queens, two-bit drug dealers, and gay Republicans.

I don't know, and I don't much care, because Joel Schumacher's *Flawless* is more fable than slice-of-life, and all these people and props give Robert De Niro and Philip Seymour Hoffman their opening to create two screwy characters from opposite ends of the great personality divide. The only reason you can't say they deserve each other is that nobody deserves Walt Koontz.

Koontz is the De Niro character, a security guard who was a hero back in 1988 during a hostage crisis. Now he's getting too old for the work. One night he gets involved in a disturbance in the flophouse where he lives. A stroke leaves him partially paralyzed; his speech is slurred and his walk is a lurch from one handhold to the next. His life seems over. It looked pretty drab to begin with. One night a week he went to a dance hall and paid for dances with Karen (Wanda De Jesus), and we sense the screenplay using heroic restraint to avoid the words, "Come on, big boy—10 cents a dance."

Walt's reaction to the stroke is despair, which he presents as anger. His buddies from work come to see him, but he's not interested. He retreats inside a shell. This is a man who had few enough resources for keeping himself amused before the stroke, and now his pastime of choice is sitting and brooding. Nor can he get to know his neighbors, since most of the other residents of the flophouse seem to be hookers, drag queens, or both, and he makes no secret of his distaste for homosexuals.

One of the neighbors is a drag artist named Rusty (Philip Seymour Hoffman). Some men can transform themselves into pretty women; they study *Vogue* magazine. Others do not make pretty women and study the works of Sophie Tucker. Rusty is in the second category—a good soul stuck in a completely impractical lifestyle that involves trying to pay the rent with one-liners instead of cash.

Walt contemplates suicide. Rehabilitation therapy is suggested—singing lessons, for example, to help his speech. Rusty has a piano, and Walt swallows his fierce pride and asks for lessons. Rusty needs the money, and agrees. They make a touching couple, there on the piano bench. Walt probably figures taking singing lessons from a drag queen is marginally preferable to sticking his gun into his mouth and pulling the trigger.

The plot of *Flawless* is too busy and sometimes strays into fictional hinterlands; Rusty's posse of drag friends has a way of turning up on cue, like the factory workers in *Carmen*. The subplot about hidden drug money is a creaky distraction. But when the movie involves Walt and Rusty, it has a wacky charm. De Niro spends most of the movie locked inside a stroke-induced slur, but somehow manages to communicate despite his character's difficult speech (Rusty observes he has no troubles with the f-sound). He's a pathetic coot who begins to grow on us, and for Rusty, who is a soft touch anyway, he's an opportunity for the mother hen routine.

There's also intrigue involving two women from the dance hall—not only the money-minded Karen, but also the younger, gentler Tia (Daphne Rubin-Vega), who has one of the movie's most touching moments. When she comes to visit Walt, he says he's sure his buddy paid her to do it: "I get it. Harvey paid you. He felt sorry for me." Tia replies quietly, "Feel sorry for you? I never felt sorry for you, Walt, until now."

De Niro is a great technical actor who may have been attracted to this material because of the chance to play a stroke victim. His performance not only gets Walt's symptoms right, but also shows sympathy for the man inside. Hoffman, who played the pathetic man who made dirty phone calls in *Happiness*, shows he's one of the best new character actors, able to take a flamboyant role and find the quiet details in it. Too bad they're stuck in a jumbled plot, but as an odd couple, they work.

The Flintstones in Viva Rock Vegas ½★
PG, 90 m., 2000

Mark Addy (Fred Flintstone), Stephen Baldwin (Barney Rubble), Kristen Johnston (Wilma Slaghoople), Jane Krakowski (Betty O'Shale), Thomas Gibson (Chip Rockefeller), Joan Collins (Pearl Slaghoople), Alex Meneses (Roxie), Alan Cumming (Gazoo/Mike Jagged). Directed by Brian Levant and produced by Bruce Cohen. Screenplay by Deborah Kaplan, Harry Elfont, Jim Cash, and Jack Epps Jr.

The Flintstones in Viva Rock Vegas has dinosaurs that lumber along crushing everything in their path. The movie's screenplay works sort of the same way. Think of every possible pun involving stones, rocks, and prehistoric times, and link them to a pea-brained story that creaks and groans on its laborious march through unspeakably obvious, labored, and idiotic humor.

This is an ideal first movie for infants, who can enjoy the bright colors on the screen and wave their tiny hands to the music. Children may like it because they just plain like going to the movies. But it's not delightful or funny or exciting, and for long stretches it looks exactly like hapless actors standing in front of big rocks and reciting sitcom dialogue.

The story isn't a sequel to *The Flintstones* (1994) but a prequel, recalling those youthful days when Fred and Wilma Flintstone first met and fell in love. Fred is portrayed this time by Mark Addy, the beefiest of the guys in *The Full Monty*. His best pal, Barney Rubble, is played by Stephen Baldwin, who recites his lines as if he hopes Fred will ask him to come out and play, but is afraid he won't. As the movie opens Fred and Barney have gotten jobs at the rock quarry, and have settled down to a lifetime of quarrying rocks, which their world does not seem to need any more of, but never mind.

Meanwhile, in a parallel plot, Wilma Slaghoople (Kristen Johnston) resists the schemes of her mother (Joan Collins) to get her to marry the millionaire Chip Rockefeller (get it?). Fleeing the rich neighborhood, she ends up working in a drive-in restaurant ("Bronto King") with Betty O'Shale (Jane Krakowski), and soon the two of them have met Fred and Barney. There's instant chemistry, and the two couples grind off to a weekend in Rock Vegas. The jealous Chip (Thomas Gibson) is waiting there to foil romance and get his hands on the Slaghoople fortune. His conspirator is a chorus-line beauty named Roxie (Second City grad Alex Meneses), whose boulders are second to none. The Vegas sequence is livened by a soundtrack rendition of "Viva Las (and/or Rock) Vegas" by Ann-Margret.

Another story line involves Gazoo (Alan Cumming), an alien who arrives in a flying saucer. He looks exactly like a desperate measure to flesh out an uninteresting plot with an uninteresting character. The movie would be no better and no worse without Gazoo, which is a commentary on both Gazoo and the movie, I think.

The pun, it has been theorized, is the lowest form of humor. This movie proves that theory wrong. There is a lower form of humor: jokes about dinosaur farts. The pun is the second lowest form of humor. The third lowest form is laborious plays on words, as when we learn that the Rock Vegas headliners include Mick Jagged and the Stones.

Minute by weary minute the movie wends its weary way toward its joyless conclusion, as if everyone in it is wearing concrete overshoes, which, come to think of it, they may be. The first film was no masterpiece, but it was a lot better than this. Its slot for an aging but glamorous beauty queen was filled by Elizabeth Taylor. This time it is Joan Collins. As Joan Collins is to Elizabeth Taylor, so *The Flintstones in Viva Rock Vegas* is to *The Flintstones.*

Forces of Nature ★
PG-13, 103 m., 1999

Sandra Bullock (Sarah), Ben Affleck (Ben), Maura Tierney (Bridget), Steve Zahn (Alan), Blythe Danner (Virginia Cahill), Ronny Cox (Hadley Cahill), David Strickland (Steve), Meredith Scott Lynn (Debbie). Directed by Bronwen Hughes and produced by Susan Arnold, Ian Bryce, and Donna Roth. Screenplay by Marc Lawrence.

So I'm sitting there, looking in disbelief at the ending of *Forces of Nature*, and asking myself—if this is how the movie ends, *then what was it about?* We spend two endless hours slogging through a series of natural and man-made disasters with Sandra Bullock and Ben Affleck, and then . . . that's it?

Bronwen Hughes's *Forces of Nature* is a romantic shaggy dog story, a movie that leads us down the garden path of romance, only to abandon us by the compost heap of uplifting endings. And it's not even clever enough to give us the right happy ending. It gives us the *wrong* happy ending.

By then, of course, any ending is good news. The movie is a dead zone of boring conversations, contrived emergencies, unbelievable characters, and lame storytelling. Even then it might have worked at times if it had generated the slightest chemistry between Ben Affleck and Sandra Bullock, but it doesn't. She remains winsome and fetching, but he acts like he's chaperoning his best friend's sister as a favor.

The movie combines at least five formulas, and probably more: the Meet Cute, the Road Movie, the Odd Couple, Opposites Attract, and Getting to Know Yourself. It also cuts back and forth between a journey and the preparations for a marriage, and it tries to keep two sets of parents in play. With so much happening it's surprising that the movie finds a way to be boring, but it does, by cross-cutting between one leaden scene and another.

Affleck stars as an ad man who is flying from New York to Savannah, Georgia, for his wedding. On the plane, he's strapped in next to Bullock, who has held a lot of jobs in her time: flight attendant, wedding photographer, exotic dancer, auto show hostess. The flight crashes on takeoff, and they end up driving to Georgia together amid weather reports of an approaching hurricane.

Of course, circumstances conspire to make him pretend to be a doctor, and them to pretend they're married, and a motel to put them in the same room, and his best man to see him with this strange woman even though he tries to hide by holding his breath in a swimming pool, and so on. Rarely does the artificial contrivance of a bad screenplay reveal itself so starkly on the screen. And when the contrivances stop the revelations begin, and we learn sad things about Bullock's past that feel exactly as if Marc Lawrence, the writer, supplied them at random.

They have a lot of adventures. Arrests, crashes, trees falling on their car, hospitalizations. They take a train for a while (standing on top of one of the cars in a shamelessly pandering shot). And they take a bus (with condo-shopping oldsters). And a Spinning Sombrero ride. At one point they both find themselves performing onstage in a strip club—not quite the kind of club you have in mind. This scene would seem to be foolproof comedy, but the timing is off and it sinks.

Despite my opening comments, I have not actually revealed the ending of the movie, and I won't, although I will express outrage about it. This movie hasn't paid enough dues to get away with such a smarmy payoff. I will say, however, that if the weatherman has been warning for three days that a hurricane is headed thisaway, and the skies are black and the wind is high and it's raining, few people in formal dress for a wedding would stand out in the yard while umbrellas, tables, and trees are flying past. And if they did, their hair would blow around a little, don't you think?

For Love of the Game ★ ½
PG-13, 128 m., 1999

Kevin Costner (Billy Chapel), Kelly Preston (Jane Aubrey), John C. Reilly (Gus Sinski), Jena Malone (Heather), Brian Cox (Gary Wheeler), J. K. Simmons (Frank Perry), Vin Scully (Himself), Steve Lyons (Himself). Directed by Sam Raimi and produced by Armyan Bernstein and Amy Robinson. Screenplay by Dana Stevens, based on the novel by Michael Shaara.

You know those quizzes they run in women's magazines about testing your relationship? *For Love of the Game* is about the kinds of people who give the wrong answers. It's the most lugubrious and soppy love story in many a moon, a step backward for director Sam Raimi after *A Simple Plan,* and yet another movie in which Kevin Costner plays a character who has all the right window dressing but is neither juicy nor interesting.

Costner plays Billy Chapel, a forty-year-old pitcher for the Detroit Tigers, facing retirement at the end of a mediocre season. As the film opens, he's set the stage for a candlelit dinner in his New York hotel, but his date never arrives, he drinks the champagne and all the booze in the minibar, and next day he wakes up with a hangover and learns (a) crusty old Mr. Wheeler is selling the team because his sons don't want it, (b) he's being traded, and

(c) Jane, the girl he was waiting for, is leaving him and taking a job in London because "you don't need me—you're perfect with you and the ball and the diamond." Not what you want to hear when you're facing retirement.

The movie has a screenplay that lumbers between past and present like regret on a death march. Billy suits up for his final game of the season, and as he starts pitching we get the "Five Years Earlier" card, and the movie cuts back and forth between his quest to pitch a perfect game, and his memories of his love affair with Jane. Will he pitch the perfect game and save the relationship? Or will he throw a home-run pitch in the bottom of the ninth, while the girl disappears? What's your best guess?

Five Years Earlier, he first encountered Jane (Kelly Preston) in a Meet Cute, when he saw her kicking her rented VW by the side of the expressway. He's able to get the car running again, and likes her at first sight—even though she doesn't know who he is until the tow-truck guy says, "Hey—you're Billy Chapel!" He is indeed a baseball great, and soon she's complaining, "I need a regular guy. Not the guy in the Old Spice commercials." "It was Right Guard," he says. "I was being metaphorical," she says. She's also not thrilled by kids who collect his picture on bubble-gum cards. "They buy them for the gum," he says, revealing he's seriously out of touch. Today's wise child preserves the original wrappers, and finances his college education by selling them on eBay.

The rhythm of their relationship quickly grows sour. She keeps turning up, and he keeps pushing her away and then needing her when she's gone. She weeps when they're together, he weeps when they're apart. Typical crisis: One winter weekend, he's unwisely sawing some lumber with a rotary saw and cuts his hand. She packs it in snow, but isn't allowed on the medevac helicopter, is dissed by the obligatory rude nurse in the ER ("Are you his wife?"), and is crushed when Billy tells her the team trainer is "the most important person for me right now."

Another crisis. He's in Boston for a game and gets a panic call: Her daughter has run away from home and gone to Boston to seek her dad, who wasn't at home, so now she's alone in the big city. Billy didn't know she had a daughter. "What's her name?" he asks. "Freedom," she says. "Scared you, didn't I? It's Heather." Just the sort of quip a mother would make during a panic call. (In a wittier movie, she would have said, "Heather. Scared you, didn't I? It's Freedom.")

The screenplay, written by Dana Stevens and based on a novel by Michael Shaara, includes getting-to-know-you stuff ("Do you like white meat or dark?"), jealousy ("She's my masseuse."), and sports lore ("All the guys are here for you, Billy."). Some of the sports scenes consist of Costner on the mound, lost in thought (at one point the catcher is concerned because he's staring at clouds), but there are some nice details when he shuts out all the crowd noises, and when he directs a running monologue at each batter he faces. And of course no sports movie has any trouble building suspense at the end of the big game.

The ending is routine: false crisis, false dawn, real crisis, real dawn. Only a logician would wonder why two people meet in a place where neither one would have the slightest reason to be. Thinking back through the movie, I cannot recall a single thing either character said that was worth hearing in its own right, apart from the requirements of the plot. No, wait: She asks him, "What if my face was all scraped off and I was basically disfigured and had no arms and legs and no (something else, can't read my handwriting). Would you still love me?" And he replies, "No. But we could still be friends."

42 Up ★ ★ ★ ★
NO MPAA RATING, 139 m., 2000

A documentary series directed and produced by Michael Apted.

"Give me the child until he is seven, and I will show you the man."
—Jesuit saying

In 1964, a British television network began an intriguing experiment. They would interview a group of seven-year-olds, asking them what they wanted to do in life and what kind of a future they envisioned. Then these same subjects would be revisited every seven years to see how their lives were turning out. It was an intriguing experiment, using film's unique ability to act as a time machine—"the most remarkable nonfiction film project in the history of the medium," wrote Andrew Sarris.

Now here is *42 Up*, the sixth installment in the series. I have seen them all since *14 Up*, and every seven years the series measures out my own life too. It is impossible to see the films without asking yourself the same questions—without remembering yourself as a child and a teenager, and evaluating the progress of your life.

I feel as if I know these subjects, and indeed I do know them better than many of the people I work with every day, because I know what they dreamed of at seven, their hopes at fourteen, the problems they faced in their early twenties, and their marriages, their jobs, their children, even their adulteries.

When I am asked for career advice, I tell students that they should spend more time preparing than planning. Life is so ruled by luck and chance, I say, that you may end up doing a job that doesn't even exist yet. Don't think you can map your life, but do pack for the journey. Good advice, I think, and yet I look at *42 Up* and I wonder if our fates are sealed at an early age. Many of the subjects of the series seemed to know at seven what they wanted to do and what their aptitudes were, and they were mostly right. Others produce surprises, and keep on producing them right into middle age.

Michael Apted could not have predicted that his future would include a lifelong commitment to this series. He was a young man at the beginning of his career when he worked as a researcher on *7 Up*, choosing the fourteen subjects who would be followed. He became the director of *14 Up*, and has guided the series ever since, taking time off from a busy career as the director of feature films (*Coal Miner's Daughter, Gorillas in the Mist*). In his introduction to a new book about the series, he says he does not envy his subjects: "They do get notoriety and it's the worst kind of fame—without power or money. They're out in the street getting on with their lives and people stop them and say, 'Aren't you that girl?' or 'Don't I know you?' or 'You're the one,' and most of them hate that."

The series hasn't itself changed their lives,

he believes. "They haven't got jobs or found partners because of the film, except in one case when a friendship developed with dramatic results."

That case involves Neil, who for most long-time followers of the series has emerged as the most compelling character. He was a brilliant but pensive boy, who at seven said he wanted to be a bus driver, so he could tell the passengers what to look for out the windows; he saw himself in the driver's seat, a tour guide for the lives of others. What career would you guess for him? An educator? A politician?

In later films he seemed to drift, unhappy and without direction. He fell into confusion. At twenty-eight, he was homeless in the Highlands of Scotland, and I remember him sitting outside his shabby house trailer on the rocky shore of a loch, looking forlornly across the water. He won't be around for the next film, I thought: Neil has lost his way. He survived, and at thirty-five was living in poverty on the rough Shetland Islands, where he had just been deposed as the (unpaid) director of the village pageant; he felt the pageant would be going better if he were still in charge.

The latest chapter in Neil's story is the most encouraging of all the episodes in *42 Up*, and part of the change is because of his fellow film subject Bruce, who was a boarding school boy, studied math at Oxford, and then gave up a career in the insurance industry to become a teacher in London inner-city schools. Bruce has always seemed one of the happiest of the subjects. At forty, he got married. Neil moved to London at about that time, was invited to the wedding, found a job through Bruce, and today—well, I would not want to spoil your surprise when you find the unlikely turn his life has taken.

Apted says in his introduction to the book *42 Up* (The New Press, $16.95) that if he had the project to do again, he would have chosen more middle-class subjects (his sample was weighted toward the upper and working classes), and more women. He had a reason, though, for choosing high and low: The original question asked by the series was whether Britain's class system was eroding. The answer seems to be: yes, but slowly. Sarris, writing in the *New York Observer*, delivers this verdict: "At one point, I noted that the upper-class kids, who sounded like twits at 7 compared to the more spontaneous and more lovable lower-class kids, became more interesting and self-confident as they raced past their social inferiors. It was like shooting fish in a barrel. Class, wealth, and social position did matter, alas, and there was no getting around it."

None of the fourteen have died yet, although three have dropped out of the project (some drop out for a film and are back for the next one). By now many have buried their parents. Forced to confront themselves at seven, fourteen, twenty-one, twenty-eight, and thirty-five, they seem mostly content with the way things have turned out. Will they all live to forty-nine? Will the series continue until none are alive? This series should be sealed in a time capsule. It is on my list of the ten greatest films of all time, and is a noble use of the medium.

Freddy Got Fingered no stars
R, 93 m., 2001

Tom Green (Gord Brody), Rip Torn (Jim Brody), Harland Williams (Darren), Julie Hagerty (Julie Brody), Marisa Coughlan (Betty), Eddie Kaye Thomas (Freddy). Directed by Tom Green and produced by Larry Brezner, Lauren Lloyd, and Howard Lapides. Screenplay by Green and Derek Harvie.

It's been leading up to this all spring. When David Spade got buried in crap in *Joe Dirt*, and when three supermodels got buried in crap in *Head Over Heels*, and when human organs fell from a hot-air balloon in *Monkey Bone* and were eaten by dogs, and when David Arquette rolled around in dog crap and a gangster had his testicles bitten off in *See Spot Run*, and when a testicle was eaten in *Tomcats*, well, somehow the handwriting was on the wall. There had to be a movie like *Freddy Got Fingered* coming along.

This movie doesn't scrape the bottom of the barrel. This movie isn't the bottom of the barrel. This movie isn't below the bottom of the barrel. This movie doesn't deserve to be mentioned in the same sentence with barrels.

Many years ago, when surrealism was new, Luis Buñuel and Salvador Dali made a film so shocking that Buñuel filled his pockets with stones to throw at the audience if it attacked him. Green, whose film is in the surrealist tradition, may want to consider the same tactic. The day may come when *Freddy Got Fingered* is seen as a milestone of neosurrealism. The day may never come when it is seen as funny.

The film is a vomitorium consisting of ninety-three minutes of Tom Green doing things that a geek in a carnival sideshow would turn down. Six minutes into the film, his character leaps from his car to wag a horse penis. This is, we discover, a framing device—to be matched by a scene late in the film where he sprays his father with elephant semen, straight from the source.

Green plays Gord Brody, a twenty-eight-year-old who lives at home with his father (Rip Torn), who despises him, and his mother (Julie Hagerty), who wrings her hands a lot. He lives in a basement room still stocked with his high school stuff, draws cartoons, and dreams of becoming an animator. Gord would exhaust a psychiatrist's list of diagnoses. He is unsocialized, hostile, manic, and apparently retarded. Retarded? How else to explain a sequence where a Hollywood animator tells him to "get inside his animals," and he skins a stag and prances around dressed in the coat, covered with blood?

His romantic interest in the movie is Betty (Marisa Coughlan), who is disabled, and dreams of rocket-powered wheelchairs and oral sex. A different kind of sexual behavior enters the life of his brother, Freddy, who gets the movie named after him just because, I suppose, Tom Green thought the title was funny. His character also thinks it is funny to falsely accuse his father of molesting Freddy.

Tom Green's sense of humor may not resemble yours. Consider, for example, a scene where Gord's best friend busts his knee open while skateboarding. Gord licks the open wound. Then he visits his friend in the hospital. A woman in the next bed goes into labor. Gord rips the baby from her womb and, when it appears to be dead, brings it to life by swinging it around his head by its umbilical cord, spraying the walls with blood. If you wanted that to be a surprise, then I'm sorry I spoiled it for you. ☞

Frequency ★ ★ ★ ½
PG-13, 117 m., 2000

Dennis Quaid (Frank Sullivan), Jim Caviezel (John Sullivan), Andre Braugher (Satch DeLeon), Elizabeth Mitchell (Julia Sullivan), Noah Emmerich (Gordo Hersch), Shawn Doyle (Jack Shepard), Jordan Bridges (Graham Gibson), Melissa Errico (Samantha Thomas), Daniel Henson (Johnny Sullivan [Six]). Directed by Gregory Hoblit and produced by Hawk Koch, Hoblit, Bill Carraro, and Toby Emmerich. Screenplay by Emmerich.

I know exactly where the tape is, in which box, on which shelf. It's an old reel-to-reel tape I used with the tape recorder my dad bought me in grade school. It has his voice on it. The box has moved around with me for a long time, but I have never listened to the tape since my dad died. I don't think I could stand it. It would be too heartbreaking.

I thought about the tape as I was watching Gregory Hoblit's *Frequency*. Here is a movie that uses the notion of time travel to set up a situation where a man in 1999 is able to talk to his father in 1969, even though his father died when the man was six. The movie harnesses this notion to a lot of nonsense, including a double showdown with a killer, but the central idea is strong and carries us along. There must be something universal about our desire to defeat time, which in the end defeats us.

The father in 1969 is named Frank Sullivan (Dennis Quaid). He is a fireman, and he dies heroically while trying to save a life in a warehouse fire. The son in 1999 is named John Sullivan (Jim Caviezel), and he has broken with three generations of family tradition to become a policeman instead of a fireman. One night he's rummaging under the stairs of the family house where he still lives, and finds a trunk containing his dad's old ham radio. The plot provides some nonsense about sunspots and the northern lights, but never mind: What matters is that the father and the son can speak to each other across a gap of thirty years.

The paradox of time travel is familiar. If you could travel back in time to change the past in order to change the future, you would already have done so, and therefore the changes would have resulted in the present that you now occupy. Of course, the latest theories of quantum physics speculate that time may be a malleable dimension, and that countless new universes are splitting off from countless old ones all the time—we can't see them because we're always on the train, not in the station, and the view out the window is of this and this and this, not that and that.

But *Frequency* is not about physics, and the heroes are as baffled as we are by the paradoxes they get involved in. Consider a scene where the father uses a soldering iron to burn into a desk the message: "I'm still here, Chief." His son sees the letters literally appearing in 1999 as they are written in 1969. How can this be? If they were written in 1969, wouldn't they have already been on the desk for thirty years? Not at all, the movie argues, because every action in the past *changes* the future into a world in which that action has taken place.

Therefore—and here is the heart of the story—the son, knowing what he knows now, can reach back in time and save his father's life by telling him what he did wrong during that fatal fire. And the father and son can exchange information that will help each one fight a serial killer who, in various time-line configurations, is active now, then, and in between, and threatens both men and, in some configurations, the fireman's wife. How do the voices know they can trust each other? The voice in the future can tell the voice in the past exactly what's going to happen with the Amazing Mets in the '69 Series.

Are you following this? Neither did I, half the time. At one point both the father and the son are fighting the same man at points thirty years separated, and when the father shoots off the 1969 man's hand, it disappears from the 1999 version of the man. But then the 1999 man would remember how he lost the hand, right? And therefore would know—but, no, not in this time line he wouldn't.

There may be holes and inconsistencies in the plot. I was too confused to be sure. And I don't much care, anyway, because the underlying idea is so appealing—that a son who doesn't remember his father could talk to him by shortwave and they could try to help each other. This notion is fleshed out by the father's wife (Elizabeth Mitchell), who must also be saved by the time-talkers, by partners in the

fire and police department, and so on. By the end of the movie, the villain (Shawn Doyle) is fighting father and son simultaneously, and there is only one way to watch the movie, and that is with complete and unquestioning credulity. To attempt to unravel the plot leads to frustration if not madness.

Moviegoers seem to like supernatural stories that promise some kind of escape from our mutual doom. *Frequency* is likely to appeal to the fans of *The Sixth Sense, Ghost,* and other movies where the characters find a loophole in reality. What it also has in common with those two movies is warmth and emotion. Quaid and Caviezel bond over the radio, and we believe the feelings they share. The ending of the movie is contrived, but then of course it is: The whole movie is contrived. The screenplay conferences on *Frequency* must have gone on and on, as writer Toby Emmerich and the filmmakers tried to fight their way through the maze they were creating. The result, however, appeals to us for reasons as simple as hearing the voice of a father you thought you would never hear again.

Friends & Lovers ½★

NO MPAA RATING, 102 m., 1999

Stephen Baldwin (Jon), Danny Nucci (David), George Newbern (Ian), Alison Eastwood (Lisa), Claudia Schiffer (Carla), Suzanne Cryer (Jane), David Rasche (Richard), Neill Barry (Keaton), Robert Downey Jr. (Hans). Directed by George Haas and produced by Josi W. Konski. Screenplay by Haas.

I don't want to review *Friends & Lovers;* I want to flunk it. This movie is not merely bad, but incompetent. I get tapes in the mail from tenth-graders that are better made than this.

Recently I hosted the first Overlooked Film Festival at the University of Illinois, for films that have been unfairly overlooked. If I ever do a festival of films that deserve to be overlooked, here is my opening night selection. The only possible explanation for the film being released is that there are stars in the cast (Stephen Baldwin, Claudia Schiffer, Alison Eastwood, Robert Downey Jr). They should sue their agents.

The story involves a group of friends spending the holidays in a Park City ski chalet. They're involved in what an adolescent might think were adult relationships. Much time is spent in meaningless small talk. We also get the ultimate sign of writer desperation: characters introducing themselves to each other.

If I were marking this as a paper, I would note:

—Director George Haas often lines up actors so they awkwardly face the camera and have to talk sideways to one another.

—Much of the dialogue is handled by cutting to each character as he speaks. This is jarring because it reveals that the movie knows when each character will speak. Professional movies overlap sound and image so that dialogue begins offscreen, before a cut to the speaker.

—The characters frequently propose toasts, as if the movie is a social occasion.

—Pregnant girl looks like she has a pillow stuffed down her dress. Self-consciously holds her belly with both hands in many scenes.

—Dad puts tin can in microwave. Can explodes, and whole chalet is plunged into darkness. I am not surprised that a character in this movie would be stupid enough to microwave an unopened can, but why would the explosion blow every fuse?

—Characters gossip that one character has a big penis. Everyone strips for the Jacuzzi. Movie supplies close-up of penis. Since this is the first nudity of any kind in the movie, audience is jolted. In a light comedy, a close-up of a penis strikes a jarring note. An amazed reaction shot might work, but represents a level of sophistication beyond the reach of this film.

—The general preoccupation with sex and size reminds me of conversations I had when I was eleven. One guy says a female character has two-inch nipples. No one questions this theory. I say two-inch nipples are extremely rare among bipeds.

—Dad says, "My generation thought that working was the best way to support a family." Dad doesn't even know what generation he belongs to. Dad is in his fifties, so is a member of the sixties generation. He is thinking of his parents' generation.

—All dialogue on ski slopes involves ludicrous echoing effects. Yes, a yodel will echo in the Alps. No, conversational levels will not echo in Utah.

—David seems to be a virgin. Friend asks, "You have never done the dirty deed?" David asks, "How exactly would you define that?" Friend makes circle with thumb and finger, sticks another finger through it. Most twentysomething movie characters have advanced beyond this stage.

—Automobile scenes are inept. One "crash" is obviously faked to avoid damaging either vehicle. In a scene that cuts between girl walking by road while a guy drives beside her and talks through open window, the girl is walking at a slower rate of speed than car.

I have often asked myself, "What would it look like if the characters in a movie were animatronic puppets created by aliens with an imperfect mastery of human behavior?" Now I know.

Frogs for Snakes no stars
R, 98 m., 1999

Barbara Hershey (Eva), Robbie Coltrane (Al), Harry Hamlin (Klench), Ian Hart (Quint), David Deblinger (UB), John Leguizamo (Zip), Ron Perlman (Gascone), Lisa Marie (Myrna), Debi Mazar (Simone). Directed by Amos Poe and produced by Phyllis Freed Kaufman. Screenplay by Poe.

Amos Poe's *Frogs for Snakes* is not a film so much as a filmed idea. That could be interesting, but alas, it is a very bad idea. The film is about a group of Manhattan actors who support themselves between roles by acting as gangsters and hit men, and as the film opens they turn their guns on one another. This is a movie that gives new meaning to the notion of being willing to kill for a role.

Barbara Hershey stars, as a waitress and debt collector who used to be married to crime kingpin Al (Robbie Coltrane), who doubles as a theater producer and is preparing a production of Mamet's *American Buffalo*. She and several other characters spend much of their time hanging out in a diner and talking about absent friends. So much time is spent in the diner, indeed, that *Frogs for Snakes* begins to resemble a one-set play, until there are excursions to pool halls, apartments, and even a theater.

Sample dialogue from a pool hall:

"What are you doing here?"

"We heard you were doing *True West*."

"Well, you heard wrong. We're doing *American Buffalo*."

(Shoots him)

Not a single one of the characters is even slightly convincing as anything other than an artificial theatrical construction. Is that the point? I haven't a clue. Much of their dialogue is lifted intact from other movies, sometimes inappropriately (Lisa Marie plays a buxom sex bomb who recites Harry Lime's speech about cuckoo clocks from *The Third Man*). Other speeches come from *Night and the City, Sex, Drugs and Rock 'n' Roll, The Hustler, The Apartment, Repo Man, I Am a Fugitive from a Chain Gang,* and several more. (The film ends by crediting the screenplays, just as most films end with a scroll of the songs on the sound track.)

"Today they write dialogue about cheeseburgers and big special effects," one of the characters says, contrasting the quoted classics with *Pulp Fiction*. Yes, but Tarantino's cheeseburger dialogue is wonderful comic writing, with an evil undercurrent as the hit men talk while approaching a dangerous meeting; no dialogue in this movie tries anything a fraction as ambitious, or risks anything.

Seeing the cast of familiar actors (not only Hershey and Coltrane but Harry Hamlin, Ian Hart, Debi Mazar, John Leguizamo, and Ron Perlman), I was reminded of *Mad Dog Time* (1996), another movie in which well-known actors engaged in laughable dialogue while shooting one another. Of that one, I wrote: "*Mad Dog Time* is the first movie I have seen that does not improve on the sight of a blank screen viewed for the same length of time." Now comes *Frogs for Snakes,* the first movie I have seen that does not improve on the sight of *Mad Dog Time*.

G

Galaxy Quest ★ ★ ★
PG, 102 m., 1999

Tim Allen (Nesmith/Taggart), Sigourney Weaver (Gwen DeMarco/Tawny Madison), Alan Rickman (Alexander Dane/Dr. Lazarus), Tony Shalhoub (Fred Kwan/Tech Sergeant Chen), Sam Rockwell (Guy Fleegman), Daryl Mitchell (Tommy Webber/ Laredo), Enrico Colantoni (Mathesar), Robin Sacgs (Sarris). Directed by Dan Parisot and produced by Mark Johnson and Charles Newirth. Screenplay by David Howard and Robert Gordon.

One of my favorite moments in *Galaxy Quest* takes place as a red digital readout is ticking off the seconds until a spaceship is blown to smithereens. The only person who can save it is a teenage science-fiction fan far away on Earth—and he has just been ordered by his mother to take out the garbage. But then the ship is saved! How? I won't spoil the moment, except to say the ship is modeled in every possible respect on a ship that appears on a TV show, and that includes a digital readout that is also consistent with TV clichés.

Galaxy Quest begins at a convention for the fans of a cult TV program not a million light years removed from *Star Trek*. Anyone who has seen *Trekkies,* the documentary about *Star Trek* fans, will recognize this world at once—a world of fanatics who take the show very seriously indeed, packing hotel ballrooms to screen classic episodes of the show and get autographs from its now aging cast members.

Backstage in a dressing room, Alexander Dane (Alan Rickman), who played an alien who was a doctor on the show, vows, "I won't say that stupid line one more time." Other cast members are enraged that the show's star is late as usual. He is Jason Nesmith (Tim Allen), who plays Commander Peter Quincy Taggart and is not a million light years removed from William Shatner. The heroine is Gwen De-Marco (Sigourney Weaver), who plays Lieutenant Tawny Madison and complains that *TV Guide* interviewed her only about her boobs.

Something strange is about to happen. A race of aliens, who have intercepted broadcasts of the show in outer space and mistaken them for "historical documents," arrives on Earth and transports the entire crew into space, placing them on board a spaceship that has been carefully modeled on the sets of the show. Taggart, who is hung over and thinks he's at another fan event, is impressed by the ship: "Usually it's just something made out of cardboard in someone's garage."

The plot: A race of enemy aliens has attacked the home of the friendly aliens, who are led by Mathesar (Enrico Colantoni). The good guys actually look like many-tentacled octopi, but have a gizmo that gives them human form and even translates their speech. (One of their females and a human cast member fall in love, and a necking session gets interesting when she relapses into a few friendly tentacles.)

The original TV show of course looks cheesy, and the spaceship *Protector* looks as unconvincing as the command deck of the original *Enterprise*. But the enemy aliens, designed by Stan Winston, look fearsomely good, and no wonder: They're supposed to be real, not clones of TV aliens. Of course, all of the cast members turn out to be able to command and operate the ship the aliens have built for them, since it works just like the one on TV. And they find themselves repeating their familiar roles. When the onboard computer speaks, Tawny Madison (Weaver) repeats the words. It's not necessary, but: "That's my one job on the show!" Like any actor she's not about to cut her lines.

The movie's humor works best when the illogic of the TV show gets in the way. There is onboard, for example, a passageway blocked by alternating vertical and horizontal clappers that smash back and forth across the passageway. Negotiating it could be fatal. Why are they there? No reason. Just because they look good on TV.

The General ★ ★ ★ ½
R, 129 m., 1999

Brendan Gleeson (Martin Cahill), Jon Voight (Inspector Ned Kenny), Adrian Dunbar (Noel Curley), Sean McGinley (Gary), Maria Doyle Kennedy (Frances), Angeline Ball (Tina), Eanna

MacLiam (Jimmy), Tom Murphy (Willie Byrne). Directed by and produced John Boorman. Screenplay by Boorman.

There is a certain honor in sticking to your guns, even if they are the wrong guns. Martin Cahill, the subject of John Boorman's *The General,* was for many years the most famous professional criminal in Ireland, a man who copied Robin Hood, up to a point: He stole from the rich and gave to himself. He was as stubborn a man as ever was born, and so clever that even though he was a villain, he inspired grudging admiration even from the police. He was shot dead in 1994 by the IRA, after getting involved in politics, the one thing in Ireland more dangerous than crime.

Boorman, whose films have ranged from *Deliverance* to *Excaliber,* had one close brush with Cahill, who broke into his house and stole the gold record he was awarded for "Dueling Banjos." The movie includes that episode; when Cahill gets the record home and finds it is not really made of gold, it confirms his low regard for straight society. Most of the time he was more lucky; his lifetime haul is estimated at $60 million.

Cahill is played in *The General* by Brendan Gleeson, an expert Irish actor (he was Hamish, Mel Gibson's sidekick, in *Braveheart*) who succeeds in doing two things not easy for an actor: He creates the illusion that we are looking at Cahill himself, and he makes us admit we like him even despite his vicious streak. Gleeson and Boorman, who wrote his own screenplay, look unblinkingly at horrors, and then find the other side of the coin.

Consider, for example, a scene where Cahill suspects a longtime partner of ratting to the cops. To get a confession out of him, he nails him to a snooker table. The man protests his innocence. Finally Cahill pulls out the nails, observing, "No one can stand that much pain without talking." Then he personally takes him to the hospital, reassuring him, "You came through with flying colors." Look on the positive side: Cahill at least has the integrity to pound the nails himself and not leave it to a flunky. And he's man enough to admit his mistake.

Cahill is, in fact, a charming rogue, able to bestir shreds of admiration even in the heart of his archenemy, police inspector Ned Kenny

(Jon Voight). He embodies a certain style in his planning. Trying to buy a house, for example, he is told the agent cannot accept cash. So he takes 80,000 pounds to the bank and purchases a bank draft. He puts the draft in his pocket and walks across the street to the police station, where he is in conversation with Inspector Kenny at the very moment when, wouldn't you know, two masked men approach the very same teller and rob her of all the money in her drawer.

The General opens with Cahill as a young boy, stealing from a local merchant and being sent to reform school (where he socks a would-be molester). As an adult, he was a man who attracted enormous publicity even while obsessively guarding his privacy (he hides his face inside hooded sweatshirts, and invariably holds a hand over his face, peering out from between the fingers). His jobs included knocking over Dublin's largest jewelers, and stealing Old Masters from an Irish country house. In both cases, he uses a devious plan rather than a frontal assault.

Boorman finds subtle humor in Cahill's domestic arrangements; he was married to one woman (Maria Doyle Kennedy) but also shared his bed with her sister (Angeline Ball) and had children by both—apparently a satisfactory arrangement, perhaps because if you were going to be Cahill's sister-in-law you were in bed with him anyway, in one way or another. With his son he shares a delight in pigeons, and one of the low blows struck him by the Dublin police involves setting a ferret loose to kill his prized birds.

Cahill was not a political man, and the way he runs afoul of the IRA is presented in the movie as a lapse of strategy: He did a deal he shouldn't have. In real life, I learn, Cahill's problems came when he interfered in the IRA's drug trade, but such an inference is no doubt still too hot a potato for a director who hopes to film again in Ireland.

Boorman's film is shot in wide-screen black and white, and as it often does, black and white emphasizes the characters and the story, instead of setting them awash in atmosphere. And Boorman's narrative style has a nice offhand feel about it. Instead of explaining everything in neat little simpleminded setups, he lets us discover for ourselves that Cahill is living with both women. As the general unfolds his devious criminal schemes, we see them as they develop, instead of getting those clichéd crime movie chalk talks.

Part of Cahill's charm comes in the way he insists that crime is not his vice, but his occupation. After his neighborhood is torn down by city planners (over his stubborn protests), he demands to be relocated to "a nice neighborhood." A public official sneers: "Wouldn't you sooner live closer to your own kind?" Cahill replies, "No, I'd sooner live closer to my work."

The General's Daughter ★ ★ ½

R, 115 m., 1999

John Travolta (Paul Brenner), Madeleine Stowe (Sarah Sunhill), James Cromwell (General Joe Campbell), Timothy Hutton (Colonel William Kent), James Woods (Colonel Robert Moore), Clarence Williams III (Colonel Fowler), Leslie Stefanson (Captain Elisabeth Campbell), Daniel Van Bargen (Chief Yardley). Directed by Simon West and produced by Mace Neufeld. Screenplay by William Goldman and Christopher Bertolini, based on the novel by Nelson DeMille.

"Elisabeth once told me she was conducting a field investigation in psychological warfare, and the enemy was Daddy."

So speaks one of the friends of the late Captain Elisabeth Campbell, whose bizarre death is the centerpiece of *The General's Daughter*. Her army job is to teach "psychological operations"—or, as she explains to a guy whose tire she helps to change, to mess with people's minds. Nobody's mind has been messed with more than her own.

The friendly guy is Warrant Officer Paul Brenner, played by John Travolta—first as a slow-talking redneck, and then, after he drops the undercover masquerade, as an aggressive army cop. He meets Elisabeth Campbell (Leslie Stefanson) just that once before her naked corpse is found staked spread-eagled to the ground, having been strangled. And if you blinked at that description of her dead body, well, so did I. The circumstances of the victim's death are so bizarre and unlikely that they derail most of the scenes they involve.

The General's Daughter is a well-made thriller with a lot of good acting, but the death of Elisabeth Campbell is so unnecessarily graphic and gruesome that by the end I felt sort of unclean. If this had been a documentary, or even a fiction film with serious intentions, I would have accepted it. But does entertainment have to go this far just to shake us up?

The movie is based on a page-turner by Nelson DeMille, adapted for the screen by William Goldman and Christopher Bertolini, who along the way provide a dialogue scene for Travolta and James Woods that's sharp-edged and crisply delivered; one-on-one, they fence with words and the theater grows as quiet as if it were a sex scene. Simon West, the director, creates a gloomy southern Gothic atmosphere for his film, which is set at an "urban warfare center," an army base that includes mock-ups of civilian architecture, and an antebellum mansion for the general to occupy.

The general (James Cromwell) seems to have lived there quite some time, judging by the furnishings, which make the interiors look like pages from *Architectural Digest*. General Campbell occupies rooms filled with wood, leather, brass, crystal, weapons, and flags, and is doted on by his loyal aide-de-camp, Colonel Fowler (Clarence Williams III). Campbell is a war hero now considered vice-presidential timber, although of course the messy murder of his daughter may put an end to that, especially if he had anything to do with it.

He is not the only suspect. With the efficiency of all good police procedurals, every single main character is a suspect, except for those deployed for local color and comic effect (and you can never be sure about them). Travolta's warrant officer is assigned to the case and partnered with another army cop, Sarah Sunhill (Madeleine Stowe); they had an affair once in Brussels, which gives them something to talk about—just as well, since the primary function of her character is to wait around in hopes that the screenplay will hurl her into a dangerous and threatening situation.

They quiz Captain Moore (Woods), who describes himself as Elisabeth's mentor in psychological warfare, and Colonel Kent (Timothy Hutton), the provost marshal, who seems awfully nosy if he has nothing to hide. The local police chief insulted Travolta while he was undercover, and now Travolta insults him back, and finds out that the chief's son and deputy was dating the dead woman.

He had a lot of company. Travolta finds a secret room in the woman's basement that contains S&M props and equipment, an automatic video system, and lots of incriminating tapes. The sweet blonde who changed Travolta's tire apparently spent her evenings tightening more than lugs. Travolta finds out from the tapes (and from gossip universally offered) that the general's daughter had apparently slept with more or less everyone on the general's staff.

We know from long experience with other thrillers that present problems always have their explanations in lurid flashbacks. Travolta discovers that something unspeakable happened to Captain Campbell during her third year at West Point. What that is, and how it leads to the death of the general's daughter, I leave to you to discover. The explanation does not speak highly for the psych courses at the Point, however, since Elisabeth apparently learned that the way to exorcise a traumatic memory is to reenact the events that produced it.

The General's Daughter is, as I have said, a well-made film. It is populated by edgy performances, and we get a real feeling for the characters played by Woods, as a career man with a secret to hide, Cromwell, as an unbending officer and father, and Williams, as a man who hero-worships the general to a fault. Travolta demonstrates again, as he did in *A Civil Action* and *Primary Colors,* that he has developed into a fine actor.

I also admired the darkly atmospheric look of the film, and the way it sustains its creepy mood. But I cringed when the death of the general's daughter was played out. Did the details have to be so graphic? Did we need to linger on the sight of a terrified woman? Did the filmmakers hesitate before supplying actual shots of her being strangled? Can anything be left to the imagination? I believe that any subject matter is legitimate for artistic purposes, but this isn't art. It's a thriller that could have spared us the details of that woman's horrible death.

Genghis Blues ★ ★ ★ ½
NO MPAA RATING, 88 m., 1999

A documentary featuring Paul Pena and Kongar-ol Ondar. Directed by Roko Belic and produced by Roko Belic and Adrian Belic. Screenplay by Roko Belic.

This is the kind of story that has to be true because no novelist would dare to dream it up. In San Francisco lives a blind blues singer named Paul Pena. He plays and sings backup for such legends as Muddy Waters and B. B. King. Late at night when he cannot sleep, he listens to the world on a shortwave radio. We see his fingers delicately touching the dial, rotating it just a little at a time, seeking stations hidden in the bandwidth.

One night he hears strange, haunting music on Radio Moscow. He tracks it down. It is called "khoomei," or "throat-singing," and is practiced in the tiny Republic of Tuva, which you can find on the map between Mongolia and Siberia. Tuvan throat-singing, he learns, involves creating an eerie sound that combines different and distinct notes at the same time.

For years Paul Pena studies throat-singing, just for the love of it. He translates the lyrics using two Braille dictionaries, one to get them from Tuvan to Russian, and the other from Russian to English (we are not amazed to learn there are no Tuvan-English dictionaries in Braille). He becomes possibly the only throat singer not born in Tuva, all this time without ever meeting anyone else who knows what he is doing.

Now it is 1993. A touring group from Tuva performs in San Francisco. He visits them backstage, and sings their songs—in their style, in their language. They are thunderstruck. In 1995, Pena is invited to Tuva for the annual khoomei competition. He is accompanied by the sound engineer Lemon DeGeorge ("I am basically a tree-trimmer"), a San Francisco deejay named Mario Casetta, and Roko and Adrian Belic, from Evanston, Illinois, who are documentarians. They return with this film.

But so far we have touched only on the amazing facts of *Genghis Blues.* If the film were only about Pena learning throat-singing and going to Tuva, it would be a travelogue. It is about much more. About the way we communicate with music. About the way Paul Pena is clearly an extraordinary person—warm, funny, beset by the demon of depression but singing his way free of it. And about the friend he makes in Tuva, a man named Kongar-ol Ondar, who is the leading throat singer and becomes Paul Pena's close friend in no time at all.

The Tuvans have not had an easy time of it, with the Soviets trying their best to dismantle the national customs, music, and costumes. Now communism has collapsed, and in Tuva they are returning to the old customs with a fierce joy. To think that a man in San Francisco was listening to them on the radio! That he has written a throat-song about friendship in the Tuvan language!

Things happen along the way. Torrential rains. Illness. Competitions. Parades. Feasts. The peculiar way that the legendary physicist Richard Feynman was involved in this Tuvan story. They are all incidents, many colorful, that would be just as interesting in any other film. The heart of *Genghis Blues* is in the music and its singers. Throat-singing sounds as if it were discovered and perfected by musicians like Paul Pena, awake in the middle of the night, searching the dials of their minds for the stations between the numbers.

George Washington ★ ★ ★ ★
NO MPAA RATING, 89 m., 2001

Candace Evanofski (Nasia), Donald Holden (George), Curtis Cotton III (Buddy), Eddie Rouse (Damascus), Paul Schneider (Rico Rice), Damian Jewan Lee (Vernon), Rachael Handy (Sonya), Jonathan Davidson (Euless), Janet Taylor (Ruth). Directed by David Gordon Green and produced by Green, Sacha W. Mueller, and Lisa Muskat. Screenplay by Green.

There is a summer in your life that is the last time boys and girls can be friends until they grow up. The summer when adolescence has arrived, but has not insisted on itself. When the stir of arriving sexuality still makes you feel hopeful instead of restless and troubled. When you feel powerful instead of unsure. That is the summer *George Washington* is about, and all it is about. Everything else in the film is just what happened to happen that summer.

This is such a lovely film. You give yourself to its voluptuous languor. You hang around with these kids from the poor side of town, while they kill time and share their pipe dreams. A tragedy happens, but the movie is not about the tragedy. It is about the discovery that tragedies can happen. In the corresponding summer of my life, a kid tried to be a daredevil by riding his bicycle up a ramp, and fell off and broke his leg, and everybody blamed that when he got polio. I tell you my memory instead of what happens in this film, because the tragedy in the film comes so swiftly, in the midst of a casual afternoon, that it should be as surprising to you as to the kids.

The movie takes place in a rusting industrial landscape, which the weeds are already returning to nature. It is in North Carolina. We meet some black kids, between ten and thirteen, and a few white kids. They're friends. They are transparent to one another. They are facts of life. You wake up every morning and here they are, the other kids in your life. They are waiting to grow up. There are some adults around, but they're not insisted upon. Some of them are so stranded by life they kill time with the kids. Nothing better to do.

Buddy (Curtis Cotton III) has a crush on Nasia (Candace Evanofski). She leaves him for George (Donald Holden). This is all momentous because it is the first crush and the first leaving of their lives. Buddy asks for one last kiss. "Do you love me?" asks Nasia. Buddy won't say. He wants the kiss voluntarily. No luck. George has his own problems: The plates in his skull didn't meet right, and he wears a football helmet to protect his skull. "When I look at my friends," Nasia muses, "I know there's goodness. I can look at their feet, or when I hold their hands, I pretend I can see the bones inside."

George fears for his dog because his Uncle Damascus (Eddie Rouse) doesn't like animals. "He just don't like to get bothered," says Aunt Ruth (Janet Taylor). "Do you remember the first time we made love to this song?" Damascus asks Ruth. "We were out in that field. You buried me in that grass." "Why is it," Ruth asks him, "every time you start talkin', you sound like you gonna cry?"

The heat is still, the days are slow, there is not much to do. A kid with freckles gets in trouble in the swimming pool and George jumps in to save him, even though he's not supposed to get his head wet. Then George starts wearing a cape, like a superhero. Buddy wears a Halloween dinosaur mask while he stands in a rest room, which is one of their hangouts, and delivers a soliloquy that would be worthy of Hamlet, if instead of being the prince of Denmark, Hamlet had been Buddy. Buddy disappears. Nasia thinks he ran away "because he still has his crush on me." Others know why Buddy disappeared but simply do not know what to do with their knowledge. Vernon (Damian Jewan Lee) has a soliloquy beginning with the words "I wish," that would be worthy of Buddy, or Hamlet.

The film has been written and directed by David Gordon Green. The cinematography, by Tim Orr, is the best of the year. The mood and feel of the film has been compared to the work of Terence Malick, and Green is said to have watched *The Thin Red Line* over and over while preparing to shoot. But this is not a copy of Malick; it is simply in the same key. Like Malick's *Days of Heaven,* it is not about plot, but about memory and regret. It remembers a summer that was not a happy summer, but there will never again be a summer so intensely felt, so alive, so valuable.

Get Bruce ★ ★ ★
R, 72 m., 1999

Appearing as themselves: Bruce Vilanch, Whoopi Goldberg, Billy Crystal, Bette Midler, Robin Williams, Nathan Lane, Lily Tomlin, Raquel Welch, Michael Feinstein, and Shirley MacLaine. Directed and produced by Andrew J. Kuehn.

Get Bruce is exactly the kind of documentary we all want to have made about ourselves, in which it is revealed that we are funny, smart, beloved, the trusted confidant of famous people, the power behind the scenes at great events, and the apple of our mother's eye. That all of these things are true of Bruce Vilanch only adds to the piquancy. I have known him for thirty years. If there is a dark side to his nature, I believe it shows itself mostly when he can't decide which T-shirt to wear.

Vilanch writes "specialized material" for Hollywood stars. When Whoopi emcees, when

Billy does the Oscars, when Better Midler opens a new show at Radio City Music Hall, much of what they say (and most of the funniest stuff) has passed through Bruce's laptop computer. He has written the recent Oscarcasts, and can be found backstage at almost every big Hollywood awards show or charity benefit, suggesting "improvised" one-liners as the host dashes onstage between acts. His greatest triumph was arguably the night Jack Palance did the one-armed push-ups, and Billy Crystal milked it for the whole evening.

It is not that Billy, Robin, Whoopi, Bette, and the others are idiots who need Vilanch to put words in their mouths. Quite the opposite, as this film shows in some fascinating footage of them at work. Vilanch is a foil, a collaborator, a dueling partner, a lateral thinker able to help them move in the direction they want to go. Only when some clients are insecure or truly at sea does he become a ventriloquist.

I knew him a long time ago in Chicago when he worked for the *Tribune,* the film says, although I recall, perhaps imperfectly, that it was *Chicago Today.* He was very funny then. He looked about the same: large, always wearing a well-stretched T-shirt, his face a cartoon made of a mass of hair, a Santa beard, and glasses. He wrote wonderful celebrity profiles, and that's how he met Bette Midler at Mister Kelly's and went from rags to riches.

I may not have actually been present when they met, but I was there at Kelly's one night at about the same time. Mort Sahl was on the stage. I was in the booth next to the runway to the dressing rooms. I heard a voice. "Why do I have to open for this guy?" It was Bette Midler. Another voice. "Why do I have to be your piano player?" Her piano player was Barry Manilow.

The world was young then and Bruce flirted briefly with the possibility that he could build a performing career of his own. He actually opened at Kelly's as a stand-up comic. This was in the days before comedy clubs, and it took nerve to stand up in front of a room of friends and critics (the friends were more frightening) and try to be funny. I do not recall that he was a hit. I can see from *Get Bruce,* however, that he's good in front of a crowd these days, no doubt because he has a lot more confidence and because his persona is familiar to his audiences.

"There isn't a show in town that can be held without him," says one of the subjects of *Get Bruce*. He recalls, usually with the perpetrators, how specific material was generated. Not just the triumphs (Palance's push-ups) but the disasters like Ted Danson's appearance in blackface at the Friar's Club roast for Whoopi Goldberg. Vilanch wrote a lot of Danson's material, which went over so badly it occupied the entire front page of the *New York Daily News* the next day, but Goldberg defends him: "It was my idea. All my idea."

I remember when he left for the coast. There was a farewell party at Larry Dieckhaus's and we all sat on the floor around a coffee table, eating pizza and weeping with laughter. At first it was slow going in L.A. He got a job on the *Brady Bunch Variety Hour,* and then interviewed with Donny and Marie. What he said to Donny during their unsuccessful meeting cannot be quoted here, but will be much quoted elsewhere. He also recalls some of the people he did not write for; he is well paid, we learn, and Barbra Streisand's offer was so low he told her, "Jim Bailey offered me more to write the drag version of this act."

Some of the film's best sequences have Vilanch bouncing lines back and forth with Crystal and Williams. He works differently with each client. With some he's a counselor, a source of calm reassurance. With others he's a competitor, a one-upper. Lots of funny lines are generated, and he remembers a few that went too far and were wisely left out of the script.

Where does he get his humor? Maybe from his mother back on Long Island, whose every statement is hilarious—apparently unintentionally, although we sense she knows exactly what she's doing. Bruce was adopted, she confides, but "he's more like me than any child who was ever naturally born." High praise. Deserved.

Get Real ★ ★ ★
R, 110 m., 1999

Ben Silverstone (Steven Carter), Brad Gorton (John Dixon), Charlotte Brittain (Linda), Stacy A. Hart (Jessica), Kate McEnery (Wendy), Patrick Nielsen (Mark), Tim Harris (Kevin), James D. White (Dave). Directed by Simon Shore and produced by Stephen Taylor. Screenplay by Patrick Wilde, based on the play *What's Wrong with Angry?* by Wilde.

Get Real tells the story of a teenage boy who has become sexually active at sixteen. That is, of course, the fodder for countless teenage sexcoms, in which the young heroes raid the brothels of Tijuana, are seduced by their French governesses, or have affairs with their teachers. The difference is that the hero in *Get Real* is gay, and so no doubt some critics will be offended by the film's assumptions.

I am thinking, for example, of a columnist for my own newspaper who doesn't think gays should be allowed into the Boy Scouts. His opposition to abortion clinics is matched only by his outrage at the birth control information supplied on a Planned Parenthood Web page; the logical result of his arguments is teenage childbearing. While it may be true that in his ideal world everyone is straight and they never have sex until they have been united by clergy, the real world is filled with young people who must deal every day with strong emotional and sexual feelings. Some of them have sex. This is a fact of life.

Such a person is Steven Carter (Ben Silverstone), the young British student who is the subject of *Get Real*. He has known he was gay since he was eleven. He keeps it a secret because in his school, you can be beaten for being gay. He's picked on anyway by insecure kids who deal with their own sexual anxiety by punishing it in others. The cards are stacked against him, he tells a girl who's his best friend: "I don't smoke or play football, and I have an IQ over 25."

One day Steven visits a local park where gays are known to meet, and is surprised to find that John Dixon (Brad Gorton), an athletic hero at his school, is hanging out there, too—and apparently for the same reason. John is far from out of the closet. He's attracted to Steven, and then runs away, and then comes creeping curiously back, and then denies his feelings. There is a heartbreaking scene (after they have become lovers) where he beats up Steven in the locker room, just to keep his cover in front of a gang of gay-bashers.

The movie deals with this material in a straightforward way, but is not sexually graphic and it somehow finds humor and warmth even while it shows Steven's lonely, secretive existence. In its general outlines, it's a typical teenage comedy like the ones that have been opening every weekend all spring, where the shy outsider is surprised to attract the most popular boy in class. This time the outsider is not played by Drew Barrymore, Rachel Leigh Cook, or Reese Witherspoon. And when Steven and John go to the school dance, they both dance with girls, while their eyes meet in hopeless longing.

Much of the humor in the film comes from Linda (Charlotte Brittain), Steven's plump best friend and for a long time the only one who knows he is gay. She acts as a confidante and cover, and even obligingly faints at a wedding when he needs to make a quick getaway. He's known her since the early days when everything he knew about sex was learned from his dad's hidden porno tapes ("I thought babies were made when two women tie a man to a bed and cover his willy with ice cream").

There is also Jessica (Stacy A. Hart), an editor on the school magazine, who likes Steven a lot and wants to be his girlfriend. He would like to tell her the truth, but nobody guesses it, certainly not his parents, and he lacks the courage. Then the relationship with John helps him to see his life more clearly, to grow tired of lying, and he writes an anonymous article for the magazine that is not (as he must have known) destined to remain anonymous for long.

The film takes a bit long to arrive at its obligatory points, and Steven's brave decision at the end is probably unlikely—he acts not as a high school boy probably would, but as a screenwriter requires him to. But the movie is sound in all the right ways; it argues that we are as we are, and the best thing to do is accept that. I doubt if movies have much influence on behavior, but I hope they can help us empathize with those who are not like us. There were stories that the Colorado shooters were taunted (inaccurately, apparently) for being gay. Movies like *Get Real* might help homophobic teenagers and adults become more accepting of differences. Certainly this film has deeper values than the mainstream teenage comedies that retail aggressive materialism, soft-core sex, and shallow ideas about "popularity."

Getting to Know You ★ ★ ★
NO MPAA RATING, 96 m., 2000

Heather Matarazzo (Judith), Zach Braff (Wesley), Michael Weston (Jimmy), Bebe Neuwirth (Trix [Judith's Mom]), Mark Blum (Darrell [Judith's Dad]), Bo Hopkins (Officer Caminetto, Tristine Skyler (Irene), Christopher Noth (Sonny), Jacob Reynolds (Lamar Pike Jr.). Directed by Lisanne Skyler and produced by Laura Gabbert and George LaVoo. Screenplay by Tristine Skyler and Lisanne Skyler, based on stories by Joyce Carol Oates.

The work of Joyce Carol Oates is populated with characters who live in a lonely landscape, filled with hurt and shame. She has written so much about them, and knows them so well, that we are at a loss to understand the springs of her invention; she reminds me of a story I read long ago about a man who was telepathic, and went mad because he could not drown out the incoming pain and cries for help.

Getting to Know You is a film based on several of Oates's stories, held together by the linking device of some people waiting in a small bus station: a sixteen-year-old girl named Judith, her brother Wesley, a boy named Jimmy who hangs around the station, a security guard, and some others. Judith and Wesley (Heather Matarazzo and Zach Braff) have clung together in the wreckage of their parents' alcoholic marriage; Jimmy is a kid who makes up stories about himself and about the strangers he sees in the bus station, and in a way he represents Oates.

The kids' parents are Trix (Bebe Neuwirth) and Darrell (Mark Blum), two drinkers and ballroom dancers who live in a world of their own. In a flashback, the kids sit on a staircase, peering down at their parents drifting across a living room that has become, in their minds, a ballroom. Going through old family photo albums, they notice that the pictures stop at about the time they were born. Now, we learn, Trix is in an institution, maybe with wet brain, and when Judith calls her dad, he doesn't want her to call anymore—he has "canceled all debts."

When the bus arrives, Wesley will be off to college, and then Judith will be going to a foster home. Wesley spends most of the movie buried in textbooks, obviously determined to learn his way out of despair. Judith starts talking to Jimmy, who singles out people in the bus station and tells her stories about them. He says the security guard (Bo Hopkins), for example, left the police force after his partner was killed on a day off in what may have been an unnecessary way.

A movie like this runs the risk of feeling cut up and episodic, but director Lisanne Skyler, who cowrote the screenplay with her actress sister Tristine, makes the episodes vivid. One stars Tristine and Chris Noth in the story of a girl who meets a gambler in an Atlantic City casino. He wins $75,000 and is charming, expansive, blessed, and it's love for a night. Then he's drawn back to the tables, and his sad need to lose draws shadows over his face, and she is frightened. Another story involves a scrawny, deep-voiced boy named Lamar Jr. (Jacob Reynolds), and his dad, and an ax.

Heather Matarazzo is at the center of the film, her first major role since *Welcome to the Dollhouse* (1995). The camera likes to regard her; she has a repose and inwardness that attracts our attention. Like Lili Taylor or Shelley Duvall, she is not conventionally pretty, although she glows and is more entrancing than the teen-mag beauties who pass for stars in Friday night specials. Her character Judith takes a . . . care with life. When she touches something, you can't tell if she doesn't want to harm it, or is afraid of being burned. She is poised on the edge of a life when things like she's heard about today could happen to her.

The history of this film is intriguing. It played first on the Sundance Channel, and is now going out theatrically. Another good film, *Panic,* also went to cable after winning a warm reception in festivals. Mass distribution is so dominated by 3,000-screen f/x extravaganzas that smaller films get lost in the noise, and perhaps the cable exposure will act like a sneak preview, as people tell each other about the film they discovered and admired. Movies about people are being drowned out these days by movies about things, which can give you insights about yourself only if you are a cyborg. Here is a film about people.

Ghost Dog: The Way of the Samurai ★ ★ ★
R, 116 m., 2000

Forest Whitaker (Ghost Dog), Henry Silva (Ray Vargo), Richard Portnow (Handsome Frank), Tricia Vessey (Louise Vargo), John Tormey (Louie), Cliff Gorman (Sonny Valerio), Victor Argo (Vinny). Directed by Jim Jarmusch and produced by Jarmusch and Richard Guay. Screenplay by Jarmusch.

It helps to understand that the hero of *Ghost Dog* is crazy. Well, of course he is. He lives in a shack on a rooftop with his pigeons. He dresses like a homeless man. "He has no friends and never talks to anybody," according to the mother of the little girl in the movie. Actually, he does talk: to the little girl and to a Haitian ice-cream man. The Haitian speaks no English and Ghost Dog speaks no French, so they simply speak in their own languages and are satisfied with that. What's your diagnosis?

Ghost Dog (Forest Whitaker) is a killer for the mob. He got into this business because one day a mobster saved his life—and so, since he follows "The Way of the Samurai," he must dedicate his life to his master. The mobster is named Louie (John Tormey). He orders hits by sending Ghost Dog messages by carrier pigeon. The Dog insists on being paid once a year, on the first day of autumn. When the mob bosses want Ghost Dog rubbed out, they're startled to discover that Louie doesn't know his name or where he lives; their only contact is the pigeons.

It seems strange that a black man would devote his life to doing hired killing for a group of Italian-American gangsters after having met only one of them. But then it's strange, too, that Ghost Dog lives like a medieval Japanese samurai. The whole story is so strange, indeed, that I've read some of the other reviews in disbelief. Are movie critics so hammered by absurd plots that they can't see how truly, profoundly weird *Ghost Dog* is? The reviews treat it matter-of-factly: Yeah, here's this hit man, he lives like a samurai, he gets his instructions by pigeon, blah, blah . . . and then they start talking about the performances and how the director, Jim Jarmusch, is paying homage to Kurosawa and *High Noon.*

But the man is insane! In a quiet, sweet way, he is totally unhinged and has lost all touch with reality. His profound sadness, which permeates the touching Whitaker performance, comes from his alienation from human society, his loneliness, his attempt to justify inhuman behavior (murder) with a belief system (the samurai code) that has no connection with his life or his world. Despite the years he's spent studying "The Way of the Samurai," he doesn't even reflect that since his master doesn't subscribe to it, their relationship is meaningless.

I make this argument because I've seen *Ghost Dog* twice, and admired it more after I focused on the hero's insanity. The first time I saw it, at Cannes, I thought it was a little too precious, an exercise in ironic style, not substance. But look more deeply, and you see the self-destructive impulse that guides Ghost Dog in the closing scenes, as he sadly marches forth to practice his code in the face of people who only want to kill him (whether he survives is not the point).

Jarmusch is mixing styles here almost recklessly, and I like the chances he takes. The gangsters (played by colorful character actors like Henry Silva, Richard Portnow, Cliff Gorman, and Victor Argo), sit in their clubhouse doing sub-Scorsese while the Louie character tries to explain to them how he uses an invisible hit man. Ghost Dog meanwhile mopes sadly around the neighborhood, solemnly recommending *Rashomon* to a little girl ("you may want to wait and read it when you're a little older"), and miscommunicating with the ice-cream man. By the end, Whitaker's character has generated true poignance.

If the mobsters are on one level of reality and Ghost Dog on another, then how do we interpret some of the Dog's killings, particularly the one where he shoots a man by sneaking under his house and firing up through the lavatory pipe while the guy is shaving? This is a murder that demands Inspector Clouseau as its investigator. Jarmusch seems to have directed with his tongue in his cheek, his hand over his heart, and his head in the clouds. The result is weirdly intriguing.

The Gift ★ ★ ★

R, 110 m., 2001

Cate Blanchett (Annie Wilson), Giovanni Ribisi (Buddy Cole), Keanu Reeves (Donnie Barksdale), Greg Kinnear (Wayne Collins), Hilary Swank (Valerie Barksdale), J. K. Simmons (Sheriff Pearl Johnson), Michael Jeter (Defense Attorney), Gary Cole (David Duncan). Directed by Sam Raimi and produced by James Jacks, Tom Rosenberg, and Robert G. Tapert. Screenplay by Billy Bob Thornton and Tom Epperson.

Psychics and hairdressers have three things in common: They can appoint themselves, they can work out of their homes, and they don't have a lot of overhead—a Tarot deck, shampoo, candles, scissors, incense, mousse. It helps if they have a reassuring manner, because many of their clients want to tell their troubles and receive advice.

Poor neighborhoods have a lot of women working as beauticians or soothsayers. If you're a woman with few options, no husband, and a bunch of kids, you can hang out the shingle and support yourself. The advice dispensed by these professionals is often as good as or better than the kind that costs $200 an hour, because it comes from people who spent their formative years living and learning. The problems of their clients are not theoretical to them.

Consider Annie Wilson (Cate Blanchett), the heroine of *The Gift*. Her husband was killed in an accident a year ago. She has three kids. She gets a government check, and supplements it by reading cards and advising clients. She doesn't go in for mumbo jumbo. She takes her gift as a fact of life; her grandmother had it, and so does she. She looks at the cards, she listens to her clients, she feels their pain, she tries to dispense common sense. She is sensible, courageous, and good.

She lives in a swamp of melodrama; that's really the only way to describe her hometown of Brixton, Georgia, which has been issued with one example of every standard Southern Gothic type. There's the battered wife and her redneck husband; the country club sexpot; the handsome school principal; the weepy mama's boy who is afeared he might do something real bad; the cheatin' attorney; the salt-of-the-earth sheriff; and various weeping willows, pickup trucks, rail fences, country clubs, shotguns, voodoo dolls, courtrooms, etc. When you see a pond in a movie like this, you know that sooner or later it is going to be dragged.

With all of these elements, *The Gift* could have been a bad movie, and yet it is a good one, because it redeems the genre with the characters. Cate Blanchett's sanity and balance as Annie Wilson provide a strong center, and the other actors in a first-rate cast go for the realism in their characters, instead of being tempted by the absurd. The movie was directed by Sam Raimi and written by Billy Bob Thornton and Tom Epperson. They know the territory. Raimi directed Thornton in *A Simple Plan* (1998), that great movie about three buddies who find a fortune and try to hide it; and Thornton and Epperson wrote *One False Move* (1991), about criminals on the run and old secrets of love.

The Gift begins by plunging us into the daily lives of the characters, and then develops into a thriller. One of Annie's kitchen-table clients is Valerie Barksdale (Oscar winner Hilary Swank), whose husband, Donnie (Keanu Reeves), beats her. Another is Buddy Cole (Giovanni Ribisi), who is haunted by nightmares and is a seething basket case filled with resentment against his father. Annie advises Valerie to leave her husband before he does more harm, and then Keanu Reeves has two terrifying scenes—one threatening her children, the other a midnight visit where he uses the voodoo doll as a prop.

Social interlude: Annie attends a country club dance, where she has a flirty conversation with the school principal (Greg Kinnear). He's engaged to Jessica King (Katie Holmes), a sultry temptress (i.e., country club slut) who Annie accidentally sees having a quickie with another local man. Not long after, Jessica disappears, and Sheriff Pearl Johnson (J. K. Simmons), frustrated by an absence of clues, appeals to Annie for some of her "hocus-pocus."

Annie has a dream that leads the law to Donnie Barksdale's pond, where the dead body is found, and Donnie looks like the obvious killer, but Annie's visions don't stop, and we are left (1) with the possibility that the murder may have been committed by several

other excellent candidates, and (2) with suspicion falling on the psychic herself.

The movie is ingenious in its plotting, colorful in its characters, taut in its direction, and fortunate in possessing Cate Blanchett. If this were not a crime picture (if it were sopped in social uplift instead of thrills), it would be easier to see the quality of her work. By the end, as all hell is breaking loose, it's easy to forget how much everything depended on the sympathy and gravity she provided in the first two acts. This role seems miles away from her Oscar-nominated *Elizabeth* (1998), but after all isn't she once again an independent woman surrounded by men who want to belittle her power, seduce her, frame her, or kill her? A woman who has to rely on herself and her gifts, and does, and is sufficient. ☞

Girlfight ★ ★ ★ ½
R, 122 m., 2000

Michelle Rodriguez (Diana), Jaime Tirelli (Hector), Ray Santiago (Tiny), Paul Calderon (Sandro), Santiago Douglas (Adrian), Louis Guss (Don), J. P. Lipton (Mr. Price). Directed by Karyn Kusama and produced by Sarah Green, Martha Griffin, and Maggie Renzi. Screenplay by Kusama.

After the screening of *Girlfight* at Cannes, I was talking to the two leads: Michelle Rodriguez, who plays Diana, a troubled Brooklyn girl who solves some of her problems by training to become a boxer, and Santiago Douglas, who plays her boyfriend and (improbably but with much suspense) her rival in the ring.

"There was a blooper in the big fight," Rodriguez told me. "He hit me by mistake. Really hit me."

"Don't start," said Douglas.

"I got mad and I jumped at him. So I had to leave the ring and just compose myself and just breathe."

"When I hit Michelle," Douglas said, "it wasn't a mistake. She'd won all of her fights in the story so far. I realized there was no fear in her eyes. She was overconfident."

"You did that on *purpose?*" said Michelle.

"I did."

There was a little silence, while Rodriguez absorbed that information, and I began to understand why, under the craft and drama of *Girlfight,* there was a certain real feeling of danger and risk.

Rodriguez told me she trained as a boxer for the movie, and enjoyed it, but finally, "I had to stop the boxing because your ego flies all over the place, and I started to actually welcome the challenge of someone in the street stepping up to me."

Yes, and that would fit, because Michelle Rodriguez is ideally cast in the movie, not as a hard woman or a muscular athlete, but as a spirited woman with a temper, and fire in her eyes. We need that for the picture to work. Consider one of her first scenes. Diane gets in an argument over a boy in the hallways at high school. It's her fourth fight this semester. She's threatened with expulsion. In her eyes we can see resentment and outrage—the world is against her.

Later she's at the gym where her brother Tiny (Ray Santiago) takes lessons without much enthusiasm. A sparring partner hits Tiny with a sucker punch, and Diana jumps in the ring and clocks him. And likes the feeling.

Girlfight looks like a sports picture, but it's really more of a character study, in which boxing is the way that Diana finds direction in her life. She and Tiny live at home with their dad (Paul Calderon). Old angers simmer about the death of their mother. It's a traditionally macho Latin household in which Tiny's boxing lessons are paid for even though he has no interest in the sport. Diana does, and eventually her brother gives her his boxing money: "I'm a geek. I'll do something constructive with my time."

At the gym Diana meets Adrian, who seems to be going with another girl but maybe not. They go to dinner. She says she likes boxing. "It's a dangerous sport," he says. "I didn't make the cheerleading team," she says, and the tone of her voice says more.

Yes, the movie leads up to the obligatory big fight. But what is proven in the fight settles more about the characters and their relationships than it does about the plot. This is a story about a girl growing up in a macho society and, far from being threatened by its values, discovering she has a nature probably more macho than the men around her. Since the movie (written, directed, and produced by women) is deeply aware of that theme, it's always about more than boxing.

Karyn Kusama was named Best Director at Sundance for *Girlfight* (which also won the Grand Jury Prize), and she wisely realizes many of the changes in the story have to be embodied in the performances (it would be fatal to spell out the themes in dialogue). Rodriguez, a newcomer, seems to have a natural affinity for the camera. Her Diana hungers, she cares, she is easily wounded and quick to defend herself, and all of those qualities are simply there in every scene; they don't need to be underlined, because Rodriguez brings them along.

"Making this movie was good for me," Rodriguez told me that day in Cannes. "I learned discipline. I'm a very irresponsible person with a short attention span. I learned to dedicate myself to something." Was she talking about herself, or her character? The movie is stronger because that's such a close call.

Girl, Interrupted ★ ★ ½
R, 125 m., 2000

Winona Ryder (Susanna), Angelina Jolie (Lisa), Clea Duvall (Georgina), Brittany Murphy (Daisy), Elisabeth Moss (Polly), Jared Leto (Tobias Jacobs), Whoopi Goldberg (Valerie [nurse]), Jeffrey Tambor (Dr. Potts), Vanessa Redgrave (Dr. Wick). Directed by James Mangold and produced by Douglas Wick and Cathy Konrad. Screenplay by Mangold, Lisa Loomer, and Anna Hamilton Phelan, based on the book by Susanna Kaysen.

In the spring of 1967, while everyone else in her senior class seems to be making plans for college, Susanna consumes a bottle of aspirin and a bottle of vodka. "My hands have no bones," she observes. Soon, with a push from her family, she has committed herself to Claymoore, an upscale psychiatric institution. The diagnosis? "Borderline personality disorder," say the shrinks. A supervising nurse played by Whoopi Goldberg offers her own diagnosis: "You are a lazy, self-indulgent little girl who is driving herself crazy."

Winona Ryder plays Susanna Kaysen, whose real-life memoir tells of how she lost two years of her life by stumbling onto the psychiatric conveyor belt. Although mental illness is real and terrifying, the movie argues that perfectly sane people like Susanna can become institutionalized simply because once they're inside the system there is the assumption that something must be wrong with them. Goldberg's nurse has seen this process at work and warns Susanna: "Do not drop anchor here."

But Susanna fits easily into the cocoon of Claymoore, where the other women include a rebel misfit named Lisa (Angelina Jolie), a roommate named Georgina (Clea Duvall) who would like to live in the land of Oz, the burn victim Polly (Elisabeth Moss), and the deeply troubled Daisy (Brittany Murphy). The staff is headed by a bureaucrat (Jeffrey Tambor) and an intelligent but detached psychiatrist (Vanessa Redgrave).

The film unfolds in an episodic way, like the journal it's based on. Themes make an appearance from time to time, but not consistently; the film is mostly about character and behavior, and although there are individual scenes of powerful acting, there doesn't seem to be a destination. That's why the conclusion is so unsatisfying: The story, having failed to provide itself with character conflicts that can be resolved with drama, turns to melodrama instead.

One problem is the ambivalent nature of Susanna's condition ("ambivalent" is one of her favorite words). She isn't disturbed enough to require treatment, but she becomes strangely absorbed inside Claymoore, as if it provides structure and entertainment she misses on the outside. Certainly Lisa is an inspiration, with her cool self-confidence masking deep wounds. Instead of being in a women's dorm at college, Susanna is in a women's dorm at Claymoore, where her subject of study is herself. Susanna is not therefore a captive of an evil system, but someone seduced by a careless one, and there is the temptation to suspect she deserves what she gets.

Even a feminist argument with her psychiatrist (Redgrave) lacks power. They argue over the definition of promiscuity; Susanna points out that women are labeled promiscuous after much less sexual experience than men. Susanna has indeed slept in one day with both her boyfriend and an orderly, but under the circumstances is that promiscuity or opportunism?

Jared Leto plays her boyfriend, Toby, whose number is up in the draft lottery. He wants them to run away to Canada. She is no longer much interested in steering her future into their relationship, and prefers her new friends in Claymoore. "Them?" says Toby. "They're eating grapes off of the wallpaper." Susanna chooses solidarity: "If they're insane, I'm insane." Wrong. They're insane and she isn't, and that deprives the film of the kind of subterranean energy that fueled its obvious inspiration, *One Flew Over the Cuckoo's Nest*.

Two reasons to see the film: Winona Ryder and Angelina Jolie. Their characters never really get a plot to engage them, and are subjected to a silly ending, but moment to moment they are intriguing and watchable. Jolie is emerging as one of the great wild spirits of current movies, a loose cannon who somehow has deadly aim. Ryder shows again her skill at projecting mental states; one of her gifts is to let us know exactly what she's thinking, without seeming to. Their work here deserves a movie with more reason for existing.

The Girl on the Bridge ★ ★ ★ ½
R, 92 m., 2000

Daniel Auteuil (Gabor), Vanessa Paradis (Adele), Claude Aufaure (Suicide Victim), Bertie Cortez (Kusak), Giorgios Gatzios (Barker), Demetre Georgalas (Takis), Catherine Lascault (Irene), Mireille Mosse (Miss Memory). Directed by Patrice Leconte and produced by Christian Fechner. Screenplay by Serge Frydman.

The hero of *The Girl on the Bridge* hangs around bridges in Paris, looking for girls who are about to jump. Then he offers them a deal. Suicide is a permanent solution to a temporary problem, so perhaps they will consider working for him. He is a knife thrower. There is always the possibility he will miss. If he doesn't, they get an interesting job with lots of travel. If he does hit them, well, what do they have to lose?

This logic proves persuasive to Adele (Vanessa Paradis), who signs on with Gabor (Daniel Auteuil). Well, not immediately; first she jumps, or perhaps slips, into the water, and he has to jump in and save her life. That will get a girl's attention. They travel from one venue to another, at first in the south of France, as he straps her to a cork backdrop and hurls knives at her. There are variations. He straps her to a spinning wheel. Sometimes he is blindfolded, or she is concealed beneath a sheet. They are booked on cruise ships, where the rocking of the waves adds a risk factor.

Gabor complains that his eyes are failing him ("past forty, knife throwing becomes erratic"), but he is really very good, a skill revealed by the fact that this film is not a short subject. If he is good at knives, she is good at roulette, and in the casinos in the towns where they appear she has an extraordinary run of good luck. His luck has turned good, too; they're making better money, finding better bookings, and they become so closely in synch they can even hear each other's thoughts.

The Girl on the Bridge was directed by Patrice Leconte, a French filmmaker whose work includes *Monsieur Hire* (1989), *The Hairdresser's Husband* (1990), and *Ridicule* (1996). He is fascinated by the hoops that his characters will jump through in their search for sexual fulfillment. Monsieur Hire is a bald little man of solemn visage who is a voyeur. He meekly worships the woman in the apartment across the way, who is not oblivious to his attentions, but his haplessness is his undoing. *The Hairdresser's Husband,* on the other hand, is about a man who became fixated in adolescence on hairdressers, and wants only to be present while the woman of his dreams cuts hair. Now comes the knife thrower.

Leconte's movies almost always involve a deep, droll humor (it is hard to see in *Monsieur Hire,* but it is there). He's amused by human nature. His characters in *The Girl on the Bridge* aren't oblivious to the humor in their situation; their love and luck seem to depend on earning their living by seeing how close they can come to disaster. Much of their appeal comes from the human qualities of the performers. Auteuil, he of the crooked nose and mournful countenance, is a man who can hardly believe good fortune, and Paradis is a woman who can see that during many of her orgasms the joke is on her.

The movie begins by taking an absurd situation rather seriously, and then lets the seriousness melt away; by the time the lovers have voluntarily gotten themselves into a rowboat in the middle of the ocean, we are almost in Looney Tunes territory.

Leconte's own adolescent fixation seems to be with exotic Turkish harem music, which he gets around to with amazing frequency in his movies. In *The Hairdresser's Husband,* so great was the husband's exuberance that he would sometimes put Turkish music on the phonograph and dance about the shop. In *The Girl on the Bridge,* the lovers work through the French and Italian Rivieras, and then move on by sea to Istanbul—perhaps for no better reason than so Leconte can slip his favorite music onto the sound track.

What's best about the movie is its playfulness. Occupations like knife throwing were not uncommon in silent comedy, but modern movies have become depressingly mired in ordinary lifestyles. In many new romantic comedies, the occupations of the characters don't even matter, because they are only labels; there's a setup scene in an office, and everything else is after hours. Here knife throwing explains not only the man's desperation to meet the woman, but the kind of woman he meets, and the way they eventually feel about each other. Dr. Johnson said that the knowledge that you will be hanged in the morning concentrates the mind wonderfully. There is nothing like being partners in a knife-throwing act to encourage a man and a woman to focus on their relationship.

Gladiator ★ ★
R, 150 m., 2000

Russell Crowe (Maximus), Joaquin Phoenix (Commodus), Connie Nielsen (Lucilla), Oliver Reed (Proximo), Richard Harris (Marcus Aurelius), Derek Jacobi (Gracchus), Djimon Hounsou (Juba), David Schofield (Falco). Directed by Ridley Scott and produced by Douglas Wick, David Franzoni, and Branko Lustig. Screenplay by Franzoni, John Logan, and William Nicholson.

Maximus: *I'm required to kill—so I kill. That's enough.*
    Proximo: *That's enough for the provinces, but not for Rome.*

A foolish choice in art direction casts a pall over Ridley Scott's *Gladiator* that no swordplay can cut through. The film looks muddy, fuzzy, and indistinct. Its colors are mud tones at the drab end of the palate, and it seems to have been filmed on grim and overcast days. This darkness and a lack of detail in the long shots helps obscure shabby special effects (the Coliseum in Rome looks like a set from a computer game), and the characters bring no cheer: They're bitter, vengeful, depressed. By the end of this long film, I would have traded any given gladiatorial victory for just one shot of blue skies. (There are blue skies in the hero's dreams of long-ago happiness, but that proves the point.)

The story line is *Rocky* on downers. The hero, a general from Spain named Maximus (Russell Crowe), is a favorite of emperor Marcus Aurelius (Richard Harris). After Maximus defeats the barbarians, Marcus names him protector of Rome. But he is left for dead by Marcus's son, a bitter rival named Commodus (the name comes from the Latin for "convenient" and not what you're thinking). After escaping and finding that his wife and son have been murdered, Maximus finds his way to the deserts of North Africa, where he is sold as a slave to Proximo (the late Oliver Reed), a manager of gladiators. When Commodus lifts his father's ban on gladiators in Rome, in an attempt to distract the people from hunger and plagues, Maximus slashes his way to the top, and the movie ends, of course, with the Big Fight.

This same story could have been rousing entertainment; I have just revisited the wonderful *Raiders of the Lost Ark,* which is just as dim-witted but twelve times more fun. But *Gladiator* lacks joy. It employs depression as a substitute for personality, and believes that if the characters are bitter and morose enough, we won't notice how dull they are.

Commodus (Joaquin Phoenix) is one of those spoiled, self-indulgent, petulant Roman emperors made famous in the age of great Roman epics, which ended with *Spartacus* (1963). Watching him in his snits, I recalled Peter Ustinov's great Nero, in *Quo Vadis* (1951), collecting his tears for posterity in tiny crystal goblets. Commodus has unusual vices even for a Caesar; he wants to become the lover of his older sister Lucilla (Connie Nielsen), whose son he is raising as his heir.

The ethical backbone of the story is easily mastered. Commodus wants to be a dictator, but is opposed by the Senate, led by such as Gracchus (Derek Jacobi). The senators want him to provide sewers for the city's Greek district, where the plague is raging, but Commodus decides instead on a season of games. Proximo arrives with his seasoned gladiators from Africa, who prove nearly invincible, and threaten the emperor's popularity. The moral lesson: It is good when gladiators slaughter everyone in sight, and then turn over power to the politicians.

The Coliseum productions play like professional wrestling. Events are staged to re-create famous battles, and after the visitors wipe out the home team, a puzzled Commodus tells his aide, "My history's a little hazy—but shouldn't the barbarians *lose* the battle of Carthage?" Later, an announcer literally addresses the crowd in these words: "Caesar is pleased to bring you the only undefeated champion in Roman history—the legendary Tiger!"

The battle sequences are a pale shadow of the lucidly choreographed swordplay in *Rob Roy* (1995); instead of moves we can follow and strategy we can appreciate, Scott goes for muddled close-ups of fearsome but indistinct events. The crowd cheers, although those in the cheaper seats are impossible to see because of the murky special effects.

When Maximus wins his first big fight, it's up to Commodus to decide whether he will live or die. "Live! Live!" the fans chant, and Commodus, bowing to their will, signals with a "thumbs up." This demonstrates that Commodus was not paying attention in Caesar School, since the practice at the Coliseum at that time was to close the thumb in the fist to signal life; an extended thumb meant death. Luckily, no one else in the Coliseum knows this either.

Russell Crowe is efficient as Maximus; bearded, taciturn, brooding. His closest friend among the gladiators is played by Djimon Hounsou, who played the passionate slave in *Amistad.* Since protocol requires him to speak less than Maximus, he mostly looks ferocious, effectively. Connie Nielsen shows the film's most depth as the sister. Phoenix is passable as Commodus, but a quirkier actor could have had more fun in the role. Old pros Harris, Jacobi, and Reed are reliable; Scott does some fancy editing and a little digital work to fill the gaps left when Reed died during the production.

243

Gladiator is being hailed by those with short memories as the equal of *Spartacus* and *Ben Hur*. This is more like *Spartacus Lite*. Or dark. It's only necessary to think back a few months to Julie Taymor's *Titus* for a film set in ancient Rome that's immeasurably better to look at. The visual accomplishment of *Titus* shames *Gladiator*, and its story is a whole heck of a lot better than the *Gladiator* screenplay, even if Shakespeare didn't make Titus the only undefeated champion in Roman history. 　☞

The Gleaners and I ★ ★ ★ ★

NO MPAA RATING, 82 m., 2001

A documentary by Agnes Varda.

In our alley we see men searching through the garbage for treasure. *The Gleaners and I* places them in an ancient tradition. Since 1554, when King Henry IV affirmed the right of gleaning, it has been a practice protected by the French constitution, and today the men and women who sift through the Dumpsters and markets of Paris are the descendants of gleaners who were painted by Millet and van Gogh.

Gleaners traditionally follow the harvest, scavenging what was missed the first time around. In Agnes Varda's meditative new film we see them in potato fields and apple orchards, where the farmers actually welcome them (tons of apples are missed by the first pickers, because the professionals work fast and are not patient in seeking the hidden fruit). Then we meet urban gleaners, including an artist who finds objects he can make into sculpture, and a man who has not paid for his food for more than ten years.

Everybody seems to know this practice is protected by law, but no one seems to know quite what the law says. Varda films jurists standing in the fields with their robes and law books, who say gleaning must take place between sunup and sundown, and she shows oyster-pickers in rubber hip boots, who say they must come no closer than ten, or twenty, or twelve, or fifteen yards of the oyster beds, and cannot take more than eight, or twenty, or ten pounds of oysters—not that anybody is weighing them.

In a provincial city, Varda considers the case of young unemployed people who overturned the Dumpsters of a supermarket after the owner drenched the contents with bleach to discourage them. Perhaps both parties were violating the law; the young people had the right to glean, but not to vandalize. But as she talks to the young layabouts in the town square, we realize they don't have the spirit of the other gleaners, and in their own minds see themselves as getting away with something instead of exercising a right. They have made themselves into criminals, although the French law considers gleaning a useful profession.

The true gleaner, in Varda's eyes, is a little noble, a little idealistic, a little stubborn, and deeply thrifty. We meet a man who gleans for his meals and to find objects he can sell, and follow him back to a suburban homeless shelter where for years he has taught literature classes every night. We look over the shoulders of him and his comrades as they find perfectly fresh tomatoes left after a farmer's market. Varda and her cinematographer find a clock without hands—worthless, until she places it between two stone angels in her house, and it reveals a startling simplicity of form.

Agnes Varda, of course, is a gleaner herself. She is gleaning the gleaners. And in what appears to be a documentary, she conceals a tender meditation about her own life, and life itself. Who is this woman? I have met her, with her bangs cut low over her sparkling eyes in a round and merry face, and once had lunch in the house she shared with her late husband, the director Jacques Demy (*The Umbrellas of Cherbourg*). The house itself was in the spirit of gleaning: not a luxury flat for two famous filmmakers, but a former garage, with the bays and rooms around a central courtyard parceled out, one as a kitchen, one as Jacques's office, one a room for their son, Mathieu, one Agnes's workroom, etc.

Varda is seventy-two and made her first film when she was twenty-six. She was the only woman director involved in the French New Wave, and has remained truer to its spirit than many of the others. Her features include such masterpieces as *One Sings, the Other Doesn't, Vagabond,* and *Kung Fu Master* (which is not about kung fu but about love). Along the way she has made many documentaries, including *Uncle Yanco* (1968), about her uncle who lived on a houseboat in California and was a gleaner of sorts, and *Daguerreotypes* (1975), about the other people who live on her street. Her *A Hundred and One Nights* (1995) gleaned her favorite moments from a century of cinema.

In *The Gleaners and I*, she has a new tool—a modern digital camera. We sense her delight. She can hold it in her hand and take it anywhere. She is liberated from cumbersome equipment. "To film with one hand my other hand," she says, as she does so with delight. She shows how the new cameras make a personal essay possible for a filmmaker—how she can walk out into the world and, without the risk of a huge budget, simply start picking up images as a gleaner finds apples and potatoes.

"My hair and my hands keep telling me that the end is near," she confides at one point, speaking confidentially to us as the narrator. She told her friend Howie Movshovitz, the critic from Boulder, Colorado, how she had to film and narrate some scenes while she was entirely alone, because they were so personal. In 1993, she directed *Jacquot de Nantes*, the story of her late husband, and now this is her story of herself, a woman whose life has consisted of moving through the world with the tools of her trade, finding what is worth treasuring.

Go ★ ★ ★
R, 100 m., 1999

Katie Holmes (Claire Montgomery), Sarah Polley (Ronna Martin), William Fichtner (Burke), Desmond Askew (Simon Baines), Taye Diggs (Marcus), Scott Wolf (Adam), Jay Mohr (Zack), Timothy Olyphant (Todd Gaines), Jane Krakowski (Irene). Directed by Doug Liman and produced by Paul Rosenberg, Mickey Liddell, and Matt Freeman. Screenplay by John August.

Sooner or later the statute of limitations has to run out on comparisons between new movies and *Pulp Fiction*. Quentin Tarantino's 1994 film mesmerized the Sundance generation, who have been doing riffs ever since on its interlocking time lines, its quirky sex and violence, its pop culture expertise, its familiarity with drugs, its squirmy comedy, its black-white friendships, its ironic profundity, and its revelations in all-night diners. Those who haven't seen it must wonder why it's cited in so

many movie reviews; has no other movie been made in the interim?

Well, no, not one that staked out the territory so firmly. Consider, for example, Doug Liman's *Go*. This is an entertaining, clever black comedy that takes place entirely in Tarantino-land. Liman is a talented director who works as his own cinematographer and finds a nice off-center humor. His *Swingers* (1996) was an accomplished debut film, and here, with a screenplay by John August, he does more, and better, and yet the shadow of QT falls on many scenes.

When his characters deliberately create a flesh wound with a gunshot, for example, the setup and payoff reminds us of the needle plunging into the heart in *Pulp Fiction* (and of the deliberate blade wound in *Gridlock'd*). And when two of his characters sit in a diner and have a conversation about the comic strip *Family Circus*, we think of Uma Thurman and John Travolta sharing pop lore over their milk shakes in *PF*. We're also reminded of *Pulp* in scenes involving a laconic drug dealer, a crisis involving body disposal, an unintended drug overdose, the way its story lines branch off and then join up again, and even in an unusual character name, Zack.

Tarantino has created a generation of footnoters and cross-referencers. I'm not saying *Go* couldn't have been made without the example of *Pulp Fiction*, but it can't be seen without thinking of it. What it adds is a grittier feel; Liman's characters are closer to ground level.

The story begins in a supermarket, where Ronna the checkout girl (Sarah Polley) takes a shift for her friend Simon (Desmond Askew), a part-time drug dealer who wants to go to Vegas. She needs rent money. When two customers named Adam and Zack (Scott Wolf and Jay Mohr) want to score some ecstasy, she goes to Simon's usual dealer (Timothy Olyphant) to get twenty hits. Olyphant, lounging bare-chested in his apartment hideaway, stroking his girlfriend and his cat, working the phone, supplies the legal expertise such stories always require: "Twenty hits! The magic number where intent to sell becomes trafficking."

Without revealing too much of the plot, which depends on surprises and connections, I can say that the other main stories involve

(1) Simon's adventures in Las Vegas, where he and his black friend Marcus (Taye Diggs) get into big trouble with the owners of a topless bar, and (2) the relationship between Adam, Zack, and a cop named Burke (William Fichtner), who invites the two men over to Christmas dinner with his wife (Jane Krakowski). This couple is extremely open to sexual adventures with strangers, but turns out to have another even stronger obsession; there is nothing like a pyramid scheme to bring out fanaticism.

Trouble in Vegas leads to more trouble in Los Angeles, where the stories of the checkout clerk and the two young men also meet again, unexpectedly. The plot, of course, is a complete contrivance, but Liman and August have a lot of fun with the details, including a "Macarena" dance in an unlikely setting, a telepathic cat, and a scene with echoes of *Blood Simple,* in which some characters try to leave a hotel room while others are trying to break in.

Go has energy and wit, and the performances are right for the material—especially Sarah Polley, who thinks fast and survives harrowing experiences, and Fichtner, the cop who is so remarkably open to new experiences. The movie is ruthless in its attitude toward the apparently dead or dying, but then grisly indifference is central to the self-centered values without which these characters would have no values at all. Liman shows here, as he did in *Swingers,* that he has a good eye and can create screwy characters. Can he break out of QT-land?

God Said, 'Ha!' ★ ★ ★ ½
PG-13, 85 m., 1999

Directed and performed by Julia Sweeney and produced by Rana Joy Glickman. Screenplay by Sweeney, based on the stage play directed by Greg Kachel.

There is a kind of luminous quality in the way Julia Sweeney talks about her life and family in *God Said, 'Ha!'* She wanders the stage for an hour and a half, talking about a year in her life when her brother, Mike, was dying of cancer. This is a sad subject, painful to her, and yet she makes humor of it. She is a comedian, and, like the hero of *Life Is Beautiful,* she deals with life with the gifts at her command.

What she weaves out of her memories is a funny love poem to Mike and her parents—who all moved into her small house for the duration of the crisis. She sees their human weaknesses, she smiles at their goofy logic, she lets their habits get on her nerves, but above all she embraces them. And when, midway through the year, even more bad news descends upon her, she is able to transform that, too, into truth and fond humor.

Sweeney may be familiar to you as a former cast member of *Saturday Night Live.* Her androgynous character "Pat" was a regular on the show, and later appeared in a movie. She began in show business as an accountant, keeping the books for *Rainman,* and edged into performance through local comedy clubs. After the *SNL* gig was over, she moved to Los Angeles, looking for work in movies and sitcoms, and bought her own house. Soon she was sharing it with her parents and Mike, and "the lines started to cross about whose house it really was."

Mike had lymphoma. He got worse and then he got better and then he got even worse, and then he got a little bit better—she charts the progress of an implacable foe. But there is laughter, too, especially from Mike, who found wry material in the doctor's decision to administer chemotherapy by inserting a permanent "shunt" into his body: Should it be called a faucet? A spigot? Where should it go? The possibilities were endless.

Sweeney's parents come across as nice people who, in their well-meaning attempts to stay out of the way, are usually in the way. When a light goes out in the bathroom, her mother reports, "I found a bulb—but I didn't know if there was some special way to screw it in."

During Mike's illness, Sweeney began talking about what she was going through as part of her act. "It must be hard," Mike joked, "you being an actress, and me in the cancer spotlight." It was hard for Mike, too—who now spent much of his time in a bed in her living room, and who as a child so valued his privacy that he installed a doorbell on his bedroom door.

Sweeney and other family members would take him to the UCLA Medical Center several times a week for chemotherapy, and as they met patients with many kinds of cancer, they began to muse on why cancer only seemed to strike vital organs. "Why can't there be cancer of the fat?" she wondered, only to find out that there was—and that you don't want it, either.

Watching *God Said, 'Ha!'*, I wished that I could show it to people who wondered why I didn't approve of *Patch Adams*. This film has a dignity, an underlying taste, in the way it deals with subjects like cancer and dying. It doesn't simply use the subjects as an occasion for manipulative sentiment. At the end of the film, we feel we've been through a lot with Julia and Mike Sweeney and their family. We're sad, but we're smiling. I was thinking: Life's like that.

The Golden Bowl ★ ★ ★
R, 130 m., 2001

Nick Nolte (Adam Verver), Kate Beckinsale (Maggie Verver), Uma Thurman (Charlotte Stant), Jeremy Northam (Prince Amerigo), Anjelica Huston (Fanny Assingham), James Fox (Bob Assingham). Directed by James Ivory and produced by Ismail Merchant. Screenplay by Ruth Prawer Jhabvala, based on the novel by Henry James.

There are four good people in *The Golden Bowl* and four bad people, making, in all, four characters. The genius of Henry James's greatest novel is that these four people have placed themselves in a moral situation that alters as you rotate them in your view. If you come to the movie without reading the book, you may find yourself adrift; it's not easy to know who to like when everyone is a sinner, and all have their reasons.

The story involves two marriages, with the same dreadful secret hidden at the heart of both of them. Adam Verver (Nick Nolte), an American billionaire, has been traveling in Europe with his daughter, Maggie (Kate Beckinsale), buying things. Having grown rich on the backs of his workers (he frets about their long hours), he now vows to brighten their lives by filling a museum with his treasures, which they can admire while he no doubt feels virtuous. Having purchased innumerable statues, houses, and paintings, he finds it time to buy Maggie

a husband. Prince Amerigo (Jeremy Northam) seems a good investment: He is handsome and refined, and his old Italian family occupies the Pallazzo Ugolini in Florence. The prince needs Verver's money, and will provide a title for his grandson; Maggie is swayed by his charm.

There is a complication, which is revealed in the very first scene of the movie. The prince was long involved in an affair with Charlotte Stant (Uma Thurman), Maggie's best friend. Since the story takes place in 1902, when such affairs could ruin reputations, it has been a secret—even from Maggie. The prince is prepared to marry Maggie for her father's money, and also because she is lithe and fragrant. But where does that leave poor Charlotte?

In her drawing room in London, Fanny Assingham (Anjelica Huston) thinks she knows the answer. She's one of those middle-aged American exiles, much beloved by James, who lurks at the center of a web of social connections, waiting for twitches. She boldly suggests that the widower billionaire Verver is the perfect match for Charlotte. That will mean that the father and daughter will be married to former lovers, a fact known to Mrs. Assingham, who can live with it.

Now, does that make Charlotte and the prince dishonest? Yes, they share a secret. But both the prince and Charlotte must, because they are poor, marry money. They are marrying people who want them. Perhaps they are making a sacrifice—especially if they behave themselves, which they are determined to do. Or are Maggie and her father dishonest, since she is marrying to please her father and he is marrying her best friend to please his daughter? No one at the altar is blameless. But no one is marrying for love, except Maggie, whose definition of love is too specialized to be entirely idealistic.

Soon the two couples settle into a routine that satisfies Maggie and Mr. Verver, who dote on each other and spend all of their time together, to the dissatisfaction of their mates. Charlotte complains that her husband and his daughter are always together. "What becomes of me when they're so happy?" she asks the prince. "And what becomes of you?" Soon enough the two former lovers find themselves at a house party in the country without their spouses, and one thing apparently leads to another (it is difficult to be sure with James, since no novelist ever used the word "intercourse" more frequently without quite making it clear what he meant by it).

It is not sexual infidelity that causes trouble, however, but the slight shade of suspicion—and then a darker shade, when a golden bowl in an antique shop provides Maggie with absolute proof that the prince and Charlotte knew each other before they had, presumably, met. Now comes the diabolical unfolding of James's plan, since at no time do the four people ever openly discuss what each one of them privately knows. Instead, wheels of unspoken priorities grind mercilessly, and Charlotte, in my opinion, becomes the character we have most reason to pity.

The Golden Bowl would seem to be an ideal project for director James Ivory, producer Ismail Merchant, and screenwriter Ruth Prawer Jhabvala; they specialize in literary adaptations, and previously collaborated on James's *The Europeans* and *The Bostonians*. But here they've taken on the most difficult of James's novels—a story told largely through what remains unsaid. James has not made it easy for the modern moviegoer who expects good and evil to be clearly labeled and lead to a happy ending. His villain is a system based on wealth and class, which forces the poor to deal on the terms of the rich and then sometimes spits them out anyway—or, in Charlotte's case, buries her alive. That James spent his career chronicling people like these characters does not mean he loved them, and in a novel like *The Ambassadors* you can hear him cheering as a female version of Verver is frustrated in her desire to control her son.

I admired this movie. It kept me at arm's length, but that is where I am supposed to be; the characters are, after all, at arm's length from one another, and the tragedy of the story is implied but never spoken aloud. It will help, I think, to be familiar with the novel, or to make a leap of sympathy with the characters; they aren't dancing through a clockwork plot, but living their lives according to rules which, once they accept them, cannot ever be broken.

Gone in 60 Seconds ★ ★
PG-13, 119 m., 2000

Nicolas Cage (Memphis Raines), Delroy Lindo (Detective), Giovanni Ribisi (Kip Raines), Robert Duvall (Otto Halliwell), Angelina Jolie ("Sway" Wayland), Christopher Eccleston (Raymond Calitri), T. J. Cross (Mirror Man), William Lee Scott (Toby), Scott Caan (Tumbler), James Duval (Freb), Will Patton (Atley Jackson). Directed by Dominic Sena and produced by Jerry Bruckheimer and Mike Stenson. Screenplay by Scott Rosenberg.

Gone in 60 Seconds is like a practice game between the varsity and the reserves. Everybody plays pretty well, but they're saving up for Saturday. First team is Nicolas Cage, Delroy Lindo, and Robert Duvall. Second team is Giovanni Ribisi, Will Patton, and Angelina Jolie, who gets second billing but not much playing time. There are lots of subs who come off the bench for a play or two. This is the kind of movie that ends up playing on the TV set over the bar in a better movie.

Nicolas Cage plays Memphis Raines, who used to be the greatest car thief in Los Angeles ("I didn't do it for the money. I did it for the cars"). Now he has retired to the desert to run a gas station and go-cart track. He retired because his mom asked him to. She was afraid his younger brother Kip (Ribisi) would become a thief too. Kip became a thief anyway. Kip steals a car, recklessly leads the cops to a chop shop, and angers a vile crime lord named Raymond (Christopher Eccleston), who, according to a line Robert Duvall successfully says out loud without laughing, is "a jackal tearing at the soft belly of our fair city."

Memphis learns about Kip's screwup from one of his old crew members. He visits Raymond to try to set things right, but Raymond has Kip handcuffed inside a car and threatens to crush him and sell him as scrap metal. Memphis can save him by stealing fifty hard-to-find cars. Memphis recruits an old pal (Duvall); together they assemble a very large team in a very long and boring sequence that produces so many car thieves we can't keep them all straight. It looks like they sent out contracts to a lot of actors and were surprised when they all said yes.

The pros try to steal the fifty cars. Delroy Lindo, as the cop, knows who they are and what they plan to do, but wants to catch them at it. He intuits that the key theft will be of a 1967 Shelby GT 350 Mustang, a car Memphis both loves and fears. "He'll save that for the last," says Lindo, planning to nab him in the act. This decision means that forty-nine cars will *already* have been stolen before Memphis moves on the Mustang. I am reminded of the line from *Fargo* when Marge tells her deputy, "I'm not sure I agree with you a hundred percent on your police work there, Lou."

There isn't much time for character development. Cage walks on-screen with his character already established from *The Rock* and *Con Air*. Duvall is . . . Duvall. Angelina Jolie's rare appearances are reminders she is still in the picture. After the confusions of the recruitment scenes and the puzzlement about who all these guys are, it's a relief when the movie goes on autopilot with a fabulous chase sequence and an obligatory final confrontation inside a flame and steam factory.

We have discussed flame and steam factories before. They are cavernous industrial locations with flame and steam in the background and no people around. The moment I saw the first shower of sparks, I predicted that Memphis and Raymond would eventually be climbing around on high catwalks while shooting at one another, that Memphis would inevitably cling to a catwalk by his fingers, and that Raymond would fall to his death. See how well your own predictions turn out.

The chase sequence is fine. Memphis hurtles the Mustang down city streets and alleys and hits 160 mph in a drainage ditch, outsmarting a police helicopter by taking the tunnel under the airport while the copter is waved away from commercial airspace. There is a stunt jump that would have made Evel Knievel famous, and dead. All of this is done in weirdly underlit, saturated dark colors; the movie desperately yearns to be in sepiatone, and some of its skies are so dark you're looking for the twister.

Movies like this are what they are. *Gone in 60 Seconds* is a prodigious use of money and human effort to make a movie of no significance whatever, in which the talents of the artists are subordinated to the requirements of the craftsmen. Witnessing it, you get some thrills, some chuckles, a few good one-liners, and after 119 minutes are regurgitated by the theater not much the worse for wear.

Goodbye, Lover ★
R, 102 m., 1999

Patricia Arquette (Sandra), Dermot Mulroney (Jake), Don Johnson (Ben), Mary-Louise Parker (Peggy), Ellen DeGeneres (Detective Rita Pompano), Ray McKinnon (Detective Rollins). Directed by Roland Joffe and produced by Arnon Milchan. Screenplay by Ron Peer, Joel Cohen, and Alec Sokolow.

I've just transcribed no less than eleven pages of notes I scribbled during *Goodbye, Lover,* and my mind boggles. The plot is so labyrinthine that I'd completely forgotten the serial killer named The Doctor, who murders young women by injecting curare into their veins with a syringe. When a character like The Doctor is an insignificant supporting character, a movie's plate is a little too full, don't you think?

Goodbye, Lover is not so much a story as some kind of a board game, with too many pieces and not enough rules. The characters careen through the requirements of the plot, which has so many double-reverses that the real danger isn't murder, it's being disemboweled by G-forces. There's no way to care about the characters, because their fates are arbitrary—determined not by character, not by personality, but by the jigsaw puzzle constructed by the screenwriters (there are three of them—which, for this material, represents a skeleton crew).

And yet the film does have a certain audacity. It contains a character played by Patricia Arquette who is the most enthusiastic sexual being since Emmanuelle, and another, played by Don Johnson, who just plain gets tuckered out by her demands. (At one point, they've taken the collection in church and are walking down the aisle with the offering, and she's whispering that he should meet her for sex tomorrow, or else.) There's also a droll supporting role for Ellen DeGeneres, as a police detective who keeps picking on her partner, a Mormon man who doesn't, I hope, understand most of her jokes. One of her key clues comes with the discovery of a *Sound of Music* tape, which arouses her suspicions: "I don't trust anybody over the age of ten who listens to 'The Sound of Music.'"

The movie opens with phone sex and never looks back. We meet Sandra (Arquette), a Realtor who memorizes Tony Robbins self-help tapes, treasures *The Sound of Music* as her favorite movie, and likes to whisper, "I'm not wearing any underwear." She is having an affair with Ben (Johnson), and at one point handcuffs him with some sex toys she finds in a house she's selling. When the clients return unexpectedly, poor Ben barely has time to release himself and hide the cuffs in his pants pocket. (The Foley artists, concerned that we may have missed the point, cause the cuffs to rattle deafeningly, as if Ben had a tambourine concealed in his underwear.)

Sandra is married to Jake (Dermot Mulroney), who is Ben's brother. Ben is the straight arrow who runs an ad agency, and Jake is the unkempt alcoholic who nevertheless is a brilliant copywriter. Why is Sandra cheating on Jake? The answer is not only more complicated than you might think—it's not even the real answer. This is one of those plots where you might want to take a night school class about double-indemnity clauses in insurance policies before you even think about buying a ticket.

My space is limited, but I must also mention the GOP senator who is caught with a transvestite hustler; the struggle on the condo balcony; the motorcycle-car chase; the sex scene in a church's organ loft; the black leather mask; the Vegas wedding chapel ploy; Mike, the professional killer (not to be confused with The Doctor); and Peggy, Ben's secretary, who is played by Mary-Louise Parker as the kind of woman who would be a nymphomaniac in any other movie, but compared to Sandra is relatively abstentious.

There is a part of me that knows this movie is very, very bad. And another part of me that takes a guilty pleasure in it. Too bad I saw it at a critic's screening, where professional courtesy requires a certain decorum. This is the kind of movie that might be materially improved by frequent hoots of derision. All bad movies have good twins, and the good version

of *Goodbye, Lover* is *The Hot Spot* (1990), which also starred Don Johnson, along with Virginia Madsen and Jennifer Connelly, in a thriller that was equally lurid but less hyperkinetic. *Goodbye, Lover* is so overwrought it reminds me of the limerick about that couple from Khartoum, who argued all night, about who had the right, to do what, and with which, and to whom.

Gossip ★ ★
R, 90 m., 2000

James Marsden (Derrick), Lena Headey (Jones), Norman Reedus (Travis), Kate Hudson (Naomi Preston), Joshua Jackson (Beau Edson), Marisa Coughlan (Sheila), Edward James Olmos (Detective Curtis), Sharon Lawrence (Detective Kelly), Eric Bogosian (Professor Goodwin). Directed by Davis Guggenheim and produced by Jeffrey Silver and Bobby Newmyer. Screenplay by Gregory Poirier and Theresa Rebeck.

Gossip stays in the game until the bottom of the ninth, and then blows it. The trick ending is a kick in the teeth. The movie tells a story worth telling, and then cops out with an ironic gimmick that's like a sneer at the craft of storytelling. *Usual Suspects* had the grace to earn its surprise ending, but *Gossip* pulls a 180 just for the hell of it. Chop off the last two or three minutes, fade to black, and you have a decent film.

The premise is promising. We meet three college roommates who decide to start a rumor just to see how far it will go. They spread the news that a couple had sex in an upstairs bedroom at an off-campus party. Problem is, the rich girl in the bedroom was drunk and passed out. She hears the gossip, assumes it's true, and brings rape charges against her date. And then it gets a lot more complicated than that, until simply telling the truth won't mend things anymore.

The story takes place on the kind of campus that would be designed by the ad agency for Bennetton. The roommates are Jones (Lena Headey), independent and smart, who seems to cast herself in a real-time version of *Murder, She Wrote*, Derrick (James Marsden), a ladies' man with easy charm and something wrong inside, and Travis (Norman Reedus), who creates strange art out of graphics and photographs, and has trouble expressing himself. The roomies share a luxurious loft, where they spend more time drinking than Nick and Nora Charles in the *Thin Man* movies. My guess is that less booze and at least some drugs would be involved with characters like these, but it's glug, glug, glug, scene after scene.

The film is heavy on style, and knows what it's doing. Cinematographer Andrzej Bartkowiak *(Speed, Species)* deepens the colors and photographs the actors like models, which works because great though he makes them look, they can still act. Jones is the catalyst. She agrees to spread the rumor, and then develops a conscience when the gossip goes wrong. She also gets to perform the obligatory high school yearbook scene, in which secrets from the past are obligingly revealed.

As the seriousness of the situation escalates, the student charged with rape (Joshua Jackson) is led away in handcuffs, and his date (Kate Hudson) hits the bottle as if she were Dorothy Malone in a 1950s weeper. Edward James Olmos knocks on the door and introduces himself as the detective on the case, and he's good at his role, brushing aside Derrick's alibis and self-assurance as if shooing a fly. Eric Bogosian has a juicy role as one of those showboat professors who conducts lectures like a talk show and is filled with a deep appreciation of himself.

And then the movie self-destructs. The material was here, in Gregory Poirier and Theresa Rebeck's screenplay, for a movie that had something interesting to say about date rape and gossip. But it all derails in a self-indulgent exercise, as director Davis Guggenheim ducks responsibility to the story and gives us a cop-out instead. I really got into this film. If I hadn't, maybe the ending wouldn't have annoyed me so much.

Goya in Bordeaux ★ ★
R, 98 m., 2000

Francisco Rabal (Goya), Jose Coronado (Goya as a Young Man), Dafne Fernandez (Rosario), Maribel Verdu (Duchess of Alba), Eulalia Ramon (Leocadia), Joaquin Climent (Moratin), Cristina Espinosa (Pepita Tudo), Jose Maria Pou (Godoy). Directed by Carlos Saura and produced by Andres Vincent Gomez. Screenplay by Saura.

Lushly photographed and grandly conceived, Carlos Saura's *Goya in Bordeaux* never comes alive. It is an homage to the great Spanish painter, but we must come to the film already fascinated by Francisco Goya; if we do not, the film will not convince us. It is too much a study and an exercise, not enough a living thing.

The film opens with an extraordinary image: a cow's carcass, dragging itself to a scaffold and then hoisted up so that we can regard animal flesh and meditate that thus are we all. Then the details of muscle and fat begin to run like paint, until they reveal the ruined face of an old man. This is Goya on his deathbed.

The old man rises up, confused. Where is he? Who brought him here? He wanders from his bed, and a shift in the lighting reveals the walls of his room as a scrim. We can see him through the walls, and then find him wandering bewildered in the street, until he is found and taken home by his daughter, Rosario. For the rest of the film he will relate his memories to Rosario, and we will see many of them in flashback, as well as his nightmares and fantasies.

The cinematographer is Vittorio Storaro, who has worked with Saura frequently. *Tango* (1999) is a recent collaboration, the story of a man trying to make a film in Argentina, caught in a labyrinth of love, politics, and music. *Goya in Bordeaux* is as good-looking but not as fruitful.

Goya has fled to France, we gather, because of troubles at home, linked to the fate of the woman of his dreams, Cayetano, Duchess of Alba (Maribel Verdu). She unwisely opposed Queen Maria Luisa and paid with her life; now Goya, in exile, likes the scenery and the wine but misses his villa in Madrid.

As Rosario sits by his side, her attention sometimes drifting (as ours does), Goya recalls his earlier years, his experiments with paint and lighting, the illness that made him deaf. Played as an old man by Francisco Rabal and in middle age by Jose Coronado, he finds it difficult to draw a line between his work and his life. Cayetano emerges from a painting to cast a shadow over him, one that eventually will mark his life's end. Other death's-head specters also emerge from his canvases, or his memories of them, to haunt his dreams.

There are better films about how a painter works (Rivette's *La Belle Noiseuse* from 1991 is incomparable), and better films about old men remembering their lives. Goya, younger and older, shuffles through morose regrets and rueful memories. He does not seem to have created his paintings so much as become their innocent victim. This is not a stand-alone film so much as a visual aid to the study of Goya; I could imagine an old 16mm projector clacking away in the back of art appreciation class.

Grass ★ ★
R, 80 m., 2000

A documentary directed and produced by Ron Mann. Narrated by Woody Harrelson. Screenplay by Solomon Vesta.

It is agreed by reasonable people that one of the results of antidrug laws is to support the price of drugs and make their sale lucrative. If drugs were legalized, the price would fall, and the motive to promote them would fade away. Since anyone who wants drugs can already get them, usage would be unlikely to increase. Crime would go down when addicts didn't have to steal to support their habits, and law enforcement would benefit from the disappearance of drug-financed bribery, payoffs, and corruption.

All of this is so obvious that the opposition to the legalization of drugs seems inexplicable—unless you ask who would be hurt the most by the repeal of drug laws. The international drug cartels would be put out of business. Drug enforcement agencies would be unnecessary. Drug wholesalers and retailers would have to seek other employment. If it is true (as often charged) that the CIA has raised money by dealing in drugs, it would lose this source of funds free from congressional accounting. Who would *benefit* if drugs were legalized? The public—because both drug usage and its associated crimes would diminish.

Despite the logic of this argument, few political candidates have had the nerve to question the way that our drug laws act as a price support system, and encourage drug usage. *Grass*, a new documentary by Ron Mann, traces

the history of the laws against one drug—marijuana—back to their origins in anti-Mexican prejudice at the turn of the century, and forward through periods when marijuana was seen as part of the Red conspiracy. When New York Mayor Fiorello LaGuardia commissioned a study of the weed, his commission found the "sociological, psychological, and medical" threat of the substance was "exaggerated." He called for its decriminalization. So, many years later, did President Jimmy Carter—until he had to lay low after an aide was nabbed on cocaine charges.

Other presidents, of course, have enthusiastically supported antidrug laws (Nixon going so far as to swear in Elvis Presley in the war against narcotics). *Grass* traces much of our national drug policy to one man, Harry J. Anslinger, the first drug czar, who like J. Edgar Hoover, created a fiefdom that was immune to congressional criticism.

Grass is not much as a documentary. It's a cut-and-paste job, assembling clips from old and new antidrug films, and alternating them with prodrug footage from the Beats, the flower power era, and so on. The narration by prohemp campaigner Woody Harrelson is underlined by the kind of lurid graphics usually seen on 1940s coming attractions trailers.

The film is unlikely to tell many of its viewers anything they don't already know, and unlikely to change our national drug policy. The situation will continue indefinitely, corrupting politicians and whole nations with billions of dollars of illegal profits. Those who use drugs will continue to do so. Others will abstain, die, or find a way to stop, just as they do now. Prohibition proved that when the government tries to come between the people and what the people want to do, laws are not effective; statistically, Prohibition coincided with a considerable increase in drinking.

Am I in favor of drugs? Not at all. Drug abuse has led to an epidemic of human suffering. Grass seems relatively harmless, but I have not known anyone who used hard drugs and emerged undamaged. Still, in most societies throughout human history, drug use has been treated realistically—as a health problem, not a moral problem. Have our drug laws prevented anyone from using drugs? Apparently not. Have they given us the world's largest prison population, cost us billions of dollars, and helped create the most violent society in the First World? Yes. From an objective point of view—what's the point?

The Green Mile ★ ★ ★ ½
R, 182 m., 1999

Tom Hanks (Paul Edgecomb), David Morse (Brutus "Brutal" Howell), Michael Clarke Duncan (John Coffey), Doug Hutchison (Percy Wetmore), Michael Jeter (Eduard Delacroix), Sam Rockwell (William Wharton), Bonnie Hunt (Jan Edgecomb), James Cromwell (Warden Hal Moores), Graham Greene (Arlen Bitterbuck), Patricia Clarkson (Melinda Moores). Directed by Frank Darabont and produced by David Valdes and Darabont. Screenplay by Darabont, based on the novel by Stephen King.

"We think of this place like an intensive care ward of a hospital." So says Paul Edgecomb, who is in charge of death row in a Louisiana penitentiary during the Depression. Paul (Tom Hanks) is a nice man, probably nicer than your average Louisiana death row guard, and his staff is competent and humane—all except for the loathsome Percy, whose aunt is married to the governor, and who could have any state job he wants, but likes it here because "he wants to see one cook up close."

One day a new prisoner arrives. He is a gigantic black man, framed by the low-angle camera to loom over the guards and duck under doorways. This is John Coffey ("like the drink, only not spelled the same"), and he has been convicted of molesting and killing two little white girls. From the start it is clear he is not what he seems. He is afraid of the dark, for one thing. He is straightforward in shaking Paul's hand—not like a man with anything to be ashamed of.

This is not a good summer for Paul. He is suffering from a painful infection, and suffering, too, because Percy (Doug Hutchison) is like an infection in the ward: "The man is mean, careless, and stupid—that's a bad combination in a place like this." Paul sees his duty as regulating a calm and decent atmosphere in which men prepare to die.

The Green Mile (so called because this death row has a green floor) is based on a novel by Stephen King, and has been written and directed by Frank Darabont. It is Darabont's first film since the great *Shawshank Redemption* in 1994. That, too, was based on a King prison story, but this one is very different. It involves the supernatural, for one thing—in a spiritual, not creepy, way.

Both movies center on relationships between a white man and a black man. In *Shawshank* the black man was the witness to a white man's dogged determination, and here the black man's function is to absorb the pain of whites—to redeem and forgive them. By the end, when he is asked to forgive them for sending him to the electric chair, the story has so well prepared us that the key scenes play like drama, not metaphor, and that is not an easy thing to achieve.

The movie is told in flashback as the memories of Paul as an old man, now in a retirement home. "The math doesn't quite work out," he admits at one point, and we find out why. The story is in no haste to get to the sensational and supernatural; it takes at least an hour simply to create the relationships in the prison, where Paul's lieutenant (David Morse) is rock-solid and dependable, where the warden (James Cromwell) is good and fair; and where the prisoners include a balmy coot named Delacroix (Michael Jeter) and a taunting monster named Wharton (Sam Rockwell).

Looming over all is the presence of John Coffey (Michael Clarke Duncan), a man whose own lawyer says he seems to have "dropped out of the sky." Coffey cannot read or write, seems simpleminded, causes no trouble, and exudes goodness. The reason Paul consults the lawyer is because he comes to doubt this prisoner could have killed the little girls. Yet Coffey was found with their broken bodies in his huge arms. And in Louisiana in the 1930s a black man with such evidence against him is not likely to be acquitted by a jury. (We might indeed question whether a Louisiana death row in the 1930s would be so fair and hospitable to a convicted child molester, but the story carries its own conviction, and we go along with it.)

There are several sequences of powerful emotion in the film. Some of them involve the grisly details of the death chamber, and the process by which the state makes sure that a condemned man will actually die (Harry Dean

253

Stanton has an amusing scene as a stand-in at a dress rehearsal with the electric chair). One execution is particularly gruesome, and seen in some detail; the R rating is earned here despite the film's generally benevolent tone. Other moments of great impact involve a tame mouse that Delacroix adopts, a violent struggle with Wharton (and his obscene attempts at rabble-rousing), and subplots involving the wives of Paul (Bonnie Hunt) and the warden (Patricia Clarkson).

But the center of the movie is the relationship between Paul and his huge prisoner, Coffey. Without describing the supernatural mechanism that is involved, I can explain in Coffey's own words what he does with the suffering he encounters: "I just took it back, is all." How he does that, and what the results are, all set up the film's ending—in which we are reminded of another execution some 2,000 years ago.

I have started to suspect that when we talk about "good acting" in the movies, we are really discussing two other things: good casting, and the creation of characters we react to strongly. Much of a performance is created in the filmmaking itself, in photography and editing and the emotional cues of music. But an actor must have the technical and emotional mastery to embody a character and evoke him persuasively, and the film must give him a character worth portraying. Tom Hanks is our movie everyman, and his Paul is able to win our sympathy with his level eyes and calm, decent voice. We get a real sense of his efficient staff, of the vile natures of Percy and Wharton, and of the goodness of Coffey—who is embodied by Duncan in a performance that is both acting and being.

The movie is a shade over three hours long. I appreciated the extra time, which allows us to feel the passage of prison months and years. Stephen King, sometimes dismissed as merely a best-seller, has in his best novels some of the power of Dickens, who created worlds that enveloped us, and populated them with colorful, peculiar, sharply seen characters. King in his strongest work is a storyteller likely to survive as Dickens has, despite the sniffs of the litcrit establishment.

By taking the extra time, Darabont has made King's *The Green Mile* into a story that develops and unfolds, that has detail and space. The movie would have been much diminished at two hours—it would have been a series of episodes without context. As Darabont directs it, it tells a story with beginning, middle, end, vivid characters, humor, outrage, and emotional release. Dickensian.

Groove ★ ★
R, 86 m., 2000

Lola Glaudini (Leyla), Hamish Linklater (David), Denny Kirkwood (Colin), MacKenzie Firgens (Harmony), Vince Riverside (Anthony), Rachel True (Beth), Steve Van Wormer (Ernie), Nick Offerman (Sergeant), Ari Gold (Cliff). Directed by Greg Harrison and produced by Danielle Renfrew. Screenplay by Harrison.

Groove provides a cleaned-up, innocuous version of the rave scene, showing it as a life-affirming voyage of discovery instead of what it often is, a stop-and-shop ticket to troubles with Ecstasy. Like drug movies from the 1960s, it's naive, believing that the problems of the straight life can be solved by dropping out and tuning in. It somehow manages not to have any of its characters actually say, "After that night, nothing was ever the same again," but I have a feeling they're thinking it.

The movie opens with a raid on an abandoned warehouse by the rave-master Ernie (Steve Van Wormer), who is seeking a venue for his next rave. Ernie sees himself as a sort of public servant; he charges only $2 a head because he *believes* in raves. When he is asked, toward dawn, why he risks arrest on all sorts of charges, he explains he does it for "the nod." The nod? Yes, the nod he gets at least once every party from someone who tells him, "Thanks, man. I feel like I really needed this."

If that's a tad simpleminded as a rationale for the zealous promotion of a drug-soaked venue, consider one of the film's self-proclaimed amateur narcotics experts, who offers advice like, "Never take drugs on an empty stomach." These characters are living in a neverland of idealism and bliss, and I look forward to other rave movies to document what must be the underside of their dream.

The movie's characters are barely sketched. We meet an experienced raver named Colin

(Denny Kirkwood), who convinces his straight-arrow brother David (Hamish Linklater) to attend a rave against his own better judgment. David meets a woman named Leyla (Lola Glaudini) at the party and gets past her somewhat forbidding exterior to discover he likes her. She gives him Ecstasy and advises him to "drink a lot of water," although I am not sure if the water intake is associated with the drug use, or is simply her ingrained mantra (she seems like one of those women who never goes anywhere without two liters of Evian, and lectures you on the ominous threat of dehydration). By dawn David and Leyla have arrived at an understanding that, I hope for their sake, will allow them to move in together and quit the rave singles scene.

What is a rave, anyway, but an all-night party where you get high and dance? And what is very new about that? What sets raves apart from disco parties, be-ins, beer blasts, and all the earlier manifestations of the same thing is that they've become professionalized; word is spread on the Internet, and with his $2 admissions Ernie has somehow been able to afford a series of famous DJs, who trundle their turntables and vinyl on and off the scene without ever inspiring the curiosity of the filmmaker, Greg Harrison. We see a lot of them, but learn little about them—but then the film itself is very thin, with dance and music sequences stretched out to cover the lack of dramatic substance.

I liked the music. I would rather have the movie's sound track than see it again—or at all. I know that every generation goes through its rites of passage, and having partied until the dawn more than a time or two myself, I am in sympathy. But the filmmaker has a different responsibility than his subjects. While their job is to be young, get high, meet a sexual partner, and possibly find someone they can stand to live with, the job of the director is to see beyond these immediate goals. I don't ask that he take a long-term view. Even a taste of the middle distance would do.

Guinevere ★ ★ ★ ½
R, 107 m., 1999

Sarah Polley (Harper Sloane), Stephen Rea (Connie Fitzpatrick), Carrie Preston (Patty), Tracy Letts (Zack), Gina Gershon (Billie), Jean Smart (Deborah Sloane), Emily Procter (Susan), Sharon McNight (Leslie). Directed by Audrey Wells and produced by Jonathan King and Brad Weston. Screenplay by Wells.

Despite all the piety of conventional opinion, people will insist sometimes on falling in love with inappropriate partners. No thoughtful person is ever looking for an appropriate partner in the first place—they're looking for the solution to their own needs and dreams. If you find who you need, then that's the partner you want, no matter what your parents or society tell you. Heaven help the spouse who has been chosen for appropriateness.

Guinevere is a love story involving a twenty-one-year-old woman who is fresh, blond, and vulnerable, and a man in his fifties who is a wet-eyed, hangdog drunk. "He was the worst man I ever met—or maybe the best," she remembers four years after their affair ended. "If you're supposed to learn from your mistakes, then he was the best mistake I ever made." They are not a good match or even a reasonable one, but at that time, and for her needs, he was a better choice than some college boy.

The woman's name is not Guinevere but Harper. He calls all of his women Guinevere. His name is Connie Fitzpatrick, and he's a talented but alcoholic photographer who lives in a loft in San Francisco and specializes in mentoring young women. He also sleeps with them, but we sense that the sex is secondary to the need for protégés. Harper arrives at his loft as the previous Guinevere is tearfully leaving, and later in the film Connie is presented with a group portrait of five of his former lovers: "Your life work," they tell him.

Harper (Sarah Polley) meets Connie at a particular time in her life. Her family is rich and cold. She is on track for Harvard but feels no calling to go there. There is no boy in her life. Anger, irony, and cynicism circle the family dining table. She wants to break with this and find a partner who allows her to express her idealism. Writing those words, I realized that *Guinevere* tells the same story as *American Beauty*, with the ages and sexes reversed: The middle-aged Kevin Spacey character lusts for a high school cheerleader for the same reason that Harper knocks on the photographer's door;

what they both seek is affirmation that they are good, unique, and treasured. If you can find that in a lover, you can put up with a lot.

Connie (Stephen Rea) is, we are told, a great photographer. We are told by him. We see a few of his pictures, which are good enough, and we hear some of his beliefs, such as, "Take a picture when it hurts so bad you can't stand it." Well, that's easy enough to say. He supports himself as a wedding photographer, which would seem to contradict his rule, but since it hurts really bad when he doesn't have enough money to buy booze, maybe the rule applies.

Connie's need is to find unformed young women and teach them. "You have to create something," he tells Harper when she moves in. He makes her read. And she is included in his boozy philosophical roundtable at the neighborhood tavern. His tragedy is that when his Guineveres learn enough, they know enough to leave. There is a horrible, perfect, brilliant moment in this film when Harper's society-bitch mother (Jean Smart) finds out about their relationship, and comes to call. She stalks the shabby loft in her expensive clothes, she smokes a cigarette with such style that he puts his own out, and in icy disdain she says, "What do you have against women your own age?" And answers her own question: "I know exactly what she has that I haven't got. Awe."

She's right, but can you blame him? To be regarded with awe can be a wondrous aphrodisiac. And he does care, really care, for her—for all the Guineveres. In her first night at his place, he lets her have the sleeping loft and he sleeps on the floor of his darkroom. "There's lots of reading matter here," he says. The book on top of the stack is the photography of Alfred Steiglitz. It falls open to a page. "That's Georgia O'Keeffe," she says. He tells her: "When they met, he was a famous photographer, and she was about your age." If the movie had been fifteen seconds longer, there could have been a scene showing him placing that educational volume on top of the reading matter.

The film was written and directed by Audrey Wells, who wrote the inspired romantic comedy *The Truth About Cats and Dogs*. She does not cast stones or lay blame. Wells is far beyond judging this relationship on grounds of conventional morality; it would be less moral for either one of them to settle for whoever society puts in their path.

Sarah Polley played the teenage girl in *The Sweet Hereafter* who surprised everyone with her testimony. She contains depths of feeling. She does not use cheap effects. There is a moment in *Guinevere* when Connie calls her his "good girl," and I was fascinated by the subtle play of emotions on her face. The words mean a lot to her, not altogether pleasant. She is tired of being a good girl at home. Tired of being condescended to. He uses the words in a different context. She is not sure she likes that context, either, but she understands why he has to say them. There is a one-act play in the way she uses her face in that scene.

Stephen Rea, from *The Crying Game*, has a more thankless role, because he is shabby and sad. His Connie is never going to be happy (or sober), but he knows how to give a push to a shy girl with low self-esteem. One of his most touching scenes involves a carefree moment cut short by a catastrophe: His false teeth break loose. On any scale of male vanity, this ranks well above impotence. He has another scene, at the end of a disastrous trip to Los Angeles, that ranks in poignancy with some of the moments in *Leaving Las Vegas*.

Guinevere is not perfect. Like many serious modern movies, it lacks the courage to use the sad ending it has earned. There is an absurd final fantasy scene that undoes a lot of hard work. But the movie's heart is in the right place. This movie isn't really about an old man and a younger woman at all. It's about everyone's dream of finding a person who, in the words of the old British beer commercial, refreshes the parts the others do not reach.

H

Hamlet ★ ★ ★
R, 111 m., 2000

Ethan Hawke (Hamlet), Kyle McLachlan (Claudius), Diane Venora (Gertrude), Sam Shepard (Ghost), Bill Murray (Polonius), Liev Schreiber (Laertes), Julia Stiles (Ophelia), Karl Geary (Horatio), Steve Zahn (Rosencrantz), Dechen Thurman (Guildenstern). Directed by Michael Almereyda and produced by Andrew Fierberg and Amy Hobby. Screenplay by Almereyda, based on the play by William Shakespeare.

I've seen Hamlet as an intellectual,
And I've seen Hamlet as an ineffectual,
And I've seen Hamlet as a homosexual,
And I've seen Hamlet ev'ry way but textual....
— "I've Seen Shakespeare," by Weeden, Finkle, and Fay

And now the melancholy Dane is a Manhattan techno-nerd, closeted with his computers, his video-editing gear, and his bitter thoughts. His father's company, the Denmark Corp., has made the front page of *USA Today* after a boardroom takeover by the scheming Claudius. Hamlet's mother has married the usurper. And the ghost of Hamlet's father appears on security cameras and materializes in a form transparent enough for Hamlet to see the Pepsi machine behind him.

Michael Almereyda's *Hamlet,* with Ethan Hawke as the prince and Bill Murray as Polonius, is both a distraction and a revelation. Sometimes the modern setting works against the material, sometimes it underlines it, and at all times it proves that *Hamlet* no more belongs in medieval Denmark than anywhere else. However it is staged, wherever it is set, it takes place within Hamlet's mind.

There are few thoughts worth having about life, death, and existence that *Hamlet* does not express in the fewest and most memorable words. "To be, or not to be" is the central question of human life, and Shakespeare asked it 400 years before the existentialists, and better than the Greeks. If man is the only animal that knows he must die, *Hamlet* is the distillation of that knowledge. This twenty-first-century

Hamlet, with its concealed microphones, answering machines, videotapes, and laptops, is as much Shakespeare's as Olivier's in medieval dress was, or Burton's in business suits, or Branagh's in nineteenth-century Blenheim Castle, or Mel Gibson's in a Scottish castle. It is Shakespeare because it respects his language, just as Baz Luhrmann's *Romeo + Juliet* (1996) was not because it did not.

Ethan Hawke plays Hamlet as a restless, bitter neurotic, replaying his memories on video machines and doing dry runs of his big speeches on a PixelVision camera he aims at himself. "To be, or not to be" is sketchily seen on Hamlet's own video, and finally reaches its full ironic flower in the "Action" corridor of a Blockbuster store. When Polonius (Murray) asks his daughter Ophelia (Julia Stiles) to sound out Hamlet, he supplies her with a concealed tape recorder—and Hamlet discovers the bug. When Hamlet denounces Ophelia, there is a reprise on her answering machine. The play within a play is Hamlet's own video production, presented in a screening room.

Kyle McLachlan and Diane Venora play Claudius and Gertrude, as reasonable as any modern materialist parents or stepparents (indeed, Gertrude is so modern she might be literature's first corporate wife). They are a couple comfortable in their affluence, content in their compromises, annoyed as much as disturbed by Hamlet's whingeing. He has had every opportunity, and now look at him, holed up with his resentments and driving his girlfriend crazy. Even Hawke's wardrobe strikes the right note: He wears an ugly knit ski hat that looks a little like a Norse helmet and a lot like the deliberately gauche clothes that teenagers choose to show they reject such middleclass affectations as taste.

Bill Murray is a good choice as Polonius, although Almereyda should have simply let him deliver his great speech to Laertes ("Neither a borrower nor a lender be . . .") without so much unnecessary business on the sound track. Liev Schreiber, as Laertes, is the wellmeaning brother of Ophelia, helpless to intervene because his common sense provides no strategy for dealing with madness. Steve Zahn and Dechen Thurman, as Rosencrantz and

Guildenstern, are the neighborhood layabouts, and it is a nice touch when Hamlet hacks into their laptop, changing their instructions so they, not he, will be murdered.

I like the way the material has truly been "adapted" to its modern setting without the language being adulterated. Yes, the play has been shortened (Branagh's *Hamlet* is one of the rare uncut versions, and runs 238 minutes). But it demonstrates how Shakespeare, who in a way invented modern English, has so dominated it ever since that his meanings are always broadly clear to us, even despite unfamiliar usages.

The purpose of this staging of the play is not simply to tart up *Hamlet* in modern dress, but to see him as the young man he was (younger than almost all of the great actors who have played him)—a seething bed of insecurities, guilt, unformed resolution, lust, introspection, and self-loathing. It was his misfortune that he was able to express his feelings so clearly that, once stated, they could not be evaded.

He marches here as he marched in Shakespeare's mind, toward an ending to life that settles nothing, that answers no questions, that contains victory for no one and confusion for all. The ultimate irony of Shakespeare's final scene, in which the dead king's successor steps over the bloody corpses and prepares for business as usual, is richly ironic in this modern corporate setting. Executives are eviscerated, their wives go down with them, their children die in grand, senseless gestures, new management comes in, and the stock price goes up. It happens every day.

Hanging Up ★ ★
PG-13, 99 m., 2000

Meg Ryan (Eve), Diane Keaton (Georgia), Lisa Kudrow (Maddy), Walter Matthau (Lou), Adam Arkin (Joe), Cloris Leachman (Pat). Directed by Diane Keaton and produced by Laurence Mark and Nora Ephron. Screenplay by Delia and Nora Ephron, based on the book by Delia Ephron.

"I live half my life in the real world and half on the telephone," Delia Ephron's father once told her. He was Henry Ephron (1911–1992), the successful writer of such comedies as *Desk Set* and *Daddy Longlegs*. He was always on the phone with his daughters, and they were al-

ways on the phone with one another, and now we have *Hanging Up*, a movie inspired by his last days, in which Walter Matthau plays the father as a man who probably should have lived more of his life in the real world.

The movie is based on Delia's 1995 novel, has been adapted by Delia and her sister Nora, and directed by Diane Keaton, who stars with Meg Ryan and Lisa Kudrow. It is so blonde and brittle, so pumped up with cheerful chatter and quality time, so relentless in the way it wants to be bright about sisterhood and death, that you want to stick a star on its forehead and send it home with a fever.

Lou, the Matthau character, is in the hospital dying of one of those diseases that only leaves you with enough strength for one-liners. He's been in show business for centuries. He wants constant reassurance from his daughters, who are racing in three different directions and keep in touch through an amazing number of telephones. The oldest, Georgia (Diane Keaton), runs her own magazine, which is named *Georgia* and is apparently a cross between *George* and *Lear*. The middle daughter, Eve (Meg Ryan), is a party planner and mother. The youngest, Maddy (Lisa Kudrow), is an actress on a soap opera that she takes at least as seriously as any of its fans. They love telephone round-robins, where one will tell something to the second, who immediately has to tell the third.

The film is really more about the lifestyles of the women than about their parting from their father, and he sort of understands this; this family has been raised as if it's on a stage, putting on a performance for the world, and the show must go on. There is a moment when Eve recruits Georgia to speak at an event she is coordinating, and Georgia starts talking about her sick father, and does something that can only be described as faking real tears. Yes, she is snuffling on demand, for dramatic purpose, at a key moment in her remarks—but just because you can turn an emotion on and off at will doesn't mean it isn't real. Of course, the attitudes she is expressing are really Eve's ("You take my life and you use it"), but borrowed real emotion is still real, right?

Delia Ephron and her sister Nora have lived in worlds not unlike this film, and so, of course, have Keaton, Ryan, and Kudrow. There are moments of sharp observation, as when we sense that these pretty, chic women dress for their meetings with one another at least as carefully as a boxer tapes his wrists. The best scenes are the ones in which the daughters are performing as themselves—projecting the images they use in order to carve out psychic space within the family. Georgia must be dominant because oldest. Eve must be accommodating and commonsensical because middle. Maddy must be dotty because youngest. If the movie hadn't been based on *Hanging Up,* it could have been based on Gail Sheehy's *Passages.*

The peculiar thing about the Matthau character is that he doesn't seem to be sick so much as waiting in a hospital bed for his dialogue to arrive. This is not a movie about true dying heartbreak (for that, see *Unstrung Heroes,* Keaton's wonderful 1995 film, much wiser about death and about the children it leaves behind). *Hanging Up* is more about continuing the legend of the irascible but lovable old man into the grave, if necessary.

Matthau is of course an invaluable actor, lined and weathered, a perfect fit, a catcher's mitt that has seen us through many a good season. Matthau has himself been very ill, and could no doubt have drawn on that experience for enough cries and whispers to furnish a Bergman movie. But he's read the script and understands it, and doesn't embarrass himself by providing more authenticity than the material can carry.

And the movie doesn't really want to be all that heartbreakingly true. It's a facile comedy of manners, a story in which the three daughters have somehow been taught by their upbringing to put a consistent face on everything. Their incessant telephoning is like a way of staying in tune. There are a couple of other characters in the film, an Iranian doctor and his salt-of-the-earth mother, who at first seem inexplicable, until you realize they function as a reality check. They're phoning in from the real world.

Hannibal ★ ★ ½
R, 131 m., 2001

Anthony Hopkins (Hannibal Lecter), Julianne Moore (Clarice Starling), Ray Liotta (Paul Krendler), Frankie R. Faison (Barney), Giancarlo Giannini (Pazzi), Francesca Neri (Signora Pazzi), Zeljko Ivanek (Dr. Cordell Doemling), Hazelle Goodman (Evelda Drumgo). Directed by Ridley Scott and produced by Dino De Laurentiis and Martha De Laurentiis. Screenplay by David Mamet and Steven Zaillian, based on the novel by Thomas Harris.

Ridley Scott's *Hannibal* is a carnival geek show elevated in the direction of art. It never quite gets there, but it tries with every fiber of its craft to redeem its pulp origins, and we must give it credit for the courage of its depravity; if it proves nothing else, it proves that if a man cutting off his face and feeding it to his dogs doesn't get the NC-17 rating for violence, nothing ever will.

The film lacks the focus and brilliance of *The Silence of the Lambs* for a number of reasons, but most clearly because it misplaces the reason why we liked Hannibal Lecter so much. He was, in the 1991 classic, a good man to the degree that his nature allowed him to be. He was hard-wired as a cannibal and mass murderer, true, but that was his nature, not his fault, and in his relationship with the heroine, FBI Agent Clarice Starling, he was civil and even kind. He did the best he could. I remember sitting in a restaurant with Anthony Hopkins as a waitress said, "You're Hannibal Lecter, aren't you? I wish my husband was more like you."

Hopkins returns here as Lecter, although Jodie Foster has been replaced by Julianne Moore as Clarice. We do not miss Foster so much as we miss her character; this Clarice is drier, more cynical, more closed-off than the young idealist we met ten years ago. A decade of law enforcement has taken the bloom off her rose. She is credited, indeed, by the *Guinness Book* as having killed more people than any other female FBI agent, although like all cops in movies, she still doesn't know what to say when her boss demands her badge and her gun. (Suggestion: "I ordered the D.C. police to stand down, and they opened fire anyway.")

Exiled to a desk job, she soon finds herself invited back to the chase by Lecter himself, who writes her from Florence, where he is now a wealthy art curator. On his trail is another millionaire, Mason Verger, who wants revenge. Verger was a child molester assigned to Dr.

Lecter for therapy, which Lecter supplied by drugging him and suggesting he cut off his face and feed it, as mentioned, to the dogs. Now horribly disfigured, with no eyelids or lips, he remembers: "It seemed like a good idea at the time." (Verger is played with repellent ooze by an uncredited and unrecognizable star; search the end credits.)

A Florence policeman named Pazzi (Giancarlo Giannini) suspects that the curator is actually Hannibal Lecter, and decides to shop him to Verger for a $3 million reward. This turns out to be a spectacularly bad idea, he realizes, as he ends up spilling his guts for Lecter. Giannini has always had sad eyes, never sadder than in his big scene here.

But do we like Lecter on the loose? It was the whole point of *Silence* that he could never hope to escape. Clarice descended seven flights of stairs and passed through seven locked doors before arriving at the Plexiglas wall that contained his shackled body. Only his mind was free to roam and scheme; the only way he could escape was to think himself out. In *Hannibal*, Lecter can move freely, and that removes part of the charm. By setting him free to roam, the movie diminishes his status from a locus of evil to a mere predator. He can escape from traps seemingly at will, but that misses the point. He is never more sympathetic here than when he's strapped to a cruciform brace and about to be fed, a little at a time, to wild boars. His voice at that point sounds a note of pity for his tormentors, and we remember the earlier Lecter.

Having read the Harris novel, I agreed with earlier reviewers who doubted it could be filmed in its original form. What is amazing is that Ridley Scott, with screenwriters David Mamet and Steven Zaillian, has kept most of the parts I thought would have to go. Verger's muscle-bound lesbian dominatrix sister is missing, along with her electric eel, and the very ending of the novel is gone, perhaps to spare Clarice irreversible humiliation in case there is a sequel. But the face-eating and voracious boars are still here, along with the man whose skull is popped open so that nonessential parts of his brain can be sliced off and sautéed for his dinner.

Many still alive will recall when a movie like this could not be contemplated, let alone filmed

and released. So great is our sophistication that we giggle when earlier generations would have retched. The brain-eating scene is "special effects," the face-eating is shot in deep shadow and so quickly cut that you barely see the dogs having their dinner, and Julianne Moore explains in interviews that the story is a fable of good and evil (although she cautions that she "actually talked to my shrink about it").

I cannot approve of the movie, not because of its violence, which belongs to the Grand Guignol tradition, but because the underlying story lacks the fascination of *The Silence of the Lambs*. Lecter on the loose loses power, Clarice is harder and less likable, the story unsuccessfully joins its depravity with its police procedural details, and the movie is too bold in its desire to shock (*Silence* somehow persuaded us the shocks were forced upon it).

Still, I'm left with admiration for Scott's craft in pulling this off at all, and making it watchable and (for some, I'm sure) entertaining. The Mason Verger character is a superb joining of skill and diabolical imagination, Julianne Moore's agent is probably an accurate portrait of how Clarice would have changed in ten years, and Anthony Hopkins makes Lecter fascinating every second he is on the screen. The old cannibal still has his standards. "He said that whenever possible," his former jailer Barney recalls, "he preferred to eat the rude—the free-range rude." ☞

Happy, Texas ★ ★ ★
PG-13, 104 m., 1999

Jeremy Northam (Harry Sawyer), Steve Zahn (Wayne Wayne Wayne Jr.), William H. Macy (Sheriff Chappy Dent), Ally Walker (Josephine McLintock), Illeana Douglas (Ms. Schaefer), M. C. Gainey (Bob), Ron Perlman (Nalhober), Tim Bagley (David), Michael Hitchcock (Steven), Paul Dooley (Judge). Directed and produced by Mark Illsley. Screenplay by Ed Stone, Illsley, and Phil Reeves.

There is a moment early in *Happy, Texas* when an escaped convict looks at a roomful of five-year-old beauty pageant contestants and asks them if they know the words to "Ninety-nine Bottles of Beer on the Wall." They look at him with curiosity. After all, he is the out-of-town pageant consultant, hired to prepare them for the Little Miss Fresh-Squeezed Pre-Teen Beauty Pageant.

The convict's name is Wayne Wayne Wayne Jr. (Steve Zahn). He and Harry Sawyer (Jeremy Northam) have escaped from an overturned prison van, cut through their handcuffs, and stolen a van at a gas station. What they discover belatedly is that the van belongs to two gay men who travel around Texas consulting on beauty contests. "Lots of folks are looking for you," says Happy's sheriff Chappy Dent (William H. Macy) as he stops them outside of town.

They think they're being arrested. Not at all. They're being hired. And they decide to stay in the town after they meet the local bank president (Ally Walker) and realize a bank heist might be a pushover. That requires them to impersonate pageant consultants, in a plot that brings together three of the oldest dodges in the screenwriter's arsenal (Fish Out of Water, Mistaken Identities, Love Under False Pretenses). What saves the movie is that it doesn't really depend on the plot wheezes. They're taken for granted, in a comedy that's really about human nature.

Since Wayne and Harry are assumed by everyone in town to be a gay couple, that makes them safe "friends" for two local women—Walker, as Jo the bank president, and Illeana Douglas, as Ms. Schaefer, the teacher in charge of the little contestants. We get the obligatory dialogue passages in which the women are talking about one thing and the men about another, but we don't care, because the actors sell the situation so amusingly—and warmly. Zahn's performance is especially funny; he's rough-hewn, unsophisticated, and not very bright, and he quickly falls desperately in love with "Ms. Schaefer." The hurdle of his sexual orientation? No problem: "That whole gay thing is just like a hobby."

Harry quickly sees that pretending to be gay is a way to get close to Jo, but there's another complication: Sheriff Chappy Dent has a crush on Harry and asks him out for a date, leading to an evening in a cowboy gay bar, where Harry follows and Chappy leads ("Now I'm gonna spin ya!").

Macy's performance as the quietly, earnestly in love sheriff is the most touching in the movie, another role in which he gets laughs by finding the truth beneath the humor. Steve Zahn's work gets the loud laughs. In the division of labor between the two escaped cons, Harry takes over the bank job and Wayne's task is to pose as a choreographer. Completely without a clue, he studies videotapes and then tries to teach the same steps to the dutiful little girls, and discovers, amazingly, that he is not without talent at the pageant business. ("I'm trying to figure out if slip-stitching or basting is the best way to sew on a sparkly heart.")

There's boundless good nature in the work by Douglas and Zahn. Macy lets his eyes carry scenes where no dialogue would have worked. And watching Jeremy Northam is a revelation: Here is the slick, urbane British gentleman of *Emma, The Winslow Boy,* and *An Ideal Husband,* playing a Texas convict and not missing a beat. Mark Illsley, who produced, directed, and cowrote the script, had his choice of two endings: the big pageant or the bank job. I would have liked more pageant and less of the bank, but the movie is so good-humored it hardly matters. This is one of those comedies that doesn't pound us on the head with the obvious, but simply lets us share vast amusement.

The Harmonists ★ ★ ★
R, 115 m., 1999

Ben Becker (Robert Biberti), Heino Ferch (Roman Cycowski), Ulrich Noethen (Harry Frommermann), Heinrich Schafmeister (Erich A. Collin), Max Tidof (Ari Leschnikoff), Kai Wiesinger (Erwin Bootz), Meret Becker (Erna Eggstein), Katja Riemann (Mary Cycowski). Directed by Joseph Vilsmaier and produced by Reinhard Kloos, Hanno Huth, and Danny Krausz. Screenplay by Klaus Richter.

The Harmonists tells the story of the rise and fall of a vocal group that was wildly popular in Germany before it was disbanded in 1934 as part of the mounting persecution of Jews. The Comedian Harmonists, who did comic and romantic songs in intricate harmony, were popular and beloved. Even members of the Nazi hierarchy were among their fans. But eventually they were forbidden to sing songs by Jewish composers—and finally, because three of their members were Jewish, they were banned from performing in public.

Given the suffering created by the Nazis, the fate of the Harmonists ranks low on the scale. But as one of the countless little stories that add up to the plague of Nazism, they deserve an entry in the chronicle of despair. And it is revealing how, like many of their countrymen both Jewish and gentile, they were blind until the last moment to the actual intentions of the Nazis. There is a moment in the film when the Harmonists are performing in New York and consider staying in America. But they do not. The handwriting was on the wall, but it was not yet sufficiently clear.

The arc of the film leads from early cheerfulness to eventual defeat, but for much of the time *The Harmonists* plays like a standard showbiz biopic. We meet the founder of the group, Harry Frommermann (Ulrich Noethen), who in 1927 hears a record by a black American jazz group named the Revellers. Entranced by the beauty of their close harmony, he determines to start a German group that would sing in the same style. It's slow-going at first, but after the brash, confident Robert Biberti (Ben Becker) joins him, they find the other recruits and end up with five singers and a piano player.

The first agent they audition for tells them their music sounds "funereal." That night, the pianist plays around with a faster tempo, and they find their style. I've never heard the Revellers, but the Harmonists remind me of the Mills Brothers, and they do something the Mills Brothers also did: They use their voices, hands, and breath control to imitate the sound of musical instruments. There's an instrumental solo in the film done entirely without instruments.

As the six men work and travel together, tensions of course develop, and the most delicate involves the fact that Harry and Robert are both in love with the same woman, a comely music store clerk named Erna (Meret Becker). She likes Harry (indeed, she makes sure she's up on a ladder with a little of her slip and a lot of her leg showing when he enters the store). He likes her, too, enough to propose marriage even though he's Jewish and she isn't. (He visits his parents' grave to tell them, "God will forgive me—after all; it's his job.")

But Harry is a complicated man—distracted, driven, inattentive, forgetful, maddening. Robert, on the other hand, is as solid as a Teutonic rock, and looks a little like Mencken with the stogie he keeps planted in his mouth. Robert is not Jewish, but he's not a Nazi, either, and his decency helps hold the Harmonists together.

There are a lot of entertaining musical numbers in the film, and an ominous low-key, background treatment of the way that Nazism and anti-Semitism change the fabric of German society even while many of the characters are busy denying it. (When ugly slogans are painted on the window of the music store, the grandmotherly owner says it's "just kids.")

Eventually the situation can no longer be ignored. There's an electrifying scene just before the group sails for New York; a high Nazi official asks them to perform at his home, which they do, but when he requests a German folk song with Nazi associations, Harry says he "just cannot sing it." Their fate as a group is sealed at that moment, although it would have been sealed sooner or later anyway. Roman Cycowski (Heino Ferch), another Jewish member, announces eventually, "No power on Earth can force me to sing in this country again."

After they break up, the three Jewish Harmonists regroup outside Germany, and the three Germans start a new group at home. But what made them special fades away, and their music somehow seems like a reproach to the rising tide of war. An epilogue reveals what eventually happened to all the Harmonists. One moved to California and became the oldest active cantor in America. Others did not end so happily.

The Haunting ★ ★ ★
PG-13, 113 m., 1999

Lili Taylor (Nell), Liam Neeson (Dr. David Marrow), Catherine Zeta-Jones (Theo), Owen Wilson (Luke Sanderson), Bruce Dern (Mr. Dudley), Marian Seldes (Mrs. Dudley), Alix Koromzay (Mary Lambetta), Todd Field (Todd Hackett), Virginia Madsen (Jane). Directed by Jan De Bont and produced by Susan Arnold, Donna Arkoff Roth, and Colin Wilson. Screenplay by David Self, based on a novel by Shirley Jackson.

To my surprise, I find myself recommending *The Haunting* on the basis of its locations, its sets, its art direction, its sound design, and the overall splendor of its visuals. The story is a mess, but for long periods of time that hardly matters. It's beside the point, as we enter one of the most striking spaces I've ever seen in a film.

That space is Hill House, the haunted manor selected by a psychology professor (Liam Neeson) for an experiment in the mechanics of fear. He recruits three people who are told they'll get help for insomnia, and installs them in the ornate and gloomy Gothic pile, where alarming things start to happen immediately. We assume the frightening manifestations are manufactured by the professor (last name: Marrow), but perhaps not.

The three patients are played by Lili Taylor, Catherine Zeta-Jones, and Owen Wilson. Professor Marrow is joined by two assistants, but in one of the screenplay's several clumsy moves, one of them is injured the first night, the other takes her to the hospital, and that's the last we ever see of them. Taylor's character, named Nell, is the key figure in the film, a woman whose life has been on hold until the ghosts of Hill House start to tell their story.

The exteriors of Hill House were shot at Harlaxton Manor in Nottinghamshire. Its architectural details look like a shriek from hell; now I know what a building looks like with its hair standing on end. (It's a bit of an anticlimax to discover that the building is currently used as a foreign campus of the University of Evansville, Indiana.) The interiors I gather are mostly sets, although some of them are inspired by Harlaxton and Belvoir Castle in Leicestershire.

The production design is by Eugenio Zanetti *(What Dreams May Come, Restoration)* and he has done a masterful job of creating interiors that seem to be alive with menace. One of the great moments in the film comes when Taylor and Zeta-Jones explore their bedrooms, which are so rich with detail that you want to wallow in them. The great hall of the house features a walk-in fireplace not unlike the one in *Citizen Kane*'s Xanadu, and indeed when Zeta-Jones first enters Hill House, she murmurs, "It's like Charles Foster Kane meets the Munsters."

The horror story itself is based on things that go thump (and bang and wheeze) in the night. The cavernous halls and ominous corridors reverberate with great groaning, echoing noises, as if the house has gas pains. Doors are hammered on. Ghostly manifestations appear. One or two moments are truly scary, including a recycled version of the classic *Carrie* end shot. We enter this space and feel enclosed by it; it's not like a set, but more like a virtual reality.

Lili Taylor struggles valiantly with her character, the movie's juiciest, and has some effective scenes, mostly by herself. "I can be a victim or I can be a volunteer," she tells herself when the going gets really rough. The rest of the characters are underwritten, including Catherine Zeta-Jones's beautiful Theo, who does some bisexual lip-smacking at the outset but never follows up, and spends most of her time running to the rescue. Owen Wilson, as the guy, asks obvious questions and helps tug open doors, etc., but is not made much of, and neither is Liam Neeson's professor, whose motivations are explained in some flat opening scenes, and who then goes adrift in the plot ("All right, you two! Enough about pharmaceuticals!").

But the special effects are original and effective, evoking a haunted house in unexpected ways. A floor-level gliding camera is insinuating. Scenes set in a huge old conservatory are creepy in the way they use dead vegetation, and there's a nice scene on a shaky spiral staircase. To enter these rooms, to move among them, to feel their weight and personality, is an experience. I am reminded of the abandoned subway station in *The Mimic* (1997), another space with a personality of its own.

The movie often edges so close to being truly scary that you wonder why they didn't try just a little harder to write more dimensional characters and add the edge of almost plausible realism that distinguished Shirley Jackson's original novel. The movie does not, alas, succeed as a horror film. But it succeeds as a film worth watching anyway, and that is no small achievement.

Head Over Heels ★ ½
PG-13, 91 m., 2001

Monica Potter (Amanda Pierce), Freddie Prinze Jr. (Jim Winston), Shalom Harlow (Jade), Ivana

Milicevic (Roxana), Sarah O'Hare (Candi), Tomiko Fraser (Holly), Raoul Ganeev (Harold). Directed by Mark S. Waters and produced by Julia Dray and Robert Simonds. Screenplay by Ron Burch and David Kidd.

Head Over Heels opens with fifteen funny minutes and then goes dead in the water. It's like they sent home the first team of screenwriters and brought in Beavis and Butt-Head. The movie starts out with sharp wit and edgy zingers, switches them off, and turns to bathroom humor. And not funny bathroom humor, but painfully phony gas-passing noises, followed by a plumbing emergency that buries three supermodels in a putrid delivery from where the sun don't shine. It's as if the production was a fight to the death between bright people with a sense of humor and cretins who think the audience is as stupid as they are.

Monica Potter and Freddie Prinze Jr. star, in another one of those stories where it's love at first sight and then she gets the notion that he's clubbed someone to death. The two characters were doing perfectly well being funny as *themselves,* and then the movie muzzles them and brings in this pea-brained autopilot plot involving mistaken identities, dead bodies, and the Russian mafia.

Why? I wanted to ask the filmmakers. Why? You have a terrific cast and the wit to start out well. Why surrender and sell out? Isn't it a better bet, and even better for your careers, to make a whole movie that's smart and funny, instead of showing off for fifteen minutes and then descending into cynicism and stupidity? Why not make a movie you can show to the friends you admire, instead of to a test audience scraped from the bottom of the IQ barrel?

Monica Potter is radiant as Amanda, an art restorer at the Museum of Modern Art. She has been betrayed by a boyfriend, and vows to focus on her job. "I love art better than real life," she says, because the people in paintings "stay in love forever." True of the Grecian urn, perhaps, if not of Bosch, but never mind; her latest challenge is to restore a priceless Titian, which the curator hauls into the room with his fingers all over the paint, banging it against the doorway.

Moving out from her faithless boyfriend, she finds a $500-a-month room (i.e., closet) in a vast luxury apartment occupied by "the last four nonsmoking models in Manhattan" (Shalom Harlow, Ivana Milicevic, Sarah O'Hare, and Tomiko Fraser). And then she falls head over heels in love with a neighbor, Jim (Prinze), who walks a big dog that knocks her over and sets up a conversation in which she says all of the wrong things. That's the dialogue I thought was so funny.

In a film with more confidence, the comedy would continue to be based on their relationship. This one prefers to recycle aged clichés. She thinks she sees him club someone to death. We know he didn't, because—well, because (a) it happens in silhouette, so the movie is hiding something, and (b) Freddie Prinze is not going to play a *real* club-murderer, not in a movie with a cute dog. Idiot Plot devices prevent either one of them from saying the two or three words that would clear up the misunderstanding. Meanwhile, the exhausted screenwriters haul in the Russian mafia and other sinister characters in order to make this movie as similar as possible to countless other brain-dead productions.

As my smile faded and I realized the first fifteen minutes were bait-and-switch, my restless mind sought elsewhere for employment. I focused on Amanda's job, art restoration. Her challenge: An entire face is missing from a grouping by Titian. She "restores" it by filling the gap with, yes, Freddie Prinze's face and head, complete with a haircut that doesn't exactly match the Renaissance period.

But never mind. Give the movie the benefit of the doubt. Maybe one of those Renaissance geniuses like Michelangelo invented Supercuts clippers at the same time he invented bicycles and submarines. What's really odd is that the face is not in the style of Titian, but in the style of Norman Rockwell. Obviously it was only with the greatest restraint that Amanda was able to prevent herself from adding a soda fountain to the background.

Now what about that eruption of unspeakable brown stuff that coats the supermodels as they hide behind a shower curtain in a bathroom? Why was that supposed to be funny? The scene betrays a basic ignorance of a fundamental principle of humor: It isn't funny when innocent bystanders are humiliated. It's funny when they humiliate themselves. For example, *Head Over Heels* would be funny if it were about the people making this movie.

Heartbreakers ★ ★ ★
PG-13, 123 m., 2001

Sigourney Weaver (Max), Jennifer Love Hewitt (Page), Ray Liotta (Dean Cumanno), Jason Lee (Jack), Gene Hackman (William B. Tensy), Anne Bancroft (Gloria Vogal/Barbara), Nora Dunn (Miss Madress). Directed by David Mirkin and produced by John Davis and Irving Ong. Screenplay by Robert Dunn, Paul Guay, and Stephen Mazur.

Heartbreakers is *Dirty Rotten Scoundrels* plus Gene Hackman as W. C. Fields, plus Jennifer Love Hewitt and Sigourney Weaver walking into rooms wearing dresses that enter about a quarter of an inch after they do. I guess that's enough to recommend it. It's not a great comedy, but it's a raucous one, hardworking and ribald, and I like its spirit.

Weaver and Hewitt play Max and Page, a mother-and-daughter con team. Their scam: Max (Weaver) marries a rich guy and then surprises him in a compromising position with Page (Hewitt), after which there's a big divorce settlement. This has worked thirteen times, according to Max, whose latest victim is Dean (Ray Liotta), a chop-shop owner who falls for what my old buddy Russ Meyer would describe as Hewitt's capacious bodice.

Hewitt spends the entire film with her treasures on display, maybe as product placement for the Wonder Bra, and for that matter, Heather Graham is identically costumed in *Say It Isn't So*. The moviegoers of America owe something, possibly gratitude, to Erin Brockovich, the most influential movie style-setter since Annie Hall.

Weaver and Hewitt attack their roles with zeal, but the movie doesn't really start humming until Hackman enters. He plays William B. Tensy, a chain-smoking tobacco zillionaire who lives on the water in Palm Beach with a draconian housekeeper (Nora Dunn) and lots of ashtrays. He believes everyone, especially children, should take up smoking, and has a cigarette in his mouth at all times except when violently choking with bronchial spasms, which is frequently.

My guess is that Hackman decided to take the role when he hit on the approach of playing Tensy as W. C. Fields. There is nothing in the role as written that suggests Fields, but everything in the role as played, including Hackman's recycling of Fields's wardrobe from the famous short *The Golf Specialist* (1930).

Weaver seems tickled by the sheer awfulness of Tensy, a man most women would cross not only the room but perhaps the state to avoid. With the Liotta character she was within the guidelines of traditional farce, but with Hackman she's working without a net: What strategy *can* a woman adopt in dealing with such an astonishing combination of the gauche and the obnoxious? Their relationship concludes with a sight gag involving, of course, cigarette smoke; I wouldn't dream of revealing one more thing about it.

Weaver's approach to Tensy is a devious one; she pretends to be Russian, which leads into a precarious situation when she's called up on the stage in a Russian nightclub and expected to sing; her response to this emergency is inspired. Not so brilliant is another strategy she and her daughter use. In restaurants, they sneak broken glass onto their salads and then complain loudly, refusing to pay. Nice, but wiser if they'd eat some of the salad course before complaining; by dropping the glass immediately, they defeat the purpose.

Anyway. While Max courts the disgusting Tensy, Hewitt, as Page, is developing a relationship with Jack (Jason Lee), the owner of a Palm Beach bar. She's torn between falling in love with him and fleecing him, especially after she learns he's been offered 3 million bucks for his bar and its waterfront property. This is the moment that will get the biggest laughs in Palm Beach, where the last time this much ocean frontage went for $3 million was when Roxanne Pulitzer was taking trumpet lessons. That both Jack and Page are dumb enough to be dazzled by the offer is a hint that they may be made for each other.

The movie has been directed by David Mirkin, who made the sly and charming *Romy and Michele's High School Reunion* (1997). *Heartbreakers* is not as sly and has no ambition to be charming, but in a season of dreary failed comedies it does what a comedy must: It makes us laugh.

Here on Earth ★ ★

PG-13, 97 m., 2000

Chris Klein (Kelley), Leelee Sobieski (Samantha), Josh Hartnett (Jasper), Bruce Greenwood (Earl Cavanaugh), Annette O'Toole (Jo Cavanaugh), Michael Rooker (Malcolm Arnold), Annie Corley (Betsy Arnold). Directed by Mark Piznarkski and produced by David T. Friendly. Screenplay by Michael Seitzman.

When we see the sweet advertising art for *Here on Earth,* we suspect this may be another movie about angels walking among us, and it is—but these are human angels, not heavenly ones. It is about characters so generous, understanding, forgiving, and just doggone nice that they could have been created by Norman Rockwell, just as their town seems to have been.

The movie begins, however, on a sour note, as a snotty prep school boy named Kelley (Chris Klein) gets a new Mercedes convertible from his rich dad, and takes some friends slumming at the diner in the nearby small town. He gets smart with Samantha, the waitress (Leelee Sobieski), and has words with her boyfriend, Jasper (Josh Hartnett). That leads to a drag race during which Kelley and Jasper crash their cars into a gas pump and burn down the gas station and the diner, which are owned by Samantha's parents.

Kelley has come across up until this point as an arrogant brat. Sure, he's the class valedictorian, but he doesn't care about stuff like that. All he cares about is expanding the family fortune. So maybe it will teach him a lesson when the judge orders Kelley and Jasper to help rebuild the diner during the summer ahead. And maybe Samantha is right to see something good hidden beneath his cynical defiance. Consider the scene where he sneaks through the woods to eavesdrop on the substitute valedictorian's speech (he's been banned from graduation), and she tiptoes behind him and watches as he gives his own speech to the trees and the birds. It's a sweet scene. Unlikely in its logistics, but sweet.

Kelley isn't easy to like ("My probation doesn't say anything about sitting around and spitting out watermelon seeds with you people"). But as the summer meanders along, the boys get tans and develop muscles, and Samantha and Kelley fall in love, while good-hearted Jasper looks on helplessly. Read no further if you don't want to know . . . that Samantha, alas, has received bad news from her doctor. The cancer has spread from her knee to her liver, nothing can be done, and besides, "So I lived another year or two. It's not worth it."

Not worth it? When you're young and smart and in love? I would personally endure a good deal of pain just to live long enough to read tomorrow's newspaper. But Samantha fades away, another victim of Ali MacGraw's Disease (first identified many years ago in *Love Story*), which makes you more beautiful the sicker you get.

By now the film has become fairly unbelievable. Jasper is telling Kelley that although it kills him to see the woman he loves in the arms of another man, whatever makes her happy is all he wants for her. And Kelley is softening up and telling his rich dad that money isn't the only thing in life, and that you can be just as happy with a poor girl as a rich one.

But then comes a scene that clangs with a harsh false note. (Once again: Spoiler warning.) While Samantha bravely faces death and nobly smiles upon all around her, Kelley, the rat, suddenly announces he "has a life to get back to," and leaves town. This seems to be an utterly unmotivated act, but actually it has a splendid motivation: He has to leave so that he can come back. The plot requires a crisis before the dawn. The fact that his action is unconvincing and inexplicable doesn't bother the filmmakers, any more than it bothers the saintly and forgiving Samantha.

Leelee Sobieski is really very good in this movie. Still only nineteen, she was wonderful in *A Soldier's Daughter Never Cries* and *Eyes Wide Shut,* and in lesser movies like *Deep Impact* and *Never Been Kissed*. I didn't see her TV version of *Joan of Arc,* but with her deep, grave voice and unforced presence, I have a feeling she was equal to the role. The cast is filled with other winning actors: Klein and Hartnett, and Bruce Greenwood and the undervalued Annette O'Toole as Samantha's parents. But they need a little more reality to kick against. *Here on Earth* slides too easily into its sentimentality; the characters should have put up more of a struggle.

Hideous Kinky ★ ★ ★
R, 99 m., 1999

Kate Winslet (Julia), Said Taghmaoui (Bilal), Bella Riza (Bea), Carrie Mullan (Lucy), Pierre Clementi (Santoni), Abigail Cruttenden (Charlotte), Ahmed Boulane (Ben Said), Sira Stampe (Eva). Directed by Gillies MacKinnon and produced by Ann Scott. Screenplay by Billy MacKinnon, based on the novel by Esther Freud.

In the 1970s, there were movies about the carefree lives of hippies and flower people, and on the screen you could see their children, longhaired, sunburned, and barefoot, solemn witnesses at rock concerts and magical mystery tours. Remember the commune in *Easy Rider.*

Now it is the 1990s and those children have grown up to make their own movies and tell their side of the story. *A Soldier's Daughter Never Cries* (1998) was based on an autobiographical novel by Kaylie Jones, whose novelist father, James, raised his family in bohemian freedom as exiles in Paris. Now here is *Hideous Kinky,* based on an autobiographical novel by Esther Freud, whose father is the British painter Lucien Freud. I'm not sure how much of the story is based on fact, but presumably the feelings are accurately reflected, as when a child tells her hippie mother: "I don't need another adventure, Mom! I need to go to school. I want a satchel!"

The film stars Kate Winslet, in an aboutface after *Titanic,* as a thirtyish British mom named Julia, who has journeyed to Marrakech in 1972 with her two young daughters, Bea (Bella Riza) and Lucy (Carrie Mullan). She is seeking the truth, she says, or perhaps she is making a grand gesture against her husband, a London poet whom she caught cheating. Well, actually, he's not officially her husband, although he is the father of the children, and is sending them packages and checks from time to time, although sometimes they get packages intended for his other family, and the bank doesn't often receive the checks.

Julia is not a bad woman—just reckless, naive, foolishly trusting, and seeking truth in the wrong places, times, and ways. She doesn't do drugs to speak of, drinks little, wants to study Sufi philosophy. Her children, like most children, are profoundly conservative in the face of anarchy. They want a home, school, "real shirts." They're tired of Julia's quest, and ask, "Mom, when can we have rice pudding again?" The movie's tension comes from our own uneasiness about the mother, who with the best intentions seems to be blundering into trouble.

The film, directed by Gillies MacKinnon, fills its canvas with details about expatriate life in the time of flower power. Moroccan music blends with psychedelic rock, and they meet a teacher from the School of the Annihilation of the Ego. The expatriate American novelist Paul Bowles is presumably lurking about somewhere, writing his novel *The Sheltering Sky,* which is about characters not unlike these. One day in the bazaar the family encounters Bilal (Said Taghmaoui), a street performer who possibly has some disagreements with the police, but is humorous and friendly, and is soon Julia's lover.

Bilal is not a bad man, either. *Hideous Kinky* is not a melodrama or a thriller, and doesn't need villains; it's the record of a time when idealism led good-hearted seekers into danger. Some of the time Julia doesn't have enough food for her children, or a place for them to stay, and her idea for raising money is pathetic: She has them all making dolls to sell in the marketplace. Their trip to the desert leads to a nearly fatal ride with a sleepy truck driver, and to an uneasy meeting with a woman who may or may not be Bilal's wife.

In Marrakech, invitations come easily. They meet a Frenchman (Pierre Clementi, who played young hippies himself in the 1960s and 1970s) who invites them to his house: "I have lots of rooms." There they get involved in a strange ménage. Later, incredibly, Julia leaves Bea with them for safekeeping, only to discover that the household has broken up and her child has disappeared. She finds Bea in the keeping of an earnest Christian woman who runs an orphanage and doesn't seem inclined to surrender the child. "It's what Bea always wanted," she tells Julia. "To be an orphan?" "To be normal."

The movie is episodic and sometimes repetitive; dramatic scenes alternate with music and local color, and then the process repeats itself. What makes it work is Winslet's performance, as a sincere, good person, not terrifically

267

smart, who doggedly pursues her dream and drags along her unwilling children. Parents, even flower-child moms, always think they know what's best for their kids. Maybe they do. Look at it this way: To the degree that this story really is autobiographical, Julia raised a daughter who wrote a novel and had it made into a movie. Bea might not have turned out quite so splendidly by eating rice pudding and carrying a satchel to school.

High Fidelity ★ ★ ★ ★
R, 120 m., 2000

John Cusack (Rob), Iben Hjejle (Laura), Todd Louiso (Dick), Jack Black (Barry), Lisa Bonet (Marie), Catherine Zeta-Jones (Charlie), Joan Cusack (Liz), Tim Robbins (Ian). Directed by Stephen Frears and produced by Tim Bevan and Rudd Simmons. Screenplay by D. V. Devincentis, Steve Pink, John Cusack, and Scott Rosenberg, based on the book by Nick Hornby.

In its unforced, whimsical, quirky, obsessive way, *High Fidelity* is a comedy about real people in real lives. The movie looks like it was easy to make—but it must not have been, because movies this wry and likable hardly ever get made. Usually a clunky plot gets in the way, or the filmmakers are afraid to let their characters seem too smart. Watching *High Fidelity*, I had the feeling I could walk out of the theater and meet the same people on the street—and want to, which is an even higher compliment.

John Cusack stars as Rob, who owns a used-record store in Chicago and has just broken up with Laura, his latest girlfriend. He breaks up a lot. Still hurting, he makes a list of the top five girls he's broken up with, and cackles that Laura didn't make it. Later he stands forlornly on a bridge overlooking the Chicago River and makes lists of the top five reasons he misses her.

The key design elements in Rob's apartment are the lumber bookshelves for his alphabetized vinyl albums. He has two guys working for him in his store. Each was hired for three days a week, but both come in six days a week, maybe because they have no place else to go. These guys are the shy, sideways Dick (Todd Louiso) and the ultraconfident Barry (Jack Black). They are both experts on everything, brains stocked with nuggets of information about popular culture.

Rob is the movie's narrator, guiding us through his world, talking directly to the camera, soliloquizing on his plight—which is that he seems unable to connect permanently with a girl, maybe because his attention is elsewhere. But on what? He isn't obsessed with his business, he isn't as crazy about music as Dick and Barry, and he isn't thinking about his next girl—he's usually moping about the last one. He seems stuck in the role of rejected lover, and never likes a girl quite as much when she's with him as after she's left.

Laura (Iben Hjejle) was kind of special. Now she has taken up with an unbearably supercilious, ponytailed brainiac named Ian (Tim Robbins), who comes into the store to "talk things over" and inspires fantasies in which Rob, Dick, and Barry dream of kicking him senseless. "Conflict resolution is my job," he offers helpfully. Whether Ian is nice or not is of no consequence to Rob; he simply wants Laura back.

The story unspools in an unforced way. Barry and Dick involve Rob in elaborate debates about music minutiae. They take him to a nightclub to hear a new singer (Lisa Bonet). Rob gets advice from Laura's best friend (Joan Cusack), who likes him but is fed up with his emotional dithering. Rob seeks out former girlfriends like Charlie (Catherine Zeta-Jones), who tells him why she left him in more detail than he really wants to hear. Rob decides that his ideal girl would be a singer who would "write songs at home and ask me what I thought of them—and maybe even include one of our private little jokes in the liner notes."

High Fidelity is based on a 1995 novel by Nick Hornby, a London writer, and has been directed by Stephen Frears, also British. Frears and his screenwriters (D. V. Devincentis, Steve Pink, Cusack, and Scott Rosenberg) have transplanted the story to Chicago so successfully that it feels like it grew organically out of the funky soil of Lincoln Avenue and Halsted, Old Town and New Town, Rogers Park and Hyde Park, and Wicker Park, where it was shot—those neighborhoods where the workers in the alternative lifestyle industry live, love, and labor.

This is a film about, and also for, not only obsessed clerks in record stores, but the video store clerks who have seen all the movies, and the bookstore employees who have read all the books. Also for bartenders, waitresses, greengrocers in health food stores, kitchen slaves at vegetarian restaurants, the people at GNC who know all the herbs, writers for alternative weeklies, disc jockeys on college stations, salespeople in retro-clothing shops, tattoo artists and those they tattoo, poets, artists, musicians, novelists, and the hip, the pierced, and the lonely. They may not see themselves, but they will recognize people they know.

The Cusack character is someone I have known all my life. He is assembled out of my college friends, the guys at work, people I used to drink with. I also recognize Barry, the character played by Jack Black; he's a type so universal it's a wonder he hasn't been pinned down in a movie before: a blowhard, a self-appointed expert on all matters of musical taste, a monologuist, a guy who would rather tell you his opinion than take your money. Jack Black is himself from this world; he's the lead singer of the group Tenacious D, and it is a measure of his acting ability that when he does finally sing in this movie, we are surprised that he can.

The women I recognize too. They're more casual about romance than most movie characters, maybe because most movies are simpleminded and pretend it is earthshakingly important whether this boy and this girl mate forever, when a lot of young romance is just window-shopping and role-playing, and everyone knows it. You break up, you sigh, you move on. The process is so universal that with some people, you sigh as you meet them, in anticipation.

I am meandering. All I want to say is that *High Fidelity* has no deep significance, does not grow exercised over stupid plot points, savors the rhythms of these lives, sees how pop music is a sound track for everyone's autobiography, introduces us to Rob and makes us hope that he finds happiness, and causes us to leave the theater quite unreasonably happy.

Hilary and Jackie ★ ★ ★ ½
R, 121 m., 1998

Emily Watson (Jacqueline du Pre), Rachel Griffiths (Hilary du Pre), David Morrissey (Kiffer Finzi), James Frain (Daniel Barenboim), Charles Dance (Derek du Pre), Celia Imrie (Iris du Pre), Rupert Penry-Jones (Piers du Pre), Bill Paterson (Jackie's Cello Teacher). Directed by Anand Tucker and produced by Andy Paterson and Nicolas Kent. Screenplay by Frank Cottrell-Boyce, based on the book *A Genius in the Family* by Hilary and Piers Du Pre.

Jackie to Hilary: "The truth is, you're not special."

Hilary to Jackie: "If you think that being an ordinary person is any easier than being an extraordinary one, you're wrong. If you didn't have that cello to prop you up, you'd be nothing."

And yet the two sisters love each other with a fierceness that stands beside their lifelong rivalry. *Hilary and Jackie* is the story of two gifted musicians, who in a way were always playing for (or against) each other, and how one of them was struck down by disease. "I have a fatal illness," Jackie says, "but the good news is, I have a very mild case."

Jacqueline du Pre (Emily Watson) was one of the most gifted cellists of her time, and her brilliant marriage to the pianist and conductor Daniel Barenboim was a celebrated musical and romantic liaison. Hilary du Pre (Rachel Griffiths), her older sister, played the flute and might perhaps have been as gifted as her sister. But that we will never know, because a music teacher beat down her talent and crushed her spirit. Perhaps she had a happier life as a result.

Hilary and Jackie is an extraordinary film about riding the tiger of genius, and how that cuts through conventional rules and invests the rider with special license. That Jackie's long illness and too-young death was tragic there is no doubt, but she played such beautiful music that it is our tragedy as well as hers. And yet to those close to the story, there is always another side and more personal feelings. *Hilary and Jackie*, directed by Anand Tucker, is based on a memoir written by Hilary and her brother, Piers du Pre, and it is unusually knowing for a biopic.

It opens with a long section seen from Hilary's point of view. We see the two young sisters playing at the beach and practicing their instruments. Hilary is the talented one, applauded at family gatherings, while Jackie smolders ignored in the corner. But when Hilary is asked to play on a BBC children's concert, she won't go without Jackie. And when Jackie is not very good, they're told by their mother: "If you want to be together, you've got to be as good as each other."

That line of instruction may have been the turning point in Jacqueline du Pre's musical career, inspiring her to practice obsessively until she was not only as good as Hilary, but better. It was her fortune to find teachers who supported her, while Hilary was driven off the stage by pressures mostly engendered by her teacher. Both young women moved freely while playing; Jackie's onstage enthusiasm helped make her famous, but Hilary was ordered to stand still: "It is impossible to produce a proper tone without proper deportment."

She freezes during an audition and abandons any hope of a concert career. Luckily, she finds a man who believes in her: Kiffer Finzi (David Morrissey). Jackie also finds love with "Danny" (James Frain), and they are happy, but there comes a time when Jackie walks off a concert stage and goes to Hilary's farm and demands to be allowed to make love to her husband: "You don't mind, do you, Sis?"

Her arrival, her demand, and her behavior ("bonkers") are all seen from Hilary's point of view. Then the film's next section, seen through Jackie's eyes, details the early warning signs of multiple sclerosis. The film follows through to the unhappy end, showing the destruction of a career, a personality, and a life. It stays tactfully at arm's-length in the way it handles Jacqueline's troubled relationship with Barenboim, and looks mostly through Hilary's eyes as the sad story unfolds.

A film like this lives in its performances. Emily Watson is fiery and strong willed as Jackie; we see the fierce stubbornness of her character in *Breaking the Waves* now wedded to talent and neurosis. The key performance, however, is Rachel Griffiths's, as Hilary, the witness, the person who senses on an almost telepathic level what her sister thinks and feels. Griffiths, not yet well known, is able to convey penetrating intelligence in a look; in a film named *My Son the Fanatic,* she plays a prostitute whose sense of herself and her occupation is almost scarily perceptive.

The film has details that only a family member could supply, such as the few but significant scenes involving the parents: the mother who engenders competition, the father (Charles Dance) who doesn't want his girls living near Soho for fear they will be snatched for the white slave trade. Although the brother, Piers, is coauthor of the book, he has hardly any dialogue in the movie; it is the sisters' story.

The movie makes no attempt to soften the material or make it comforting through the clichés of melodrama; it is instructive to see it side by side with *At First Sight.* One takes true experience and masks it with scenes that could literally be in any romantic melodrama; *Hilary and Jackie* feels as if every scene was newly drawn out of the sharp memories of actual lifetimes.

There is, of course, a lot of music in the film, and the sound track will be good to have; but it is not a film about performances, it is a film about performing: about how physically and emotionally difficult it is to travel from city to city, adored by strangers, far from friends, and find every night the ability to play the cello as well as it can be played. "Would you still love me if I couldn't play?" Jacqueline asks her husband. "You wouldn't be you if you didn't play," he replies, and that is the simple truth made clear by this film. We are what we do.

The Hi-Lo Country ★ ★
R, 114 m., 1999

Billy Crudup (Pete Calder), Woody Harrelson (Big Boy Matson), Patricia Arquette (Mona), Penelope Cruz (Josepha O'Neil), Sam Elliott (Jim Ed Love), Cole Hauser (Little Boy Matson), James Gammon (Hoover Young), Lane Smith (Steve Shaw), Katy Jurado (Meesa), Don Walser (Singer). Directed by Stephen Frears and produced by Barbara De Fina, Martin Scorsese, Eric Fellner, and Tim Bevan. Screenplay by Walon Green.

When poker players want to make the game a little more interesting, they either raise the stakes or declare a wild card. Woody Harrelson has the same effect on a movie. He has a reckless, risky air; he walks into a scene and you can't be sure what he'll do. He plays characters who are a challenge to their friends, let alone their enemies.

In Stephen Frears's *The Hi-Lo Country,* Harrelson has an energy the rest of the film lacks. He plays a variation on that old theme, the Last of the Cowboys, but does it with a modern irony. Watching his character tame unruly horses and strut into bars, I was reminded of a line from a completely different kind of movie, *A New Leaf,* where the aging playboy is told, "You are carrying on in your own lifetime a way of life that was dead before you were born."

Harrelson plays Big Boy Matson, a man's man in the arid Hi-Lo country of New Mexico. He's seen through the eyes of the film's narrator and nominal hero, Pete Calder (Billy Crudup), who returns to the area after serving in World War II and plans to raise cattle. He's advised against it by the rich local rancher Jim Ed Love (Sam Elliott), who says the days of the independent herds are over and gone. "People still drive cattle to railheads," Pete tells him. "Only in the movies," Jim Ed says.

The movie evokes the open space of New Mexico with a bright, dusty grandeur; Oliver Stapleton's camera places the characters in a wide-screen landscape of weathered buildings, lonesome windmills, and distant mountains. There do not seem to be enough people around; the inhabitants of the small town live in each other's pockets, and there are no secrets.

One secret that would be hard to keep is the allure of Mona (Patricia Arquette), a local man's wife who dances on Saturday nights at the tavern as if she might go home with the next man who takes her out on the floor. Mona likes Pete. Indeed, the first time she sees him after the war, at the tavern, she all but propositions him: "Am I keepin' you from something? Or someone? You look good, Pete. Real good." Pete dances with her, and confides in a voice-over, "She was right. I was lookin' for someone. She came up against me like silver foil, all fragrance and warm pressure."

That's not the sort of line a New Mexico cowboy is likely to use in 1946, but there's a kind of distance between the hard-boiled life of the Hi-Lo country and the poetry of the film, which wants the characters steeped in nostalgia and standing for a vanishing way of life. The screenplay is by Walon Green, who also wrote *The Wild Bunch,* which was more hard-boiled about nostalgia.

Mona's problem is, as good as Pete looks to her, Big Boy looks better. That's who she really loves, and who really loves her. But Big Boy is untamed, just like Old Sorrel, the unruly horse he bought from Pete. And Big Boy is incautious in his remarks. Even though Mona is married to a man with friends who have guns, Big Boy makes reckless announcements for the whole bar to hear, like "A good woman's like a good horse—she's got bottom. Mona's gonna make me a partner to go along with Old Sorrel."

The romantic lines grow even more tangled because there is, as there always is in a Western, a Good Woman who steadfastly stands by the hero even while he hangs out with the boys and the bad girls. This is Josepha (Penelope Cruz), a Mexican-American Pete was seeing before the war. She loves Pete, and Pete says he loves her (he lies), and she knows about Mona: "She's a cheap ex-prostitute and a phony."

Mona may be, but she's sincere in her love for Big Boy, and in one way or another that drives most of the plot. The underlying psychology of the film is in the tradition of those Freudian Westerns of the 1950s, in which a man was a man but a gun was sometimes not simply a gun. There's a buried attraction between Big Boy and Pete, who not only sleep with the same woman (and know they do) but engage in roughhouse and camaraderie in a way that suggests that no woman is ever going to be as important to them as a good buddy (or a horse). Jim Ed Love, of course, represents patriarchal authority: He stands for wisdom, experience, and money, and for telling boys to stop that fooling around and grow up.

Stephen Frears is an Irish director who therefore grew up steeped in the lore of the American West (country-and-western music is more popular in Irish pubs than in some states of the union). He's seen a lot of revisionist modern Westerns (especially *Giant*), and he gets the right look and feel for his film. But I think he brings a little too much taste and restraint to it. If he'd turned up the heat under the other characters, they could have matched Big Boy's energy, and the movie could have involved us in the way a good Western can.

Instead, *The Hi-Lo Country* is reserved and even elegiac. It's about itself, rather than about its story. The voice-over narration insists on that: It stands outside and above the story, and elevates it with self-conscious prose. By the end, we could be looking at Greek tragedy. Maybe that's the idea. But Harrelson suggests another way the movie could have gone. With his heedless energy and his sense of complete relaxation before the camera (he glides through scenes as easily as a Cary Grant), he shows how the movie might have been better off staying at ground level and forgetting about the mythological cloud's-eye view.

Note: Two small scenes deserve special mention. One involves the legendary Mexican-American actress Katy Jurado, as a fortune-teller. When the boys visit her, she's asked if "all of us who are here will be alive and prosperous next year." They get their money's worth: "No." The other showstopper is a C&W singer named Don Walser, whose high, sweet voice provides a moment when the movie forgets everything and just listens to him.

Hollow Man ★ ★
R, 114 m., 2000

Elisabeth Shue (Linda McKay), Kevin Bacon (Sebastian Caine), Josh Brolin (Matthew Kensington), Kim Dickens (Sarah Kennedy), Greg Grunberg (Carter Abbey), Joey Slotnick (Frank Chase), Mary Jo Randle (Janice Walton), William Devane (Dr. Kramer). Directed by Paul Verhoeven and produced by Douglas Wick and Alan Marshall. Screenplay by Andrew W. Marlowe.

Hollow Man deserves a niche in the Underachievement Hall of Fame right next to *Jack Frost.* That was the movie, you will recall, where a dead father came back as a snowman, and all he could think of to do was advise his kid about a bully at school. Now we get a scientist who becomes invisible, and all he can become is a mad slasher. Does Paul Verhoeven, who directed *Hollow Man,* have such a low opinion of his audience that he thinks all we want is to see (or not see) the invisible man go berserk?

Although the movie will be compared with the 1933 Claude Rains classic, a better parallel is with *The Fly,* David Cronenberg's 1986 film about a scientist who tests his theories on himself and becomes trapped in the nature of the creature he becomes. That film was charged with curiosity. *Hollow Man* uses the

change simply as a stunt: Scientist becomes invisible, becomes sex fiend, goes berserk, attacks everyone.

Have today's audiences lost all interest in anything except mayhem, or does Hollywood only think they have? *Hollow Man* stars Kevin Bacon, who in *Flatliners* (1990) was one of a group of medical students who dared to see how close they could come to death and still return to tell the story. That was a film with genuine curiosity. Now he plays Dr. Sebastian Caine, a scientist who perfects an invisibility formula, tests it on animals, and then injects it into himself. But then *Hollow Man* can think of nothing more interesting for him to do than spy on his girlfriend and assault his neighbor.

Too bad. Really too bad, because the movie is supported by some of the most intriguing special effects I've seen. Early in the film, a chemical is pumped into the bloodstream of an invisible gorilla, and we see it racing up an artery to the heart and then fanning out into the circulatory system while the body remains invisible: It's like a road map of the veins. Later we see both the gorilla and the scientist as they gradually lose layers of visibility and then slowly regain them; the intermediate stages are like those see-through pages in high school biology textbooks (exactly like them, even to the see-through genitals).

These effects are astonishing. The movie also has fun with the attempts of the characters to make the invisible visible: They spray him with fire-fighting chemicals, turn on the sprinkler system, splash blood around. All very ingenious, but by then the movie is just a slasher film with a science gimmick.

Why, I'm wondering, would the Pentagon spend a fortune on a secret underground lab to invent this process anyway? It's clear that the invisible man can be sensed by motion and heat detectors. That makes him vulnerable to any security system. Yes, he could sneak into secret meetings, but isn't it cheaper to use spies or electronic bugs? Logical quibbles are out of place in this movie, anyway. It ends with a fireball exploding up an elevator shaft until the flames lick the ankles of the fleeing heroine; a superheated jet of hot gas should reasonably be pushed above the visible flames, incinerating her, but not in this movie.

The heroine, by the way, is Dr. Linda

McKay—played by Elisabeth Shue, who won an Oscar nomination for *Leaving Las Vegas*. Here both she and Kevin Bacon do what they can with their roles, which isn't much. The screenplay builds in some jealousy between Dr. Caine, who is McKay's former lover, and Josh Brolin, as her current squeeze. Apparently the invisibility process makes Bacon more animalistic, so that when he spies them together, he goes berserk. Anything will do as the excuse for a twenty-five-minute action sequence in which the monster chases the scientist around the lab like someone who has spent a lot of time studying *The Thing*.

At some kind of mechanical level I suppose the movie works. But it brings nothing to the party except the most simplistic elements. Paul Verhoeven is the director of *RoboCop, Total Recall,* and *Basic Instinct,* films with imagination and wit. *Hollow Man* follows his *Starship Troopers,* in which mankind ventures to the stars in order to squish bugs. Here's a guy who needs an injection of idealism.

Holy Smoke! ★ ★ ½
R, 114 m., 2000

Kate Winslet (Ruth Barron), Harvey Keitel (P. J. Waters), Julie Hamilton (Miriam [Mum]), Tim Robertson (Gilbert [Dad]), Sophie Lee (Yvonne), Dan Wyllie (Robbie), Paul Goddard (Tim), George Mangos (Yani), Pam Grier (Carol). Directed by Jane Campion and produced by Jan Chapman. Screenplay by Anna and Jane Campion.

Holy Smoke! begins as a movie about the deprogramming of a cult member and ends with the deprogramming of the deprogrammer. It's not even a close call. The cult member is Ruth (Kate Winslet), an Australian who has gone to India and allied herself with a guru. And the deprogrammer is Harvey Keitel, summoned by Ruth's parents; he stalks off the plane like his no-nonsense fix-it man in *Pulp Fiction* and then starts falling to pieces. The movie leaves us wondering why the guru didn't become Ruth's follower too.

The film isn't really about cults at all, but about the struggle between men and women, and it's a little surprising, although not boring, when it turns from a mystic travelogue into a feminist parable. The director is Jane Campion (*The Piano*), who wrote the screenplay with her sister Anna. Like so many Australian films (perhaps even a majority), *Holy Smoke!* suggests that everyone in Australia falls somewhere on the spectrum between goofy and eccentric, none more than characters invariably named Mum and Dad. Parents are totally unhinged beneath a facade of middle-class conventionality; their children seem crazy but like many movie mad people are secretly saner than anyone else. Campion's first film, *Sweetie,* was an extreme example; *Holy Smoke!* reins in the strangeness a little, although to be sure there's a scene where Keitel wanders the Outback wearing a dress and lipstick, like a passenger who fell off *Priscilla, Queen of the Desert.*

Ruth, the Winslet character, journeys to India and falls under the sway of a mystic guru. Her parents trick her into returning, and hire P. J. Waters (Keitel) to fly over from America and deprogram her. At this point I was hoping perhaps for something like *Ticket to Heaven* (1981), the powerful Canadian film about the struggle for a cult member's mind. But no. The moment Ruth and P.J. face off against each other, their struggle is not over cult beliefs but about the battle between men and women. And P.J., with his obsolete vocabulary of sexual references, is no match for the strong-willed young woman who overwhelms him mentally, physically, and sexually.

Winslet and Keitel are both interesting in the film, and indeed Winslet seems to be following Keitel's long-standing career plan, which is to go with intriguing screenplays and directors and let stardom take care of itself. That may mean he doesn't get paid $20 million a picture, but $20 million roles, with rare exceptions, are dog's bones anyway—because they've been chewed over and regurgitated by too many timid executives. A smaller picture like this, shot out of the mainstream, has a better chance of being quirky and original.

And quirky it is, even if not successful. Maybe it's the setup that threw me off. Ruth comes onscreen as one kind of person—dreamy, escapist, a volunteer for mind-controlling beliefs—and then turns into an articulate spokeswoman for Jane and Anna Campion's ideas. It's also a little disappointing that the film didn't penetrate more deeply into the Indian scenes, instead of using them mostly just as setup for the feminist payoff. And it's difficult to see how the Ruth at the end of the film could have fallen under the sway of the guru at the beginning. Not many radical feminists seek out male gurus in patriarchal cultures.

The House of Mirth ★ ★ ★ ½
PG, 140 m., 2000

Gillian Anderson (Lily Bart), Eric Stoltz (Lawrence Selden), Dan Aykroyd (Gus Trenor), Eleanor Bron (Mrs. Peniston), Terry Kinney (George Dorset), Anthony LaPaglia (Sim Rosedale), Laura Linney (Bertha Dorset), Jodhi May (Grace Stepney), Elizabeth McGovern (Carrie Fisher). Directed by Terence Davies and produced by Olivia Stewart. Screenplay by Davies, based on the novel by Edith Wharton.

Like the Edith Wharton novel that inspired it, Terence Davies's *The House of Mirth* conceals rage beneath measured surface appearances. This is one of the saddest stories ever told about the traps that society sets for women. Perhaps its characters fear that if they ever really spoke their thoughts, their whole house of cards, or mirth, would tumble down. And so they speak in code, and people's lives are disposed of with trivial asides and brittle wit.

The movie tells the story of Lily Bart (Gillian Anderson), a respectable member of New York society in her late twenties, who keenly feels it is time for her to be married. Is there nothing else she can do? Apparently not; her upbringing has equipped her for no trade except matrimony, and even Lawrence Selden (Eric Stoltz), her best friend, observes dispassionately: "Isn't marriage your vocation? Isn't that what you were brought up for?"

Lily is alone in the world except for a rich maiden aunt, whom she expects to inherit from. She lives in a world of lunches and teas, house parties and opening nights, where she is no longer a fresh face: "I've been about too long. People are getting tired of me." But her life is not unpleasant until a chain of events destroys her with the thoroughness and indifference of a meat grinder.

She goes to tea at Selden's house, and is seen leaving by Mr. Rosedale (Anthony LaPaglia).

He knows only bachelors live in the building. For a woman to go unaccompanied to a man's rooms is not proof she is a tramp, but might as well be. Mr. Rosedale guesses something of Lily's financial situation, and makes her an offer she refuses. So, in a different way, does Gus Trenor (Dan Aykroyd), playing one of those rich men who offer investment advice to desirable women as if they have only benevolence on their minds.

Lily's social world includes George and Bertha Dorset (Terry Kinney and Laura Linney). Bertha flaunts her infidelities, and George is too timid, or well-mannered, to rise to the bait. She all but insists Lily accompany them on their yacht in the Mediterranean, and then gets herself out of a tight spot by a subterfuge against Lily so cruel and unfair it almost rips the fabric of the film. After that, Lily is all but done for, although her descent is gradual.

"Men have minds like moral flypaper," Lily's plain cousin Grace observes. "They will forgive a woman almost anything except the loss of her good name." As Lily finds her credit in society running out, she turns to the resources she has left—or thinks she has—and we see finally that she is defeated. She is prepared for two things in life, to be a rich man's wife, or to do piecework at poverty wages. The vise that closes on her in the final scenes is inexorable.

And yet she could have prevented her fate. There is the matter of a debt to Gus Trenor. We modern viewers are thinking that she need not repay it, that he is a louse and she can save herself, but that is not the sort of thing that would occur to Lily Bart. Nor can she accept a liaison of convenience with Mr. Rosedale. She cannot keep a job as a rich woman's companion because her reputation is wanting. Everyone knows the truth about her—that she is not a bad woman but an admirable one—and yet no one will act on it, because perceptions are more important than reality. What finally defeats Lily Bart is her own lack of imagination, her inability to think outside the envelope she was born within.

Gillian Anderson seems an unexpected choice as Lily. Apparently Terence Davies saw a still of her in *The Mighty* (1998) and made her his first choice. Her success on *The X-Files* might seem to disqualify her, but Anderson's talent has many notes, and I liked the presence she brought to Lily Bart. It would be wrong, I think, to cast the role as a fragile flower; Lily is a strong, healthy, and competent woman who has everything she needs to lead a long and happy life except (1) a husband, or (2) a society that provides for independent women.

Edith Wharton, a sharp and unforgiving chronicler of New York society, knew that, and knew that her own independence was based on her self-employment as a novelist. It is ironic that Virginia Woolf, in *A Room of One's Own*, writes about Jane Austen and other earlier women writers as finding the only profitable and challenging female occupation that could be undertaken in a drawing room, and Wharton was still illustrating that a century later.

The House of Mirth will be compared with Scorsese's *The Age of Innocence,* also based on a Wharton novel. The two directors focus on different sides of Wharton's approach. Wharton as a writer was a contemporary of her great friend Henry James, and also of the rising group of realists like Theodore Dreiser. *The Age of Innocence* is a Jamesian novel, but *The House of Mirth* is more like Dreiser, like an upper-class version of *Sister Carrie,* in which a woman's life is defined by economic determinism. (If Lily had read *Sister Carrie,* indeed, it might have given her some notions about how to survive.) The movie will seem slow to some viewers, unless they are alert to the raging emotions, the cruel unfairness, and the desperation that are masked by the measured and polite words of the characters.

Human Resources ★ ★ ★

NO MPAA RATING, 100 m., 2000

Jalil Lespert (Frank), Jean-Claude Vallod (Father), Chantal Barre (Mother), Veronique de Pandelaere (Sylvie), Michel Begnez (Olivier), Lucien Longueville (Chief Executive), Danielle Melador (Mrs. Arnoux), Pascal Semard (Head of Human Resources). Directed by Laurent Cantet and produced by Caroline Benjo and Carole Scotta. Screenplay by Cantet and Gilles Marchand.

"This is my machine," the father tells his son. He explains its workings. It rotates like this, he says, and then he adds a part, he pushes a lever,

and the machine performs a function. "I can do 700 an hour," he says with quiet satisfaction. He has been doing it for thirty years. His body is permanently stooped as if bowing to the machine. He seems hypnotized by continuity: As long as he stays here, doing this, he is alive and serves a function.

His son has broken out of the family's class. He has gone to college, and now has returned to their small French town as a trainee in the personnel division. The night before his first job interview, his father fearfully briefs him to respect his boss and to play down his own opinion. The father's spirit has long since been broken down into timid subservience.

Human Resources, written and directed by Laurent Cantet, follows the son during his first weeks on the job, gradually revealing itself as an angry and unforgiving look at the way factories can treat employees as machines, and sometimes scrap them. More class-conscious than an American film would be, it shows the son torn between tempting management opportunities and his sense of fairness. He begins to realize that "human resources" is not a benevolent term, but belongs on the same list with "raw materials resources." Humans are simply an element in a production flow chart.

Management is thinking of scaling back. Frank (Jalil Lespert), the son, is involved in the discussions, and suggests a questionnaire that might help employees feel they have input. Mrs. Arnoux (Danielle Melador), the Communist shop steward, is having none of it. She chairs an angry meeting, but her very anger discredits her, and her warnings aren't heeded. Then Frank, poking around on his boss's computer, discovers his questionnaire has been used as a rationale for layoffs, and his dad will be one of those to be fired.

The film is not really driven by specific plot elements. It's not so much about what management does and how the workers fight back as it is about feelings. Consider, for example, that the father (Jean-Claude Vallod) will not strike even after he learns he is going to be fired. He doggedly marches back to his machine like an animal that has learned only one trick. On his days off, he works on another machine in his garage—he seems to have no identity without a machine to give his life a symbiotic partner.

275

In the town, Frank finds a barrier growing between himself and old friends. There's a shoving match in a bar. He is seen as a sellout. At the same time, he sees through the efforts of his bosses to recruit him to their view. Most of those being fired would have qualified for retirement in a few years, but now won't. That's a particularly vile and common misuse of "human resources," not just in France. When Frank's dad is offered a pension, however, Frank sees the irony: The factory has so broken his father than the old man cannot live without serving his machine. A pension has nothing to do with it.

And yet—Frank doesn't feel merely pity for his father. He also feels shame. Moving up on the class ladder has separated him from his father's tunnel vision, and to his educated eyes, the old man seems pathetic. He is a man almost robbed of speech, of imagination, and when he cries, his wife finds that a wonder rather than a shame.

American films are hardly ever about work, especially hard work, factory work. The most common employment areas in American movies are probably law enforcement, crime, medicine, the law, prostitution, and bartending. The movies have no curiosity about people who get up every day and go out to work hard and earn a living. *Human Resources* is a valuable, heartbreaking film about the way those resources are plugged into a system, drained of their usefulness, and discarded.

Human Traffic ★ ★

R, 84 m., 2000

John Simm (Jip), Lorraine Pilkington (LuLu), Shaun Parkes (Koop), Nicola Reynolds (Nina), Danny Dyer (Moff), Dean Davies (Lee). Directed by Justin Kerrigan and produced by Allan Niblo and Emer McCourt. Screenplay by Kerrigan.

"Act like an adult. Be fake."

So says one of the feckless heroes of *Human Traffic*, a sad comedy about druggies in Wales. This movie is about how he and his friends are already acting like adults. They're right that many adults are fakes, but some adults at least know when they're faking it. These kids are clueless.

They know how to take drugs and feel good.

That doesn't require cleverness. When they don't take drugs they don't feel good, partly because of withdrawal, partly because they lack any other avenue to happiness. They possess, for the time being, youth. It is their only capital, and when it is spent, they will lead the rest of their lives empty-handed. They're sheep marching into the slaughter of middle age.

The film takes place in Cardiff, and is mostly about five friends who have jobs of stultifying boredom. They live for the weekends, when they can go out to rave clubs, use ecstasy, heroin, and whatever else they can get their hands on, and pretend for forty-eight hours that they are free. They have high spirits, and their speech possesses the style and wit that can still be heard in those pockets of verbal invention (Ireland is another) where conversation is an art form.

They are, in fact, likable. That's why their comedy is so sad. There must, we think, be something more for them than this dead-end lifestyle. The movie remembers how at a certain age, hanging out with your friends, feeling solidarity against the nine-to-five world, creates a fierce inner joy. They laugh at each other's self-destructiveness. It is funny to get wasted, to almost overdose, to do reckless things, to live dangerously, to flirt with crime and drugs. Why is it funny? Because they're getting away with it. The odds don't apply to them. They're immune. Fate has said they can put unknown substances into their systems and survive. Fate, of course, is a practical joker with a nasty streak, but tell them that.

The director of the film, Justin Kerrigan, is twenty-five. He sees his story from the inside. It's based on his friends. There is no perspective, no angle: He sympathizes with his characters. But he's already escaped their fate. He isn't working in a fast-food outlet at minimum wage. He's a movie director.

I was reminded of Mark Borchardt, the subject of the tragicomic documentary *American Movie*, who dropped out at thirteen or fourteen and started drinking with his friends in the basements of their houses. "I was always watching them, always fascinated by them," he remembers, and today, at thirty-four, while he still plays the same role, he does it on the *Letterman* show, while his friends are still in the basement, or the ground.

Human Traffic is narrated as a pseudo-documentary; the characters take us on a tour of their world, but the real narrator is the director, who could not make the film if he lived as his heroes do. The characters have names, and there is a plot—a plot and a half, in fact. I could name them (all right: Jip, Lulu, Koop, Nina, and Moff). I could describe the plot. But every weekend has its own plot, and every plot has its own unhappy ending, which is known as Monday morning.

Stories like this can transcend. *Trainspotting* had a certain charm. *SLC Punk* had more wit and fewer drugs. *Kicking and Screaming* was enlightening because it showed that kids of about the same age, given a chance at a decent education, were more interesting and better at entertaining themselves. For the characters in *Human Traffic*, these weekends are as good as it's going to get.

"There is definitely more to their relationships than just going out, taking drugs, and having a good time," says Nicola Reynolds, an actress in the film. "They are strong, strong friendships. The more you go through things together, the more you bond those relationships." Uh-huh. You know the difference between a real friend and a party friend? You have a flat tire. The real friend goes outside in the rain and helps you change it. The party friend says, "Bummer," and buys you a drink.

The Hurricane ★ ★ ★ ½
R, 125 m., 2000

Denzel Washington (Rubin Carter), Vicellous Reon Shannon (Lesera Martin), Deborah Kara Unger (Lisa Peters), Liev Schreiber (Sam Chaiton), John Hannah (Terry Swinton), Dan Hedaya (Della Pesca), Debbie Morgan (Mae Thelma), Clancy Brown (Lieutenant Jimmy Williams), David Paymer (Myron Beldock), Harris Yulin (Leon Friedman), Rod Steiger (Judge Sarokin), Garland Whitt (John Artis). Directed by Norman Jewison and produced by Armyan Bernstein, John Ketcham, and Jewison. Screenplay by Bernstein and Dan Gordon, based on *The 16th Round* by Rubin "Hurricane" Carter and *Lazarus and the Hurricane* by Sam Chaiton and Terry Swinton.

The key moment in *The Hurricane*, which tells the story of a boxer framed for murder, takes place not in a prison cell but at a used-book sale in Toronto. A fifteen-year-old boy named Lesera spends twenty-five cents to buy his first book, the autobiography of the boxer Rubin "Hurricane" Carter. As he reads it, he becomes determined to meet the boxer and support his fight for freedom, and that decision leads to redemption.

The case and cause of Hurricane Carter are well known; Bob Dylan wrote a song named "The Hurricane," and I remember Nelson Algren's house sale when the Chicago novelist moved to New Jersey to write a book about Carter. Movie stars and political candidates made the pilgrimage to Carter's prison, but his appeals were rejected and finally his case seemed hopeless.

This film tells his story—the story of a gifted boxer (Denzel Washington) who was framed for three murders in Patterson, New Jersey, and lost nineteen years of his life because of racism, corruption, and—perhaps most wounding—indifference. In the film, the teenage boy (Vicellous Reon Shannon), who is from New Jersey, enlists his Canadian foster family to help Carter, and they find new evidence for his defense attorneys that eventually leads to his release. The villain is a cop named Pesca (Dan Hedaya), who essentially makes it his lifelong business to harm Carter.

Norman Jewison's film starts slowly, with Carter's early years and his run-ins with Pesca. In my notes I wrote: "If this is going to be the story of a persecuting cop, we need to know him as more than simply the instrument of evil"—as a human being rather than a plot convenience. We never do. Pesca from beginning to end is there simply to cause trouble for Carter. Fortunately, *The Hurricane* gathers force in scenes where Carter refuses to wear prison clothing, and learns to separate himself mentally from his condition. Then young Lesera enters the picture, and two people who might seem to be without hope find it from one another.

This is one of Denzel Washington's great performances, on a par with his work in *Malcolm X*. I wonder if *The Hurricane* is not Jewison's indirect response to an earlier controversy. Jewison was preparing *Malcolm X* with Washington when Spike Lee argued that a white man should not direct that film. Jewison stepped aside, Lee made a powerful film with

Washington—and now Jewison has made another. Washington as Hurricane Carter is spare, focused, filled with anger and pride. There is enormous force when he tells his teenage visitor and his friends, "Do not write me. Do not visit me. Find it in your hearts to not weaken me with your love."

But the Canadians don't obey. They move near to Trenton State Prison, they meet with his lead defense attorneys (David Paymer and Harris Yulin), they become amateur sleuths who help take the case to the New Jersey Supreme Court in a do-or-die strategy. It always remains a little unclear, however, just exactly who the Canadians are, or what their relationship is. They're played by Deborah Kara Unger, Liev Schreiber, and John Hannah, they share a household, they provide a home for Lesera, a poor African-American kid from a troubled background, and we wonder: Are they a political group? An unconventional sexual arrangement?

I learn from an article by Selwyn Raab, who covered the case for the *New York Times,* that they were in fact a commune. Raab's article, which appeared the day before the film's New York opening, finds many faults with the facts in *The Hurricane.* He says Carter's defense attorneys deserve much more credit than the Canadians. That Carter was not framed by one cop with a vendetta, but victimized by the entire system. That Carter's codefendant, John Artis (Garland Whitt), was a more considerable person than he seems in the film. That events involving the crime and the evidence have been fictionalized in the film. That Carter later married the Unger character, then divorced her. That Lesera broke with the commune when it tried for too much control of his life.

News travels fast. Several people have told me dubiously that they heard the movie was "fictionalized." Well, of course it was. Those who seek the truth about a man from the film of his life might as well seek it from his loving grandmother. Most biopics, like most grandmothers, see the good in a man and demonize his enemies. They pass silently over his imprudent romances. In dramatizing his victories, they simplify them. And they provide the best roles to the most interesting characters. If they didn't, we wouldn't pay to see them.

The Hurricane is not a documentary but a parable, in which two lives are saved by the power of the written word. We see Carter's concern early in the film that the manuscript of his book may be taken from his cell (it is protected by one of several guards who develop respect for him). We see how his own reading strengthens him; his inspirations include Malcolm X. And we see how his book, which he hoped would win his freedom, does so—not because of its initial sales, readers, and reviews, but because one kid with a quarter is attracted to Hurricane's photo on the cover. And then the book wins Lesera's freedom too.

This is strong stuff, and I was amazed, after feeling some impatience in the earlier reaches of the film, to find myself so deeply absorbed in its second and third acts, until at the end I was blinking at tears. What affects me emotionally at the movies is never sadness, but goodness. I am not a weeper, and have only really lost it at one film *(Do the Right Thing),* but when I get a knot in my throat it is not because Hurricane Carter is framed, or loses two decades in prison, but that he continues to hope, and that his suffering is the cause for Lesera's redemption.

That is the parable Norman Jewison has told, aiming for it with a sure storyteller's art and instinct. The experts will always tell you how a movie got its facts wrong (Walter Cronkite is no doubt correct that Oliver Stone's *JFK* is a fable). But can they tell you how they would have made the movie better? Would *The Hurricane* have been stronger as the story of two selfless lawyers doing pro bono work for years? And a complex network of legal injustice? And a freed prisoner and a kid disillusioned with a commune? Maybe. Probably not.

I

An Ideal Husband ★ ★ ★
PG-13, 97 m., 1999

Cate Blanchett (Gertrude Chiltern), Minnie Driver (Mabel Chiltern), Rupert Everett (Lord Goring), Julianne Moore (Mrs. Cheveley), Jeremy Northam (Sir Robert Chiltern), John Wood (Lord Caversham), Lindsay Duncan (Lady Markby), Peter Vaughan (Phipps). Directed by Oliver Parker and produced by Barnaby Thompson, Uri Fruchtmann, and Bruce Davey. Screenplay by Parker, based on the play by Oscar Wilde.

A play like Oscar Wilde's *An Ideal Husband* works because it takes place in a society bound by inflexible rules and social inhibitions. Here is a story in which a marriage, a romance, a fortune, and government policy all rest on such foundations as a man's obligation to act like a gentleman. (Of course, he doesn't need to *be* a gentleman—that's where the story comes in.)

In the play, an incriminating letter is sent in the belief that it will never be revealed. Suspicions are aroused, but they don't inspire questions—because they involve matters it would be unseemly to ask a gentleman about. As long as everyone plays by the rules in public, they can be broken in private. But then an entire society is threatened by the willingness of one character to act as she should not.

The play tells the story of Sir Robert Chiltern (Jeremy Northam), a rising parliamentary star who has been a paragon of honesty all of his career—except right at the first, when he shopped some secret government information to a baron, who paid him handsomely. Sir Robert is adored by his wife (Cate Blanchett), whose high standards would not permit her to be married to a cheat and liar. An old acquaintance of theirs reappears in London: Mrs. Cheveley (Julianne Moore), who was once married to the baron and possesses the letter in which Chiltern leaked the information. She blackmails him. Either he will change his position on an upcoming piece of legislation, thus protecting her investments, or she will reveal him as a fraud.

It is even more complicated than that. Chiltern's best friend is Lord Goring (Rupert Everett), a rich and idle bachelor. Chiltern begs him to subtly prepare Lady Chiltern for bad news: to help her understand, in a general way, how a chap could do a bad thing and then lead a spotless life ever since. In the course of the plot machinations, romance appears: Goring falls in love with Chiltern's younger sister Mabel (Minnie Driver), and Mrs. Cheveley decides that Goring would be a splendid choice for her own third husband.

Would a man marry a woman he did not love simply to protect a friend or keep a confidence? Today that would be unlikely, but for the original audiences of *An Ideal Husband* it was plausible enough to keep the entire plot suspended over an abyss of misunderstandings.

In another sense, of course, neither Wilde nor his audience cared a fig about the letter, the bribe, the blackmail, or the romance. They were all just cogs in a complicated windup mechanism to keep several charming people on stage for three hours, and provide them with an excuse for saying witty things (this is the play where Goring observes, "To love oneself is the beginning of a lifelong romance"). I do not know if the British upper classes of a century ago were actually capable of standing handsomely in drawing rooms while trading elegant epigrams, and I suspect many of them were not, but I don't care—just so they do it on the stage.

An Ideal Husband works because Wilde created an expert mechanism (kind of slow-motion, serious screwball comedy) for manipulating the plot and characters. But of course the actors are indispensable: They have to make characters plausible while negotiating a plot of pure contrivance, and they have to be charming even while lying, scheming, and blackmailing. The two leading men, Northam and Everett, are smooth and charming—Northam's Sir Robert more realistic and serious about his life, Everett's Lord Goring like a Wildean visitor from outside the plot, who sees everything clearly, is amused, and hardly believes it when Mrs. Cheveley almost snares him in her net.

Women in the plays of a century ago were technically powerless; they lived through their husbands, and spent much of their time speculating on what the men were really up to or waiting for news. At the same time, the plays were really about them, and everything the men did was designed to win their love, admiration, or forgiveness. It is important that we believe Lady Chiltern (Blanchett) loves her husband but loves his upright character even more, and will leave him if she discovers his sins. And important to believe that Mabel (Driver), Sir Robert's sister, could fall in love with Goring in an instant. Well, of course she could. Modern critics who complain they fall in love too suddenly have forgotten that she would have spent months or years making up her mind about every eligible man in her universe.

As we leave the twentieth century there seems to be a powerful nostalgia for the British ninetenth. Every year brings three or four of these literate comedies (or melodramas) set in London. Life was more exciting when you were the entertainment in your own living room and didn't have to watch it on TV.

Idle Hands ★ ★ ½
R, 92 m., 1999

Devon Sawa (Anton), Seth Green (Mick), Elden Henson (Pnub), Jessica Alba (Molly), Christopher Hart (The Hand), Vivica A. Fox (Debi), Jack Noseworthy (Randy), Katie Wright (Tanya). Directed by Rodman Flender and produced by Suzanne Todd, Jennifer Todd, Andrew Licht, and Jeffrey A. Mueller. Screenplay by Terri Hughes and Ron Milbauer.

Idle Hands samples other teen horror movies like a video DJ with a tape deck, exhibiting high spirits and a crazed comic energy. It doesn't quite work, but it goes down swinging—with a disembodied hand. The hand, which has a mind of its own, is chopped off the arm of a teenage kid who is the victim of some kind of weird Halloween demonic possession.

The film involves the adventures of Anton (Devon Sawa), a pothead so addled he doesn't notice for a few days that his parents are dead—the victims of an evil power that writes, "I'm under the bed," on the ceiling of their bedroom, and is. Anton's chief occupations are getting high and hanging out with his friends Mick and Pnub, who live in a nearby basement. The three of them are dropouts

from all possible societies, and their world is like a cross between *SLC Punk* and *Evil Dead 2*. (If neither one of those titles rings a bell, the movie undoubtedly won't, either.)

The possessed killer hand is, of course, lifted from *Evil Dead 2*, but it wasn't original there, and has its origins in such films as *The Hand* and *The Beast with Five Fingers*. Rodman Flender, who directed this film, has fun with it in a scene where Anton is on a date with the babe of his dreams, Molly (Jessica Alba), and tries to fight down the hand as it tries to throttle her. Finally, he ties it to the bed. Molly, who is not very observant, translates this as kinky.

Anton finally rids himself of the hand (it's chopped off in the kitchen, with the wound cauterized by an iron). His pals Mick (Seth Green) and Pnub (Elden Henson, from *The Mighty*) have worse luck. Mick is taken out by a beer bottle, which remains embedded in his skull for the rest of the movie. Pnub loses his head altogether, and carries it in his hands until Anton figures out how to mount it on his shoulders using a barbecue fork. Don't ask. Both of them continue through the entire film as the living dead.

Vivica A. Fox plays the demonbuster, tracking down alarming manifestations and delivering the single best line of dialogue: "Well, my work here is done. Time for the ritualistic sex." The plot involves her pursuit only absentmindedly, however, since most of the big scenes involve comic gore: disembodied eyeballs, unusual biological processes, body parts discovered in unexpected ways, etc. There's no really convincing comic inspiration behind the f/x scenes, however, and although we might laugh at some of the goofiness, a movie like this works best when the effects are a means, not an end.

The movie has energy and is probably going to attract a young audience, especially on video, since the R rating will keep away some viewers in its target audience, which is junior high school boys. After the Colorado tragedy, some commentators have wondered if movies like this aren't partly responsible. I don't think we have to worry about *Idle Hands*. Kids understand this kind of macabre comedy, which is in the ancient horror spoof tradition, and don't take it seriously; any viewer capable of being influenced by such silly gags would have to be deeply disturbed already. The only thing this movie is likely to inspire a kid to do is study *Fangoria* magazine to find out how the special effects were achieved.

I Dreamed of Africa ★ ★
PG-13, 112 m., 2000

Kim Basinger (Kuki Gallmann), Vincent Perez (Paolo Gallmann), Liam Aiken (Emanuele [Seven]), Garrett Strommen (Emanuele [Seventeen]), Eva Marie Saint (Franca), Daniel Craig (Declan Fielding), Lance Reddick (Simon), Connie Chiume (Wanjiku). Directed by Hugh Hudson and produced by Stanley R. Jaffe and Allyn Stewart. Screenplay by Paula Milne and Susan Shilliday, based on the book by Kuki Gallmann.

It's strange to see *I Dreamed of Africa* at a time when the papers are filled with stories of white farmers being murdered in Zimbabwe. Here is the story of an Italian couple who move to the highlands of Kenya in 1972, buy a ranch near the Great Rift Valley, and lead lives in which the Africans drift about in the background, vaguely, like unpaid extras. Is it really as simple as that? The realities of contemporary Africa are simply not dealt with.

A shame, since Kuki Gallmann is a real woman and still lives on Ol Ari Nyiro, a 100,000-acre ranch in Kenya that she has made into a showcase farm and a wildlife conservancy. I know this because of her Web page (www.gallmannkenya.org); the movie never makes it very clear how the Gallmanns support themselves—it's not by working, apparently. Paolo is away for days at a time, hunting and fishing with his friends, and Kuki doesn't seem deeply engaged with the land, either (her attempt to create a dirt dam begins when she inadvertently pulls down a barn, and ends with the tractor stuck in the mud).

The real Kuki Gallmann must have arrived at an accommodation with Africa and Africans, and with the Kenyan government. The Kuki in the movie has a few brief conversations in Swahili with her farm foreman and laborers, but devotes most of her attention to the landscape, which is indeed breathtaking (the film was shot on the ranch and in South African game preserves). The only social commentary we get, repeated three times, is, "Things have a different rhythm here."

Kuki is played by Kim Basinger, who is ready to do more than the screenplay allows. She is convincing throughout, especially in a scene where trouble strikes her son, Emanuele (Garrett Strommen)—her panic is real, but so is her competence as she tries to deal with the emergency. Her frustration with her husband, Paolo (Vincent Perez), is also real, but mundane (frustrated at his extended hunting trips and general irresponsibility, she throws a handful of pasta at him).

Her life is interrupted from time to time by visits from her mother (Eva Marie Saint), who begs her to return to Italy, but no, she belongs to the land, learns from experience, and tries to bring good out of the tragedies in her life by becoming a conservationist and a leader in the fight against poaching.

All admirable. But Hugh Hudson's film plays curiously like a friendly documentary of her life, especially with the voice-over narration that sounds like it belongs in an idealistic travelogue. There is a lack of drama and telling detail. When events happen, they seem more like set pieces than part of the flow. Consider the big storm that blows up, toppling the windmill and blowing the thatch from the ranch house roof. It strikes, it is loud and fierce, and then it is over, and after one more shot, it is forgotten. An entry in a diary, growing from nothing, leading to nothing, but occupying screen time. As is the scene where Kuki, Paolo, and her mother drive a Range Rover down a rough road and it gets stuck in the mud (that happens to her a lot). What to do? They get out and walk home. The film doesn't even show them arriving there.

Watching *I Dreamed of Africa,* I was reminded that one often meets people who have led fascinating lives, but only rarely people who can tell fascinating stories. The events don't make the story; the storytelling does. Russell Baker or Frank McCourt can make human sagas out of everyday memories. Generals who have led thousands into battle can write memoirs of stultifying dullness. Kuki Gallmann has led a fascinating life, yes, but either she's not remembering the whole truth, or she should have made up more. The film

281

doesn't sing with urgency and excitement, and we attend it in the same way we listen politely to the stories of a hostess who must have really been something in her day.

In Dreams ★ ½
R, 100 m., 1999

Annette Bening (Claire Cooper), Robert Downey Jr. (Vivian), Aidan Quinn (Paul Cooper), Stephen Rea (Dr. Silverman), Paul Guilfoyle (Detective Jack Kay), Dennis Boutsikaris (Dr. Stevens), Katie Sagona (Rebecca Cooper), Krystal Benn (Ruby). Directed by Neil Jordan and produced by Stephen Woolley and Redmond Morris. Screenplay by Bruce Robinson and Jordan, based on the novel *Doll's Eyes,* by Bari Wood.

In Dreams is the silliest thriller in many a moon, and the only one in which the heroine is endangered by apples. She also survives three falls from very high places (two into a lake, one onto apples), escapes from a hospital and a madhouse, has the most clever dog since Lassie, and causes a traffic pileup involving a truck and a dozen cars. With that much plot, does this movie really need the drowned ghost town, the husband's affair with an Australian woman, the flashbacks to the dominatrix mom, and the garbage disposal that spews apple juice?

All of this goofiness is delivered with style and care by a first-rate team; this is a well-made bad movie. The heroine, named Claire, is portrayed by Annette Bening as a woman in torment. She begins to dream of horrible things, and realizes an evil killer is causing her nightmares ("He's inside my head!"). Her husband (Aidan Quinn) goes to the cops with her premonitions, but gets the brush-off. A frequent dream involves harm to a child; it turns out to be her own.

Eventually she falls into the hands of a psychiatrist (Stephen Rea) who is wise, kindly, and patient, and locks her up in two cruel institutions. One has a padded cell and is guarded by a Nurse Ratchet clone. The other looks like the original snake pit crossed with a dorm at summer camp. The psychiatrist isn't even the villain.

In Dreams is the kind of movie where children's nursery rhymes and sayings are underscored like evil omens. "Mirror, mirror, on the wall . . ." we hear, while the sound track vibrates with menace, and a mother, a daughter, and their dog walk on the banks of a reservoir that was, we learn, created in 1965 by flooding a village that still lurks beneath the waters, a ghost town. Scuba divers explore it, and we see that the napkin dispensers are still on the counters in the diner, while holy statues float around the church.

Was the villain (Robert Downey Jr.) drowned in this town? It's not that simple. The explanation of this movie contains more puzzles than the plot itself. Let's say we grant the premise that the villain can indeed project his dreams into the mind of poor Claire. In addition to being clairvoyant, is he also telekinetic? Can he make children's swings move on their own, and turn on boom boxes at a distance, and project words onto a computer screen, and control garbage disposals?

And does he control the family dog, which has an uncanny ability to find its masters anywhere, anytime? (This is such a clever dog it should know better than to lure Claire into the middle of that highway—unless, of course, its dreams are also under remote control.) And what does the buried village have to do with anything? And although the killer was abused as a child by his mother, whose high heels supply a central image, what does that have to do with the nursery rhyme about how "My father was a dollar"?

I dunno. The movie was directed by Neil Jordan, who has done a whole lot better (*Mona Lisa, The Crying Game, Interview With the Vampire*). Here he navigates uncertainly through a script that is far too large for its container. Whole subplots could have been dumped; why even bother with the other woman in Australia? Although the drowned village supplies some vivid images, wasn't it a huge expense just for some atmosphere? And how many viewers will be able to follow the time-shifted parallels as Claire's escape from a hospital is intercut with the killer's?

In *my* dreams, I'm picturing Tony Lawson's first day on the job. He was the editor of this picture. His survey of the unassembled footage must have been a real horror story.

Inside/Out ★ ★ ½
NO MPAA RATING, 115 m., 1999

Berangere Allaux (Monica), Tom Gilroy (Priest), Stefania Rocca (Organist), Frederic Pierrot (Jean), Steven Watkin (Roger). Directed by Rob Tregenza and produced by Gill Holland. Screenplay by Tregenza.

It happens that within two days I've seen a 52-minute film that seemed bursting with content, and now a 115-minute film that inspires admiration, but also restlessness. The shorter film *(See the Sea)*, played just long enough to deliver its horrifying punch line. The longer one *(Inside/Out)* has no punch line, and indeed not much of a plot; it's about the arid passage of time in a mental hospital. A director approaching such a subject can either suggest the emptiness and ennui, or attempt to reproduce it. Rob Tregenza, who wrote, directed, photographed, and edited *Inside/Out,* chooses the second approach.

His film takes place in the late 1950s, in a cold and lifeless autumn or early spring, in a mental hospital of whitewashed walls and barren interiors. The institution isn't on the cutting edge of treatment; it's more like a holding cell for patients, a waiting room before death. The patients wander the grounds, sometimes try to run away, line up for their pills, are angry or morose, mill about aimlessly at a dance, attend religious services, and stand stock-still as if lost in thought.

Their actions are watched by Tregenza on the Cinemascope screen, the widest gauge available. The film covers an enormous expanse of screen, and is often photographed in long shots, so that the characters seem isolated within vast, empty spaces. In one sequence two men shoot some baskets (one is completely uninvolved), and in the background there is a man dressed in black who simply stands, swaying slightly, the whole time.

One point of the wide screen may be to emphasize how little contact these people have with one another. They're looked over by nuns (Episcopalian, I gather) who give them their pills, issue instructions ("No sitting on the tables!"), and enforce standards (a female character undresses and tries to snuggle up to another inmate, only to be yanked away by a nun hissing, "You little whore!"). The lives of the people on the screen—patients and caretakers—seem bereft of happiness.

Dialogue is heard only in snatches. There are no word-driven relationships. Visuals make the point. The institution's priest works in a plain little chapel that reminded me of the church in Bergman's *Winter Light,* in the feeling that it was a place little frequented by God.

Some of the scenes have the same kind of deadpan visual punning we find, in another tone, in the films of Jacques Tati. Two men struggle on a train track, and we hear the whistle and roar of the approaching train—which arrives, passes, and disappears, invisibly. In an opening shot, two patients run across the crest of a hill, we hear dogs barking, and they reappear chased by the dogs—and by figures on horseback. It is a hunt.

Tregenza's handling of a "party" scene makes full use of his wide-screen camera. In a barren, low-ceilinged room, too big for the people in it, volunteers arrange clusters of balloons. Crepe paper hangs thinly from beams. An inept rock band sets up. Patients mill about endlessly (one darts across screen and up some stairs). The band starts playing and is accompanied by a patient who rhythmically bangs a folding chair open and closed. Finally, incongruously, a harpist begins to play, and the camera circles the room, which is stilled by the quiet music.

I admired *Inside/Out* in its moments, in individual scenes. I would recommend the party scene to film students, who could learn from it. But I was kept outside the film by the distanced, closed-off characters. That's the idea, I know—but Tregenza succeeds all too well with it. Seeing the movie is like paying dues to his vision. We are witnesses that he accomplished what he set out to do. He does it in his own time and space. He's as little interested in us as his characters would be. We're like guests on visiting day, sitting restlessly on chairs along the side of the room. If anyone asked us, we'd say we were having a good time. But we're thinking restlessly of how long we have to stay, and where we can go next.

The Insider ★ ★ ★ ½

R, 148 m., 1999

Al Pacino (Lowell Bergman), Russell Crowe (Jeffrey Wigand), Christopher Plummer (Mike Wallace), Diane Venora (Liane Wigand), Philip Baker Hall (Don Hewitt), Lindsay Crouse (Sharon Tiller), Debi Mazar (Debbie De Luca), Stephen Tobolowsky (Eric Kluster), Gina Gershon (Helen Caperelli). Directed by Michael Mann and produced by Mann and Pieter Jan Brugge. Screenplay by Eric Roth and Mann, based on the *Vanity Fair* article "The Man Who Knew Too Much" by Marie Brenner.

Michael Mann's *The Insider* makes a thriller and exposé out of how big tobacco's long-running tissue of lies was finally exposed by investigative journalism. At its center stands Lowell Bergman, a producer for *60 Minutes*, the CBS News program where a former tobacco scientist named Jeffrey Wigand spilled the beans. First Bergman coaxes Wigand to talk. Then he works with reporter Mike Wallace to get the story. Then he battles with CBS executives who are afraid to run it—because a lawsuit could destroy the network. He's a modern investigative hero, Woodward and Bernstein rolled into one.

Or so the film tells it. The film is accurate in its broad strokes. Wigand did indeed reveal secrets from the Brown and Williamson laboratories that eventually led to a $246 billion settlement of suits brought against the tobacco industry by all fifty states. *60 Minutes* did eventually air the story, after delays and soul-searching. And reporting by the *Wall Street Journal* was instrumental in easing the network's decision to air the piece.

But there are ways in which the film is misleading, according to a helpful article in *Brill's Content*. Mike Wallace was more of a fighter, less Bergman's puppet. *60 Minutes* producer Don Hewitt didn't willingly cave in to corporate pressure, but was powerless. The *Wall Street Journal's* coverage was not manipulated by Bergman, but was independent (and won a Pulitzer Prize). Bergman didn't mastermind a key Mississippi lawsuit, or leak a crucial deposition. And the tobacco industry did not necessarily make death threats against Wigand

(his former wife believes he put a bullet in his mailbox himself).

Do these objections invalidate the message of the film? Not at all. And they have no effect on its power to absorb, entertain, and anger. They go with the territory in a docudrama like this, in which characters and narrative are manipulated to make the story stronger. The *Brill's Content* piece, useful as it is, makes a fundamental mistake: It thinks that Lowell Bergman is the hero of *The Insider* because he fed his version of events to Mann and his cowriter, Eric Roth. In fact, Bergman is the hero because he is played by Al Pacino, the star of the film, and thus must be the hero. A movie like this demands only one protagonist. If Pacino had played Mike Wallace instead, then Wallace would have been the hero.

The decision to center on a producer, to go behind the scenes, is a good one, because it allows the story to stand outside Wallace and Hewitt and consider larger questions than tobacco. The movie switches horses in midstream, moving from the story of a tobacco cover-up to a crisis in journalistic ethics. Did CBS oppose the story only because it feared a lawsuit, or were other factors involved, such as the desire of executives to protect the price of their stock as CBS was groomed for sale to Westinghouse?

The movie is constructed like a jigsaw puzzle in which various pieces keep disappearing from the table. It begins when Bergman hires Jeffrey Wigand (Russell Crowe) as a consultant on another tobacco story. He learns that Wigand possesses information from the tobacco industry not only proving that nicotine is addictive (which the presidents of seven cigarette companies had denied under oath before Congress), but that additives were used to make it more addictive—and one of the additives was a known carcinogen! Wigand has signed a confidentiality agreement with B&W, and Bergman somehow has to get around that promise if the truth is going to be revealed.

Mann is able to build suspense while suggesting what a long, slow, frustrating process investigative journalism can be. Wigand dances toward a disclosure, then away. Bergman works behind the scenes to manipulate lawsuits and the coverage of the *Wall Street Journal* (these scenes are mostly fictional, we learn). He hopes to leak parts of the story in truncated form so that he's free to expose its full glory. Mike Wallace (Christopher Plummer) is beside him all the way, finally zeroing in on Wigand in one of those interviews where shocking statements are given little pools of silence to glisten in. Then a corporate lawyer (Gina Gershon) explains the law to the *60 Minutes* gang: The more truthful Wigand's statements, the more damaging in a lawsuit. *60 Minutes* boss Don Hewitt (Philip Baker Hall) sides with the network, and Bergman is blindsided when Wallace at first sides with Hewitt.

It's then that Bergman goes to work behind the scenes, leaking information and making calls to competitors to blast the story loose from legal constraints. And these are the scenes that owe the most to Hollywood invention; the chronology is manipulated, and actions of key players get confused. There is an underlying truth, however: *60 Minutes* did eventually find a way to air its original story, through the device of reporting about how it couldn't—a report that had the effect of breaking the logjam.

Hewitt, one of the patron saints of investigative journalism, is portrayed as too much of a corporate lackey, but Wallace's image emerges intact in a wonderful scene where Hewitt says the whole matter will blow over in fifteen minutes, and Wallace says, "No, that's fame. You get fifteen minutes of fame. Infamy lasts a little longer."

Pacino's performance underlies everything. He makes Bergman hoarse, overworked, stubborn, and a master of psychological manipulation who inexorably draws Wigand toward the moment of truth. Pacino can be flashy, mannered, over the top, in roles that call for it; this role calls for a dogged crusader, and he supplies a character who is always convincing.

There is, I admit, a contradiction in a film about journalism that itself manipulates the facts. My notion has always been that movies are not the first place you look for facts anyway. You attend a movie for psychological truth, for emotion, for the heart of a story and not its footnotes. In its broad strokes, *The Insider* is perfectly accurate: Big tobacco lied, one man had damning information, skilled journalism developed the story, intrigue helped blast it free. *The Insider* had a greater impact on me than *All the President's Men*, because you know what? Watergate didn't kill my parents. Cigarettes did.

Inspector Gadget ★ ½
PG, 80 m., 1999

Matthew Broderick (Brown/Gadget/ RoboGadget), Rupert Everett (Scolex/Claw), Joely Fisher (Brenda/RoboBrenda), Michelle Trachtenberg (Penny), Andy Dick (Kramer), Cheri Oteri (Mayor Wilson), Michael G. Hagerty (Sikes), Dabney Coleman (Chief Quimby). Directed by David Kellogg and produced by Jordan Kerner, Roger Birnbaum, and Andy Heyward. Screenplay by Kerry Ehrin and Zak Penn, based on a story by Dana Olsen and Ehrin.

Inspector Gadget was an afternoon TV cartoon in the 1980s, much-loved by some, unseen by me, which has now inspired a high-tech live-action retread that has *Gadget* fans on the Internet furious because, apparently, they do not want to see the face of Dr. Claw. If Dr. Claw went unseen in the cartoon, their reasoning goes, it is no consolation that he is brought to life here by Rupert Everett. One person who might agree with them is Rupert Everett himself, who was on a winning streak until this movie came along.

Matthew Broderick stars, first as a security guard named John Brown, then as a bionic supercop named Inspector Gadget: "Colombo and Nintendo all rolled into one," quips Police Chief Quimby (Dabney Coleman). Broderick also plays an anti-Gadget look-alike, the bad guy RoboGadget, who impersonates the inspector and sets half the city on fire in an attempt to discredit him.

The gimmick with Gadget is that he has been equipped with a body, a suit, and (especially) a hat that are all stuffed with gadgets. All he has to say is, "Go-go gadget," and then name the gadget he wants, and it materializes, although it can be difficult remembering the right go-go word while falling from the top of a skyscraper. His gadgets include hands that spray toothpaste (Gadget) and fire (RoboGadget), a hat that turns into a helicopter, and legs that extend into long steel stilts, allowing him to leapfrog traffic and cover a lot of ground in a hurry. Also about a zillion other gadgets.

His partner in the movie, Brenda (Joely Fisher), is the daughter of an inventor who figured out how to join flesh and technology. The enemy, Claw, wants to steal the technology for himself. Local officials get involved when the warfare escalates into a safety hazard, and there are also key roles for cats, mayors, and nieces.

Obviously I would be better armed to deal with this stuff had I ever seen an *Inspector Gadget* cartoon. I could discuss how the movie does or doesn't live up to, or down to, the original. As it is I'm stuck with the movie as a stand-alone, and I'm pretty underwhelmed. Perhaps younger kids will like it more. I didn't care about the action because it made no difference to me who won or lost. The plot was an arbitrary concoction. The bad guy is played by Everett as a man fastidiously keeping a certain distance from the jokes. There are all sorts of pop culture references, but so what? There are admittedly some individual funny lines. (When the Dabney Coleman character sees John Brown in a head-to-toe body cast, he calls him "The English Patient.")

The funniest moment in the movie comes at the end, as a credit cookie during the closing titles. It's a shot of a "Minion Support Group," showing Claw's sidekick twelve-stepping with other famous evil minions (I spotted Richard Kiel's "Jaws" and perhaps Odd Job). Now *that* is an idea for a comedy.

Question: Since the movie is only eighty minutes long, would it have killed them to add a real *Inspector Gadget* cartoon to the program as a warm-up and scene-setter?

Instinct ★ ½

R, 124 m., 1999

Anthony Hopkins (Ethan Powell), Cuba Gooding Jr. (Theo Caulder), Donald Sutherland (Ben Hillard), Maura Tierney (Lyn Powell), George Dzundza (Dr. John Murray), John Ashton (Guard Dacks), John Aylward (Warden Keefer), Thomas Q. Morris (Pete). Directed by Jon Turteltaub and produced by Michael Taylor and Barbara Boyle. Screenplay by Gerald Di Pego, suggested by the novel *Ishmael* by Daniel Quinn.

If there's anything worse than a movie hammered together out of pieces of bad screenplays, it's a movie made from the scraps of good ones. At least with the trash we don't have to suffer through the noble intentions. *Instinct* is a film with not one but four worthy themes. It has pious good thoughts about all of them, but undermines them by slapping on obligatory plot requirements, thick. Nothing happens in this movie that has not been sanctioned by long usage in better films.

This is a film about (1) why Man should learn to live in harmony with Nature; (2) how prison reform is necessary; (3) how fathers can learn to love their children; (4) why it is wrong to imprison animals in zoos. The film doesn't free the beasts from their cages, but it's able to resolve the other three issues—unconvincingly, in a rush of hokey final scenes.

Instinct, directed by John Turteltaub (*Phenomenon*), is all echoes. It gives us Anthony Hopkins playing a toned-down version of Hannibal Lector, Cuba Gooding Jr., reprising his nice-guy professional from *As Good As It Gets,* Donald Sutherland once again as the wise and weary sage, and John Ashton (you'll recognize him) as a man who is hateful for no better reason than that the plot so desperately needs him to be.

Oh, and the settings are borrowed from *Gorillas in the Mist* and *One Flew Over the Cuckoo's Nest.*

The movie's just so darned uplifting and clunky as it shifts from one of its big themes to another while groaning under the weight of heartfelt speeches. The photography labors to make it look big and important, and the music wants to be sad and uplifting at the same time, as if to say it's a cruel world but that's not entirely our fault.

Hopkins stars as Ethan Powell, an anthropologist who went missing in 1994 in an African jungle and surfaced two years later while murdering two rangers and injuring three others. After a year in chains, he's returned to the United States and locked up in a brutal psycho ward. His interrogation is set to be conducted by an eminent psychiatrist (Donald Sutherland), who instead assigns his famous prisoner to Theo Caulder (Gooding), a student just completing his final year of residency. Why give this juicy patient to a kid who admits he wants to write a best-seller about him? Because Cuba Gooding is the star of the movie, that's why, and Donald Sutherland, who cannot utter a word that doesn't sound like God's truth, always has to play the expert who waits in an oak-paneled study, passing around epigrams and brandy.

Powell's hair and beard make him look like the wild man of Borneo—with reason, since he lived with a family of gorillas in the jungle. He has been mute since the murders, but Caulder thinks he can get him to talk—and can he ever. Hopkins faces one of his greatest acting challenges, portraying a character who must seem reluctant to utter a single word while nevertheless issuing regular philosophical lectures. "I lived as humans lived 10,000 years ago," he explains. "Humans knew how to live then." Even 10,000 years ago, don't you suppose humans were giving gorillas lots of room?

Caulder believes that if he can get Powell to talk about what he did, and why, he can "get him out of there." No matter that Powell *did* kill two men; to understand is to forgive. In his struggle to comprehend his patient, Caulder meets Powell's bitter daughter (Maura Tierney, in a good performance). She is angry with her father. Her father doesn't want to talk about her. "Leave it," he snaps, menacingly. What dire issues stand between them? The movie disappoints us with a reconciliation that plays like a happy ending on the Family Channel. One should always have time for one's children, Powell learned (from the gorillas).

The prison is a snake pit of brutality, run by cruel guards and presided over by a sadistic warden and a weak psychiatrist. Each man is supposed to get thirty minutes a day outdoors. Because this is too much trouble, the guards hand out cards, and the man with the ace of diamonds gets to go outside. The toughest prisoner beats up anyone who won't give him the card. Dr. Caulder sees that this is wrong, and institutes a fair lottery, over the objections of the sadistic guards, but with the prisoners chanting their support. The entire business of the ace of diamonds, which occupies perhaps twenty minutes, is agonizingly obvious, contrived, and manipulative; the prison population, colorful weirdos of the *Cuckoo's Nest* variety, responds with enthusiastic overacting.

Ethan Powell, of course, sees through the entire system. Superhumanly strong and violent, he puts Caulder through a brief but painful education in the laws of the wild. What he is able to do at the end of the film, and where he is finally able to do it, I leave you to explain, since the film certainly cannot. I also have the gravest doubts about the thank-you note from Powell, which reads not like something that would be written by a man who had lived with the gorillas and killed two men, but by a marketing expert concerned that audiences feel real good when they leave the theater.

In the Mood for Love ★ ★ ★
PG, 97 m., 2001

Tony Leung (Chow Mo-wan), Maggie Cheung (Su Li-zhen), Rebecca Pan (Mrs. Suen), Lai Chin (Mr. Ho), Siu Ping-lam (Ah Ping), Cin Tsi-ang (The Amah). Directed and produced by Wong Kar-wai. Screenplay by Wong.

They are in the mood for love, but not in the time and place for it. They look at each other with big damp eyes of yearning and sweetness, and go home to sleep by themselves. Adultery has sullied their lives: His wife and her husband are having an affair. "For us to do the same thing," they agree, "would mean we are no better than they are."

The key word there is "agree." The fact is, they do not agree. It is simply that neither one has the courage to disagree, and time is passing. He wants to sleep with her and she wants to sleep with him, but they are both bound by the moral stand that each believes the other has taken.

You may disagree with my analysis. You may think one is more reluctant than the other. There is room for speculation, because whole continents of emotions go unexplored in Wong Kar-wai's *In the Mood for Love*, a lush story of unrequited love that looks the way its songs sound. Many of them are by Nat King Cole, but the instrumental "Green Eyes," suggesting jealousy, is playing when they figure out why her husband and his wife always seem to be away at the same times.

His name is Mr. Chow (Tony Leung). Hers is Su Li-zhen (Maggie Cheung). In the crowded Hong Kong of 1962, they have rented rooms in apartments next to each another. They are not poor; he's a newspaper reporter, she's an executive assistant, but there is no space in the crowded city and little room for secrets.

Cheung and Leung are two of the biggest stars in Asia. Their pairing here as unrequited lovers is ironic because of their images as the usual winners in such affairs. This is the kind of story that could be remade by Tom Hanks and Meg Ryan, although in the Hollywood version there'd be a happy ending. That would kind of miss the point and release the tension, I think; the thrust of Wong's film is that paths cross but intentions rarely do. In his other films, like *Chungking Express*, his characters sometimes just barely miss connecting, and here again key things are said in the wrong way at the wrong time. Instead of asking us to identify with this couple, as an American film would, Wong asks us to empathize with them; that is a higher and more complex assignment, with greater rewards.

The movie is physically lush. The deep colors of *film noir* saturate the scenes: reds, yellows, browns, deep shadows. One scene opens with only a coil of cigarette smoke, and then reveals its characters. In the hallway outside the two apartments, the camera slides back and forth, emphasizing not their nearness but that there are two apartments, not one.

The most ingenious device in the story is the way Chow and Su play-act imaginary scenes between their cheating spouses. "Do you have a mistress?" she asks, and we think she is asking Chow, but actually she is asking her husband, as played by Chow. There is a slap, not as hard as it would be with a real spouse. They wound themselves with imaginary dialogue in which their cheating partners laugh about them. "I didn't expect it to hurt so much," Su says, after one of their imaginary scenarios.

Wong Kar-wai leaves the cheating couple offscreen. Movies about adultery are almost always about the adulterers, but the critic Elvis Mitchell observes that the heroes here are "the characters who are usually the victims in a James M. Cain story." Their spouses may sin in Singapore, Tokyo, or a downtown love hotel, but they will never sin on the screen of this movie, because their adultery is boring and commonplace, while the reticence of Chow and Su elevates *their* love to a kind of noble perfection.

Their lives are as walled in as their cramped living quarters. They have more money than places to spend it. Still dressed for the office, she dashes out to a crowded alley to buy noodles. Sometimes they meet on the grotty staircase. Often it is raining. Sometimes they simply talk on the sidewalk. Lovers do not notice where they are, do not notice that they repeat themselves. It isn't repetition, anyway—it's reassurance. And when you're holding back and speaking in code, no conversation is boring, because the empty spaces are filled by your desires.

Invisible Circus ★ ½
R, 98 m., 2001

Jordana Brewster (Phoebe), Christopher Eccleston (Wolf), Cameron Diaz (Faith), Blythe Danner (Gail), Patrick Bergin (Gene), Camilla Belle (Young Phoebe), Isabelle Pasco (Claire), Moritz Bleibtreu (Eric). Directed by Adam Brooks and produced by Julia Chasman and Nick Wechsler. Screenplay by Brooks, based on the book by Jennifer Egan.

Adam Brooks's *Invisible Circus* finds the solution to searing personal questions through a tricky flashback structure. There are two stories here, involving an older sister's disappearance and a younger sister's quest, and either one would be better told as a straightforward narrative. When flashbacks tease us with bits of information, it has to be done well, or we feel toyed with. Here the mystery is solved by stomping in thick-soled narrative boots through the squishy marsh of contrivance.

Jordana Brewster stars as Phoebe, eighteen years old in 1976. In the summer of 1969, she tells us in her narration, her sister Faith went to Europe and never came back. The story was that Faith (Cameron Diaz) killed herself in Portugal. Phoebe doesn't buy it. After a heart-to-heart with her mother (Blythe Danner), Phoebe sets off on a quest to solve the mystery, message, meaning, method, etc., of Faith's disappearance.

The search begins with Wolf (Christopher Eccleston), Faith's old boyfriend, now engaged and living in Paris. Since Wolf knows all the answers, and that's pretty clear to us (if not to Phoebe), he is required to be oblique to a tiresome degree. And there is another problem. In any movie where a lithesome eighteen-year-old confronts her older sister's lover, there is the inescapable possibility that she will sleep with him. This danger, which increases alarmingly when the character is named Wolf, is to be avoided, since the resulting sex scene will usually play as gratuitous, introducing problems the screenplay is not really interested in exploring. I cringe when a man and a woman pretend to be on a disinterested quest, and their unspoken sexual agenda makes everything they say sound coy.

Wolf and Faith, we learn, were involved in radical 1960s politics. Faith was driven by the death of her father, who died of leukemia caused by giant corporations (the science is a little murky here). Phoebe feels her dad always liked Faith more than herself. What was Dad's reason? My theory: Filial tension is required to motivate the younger sister's quest, so he was just helping out.

The movie follows Faith, sometimes with Wolf, sometimes without, as she joins the radical Red Army, becomes an anarchist, is allowed to help out on protest raids, fails one test, passes another, and grows guilt-ridden when one demonstration has an unexpected result. Phoebe traces Faith's activities during an odyssey/travelogue through Paris, Berlin, and Portugal, until we arrive at the very parapet Faith jumped or fell from, and all is revealed.

I can understand the purpose of the film, and even sense the depth of feeling in the underlying story, based on a novel by Jennifer Egan. But the clunky flashback structure grinds along, doling out bits of information, and it doesn't help that Wolf, as played by Eccleston, is less interested in truth than in Phoebe. He is a rat, which would be all right if he were a charming one.

There is a better movie about a young woman who drops out of sight of those who love her and commits to radical politics. That movie is *Waking the Dead* (2000). It has its problems, too, but at least it is unclouded by extraneous sex, and doesn't have a character who withholds information simply for the convenience of the screenplay. And its Jennifer Connelly is much more persuasive than Cameron Diaz as a young woman who becomes a radical; she enters a

kind of solemn holy trance, unlike Diaz, who seems more like a political tourist.

The Iron Giant ★ ★ ★ ½
PG, 81 m., 1999

Voices of: Jennifer Aniston (Annie Hughes), Eli Marienthal (Hogarth Hughes), Harry Connick Jr. (Dean McCoppin), Vin Diesel (The Iron Giant), James Gammon (Marv and Floyd), Cloris Leachman (Mrs. Tensedge), Christopher McDonald (Kent Mansley), John Mahoney (General Rogard), M. Emmet Walsh (Earl Stutz). Directed by Brad Bird and produced by Allison Abbate and Des McAnuff. Screenplay by Tim McCanlies and Bird, based on the book *The Iron Giant* by Ted Hughes.

Imagine *E.T.* as a towering metal man and you have some of the appeal of *The Iron Giant,* an enchanting animated feature about a boy who makes friends with a robot from outer space. The giant crash-lands on a 1957 night when America is peering up at the speck of *Sputnik* in the sky, and munches his way through a Maine village, eating TV antennas and cars, until he finds a power plant. That's where young Hogarth Hughes finds him.

Hogarth, with a voice by Eli Marienthal, is a nine-year-old who lives with his single mom (Jennifer Aniston) and dreams of having a pet. His mom says they make too much of a mess around the house, little dreaming what a 100-foot robot can get into. One night Hogarth discovers their TV antenna is missing and follows the Iron Giant's trail to the power plant, where he saves the robot from electrocution after it chomps on some live wires. That makes the Giant his friend forever, and now all Hogarth has to do is keep the robot a secret from his mom and the federal government.

The Iron Giant is still another example of the freedom that filmmakers find in animation: This would have been a $100 million live-action special-effects movie, but it was made for a fraction of that cost because the metal man is drawn, not constructed. And here is a family movie with a message: a Cold War parable in which the Iron Giant learns from a little boy that he is not doomed to be a weapon because "you are what you choose to be."

The movie is set in the 1950s because that's

the decade when science fiction seemed most preoccupied with nuclear holocaust and invaders from outer space. It includes a hilarious cartoon version of the alarming *Duck and Cover* educational film in which kids were advised to seek shelter from H-bombs by hiding under their desks. And the villain is a Cold Warrior named Kent Mansley (voice by Christopher McDonald), a G-man who, of course, sees the Iron Giant as a subversive plot and wants to blast it to pieces.

That political parable is buried beneath a lot of surface charm; the film's appeal comes from its *E.T.*-type story about a boy trying to hide an alien from his mom. The Iron Giant is understandably too big to conceal in the closet, but there's a funny sequence where Hogarth brings the creature's hand into the house and it scampers around like a disobedient dog.

Like the new Japanese animated films, *The Iron Giant* is happy to be a "real movie" in everything but live action. There are no cute little animals and not a single musical number: It's a story, plain and simple. The director, Brad Bird, is a *Simpsons* veteran whose visual look here, much more complex than the *Simpsons*, resembles the "clear line" technique of Japan's Hayao Miyazaki *(My Neighbor Totoro)*. It works as a lot of animation does, to make you forget from time to time that these are moving drawings, because the story and characters are so compelling.

As for the Iron Giant himself, he's surprisingly likable. He can't speak English at first, but is a quick study, and like E.T. combines great knowledge with the naïveté of a stranger in a puzzling land. His voice is by Vin Diesel, and sounds like it has been electronically lowered. He looks unsophisticated—something like a big Erector Set construction with a steamshovel mouth. But as we get to know him he turns into a personality before our very eyes—a big lunk we feel kind of sorry for. By the climax (which, also like *E.T.*, involves a threat from bureaucrats and technocrats), we're hoping Hogarth can help save his friend once again.

It must be tough to get a movie like this made. Disney has the traditional animation market locked up, but other studios seem willing to throw money at Disney musical lookalikes (like *The King and I*) even though they might have a better chance moving in the op- posite direction—toward real stories told straight. *The Iron Giant*, based on a book by the late British poet laureate Ted Hughes, is not just a cute romp but an involving story that has something to say.

Isn't She Great? ★
R, 95 m., 2000

Bette Midler (Jacqueline Susann), Nathan Lane (Irving Mansfield), Stockard Channing (Florence Maybelle), David Hyde Pierce (Michael Hastings), John Cleese (Henry Marcus), John Larroquette (Maury Manning), Amanda Peet (Debbie). Directed by Andrew Bergman and produced by Mike Lobell. Screenplay by Paul Rudnick, based on an article by Michael Korda.

Perhaps it's appropriate that Jacqueline Susann's biopic has been written by Paul Rudnick, whose alter ego, "Libby Gelman-Waxner," waxes witty and bitchy in her *Premiere* magazine column every month. It was Truman Capote who said on a talk show that Jackie Susann "looks like a truck driver in drag," but whenever that image swims into view, it somehow seems to have the Gelman-Waxner byline attached.

Susann became famous writing potboilers about the sex and drug lives of the stars. Identifying the real-life models for her thinly veiled characters grew into a parlor game, and her *Valley of the Dolls* became the best-selling novel of all time. She also became famous for revolutionizing book retailing; Susann and her agent husband, Irving Mansfield, turned the book tour into a whistle-stop of America, and there was scarcely a bookseller, interviewer, or indeed shipping dockworker who didn't get the Susann treatment.

So tireless was her publicity that she even talked to me, at a time when I was twenty-three years old and had been on the *Sun-Times* for ten minutes. Jackie, Irving, and I had lunch at Eli's the Place for Steak, although all I can recall of the conversation is that she said, "I'm like Will Rogers. I never met a dog I didn't like." Full disclosure: Three years later I wrote the screenplay for the parody *Beyond the Valley of the Dolls*, and a few years after that, the Fox studio was sued by Mansfield on the grounds that the film diminished his wife's literary reputation. (Had I been called to testify, I would have expressed quiet pride in whatever small part I had played in that process.)

Susann's life would seem to be the perfect target for the Libby Gelman-Waxner sensibility; who better to write about the woman whose prose one reader described as "like overhearing a conversation in the ladies' room." My hopes soared when I learned that Andrew Bergman, who made the wacky comedies *Honeymoon in Vegas* and *Soapdish*, would be directing—and that John Cleese would play her publisher. I was hoping for satire, but they've made a flat and peculiar film that in its visual look and dramatic style might be described as the final movie of the 1950s.

Maybe that was the purpose. Maybe the whole look, feel, and sensibility of *Isn't She Great?* is part of the joke. It's a movie that seems to possess the same color scheme and style sense as *Valley of the Dolls,* but, alas, without Jackie's dirty mind. So devout is this story that when Irving (Nathan Lane) walks out on Jackie (Bette Midler), we don't even find out why he really left. Jackie would have given us the scoopola.

And when they get back together again, is it with tearful recriminations and shocking accusations? Not at all. There is a tree in Central Park that they hold precious, because to them it represents God, and one day when Jackie visits the tree Irving is there already talking to God. To prove how much he loves her, on this and another occasion, he even wades into the Central Park lagoon. I think, although the movie isn't clear, that Irving left her not because of another person, but because the diamond brooch he bought for Jackie at the height of her success was upstaged by the diamond necklace given by her publisher. As her agent, shouldn't his gift be only 10 percent as expensive as her publisher's?

Money brings up another point: their lifestyle. Once Jackie makes it big time, they have a lot of money. But even before then, they live in Mansfield's lavishly expensive Manhattan apartment, reproduced on one of those spacious Hollywood sets where people make dramatic entrances and exits and the interior decorators have taste as vague as their budgets. Where did Mansfield get the money to live like this? When they first meet, he drops names like Perry Como and Frank Sinatra,

but it turns out he represents their distant relatives.

Never mind. Factual accuracy is not what we're looking for anyway. What we want, I think, is the portrait of a funny trash-talker, not a secular saint who bravely bore the birth of an autistic son (visited on weekends in a luxury care center) and later battled cancer. Bette Midler would seem to be the right casting choice for Jackie, but not for this Jackie, who is not bright enough, vicious enough, ambitious enough, and complicated enough to be the woman who became world-famous through sheer exercise of will. Stockard Channing, who plays Jackie's boozy best friend, does a better job of suggesting the Susann spirit.

Jackie Susann deserved better than *Isn't She Great?* A woman who writes *Valley of the Dolls* shouldn't be punished with a biopic that makes her look only a little naughtier than Catherine Cookson. There's a scene here where Jackie and Irving visit with Jackie and Aristotle on the Onassis yacht. Consider for a moment what Susann could have done with that. Then look at the tepid moment where Ari sighs fondly, "Perhaps I married the wrong Jackie." Uh, huh. Here is a movie that needed great trash, great sex, and great gossip, and at all the crucial moments Susann is talking to a tree.

It All Starts Today ★ ★ ★
NO MPAA RATING, 117 m., 2001

Philippe Torreton (Daniel), Maria Pitarresi (Valeria), Nadia Kaci (Samia), Veronique Ataly (Mrs. Lienard), Nathalie Becue (Cathy), Emmanuelle Bercot (Mrs. Tievaux), Francoise Bette (Mrs. Delacourt), Lambert Marchal (Remi). Directed by Bertrand Tavernier and produced by Alain Sarde and Frederic Bourboulon. Screenplay (in French, with English subtitles) by Dominique Sampiero, Tiffany Tavernier, and Bertrand Tavernier.

Daniel, the kindergarten teacher in *It All Starts Today,* finds himself doing a lot more than teaching. He is also expected to be a social worker, child abuse investigator, hot lunch provider, political activist, fund-raiser, administrator, son, and lover, and now his girlfriend wants him to become a father as well. Philippe

Torreton plays the role with a kind of desperate energy, relaxing only with the kids in the schoolroom and one night when he dances at a birthday party.

There is not much good cheer in the town where he teaches, a depressed mining village in the very area of France that inspired Zola's great exposé of mine conditions, *Germinal*. Today the typical miner is more like Daniel's dad, a broken figure who shuffles through the living room with his oxygen tank strapped to his back. Unemployment is widespread, government funds are lacking, and the mayor complains that schools and social services eat up his budget.

Not that the services are that good. Early in the film, Daniel locks out a social worker (Nadia Kaci) after she hangs up on him. Later they get to be friends and bend a few rules to make things happen. But what can they do about the pathetic mother who pushes her baby carriage into the schoolyard to pick up her preschooler, collapses on the asphalt, and then runs away, leaving behind both her baby and her little girl?

"She reeked of red wine," another teacher tells Daniel (the French would note the color). He visits her home, to find that the power has been turned off. It is winter, and cold. It's against the law to turn off a customer's power in the winter, but the power company gets around that by turning it off in the autumn. This woman, her kids, and her dispirited husband have no money, no hope, no plans.

The movie is a tender and passionate protest, not without laughter, by Bertrand Tavernier—a director who is not only gifted but honorable, and who since his debut with the wonderful *The Clockmaker* in 1973 has never put his hand to an unworthy film. He works all over the map, from the fantasy of *Death Watch* to the politics of *The Judge and the Assassin* to the character study *A Week's Vacation* to the jazz biopic *'Round Midnight* to

the heartbreaking *Daddy Nostalgia* and the angry *L.627*, about the impossibility of being an effective drug cop.

It All Starts Today has most in common with *L.627*. Both films are about talented professionals who are hamstrung by the French bureaucracy and driven to despair by the untidy lives of their citizen clients. The screenplay, written by Tavernier with his daughter Tiffany and a schoolteacher named Dominique Sampiero, works by looking at everyday challenges. What is Daniel to say, for example, when the schoolyard woman and her husband explain that their son has stopped coming to school because it is just too much effort for them to set the alarm and get him out of bed? Irresponsible? Or would you also be defeated by months without heat and light?

The movie sketches Daniel's run-ins with a world that seems determined to make it impossible for him to be a good kindergarten teacher. He is considered a troublemaker, but what can he do? Consider the insufferable school inspector who advises him not to "move among groups" while teaching. "What should I do about the other three groups?" Daniel asks. "Make them self-reliant," advises the inspector, who obviously knows little about the self-reliance skills of two- to five-year-olds.

Maria Pitarresi plays Daniel's girlfriend, a sculptor with a young son who resents him. Her character seems a little unlikely, especially when she dreams up the school fete that ends the film, with classrooms filled with sand and Berber tents made from sheets, and a schoolyard filled with a maze of brightly colored bottles. As the town band plays and the children dance, we're aware that the upbeat ending changes absolutely nothing about the grim prospects for these kids when they someday look for work in this dying region. They'll end up paralyzed in front of the TV, like their parents. No wonder two of the students are named Starsky and Hutch.

J

Jakob the Liar ★ ★
PG-13, 114 m., 1999

Robin Williams (Jakob), Alan Arkin (Frankfurter), Bob Balaban (Kowalski), Mathieu Kassovitz (Herschel), Armin Mueller-Stahl (Kirschbaum), Liev Schreiber (Mischa), Hannah Taylor Gordon (Lina), Nina Siemaszko (Rosa), Michael Jeter (Avron). Directed by Peter Kassovitz and produced by Marsha Garces Williams and Steven Haft. Screenplay by Kassovitz and Didier Decoin, based on the book by Jurek Becker.

The last shot of *Jakob the Liar* (don't worry, it has nothing much to do with the rest of the film) shows an American jazz band playing in a field near the death camps of World War II. Three women who resemble the Andrews Sisters are singing. This shot is a fantasy, imagined by a character who wouldn't have the slightest notion what such a performance would look like. What is it doing in the movie? I fear it is there for one reason only, to provide an uplifting conclusion even if it has to be hauled in by the ears.

The first shots of the film show a man chasing a newspaper. Special effects give the paper a mind of its own. Every time the man is almost ready to pounce on it, a gust of wind comes along and blows it away. Hither and yon it blows, more versatile even than the feather at the beginning of *Forrest Gump* (which is, I suspect, its inspiration). Why is it so tantalizingly out of reach? It is a metaphor for the movie, which is about a man who pursues the illusive goal of news about the war.

These two contrived images bracket a movie that reflects their manipulative sensibility. *Jakob the Liar* takes place inside the ghetto of an unnamed Polish city where Nazis have walled off the streets and installed searchlights and guards with machine guns. Inside, Jewish captives live crowded into tiny apartments, waiting for news. The news they fear most is that they're going to be shipped to concentration camps, never to be heard of again.

Early in the film, a Jew named Jakob (Robin Williams) finds himself inside Nazi headquarters and accidentally overhears a news broadcast indicating that the war is going badly for Germany. He shares this news with his fellow captives, and it gives them hope. If the war is going to end soon, then perhaps it's worth holding on against despair and suicide.

Rumors spread that Jakob has a radio. Using the bigmouthed former boxer Mischa (Liev Schreiber) as a conduit, Jakob reluctantly leaks hints of more bad news for the Nazis. He's making it all up, of course, but in a situation like this every shred of hope could save lives. We meet various other members of the population: an old doctor (Armin Mueller-Stahl), an actor (Alan Arkin), a deeply depressed man (Bob Balaban), and a ten-year-old girl named Lina (Hannah Taylor Gordon), who was helped to escape from a death train by her parents and found by Jakob, who is hiding her.

That Jakob has room to hide both a girl and an imaginary radio is odd in a ghetto where most apartments house a dozen people. Also contrived is the way the Jews and the Nazis share a closed universe in which all important activities are limited to a few broadly drawn characters with stage accents and simple personality traits. There is little sense that a real war is lurking outside the frame.

Such a parable invites comparison with Roberto Benigni's *Life Is Beautiful,* the 1998 film about a clown who tries to use his gift of humor and imagination to save his little boy in a Nazi camp. *Jakob,* directed by Peter Kassovitz, was not inspired by Benigni's success; based on a 1975 East German movie, it was filmed before *Life Is Beautiful* was released, and (if you were wondering, and I'll bet you were) before Williams's schmaltzfest *Patch Adams.*

Both films are about extroverts using imagination as a weapon against the Holocaust. I prefer *Life Is Beautiful,* which is clearly a fantasy, to *Jakob the Liar,* which is just as contrived and manipulative but pretends it is not. You have to earn the dividends of realism. *Life Is Beautiful* is all of a piece, the opening hour showing us the limitations the hero will have to work with once he's inside the camp. *Jakob the Liar* wants the freedom of the Benigni film but doesn't want to pay the dues.

Williams is a talented performer who moves me in the right roles but has a weakness for the wrong ones. He needs a director like Billy Wilder, who once asked Jack Lemmon for "Less! Less! A little less!" so many times that Lemmon finally exploded: "Whaddaya want? Nothing?" To which Wilder replied, "Please God!" If less is more, then Williams often demonstrates that more is less.

Movies as different as *The Dead Poets Society* and *Patch Adams* have been brought to a halt by interludes in which Williams darts in a frenzy from one character and accent to another. Here, in a scene that passes for restrained, he imitates Churchill, and uses a kitchen funnel and a flour can to create sound effects (only sneezing a little because of the flour). These scenes demonstrate that Williams cannot use shtick in a serious movie without damaging the fabric.

The other actors do their best (Schreiber is convincing, although hampered by a hat with funny ear flaps), but the screenplay and direction are lugubrious, as the characters march in their overwritten and often overacted roles toward a foregone conclusion. And then the Andrews Sisters. What a cheap shot. I wonder if it was forced on the director. It denies the truth of the film; is the audience supposed to be much relieved as it taps its feet to the tune?

I can imagine this material in black-and-white, grubbier, without stars, with subtitles to spare us the accents. It could work. Maybe I'm actually describing the 1975 East German film, which won the Silver Bear at the Berlin Film Festival. When this one opened at the Toronto festival, Williams got more applause for walking out on the stage before the screening than the whole movie got afterward.

Jawbreaker ★ ½
R, 91 m., 1999

Rose McGowan (Courtney), Rebecca Gayheart (Julie), Julie Benz (Marcie), Judy Evans Greer (Fern Mayo), Chad Christ (Zach), Charlotte Roldan (Liz Purr), Pam Grier (Detective Vera Cruz), Ethan Erickson (Dane Sanders). Directed by Darren Stein and produced by Stacy Kramer and Lisa Tornel. Screenplay by Stein.

I knew high school comedies were desperate for new ideas, but *Jawbreaker* is the first one I've seen where the bad girl is stoned with corsages. The movie is a slick production of a lame script, which kills time for most of its middle hour. If anyone in the plot had the slightest intelligence, the story would implode.

The film opens with an accidental death. The "Fearless Four" are the coolest girls in Reagan High School (and no wonder, since they look well into their twenties). One morning three of them surprise their friend Liz by sticking a jawbreaker into her mouth, taping it shut, and locking her in a car trunk for a ride to a restaurant where they plan a birthday breakfast. Liz chokes to death.

What to do? Cover it up, of course. The ringleader is Courtney (Rose McGowan), a rhymes-with-witch who fakes a phone call from Liz's mother, saying she'll be absent from school. Then she has her pals Julie (Rebecca Gayheart) and Marcie (Julie Benz) help her carry the corpse back to Liz's bed, where they fake a rape scene. Meanwhile, a school wallflower named Fern Mayo (Judy Evans Greer) delivers Liz's homework to her house, overhears the girls talking, and learns of their crime.

What to do? Part II. Make Fern one of them, of course, by giving her a beauty makeover, a new name (Vylette), and instructions on how to be a babe ("Never, ever, eat at lunch—period!"). Vylette, of course, turns out to be even more spiteful than the other girls, and indeed one of the original team, Julie (Rebecca Gayheart), drops out of the clique because she's disgusted with the whole deception.

Once poor Liz is dead and the cover-up begins, the film has to delay the obvious resolution of the situation in order to sketch in two tired subplots: Julie's romance with the star drama student (Chad Christ) and Fern/ Vylette's transformation into a monster. Julie could end it all by speaking out, but she delays, because that would not be convenient for the plot.

Another problem. A local detective is investigating the death. She's played by Pam Grier, so cloaked in vast black garments and long hair that she seems to be peeking out from behind the wardrobe department. She has a scene where she's strong and angry, and then the movie forgets that personality trait and makes her into a stooge who listens to unbelievable stories. She arrests a man as a suspect in the case, disregarding a crucial clue: The school received that call from Liz's "mother," and since Liz's real mother didn't make it, it must have come from a female who knew what school Liz went to. Thus, probably not a random male rapist.

And on and on. The movie's fugitive pleasure is Rebecca Gayheart as the good girl; she is wonderfully photogenic, we reflect, as she and the rest of the cast founder in amateur-night dialogue and a plot that desperately stretches its thin material and still barely struggles to the ninety-one-minute mark—and that's counting end credits and various songs including, inexplicably, Frank Sinatra's "Young at Heart."

Jesus' Son ★ ★ ★ ½
R, 110 m., 2000

Billy Crudup (FH), Samantha Morton (Michelle), Denis Leary (Wayne), Jack Black (Georgie), Will Patton (John Smith), Greg Germann (Dr. Shanis), Holly Hunter (Mira), Dennis Hopper (Bill). Directed by Alison Maclean and produced by Elizabeth Cuthrell, Lydia Dean Pilcher, and David Urrutia. Screenplay by Cuthrell, Urrutia, and Oren Moverman, based on stories by Denis Johnson.

Thinking at first I am seeing still one more road movie about a druggie, I find I am wrong. *Jesus' Son* surprises me with moments of wry humor, poignancy, sorrow, and wildness. It has a sequence as funny as any I've seen this year, and one as harrowing, and it ends in a bittersweet minor key, as it should, because to attach this story to a big climax would be a lie, if not a crime. Like all good films, it is not for everybody (only bad films are for everybody).

The story revolves around the time and place of Iowa City, circa 1971, although the hero does a lot of traveling all over the country, and in his own memories. His name is FH, which is short for guess what, and in the beginning he is one of those college town layabouts with no plans and not many problems. One day on a bench he meets Michelle. They

talk a little and he asks, "Do I kiss you now?" Later, she asks him, "You ever seen anybody shoot up before?" He has not, but soon heroin is running his life.

But this is not a drug movie like any you've seen. It doesn't glamorize drugs or demonize them, but simply remembers them from the point of view of a survivor. FH (Billy Crudup) narrates the story, sometimes doubling back to fill in gaps or add overlooked details. He isn't a hero or an antihero, just a fairly clueless guy with good intentions who gets muddled by the drug lifestyle—which creates a burden the mind is not really designed to endure.

The movie's director is Alison Maclean, a New Zealander whose screenplay (by Elizabeth Cuthrell, David Urrutia, and Oren Moverman) is based on short stories by the American Denis Johnson. Some will complain that the episodes jostle too loosely against one another (it's "a barbiturate-driven version of *Pulp Fiction*, in which the guns misfire and the cars don't have brakes," writes *Salon*'s Andrew O'Hehir, in a negative but somehow affectionate review). I think short stories are right for a story about druggies. Their lives are too episodic to add up to a novel; the highs and lows settle out into disconnected adventures and anecdotes, separated by voids and blackouts.

The thing about FH and Michelle (Samantha Morton) is that they love each other, in a fashion, but are inhabiting a lifestyle that has too many distractions for any kind of continuity. Drugs or love: You sort of have to choose one or the other, because you can't pay attention to both. Their romance, when it is working, has a kind of tenderness that grows out of their suffering. They are so screwed up that when the movie lingers on the sight of them kissing, we realize with a stir that their kissing is direct and needy, not movie-stylized. They aren't putting on a show for the camera, but feeding at each other's lips.

Samantha Morton you will remember from Woody Allen's *Sweet and Lowdown*, where she played a mute. Here she plays a woman who is more or less the result of the situation she's gotten herself into: If you are going to use drugs and don't have infinite money, you are going to have to make some compromises. Crudup is a good partner for her, coming in

295

under her radar, ready for whatever she has in mind.

But the movie is not just about (or even really about) FH and Michelle. It's episodic, and there are moments that stand out like sharp memories in a confused time. Like the fat kid who races after their car and runs into the pole. Or the naked woman parasailing. "That's my wife," says FH's newfound barroom buddy Wayne (Denis Leary). No further explanation. They spend an afternoon stripping the copper wires out of an empty house. "How much money do you think we can make from this?" FH asks. "Enough to go to bed drunk tonight," says Wayne.

FH eventually gets a job as an orderly in a hospital, and that leads to a sequence that combines the gruesome and the comic as memorably as the needle to the heart in *Pulp Fiction*. A patient comes in with a knife sticking out of his eye socket. The ER nurse tells him, "We better get you lying down." I liked the way the man's condition is diagnosed: "Patient complains of knife in head." FH's fellow orderly is Jack Black (the larger of the two clerks in *High Fidelity*). When a doctor hesitates, he knows what to do.

The last third of the film is one bemusement and perplexity after another. FH goes into rehab, and gives a shave to a patient (Dennis Hopper) whose sentences summarize decades. He has a little romance with a woman (Holly Hunter) who just plain has bad luck with her husbands. He gets a job as the editor of a newsletter at an old folks' home. ("This job includes a lot of touching," he's told. "We want to see you touching the patients.") He falls in love with the overheard voice of a Mennonite woman, singing in her shower—and observes the complexities of the situation where her husband tells him, "Take what you need."

The movie's title is not intended to be a literal description of FH ("Jesus' Son" is a line from a Lou Reed song), but I see what it's getting at: A lot of great men have sons who plug away at the family business but just don't have the knack. FH's story is not a cautionary tale, a parable, or a fable. It is just what happened to him. He's not a bad guy. He should play more of an active role in his life, instead of just letting it happen to him. And when he's asked if he's ever seen anybody shoot up before, he should ask himself if he hasn't been getting along more or less okay without having had that experience.

Joe Dirt ★ ½
PG-13, 93 m., 2001

David Spade (Joe Dirt), Brittany Daniel (Brandy), Dennis Miller (Zander Kelly), Adam Beach (Kicking Wing), Christopher Walken (Clem), Jaimie Pressly (Jill), Kid Rock (Robby), Erik Per Sullivan (Little Joe Dirt), Carson Daly (Himself). Directed by Dennie Gordon and produced by Robert Simonds. Screenplay by David Spade and Fred Wolf.

I wrote the words *Joe Dirt* at the top of my notepad and settled back to watch the new David Spade movie. Here is the first note I took: "Approx. 6 min. until first cow fart set afire." *Joe Dirt* doesn't waste any time letting you know where it stands.

This is the kind of movie where the hero finds two things that have fallen from the skies—a meteor and an atomic bomb—and both turn out to be a case of mistaken identity. Yes, the meteor is actually a large chunk of frozen treasure from an airplane lavatory, and the bomb is actually a large human waste storage unit.

We professional movie critics count it a banner week when only one movie involves eating, falling into, or being covered by excrement (or a cameo appearance by Carson Daly). We are not prudes. We are prepared to laugh. But what these movies, including *Joe Dirt*, often do not understand is that the act of being buried in crap is not in and of *itself* funny.

Third-graders might think so (they're big on fart jokes, too), but trust me: When Joe Dirt thinks he has an atom bomb until the cap gets knocked off and a geyser of brown crud pours out, and he *just stands there* while it covers him—that's not funny. Especially since we know he's only standing there to be sure we get the joke. Otherwise, he would move to avoid being entirely covered. Wouldn't you? (Direct quote from the press release, in connection with a scene where Spade is nearly eaten by an alligator: "David Spade performed his own stunts with the animatronic reptile.

Trapped in a tangle of cable while lodged in the beast's mouth, he joked to the crew that he hoped he'd never have to get a job at a zoo." To which I can only add, "What? And leave show business?!")

Spade plays Joe Dirt, who is white trash. The movie uses that expression constantly, even observing at one point that his facial hair has grown in "white trash style" without the need for trimming. Joe's haircut is one of those 1970s mullet jobs; we learn it's not real hair but a wig supplied by his parents to cover a crack in his infant head that exposed his brain (Note: This is also supposed to be funny). The wig is a rare gift from his parents, who apparently abandoned him at the Grand Canyon when he was eight and happily playing in a garbage can.

Joe's origins and adventures are related many years later, when he happens into the studio of a talk jock played by Dennis Miller, whose own facial hair makes him look uncannily like the BBC's recent computer reconstruction of historical Jesus. Little Joe has been on his own ever since he was eight, he says, wandering the country as kind of a low-rent Forrest Gump, stumbling into interesting people and strange experiences. Where Forrest might meet a president, however, Joe is more likely to accidentally find himself in the gondola of a hot-air balloon in the shape of a tooth.

The movie's production notes further inform us: "Spade says this is the first time he has ever played a character that is likable. 'It's a big switch for me,' he says." I think he may still have his first likable character ahead of him. Joe Dirt is so obviously a construction that it is impossible to find anything human about him; he is a concept, not a person, and although Spade arguably looks better in the mullet wig than he does with his trademark mop-top, he still has the same underlying personality. Here is a man born to play the Peter Lorre role.

The movie has a very funny moment. (Spoiler alert!) It involves Christopher Walken, an actor with so much identity and charisma that his mere appearance on a screen generates interest in any audience (and gratitude and relief from this one). He plays a character named Clem, who has good reasons for not wanting to appear on television. Eventually he reveals that he has gone underground with a new identity and is now Gert B. Frobe.

Note: The movie's PG-13 rating is one more plaque on the Jack Valenti Wall of Shame. The press kit quotes Spade on the movie: "Honestly, I think it's kind of good for kids. I mean, here's a guy that's just trying to be a good guy. He's not mean to people, and he's not sarcastic, and he's not a jerk." That could be an apology for the mean, sarcastic jerks he's played up until now, but probably not.

Joe Gould's Secret ★ ★ ★ ½
R, 108 m., 2000

Ian Holm (Joe Gould), Stanley Tucci (Joe Mitchell), Hope Davis (Therese Mitchell), Sarah Hyland (Elizabeth Mitchell), Hallee Hirsh (Nora Mitchell), Celia Weston (Sarah), Patrick Tovatt (Harold Ross), Susan Sarandon (Alice Neel). Directed by Stanley Tucci and produced by Elizabeth W. Alexander, Tucci, and Charles Weinstock. Screenplay by Howard A. Rodman, based on *Professor Seagull* and *Joe Gould's Secret* by Joseph Mitchell.

The secret of *Joe Gould's Secret* is that it is not Joe Gould's secret at all. It is Joe Mitchell's secret. Joe Gould is easy to understand, because like many madmen he is consistent from day to day—stuck in the rut of his delusions. But Joe Mitchell is a hard case, a man who hides his elusive nature behind a facade of shyness and courtly southern manners. Stanley Tucci's lovingly crafted film pretends to be about Joe Gould, and all the time its real subject is hidden right there before us in plain view.

Joseph Mitchell was a writer for the *New Yorker* in its glory days, in the 1930s and 1940s, when Harold Ross was the editor and the staff included Robert Benchley and E. B. White. He wrote stories about the people of the city, characters he encountered or heard about. One of them was Joe Gould, a bearded bohemian who marched through the streets of Greenwich Village clutching his tattered portfolio and demanding donations to the "Joe Gould Fund."

Gould claimed to be writing an oral history of New York, a million-word record of the daily conversations of the citizens, and had collected many patrons who believed him.

"Gimme a bowl of soup—I don't have all day," he announces, marching into a restaurant the first time Mitchell sees him. He gets his soup. Max Gordon of the Village Vanguard donates to the "fund," and so does the poet e. e. cummings. In the film, the painter Alice Neel (Susan Sarandon) tells Mitchell: "I have always felt that the city's unconscious is trying to speak to you through Joe Gould."

Gould (Ian Holm) is a man of swiftly changing emotional weather. He can be sweet, perceptive, philosophical, and then burst out in sudden rage. The first time he has a conversation with Joe Mitchell (Stanley Tucci), he gets right to the heart of the matter. "Say 'I may marry Mary,'" he orders Mitchell, and then, after listening to the writer's accent, asks, "How did your father feel when you didn't want to go into the tobacco industry?" He has correctly clocked Mitchell as a refugee from a southern tobacco state, who became a writer against his father's wishes.

In another scene, Mitchell brings home watermelon for his wife and daughters, and cuts it on a piece of newspaper. "My father always said this was the only thing a newspaper was good for," he recalls. "And what did you say?" his wife asks the writer. He replies evenly, "I said not a thing."

There are clues to the film's real subject all through the movie. Mitchell's opening narration observes that Joe Gould felt at home among the city's outcasts and homeless, cranks and crazies. Mitchell says he did, too, and adds, "As time went on, I would find that this was not the only thing we had in common." What else they had in common is saved for the movie's end title, and suddenly illuminates the whole film.

Stanley Tucci is a director and actor with an openhearted generosity for his characters; he loves and forgives them. His first film, *Big Night,* codirected with Campbell Scott, was a perfect little masterpiece about an Italian restaurant run with too many ideals and not enough customers. Here he's made a chamber piece of quiet scenes, acutely heard dialogue, and subterranean emotional shifts. Ian Holm's role as Joe Gould is the flashy one, and some viewers will be fooled into thinking the film is about Gould. But he isn't the one who changes. He is himself from beginning to end, repeating the same notes, sometimes touchingly, sometimes maddeningly.

The movie is about Joe Mitchell, a man who avoids confrontation with such determination that he even hesitates to finish a sentence, lest it not be to his interrogator's liking. He pauses and backtracks, stammers and corrects himself, qualifies every word, and phrases everything with elusive southern courtesy. Joe Gould enters his life like a cautionary tale. Toward the end of the film, at a Greenwich Village party, Mitchell finds himself describing the book he plans to write, and we realize (if he does not) that he is describing a version of Joe Gould's oral history. Indeed, most of Mitchell's *New Yorker* articles did what Gould claimed to do; Mitchell wandered the city, stumbling bemusedly on people and their stories.

There is a dark, deep, and sad undercurrent in the movie. There is a whole story to be extracted from Mitchell's hints about himself. We sense it from the opening moments. It tantalizes us as the subtext of most of the scenes. Where is he headed? At the movie's very end we learn that one additional piece of information about Joseph Mitchell, and everything becomes clear. Tucci and Howard A. Rodman, who wrote the screenplay, based it on Mitchell's two articles about Gould, but they discovered something unwritten in those articles that gave them the clue to this movie. Some have said the film is too quiet and slow. There is anguish here that makes *American Beauty* pale by comparison.

Joe the King ★ ★
R, 100 m., 1999

Noah Fleiss (Joe), Karen Young (Theresa), Camryn Manheim (Mrs. Basil), Austin Pendleton (Winston), John Leguizamo (Jorge), Ethan Hawke (Len Coles), Val Kilmer (Bob), Max Ligosh (Mike). Directed by Frank Whaley and produced by Robin O'Hara, Scott Macaulay, Jennifer Dewis, and Lindsay Marx. Screenplay by Whaley.

Frank Whaley's *Joe the King* has been described as "semiautobiographical," and you can feel the pain behind this story of a boy from a gloomy home whose bad luck never seems to change. What you can also sense is too much self-pity: The film is so steeped in resentment that it's not able to pull back and let us see the boy behind the shield of his misery.

The film takes place in the mid-1970s, when Joe, played for most of the film by Noah Fleiss, is a dour loner who works after school in a diner and comes home to an alcoholic father (Val Kilmer), a bitter mother (Karen Young), and an older brother who tries his best but isn't much help (Max Ligosh). Joe is one of those kids whom other kids take a sadistic satisfaction in picking on. It doesn't help that his father is the school janitor; when Joe makes up stories about his dad on Careers Day, a fellow student blurts out the truth: "He cleans our toilets."

A sadistic teacher always seems to have Joe in her sights, and one day she calls him in front of the class, pulls down his pants, and smacks his bare bottom. This scene reveals a filmmaker so angered by his memories that he goes over the top: In the 1970s, in upstate New York, would a teacher really have gotten away with this? For Joe, every day is more or less the same: a round of humiliation at school, hard labor at the diner, fights between his parents at home.

The film has been compared to Truffaut's *The 400 Blows*, also about a boy whose parents' unhappy marriage sends him out into the streets, where crime beckons. Joe would also be at home in a novel by Dickens. He is hungry a lot of the time, steals food at the diner, and moves on to petty theft. After he gets in trouble with the law, there's a touching scene where he goes to the diner, orders platefuls of food, eats what he can, is overcome by grief, and throws up.

A movie like this needs some kind of arc to suggest a future for the boy. Truffaut's hero, who has an altar to Balzac in his room, at least had his dreams; no child, however unhappy, is completely without hope if he can get his hands on good books. Joe's prospects seem barren. His parents have surrendered, the system sees no good in him, and he's such a sad sack that when he's sent to a juvenile facility it plays less like an injustice than like an opportunity.

Frank Whaley, who wrote and directed, is an actor who works a lot and has a line on creepy connivers. He played the subversive assistant to studio executive Kevin Spacey in *Swimming With Sharks* (1994), studying his moves and then taking his revenge; in the underappreciated *Homage* (1996), he was a celebrity stalker who becomes indispensable to the mother of his favorite TV star; and in *Cafe Society* (1995) he was Mickey Jelke, the rich playboy who lived for headlines and made one too many.

In those roles you can sometimes see something in his eyes that can also be glimpsed in the eyes of Joe the King. However "semiautobiographical" this movie is, its author has become a successful and talented actor. I would be interested in seeing what Joe does with the rest of his life.

Josie and the Pussycats ½★
PG-13, 95 m., 2001

Rachael Leigh Cook (Josie McCoy), Tara Reid (Melody Valentine), Rosario Dawson (Valerie Brown), Parker Posey (Fiona), Alan Cumming (Wyatt Frame), Gabriel Mann (Alan M. Mayberry), Paulo Costanzo (Alexander Cabot), Missi Pyle (Alexandra Cabot). Directed by Harry Elfont and Deborah Kaplan and produced by Tony DeRosa-Grund, Tracey E. Edmonds, Chuck Grimes, and Marc E. Platt. Screenplay by Elfont and Kaplan.

The heroines of *Josie and the Pussycats* are not dumber than the Spice Girls, but they're as dumb as the Spice Girls, which is dumb enough. They're a girl band recruited as they're crossing the street by a promoter who wants to use their songs as a carrier for subliminal messages. The movie is a would-be comedy about prefab bands and commercial sponsorship, which may mean that the movie's own plugs for Coke, Target, Starbucks, Motorola, and Evian are part of the joke.

The product placement for Krispy Kreme doughnuts is, however, an ominous development, since it may trigger a war with Dunkin' Donuts, currently the most visible product placer in the movies. With Krispy and Dunkin' dukin' it out, there may soon be no doughnut-free movies not actually featuring gladiators.

The movie, based on a comic book from the Archie stable, stars Rachel Leigh Cook as Josie McCoy, its lead singer; Tara Reid as Melody Valentine, the bubble-brained blonde; and

Rosario Dawson as Valerie Brown. None of these women have families, friends, or employers, apparently, and are free to move randomly through the plot as a unit without ever calling home. After a prologue in which a previous prefab boy band disappears in a plane crash, a nefarious record producer named Wyatt Frame (Alan Cumming, the gay villain du jour) hires them on first sight, without hearing them sing a note, to be his newest promotion.

The prologue has some vaguely *Spinal Tap* overtones (I liked the detail that its members wear headsets at all times, not just onstage). But *Josie* ignores bountiful opportunities to be a satire of the Spice Girls and other manufactured groups, and gets dragged down by a lame plot involving the scheme to control teen spending with the implanted messages. (The movie calls them "subliminal." Since they're sound waves, they're actually "subaural," but never mind; the Pussycats would probably think subaural was a kind of foreplay.)

One curiosity about the movie is its stiff and sometimes awkward dialogue; the words don't seem to flow, but sound as if the actors are standing there and reciting them. The movie's market on verbal wit is cornered by Cumming, in the Richard E. Grant role, who has one (1) funny moment in which he demonstrates how very well trained the boy band is. The rest of the time, he has the thankless task of acting as if he is funny in a plot that is not funny.

The music is pretty bad. That's surprising, since Kenneth (Babyface) Edmunds is one of the producers, and knows his way around music. Maybe it's *supposed* to sound like brainless preteen fodder, but it's not good enough at being bad to be funny, and stops merely at the bad stage.

Parker Posey has one of those supporting roles from hell, where she has to make her entrance as a cliché and then never even gets to play with the conventions of her role. She's Cummings's boss, one of the masterminds of the nefarious subaural marketing scheme, and since she is, in fact, a funny and talented actress with wicked timing, her failure to make anything of this role is proof there's nothing for her to work with. Also drifting aimlessly through the plot is a character named Alexandra Cabot (Missi Pyle), who at least has the best explanation for why she's in the movie, as well as the movie's second (2nd) funny line of dialogue. "Why are you here?" she's asked, and replies with serene logic, "I'm here because I was in the comic book."

julien donkey-boy ★ ★ ★
R, 94 m., 1999

Ewen Bremner (Julien), Chloe Sevigny (Pearl), Werner Herzog (Father), Evan Neumann (Chris), Joyce Korine (Grandma), Chrissy Kobylak (Chrissy), Alvin Law (Neighbor), Victor Varnado (Albino Rapper). Directed by Harmony Korine and produced by Cary Woods, Scott Macaulay, and Robin O'Hara. Screenplay by Korine.

Is there an audience for movies like Harmony Korine's *julien donkey-boy*? The campus film freaks who used to support underground films have migrated to slick aboveground indie productions. There's no longer a fascination with films that are difficult and experimental. They can't fill a classroom these days, let alone a theater. Korine, who at twenty-five is one of the most untamed new directors, belongs on the list with Godard, Cassavetes, Herzog, Warhol, Tarkovsky, Brakhage, and others who smash conventional movies and reassemble the pieces.

Werner Herzog, the great German free spirit, is indeed one of the stars of *julien donkey-boy*, which is the story of a schizophrenic, told more or less through his own eyes. The film's style is inspired by Dogma 95, the Danish manifesto calling for movies to be made with handheld cameras, available light and sound, and props found on location. Korine shot his basic material using that approach, and then passed it through a lot of postproduction stages, so that at times it looks like abstract art seen through a glass, murkily. (The outtakes on the Website look like straightforward digital video; the movie rarely does.)

julien doesn't always work in its individual moments, but it works as a whole. It adds up to something, unlike a lot of movies where individual shots are sensational, but they add up to nothing. The characters emerge gradually from the kaleidoscopic style. We learn that Julien (Ewen Bremner, from *Trainspotting*) is a schizophrenic who lives at home with his bizarre father (Herzog), his fairly normal brother, Chris (Evan Neumann), and a sister, Pearl (Chloe Sevigny), who is carrying his child.

Life in this household consists of mind games, wrestling matches, and family fights. Herzog, as the father, is the ringleader. At various times he listens to bluegrass music while wearing a gas mask, lectures on the world championship for talking birds, praises *Dirty Harry* movies, and belittles his daughter's musical ambitions: "Why don't you tell your sister she is never going to learn to play this harp? She's a dilettante and a slut."

Sometimes this is funny. Sometimes it is sad. Some of it takes place so completely within Julien's mind that we can't be sure what really happens—the opening scene involving an attack on a boy and his pet turtle, for example. Other scenes take on a heartbreaking realism, as when Pearl has a miscarriage at an ice rink and Julien takes the stillborn infant in his arms, carries it home with him on the bus, and hides under his covers, cradling it and weeping.

The experience of seeing a movie like this is shocking for most moviegoers, and while some are stimulated by it, most resist and resent it. That's as it should be. No movie is made for everybody. *julien donkey-boy* is hardly made for anybody. It seems at first to be merely a jumble of discordant images (*Freaks* shot by the *Blair Witch* crew), but then, if you stay with it, the pattern emerges from the jumble.

You understand, first of all, that the point of view is that of a schizophrenic person. Second, that the family is dysfunctional to any outside observer but functions in its own way for its members. Third, that the story is filled with genuine emotion and even love (the movie is dedicated to Korine's schizophrenic uncle). An operatic aria plays in snatches throughout the film, and when it swells up at the end, it is a sad lament for the suffering of these characters.

Korine's background is well known. He was a skateboarder in New York when his screenplay about his friends was made into Larry Clark's *Kids* (1995), a harrowing portrait of street kids and their society. His second film, *Gummo*, unseen by me, won festival prizes at Venice and Rotterdam and was despised by a good majority of mainstream critics. Now comes *julien*, and it demonstrates that Korine is the real thing, an innovative and gifted

filmmaker whose work forces us to see on his terms.

To be sure, Korine is sometimes too willing to shock for fun. A talent show at a school for the blind is excessive, especially the cigarette-eating act; and appearances by an armless drummer and a black albino rap artist are not persuasively integrated into the rest of the film. But a scene in an African-American gospel church service begins as tourism and then deepens into something very moving, as Julien's eyes brim with tears. The odds are good that most people will dislike this film and be offended by it. For others, it will provoke sympathy rather than scorn. You know who you are.

Note: In a "confession" published on the movie's Website, Korine kids Dogma 95 at the same time he genuflects to it. He admits that although Dogma requires all props to be found on location, he imported a can of cranberries from a supermarket. And he apologizes that Chloe Sevigny, his real-life girlfriend, was not really pregnant in the movie ("I did try, though"), but only had a pillow stuffed under her clothes. He proudly adds that the pillow was found on the location, in his grandmother's bedroom closet. All this and more at www.juliendonkeyboy.com.

Just Visiting ★ ★ ★
PG-13, 88 m., 2001

Jean Reno (Thibault), Christina Applegate (Rosalind/Julia), Christian Clavier (André), Matthew Ross (Hunter), Tara Reid (Angelique), Bridgette Wilson-Sampras (Amber), John Aylward (Byron), George Plimpton (Dr. Brady), Malcolm McDowell (Wizard). Directed by Jean-Marie Poire and produced by Patrice Ledoux and Ricardo Mestres. Screenplay by Poire, Christian Clavier, and John Hughes.

A medieval sorcerer accidentally sends a French knight and his serf on a trip into the future—landing them in today's Chicago, where the elevated trains terrify them. But they grow to like the city, and when the sorcerer prepares to return them to the Middle Ages, the serf is against it: "I want to stay here, where I can eat doughnuts, and wear exciting men's fashions at rock-bottom prices."

Just Visiting, which tells their story, is one of

those rare American remakes of a French film that preserves the flavor of the original and even improves upon it. The movie is a remake of *The Visitors,* or *Les Visiteurs* (1993), which was the top-grossing comedy in French history, but did only moderate business in America. Like the original, it's broad and swaggering, but somehow it plays better in English—maybe because the fish-out-of-water concept works better with French and American accents, instead of everybody speaking in subtitles.

The movie, directed by Jean-Marie Poiré, wisely centers on its two original French stars, Jean Reno (of *Mission: Impossible* and *Godzilla*) and Christian Clavier. They look and sound the part; I can imagine the roles being assigned to Adam Sandler and David Spade, but I don't want to. Reno is Sir Thibault, a French knight who goes to Sussex to marry the beautiful Rosalind (Christina Applegate). His vassal André (Clavier) follows along, trotting obediently behind the cart and being whacked occasionally just to honor the class divide.

After a setup heavy on special effects and overacting, involving witches, cauldrons, and royal schemers, Thibault convinces a sorcerer (Malcolm McDowell) to jump them back a little in time, so they can get things right on a second try. The wizard, alas, miscalculates and sends them to modern Chicago, where the knight and serf are terrified by semis, awestruck by skyscrapers, and soon involved in the life of Thibault's great-great-great-great-great (I think) granddaughter Julia (Applegate again).

She's the heir to the family's old European fortune, founded all those years ago by Thibault, and the spitting image of his beloved Rosalind. But her boyfriend, the sneering Hunter (Matthew Ross) wants her to sell the family's European estate, so he can get his claws on the money. Thibault and André understandably have difficulty convincing Chicagoans they are really from the twelfth century, but their behavior certainly seems authentic enough (in a restaurant, Thibault expects André, as his servant, to eat off the floor).

Thibault cannot actually fall in love with Julia, since she is his great, etc., granddaughter, but since she looks exactly like the woman he loved, he cares for her deeply, and tries to protect her from Hunter's schemes while

schooling her in the ways of medieval gallantry. This involves a sword-fighting lesson in which they slice up refrigerators and Dumpsters, and a horsemanship adventure in which they actually ride their horses up the stairs, across an L platform, and onto the train.

André meanwhile falls in love with Angelique (Tara Reid), providing a counterpoint to the courtly idealism of his master. And every day is an adventure. Their first ride in a car, for example, is a terrifying experience. "Slower! Slower!" cries Thibault, as the car creeps at twenty miles per hour and both visitors hurl out the windows.

Is it only because the movie is in English that I like it more than the original? I hope I'm not that provincial. It strikes me that *Just Visiting* is brighter and sprightlier than *Les Visiteurs,* and the contrasts are funnier. Modern Europe is filled with Gothic and medieval piles, but in Chicago, when the visitors go looking for castles and turrets, they find them in the architecture of bars—where the regulars are always ready to drink with a man in armor, as long as he pays for his round.

There's something else too. *Just Visiting* isn't low and dumb like so many recent American comedies. It depends on the comedy of personality and situation, instead of treading meekly in the footsteps of the current gross-out manure-joke movies. Jean Reno, who usually plays a tough guy (remember him in *The Professional?*), plays Thibault more or less straight, taking his chivalric code seriously. Both he and Clavier try to appear truly baffled by what they see, instead of going straight for the gags.

Note: It must be said, all chauvinism aside, that the city of Chicago itself makes an important contribution. John Hughes, who sets almost all of his movies here, is one of the movie's producers and cowriters, and he knows the town better than any other director (maybe it's a tie with Andrew Davis). Chicago locations have not been better used in any movie since Davis's Code of Silence *and* The Fugitive *and Hughes's* Ferris Bueller's Day Off, *and they work not simply as backdrops but as dramatic settings. Given a knight on a horse in a city with elevated trains, it may seem inevitable that sooner or later he'd ride the horse onto the train, but it certainly looked like an inspired idea to me.*

K

Kadosh ★ ★ ★
NO MPAA RATING, 110 m., 2000

Yael Abecassis (Rivka), Yoram Hattab (Meir),
Meital Barda (Malka), Uri Ran Klausner
(Yossef), Yussef Abu Warda (Rav Shimon),
Sami Hori (Yaakov), Lea Koenig (Elisheva).
Directed by Amos Gitai and produced by
Laurent Truchot, Michel Propper, and Amos
Gitai. Screenplay by Amos Gitai, Eliette
Abecassis, and Jacky Cukier.

Kadosh is an Israeli film about the ultraorthodox
Jewish sect of Hassidim, where men make the
decisions and women are seen, narrowly, as
vessels for the production of more sons. It is a
very angry film, and has caused much discussion in Israel and within American Jewish circles, where most share its anger. Tolerance is
not the strong point of the Hassidim, and a
Jewish friend of mine was much saddened when
his family was spat upon in Jerusalem for mistakenly entering a place where they were not
welcome.

The film takes place in Mea Shearim, an
area of Jerusalem where life is regulated according to ancient and unwavering laws. It
tells the stories of two sisters, one married and
one single but in love with an unacceptable
man. Rivka and her husband, Meir, have been
married for ten years and still have no children, a fact that preys on the mind of Meir's
father, a rabbi. "The only task of a daughter of
Israel is bringing children into the world," he
believes, and eventually he orders his son to
divorce his wife and marry a younger woman
who might give him children. Meir protests—
he loves his wife—but eventually he obeys.
(Rivka has learned that her husband is sterile,
but cannot share this information because such
tests are forbidden.)

The other sister, Malka, has been in love for
years with a man named Yaakov (Sami Hori),
who was once a member of the sect but had to
leave it when he joined the Israeli army; his religion did not permit him to serve. There is
great family pressure on her to marry another
man, a religious zealot who cruises the streets
with a loudspeaker attached to his car, exhorting his listeners at deafening volume to see
things his way.

The film, directed by a longtime Israeli
documentarian named Amos Gitai, sees the
story largely through the eyes of the women,
who sometimes share rebellious thoughts like
naughty schoolgirls: Their men spend their
days in the study of the Torah, they observe, but
women are not allowed to read it—perhaps because they might not agree that it prescribes
such a limited life for women. Although some
marriages, like Rivka's, are happy, women are
actually told that their primary function in
life is to bear as many children as possible, to
"help vanquish the secular movement"—which
includes Jews whose observance does not mirror the strict ways of the sect.

The women are restive, but obedient. Rivka
leaves her house and goes to live alone, sinking into solitude and depression. Malka marries the zealot, and her wedding night brings
into cruel focus the definition of husbandly
duties. Their mother does not agree with what
has happened to them but dares not oppose
her husband. The men spend their days closed
off together in ceaseless study and debate, even
over the details for brewing (or not brewing)
tea on the Sabbath. (This particular discussion
seems more interested in finding theological
loopholes than in honoring the underlying
ideas.)

As I watched the film, I was reminded of
Two Women, an Iranian film I saw recently, in
which a woman was given a brief taste of freedom before being yanked out of college and
married to her father's choice of a mate. Extreme forms of belief in both films seem designed to rationalize a fear of sex and distrust
of women. My own notion is: I would be more
persuaded by religious laws that are harder on
the enforcers than on those under their authority, but it never seems to work out that
way.

It occurred to me, during *Kadosh,* that while
the Hassidim are a sect, the men within it have
essentially formed a cult—excluding women,
suspicious of others, dressing in such a way
that they cannot mix unnoticed with outsiders,
denying their own natures and instincts in

order to follow their leaders. Although I am sure happy lives can be led and happy marriages created within such boundaries—and I realize the story of *Kadosh* may be an extreme example, not typical—I left the film with the thought that if God in his infinite love cannot gather both sexes into his arms equally, then I would like to sit down with him and ask him, respectfully, what his problem is.

Keeping the Faith ★ ★ ★
PG-13, 129 m., 2000

Ben Stiller (Jake), Edward Norton (Brian), Jenna Elfman (Anna), Anne Bancroft (Ruth), Eli Wallach (Rabbi Lewis), Ron Rifkin (Larry Friedman), Lisa Edelstein (Ali Decker), Milos Forman (Father Havel), Holland Taylor (Bonnie Rose), Rena Sofer (Rachel Rose). Directed by Edward Norton and produced by Hawk Koch, Norton, and Stuart Blumberg. Screenplay by Blumberg.

Edward Norton's *Keeping the Faith* is a profoundly secular movie about the love lives of a priest and a rabbi. It shares the universal Hollywood presumption that love should conquer all—that gratification of immediate emotional needs is more important than ancient values. Both the rabbi and the priest are in love with the same girl, and if only priests were allowed to marry, or if only Jews didn't mind a rabbi with a gentile wife, their problems would be over—except for the problem of which one the girl chooses.

We in the audience have been trained by a multitude of other movies to cheer for romance, especially when the girl is played by the sunny and lovable Jenna Elfman, and the boys are Rabbi Ben Stiller and Father Ed Norton. The movie does finally nod toward tradition at the end, with a loophole in the form of one brief dialogue exchange that is easily missed. But make no mistake: Both of these boys are ready to sleep with this girl no matter what their theology teaches.

The screenplay by Stuart Blumberg, of course, casts the story as a romantic comedy, not an ethical dilemma, and on that level I enjoyed it, especially since the dialogue makes the characters more thoughtful than we might expect. The story begins when all three characters are best friends as children. They go everywhere together, share everything, and then the parents of Anna (Elfman) move to California. Jake (Stiller) grows up to be a rabbi, Brian (Norton) grows up to be a priest, and they remain best friends whose church and synagogue even share development of a community center. Then Anna moves back to New York.

She's very successful. "I'm like a plumber except I fix leaky corporations," she explains. The three old friends go out together to dinner and the movies, and it's clear both guys are thunderstruck with love. But Jake is the one she likes, although she also has a conversation with Brian about the "sex thing" that, in his mind at least, contains faint echoes of invitation.

Written by a Jew and directed by a Catholic, the film has an evenhanded approach where possible. But there is one imbalance. The priest, with his vow of chastity, is not supposed to date or marry. The rabbi, who is not getting any younger and is still a bachelor, is under enormous pressure from his mother (Anne Bancroft) and his entire congregation to date and marry a Jewish woman. Indeed, his job depends on it. And since the mechanics of the screenplay require him to love only Anna, it follows that he is unable to find a Jewish woman he likes enough to marry.

This dilemma leads to a series of scenes in which romantic candidates are paraded before him like exhibits from a bachelor's nightmares. We meet Ali, the pushy physical fitness nut (Lisa Edelstein), and Rachel (Rena Sofer), the glamorous ABC correspondent, and lots of other available women, who all seem to crowd the lens and gush all over the film, with their mothers smiling and nodding behind them. We get the point, but we question it: Isn't it possible to write a movie in which Jake just plain loves Anna, period—without making every visible Jewish girl obnoxious? My guess is that if Anna had stayed in California, Jake would have been crawling through broken glass to date the ABC correspondent.

These are the kinds of thoughts that occur after the film. During the film, we're swept up in the story's need to find a happy ending. In conservative moral terms, the happiest ending, of course, would be: (1) priest remains celibate, offers up his sacrifice; (2) rabbi explains "two different worlds we come from," wishes Anna well, marries nice Jewish girl, and (3) Anna returns to California, where all things are possible. It is safe to say that no audience would accept this ending, however, as there is an emotional conservatism that runs much deeper in movie audiences than any other form of belief, and which teaches: If a movie shows us a boy and a girl who are really in love, there *must* be a happy ending.

What helps is that all of the major characters in the movie are good people—yes, even Jake's mother, who is played gently by Anne Bancroft as a woman willing to admit her mistakes and learn from them. And I like the way the filmmakers bring in older role models for the two young men. Jake turns to old Rabbi Lewis (Eli Wallach) and the wise Larry Friedman (Ron Rifkin), the head of his congregation. Brian turns to old Father Havel (Milos Forman), who confesses to having fallen in love, big time, at least every decade of his priesthood.

Why are love stories comedies and not tragedies? Because it is funny when we lose control of ourselves despite our best efforts to remain dignified. A man in love has stepped on an emotional banana peel. When a woman falls in love with an unavailable man, he *is* a banana peel.

Keep the River on Your Right ★ ★ ★
R, 110 m., 2001

A documentary directed and produced by David Shapiro and Laurie Gwen Shapiro.

In the mid-1950s, a New York artist and anthropologist named Tobias Schneebaum walked into the rain forests of Peru, planning to paint some pictures there. His geographical knowledge was limited to the advice: Keep the river on your right. A year later, he walked out of the jungle naked, covered with body paint, having found and lived with an Indian tribe.

At some point during that year, the tribe went on a raid, killed enemies, and ate them. Schneebaum joined them in consuming human flesh. "Didn't you try to stop them?" someone asks him in this documentary. It is the kind of question asked by a person who has never had to live with cannibals, on their terms.

Schneebaum is not the kind of man you would immediately think of in connection with this adventure. Seventy-eight when the film was made, he is a homosexual aesthete who lectures on art and works as a tour guide on cruise ships. Yet his adventures were not limited to Peru, and in the extraordinary documentary *Keep the River on Your Right: A Modern Cannibal Tale,* he also revisits the jungles of New Guinea, where he lived with a tribe, took a male lover, and has a reunion with his old friend. Many years have passed, but the friend accepts him as warmly as if he'd been away for a week or two.

The visits to his old homes in New Guinea and Peru are not without hazards. Schneebaum isn't worried about jungle animals or diseases, but has more practical concerns on his mind, like breaking a hip: "If I slip on the mud, I've had it."

The movie is the work of a brother and sister, David Shapiro and Laurie Gwen Shapiro, who learned about Schneebaum and became determined to make a movie about him. It is a story he has been telling for years; he wrote a memoir about his adventures, and we see clips of him chatting about the book with Mike Douglas and Charlie Rose. He also, I imagine, gets good mileage out of his stories on those cruise ships, although he is not particularly eager to discuss cannibalism, and we sense pain that his dry, laconic style tries to mask. Asked how people taste, he answers shortly, "I don't remember." At another point, in another context, he observes: "I kind of died. Something I had that was made of me, and then it was gone after the Peruvian experience."

Can we speculate that he penetrated so close to the fault line of human existence that he lost the unspoken security we walk around with every day? Things may get bad for us, even hopeless, but we will not be naked in the jungle, face-to-face with life's oldest and most implacable code, eat or be eaten. Schneebaum doesn't strike us as the Indiana Jones sort. He didn't go into the jungle as a lark. Whatever happened there he prefers to describe in terms of its edges, its outside.

The sexuality he encountered in New Guinea is another matter, and there he cheers up. The men of the tribe he lived with have sex with both men and women and consider it natural.

We sense this is not the kind of sex people go looking for in big Western cities, but more of a pastime and consolation among friends. There is a certain shy warmth in the reunion with his former lover, but subtly different on Schneebaum's side than on the other man's, because sex between men means something different to each of them.

Tobias Schneebaum could probably develop a stand-up act based on his adventures, but he is more of a muser and a wonderer. "You're there to study them, not to play with them," he says sharply at one point. I met him at the 2000 Toronto Film Festival, where in interview and question sessions he answered as if he were a teacher or a witness, not a celebrity. We get glimpses of his earlier life in Greenwich Village (former neighbor Norman Mailer remembers him as "our house homosexual—terrified of a dead mouse"), and learn something of his painting and his books.

But mostly we are struck by the man. *Keep the River on Your Right* could have been quite a different kind of film, but the Shapiros wisely focus on the mystery of this man, who was spectacularly ill-prepared for both of his jungle journeys, and apparently walked away from civilization prepared to rely on the kindness of strangers. Perhaps it was his very naïveté that shielded him. The cannibals obviously had nothing to fear from him. Today, we learn, they no longer practice cannibalism, and indeed are well on their way down the capitalist assembly line, shedding their culture and learning to eat fast food. Tobias Schneebaum was not only their first visitor from "civilization," but their most benign.

Note: The flywheels at the MPAA Ratings Board have given this sweet and innocent movie an R rating, explaining "mature thematic material." Yes, but the cannibalism is not seen, only discussed. How can this film and Freddy Got Fingered, *with Tom Green biting a newborn baby's umbilical cord in two, deserve the same rating?*

Kikujiro ★ ★ ½
PG-13, 116 m., 2000

Beat Takeshi (Kikujiro), Yusuke Sekiguchi (Masao), Kayoko Kishimoto (Kikujiro's Wife), Yuko Daike (Masao's Mother), Kazuko Yoshiyuki (Masao's Grandmother), Beat Kiyoshi (Man at Bus Stop), Great Gidayu (Biker/Fatso), Rakkyo Ide (Biker/Baldy). Directed by Takeshi Kitano and produced by Masayuki Mori and Takio Yoshida. Screenplay by Kitano.

The little boy lives with his grandmother, who leaves food for him before she goes to work. The summer days stretch long, and the streets are empty. He is lonely, and finds the address of his mother, who works far away. He wants to visit her. The grandmother has a friend who has a husband who is a low-level gangster. The gangster is assigned to take the kid to find the mother, and that's the setup for *Kikujiro*, which is a lot of things, although one of them is not a sweet comedy about a gangster and a kid.

The movie was made by Takeshi Kitano, currently Japan's most successful director, and he stars in it under the name he uses as an actor, Beat Takeshi. Kitano is a specialist in taut, spare crime dramas where periods of quiet and tension are punctuated by sharp bursts of violence. *Kikujiro* is the last sort of film you would expect him to make—even though he skews the material toward his hard-boiled style and away from the obvious opportunities for sentiment.

Kikujiro, known only as "Mister" to the little boy, is played by Kitano as a man who is willing to seem a clown, but keeps his thoughts to himself. His dialogue to the kid is not funny to the kid, but might be funny to a third party, and since there is none (except for the audience), it seems intended for self-amusement. Unlike *Gloria* or *Little Miss Marker*, this movie's kid doesn't have much of a personality; he pouts a lot, and looks at Mister as if wondering how long he will have to bear this cross.

The two of them are essentially broke for most of the movie, after Mister trusts the kid's ability to pick the winners at a bicycle race track. The kid guesses one race right and all the others wrong, and so the man and the boy are reduced to hitching to the remote city where the mother may live. This turns the movie into a road picture that develops slapstick notes, as when Mister tries to stop cars by lying down in the road or positioning nails to cause flat tires. (His efforts produce one puncture, which results in a great sight gag.)

Some of the adventures, like the kid's run-in

with a child molester in a park, are fairly harrowing; the movie is rated only PG-13, but we can see why one paper mistakenly self-applied an R rating; scenes like this would be impossible in an American comedy, and it's all Kitano can do to defuse them enough to find comedy (very little, it is true) in them. Other scenes are funnier, including a road relationship with a couple of Hells Angels named "Baldy" and "Fatso," who despite their fearsome appearance are harmless. One extended sequence, when the man and boy are stranded at a remote bus stop, has a Chaplinesque quality.

If the movie finally doesn't work as well as it should, it may be because the material isn't a good fit for Kitano's hard-edged underlying style. Japanese audiences would know he is a movie tough guy (Clint Eastwood's Dirty Harry is our equivalent), and so they'd get the joke that he seems ineffectual and clueless. Western audiences, looking at the material with less of the context, are likely to find some scenes a little creepy, even though the cheerful music keeps trying to take the edge off. This same movie, remade shot-for-shot in America, wouldn't work at all, and only its foreign context blunts the bite of some scenes that are a little cruel or gratuitous.

Still, Takeshi Kitano is a fascinating filmmaker—a man with a distinctive style that's comfortable with long periods of inactivity. As an action director, he relishes the downtime, and keeps the action to a minimum; there is a relaxed rhythm, a willingness to let scenes grow at their own speed instead of being pumped out at top volume. I like the director and his style, but the material finally defeats him. You can't smile when you keep feeling sorry for the kid—who is not, after all, in on the joke.

Kingdom Come ★ ★

PG, 95 m., 2001

LL Cool J (Ray Bud Jr.), Jada Pinkett Smith (Charisse), Vivica A. Fox (Lucille), Loretta Devine (Marguerite), Anthony Anderson (Junior), Toni Braxton (Juanita), Cedric the Entertainer (Reverend Hooker), Whoopi Goldberg (Raynelle Slocumb), Darius McCrary (Royce). Directed by Doug McHenry and produced by Edward Bates and John Morrissey.

Screenplay by David Dean Bottrell and Jessie Jones, based on their play Dearly Departed.

In an opening scene of Kingdom Come, Whoopi Goldberg's husband drops dead at the breakfast table. This triggers a funeral, and Raynelle Slocumb (Goldberg) welcomes her children, in-laws, and descendants to a disorganized family reunion in which three or four subplots jostle for attention.

The movie is based on the play Dearly Departed, much performed by local theater groups, and has been adapted by the playwrights, David Dean Bottrell and Jessie Jones. The director, Doug McHenry, also has a long list of credits; as a producer or director he's been involved with New Jack City, House Party II, Jason's Lyric, and The Brothers. Together, they've made a movie that has generated a terrific trailer, making the film look like a warmhearted comedy. But the movie doesn't match the trailer.

Somewhere along the line a curious disconnect has taken place between the Whoopi Goldberg character and the others. She doesn't seem like their mother, their relative, or even an inhabitant of the same social milieu as the other members of her family. She's more like a wise, detached oracle, and when she's given comedy lines, they just don't fit. Early on, for example, she declares that her late husband was "mean as a snake, and surly." Later she insists that "Mean and Surly" be engraved on his tombstone. But she doesn't seem to hear them or feel them; they're words for another character in another movie, and have no connection to how she, or her children, feel about the dearly departed. With those and certain other lines, it's as if she's quoting a stranger.

We meet the family members, played by an all-star cast that never seems to mesh. Raynelle's son Ray Bud Jr. (LL Cool J) is married to Lucille (Vivica A. Fox). She's a scold; he's a good guy trying to handle a drinking problem. Her daughter Charisse (Jada Pinkett Smith) is married to another Junior (Anthony Anderson), who cheats on her. She's over the top in most of her scenes, which aren't played to the scale of the other performances. Another daughter, Marguerite (Loretta Devine), has her hands full with her son Royce (Darius McCrary), who apparently plans to nap through life, and taunts his mother with his shiftlessness. Then there's rich Cousin Juanita (Toni Braxton), and the pious Reverend Hooker (Cedric the Entertainer), who must officiate at the funeral and keep the peace.

Reverend Hooker makes some unwise dietary choices shortly before the funeral begins and farts all the way through it, causing the congregation to break up at this solemn moment. This material is an example of the movie's approach, which is all over the map. Fart jokes have their place, I concede, when the Klump family is at the dinner table. They may even have their place at a funeral—but not one where Raynelle has so recently had a heart-to-heart with Ray Bud Jr. The film changes tone so quickly we get whiplash.

There are times when the movie plays like a pilot for a TV comedy. Each family unit is given a costume, speaking style, and lifestyle that seems self-contained, so that when they assemble it's like a collision involving separate sitcoms. Some of the humor is broad and bawdy, some is observational, some is whimsical, and sometimes the humor collapses into sentiment. The central problem is that the movie seems unsure whether the late Bud Slocumb was indeed mean and surly—and if he was, how it feels about it. Is his death a loss or a liberation?

The pieces are here for a better movie. The cast is capable. A rewrite or two might have helped. *Kingdom Come* has passably funny moments, but they don't connect; it might work on video for viewers who glance up at the screen from time to time. The more attention you pay to it, the less it's there.

The King Is Alive ★ ★ ★

R, 105 m., 2001

Jennifer Jason Leigh (Gina), Miles Anderson (Jack), Romane Bohringer (Catherine), David Bradley (Henry), David Calder (Charles), Bruce Davison (Ray), Brion James (Ashley), Peter Khubeke (Kanana), Vusi Kunene (Moses), Janet McTeer (Liz). Directed by Kristian Levring and produced by Patricia Kruijer and Vibeke Windelov. Screenplay by Anders Thomas Jensen and Levring, based on *King Lear* by William Shakespeare.

In the Namibian desert in southwest Africa, a tourist bus strays far off course and runs out of petrol. The passengers stumble into the blinding sun and find themselves at an abandoned German mining station, its only occupant an old African who surveys them impassively. Jack (Miles Anderson) is the only passenger with any desert experience. He lectures them: There are five things you need to survive in the desert, and in descending order of importance they are water, food, shelter, making yourself visible, and keeping up your spirits.

Well, there is food here (rusted cans of carrots), water (they can collect the morning dew), and old buildings. They tend a signal fire at night. Jack walks off in search of help. Those left behind consider a suggestion by Henry (David Bradley) that they rehearse a production of *King Lear* to keep their spirits up. *Lear* is not the first play one thinks of when spirits sink, but perhaps in this desolate landscape it is a better choice than *The Producers*.

We meet the tourists, without ever discovering what they were seeking in Namibia (they took the bus after their flight was canceled). Many seem more appropriate for a play by Beckett, and Ray and Liz (Bruce Davison and Janet McTeer) are a squabbling couple out of Albee (when Ray asks her what *King Lear* is about, she replies: "You don't have to worry, you know. Nobody has to fall in love and everybody gets to die in the end").

Hardly anybody dies in the end of the movie, but a lot of them have sex, which seems inspired less by pleasure than by the desire to annoy. There are moments of truth and despair, marital crises, denunciations, renunciations, false hopes, and raving madness. Henry writes out the roles for the play (chosen, we suspect, simply because he happened to know it by heart), there are rehearsals, and finally a performance of sorts. But although the movie's credits say "Based on *King Lear* by William Shakespeare," I was unable to sift through the cast finding specific characters who represented Cordelia, Regan, Kent, the Fool, etc. I think perhaps the play acts more as a mirror; like Lear, they are lost in the wilderness and no longer have faith in goodness.

The King Is Alive is the fourth of the Dogma 95 movies, so called because of a "vow of chastity" signed by the four Danish directors Kristian Levring (who directed this one), Thomas Vinterberg *(Celebration)*, Søren Kragh-Jacobsen *(Mifune)*, and Lars von Trier *(The Idiots)*. Dogma wanna-bes have been produced by Harmony Korine *(julien donkey-boy)*, and von Trier made a half-Dogma, half-musical *(Dancer in the Dark)*. What they have in common is a rough, immediate feel: The drama isn't too formed, the dialogue isn't tamed, the lighting and music are found on the set, the performances seem raw and improvisational.

In *The King Is Alive,* the Dogma approach helps the film look like what might have resulted if one of the characters had used a digital camera. It has the same relationship to a commercial film that their production of *King Lear* has to a conventional staging. It's built from raw materials, needs, and memories, instead of off-the-shelf parts from the movie store.

On one level, of course, we're aware of the artifice. It's an old dramatic formula to strand a group of characters somewhere and have them try to survive while conditions edge toward the primitive. Cross *Lord of the Flies* with *Flight of the Phoenix* and add *Lifeboat* and you have this film's second cousin. On another level, this kind of story gives great opportunities to actors, who can test their emotional range. But what does the audience get out of it?

I imagine many people would be actively hostile to *The King Is Alive*. It doesn't make the slightest effort to cater to conventional appetites. But the more you appreciate what they're trying to do, the more you like it. I saw it for the first time at Cannes in May 2000, and it stuck with me. It didn't fade in the memory. Ungainly, ill-formed, howling, and desperate, it was there and endured—while, of the more forgettable films, I could observe with Lear that nothing will come of nothing.

The King of Masks ★ ★ ★
NO MPAA RATING, 101 m., 1999

Zhu Xu (Bian Lian Wang), Zhou Ren-Ying (Doggie), Zhang Riuyang (Tien Che), Zhao Zhigang (Liang Sao Lang). Directed and produced by Wu Tianming. Screenplay by Wei Minglung.

In a remote area of China, in the 1930s, we meet an old street performer. His profession is humble but his secrets are a great prize. One day a famous female impersonator from the Sichuan opera sees him performing, gives him a big coin, invites him to tea, and offers him a job in his troupe. But the old man, whose name is Wang, refuses this offer because it is a tradition in his family that the secrets are passed only from father to son.

Alas, Wang (played by Zhu Xu with touching appeal) has no son. And at his age, traveling the rivers in his little houseboat from one town to another, it is unlikely he will ever have one. The female impersonator begs him: "Do not die without an heir, or your magic will die too." Wang takes this advice to heart. It is a time of floods and homelessness, and in the next city there is a baby market where desperate parents look for homes for their hungry children—and cash. Wang is about to leave when an urchin cries out "Grandpa!" and captures his heart. He pays $10 for the eight-year-old, returns with him to his boat, and nicknames him Doggie. Together they will study the ancient art of silk masks, by which a man's face can take on a new and startling visage in the flash of a second.

That's the setup for *The King of Masks,* a new Chinese film of simplicity, beauty, and surprising emotional power. Like *Central Station,* it tells the story of a journey involving an old curmudgeon and a young child in search of a father. The difference is that the curmudgeon can become the father, if he chooses. And another one: Doggie is not a little boy, but a little girl.

Girls are not highly valued in China. When he discovers the deception, Wang feels cheated and wants to send Doggie away, but Doggie tearfully explains that she pretended to be a boy because she had been sold seven times already: The man who sold her was not her father, but a man who beat her. She promises to scrub the deck, do the cooking, and be a good doggie. The little girl, played with utter simplicity and solemnity by Zhou Ren-Ying, has already touched the old man's heart and he allows her to stay.

The King of Masks benefits by the survival of ancient ways into modern times. Today a street performer might be scorned, but in the 1930s he was seen as a member of an elite fraternity. Wang has a certain fame in the cities where he appears, and gains respect from his colleagues—even the female impersonator who is a great opera star, doted on by army generals. (The character, Liang, who dresses elegantly and travels in state, is played by the opera star Zhao Zhigang; we recall the tradition of female impersonators in Chinese opera from *Farewell, My Concubine.*)

Wang's life is happy, but he frets for a son and visits Buddhist temples (where Doggie plays happily among the toes of vast statues hewn from the hillside). One day Doggie comes upon a homeless little boy, and brings him home as a prize for old Wang, who is overjoyed. But the boy comes attached to great complications, and soon only Doggie can save Wang from imprisonment.

The King of Masks was directed by Wu Tianming, who as a studio head in the 1980s helped bring the Fifth Generation of Chinese filmmakers to prominence. After Tiananmen Square he moved to the United States, and returned only in 1995. This is his first film after his homecoming, and although it has no overt political message, perhaps it is no accident that its hero is a stubborn old artist who clings to his secrets.

Like so many recent Chinese films, it benefits enormously from the beauty of the setting, the costumes, and the customs. It's poignant to realize that a society of such unique beauty existed so recently. The river life of Wang and Doggie may be at the poverty level, but it has a quality that no modern rich man can afford. The story contains elements of fable (the changeling, ancient secrets), but gains weight because we know that to Wang it makes a great difference whether Doggie is a boy or a girl. And Doggie's heroics at the end seem like melodrama until we reflect that, trained by a street artist, she would have known what she was doing.

Note: The King of Masks *is being marketed as an art film for grown-ups. But as I watched it, I realized it would be an absorbing experience for bright children. Yes, there are subtitles, but no words a good reader wouldn't know. And the focus on the eight-year-old girl (not to mention Wang's beloved pet monkey) make this a magical film for third-graders and up. If you know the right child, this is the right film.*

A Knight's Tale ★ ★ ★
PG-13, 132 m., 2001

Heath Ledger (William), Rufus Sewell (Count Adhemar), Shannyn Sossamon (Jocelyn), Paul Bettany (Chaucer), Laura Fraser (Kate), Mark Addy (Roland), Alan Tudyk (Wat), Berenice Bejo (Christiana). Directed and produced by Brian Helgeland. Screenplay by Helgeland.

It is possible, I suppose, to object when the audience at a fifteenth-century jousting match begins to sing Queen's "We Will Rock You" and follows it with the Wave. I laughed. I smiled, in fact, all through Brian Helgeland's *A Knight's Tale*, which tells the story of a low-born serf who impersonates a knight, becomes a jousting champion, and dares to court the daughter of a nobleman.

Some will say the movie breaks tradition by telling a medieval story with a sound track of classic rock. They might as well argue it breaks the rules by setting a 1970s rock opera in the Middle Ages. To them I advise: Who cares? A few days after seeing this movie, I saw Baz Luhrmann's *Moulin Rouge,* which was selected to open the Cannes Film Festival despite being set in 1900 and beginning with the hero singing "The Sound of Music." In the case of *A Knight's Tale,* Helgeland has pointed out that an orchestral score would be equally anachronistic, since orchestras hadn't been invented in the 1400s. For that matter, neither had movies.

The film stars Heath Ledger, said to be the next big thing on the Australian sex symbol front, as William, a servant to a knight. The knight is killed, and his servants will be eating parboiled hedgehogs unless someone comes up with an idea. Along happens a desperate and naked man who makes them an offer: "Clothe, feed, and shoe me, and I'll give you your patents!" *Brewer's Dictionary* teaches us that "letters patent" are documents signed by a sovereign, conferring such rights as a title of nobility. The man offering to forge them introduces himself as Chaucer (Paul Bettany), and indeed, *A Knight's Tale* is a very, very, *very* free adaptation of one of his *Canterbury Tales.*

With the forged patents and the dead knight's suit of armor to disguise him, William and his sidekicks Roland and Wat (Mark Addy and Alan Tudyk) put themselves through one of those standard movie training montages and are soon ready to enter a joust, which is the medieval version of golf, with your opponent as the ball. There are many fearsome jousting matches in the movie, all of them playing with perspective and camera angles so that the horses and their riders seem to thunder at high speed for thirty seconds down a course that would take about five, until one knight or the other unseats his opponent three times and takes the victory.

This is not handled with great seriousness but in the spirit of high fun, and there is the evil Count Adhemar (Rufus Sewell) as an opponent. Since the knights wear armor guarding their faces, it might seem hard to distinguish them, but since time immemorial the movies have solved this dilemma by giving good knights attractive facial armor, and bad knights ugly little asymmetrical slits to peer through. I imagine a bad knight going into the armor store and saying, "I want the ugliest facial mask in the place!" Darth Vader is the only villain in the movies with a cool face plate.

Anyway, there are lots of babes in jousting land, especially the lady Jocelyn (Shannyn Sossamon), whose father is the ruler (at a banquet after the first tournament, she dances with William as David Bowie sings "Golden Years"). There is also a cute blacksmithess named Kate (Laura Fraser), who must be good, as she has obviously not been kicked in the head much.

The movie is centered around a series of jousting matches, alternating with threats to unveil the secret of William's identity. Finally we arrive at the World Championships in London, alas without the movie supplying a definition of what in these pre-Columbian times is considered the "world." My guess is that the World Championship of Jousting is to England as the World Series is to North America. Another thing they have in common: Both events feature "The Boys Are Back in Town."

The movie has an innocence and charm that grows on you. It's a reminder of the days before films got so cynical and unrelentingly violent. *A Knight's Tale* is whimsical, silly, and romantic, and seeing it after *The Mummy Returns* is like taking Tums after eating the Mummy. ☞

L

La Ciudad (The City) ★ ★ ★
NO MPAA RATING, 88 m., 2000

Bricks—Ricardo Cuevas (Man), Anthony Rivera (Boy), Joe Rigano (Contractor). *Home*—Cipriano Garcia (Young Man), Leticia Herrera (Young Woman). *The Puppeteer*—Jose Rabelo (Father), Stephanie Viruet (Daughter). *Seamstress*—Silvia Goiz (Seamstress), Rosa Caguana (Friend), Guillermina de Jesus (Friend). Directed by David Riker and produced by Riker and Paul S. Mezey. Screenplay by Riker.

Those who leave their native land and immigrate to another are often, almost by definition, the boldest and most capable, able to imagine a new life for themselves. Arriving in a new land without language or connections, they are likely to be shuttled into low-paying jobs and scorned by the lucky citizens who are already onboard. They earn their living by seizing opportunities.

Consider the puppeteer (Jose Rabelo), who is the third subject of David Riker's *La Ciudad (The City)*. He lives in a station wagon with his daughter (Stephanie Viruet). He supports them both by performing Punch and Judy shows for city kids, whose video games must make this entertainment look quaint. His daughter loves to read, is bright, wants to go to school. He tries everything to get her accepted. Every child is guaranteed a place in school, he has been told, but there is a hitch: He needs a receipt for rent or a telephone to show where he lives. And, of course, he lives in a car.

His story is one of four in *The City*, a direct, spare, touching film developed by Riker during six years of acting workshops with immigrants in New York City. His characters come from the Spanish-speaking lands to the south, have arrived in New York filled with hope, and now are exploited as cheap labor.

The first of his stories, *Bricks*, is about day laborers. They're hired a truckload at a time to be carted out to a work site, where they're promised $50 a day only to find out that is a theoretical sum and the job is piecework—fifteen cents for every brick they chip clean of mortar. A man (Ricardo Cuevas) wants to bring along his boy (Anthony Rivera). "This isn't a

day-care center," growls the foreman. But if the man is to work, is the boy to wait alone on the streets? There is an accident at the construction site, and we see how expendable these day workers are considered to be.

The second story, named *Home*, is the most bittersweet because it suggests the possibility of hope, even love. A young man (Cipriano Garcia) arrives in the city from Mexico. He crashes a party and finds himself dancing with a woman (Leticia Herrera) who, wonder of wonders, is from his hometown. He confesses to her: "My whole life is in this bag I am carrying." She responds with sweet formality, "I invite you to my home." They have the promise of happiness. And then, in an O. Henry ending, the man's hand closes on air.

Seamstress, the final story, is about a woman (Silvia Goiz) who has left her village and country to earn money to buy medicine for a sick child. Now she works in a sweatshop where no wages have been paid for weeks—and when she asks for her pay, she is fired. The other workers listen silently and glance out of the corners of their eyes. They have no job security, and they need this work desperately; will they express solidarity with her?

The Italian neorealists Rossellini and De Sica believed that everyone could play at least one role in a movie—himself. The movie camera is an effortless recorder of authenticity (it does just as well when exposing the false), and in *The City* we sense in the faces and voices of the performers an experience shared at firsthand. Their stories may be fictional, but their knowledge of them is true. The film is in black and white, as it must be; these spare outlines would lose so much power in color. Riker does an interesting thing with his writing: He never quite closes a story. The open endings are a way of showing that these lives continue from one trouble to another, without happy endings.

I saw this film at its first public screening at the 1998 Toronto Film Festival. Finally it is making its way around the country, at venues like the Film Center of the Art Institute of Chicago. It is a film that would have great power for Spanish-speaking working people, who, of course, are not likely to find it at the Art Institute. Eventually, on television, it may find broader audiences. It gives faces to the faceless, and is not easily forgotten.

La Cucaracha ★ ★ ★
R, 94 m., 1999

Eric Roberts (Walter), Tara Crespo (Lourdes), Alejandro Patino (Fruit Vendor), Joaquim de Almeida (Jose Guerras). Directed by Jack Perez and produced by Michael A. Candela and Richard Mann. Screenplay by James McManus.

One moment Walter is sleeping the sleep of the damned. The next moment his eyes snap open, he sits bolt upright, and runs in terror out of his shack, running through the sagebrush to the nearest cantina, where he gasps out an order for cerveza. Lots of cerveza. Eventually he is passed out at his table, sleeping now the sleep of a man who keeps terror at bay with drunkenness.

The title of La Cucaracha is possibly inspired by Walter, who like a cockroach hides in cracks and crannies and lives on the crumbs he picks up in bars. Once he was a would-be novelist, and sometimes he writes (or hallucinates that he writes) letters back home about how he cannot write his novel. He claims he is hiding out in Santiago, Mexico, because he killed a man. Unlikely. Like the consul who is the hero of Malcolm Lowry's great novel Under the Volcano, reality and fantasy both look the same to him.

Walter is played by Eric Roberts, often an intense and passionate actor, rarely more so than here, where with a bandage holding his broken glasses together, he peers out at a world that terrifies him. He is at the end of his rope, so strung out on booze that sobriety is only an invitation for the DTs. How does a man arrive at such a dead end, so far from home? By accident, bad habits, and rotten luck.

There is a beautiful woman in the town. He yearns for her. He stands in the night and watches her inside her house. He has nothing to offer her. A stranger approaches him in the bar with an offer of $100,000 if he will kill a man. A man, he is told, who is a child killer. He is not sure he can kill, but he is sure he needs $100,000. Soon he is holding a gun on the man he has been paid to kill. He does not pull the trigger.

"If you were worth the money they paid you, I would be dead five minutes ago," the man tells him. "Please—do what you came for." He hesitates. Now the man says: "The man who really killed the boy was the man who hired you. He could not stand the idea that his son was a homosexual."

Does he pull the trigger? The beauty of La Cucaracha is that it doesn't matter. This is a movie gloriously free of plot, and all the boring obligatory twists and turns that plot drags along with it. It is a character study about a man in peril. It was directed by Jack Perez and written by James McManus, who at one point includes dialogue mentioning Hemingway, Lowry, and Graham Greene—who wrote about men at the end of the line, drunken writers and whiskey priests. Walter is in that tradition.

The movie won the Austin Film Festival in 1998 and then disappeared until its current limited release. Perez's two earlier credits are The Big Empty (1997), which despite its promising title apparently never opened anywhere, and America's Deadliest Home Video, which went straight to same.

Now comes this intriguing, stylish little film. In superficial ways it's like El Mariachi, the film that made Robert Rodriguez's reputation, except that it lacks a strong marketing push, is not as cheaply made, and is more interested in character than action. It also has a wicked strain of humor, leading to such lines as, "If it's any consolation, this money will now be spent to build a pediatric ward in Santiago hospital."

It must have required a certain courage for Eric Roberts to take a role like this. It's not a prestigious job for a former Oscar nominee. But it's a juicy role for an actor whose career has meandered recently (what was he doing in Best of the Best 2?). His performance evokes some of the same desperation and determination as Warren Oates's work in Peckinpah's great Bring Me the Head of Alfredo Garcia. He's willing to go over the top with it—and yet his performance is not the manic hyperactivity we sometimes see from him; he finds a sadder, more controlled note.

The movie is not for everybody. Some people will no doubt find it silly, or yearn for the consolations of formula and genre. But the more you're into nuance and atmosphere, the more you appreciate a movie that evokes instead of explains, the more you might like it.

The Ladies Man ★
R, 84 m., 2000

Tim Meadows (Leon Phelps), Karyn Parsons (Julie), Billy Dee Williams (Lester), Tiffani Thiessen (Honey DeLune), Lee Evans (Barney), Will Ferrell (Lance), Julianne Moore (Bloopie). Directed by Reginald Hudlin and produced by Lorne Michaels. Screenplay by Tim Meadows, Dennis McNicholas, and Andrew Steele.

The Ladies Man is yet another desperately unfunny feature-length spin-off from *Saturday Night Live,* a TV show that would not survive on local access if it were as bad as most of the movies it inspires. There have been good *SNL* movies, like *Wayne's World, The Blues Brothers,* and *Stuart Saves His Family.* They all have one thing in common: *SNL* producer Lorne Michaels was not primarily responsible for them.

Michaels had nothing to do with *Stuart* and *Brothers.* Credit for the glories of the *Wayne's World* pictures, which he did produce, should arguably go to their directors and stars. Mike Myers went on to *Austin Powers.* Michaels went on to *Coneheads, Superstar, A Night at the Roxbury,* and now *The Ladies Man.*

If I were a Hollywood executive, I would automatically turn down any Michaels *SNL* project on the reasonable grounds that apart from the Mike Myers movies he has never made a good one. He doesn't even come close. His average star rating for the last four titles is 1.125. Just to put things in perspective, the last three Pauly Shore movies I reviewed scored 1.5.

The Ladies Man, directed by Reginald *(House Party)* Hudlin, stars Tim Meadows as Leon Phelps, a boundlessly enthusiastic seducer who seems stylistically and ideologically stuck in the sexist early 1970s. The character, with his disco suits and giant Afro, is funny on TV—but then so are most of the reoccurring *SNL* characters; that's why the show recycles them. At feature length, Leon loses his optimistic charm and slogs through a lamebrained formula story that doesn't understand him.

He plays a radio talk show host in Chicago (i.e., Toronto with CTA buses), who offers late-night advice to the sexually challenged. (To one lonely lady who can't seem to meet the right guy: "Take yo panties off and hang out at the bus station.") In real life he has extraordinary luck picking up girls, for reasons perhaps explained in one scene where he displays his equipment to a girl he's just met. We can't share the sight because he's standing on the other side of the bar, but from the way her face lights up while angelic music swells on the sound track, his pants obviously contain a spotlight and the Mormon Tabernacle Choir.

Leon gets into trouble for what he says on the radio, is fired, and lands briefly at a Christian station, where he tries to sound devout but finds the struggle is too much for him. Following him loyally is his producer Julie (Karyn Parsons), who likes him because she can see he's a nice guy inside. Tiffani Thiessen costars as one of Leon's admirers, Billy Dee Williams is the bartender and narrator, and Julianne Moore has an inexplicable scene as the lustful Bloopie the Clown.

There is a painfully bad sequence involving bets in a bar about who is willing to eat what; it exists *only* to get a merde-eating scene into the movie. Meanwhile, a posse of outraged husbands forms on the Internet and wants to hunt Leon down for seducing their wives. They know they're all looking for the same guy because he has a smiley face tattooed on his butt. At one point the outraged husbands have a song-and-dance scene. The movie makes the mistake of thinking it is funny *that* they sing and dance; next-level thinking would have suggested their song and dance be funny in itself.

All of the outraged husbands but one are white. Leon is black. The movie makes no point of this, for which we can be grateful, since lynch mobs are very hard to make amusing. Spike Lee's *Bamboozled* would have been funnier if this very movie, rather than a blackface minstrel show, had been offered as an example of black stereotypes marketed by white executives. While Lee's fictitious TV show could never conceivably be aired, *The Ladies Man* has been made and distributed and is in theaters as proof that Lee's pessimism is not exaggerated.

Lakeboat ★ ★ ★
R, 98 m., 2001

Charles Durning (Skippy), Peter Falk (The Pierman), Denis Leary (The Fireman), Robert Forster (Joe Pitko), J. J. Johnston (Stan), Tony Mamet (Dale Katzman), Jack Wallace (Fred), George Wendt (First Mate Collins), Andy Garcia (Guigliani). Directed by Joe Mantegna and produced by Tony Mamet, Mantegna, and Morris Ruskin. Screenplay by David Mamet.

Lakeboat was the tenth play by David Mamet to be produced, but it feels like the wellspring. Here in the rough, awkward, poetic words of the crew members of a Lake Michigan ore boat, he finds the cadences that would sound through his work. The play was first produced in 1981, and three years later came *Glengarry Glen Ross.* Both draw from his early jobs, when as a college student he supported himself working on a lake steamer and as a real-estate salesman. Both are unusual because their young protagonists are not heroes, but witnesses. These plays are not about a young man coming of age, but about older men who have come of age. In *Lakeboat,* a veteran crew member, a thoughtful loner who spends all of his free time reading books, tells the young cook, "You got it made."

We sense that men like these taught the young Mamet how his characters would think and talk. They're not narrow proletarians but men confident of themselves and their jobs, and yet needful of the isolation and loneliness of long lake voyages. No one quotes Melville, who said a ship was his Yale and his Harvard, but his words must have been in Mamet's mind as he created Dale Katzman, a second-year graduate student from "a school outside Boston," who signs on as a cook and sails with the *Seaway Queen.*

Dale is played by Tony Mamet, David's brother. The music is by Bob Mamet, another brother. The screenplay adaptation is by David and the direction is by Joe Mantegna, who has appeared in countless Mamet plays. The key actors include two who have been with him from the beginning, Jack Wallace and J. J. Johnston, and others who show how the poignancy and rhythm of the material allows them living space inside the words: Robert Forster, Charles Durning, Peter Falk, George Wendt, Denis Leary, Andy Garcia. I once taught a class on Mamet's films. I wish I could have opened it with this one, because for Mamet it all starts here.

It is important to note that nothing "happens" in the film in conventional movie-plot terms. It is not about a storm, a mutiny, a personal conflict, an old grudge. There is some mystery about why the regular cook, Guigliani (Garcia), is missing on the voyage, but he makes a space for Dale to be hired, and when the ship sails there is nothing much to be done but get the ore to the other end. Denis Leary plays the fireman, who tells Dale: "I keep my eye on the gauges. I watch them constantly." Yes, and studies porno magazines, although why a man would sign on for a world without women and then yearn for them is a question Mamet asks just by creating the character.

Another crew member with theories about women is Fred, played by Jack Wallace in a performance of such crude sweetness you can hear echoes of those very first Mamet plays, when Wallace was onstage in church basements and rented storefronts. Like most limited men, Fred knows a few things very well, and repeats them often to give himself the air of an expert. He thinks he knows all about women (they like to be smacked around a little, so they can see that the guy really cares). Fred delivers a meditation on the use of the f-word that could be printed as an introduction to Mamet's plays.

If Fred's obsession is with women, Stan (J. J. Johnston) is fascinated and baffled by drink. Booze too is a companion, always there to underline the good times and drown the bad ones, and Stan lectures Dale on drink the way Fred does on women. Both of them give extraordinarily bad advice, but not without having given their subjects a good deal of misguided thought.

The captain (Charles Durning) and first mate (George Wendt) are heavy-set men whose weight makes their movements into commitments. They have worked together a long time, long enough so that the skipper can ask the mate to make him a sandwich without giving offense. Without being sexual, their relationship seems domestic. They fiercely love their jobs.

It is the crew member Joe Pitko (Robert Forster) who is young Dale's mentor, the one he will remember with the most affection many years later. This is a working man who hungers for the life of the mind, and who leads two parallel lives, one in his work, the other in his books. There was perhaps a turning point in his life when he might have gone to school or tested some secret dream, but he took the safe bet of a regular paycheck and now finds himself working with men he cannot have nourishing conversations with. The college boy is a godsend. Pitko, in an unspoken way, gives his blessing to the fact that the boy may someday turn this summer of work into a story or a play. Pitko is not so narrow that he sees himself only as the subject for something the kid might write: He also sees himself as audience and critic.

The lakeboat sails on. Mantegna gives us just enough detail, enough exterior shots, so that we feel we're on a ship. All the rest is conversation and idleness. What do men think about on a long uneventful voyage? The routine of their work, the personalities of their crewmates, the certainty of their paychecks, the elusiveness of their dreams, the rhythms of their anecdotes, and sex. The lakeboat is a lot like life.

Lake Placid ★

R, 82 m., 1999

Bridget Fonda (Kelly Scott), Bill Pullman (Jack Wells), Oliver Platt (Hector Cyr), Brendan Gleeson (Sheriff Keough), Betty White (Mrs. Bickerman), Meredith Salenger (Deputy Sharon Gare). Directed by Steve Miner and produced by David E. Kelley and Michael Pressman. Screenplay by Kelley.

"What an animal does in the water is his own business—unless he does it to man." So says Sheriff Keough, one of the crocbusters of *Lake Placid*. I couldn't disagree with him more. The thirty-foot crocodile in this movie stays peacefully in the water, contentedly munching on bears and cows, until scuba-diving beaver-taggers invade his domain. It's their own fault that the beast gets mad and eats a scientist and half a game warden.

The croc inhabits Black Lake in Maine. (There is no Lake Placid in the movie, which may be its most intriguing mystery.) It is, we learn, an Asian crocodile. "How did he swim across the sea?" a lawman asks, not unreasonably. "They conceal information like that in books," one of the movie's croc lovers answers sarcastically. I dunno; I thought it was a pretty good question.

As the movie opens, two game wardens are tagging beavers to study their movements. Suddenly they're attacked by an underwater camera, which lunges at them in an unconvincing imitation of an offscreen threat. It becomes clear that Black Lake harbors more than beavers, although for my money the scenes involving beavers were the scariest in the movie. Can you imagine being underwater inside a beaver dam with angry animals the size of footstools whose teeth can chomp through logs?

When it becomes clear that Black Lake harbors a gigantic beast, an oddly assorted crew assembles to search for it. There's fish warden Jack Wells (Bill Pullman), museum paleontologist Kelly Scott (Bridget Fonda), Sheriff Keough (Brendan Gleeson), and millionaire croc-lover Hector Cyr (Oliver Platt), a mythology professor who believes "crocodiles are divine conduits." Oh, and there's Mrs. Bickerman (Betty White), who lives in a cute little farm cottage on the shores of the lake and lost her husband a few years ago. That's her story, anyway.

Whether the movie was intended at any point to be a serious monster thriller, I cannot say. In its present form it's an uneasy compromise between a gorefest and a comedy—sort of a failed *Anaconda*. One peculiar aspect is the sight of an expensive cast in such a cheap production. We're looking at millions of dollars' worth of actors in the kind of aluminum boat you see on display outside Sam's Club. Given the size of the crocodile, this movie lends a new meaning to the classic *Jaws* line, "We're going to need a bigger boat."

There's tension between the locals and the visitors, between the croc lovers and the croc killers, between the sheriff and the state game officials, between the sexes, and between everybody else and Betty White, who uses language that would turn the Golden Girls green. Almost all of the disagreements involve incredibly stupid decisions (would you go scuba-diving in a lake with a hungry giant crocodile?). New meaning also is given to the disclaimer "no animals were harmed during the filming of this movie" by a scene where a cow is dangled from a helicopter as bait for the crocodile. I believe the cow wasn't harmed, but I'll bet she was really upset.

Occasional shots are so absurd they're just plain funny. Consider the way thousands of perch jump into the air because they're scared of the crocodile. What's their plan? Escape from the lake? I liked the way the croc's second victim kept talking after he'd lost half his body. And the way the Fonda character was concerned about toilet and tent facilities in their camp; doesn't she know she's an hour's drive from Freeport, Maine, where L.L. Bean can sell her a folding condo?

The movie is pretty bad, all right. But it has a certain charm. It's so completely wrongheaded from beginning to end that it develops a doomed fascination. We can watch it switching tones within a single scene—sometimes between lines of dialogue. It's gruesome, and then camp, and then satirical, and then sociological, and then it pauses for a little witty intellectual repartee. Occasionally the crocodile leaps out of the water and snatches victims from the shore, looking uncannily like a very big green product from the factory where they make Barney dolls. This is the kind of movie that actors discuss in long, sad talks with their agents.

Lara Croft Tomb Raider ★ ★ ★
PG-13, 96 m., 2001

Angelina Jolie (Lara Croft), Daniel Craig (Alex Marrs), Leslie Phillips (Wilson), Mark Collie (Larson), Rachel Appleton (Young Lara), Chris Barrie (Hilary the Butler), Iain Glen (Manfred Powell), Julian Rhind-Tutt (Pimms), Jon Voight (Lord Croft). Directed by Simon West and produced by Colin Wilson, Lawrence Gordon, and Lloyd Levin. Screenplay by Patrick Massett, West, and John Zinman.

Lara Croft Tomb Raider elevates goofiness to an art form. Here is a movie so monumentally silly, yet so wondrous to look at, that only a churl could find fault. And please don't tell me it makes no sense. The last thing I want to see is a sensible movie about how the Illuminati will reunite the halves of the severed triangle in order to control time in the ruins of the ancient city that once rose in the meteor crater—if, and it's a big "if," the clue of the all-seeing eye inside the hidden clock can be used at the moment of planetary alignment that comes every 5,000 years, and if the tomb raiders are not destroyed by the many-armed Vishnu figure and the stone monkeys. The logic is exhausting enough even when it doesn't make sense.

This is, at last, a real popcorn movie. I have been hearing for weeks from fans of *The Mummy Returns* and *Pearl Harbor,* offended that I did not like those movies—no, not even as "popcorn movies." I responded that *The Mummy* was a good popcorn movie, but *The Mummy Returns* was a bad popcorn movie. It is my job to know these things. That *Pearl Harbor* is even discussed in those terms is depressing.

The plot of *Lara Croft Tomb Raider* exists as a support system for four special-effects sequences. Right away you can see that the movie is relatively advanced; *The Mummy Returns* had no plot and one special-effects sequence, which was 121 minutes long.

The film opens with Lara Croft doing desperate battle with a deadly robot, in what turns out to be an homage to the openings of the *Pink Panther* movies where Clouseau took on Kato. When the dust settles, we learn that she is Lady Lara Croft (Angelina Jolie), daughter of the tomb raider Lord Croft (Jon Voight), whose memorial stone sadly informs us, "Lost in the Field, 1985." Lady Lara lives in a vast country estate with a faithful butler and a private hacker and weapons system designer. Elaborate research-and-development and manufacturing facilities must be tucked away somewhere, but we don't see them.

Lara Croft is a major babe with a great set of ears. She hears a faint ticking under the stairs, demolishes the ancient paneling (with her bare hands, as I recall), and finds an old clock that conceals the all-seeing eye. This is the key to whatever it is the Illuminati plan to do with the lost city, etc., in their plan to control time, etc. Why they want to do this is never explained. A letter from her father is discovered sewn into the binding of an old edition of William Blake; "I knew you would figure out my clues," it says. And a good thing, too, since fate hangs in the balance while she plays his parlor games.

We now visit "Venice, Italy," where the Illuminati gather, and then there is an expedition to the frozen northern land where the ancient city awaits in a dead zone inside the crater created by the meteor that brought the key to time here to Earth—I think. Machines do not work in the dead zone, so Lara and the others have to use dogsleds. It is cold on the tundra, and everyone wears fur-lined parkas. Everyone but Lara, whose light gray designer cape sweeps behind her so that we can admire the tight matching sweater she is wearing, which clings tightly to those parts of her body which can be found a foot below and a little to the front of her great ears.

The inside of the city is an inspired accomplishment in art direction, set design, and special effects. A giant clockwork model of the universe revolves slowly above a pool of water, and is protected by great stone figures that no doubt have official names, although I think of them as the "crumbly creatures," because whenever you hit them with anything, they crumble. They're like the desert army in *The Mummy Returns* and the insect alien soldiers in *Starship Troopers*—they look fearsome, but they explode on contact, just like (come to think of it) targets in a video game.

Angelina Jolie makes a splendid Lara Croft, although to say she does a good job of playing the heroine of a video game is perhaps not the highest compliment. She looks great, is supple and athletic, doesn't overplay, and takes with great seriousness a plot that would have reduced a lesser woman to giggles. In real life she is a good actress. Lara Croft does not emerge as a person with a personality, and the other actors are also ciphers, but the movie wisely confuses us with a plot so impenetrable that we never think about their personalities at all.

Did I enjoy the movie? Yes. Is it up there with the *Indiana Jones* pictures? No, although its art direction and set design are (especially in the tomb with all the dead roots hanging down like tendrils). Was I filled with suspense? No. Since I had no idea what was going to happen, should happen, shouldn't happen, or what it meant if it did happen, I could hardly be expected to care. But did I grin with delight at the absurdity of it all? You betcha.

The Last Days ★ ★ ★ ½
NO MPAA RATING, 88 m., 1999

A documentary directed by James Moll and produced by June Beallor and Ken Lipper for Steven Spielberg's Survivors of the Shoah Visual History Foundation. Featuring U.S. representative Tom Lantos, Alice Lok Cahana, Renee Firestone, Bill Basch, and Irene Zisblatt.

The Holocaust is so overwhelming that it threatens literally to become unthinkable—to become an abstraction of evil. *The Last Days* and other documentaries make it real by telling some of the countless small stories that make up the larger ones. To say that 6 million died is one thing. To listen to a woman's memories of her girlhood, when she hid from her father in a Nazi death camp because she wanted to spare them both the sight of each other—and how their eyes nevertheless met for a last time as he was marched to his death—is another thing altogether.

Steven Spielberg's Survivors of the Shoah Visual History Foundation is engaged in making a record of as many such memories as can be recorded from those who saw the tragedy with their own eyes. The eventual goal is 50,000 taped interviews. *The Last Days* features five of those survivors and others, telling their own stories. It focuses on the last year of the war, when Hitler, already defeated and with his resources running out, revealed the depth of his race hate by diverting men and supplies to the task of exterminating Hungary's Jews. At that late point, muses one of the witnesses in this film, couldn't the Nazis have just stopped? Used their resources where they were needed for the war effort? Even gotten some "brownie points" by ending the death camps?

No, because for the fanatic it is the fixed idea, not the daily reality, that obsesses the mind. Those apologists like the British historian David Irving, who argue that Hitler was not personally aware of many details of the Holocaust, are hard pressed to explain why his military mind could approve using the dwindling resources of a bankrupt army to kill still more innocent civilians.

In Spielberg's *Schindler's List* there are the famous shots of the little girl in the red coat (in a film otherwise shot in black and white).

Her coat acts as a marker, allowing us to follow the fate of one among millions. *The Last Days,* directed by James Moll, is in a way all about red coats—about a handful of survivors, and what happened to them.

One describes the Nazis' brutality toward children, and says, "That's when I stopped talking to God." Another, Renee Firestone, confronts the evasive Dr. Hans Munch, who was acquitted in war crimes trials; his defense was that he spared the lives of some prisoners by conducting harmless medical experiments on them. But Firestone believes he was responsible for the death of her sister, Klara, and when he grows vague in his answers, she grows angry. Anyone who worked in a death camp has much to be vague about.

There is another passage where a woman, now around seventy, remembers instructions to Hungarian Jews to gather up their belongings for a trip by train. She took along a precious bathing suit, one she looked forward to wearing at the pool as any teenage girl might, and as she describes the fate of that suit, and of herself and her family, we hear a lifelong regret: In a moment, she was denied the kind of silly, carefree time a teenage girl deserves.

There is a final passage of joy that affected me with the same kind of emotional uplift as the closing scenes in *Schindler's List.* We have met during the film the only Holocaust survivor to be elected to the U.S. Congress—Representative Tom Lantos, whose wife is also a survivor. Both lost all of the members of their families. But they had two daughters, who came to them with the promise of a gift: They would have a lot of children. And then there is a shot of the Lantos family and its seventeen grandchildren.

That scene provides release after a harrowing journey. The movie contains footage of the survivors as they looked on the day their camps were liberated by the Allies—walking skeletons, whose eyes bear mute witness to horror. And the film has angry memories of an aftermath. One witness, an American soldier, describes shooting an unarmed German dead in cold blood, after being spat at. The film doesn't follow up on the implications of that, and because we can understand his rage, perhaps we let it go. But I feel the film should have either left out that memory or dealt with

it. The soldier was wrong for the same reason the Holocaust was wrong.

The Holocaust is the most tragic and deadly outburst of the once useful, now dangerous, human trait of tribalism, in which we are right and you are wrong because we are we and you are not. In recent years in Serbia, in Africa, in Cambodia, in Northern Ireland, the epidemic is alive and well. Just the other day in Israel, Orthodox Jewish students booed and insulted visiting Reform rabbis who hoped to pray at the Western Wall, and the *New York Times* reported that some of the attackers "screamed that the rabbis should 'go back to Germany,' to be exterminated, one explained later." Any belief that does not allow others the right to believe something else is based more on fear than on faith. If that is not the lesson of the Holocaust, then what has been learned?

Last Night ★ ★ ★
R, 93 m., 1999

Don McKellar (Patrick), Sandra Oh (Sandra), Callum Keith Rennie (Craig), Sarah Polley (Jennifer), David Cronenberg (Duncan), Tracy Wright (Donna), Genevieve Bujold (Mrs. Carlton), Roberta Maxwell (Patrick's Mother). Directed by Don McKellar and produced by Niv Fichman and Daniel Iron. Screenplay by McKellar.

I am writing in the closing days of December 1999. There are those who expect an apocalypse in a week or so, when Y2K shuts down the power grid and roving bands of carnivorous Americans stalk heavily armed into the streets to steal one another's Christmas presents. My own guess is that New Year's Eve will be more uneventful than usual, as most of us pause, awestruck, at the chiming of the millennium clock.

Don McKellar's *Last Night* is a Canadian film about the end of the world, and paints a picture more bittersweet than violent. While American fantasies run toward riot, rape, and pillage, life will end in Toronto, we learn, with farewell dinners, favorite songs, and people deciding they have put off far too long their intention to sleep with one another.

The movie wisely offers no explanation for the coming apocalypse. All we know is that the world will end at midnight precisely, and that darkness never comes. As a soft, early evening twilight hangs late over the city, radio stations count down the 500 top songs of all time, revelers in a city square treat the event like New Year's Eve, and we meet a small group of people as they try to face the end with a certain grace and dignity.

One couple meets by accident. Sandra (Sandra Oh) is marooned in a distant part of the city with no way to get back for a planned final meal with her husband. She asks a stranger named Patrick (McKellar) for the use of his phone, but can't find her husband at home or his office. And she has lost her car. Now they sit there in his apartment, two strangers. He has planned to spend this evening alone. What is the etiquette for two people in a situation like this?

We meet other characters. One is Craig (Callum Keith Rennie), who has a rendezvous with his high school teacher (Genevieve Bujold). We sense they'd always been attracted to each other, but never acted on their impulses. Now years have passed and it is time to take care of unfinished business. Turns out Patrick knows Craig, and thinks perhaps he might loan Sandra a car. Craig protests that his cars are not just any cars, but valuable antiques. As if it makes a difference.

Downtown in an office building, an employee of the gas company (David Cronenberg) reassures customers their service will continue until the end. Elsewhere in town, a mother holds a Christmas dinner, since Christmas will not come, and gives her children the favorite toys she has saved for since they were children. Many of these characters turn out to be connected in one way or another.

Perhaps nothing tests our dignity more than how we behave when we know for certain the hour of our death. That knowledge must be the worst thing about being on death row—worse than the gallows itself. Better to die suddenly, or in oblivion. What makes life bearable is our personal conviction that we will never die—or at least, not yet.

As the final hour approaches for the characters in *Last Night,* there are moments of startling poignancy. Sandra and Patrick, for example, find themselves stranded together, their plans for the end interrupted. She suggests they tell each other the stories of their lives. He lists the usual biographical details. "You'd better hurry up," she tells him. "Tell me something to make me love you."

Note: On a talk show in Toronto, I was asked to define the difference between American and Canadian films, and said I could not. Another guest was Wayne Clarkson, the former director of the Toronto Film Festival. He said he could, and cited this film. "Sandra Oh goes into a grocery story to find a bottle of wine for dinner," he said. "The store has been looted, but she finds two bottles still on the shelf. She takes them down, evaluates them, chooses one, and puts the other one politely back on the shelf. That's how you know it's a Canadian film."

Last Resort ★ ★ ★

NO MPAA RATING, 76 m., 2001

Paddy Considine (Alfie), Dina Korzun (Tanya), Artiom Strelnikov (Artiom), Lindsay Honey (Les). Directed by Pawel Pawlikowski and produced by Ruth Caleb. Screenplay by Pawlikowski and Rowan Joffe.

Tanya's fiancé was going to meet them in England, but he is not at the airport, the rat. The Russian woman with the small boy and the uncertain English tries to deal with British immigration officials, who are not unkind but have seen this scenario countless times before. She talks about her fiancé, she cites vague employment plans, and finally, in desperation, she requests political asylum.

Asylum is not really what she wants, but it's what she gets: asylum inside the British bureaucracy, which ships Tanya (Dina Korzun) and her son, Artiom (Artiom Strelnikov), to a bleak and crumbling seaside resort named Dreamland, where she's given some food coupons and a barren apartment, and told to wait for a decision that may take months, or years.

Tanya learns over the telephone that the fiancé is never going to show. But in making the call she has also made a crucial connection; using an unfamiliar phone card at a run-down seaside arcade, she meets its owner, Alfie (Paddy Considine). He is an enigma, a seemingly nice man who perhaps has a subtle romantic agenda, or perhaps simply feels sorry for her and wants to help. Having been betrayed by her fiancé, Tanya is not much interested in a new man. But Alfie doesn't push it.

The movie was directed for the BBC films division by Pawel Pawlikowski, who has a background in documentaries and does a good job of sketching in everyday life in the area, where the cold concrete and joblessness of a housing project has bred a generation of young outlaws. It's not clear whether the barbed wire is to keep people out, keep them in, or simply supply a concentration camp decor.

Young Artiom is an enterprising lad who makes friends with Alfie more quickly than his mother will, and is soon hanging out in the arcade, finding his niche in the Dreamland ecology. ("Mom, why can't we stay here with him?") His mother, desperately poor, fields a job offer from a pornographer named Les (Lindsay Honey) who wants to pay her to writhe on a bed for his Internet customers (he demonstrates with a teddy bear, in a scene balancing humor and the grotesque). Les is a sleazeball but a realist, the heir to generations of Cockney enterprisers. He points out that Tanya at least will not have to see, or be touched by, any of her "clients," and that the money's not bad. Such employment would be a change; in Russia, Tanya was an illustrator of children's books.

It's intriguing the way Pawlikowski keeps his hand hidden for most of the movie. We can't guess where things are headed. The movie is not on a standard Hollywood romantic arc in which the happy ending would be Alfie and Tanya in each other's arms. That's only one of several possibilities, and economic factors affect everything. Dina Korzun's performance holds our interest because she bases every scene on the fact that her character is a stranger in a strange land with no money and a son to protect. *Last Resort* avoids all temptations to reduce that to merely the setup for a romantic comedy; it's the permanent condition of her life.

Some movies abandon their soul by solving everything with their endings. Life doesn't have endings, only stages. To pretend a character's problems can be solved is a cheat—in a realistic film, anyway (comedies, fantasies, and formulas are another matter). I like the way *Last Resort* ends, how it concludes its emotional

journey without pretending the underlying story is over. You walk out of the theater curiously touched.

The Last September ★ ★
R, 104 m., 2000

Maggie Smith (Lady Myra), Michael Gambon (Sir Richard Naylor), Jane Birkin (Francie Montmorency), Fiona Shaw (Marda Norton), Lambert Wilson (Hugo Montmorency), David Tennant (Captain Gerald Colthurst), Richard Roxburgh (Daventry), Keeley Hawes (Lois Farquar), Gary Lydon (Peter Connolly). Directed by Deborah Warner and produced by Yvonne Thunder. Screenplay by John Banville, based on the novel by Elizabeth Bowen.

Years ago I visited one of the great country houses built by the Anglo-Irish in Ireland. It was Lissadell, the very one Yeats wrote about, its "great windows open to the south." The Gore-Booth family lived there; one of its daughters, Constance, Countess Markiewicz, was a leader in the Easter Rebellion of 1916, which marked the beginning of the Irish republic and the end for the Anglo-Irish. I went with an Irish friend whose family had grown up nearby. The tour was conducted by a distant relative of the family. As we left, my friend chortled all the way down the drive—that the gentry had so fallen that the son of a working-man could drop some coins in the collection pot near the door.

Deborah Warner's *The Last September* is set during the slow decline of the Anglo-Irish. It takes place in 1920 in county Cork, where Sir Richard Naylor and his wife, Lady Myra, preside over houseguests who uneasily try to enjoy themselves while the tide of Irish republicanism rises all around them. British Army troops patrol the roads and hedgerows, and Irish republicans raid police stations and pick off an occasional soldier. It is the time of the Troubles.

We meet the owners of the great house: pleasant and befuddled Sir Richard (Michael Gambon) and Lady Myra (Maggie Smith), a sharp and charming snob. She notices that her niece, Lois (Keeley Hawes), is sweet on Gerald Colthurst, a British captain (David Tennant), and warns her that, socially, the match won't do. It would be bad enough if the captain's parents were "in trade," but that at least would produce money; it is clear to Lady Myra that the suitor is too poor to afford thoughts of Lois.

Lois keeps her own thoughts to herself, and knows that Peter Connolly (Gary Lydon), a wanted Irish killer, is hiding in the ruined mill on their property. She brings him food, but he wants love, too, and she is not so sure about that—although she returns despite his roughness. Does she love either man? She is maddeningly vague about her feelings, and may simply be entertaining herself with their emotions.

Also visiting: Hugo and Francie Montmorency (Lambert Wilson and Jane Birkin), who have had to sell their place and become full-time guests, and Marda Norton (Fiona Shaw), a woman from London who is uncomfortably aware that she is approaching her sell-by date. She and Hugo were once lovers; she wouldn't marry him, Francie would, and now volumes go unspoken between them.

The weakness of the movie is that these characters are more important as types than as people. The two older women, Marda and Lady Myra, are the most vivid, the most sure of who they are. Hugo is an emasculated free-loader, and Captain Colthurst is a young man in love with infatuation. As for Connolly, the IRA man, he is a plot device.

The movie is based on a novel by Elizabeth Bowen, whose stories of London during the Blitz capture the time and place exactly. She grew up at Bowen's Court, a country house in county Cork, was a member of an Anglo-Irish family, and would have been twenty-one in 1920—about the same age as Lois. But if Bowen modeled Lois on herself, she did herself no favor; Lois is bright and resourceful and likes attention, but is irresponsible and plays recklessly at a game that could lead to death.

The movie is elegantly mounted, and the house is represented in loving detail, although the opening scenes allow so much of the red-gold sunset to pour into the drawing room that we fear the conservatory is on fire. The tone is one of languid hedonism; life is pleasant for these people, who speak of themselves as Irish even though to the native Irish they are merely trespassers for the British empire. I'm not sure the movie should have pumped up the melodrama to get us more interested, but something might have helped.

Left Luggage ★ ★
NO MPAA RATING, 100 m., 2001

Laura Fraser (Chaja), Isabella Rossellini (Mrs. Kalman), Maximilian Schell (Chaja's Father), Marianne Sagebrecht (Chaja's Mother), Jeroen Krabbe (Mr. Kalman), Adam Monty (Simcha), Chaim Topol (Mr. Apfelschnitt). Directed by Jeroen Krabbe and produced by Ate de Jong, Hans Pos, and Dave Schram. Screenplay by Edwin de Vries.

Left Luggage is one of those movies where the audience knows the message before the film begins and the characters are still learning it when the film ends. No matter how noble a film's sentiments, it's wearying to wait while elementary truths dawn gradually on slow learners. Add to this yet one more tiresome story in which the women possess all the wisdom and humanity and the men are cruel, stubborn, and crazed, and you have a long slog through a parched landscape.

The movie takes place in 1972 in Antwerp, where a young woman named Chaja (Laura Fraser) gets a job as a nanny for the Kalmans, a family of Hasidic Jews. Chaja is a Jew herself, but so indifferent to her identity that one of her best friends doesn't even realize she's Jewish. She finds the Hasidim, with their traditional black garments, strict observances, and unyielding patriarchy, absurd throwbacks. But she needs the money and takes the job, and soon bonds with Mrs. Kalman (Isabella Rossellini) and her children, especially a four-year-old named Simcha (Adam Monty).

Simcha has not started to speak. One reason for this may be the fierce tyranny with which Mr. Kalman (Jeroen Krabbe, the film's director) rules his family. He is strict, forbidding, and unforgiving, in accordance with the convention in which most movie fathers are deeply flawed repositories of character defects, while their wives are bubbling reservoirs of life, wit, and humanity. Gene Siskel called this the Bad Dad Syndrome, noting that we could go months at a time between films where a father was smart, gentle, and caring.

At home, Chaja's parents are stuck in their own pasts. Both her father and mother (Maximilian Schell and Marianne Sagebrecht) are Holocaust survivors whose lives are still governed by the experience. The mother compulsively bakes cakes and endlessly tries to feed them to everyone within sight. The father prowls Antwerp with a map and a shovel, trying to find the spot where he buried two precious suitcases before being shipped off by the Nazis. "They're probably all moldy by now," his wife warns—and so is the labored plot device. Surely there is a more creative way to suggest a search for lost roots than to have poor Maximilian Schell up to his armpits in holes he is frantically digging in Antwerp's gardens and backyards.

Chaja becomes close with little Simcha, who eventually reveals that he can indeed speak. His first word is "quack." It is inspired by a toy duck he pushes along so that it quacks too. It goes without saying that the toy duck arouses the ire of Mr. Kalman, who wants to banish it from the house ("My son is saying 'quack, quack' when he should be asking the four questions for the Seder"). Later, when Chaja teaches little Simcha the four questions (remember, this is a child who was thought to be mute), the beast of a father criticizes a mistake and the kid pees in his pants. My notion is that a great many Hasidic fathers succeed in combining their religion with love and kindness for their children, and that this particular father is an example of melodramatic overkill crossed with gender bias.

Ah, but there's more. The Kalmans have succeeded in being the only family still resident in a building where the concierge is a vicious anti-Semite. This is no doubt a great convenience for the plot, since by stationing him at the door to hiss and swear at the Jews every time they enter or leave, the screenplay doesn't have to waste valuable screen time importing anti-Semites from elsewhere. And then there is a development at the end which, as tearjerking goes, is shameless.

In the midst of this contrivance, both Isabella Rossellini and Laura Fraser give solid and affecting performances, and Schell makes his character less of a caricature than he might

have been. But the very last shot of the film, intended as uplifting, seems to solve nothing and to condemn the characters to continue to let the past destroy their present and future. With limitless possibilities for stories involving essentially these same characters, Krabbe and his writer, Edwin de Vries, are trapped by sentimentality and awkward contrivance.

The Legend of Bagger Vance ★ ★ ★ ½
PG-13, 127 m., 2000

Will Smith (Bagger Vance), Matt Damon (Rannulph Junuh), Charlize Theron (Adele Invergordon), Bruce McGill (Walter Hagen), Joel Gretsch (Bobby Jones), J. Michael Moncrief (Hardy Greaves), Peter Gerety (Neskaloosa), Lane Smith (Grantland Rice), Jack Lemmon (Old Hardy). Directed by Robert Redford and produced by Redford, Michael Nozik, and Jake Eberts. Screenplay by Jeremy Leven, based on the novel by Steven Pressfield.

Look how silky this movie is, and how completely in command of its tone. Robert Redford's *The Legend of Bagger Vance* could be a movie about prayer, music, or mathematics, because it is really about finding yourself at peace with the thing you do best. Most of the movie is about an epic golf tournament, but it is not a sports movie in any conventional sense. It is the first Zen movie about golf.

I watched it aware of what a delicate touch Redford brings to the material. It could have been punched up into clichés and easy thrills, but no: It handles a sports movie the way Billie Holiday handled a trashy song, by finding the love and pain beneath the story. Redford and his writer, Jeremy Leven, starting from a novel by Steven Pressfield, are very clear in their minds about what they want to do. They want to explain why it is possible to devote your life to the love of golf, and they want to hint that golf and life may have a lot in common.

I am not a golfer. It doesn't matter. Golf or any game is not about the rules or tools, but about how you conduct yourself. Civilized games make civilized societies. You look at the movie and you see that if athletes are not gentlemen and gentlewomen, there is no reason to watch them. Michael Jordon is a gentleman. Roger Clemens is not. You see how it works.

The Legend of Bagger Vance takes place in Savannah, Georgia, in the first years of the depression. A man builds a great golf course, goes broke, and shoots himself. His daughter Adele (Charlize Theron) faces ruin, but risks everything on a $10,000 tournament. She invites the two greatest golfers in the world: Bobby Jones (Joel Gretsch) and Walter Hagen (Bruce McGill). And she also invites Rannulph Junuh (Matt Damon), who was the greatest player in Savannah until he went off to World War I and something broke inside. He spent the 1920s drinking and playing poker.

Junuh doesn't much want to return to golf, which for him also means returning to civilization and to his own better nature. Three people encourage him. One is Adele. Before the war they were in love. One is a young boy named Hardy (J. Michael Moncrief) who dreams about golf. And one is Bagger Vance (Will Smith), a caddy who appears out of nowhere and assigns himself to the rehabilitation and education of Rannulph Junuh.

We have here the elements for a cruder movie. We can imagine how Jones and Hagen could be painted as hard-edged professionals, how the caddy could be sketched with broad strokes like some kind of an angel in a sitcom, how the little kid could be made insufferable and cute, how Adele and Junuh could fight and make up and fight, all according to the outlines they hand out in screenwriting class.

That's not how this movie goes. Nothing in it is pushed too far; it is a masterpiece of tact. Not even the outcome of the tournament is pumped up for effect; quietly, the movie suggests that how the tournament is won is more important than who wins it. As for the romance, it's in a minor key good for regret and tremulous hope; Charlize Theron's wise, sweet Adele handles Junuh like a man she wants to teach about tenderness.

Every actor makes the point, and then pauses, content. Matt Damon's Junuh is not a comeback hero but a man who seems surprised to be playing golf. Jones and Hagen are not the good cop and the bad cop. They're both good—sportsmen who love the game but don't talk a lot about it. Jones is handsome, a golden boy.

Hagen is dark and has a gut and smokes all the time. Jones plays a beautiful game. Hagen is always getting into trouble and saving himself. Both of them are . . . having fun. Just having fun.

Will Smith could make Bagger Vance insufferable, but the part is written and played to make it more of a bemused commentary. He has theories about golf, and ways of handling his player, and advice, but it is all oblique and understated. No violins. Is he a real person or a spirit? You tell me. Oh, and the kid: He's necessary because he has to grow up and become an old man (Jack Lemmon) and tell the story, so that you can see that lessons were learned.

The photography by Michael Ballhaus makes the great course look green, limitless, and sad—sad that every shot must fall and every game must end. There is a dusk here that is heartbreaking, like the end of every perfect summer day. The spectators do not make spectacles of themselves, but seem to identify with the aspirations of the players. Hagen and Jones know each other well, and during the marathon tournament they watch Junuh carefully, and decide that he will do. Redford found the same feeling in *A River Runs Through It*, where the standards a man forms through his pastime give value to his whole life. Golf, Bagger tells Junuh, is "a game that can't be won, only played." ☞

The Legend of 1900 ★ ★ ½
R, 110 m., 1999

Tim Roth (1900), Pruitt Taylor Vince (Max), Bill Nunn (Danny Boodmann), Clarence Williams III (Jelly Roll Morton), Melanie Thierry (The Girl), Cory Buck (Younger 1900), Easton Gage (Youngest 1900). Directed by Giuseppe Tornatore and produced by Francesco Tornatore. Screenplay by Giuseppe Tornatore, based on a dramatic monologue by Alessandro Baricco.

Because life is at such hazard, we value those who lead their lives all in one place, doing one thing. Such continuity is reassuring. We are buffeted by the winds of fate, but the Trappist tills his field and the blacksmith stands beneath his tree. There is a certain charm in the notion of a man who is born on board an ocean liner and never gets off. He does not move, yet is never still.

The man's full name is Danny Boodmann T. D. Lemon 1900. That is because as a squawling infant he was discovered on the luxury liner *Virginian* by a man named Boodmann, in a lemon box, in the year 1900. He is raised in the engine room, his cradle swaying as the ship rolls, and as an adult plays piano in the ship's lounge. And what piano! So great is his fame that even the great Jelly Roll Morton comes on board for a duel.

1900 is played as an adult by Tim Roth, he of the sad eyes and rueful grin. Night after night he sits at his keyboard, as crews change and ports slip behind. His best friend is Max (Pruitt Taylor Vince), a trumpet player in the ship's orchestra, and his story is told through Max's eyes. It begins almost at the end, when Max finds an old wax recording in an antique shop and recognizes it as 1900's love melody to the only woman who almost got him to leave the ship.

The movie has been directed by Giuseppe Tornatore, whose *Cinema Paradiso* was much beloved in 1988. Like a lot of European directors, he despairs of ever finding large American audiences with subtitles, and shot this movie in English. (Europeans do not object to dubbing.) *The Legend of 1900* nevertheless seems mournfully, romantically Italian, and could be an opera. There is something heroic about a man whose whole life is ruled by the fixed idea that he must not step foot on dry land.

There is also something pigheaded and a little goofy. That side of 1900 seems to lurk just out of sight in scenes like the one where he and Jelly Roll pound out tunes in what seems more like a test of speed and volume than musicianship. We sense, as 1900 plays, that he loves music less than himself—that he is defending not his ability as a pianist but his decision to stay on the ship: See, he seems to be saying, I never went to New Orleans and yet look at my fingers fly.

Decades come and go. Fashions change. 1900 remains steadfast even during the war. Then one day something happens to stir him to his fundament. A woman comes on board. The Girl, for so she is called, is played by Melanie Thierry as an angelic vision who never pauses on the deck unless she is perfectly framed by a porthole directly in the sight line of the moody pianist. It is true love. It must be: It gets him halfway down the gangplank.

There is a mystery to an ocean liner. It is vast, yet self-contained. It has secrets, but they can be discovered. Somewhere even today, hidden on the *Norway,* which used to be the *France,* is a private first-class courtyard. You can find it. 1900 is the secret of the *Virginian,* whose shadows and secret passages he haunts like the hunchback of Notre Dame or the phantom of the opera.

His story was originally written not as a screenplay or a novel, but as a dramatic monologue by Alessandro Barrico. The film has inevitably been compared to *Titanic,* but has more in common with the little-known French film *A Chambermaid on the Titanic* (1997), about a man who wins a free ticket on the *Titanic.* The night before sailing, he is seduced by a woman who says she works on the ship. Does she? Or does she only want to steal his ticket? The monologue he makes of his experience grows in popularity until he has to perform it professionally. You see how ships can make us storytellers.

The Legend of 1900 has moments of great imagination: a scene, for example, where the piano rolls back and forth across the polished dance floor in a storm, and 1900 keeps on playing. But it never quite develops the conviction we expect. What does it think of this man? Is he crazy or heroic? Nice or narcissistic? At the end we are left with Max the trumpet player, treasuring the sound of an old recording and assuring the antique dealer that this was some kinduva guy. Yes, but what kinduva guy? And why?

The Legend of Rita ★ ★ ★ ½
NO MPAA RATING, 101 m., 2001

Bibiana Beglau (Rita), Martin Wuttke (Hull), Nadja Uhl (Tatjana), Harald Schrott (Andi), Alexander Beyer (Jochen), Jenny Schily (Friederike), Mario Irrek (Klatte), Thomas Arnold (Gerngross). Directed by Volker Schlondorff and produced by Arthur Hofer and Emmo Lempert. Screenplay by Wolfgang Kohlhasse and Schlondorff.

It's said that European films are about adults, Hollywood films about adolescents. For evidence, compare two recent films: *The Legend of Rita* and *Invisible Circus*. Both are about young women who become involved with German terrorist gangs. The German film is told through the eyes of a woman who tries to remain true to her principles while her world crumbles around her. The American film is told through the eyes of a kid sister, who seeks the truth of her older sister's death, and ends up sleeping with her boyfriend, etc. The German woman is motivated by political beliefs. The American woman is motivated by family sentiment, lust, and misguided idealism, in keeping with Hollywood's belief that women are driven more by sex than ideas, and that radicalism is a character flaw.

The Legend of Rita, directed by the gifted German Volker Schlondorff *(The Tin Drum),* won two acting prizes and the award as best European film at the 2000 Berlin Film Festival. It stars Bibiana Beglau as Rita, a West German who belongs to a left-wing terrorist group in the 1970s. The group robs banks, kills people, and inspires a dragnet after a jailbreak. The movie doesn't make it easy for us: Rita is not an innocent bystander, and kills a policeman herself. But this isn't a simplistic parable about her guilt or motivation; it's about the collapse of belief during the last decade of the Cold War. Schlondorff believes his audience may be grown-up enough to accept a story about a woman who is not a heroine. Imagine that.

The setup comes as Rita, who has been in Lebanon, attempts to enter East Germany with a revolver in her luggage. She is questioned by Hull (Martin Wuttke), an agent for Stasi, the East German secret police, and allowed to enter the country with the weapon but without her bullets. Later, because Hull (and Stasi, it is implied) sympathizes with her group's opposition to capitalism, she is offered a new identity.

Cutting her ties to her name, her past and everyone she knows, Rita becomes a cog of the working class. This is all right with her: She isn't a naive hobbyist but seriously believes in socialism. With a new name and identity, she goes to work in a textile factory and becomes friendly with a fellow worker named Tatjana (Nadja Uhl); their affection nudges toward a love affair, but when her identity is discovered, Hull yanks her into another life, this time running a summer camp for the children of factory workers. Here she falls in love with a man. But can she marry a man who doesn't know who she really is?

The movie isn't about love, unrequited or not. It's about believing in a cause after the cause abandons you. Here the intriguing figure is Hull, who is not the evil East German spy of countless other movies, but a bureaucrat with ideals who likes Rita and believes he is doing the right thing by protecting her. When the Berlin Wall collapses, there is an astonishing exchange between Hull and the general who is his superior. The general says West Germany demands the extradition of Rita and other terrorists.

"How did they know they were here?" asks Hull.

"They always knew," says the general.

"How did they find out?"

"From us, perhaps."

The Legend of Rita shows a lot of everyday East Germans, workers and bureaucrats, who seem unanimously disenchanted by the people's paradise. Rita's original cover story was that she moved to the East from Paris because of her ideals; not a single East German can believe that anyone from the West would voluntarily move to their country. In the last days of the East, as the wall is coming down, Rita makes a touching little speech in the factory cafeteria, saying the ideals of socialism were good, even if they were corrupted in practice. The East German workers look at her as if she's crazy.

The Legend of Rita doesn't adopt a simplistic political view. It's not propaganda for either side, but the story of how the division and reunification of Germany swept individual lives away indifferently in its tide. In 1976, Schlondorff and his wife, Margarethe von Trotta, made another strong film, *The Lost Honor of Katharina Blum,* set in West Germany. It was about an innocent bystander caught in the aftermath of raids by the Baader-Meinhof Gang, the same group Rita presumably belongs to. From West or East, from right or left, his stories have the same message: When the state's interests are at stake, individual rights and beliefs are irrelevant.

The Legend of Drunken Master ★ ★ ★ ½
R, 101 m., 2000

Jackie Chan (Wong Fei Hung), Ti Lung (Wong's Father), Anita Mui (Wong's Mother), Felix Wong (Tsang), Lau Ka Leung (Master Fu), Low Houi Kang (John), Chin Ka Lok (Fo Sang), Ho Sung Pak (Henry), Tsung Chi Kwong (Tso). Directed by Lau Ka Leung and produced by Eric Tsang, Edward Tang, and Barbie Tung. Screenplay by Tang, Tong Man Ming, and Yeun Chieh Chi.

Jackie Chan's *The Legend of Drunken Master* is quite simply amazing. It involves some of the most intricate, difficult, and joyfully executed action sequences I have ever seen. If you have any interest in seeing a Jackie Chan martial arts film, then this is the one to see. Filmed in 1994 but not given a wide North American release until now, it is considered by those who have seen most of Chan's seventy-plus films to be one of his two or three best.

When I did a seminar at the Hawaii Film Festival several years ago, comparing the physical comedy of Chan and Buster Keaton, martial arts fans brought in their bootleg Hong Kong laser discs of this film and told me that I had to see the final twenty-minute fight sequence. They were correct. Coming at the end of a film filled with jaw-dropping action scenes, this extended virtuoso effort sets some kind of benchmark: It may not be possible to film a better fight scene.

But before I describe it, some general comments:

1. Most of Jackie Chan's plots exist only as clotheslines on which to hang the action scenes. Characters are thin, the dubbed dialogue ranges from rudimentary to inane, and the climax comes not at the end of the story but during the outtakes, when we see Jackie *really* getting hit, burned, dropped, slammed, etc. The man seems to spend half of his life on a hospital stretcher or having fire extinguishers aimed at him.

2. At least half the running time consists of violence, but this is curiously innocent, harmless violence—not the brutal and ugly stuff of many Hollywood action pictures. There are villains and heroes—a fight needs two sides— but everyone on both sides is in superb physical condition, and seems to be fighting largely for the fun of it. Between the action, Jackie hams it up with broad humor. To rate this movie R is to be terminally clueless.

3. The pleasure of the fight sequences comes not in seeing people get hit, but in watching physical coordination and precise choreography. Chan himself routinely does little throwaway things like running up walls, leaping into train windows, and making tricky twist-and-jumps.

4. The whole point is that Chan and the other actors *actually do most of the stunts.* Yes, there are certain special effects, and camera angles and editing make it appear that things happen in a way they perhaps did not. But when Jackie Chan falls into a pit of burning coals in this movie, that is really Jackie Chan, and the coals are really burning, and Chan insisted on doing the stunt three times until he got it right (the third time was when he burned himself and got those nasty scars you can still see on his arm).

Chan was forty when *The Legend of Drunken Master* was made, and although he is still in superb shape, he is reaching the age when he might want to produce and direct these movies instead of starring in them. It is all rather academic, sadly, because computerized special effects have made the authenticity of his physical skills sort of obsolete. When you see bodies whirling in midair in *The Matrix,* you don't think about computers, you simply accept them. But what Chan does, he is more or less, one way or another, actually doing.

The movie's plot is nonsense about Jackie battling with ambassadorial thieves who would steal precious Chinese national treasure. The title comes from the notion that pretending to be drunk, or being just drunk enough (without being too drunk) can make one a better fighter. Chan gets some low physical humor out of drunk jokes during the action scenes (he seems able to lean over at impossible angles). The sets are elaborate, the photography is elegant, and at the end, in the twenty-minute sequence, Chan faces his own bodyguard (filling in after another actor was injured) in one of the most remarkably sustained examples of martial arts choreography ever filmed. (I *think* the bodyguard is named Lo Wai Kwong, although the credits are confusing.)

Jackie Chan became a worldwide star because of word of mouth. Hollywood discovered him belatedly. There is a kind of innocence in his films, an exuberance, that can't be faked. Some people love Jackie; others have no interest in ever seeing his films because they think they know what they will see. The bottom line is: Chan deserves a place in movie history somewhere in the same hall of fame that also houses the other great physical performers who really did their stuff themselves: Buster Keaton, Douglas Fairbanks Sr., Fred Astaire, Gene Kelly, and, yes, Jackie Chan.

L'Humanite ★ ★ ★ ½
NO MPAA RATING, 148 m., 2000

Emmanuel Schotte (Pharaon De Winter), Severine Caneele (Domino), Philippe Tullier (Joseph), Ghislain Ghesquiere (Commandant), Ginette Allegre (Eliane). Directed by Bruno Dumont and produced by Rachid Bouchareb and Jean Brehat. Screenplay by Dumont.

Bruno Dumont's *L'Humanite* has the outer form of a police movie, but much more inside. It is not about a murder, but about the policeman in charge of the investigation. It asks us to empathize with the man's deepest feelings. I saw the film a week after *Shaft*. Both films are about cops driven to the edge of madness by a brutal crime. *Shaft* is about the story; *L'Humanite* is about the character.

It is not an easy film and is for those few moviegoers who approach a serious movie almost in the attitude of prayer. A great film, like a real prayer, is about the relationship of a man to his hopes and fate.

The man this time is named Pharaon De Winter. He is played by Emmanuel Schotte as a man so seized up with sadness and dismay that his face is a mask, animated by two hopeless eyes. He lives on a dull street in a bleak French town. Nothing much happens. He once had a woman and a child, and lost them. We know nothing else about them. He lives with his mother, who treats him like a boy. Domino (Severine Caneele) lives next door. She has an intense physical relationship with her lover,

Joseph, that gives her no soul satisfaction. It is impossible to guess if Joseph even knows what that is.

There is a scene where Pharaon walks in as they are making love, and regards them silently. Their lovemaking is not erotic or tender, but just a matter of plumbing arrangements. Domino sees him standing in the doorway. Later she asks him, "Get an eyeful?" He mumbles a lame excuse. She says something hurtful and leaves. Then she returns, touches him lightly, and says, "I'm sorry." When she leaves again, he pumps his fists in the air with joy.

Why? Because he loves her or wants her? It isn't that simple. He is like those children or animals who go mad from lack of touching and affection. His sadness as he watched them was not because he wanted sex, but because they were getting nothing out of it. His joy was because she touched him and indicated that she knew how he felt, and that she had hurt him.

He is a policeman, but he has no confidence or authority. The opening shots show him running in horror from a brutal murder scene, and falling inarticulate on the cold mud. He tells his chief how upset he is by the crime. He doesn't have the chops to be a cop. He watches a giant truck race dangerously through the narrow lanes of the little town, and then exchanges a sad shrug with the old lady across the street. His police car is right there, but he doesn't give chase.

His relationship with Domino and Joseph is agonizing. He goes along with them on their dates for sad reasons: He has nothing else to do, they have nothing to talk about with each other, he's no trouble. Because Joseph is the dominant personality, he enjoys flaunting the law in front of Pharaon, who is so cowed he can't or won't stop him. There's a scene with the three of them in a car, Joseph speeding and running stop signs and Pharaon impotently saying he shouldn't. Domino listens, neutral. And a scene where Joseph behaves piggishly to bystanders, and Pharaon is passive. The dynamic is: Joseph struts so that Domino can observe that he is more of a man than Pharaon the cop. Pharaon implodes with self-loathing.

The murder investigation continues, sending Pharaon to England and to an insane asylum. His efforts are not really crucial to the solution of the case. In a way, the rape and death of the girl at the beginning is connected with his feelings for Domino—because she offers him sex (in a friendly way) and he cannot separate her body from the memory of the victim in the field. The rapist has taken away Pharaon's ability to see women in a holy light.

The movie is long and seemingly slow. The actors' faces can be maddening. We wait for something to happen, and then realize, something *is* happening—*this* is happening. In the spiritual desert of a dead small town, murder causes this cop to question the purpose of his life. Eventually he goes a little mad (notice the way he sniffs at the possible drug dealer).

The film won the Grand Jury Prize at the 1999 Cannes Film Festival; Emmanuel Schotte won as Best Actor, and Severine Caneele shared the Best Actress Award. On stage, Schotte seemed as closed-off as in the film. Perhaps Bruno Dumont cast him the way Robert Bresson sometimes cast actors—as figures who did not need to "act" because they embodied what he wanted to communicate.

The Cannes awards were not popular. Well, the movie is not "popular." It is also not entirely successful, perhaps because Dumont tried for more than he could achieve, but I was moved to see how much he was trying. This is a film about a man whose life gives him no source of joy, and denies him the consolation of ignorance. He misses, and he knows he misses. He has the willingness of a saint, but not the gift. He would take the suffering of the world on his shoulders, but he is not man enough. The film is not perfect but the character outlives it, and you will not easily forget him.

Liberty Heights ★ ★ ★ ½
R, 122 m., 1999

Adrien Brody (Van), Ben Foster (Ben), Rebekah Johnson (Sylvia), Carolyn Murphy (Dubbie), Joe Mantegna (Nate), Orlando Jones (Little Melvin), Bebe Neuwirth (Ada), David Krumholtz (Yussel), Richard Kline (Charlie), Vincent Guastaferro (Pete). Directed by Barry Levinson and produced by Levinson and Paula Weinstein. Screenplay by Levinson.

Baltimore, 1955. Integration is the law of the land, and none too soon for Ben Kurtzman and his best pals, who are freshmen in high school. They regard the sign outside a municipal swimming pool: "No Jews, dogs, or colored." Dogs they understand. They ask themselves why Jews are listed first, and decide it's because "you never see any colored at the beach, so it must be directed mainly at Jews." Not deep, analytical thinking, but they are distracted by the girls on the other side of the chain-link fence, their plump bits displayed in frilly bathing suits. This will be a year of discovery for Ben, and by the time it is over, he will understand more about Negroes, Jews, segregation, and himself.

Ben (Ben Foster) has been raised in a neighborhood so Jewish that when he is offered the gentile staff of life, Wonder Bread, he looks at it in amazement: "I've never seen raw bread before. We toast it." At school, he is interested in Sylvia (Rebekah Johnson), an African-American girl whose presence in their classroom is an aftershock from the earthquake of *Brown vs. the Board of Education*. The morning begins with the recitation of the Twenty-third Psalm, and Ben notices that Sylvia closes her eyes and really seems to be praying, and that touches him.

Liberty Heights understands in that scene an important element of adolescent romance: It can be based more on idealism than lust. Yes, in locker rooms teenage boys make crude remarks about girls. But in their hearts the girl they idealize is perfect, blessed, the embodiment of their most fervent desire (which is to be noticed and loved by the girl they have chosen for sainthood). Ben thinks Sylvia is "pretty attractive," he tells his mother, who is stopped in her tracks that her son would say this of a Negro girl: "Just kill me now!" Ben backtracks: "I said she was attractive. That doesn't mean that I'm necessarily attracted to her."

But he is. Yet *Liberty Heights* is not so much about romance, interracial or otherwise, as about coming of age and finding your own two feet in the world. Ben's older brother, Van (Adrien Brody), is also in love, with a gentile girl he has seen at a party. She is Dubbie (Carolyn Murphy), a blond Cinderella to his eyes, and he spends much energy trying to get an introduction through a WASP friend. Will either Van or Ben end up marrying a girl who is not Jewish? Not the point. The point is that the residential and social segregation that raised walls between all of Baltimore's communities is coming to an end.

Liberty Heights is the fourth of Barry Levinson's films set in his hometown of Baltimore (the others are *Diner, Tin Men,* and *Avalon*). He makes big Hollywood films *(Rain Man, Sphere, Good Morning, Vietnam)* and then he makes these more personal Baltimore pieces, and you can feel the love and nostalgia in them.

I assume the character of Ben is based on Levinson himself, or someone he knew very well. The best thing about Ben is that he doesn't know then what we all know now. The movie doesn't give itself the benefit of hindsight: It remembers the racial divides of forty-five years ago, but it also remembers the innocence of a time when a high school freshman would probably not have smoked, would know nothing of drugs, would have little sexual experience, would be big-eyed with wonder at the unfolding world.

For me, the truest scene is the one where Ben goes over to Sylvia's house and they listen to Redd Foxx records (probably her father's). In the time just before rock 'n' roll broke loose, it was not so much music as comedy albums that spoke to young teenagers of freedom, risk, and daring. That scene ends with Sylvia's father, a doctor, coming home early, and Ben hiding in the closet. The doctor's conversation with the closed closet door is funny and terrifying at the same time.

We meet Ben's parents, Nate and Ada (Joe Mantegna and Bebe Neuwirth), and the rest of his family. We see family dinners interrupted by mysterious phone calls. "What does Dad *do?*" asks one of the kids. Mantegna runs a burlesque house and a numbers game, yet is a good provider and faithful family man, and scrupulously honest—so honest that he risks losing everything when a lowlife named Little Melvin (Orlando Jones) wins a $100,000 lottery that Nate unwisely tacked on top of the numbers payoff in the expectation that no one would ever get lucky.

One of the film's best sequences involves a sort of date that Sylvia and Ben go on, separately. A young singer named James Brown is playing at the Royal, and both kids want to see him. They dare not go as a couple. So they both go with their best friends, sitting a few rows apart, loving the music, happy to be in the same balcony together.

The film leads to a final scene that is one of those perfect public displays of poetic justice. I didn't quite believe it, but I'm glad it was there anyway, especially in the way it plays against the parents without making them the bad guys.

The film has some weaknesses. I thought the Little Melvin character was too broadly drawn, and I thought the whole subplot about how he tries to collect his winnings could not unfold as it does here. (The Mantegna character comes across not merely as a nice guy, but positively Gandhi-like.) But those flaws are not fatal, and the movie emerges as an accurate memory of that time when the American melting pot, splendid as a theory, became a reality.

Life ★ ★ ★
R, 100 m., 1999

Eddie Murphy (Ray Gibson), Martin Lawrence (Claude Banks), Obba Babatunde (Willie Long), Ned Beatty (Dexter Wilkins), Bernie Mac (Jangle Leg), Rick James (Spanky), Miguel A. Nunez Jr. (Biscuit), Clarence Williams III (Winston Hancock), Bokeem Woodbine (Can't Get Right). Directed by Ted Demme and produced by Brian Grazer and Eddie Murphy. Screenplay by Robert Ramsey and Matthew Stone.

Eddie Murphy and Martin Lawrence age more than fifty years in *Life,* the story of two New Yorkers who spend their adult lives on a Mississippi prison farm because of some very bad luck. It's an odd, strange film—a sentimental comedy with a backdrop of racism—and I kept thinking of *Life Is Beautiful,* another film that skirts the edge of despair. *Life Is Beautiful* avoids it through comic inspiration, and *Life* by never quite admitting how painful its characters' lives must really have been.

The movie is ribald, funny, and sometimes sweet, and very well acted by Murphy, Lawrence, and a strong supporting cast. And yet the more you think about it, the more peculiar it seems. Murphy created the original story line, and Ted Demme *(The Ref)* follows his lead; the result is a film that almost seems nostalgic about what must have been a brutal existence. When was the last time a movie made prison seem almost pleasant?

Life opens in 1932 in a Harlem nightclub, with a chance encounter between a bank teller named Claude (Lawrence) and a pickpocket named Ray (Murphy). They both find themselves in big trouble with Spanky, the club owner (Rick James), who is in the process of drowning Claude when Ray saves both their lives by talking them into a job: They'll drive a truck to Mississippi and pick up a load of moonshine.

The trip takes them into Jim Crow land, where Claude is outspoken and Ray more cautious in a segregated diner that serves "white-only pie." Then they find the moonshiner, load the truck, and allow themselves to get distracted by a local sin city, where Ray loses all his money to a cheat (Clarence Williams III) and Claude goes upstairs with a good-time girl. The cheat is found dead and Claude and Ray are framed by the sheriff who actually killed him, and given life in prison.

The early scenes move well (although why was it necessary to send all the way to Mississippi for moonshine, when New York was awash in bootleg booze during Prohibition?). The heart of the movie, however, takes place in prison, where after an early scene of hard physical labor, life settles down into baseball games, talent shows, and even, at one point, a barbecue. Bokeem Woodbine plays Can't Get Right, a retarded prisoner who hits a homer every time at the plate, and Ray and Claude become his managers, hoping to get a free ride out of prison when he's recruited by the Negro Leagues.

But it doesn't work that way, and life goes on, decade after decade, while the real world is only hearsay. Demme has two nice touches for showing the passage of time: Prison inmates are shown simply fading from the screen, and in the early 1970s Claude gets to drive the warden (Ned Beatty) into nearby Greenville, where he sees hippie fashions and his first Afro. Meanwhile, Rick Baker's makeup gradually and convincingly ages the two men, who do a skillful job of aging their voices and manners.

All of this time, of course, they dream of escaping. And they maintain the fiction that they don't get along, although in fact they've grown close over the years (comparisons with *The Shawshank Redemption* are inevitable). Ray remains the realist and compromiser, and Claude remains more hotheaded; the warden likes them both, and eventually assigns them to his house staff.

But what are we to make of their long decades together? That without the unjust prison term, they would never have had the opportunity to enjoy such a friendship? That prison life has its consolations? That apart from that unfortunate lifetime sentence, the white South was actually pretty decent to the two friends? *Life* simply declines to deal with questions like that, and the story makes it impossible for them to be answered. It's about friendship, I guess, and not social issues.

Murphy and Lawrence are so persuasive in the movie that maybe audiences will be carried along. Their characters are likable, their performances are touching, they age well, they survive. And their lives consist of episodes and anecdotes that make good stories—as when the white superintendent's daughter has a black baby, and the super holds the kid up next to every convict's face, looking for the father. That's a comic scene in the movie; real life might have been different. But life flows along and we get in the mood, and by the end we're happy to see the two old-timers enjoying their retirement. After all, they've earned it.

Light It Up ★ ★ ½
R, 103 m., 1999

Usher Raymond (Lester Dewitt), Forest Whitaker (Officer Dante Jackson), Rosario Dawson (Stephanie Williams), Robert Ri'chard ("Ziggy" Malone), Judd Nelson (Ken Knowles), Vanessa L. Williams (Audrey McDonald), Fredro Starr (Rodney J. Templeton), Sara Gilbert (Lynn Sabatini), Clifton Collins Jr. (Robert "Rivers" Tremont). Directed by Craig Bolotin and produced by Tracey E. Edmonds and Kenneth Edmonds. Screenplay by Bolotin.

As recently as 1985, our view of high school was so innocent that a movie like *The Breakfast Club* could involve five teenage troublemakers working things out in unsupervised detention. Now look at *Light It Up*. The same kinds of kids take hostages and get involved in an armed standoff with the police.

The movie takes place at an inner-city high school where the heat doesn't work, the winter wind blows in through broken windows, and most students don't have copies of the textbook. But the students are basically good kids—not the crazed dopers and gang bangers depicted in so many movies about high schools in trouble.

The ingredients for a tragedy are assembled early. A new security guard with the ominous name of Dante Jackson (Forest Whitaker) has come to work. He's got problems. One student pegs him: "A $5 cop with a $50 attitude." Meanwhile, a teacher named Knowles (Judd Nelson, from the original *Breakfast Club*) is wandering the halls with his students, looking for a heated classroom. He eventually takes them to a fast-food restaurant. Misunderstandings multiply when they return to the school. The guard gets into a shoving match with some of the students, his gun goes off and wounds him, and a routine day turns into a hostage crisis.

The ringleader is a good student and star athlete named Lester, played by R&B singer Usher Raymond, who shows real screen presence. Other students include Rosario Dawson, as a girl who counsels moderation; Sara Gilbert, as a girl so steeped in misery she's basically just along for the ride; Robert Ri'chard as a goofy kid who unwittingly starts the trouble; Fredro Starr as a hothead with a police record; and Clifton Collins Jr. as Lester's lieutenant.

As these six students barricade themselves in the library with the wounded guard, we're reminded of the young actors in *The Breakfast Club*'s library: Emilio Estevez, Anthony Michael Hall, Judd Nelson, Molly Ringwald, and Ally Sheedy. Although their careers have had ups and downs, they all became stars, and the *Light It Up* cast is similarly promising.

The arc in the movie is predictable—so predictable that it keeps it from truly generating suspense (*The Breakfast Club* wisely went for discovery and revelation instead). Cops surround the school, which is in New York (although the movie was filmed in Chicago). Searchlights bathe it, Vanessa L. Williams plays the hostage negotiator who gets Lester on the telephone. Of course, the library is equipped with computers, and soon the students are e-mailing their defense to CNN.

I am not sure I buy the way the movie thinks the crisis would play out. With the hostage-takers portrayed on TV as good kids, with their friends demonstrating their support, with even their teacher (Nelson) backing them, is it possible a hothead cop would seize control from the negotiator "because we want this wrapped up before the morning news"? Maybe that's necessary because in these souped-up times, a more rational conclusion is unthinkable. *The Breakfast Club* ended with the students, slightly older and wiser, driving off with their parents. This one has a SWAT team poised in a stairwell while the gang members prepare Molotov cocktails. Connect the dots.

The movie was directed by Craig Bolotin and produced by musician Kenneth (Babyface) Edmonds and his wife, Tracey. It has a refreshing lack of heated racial attitudes. Twenty years ago, there would have been some kind of obligatory shouting match in the library between the white girl and the black one. The teacher might not have been white. The principal would have been. The negotiator might not have been black. Bolotin's screenplay considers the characters as individuals, and they're not color-coded. Obligatory racial side-taking and name-calling is gradually (too gradually) being phased out of situations like this, in fiction and life, at the end of the century.

If I can't quite recommend the movie, it's because so much of the plot is on autopilot. The dialogue spells out too much that doesn't need to be said. The dynamic of the Internet-media angle is not really exploited. The final scenes seem contrived to supply action where it is not needed or convincing. But there's a lot in the movie that's good, including its introduction of a cast of gifted newcomers.

Limbo ★ ★ ★ ½
R, 126 m., 1999

Mary Elizabeth Mastrantonio (Donna De Angelo), David Strathairn (Joe Gastineau), Vanessa Martinez (Noelle De Angelo), Casey Siemaszko (Bobby Gastineau), Kris Kristofferson (Smilin' Jack), Kathryn Grody (Frankie), Rita Taggart (Lou). Directed and edited by John Sayles and produced by Maggie Renzi. Screenplay by Sayles.

Limbo sure isn't heaven and it's too cold to be hell.
—From the diary read by Noelle

Juneau is the only state capital with roads that lead nowhere. Every highway out of town ends in the wilderness. That serves as a metaphor for the characters in John Sayles's *Limbo,* a movie about people whose lives are neither here nor there, but stuck in between. It also helps explain the movie's surprising story structure, which doesn't obediently follow our expectations, but reflects the way a wilderness like Alaska can impose its own abrupt reality.

We meet a local handyman named Joe (David Strathairn), who was a high school All-American until he wrecked his knee, and a fishing boat skipper until he lost two lives and quit the trade. And we meet a singer named Donna (Mary Elizabeth Mastrantonio), whose career on the club circuit has ended her up at the Golden Nugget Lounge, pretty much the end of the line. She's had bad luck with men, and we see her breaking up with her latest guy at a wedding reception. Joe gives her a lift back to town.

The movie seems to be announcing it is about a relationship. We meet Donna's daughter, Noelle (Vanessa Martinez), who is exasperated by her mom's taste in men but begins to like Joe. The backdrop also seems to fall into place. We learn about local campaigns to save the environment, and about ways to get around them ("Quit with the chain saws when you get to where people can see"). We meet some of the local fauna, including the high-spirited lesbian couple, Lou (Rita Taggart) and Frankie (Kathryn Grody), who have taken over a valued commercial fishing license.

Mastrantonio is a splendid presence in her role. She can sing well and talks about how sometimes in a song she'll find a moment of grace. She doesn't know what she's doing in Alaska: "Anything where you need equipment instead of clothing, I don't do." Strathairn's character has lived in Alaska most of his life, and it has taught him not to hope for much, and to expect anything. But just now it's summer, and the living looks easy. A romance seems to be forming.

We assume we're in familiar John Sayles territory; he likes to populate his stories with large, interlocking casts, and then show how the local politics and economy work. That's what he did in *City of Hope* (1991), set in New Jersey, and the great *Lone Star* (1996), set on the Tex-Mex border. But he has a surprise ready for us. (Although the ads and review clips reveal it, you might not want to read beyond this point before seeing the movie.)

The surprise is a complete overthrow of all of our expectations for the story, a sharp turn in the narrative that illustrates how Alaska is domesticated only up to a point—that the wilderness is only a step away, and death only a misstep. I was reminded of the chilling book *Into the Wild,* about the young dropout who went on an Alaskan camping trip where everything went wrong.

Joe has a half-brother named Bobby (Casey Siemaszko), who talks him into crewing his boat on a "business trip." Joe innocently invites Donna and Noelle along. The purpose of the trip is far from innocent. After narrowly surviving a storm, Joe guides the boat into an inlet where few boats ever come. And then there are more unexpected developments, and three of them (Joe, Donna, and Noelle) find themselves castaways on an island far from anyone else.

What I liked so much about this story structure is that it confounded my expectations at every step. I expected the story to stay in Juneau, but it didn't. When it took a turn toward adventure, I thought the threat would come from nature—but it comes from men. After the three characters are stranded, I expected—I don't know what, maybe Swiss Family Robinson–style improvisation.

But Sayles gradually reveals his buried theme, which is that in a place like the Alaskan wilderness you can never be sure what will happen next. And that optimism, bravery, and ingenuity may not be enough. Some of the best dialogue passages in the film involve Joe's quiet realism. He refuses to raise false hopes. And of course even the hope of rescue comes with a hidden barb: Will they be found by friends, or death?

The movie leaves conventional plot structure behind and treks off into the wilderness itself. There's even a story within the story, based on a journal Noelle finds—and it contains a surprise too. Then comes the film's ending. Watching the screen, I felt confident that I knew exactly what would have to happen. What, and how, and why. And I was wrong. The more you think about the way *Limbo* ends, the more you realize that any other ending would betray the purpose of the story. Sayles has started with a domestic comedy, and led us unswervingly into the heart of darkness.

The Limey ★ ★ ★
R, 89 m., 1999

Terence Stamp (Wilson), Lesley Ann Warren (Elaine), Luis Guzman (Ed), Peter Fonda (Valentine), Barry Newman (Avery), Joe Dallesandro (Uncle John), Nicky Katt (Stacy), Amelia Heinle (Adhara). Directed by Steven Soderbergh and produced by John Hardy and Scott Kramer. Screenplay by Lem Dobbs.

If you live like a villain all your life, sooner or later you will be sixty and still being shot at. Although violence may be a way of life for the poor, it is a nuisance to the rich, and they try to hire out the work wherever possible. Steven Soderbergh's *The Limey* is the story of two older guys who hire their killers, and another who is a do-it-yourselfer. In its quiet and murderous way, it is like the delayed final act of an old movie about drugs, guns, and revenge.

The movie opens with close-ups of Terence Stamp's tight, closed, angry face. His features were chiseled in those Westerns he made thirty years ago, and you can still see the skull beneath the skin. He has been released from a British prison, and is flying to Los Angeles to seek revenge for the murder of his daughter. He is not a sophisticate, but a smart, working criminal who amuses himself with Cockney slang.

He believes a man named Valentine has killed the girl. Valentine, played by Peter Fonda, is a legendary record producer who lives in an architectural showcase in the hills above L.A.— one of those places with a swimming pool cantilevered out over the valley. It is a nice irony that both Valentine and Wilson (the Stamp character) made their money from rock music: Valentine by selling the tickets, Wilson by stealing the receipts of a Pink Floyd concert.

Valentine's security problems are dealt with, we learn, by Avery (Barry Newman), also around sixty, with the expensive suit and the tinted glasses. The men have recently been involved in a drug deal. Valentine is nervous; he doesn't want anything to "touch" him. Avery is paid well to reassure him: "The goods have been turned around, the money's been laundered, the guys are dead. This is a *good* thing." The two men have the kind of relationship you sometimes see between two business partners who have long since lost interest in their business or each other, but stay together because they need to drive a Mercedes.

Soderbergh's direction of the film takes the underlying story, which is basic Ross Macdonald, and uses the visuals to add an ironic amusement. Notice, for example, the scene where Wilson and *his* acting security guy (a big, tough Mexican-American played by Luis Guzman) arrive for a party at Valentine's house. We get a POV shot through binoculars, which is standard, and shows guests arriving at the hilltop house. But now listen to Wilson, who has never seen valet parkers before, and thinks all those guys in uniforms are minders and bodyguards.

And watch a later scene, where Wilson has a run-in with one of Valentine's actual bodyguards, a tough guy dispatched by Avery to bounce him out of the party. Wilson throws him over the edge of the swimming deck and to his death on the hillside below. Standard. But the cinematographer, Ed Lachman, keeps it in a long shot, in the background; the foreground is filled with Valentine relaxing in what he thinks is safety. Neat.

Avery realizes he needs to have Wilson killed, and goes to a pool hall to hire a hit man. The hired hand is one of those wise guys who always has the verbal commentary going. "I embrace my lifestyle," he says. We realize he isn't a kid, either. Forty, maybe. In Southern California youth is eternal, and these guys, with their tans and haircuts and clothes and cars and young girlfriends, believe their own images and think they're still nimble and tough.

Soderbergh makes full use of the screen history of both Terence Stamp and Peter Fonda. We get flashbacks of Wilson as a young man— actually Stamp in the movie *Poor Cow* (1968). If the Fonda character in *Easy Rider* had lived, he might have turned out like this. We learn the Valentine character "took the whole sixties Southern California zeitgeist and ran with it."

What is *The Limey* about? Drugs, girls, guns, and revenge? Not at all. It's about retirement. It's about tough guys who talk big but are past their sell-by dates. They're not fast enough for the ageless limey, who was cured in prison like beef jerky, and comes in low and fast. Soderbergh's visuals place them in the eternal world of California wealth and sun, heaven's waiting room, where the old look young until they look dead. When Wilson gets off the plane from London, they might as well take their zeitgeist and stick it where the zeit don't geist.

Little Nicky ★ ★ ½
PG-13, 93 m., 2000

Adam Sandler (Nicky), Patricia Arquette (Valerie), Harvey Keitel (Satan), Rodney Dangerfield (Satan's Dad), Tommy "Tiny" Lister Jr. (Cassius), Rhys Ifans (Adrian), Quentin Tarantino (Blind Preacher), Robert Smigel (Bulldog), Ozzy Osbourne (Himself), Reese Witherspoon (Angel). Directed by Steven Brill and produced by Jack Giarraputo and Robert Simonds. Screenplay by Adam Sandler, Tim Herlihy, and Brill.

I've met Adam Sandler a couple of times and he's a nice guy, smart and personable. Considering what I've written about his movies, he could also be described as forgiving and tactful. What I cannot understand is why he has devoted his career to finding new kinds of obnoxious voices and the characters to go along with them.

Consider Nicky, the star of his new film, *Little Nicky.* Nicky may be the spawn of Satan, but his two brothers, Cassius (Tiny Lister) and Adrian (Rhys Ifans) are reasonably presentable. Nicky, on the other hand, looks like the star of a low-rent road company version of *Richard III,* has a face twisted out of plumb (one of his brothers socked him in the head with a shovel), and speaks in yet another bizarre Sandler voice—sort of a mush-mouthed lisping whine.

Thinking back over the movie, I'm not sure why. Nicky is an intriguing comic character, whose appeal doesn't depend on how he talks or looks—Sandler's contributions, indeed, detract from the character. I try to imagine the movie with Nicky played as a more ordinary guy, and I think it would benefit (hundreds of millions of dollars of Sandler box-office grosses suggest I could be wrong).

Anthony Hopkins talks about how he needs to find a character's "mask" before he can play him. Many actors find it painful to play themselves, and are comfortable only after they find the right mask or persona to occupy. Is it that way with Sandler? I dunno, but for his next movie I suggest a mask that allows him to play an adult, instead of an infantile grotesque.

The movie surrounding Nicky is actually pretty good—the best Sandler movie to date. The premise: Satan (Harvey Keitel) has been on the job for 10,000 years and is thinking of retiring. The changes in Hell roil up Cassius and Adrian, who bolt for New York and freeze the gates of Hades behind them. Without fresh souls to feed on, Satan starts to disintegrate, literally. First an ear falls off, and then it's one thing after another until he's reduced to two hands holding his mouth. (It's Keitel's most piecemeal performance, ho, ho.)

Worried about his old man, Little Nicky is able to follow his brothers to Manhattan, where a talking bulldog named Beefy befriends him. Soon he is occupying an authentic New York–style hell (i.e., his roommate is an actor), but he meets a fetching young woman (Patricia Arquette) who somehow likes him, even though he occasionally blurts out disgusting things. His excuse: The devil made him do it.

The plot is populated with large numbers of stars in cameo roles: Rodney Dangerfield as Nicky's grandfather, Ozzy Osbourne as himself, Quentin Tarantino as a blind preacher, supplying yet another reminder that he should be directing movies, not infiltrating them. The best cameo is by Reese Witherspoon, as an angel with dubious genes, who talks like a Valley Girl and knows God: "He's so smart!" she says. "Like—*Jeopardy!* smart!"

Newscasts chart the progress as Hell's ambassadors change New York. The city motto, "I Love NY," becomes "I love hookers," the drinking age is lowered to ten (setting up the obligatory projectile vomiting scene without which no Sandler movie is complete), and—my favorite—the Harlem Globetrotters start being called for traveling violations and technical fouls.

All of this is kinda fun, and some of it more than that. I can see how *Little Nicky* could have worked. It's just that Sandler, at the center, is a distraction; he steals scenes, and we want him to give them back. He's thirty-five now. I know you can play an adolescent all of your life (consider Jerry Lewis), but isn't it time for us to see the real Adam Sandler? When I met him, I thought to myself, this guy has movie star potential.

The Little Vampire ★ ★
PG, 97 m., 2000

Jonathan Lipnicki (Tony Thompson), Richard E. Grant (Frederick), Jim Carter (Rookery), Alice Krige (Freda), Rollo Weeks (Rudolph), John Wood (Lord McAshton), Pamela Gidley (Dottie Thompson), Tommy Hinkley (Bob Thompson), Anna Popplewell (Anna). Directed by Uli Edel and produced by Richard Claus. Screenplay by Karey Kirkpatrick and Larry Wilson, based on the novel by Angela Sommer-Bodenburg.

The Little Vampire is a dim-witted but visually intriguing movie about a kid from San Diego who moves to Scotland with his mom and dad and befriends a family of vampires. It is based on a popular children's book by the German author Angela Sommer-Bodenburg, but those cute round wire frames on the hero's glasses are a clue that the Harry Potter books are at least as much to blame.

As the film opens, young Tony (Jonathan Lipnicki) doesn't much like Scotland, where his dad (Tommy Hinkley) has moved to construct a golf course for Lord McAshton (John Wood). The local kids pick on him at school, they're isolated in the middle of nowhere, etc., and his parents are impatient with his nightly dreams of vampires.

Then one night things pick up when a bat flies into Tony's fireplace and turns into a boy named Rudolph (Rollo Weeks), who is lonely too, as what vampire boy would not be. Rudy takes Tony on a flight to visit a vampire family that has been in hibernation for 300 years, waiting for a comet to cross the Moon and send a beam of light to a magic amulet—of which, alas, Rudy's dad (Richard E. Grant) possesses only half.

Touring the neighborhood is a scabby vampire hunter named Rookery (Jim Carter),

whose personal appearance and demeanor and his giant truck (with searchlights, drills, cages, neon crucifixes, etc.) suggest he should be paying royalties to the character of Snowplow Man (Chris Elliott) in *Snow Day.*

The movie is aimed at kids but filmed with an adult sensibility, which leads to peculiar scenes like the one where Rudy's vampire sister Anna (Anna Popplewell) presents him with a dead mouse, explains it is a charm to get him out of trouble, and adds: "If you ever need me, just whistle. You know how to whistle, don't you? Just whistle." Puckering your lips and blowing might be too risqué, I assume. (Miss Popplewell is refreshingly frank in comments about the film which she has posted on the Internet Movie Database: "My brother and sister, five and nine, both loved it and so did an audience full of children at the test screening. It is true that children above twelve may find it a little babyish.")

The movie has first-rate credits, from the director Uli Edel *(Last Exit to Brooklyn)* to the writers Karey Kirkpatrick *(James and the Giant Peach)* and Larry Wilson *(Beetlejuice)* to the cast (Lipnicki played the kid in *Jerry Maguire* and *Stuart Little).* The costumes are neat, the photography looks great—all the pieces are on hand, but they don't fit.

One problem is that the movie's saddled with too many elements. The vampires, we discover, want to become human again, and all of them but the father are vegetarians (lacto-ovo variety, if you were wondering). Fine, but then there's the complication of Lord McAshton's sinister plans, and the mumbo-jumbo about the comet and the beam of light and the amulet, and then the unwelcome periodic appearances of the spectacularly unfunny vampire hunter, and then Tony's problems in communicating his amazing discoveries to his parents.

Occasionally there's a flash of wit to suggest what would have gone right. The vampire dad says, "We need darkness, dampness, and decay," and Tony, who misses southern California, replies, "Then you need our cellar." There's a herd of flying vampire cows that caught my attention. And a scene set atop a giant blimp that sounds James-and-the-Peachian notes. All the same, children over twelve may indeed find it babyish, and those under twelve may find it not babyish enough.

Live Nude Girls Unite! ★ ★ ★

NO MPAA RATING, 70 m., 2001

A documentary directed by Julia Query and Vicky Funari and produced by Query and John Montoya. Screenplay by Query and Funari.

This Union Maid was wise,
To the tricks of company spies.
She couldn't be fooled by company stools—
She'd always organize the guys.
—Old labor song

And not only the guys. When the strippers at the Lusty Lady, a San Francisco peep emporium, decided to organize themselves into a labor union, there were jolly news stories all over the country. People thought it was hilarious. This may be because in the popular mind strippers do not really work.

Opposing the strike, the management of the Lusty Lady argued that taking off your clothes in a peep show is not real labor so much as an enjoyable part-time job. The women putting in ten-hour shifts didn't see it that way—but their customers did. "What's your job?" one of the clients asks one of the girls. "I'm a stripper," she says. "I mean," he says, "how do you earn a living?"

There is the curious notion that strippers and prostitutes do what they do because they enjoy it. This is a fiction that is good for business. I am sure that some strippers and hookers do sometimes enjoy what they do, but not that they do it over and over, all day long, week after week, for a living. By way of illustration, it is possible to take pleasure in making a ham sandwich, but you might not want to work behind the counter at Mr. Submarine, especially when the customers always leave with the sandwiches.

When you think of strippers, you think of a stage, but the strippers at the Lusty Lady work in a small mirrored room. The clients enter little booths surrounding the room and put a quarter in a slot; a panel slides up and they can see the girls for fifteen seconds. Another quarter, another fifteen seconds. It's enough to

bring back the silver dollar. The veteran girls make $20 an hour, and there are always two to four on duty, which makes you realize that the hardest job at the Lusty Lady belongs to the guy who collects the quarters.

Live Nude Girls Unite! is a documentary made by Julia Query, a stripper at the club, and Vicky Funari. It is an advertisement for the possibilities of the consumer digital video camera. It's not slick, it has some lapses, it sometimes looks like a home movie, but it's never boring. It follows some eighty strippers as they hire a lawyer, demand a contract, and threaten to strike. Query, Funari, and two other filmmakers simply took the camera along with them and shot whatever happened.

Miss Query is not your average stripper—but then no stripper ever is. She dropped out of graduate school, has worked as a dominatrix, and has a mother who is a famous public health advocate. The mother pilots a van around Manhattan handing out free condoms to hookers, and tells Barbara Walters in a *20/20* segment that her group facilitates 500,000 safe sex acts a year. "Peppermint?" Miss Walters asks, holding up one of the condoms.

When Julia turns up as a speaker and stand-up comic at the same conference where her mother is delivering a paper, the result is one of the more unusual mother-daughter arguments in movie history. Julia was raised to "do the right thing" and expects her mother to be proud of her as a union organizer, but the mother somehow cannot get around the stripping. This although Query tries to stir indignation about the club's discrimination against strippers who are not white (or, for that matter, white but not blond).

Julia is a disarmingly honest narrator. When she decided to earn money by stripping, she says, she was terrified by the thought of going on the stage, because "I can't dance." The mirrored room at the Lusty Lady, which reminded her of an aquarium, seemed less of a challenge, especially since it has silver poles in it. The other girls use these for posing, but we gather Julia may need to grab one to keep from falling down. Still, she's a spirited Union Maid, and she and her sister organizers make labor history. She's the kind of woman Studs Terkel was born to interview.

Lock, Stock and Two Smoking Barrels
★ ★ ★
R, 106 m., 1999

Jason Flemyng (Tom), Dexter Fletcher (Soap), Nick Moran (Eddy), Jason Statham (Bacon), P. H. Moriarty (Hatchet Harry), Lenny McLean (Barry the Baptist), Steven Mackintosh (Winston), Sting (JD), Nicholas Rowe (J), Vinnie Jones (Big Chris). Directed by Guy Ritchie and produced by Matthew Vaughn. Screenplay by Ritchie.

Lock, Stock and Two Smoking Barrels is like Tarantino crossed with the Marx Brothers, if Groucho had been into chopping off fingers. It's a bewilderingly complex caper film, set among the lowlifes of London's East End, and we don't need to be told that the director used to make TV commercials; we figure that out when a cook throws some veggies into water, and the camera shoots up from the bottom of the pot.

The movie is about a poker player named Eddy (Nick Moran), who is bankrolled by three friends for a high-stakes game with Hatchet Harry (P. H. Moriarty), a gambling and porn kingpin. Harry cheats, Eddy runs up an enormous debt, and Harry's giant enforcer, Barry the Baptist (Lenny McLean), explains that he will start chopping fingers if the friends don't pay up—or hand over a pub belonging to Eddy's father (Sting).

What to do? Eddy and his mates eavesdrop on neighbors in the next flat—criminals who are planning to rob a rich drug dealer. Meanwhile, Barry assigns two dimwits to steal a couple of priceless antique shotguns for Harry. The shotguns end up in the hands of Eddy and friends, who steal the drug money from the other thieves, and then—but you get the idea.

Or maybe you don't. The movie, which is an enormous hit in Britain, had its American premiere at the Sundance Film Festival, where I lost track of the plot and some of the dialogue. Seeing it again recently, I found the dialogue easier to understand, and the labyrinthine plot became a little clearer—although it's designed to fold back upon itself with unexpected connections.

The actors seem a little young for this milieu; they seem to be playing grown-up. Tarantino's *Reservoir Dogs* had characters with mileage on them, played by veterans like Harvey Keitel, Lawrence Tierney, and Michael Madsen.

But the heroes of *Lock* (Jason Flemyng, Dexter Fletcher, Jason Statham, and Moran) seem a little downy-cheeked to be moving in such weathered circles. And as the cast expands to include the next-door neighbors and the drug dealers, there are times when, frankly, we wish everybody would wear name tags ("Hi! I'm the effete ganja grower!").

I was convinced, however, by Harry and Barry—and also by Harry's collector, Big Chris, who is played by a soccer star named Vinnie Jones who became famous for squeezing in his vicelike grip that part of an opponent's anatomy that most quickly gains his full attention. They seemed plausible as East End vice retailers—seamy, cynical, middle-aged professionals in a heartless business.

I also liked the movie's sense of fun. The sound track uses a lot of rock music and narration to flaunt its attitude, it keeps most of the violence offscreen, and it's not above throwaway gags. While Eddy plays poker, for example, his three friends go next door to a pub. A man on fire comes staggering out of the door. They look at him curiously, shrug, and go in. The pub is named Samoa Joe's, which seems like a sideways nod to *Pulp Fiction* (Big Kahuna burgers crossed with Jack Rabbit Slim's restaurant). The guys sip drinks with umbrellas in them.

I sometimes feel, I confess, as if there's a Tarantino reference in every third movie made these days. *Lock, Stock and Two Smoking Barrels* is the kind of movie where you naturally play Spot the Influence: Tarantino, of course, and a dash of Hong Kong action pictures, and the old British crime comedies like *The Lavender Hill Mob*. The director, Guy Ritchie, says his greatest inspiration was *The Long Good Friday* (1980), the Cockney crime movie that made a star out of Bob Hoskins. Lurking beneath all the other sources, I suspect, is *Night and the City* (1950), Jules Dassin's masterful noir, also about crime in the East End, also with a crime kingpin who employs a giant bruiser.

By the end of it all, as you're reeling out trying to make sense of the plot, *Lock, Stock, etc.*

seems more like an exercise in style than anything else. And so it is. We don't care much about the characters (I felt more actual affection for the phlegmatic bouncer, Barry the Baptist, than for any of the heroes). We realize that the film's style stands outside the material and is lathered on top (there are freeze-frames, jokey subtitles, speed-up, and slo-mo). And that the characters are controlled by the demands of the clockwork plot. But it's fun, in a slapdash way; it has an exuberance, and in a time when movies follow formulas like zombies, it's alive.

Loser ★ ★
PG-13, 97 m., 2000

Jason Biggs (Paul Tanneck), Mena Suvari (Dora Diamond), Greg Kinnear (Professor Edward Alcott), Dan Aykroyd (Paul's Father). Directed by Amy Heckerling and produced by Heckerling and Twink Caplan. Screenplay by Heckerling.

Love is blind, and movies about that blindness can be maddening. *Loser,* for example, is about Paul, a college student of almost surreal niceness, who falls in love with Dora, a college student who persists in the wrong romantic choice almost to the point of perversion. When a movie character does something against her best interests and beneath her intelligence, I get restless. When it's clear she is persisting only because the plot requires her to, I grow unhappy. *Loser* is not a love story so much as an exercise in postponing the obvious.

Paul is played by Jason Biggs, the star of *American Pie.* Dora is played by Mena Suvari, the pom-pom girl who electrified Kevin Spacey's libido in *American Beauty.* Here he doesn't look as goofy and she looks grungier, like a college girl who dresses down as a lifestyle decision. They make a sweet couple, or would if she were not stupidly in love with Professor Alcott (Greg Kinnear), the arrogant prig who lets her do his typing, grade his papers, serve his tea, and share his bed, but values her about as much as a handy household appliance.

We buy the premise of the movie. He loves her but is a small-town boy who feels his case is hopeless. She likes him as a friend but is blind to his love because of her fantasies about the professor. He could expose the professor as a cruel fraud, but doesn't want to hurt her and figures he doesn't have a chance anyway. She is not so much blind to the professor's flaws as masochistically willing to endure them. We wait patiently for her to wake up and smell the coffee.

The movie is set in New York City, where Paul is categorized as a hick and even the lovely Dora is one of those "bridge and tunnel girls—they sleep around to avoid the commute." Paul gets a job in an animal hospital, Dora likes the animals (and a place where she can sleep over and avoid the commute). Paul's friends are keen amateur chemists who spike the drinks with date-rape drugs at their parties, which leads to a crisis when Dora nearly overdoses and the professor reveals how heartless he really is. Kinnear is wonderfully loathsome as the professor—and allowed to be as smart as he should be.

Watching this movie, I was reminded of *High Fidelity,* which has raised the bar for romantic comedies about twenty-somethings. The characters there were so accurately observed that we felt a stir of recognition. *Loser* wants to have that kind of perception, but doesn't trust itself. The movie, written and directed by Amy Heckerling *(Fast Times at Ridgemont High, Clueless),* has moments of truth, especially in the dialogue ("I love self-loathing complaint rock you can dance to," Dora tells Paul). But Dora is so obtuse in her inability to see through the professor and accept her love for Paul that eventually we grow impatient with her: She's sweet, smart, and cute, but she's simply not an interesting enough character to justify the wait while she figures things out.

Note: Ever since American Graffiti, *movies about kids in school have often ended with freeze frames telling us what happened to them later in life. Loser's bio notes are lame, and it is not encouraging when a college movie means "aid" but spells it "aide."* ☞

The Loss of Sexual Innocence ★ ★ ★ ½
R, 101 m., 1999

Julian Sands (Adult Nic), Johanna Torrel (His Wife), Saffron Burrows (Twins), Stefano Dionisi (Lucca), Kelly MacDonald (Susan), Jonathan Rhys-Meyers (Nic, Age Sixteen), Hanne Klintoe

(Eve), Femi Ogumbanjo (Adam). Directed by Mike Figgis and produced by Figgis and Annie Stewart. Screenplay by Figgis.

Mike Figgis, who pays so much attention to the music in his films, has made one that plays like a musical composition, with themes drifting in and out, and dialogue used more for tone than speech. *The Loss of Sexual Innocence* is built of memory and dreams, following a boy named Nic as he grows from a child into a man, and intercutting his story with the story of Adam and Eve. Not all of it works, but you play along, because it's rare to find a film this ambitious.

Figgis knows how to tell a story with dialogue and characters (*Leaving Las Vegas* is his masterpiece), but here he deals with impressions, secrets, desires. His story is about the way the world breaks our own Gardens of Eden, chopping down the trees and divesting us of our illusions. The process begins early for Nic, a British boy being raised in Kenya in 1953, when through a slit in a window he observes an old white man watching while a young African girl, dressed only in lingerie, reads to him from the Bible.

We move forward ten years or so to England, where Nic, now sixteen or so, is ignored by his girlfriend, Susan, at a family function. Susan gets drunk, and Nic discovers her upstairs, necking with an older man on the bed. Later there is an earlier scene from their courtship, when Nic and Susan are younger and steal into her house at night. She makes him coffee, they kiss by the fire, and then her father enters. He doesn't "catch" them and hardly notices them; he is in pain, and takes pills. Their young love is contrasted with the end that awaits us all.

These episodes are intercut with "Scenes from Nature," as Adam and Eve (Femi Ogumbanjo and Hanne Klintoe) emerge from a pond and explore the world, and their own bodies, with amazement. The nudity here, while explicit, is theologically correct; we didn't need clothing until we sinned. The whole Eden sequence could have been dispatched with, I think (its surprise payoff tries too hard to make a point that the ending of *Walkabout* made years ago). Yet the Eden scenes are so beautifully photographed that you enjoy them even as you question them. (The first shot of Eden is a breathtaking optical illusion.)

Nic's story, as it unfolds, reveals unhappiness. As he becomes an adult, now played by Julian Sands, we see glimpses of a marriage underlined with tension. He is a film director, and there is a trip to Tunisia that ends with a surprise development that is a sudden, crushing loss of innocence. And Figgis also weaves in a strand involving twins (played by Saffron Burrows) who are separated shortly after birth, and come face-to-face with one another in an airport years later. To look at your own face on another person is a fundamental loss of innocence, because it deprives you of the assumption that you are unique.

The film has no particular statement to make about its material (apart from the symbolism of the Eden sequence). It wants to share feelings, not thoughts. A lot of the dialogue sounds remembered, or overheard from a distance. (I was reminded of the dialogue treatment in *Bonnie and Clyde* when Bonnie goes to a family picnic and talks with her mother). We get the points that are being made, but this movie isn't about people talking to one another.

The film itself moves forward, but there are flashbacks of memory, as Nic, driving, recalls scenes from earlier life. There are two dream sequences—one for him, one for his wife, played by Johanna Torrel. Hers is about his indifference as he plays the piano while she makes love with another man. His is about his own death. We don't know if this material comes from Mike Figgis's life, but we're sure it comes from his feelings.

The Loss of Sexual Innocence is an "art film," which means it tries to do something more advanced than most commercial films (which tell stories simple enough for children, in images shocking enough for adults). It wants us to share in the process of memory, especially sexual memory. It assumes that the moments we remember most clearly are those when we lost our illusions—when we discovered the unforgiving and indifferent nature of the world. It's like drifting for a time in the film's musings, and then being invited to take another look at our own.

Lost & Found ★
PG-13, 98 m., 1999

David Spade (Dylan), Sophie Marceau (Lila), Artie Lange (Wally), Patrick Bruel (Rene), Mitchell Whitfield (Mark), Martin Sheen (Millstone), Jon Lovitz (Uncle Harry). Directed by Jeff Pollack and produced by Wayne Rice, Morrie Eisenman, Andrew A. Kosove, and Broderick Johnson. Screenplay by J. B. Cook, Marc Meeks, and David Spade.

Lost & Found is a movie about characters of limited intelligence who wander through the lonely wastes of ancient and boring formulas. No one involved seems to have had any conviction it could be great. It's the kind of movie where the hero imitates Neil Diamond—and he's not making fun of him, he's serious.

In asking us to believe David Spade as a romantic lead, it miscalculates beyond all reason. Spade is wrong by definition for romantic leads, because his persona is based on ironic narcissism and cool detachment. A girl has to be able to believe it when a guy says he loves her more than anything else in the world. When Spade says it, it means he doesn't love anything else in the world, either.

Spade plays the owner of an Italian restaurant in Los Angeles. Like not very many owners of Italian restaurants, his name is Dylan. I have three hints for Dylan: (1) Unless you know them very well, customers do not like to be caressed on their arms as you pass their tables. (2) Although waiters must touch plates while serving them, it is bad form for the owner to put his thumb on a plate while it is being eaten from. (3) During renovations, do not seat customers directly below drywall with holes ripped in it.

Most L.A. restaurant owners do not live in colorful apartment buildings where all the neighbors know each other and little old ladies play strip poker. But the screenplay throws in the colorful rental units as a way of supplying recycled sitcom characters, and to place Dylan near the apartment of Lila (Sophie Marceau), a French cellist. She has a former boyfriend named Rene (Patrick Bruel), whose function is to look pained and supply straight lines to Dylan. And she has a dog named Jack, who is treated as much like the dog in *There's Something About Mary* as is possible without actually including clips from the other movie.

Dylan and Lila have a Meet Cute. She runs into him and knocks him flat, with her landing on top, which is about the cheapest Meet Cute you can buy at the Movie Cliché Store. He falls in love with Lila, gets nowhere, and steals her dog so that he can claim to have found it and thus win her love. Lila is so unobservant that Dylan often carries the dog past her windows, and even walks it in a nearby park, without Lila ever seeing them together. When the dog needs to poop, Dylan wears one of those tool belts you see on power company linemen, with eight or nine bright plastic pooper-scoopers dangling from it. Supplying a character with too much equipment is a creaky comedy wheeze; in a good movie, they'd give him one pooper-scooper and think of something funny to do with it.

Anyway. Dylan has an employee at the restaurant named Wally (Artie Lange), who is tall, fat, and dumb, sleeps over one night, and ends up in Dylan's bed because he gets scared. As they leap to attention in the morning, they can't even think of a funny payoff (such as Steve Martin in *Planes, Trains & Automobiles*, shouting at John Candy, "That wasn't a pillow!"). Instead, when Lila rings the doorbell, they both answer the door in their underpants and she assumes they're gay. Ho, ho.

Meanwhile, Jack the dog eats junk food and throws up. When Dylan comes home, we get a nauseated-dog's-eye-view of an optically distorted Dylan dressed in 1970s disco gear while dancing to a record on the sound track. Don't ask how a dog could have this hallucination; be thankful instead that the dog's fantasies are more interesting than any other visual in the movie.

Lost & Found ends at a big lawn party for rich people, which in movies about people over twenty-one is the equivalent of the Senior Prom scene in all other movies. There is a role for Martin Sheen, as Mr. Millstone, the tight-fisted banker who wants to fly in Neil Diamond as a surprise for his wife. In 1979, Martin Sheen starred in *Apocalypse Now*. In 1999, he plays Mr. Millstone. I wish he had taken my advice and gone into the priesthood.

As for the Neil Diamond imitation, my best guess is that David Spade secretly thinks he could have a parallel career as a Las Vegas idol, and is showing us how he can do Neil Diamond better than Diamond himself. All that's lacking is for Spade to take that hank of hair that hangs in front of his eyes and part it, so that it hangs over his ears.

Truth in Criticism: The movie has one funny scene, starring Jon Lovitz, as a dog whisperer.

Lost Souls ★ ★

R, 102 m., 2000

Winona Ryder (Maya Larkin), Ben Chaplin (Peter Kelson), John Hurt (Father Lareaux), Sarah Wynter (Claire Van Owen), Elias Koteas (John Townsend), John Diehl (Henry Birdson), James Lancaster (Father Jeremy), Victor Slezak (Father Thomas), Philip Baker Hall (Father James), Alfre Woodard (Psychiatrist). Directed by Janusz Kaminski and produced by Meg Ryan and Nina R. Sadowsky. Screenplay by Pierce Gardner.

Lost Souls possesses the art and craft of a good movie, but not the story. For a thriller about demonic possession and the birth of the antichrist, it's curiously flat. Strange, how a trashy Satanic movie like *End of Days* is filled with a fearful intensity, while this ambitious stab at the subject seems to lack all conviction. All through the movie I found myself thinking about how well it was photographed. Not a good sign.

Winona Ryder stars as Maya Larkin, a woman who was once possessed by the devil. Now she teaches children at a church school. One day her former exorcist squad summons her to the cell of a serial killer (John Diehl) who is also possessed. "He's in torment," Father Lareaux (John Hurt) tells her, "the way you were when I met you." The exorcism goes so badly that Hurt is hospitalized and the victim goes into a coma.

It is revealed during the exorcism that the devil will appear soon in human form. Ryder comes away with pages of numbers from the possessed man—long legal pads of figures. Smoking lots of cigarettes, she massages the encryption until she breaks it. As nearly as I could tell, looking over her shoulder, every

number stood for a letter of the alphabet. When I was a kid I had a Lone Ranger Decoder Ring that could have saved her a lot of trouble.

What the message tells her is that Peter Kelson (Ben Chaplin), a best-selling author of true crime books, will be reborn on his thirty-third birthday as the antichrist. Maya tries to warn Peter, who at first thinks she's a nut and then, after a series of strange events and revelations, decides she may very well be right. There's lots of stuff about being born in incest, and blood types that don't match, and dreams in which he sees the letters XES. He's slow to catch on, he admits, when it's pointed out that XES is "sex" spelled backward. And that's not all. Those are also the Greek letters for 600, 60, and 6, a psychic tells him, and that spells 666—the mark of Satan.

These events and others are related in a downbeat, intense, gloomy narrative that seems better suited to a different kind of story. Even the shock moments are somewhat muted, as if the movie is reluctant to 'fess up to its thriller origins. The director is Janusz Kaminski, the Academy Award–winning cinematographer *(Schindler's List, Saving Private Ryan)*, and he and *his* cinematographer, Mauro Fiore, create a masterful look for the film—denatured blues and browns, filmed in shadow with lots of backlighting and a certain dreaminess around the edges.

The performers are convincing in the moment, even if the arc lets them down. Ryder, always able to suggest intelligence, also hints at the terrors of a child whose parents were murdered. Chaplin perhaps doesn't take his impending transformation urgently enough, but what would you do? The priests, including not only John Hurt with his sorrowful eyes but also Philip Baker Hall with his underpriced charm, are convincing as spiritual pros—when an exorcism team goes on assignment, the camera is low-angle to show the thick-soled, black business shoes beneath their cassocks.

Without revealing the ending, I will give it credit for being absolutely consistent with the logic of the material. No wedge-brained focus groups got their philistinic little hands on this material. But when it's all over, we're left without much to talk about in our next confession. What surprises me, in one Satanic movie after another, is how vulnerable Satan seems to be. He's terrific at grabbing control of minds and making his victims speak in foul tones, and he puts a lot of wear and tear on the priests, but in the end he's always defeated by lowly humans. Here's a being who once declared war on God, and is now facing Winona Ryder. What a comedown.

Love & Basketball ★ ★ ★
PG-13, 118 m., 2000

Sanaa Lathan (Monica Wright), Omar Epps (Quincy McCall), Alfre Woodard (Camille Wright), Dennis Haysbert (Zeke McCall), Debbi Morgan (Mona McCall), Harry J. Lennix (Nathan Wright), Kyla Pratt (Young Monica), Glenndon Chatman (Young Quincy), Jess Willard (Jamal), Chris Warren Jr. (Kelvin), Naykia Harris (Young Lena). Directed by Gina Prince-Bythewood and produced by Spike Lee and Sam Kitt. Screenplay by Prince-Bythewood.

Love & Basketball is about how you can either be in love or play basketball, but it's tricky to do both at the same time. It may be unique among sports movies in that it does *not* end with the Big Game. Instead, it's a thoughtful and touching story about two affluent black kids, a boy and a girl, who grow up loving each other, and the game.

Monica is a tomboy. Her parents and older sister despair of getting her to act like a girl. She'd rather shoot baskets. In 1981, when she's about twelve, her family moves into a new house in Baldwin Hills, a good Los Angeles neighborhood. Next door lives a star for the L.A. Clippers and his son, Quincy. The first time the kids meet, they play a pickup game. Monica goes for a score, Quincy pushes her, and she gets a little scar that will be on her right cheek for the rest of her life.

He likes her. "You wanna be my girl?" he asks. She wants to know what that means. "We can play ball and ride to school together and when you get mad I gotta buy you flowers." She doesn't like flowers, she says. But she kisses him (they count to five), and the next day he wants her to ride to school on the handlebars of his bike. She wants to ride her own bike. This will be the pattern of a lifetime.

Flash forward to 1988. Monica, now played by Sanaa Lathan, and Quincy (Omar Epps) are high school stars. They're not dating but they're friends, and when Quincy's parents (Dennis Haysbert and Debbi Morgan) start fighting, he slips out his bedroom window and sleeps on the floor of her room. In a sequence of surprising effectiveness, she takes the advice of her mom and sister to "do something" with her hair, and goes to a school dance with a blind date. Quincy is there too. They dance with their dates but they keep looking at each other. You know how it is.

They're both recruited by USC, and both turn into college basketball stars, although Monica, on the women's team, feels she's penalized for an aggression that would be rewarded on the men's team. Their romance has its ups and downs, and eventually they're both playing in the pros—he in America, she in Spain. The ending reunites them a little too neatly.

But these bare bones of the plot don't convey the movie's special appeal. Written and directed by first-timer Gina Prince-Bythewood (and produced by Spike Lee), it is a sports film seen mostly from the woman's point of view. It's honest and perceptive about love and sex, with no phony drama and a certain quiet maturity. And here's the most amazing thing: It considers sports in terms of career, training, motivation, and strategy. The Big Game scenes involve behavior and attitude, not scoring. The movie sees basketball as something the characters do as a skill and a living, not as an excuse for audience-pleasing jump shots at the buzzer.

Omar Epps is an accomplished actor, effective here if a little too old (twenty-seven) to be playing a high schooler. Sanaa Lathan is the discovery. This is her sixth movie (she was in the look-alike films *The Wood* and *The Best Man*) and her chance to flower, and she does, with a combination of tomboy stubbornness and womanly pride. She has some wonderful scenes with her mother (Alfre Woodard), a housewife who defends her choices in life against her daughter's half-formed feminist notions.

Epps has effective scenes, too, with his parents. His dad retires from pro ball and is socked with a paternity suit, and Quincy has to reevaluate how he feels about both parents in a couple of strong truth-telling scenes.

343

The movie is not as taut as it could have been, but I prefer its emotional perception to the pumped-up sports clichés I was sort of expecting. Like Robert Towne's *Personal Best*, it's about the pressures of being a star athlete—the whole life, not the game highlights. I'm not sure I quite believe the final shot, though. I think the girl suits up for the sequel.

Love & Sex ★ ★

NO MPAA RATING, 82 m., 2000

Famke Janssen (Kate Welles), Jon Favreau (Adam Levy), Noah Emmerich (Eric), Cheri Oteri (Mary), Ann Magnuson (Ms. Steinbacher). Directed by Valerie Breiman and produced by Timothy Scott Bogart, Martin J. Barab, Brad Wyman, and Darris Hatch. Screenplay by Breiman.

If *Love & Sex* contained nothing else, it would pass into memory for a pickup line that is either fatal or inspired—I am still trying to decide which: "You have those long E.T. fingers, like a tree frog." These words are spoken by Adam, an artist, to Kate, a bimbo savant, on their first date. She fires back by telling him his head is too big. It will be like this for most of the movie: Love at first sight reduces itself to second thoughts and one-liners. If it weren't being released unrated, which translates to adults only, the movie might be fun for younger teenagers who want to be reassured that people in their thirties still behave like younger teenagers.

Kate is played by Famke Janssen, from *X-Men* and the Bond pic *GoldenEye*, who confesses she wears a size 11 shoe—a line usually reserved for the man in a movie like this. Adam is played by Jon Favreau, a versatile actor recently seen as the pit-bull lineman in *The Replacements*. Both of them show they can play characters a lot smarter than we associate them with. They don't play them, but they show they can.

Their dialogue examines the mechanics and technicalities of sex and love in the same way HBO's *Sex and the City* does, but at a reduced level of sophistication and self-knowledge. Kate and Adam may be chronologically adult, but they behave on dates the way they probably did in high school.

Kate is a magazine writer, recently fired by the editor of a women's magazine for writing an article about oral sex that presumed to describe it rather than snicker about it. Ironic, since in its own consideration of sex the movie also snickers and withdraws. She goes to an art opening with her current squeeze, a stand-up comic, and Adam falls in love with her from across the room. He red dogs her, and soon they're having dinner, exchanging insults, and sharing intimate moments, like passing gas in bed and having conversations like:

"When I look at you like this, it looks like you only have one eye."

"Thank you."

The film is told from Kate's point of view. It's a cautionary tale about love (which, she explains, we fall into because nothing feels better) and relationships, which, we gather, end because nothing feels worse. In an early sharing of confidences, they reveal how many sexual partners they've had. Adam has had two. Kate has had thirteen. My best guess is they're both lying, but never mind: Adam can't get over Kate's cheerful promiscuity. It becomes clear that his feelings are clouded and she intuits: "It's the thirteen guys, isn't it?" Then she starts dating a basketball player, just to make him jealous.

The thing is, nothing's at stake here. Adam and Kate don't have enough weight and complexity for us to care about them. They're pawns in the hands of writer-director Valerie Breiman, who hides them in a thicket of sitcom clutter. When they break up and he sends a drum-pounding midget to her office with an apologetic offering, we're not seeing Kate and Adam, but Lucy and Ricky. A movie like John Cusack's *High Fidelity* acts as a rebuke to *Love & Sex* by showing the real quirks and self-punishments of the romantically unsuccessful.

As for Favreau and Janssen, it would be unfair to say there's no chemistry between them, because that would blame the actors, when in fact the screenplay gives them little to have chemistry with, for, or about. The film seems shy of sexual intimacy and physical delight, and the lovers approach each other with all the perplexity of a jigsaw fanatic who has just discovered pieces are missing. In successful screen romance, there needs to be the sense that the partners are happy simply to be *there* with each other, that there is a physical yearning, and not simply the need to talk fast enough to stay ahead of the one-liners.

Lovers of the Arctic Circle ★ ★ ★
R, 112 m., 1999

Fele Martinez (Otto), Najwa Nimi (Ana), Nancho Novo (Alvaro), Maru Valdivielso (Olga), Peru Medem (Otto [Child]), Sara Valiente (Ana [Child]), Victor Hugo Oliveira (Otto [Teenager]), Kristel Diaz (Ana [Teenager]). Directed by Julio Medem and produced by Fernando Bovaira and Enrique Lopez Lavigne. Screenplay by Medem.

palindrome, n. Word, verse, sentence, etc., that reads the same backward as forward (e.g., madam, radar).

There is a certain kind of mind that enjoys difficulties. It is not enough to reach the objective; one must do it in a certain way. We begin by not stepping on the cracks in the sidewalk. Some never stop. Ernest Wright wrote an entire novel without using the letter "e." Hitchcock made a film without a single visible edit. There are paintings made of dots, piano compositions for one hand, and now here is a strange and haunting movie that wants to be a palindrome.

Lovers of the Arctic Circle tells the story of Ana and Otto, whose names are palindromes, and whose lives seem governed by circular patterns. Events at the beginning are related to events at the end. The movie is about love—or, rather, about their grand ideas of romance. It is comforting to think that we can love so powerfully that fate itself wheels and turns at the command of our souls.

Ana and Otto are seen at three periods of their lives. When they are small, they have a chance meeting in the woods, and Otto falls in love with Ana. A message he writes on a paper airplane leads to a meeting between their parents, who fall in love, and there is a marvelous shot of Otto's face when he realizes that the girl he loves is going to become his stepsister. As teenagers, they are lovers. As adults, they are separated—although for one heart-stopping moment they sit back to back in a Spanish café, each unaware of the other. And then fate takes them both to Finland, where the great circles of their lives meet again.

Julio Medem, who wrote and directed *Lovers of the Arctic Circle,* suggests that plot alone is not enough to explain a great love; faith is necessary, and an almost mystical belief that one is destined to share life with a single chosen person. His film more or less begins when Ana and Otto are young, and ends when they are older, but the story line is intercut with scenes and images that move back and forth in time and only gradually reveal their meanings. The shot at the beginning, for example, when one character is reflected in the eyes of another—we find out what that means at the end. And there are moments when a car either does, or does not, crash into a red bus. All becomes clear.

When you have a metaphysical system tiptoeing through a film, it's important that the actors provide a grounding of reality; otherwise, we're down the rabbit hole. There are many stretches in *Lovers of the Arctic Circle* that play just like ordinary drama, as we see the children growing up, we see their parents falling in love, we share the anger of Otto's mother when his father chooses the other woman, and we sense her hurt when Otto announces he wants to move in with the other family (it's not that he doesn't love his mother—but that he loves Ana more). There's even room for Ana's discovery that her mother may not be entirely faithful.

The romance between Ana and Otto (played by three sets of actors) is seen growing over many years, from a moment when young Otto wants to tell Ana he loves her, to a moment when he touches her leg, to a moment in their adolescence when she sends him a note: "Come to me tonight! Jump through the window. Be brave!" The movie doesn't linger on sexual details, but is interested instead in the whole arc of a life. It reminded me of the Kieslowski films in which characters are buffeted by chance, fate, and coincidence. And of Vincent Ward's *A Map of the Human Heart.* Yes, we have free will, such films are saying, and can choose as we want—but what ungoverned forces produce the choices we choose from?

Everything in the film is connected. A German pilot in World War II is linked to another pilot, years later. A story in a newspaper changes its meaning the more we learn. Who steps into the street at the wrong moment, and what happens then? It would be unfair to the film to tell. This is not the sort of movie where you can give away the ending. It is all ending. "In my end is my beginning," T. S. Eliot wrote. By now you are either confused by my description of the film, or intrigued by it. There is a certain kind of mind that enjoys difficulties. Are we not drawn onward to a new era? Give or take an "a"?

The Lovers on the Bridge ★ ★ ★
R, 125 m., 1999

Juliette Binoche (Michele Stalens), Denis Lavant (Alex), Klaus-Michael Gruber (Hans). Directed by Leos Carax and produced by Alain Dahan. Screenplay by Carax.

Leos Carax's *The Lovers on the Bridge* arrives trailing clouds of faded glory. It was already one of the most infamous productions in French history when it premiered at the Cannes festival in 1992, where some were stunned by its greatness and more were simply stunned. Its American release was delayed, according to Carax, because its distributor vindictively jacked up the asking price. Now it has arrived at last, a film both glorious and goofy, inspiring affection and exasperation in about equal measure.

The story could have been told in a silent melodrama, or on the other half of a double bill with Jean Vigo's great *L'Atalante* (1934), which was Carax's inspiration. On the ancient Pont-Neuf, the oldest bridge in Paris, two vagrants discover one another. One is Michele (Juliette Binoche), an artist who is going blind. The other is Alex (Denis Lavant), a drunk and druggie who supports himself by fire-breathing. The bridge has been closed for a year for repairs, bags of cement and paving blocks are tossed about, and they make it their home for the summer; their landlord, so to speak, is a crusty old bum named Hans (Klaus-Michael Gruber).

This three-hander could have made a nice little film in other hands, but Carax's production costs became legendary. His permission to shoot on the Pont-Neuf ran out while delays stalled his production; Lavant broke his leg, which held up the film a year, according to

some sources, although since he uses a crutch and wears a cast in the film, one wonders why. (The broken leg is simply explained: Alex passes out in the middle of a boulevard late one night.) Thrown off the real bridge, Carax moved his entire production to the South of France and built a giant set of the Pont-Neuf, including the facades of three buildings of the famous Samaritaine department store. This was not cheap.

The lovers are both reckless and secretive. Michele, who wears a dressing over one eye, doesn't reveal for a long time that she is going blind. Alex loves her and yet would rather read her mail and break into her former home than ask her flat-out about herself. The bum keeps trying to throw her off the bridge ("It's all right for Alex, but not for a young girl like you"), but when he finally shares his own story, it opens the floodgates for all three.

There is much here that is cheerfully reckless, as when Alex does cartwheels on the bridge parapet above the Seine (did no authorities see him?). Or when the two of them steal a police speedboat so she can water-ski past the fireworks display on the night of the French bicentennial. Alex raises money by his fire-eating, his sweaty torso dancing in the middle of smoke and flames, and she pours drugs into the drinks of tourists to steal their money.

All well and good in a different kind of film. But other scenes break with the gritty reality and go for Chaplinesque bathos. Posters go up all over Paris—*all* over, on every Metro wall and construction site—and Alex sets them afire (why is there no one else in the Metro?). Then he torches the van of the man who is hanging the posters, and the man burns alive. This melodramatic excess leads, after a time, to a romantic conclusion that seems to dare us to laugh; Carax piles one development on top of another until it's not a story; it's an exercise in absurdity.

All of this is not without charm. Juliette Binoche, from *The English Patient,* the Kieslowski Red-White-Blue trilogy, and Louis Malle's *Damage,* dares to play her character with the kind of broad strokes you'd find in a silent film, and old Klaus-Michael Gruber has a touching moment of confession as Hans. Denis Lavant is not a likable Alex, but then how could he be? His approach to romance is simple: He makes his most dramatic demonstration of love in her absence, by burning the posters so she will not leave him; when she's there, he's likely to be sullen, petulant, or drunk. For two strong young people to embrace their lifestyle is itself an exercise in stylish defeatism; they have to choose to be miserable, and they do, wearing it well.

I felt a certain affection for *The Lovers on the Bridge*. It is not the masterpiece its defenders claim, nor is it the completely self-indulgent folly described by its critics. It has grand gestures and touching moments of truth, perched precariously on a foundation of horsefeathers.

So troubled was its distribution history that Carax waited seven years to make another film, which confirmed his unshakably goofy worldview. That was *Pola X*, which opened the 1999 Cannes festival, and was a modern telling of Melville's nineteenth-century novel *Pierre*, about a young man's idyllic relationship with his mother and his happy plans for marriage, all destroyed by the appearance of a strange, dark woman who claims to be his father's secret daughter. The movie "exists outside the categories of good and bad," I wrote from Cannes; "it is a magnificent folly."

The Lovers on the Bridge, on the other hand, exists just inside the category of good. I am not sure, thinking about the two films, that I don't prefer *Pola X*. If you have little taste or discipline as a filmmaker but great style and heedlessness, it may be more entertaining to go for broke than to fake a control you don't possess.

Love's Labour's Lost ★ ★ ½
PG, 95 m., 2000

Kenneth Branagh (Berowne), Alessandro Nivola (King), Nathan Lane (Costard), Adrian Lester (Dumaine), Matthew Lillard (Longaville), Natascha McElhone (Rosaline), Alicia Silverstone (Princess), Timothy Spall (Don Armado), Carmen Ejogo (Maria), Emily Mortimer (Katherine). Directed by Kenneth Branagh and produced by David Barron and Branagh. Screenplay by Branagh, based on the play by William Shakespeare.

Shakespeare supplies not so much the source of Kenneth Branagh's *Love's Labour's Lost* as the clothesline. Using the flimsy support of one of the least of the master's plots, Branagh strings together ten song-and-dance numbers in a musical that's more like a revue than an adaptation. After daring to film his great version of *Hamlet* using the entire, uncut original play (the first time that had been done), Branagh here cuts and slashes through Shakespeare's text with an editorial machete.

What is left is winsome, charming, sweet, and slight. It's so escapist it escapes even from itself. The story pairs off four sets of lovers, supplies them with delightful songs and settings, and calls it a day. The cast is not especially known for being able to sing and dance (only the British Adrian Lester and the Broadway veteran Nathan Lane are pros in those departments), but that's part of the charm. Like Woody Allen's *Everyone Says I Love You*, this is one of those movies were real people are so seized with the need to break into song that a lack of talent can't stop them.

Not, in fact, that they are untalented. The songs here are well within the abilities of the cast to sing them, and indeed several of them were originally sung on the screen by Fred Astaire, whose vocal range was as modest as his footwork was unlimited. (Most of the songs have been recorded on albums by the British singer Peter Skellern, who can hit a note and the one below it and the one above it, and that's about it—and he makes them entertaining too.)

The plot: The king of Navarre (Alessandro Nivola) has declared that he and three of his comrades (Kenneth Branagh, Adrian Lester, Matthew Lillard) will withdraw from the world for three years of thought and study. During this time, they will reject all worldly pleasures, most particularly the company of women. No sooner do they make their vow and retire to their cloister than the princess of France (Alicia Silverstone) arrives for a visit, accompanied by three friends (Natascha McElhone, Carmen Ejogo, Emily Mortimer).

The men find it acutely poignant that they have sworn off the company of women (with a severe penalty for the first who succumbs). They search for loopholes. Perhaps if the ladies camp *outside* the palace walls, that won't count as a visit. Perhaps if the visit is a state occasion, it is not a social one . . .

All of these rationalizations collapse before the beauty of the women, and the eight men and women pair off into four couples so quickly it's like choosing sides for a softball game. Then we get the songs, some of them wonderfully well staged, as when "Cheek to Cheek" (with its line "Heaven . . . I'm in heaven . . .") has them floating in midair beneath the stars painted on the underside of the dome of the king's library.

The eight starters are joined by low-comedy relief pitchers, in the tradition of all Shakespeare comedies. They include Timothy Spall as a Spaniard whose "I Get a Kick Out of You" is a charmer, and Nathan Lane (who does a nice slow-tempo "There's No Business Like Show Business"). Alicia Silverstone is the lead among the women, who playfully do a synchro-swimming version of "Fancy Free," and Branagh gives himself the best male role, although not tilting the scales to an unseemly degree.

All is light and winning, and yet somehow empty. It's no excuse that the starting point was one of the weaker of Shakespeare's plays. *Love's Labour's Lost* is hardly ever performed on the stage and has never been previously filmed, and there is a reason for that: It's not about anything. In its original form, instead of the songs and dances we have dialogue that's like an idle exercise in brainy banter for Shakespeare.

It's like a warm-up for the real thing. It makes not the slightest difference which boy gets which girl, or why, and by starting the action in 1939 and providing World War II as a backdrop, Branagh has not enriched either the play or the war, but fit them together with an awkward join. There's not a song I wouldn't hear again with pleasure, or a clip that might not make me smile, but as a whole, it's not much. Like cotton candy, it's better as a concept than as an experience.

Loving Jezebel ★ ★ ½

R, 85 m., 2000

Hill Harper (Theodurus Melville), Laurel Holloman (Samantha), Lysa Aya Trenier (June), Gabe Parks (David), Nicole Ari Parker (Frances), David Moscow (Gabe), Phylicia Rashad (Alice Melville), Sandrine Holt (Mona). Directed by Kwyn Bader and produced by David Lancaster. Screenplay by Bader.

"I've spent my life," Theodurus Melville tells us, "loving other men's women." That would make him a Casanova, but the title of *Loving Jezebel* puts the blame on the women: A jezebel, we learn from a definition on the screen, is a woman who fools around with lots of men.

Either definition would set up a sex romp, I suppose, but this movie is not quite what you'd expect. Within its romantic comedy we find a character who is articulate and a little poignant, and we realize Theodurus doesn't so much seek out other men's women as have them, so to speak, thrust upon him.

That's because he knows how to listen to women, and meets many women whose men are intoxicated only by their own words. We're reminded of *The Tao of Steve,* and Steve's strategy for seduction: "Men and women both want to have sex, but women want to have sex fifteen minutes after us, so if you hold out for twenty, she'll be chasing you for five."

Theodurus is the son of an interracial marriage, whose romantic conquests range from blonde to Trinidadian, from a ballerina who looks perhaps Eurasian to one, who is, he says, and we can hear the savor in his voice, "Afro-Filipino-Bavarian." One of the movie's not incidental pleasures is what beautiful women Theodorus seems to attract.

The movie is narrated by Theodurus (Hill Harper), who explains that his lifelong dilemma began in first grade, when he was kissed by a girl and was blissful for thirty seconds, until he realized she kissed all the boys in the class. Flash forward to 1985, with Theodurus in college, where he yearns for the fragrant Frances (Nicole Ari Parker), who lays down the rules (no kissing, no sex, she's a virgin) and then turns out to like sex, has a boyfriend, and warns him, "You know I like to play the crowd."

Other women turn up, including Mona (Sandrine Holt) from Trinidad, and Samantha (Laurel Holloman), who mopes at the corner table in the café where he works, sipping cappuccino and writing, or trying to write, poetry. She has a husband named Gabe (David Moscow) who seems obtuse even for a chauvinist pig.

In a film filled with beautiful women, the distributors seem determined to overlook the most stunning. This is Lysa Aya Trenier, who plays June, a bartender and ballerina, who wonders if she will ever be able to dance well enough to become a prima. Trenier is one of those women who pop off the screen with stardom written all over her; whether she will become a successful actress I cannot predict, but she was born to be a Bond girl, and I mean that as a sincere compliment.

Strangely enough, her name is not included in the movie's press material, or on its official Website, or in the Internet Movie Database, and it is a measure of her unknown status that even Google, mightiest of the search engines, turns up absolutely no references to her. So anyone searching for her will be led, I assume, straight to this review, where all I can tell you is: I know why you're searching.

Hill Harper, seen before now on TV and in movie supporting roles (He Got Game), is an engaging actor, able to sound absolutely convincing as he fast-talks his would-be conquests. No wonder he sounds smart; after graduating from Brown, he got graduate degrees in law and government from Harvard. He sounds like he knows what he's talking about even when he doesn't; I was fascinated by his theory about the egg-stealing activities of the bluebird (which I think he has confused with the cuckoo, although that doesn't slow him down).

The movie's problem is a fundamental lack of substance. None of the women are really developed in any depth except Samantha, so what we get is Theodurus as a tour guide through his romantic conquests and failures. He's like a guy paging through his college yearbook and telling us who he has, or would like to have, made love to: interesting for him, less interesting for us. Still, if the movie treats its women like pretty faces, at least it has good taste in pretty faces.

The Low Down ★ ★ ★
NO MPAA RATING, 96 m., 2001

Aidan Gillen (Frank), Kate Ashfield (Ruby), Dean Lennox Kelly (Mike), Tobias Menzies (John), Rupert Proctor (Terry), Samantha Power (Lisa), Dena Smiles (Susan), Maggie Lloyd Williams (Jean). Directed by Jamie Thraves and produced by John Stewart and Sally Llewellyn. Screenplay by Thraves.

You probably went through a time in your life like the one Frank is going through in *The Low Down*. I know I did. You may be going through it now. It passes. At the time, you hardly notice it. Later, you look back and wonder how you could have been so clueless. Frank is stuck. He should have quit his job, changed his apartment, and found a steady girl a long time ago, but he drifts in vagueness, unable to act. There are times when he may be terrified in social situations, but we can't be sure—and maybe he can't, either.

Frank (Aidan Gillen) works with Mike (Dean Lennox Kelly) and John (Tobias Menzies) in a London shop where they manufacture jokey props for TV shows and magic acts. He lives in a grotty walk-up above a hairdresser's and next door to a crack house. All night long junkies stand on the sidewalk beneath his window, shouting "Paul! Paul!" to their dealer. Frank knows he should move, but jokes about buying Paul a doorbell.

Thinking it is time to buy his own flat, he goes to a real-estate office and meets Ruby (Kate Ashfield). As they look at apartments together, they begin to like each other. The writer-director, Jamie Thraves, uses freeze-frames to show how they're struck with each other. A stylistic device like that leaps out because the movie is so low-key. It has no plot, no objective, no purpose other than to show a few days in the lives of a group of friends. They work, they gossip, they hang out, they go to parties, they sit on each other's beds and talk, and Frank and Ruby draw as close to each other as Frank can stand before he has to retreat. There is a subtle subplot about how he has stopped drinking, and starts again.

The British critics said the movie was about nothing. Depends on how you see it. I think it's about Frank's paralyzing inability to move, socially or any other way. The more you look at this guy, the more you realize he's trembling inside. Aidan Gillen is handsome in a Richard Gere–Timothy Hutton sort of way, and can be charming at first, but soon Ruby is looking at him strangely because he seems distant and tentative. He has a way of breaking dates, or turning up late; once he hides and watches her waiting for him.

The movie provides key scenes which are like tests. In one of them, he plays handball with a stranger he meets at the court, and then they have a drink together and it is possible that the other man wants to know if Frank is gay, and interested. I say "possible" because Frank is not receiving on that frequency. In another scene, he's in a pub with a friend at closing time, and an ugly drunk gets in Frank's face and Frank avoids a fight by meekly saying what the drunk wants to hear. A little later, when one of Frank's coworkers screws up by spilling paint on a prop, Frank attacks him violently for no real reason; the poor sap gets to stand in for the drunk, I guess.

Two other scenes intrigued me. Both involve encounters with a street woman who wants money. Frank gives the money both times. The second time, the woman offers her body in payment. Frank turns her down. But watch his body language. He takes her up to his flat, and when he goes into the bedroom to get the money, he straightens the cover on the bed, and runs his hand through his hair. Why? Because he doesn't really know if he will have sex with her or not. And, despite the fact that she's a junkie offering her body, she activates old habits and "manners" involving his uncertainty about women.

A movie like *The Low Down* gets better the more attention you pay. To say "nothing happens" is to be blind to everyday life, during which we wage titanic struggles with our programming. Someday a woman (or a man) will come along who can blast Frank out of his bunker. Someday he will give up the after-college job and find his real work. At the end of the film he at least moves to a different apartment. From time to time, he will remember Ruby, and wonder what went wrong—wonder, for a fleeting moment, if he had anything to do with it.

Lucie Aubrac ★ ★ ½
R, 116 m., 1999

Carole Bouquet (Lucie), Daniel Auteuil (Raymond), Patrice Chereau (Max), Jean-Roger Milo (Maurice), Eric Boucher (Serge), Heino Ferch (Barbie), Bernard Verley (Charles-Henri), Jean Martin (Paul Lardanchet), Marie Piller (Marie). Directed and produced by Claude Berri. Screenplay by Berri, based on the novel *Ils partiront dans l'ivresse* by Lucie Aubrac.

Lucie Aubrac is set in Lyon in 1943, and tells the story of a brave, pregnant woman who leads a daring raid to free her husband, a Resistance leader who has been condemned to death by the Gestapo. It is based on a novel by the real Lucie Aubrac, who says in a final screen note that she chose Claude Berri to direct the film because of his support for a foundation that commemorates the Resistance. It is a quiet and bitter joke in France, of course, that once the war was over everyone turned out to have been in the Resistance; the Nazis ran things with no help at all.

The opening titles tell us that *Lucie Aubrac* is based on fact, although "certain liberties" have been taken for the purposes of drama. On a whim, I searched for Raymond and Lucie Aubrac on the Web, and turned up many pages from *Liberation*, the Paris daily, involving a controversy over the most basic facts of all. Were the Aubracs indeed Resistance heroes, as her novel presents them, or did Raymond crack under Gestapo torture and identify the Resistance leader Jean Moulin? Detractors point to the coincidence that soon after Raymond's escape, Moulin was betrayed.

I don't have a clue about these facts, any of them. I doubt Lucie Aubrac would draw the attention of a novel and film to her story if she felt it could be disproved. At this point the Gestapo witnesses involved are certainly dead (among them Klaus Barbie, the "Butcher of Lyon," who makes a brief appearance here). What we are left with is a story which, if true, is certainly heroic. But since we are attending a movie and not a benefit, we must ask if we are moved and entertained.

I must say, not enough. There are some moments of true tension, as when Lucie (Carole Bouquet) confronts local Nazi officials and claims she is pregnant by the man they are holding prisoner, and wants to be married so her child can have a name. And more tension when she is permitted to meet with her husband in front of the Nazis. He has claimed to be somebody else, has denied he knows her, and now must somehow intuit that the time is right to admit his real identity—since her plan involves hijacking the truck that would carry him from prison to the wedding ceremony.

Those scenes work. Other scenes, including the planning and execution of the snatch, would not be remarkable if we saw them in a fiction film. They take on a certain interest because they are based on fact, yes, but the bones of the action are not very meaty. A map is drawn, showing an intersection of two streets. A plan is devised: Partisans will drive their cars in front of the truck, blocking it. Others will shoot the driver and guards. Raymond Aubrac and his fellow prisoners will escape. This is not the stuff of a caper movie.

Raymond is played by Daniel Auteuil, who has the best nose among French actors, ahead even of Depardieu (whose nose has been broken more often than Auteuil's but with less dramatic effect). He is a wonderful actor *(A Heart in Winter, My Favorite Season, Les Voleurs)*. Here he seems constrained by the tradition of brave understatement that inflicts so many movie Resistance heroes. He is tender in quiet, private moments with his wife, but otherwise essentially a pawn in her scheme.

Bouquet is an enigma. A beautiful woman, she somehow lacks juice in this role. She is too perfectly coiffed, dressed, made up; there should be more smudges on a girl who has been seduced and abandoned. Opportunities are lost in her meetings with Nazi officials, including one beefy general who in civilian life could have been typecast as a real butcher, in Lyon or anywhere. The confrontations are too dry, too restrained by unexpressed hostility. The movie has too much docudrama and not enough soul.

As a heroine, Lucie Aubrac has much to recommend her. After the screening I informed my wife that in the event of my being taken prisoner by villains, I would expect her, like Lucie, to lead a raid to free me. She agreed. I hope she springs me before I crack under torture.

Lucky Numbers ★ ★
R, 105 m., 2000

John Travolta (Russ Richards), Lisa Kudrow (Crystal Latroy), Tim Roth (Gig), Ed O'Neill (Dick Simmons), Michael Rapaport (Dale), Bill Pullman (Lakewood), Michael Moore (Walter), Daryl Mitchell (Chambers), Michael Weston (Larry). Directed by Nora Ephron and produced by Sean Daniel, Ephron, Jonathan D. Krane, and Andrew Lazar. Screenplay by Adam Resnick.

Lucky Numbers, starring John Travolta as a TV weatherman who tries to rig the lottery, tells too much story at not enough energy. It should have been cut back and cranked up. Instead, it keeps introducing new characters until the plot becomes a juggling act just when it should be a sprint. And there's another problem: Is it intended as a comedy, or not?

I ask because there are funny things in it, and then gruesome things, sad things and brutal things. Quentin Tarantino was able to cover that spread in *Pulp Fiction.* But Nora Ephron *(Sleepless in Seattle, You've Got Mail)* doesn't find a way. She has Travolta and Tim Roth from *Pulp Fiction,* but they didn't bring their notes.

Consider a scene involving Lisa Kudrow and Michael Moore (yes, Michael Moore). Kudrow with the right material is one of the funniest actresses around; see her in *The Opposite of Sex* or *Romy and Michele's High School Reunion.* Here she plays a daffy model who draws the winning lottery numbers on TV. Moore is her sad-sack cousin, recruited to front as the purchaser of the winning number. He has asthma. When he won't tell her where the ticket is, she bounces on his chest until he has an asthma attack, and then won't give him his inhaler.

Up to a certain point this could be funny (it doesn't sound funny, but trust me). The movie takes it beyond that point, until we want to cringe. Ephron doesn't actually show the poor guy's tongue turning purple, but Kudrow can't make the payoff anything but pathetic, and neither could any other actress. When you add in the rest of the movie's violence, it looks like a black comedy that needed to go either blacker or funnier, instead of each approach undercutting the other.

Travolta and Kudrow work at a TV station managed by Ed O'Neill. Both men are having affairs with her, which makes her a two-way conduit of knowledge, among other things. Travolta is in debt because his snowmobile business is failing (it's the warmest winter in years). He and Kudrow plot with Tim Roth, the owner of a strip club, to rig the lottery, and the plan works, up to a point. But then so many characters want a cut of the action that, Travolta complains, he'll be back in debt again.

The movie has fun establishing the weatherman character as a big celebrity in the small pond of Harrisburg, Pennsylvania. He has a parking space with his name on it at Denny's, a private booth protected by a red velvet rope, and an omelet named after him. Travolta is wonderful at projecting a sunny joy in his own fame, but less successful later in the film as he goes into guilty meltdown.

The O'Neill character has his own agenda, but so do several other characters, including Roth, Dale the thug (Michael Rapaport), Lakewood the cop (Bill Pullman), Lakewood's partner Chambers (Daryl Mitchell), Larry the snowmobile salesman (Michael Weston), and a local numbers game operator. New characters are introduced as the story moves along, and the narrative gets expansive and gabby.

So much depends on tone in a movie. Either you find the right one and stick with it, or you're in trouble (unless, like Tarantino, you really know what you're doing). If we're supposed to like these people, then there's a point beyond which they should not go in their villainy. If we're not, then the scenes where they're nice should have more irony. Kudrow figures out her own character and sticks with it successfully from beginning to end (apart from the unfortunate asphyxiation episode). I like the way she keeps glancing down at her body to be sure it still looks sexy.

Travolta as a person wants to be nice, and to be seen as nice, in every atom of his being, and that causes a tension the movie never resolves. He needs to be a little nastier. Instead of starting with a nice guy and getting him in trouble, it might have been a better idea to start with a tough guy and show him trying to be nice (Robert De Niro's character in *Meet the Parents* comes to mind).

By the end of the film, we're less entertained than relieved. Lots of stuff happened, and much of it might have been interesting in a different kind of film. Here we get the curious sense that the characters are racing around Harrisburg breathlessly trying to keep up with the plot. There is, however, good news. Travolta survived this experience with his sense of humor still intact. How can I be sure? He has announced he wants to make a sequel to *Battlefield Earth*.

The Luzhin Defence ★ ★ ½
PG-13, 108 m., 2001

John Turturro (Alexander Luzhin), Emily Watson (Natalia), Geraldine James (Vera), Stuart Wilson (Valentinov), Christopher Thompson (Jean de Stassard), Fabio Sartor (Turati), Peter Blythe (Ilya), Orla Brady (Anna). Directed by Marleen Gorris and produced by Stephen Evans, Philippe Gulz, and Caroline Wood. Screenplay by Petter Berry, based on the novel by Vladimir Nabokov.

"There is a pattern emerging!" cries the eccentric chess genius Alexander Luzhin. "I must keep track—every second!" To which the woman he loves can only reply, "It sounds like such a lonely battle." It is the 1920s in Italy, and they've met at a chess tournament, where Luzhin has the ability to become world champion, if his demons do not drive him mad. As anyone who has played chess knows, the game is utterly absorbing, driving out thoughts of anything else. The better you play, the deeper it becomes, until finally, among the very strongest players, it becomes an abyss. Some fall in. Where is Bobby Fischer?

The Luzhin Defence, based on a novella by Vladimir Nabokov, is about love, genius, and madness, but it is also about life among the wealthy emigrés of Europe in the years after World War I. They dress and move with elegance, their wealth preserving around them an illusion of the social order that was destroyed by the guns of August. They move from spa to spa, and although I am not sure where the movie is set, its villa looks as if it could be on the shore of Lake Como.

Here chess masters arrive from all over the world, as well as the debutante Natalia (Emily Watson) and her socially ambitious mother,

Vera (Geraldine James). Alexander Luzhin (John Turturro) wanders in like a dreamer from another planet, absentminded, careless of his dress, in a world of his own. "That man is a genius," an onlooker whispers to Natalia. "He can accomplish anything he sets his mind to."

Well, perhaps. He sets his mind on Natalia. After having had no real conversation with her, he approaches her and announces, "I want you to be my wife. I implore you to agree." She doesn't turn him down as a madman, but asks for time to consider, and then agrees. She is won by his absolute simplicity and honesty. She is repelled by the corrupt marriage candidates sponsored by her mother. And something in her needs to protect Alexander.

The film follows a match between Luzhin and a grandmaster whose patience for chess is equaled only by his patience for Luzhin. But there is an evil presence on the premises: Valentinov (Stuart Wilson), who was the boy's chess teacher. The older man has never forgiven young Alexander for crushing him time and again at the board—emasculating him, ignoring him—and has tried for years on end to sabotage the dreamer's chess career. Now he turns up at the villa with more schemes. At one point, totally absorbed by a chess problem, Luzhin is driven away from the tournament by a chauffeur paid by Valentinov. Luzhin solves the problem and gets out of the car, belatedly noticing that he is stranded in the countryside.

The film is elegiac and sad, beautifully mounted, but not as compelling as it should be. It was directed by Marleen Gorris, whose *Antonia's Line* is what *Chocolat* wanted to be in its celebration of a female life-spirit. Here she captures Nabokov's elegance but not his passion. Perhaps we are never convinced by the bond between Alexander and Natalia. She pities him, she cares for him, she tries to protect him—but their relationship is so new we cannot understand the depth of her devotion, unless it involves madness too. And his love for her, after its first dramatic flourish in the marriage proposal, seems to recede into the clutter of his mind and its systems and patterns.

Turturro does something in his performance that demands more of an anchor than the film provides. He is floating in Luzhin's own interior monologue, entranced by the infinity of chess, and to the outer world seems childlike, innocent, incapable of protecting himself. At one point a doctor says he must stop playing to save his life. But it is never the Luzhins who are burnt out by chess. It is their opponents. The mad geniuses play on obsessively, while their opponents play at a level only high enough to understand how much higher there is to go. Turturro looks uncannily like Bobby Fischer, and I irreverently wish Gorris had abandoned Nabokov and his world and used Turturro in a movie about the match between Fischer and Spassky in Iceland in 1972. I see Bjork as Natalia.

M

Madadayo ★ ★ ★
NO MPAA RATING, 134 m., 2000

Tatsuo Matsumura (Hyakken Uchida), Kyoko Kagawa (Uchida's Wife), Hisashi Igawa (Takayama), George Tokoro (Amaki). Directed by Akira Kurosawa and produced by Hisao Kurosawa. Screenplay by Akira Kurosawa.

Made in 1993 when he was eighty-three, *Madadayo* is the last film by the Japanese master Akira Kurosawa, one of the greatest of all filmmakers, who died in 1998. And yet the very title of the film argued against death; "Madadayo" means "not yet!" That is the ritual cry that the film's old professor shouts out at the end of every one of his birthday parties, and it means that although death will come and may be near, life still goes on.

This is the kind of film we would all like to make, if we were very old and very serene. There were times when I felt uncannily as if Kurosawa were filming his own graceful decline into the night. It tells the story of the last two decades in the life of Hyakken Uchida, a writer and teacher who retires in the war years of the early 1940s. He was the kind of teacher who could inspire great respect and affection from his students, who venerate him and, as a group, help support him in his old age.

In Japan they have a tradition of "living national treasures"—people who because of their gifts and knowledge are treated like national monuments. Uchida is such a man, who has taught all his life and now finds that his books are selling well enough that he can move with his wife to a pretty little house, and sit in the entranceway: "That will be my study, and at the same time I will be the gatekeeper."

Kurosawa's career itself spanned some sixty years, and the titles of his films are spoken with awe by those who love them. Consider that the same man made *Rashomon, Yojimbo, Ikiru, The Seven Samurai, The Hidden Fortress, Red Beard, Throne of Blood, Kagemusha, Ran,* and twenty-five more. His movies have been filled with life and spectacle, but here, in *Madadayo,* he has made a film in the spirit of his near-contemporary Yasujiro Ozu, whose domestic dramas are among the most quietly observant and contemplative of all films.

Very little happens in *Madadayo.* The old man (Tatsuo Matsumura) and his wife (Kyoko Kagawa) are feted by his students on his sixtieth birthday, and go to live in the fine little house. The house is destroyed in an air raid. They move to a little hut, hardly more than a room and a half, and there the professor also sits in the doorway and writes. His students come to see him, and every year on his birthday they have the ritual party at which he downs a big glass of beer and cries out "not yet!"

The students conspire to find the professor a larger house. Then something very important happens. A cat named Nora wanders into their house, and the professor and his wife come to love it. Nora disappears. The professor is grief-stricken. Leaflets are circulated, and his students, now middle-aged businessmen, scour the neighborhood for Nora, without success. Then another cat walks into their house, and the wound is healed.

At the professor's seventy-seventh birthday dinner, we see that things have changed. The early events were held Japanese-style, with men only. Now women are present, too: wives, daughters, even grandchildren, in a Western-style banquet room. And still the cry is "not yet!"

Like Ozu, Kurosawa is content to let his camera rest and observe. We never quite learn what sorts of things the professor writes (the real Uchida was in fact a beloved essayist), but we know he must be a great man because his students love him so. We learn few intimate details about his life (not even, if I recall, his wife's first name). We see him mostly seated in his front door, as a stranger might.

Like his students, we are amused by his signs forbidding visitors and warning away those who would urinate on his wall. We learn about the burglar-proofing strategies in his first, larger, house: He leaves a door open, with a sign saying "Burglar's Entrance." Inside, signs indicate "Burglar's Passage," "Burglar's Recess Area," and "Burglar's Exit." He guesses right that burglars would prefer to operate in a house that grants them more anonymity.

The movie is as much about the students as

the professor, as much about gratitude and love as about aging. In an interview at the time of the film's release, Kurosawa said his movie is about "something very precious, which has been all but forgotten: the enviable world of warm hearts." He added, "I hope that all the people who have seen this picture will leave the theater feeling refreshed, with broad smiles on their faces."

Magnolia ★ ★ ★ ★
R, 179 m., 2000

Jason Robards (Earl Partridge), Julianne Moore (Linda Partridge), Tom Cruise (Frank Mackey), Philip Seymour Hoffman (Phil Parma), John C. Reilly (Officer Kurring), Melora Walters (Claudia Gator), Jeremy Blackman (Stanley Spector), Michael Bowen (Rick Spector), William H. Macy (Donnie Smith), Philip Baker Hall (Jimmy Gator), Melinda Dillon (Rose Gator), April Grace (Reporter). Directed by Paul Thomas Anderson and produced by Joanne Sellar. Screenplay by Anderson.

Magnolia is operatic in its ambition, a great joyous leap into melodrama and coincidence, with ragged emotions, crimes and punishments, deathbed scenes, romantic dreams, generational turmoil, and celestial intervention, all scored to insistent music. It is not a timid film. Paul Thomas Anderson here joins Spike Jonze *(Being John Malkovich),* David O. Russell *(Three Kings),* and their master, Martin Scorsese *(Bringing Out the Dead),* in beginning the new decade with an extroverted self-confidence that rejects the timid postmodernism of the 1990s. These are not movies that apologize for their exuberance or shield themselves with irony against suspicions of sincerity.

The movie is an interlocking series of episodes that take place during one day in Los Angeles, sometimes even at the same moment. Its characters are linked by blood, coincidence, and by the way their lives seem parallel. Themes emerge: the deaths of fathers, the resentments of children, the failure of early promise, the way all plans and ambitions can be undermined by sudden and astonishing events. Robert Altman's *Short Cuts* was also a

group of interlinked Los Angeles stories, and both films illustrate former district attorney Vincent Bugliosi's observation in *Till Death Do Us Part* that personal connections in L.A. have a way of snaking around barriers of class, wealth, and geography.

The actors here are all swinging for the fences, heedless of image or self-protective restraint. Here are Tom Cruise as a loathsome stud, Jason Robards looking barely alive, William H. Macy as a pathetic loser, Melora Walters as a despairing daughter, Julianne Moore as an unloving wife, Michael Bowen as a browbeating father. Some of these people are melting down because of drugs or other reasons; a few, like a cop played by John C. Reilly and a nurse played by Philip Seymour Hoffman, are caregivers.

The film's opening sequence, narrated by an uncredited Ricky Jay, tells stories of incredible coincidences. One has become a legend of forensic lore; it's about the man who leaps off a roof and is struck by a fatal shotgun blast as he falls past a window before landing in a net that would have saved his life. The gun was fired by his mother, aiming at his father and missing. She didn't know the shotgun was loaded; the son had loaded it some weeks earlier, hoping that eventually one of his parents would shoot the other. All (allegedly) true.

This sequence suggests a Ricky Jay TV special, illustrating weird coincidences. But it is more than simply amusing. It sets up the theme of the film, which shows people earnestly and single-mindedly immersed in their lives, hopes, and values, as if their best-laid plans were not vulnerable to the chaotic interruptions of the universe. It's humbling to learn that existence doesn't revolve around us; worse to learn it revolves around nothing.

Many of the characters are involved in television, and their lives reflect on one another. Robards plays a dying tycoon who produces many shows. Philip Baker Hall, also dying, is a game show host. Cruise is Robards's son, the star of infomercials about how to seduce women; his macho hotel ballroom seminars could have been scripted by Andrew Dice Clay. Walters is Hall's daughter, who doesn't believe anything he says. Melinda Dillon is Hall's wife, who might have been happier without his compulsion for confession. Macy plays "former quiz kid Donnie Smith," now a drunk with a bad job in sales, who dreams that orthodontics could make him attractive to a burly bartender. Jeremy Blackman plays a bright young quiz kid on Hall's program. Bowen plays his father, a tyrant who drives him to excel.

The connections are like a game of psychological pickup sticks. Robards alienated Cruise, Hall alienated Dillon, Bowen is alienating Blackman. The power of TV has not spared Robards or Hall from death. Childhood success left Macy unprepared for life, and may be doing the same thing for Blackman. Both Hall and Robards have employees (a producer, a nurse) who love them more than their families do. Both Robards and Hall cheated on their wives. And around and around.

And there are other stories with their own connections. The cop, played by Reilly, is like a fireman rushing to scenes of emotional turmoil. His need to help is so great that he falls instantly in love with the pathetic drug user played by Walters; her need is more visible to him than her crime. Later, he encounters Macy in the middle of a ridiculous criminal situation brought about to finance braces for his teeth.

There are big scenes here for the actors. One comes as Cruise's cocky TV stud disintegrates in the face of cross-examination from a TV reporter (April Grace). He has another big scene at Robards's deathbed. Philip Baker Hall (a favorite actor of Anderson's since *Hard Eight*) also disintegrates on TV; he's unable to ask, instead of answer, questions. Julianne Moore's breakdown in a pharmacy is parallel to Walters's nervousness with the cop: Both women are trying to appear functional while their systems scream because of drugs.

All of these threads converge, in one way or another, upon an event there is no way for the audience to anticipate. This event is not "cheating," as some critics have argued, because the prologue fully prepares the way for it, as do some subtle references to Exodus. It works like the hand of God, reminding us of the absurdity of daring to plan. And yet plan we must, because we are human, and because sometimes our plans work out.

Magnolia is the kind of film I instinctively respond to. Leave logic at the door. Do not expect subdued taste and restraint but instead a kind of operatic ecstasy. At three hours it is even operatic in length, as its themes unfold, its characters strive against the dying of the light, and the great wheel of chance rolls on toward them.

Malena ★ ★
R, 105 m., 2000

Monica Bellucci (Malena Scordia), Giuseppe Sulfaro (Renato Amoroso), Luciano Federico (Renato's Father), Matilde Piana (Renato's Mother), Pietro Notarianni (Professor Bonsignore). Directed by Giuseppe Tornatore and produced by Harvey Weinstein and Mario Cotone. Screenplay by Tornatore, based on a story by Luciano Vincenzoni.

Giuseppe Tornatore's *Malena* tells the story of a woman whose life is destroyed because she has the misfortune to be beautiful and have a great butt. The film tortuously tries to transform this theme in scenes of comedy, nostalgia, and bittersweet regret, but somehow we doubt its sincerity, maybe because the camera lingers so lovingly on the callipygian charms of the actress Monica Bellucci. There is nothing quite so awkward as a film that is one thing while it pretends to be another.

The setup scenes are like low-rent Fellini. In a small Italian town in 1940, a group of adolescent boys wait for the beautiful Malena to pass by. She is all they can imagine a woman could be, arousing their imaginations, and more, with her languorous swaying passage. Malena, who is a schoolteacher and of at least average intelligence, must be aware of her effect on the collective local male libido, but seems blissfully oblivious; her role is not so much dramatic as pictorial (a word I am using in the *Playboy* sense).

The story is told by Renato (Giuseppe Sulfaro), who as the movie opens is admitted to the local fraternity of girl-watchers. They use Malena as subject matter for their autoerotic pastimes, but for Renato she is more like a dream, like a heroine, like a woman he wants to protect from herself—with his bare hands, hopefully.

The story involves Malena's bad luck after her husband is called up by the army and her good name is sullied by local gossip. She's eventually reduced by wartime poverty to dating German soldiers. This descent in the world requires her to spend a great deal of time half-dressed before Tornatore's appreciative camera. She continues to shine brightly in Renato's eyes, however, even after his field of knowledge is broadened when his father takes him to a bordello for the old "I give you the boy—give me back the man" routine.

Fellini's films often involve adolescents inflamed by women who embody their carnal desires. (See *Amarcord* and *8½*. Please.) But Fellini sees the humor that underlies sexual obsession, except (usually, but not always) in the eyes of the participants. *Malena* is a simpler story, in which a young man grows up transfixed by a woman, and essentially marries himself to the idea of her. It doesn't help that the movie's action grows steadily gloomier, leading to a public humiliation that seems wildly out of scale with what has gone before, and to an ending that is intended to move us much more deeply, alas, than it can.

Man of the Century ★ ★ ★
R, 78 m., 1999

Gibson Frazier (Johnny Twennies), Susan Egan (Samantha Winter), Anthony Rapp (Timothy Burns), Cara Buono (Virginia Clemens), Brian Davies (Victor Young), Dwight Ewell (Richard Lancaster), Frank Gorshin (Roman Navarro), David Margulies (Mr. Meyerscholtz), Bobby Short (Chester), Marisa Ryan (Gertrude). Directed by Adam Abraham and produced by Gibson Frazier and Abraham. Screenplay by Frazier and Abraham.

I have a friend named Jay Robert Nash who seems to be a character written by Ben Hecht. He embodies a personal style of speech and dress that would be at home in a classic old crime film or screwball comedy, and indeed he is an expert on both; he has penned encyclopedias on both film and crime. Nash talks with a cigarette bobbing in his mouth, likes to wear fedoras, and calls you "mug." Not only did he write a book proving that the FBI didn't kill John Dillinger outside the Biograph Theater, he actually met Dillinger in the 1960s ("I could see him through the screen door—an

old man now, a hand on the heavy gat in his bathrobe pocket . . .").

Nash is a work of art, and the only person I know who does not need to see *Man of the Century*. This film is about a man with the style of a character in a 1920s wisecracking movie, who lives in the 1990s. Johnny Twennies (Gibson Frazier) walks, talks, dresses, behaves, and thinks like a character that might have been played by Jimmy Cagney or Pat O'Brien.

He writes a column for a modern New York newspaper, but on his desk there's a battered old Smith-Corona typewriter. There's no smoking in the office, of course, but Johnny always has one lit. When he grabs the phone, it's to say things like, "Hello, sweetheart! Give me rewrite!" And when he takes a date to a nightclub, a song and dance number breaks out and the movie stops to savor it.

Johnny lives in a world of street crime and casual four-letter vulgarity, but he doesn't seem to notice the shocking language that surrounds him. When he wants to ask his "best girl" out on a date, he sends her a telegram. His girl, Samantha (Susan Egan), runs an art gallery in SoHo and is a liberated woman, who finds it peculiar that Johnny hasn't made a move. One night she pins him to the sofa and tries to get a kiss, but—hey, what kindofa guy does she think he is?

Johnny writes his column about no-news stories like a ribbon-cutting at a library. But readers love it because of its innocence. The paper assigns him a photographer named Tim (Anthony Rapp) who is gay, but Johnny doesn't comprehend homosexuality, or indeed much of anything else in the modern world. When he sees a mugging under way, he breaks it up instead of Not Getting Involved.

Gibson Frazier, who not only stars but cowrote the screenplay with director Adam Abraham, has a natural affinity for this material. You can't fake rapid-fire screwball dialogue. It has to be in your blood. *Man of the Century* is a peculiar delight, a one-of-a-kind movie that was obviously inspired by his love of old movies.

Watching those old films, I wonder if anybody ever really talked that way. And then I remember a story about Ben Hecht, who wrote dozens of crime movies, and realized that gangsters were learning how to talk by studying his movies. Stylized speech and behavior in the movies took a body blow from the Method, which prized realism above mannerism. *Man of the Century* is like a prizefight between the two acting styles, as if a character from *The Front Page* has been teleported into a movie from 1999. You review a movie like this, and you don't want to e-mail it to the office. You want to get on the horn and ask for rewrite, sister—on the double, see?

Man on the Moon ★ ★ ★ ½
R, 118 m., 1999

Jim Carrey (Andy Kaufman), Courtney Love (Lynne Margulies), Paul Giamatti (Bob Zmuda), Danny DeVito (George Shapiro), Jerry Lawler (Himself). Directed by Milos Forman and produced by Danny DeVito, Michael Shamberg, and Stacey Sher. Screenplay by Scott Alexander and Larry Karaszewski.

Our inner child embraces Andy Kaufman. We've been just like that. Who cannot remember boring our friends for hour after hour after *hour* with the same dumb comic idea, endlessly insisted on? Who hasn't refused to admit being wrong? "I won't give up on this," we're saying, "until you give up first. Until you laugh, or agree, or cry 'uncle.' I can keep this up all night if necessary."

That was Andy Kaufman's approach to the world. The difference was, he tried to make a living out of it, as a stand-up comedian. Audiences have a way of demanding to be entertained. Kaufman's act was essentially a meditation on the idea of entertainment. He would entertain you, but you had to cave in first. You had to laugh at something really dumb, or let him get away with something boring or outrageous. If you passed the test, he was like a little kid, delighted to be allowed into the living room at last. He'd entertain, all right. But you had to pass the entry exam.

He was not the most successful comedian of his time. The last years of his life, his biographer Bill Zehme tells me, were spent in mostly unemployed showbiz free-fall. But Kaufman enjoyed that, too: He was fascinated by the relationship between entertainer and audience, which is never more sincere than when the entertainer is hated. It is poetic justice that Andy

Kaufman now has his own biopic, directed by Milos Forman and starring Jim Carrey. He wins. Uncle.

What is most wonderful about *Man on the Moon,* a very good film, is that it remains true to Kaufman's stubborn vision. Oh, it brightens things up a little (the cookie-and-milk evening at Carnegie Hall wasn't his farewell concert, because by then he was far too unemployable for a Carnegie booking). But essentially it stays true to his persona: a guy who would test you, fool you, lie to you, deceive you, and stage elaborate deceptions, put-ons, and hoaxes. The movie doesn't turn him into a sweet, misunderstood guy. And it doesn't pander for laughs. When something is not working in Kaufman's act, it's not working in the movie either, and it's not funny; it's painful.

The film has a heroic performance from Jim Carrey, who successfully disappears inside the character of Andy Kaufman. Carrey is as big a star as Hollywood has right now, and yet fairly early in *Man on the Moon,* we forget who is playing Kaufman and get involved in what is happening to him. Carrey is himself a compulsive entertainer who will do anything to get a laugh, who wants to please, whose public image is wacky and ingratiating. That he can evoke the complexities of Kaufman's comic agonies is a little astonishing. That he can suppress his own desire to please takes a kind of courage. Not only is he working without his own net, but he's playing a guy who didn't use a net.

The film, directed by Forman and written by Scott Alexander and Larry Karaszewski, begins with Kaufman as a troublesome kid in his room, refusing to go out and play, preferring to host his own TV variety program for the cameras he believed were hidden in his bedroom walls. His material was inspired by shabby nightclub and lounge acts. He understood that a live performance is rarely more fascinating than when it is going wrong.

I myself, for example, have seldom been more involved than I was one night at a thirty-six-seat theater in London during a performance of a one-man show called "Is It Magic—or Is It Manilow?" The star was a bad magician who did a bad imitation of Barry Manilow, alternating the two elements of his act. There were twelve people in the audience, and we were desperately important to him. The program notes said he had once been voted most popular entertainer on a cruise ship out of Goa. Andy Kaufman would have been in ecstasy.

The movie follows Kaufman into the L.A. stand-up circuit, where a talent manager (Danny DeVito) sees something in his act and signs him. Kaufman is soon a sitcom star, a regular on *Taxi* (we see cast veterans Marilu Henner, Carol Kane, Christopher Lloyd, and Judd Hirsch playing themselves—DeVito, of course, is otherwise engaged). He insists on "guest bookings" for his "protégé," an obnoxious lounge act named Tony Clifton, who is played behind impenetrable makeup by Kaufman and sometimes by his accomplice Bob Zmuda. Kaufman steadfastly refuses to admit he "is" Clifton, and in a way, he isn't.

The parabolas of Kaufman's career intersect as *Taxi* goes off the air. He has never been more famous, or had bleaker prospects. He's crying wolf more than the public is crying uncle. He starts wrestling women in his nightclub act, not a popular decision, and gets involved in a feud with Memphis wrestling star Jerry Lawler. They fight on the Letterman show. It looks real. The movie says it was staged (Lawler plays himself). Okay, so it was staged—but Lawler's blow to Kaufman's head was real enough to tumble him out of his chair. And no doubt Kaufman made Lawler vow to hit him that hard. He always wanted to leave you in doubt.

Courtney Love is back in her second Milos Forman movie in a row, playing the lover of an impossible man (she was the *Hustler* publisher's lover in Forman's *The People vs. Larry Flynt*). She comes to wrestle Kaufman and stays to puzzle at him. She likes him, even loves him, but never quite knows who he is. When he tells her he's dying of cancer, her first reaction is anger that he would toy with her feelings in yet another performance piece. Love shows again here that she is a real actress and can, if she wants to, give up the other job.

What was it with Kaufman? The movie leaves us with a mystery, and it should. In traditional Hollywood biopics, there would be Freudian shorthand to explain everything. Nothing explains Andy Kaufman. If he had been explicable, no one would have wanted to make a movie about him.

The Chicago talk jock Steve Dahl told me the other day that Kaufman once recruited him for a performance. "He told me I would be inside a box on the stage, and people would try to guess what was in the box," Dahl recalled. "He gave me a six-pack of Heinekens to keep me company. What he didn't tell me was that I would be in the box for three hours. There I was in the dark, trying to pee back into the can." Dahl thought he was in the show, but from Kaufman's point of view, he was the ideal member of the audience.

Mansfield Park ★ ★ ★ ★
PG-13, 110 m., 1999

Embeth Davidtz (Mary Crawford), Jonny Lee Miller (Edmund Bertram), Alessandro Nivola (Henry Crawford), Frances O'Connor (Fanny Price), Harold Pinter (Sir Thomas Bertram), Lindsay Duncan (Lady Bertram/Mrs. Price), Sheila Gish (Mrs. Norris), James Purefoy (Tom Bertram), Hugh Bonneville (Mr. Rushworth), Justine Waddell (Julia Bertram), Victoria Hamilton (Maria Bertram), Sophia Myles (Susan), Hilton McRae (Mr. Price), Hannah Taylor Gordon (Young Fanny), Charles Edwards (Yates). Directed by Patricia Rozema and produced by Sarah Curtis. Screenplay by Rozema, based on the novel by Jane Austen, her letters, and early journals.

Patricia Rozema's *Mansfield Park* makes no claim to be a faithful telling of Jane Austen's novel, and achieves something more interesting instead. Rozema has chosen passages from Austen's journals and letters and adapted them to Fanny Price, the heroine of *Mansfield Park*, and the result is a film in which Austen's values (and Fanny's) are more important than the romance and melodrama.

The film begins with a young girl whispering a lurid story into the ear of her wide-eyed little sister. This is Fanny (Hannah Taylor Gordon), whose family lives in poverty in a dockside cottage in Portsmouth. Fanny's mother married unwisely for love. Her sister Lady Bertram married for position, and now lives in the great country estate Mansfield Park. Lady Bertram spends her days nodding in a haze of laudanum, but rouses herself sufficiently to send for one of her nieces, and so with no warning Fanny is bundled into a carriage and taken away from her family. "It seems that mother has given me away," she writes her sister. "I can augur nothing but misery with what I have seen at Mansfield Park."

The narrative springs forward, and we meet a twentyish Fanny, now played by Frances O'Connor. Great English country houses in those days were truly family seats, giving shelter and employment to relatives, dependents, and servants, and we meet Lord Bertram (the playwright Harold Pinter, magisterial and firm), his drug-addled wife (Lindsay Duncan), his drunken older son, Tom (James Purefoy), his likable younger son, Edmund (Jonny Lee Miller), his two inconsequential daughters, and the attractive Crawfords, Henry and his sister, Mary (Alessandro Nivola and Embeth Davidtz). The Crawfords have rented the estate's parsonage with the aim of marrying into the Bertram family.

This may seem like a large cast (I have left out three or four characters), but it is important to understand that in that time and place, it would have seemed a small enough one, because these were literally the only people Fanny Price could expect to see on a regular basis. If she is to marry, her husband will probably come from among them, and nobody has to tell her that the candidates are Tom, Edmund, and Henry. All of Austen's novels, in one way or another, are about capable young women trapped in a strata of country society that assigns them to sit in drawing rooms looking pretty while they speculate on their matrimonial chances and risks.

In crossing this theme with the idea that Fanny is a writer, Rozema cuts right to the heart of the matter. We assume that women have always written, but actually until 200 years ago women authors were rare; Austen found her own way into the profession. Most women did not have the education, the freedom, or the privacy to write. Virginia Woolf is eloquent about this in A Room of One's Own, speculating that someone like Austen might literally have never been alone in a room to write, but should be pictured in the corner of a drawing room containing all the other members of her household—writing her novels while conversation and life carried on regardless, dogs barked and children urped.

In *Mansfield Park,* we see Fanny thrilled to receive a quire of writing paper, and sending letters to her sister Susie that contain a great deal more observation and speculation than family correspondence really requires. This young woman could grow up to write—well, *Pride and Prejudice.* We are so accustomed to the notion of Austen's wit and perception that we lose sight of the fact that for her to write at all was a radical break with the role society assigned her.

Women in the early years of the nineteenth century were essentially commodities until they were married, and puppeteers afterward, exerting power through their husbands and children and in the management of their households. Thus all of Austen's novels (and those of George Eliot, Mrs. Gaskell, and the Brontës) can be seen as stories about business and finance—for a woman's occupation and fortune came through marriage.

The key thing about Fanny Price, and about many of Austen's heroines, is that she is ready to say no. Her uncle, Lord Bertram, informs her that Henry Crawford has asked for her hand, and "I have agreed." Fanny does not love Henry. She loves her cousin Edmund, who is engaged to the worthless Mary Crawford. When she says she does not trust Henry, there is a ruthless exchange with her uncle. "Do you trust me?" he asks. "Yes, sir." "Well, I trust him, and you will marry him."

Later in the film there is a bloodcurdling scene in the drawing room after a scandal has threatened the family's reputation. Without revealing too much, let me ask you to listen for Mary Crawford's chilling analysis of the emergency and her plan for what must be done. To modern ears it sounds crass and heartless. In 1806, just such conversations would have sounded reasonable to people schooled to think of the family fortune above any consideration of love or morality.

Mansfield Park is a witty, entertaining film, and I hope I haven't made it sound too serious. Frances O'Connor makes a dark-haired heroine with flashing eyes and high spirits. Harold Pinter is all the country Tory one could possibly hope for. Alessandro Nivola makes a rakish cad who probably really does love Fanny, after his fashion. And Embeth Davidtz's cold-blooded performance as Mary strips bare the pretense and exposes the family for what it is—a business, its fortune based on slave plantations in the Caribbean. This is an uncommonly intelligent film, smart and amusing, too, and anyone who thinks it is not faithful to Austen doesn't know the author but only her plots.

The Man Who Cried ★ ★ ★

R, 97 m., 2001

Christina Ricci (Suzie), Cate Blanchett (Lola), John Turturro (Dante), Johnny Depp (Cesar), Harry Dean Stanton (Felix), Claudia Lander-Duke (Young Suzie), Oleg Yankovsky (Father), Danny Scheinman (Man in Suit). Directed by Sally Potter and produced by Christopher Sheppard. Screenplay by Potter.

Sally Potter makes movies about women who use art and artifice to escape from the roles society has assigned them. *Orlando* (1993) is about a character who lives for four centuries, first as a man, then as a woman. *The Tango Lesson* (1997) is about a British film director (Potter herself) who becomes a tango dancer. Now here is *The Man Who Cried,* about a little Jewish girl from Russia who becomes a little British girl and then a Parisian dancing girl and then a wartime refugee, and finally, once again, her father's daughter.

This is an amazingly ambitious movie, not so much because of the time and space it covers (a lot), but because Potter trusts us to follow her heroine through one damn thing after another. There is a moment when Suzie is on a bicycle, chasing Gypsy horsemen through the streets of Paris, and I thought: Yes, of course, realism at last—a woman in that situation *would* use a bicycle to chase a man on a horse. By the time a ship is torpedoed near the end of the film, we're reflecting that most movies are too timid to offend the gods of plausibility.

Potter puts her money where her mouth is. If she personally, in her forties, can go to Argentina and become a tango dancer, then we can't complain about anything that happens to Suzie. Not that we'd want to. The story begins in Russia in 1927, when the girl's father determines to move the family to America. The girl and her father are separated, the girl is mislabeled by adults, and ends up being adopted by a well-meaning but grim British couple. When she sees Gypsies in the lanes of Britain, she is reminded of her own Jewish community in Russia.

Britain cannot hold a spirit like this. In Paris, Suzie is taken under the arm of a gold-digging showgirl named Lola (Cate Blanchett), who wants to marry well, and has her eyes on a famous opera singer named Dante (John Turturro). Suzie meanwhile falls for Cesar (Johnny Depp), the Gypsy on the white horse, and finds that he is a ride-on extra in Dante's current production. As the clouds of World War II gather, Dante reveals himself as a supporter of Mussolini and a hater of Gypsies and Jews, and Lola's appetite begins to fade.

Potter drenches her movies in bold, romantic music, and in wildly involved visuals. Her camera (here choreographed by the great European veteran Sacha Vierny) does not observe but joins. She loves rich images, unexpected whirls, camera movements that join unexpected elements. The music this time is mostly opera, evoking grand emotions that the action mirrors. *The Man Who Cried* is like an arthouse companion for *Moulin Rouge.*

Some of the actors are indulged, others reined in. Turturro's Dante is a character basking in his own glory, an ego with a voice, less an artist than a man who knows which way the wind is blowing. Blanchett uses a thick accent as a tart with a heart of pawned gold (consider the reach between this role and her Appalachian fortune-teller in *The Gift*). Depp more or less imports his soulful Gypsy from *Chocolat,* sensitive and moody. Christina Ricci's Suzie is at the still center, and very still herself; can a heroine ever have had less dialogue in a talking picture? And here is Harry Dean Stanton as the Parisian opera impresario. Yes, Harry Dean Stanton. Well, why not?—and with a scene where he takes a stand no matter what it costs him.

The Man Who Cried himself does not turn up until very late in the movie. He might once have cried for other reasons, but by then he is crying mostly for himself. He has paid a price for his decisions. As for Suzie, she ends up in Hollywood—and no, that is not giving away the ending. No doubt she grew old and became one of those strange women I would sometimes meet up in the Hollywood Hills, when David Bradley threw his dinner parties for the survivors of the silent era, or at Telluride, where they were the widows of legendary emigrés. Old women who told their stories and said, "But you'll never believe this."

A Map of the World ★ ★ ★ ½
R, 127 m., 2000

Sigourney Weaver (Alice Goodwin), Julianne Moore (Theresa Collins), David Strathairn (Howard Goodwin), Ron Lea (Dan Collins), Arliss Howard (Paul Reverdy), Chloe Sevigny (Carole Mackessy), Louise Fletcher (Nellie), Sara Rue (Debbie), Aunjanue Ellis (Dyshett). Directed by Scott Elliott and produced by Kathleen Kennedy and Frank Marshall. Screenplay by Peter Hedges and Polly Platt, based on the novel by Jane Hamilton.

There is a pounding that starts inside the heads of certain kinds of people when they're convinced they're right. They know in theory all about being cool and diplomatic, but in practice a great righteous anger takes hold, and they say exactly what they think in short and cutting words. Later they cool off, dial down, and vow to think before they speak, but then the red demon rises again in fury against those who are wrong or stupid—or seem at the moment to be.

Alice Goodwin, the Wisconsin farm woman played by Sigourney Weaver in *A Map of the World*, is a woman like that. She has never settled comfortably inside her own body. She is not entirely reconciled to being the wife of her husband, the mother of her children, the teacher of her students. She is not even sure she belongs on a farm. You sense she has inner reservations about everything, they make her mad at herself, and sometimes she blurts out exactly what she's thinking, even when she shouldn't be thinking of it.

This trait leads to a courtroom scene of rare fascination. We've seen a lot of courtrooms in the movies, and almost always we know what to expect. The witnesses will tell the truth or lie, they will be effective or not, and suspense will build if the film is skillful. *A Map of the World* puts Alice Goodwin in the witness box, and she says the wrong thing in the wrong way for reasons that seem right to her but nobody else. She'd rather be self-righteous than acquitted.

This quality makes her a fascinating person, in one of the best performances Weaver has given. We can't take our eyes off her. She is not the plaything or the instrument of the plot. She fights off the plot, indeed: The movement of the film is toward truth and resolution, but she hasn't read the script and is driven by anger and a deep wronged stubbornness. She begins to speak and we feel enormous suspense. We care for her. We don't want her to damage her own case.

The plot involves her in a situation that depends on two unexpected developments, and I don't feel like revealing either one. Neither one is her fault, morally, but bad things happen all the same. She's smart enough to see why she's not to blame for the first event, but human enough to feel terrible about it anyway. And the second development is sort of a combination of the first, plus her own big mouth. Her family is terrified. Her husband doesn't know what to make of her, and her kids don't have the comfort of thinking of their mom as an innocent in an unfair world, because she doesn't act like a victim—she acts like a woman who plans to win the game in the last quarter.

There are good performances all through the movie, which was directed by Scott Elliott and written by Peter Hedges and Polly Platt. David Strathairn plays Howard, Alice Goodwin's husband, and Julianne Moore and Ron Lea play their farm neighbors—just about their only friends. When Alice spends time in prison, she gets a hard time from an inmate (Aunjanue Ellis), who senses (correctly) that this woman may have dug her own grave. And there is a small but crucial role for Chloe Sevigny, who in several recent movies (*Boys Don't Cry, julien donkey-boy, American Psycho*) shows an intriguing range. As for Julianne Moore, see Stanley Kauffmann's praise in his *New Republic* review, where he finds her grief "a small gem of truthful heartbreak."

The movie is not tidy. Like its heroine, it doesn't follow the rules. It breaks into parts. It seems to be a family story, and then turns into a courtroom drama, and then into a prison story, and there is intercutting with romantic intrigue, and there aren't any of the comforting payoffs we get in genre fiction. I'm grateful for movies like this; *Being John Malkovich* and *Three Kings,* so different in every other way, resemble *A Map of the World* in being free—in being capable of taking any turn at any moment, without the need to follow tired conventions. And in Sigourney Weaver, the movie has a heroine who would be a lot happier if she weren't so smart. Now there's a switch.

The Matrix ★ ★ ★
R, 135 m., 1999

Keanu Reeves (Neo), Laurence Fishburne (Morpheus), Carrie-Anne Moss (Trinity), Hugo Weaving (Agent Smith), Joe Pantoliano (Cypher), Gloria Foster (Oracle). Directed by Larry and Andy Wachowski and produced by Joel Silver and Dan Cracchiolo. Screenplay by Larry and Andy Wachowski.

The Matrix is a visually dazzling cyberadventure, full of kinetic excitement, but it retreats to formula just when it's getting interesting. It's kind of a letdown when a movie begins by redefining the nature of reality and ends with a shoot-out. We want a leap of the imagination, not one of those obligatory climaxes with automatic weapons fire.

I've seen dozens if not hundreds of these exercises in violence, which recycle the same tired ideas: Bad guys fire thousands of rounds, but are unable to hit the good guy. Then it's down to the final showdown between good and evil—a martial arts battle in which the good guy gets pounded until he's almost dead, before he finds the inner will to fight back. Been there, seen that (although rarely done this well).

Too bad, because the setup is intriguing. *The Matrix* recycles the premises of *Dark City* and *Strange Days,* turns up the heat and the volume, and borrows the gravity-defying choreography of Hong Kong action movies. It's fun, but it could have been more. The directors are Larry and Andy Wachowski, who know how to make movies (their first film, *Bound,* made my ten best list in 1996). Here, with a big budget and veteran action producer Joel Silver, they've played it safer; there's nothing wrong with going for the Friday night action market, but you can aim higher and still do business.

Warning; spoilers ahead. The plot involves Neo (Keanu Reeves), a mild-mannered soft-

ware author by day, a feared hacker by night. He's recruited by a cell of cyber-rebels, led by the profound Morpheus (Laurence Fishburne) and the leather-clad warrior Trinity (Carrie-Anne Moss). They've made a fundamental discovery about the world: It doesn't exist. It's actually a form of Virtual Reality, designed to lull us into lives of blind obedience to the "system." We obediently go to our crummy jobs every day, little realizing, as Morpheus tells Neo, that "Matrix is the wool that has been pulled over your eyes—that you are a slave."

The rebels want to crack the framework that holds the Matrix in place and free mankind. Morpheus believes Neo is the Messianic "One" who can lead this rebellion, which requires mind power as much as physical strength. Arrayed against them are the Agents, who look like Blues Brothers. The movie's battles take place in Virtual Reality; the heroes' minds are plugged into the combat. (You can still get killed, though: "The body cannot live without the mind.")

"Jacking in" like this was a concept in *Strange Days* and has also been suggested in novels by William Gibson *(Idoru)* and others. The notion that the world is an artificial construction, designed by outsiders to deceive and use humans, is straight out of *Dark City.* Both of those movies, however, explored their implications as the best science fiction often does. *Dark City* was fascinated by the Strangers who had a poignant dilemma: They were dying aliens who hoped to learn from human methods of adaptation and survival.

In *Matrix,* on the other hand, there aren't flesh-and-blood creatures behind the illusion—only a computer program that can think and learn. The Agents function primarily as opponents in a high-stakes computer game. The movie offers no clear explanation of why the Matrix-making program went to all that trouble. Of course, for a program, running is its own reward—but an intelligent program might bring terrifying logic to its decisions.

Both *Dark City* and *Strange Days* offered intriguing motivations for villainy. *Matrix* is more like a superhero comic book in which the fate of the world comes down to a titanic fistfight between the designated representatives of good and evil. It's cruel, really, to put tantalizing ideas on the table and then ask the audience to be satisfied with a shoot-out and a martial arts duel.

Let's assume Neo wins. What happens then to the billions who have just been "unplugged" from the Matrix? Do they still have jobs? Homes? Identities? All we get is an enigmatic voice-over exhortation at the movie's end. The paradox is that the Matrix world apparently resembles in every respect the pre-Matrix world. (I am reminded of the animated kid's film *Doug's 1st Movie,* which has a VR experience in which everything is exactly like in real life, except more expensive.)

Still, I must not ignore the movie's virtues. It's great-looking, both in its design and in the kinetic energy that powers it. It uses flawlessly integrated special effects and animation to visualize regions of cyberspace. It creates fearsome creatures, including mechanical octopi. It morphs bodies with the abandon of *Terminator II.* It uses f/x to allow Neo and Trinity to run horizontally on walls, and hang in the air long enough to deliver karate kicks. It has leaps through space, thrilling sequences involving fights on rooftops, helicopter rescues, and battles over mind control.

And it has performances that find the right notes. Keanu Reeves goes for the impassive Harrison Ford approach, "acting" as little as possible. I suppose that's the right idea. Laurence Fishburne finds a balance between action hero and Zen master. Carrie-Anne Moss, as Trinity, has a sensational title sequence, before the movie recalls that she's a woman and shuttles her into support mode. Hugo Weaving, as the chief Agent, uses a flat, menacing tone that reminded me of Tommy Lee Jones in passive-aggressive overdrive. There's a well-acted scene involving Gloria Foster as the Oracle, who like all oracles is maddeningly enigmatic.

The Matrix did not bore me. It interested me so much, indeed, that I wanted to be challenged even more. I wanted it to follow its material to audacious conclusions, to arrive not simply at victory, but at revelation. I wanted an ending that was transformational, like *Dark City's,* and not one that simply throws us a sensational action sequence. I wanted, in short, a third act.

Meet the Parents ★ ★ ★
PG-13, 108 m., 2000

Robert De Niro (Jack Byrnes), Ben Stiller (Greg Focker), Teri Polo (Pam Byrnes), Blythe Danner (Dina Byrnes), Nicole DeHuff (Debbie Byrnes), Jon Abrahams (Denny Byrnes), Owen Wilson (Kevin Rawley), Tom McCarthy (Bob Banks), Phyllis George (Linda Banks), Kali Rocha (Flight Attendant). Directed by Jay Roach and produced by Nancy Tenenbaum, Jane Rosenthal, Robert De Niro, and Roach. Screenplay by Jim Herzfeld and John Hamburg, based on a story by Greg Glienna.

Ben Stiller has a good line in embarrassment and chagrin. His chiseled face looks so earnest, so willing to please, and turns incredulous as the world conspires against him. In *There's Something About Mary* and again in *Meet the Parents,* he plays a young man who desperately wants to impress the girl he loves, and plunges into a series of humiliating miscalculations. He doesn't have anything hanging from his ear in this picture, but he acts as if he thinks he might.

In *There's Something About Mary,* Stiller played a character who managed to set a beloved dog afire. *Meet the Parents* is not a clone or imitation of *Mary*—it has its own original inspiration—but it does get Stiller into a lot of trouble over a beloved pet cat, and even funnier trouble over another cat, entirely imaginary, which he claims to have milked.

Why would a man claim to have milked a cat? The screenplay, by Jim Herzfeld and John Hamburg, gets a lot of its laughs out of the way Stiller's character tells thoughtless little social lies and then, when he's caught, improvises his way into bigger, outrageous lies. The development is like a comic pyramid: The base is a casual claim that he was raised on a farm. It is revealed he was actually raised in Detroit. Well, yes, he says, he was. Then why did he claim to have experience at milking? Well, he had a cat, which "birthed" thirty kittens, including one little fellow who could never get his turn at the table, and . . . by this time Stiller is demonstrating how he used his fingers on the mother cat's itsy-bitsy little nipple, and everyone in the room is regarding him as a madman.

In *Meet the Parents,* he plays the unfortunately named Greg Focker. That's not his real name; Focker is, Greg isn't. He is in love with a Chicago schoolteacher named Pam (Teri Polo), who takes him home to meet her parents on Long Island. Her dad, Jack, is played by Robert De Niro as the nightmare of every hopeful groom. He is a reasonable man, his reason operating like a steel vise to clamp down on every contradiction and improbability in Greg's conversation, and there is no shortage of them. He is also a man with a great love for his cat, which he has toilet-trained, but which, ominously, "has no outdoor survival skills."

What are the odds that Greg will let the cat outdoors? And that the cat will turn out to be better toilet-trained than Greg? *Meet the Parents* builds brilliantly on interlocking comic situations, until Greg has involved himself in a counterfeit cat, set the house afire, and flooded the lawn (where Pam's sister is about to be married) with an overflowing septic tank.

Pam's mom, Dina (Blythe Danner), understands that her husband can be hard on a young man. "Go easy on this one, Jack," she tells De Niro. "I think Pam really likes him." But Pam has really liked other young men—a lot of them, we gather. One that we meet is her ex-fiancé Kevin (Owen Wilson), a blond multimillionaire who, for the sister's wedding, has carved an altar out of a solid block of wood. The thing with Kevin was "strictly physical," Pam assures Greg, who is far from assured by information like that.

Eventually it begins to appear, even to Greg, that he is a dangerous, lying maniac. The simplest situations conceal hidden traps. He is asked by Jack to say grace at dinner. "Greg is Jewish," Jack is told. "I'm sure Jews bless their food," Jack smiles, and Greg launches into a tortured prayer that segues, to his own horror, into lyrics from *Godspell.* (He has bad luck with lyrics; it is the wrong idea to chat with Jack about the various possible meanings of "Puff, the Magic Dragon.")

The De Niro character conceals secrets and sentimentalities. He loves his cat, he treasures the ashes of his dead mother, he is suspicious of anyone who wants to marry his daughter, and he has a wide range of double takes, frowns, lifted eyebrows, significant pauses, chilling asides, and subtle put-downs. He isn't a vulgarian, but a self-confident man who serenely enforces a set of standards that Greg violates, one by one, until finally everything has gone horribly wrong and Greg goes berserk—not in Pam's home, but at the airport, where he is pushed over the edge by a flight attendant (Kali Rocha) on autopilot.

Meet the Parents was directed by Jay Roach, who made the *Austin Powers* movies and here shows he can dial down from farce into a comedy of (bad) manners. His movie is funnier because it never tries too hard; De Niro, in particular, gets laughs by leaning back and waiting for them to come to him. And Stiller is like the target in a dunk-the-clown game, smiling while the world falls out from under him.

Memento ★ ★ ★

R, 113 m., 2001

Guy Pearce (Leonard), Carrie-Anne Moss (Natalie), Joe Pantoliano (Teddy), Mark Boone Junior (Burt), Stephen Tobolowsky (Sammy), Jorja Fox (Leonard's Wife), Harriet Harris (Mrs. Jankis). Directed by Christopher Nolan and produced by Jennifer Todd and Suzanne Todd. Screenplay by Christopher Nolan, based on the short story by Jonathan Nolan.

I have here a message from Vasudha Gandhi of Queens Village, New York, about the movie *Memento:*

"Although I loved the film, I don't understand one key plot point. If the last thing the main character remembers is his wife dying, then how does he remember that he has short-term memory loss?"

Michael Cusumano of Philadelphia writes with the same query. They may have identified a hole big enough to drive the entire plot through. Perhaps a neurologist can provide a medical answer, but I prefer to believe that Leonard, the hero of the film, has a condition similar to Tom Hanks's "brain cloud" in *Joe vs. the Volcano*—Leonard suffers from a condition brought on by a screenplay that finds it necessary, and it's unkind of us to inquire too deeply.

Leonard is played by Guy Pearce, in a performance that is curiously moving, considering that by definition it has no emotional arc. He has witnessed the violent death of his wife, and is determined to avenge it. But he has had short-term memory loss ever since the death, and has to make copious notes—he even has memos tattooed to his body in order.

If Leonard keeps forgetting what has already happened, we in the audience suffer from the opposite condition. We begin at the end, and work our way back toward the beginning, because the story is told backward. Well, not exactly; it begins with a brilliant idea, a Polaroid photograph that fades instead of developing, but every individual scene plays with time running forward, and there are some lateral moves and flashbacks that illuminate, or confuse, the issue. Essentially, Leonard is adrift in time and experience, and therefore so are we.

The idea of a narrative told backward was famously used by Harold Pinter in the 1983 film *Betrayal,* based on his play. He told a story of adultery and betrayed friendship, beginning with the sad end and then working his way back through disenchantment to complications to happiness to speculation to innocence. His purpose was the opposite of the strategy used by writer-director Christopher Nolan in *Memento.* Pinter's subject was memory and regret, and the way adulteries often begin playfully and end miserably. There was irony in the way the characters grew happier in each scene, while the audience's knowledge of what was ahead for them deepened.

Nolan's device of telling his story backward, or sort of backward, is simply that—a device. It does not reflect the way Leonard thinks. He still operates in chronological time, and does not know he is in a time-reversed movie. The film's deep backward and abysm of time is for our entertainment and has nothing to do with his condition. It may actually make the movie too clever for its own good. I've seen it twice. The first time, I thought I'd need a second viewing to understand everything. The second time, I found that greater understanding helped on the plot level, but didn't enrich the viewing experience. Once is right for this movie. Confusion is the state we are intended to be in.

That said, *Memento* is a diabolical and absorbing experience, in which Pearce doggedly plays a low-rent Fugitive who patiently makes maps, jots notes, and explains over and over that he has to talk fast, because in a few minutes he'll start forgetting the conversation. A motel clerk takes advantage of his condition to charge him for two rooms at the same time, and cheerfully admits his fraud, pointing out Leonard will forget it. "Even if you get revenge, you're not going to remember it," he's told at one point, but his reply has a certain logic: "My wife deserves revenge whether or not I remember it."

One striking element of the film is a series of flashbacks to a case Leonard investigated when he worked for an insurance company. This involves a man named Sammy, who appears to have memory loss, although he seems otherwise just like good old Sammy. His wife, a diabetic, can't be sure he isn't faking his condition, and arranges a test I will not reveal. This story has relevance to Leonard's own plight, in an indirect way.

The other major characters are Natalie (Carrie-Anne Moss) and Teddy (Joe Pantoliano). Of Natalie, he has a Polaroid inscribed: "She has also lost someone. She will help you out of pity." Their relationship keeps starting over from the beginning. As for Teddy, his identity and role shifts mysteriously.

The purpose of the movie is not for us to solve the murder of the wife. ("I can't remember to forget you," he says of her.) If we leave the theater not sure exactly what happened, that's fair enough. The movie is more like a poignant exercise in which Leonard's residual code of honor pushes him through a fog of amnesia toward what he feels is his moral duty. The movie doesn't supply the usual payoff of a thriller (how can it?), but it's uncanny in evoking a state of mind. Maybe telling it backward is Nolan's way of forcing us to identify with the hero. Hey, we all just got here. ☞

Me, Myself & Irene ★ ½
R, 116 m., 2000

Jim Carrey (Charlie/Hank), Renee Zellweger (Irene), Robert Forster (Colonel Partington), Chris Cooper (Lieutenant Gerke), Richard Jenkins (Agent Boshane), Daniel Green (Dickie Thurman), Anthony Anderson (Jamaal), Mongo

Brownlee (Lee Harvey). Directed by Peter Farrelly and Bobby Farrelly and produced by the Farrellys and Bradley Thomas. Screenplay by the Farrellys and Mike Cerrone.

Me, Myself & Irene is a labored and sour comedy that rouses itself to create real humor, and then settles back glumly into an impenetrable plot and characters who keep repeating the same schtick, hoping maybe this time it will work. It stars Jim Carrey in a role that mires him in versions of the same gags, over and over. Renee Zellweger costars as a woman who stays at his side for no apparent reason except that the script requires her to.

The movie is by the Farrelly brothers, Peter and Bobby, whose *There's Something About Mary* still causes me to smile whenever I think about it, and whose *Kingpin* is a buried treasure. They worked with Carrey in *Dumb and Dumber,* which has some very big laughs in it, but this time their formula of scatology, sexuality, political incorrectness, and cheerful obscenity seems written by the numbers. The movie is as offensive as most of their work, which would be fine if it redeemed itself with humor. It doesn't. There is, for example, an extended passage making fun of an albino that is not funny at all, ever, in any part, but painfully drones on and on until the filmmakers cop out and make him the pal of the heroes.

Carrey plays a Rhode Island state trooper who puts up with shocking insults to his manhood and uniform and manages somehow to be a sunny Dr. Jeckyl, until he finally snaps and allows his Mr. Hyde to roam free. As the nice guy (named Charlie), he keeps smiling after his wife presents him with three black babies, fathered by a dwarf limo driver and Mensa member. He even keeps smiling when his neighbor allows his dog to defecate on his lawn, while the neighbor's wife steals his newspaper, and when the guys in the barbershop laugh at his attempts to enforce the law.

Years pass in this fashion. His wife runs off with the little genius. His sons stay with him, growing into enormous lads who are brilliant at school but use the MF-word as if it were punctuation (they learned it by watching Richard Pryor and Chris Rock videos). The movie must think all African-Americans are required by statute or genetics to repeat the word cease-lessly (it might have been funnier to have all three boys talk like Sam Donaldson).

After the evil side of his personality ("Hank") breaks free, Carrey starts kicking butt and taking no prisoners. Through twists unnecessary to describe, he hooks up with the perky, pretty Irene (Renee Zellweger), and they become fugitives from the law, pursued by the evil Lt. Gerke (Chris Cooper) for reasons that have something to do with environmental scandals, country clubs, bribery, and cover-ups; the plot is so murky we abandon curiosity and simply accept that Carrey and Zellweger are on the run, and the bad guys are chasing them.

The movie has defecation jokes, urination jokes, dildo jokes, flasher jokes, and a chicken that must be thoroughly annoyed by the dilemma it finds itself in. Not many of the jokes are very funny, and some seem plain desperate. I did laugh a lot during a sequence when Carrey tries to put a wounded cow out of its misery, but most of the time I sat quietly reflecting that the Farrelly brand of humor is a high-wire act; it involves great risks and is a triumph if they get to the other side, but ugly when they fail.

Carrey has a plastic face and body, and does remarkable things with his expressions. As Charlie he's all toothy grins and friendliness. As Hank, his face twists into an evil scowl, and his voice is electronically lowered into a more menacing register. Problem is, although it's sort of funny to see Charlie reacting to the insulting ways people treat him, it is rarely funny to see him transform himself into Hank, who then takes revenge. Hank is not really a comic character, and it's a miscalculation to allow him to dominate most of the movie.

Irene, the Zellweger character, has not been invented fresh with a specific comic purpose, but is simply a recycled version of the character she usually plays. Her job is to be loyal and sensible, lay down the law, pout, smile, and be shocked. It is a thankless task; she's like the on-screen representative of the audience.

The Farrellys are gifted and have made me laugh as loudly as anyone since the golden age of Mel Brooks. They have scored before and will no doubt score again. This time they go for broke, and get there.

Note: The film is dedicated to the late Gene

Siskel, whose enthusiasm for Kingpin *came at a crucial time for the Farrellys, encouraging them to push ahead with* There's Something About Mary.

Me Myself I ★ ★ ★
R, 104 m., 2000

Rachel Griffiths (Pamela), David Roberts (Robert), Sandy Winton (Ben), Yael Stone (Stacey), Shaun Loseby (Douglas), Trent Sullivan (Rupert), Rebecca Frith (Terri), Felix Williamson (Geoff). Directed by Pip Karmel and produced by Fabien Liron. Screenplay by Karmel.

Consider now Rachel Griffiths. I first noticed her as the best friend with the infectious grin in *Muriel's Wedding,* the quirky Australian comedy. She was the lusty pig farmer's daughter who married the earnest student in *Jude.* In *Hilary and Jackie,* she played the sister of the doomed musician, and won an Oscar nomination. She was wonderful in two films that didn't find wide distribution: *My Son, the Fanatic,* where she played a hooker who forms a sincere friendship with a middle-aged Pakistani taxi driver in the British Midlands, and *Among Giants,* where she was a backpacking rock climber who signs up for the summer with a crew of British power pylon painters. That was the movie where, on a bet, she traversed all four walls of a pub with her toes on the wainscoting, finding fingerholds where she could.

It is quite possible that Griffiths made all of these movies without coming to your attention, since none of them were big box-office winners, and a depressing number of moviegoers march off like sheep to the weekend's top-grossing hot-air balloon. She's been in one hit, *My Best Friend's Wedding,* but not so's you'd notice. I think she is one of the most intensely interesting actresses at work today, and in *Me Myself I* she does something that is almost impossible: She communicates her feelings to us through reaction shots while keeping them a secret from the other characters. That makes us conspirators.

Griffiths is not a surface beauty but a sexy tomboy with classically formed features, whose appeal shines out through the intelligence in her eyes and her wry mouth. You cannot imagine her as a passive object of affection. If Hollywood romances were about who women were rather than how they looked, she'd be one of the most desirable women in the movies. To the discerning, she is anyway.

Me Myself I is a fantasy as contrived and satisfactory as a soap opera. Griffiths plays Pamela, a professional magazine writer in her thirties who smokes too much and keeps up her spirits with self-help mantras ("I deserve the best and I accept the best"). Her idea of a date is to open a bottle of wine and look at photos of guys she dated fifteen years ago. "Why did I let you go?" she asks the photo of Robert (David Roberts). She's attracted to a crisis counselor named Ben (Sandy Winton), but finds out he is happily married, with children.

Should she have married Robert all those years ago? An unexplained supernatural transfer takes place, and she gets a chance to find out. She's hit by a car, and the other driver is—herself. After a switch, she finds herself living in an alternate universe in which she did marry Robert, and they have three children. This, of course, is all perfectly consistent with the latest theories in movie metaphysics; only the mechanism of the transfer remains cloudy.

Here is the key to the transformation scenes: Pamela knows she is a replacement for the "real" Pamela in this parallel world, and so do we, but everyone else fails to notice the substitution (except for Rupert, the youngest, who asks her bluntly, "When's Mommy gonna be home?"). There are scenes involving cooking dinner, managing the house, and copiloting for Rupert during his toilet duties. And a sex life with Robert that he finds surprising and delightful, since he and his original Pamela had cooled off considerably.

In this parallel universe, Ben is single, not married, and she takes the chance to have an affair with him, despite the complication that now she is married, not single. When she thinks Robert has been unfaithful, she is outraged, as much on behalf of the other Pamela as for herself, although in the new geometries of the universe-switch they are equally guilty, or innocent. This new Robert also has to be trained to accept an independent woman. When she announces that she needs a new computer and he says, "We'll see," she jolts him with: "I'm not asking your permission."

There are sweet scenes in the film, and touching ones. My favorite moments come when Pamela does subtle double takes when she realizes how her life is different now, and why. The plot is not remarkably intelligent, but Pamela (or Griffiths) is, and her reaction shots, her conspiratorial sharing of her thoughts with us, is where the movie has its life.

Rachel Griffiths's career is humming right along, if the criteria is that she stars in good roles in interesting movies, and is able to use her gifts and her intriguing personality. It could stand some improvement if the criteria is that she appears in big hits and makes $20 million a picture. The odds are she is too unique to ever make that much money; she isn't generic enough. And remember that the weekend box-office derby is usually won by the movie appealing to teenage boys. She doesn't play the kinds of women who are visible to them yet. All of this is beside the point for evolved moviegoers such as ourselves, who know a star when we see one.

Men of Honor ★ ★ ★
R, 128 m., 2000

Cuba Gooding Jr. (Carl Brashear), Robert De Niro (Billy Sunday), Charlize Theron (Gwen), Aunjanue Ellis (Jo), Hal Holbrook (Mister Pappy), David Keith (Captain Hartigan), Michael Rapaport (Snowhill), Powers Boothe (Captain Pullman). Directed by George Tillman Jr. and produced by Robert Teitel. Screenplay by Scott Marshall Smith.

Carl Brashear was quite a guy. A black sharecropper's son without a high school education, he signed up for the navy right after World War II. Harry Truman had integrated the services, but the navy was slow to change, and African-Americans were guided toward two job choices: They could become a cook or an officer's valet. Brashear (Cuba Gooding Jr.) wanted to be a diver. *Men of Honor* tells the story of how he became one despite everything, and then how he insisted on returning to active duty after losing a lower leg in an onboard accident.

The movie is an old-fashioned biopic, and I mean that as a compliment. It isn't pumped up with phony action scenes, but follows the curve of Brashear's life as it intersects with another man, Master Chief Billy Sunday (Robert De Niro), a redneck who at first hates Carl and then gradually changes his mind.

The most gripping scene in the movie is the reverse of the heroism in a lot of military movies. It isn't about thrills and explosions, but about tenacity, and most of it takes place within our own imaginations. To graduate from diving school, divers take a test where they have to assemble the pieces of a pump while working more or less in the dark, underwater. Brashear's test is rigged to make it almost impossible to pass. The water is so cold that long submersion could be fatal. Hour after hour, Brashear stays down there on the bottom.

De Niro's character is opposed to the idea of a black navy diver, but his master chief is first and foremost a diver, and if you love doing something enough, you come to respect others who do it well. The chief also comes from a dirt-farm background, and has another problem, alcoholism, which tests his marriage to the patient Gwen (Charlize Theron). There is also a good woman in Brashear's life: Jo (Aunjanue Ellis), the Harlem librarian who tutors him in reading when he has trouble with written exams.

The ugliest opponent of Brashear's dream is "Mister Pappy" (Hal Holbrook), the commanding officer of the group, who seems like a cross between Ahab and Queeg. "There may come a day when a colored diver graduates from this school," he thunders, "but it won't be while I'm here." I wonder if Mister Pappy needs to be such a nut job; surveying his realm from living quarters in a water tower, he is less a commanding officer than a refugee from the guys with the butterfly nets.

Cuba Gooding is the kind of actor who bubbles even when he's idling. That kind of energy wouldn't be appropriate here, and he dials down and delivers a strong, convincing performance. The secret of Carl Brashear's success is not complicated: He won't give up, he won't go away, and eventually his very presence shames navy men who cannot deny his ability.

The racism that permeated American life in the 1940s is shown in scenes like the one where all of the other navy trainees refuse to share a bunkhouse with Brashear—all except for one, Snowhill (Michael Rapaport), who stays. Snowhill's reason is not some noble liberal sentiment, but more simple and personal, and my guess is that this line, of all the dialogue in the movie, is the most likely to have been taken straight from real life. "I'm from Wisconsin," he explains.

This is the second feature by George Tillman Jr., whose *Soul Food* was a success in 1997. Here he depends on a strong story and solid performances and avoids unnecessary flash; the movie sells itself. But the screenplay betrays some evidence of knee-jerk front-office requirements. How else to explain the character of Gwen, the master chief's wife? She is simply unnecessary to the picture, and although Theron's performance is professional, it's beside the point.

Such details aren't important compared to the central strength of the film, which shows one American life, lived well and proudly. We glorify overpaid sports heroes and put them on postage stamps, but what about a man like Brashear, who wanted to serve his country and wouldn't take no for an answer?

Note: The R rating for this film, given because of salty talk by sailors, is inappropriate. This is an inspirational film for teenagers.

Message in a Bottle ★ ★
PG-13, 126 m., 1999

Kevin Costner (Garret Blake), Robin Wright Penn (Theresa Osborne), John Savage (Johnny Land), Illeana Douglas (Lina Paul), Robbie Coltrane (Charlie Toschi), Jesse James (Jason Osborne), Paul Newman (Dodge Blake). Directed by Luis Mandoki and produced by Denise Di Novi, Jim Wilson, and Kevin Costner. Screenplay by Gerald DiPego, based on the novel *The Notebook* by Nicholas Sparks.

Message in a Bottle is a tearjerker that strolls from crisis to crisis. It's curiously muted, as if it fears that passion would tear its delicate fabric; even the fights are more in sorrow than in anger, and when there's a fistfight, it doesn't feel like a real fistfight—it feels more like someone thought the movie needed a fistfight 'round about then.

The film is about a man and a woman who believe in great true love. The man believes it's behind him; the woman hopes it's ahead of her. One of their ideals in life is "to be somebody's true north." Right away we know they're in trouble. You don't just find true love. You team up with somebody, and build it from the ground up. But *Message in a Bottle* believes in the kind of love where the romantic music comes first, trembling and sweeping under every scene, and the dialogue is treated like the lyrics.

Yet it is about two likable characters—three, really, since Paul Newman not only steals every scene he's in, but puts it in the bank and draws interest on it. Robin Wright Penn plays Theresa, a researcher for the *Chicago Tribune*, who finds a letter in a bottle. It is a heartbreaking love note to "Catherine," by a man who wants to make amends to his true north.

Theresa, a divorced mother of one, is deeply touched by the message, and shares it with a columnist named Charlie (Robbie Coltrane), who of course lifts it for a column. Theresa feels betrayed. (If she thinks she can show a letter like that to a guy with a deadline and not read about it in tomorrow's paper, no wonder she's still a researcher.) The column leads to the discovery of two other letters on the same stationery. Charlie has the bottle, the cork, the stationery, and the handwriting analyzed, and figures the messages came from the Carolinas. A few calls to gift shops, and they know who bought the stationery.

It's Garret Blake (Kevin Costner). Theresa is sent out on a mission to do research about him. She meets his father (Newman), and then the man himself, a shipwright who handcrafts beautiful vessels. He takes her for a test sail. The wind is bracing and the chemistry is right. "You eat meat?" he asks her. "Red meat? I make a perfect steak. It's the best thing I do." With this kind of buildup, Linda McCartney would have tucked into a T-bone.

Soon it's time for Theresa to return home (where after she writes one column, the paper promotes her and gives her an office with a window view; at that rate, in six weeks she'll be using Colonel McCormick's ancestral commode). Of course she wants him to come and see her—to see how she lives. "Will you come and visit me?" she asks. His reply does not represent the proudest moment of the screenwriter: "You mean, inland?"

Sooner or later he's going to find out that she found his letter in a bottle and is not simply a beautiful woman who wandered onto his boat. That his secrets are known in those few places where the *Tribune* is still read. Yes, but it takes a long time, and when his discovery finally comes, the film handles it with a certain tact. It's not just an explosion about betrayal, but more complicated—partly because of the nature of the third letter.

As morose and contrived as the movie is, it has a certain winsome charm because of the personal warmth of the actors. This is Robin Wright Penn's breakthrough to a different kind of acting, and she has a personal triumph; she's been identified with desperate, hard-as-nails characters, but no more. Costner finds the right note of inarticulate pain; he loves, but doesn't feel he has the right to. Paul Newman handles his role, as Costner's ex-drunk father, with the relaxed confidence of Michael Jordan shooting free throws in your driveway. It is good to see all three of them on the screen, in whatever combination, and the movie is right to play down the sex scenes and underline the cuddling and the whispers.

But where, oh where, did they get the movie's ending? Is it in the original novel by Nicholas Sparks? Don't know. Haven't read it. The climactic events are shameless, contrived, and wildly out of tune with the rest of the story. To saddle Costner, Penn, and Newman with such goofy melodrama is like hiring Fred Astaire and strapping a tractor on his back.

The Messenger: The Story of Joan of Arc ★ ★
R, 141 m., 1999

Milla Jovovich (Joan), John Malkovich (Charles VII), Faye Dunaway (Yolande D'Aragon), Dustin Hoffman (Joan's Conscience), Pascal Greggory (Alencon), Vincent Cassel (Gilles de Rais), Tcheky Kary (Dunois), Richard Ridings (La Hire), Desmond Harrington (Aulon). Directed by Luc Besson and produced by Patrice Ledoux. Screenplay by Besson and Andrew Birkin.

Luc Besson's *The Messenger: The Story of Joan of Arc* labors under the misapprehension that Joan's life is a war story, and takes place largely on battlefields. In fact, it takes place almost entirely within the consciences of everyone involved. The movie does at least concede that a good part of Joan's legend involves her trial for heresy and her burning at the stake, and these scenes may prove educational for the test audience members who wrote on their sneak-preview cards, "Why does she have to die at the end?"

Two of the best films ever made are about Joan of Arc: *The Passion of Joan of Arc*, by Carl Dreyer (1928), and *The Trial of Joan of Arc*, by Robert Bresson (1962). Also one of the worst, *Saint Joan* (1957), by Otto Preminger, who had in common with Luc Besson the theory that Joan must look like a babe. Dreyer's Joan was Falconetti, a French actress whose haunted face mirrored one of the greatest performances in cinema—the only one she ever gave. Preminger's was Jean Seberg, found in Iowa after an international talent search. (The search for her talent continued after the film was completed, and it was finally found in Godard's *Breathless* two years later.)

Besson has cast Milla Jovovich as his Joan. She was his wife at the time they started shooting. They have since split, although he says they would still be together if they could only have made movies 365 days a year, a statement that may provide more insight than he intended. Jovovich, who also starred in Besson's *The Fifth Element*, is a healthy, cheerful, open-faced twenty-four-year-old actress who seems much too robust and uncomplicated to play Joan.

The movie is a mess: a gassy costume epic with nobody at the center. So deficient is Besson at suggesting the conscience that rules Joan's actions that the movie even uses another character, the Grand Inquisitor, as a surrogate conscience, and brings in Dustin Hoffman to play it; he is a creation of Joan's imagination. That Hoffman's performance is the best in the film should have been a nudge to the filmmaker that he could cut back on the extras and the battle scenes and make the movie about—well, about Joan.

Joan of Arc was a naive young French peasant woman, illiterate, who was told by voices that she must go to the aid of her king. France at that time was ill-supplied with kings; the best it could offer was the reluctant Dauphin (John Malkovich), later Charles VII. She informed him her destiny was to lead French troops on the battlefield against the English, who were godless (or foreign, which to the French was a negligible distinction). Legend has it she ended the siege of Orleans.

Legend may be wrong. A book published in France by the historian Roger Caratini claims "precious little of what we French have been taught in school about Joan of Arc is true." He finds scant evidence that Joan did much more than go along for the ride, and adds cruelly that she could not have raised the siege of Orleans because the city was never besieged in the first place. Her trial for heresy was not at the hands of the British but under the French Inquisition at the University of Paris, and her greatest crime may have been dressing like a boy and offending the ecclesiastical gender police. Her legend was "more or less invented" in the nineteenth century, we learn, as a tonic for emerging French nationalism, which had a "desperate need for a patriotic mascot."

Of course we do not expect *The Messenger* to be a revisionist downgrading of the French national heroine, who was burned by a schismatic branch of the church and canonized by Rome five centuries later without having, perhaps, done much to deserve either. We expect a patriotic epic, in which the heroic young woman saves her country but is destroyed by an effete ruler and a lot of grim old clerics. Even if the film is not about a battle of opposing moralities, even if it is not about conscience (as the Dreyer and Bresson films are), it can at least be as much fun as, say, *Braveheart*, wouldn't you say?

No such luck. Besson's film is a thin, uninvolving historical romp in which the only juicy parts are played by supporting characters, such as the Dauphin, made by John Malkovich into a man whose interest in the crown essentially ends with whether it fits. Faye Dunaway has fun as his stepmother, Yolande D'Aragon, who schemes against Joan as any mother would when her son falls under the sway of a girl from the wrong side of the class divide. And Dustin Hoffman is really very good as Joan's

surrogate conscience, the Inquisitor, even if his role seems inspired by the desperate need to somehow shoehorn philosophy into the film. I was reminded of the Roger Corman horror picture where holes in the plot were plugged by hiring two bit players and having one ask the other, "Now explain what all this means."

Metroland ★ ★ ★
NO MPAA RATING, 101 m., 1999

Christian Bale (Chris), Emily Watson (Marion), Lee Ross (Toni), Elsa Zylberstein (Annick), Rufus (Henri), Jonathan Aris (Dave), Ifan Meredith (Mickey), Amanda Ryan (Joanna). Directed by Philip Saville and produced by Andrew Bendel. Screenplay by Adrian Hodges, based on the novel by Julian Barnes.

There are a lot of movies about escaping from the middle class, but *Metroland* is one of the few about escaping into it. In 1968, Chris is a footloose British photographer in Paris, who has an affair with a French woman and drifts through streets alive with drugs and revolution. In 1977, Chris has become a married man with a child, living in a London suburb at the end of the Metropolitan line of the Underground. Is he happier now?

Not according to his friend Toni, who joined Chris in sixties hedonism and never looked back. Toni (Lee Ross) has just returned from America, after dropping out in Africa and Asia. He's returned to the United Kingdom for one reason only: to convince Chris (Christian Bale) to leave his family behind and join him on the road. *Metroland,* based on a 1980 novel by Julian Barnes, who became famous after *Flaubert's Parrot,* watches Chris as he is enticed by temptation and memory.

The memories are often about the two women he met in Paris that year—the one he married and the one he didn't. Annick (Elsa Zylberstein) is one of those young Parisians who live on air and use the cafés as living rooms. They meet, they flirt, they become a couple. The sound track of their romance is sixties rock, mixed with Django Reinhardt, and with Annick he learns about sex ("Is it the first time?" she asks, with reason). Then into his world drifts a visiting English girl, Marion (Emily Watson), who is sensible, cheerful, supportive, reassuring, and wholesome. She sizes him up and informs him that he will get married, probably to her, because "you're not original enough not to."

He does, and life in Metroland continues happily until Toni calls at 6 A.M. one morning. Toni tempts Chris with tastes of the life he left behind, and at a party they attend, an available girl makes him an offer so frank and inviting he very nearly cannot refuse. Yet the movie is not about whether Chris will remain faithful to Marion; it's about whether he chose the right life in the first place.

Philip Saville, who directs from a screenplay by Adrian Hodges, starts with a straightforward story of life choices (the plot could as easily be from Joanna Trollope as Julian Barnes), and slips in teasing asides, as in a scene where Toni almost has Chris and Marion believing he has "always been in love with Chris." Or when Chris daydreams about Marion telling him, "of course, I expect you to have affairs." What Saville doesn't do, mercifully, is depend on sentiment: Chris is not asked to make his decision based on loyalty to wife and daughter, but on the actual issue of his choice to live in the London outskirts and raise a family. There is a cold-blooded sense in which he could decide, objectively, dispassionately, that he took the wrong turn—that it is his right to join Toni in a life of wandering, sex, and mind-altering.

What's curious, given how everything depends on Chris, is the way the movie is really centered on the two women. Annick almost deliberately plays the role of a cliché—the brainy, liberated French woman showing the Englishman the sensual ropes. Elsa Zylberstein finds the right note: The woman proud to have "a beautiful British boyfriend," and hurt when she's dumped, but not blinded by dreams of eternal love. And then there's Marion, played by Emily Watson in a radical departure from her tormented characters in *Breaking the Waves* and *Hilary and Jackie*. Here she is cheerfully normal—an ideal wife, if that's what Chris is looking for. "No wonder you're bored," says Toni. But why did Toni come back, if he wasn't bored too?

The Mexican ★ ★ ★
R, 123 m., 2001

Brad Pitt (Jerry Welbach), Julia Roberts (Samantha Barzel), James Gandolfini (Leroy), Bob Balaban (Nayman), J. K. Simmons (Ted), David Krumholtz (Beck), Richard Coca (Car Thief), Michael Cerveris (Frank), Gene Hackman (Margolese). Directed by Gore Verbinski and produced by Lawrence Bender and John Baldecchi. Screenplay by J. H. Wyman.

The Mexican stars Brad Pitt and Julia Roberts, and involves a quirky, offbeat relationship—but it's not between Brad and Julia, it's between Julia and James Gandolfini. I like it that way. Considering how badly Jerry and Samantha, the Brad and Julia characters, get along when they're together, a whole movie involving them would be a long, shrill slog. Gandolfini comes in from left field and provides a character with dimension and surprises, bringing out the best in Roberts. Their dialogue scenes are the best reason to see the movie.

The setup: The Mexican of the title is a priceless handgun that a Mafioso named Margolese (Gene Hackman) desires above all else. Margolese is in prison for complicated reasons, and Jerry, who was sort of responsible, has been trying to work off his debt (and stay alive) by running errands for Margolese's lieutenant, Nayman (Bob Balaban). But Jerry is unreliable because he's under the thumb of the demanding Samantha. His excuse for blowing an important assignment: "When you told me to pick up the thing at the thing, well, Samantha, she wanted the car to pick up some things."

Jerry gets one more chance: Go to Mexico, meet a man in a bar, pick up the handgun, and bring it back to America. Samantha blows her top: Jerry promised to take her to Vegas. Jerry explains that if he does not do the errand, he will be killed. Samantha is unmoved and throws his clothes out the window. Jerry leaves for Mexico. Samantha says she will never speak to him again. She leaves for Vegas, and is kidnapped by Leroy, the Gandolfini character.

That means Jerry and Samantha spend most of the movie apart, and that has drawn complaints from critics who would have preferred these two megastars to share lots of screen time. But Roberts, curiously, hardly ever makes love stories involving people her age. Maybe she has so much wattage all by herself that pairing her with an equivalent dude would blow the fuses. Most of her movies involve older men (Richard Gere in *Pretty Woman*), or unavailable men (Dr. Jekyll and Mr. Hyde in *Mary Reilly*), or unacceptable men *(Runaway Bride)*, or make her the heroine of stories with less significant men *(Erin Brockovich, Notting Hill)*. She hardly ever goes knee-to-knee with a guy she's in love with.

Here Gandolfini (from *The Sopranos*) comes in as Leroy, a big bruiser who kidnaps her for reasons that start out simple and grow increasingly complicated as the plot unfolds. They're both talkers, and soon they're bathing each other in confessions and insights. She talks a lot about Jerry, who is guilty of "blame-shifting," etc., and he nods in sympathy and offers advice at least as sound as she could find in a women's magazine. Then, while they're sitting in a diner, he exchanges a look with a guy sitting at the counter, and she says, "You had a moment there. What was that about?" And then their psychobabble moves into sublime territory.

These scenes make the movie special. The screenplay, by J. H. Wyman, could have easily been one of those dreary road stories where the guy and the girl head south together on a rendezvous with steamy love scenes and lots of bloody chases. Instead, this movie is *about* something. Not something terrifically profound, to be sure, but at least it prefers style and wit to tired, old ideas.

Wyman and the director, Gore Verbinski, intercut the story with various versions of the legend of the Mexican. The movie goes to sepiatone as we learn why the handgun is so valued and legendary. None of these legends agree, which is part of the fun, and meanwhile the real Mexican in the movie runs rings about Jerry, a character so brain-swoggled by Samantha that he can think of little else.

There are lots of things I like in *The Mexican*. Jerry's idiotic attempts to change English into Spanish by adding an "o" to the end of every word. And the way a supporting character keeps explaining, "I'm just trying to do my portion." And the way Samantha zeroes in on Leroy and sees right through his defenses. And

the way the movie is amused by its plot, and keeps a wry distance from it, instead of breathlessly chasing it around the screen.

Pitt and Roberts are good, too—maybe better like this than if they were together. I don't see what purpose it serves to complain they don't have every scene together. Usually when $20 million stars are put into movies, we have to look at them every second so the producers can be sure they're getting their money's worth. *The Mexican* is more like a 1940s Warner Bros. picture where the stars get a breather while the supporting actors entertain us. If it had been a Pitt/Roberts two-hander, there wouldn't have been room for Gandolfini's wonderful character, and that would have been a shame.

Me You Them ★ ★ ★
PG-13, 107 m., 2001

Regina Case (Darlene), Lima Duarte (Osias), Stenio Garcia (Zezinho), Luiz Carlos Vasconcelos (Ciro), Nilda Spencer (Raquel). Directed by Andrucha Waddington and produced by Flavio R. Tambellini, Leonardo M. de Barros, Pedro B. de Hollanda, and Waddington. Screenplay by Elena Soarez.

Me You Them tells the story of a peasant woman who creates a happy home with three men— one a provider, one genial, one lustful—while producing children who hardly resemble their reputed father. The film has inspired the usual analysis in feminist terms, with some critics finding the woman strong and others finding her victimized. I don't think ideology has as much to do with it as poverty. In a poor and dusty backwater of Brazil, this woman and all three men find a pragmatic solution to their problems.

The movie could have been a dumb sex comedy, but cares too much for its characters, and is too intrigued by how this unlikely household came into being. It stars Regina Case, "the Oprah of Brazil," as Darlene, a strong country girl who isn't beautiful, but has an earth-mother energy that men are drawn helplessly toward. She has big teeth, she wipes her hands on her dress, she can work in the fields all day, and if she takes you to her bed, you'll have your work cut out for you.

The film opens with Darlene leaving her provincial town. Three years later she's back from the city, with a baby but no husband. She wants her grandmother to bless the child. But her grandmother is dead, and now she is bereft until Osias (Lima Duarte) offers her a deal: Marry him, and she can move into his house. "Tomorrow I'll give you an answer," she says, and her answer is yes.

Osias is not a prize. He raises goats. As a married man, he assigns Darlene to care for the goats while he swings in his hammock, listening to his portable radio. Soon another child arrives, curiously a good deal darker in hue than Osias. A local colonel may know something about this. And eventually another man drifts into Darlene's life. This is Zezinho (Stenio Garcia), Osias's cousin, who is easygoing, gets along with everybody, helps Darlene with the goats, and seems to sort of move in. Osias rationalizes this as providing a home for his cousin rather than thinking about the sexual implications, even though in due time another baby arrives, this one with blue eyes that Osias didn't supply.

Life continues peacefully, Osias listening to his radio and content to play the husband and father rather than to perform such duties in the flesh. Then down by the river Darlene encounters a sexy young man named Ciro (Luiz Carlos Vasconcelos), and feels passionate lust for the first time. When Ciro turns up at the compound, he doesn't like the arrangements, and wants Darlene to leave with him. Osias is possessive and angry, and it's up to Zezinho to explain the facts of life to him: Either they build another room for Ciro, or Darlene will leave, and then they will be lonely and sad.

Me You Them is "based on a true story," we are told, although movies should follow those words with the disclaimer, "as fictionalized according to our needs." It takes place in a remote Brazilian state of stark landscapes and scarce water, where it is usually autumn and the trees stand sad without their leaves. The director, Andrucha Waddington, has worked with cinematographer Breno Silveira to make this a place of dusty beauty, the reds, browns, and ochres fading into deep shadows. The key to the story is that these people so clearly seem to live here, to depend on this land, to have no place else to go. In a society with more movement and choice, the *Me You Them* household would lack what it has here: necessity.

It has been observed that Darlene essentially needs three men to give her one complete husband. One provides shelter, one provides companionship, one provides sex. This doesn't mean she exploits them; the movie also demonstrates that each man is given the opportunity to provide what is in his nature. That is why the household works. None of these men really wants the role of the other two. Even the jealousy of Osias is based more on pride of possession than pride of paternity; if the children are technically considered his, he is content not to have to rouse himself from his hammock to actually father them.

Me You Them, written by Elena Soarez, works because the story is sympathetic to the feelings of the characters, observes them as individuals, is not concerned with the sensational aspects of their household but in the gradual way practical matters work themselves out. In the end this is not a story about sex but about economics. The characters have probably never heard of Marx, but they find his formula useful: From each, according to his abilities; to each, according to his needs.

Michael Jordan at the Max ★ ★
NO MPAA RATING, 45 m., 2000

A documentary directed by Jim Stern and John Kempf and produced by John Kempf, Steve Kempf, and Stern.

It is awesome to see Michael Jordan on the five-story IMAX screen, and to hear the roar of the crowd in surround stereo. Any Jordan fan will enjoy *Michael Jordan at the Max* on that level. Unfortunately, that's the only level there is. As a documentary, the film plays like one of those packages NBC cobbles together before a semifinals round: game footage, talking heads, and a narrator who intones the usual mantras about His Airness.

We might as well get used to the idea that there will never be a real documentary about Michael Jordan—one made with the full tools of the filmmaker's art, with its own point of view and insights beneath the surface. *Michael Jordan at the Max*, like almost everything that has been filmed or written about Jordan, is essentially just a promotional film for Jordan as a product. It plays like a commercial for itself.

Jordan is a private man—so private, that although he talks about his dead father in this film, there is no mention of his mother, his wife, or his children. His mother is seen and heard once; his wife is (I think) glimpsed briefly. I didn't expect an intimate display of private matters, but in this film Jordan is a man who lives on the basketball court and evaporates otherwise, except when starring in commercials. The only time we see him not wearing a basketball uniform is when he's wearing a suit while walking into the dressing room.

Michael Jordan at the Max takes as its framework that remarkable final championship season, and there are moments from games we remember so well, against Indiana, Seattle, and Utah. But they aren't analytical or even very informative—just colorful shots of Michael scoring again and again (he misses two shots in the entire film). Sometimes you have to know the story to realize what you're seeing, as when we overhear Steve Kerr, during a time out, tell Michael that if he gets the ball he will not miss the shot—and then sinking his famous game-winning two-pointer. The movie shows this, but doesn't underline it or explain it.

Jordan's career is commented on in interviews with Bob Greene, Phil Jackson, Bob Costas, Johnny "Red" Kerr, and others. The professional sportswriters who covered the games are not consulted. Not a word by the others seems spontaneous; the photography is flawless, like a studio portrait, and so are their comments, which sound (even if they aren't) scripted and rehearsed. I don't think we're seeing take one. Nobody ever fumbles, or pauses, or searches for a thought. They're all so sure what they want to say—and so is Jordan, interviewed in the United Center, his words so familiar they are like a politician's basic stump speech, perfected after many deliveries.

Season after season, Gene Siskel explained the Bulls to me (and anyone else who would listen). He was smarter on basketball than anyone else I've ever encountered. He noticed small things and drew lessons from them (why Dennis Rodman missed the first free throw, why Toni Kukoc was more willing to take a bad shot than a good one). He watched the games

not only as a fan, but as an analyst. He was to fans as Jackson is to coaches.

That taste of real insight left me feeling empty after *Michael Jordan at the Max,* with its platitudes and the same familiar sentences of praise we've heard so many times before, about how hard Jordan practiced, and how fierce was his desire to win, and what a leader he was. Yes, yes, yes, but there was *strategy* at work too. Jordan outplayed his opponents on some nights. He outthought them on every night. By treating him like a god the movie diminishes the achievement of the man.

This movie has no curiosity about the way Jordan read the game and its players. It has the spirit of a promotional film. It's bright and colorful, and it makes it fun for us to revisit those cherished Bulls triumphs, but there is no bite. It's the official, authorized version. On the giant IMAX screen it has an undeniable impact, and as a Bulls fan I enjoyed it. But as a film critic I was disappointed: Shrink this to a videocassette, pop it into your VCR machine, and you might as well be looking at an NBA highlight reel.

Mickey Blue Eyes ★ ★
PG-13, 103 m., 1999

Hugh Grant (Michael Felgate), James Caan (Frank Vitale), Jeanne Tripplehorn (Gina Vitale), Burt Young (Vito Graziosi), James Fox (Philip Cromwell), Joe Viterelli (Vinnie), Scott Thompson (Agent Lewis), Paul Lazar (Ritchie Vitale). Directed by Kelly Makin and produced by Elizabeth Hurley and Charles Mulvehill. Screenplay by Adam Scheinman and Robert Kuhn.

Mickey Blue Eyes has most of the ingredients in place for another one of those married-to-the-mob comedies, but the central character has to hold it together, and Hugh Grant is wrong for the role. More than some actors, perhaps, he depends on correct casting for his appeal—and here, as an art auctioneer who gets into danger after falling in love with a mobster's daughter, he strikes one wrong note and then another.

The setup is ingenious. He's Michael Felgate, an art expert, proper, reserved, with a mid-

Atlantic accent, and he falls in love with a dazzling young woman named Gina Vitale, who loves him too—but explains they can never marry. Why not? She's reluctant to tell him, but she fears for his life if he gets too close to her dad's mob connections.

Michael blunders ahead anyway. He meets her dad (James Caan), who runs a restaurant where the customers all seem supplied by Central Casting, Gangster Division. The inimitable Joe Viterelli, who was so funny as the bodyguard in *Analyze This,* is even on hand. Michael's slow to catch on: "Your dad is some kind of mob caterer?" And he asks the wrong questions for the right reasons ("Are you mostly family?"). But before she realizes what's happening, her dad has taken a liking to Michael and the wedding is on.

Complications. The big boss (nicely played by Burt Young) doesn't know the real story. There are misunderstandings. Michael has to pose as a mobster to save his life. He gets lessons in pronunciation to learn to talk like a gangster, and these scenes are so badly handled by Grant that the movie derails and never recovers. Either he can't do a plausible mob accent, or he thought it wasn't called for. The squawks and gurgles he produces, both during the lessons and later, are so strangled and peculiar that we wonder why the other actors don't just break off and wait for the next take.

Grant is wrong for the role anyway. He has a good line in charm and wit, he can play intelligent and vulnerable, and he's likable. But there's never a moment here where he convinces us he's truly desperate or in danger. He drops into the movie like a dinner guest; we're reminded of somebody unflappable like David Niven, although Niven could play desperate when he had to.

Jeanne Tripplehorn is sufficiently convincing as the woman who loves him, although it must have seemed odd to her, being so intense in the face of his cool. James Caan and Burt Young are right at home (Young's thin lips releasing each word grudgingly), and Viterelli is a mountain of plausibility. But without a strong center, there's not enough for them to play against.

A side plot, involving James Fox as a major player in the art world, seems like an after-thought, but there is funny stuff about art in the movie. I liked the plot device of a mobster's son who paints unspeakably awful pictures (Jesus with a machine gun, etc.). They end up at auction, where they turn out to be a handy way to launder money (mob pays big for painting, son therefore has legitimate income from art). There are interesting consequences when the paintings become sought-after, especially by a sweet little old lady who is tempted by dangerous investments.

All good stuff, but it doesn't add up. Is this movie Hugh Grant's fault? I don't know. Not many actors can save themselves from wrong casting. On paper perhaps Grant looked right. But consider his success in *Notting Hill.* Even there, faced with the loss of the woman he loved, his instincts were not to scream but to apologize. Some actors can convey charm and desperation in a romantic farce (Matt Dillon comes to mind) and some need to be a little more grounded in reality. After the bite and freshness of *Analyze This, Mickey Blue Eyes* plays like an afterthought.

Mifune ★ ★ ★
R, 99 m., 2000

Anders W. Berthelsen (Kresten), Iben Hjejle (Liva), Jesper Asholt (Rud, Kresten's Brother), Sofie Grabol (Claire, Kresten's Wife), Emil Tarding (Bjarke, Liva's Brother), Anders Hove (Gerner), Paprika Steen (Pernille), Mette Bratlann (Nina). Directed by Soren Kragh-Jacobsen and produced by Birgitte Hlad. Screenplay by Kragh-Jacobsen and Anders Thomas Jensen.

Mifune is the latest work with the imprimatur of Dogma '95, a group of Danish filmmakers who signed a cinematic "vow of chastity"—reserving poverty and obedience, apparently, for TV directors. Dogma films are encouraged to use natural light and sound, real locations, no props or music brought in from outside, handheld cameras and "no directorial touches," as if the auteur theory was shamelessly immodest. Of the Dogma films I have seen (*The Idiots, Celebration*) and the Dogma wanna-be *julien donkey-boy, Mifune* is the most fun and the least dogmatic. With just a few more advances, like props, sets, lighting, music, and style, the Dogma crowd will be making real movies.

Only kidding. But in truth, Dogma '95 is as much publicity as conviction, and its films contain more, not less, directorial style. Like the American indie movement, they use small budgets and unsprung plots, but that's not a creed; it's a strategy for making a virtue of necessity. That the Dogma films have been good and interesting is encouraging, but a coincidence.

The story of *Mifune* breaks down no barriers but is in the tradition of offbeat romantic comedy, and one can imagine it being remade by Hollywood with Jeff Daniels as the hero, Martin Short as the retarded brother, and Angelina Jolie as the hooker. It is a "commercial" story, and all the more entertaining for being so, but Soren Kragh-Jacobsen's low-rent version has a freshness and spontaneity that the Hollywood version would probably lose. There's something about ground-level filmmaking that makes an audience feel a movie is getting away with something.

The story begins with the wedding of Kresten (Anders W. Berthelsen) and Claire (Sofie Grabol). If the eye contact between Kresten and Claire's sexy mother is any indication, this marriage might have soon grown very complicated, but Kresten's past catches up with him and dooms the marriage (not, luckily for Claire, before a wedding night that seems to set Guinness records). Kresten learns that his father has died, and he has avoided telling his wife and snotty in-laws about his family's ramshackle farm, his retarded brother, or his mother who hung herself on "one of the oldest trees in Denmark." ("He grew up," observes A. O. Scott, "in the Danish translation of a Tennessee Williams play.")

Kresten returns to the farm, which is a run-down shambles with water damage and animals making free use of the house, and finds his brother, Rud (Jesper Asholt), drinking under the table that bears the father's corpse. What to do? Rud cannot take care of himself, the farm is falling to pieces, and this is not the kind of situation he can bring Claire into. Desperate, Kresten hires a housekeeper named Liva, played by Iben Hjejle (she plays Laura, the lost love, in *High Fidelity*). Liva is desperate, too; we learn she was a hooker, is being pursued by an angry pimp, and receives alarming phone calls.

At this point in the story not even the most stringent application of Dogma vows can prevent the director and his audience from hurtling confidently toward the inevitable development in which Kresten and Liva fall in love and form a sort of instant family with Rud as honorary child. Dogma forbids genre conventions, but this story is made from the ground up of nothing else—and more power to it.

If the story is immensely satisfying in a traditional way, the style has its own delights. Kragh-Jacobsen feels free to meander. Every single scene doesn't have to pull its weight and move the plot marker to the next square. Asides and irrelevant excursions are allowed. Characters arrive at conclusions by a process we can follow on the screen, instead of signaling us that they are only following the script. And there is an earthiness to the unknown actors, especially Asholt as Rud, that grounds the story in the infinite mystery of real personalities.

Watching *Mifune* and the other Dogma films (except for *julien*, which is more of an exercise in video art), we're taught a lesson. It's not a new lesson; John Cassavetes taught it years ago and directors as various as Mike Leigh and Henry Jaglom demonstrate it. It has to do with the feel of a film, regardless of its budget or the faces in the cast. Some films feel free, and others seem caged. Some seem to happen while we watch, and others seem to know their own fates. Some satisfy by marching toward foregone conclusions, and others (while they may arrive at the same place) seem surprised and delighted by how they turn out.

Mifune is like a lesson in film watching. If you see enough films like this, you learn to be suspicious of high-gloss films that purr along mile after mile without any bumps. If a film like this were a car and it stalled, you could go under the hood with a wrench. When fancy films stall, you need a computer expert.

Mighty Peking Man ★ ★ ★
NO MPAA RATING, 100 m., 1977 (rereleased 1999)

Danny Lee (Li Hsiu-Hsien) (Johnny Feng), Evelyne Kraft (Samantha [Ah Wei]), Hsiao Yao (Huang Tsui-Hua), Ku Feng (Lu Tien), Lin Wei-

Tu (Chen Shi-Yu), Hsu Shao-Chiang (Ah Lung), Wu Hang-Sheng (Ah Pi), Cheng Ping (Lucy). Directed by Ho Meng-Hua and produced by Runme Shaw. Screenplay by I. Kuang.

There is an earthquake near the beginning of *Mighty Peking Man*, but unlike the earthquake in the fondly remembered *Infra-Man*, it does not unleash the Slinky-necked robots and hairy mutant footstools controlled by Princess Dragon Mom. Still, it offers attractions of its own. It disturbs a giant ape, for example, which lumbers down from its mountain home and heads for the jungles of India. And it is no ordinary tremor; it unfolds progressively.

First, a character shouts that there's an earthquake. Then we hear it, although we do not see anything alarming. Then the back-projected landscape begins to shake violently, although the foreground does not shake. Then the camera begins to shake, while the foreground still holds steady. Later, finally, Earth moves. This may be the first special effects–generated earthquake in which the back projection shakes so hard it moves Earth.

The earthquake doesn't really have an impact on the plot. It's simply an earthquake scene, just as later there is a quicksand scene, a scene where a python fights a tiger, etc. *Mighty Peking Man*, made in 1977, is being rereleased by Quentin Tarantino's Rolling Thunder Pictures, and we can only imagine young QT behind the counter of that legendary video store of his youth, watching this on the monitor and realizing he'd struck gold.

The plot involves an expedition to discover the giant apelike Peking Man, who is said at one point to be ten feet tall—although a grown man is able to stand inside one of its footprints. Later in the film, however, the creature has grown enough to knock down tall buildings, although later still it has shrunk enough to climb one.

The dialogue is to the point. After the expedition is suggested, a character says: "I know an explorer here in Hong Kong! He just lost his girl! He wants to get away!" The explorer, whose name is Johnny Feng (Danny Lee), is drunk when we first meet him; a flashback reveals that his girlfriend is having an affair with his brother. That doesn't dissuade Lu Tien, the hunt financer: "You're going to lead our expe-

dition into the Himalyan jungle! You're the only one I trust!"

Soon the expedition sets off, not in Land Rovers as we might expect, but in tall two-wheeled ox carts. There are hazards along the way. My favorite is when a Sherpa gets his leg bitten off above the knee. Johnny wants to summon medical help, but Lu Tien simply shoots the man in the head. The expedition soon encounters a blond woman named Samantha (Evelyne Kraft) who has lived in the jungle since the crash long ago of a plane carrying her family (in a flashback, we see the tot crying out, "Mama! Papa!"). Mighty Peking Man and Samantha hang out together, but are just friends.

Samantha doesn't speak English at first, but quickly learns, no doubt in the same way the other actors have learned: by speaking their usual language and having it dubbed. What is amazing is that Mighty Peking Man, when encountered, also speaks English. Samantha's savage existence has given her time to design an off-the-shoulder leopard-skin brassiere, and to find a supply of lip gloss and eyeliner. Soon Samantha and Johnny are an item.

Lu Tien sees a fortune in Mighty Peking Man, and brings him to Hong Kong, where he is displayed in a stadium before thousands of people, while chained to big trucks. Samantha meanwhile has found Johnny in bed with his original girlfriend, and races distraught to the stadium when she sees Mighty Peking Man on TV, tossing the trucks around like large toys (which they are). She desperately pleads with the implacable security forces to spare the beast because he has been misunderstood. But too late: MPM goes on a rampage through downtown Hong Kong, knocking over buildings and batting helicopters out of the sky in a sequence that was surely not an attempt to rip off Dino De Laurentiis's *King Kong*, made a year earlier.

Mighty Peking Man is very funny, although a shade off the high mark of *Infra-Man*, which was made a year earlier and is my favorite Hong Kong monster film. Both were produced by the legendary Runme Shaw, who, having tasted greatness, obviously hoped to repeat. I find to my astonishment that I gave *Infra-Man* only two and a half stars when I reviewed it. That was twenty-two years ago, but a fellow will remember a lot of things you wouldn't think he'd remember. I'll bet a month hasn't gone by since that I haven't thought of that film. I am awarding *Mighty Peking Man* three stars, for general goofiness and a certain level of insane genius, but I cannot in good conscience rate it higher than *Infra-Man*. So, in answer to those correspondents who ask if I have ever changed a rating on a movie: Yes, *Infra-Man* moves up to three stars.

The Minus Man ★ ★ ★

R, 115 m., 1999

Owen Wilson (Van), Janeane Garofalo (Ferrin), Brian Cox (Doug), Mercedes Ruehl (Jane), Dwight Yoakam (Blair), Dennis Haysbert (Graves), Sheryl Crow (Caspar). Directed by Hampton Fancher and produced by David Bushell and Fida Attieh. Screenplay by Fancher, based on the novel by Lew McCreary.

"I take the natural momentum of a person and draw it toward me," Van tells us during *The Minus Man*. He is like the narrator of a how-to tape for serial killers. In musings on the sound track, he talks about his methods, as he drifts from place to place, poisoning people. His approach is not violent, "just the minimum necessary." He is an enigma. People seem to like him, and we wonder why.

We are curious about such killers, because they fit in so easily. A mad-dog psychopath, shooting up a church or school, is clearly nuts and evil. But what about mild-mannered Van (Owen Wilson), polite and quiet, able to win the confidence of girls in bars, landlords, strangers? It is one thing to be the victim of random violence, another to welcome your killer into your life.

Van's act is that he just wants to help out and not make waves. In an opening sequence, he meets a sad addict (Sheryl Crow) in a bar, and offers her a lift. He's like a good Samaritan. He says what people want to hear, or need to hear. He's quiet; he doesn't frighten them away with loud noises or sudden moves. Even his killing method is subdued. Retracing the movements of serial killers, we often find they had contact with the law, without the law knowing who they were. Maybe part of the thrill is in edging close to capture and then

dancing away. There's a dicey scene in *The Minus Man* where Van is awakened by a cop as he sleeps in his car. A search would turn up incriminating evidence, but he's so respectful that he gets off with a warning.

Soon he's a boarder in the home of Doug and Jane (Brian Cox and Mercedes Ruehl). Doug is a postal worker. Jane is suspicious. They need the income from renting the extra room, but she warns Doug, "Don't make a boarder your guest." But Doug is lonely, and Jane is always picking on him. He needs a friend. Soon he's found Van a job he loves, at the post office. And there he meets Ferrin (Janeane Garofalo), who likes him.

All of these developments are done in low-key, understated style. The suspense beats away underneath because we know what Van is capable of. Will Doug get a pass because he provided a job? What about Ferrin? Does he like her, or is he leading her on? What is Van thinking about, in his rented room? I was reminded of the Joseph Cotten character in Hitchcock's *Shadow of a Doubt*—the man of unspeakable evil, moving blandly through small-town society. And of Joyce Carol Oates's chilling novel *Zombie*, about a character not unlike Van.

Both Van and the Oates character narrate their own stories, dwelling on methods, giving helpful advice to anyone hoping to follow in their footsteps. There's never a second's introspection. They don't ask why they kill because the question doesn't occur to them; they act according to their natures. It is for us to wonder that our species could produce a creature that will not sign the truce that makes civilization possible.

The Minus Man, based on a novel by Lew McCreary, was written and directed by Hampton Fancher, who wrote *Blade Runner*. This is his directing debut; a curious choice, but since he pulls it off he must feel a connection with it. Owen Wilson, who can look reassuring or not, depending on how much tension he allows into his face, finds the right insidious, ingratiating tone for Van. And the three closest people in his life (Garofalo's postal worker and Ruehl and Cox as the landlords) are able to meet one of an actor's trickiest challenges: to stand in harm's way and be oblivious to it.

Karl Malden told me that the most difficult scene he ever had as an actor was in *On the*

Waterfront, where he played a priest who had to make a speech while unaware that a beer can was about to be thrown at his head. The priest didn't know about the can, but the actor did. You see the problem. In *The Minus Man,* Garofolo, Ruehl, and Cox successfully spend the whole movie acting as if the can hasn't been thrown.

Miss Congeniality ★ ★
PG-13, 110 m., 2000

Sandra Bullock (Gracie Hart), Benjamin Bratt (Eric Matthews), Michael Caine (Victor "Vic" Melling), William Shatner (Stan Fields), Jennifer Gareis (Miss New Jersey), Wendy Raquel Robinson (Miss California), Candice Bergen (Kathy), Heather Burns (Miss Rhode Island). Directed by Donald Petrie and produced by Sandra Bullock. Screenplay by Marc Lawrence, Katie Ford, and Caryn Lucas.

Something about Sandra Bullock strikes me the right way. She has a warmth that gets you smiling even when the material is weak—as it sometimes is, since she has uncertain luck in choosing projects. In *Miss Congeniality,* she makes her way through a screenplay that in other hands would have been a dreary sitcom mishmash, and her presence transforms it into a less dreary sitcom mishmash.

She has the producer's credit on the movie. That means she thought this project was a good fit. Since the material is tired and routine, what was she thinking of? Maybe she's not ambitious enough. Comedies will find her; she doesn't need to go looking for them. Stars with clout usually take on personal projects to break out of their typecasting, not to reinforce it.

In *Miss Congeniality,* Bullock plays another version of a familiar role for her, in which she begins the film looking unglamorous and then undergoes a transformation. Sometimes that happens in the eye of the beholder, as it did in *While You Were Sleeping.* This time, it happens because of a big-time beauty makeover. She starts as an FBI agent and ends up as a beauty contest finalist, and although churls may argue she's not convincing as a beauty queen, they are not of this Earth.

Before she grows up to become an FBI agent, she's a tomboy who can beat up the other kids at school. As an agent, she clomps around looking hearty and graceless, pounding on punching bags and running red lights on her way to Starbucks, until she's assigned to impersonate a contestant at a beauty pageant. As an undercover agent, she can help head off a rumored terrorist threat to the event.

Uh-huh. But there are some funny scenes as Michael Caine, a disgraced but still brilliant "beauty consultant," supervises her makeover and teaches her how to dress less like a model for L.L. Bean campwear. I saw this movie and Mel Gibson's *What Women Want* within a few days of each other, and in both stories the lead characters get a lot of mileage out of their unfamiliarity with feminine beauty products. Gibson has the edge on depilatories, but Bullock does a better job of not being able to walk like a woman.

The plot also involves Candice Bergen as the founder of the beauty pageant, and Benjamin Bratt as Bullock's FBI partner. No prizes for figuring out that Bergen is up to more than she seems, and that after Bullock's transformation the scales fall from Bratt's eyes and he realizes, gosh, she cleans up real well. Bullock's character has a thing she does where she snorts through her nose—kind of a genteel barnyard sound—and she even stops doing that after a while.

Miss Congeniality is harmless fun of a silly sort. It isn't bad so much as it lacks any ambition to be more than it so obviously is. I smiled during it, and enjoyed Bullock, but then again I got to see it for free, and I'm the guy who thinks *Speed 2* is a good movie, something even Bullock doesn't believe. Opening *Miss Congeniality* against more than a dozen big-name holiday releases is kind of suicidal. With that kind of competition, you gotta be more than congenial.

Mission: Impossible 2 ★ ★ ★
PG-13, 120 m., 2000

Tom Cruise (Ethan Hunt), Dougray Scott (Sean Ambrose), Thandie Newton (Nyah Hall), Richard Roxburgh (Hugh Stamp), John Polson (Billy Baird), Brendan Gleeson (McCloy), Rade Sherbedgia (Dr. Nekhorvich), Ving Rhames

(Luther Stickell). Directed by John Woo and produced by Tom Cruise and Paula Wagner. Screenplay by Robert Towne, based on a story by Ronald D. Moore and Brannon Braga and the television series created by Bruce Geller.

If James Bond is still around at the end of the twenty-first century, he will look a lot like Ethan Hunt. The hero of the *Mission: Impossible* series is a 007 for our time.

That means: Sex is more of a surprise and a distraction than a lifestyle. Stunts and special effects don't interrupt the plot, but *are* the plot. The hero's interest in new consumer items runs more toward cybergadgets than sports cars. He isn't a patriot working for his government, but a hired gun working for a shadowy international agency. And he doesn't smoke, hardly drinks, and is in the physical condition of a triathlete.

The new Bond, in short, is a driven, overachieving professional—not the sort of gentleman sophisticate the British spy family used to cultivate. His small talk consists not of lascivious puns, but geekspeak. When he raises an eyebrow, it's probably not his, because he's a master of disguise and can hide behind plastic masks so realistic even his cinematographer doesn't know for sure.

The first *Mission: Impossible* (1996) had a plot no one understood. *Mission: Impossible 2* has a plot you don't need to understand. It's been cobbled together by the expert Hollywood script doctor Robert Towne out of elements of other movies, notably Hitchcock's *Notorious,* from which he takes the idea that the hero first falls in love with the heroine, then heartlessly assigns her to resume an old affair with an ex-lover in order to spy on his devious plans. In both films, the woman agrees to do this because she loves the hero. In *Notorious,* the hero loses respect for the woman after she does what he asks. The modern hero is too amoral to think of this.

Towne's contribution is quite skillful, especially if it's true, as I've heard, that he had to write around major f/x sequences that director John Woo had already written and fine-tuned. His strategy is to make Ethan Hunt (Tom Cruise) into a sympathetic yet one-dimensional character, so that motivation and emotion will not be a problem. He's a cousin of Clint Eastwood's Man With No Name—a hero defined not by his values but by his actions.

The villain remains in the Bond tradition: A megalomaniac who seeks power or wealth by holding the world ransom. In this case, he seeks control of a deadly virus, but the virus is what Hitchcock called a MacGuffin; it doesn't matter what it is, just so it's something everyone desires or fears. The movie wisely spends little time on the details, but is clever in the way it uses the virus to create time pressure: Twenty-four hours after you're exposed, you die, and that leads to a nicely timed showdown involving the hero, the woman he loves, the villain, the virus, and a ticking clock.

Thandie Newton plays the woman, and the most significant thing about her character is that she's still alive at the end, and apparently available for the sequel. The Bond girls have had a depressing mortality rate over the years, but remember that 007 was formed in the promiscuous 1960s, while Ethan Hunt lives in a time when even spies tend to stay with old relationships, maybe because it's so tiresome to start new ones.

Newton's character is unique in the way she plays a key role in the plot, taking her own initiative. Bond girls, even those with formidable fighting skills, were instruments of the plot; Newton's Nyah Hall not only lacks a name that is a pun, but shockingly makes a unilateral decision that influences the outcome of the movie. The playing field will be more level in the *M:I* battle of the sexes.

For Tom Cruise, the series is a franchise, like Mel Gibson's *Lethal Weapon* movies. *M:I3* is already on the drawing board, again with John Woo as director, and there's no reason the sequels can't continue as long as Cruise can still star in action scenes (or their computer-generated manifestations). This is good for Cruise. By more or less underwriting his box-office clout, it gives him the freedom to experiment with more offbeat choices like *Eyes Wide Shut* and *Magnolia.*

As for the movie itself: If the first movie was entertaining as sound, fury, and movement, this one is more evolved, more confident, more surefooted in the way it marries minimal character development to seamless action. It is a global movie, flying no flag, requiring little dialogue, featuring characters who are Pavlovian in their motivation. It's more efficient than the Bond pictures, but not as much pure fun. In this new century, I have a premonition we'll be seeing more efficiency and less fun in a lot of different areas. The trend started about the time college students decided management was sexier than literature.

Mission to Mars ★ ★ ½
PG, 113 m., 2000

Gary Sinise (Jim McConnell), Tim Robbins (Woody Blake), Don Cheadle (Luke Graham), Connie Nielsen (Terri Fisher), Jerry O'Connell (Phil Ohlmyer), Peter Outerbridge (Sergei Kirov), Kavan Smith (Nicholas Willis), Jill Teed (Renee Cote). Directed by Brian De Palma and produced by Tom Jacobson. Screenplay by Jim Thomas, John Thomas, Graham Yost, and Lowell Cannon.

Well, here it is, I guess, a science-fiction movie like the one I was wishing for in my review of *Pitch Black*. That film transported its characters to an alien planet in a three-star system and then had them chase each other around in the desert and be threatened by wicked bat-creatures. Why go to all the trouble of transporting humans millions of miles from Earth, only to mire them in tired generic conventions?

Mission to Mars is smarter and more original. It contains some ideas. It also has its flaws. It begins with an astronaut's backyard picnic so chirpy it could easily accommodate Chevy Chase. It contains conversations that drag on beyond all reason. It is quiet when quiet is not called for. It contains actions that deny common sense. And for long stretches the characters speak nothing but boilerplate.

And yet those stretches on autopilot surround three sequences of real vision, awakening the sense of wonder that is the goal of popular science fiction. The film involves a manned mission to Mars, which lands successfully and then encounters . . . something . . . that results in the death of three of the crew members, and loss of radio contact with the fourth (Don Cheadle).

A rescue mission is dispatched, led by co-pilots Tim Robbins and Gary Sinise, with Connie Nielsen as Robbins's wife and Jerry O'Connell as the fourth member. They run into a clump of tiny meteorites that puncture the hull and lead to a loss of air pressure. (It's here that the Sinise character defies logic by refusing, for no good reason, to put on his helmet and draw oxygen from his suit.) Then there's another crisis, which leads to a surprisingly taut and moving sequence in which the four characters attempt a tricky maneuver outside their ship and are faced with a life-or-death choice.

Arriving on the red planet, they find the survivor, hear his story, and then are led into a virtual reality version of a close encounter of the third kind. They learn the history of Mars, and the secret of life on Earth, and Sinise continues his journey in an unexpected way.

I am being deliberately vague here because one of the pleasures of a film like this is its visual and plot surprises. I like a little science in science fiction, and this film has a little. (The emphasis is on "little," however, and its animated re-creation of the evolution of species lost me when the dinosaurs evolved into bison—and besides, how would the makers of that animation know the outcome of the process?) The movie also has some intriguing ideas, and some of the spirit of *2001: A Space Odyssey*. Not a lot, but some. (It pays homage to Kubrick's film by giving us space suits and spaceship interiors that seem like a logical evolution of his designs.)

I watched the movie with pleasure that was frequently interrupted by frustration. The three key sequences are very well done. They are surrounded by sequences that are not—left adrift in lackluster dialogue and broad, easy character strokes. Why does the film amble so casually between its high points? Why is a meditative tone evoked when we have been given only perfunctory inspiration for it? Why is a crisis like the breached hull treated so deliberately, as if the characters are trying to slow down their actions to use up all the available time? And why, oh why, in a film where the special effects are sometimes awesome, are we given an alien being who looks like a refugee from a video game?

I can't recommend *Mission to Mars*. It misses too many of its marks. But it has extraordinary things in it. It's as if the director, the gifted Brian De Palma, rises to the occasions but the screenplay gives him nothing much to do in between them. It was old Howard Hawks who supplied this definition of a good movie: "Three great scenes. No bad scenes." *Mission to Mars* gets only the first part right.

Miss Julie ★ ★ ★
R, 100 m., 2000

Saffron Burrows (Miss Julie), Peter Mullan (Jean), Maria Doyle Kennedy (Christine), Tam Dean Burn (Servant), Heathcote Williams (Servant), Eileen Walsh (Servant). Directed by Mike Figgis and produced by Figgis and Harriet Cruickshank. Screenplay by Helen Cooper, based on the play by August Strindberg.

Mike Figgis's *Leaving Las Vegas* was about a self-destructive man who pauses briefly for sex and kindness from a Vegas call girl on his way to the grave. Now Figgis has made *Miss Julie,* a film based on the Strindberg play about the daughter of a count and her footman—two people who use sex as their instrument of self-destruction. Both films are intense, erotic, and willful; the difference is that we pity and love the characters in the first, while Strindberg and Figgis allow only pity in the second.

It is Midsummer's Eve in the house of a wealthy Swedish count. In the kitchen, there's much cheerful toing-and-froing from the downstairs staff, while upstairs a party is under way. We meet Jean, the footman, played by Peter Mullan as a compact, self-assured man who polishes boots as if they were his enemies. His fiancée, Christine (Maria Doyle Kennedy), is a plump, jolly woman who not only knows her place, but approves of it.

Miss Julie walks down the stairs. Played by Saffron Burrows, she is several inches taller than Jean, and bold, the kind of woman who learned to handle men by first mastering horses. She's come for a little sport with the servants, or because she's bored with the aristocrats upstairs, or because she has noticed how Jean looks at her, or perhaps because her fiancé has left her. He left, we learn, because she was too headstrong. On the rebound, she is angry and reckless.

For the next hour and a half, Jean and Miss Julie will engage in a duel of wills. The movie is almost exactly as long as Strindberg's one-act play, which traps them in the same time and space, and calls their mutual bluff: Each wants to prove the other doesn't have the nerve to have sex. Intimacy between them, of course, is forbidden by all the codes that apply in this kitchen: the class system, religious beliefs, the separation of servant and master, Jean's engagement to Christine, and not least the fact that they do not like each other.

Their dislike is, however, an aphrodisiac, and so is the danger they place themselves in, because a servant and a mistress who have sex can never be accepted again by the society that contains them. They must leave—flee to Paris, perhaps—or find some other kind of escape. Ah, you say, but what if no one finds out? The whole point is that they themselves will know. They've been instructed by the class system to see themselves in a certain way, and sex would destroy that way of seeing.

Of course, their danger makes it all the more enticing, and the drama is a verbal duel in which words are foreplay. There is a lot of sadomasochism in their fencing. She at first wants him to grovel, and towers over him. Then he takes the upper hand and lashes her with harsh truths about herself. When they finally do have sex, it is not pleasurable but more like a mutual wounding: As you destroy me, I destroy you.

The actors are compelling. Mullan *(My Name Is Joe)* can be a hard man, roughened by his servant's life. Burrows *(The Loss of Sexual Innocence)* is a great beauty but, like Sigourney Weaver, another tall woman, possessed of angularity: She can be soft, and then all sharp corners. They talk, they fence, they dream, they are tender, they tease, they taunt, they dance closer and closer to the film's outcome, which, once you experience it, you know you saw coming right from the first.

The Mod Squad ★ ★
R, 94 m., 1999

Claire Danes (Julie), Giovanni Ribisi (Pete), Omar Epps (Linc), Dennis Farina (Greer), Josh Brolin (Billy), Michael Lerner (Wiseman), Steve Harris (Briggs), Richard Jenkins (Mothershed), Larry Brandenburg (Eckford). Directed by Scott Silver and produced by Ben Myron, Alan Riche, and Tony Ludwig. Screenplay by Stephen Kay, Silver, and Kate Lanier.

The Mod Squad has an intriguing cast, a director who knows how to use his camera, and a lot of sly humor. Shame about the story. When you see this many of the right elements in a lame movie, you wonder how close they came to making a better one. The director, Scott Silver, cowrote the script himself, and has to take some of the blame: This is a classy production and deserves better.

The premise is from the old TV series. Three young screw-ups are interrupted at the beginning of criminal careers and recruited by a police captain to form an undercover squad. Their assignment: Infiltrate a club where prostitution and drug dealing seem to be happening. The mod squad doesn't carry guns (officially, anyway), doesn't have badges, and I'm not sure if they can make arrests; maybe they're more like high-level snitches.

The members are described by a Rod Serling–type voice over the opening credits. Julie (Claire Danes) was "a runaway—an addict at eighteen." Pete (Giovanni Ribisi) "went straight from Beverly Hills to county jail." Linc (Omar Epps) "doesn't blame his crimes on anything." (He's black, and so the implication, I guess, is that this is worthy of comment.) In the good-looking opening sequence, filmed by Ellen Kuras, they're intercut with dancers at a club, get into a fight, and then find themselves being debriefed and lectured by Captain Greer (Dennis Farina), who orders them to stand up when they talk to him, quit sitting on his desk, etc. Of course, their bad manners are a curtain-raiser to bravery, heroism, and astonishing crime-fighting skills.

The skills, alas, are astonishing because they're so bush-league. The main investigative technique in this movie consists of sneaking up on people and eavesdropping while they explain the entire plot and give away all the secrets. Julie falls for a former lover, follows him to a rendezvous with a drug kingpin (Michael Lerner), and overhears choice nuggets of conversation ("None of them have any idea I know they're cops!"). Then she follows him home and hides in his closet while the faithless louse does the rumpy-pumpy with another woman.

Petey, meanwhile, is even more clever. He creeps up on a hideout and hides behind a wall while tape-recording a full confession. It goes without saying his tape will later be played over a loudspeaker in order to incriminate the bad guys. He uses one of those little $29 microcassette recorders—you know, the kind that can record with perfect fidelity at twenty yards outdoors on a windy day.

As the mod squaders were creeping around, eavesdropping and peeping through windows, I grew restless: This is the kind of stuff they rewrote the Nancy Drew books to get rid of. Too bad, because I liked the pure acting touches that the cast brought to their roles. Ribisi (from *Friends, Saving Private Ryan,* and *The Other Sister*) has a kind of poker-faced put-upon look that's appealing, especially when he gets beat up and goes back to Beverly Hills and his dad chortles heartily at the claim that his kid is now a cop. Danes *(Romeo and Juliet)* has a quick intelligence that almost but not quite sells the dumb stuff they make her do. Epps *(Scream 2, Higher Learning)* is the dominant member of the squad, who tries to protect the others from their insane risk-taking.

And there's a small but indispensable supporting role by Michael Lerner as the crewcut evil kingpin, who intimidates his enemies by dancing with them ("I'm not a fairy—I just like to dance"). He delivers his dialogue indirectly, as an ironic commentary on the horrible things he always seems about to do.

So all of this is a good start, but the screenplay just doesn't provide the foundation. Consider Billy, the Josh Brolin character, who is Julie's once and future boyfriend. We know from the first moment we see him that he's no good. We're tipped off by how suddenly Julie goes for him; if the point were romance, the movie would let them take longer, but since the point is for her to be deceived, she has to rush in heedlessly. No girl meets a guy who dumped her and broke her heart, and immediately drags him into a toilet stall for sex. Especially not now that she's clean and sober, as Julie is (although the movie repeats the tiresome cliché that all recovering alcoholics immediately turn to drink after a setback—preferably swigging from a fifth).

What I'd love to know is how the screenplay got green-lighted. This is a top-drawer film with a decent budget and lots of care about the production values. The cast is talented and well chosen. The movie is even aware of potential clichés (before the last shoot-out, Julie says, "At least it's not going down in an abandoned warehouse"). And then what do they end up with? The most expensive Nancy Drew mystery ever filmed.

Monkeybone ★ ½
PG-13, 87 m., 2001

Brendan Fraser (Stu Miley), Bridget Fonda (Julie McElroy), Whoopi Goldberg (Death), Chris Kattan (Organ Donor), David Foley (Herb), Giancarlo Esposito (Hypnos), John Turturro (Monkeybone's Voice), Rose McGowan (Kitty). Directed by Henry Selick and produced by Mark Radcliffe and Michael Barnathan. Screenplay by Sam Hamm.

A character played by Brendan Fraser spends half of *Monkeybone* on life support, and so does the movie. Both try to stay alive with injections of nightmare juice. The movie labors hard, the special effects are admirable, no expense has been spared, and yet the movie never takes off; it's a bright idea the filmmakers were unable to breathe into life.

Fraser plays a cartoonist named Stu Miley ("S. Miley"—ho, ho). He's created a character named Monkeybone, which has become enormously popular and might soon star on its own TV show—except that Stu is one of those unsullied artists who shies away from success. He flees a fancy reception with his girlfriend Julie (Bridget Fonda), but as they're driving away a giant plastic Monkeybone toy in the backseat suddenly inflates, causing a crash. Julie is unharmed, but Stu goes into a coma, with his sister negotiating with the hospital about how soon they can pull the plug.

The coma is, in fact, action-packed. In his mind, Stu has taken an escalator to Downtown, a nightmare dreamland nightclub ruled by Hypnos (Giancarlo Esposito); it's not far from Thanatopolis, ruled by Death (Whoopi Goldberg). Here Monkeybone is the emcee, and exit passes are hard to come by. That leads to a scheme by Monkeybone ("I'm tired of being a figment!") to occupy Stu's body and escape from Downtown.

Meanwhile, on Earth, Stu's time is drawing short and his sister has her hand on the plug. Julie scans a brain chart and intuits that Stu is trapped in a "nightmare loop." She thinks

maybe an emergency injection of Nightmare Juice might scare him awake. Through a coincidental miracle of timing, Monkeybone leaves Downtown and possesses Stu's body just as the juice hits, so when he comes out of the coma and starts acting strangely, she blames it on the juice.

And so on. The plot is not exactly the issue here. *Monkeybone* was directed by Henry Selick, who also made *The Nightmare Before Christmas* and *James and the Giant Peach*. His ability to blend live action with makeup, special effects, and computer effects is about as good as it gets—and he leans away from computers and in the direction of bizarre sets and makeup and stop-action animation, which gives his work an eerie third-dimensionality unmatched by slicker computer effects.

Here he achieves technical marvels, but the movie just doesn't deliver. The Monkeybone character doesn't earn its screen time; it's just a noxious pest. Brendan Fraser has been at home before in cartoon roles *(George of the Jungle, Dudley Do-Right)*, but here he seems more like the victim of the joke than the perpetrator, and Bridget Fonda's girlfriend is earnest and plucky, but not funny (she has to look concerned about Stu all the time).

One sequence made me smile. It involves Chris Kattan, from *Saturday Night Live*, as an organ transplant donor snatched from the hospital in midoperation and lofted over the city by a hot air balloon, while spare parts fall from his incision and are greeted below by grateful dogs.

Downtown itself looks like the amusement park from (or in) hell, and there's a lot of *Beetlejuice* in the inspiration for the strange creatures, one-eyed and otherwise, who live there. But strangeness is not enough. There must also be humor, and characters who exist for some reason other than to look bizarre. That rule would include Whoopi Goldberg's Death, who is sadly underwritten, and played by Whoopi as if we're supposed to keep repeating: "Wow! Look! Death is being played by Whoopi Goldberg!" It is a truth too often forgotten that casting a famous actor in a weird cameo is the setup of the joke, not the punch line.

The Mother and the Whore ★ ★ ★ ★
NO MPAA RATING, 215 m., 1973 (rereleased 1999)

Jean-Pierre Leaud (Alexandre), Bernadette Lafont (Marie), Francoise Lebrun (Veronika), Isabelle Weingarten (Gilberte), Jean Douchet (Man at Café Flore), Jean-Noel Picq (Offenbach Lover). Directed by Jean Eustache and produced by Pierre Cottrell. Screenplay by Eustache.

When Jean Eustache's *The Mother and the Whore* was released in 1973, young audiences all over the world embraced its layabout hero and his endless conversations with the woman he lived with, the woman he was dating, the woman who rejected him, and various other women encountered in the cafés of Paris. The character was played by Jean-Pierre Leaud, star of *The 400 Blows* and two other autobiographical films by François Truffaut. In 1977, Truffaut made *The Man Who Loved Women*. This one could have been titled *The Man Who Loved to Hear Himself Talk*.

At three and a half hours, the film is long, but its essence is to be long: Make it any shorter, and it would have a plot and an outcome, when in fact Eustache simply wants to record an existence. Alexandre (Leaud), his hero, lives with Marie (Bernadette Lafont), a boutique owner who apparently supports him; one would say he was between jobs if there were any sense that he'd ever had one. He meets a blind date named Veronika (Francoise Lebrun) in a café, and subjects her to a great many of his thoughts and would-be thoughts. (Much of Lebrun's screen time consists of close-ups of her listening.) In the middle of his monologues, Alexandre has a way of letting his eyes follow the progress of other women through his field of view.

Alexandre is smart enough, but not a great intellect. His favorite area of study is himself, but there he hasn't made much headway. He chatters about the cinema and about life, sometimes confusing them ("films tell you how to live, how to make a kid"). He wears a dark coat and a very long scarf, knotted around his neck and sweeping to his knees; his best friend dresses the same way. He spends his days in cafés, holding (but not reading) Proust. "Look there's Sartre—the drunk," he says one day in Café Flore, and Eustache supplies a quick shot of several people at a table, one of whom may or may not be Sartre. Alexandre talks about Sartre staggering out after his long intellectual chats in the café, and speculates that the great man's philosophy may be alcoholic musings.

The first time I saw *The Mother and the Whore*, I thought it was about Alexandre. After a viewing of the newly restored 35mm print being released for the movie's twenty-fifth anniversary, I think it is just as much about the women, and about the way that women can let a man talk endlessly about himself while they regard him like a specimen of aberrant behavior. Women keep a man like Alexandre around, I suspect, out of curiosity about what new idiocy he will next exhibit.

Of course, Alexandre is cheating—on Marie, whom he lives with, and on Veronika, whom he says he loves. Part of his style is to play with relationships, just to see what happens. The two women find out about each other, and eventually meet. There are some fireworks, but not as many as you might expect, maybe because neither one would be that devastated at losing Alexandre. Veronika, a nurse from Poland, is at least frank about herself: She sleeps around because she likes sex. She has a passionate monologue about her sexual needs and her resentment that women aren't supposed to admit their feelings. Whether Alexandre has sex with Marie is a good question; I suppose the answer is yes, but you can't be sure. She represents, of course, the mother, and Veronika thinks of herself as a whore; Alexandre has positioned himself in the crosshairs of the classic Freudian dilemma.

Jean-Pierre Leaud's best performance was his first, as the fierce young thirteen-year-old who roamed Paris in *The 400 Blows*, idolizing Balzac and escaping into books and trouble as a way of dealing with his parents' unhappy marriage. In a way, most of his adult performances are simply that boy, grown up. Here he smokes and talks incessantly, and wanders Paris like a puppet controlled by his libido. It's amusing the way he performs for the women; there's one shot in particular, where he takes a drink so theatrically it could be posing for a photo titled, "I Take a Drink."

The genuine drama in the movie centers on Veronika, who more or less knows they are only playing at love while out of the sight of Marie. We learn a lot about her life—her room in the hospital, her schedule, her low self-esteem. When she does talk, it is from brave, unadulterated self-knowledge.

The Mother and the Whore made an enormous impact when it was released. It still works a quarter-century later, because it was so focused on its subjects and lacking in pretension. It is rigorously observant, the portrait of an immature man and two women who humor him for a while, paying the price that entails. Eustache committed suicide at forty-three, in 1981, after making about a dozen films, of which this is by far the best-known. He said his film was intended as "the description of a normal course of events without the shortcuts of dramatization," and described Alexandre as a collector of "rare moments" that occupy his otherwise idle time. As a record of a kind of everyday Parisian life, the film is superb. We think of the cafés of Paris as hotbeds of fiery philosophical debate, but more often, I imagine, they are just like this: people talking, flirting, posing, drinking, smoking, telling the truth, and lying, while waiting to see if real life will ever begin.

Moulin Rouge ★ ★ ★ ½
PG-13, 126 m., 2001

Nicole Kidman (Satine), Ewan McGregor (Christian), John Leguizamo (Toulouse-Lautrec), Jim Broadbent (Zidler), Richard Roxburgh (Duke of Monroth), Kylie Minogue (The Green Fairy), Christine Anu (Arabia), Natalie Jackson Mendoza (China Doll). Directed by Baz Luhrmann and produced by Fred Baron, Martin Brown, and Luhrmann. Screenplay by Luhrmann and Craig Pearce.

Like almost every American college boy who ever took a cut-rate flight to Paris, I went to the Moulin Rouge on my first night in town. I had a cheap standing-room ticket way in the back, and over the heads of the crowd, through a haze of smoke, I could vaguely see the dancing girls. The tragedy of the Moulin Rouge is that by the time you can afford a better seat, you've outgrown the show.

Moulin Rouge the movie is more like the Moulin Rouge of my adolescent fantasies than

the real Moulin Rouge ever could be. It isn't about tired, decadent people, but about glorious romantics who believe in the glitz and the tinsel—who see the nightclub not as a shabby tourist trap but as a stage for their dreams. Even its villain is a love-struck duke who gnashes his way into the fantasy, content to play a starring role, however venal.

The film is constructed like the fevered snapshots created by your imagination before an anticipated erotic encounter. It doesn't depend on dialogue or situation but on the way you imagine a fantasy object first from one angle and then another. Satine, the heroine, is seen not so much in dramatic situations as in poses—in postcards for the yearning mind. The movie is about how we imagine its world. It is perfectly appropriate that it was filmed on sound stages in Australia; Paris has always existed best in the minds of its admirers.

The film stars Nicole Kidman as Satine, a star dancer who has a deadly secret; she is dying of tuberculosis. This is not a secret from the audience, which learns it early on, but from Christian (Ewan McGregor), the would-be writer who loves her. Toulouse-Lautrec (John Leguizamo), the dwarf artist, lives above Christian, and one day comes crashing through the ceiling of their flimsy tenement, sparking a friendship and collaboration: They will write a show to spotlight Satine's brilliance, as well as "truth, beauty, freedom, and love." (I was reminded of Gene Kelly and Donald O'Connor's motto in *Singin' in the Rain*: "Dignity. Always dignity.") The show must be financed; enter the venal Duke of Monroth (Richard Roxburgh), who wants to pay for the show and for Satine's favors. The ringmaster is Zidler (Jim Broadbent), impresario of the Moulin Rouge.

All of these characters are seen in terms of their own fantasies about themselves. Toulouse-Lautrec, for example, is flamboyant and romantic; Christian is lonely and lovelorn; Satine has a good heart and only seems to be a bad girl; Zidler pretends to be all business but is a softy; and the duke can be so easily duped because being duped is the essence of his role in life. Those who think they can buy affection are suckers; a wise man is content to rent it.

The movie has been directed by Baz Luhrmann, an Australian with a background in opera, whose two previous films were also experiments in exuberant excess. *Strictly Ballroom* made a ballroom competition into a flamboyant theatrical exercise, and his *William Shakespeare's Romeo + Juliet* updated the play into a contempo teenage rumble. He constructs *Moulin Rouge* with the melodrama of a nineteenth-century opera, the Technicolor brashness of a 1950s Hollywood musical, and the quick-cutting frenzy of a music video. Nothing is really "period" about the movie—it's like a costume revue taking place right now, with hit songs from the 1970s and 1980s (you will get the idea if I mention that Jim Broadbent sings "Like a Virgin").

I am often impatient with directors who use so many cuts that their films seem to have been fed through electric fans. For Luhrmann and this material, it is the right approach. He uses so many different setups and camera angles that some of the songs seem to be cut not on every word of the lyrics, but on every syllable. There's no breathing room. The whole movie is on the same manic pitch as O'Connor's "Make 'Em Laugh" number in *Singin' in the Rain*. Everything is screwed up to a breakneck pitch, as if the characters have died and their lives are flashing before our eyes.

This means the actors do not create their characters but embody them. Who is Satine? A leggy redhead who can look like a million in a nightclub costume, and then melt into a guy's arms. Who is Christian? A man who embodies longing with his eyes and sighs—whose very essence, whose entire being, is composed of need for Satine. With the duke, one is reminded of silent films in which the titles said "The Duke," and then he sneered at you.

The movie is all color and music, sound and motion, kinetic energy, broad strokes, operatic excess. While it might be most convenient to see it from the beginning, it hardly makes any difference; walk in at any moment and you'll quickly know who is good and bad, who is in love and why—and then all the rest is song, dance, spectacular production numbers, protestations of love, exhalations of regret, vows of revenge, and grand destructive gestures. It's like being trapped on an elevator with the circus.

Mr. Death: The Rise and Fall of Fred A. Leuchter Jr. ★ ★ ★ ★
PG-13, 96 m., 2000

A documentary directed by Errol Morris and produced by Michael Williams, David Collins, and Dorothy Aufiero.

The hangman has no friends. That truth, I think, is the key to understanding Fred A. Leuchter Jr., a man who built up a nice little business designing death-row machines, and then lost it when he became a star on the Holocaust denial circuit. Leuchter, the subject of Errol Morris's documentary *Mr. Death: The Rise and Fall of Fred A. Leuchter Jr.*, is a lonely man of limited insight who is grateful to be liked—even by Nazi apologists.

This is the seventh documentary by Morris, who combines dreamlike visual montages with music by Caleb Sampson to create a movie that is more reverie and meditation than reportage. Morris is drawn to subjects who try to control that which cannot be controlled—life and death. His heroes have included lion tamers, topiary gardeners, robot designers, wild turkey callers, autistics, death row inmates, pet cemetery owners, and Stephen Hawking, whose mind leaps through space and time while his body slumps in a chair.

Fred Leuchter, the son of a prison warden, stumbled into the death row business more or less by accident. An engineer by training, he found himself inspired by the need for more efficient and "humane" execution devices. He'd seen electric chairs that cooked their occupants without killing them, poison gas chambers that were a threat to the witnesses, gallows not correctly adjusted to break a neck. He went to work designing better chairs, trapdoors, and lethal injection machines, and soon (his trade not being commonplace) was being consulted by prisons all over America.

Despite his success in business, he was not, we gather, terrifically popular. How many women want to date a guy who can chat about the dangers of being accidentally electrocuted while standing in the pool of urine around a recently used electric chair? He does eventually marry a waitress he meets in a doughnut shop; indeed, given his habit of forty to sixty cups of coffee a day, he must have met a lot of

389

waitresses. We hear her offscreen voice as she describes their brief marriage, and demurs at Fred's notion that their visit to Auschwitz was a honeymoon (she had to wait in a cold car, serving as a lookout for guards).

Leuchter's trip to Auschwitz was the turning point in his career. He was asked by Ernst Zundel, a neo-Nazi and Holocaust denier, to be an expert witness at his trial in Canada. Zundel financed Leuchter's 1988 trip to Auschwitz, during which he chopped off bits of brick and mortar in areas said to be gas chambers, and had them analyzed for cyanide residue. His conclusion: The chambers never contained gas. The "Leuchter Report" has since been widely quoted by those who deny the Holocaust took place.

There is a flaw in his science, however. The laboratory technician who tested the samples for Leuchter was later startled to discover the use being made of his findings. Cyanide would penetrate bricks only to the depth of a tenth of a human hair, he says. By breaking off large chunks and pulverizing them, Leuchter had diluted his sample by 100,000 times, not even taking into account the fifty years of weathering that had passed. To find cyanide would have been a miracle.

No matter; Leuchter became a favorite after-dinner speaker on the neo-Nazi circuit, and the camera observes how his face lights up and his whole body seems to lean into applause, how happy he is to shake hands with his new friends. Other people might shy away from the pariah status of a Holocaust denier. The hangman is already a pariah, and finds his friends where he can.

Just before Mr. Death was shown in a slightly different form at the 1999 Sundance Film Festival, a New Yorker article by Mark Singer wondered whether the film would create sympathy for Leuchter and his fellow deniers. After all, here was a man who lost his wife and his livelihood in the name of a scientific quest. My feeling is that no filmmaker can be responsible for those unwilling or unable to view his film intelligently; anyone who leaves Mr. Death in agreement with Leuchter deserves to join him on the loony fringe.

What's scary about the film is the way Leuchter is perfectly respectable up until the time the neo-Nazis get their hooks into him.

Those who are appalled by the mass execution of human beings sometimes have no problem when the state executes them one at a time. You can even run for president after presiding over the busiest death row in U.S. history.

Early sequences in Mr. Death portray Leuchter as a humanitarian who protests that some electric chairs "cook the meat too much." He dreams of a "lethal injection machine" designed like a dentist's chair. The condemned could watch TV or listen to music while the poison works. What a lark. There is irony in the notion that many American states could lavish tax dollars on this man's inventions, only to put him out of work because of his unsavory connections. The ability of so many people to live comfortably with the idea of capital punishment is perhaps a clue to how so many Europeans were able to live with the idea of the Holocaust: Once you accept the notion that the state has the right to kill someone, and the right to define what is a capital crime, aren't you halfway there?

Like all of Errol Morris's films, Mr. Death provides us with no comfortable place to stand. We often leave his documentaries not sure if he liked his subjects or was ridiculing them. He doesn't make it easy for us with simple moral labels. Human beings, he argues, are fearsomely complex, and can get their minds around very strange ideas indeed. Sometimes it is possible to hate the sin and love the sinner. Poor Fred. What a dope, what a dupe, what a lonely, silly man.

Mumford ★ ★ ★ ½
R, 111 m., 1999

Loren Dean (Mumford), Hope Davis (Sofie Crisp), Jason Lee (Skip Skipperton), Alfre Woodard (Lily), Mary McDonnell (Althea Brockett), Ted Danson (Jeremy Brockett), Pruitt Taylor Vince (Henry Follett), Zooey Deschanel (Nessa Watkins), Martin Short (Lionel Dillard), David Paymer (Ernest Belbanco), Jane Adams (Phyllis Sheeler). Directed by Lawrence Kasdan and produced by Charles Okun and Kasdan. Screenplay by Kasdan.

In a little town right down the imaginary road from Pleasantville and Seaside (where Truman lives), a psychologist sets up shop. His name is Mumford. The town's name is Mumford. Mumford is also the name of a great writer on towns and cities, but any connections among these Mumfords are left unexplored. Folks are too busy living their lives to spare the time.

Mumford is so carefully visualized in Lawrence Kasdan's new film that you'd sort of like to live there. Yes, it has its problems, its troubled people, and lonely lives. But the arrival of Mumford (Loren Dean) seems to help. He rents a room from Lily (Alfre Woodard), who owns the coffee shop, and begins to listen to people's problems. Soon he is the most popular psychologist in town, and it's hard to say exactly why.

His dialogue, as written by Kasdan, is so circular and comforting that at times we almost feel we're on the couch ourselves. He rarely responds directly to anything, but on the other hand he doesn't use the old professional formulas, either; you won't hear him asking, "What do *you* think about that?" Instead, he has a kind of oblique conversational style. He angles off in new directions. He encourages lateral thinking. People provide a lot of their own answers.

Kasdan has been attracted over the years to movies with large casts; like Robert Altman, he wants to know everybody in town. His credits include *The Big Chill* and *Grand Canyon*, and *Mumford* is another ensemble piece. Sooner or later most everyone wanders across Doc Mumford's path.

We meet: Sofie Crisp (Hope Davis), so chronically fatigued she's afraid to lie down on the couch for fear she may never rise again; Skip Skipperton (Jason Lee), the local Bill Gates type, a zillionaire so lonely he has a secret lab trying to develop a bionic woman; Althea Brockett (Mary McDonnell), who shops till she drops, and her husband, Jeremy (Ted Danson), who treats her badly and himself very, very well; the local druggist Henry Follett (Pruitt Taylor Vince), his fantasies inflamed by pulp magazines; Nessa Watkins (Zooey Deschanel), a troubled teenager; and Lionel Dillard (Martin Short), an attorney who is fired as a patient by Mumford and wants to get even. There are also two other local shrinks, Ernest Belbanco (David Paymer) and Phyllis Sheeler (Jane Adams), who don't violently resent Mumford's success, but would be interested to learn any scandal about him.

During the course of this movie some of these people find they are made for one another, and others find they are made for better things than they have permitted themselves to try. The film makes us feel good, and we bathe in it. There's no big climax or crisis, and we can see the secrets coming a mile away, but this isn't a plot movie anyway. It's a feeling movie, a mood movie, an evocation of the kind of interaction we sometimes hunger for. In an age when nobody has time for anybody else, when people's pockets are buzzing with urgent electronic input, when the way to get someone's attention is to walk away and call them on a cell phone, *Mumford* is about a man who listens, and whose questions are nudges in the direction of healing.

This must read like a peculiar review. Does it make you want to see the movie? There are no earthshaking payoffs here. No dramatic astonishments, vile betrayals, or sexual surprises. Just the careful and loving creation of some characters it is mostly a pleasure to meet. And at its deepest level, profoundly down there below the surface, it is something more, I think: an expression of Kasdan's humanist longings, his wish that people would listen better and value each other more. It is the strangest thing, how this movie sneaks up and makes you feel a little better about yourself.

The Mummy ★ ★ ★
PG-13, 124 m., 1999

Brendan Fraser (Rick O'Connell), Rachel Weisz (Evelyn), John Hannah (Jonathan), Kevin J. O'Connor (Beni), Arnold Vosloo (Imhotep), Jonathan Hyde (Egyptologist), Oded Fehr (Ardeth Bay), Omid Djalili (Warden). Directed by Stephen Sommers and produced by James Jacks and Sean Daniel. Screenplay by Sommers.

There is within me an unslaked hunger for preposterous adventure movies. I resist the bad ones, but when a *Congo* or an *Anaconda* comes along, my heart leaps up and I cave in. *The Mummy* is a movie like that. There is hardly a thing I can say in its favor, except that I was cheered by nearly every minute of it. I cannot argue for the script, the direction, the acting, or even the mummy, but I can say that I was not bored and sometimes I was unreasonably pleased. There is a little immaturity stuck away in the crannies of even the most judicious of us, and we should treasure it.

This is a movie about a man who fooled around with the pharaoh's mistress and lived (and died, and lived again) to regret it. As his punishment he is "mummified alive," sealed inside a sarcophagus with thousands of flesh-eating beetles (which eat flesh "very slowly," we learn). Millennia pass. In the 1920s, a French foreign legionnaire named Rick meets a librarian named Evelyn, and joins with her and her brother in an unwise quest to find Hamunaptra, the City of the Dead. (Sample dialogue: "Are we talking about *the* Hamunaptra?") They get into a race with other fortune-hunters, who have heard of untold treasure buried beneath the sands, and meanwhile the descendants of the high priests, who have guarded the city for 3,000 years, move against them.

There is good reason not to disturb the mummy, named Imhotep. If he is brought back to life, he will "arise a walking disease," we learn, and unleash the ten proverbial plagues upon Egypt, of which in the course of the movie I counted locusts, fireballs from the sky, rivers running with blood, earthquakes, and flies. Also, of course, the flesh-eating beetles, although I was not certain whether they were a plague or came with the territory.

Brendan Fraser plays Rick, a low-rent Indiana Jones who single-handedly fights his way through a bewildering series of battles. Evie (Rachel Weisz) is too clumsy to be much help (in a delightful early scene, she knocks over one bookcase and the domino effect knocks over every single bookcase in the Museum of Antiquities). Her brother Jonathan (John Hannah) is a spoiled rich kid who specializes in the sorts of asides that butlers used to make. Arnold Vosloo plays Imhotep the mummy in the later scenes, after Imhotep has absorbed the inner organs of enough victims to reconstitute himself. In the earlier scenes, Imhotep is a ghastly special-effects creature who seems made of decomposed cardboard, and lets out a cloud of dust every time Rick slices him.

None of this has anything to do with the great horror classic *The Mummy* (1932), which starred Boris Karloff in a strangely poignant performance as a long-dead priest who returns to life and falls in love with the modern reincarnation of the woman he died for. The 1932 movie contains no violence to speak of; there's hardly any action, indeed, and the chills come through slow realizations (hey, did that mummy move?). This 1999 mummy does indeed mumble something about his feelings for Evie, who may be descended from the pharaoh's mistress on her mother's side. But the bass on his voice synthesizer was set to Rumble, and so I was not quite sure what he said. It sounded vaguely affectionate, in the way that a pit bull growling over a T-bone sounds affectionate, but how can Imhotep focus on rekindling a 3,000-year-old romance when he has ten plagues to unleash?

There's a lot of funny dialogue in the movie, of which my favorite is a line of Evie's after she hears a suspicious noise in the museum library: "Abdul? Mohammed? Bob?" I liked the Goldfinger paint job on the priests in ancient Thebes. And the way a beetle burrowed in through a guy's shoe and traveled through his body, a lump under his flesh, until it could dine on his brain. And the way characters were always reading the wrong pages of ancient books, and raising the dead by accident.

Look, art this isn't. Great trash, it isn't. Good trash, it is. It's not quite up there with *Anaconda,* but it's as much fun as *Congo* and *The Relic,* and it's better than *Species.* If those four titles are not intimately familiar to you, *The Mummy* might not be the place to start.

The Mummy Returns ★ ★
PG-13, 121 m., 2001

Brendan Fraser (Rick O'Connell), Rachel Weisz (Evelyn), John Hannah (Jonathan Carnahan), Arnold Vosloo (Imhotep), Adewale Akinnuoye-Agbaje (Lock-Nah), Freddie Boath (Alex O'Connell), Oded Fehr (Ardeth Bay), Patricia Velasquez (Anck-Su-Namun), The Rock (Scorpion King). Directed by Stephen Sommer and produced by Sean Daniel and James Jacks. Screenplay by Sommer.

It is a curiosity of movie action that too much of it can be boring. Imagine yourself on a roller coaster for two hours. After the first ten minutes, the thrills subside. The mistake of *The Mummy Returns* is to abandon the characters, and to use the plot only as a clothesline for special effects and action sequences. If it were not for references to *The Mummy* (1999), this sequel would hardly have a plot at all.

Nine years have passed. Brendan Fraser is back again as Egyptologist Rick O'Connell, and Rachel Weisz, the librarian he met in the first film, is now his wife; they have an eight-year-old son named Alex (Freddie Boath). Also back are John Hannah as the twitty brother-in-law Jonathan, and Arnold Vosloo as the mummy Imhotep, whose name sounds more than ever like an ancient Egyptian chain of pancake houses. Oded Fehr is the worried sage Ardeth Bay, who begins sentences ominously with, "It is written that . . ." until Rick finally snaps, "Where is all this written?"

A good question, since much of the story involves a magical pyramid of which it is written, "No one who has seen it has ever returned alive." That logically leads us to wonder who told them about it. But logic applied to this movie will drive you mad. So will any attempt to summarize the plot, so I will be content with various observations:

1. The ads give The Rock, the WWF star, equal billing with Fraser. This is bait-and-switch. To call his appearance a "cameo" would be stretching it. He appears briefly at the beginning of the movie, is transmuted into a kind of transparent skeletal wraith, and disappears until the end of the film, when he comes back as the dreaded Scorpion King. I am not sure, at the end, if we see the real Rock, or merely his face, connected to computer-generated effects (his scorpion is blown up to giant size, which has the unfortunate effect of making him look more like a lobster tail than a scorpion). I continue to believe The Rock has an acting career ahead of him, and after seeing this movie I believe it is still ahead of him.

2. Alex, the kid, adds a lot to the movie by acting just like a kid. I particularly enjoyed it when he was kidnapped by a fearsome adversary of his parents, chained, and taken on a long journey, during which he drove his captor crazy by incessantly asking, "Are we there yet?"

3. The dialogue, "You have started a chain reaction that could bring about the next Apocalypse" is fascinating. Apparently we missed the first Apocalypse, which does not speak well for it.

4. I have written before of the ability of movie characters to outrun fireballs. In *The Mummy Returns,* there is a more amazing feat. If the rising sun touches little Alex while he is wearing the magical bracelet, he will die (it is written). But Rick, carrying Alex in his arms, is able to outrace the sunrise; we see the line of sunlight moving on the ground right behind them. It is written by Eratosthenes that Earth is about 25,000 miles around, and since there are twenty-four hours in a day, Rick was running approximately 1,041 miles an hour.

5. One of the big action sequences involves a battle between two vast armies, which stretch as far as computer-generated effects can see. One army is human. The other army is made of countless creatures named Anubis that look like giant savage dogs that stand upright and run on their hind legs (it is not done well, but one is surprised to find it done at all). These armies clash in bloody swordplay. Each dog-creature, as it is killed, reverts to the desert sand from whence it sprang. Finally all the creatures are destroyed, and we see the victors standing around feeling victorious and wishing that high-fives had been invented. And we notice that *not one single member* of the victorious army is dead or even wounded. Pathetic, that thousands of years of ancient curses and spells could engender such an incompetent army of dog-sand-creatures.

6. Several readers have argued with the rule in *Ebert's Little Movie Glossary* that teaches us: "No good movie has ever featured a hot-air balloon." To be sure, there are exceptions, but *The Mummy Returns* is not one of them. Its hot-air balloon looks like the ship that sailed to Winken, Blinken, and Nod.

7. At one point the action returns to London, and we see Tower Bridge, the dome of St. Paul's, and Big Ben clustered closely together in one shot. This is no doubt to make it easy for the geographically challenged. Perhaps adding a few snapshots from Madonna's wedding would not have been too much. ☞

393

Muppets from Space ★ ★
G, 82 m., 1999

Dave Goelz (Gonzo), Jeffrey Tambor (K. Edgar Singer), Steve Whitmire (Kermit the Frog), Bill Barretta (Pepe the Prawn), Ray Liotta (Security Guard), Hulk Hogan (Man in Black), Jerry Nelson (Robin), Brian Henson (Dr. Phil Van Neuter), Kevin Clash (Clifford), Frank Oz (Miss Piggy). Directed by Tim Hill and produced by Brian Henson and Martin G. Baker. Screenplay by Jerry Juhl, Joseph Mazzarino, and Ken Kaufman.

The funniest scene in *Muppets from Space* is the first one, where Gonzo is refused a place on Noah's Ark because he is one of a kind. Then he wakes up and realizes it was all only a nightmare. But when it's later revealed that Gonzo is, in fact, an alien from outer space, stranded on our planet, we can sympathize with his feelings: Ever since the crash landing near Roswell, New Mexico, he's been alone and lonely, the odd man out, living in a Muppet boardinghouse. Poor guy (or whatever he is).

The new Muppets movie lacks the kind of excitement the first ones generated, maybe because Muppets have become a little dated except for younger viewers, maybe because the kinds of animals in the two *Babe* movies show such an advance in special effects that we almost wonder why the Muppeteers go to all that trouble to physically manipulate their creatures.

I know that's heresy. I know we're supposed to embrace and defend Muppets because they are real, or at least more real than digital creatures, and because their personalities are more important than their special effects. But somehow *Muppets from Space* seemed a little disconsolate, a little low in energy, as if the ship (or the ark) had sailed.

Maybe that's because the best of the Muppets don't star this time. Kermit is reduced to a hop-through, Miss Piggy is a TV journalist, and most of the big moments belong to Gonzo, the weird-nosed one, who moons about looking alienated and lonely and eats alphabet cereal that spells out messages for him, like "Watch the Sky."

His space people are returning for him, forcing him to choose between Muppets and his alien relatives. This alien visit to Earth excites the attention of a government agent (Jeffrey Tambor, who plays the announcer on *The Larry Sanders Show*), and there are nudges of satire in the direction of *Men in Black* (Hulk Hogan is a man in black), but after the excitement of the human/animal interaction in *Babe* and *Babe, Pig in the City*, I dunno: It's like we've been there, done that.

I feel guilty even writing those words. I recall the charm of the original *Muppet Movie*, when Kermit actually rode a bicycle and we all gasped. I suppose it seemed then that the Muppets could continue indefinitely, with their outsize personalities and effortless interaction with human characters. But now . . . well, maybe it's just this movie. Maybe *Muppets from Space* is just not very good, and they'll make a comeback. I hope so. Because I just don't seem to care much anymore. Sorry, Miss Piggy. Really sorry.

The Muse ★ ★ ★
PG-13, 97 m., 1999

Albert Brooks (Steven Phillips), Sharon Stone (Sarah), Andie MacDowell (Laura Phillips), Jeff Bridges (Jack Warrick), Wolfgang Puck (Himself), Jennifer Tilly (Herself), Lorenzo Lamas (Himself), Cybill Shepherd (Herself), Martin Scorsese (Himself), James Cameron (Himself). Directed by Albert Brooks and produced by Herb Nanas. Screenplay by Brooks and Monica Johnson.

The Muse opens with its hero winning a humanitarian award. "Daddy," his daughter asks at bedtime, "what exactly is a humanitarian?" "It's someone who's never won the Oscar," he tells her. That ability to snatch failure from the ashes of success is common to many of Albert Brooks's characters, and in *The Muse* he plays Steven Phillips, writer of "over seventeen movies," who is fired by his studio for having lost his "edge." This is a man who is all edge, but never mind: The Hollywood executive credo is, "I fire people, therefore I am."

Steven Phillips is a man with expenses. He needs income. In desperation he visits his friend Jack (Jeff Bridges), a writer who moves from one success to another. Just as he's arriving at Jack's house, he sees a good-looking blonde on her way out. Who can this be? Is Jack having an affair? Steven presses him until Jack finally confesses that the woman is his muse: "I met her at a party a couple of years ago. Rob Reiner introduced us."

Steven begs to be introduced to the muse. Jack relents. Her name is Sarah (Sharon Stone), and she doesn't come cheap. "Bring her a gift," Jack suggests. She likes things that come in those little blue Tiffany's boxes. Soon Steven has moved her into a $1,700 suite at the Four Seasons and is fielding her midnight phone calls complaining that room service won't bring her a Waldorf salad. When Steven's wife, Laura (Andie MacDowell), finds him at the supermarket buying for Sarah that product which no man needs for himself, he confesses everything. At first Laura suspects he's having an affair. Then she realizes he's telling the truth. She knows him too well: There's no way he would bring someone a Waldorf salad just to get sex. Soon Sarah is living in Jack's guest house and receiving visitors like James Cameron ("I don't see you going back in the water," she tells him).

There is desperation in all the best Albert Brooks characters; the precision in his speech barely masks anger and melancholy. As Steven Phillips, he is a man like many others in Hollywood who has stumbled into success and now is stumbling out of it, clueless in both directions. For him, perhaps, the muse is therapeutic: If he believes she's helping him, then she is. Sarah explains early on that she doesn't do any actual writing; she just hangs around, and interesting ideas occur to her clients. This is consistent with my own belief that the muse visits during the act of creation, not before.

There is, of course, the possibility that Sarah is not a Muse, not one of the nine daughters of Zeus, but simply another Hollywood female who likes the little blue boxes and has found a sweatless way to get them. She may work as a placebo. If you believe something will help you write, it will. Ask anyone who has signed up for a screenwriting seminar. Or ask Sarah's clients; in addition to Cameron, we get a series of funny cameos starring Martin Scorsese ("I'm thinking of a remake of *Raging Bull* with a thin and angry guy"), Rob Reiner ("Thanks for *The American President*!"), and Spago chef Wolfgang Puck (after Sarah inspires a new cookie recipe for Steven's wife, Laura and Wolfgang form a partnership).

The Muse was released two weeks after *Bowfinger*, Steve Martin's comedy about desperation in Hollywood. The two movies exist in Hollywoods that never meet. Bowfinger is a mongrel stealing scraps from the feast; Phillips is a man unwilling to push back from the table. *Bowfinger* uses physical comedy; *The Muse* depends on Brooks's sharp ear for dialogue. When the studio executive rejects his screenplay using what he describes as "a form that's not insulting: It's no good," Phillips asks, "What would the insulting form be?"

The movie is good but not great Brooks; not the equal of *Lost in America* or *Mother*, but smart, funny, and—edgy. And there's something fascinating about the way Brooks, as an actor, is ingratiating and hostile at the same time. He projects the feeling of a man trying to conceal his awareness that everyone around him is stupid, or mad. Like a grade school teacher he patiently tries to lead his enemies through their lessons, while they cheerfully frustrate him. There are days and even weeks when we all feel like Steven Phillips. The sneaky thing about this movie is its insinuation that the answer is not to find a muse, but to be one.

Music of the Heart ★ ★ ★
PG, 123 m., 1999

Meryl Streep (Roberta Guaspari), Angela Bassett (Janet Williams), Aidan Quinn (Brian Sinclair), Cloris Leachman (Assunta Guaspari), Jane Leeves (Dorothea von Haeften), Kieran Culkin (Lexi "Teen"), Michael Angarano (Nick "Young"), Gloria Estefan (Isabel Vasquez), Jay O. Sanders (Dan). Directed by Wes Craven and produced by Marianne Maddalena, Walter Scheuer, Allan Miller, and Susan Kaplan. Screenplay by Pamela Gray, based on the life story of Roberta Guaspari and inspired by the documentary *Small Wonders*.

Music of the Heart is based on the true story of a violin teacher named Roberta Guaspari, who created a high school music program more or less out of thin air in East Harlem, and eventually found herself and her students on the stage of Carnegie Hall. Most movies claiming to be based on fact pour on the melodrama, but this one basically just sticks to the real story, which has all the emotional wallop that's needed.

Meryl Streep stars as Guaspari, a mother of two whose husband leaves her. On her own, she has hard times in the job market; she's gift-wrapping presents in a department store one day when she's spotted by an old friend (Aidan Quinn) who knew her in her days as a gifted music student. He tells her about a high school that might have an opening, and soon Guaspari is trying to sell a reluctant principal (Angela Bassett) on what could be accomplished with fifty violins she just happens to have purchased cheap in Greece.

The principal doesn't think so. And, of course, the school has no funds anyway (think what our society might be like if the funds spent on high school sports were used to help kids access the humanities). But Guaspari is persistent, and establishes a music program despite predictable difficulties, including the obligatory mother who complains her children are being taught the music of "dead white men." (The mother is correct, but man, could those guys compose!)

The screenplay has the courage to go easy on the scenes involving movie romance. The Quinn character is disqualified as a candidate, and although another guy (Jay O. Sanders) comes along, this movie is not so much about romance as about practice, practice, practice. Ten years pass. The program has expanded to three schools, and is so popular kids enter a lottery to get into it. Then funds are cut, and the program is threatened. "Do you know anybody who works for the *New York Times*?" Guaspari thoughtfully asks a friend, and soon an article in the *Times* leads to a benefit concert at Carnegie Hall, with violinists Isaac Stern, Itzhak Perlman, and Arnold Steinhardt playing themselves.

This second half of the film feels almost like a documentary, and no wonder; there *was* a documentary about this same material (*Small Wonders*, 1996), unseen by me, and you can guess how Guaspari must have seemed like a natural for someone like Streep to play. The movie doesn't punch up the drama, but simply shows good people trying to work together and get something done. That's why it's so effective.

Meryl Streep is known for her mastery of accents; she may be the most versatile speaker in the movies. Here you might think she has no accent, unless you've heard her real speaking voice; then you realize that Guaspari's speaking style is no less a particular achievement than Streep's other accents. This is not Streep's voice, but someone else's—with a certain flat quality, as if later education and refinement came after a somewhat unsophisticated childhood.

The movie was directed by Wes Craven, known for his horror films (*Scream, A Nightmare on Elm Street*) and he may seem like a strange choice for this material. Not at all. He is in fact a cultured man who broke into movies doing horror and got stuck in the genre; he's been trying to fight his way free from studio typecasting for twenty years, and this movie shows that he can get Meryl Streep to Carnegie Hall just as easily as a phantom to the opera.

My Best Fiend ★ ★ ★
NO MPAA RATING, 95 m., 2000

A documentary directed by Werner Herzog and produced by Lucki Stipetic.

Werner Herzog made five films starring Klaus Kinski. Few other directors wanted to work with him more than once. Midway in their first film, *Aguirre, the Wrath of God* (1972), Kinski threatened to walk off the set, deep in the Amazon rain forest, and Herzog said he would shoot him dead if he did. Kinski claims in his autobiography that he had the gun, not Herzog. Herzog says that's a lie. Kinski describes Herzog in the book as a "nasty, sadistic, treacherous, cowardly creep." Herzog says in the film that Kinski knew his autobiography would not sell unless he said shocking things—so Herzog helped him look up vile words he could use in describing the director.

And so it goes on, almost a decade after Kinski's death, the unending love-hate relationship between the visionary German filmmaker and his muse and nemesis in five films. Herzog's new documentary, *My Best Fiend*, traces their history together. They had one of the most fruitful and troubled relationships of any director-actor team.

Together they made *Aguirre,* about a mad conquistador in the Peruvian jungle; *Fitzcarraldo* (1982), about a man who used block-and-tackle to pull a steamship from one Amazonian river system to another; *Nosferatu* (1979), inspired by Murnau's silent vampire classic; *Woyzeck* (1979), about a nineteenth-century army private who seems mad to others because he sees the world in his own alternative way; and *Cobra Verde* (1988), about a slave trader in Africa. All of their collaborations contain extraordinary images, but the sight in that one of Kinski running wild inside an army of naked, spear-carrying amazons may be the strangest.

Reviewing *Woyzeck,* I wrote: "It is almost impossible to imagine Kinski without Herzog; reflect that this 'unforgettable' actor made more than 170 films for other directors—and we can hardly remember a one." Consider, too, that their strange bond began long before Herzog stood behind a camera.

Herzog told me how they met. When he was twelve, he said, "I was playing in the courtyard of the building where we lived in Munich, and I looked up and saw this man striding past, and I knew at that moment that my destiny was to direct films and that he would be the actor." Kinski was known for his scorn of both films and acting, and claimed to choose projects entirely on the basis of how comfortable he would be on the location. Yet when Herzog summoned him to the rain forest for *Aguirre,* where he would have to march through the jungle wearing Spanish armor and end up on a sinking raft with gibbering monkeys, he accepted. Why? I asked him once, and he replied grimly: "It was my fate."

Herzog believes in shooting on location, arguing that specific places have a voodoo that penetrates the film. *Fitzcarraldo* could have been shot in comfort, not 900 miles up the Amazon, and with special effects and a model boat—but Herzog insisted on isolating his crew, and in hauling a real boat up a real hill. When engineers warned him the ropes would snap and cut everyone in two, he dismissed the engineers. That's all the more intriguing when you learn that Kinski was even more hated than Herzog on the location. In *My Best Fiend,* Herzog recalls that local Indians came to him with an offer to kill Kinski. "I needed Kinski for a few more shots, so I turned them

down," he says. "I have always regretted that I lost that opportunity."

He learned early about Kinski's towering rages. The actor actually lived for several months in the same flat with Herzog's family, and once locked himself in the bathroom for two days, screaming all the while, and reducing the porcelain fixtures "to grains the size of sand." Only once, on *Aguirre,* was he able to fully contain his anger in his character—perhaps because Aguirre was as mad as Kinski—and there he gave one of the great performances in the cinema. Herzog revisits the original locations, recalling fights they had and showing the specific scenes that were shot just afterward.

There must have been good times, too, although Herzog shows only one of them—a happy day at the Telluride Film Festival. *My Best Fiend* suffers a little by not having footage to cover more of Herzog's sharpest memories (Les Blank's legendary documentary *Burden of Dreams,* shot on location during *Fitzcarraldo,* shows the two men at each other's throats). But as a meditation by a director on an actor, it is unique; most show biz docs involve the ritual exchange of compliments. *My Best Fiend* is about two men who both wanted to be dominant, who both had all the answers, who were inseparably bound together in love and hate, and who created extraordinary work—while all the time each resented the other's contribution.

My Dog Skip ★ ★ ★
PG, 95 m., 2000

Frankie Muniz (Willie Morris), Diane Lane (Ellen Morris), Luke Wilson (Dink), Kevin Bacon (Jack Morris), Mark Beech (Army Buddy), Harry Connick Jr. (Narrator). Directed by Jay Russell and produced by Broderick Johnson and Andrew Kosove. Screenplay by Gail Gilchriest, based on the book by Willie Morris.

Don't trust any critic who writes about *My Dog Skip* without remembering his childhood dog. My dog was named Blackie. He was part cocker, part beagle, and he was my friend. The sweet thing about *My Dog Skip* is the way it understands the friendship between a kid and a dog. Dogs accomplish amazing things in the movies, but the best thing Skip does is look up at his master, eager to find out what they're gonna do next.

The movie is much elaborated from a memoir by Willie Morris, who grew up in Yazoo, on the Mississippi Delta, and went on to become the editor of *Harper's* magazine. Not everything in the movie actually happened. Its embroideries remind me of Huck Finn's comment about Tom Sawyer: "He told the truth, mainly. There was things which he stretched, but mainly he told the truth."

It is probably not true, for example, that young Willie (Frankie Muniz) volunteered Skip to become an army para-puppy. Oh, I believe Willie (and Skip) saw a newsreel about the brave dogs in our fighting forces. And I believe that Willie trained Skip to become what the newsreel calls a "Yankee Doodle doggy." What I don't believe is that any kid would send his dog away to war. Let him serve on the home front.

The movie is set in the summer of 1942. Willie is a lonely child. He's no good at sports, he doesn't make friends easily, and he has a standoffish relationship with his dad (Kevin Bacon), who lost a leg in the Spanish Civil War, "and a piece of his heart." Will's mom (Diane Lane) tries to make her child happy, but look at that birthday party she throws, where all the guests are old folks, and one of them gives him a bow tie. Will's "older and only friend" is Dink (Luke Wilson), a high school sports star, who lives next door and goes off to war before he can teach Will the secrets of the curveball.

Mom decides Will needs a dog. Dad is against it. "He needs a friend," Mom says, snatching the cigar out of Dad's mouth and puffing on it herself, as a Freudian signal of her takeover. She gives the dog to Will, and Will's life is changed forever. With Skippy, he runs all over town, and the fields outside of town, and other kids want to be his friend because he has a dog.

This is some dog. It knows everybody in town, and makes a daily stop at the butcher shop for a slice of bologna. When Will makes several errors in a baseball game, Skip runs onto the field to help Will. When Will, distraught, slaps his dog, I found to my amazement that I recoiled with dismay. That's when

I discovered how the movie had gotten to me. How I had shelved a movie critic's usual reserve and just started identifying with Will and Skip. I wasn't good at sports, either, and Blackie helped me make friends.

There's a subplot about moonshiners that isn't too convincing. I don't know why they'd need to hide their booze in a cemetery crypt, and I wasn't convinced when that led to a crisis for Skip at the end. But I did remember riding my bike all over the neighborhood once when Blackie ran away, calling out his name again and again as dusk fell, and the movie has that right.

Another subplot has to do with Dink, who comes back from the war in a different mood than when he left, and tells Will, "It isn't the dying that's scary—it's the killing." And there's a scene where Will sees a deer die before his eyes. We understand that in every childhood there are lessons burned into your memory. They shape you. In Willie Morris's case, they guided him out of Yazoo and to Oxford on a Rhodes scholarship, and then to New York and a literary career. But he never forgot Skip.

A movie like this falls outside ordinary critical language. Is it good or bad? Is there too much melodrama? I don't have any idea. It triggered too many thoughts of my own for me to have much attention left over for footnotes. I realize, for example, that the movie doesn't deal in any substantial way with the racial situation in Mississippi in 1942, and I know that Will's dad undergoes a rather miraculous transformation, and that Dink seems less like a neighbor than like a symbol of lost innocence. I know those things, but they don't seem relevant to the actual experience of this movie. If there was ever a day or even a minute when your dog was not your best but your only friend, you'll see what I mean.

My Favorite Martian ★ ★
PG, 93 m., 1999

Christopher Lloyd (Uncle Martin), Jeff Daniels (Tim O'Hara), Elizabeth Hurley (Brace Channing), Daryl Hannah (Lizzie), Wallace Shawn (Coleye), Christine Ebersole (Mrs. Brown), Michael Lerner (Mr. Channing), Ray Walston (Armitan). Directed by Donald Petrie and produced by Robert Shapiro, Jerry

Leider, and Mark Toberoff. Screenplay by
Sherri Stoner and Deanna Oliver.

My Favorite Martian is slapstick and silliness,
wild sight gags and a hyped-up acting style.
The Marx Brothers would have been at home
here. The movie is clever in its visuals, labored
in its audios, and noisy enough to entertain
kids up to a certain age. What age? Low double
digits, I'd say.

It stars Jeff Daniels, a seasoned straight man
(Dumb and Dumber), as a TV producer named
Tim. He sees a flying saucer crash and is soon
adopted by its occupant, a Martian named, for
purposes of the human appearance he assumes, Uncle Martin. The Martian is played
by Christopher Lloyd with zestful looniness,
and the Martian's space suit, named Zoot, becomes a character in its own right. Both Uncle
Martin and Zoot are capable of instant shape-
shifting, and depending on what color of extraterrestrial gumball they're chewing, Martin
(and the humans) can turn into a variety of
monsters.

There's a love story in the frenzy. As the film
opens, Tim is in love with his on-air talent, a
reporter named Brace (Elizabeth Hurley). By
the end, he has come to realize that Lizzie
(Daryl Hannah), his technician, is a better
choice in every way. All of this is decided at
breakneck speed, and at one point Lizzie even
turns into a bug-eyed monster and entirely
devours a bad guy. (Soon after, defying one of
Newton's laws, I'm not sure which one, she
turns back into a lithesome young woman
who has not put on any weight.)

The villains are all government scientists,
led by Coleye (pronounced "coli," as in "e coli"),
a bureaucrat obsessed with aliens. Played by
Wallace Shawn, who often looks as if he is
about to do something immoral with a clipboard, he desperately chases Tim and Uncle
Martin because he wants to prove there is intelligent life on other planets. Uncle Martin,
on the other hand, only wants to lie low, be
friends with Tim and Lizzie, repair his spaceship, and go home. Then he discovers ice cream,
and all he wants to do is eat ice cream.

There are some good moments in *My Favorite Martian,* and the best comes right at the
top, where we see one of NASA's Martian ex-
ploratory vehicles roll up to a rock, stop, and

run out of juice just before it would have
stumbled upon an amazing sight. I also liked
the gyrations of Zoot the suit, which develops
an addiction to washing machines. And the
scene where Martin chug-a-lugs a lava lamp. I
also appreciated the information that a space
probe contained the ashes of Jerry Garcia.

It looks as if everyone who made this film
had a lot of fun. Spirits and energy are high,
mugging is permitted, dialogue is rapid-fire,
nobody walks if they can run. As kids' entertainment, it's like a live-action cartoon, and I
can recommend it on that level, although not
on a more ambitious plane. I came upon the
movie just a few days after seeing *Children of
Heaven,* a children's film from Iran that has
the power to absorb and teach any child, and I
found *My Favorite Martian* noisy and superficial by comparison. (But of *course* it's noisy
and superficial. That's its mission. I keep forgetting.)

My Life So Far ★ ★ ★
PG-13, 92 m., 1999

Colin Firth (Edward), Rosemary Harris (Gamma),
Irene Jacob (Heloise), Mary Elizabeth
Mastrantonio (Moira), Malcolm McDowell
(Uncle Morris), Robert Norman (Fraser), Tcheky
Karyo (Gabriel Chenoux), Kelly MacDonald
(Elspeth). Directed by Hugh Hudson and
produced by David Puttnam and Steve Norris.
Screenplay by Simon Donald, based on the
book *Son of Adam* by Sir Denis Forman.

It's been said that the most pleasant of all lives
were lived in the great British country houses
in the years between the wars—for those who
lived there, of course. The rest of us can only
enviously imagine those days as idealized in
the works of P. G. Wodehouse, whose characters occupy an endless summer of dotty earls,
alcoholic younger brothers, eccentric inven-
tors, ferocious aunts, hopeful suitors, and prize-
winning pigs. Their household staff functions
not as servants but as keepers.

My Life So Far, set in the late 1920s on an
estate near Argyle, Scotland, is based on the
memoirs of a real person—Sir Denis Forman,
director of the Royal Opera House. I've always
thought of the Wodehouse universe as essentially a fantasy, but perhaps not. Sir Denis's

childhood at times seems to be taking place at Plum's Blandings Castle, where Lord Emsworth doted on his blue-ribbon pig, the Empress of Blandings.

The hero of this film, a ten-year-old named Fraser Pettigrew (Robert Norman), grows up in Kiloran House, where his father, Edward (Colin Firth), invents airships and paddleboats, and commits a large part of the family fortune to the cultivation of sphagnum moss (which is, he boasts, "better than cotton wool for wounds"). Fraser's mother, Moira (Mary Elizabeth Mastrantonio), smiles indulgently and a little wearily upon her husband the enthusiast.

Her own mother (Rosemary Harris), called "Gamma" by the kids, owns the estate, which Edward hopes she will leave to him. But there is another claimant—Uncle Morris (Malcolm McDowell), Moira's brother, a hard-boiled businessman who arrives one day with his new French wife, Heloise (Irene Jacob). Soon both Fraser and (alas) his father are in love with the young woman, causing complications in Eden.

My Life So Far, directed by Hugh Hudson *(Chariots of Fire)*, is not plot-driven, and even a crisis (like the opening scene where the infant Fraser is happily climbing on the roof) is handled with a certain detachment. These are characters for whom tone is more important than content; they live their lives according to the teaching of Billy Crystal's Hernando: "It is better to look good than to feel good."

The household contains a large family, many servants, and a ceaseless stream of visitors (including Tcheky Karyo as a legendary pilot named "The Emperor of the Air"). The big scenes play out at dinner or in the drawing room before an audience of most of the other characters; these lives are so public they almost take place onstage. The reason modern American conversation has declined so sadly is because most of us no longer have fireplaces to stand before while declaiming epigrams, or dinner parties for eighteen at which precocious youngsters can suggest that the family finances could be improved if the women sold themselves into prostitution.

That is indeed a suggestion brightly made by young Fraser, who has found his father's secret library and devoured books he does not

quite understand. Meanwhile, darker currents gather as his father and his uncle jostle for position. And his father, who has seemed so carefree and steadfast for the first half of the movie, actually seems prepared to sacrifice everything—family, children, estate—for the love of Heloise, who is not even a femme fatale but only a pleasant sweetheart.

Did worlds like this exist? Yes, until death duties and taxes forced the old families to earn their own livings, while the great houses were opened to tourists and the servant quarters became tea shops. Today there are people with as much money or more, but they have had to be smart enough to earn it; they may occupy houses like this, but they lack the dreamy naïveté to enchant them. It has been a melancholy progression from the Empress of Blandings to pork bellies. Sir Denis Forman may have his knighthood and the Royal Opera House to run, but there is a poignancy that colors every scene of *My Life So Far.* He is homesick for Kiloran. So am I, and I never even lived there.

My Name Is Joe ★ ★ ★ ½
R, 108 m., 1999

Peter Mullan (Joe), Louise Goodall (Sarah), Gary Lewis (Shanks), Lorraine McIntosh (Maggie), David McKay (Liam), Anne-Marie Kennedy (Sabine), David Hayman (McGowan), Scott Hannah (Scott), David Peacock (Hooligan). Directed by Ken Loach and produced by Rebecca O'Brien. Screenplay by Paul Laverty.

His name is Joe, and he's an alcoholic. He's been sober for only ten months, and although AA advises against romance in the first year of recovery, Joe falls in love with a nurse named Sarah. She's a social worker who has seen a lot of guys like Joe, but there's something about him—a tenderness, a caring—that touches her.

They're both wounded and cautious, but a romance slowly grows at moments like the one where he invites her in for tea and plays some classical music. He explains: In his drinking days he stole some cassettes and sold them, but the classical tape didn't sell. One night he got drunk and played it, and "it was just lovely."

Joe is played by Peter Mullan, who won the 1998 Best Actor Award at Cannes. He's a compact, ginger-haired man around forty, who moves with a physical efficiency that suggests he's focused and impatient. He looks a little like Paul Newman, with the same slender energy. He keeps busy. He doesn't have work, but he manages a soccer team and picks up the members in a city van, fussing over them like a brood hen. He wears a windbreaker and sneakers, and is always in a hurry. And he takes his newfound sobriety seriously (the opening scene shows him telling his story at an AA meeting).

Joe lives in a rough neighborhood of Glasgow, where drugs and crime are a way of life. One of his friends is Liam (David McKay), a kid who did time for drugs. Liam's wife, Sabine (Anne-Marie Kennedy), dealt while Liam was inside, but now he's out and, Joe thinks, clean and sober. But it's not that simple. Sabine is using, and they're into the local druglord, McGowan, for a total of 2,000 pounds. McGowan's thugs have offered to break Liam's legs, and nobody thinks they're kidding.

My Name Is Joe takes these elements and puts them together into a story that forces Joe to choose between the twelve steps of AA and the harder, more painful steps he learned on the street. In theory, a recovering alcoholic doesn't allow himself anywhere near drink or drugs. But McGowan offers Joe a deal: If he makes two trips up north and drives back cars containing drugs, Liam's debt will be forgotten. Why doesn't McGowan simply have Liam do this? Because McGowan isn't dumb. He knows Liam can't be trusted—and he also enjoys, perhaps, compromising a community leader who no longer adorns McGowan's pub.

The film is another one of Ken Loach's tales of working-class life; like *Riff-Raff,* it is told in a regional British accent that's so thick it has been subtitled. (I understood most of it when I saw it without subtitles in Cannes, but I have to say they help.) His screenplay is ingenious in bringing together the romance, the crime elements, and the challenge of being sober in a community where drink and drugs provide the primary pastime (and employment).

The romance is all the more absorbing because it's between two streetwise people in early middle age who have no illusions. The nurse, Sarah, is played by Louise Goodall with a careworn face but a quick smile; she's had to harden herself against the sad cases she encounters as a community health worker, but she's able to be moved by Joe's spirit and sincerity.

I have made the film sound too depressing, perhaps. It is about depressing events, but its spirit is lively, and there's a lot of humor wedged here and there, including a walk-on for a bagpiper who knows three songs, plays them, and then peddles shortbread to tourists. And there's humor involving the soccer team, their bad luck and their uniforms.

Often with a film like this you think you know how it has to end. The ending of *My Name Is Joe* left me stunned. I've rarely seen a film where the conclusion is so unexpected, and yet, in its own way, so logical, and so inevitable.

My Son the Fanatic ★ ★ ★ ½
R, 86 m., 1999

Om Puri (Parvez), Rachel Griffiths (Bettina), Akbar Kurtha (Farid), Stellan Skarsgard (Schitz), Gopi Desai (Minoo), Bhasker Patel (The Maulvi), Harish Patel (Fizzy), Sarah Jane Potts (Madeleine), Judi Jones (Mrs. Fingerhut), Geoffrey Bateman (Inspector Fingerhut). Directed by Udayan Prasad and produced by Chris Curling. Screenplay by Hanif Kureishi.

My Son the Fanatic tells the story of a taxi driver of Pakistani origins, who for many years has lived in the British midlands. He works at night to make better money, and finds himself giving rides to hookers and their clients—and sometimes helping them to meet one another. There is one hooker he rather likes, because she sees him as an individual, something few other people in his life seem able to do.

The driver, whose name is Parvez, is played by Om Puri, an actor of great humor and wisdom, whose weathered face can be tough and sad. He shares an uneventful marriage with his wife, Minoo (Gopi Desai), who regards him with mute but unending disapproval. Their lives are briefly brightened when their son, Farid (Akbar Kurtha), is engaged to the daughter of the local police inspector, but then Farid breaks it off ("Couldn't you see how they

401

looked at you?" he asks his father, after a visit to the girl's parents). The son turns to fundamentalism, and is soon listening to religious tapes, wearing a costume to set himself apart from others, and asking to move a visiting guru into Parvez's home.

Real life for Parvez takes place in his cab, and we meet Bettina (Rachel Griffiths), the tough, realistic hooker he has a soft spot for. He recommends her to a visiting German businessman (Stellan Skarsgard), who has low tastes and a lot of money and treats Bettina in ways that make Parvez wince. Parvez spends long hours at work, and at home has carved out a little space in the basement that he can call his own—playing jazz records, drinking Scotch, listening to the voices upstairs of the guru and his followers, discussing their "mad ideas."

There is, of course, racial discrimination in England (I sometimes wonder if North America, for all our faults, is not the most successful multiracial society on Earth). There's an ugly scene in a nightclub, where Parvez has taken Bettina and the German, and is singled out after a comic shines a spotlight on him. And another scene, ugly in a quieter way, when Parvez takes Bettina to the big restaurant operated by his old friend Fizzy, who immigrated from Pakistan with him. Fizzy does not approve of Parvez bringing any woman not his wife (and especially not this woman) into the restaurant, and officiously sets a table for them in an empty storeroom.

The film was written by Hanif Kureishi, the novelist whose screen credits include *My Beautiful Launderette*. His stories often involve children in rebellion against the values of their parents, but here he turns the tables: It is Parvez who lives like a teenager, staying out late and cherishing his favorite albums in the basement, and his son who occupies the upstairs and preaches conservatism and religion. Parvez is not a rebel, just a realist who asks himself, "Is this it for me? To sit behind the wheel of a cab for the rest of my life and never a sexual touch?" When Bettina kisses him, says she can't remember the last time she kissed a man, and quietly reveals that her real name is Sandra, we believe them as a couple, however unlikely: In a lonely and cold world, they see each other's need.

Om Puri's performance is based on the substantial strength of his physical presence, and on his clear-sighted view of his world as an exile. When the guru comes to Parvez with requests that the son would be shocked to hear, he is not surprised: "You are so patriotic about Pakistan," he tells the guru. "That is always a sign of imminent departure." He instinctively suspects any religion, even his own, when it operates as a tribe: He is tolerant in his very bones, and dislikes religions that use costumes, fear, and peer pressure to set their members aside from the mainstream. In accepting the hooker, he accepts all outcasts and pariahs, judging them on their characters rather than their affiliations.

The movie contains a lot of humor, much of it generated by the creative differences between standard English and its variations in India and Pakistan. Parvez has a knack for putting a slight satirical spin on a phrase by not quite getting it right. When the police inspector is late to their meeting, he observes, "The law never sleeps at night!" When a man smokes in his taxi: "Please, sir! No smoking indoor! Smell is deafening."

There is humor, too, in his concern about his son's strange behavior. At first he suspects drugs rather than religion, and asks Bettina to write him out a list of the danger signals of addiction. When he tries the questions out on his son, the boy groans, "I can always tell when you have been reading *Daily Express*."

The film's director, Udayan Prasad, knows, as Kureishi does, that there are no simple solutions to the dilemmas of their story. For that reason, it is more than usually important to sit through the closing credits. The credits roll over a long shot that is not just a closing decoration, but really the resolution of the whole story, such as it is. In a way we are all exiles. In a way there is never going to be any home.

Mystery, Alaska ★ ★ ½

R, 118 m., 1999

Russell Crowe (John Biebe), Hank Azaria (Charles Danner), Mary McCormack (Donna Biebe), Burt Reynolds (Judge Walter Burns), Colm Meaney (Mayor Scott Pitcher), Lolita Davidovich (Mary Jane Pitcher), Maury Chaykin (Bailey Pruitt), Ron Eldard ("Skank" Marden).

Directed by Jay Roach and produced by David E. Kelley and Howard Baldwin. Screenplay by Kelley and Sean O'Byrne.

Mystery, Alaska is sweet, pleasant, low-key, inoffensive, and unnecessary. It sticks up for underdogs, nice people, and small towns, and doesn't like big corporations, adulterers, TV producers, and New Yorkers in general. It contains not only a big game with a thrilling finish, but also a courtroom scene, a funeral scene, an innocent teenage sex scene, a change-of-heart scene, and a lot of scenery. No one falls through the ice and almost drowns, but we can't have everything.

The movie assembles a large cast in Mystery, Alaska, a fictional town where since time immemorial life has revolved around the Saturday Game, a hockey match played on black pond ice by local boys and men, who take it very seriously indeed. A former town resident (Hank Azaria) writes an article for *Sports Illustrated* about what fierce and brilliant hockey players they all are, and soon a sports network is promoting an exhibition game between the local team and the New York Rangers.

But this is not merely a hockey movie, leading up to the big game. It has many things on its mind. A foulmouthed representative for a big retail chain comes to town and gets shot in the foot by a general-store owner. The mayor's wife fools around with one of the hockey players. A veteran team member gets kicked upstairs to the coaching job to make room for a teenage phenom. There are scenes of young and middle-aged love, visits from high-powered media stars, and a drunken driving scene involving a Zamboni.

So cluttered is the plot that Burt Reynolds, sporting a Mephistophelian beard and a black overcoat he didn't get from Eddie Bauer, plays not only the local judge but also a strict and troubled husband and father, a former hockey coach who returns to the job, and a spoilsport who turns into a good guy. Since he gets only one big scene for some of these manifestations, the screenplay is like a test of versatility.

The film was written by David E. Kelley, one of the most successful writer-producers in TV today (*Ally McBeal*), and Sean O'Byrne. They like lots of characters. Russell Crowe is the town sheriff and aging hockey star; Mary Mc-

Cormack is his sweet wife; Maury Chaykin is the local attorney; Lolita Davidovich is married to the mayor (Colm Meaney); Ron Eldard is "Skank," the local ladies' man; Judith Ivey is the judge's wife and Rachel Wilson is his daughter; Ryan Northcutt is Stevie, her boyfriend, the speed demon on ice. Mike Myers has fun with a Canadian accent and word choices as a TV color commentator; no doubt he was recruited by the director, Jay Roach, who made the *Austin Powers* movies. Hockey legends Doug McLeod, Phil Esposito, and Jim Fox are also TV announcers. I will not reveal what celebrity they recruit to sing the "Star-Spangled Banner," or what he does for an encore, because that sequence is just about perfect.

All of these people are awfully nice. I don't know how they got an R rating for their movie, which seems pretty PG-13 to me. They have a fine little village there, and darned if I wasn't rooting for the home team in the big game. This is not a bad movie so much as a meandering one, lacking in dramatic tension because no one really turns out to be a villain.

I don't require that a sports movie end when the outcome of the big game is decided, but neither do I recommend that it linger while the locals and visitors say good-bye to one another, tidy up every plot strand, and demonstrate that their hearts are in the right place. I do, however, think this same cast, in this same town, could metamorphose into an entertaining sitcom. It almost feels as if they metamorphosed out of one.

Mystery Men ★ ★
PG-13, 111 m., 1999

Geoffrey Rush (Casanova Frankenstein), Greg Kinnear (Captain Amazing), Hank Azaria (Blue Raja), Janeane Garofalo (Bowler), William H. Macy (Shoveler), Kel Mitchell (Invisible Boy), Paul Reubens (Spleen), Ben Stiller (Furious), Lena Olin (Dr. Annabel Leek), Wes Studi (Sphinx), Ricky Jay (Publicist). Directed by Kinka Usher and produced by Lawrence Gordon, Mike Richardson, and Lloyd Levin. Screenplay by Neil Cuthbert, based on the Dark Horse Comic Book Series created by Bob Burden.

Mystery Men has moments of brilliance waving their arms to attract attention in a sea of dreck. It's a long, shapeless, undisciplined mess, and every once in a while it generates a big laugh. Since many of the laughs seem totally in the character of the actors who get them, they play like ad libs—as if we're hearing asides to the audience.

The premise: Captain Amazing (Greg Kinnear) is the top-rated superhero in Champion City, a special-effects metropolis made of skyscrapers, air buses, and dirigibles. He wears sponsor badges on his leather suit (Ray-O-Vac, Pennzoil) like Indy 500 drivers, but the sponsors are growing restless because his recent exploits are tired and dumb. Consulting with his publicist (Ricky Jay), he decides to spring his archenemy from jail. Maybe Casanova Frankenstein (Geoffrey Rush) can improve his Q rating by inspiring more colorful adventures.

The problem with this strategy is that Casanova is smart and the Captain is dumb, and soon Amazing is the villain's captive. That makes an opening for second-string superheroes to try to rescue Amazing and enhance their own reputations. The B team includes the Blue Raja (Hank Azaria), who hurls forks and spoons with amazing strength; Mr. Furious (Ben Stiller), who gets bad when he gets mad; and the Shoveler (William H. Macy), who whacks people with a spade. They're joined by new hopefuls, including the Spleen (Paul Reubens), whose weapon is voluminous flatulence; the Bowler (Janeane Garofalo), whose father's skull is inside her transparent bowling ball; Invisible Boy (Kel Mitchell), whose invisibility has to be taken mostly on trust, since you can't see if he's really there; and the Sphinx (Wes Studi), whose sayings make the Psychic Friends Network look deep.

All of these characters are hurled into elaborate special-effects scenes, where they get into frenetic human traffic jams. Comedy depends on timing, and chaos is its enemy. We see noisy comic book battles of little consequence, and finally we weary: This isn't entertainment; it's an f/x demo reel.

And yet the movie has its moments. I liked William H. Macy's version of Henry V's speech on the eve of battle ("We few . . .") and his portentous line, "We've got a blind date with Destiny, and it looks like she ordered the lobster." And a lot of Janeane Garofalo's lines, as when she says: "I would like to dedicate my victory to supporters of local music and those who seek out independent films." When the smoke clears, her character is ready to retire: "Okay, now I'm going back to graduate school; that was the agreement." We share her relief.

N

Never Been Kissed ★ ★ ★
PG-13, 107 m., 1999

Drew Barrymore (Josie Geller), David Arquette (Rob Geller), Michael Vartan (Sam Coulson), Molly Shannon (Anita), Leelee Sobieski (Aldys), John C. Reilly (Gus), Garry Marshall (Rigfort), Sean Whalen (Merkin). Directed by Raja Gosnell and produced by Sandy Isaac and Nancy Juvonen. Screenplay by Abby Kohn and Marc Silverstein.

Never Been Kissed stars Drew Barrymore as a copy editor for that excellent newspaper the *Chicago Sun-Times*. I recommend its use as a recruiting film—not because it offers a realistic view of journalistic life, but because who wouldn't want to meet a copy editor like Barrymore? Even when she's explaining the difference between "interoffice" and "intraoffice," she's a charmer. The movie's screenplay is contrived and not blindingly original, but Barrymore illuminates it with sunniness and creates a lovable character. I think this is what's known as star power.

She plays a twenty-five-year-old named Josie Geller who, despite a few unhappy early experiences with spit-swapping, has indeed never *really* been kissed. At the paper, she issues copyediting edicts while hiding behind a mousy brown hairdo and a wardrobe inspired by mudslides. Her editor, played as subtly as one of the Three Stooges by Garry Marshall, likes to pound the conference table with a bat while conducting editorial meetings; he wants an undercover series on life in high school and assigns Josie because she looks young enough.

That sets up Josie's chance to return to high school and get it right. The first time around, she was known as "Josie Grossie," an ugly duckling with braces on her teeth, hair in her eyes, baby fat, and pimples. Barrymore does a surprisingly convincing job of conveying this insecure lump of unpopularity; it's one of the reasons we develop such sympathy for Josie.

Josie borrows a car from her brother Rob (David Arquette), a once-promising baseball player who now works in a store that's a cross between Kinko's and Trader Vic's. She adopts a new blond hairstyle and gets rid of the glasses. But her first day on her secret assignment gets off to the wrong start, thanks to a wardrobe (white jeans and a gigantic feather boa) that might have been Cruella DeVil's teenage costume. The popular girls mock her, but she's befriended by Aldys (Leelee Sobieski), leader of the smart kids: "How are you at calculus? How would you like to join the Denominators?" That's the math club, with matching sweatshirts.

Josie's unpopularity reaches such a height that her car is deposited by pranksters in the middle of the football field. Rob analyzes the situation and says she needs to be certified as acceptable by a popular kid. What kid? Rob himself. He enrolls in high school and is popular by lunchtime, after winning a coleslaw-eating contest. Following his example, the students accept Josie, while Rob reawakens his fantasy of playing for a state championship baseball team.

The title *Never Been Kissed* gives us reason to hope that Josie will, sooner or later, be kissed. Soon we have reason to believe that the kisser may be Mr. Coulson (Michael Vartan), the English teacher, and of course the taboo against student-teacher relationships adds spice to this possibility. Meanwhile, Josie's adventures in high school are monitored at the *Sun-Times* through a remarkable invention, a brooch pin that contains a miniature TV camera and transmits everything she sees back to the office. We do not actually have such technology at the *Sun-Times*, and thank heavens, or my editors would have had to suffer through *Baby Geniuses*.

The story develops along a familiar arc. Josie has flashbacks to her horrible high school memories, but this time around, she flowers. Unspoken romance blooms with Mr. Coulson. Comic relief comes from Josie's friend Anita (Molly Shannon), who is mistaken for a high school sex counselor and offers advice startling in its fervor. Alas, Josie gets scooped on a story about the local teenage hangout, and her editor bangs the conference table some more. We are left to marvel at the portrait of Chicago journalism in both this movie and *Message in a Bottle*, which had Robin Wright

Penn as a researcher at the *Tribune*. Apparently at both papers the way to get a big salary and your own office is to devote thousands of dollars and weeks of time to an assignment where you hardly ever write anything.

Never Been Kissed is not deep or sophisticated, but it's funny and bighearted and it wins us over. The credit goes to Barrymore. In this movie and *Ever After* (and in *The Wedding Singer*, where I liked her a lot more than the movie), she emerges as a real star—an actor whose personality and charisma are the real subject of the story. *Never Been Kissed* ends in a scene that, in any other movie, I would have hooted at. Without revealing it, I'll identify it as the five-minute wait. This scene is so contrived and artificial it could be subtitled "Shameless Audience Manipulation." But you know what? Because the wait involved Barrymore, I actually cared. Yes, I did.

The Next Best Thing ★
PG-13, 110 m., 2000

Rupert Everett (Robert), Madonna (Abbie), Benjamin Bratt (Ben), Michael Vartan (Kevin), Malcolm Stumpf (Sam), Neil Patrick Harris (David), Illeana Douglas (Elizabeth Ryder), Josef Sommer (Richard Whittaker), Lynn Redgrave (Helen Whittaker). Directed by John Schlesinger and produced by Tom Rosenberg, Leslie Dixon, and Linne Radmin. Screenplay by Thomas Ropelewski.

The Next Best Thing is a garage sale of gay issues, harnessed to a plot as exhausted as a junk man's horse. There are times when the characters don't know if they're living their lives or enacting edifying little dramas for an educational film. The screenplay's so evenhanded it has *no* likable characters, either gay or straight; after seeing this film, I wanted to move to Garry Shandling's world in *What Planet Are You From?* where nobody has sex.

Not that anybody has a lot of sex in this PG-13 film. The story hinges on a murky alcoholic night spent by Abbie (Madonna) and her gay best friend Robert (Rupert Everett). They were both in drunken blackouts, although of course by the next morning they're able to discuss their blackouts with wit and style, unlike your average person, who would be puking.

Abbie gets pregnant and decides to have the baby, and Robert announces he will be a live-in father to the child, although he doesn't go so far as to become a husband to its mother.

Both Abbie and Robert are right up-to-date when it comes to sexual open-mindedness. Robert still dates, and Abbie's okay with that, although when Abbie meets a guy named Ben (Benjamin Bratt), Robert turns into a green-eyed monster. That's because Ben wants to marry Abbie and move to New York, and where would that leave Robert? If you think this movie, which begins as a sexual comedy, is going to end up as a stultifying docudrama about child custody, with big courtroom scenes before the obligatory stern black female judge, you are no more than ordinarily prescient.

The movie's problem is that it sees every side of all issues. It sides with Robert's need to be a father, and Benjamin's need to be a husband and lover, and Abbie's need to have a best friend, a husband, a lover, a son, and a lawyer. Luckily there is plenty of money for all of this, because Abbie is a yoga instructor and Robert is a gardener, and we know what piles of money you can make in those jobs, especially in the movies. I wish the film had scaled its lifestyles to the realities of service industry workers, instead of having the characters live in the kinds of places where they can dance around the living room to (I am not kidding) Fred Astaire's "Steppin' Out With My Baby" and have catered backyard birthday parties that I clock at $10,000, easy.

In describing the plot, I've deliberately left out two or three twists that had me stifling groans of disbelief. It's not that they're implausible; it's that they're not necessary. Any movie is bankrupt anyway when it depends on Perry Mason–style, last-minute, unexpected courtroom appearances to solve what should be an emotional choice.

Rupert Everett, "openly gay," as they say, must have had to grit his teeth to get through some of his scenes. Consider a sequence where, as Abbie's best friend, he is delegated to pick up her house keys after she breaks up with her early boyfriend, Kevin ("I want to date less complicated women," Kevin tells her). Kevin is a record producer, and we see him mixing the tracks for a rap group when Robert swishes in and pretends to be his ex-lover, while there are lots of yuks from the homophobic black rappers. Give the scene credit: At least it's not politically correct.

Madonna never emerges as a plausible human being in the movie; she's more like a spokesperson for a video on alternative parenting lifestyles. She begins the movie with a quasi-British accent, but by the halfway mark we get line readings like "we can be in each other's lifes" (a Brit, and indeed many an American, would say "lives").

This and other details should have been noticed by the director, John Schlesinger, whose career has included *Midnight Cowboy, Sunday Bloody Sunday, The Falcon and the Snowman, Madame Sousatzka,* and now . . . this?

Watching the movie, I asked myself why so many movies with homosexuals feel they need to be about homosexuality. Why can't a movie just get over it? I submit as evidence the magical film *Wonder Boys,* in which the homosexuality of the character played by Robert Downey Jr. is completely absorbed into the much larger notion of who he is as a person. Nobody staggers backward and gasps out that his character is gay, because of course he's gay and everybody has known that for a long time and, hey, some people *are* gay, y'know? Watching *The Next Best Thing,* we suspect that if sexuality were banned as a topic of conversation, Abbie and Robert would be reduced to trading yoga and gardening tips.

Nico and Dani ★ ★ ★

NO MPAA RATING, 90 m., 2001

Fernando Ramallo (Dani), Jordi Vilches (Nico), Marieta Orozco (Elena), Esther Nubiola (Berta), Chisco Amado (Julian), Ana Gracia (Sonia), Myriam Mezieres (Marianne). Directed by Cesc Gay and produced by Marta Esteban and Gerardo Herrero. Screenplay by Gay and Tomas Aragay, based on the play *Krampack* by Jordi Sanchez.

Nico and Dani considers ten days in the lives of two teenage Spanish boys, during which one finds that he is gay and the other finds that he is not. Oh, but it's a lot more complicated than that. Adolescence always is. The movie takes place at a Spanish beach resort; Dani's parents have gone on vacation, leaving him with a tutor and a cook in the daytime, but on his own at night. His best friend, Nico, comes from Barcelona to spend the week.

The boys are both seventeen, both virgins, both frank about their sexual aspirations but murky about the details. They meet two girls their own age—girls they met the previous summer, but a lot can change in a year when you're a teenager. Elena (Marieta Orozco) likes Nico (Jordi Vilches), and that leaves Berta (Esther Nubiola) and Dani (Fernando Ramallo) to pair off, until Dani realizes he'd rather pair off with Nico.

If this were an American teenage sex comedy . . . but don't get me started. Thanks to the MPAA's determination to steer American teenagers toward material that is immature and vulgar, this movie would never get made except with an R or NC-17 rating. Too bad, since an observant film like *Nico and Dani* could be useful to a confused teenager, suggesting that we all have to choose our own paths in life. Teenagers masturbate and worry about it, and this movie considers the subject in a healthy and helpful way, while the MPAA prefers jokes about despoiled apple pies.

Summer at the shore is casual and aimless. The two couples meet for drinks, go to parties and dances, and visit the beach, where Nico can show off his back flips. It gradually becomes clear that all four of them have concluded that these ten days of freedom are an opportunity to lose their virginity at last. Not all of them do, but the possibility is there.

Nico and Dani return to Dani's house after an evening with the girls, feeling the universal horniness of the teenage boy. They experiment. For Nico, it's a casual, meaningless experience, but for Dani it's more than that, and Nico becomes a little alarmed at Dani's urgency. They just don't share the same feelings.

Elena, meanwhile, has an agenda of her own, which Nico doesn't discover until a night when they meet to "do it," and she reveals—well, that Nico is expected to play a role but not make any long-range plans. That's okay with Nico, who like many teenage boys will agree to almost anything if his goal is in view.

The movie is more concerned with Dani. His English teacher, Sonia (Ana Gracia), has observed subtle signs of Dani's sexuality, and tries in a quiet way to let him know his feelings are not unique in all the world. She has a gay friend, Julian (Chisco Amado), and one night they all end up at Julian's for dinner, and Dani has too much to drink. Dani knows Julian is gay, and the next morning he makes a bold, if uncertain, pass; Julian knows Dani is underage, and so does Sonia—who warns Julian to keep his hands off. This episode ends inconclusively, like so much in life.

The movie, directed by Cesc Gay, reminds me of one of Eric Rohmer's movies about teenagers on summer vacation; it has the same lightness of feeling and delicacy of touch, although it's more directly concerned with sex than Rohmer would be. It has a plot—who will lose his or her virginity, and how?—but it's not *about* the plot. It isn't so stupid as to think the answer to Who and How is the whole point, since eventually all will lose their virginity, one way or another. American teenage movies tidy things up by pairing off the right couples at the end. In Europe they know that summers end and life goes on.

Nico and Dani is more concerned with values: with what is right and wrong, ethical or not. There's the night, for example, when the boys put Valium in the sangria they serve to the girls. Wrong, and dangerous. When Berta is half-unconscious, Dani begins to take advantage of her; the technical word is rape, although here it's more of a muddle, since Dani finds he's just not that interested in a girl. Spiking the drinks is immoral. So is the way Julian casually but unmistakably makes his life available to Dani. The movie trusts us to arrive at these conclusions, and doesn't add a lot of laborious plotting to pound home the message. We've all done things that we regret; with any luck we learned something from them. Next summer, Dani and Nico will know who they are, Elena will have moved on to another boy, and Berta—well, she's already told Nico, "Elena is Elena and I'm not. I'm me." It's the way she smiles when she says it that lets Nico know what that means.

The Ninth Gate ★ ★
R, 132 m., 2000

Johnny Depp (Dean Corso), Frank Langella (Boris Balkan), Lena Olin (Liana Telfer), Emmanuelle Seigner (The Girl), Barbara Jefford (Baroness Kessler), Jack Taylor (Victor Fargas), Jose Lopez Rodero (Ceniza Brothers), Toni Amoni (Liana's Bodyguard). Directed and produced by Roman Polanski. Screenplay by Enrique Urbizu, Polanski, and John Brownjohn, based on the novel *El Club Dumas* by Arturo Perez Reverte.

Roman Polanski's *The Ninth Gate*, a satanic thriller, opens with a spectacularly good title sequence and goes downhill from there—but slowly, so that all through the first hour there is reason for hope, and only gradually do we realize the movie isn't going to pay off. It has good things in it, and I kept hoping Polanski would take the plot by the neck and shake life into it, but no. After the last scene, I underlined on my notepad: "What?"

The film stars Johnny Depp in a strong if ultimately unaimed performance, as Dean Corso, a rare-book dealer whose ethics are optional. He's hired by Boris Balkan (Frank Langella), a millionaire collector who owns a copy of *The Nine Gates of the Kingdom of the Shadows*, published in Venice in 1666 by one Aristide Torchia—who, legend has it, adapted the engravings from the work of Satan himself. Two other copies of the book survive, and Balkan wants Depp to track them down and compare the engravings.

Torchia was burned to death by the Inquisition, and indeed Andrew Telfer, one of the recent owners of the book, hangs himself in an early scene, after selling his copy to Balkan. Liana (Lena Olin), his widow, tries to appear indifferent, but has an unwholesome interest in getting the book back. Corso flies to Europe and meets the other two owners, a stately aristocrat (Jack Taylor) in Portugal and an elderly Parisian baroness (Barbara Jefford) in a wheelchair.

What's best about Corso's quest is the way he conducts it. Depp and Polanski bring a *film noir* feel to the film; we're reminded of Bogart pretending to be a rare-book buyer in *The Big Sleep*. As Corso moves from one bizarre millionaire collector to another, he narrowly avoids several threats on his life and realizes he's being followed by a young woman (Emmanuelle Seigner), whose purpose and identity remain obscure, although at one point she uses martial arts to save his life, and at another point we (but not he) see her fly.

The secret of the engravings in the three editions of the book will not be revealed here. Nor will various additional motives of Balkan, the Telfer widow, and the inexplicable young woman. Their stories are told with a meticulous attention to details, which are persuasive until we realize they are accumulating instead of adding up. If some of the engravings were indeed drawn by Satan, and if assembling them can evoke the Prince of Darkness, then that would be a threat, right? Or would it be a promise? And what happens at the end—that would be an unspeakably evil outcome, right? But why does it look somehow like a victory? And as for the woman—good or bad? Friend or foe? You tell me.

What's intriguing about the material is the way Polanski trusts its essential fascination, and doesn't go for cheesy special effects, as in the Schwarzenegger thriller *End of Days.* Satan need not show himself with external signs, but can work entirely within human nature, which is, after all, his drafting board. When Corso goes to visit the baroness in her wheelchair, I was reminded of Bogart's similar call on an elderly eccentric in *The Big Sleep,* and I relished a sequence where Corso calls on two booksellers, the twin Ceniza brothers, who in a neat f/x touch are played by one actor, Jose Lopez Rodero.

The movie does a good job of mirroring its deaths with situations from the Tarot deck, and making the Telfer widow (Olin) more sinister by (I think) inserting electronic undertones beneath her speech. I also liked the atmosphere evoked by the dialogue, which isn't too dumbed down, uses some of the jargon of the book trade, and allows us to follow Corso's process of deduction as he figures out what the engravings mean and what Balkan's true motives are. It's just that a film of such big themes should be about more than the fate of a few people; while at the end I didn't yearn for spectacular special effects, I did wish for spectacular information—something awesome, not just a fade to white.

Not One Less ★ ★ ★
G, 100 m., 2000

Wei Minzhi (Herself [Young Student]), Zhang Huike (Himself [Young Student]), Tian Zhenda (Mayor Tian), Gao Enman (Teacher Gao), Feng Yuying (TV Receptionist), Li Fanfan (TV Host). Directed by Zhang Yimou and produced by Zhao Yu. Screenplay by Shi Xiangsheng.

Not One Less is not only about the poor in China's remote rural areas, but could be dedicated to them; we sense that Zhang Yimou, the director of such sophisticated films as *Raise the Red Lantern* and *Shanghai Triad,* is returning here to memories of the years from 1968 to 1978, when he worked as a rural laborer under the Cultural Revolution. His story is simple, unadorned, direct. Only the margins are complicated.

The actors are not professionals, but local people, playing characters with their own names. Wei Minzhi, a red-cheeked thirteen-year-old who usually looks very intent, stars as Wei, a substitute teacher, also very intent. The village's schoolmaster has been called away to his mother's deathbed, and Wei's assignment is to teach his grade school class.

To assist her in this task, she is supplied with one piece of chalk for every day the teacher will be away. And she gets strict instructions: Since the school's subsidy depends on its head count, she is to return the full class to the teacher—"not one less." Keeping all the students in class is more important than anything she teaches them, and indeed she isn't a lot more advanced than her students. This isn't one of those movies where the inspired teacher awakens the minds and spirits of her class; Wei copies lessons on the board and blocks the door.

These early scenes are interesting in the way they don't exploit the obvious angles of the story. This isn't a pumped-up melodrama or an inspirational tearjerker, but a matter-of-fact look at a poor, rural area where necessity is the mother of invention and everything else.

When one of her students, Zhang (Zhang Huike), runs away to look for work in the big city, Wei determines to follow him and bring him back. This is not an easy task. It involves buying a bus ticket, and that means raising the money for the ticket. Wei puts the whole class to work shifting bricks for a local factory to earn the funds. She eventually does get to the city, Jiangjiakou, and her encounters with bureaucracy there are a child's shadow of the

409

heroine's problems in Zhang Yimou's famous film *The Story of Qui Ju* (1992).

The city scenes were not as compelling for me as the earlier ones, maybe because Wei's patience tried my own. She waits what seems like forever outside the gates of a TV studio, hoping to talk to the man in charge, and although her determination is admirable, it could have been suggested in less screen time. Once she does get on TV, there's a moment of absolute authenticity when the anchorwoman asks her a question, and Wei just stares dumbfounded at the camera.

For Chinese viewers, this film will play as a human drama (end titles mention how many children drop out of school in China every year). For Western viewers, there's almost equal interest at the edges of the screen, in the background, in the locations and incidental details that show daily life in today's China. One of the buried messages is the class divide that exists even today in the People's Republic, where TV bureaucrats live in a different world than thirteen-year-old rural schoolgirls. Zhang Yimou, whose films have sometimes landed him in trouble with the authorities, seems to have made a safe one this time. But in the margins he may be making comments of his own.

Note: Parents looking for intelligent films for children might consider Not One Less. *Like the Chinese film* King of Masks *and the Iranian film* Children of Heaven *(both available on video), it has subtitles, but none too difficult for a good young reader.*

Notting Hill ★ ★ ★
PG-13, 125 m., 1999

Julia Roberts (Anna Scott), Hugh Grant (William Thacker), Richard McCabe (Tony), Rhys Ifans (Spike), Emma Chambers (Honey), Tim McInnerny (Max), Gina McKee (Bella), Hugh Bonneville (Bernie), James Dreyfus (Martin). Directed by Roger Michell and produced by Duncan Kenworthy. Screenplay by Richard Curtis.

Well of course the moment we see Julia Roberts and Hugh Grant together on the screen, we want to see them snoggling, but a romantic comedy like *Notting Hill* is about delaying the inevitable.

After all, two different worlds they live in. Her character, Anna, is one of the most famous movie stars in the world. His character, William, runs a modest little travel bookshop in London. We know they're destined for one another, but we're always quicker to see these things than the characters are.

Notting Hill reassembles three of the key players from *Four Weddings and a Funeral* (1994), which made Hugh Grant a star: Grant, screenwriter Richard Curtis, and producer Duncan Kenworthy. In the earlier film Grant fell for a beautiful American (Andie MacDowell), and that's what happens this time too. And both films surround the romantic couple with a large, cheerful assortment of weird but lovable friends.

The film, of course, begins with a Meet Cute; she wanders into his bookstore, enjoys the way he handles a would-be shoplifter, and their eyes, as they say, meet. He tries to keep his cool, although he's as agog as if she were, well, Julia Roberts. She acknowledges his unspoken adoration, and is grateful that it remains unspoken, and although there's enough electricity between them to make their hair stand on end, she leaves. They will have to meet again. If there's one thing this movie has, luckily, it's an endless supply of Meet Cutes. The next time they meet, it's by accident, and he spills orange juice all over her. That leads to an invitation to clean up at his nearby flat, which leads to some flirtatious dialogue and a kiss, but then they separate again.

Will Anna and William never find the happiness they deserve? We slap our foreheads in frustration for them. Eventually they meet again during her press junket at the Ritz Hotel, where he is mistaken for a journalist, identifies himself as the film critic for *Horse & Hound* magazine, and quizzes her about her horses—and hounds, I think. The absurdities of a press junket are actually pretty clearly seen, allowing for some comic exaggeration, and the movie is more realistic about the world of a movie star than I expected it to be.

Anna Scott, the Julia Roberts character, is seen not simply as a desirable woman, but as a complicated one, whose life doesn't make it easy for her to be happy. There are moments of insight in the middle of this comedy that bring the audience to that kind of hushed silence you get when truths are told. One comes when Roberts looks into the camera and predicts Anna's future: "One day my looks will go, and I'll be a sad middle-aged woman who looks like someone who was famous for a while." Another comes when she kids with the bookseller that the price of her beauty was two painful operations. She points silently to her nose and her chin. Is Roberts talking about herself? Doesn't matter. The scene is based on a fact of life: Anyone who gets paid $15 million a picture is going to perform the necessary maintenance and upkeep.

To be beautiful and famous is, the movie argues, to risk losing ordinary human happiness. The first "date" between Anna and William is at his sister's birthday party, where a mixed bag of friends take her more or less at face value, and allow her to enjoy what is arguably the first normal evening she's had in years. There are other moments when they are basically just a boy and a girl, hand in hand, wandering at night through London. And then her "real life" kicks in, complete with a movie star boyfriend (Alec Baldwin) who thinks William is from room service.

From *Four Weddings*, we remember the extended family and friends such as Simon Callow, so good as the gay friend who has the heart attack. In *Notting Hill* William's circle includes his airhead sister Honey (Emma Chambers); his best friend Max (Tim McInnerny); Max's beloved wife, Bella (Gina McKee), who is in a wheelchair; and his stockbroker pal Bernie (Hugh Bonneville), who is like one of those friends we all accumulate—boring, but reassuring to have around. William also has a Welsh roommate named Spike (Rhys Ifans), who seems to regard his bodily functions as performance art. These friends and others, like a restaurant owner, represent a salt-of-the-earth alternative to Anna's showbiz satellites.

The movie is bright, the dialogue has wit and intelligence, and Roberts and Grant are very easy to like. By the end, as much as we're aware of the ancient story machinery groaning away below deck, we're smiling. I have, however, two quibbles. The first involves the personality of Grant's character. Nobody is better at being diffident, abashed, and self-effacing than Hugh Grant, but there comes a point here where the diffidence becomes less a manner, more of a mannerism. Hint: Once a woman spends the night with you, you can stop apologizing for breathing in her presence.

My other problem is with the sound track, which insists on providing a running commentary in the form of song lyrics that explain everything. There is a moment, for example, when Anna disappears from William's life, and he is sad and lonely and mopes about the city. A few violins and maybe some wind in the trees would have been fine. Instead, the sound track assaults us with "Ain't No Sunshine When She's Gone," which is absolutely the last thing we need to be told.

Nurse Betty ★ ★ ★
R, 112 m., 2000

Morgan Freeman (Charlie), Renee Zellweger (Betty), Chris Rock (Wesley), Greg Kinnear (Dr. David Ravell), Aaron Eckhart (Del), Tia Texada (Rosa), Crispin Glover (Roy), Pruitt Taylor Vince (Ballard). Directed by Neil LaBute and produced by Gail Mutrux and Steve Golin. Screenplay by John C. Richards and James Flamberg.

Neil LaBute's *Nurse Betty* is about two dreamers in love with their fantasies. One is a Kansas housewife. The other is a professional criminal. The housewife is in love with a doctor on a television soap opera. The criminal is in love with the housewife, whose husband he has killed. What is crucial is that both of these besotted romantics are invisible to the person they are in love with.

Morgan Freeman is Charlie, the killer, and Renee Zellweger is Betty, the housewife and waitress. Their lives connect because Del (Aaron Eckhart), Betty's worthless husband, tries to stiff Charlie on a drug deal. Charlie and Wesley (Chris Rock) turn up at his house, threaten him, scalp him, and kill him. Well, Charlie kills him only because Wesley scalps him—and then what you gonna do?

Betty witnesses the murder, but blanks it out of her memory. Her husband was a rat, she doesn't miss him, and in her mind his death frees her to drive out to Los Angeles to meet her "ex-fiancé," a doctor on a soap opera. Charlie and Wesley trail her, and in the course of their pursuit Charlie's mind also jumps the track. Under the influence of Betty's sweet smile in a photograph, he begins to idealize her—he speaks of her "grace"—and to see her as the bright angel of his lost hopes.

In Los Angeles, Betty meets George (Greg Kinnear), the actor who plays the doctor. She relates only to the character, and as she talks to "Dr. David Ravell" at a charity benefit, George and his friends think they're witnessing a brilliant method audition. Charlie and Wesley meanwhile arrive in Los Angeles with Charlie increasingly bewitched by fantasies about Betty. When they started chasing her, she was an eyewitness to murder who was driving a car her husband had hidden their drugs in. Now Charlie thinks of her more as a person who would sympathize with his own broken ideals.

I'm spending so much time on the plot of *Nurse Betty* because I think it's possible to misread. When the film premiered at Cannes in May, some reviews didn't seem to understand that Betty and Charlie are parallel characters, both projecting their dreams on figures they've created in their own fantasies. Look at this movie inattentively, especially if you're looking for Hollywood formulas, and all you see is a mad woman pursued by some drug dealers—kind of a high-rent *Crazy in Alabama*. But it's more, deeper, and more touching than that. Zellweger plays Betty as an impossibly sweet, earnest, sincere, lovable, vulnerable woman—a "Doris Day type," as Charlie describes her. She has unwisely married Del, a vulgar louse who orders her around and eats her birthday cupcake. Her consolation is the daily soap opera about her fantasy lover, Dr. Ravell. When Charlie and Wesley turn up, nobody knows she's home. She glimpses the murder from the next room, and her response is to hit the rewind button for a crucial soap opera scene she's missed. A therapist tells the local sheriff (Pruitt Taylor Vince) she remembers nothing; she's in an "altered state—that allows a traumatized person to keep on functioning."

Betty heads west in the fatal Buick LeSabre with the drugs in the trunk, and outside a roadside bar she experiences a fantasy in which Dr. Ravell proposes marriage. Not long after, hot on her trail, Charlie pauses in the moonlight on the edge of the Grand Canyon and fantasizes dancing with Betty. Charlie has never met Betty and Betty has never met the "doctor"; both of their dream-figures are projections of their own needs and idealism.

Morgan Freeman has a tricky role. His Charlie is a mean guy, capable of killing but looking forward to retirement in Florida after one last "assignment." He has great affection for Wesley, a loose cannon, and tries to teach him lessons Wesley is not much capable of learning. Charlie has led a life of crime but has now gone soft under the influence of Betty, whose smile in a photo helps him to mourn his own lost innocence.

Betty is even further gone. Traumatized by the murder, she has no understanding that the soap opera is a TV show, and her first scene with Kinnear is brilliantly acted by both of them, as she cuts through his Hollywood cynicism with unshakable sincerity. Kinnear is deadly accurate in portraying an actor who has confused his ego with his training, and a scene where Betty is offered a role in the show is handled with cruel realism.

LaBute previously wrote and directed *In the Company of Men* and *Your Friends and Neighbors,* films with a deep, harsh cynicism. *Nurse Betty,* written by John C. Richards and James Flamberg, is a comedy undercut with dark tones and flashes of violence. Heading inexorably toward a tidy happy ending, LaBute sidesteps clichés like a broken-field runner. As for Charlie, his final scene, his only real scene with Betty, contains some of Freeman's best work. "I'm a garbageman of the human soul," he tells her, "but you're different." He is given an almost impossible assignment (heartfelt wistfulness in the midst of a gunfight) and pulls it off, remaining attentive even to the comic subtext.

Nurse Betty is one of those films where you don't know whether to laugh or cringe, and find yourself doing both. It's a challenge: How do we respond to this loaded material? Audiences lobotomized by one-level stories may find it stimulating, or confusing—it's up to them. Once you understand that Charlie and Betty are versions of the same idealistic delusions, that their stories are linked as mirror images, you've got the key.

Nutty Professor II: The Klumps ★ ★ ★
PG-13, 110 m., 2000

Eddie Murphy (Klumps/Lance Perkins/Buddy Love), Janet Jackson (Denise), Larry Miller (Dean Richmond), John Ales (Jason), Richard Gant (Denise's Father), Anna Maria Horsford (Denise's Mother), Melinda McGraw (Leanne Guilford), Jamal Mixon (Ernie Klump Jr.). Directed by Peter Segal and produced by Brian Grazer. Screenplay by Barry W. Blaustein, David Sheffield, Paul Weitz, and Chris Weitz, based on a story by Steve Oedekerk, Blaustein, and Sheffield.

My guess is, most of the reviews of *Nutty Professor II: The Klumps* will deliver perfunctory praise to the makeup and move on quickly to the comedy. But we're not talking garden-variety "makeup" here. We're talking about a rather astonishing creative collaboration between Eddie Murphy and makeup artist Rick Baker, with considerable help from director Peter Segal and cinematographer Dean Semler, to populate the movie with eight different characters, all played by Murphy, all convincing, each with its own personality. This is not just a stunt. It is some kind of brilliance.

Yes, it appears in a comedy of determined vulgarity. Yes, some of those long sessions of five hours in makeup were put at the service of scenes involving giant hamster sex and flammable farts. Yes, the story meanders. But yes, *Nutty II* is often very funny and never less than amazing when you consider the work and imagination that went into Murphy's creation of the Klump family (Sherman, Granny, Mama, Papa, Papa when he was younger, and Ernie) and two other characters, Lance Perkins and the diabolical alter ego Buddy Love.

Murphy has an uncanny gift for mimicry, for creating new characters out of thin air. That showed as early as *Saturday Night Live*, of course. In Steve Martin's underappreciated *Bowfinger* (1999), he plays two characters more or less without help from makeup: the movie superstar Kit Ramsey, who looks a lot like Murphy, and a doofus named Jiff, who looks a lot like Kit and is hired to play his double. This isn't simply a double role. Kit and Jiff are two different people, and Jiff is actually the funnier and more involving one; he was so abashed

when he found out they wanted to put him in a movie that we couldn't help but like him.

The many Klumps played by Murphy in *Nutty II* are, of course, much broader characters, and yet Professor Sherman Klump, the family hero, also has that strain of sweetness: He is likable, vulnerable, and naive, and we can understand why his research assistant Denise (Janet Jackson) might want to marry him. We understand even better when he hires a Mexican band to stand under her window while he serenades her, although that touching scene is interrupted when Buddy Love takes over his personality.

Buddy Love is essentially Tourette's syndrome personified. Buddy appears without warning, taking over Sherman's personality, spewing insulting comments and embarrassing the professor in public. His nuisance value multiplies when Sherman tries a risky genetic split, externalizing Buddy but causing his own intelligence to start shrinking. One of the funniest twists in this movie is the way the tables are turned on Buddy. A strand of his DNA gets crossed with the genetic code of a dog, forcing Buddy to exhibit instinctual doggie behavior at all the most inconvenient moments. It's sort of wonderful when Sherman can distract his nemesis by forcing him to fetch.

Animal jokes have been obligatory in raunchy comedies since *There's Something About Mary*, and *Nutty II* builds to some kind of a crescendo as Dean Richmond (Larry Miller), Sherman's superior at the university, is assaulted by a giant hamster. How this happens and why is immaterial; what is important is the way it leads up to the line, "Do you think he'll call?"

Eddie Murphy has been a star since the 1970s, a movie star since *48 Hrs.* (1982). He started strong but has made more than his share of bad movies (*Vampire in Brooklyn* was perhaps the low point). In *Bowfinger* and *Nutty II*, he seems to be in a new flowering of his career. He seems more at ease with his comedy, willing to disappear inside characters, ready to find laughs with behavior and personality instead of forcing them with punch lines. Not only does he play eight different characters here, but he makes them distinct and (within the broad requirements of the story) plausible.

Sherman, of course, is the central character,

413

a research professor who is brilliant, innocent, and fat. We like him and feel for him. Janet Jackson is warm and supportive as his girlfriend, and they have some touching moments together (borrowed from *Charley*) when his intelligence starts to dwindle and his genius to fade. In a movie so raucous, so scatological, so cheerfully offensive, it is a little surprising to find yourself actually caring for a character who is made mostly out of latex makeup, but there you have it. ☞

O

O Brother, Where Art Thou? ★ ★ ½
PG-13, 103 m., 2000

George Clooney (Ulysses Everett McGill), John Turturro (Pete), Tim Blake Nelson (Delmar), Charles Durning (Pappy O'Daniel), John Goodman (Big Dan Teague), Michael Badalucco (George Babyface Nelson), Holly Hunter (Penny Wharvey), Stephen Root (Radio Station Man), Chris Thomas King (Tommy Johnson). Directed by Joel Coen and produced by Ethan Coen. Screenplay by Ethan Coen and Joel Coen, based upon *The Odyssey* by Homer.

The opening titles inform us that the Coen brothers' *O Brother, Where Art Thou?* is based on Homer's *The Odyssey*. The Coens claimed their *Fargo* was based on a true story, but later confided it wasn't; this time they confess they haven't actually read *The Odyssey*. Still, they've absorbed the spirit. Like its inspiration, this movie is one damn thing after another.

The film is a Homeric journey through Mississippi during the depression—or rather, through all of the images of that time and place that have been trickling down through pop culture ever since. There are even walk-ons for characters inspired by Babyface Nelson and the blues singer Robert Johnson, who speaks of a crossroads soul-selling rendezvous with the devil.

Bluegrass music is at the heart of the film, as it was of *Bonnie and Clyde*, and there are images of chain gangs, sharecropper cottages, cotton fields, populist politicians, river baptisms, hoboes on freight trains, patent medicines, 25-watt radio stations, and Klan rallies. The movie's title is lifted from Preston Sturges's 1941 comedy *Sullivan's Travels* (it was the uplifting movie the hero wanted to make to redeem himself), and from Homer we get a Cyclops, Sirens bathing on the rocks, a hero named Ulysses, and his wife, Penny, which is no doubt short for Penelope.

If these elements don't exactly add up, maybe they're not intended to. Homer's epic grew out of the tales of many storytellers who went before; their episodes were timed and intended for a night's recitation. Quite possibly no one before Homer saw the developing work as a whole. In the same spirit, *O Brother* contains sequences that are wonderful in themselves—lovely short films—but the movie never really shapes itself into a whole.

The opening shot shows three prisoners escaping from a chain gang. They are Ulysses Everett McGill (George Clooney), Pete (John Turturro), and Delmar (Tim Blake Nelson). From their peculiar conviction that they are invisible as they duck and run across an open field, we know the movie's soul is in farce and satire, although it touches other notes, too—it's an anthology of moods. Ulysses (played by Clooney as if Clark Gable were a patent medicine salesman) doesn't much want company on his escape, but since he is chained to the other two, he has no choice. He enlists them in his cause by telling them of hidden treasure.

What was *The Odyssey*, after all, but a road movie? *O Brother* follows its three heroes on an odyssey during which they intersect with a political campaign, become radio stars by accident, stumble upon a Klan meeting, and deal with Ulysses' wife, Penny (Holly Hunter), who is about to pack up with their seven daughters and marry a man who won't always be getting himself thrown into jail.

Hunter and Turturro are veterans of earlier Coen movies, and so is John Goodman, who plays a slick-talking Bible salesman. Charles Durning appears as a gubernatorial candidate with the populist jollity of Huey Long, and the story strands meet and separate as if the movie is happening mostly by chance and good luck—a nice feeling sometimes, although not one that inspires confidence that the narrative train has an engine.

The most effective sequence in the movie is the Klan rally (complete with a Klansman whose eye patch means he needs only one hole in his sheet). The choreography of the ceremony seems poised somewhere between Busby Berkeley and *Triumph of the Will*, and the Coens succeed in making it look ominous and ridiculous at the same time. (There are echoes here of *The Wizard of Oz*.)

Another sequence almost stops the show, it's so haunting in its self-contained way. It occurs when the escapees come across three women doing their laundry in a river. The

Sirens, obviously. They sing "Didn't Leave Nobody but the Baby" while moving in a slightly slowed motion, and the effect is—well, what it's supposed to be, mesmerizing.

I also like the sequence of events beginning when the lads perform on the radio as the Soggy Mountain Boys. By now they have recruited a black partner, Tommy Johnson (Chris Thomas King), and later when the song becomes a hit they're called on to perform before an audience that is hostile to blacks in particular and escaped convicts in general. They wear false beards. Really false beards.

All of these scenes are wonderful in their different ways, and yet I left the movie uncertain and unsatisfied. I saw it a second time, admired the same parts, left with the same feeling. I do not demand that all movies have a story to pull us from beginning to end, and indeed one of the charms of *The Big Lebowski*, the Coens' previous film, is how its stoned hero loses track of the thread of his own life. But with *O Brother, Where Art Thou?* I had the sense of invention set adrift: of a series of bright ideas wondering why they had all been invited to the same film.   ☞

October Sky ★ ★ ★ ½
PG, 108 m., 1999

Jake Gyllenhaal (Homer Hickam), Chris Cooper (John Hickam), Laura Dern (Miss Riley), Chris Owen (Quentin), William Lee Scott (Roy Lee), Chad Lindberg (Odell), Natalie Canerday (Elsie Hickam), Scott Thomas (Jim Hickam), Chris Ellis (Principal). Directed by Joe Johnston and produced by Charles Gordon and Larry Franco. Screenplay by Lewis Colick, based on the book *Rocket Boys* by Homer H. Hickam Jr.

Like the hero of *October Sky*, I remember the shock that ran through America when the Russians launched *Sputnik* on October 4, 1957. Like the residents of Coalwood, West Virginia, in the movie, I joined the neighbors out on the lawn, peering into the sky with binoculars at a speck of moving light that was fairly easy to see. Unlike Homer Hickam, I didn't go on to become a NASA scientist or train astronauts. But I did read Willy Ley's *Rockets, Missiles and Space Travel* three or four times, and Arthur Clarke's *The Making of a Moon*. I got their au-

tographs, too, just as Homer sends away for a signed photo of Werner von Braun.

That first shabby piece of orbiting hardware now seems like a toy compared to the space station, the shuttle, and the missions to the moon and beyond. But it had an impact that's hard to describe to anyone who takes satellite TV for granted. For the first time in history, man had built something that went up, but did not come down—not for a long time, anyway. *Sputnik* was a tiny but audacious defiance of the universe.

October Sky tells the story of four boys in a poverty-stricken corner of Appalachia who determine to build their own rocket and help get America back in the "space race." It's seen through the eyes of their leader, young Homer Hickham (Jake Gyllenhaal), who sees the speck of light in the sky and starts reading the science fiction of Jules Verne. Homer is a good student, but math and science are his weak points. He knows he needs help, and breaks all of the rules in the school lunchroom by approaching the class brain, an outcast named Quentin (Chris Owen).

They talk about rocket fuel, nozzles, velocity. Two other boys get involved: Roy Lee (William Lee Scott) and Odell (Chad Lindberg). Their first rocket blows a hole in the picket fence in front of Homer's house. The second one narrowly misses some miners at the coal mine, and Homer's dad, John (Chris Cooper), the mine supervisor, forbids further experimentation and confiscates all of the "rocket stuff" from the basement. But the kids labor on in an isolated patch of woods, building a shelter to protect themselves from exploding rockets. They talk a machinist at the mine into building them a rocket casing of stronger steel, and they use alcohol from a moonshiner as an ingredient in the fuel.

The tension in the movie is not between the boys and their rockets, but between the boys and those who think that miners' sons belong down in the mines and not up in the sky. Homer's father is not a bad man; he fights for the jobs of his men, he rescues several in a near-disaster, he injures his eye in another emergency. He wants Homer to follow in his footsteps. The mine may seem an unhealthy and hateful place to some, but when John takes Homer down for his son's first day on the job, his voice glows with poetry: "I know the mine like I know a man. I was born for this."

The high school principal (Chris Ellis) believes the job of the school to is send miners' sons down to the coal face. But a young teacher (Laura Dern) tells Homer she feels her life will have failed if some of the kids don't get out and realize their dreams. Then there's a crisis (did a rocket set a forest fire?), and a scene in which Homer and his friends use trigonometry to argue their innocence.

There have been a lot of recent movies set in high school: *She's All That, Varsity Blues, Jawbreaker*. In those movies, even the better ones, "teenagers" who look like soap stars in their twenties have lives that revolve around sex and popularity. The kids in *October Sky* look like they're in their mid-teens, and act that way too. Watching Homer get out the trig book, I was reminded how rarely high school movies have anything to do with school—with how an education is a ticket to freedom.

Perhaps because *October Sky* is based on a real memoir, Homer Hickam's *Rocket Boys*, it doesn't simplify the father into a bad guy or a tyrant. He understandably wants his son to follow in his footsteps, and one of the best elements of the movie is when the son tries to explain that in breaking free, he is respecting his father. This movie has deep values.

Office Space ★ ★ ★
R, 90 m., 1999

Ron Livingston (Peter), Jennifer Aniston (Joanna), Stephen Root (Milton), Gary Cole (Bill Lumbergh), David Herman (Michael Bolton), Ajay Naidu (Samir), Richard Riehle (Tom Smykowski), Diedrich Bader (Lawrence), Alexandra Wentworth (Anne). Directed by Mike Judge and produced by Michael Rotenberg and Daniel Rappaport. Screenplay by Judge, based on his *Milton* animated shorts.

Mike Judge's *Office Space* is a comic cry of rage against the nightmare of modern office life. It has many of the same complaints as *Dilbert* and the movie *Clockwatchers*—and, for that matter, the works of Kafka and the Book of Job. It is about work that crushes the spirit. Office cubicles are cells, supervisors are the wardens, and modern management theory is skewed to employ as many managers and as few workers as possible.

As the movie opens, a cubicle slave named Peter (Ron Livingston) is being reminded by his smarmy supervisor (Gary Cole) that all reports now carry a cover sheet. "Yes, I know," he says. "I forgot. It was a silly mistake. It won't happen again." Before long another manager reminds him about the cover sheets. "Yes, I know," he says. Then another manager. And another. Logic suggests that when more than one supervisor conveys the same trivial information, their jobs overlap, and all supervisors after the first one should be shredded.

Peter hates his job. So do all of his coworkers, although one of them, Milton (Stephen Root), has found refuge through an obsessive defense of his cubicle, his radio, and his stapler. Milton's cubicle is relocated so many times that eventually it appears to have no entrance or exit; he's walled in on every side. You may recognize him as the hero of cartoons that played on *Saturday Night Live*, where strangers were always arriving to use his cubicle as storage space for cardboard boxes.

Mike Judge, who gained fame through TV's *Beavis and Butt-head*, and made the droll animated film *Beavis and Butt-head Do America* (1996), has taken his *SNL Milton* cartoons as an inspiration for this live-action comedy, which uses Orwellian satirical techniques to fight the cubicle police: No individual detail of office routine is too absurd to be believed, but together they add up into stark, staring insanity.

Peter has two friends at work: Michael Bolton (David Herman) and Samir (Ajay Naidu). No, not that Michael Bolton, Michael patiently explains. They flee the office for coffee breaks (demonstrating that Starbucks doesn't really sell coffee—it sells escape from the office). Peter is in love with the waitress at the chain restaurant across the parking lot. Her name is Joanna (Jennifer Aniston), and she has problems with management too. She's required to wear a minimum of fifteen funny buttons on the suspenders of her uniform; the buttons are called "flair" in company lingo, and her manager suggests that wearing only the minimum flair suggests the wrong spirit (another waiter has "forty-five flairs" and looks like an exhibit at a trivia convention).

The movie's dialogue is smart. It doesn't just chug along making plot points. Consider, for example, Michael Bolton's plan for revenge against the company. He has a software program that would round off payments to the next-lowest penny and deposit the proceeds in his checking account. Hey, you're thinking—that's not original! A dumb movie would pretend it was. Not *Office Space*, where Peter says he thinks he's heard of that before, and Michael says, "Yeah, they did it in *Superman 3*. Also, a bunch of hackers tried it in the seventies. One got arrested."

The movie's turning point comes when Peter seeks help from an "occupational hypnotherapist." He's put in a trance with long-lasting results; he cuts work, goes fishing, guts fish at his desk, and tells efficiency experts he actually works only fifteen minutes a week. The experts like his attitude and suggest he be promoted. Meanwhile, the Milton problem is ticking like a time bomb, especially after Milton's cubicle is relocated into a basement storage area.

Office Space is like the evil twin of *Clockwatchers*. Both movies are about the ways corporations standardize office routines so that workers are interchangeable and can be paid as little as possible. *Clockwatchers* was about the lowest rung on the employment ladder— daily temps—but *Office Space* suggests that regular employment is even worse, because it's a life sentence. Asked to describe his state of mind to the therapist, Peter says, "Since I started working, every single day has been worse than the day before, so that every day you see me is the worst day of my life."

Judge, an animator until now, treats his characters a little like cartoon creatures. That works. Nuances of behavior are not necessary, because in the cubicle world every personality trait is magnified, and the captives stagger forth like grotesques. There is a moment in the movie when the heroes take a baseball bat to a malfunctioning copier. Reader, who has not felt the same?

Once in the Life ★ ★
R, 111 m., 2000

Laurence Fishburne (20/20 Mike), Titus Welliver (Billy ["Torch"]), Eamonn Walker (Tony the Tiger), Dominic Chianese Jr. (Freddie Nine Lives), Michael Paul Chan (Buddha), Paul Calderon (Manny Rivera), Annabella Sciorra (Maxine), Gregory Hines (Ruffhouse). Directed by Laurence Fishburne and produced by David Bushell, Fishburne, and Helen Sugland. Screenplay by Fishburne.

Once in the Life tells the story of two half-brothers, one black, one white, one just out of prison, the other a heroin addict, who are in danger from a drug lord, and find themselves sharing a hideout with a man who may be their friend or their executioner. The key word here is "hideout." This is a film made from a play, and like many filmed plays it tried to cover its traces by limiting most of the action to one room, which we are not supposed to think of as the stage.

The play is by Laurence Fishburne, who also directs the film and stars as 20/20 Mike, an ex-con who says he has eyes in the back of his head—and apparently does. His half-brother, Billy (Titus Welliver), claims he has cleaned up from his habit, but may be lying. Mike and Billy have a lot of unresolved issues about their father. As for Tony the Tiger (Eamonn Walker), he and 20/20 became friends in prison. That's why 20/20 is asking for help now, not realizing that Tony is working for Manny (Paul Calderon), the drug lord whose henchman Freddie Nine Lives (Dominic Chianese Jr.) he has offended, and whose nephew he has killed.

These plot elements are standard stuff. Drugs themselves seem almost exhausted as a plot device for all but the most inventive movies; we've seen so many variations of their sale, use, trade, and theft, and the violence they inspire. But Fishburne's film and play aren't about drugs; they're the Maguffin, and the play is really about . . . well, the desired answers are "brothers" or "trust," but I'm afraid a better answer is "dialogue."

This is a film of words, especially once the three key characters hole up in a slum room that looks like the set decorator was given too much money. No abandoned room should look this atmospheric, unless it deliberately wants to resemble a stage set. In the room, the three go round and round, settling old scores, reopening old wounds, gradually learning the truth of the situation, and from time to time someone goes to the window and looks to see who's outside—an ancient device in movies based on plays. Among the people outside, or in other locations, are Ruffhouse (Gregory Hines), a spotter and enforcer (I think; his role is not very clear), and Annabella Sciorra as Maxine, Tony's threatened wife.

I imagine this material worked on the stage, where it was titled *Riff Raff* (it was produced at the Circle Repertory Company in lower Manhattan). But stage plays are about the voices and physical presence of the actors, and we supply the necessary reality. Movies have a tendency to be literal, no matter what the intention of their makers, and stylized dialogue and acting is hazardous—it calls attention to itself, and clangs. Consider, for example, a poem that Tony recites. It brings the movie to an awkward halt.

Fishburne is a powerful actor, and he has assembled a talented cast, but the movie remains an actor's exercise—too much dialogue, too much time in the room, too much happening offstage, or in the past, or in memory, or in imagination. Billy's meltdown provides a real-time reality check, but for most of the time we're waiting for the payoff, and when it comes, I'm afraid, it's not very satisfying.

One Day in September ★ ★ ★
R, 92 m., 2001

A documentary featuring Ankie Spitzer, widow of Israeli fencing coach Andre Spitzer; terrorist Jamal Al Gashey; ITN News reporter Gerald Seymour; Alex Springer, son of Jacov Springer, Israeli and judge; and Gad Zabari, Israeli wrestler who escaped from the terrorists. Directed by Kevin Macdonald and produced by John Battsek and Arthur Cohn.

In September 1972, Palestinian terrorists invaded the athletes' quarters of the Munich Olympiad and took Israeli athletes hostage. By the following evening, eleven Israelis and five of the eight terrorists were dead. Kevin Macdonald's documentary *One Day in September* retells these events in the style of a thriller, which is a little unsettling. It's one thing to see a fictional re-creation of facts, such as the re-creation of the Cuban missile crisis in *Thirteen Days,* and another to see facts tarted up like fiction. Oh, it's exciting, all right, but do we feel ennobled to be thus entertained?

Macdonald brings remarkable research to the film. He has managed to obtain interviews with most of the key figures who are still alive, including the one surviving terrorist, Jamal Al Gashey, now in hiding "in Africa" (the two other survivors were killed by Israeli assassination squads). He talks to an Israeli athlete who escaped, the son of another, and the widow of a third, to Israeli coaches and security experts, to German generals and policemen, to journalists who covered the event. His reporting is extraordinary, as he relentlessly builds up a case against the way the Germans and the International Olympic Committee handled the crisis.

Much is made of "German efficiency," Macdonald observes, but the Germans were so inefficient that they had no trained antiterrorist squad, no security around the compound, no contingency plans, not even effective communication (a police sniper and a helicopter pilot were shot by German police who had not been told where they were). In a development that would be funny if it were not so sad, the Germans stationed a 747 on an airport runway as a getaway plane for the terrorists, and staffed it with cops dressed as the plane's crew, but minutes before the plane was to be used, the cops took a vote, decided they were not competent to handle the assignment, and walked off the plane.

In a film filled with startling charges, the most shocking is that the three captured terrorists escaped from custody as part of a secret deal with the German government, which essentially wanted the whole matter to be over with. A German aircraft was hijacked by Palestinians, who demanded that the three prisoners be handed over, which they were, with "indecent haste." The film says the plane suspiciously contained only twelve passengers, none of them women or children; now Jamal Al Gashey confirms it was a setup.

As for the Olympic committee, at first it intended to continue the Games during the hostage crisis, and we see athletes of other nations training and relaxing within sight of the dorms where the Israelis were being held. After

419

the Games were suspended, thousands watched the standoff as if it were a show, while the Germans continued to bungle (officers crept onto the roof of the building, but the scene was broadcast live on TV, and the terrorists, of course, were watching the news).

The death of the innocent athletes was an avoidable tragedy, we conclude. If the Israeli secret service had been able to stage a raid as they wanted, it's likely many lives would have been saved. The final bloodbath resulted more from German bumbling than from anything else.

Still, one wonders why newsreel shots of Hitler and reminders of the Nazi past are necessary in a film that has almost no time at all to explain who the Palestinians were or why they made such a desperate raid. The raid had nothing to do with the Nazi past, and the current Germans seemed like comic-opera buffoons from a Groucho Marx comedy. If the purpose of a documentary is to inform, it could be argued that audiences already know a great deal about Hitler but are not likely to learn much from a couple of perfunctory shots of Palestinian refugee camps.

One Day in September grips the attention and is exciting and involving. I recommend it on that basis—and also because of the new information it contains. I was disturbed, however, by Macdonald's pumped-up style, and by a tasteless conclusion in which images of action, bloodshed, and corpses are cut together into a montage and backed with rock music. What was he thinking of?

Note: When One Day in September *won the Academy Award in 2000, its producer, Arthur Cohn, held up the Oscar and boasted, "and I won this without showing it in a single theater!" The documentary community is still angry about that remark. Cohn exhibits his Oscar entries at screenings peopled largely by those on his invitation list, and to as few other people as possible. Under the Academy bylaws, only those who have seen all five docs can vote, and by limiting those who have seen his, Cohn shrinks the voting pool and improves his odds. Documentary groups and many individual filmmakers have protested this Oscar to the Academy.*

Onegin ★ ★ ½
NO MPAA RATING, 106 m., 2000

Ralph Fiennes (Evgeny Onegin), Liv Tyler (Tatyana Larin), Toby Stephens (Vladimir Lensky), Lena Headey (Olga Larin), Martin Donovan (Prince Nikitin), Irene Worth (Princess Alina). Directed by Martha Fiennes and produced by Simon Bosanquet and Ileen Maisel. Screenplay by Michael Ignatieff and Peter Ettedgui, based on the novel by Alexander Pushkin.

Onegin is a man bemused by his own worthlessness. He has been carefully prepared by his aristocratic nineteenth-century upbringing to be unnecessary—an outside man, hanging on, looking into the lives of others. Even when he's given the opportunity to play a role, after he inherits his uncle's estate, his response is to rent the land to his serfs. In another man, this would be seen as liberalism. In Evgeny Onegin, it is more like indifference.

Onegin is a leisurely, elegant, detached retelling of Pushkin's epic verse novel, with Ralph Fiennes as the hero. It is the kind of role once automatically assigned to Jeremy Irons. Both men look as if they have stayed up too late and not eaten their greens, but Irons in the grip of passion is able to seem lost and heedless, while Fiennes suggests it is heavy lifting, with few rewards. "I am not one who is made for love and marriage," his Onegin says soulfully.

As the film opens, Onegin is returning to inherit his uncle's estate outside St. Petersburg, after having lost his own fortune at the gambling tables. He is welcomed by receptions, teas, and balls, and embraced by his neighbor, Lensky (Toby Stephens). Lensky has a young bride named Olga (Lena Headey), and she has an older sister named Tatyana (Liv Tyler), who is a lone spirit and visits Onegin's estate to borrow books from his library.

Tyler has the assignment of suggesting passionate depths beneath a cool exterior, and succeeds: She is grave and silent, with an ethereal quality that is belied by her bold use of eye contact. Onegin probably falls in love with her the first time he sees her, but is not, of course, made for love, and shrugs off his real feelings in order to enter into a flirtation with Olga, who is safely married.

Tatyana's waters run deep. She declares herself in a passionate love letter to Onegin (the moment she saw his face, she knew her heart was his, etc.), but such passion only alarms him. "Any stranger might have stumbled into your life and aroused your romantic imagination," he tells her tactlessly. "I have no secret longing to be saved from myself." "You curse yourself!" she cries, rejected. The heartless Onegin continues his dalliance with Olga. This leads to a duel with Lensky. His heart is broken when he kills his friend; that will teach him to call a nineteenth-century Russian nobleman's wife "easy."

Onegin flees to exile (or Paris, which are synonymous). Six years pass. He returns to St. Petersburg and sees Tatyana again, at a ball. But now the tables are turned, in ironic revelations and belated discoveries, and Onegin pays the price for his heartlessness.

There is a cool, mannered elegance to the picture that I like, but it's dead at its center. There is no feeling that real feelings are at risk here. Liv Tyler seems sincere enough, but Fiennes withholds too well. And the direction, by his sister Martha Fiennes, is deliberate and detached when it should perhaps plunge into the story. The visuals are wonderful, but the drama is muted.

There is a tendency to embalm classics, but never was literature more tempestuous and heartfelt than in nineteenth-century Russia. Characters joyously leap from the pages of Pushkin, Dostoyevsky, and Tolstoy, wearing their hearts on their sleeves, torn between the French schoolmasters who taught them manners, and the land where they learned passion—inhaled it, absorbed it in the womb. I know *Eugene Onegin* is a masterpiece, but the story it tells is romantic melodrama, and requires some of the same soap-opera zest as David Lean's *Dr. Zhivago*. This film has the same problem as its hero: Its manners are so good it doesn't know what it really feels.

102 Dalmatians ★ ★ ½
G, 101 m., 2000

Glenn Close (Cruella De Vil), Alice Evans (Cloe), Ioan Gruffudd (Kevin), Tim McInnerny (Alonso), Gérard Depardieu (Monsieur Le Pelt), Tony Robinson (Cruella De Vil's Sidekick). Directed by Kevin Lima and produced by Edward S. Feldman. Screenplay by Kristen Buckley, Brian Regan, Bob Tzudiker, and Noni White, based on the novel by Dodie Smith.

Pavlov, you will recall, conditioned dogs to salivate at the ringing of a bell. It is only fitting that his namesake, a modern scientist in *102 Dalmatians,* is able to condition Cruella De Vil to feel affectionate when she sees a dog. As *102 Dalmatians* opens, the famous dognapper and fur enthusiast has been transformed into a dog lover by Dr. Pavlov's secret methods.

Released on probation, Cruella (Glenn Close) is assigned to a parole officer named Cloe (Alice Evans), who is a Dalmatian lover and doesn't believe Cruella has really been reformed. But Cruella seems to have turned over a new leaf, and even gets involved in the activities of a shelter for homeless animals run by Kevin (Ioan Gruffudd), who for his part has eyes for Cloe. Then, alas, a Pavlovian bell rings (it is no less than Big Ben) and Cruella reverts to type.

Such is the setup for *102 Dalmatians,* a movie in which it follows as the night the day that Cruella sooner or later goes back to her old dog-hating ways. While the 1996 live-action version of *101 Dalmatians* had the original animated film to supply much of its story, this sequel is an original, with new characters, most memorably Monsieur Le Pelt (Gérard Depardieu), a fur designer who wears a quasi-medieval costume influenced by Depardieu's other recent film, *Asterix.* There are also new dogs, including a puppy named Oddball who is depressed because it has been born with no spots.

The film is made with formidable resources, including Cruella's home with its secret fur-storage rooms and dungeons. The good characters are portrayed as plucky and cheerful, the evil ones gnash their teeth more than the dogs, and Cruella's hairstyle, half-black and half-silver, is in itself a wonder, as are her gowns, her nails, and her bizarre makeup (the character is so seriously kinky I have always wondered what an R-rated version might have to offer us). It is a movie made with style and energy.

And yet whether you like it or not depends largely, I think, on how you feel about the dogs. Oddball is cute, yes, but he and the other dogs suffer somewhat because they are—well, real. The Disney animal classics, including *Lady and the Tramp* and the animated *101 Dalmatians,* were able to make their dogs into stars; in a live-action movie, they're reduced to supporting characters. Smaller children aren't likely to understand Cruella and Le Pelt except as adults who are mean to dogs. There are some joys in chases and thrilling escapes, but taking the dogs out of the central roles leaves you with seriously weird humans and not enough puppy love.

Glenn Close does what can be done with the role. Indeed, she does more than can be done; Cruella is almost too big for a live-action film, and requires animation to fit her operatic scale. The Le Pelt character is not really necessary, and although Cloe and Kevin (and Cruella's timid servant Alonso) do what they can, the film itself doesn't really seem necessary, either.

Yet Cruella De Vil has possibilities. I wonder why movies like this stay so close to their origins. Wouldn't it be intriguing to lift Cruella entirely out of dog roles and put her back into animation as the star of a cartoon version of *Sunset Boulevard*? She's still big. It's live action that got small.

Note: I have here an urgent message from a dog lover urging me to emphasize in my review that Dalmatians are sensitive and demanding animals who require dedicated owners. The earlier Dalmatian films apparently inspired countless dog lovers to adopt Dalmatians they were not quite ready for, causing overbreeding and consequent homelessness; my correspondent will be happy to learn (1) the movie itself ends with a request that puppies be adopted only by owners prepared to be responsible and committed, and (2) if a movie hasn't yet driven you to acquire a Dalmatian, 102 Dalmatians is unlikely to do the trick.

One Night at McCool's ★ ★ ½
R, 93 m., 2001

Liv Tyler (Jewel Valentine), Matt Dillon (Randy), John Goodman (Detective Dehling), Paul Reiser (Lawyer Carl), Michael Douglas (Mr. Burmeister), Andrew Dice Clay (Utah/Mormon Brother), Reba McEntire (Carl's Psychiatrist), Richard Jenkins (Priest). Directed by Harald Zwart and produced by Michael Douglas and Allison Lyon Segan. Screenplay by Stan Seidel.

When a man tells a woman she's the one he's been searching for, this is not a comment about the woman but about the man. The male mind, drenched in testosterone, sees what it needs to see. *One Night at McCool's,* a comedy about three men who fall for the same woman, shows how the wise woman can take advantage of this biological insight.

The movie stars Liv Tyler as Jewel Valentine, a woman who walks into a bar one night and walks out, so to speak, with the hearts of three men. Each one sees a different woman. For Randy the bartender (Matt Dillon), she's the sweet homemaker he has yearned for ever since his mother died and left him a house. For Carl the lawyer (Paul Reiser), she's a sexpot with great boobs and legs that go all the way up to here. When Dehling the detective (John Goodman) sees her a few days later, she's like an angel, backlit in soft focus, as if heaven has reincarnated his beloved dead wife.

Much of the humor of the case comes because when Jewel looks at Randy, Carl, and Dehling, she sees three patsys—men who can feed her almost insatiable desire for consumer goods. She may sorta like them. She isn't an evil woman; she's just the victim of her nature. She's like the Parker Posey character in *Best in Show* who considers herself "lucky to have been raised among catalogs."

Like movie sex bombs of the past, Tyler plays Jewel not as a scheming gold digger, but as an innocent, almost childlike creature who is delighted by baubles (and by DVD machines, which she has a thing for). At least, I think that's what she does. Like the audience, I have to reconstruct her from a composite picture made out of three sets of unreliable testimony. Perhaps there is a clue in the fact that the first time we see her, she's with a big, loud, obnoxious, leather-wearing, middle-aged hood named Utah (Andrew Dice Clay). On the other hand, perhaps Utah is a nicer guy, since we see him only through the eyes of his rivals.

We see everything in the movie through secondhand testimony. Like Kurosawa's *Rashomon,* the film has no objective reality; we depend on what people tell us. Jewel Valentine waltzes into each man's life and gets him to do more or less what she desires, and what she desires is highly specific and has to do with her relationship to the consumer lifestyle (to reveal more would be unfair). Each guy, of course, filters her behavior through the delusion that she really likes him. And each guy creates a negative, hostile mental portrait of the other two guys.

Each witness has someone to listen to him. Randy the bartender confides in Mr. Burmeister (Michael Douglas, buck-toothed and in urgent need of a barber). He's a hit man Randy wants to pay to set things straight. Carl the lawyer talks to his psychiatrist (Reba McEntire), who thinks the whole problem may be related to his relationship with his mother, and may be right. And Dehling the detective talks to his brother the priest (Richard Jenkins).

Jewel is not the only character who is seen in three different ways. Consider how Randy the bartender comes across as a hardworking, easygoing, nice guy in his own version, but appears to others as a slow-witted drunk and a letch.

The movie isn't only about three sets of testimony. Far from it. Jewel has a scam she's had a lot of luck with, and enlists Randy in helping her out—against his will, since he sees her as a sweet housewife. He can't imagine her as a criminal, and neither can the cop, who tortuously rewrites the evidence of his own eyes in order to make her into an innocent bystander who needs to be rescued by—well, Detective Dehling, of course.

One Night at McCool's doesn't quite work, but it has a lot of fun being a near miss. It misses, I think because it is so busy with its crosscut structure and its interlocking stories that it never really gives us anyone to identify with—and in a comedy, we have to know where everybody stands in order to figure out what's funny, and how, and to whom. The same flaw has always bothered me about

Rashomon—a masterpiece, yes, but one of conception rather than emotion.

We enjoy the puzzle in *McCool's,* and Tyler and her costars do a good job of seeming like different things to different people, but it's finally an exercise without an emotional engine to pull it, and we just don't care enough. Does it matter if we don't care about a comedy? Yes, I think, it does: Comedy needs victims, and when everybody is innocent in their own eyes, you don't know where to look while you're laughing.

On the Ropes ★ ★ ★ ★
NO MPAA RATING, 90 m., 1999

A documentary featuring boxers Tyrene Manson, George Walton, Noel Santiago, trainer Harry Keitt, manager Mickey Marcello, and Randy Little. Directed and produced by Nanette Burstein and Brett Morgen.

On the Ropes tells the true stories of three young boxers. One of them is sent to prison although she is apparently innocent. We watch as she is represented by an incompetent lawyer, crucified by uncaring prosecutors, and sentenced by a judge who exhibits the worst kind of barbarism: indifference to those whose lives he has power over.

The most amazing thing about the trial and conviction of Tyrene Manson is not that it happened. Justice miscarries all the time in America, frequently when poor black defendants are involved. The new movie *Hurricane* tells the true story of a boxer much more famous than Manson, who was railroaded for life on three fabricated murder convictions.

No, what is amazing is that the lawyer, the prosecutors, and the judge allowed themselves to be filmed as they toyed recklessly with Tyrene Manson's life. You'd think that even the most indifferent of jurists would be on good behavior before the camera. Perhaps the camera itself explains their lack of prudence. *On the Ropes* was filmed by Nanette Burstein and Brett Morgen with a low-tech Sony Handycam; its subjects might not have expected a real movie to result. But it did, and it won the Special Jury Award at Sundance. Now they know.

On the Ropes is a sports documentary as gripping, in a different way, as *Hoop Dreams.*

Both films are about ambitious young people from the ghetto who see sports as a road out of poverty. *On the Ropes* centers on the New Bed-Stuy Gym in New York, where a wise trainer, himself a survivor of hard times, guides the careers of three boxers.

The trainer's name is Harry Keitt, and his story will also figure here. The boxers are Tyrene Manson, a young Golden Gloves contender who has already knocked out the defending champion; George Walton, who seems to have genuine professional potential; and Noel Santiago, who is quick and promising, but easily discouraged. As they prepare for upcoming fights, we learn something of their stories.

Tyrene Manson's is the most inspiring— and therefore most heartbreaking. She is determined to be "the first member of my family to make something of myself." Trapped in poverty, she lives in a house with assorted other family members, and is raising two nieces who belong to her Uncle Randy, described in the movie as a crackhead. During her training for the Golden Gloves, disaster strikes when Randy is arrested for selling drugs to undercover police. They search the house, find cocaine in a bedroom, and charge Tyrene with possession with intent to sell.

Now pause a moment for Tyrene's story, which is more than the court did. She is a woman with no previous history of drug crimes. She does not use drugs. Five people shared that bedroom as their sleeping quarters. There was no lock on the door. She had been trying desperately to find other houses for herself and her nieces, to get them away from the crackhead and his life. Why was she the one charged? Because she was there.

Now follow the progress of the court case. Because her court-appointed attorney forgets a key appointment, her trial is postponed until four days before the Golden Gloves. She asks for a postponement so she can fight. Request denied. On the very day of her cancelled fight, she is sentenced to four and a half to nine years, after a "trial" that is an incompetent assembly-line procedure. One wonders if the judge even really saw her. Certainly he took no notice of her story. Her lawyer is so inept we want to shout obvious suggestions from the audience. Her own tearful speech in her own defense does her no good.

The message is clear: The drug epidemic is so widespread and the courts so overburdened and cynical that a defendant without a competent lawyer is more or less routinely doomed to be locked up. In this case, the evidence suggests that Tyrene Manson was innocent. But to be cynical, even if she were guilty, if she had been white, rich, or well represented, she would never have done a day because of the tainted evidence trail.

There is more heartbreak in the film. We watch as George Walton shows such promise that he gets a shot at the big time, and promptly allows himself to be fast-talked by Vegas types, while hardworking Harry Keitt gets left behind. We see how hard Harry works to help Noel Santiago find direction in his life. We learn something about Harry himself, his own past history of drug problems, his homelessness, and how the gym represents his own comeback. And we see the almost unimaginable disappointments he has to bear.

Note: In one of those notes of irony that life produces so freely, Tyrene Manson was given a brief pass out of prison to attend the Oscars when On the Ropes *was nominated for an Academy Award.*

The Opportunists ★ ★ ★
R, 89 m., 2000

Christopher Walken (Victor Kelly), Peter McDonald (Michael Lawler), Cyndi Lauper (Sally Mahon), Vera Farmiga (Miriam Kelly), Donal Logue (Pat Duffy), Jose Zuniga (Jesus Del Toro), Tom Noonan (Mort Stein), Anne Pitoniak (Aunt Diedre), Olek Krupa (Ted Walikaki). Directed by Myles Connell and produced by John Lyons and Tim Perell. Screenplay by Connell.

Crime movies always seem to have neat endings. There's a chase or a shoot-out, a trial or a confession. *The Opportunists* is messier than that. It is less a matter of the big payoff than the daily struggle. In the movies, most safecrackers are egotistical geniuses who do it for the gratification. In life, I imagine they're more like Victor Kelly, and they're in it for the money. Not much money at that.

Kelly is played in *The Opportunists* by Christopher Walken, and it's one of his best performances. He's a guy who once screwed up big time, and now he's trying to keep his head down and stay on the straight and narrow. He's dutiful. He visits his Aunt Diedre, he brings her home from the geriatric hospital for a day out, and he tries his best with his daughter, Miriam. He has an auto repair shop, and is just scraping by.

Enter a visitor from Ireland, Michael Lawler (Peter McDonald), who says he is a cousin. He has heard all about the great master criminal Victor Kelly and wants to team up with him on a job. Victor is not interested, but gives the kid a cluttered mobile home to live in. Things take a turn for the worse. Victor's check bounces at the geriatric hospital, his aunt is about to be evicted, and from the way he says, "I had a setback at work," you can tell that setbacks are his way of life. It isn't long until he has agreed to join Michael and two neighbors (played by Donal Logue and Jose Zuniga) in going after a safe.

The structure of the movie is like a low-rent version of the usual caper film. There is the obligatory rehearsal scene, but held while they're sitting on the living room floor. And the attempt to crack the safe itself is less cool than confused. When things do not go right, watch the way Christopher Walken's face absorbs and accepts the inevitable. He isn't even angry. It's more like he knew all along this thing would end badly. Instead of suspense and action, the movie links together a series of uh-oh moments, done with perfect pitch.

The sad thing is, there's a woman who loves him or could if he gave her a chance, and would have helped him out if he'd let her. That's Sally Mahon, played straight from the shoulder by Cyndi Lauper. But, no, Victor has to make the same mistakes. Meanwhile, Michael from Ireland is getting friendly with Victor's daughter (Vera Farmiga), and that may not end well, either.

It's here the movie resolutely refuses to fly on autopilot. We have seen more than a few crime movies and we expect things to happen in certain ways. They don't. Without getting into the details, I'll say that a criminal named Mort (Tom Noonan) supplies a kind of input that's refreshingly realistic, and that the aftermath of the safecracking job is not at all like Victor, or the police, expect it to be. The final notes of the movie are not tragic or triumphant, but kind of a quiet comeuppance.

The Opportunists was written and directed by Myles Connell, an Irishman who developed the project at the Sundance Institute, and you wonder if there's a touch of his character Michael Lawler in him—not the bad stuff, just the knowledge about neediness and the willingness to believe unlikely stories. Certainly he helps Walken create a touching character.

Walken has been so good for so long we take him for granted. Sometimes he plays weirdos and we smile because we know he'll sink his teeth into the role. But he is a gifted classical actor (the first time I saw him, he was in an O'Neill play), and here he understands Victor Kelly from the inside out. Victor is not a hero, not a wise guy, not a colorful character, but a working man who keeps repeating the same mistakes. There is a gentleness to the way the movie regards him. And a tact in the way Walken plays this sad and dignified character without ever feeling sorry for him.

The Original Kings of Comedy ★ ★ ★
R, 117 m., 2000

With Steve Harvey, D. L. Hughley, Cedric the Entertainer, and Bernie Mac. A documentary directed by Spike Lee and produced by Lee, Walter Latham, and David M. Gale.

Could *Titanic* have been an African-American film? Not very likely, says the comedian Steve Harvey. What black band would have been so foolish as to remain on deck, playing "Nearer My God to Thee" while the icy waters rose around their knees? "Kool and the Gang would have been unplugged in no time," he says, during an early monologue in *The Original Kings of Comedy.* What would any sensible *Titanic* passenger do? Grabbing a small wooden table that's onstage, he upends it, climbs aboard, grabs a table napkin, and blows into it to make a sail.

Harvey is the emcee of Spike Lee's new concert film, which documents a Charlotte, North Carolina, stop on a concert tour called Kings of Comedy, which has become one of the top-grossing arena acts in the country. He and three other black stand-up comics pack houses with routines that all owe something, sometimes a lot, to Richard Pryor and Eddie Murphy, who have now achieved classic status.

The other three performers are D. L. Hughley, Cedric the Entertainer, and Bernie Mac, all different in style, all using material based on African-American life in America and black-white differences. Harvey is the smoothest of the performers, although the most aggressive toward the audience, picking targets in the front row for comments on their hair, clothes, and career prospects. Bernie Mac is the most hard-edged, and some of his material ventures away from comedy and into the wounds of real life.

He seems, at times, to be working directly from his autobiography, as when he says he's raising his sister's three kids ("she had some drug problems—you know how that is"). They're aged two, four, and six, he says, running down their problems and proclivities with a bluntness that seems to come not so much from comedy as from exhaustion. We wince a little as he describes the kids and wonder (since we don't know) if they're real, or fictional, or adapted for purposes of the act. No matter; his material skates close to the edge, as Pryor's did, and we realize what the poet meant when he said we laugh, that we may not cry.

Cedric the Entertainer is perceptive in pointing out the subtle fault lines between black and white culture, and does an extended riff on the difference between what a white person means by "hope" and a black person means by "wish." "Hope" here comes across as a bland and pious yearning for the best, while "wish" comes across more as an ultimatum or a dare. To hope someone is on time is to think positively for them; to wish they turn up on time is to yearn for them to get what's coming to them. It's hard to explain, but somehow Cedric's tone of voice does all the lifting.

D. L. Hughley does a very funny explanation of why black people are not enthusiastic bungee jumpers. His material is accessible and mainstream, as when he speculates that Jesus was black, just on the basis of his miracle at the wedding feast: Turning water into wine, he imagines Jesus explaining, "Normally, you know, I don't do this—but go on, keep the party goin'!"

Harvey comes on between every act and does a tightwire act with the audience's affection. There is a point beyond which you cannot kid an audience before it feels picked on, and there's tension in the way Harvey approaches that point and then smiles and releases the tension. He asks one young man in the front row what he does for a living. "Computer school," the guy says, and Harvey tells him that nothing about him seems to say "computer" or "school." This could turn bad, but Harvey is a master of timing and tone, and gets away with it.

The Original Kings of Comedy doesn't have the theatrical subtext or, let it be said, the genius of Richard Pryor. But then again, Pryor went out for an hour or ninety minutes and just talked. These guys are working in a revue format. I got the feeling that Bernie Mac, working open-ended, free to improvise, would end up in some strange and fraught places, some funny, some just true.   ☞

Orphans ★ ★ ½
NO MPAA RATING, 102 m., 2000

Gary Lewis (Thomas), Douglas Henshall (Michael), Rosemarie Stevenson (Sheila), Stephen McCole (John), Frank Gallagher (Tanga), Alex Norton (Hanson). Directed by Peter Mullan and produced by Frances Higson. Screenplay by Mullan.

How seriously does *Orphans* intend to be taken? On one hand it tells the gritty story of three Glasgow brothers and their handicapped sister in the twenty-four hours after their mother dies. On the other hand, it involves events that would be at home in a comedy of the absurd. When the sister's wheelchair topples a statue of the Virgin Mary and the damage is blamed on high winds that lifted the roof off a church, we have left the land of realism.

We have not, however, entered the land of boredom. *Orphans* is a film of great intensity and weird events, in which four suddenly parentless adults come unhinged in different ways. For Thomas, the oldest, the mother's death is an occasion for piety, and he spends the night with her coffin in the church and later tries to carry it on his back to the grave. For Michael, it's an occasion for boozing, a pub fight, and a spiral of confusion after he gets knifed. For John, the youngest, it provides a mission: to find and kill the man who stabbed Michael. And for Sheila, in the wheelchair, it leads to an act of defiance as she ventures out into the night alone.

The movie was written and directed by Peter Mullan. You may remember him as the title character in *My Name Is Joe*, Ken Loach's heartrending film about a recovering alcoholic in Glasgow. He won the Best Actor prize at Cannes for that role, and with *Orphans* focuses on at least two characters in urgent need of AA.

It's one of those sub–Eugene O'Neill family dramas in which a lifetime of confusion and anguish comes to a head during a family crisis. We see how each brother has hewn out his space in the family in reaction to the others, while the sister basically just wants out. The brothers Michael and John inhabit a world of hard characters and pub desperadoes (sample dialogue: "We'd cut your legs off for twenty Silk Cut [cigarettes] and a rubber bone for his dog"). Thomas likes to see himself as older, wiser, saner, more religious, and yet he's the maddest of them all. And the movie staggers like its drunken characters from melodrama to revelation, from truth-telling to incredible situations, as when Michael finds himself used as a dart board by a pub owner.

How are we to take this? There are times when we want to laugh, as when Thomas tries to glue the shattered Virgin back together with hot wax candle drippings ("She's a total write-off," he observes morosely). We see the roof lifting off the church in a nice effects shot, but why? To show God's wrath, or simply bad weather conditions? It's a nice point when the funeral goes ahead inside the ruined church—but wouldn't the insurance company and public safety inspectors have something to say about that?

Maybe we're not supposed to ask such realistic questions, but we can't resist. Yet other moments seem as slice-of-life as anything in *My Name Is Joe*. My guess is that Mullan never decided what tone his film should aim for; he fell in love with individual sequences without asking how they fit together.

Note: Because of its Glasgow accents, the film has been subtitled. But we can understand most of what the characters say, and that leads to disconnections, since the subtitles are reluctant to use certain four-letter Anglo-Saxonisms we can clearly hear being uttered by the characters.

The Other Sister ★
PG-13, 130 m., 1999

Juliette Lewis (Carla), Diane Keaton (Elizabeth), Tom Skerritt (Radley), Giovanni Ribisi (Danny), Poppy Montgomery (Caroline), Sarah Paulson (Heather), Linda Thorson (Drew), Joe Flanigan (Jeff). Directed by Garry Marshall and produced by Mario Iscovich and Alexandra Rose. Screenplay by Marshall and Bob Brunner.

The Other Sister is shameless in its use of mental retardation as a gimmick, a prop, and a plot device. Anyone with any knowledge of retardation is likely to find the film offensive. It treats the characters like cute little performing seals—who always deliver their "retarded" dialogue with perfect timing and an edge of irony and drama. Their zingers slide out with the precision of sitcom punch lines.

The film stars Juliette Lewis as Carla, a rich San Francisco girl of seventeen or eighteen who has just returned home after several years in an institution. Her ambition is to train as a veterinarian's assistant. Her father (Tom Skerritt) thinks she should go for it, but her mother (Diane Keaton) is opposed. If there is a convincingly retarded character in the movie, it's the mother. She's borderline hysterical in insisting her daughter is not ready for junior college, dating, dancing, sex, living in her own apartment, or anything else.

In flashbacks to the girl's childhood, we see the mother crying out, "I don't want her to be retarded!" Now she doesn't want her to be anything else. Her opposition to any sign of Carla's independence is handled oddly, however. Every once in a while, she has a brief moment of humanity, in which she softens and says sensible things like, "I'll try to see it your way." These interludes play suspiciously as if they were inserted into the script to lighten the character and make her less of a harridan. Then it's back to bullheaded denial again.

Carla does eventually get into the local polytechnic, where she makes a friend of Danny (Giovanni Ribisi). The two of them are the butts of some cruel treatment, but Danny has found a haven in the music department, where, he proudly tells Carla, he has a real job: "cleaning the marshmallows out of the tubas."

That's because at football games students throw marshmallows at the tubas in the marching bands. I am prepared to believe they do that, but not so prepared to believe that something equally cute comes up at every juncture, as when Carla and her mother attend a benefit at a dog shelter and Carla starts barking at the strays and releases them, disrupting a reception. Or when she gets a free beauty makeover at the mall and is surprised to find it covers only half her face. Or when she's garbed in an absurd swan costume for a social event. Or when she and Daniel, alone at last, study positions in *The Joy of Sex.*

The movie's dialogue knows it's funny—a fatal error. "I wonder who thought up sex in the first place?" one of them muses, studying the sex books. The answer: "I think it was Madonna." Sure, that's exactly what would be said. And how about when Daniel tells Carla, "I love you more than band music and cookie making." All of their words are pronounced as if the characters have marbles in their mouths, and when they walk, it's a funny little modified duck walk. It's like they learned how to act retarded by studying under Jerry Lewis.

Moment after moment is utterly false. Take the climax at the country club, where a bartender keeps pouring triple shots of green Chartreuse for Danny. Not likely, because: (1) Danny is obviously a novice drinker. (2) He is obviously underage. (3) Green Chartreuse is one of the strongest liquors in the world, so that several full snifters would paralyze an inexperienced drinker. And (4) country club bartenders like their jobs and know they can get fired for getting underage drinkers blind drunk.

Of course, Danny doesn't get *really* drunk—only drunk enough to make a speech that is cunningly calculated to offend those who need to be offended, please those who need to be pleased, and move the wheels of the plot. All in "retarded" language that is perfectly chosen and timed, of course.

Am I getting too technical here? I don't think so. The truth is in the details. The details of *The Other Sister* show a movie with no serious knowledge of retardation and no interest in learning or teaching. I never tire of quoting

Godard, who tells us that the way to criticize a movie is to make another movie. The movie that shames *The Other Sister* was made in 1988 by Robert M. Young. It is called *Dominick and Eugene,* and it stars Tom Hulce and Ray Liotta in the story of a retarded man and his brother. See that, and you will cringe when you compare it to *The Other Sister.*

The Out-of-Towners ★ ½
PG-13, 91 m., 1999

Steve Martin (Henry Clark), Goldie Hawn (Nancy Clark), John Cleese (Hotel Manager), Tom Riis Farrell (Mugger). Directed by Sam Weisman and produced by Robert W. Cort, Robert Evans, and Christine Forsyth-Peters. Screenplay by Marc Lawrence, based on the screenplay by Neil Simon.

The Out-of-Towners jogs doggedly on the treadmill of comedy, working up a sweat but not getting much of anywhere. It's a remake of the 1970 Neil Simon screenplay, with Steve Martin and Goldie Hawn now taking the roles played by Jack Lemmon and Sandy Dennis. The most valuable addition to the cast is John Cleese, as the hotel manager; he's doing his character from *Fawlty Towers,* but at least it's a role worth repeating.

Martin and Hawn play the Clarks, Henry and Nancy, who are empty nesters in Ohio now that their daughter has moved to New York and their son is studying abroad. Henry has a secret: He's been fired at his ad agency. He flies to New York for a job interview, Nancy tags along, and we sense the movie's desperation in a scene on the plane. She's seated several rows behind him, and asks the passengers in between to pass up his Foot Chums and rash ointment. A woman like that deserves to be in an empty nest all by herself.

But the thing is, Nancy isn't really that lamebrained. She can be smart, or tender, or goofy, or stubborn—or whatever the screenplay requires from moment to moment. That's because she isn't really anybody at all, and neither is Henry. They're devices to be manipulated by the film—figures on a chessboard.

Lots of things go wrong on the trip, which is taken by plane, train, and automobile, providing a melancholy reminder of Martin's much better 1987 movie—and also of *Forces of Nature*, in which Ben Affleck and Sandra Bullock go through a similar ordeal. The trick in a film like this is to keep the characters consistent as the situations change. If both the characters and the situations are slippery, there's no place to stand. And if you're determined to have a sweet, uplifting ending, all is lost.

It helps to observe situations closely, to find humor in the details rather than trusting the general scene. Consider, for example, a sequence where Henry and Nancy blunder into a meeting of Sex Addicts Anonymous because they're starving and spot the free sweet rolls. They don't realize what kind of a meeting it is, and the movie thinks that's joke enough, so it doesn't really "see" the other people at the meeting. I'm reminded of a scene in John Waters's *Polyester,* where Tab Hunter blunders into an AA meeting and is asked to introduce himself. He gives his name. "And?" ask the assembled members. "AND? AAANNNDDD???" They're shot with a fish-eye lens as they peer at him, waiting for the magic words, "and I'm an alcoholic."

In *The Out-of-Towners,* the filmmakers think it's funny enough that the sex addicts are creepy, and Henry and Nancy are grossed out by their stories. That misses the point. In comedy, you figure out what the objective is, and go for it single-mindedly. Why are Henry and Nancy at the meeting? Because they want those sweet rolls! So what should they do? Win the sweet rolls by any means necessary, telling the members whatever they want to hear. I can imagine Martin and Hawn improvising sexual addictions all night long. But not in this movie, which skims the surface.

There are a couple of sequences that work. I liked the absurdity of the scene where they're approached on the street by a well-dressed, well-spoken man (Tom Riis Farrell) who asks for $5 to get to a business meeting. He doesn't look like a panhandler, and his British accent is curious. Nancy finally asks, "Aren't you . . . Andrew Lloyd Webber?" Well, yes, he confesses, it's embarrassing to be caught short of funds, but yes, he is. The scene develops nicely.

And then there is John Cleese, who perhaps had a hand in the precise wording of some of his own dialogue, which spins easily between ingratiating toadiness and loathsome sneering.

There are few things funnier than Cleese playing a snob who is pretending to be a democrat.

But even some of the movie's surefire ideas don't seem to work. There's a moment, for example, when the Clarks are embracing on the grass in Central Park, and are suddenly hit with spotlights and seen by dozens of people inside the Tavern on the Green, including Mayor Rudy Giuliani, playing himself. Incredible as it may seem, this is not funny.

We observe that, yes, it's the mayor. We understand that the Clarks are embarrassed. But the movie stands flat-footed and smugly regards the situation, instead of doing something with it. If you're going to have a celebrity in your movie, make him work for his cameo. Why not have Giuliani personally take charge of the police investigation? Or claim the spectacle as an example of how people-friendly the park is? Or get turned on?

As it became increasingly clear that *The Out-of-Towners* was not a proud moment in the often inspired careers of Martin and Hawn, I started looking for evidence of little moments of genius that the stars may have slipped into the crevices of the movie on their own. Surely it was Martin's idea to suggest renting advertising space on the tongues of dogs to tattoo the word "Alpo."

Outside Providence ★ ½
R, 102 m., 1999

Shawn Hatosy (Tim Dunphy), Alec Baldwin (Old Man Dunphy), Amy Smart (Jane Weston), Jon Abrahams (Drugs Delaney), Tommy Bone (Jackie Dunphy), Jonathan Brandis (Mousy), Jack Ferver (Irving Waltham), Gabriel Mann (Jack Wheeler). Directed by Michael Corrente and produced by Corrente, Peter Farrelly, Bobby Farrelly, and Randy Finch. Screenplay by Peter Farrelly, Corrente, and Bobby Farrelly, based on the novel by Peter Farrelly.

The brothers Farrelly, Peter and Bobby, have had stupendous success with their comedies *Dumb and Dumber* and *There's Something About Mary.* So much success they have the clout to get a project made just because they want to make it. Their wish is Miramax's command—which suggests a valuable exhortation: Be careful what you wish for, because you might get it.

This is a coming-of-age movie, set in the 1970s, about a working-class kid from Pawtucket, Rhode Island, who gets in trouble and then, because his dad's mob friend knows a judge, gets sent to a private academy for his last year of high school. Here he's a fish out of water (instead of luggage, he arrives with his clothing in a plastic garbage bag). But soon he's dating the most popular girl in school, getting into and out of trouble, learning life's lessons, and having the kinds of experiences people must really actually have, since so many movies have been made about them.

If it had been well made, *Outside Providence* might have overcome its genre and amounted to something. Alas, it is badly written and severely miscast; Alec Baldwin, as a working-class stiff with a Rhode Island accent, sweats over every syllable. Its construction is so amateurish that a basic character change (the hero stops screwing around and starts studying) is blown off with a film-school montage (reads books, gets approving nod from teacher, etc.). And the school faculty contains nothing but archetypes (a befuddled Mr. Chips, a vindictive martinet).

The movie was directed by Michael Corrente and written by Corrente and the Farrellys, based on a novel by Peter Farrelly. Corrente can direct (I liked his 1995 film *Federal Hill,* set in Providence), but this time he has an underdone screenplay and compensates by pushing too hard. What are we to make of a scene where the characters are smoking dope in a car, and an exterior shot shows the car trailing so much smoke it looks on fire? In Cheech and Chong, yes. In the real world, no. I could also have done without the little brother in the wheelchair and the three-legged family dog with an eye patch. The kid brother would have been okay if he'd been better developed as a character, not just window dressing and a setup for one-liners ("We were playing touch football and he fell off the roof").

The hero is a Pawtucket teenager named Tim Dunphy (Shawn Hatosy), whose father (Baldwin) calls him "Dildo"—the kind of detail that could be true in life but never feels true in the movies. "Dunph" (as he understandably prefers to be called) hangs out with his dopehead friends, smoking reefer atop the local water tower (surely the police would never notice them there). Sent away to an exclusive Connecticut boarding school, he finds richer versions of the same kinds of friends; now they smoke dope on the roof outside their dorm windows.

The screenplay lumbers from one obligatory scene to the next, pausing most painfully at a big dramatic climax where Dunph and his dad have a heart-to-heart about his dead mother. What happened, and why, and should Dunph blame his father? We hardly care, because the dialogue is so ham-handed that the illusion of reality is broken and we can see the acting itself; we're aware of Baldwin and Hatosy struggling with lines that contain information but don't put it in context—it's payoff without setup, bathos when it should be pathos.

There's an uneasy truce between the heartfelt family stuff and the standard prep school high jinks. When Dunph gets in big trouble for having Jane in his room, it's handled as a life-changing experience on the one hand, and as a sitcom opportunity on the other. Which is it? Moment of decision, or setup for a silly scene where he hops up and down outside a dean's window to get his attention?

Outside Providence is so unsuccessful in so many different ways that maybe the whole project was doomed. At the least, the screenplay should have been rewritten in a consistent tone, and Old Man Dunphy should have been recast with a grittier actor and rewritten into a real father and not just a collection of blue-collar clichés. *Outside Providence* no doubt embodies many memories that are sacred to the Farrelly brothers, but in this form it might prudently have been left unmade.

P

Panic ★ ★ ★ ★
R, 88 m., 2001

William H. Macy (Alex), John Ritter (Josh Parks), Neve Campbell (Sarah), Donald Sutherland (Michael), Tracey Ullman (Martha), Barbara Bain (Deidre), David Dorfman (Sammy). Directed by Henry Bromell and produced by Andrew Lazar, Lori Miller, and Matt Cooper. Screenplay by Bromell.

"I've got two jobs. I run a small mail-order business out of the house. Lawn ornaments, kitchen geegaws, sexual aids—things like that."
"And the rest of the time?"
"I work for my father. I kill people."

The sad-eyed patient speaks calmly. His psychiatrist says, "You're kidding, right?" No, he is not kidding. He was raised in the family business. His father was a hit man, and he's a hit man too. Not even his wife knows; she believes the mail-order story. But now he's in his forties, has a young son he loves, and wants to stop murdering for a living.

It tells you something—it may even tell you enough—that the man, named Alex, is played by William H. Macy. This wonderful actor has a gift for edgy unhappiness, repressed resentment, and in *Panic* he speaks too calmly and moves too smoothly, as if afraid of trip wires and booby traps. He spent his childhood afraid to stand up to his father, and in a sense his childhood has never ended.

Henry Bromell's *Panic* seeps with melancholy, old wounds, repressed anger, lust. That it is also caustically funny and heartwarming is miraculous: How does it hit so many different notes and never strain? It has a relationship between Alex and his son, Sammy, that reminds us of *The Sixth Sense*, and one between Alex and the sexy young Sarah (Neve Campbell) that evokes *American Beauty*. And Alex himself, trying to keep everyone happy, trying to keep secrets, trying to separate the compartments of his life, has the desperation of the character Macy played in *Fargo*.

But this is not a movie assembled from spare parts. Bromell began as a writer *(North-*

ern Exposure, Chicago Hope), and this is a first film made with joy and with a writer's gift for character and dialogue. It involves a situation rich with irony and comic possibilities but isn't cynical about it; it's the kind of story that is funny when you hear about it from someone else, but not funny if it happens to you.

Alex was raised by his father, Michael (Donald Sutherland), to be a hit man. They started with squirrels and worked up from there. Alex didn't like killing squirrels, and in all of his killings since, it has been his father's finger pulling the trigger of Alex's tortured psyche. Alex is good at his job. But it makes him sick.

In the waiting room of his psychiatrist (John Ritter), he meets the patient of another doctor. This is Sarah, played by Neve Campbell as bright, cheeky, and with a gift for sharp observation. She has a complicated love life, is aware of her appeal, asks Alex if he's a guy in midlife crisis who thinks a sexy young girl might be just the ticket. In *American Beauty,* Kevin Spacey did indeed think that about the pom-pom girl, but Alex is looking not for sex but for approval, forgiveness, redemption; sex with Sarah would be less lust than rehab.

There are other important women in the picture. Tracey Ullman is Martha, Alex's wife, and Barbara Bain is Deidre, his mother. Martha has no idea how Alex really earns his living. Deidre knows all about everything, and when Alex confides that he wants out, she delivers a merciless lecture about how his father spent his whole life building up the family business, and Alex is an ungrateful child to destroy that dream. Yes, this is ironic, discussing murder in business terms, but it is so easy to separate success from morality. This could be any business in which the father insists that the son surrender his own dreams for the old man's.

Alex doesn't confide much in his wife; his secrets have built a wall. He loves her, but hopelessly, and he loves his son (David Dorfman, the little boy in *Bounce*). Their talks at bedtime are long and rich, and Sammy sees that something is deeply troubling his father: "Dad, are you all right?"

The movie takes these strands and weaves them into an emotional and logistical trap for

Alex. His relationship with Sarah, a complicated girl, creates more issues than it solves. His father assigns him to perform an execution that demonstrates the old man's inexorable power over his son. Flashbacks show Alex's anguish as a child, and there is also a flashback showing how he met his wife, and how he was attracted to her goofiness.

The elements of the movie stand on their own. The Neve Campbell character is not simply the younger woman in Alex's life, but creates plot space of her own, where Alex is a visitor. The parents, Michael and Deidre, have a relationship that depends on their son but excludes him. Alex and Sammy have a private bond. We come to see Alex as a desperate man running from one secret compartment to another, seeking a place where he can hide.

Macy is as easy to identify with as any actor working. He doesn't push it. As Alex, he approaches his problems doggedly, sometimes bravely, hoping for a reprieve. Sutherland makes the old hit man into a particularly unlikable person: There's something about the way he gobbles an outdoor meal, his hat askew, that sets our teeth on edge. Bain's mother in her cold confidence is even more hateful. Ullmann, that gifted character actress, creates a woman who knows her life is coming apart but doesn't know what her life is. Neve Campbell takes a tricky role and enriches it, brings it human dimension instead of being content with the "sexpot" assignment. And the little boy is heartbreaking, particularly in a conversation late in the movie. This is one of the year's best films.

Note: Panic *was a success at Sundance 2000, but didn't get a major release after a test audience disliked it. I don't blame the test audience; this is not a look-alike movie. But the executives who believed the audience instead of their own eyes should be ashamed of themselves. Now the film has won a national release and, like* Croupier, *could be discovered by filmgoers who make up their own minds.*

Paradise Lost 2: Revelations ★ ★ ★
NO MPAA RATING, 2000

A documentary directed by Joe Berlinger and Bruce Sinofsky.

Three second-graders were brutally murdered on May 5, 1993, in West Memphis, Arkansas, and three young men are still in prison for the crimes, convicted in a climate that stereotyped them as members of a satanic cult.

The possibility that they are innocent gnaws at anyone who has seen *Paradise Lost: The Child Murders at Robin Hood Hills.* That 1996 documentary argued they were innocent, and implied that the father of one of the victims might have been involved. He even supplied a knife to the filmmakers that seemed to match the profile of the murder weapon, but DNA tests on bloodstains were botched.

When *Paradise Lost* played on HBO, it inspired a national movement to free the three prisoners—Damien Echols, now twenty-four, under sentence of death, and Jessie Misskelley, twenty-three, and Jason Baldwin, twenty-one, with life sentences. Now comes *Paradise Lost 2: Revelations,* a sequel that involves their appeals, and also features extraordinarily creepy footage of Mark Byers, the father under suspicion, whose wife has died in mysterious circumstances in the meantime.

The new documentary is directed like the first by Joe Berlinger and Bruce Sinofsky. There is unlikely to be anything else on TV more disturbing than this film. Watching it, you feel like an eyewitness to injustice.

Among new evidence introduced on appeal is the finding that human bite marks, found on one of the child's bodies, do not match the bites of the three defendants. The film points out that Mark Byers had his teeth extracted in 1997, four years after the murders, although on camera he places the extraction much earlier, and gives several contradictory reasons for it.

What does this prove? Not much to prosecution forensic experts, who testify the bite marks were caused by a belt.

Byers spends a lot of time on-camera (he accepted a payment for appearing in this film). He is described by Echols as "the fakest creature to ever walk on two legs," and that seems the simple truth: He has an odd way of speaking in rehearsed sound bites, avoiding eye contact while using lurid prose that sounds strikingly insincere. Visiting the murder scene, he stages a mock burial and cremation of the three defendants, saying, "There's your head-marker, you animal," and then pouring on charcoal lighter, chortling, "Now we're gonna have some fun," and lighting his cigar before dropping the match.

Did he do it? We hear a litany of his problems: a brain tumor, manic depression, bad checks, drug abuse, DUIs, hallucinations, blackouts, neighbors who got a restraining order after he spanked their child, and the death of his wife. Byers rants about those who accused him of her death and says she died in her sleep of natural causes. Later, possibly in a Freudian slip, he says, "after my wife was murdered."

The legal establishment in West Memphis seems wedded to their shaky case—dug in too deep to reconsider. Echols's new attorney claims the original defense was underfunded and incompetent, and indeed we find that one attorney was paid only $19 an hour, and the defense was limited to $1,000 for tests and research in a case dripping with forensic evidence.

Questions remain. If the victims were killed in the wooded area where they were found, why was there no blood at the scene? Can a confession by Misskelley be trusted? He has an IQ of 72, was questioned by police for twelve hours without a parent or attorney present, and then was tape-recorded only long enough to recite a statement, which he later retracted.

On June 17, 2000, the appeal was turned down by the same judge who officiated at the original trial. A federal habeus corpus motion is the defendants' last chance.

Near the end of the film, Byers takes a lie detector test and passes. The film notes that at the time he was on five mood-altering medications. The last shots show him singing "Amazing Grace," very badly.

Pariah ★ ★ ★

NO MPAA RATING, 105 m., 1999

Damon Jones (Steve), Dave Oren Ward (Crew), David Lee Wilson (David Lee), Aimee Chaffin (Sissy), Angela Jones (Angela), Anna Padgett (Lex), Dan Weene (Joey), Ann Zupa (Babe), Brandon Slater (Doughboy), Jason Posey (Kewvin), Elexa Williams (Sam). Directed by Randolph Kret and produced by Scott Grusin, David J. Hill, Shaun Hill, and Vince Rotonda. Screenplay by Kret.

Godard said that one way to criticize a movie is to make another movie. *Pariah*, a raw and unblinking look at the skinhead subculture, is a movie I'd like to show to those admirers of *Fight Club* who have assured me of their movie's greatness. This is the real thing, with *Fight Club*'s implicit skinhead doom-worship made visible. Its characters don't take the high road in rejecting straw targets like "consumerism," but the low road, in rejecting everything outside their small, infected circle of hate. The movie understands that it's not what you reject that defines you, but the act of rejection—the very decision to scorn and offend. *Fight Club* is *Pariah* made palatable.

To be sure, the demented subjects of *Pariah* are racists, and the heroes of *Fight Club* are not. But there are scenes in *Pariah* that look uncannily like scenes in *Fight Club*, except that they are uglier, more violent, and more brutal. And the group dynamic is similar: Society is corrupt, so we will set ourselves against society, behaving in such a way that citizens will fear and hate us.

Pariah takes place within a Los Angeles neighborhood mostly devoid of ordinary people. Everyone seems to live by violence and fear. If the skinheads attack gays and attempt the murder of a transvestite in a park—well, there is a gay gang, too, to pound the skinheads with baseball bats. And if white gangs attack interracial couples because the woman is black, black gangs attack them because the man is white. When not enforcing their dating theories, the gangs fight with each other.

As the film opens, we meet Steve (Damon Jones), a peaceable white guy who dates a black woman (Elexa Williams). They are attacked by skinheads in a parking garage, and he is beaten and then made to watch while she is raped. He attempts to comfort her, in an observant if somewhat awkward scene, but she is beyond comfort. Rage then transforms Steve into an instrument of vengeance, and he becomes a skinhead, tattooed, belted, and booted, and joins the gang that attacked them. He wants revenge, especially against David Lee (David Lee Wilson), who led the attack, and Crew (Dave Oren Ward), the pack's top dog.

Only the reasonable would point out that once Steve identifies the gang, it would be fairly easy for him to kill David without going through the painful and dangerous ordeal of trying to ingratiate himself. But then there would be no movie—and also no opportunity for Randolph Kret, the writer-director, to show us Steve gradually becoming brutalized by the skinhead culture. He doesn't change his ideas, but he becomes comfortable within a world of hate-talk, rough sex, and fights that lead to bonding and friendship (ahem).

Pariah is sometimes an ungainly movie, carelessly constructed and too long, but it contains the seed of truth, and that redeems it. It shows us a male-dominated group in which sex is uninteresting unless forced, in which women are treated as slaves and receptacles, in which the rhetoric of white supremacy begs the question: How do these people not see that their values reflect pathology and zero self-esteem?

The dynamic of the skinheads and *Fight Club* is similar. Society is corrupt and unworthy, and its values are boring and materialistic. Only by a descent to the animal level can men regain self-respect. (Yes, *Fight Club* rejects this message, but its imagery makes it fleetingly attractive; *Pariah* does a better job of not making seductive what it is against.) To spend time in this movie is to reap the harvest of cruel childhoods, broken parents, poverty, ignorance, and despair. You would need to think yourself desperately without resources to turn to skinheads for improvement.

Will the film cause the kind of behavior it opposes? (It opened in Los Angeles in spring 1999, then was withdrawn after Columbine.) I doubt that any film can persuade anybody to do what he is not already fully prepared to do. Films may suggest methods, but do not force decisions. What it does do is show *Fight Club* fans what their movie is really about. I received an actual e-mail, which I believe to be genuine, from a *Fight Club* admirer who complained: "My generation was denied a war in which to test itself. We need movies like this."

Passion of Mind ★ ★
PG-13, 105 m., 2000

Demi Moore (Marie/Marty), Stellan Skarsgard (William), William Fichtner (Aaron), Sinead Cusack (Jessie), Peter Riegert (Dr. Peters), Joss Ackland (Dr. Langer), Gerry Bamman (Edward Youngerman), Julianne Nicholson (Kim). Directed by Alain Berliner and produced by Carole Scotta, Tom Rosenberg, and Ron Bass. Screenplay by Bass and David Field.

When Marie is asleep in France, Marty is awake in New York. When Marty is asleep in New York, Marie is awake in France. Both women are played by Demi Moore in Alain Berliner's *Passion of Mind,* a film that crosses the supernatural with "an interesting case of multiple personality," as one of her shrinks puts it. She has two shrinks. She needs them. She doesn't know which of her lives is real and which is the dream. Whenever she goes to sleep in one country, she wakes up in the other. Multiple personalities are bad enough, but at least she doesn't have eager kidneys; getting up in the middle of the night to go to the bathroom could lead to whiplash.

The movie uses its supernatural device to show Moore's characters living two contrasting lifestyles. In France, she leads a quiet life as a book reviewer and raises her two daughters. In New York, she's a powerful literary agent who dedicates her life to her career. In France, she meets William (Stellan Skarsgard). In New York, she meets Aaron (William Fichtner). They both love her. Each of her personalities, Marty and Marie, is aware of the other and remembers what happens in the other's life.

Like *Me Myself I,* the recent movie starring Rachel Griffiths, this movie is about a woman's choice between family and career. In the Griffiths film, a busy single writer is magically transported into a marriage with a husband and three kids. If she could have led both lives at once, as Marie/Marty does, I think she would have been okay with that. And as Marty and Marie trudge off to complain to their shrinks, I was wondering why it was so necessary to solve their dilemma. If you can live half of your life quietly in France and the other half in the fast lane of Manhattan, enjoy parenthood and yet escape the kids, and be in love with two great guys without (technically) cheating on either one—what's the problem? When you're not with the one you love, you love the one you're with. If it works, don't fix it.

Of course it doesn't work. If one of the worlds is real and the other is a dream, and if you cannot be in love with two men at once, then what happens if you commit to the dream man and lose the real one? This preys on the mind of Marie/Marty, who also dreads what could happen if the two worlds mix in some way. She won't let one guy spend the night, because "if someone were to be with me and wake me up, something bad might happen."

It is that very problem that the movie never quite solves logically. Forgive me for being literal. The time difference between New York and France is six hours. How does that fit into your sleep schedule? If she is awake until midnight in France, does that mean she's asleep all day in New York, and wakes up at six P.M.? Are there twenty-four hours in a day for both characters?

These questions are cheating. Forgive me for thinking of them. They obviously occurred to the screenwriters, Ron Bass and David Field, who just as obviously decided to ignore them. The movie is not about timetables but life choices, and to a degree it works. We see Marty/Marie pulled between two worlds, in love with her children, attracted to the two guys. The problem is, that's it. We master the situation in the first forty minutes, and then the wheels start spinning. What's needed is a way to take the story through some kind of U-turn.

Why not have the woman accept her situation, work with it, willfully experiment with her two lives, self-consciously engage with it? Don't make her a victim but a psychic explorer. Why, if we are dealing with a woman who is liberated half of the time from each lifestyle, does the movie fall back on the tired formula that there is something wrong with her, and she must seek psychiatric help to cure it? The joy in *Me Myself I* is that the woman self-reliantly deals with the vast change in her life, instead of diagnosing herself as a case study.

Another difficulty in *Passion of Mind* is with the men. Stellan Skarsgard and William Fichtner bring more to the movie than is needed. These are complex actors with subtly disturbing undertones. They both play nice guys, but we can't quite believe them. We suspect secrets or hidden agendas. They smile, they're warm and pleasant and supportive, and we're wondering, what's their angle? For this particular story, it might have been better to cast actors who were more bland and one-dimensional,

so that they could represent only what is needed (two nice guys) rather than veiled complications.

Demi Moore does what she can with a screenplay that doesn't seem confident about what to do with her. She is convincing as either woman, but not as both, if you see what I mean. She makes a wonderful mother in France and a convincing businessman in Manhattan, but when she is either one, we wonder where she puts the other one. The screenplay doesn't help her.

By the end of the film, which is unconvincingly neat, I was distracted by too many questions to care about the answers. The structure had upstaged the content. It wasn't about the heroine; it was about the screenplay. In *Me Myself I*, which has a much simpler premise (the woman goes from one life to another with an unexplained magical zap), there was room for a deeper and more human (and humorous) experience. First the heroine was one, then the other. In *Passion of Mind*, by being both, she is neither. Is her problem a split personality, or psychic jet lag?

The Patriot ★ ★ ★
R, 157 m., 2000

Mel Gibson (Benjamin Martin), Heath Ledger (Gabriel Martin), Joely Richardson (Charlotte Selton), Jason Isaacs (Colonel William Tavington), Chris Cooper (Colonel Harry Burwell), Tcheky Karyo (Jean Villeneuve), Rene Auberjonois (Reverend Oliver), Lisa Brenner (Anne Howard), Tom Wilkinson (General Cornwallis). Directed by Roland Emmerich and produced by Mark Gordon and Gary Levinsohn. Screenplay by Robert Rodat.

The Patriot is a fable arguing the futility of pacifism, set against the backdrop of the Revolutionary War. It is rousing and entertaining and you get your money's worth, but there isn't an idea in it that will stand up to thoughtful scrutiny. The British are seen as gentlemanly fops or sadistic monsters, and the Americans come in two categories: brave or braver. Those who have a serious interest in the period will find it a cartoon; those raised on summer action pictures will find it more stimulating than most.

Mel Gibson stars, in a powerful and effective performance, as a widower named Benjamin Martin with seven children. He saw enough of battle in the French and Indian War, and was frightened by what he learned about himself. He counsels a treaty with King George. Asked about his principles by an old comrade in arms (Chris Cooper), he replies, "I'm a parent. I haven't got the luxury of principles." But he gets some in a hurry after the monstrous British Colonel Tavington (Jason Isaacs) arrests Martin's eldest son, Gabriel (Heath Ledger), and takes him away to be hanged, after first shooting another of Martin's sons just for the hell of it, and then burning down his house.

Since Martin had just been treating the wounded of both sides in his home, this seems excessive, and in the long run turns out to be extremely unwise for the British, since Martin goes on to more or less single-handedly mastermind their defeat. There must have been many British officers less cruel—but none would have served the screenplay's purpose, which is to show Martin driven berserk by grief, rage, and the need for revenge.

The following sequence is the film's most disturbing. Martin and his sons hide in the woods and ambush Tavington and his soldiers; eventually the battle comes down to hand-to-hand fighting (Martin wielding a tomahawk). Gabriel is freed, and the younger adolescent boys get a taste for blood ("I'm glad I killed them!" one of the tykes cries. "I'm glad!"). The movie's scenes of carnage have more impact than the multiple killings in a film like *Shaft,* because they are personal, not technical; individual soldiers, frightened and ill-prepared, are fighting for their lives, while in the modern action pictures most of the victims are pop-up arcade targets.

The big players in the war (George Washington, King George) are far offscreen, although we do meet General Cornwallis (Tom Wilkinson), a British leader who counsels a "gentlemanly" conduct of the war and rebukes Tavington for his brutality. Still, when the Americans refuse to "fight fair" and adopt hit-and-run guerrilla tactics against the British (who march in orderly ranks into gunfire), he bends enough to authorize the evil colonel to take what steps are necessary to bring down Martin (by now legendary as "the Ghost").

The movie's battle scenes come in two flavors—harrowing and unlikely. Two battles near the beginning of the film are conveniently fought in open fields overlooked by the upper windows of houses, so onlookers have excellent seats for the show and can supply a running narration. No doubt revolutionary battles were fought right there in the pasture, but would Benjamin Martin allow his kids to stand in the windows, or tell them to hide in the barn?

The "real" battles are grueling tests of men and horses, as soldiers march into withering fire and the survivors draw their swords or fix their bayonets for blood-soaked combat in close quarters. These battles seem anarchic and pitiless, and respect the movie convention that bitter rivals will sooner or later find themselves face-to-face. The scenes are well staged by the director, Roland Emmerich, working from a screenplay by Robert Rodat, the same man who wrote *Saving Private Ryan,* with its equally appalling battle scenes.

Hollywood movies are at pains these days to provide a role for a heroic African-American or two. A role for a black sailor was found in the segregated U.S. Navy submarine corps in *U-571* (he was a mess orderly). Now we have a black slave who fights beside white men (even those who hate him) because General Washington has decreed freedom for all slaves who fight for a year. Good enough, but why not go all the way and give this character dialogue and a real role to play, instead of demeaningly using him only to count down the months and days until his freedom? When the former slave finally gets two whole sentences in a row, at the end, he quotes Martin's son: "Gabriel said if we won the war, we could build a whole new world. We could get started right here with your home." Uh-huh. Why not get started with your own home?

The movie has light comic relief to ease the tension (Martin's handmade chairs keep collapsing beneath him), and a love story (Gabriel loves Anne, a plucky colonial girl who catches his eye with a patriotic speech). Anne's father is a deaf man who misunderstands things. When Gabriel asks permission to write Anne, the old man at first takes offense. Then he says, "Oh . . . *write* her! Of course you may." What did he think Gabriel had asked? Meanwhile, there's even female company for hard-bitten Benjamin Martin, who asks the sister of his dead wife, "May I sit here?" Her answer got laughs in the screening I attended: "It's a free country—or at least, it will be."

These passages and others (including The Dead Man Who Is Not Really Dead) have been trucked directly into *The Patriot* from the warehouse of timeless clichés. They betray the movie's lack of serious intentions. It basically wants to be a summer action movie with a historical gloss. At that, it succeeds. I enjoyed the strength and conviction of Gibson's performance, the sweep of the battle scenes, and the absurdity of the British caricatures. None of it has much to do with the historical reality of the Revolutionary War, but with such an enormous budget at risk, how could it?

Payback ★ ★ ★
R, 102 m., 1999

Mel Gibson (Porter), Gregg Henry (Val), Maria Bello (Rosie), David Paymer (Stegman), Deborah Kara Unger (Lynn), William Devane (Carter), Bill Duke (Detective Hicks), Kris Kristofferson (Bronson), James Coburn (Mr. Fairfax), Lucy Liu (Pearl). Directed by Brian Helgeland and produced by Bruce Davey. Screenplay by Helgeland and Terry Hayes, based on the novel *The Hunter* by Richard Stark.

"Not many people know what their life's worth," the hero of *Payback* tells us right at the beginning. "I do. Seventy grand. That's what they took from me. And that's what I'm gonna get back." If you absorb that statement and take a close look at the title, you'll have a good idea of what the movie's about. The only remaining question: Is it about it entertainingly? Yes.

The movie's publicity makes much of the fact that the hero, named Porter, is a bad guy. It quotes the director, Brian Helgeland: "I wanted to see a bad guy as the hero, but I didn't want to make excuses for him." Of course, if the bad guy is played by Mel Gibson, you don't have to make the same kinds of excuses as if he's played by, say, James Woods. Gibson has a whimsical charm, a way of standing outside material like this and grinning at it. Oh, he's earnest and angry, blood-soaked and beaten nearly to death. But inside, there's a grin. His fundamental personality is comic—he's a joker

and a satirist—and he only rarely makes an effort to hide that side (as he did, say, in *The Year of Living Dangerously*).

Brian Helgeland has a sense of style, too (he wrote *L.A. Confidential*), and we get the sense that *Payback* is more interested in style than story; it wants to take a criminal's revenge and make it the story of a guy whose mission edges into monomania. He wants exactly $70,000, no more, no less. More than once in the movie, Porter's enemies try to pay him more than $70,000. They're missing the point. (Porter could save himself a lot of wear and tear by taking $130,000 and mailing the rest back, but you know how it is.)

The setup contains a fundamental double-cross that I dare not reveal, and that will make it a little hard to discuss certain other aspects of the story. Perhaps selected details will give you the flavor. As when Porter's friend Val (Gregg Henry) shows him the weekly routine of some Chinese mobsters picking up cash. "They're not wearing their seat belts," Porter observes, and of course that leads to the logical conclusion that the way to get their money is to crash head-on into their car.

There are also action gags involving severed gas lines on a car, a trick telephone, blackmail by cell phone, kidnapping, and a scene in which Porter comes closer than anyone since James Bond to being killed crotch-first. The film also contains a hooker with a heart of gold (Maria Bello), a two-timing dame (Deborah Kara Unger), a laconic cop (Bill Duke), a big mobster (Kris Kristofferson), and an even bigger one (James Coburn).

Writing a screenplay like this essentially involves finding new bottles for old wine. Tricking the enemy is routine, but doing it in a new way is fun. Turning the tables is standard, but not when you don't expect when, and how, they'll be turned. And cinematographer Ericson Core finds a nice blue-green grittiness in the streets of Chicago, where the exterior scenes are punctuated by elevated trains rumbling past on such a frequent schedule that actual el riders will be chuckling to themselves.

There is much cleverness and ingenuity in *Payback*, but Mel Gibson is the key. The movie wouldn't work with an actor who was heavy on his feet, or was too sincere about the material. Gibson is essentially an action comedian, who enters into violence with a bemused detachment *(Mad Max Beyond Thunderdome)*. Here he has fun as the movie goes over the top, as when a doctor operates on him for gunshot wounds, using whiskey as a painkiller (for the doctor, not Gibson). Or when he helps himself to the dollars from a beggar's hat. Or when, and how, he recites "This little piggy."

Pay It Forward ★ ★ ½
PG-13, 122 m., 2000

Kevin Spacey (Eugene Simonet), Helen Hunt (Arlene McKinney), Haley Joel Osment (Trevor McKinney), Jay Mohr (Chris Chandler), James Caviezel (Jerry), Jon Bon Jovi (Ricki), Angie Dickinson (Grace). Directed by Mimi Leder and produced by Peter Abrams, Robert Levy, and Steven Reuther. Screenplay by Leslie Dixon.

Someone does you a good turn. You pass it on to three other people. They pass it on. And what a wonderful world this will be. That's the theory behind *Pay It Forward,* a movie that might have been more entertaining if it didn't believe it. It's a seductive theory, but in the real world altruism is less powerful than selfishness, greed, nepotism, xenophobia, tribalism, and paranoia. If you doubt me, take another look at the front pages.

Consider Las Vegas, the setting of the movie. If every person in trouble there paid it forward to three more people, there would be more Gamblers Anonymous members than gamblers. An intriguing premise, but not one that occurs to this movie—although Alcoholics Anonymous plays a supporting role, and paying it forward is, of course, the twelfth step.

The movie has its heart in the right place, but not its screenplay. It tells a story that audience members will *want* to like, but it doesn't tell it strongly and cleanly enough, it puts too many loops into the plot, and its ending is shamelessly soapy for the material. Two or three times during the film I was close to caving in and going with the flow, but the story lost the way and I was brought back up to the surface again.

Haley Joel Osment, the gifted young actor from *The Sixth Sense,* stars as Trevor, a re-

sourceful latchkey kid whose father has disappeared and whose mother, Arlene (Helen Hunt), works two jobs as a Vegas cocktail waitress. She's a recovering alcoholic with a few relapses still to go. At school, Trevor is impressed by the grave, distant presence of his new teacher, Mr. Simonet (Kevin Spacey), whose face is scarred by burns.

Mr. Simonet doesn't want to win any popularity contests. "Do I strike you as someone falsely nice?" he asks Trevor. "No," the boy replies thoughtfully, "you're not even *really* all that nice." But Trevor responds to the lack of condescension in the teacher's manner: Mr. Simonet has standards, and applies them in the classroom. On the first day of school, he writes the year's assignment on the blackboard: "Think of an idea that could change the world."

Trevor thinks. Things happen in his life to help him think and guide his thinking, and before long his mother discovers that a homeless man (James Caviezel) is living in their garage. It was Trevor's idea to invite him in. Then he can pay it forward.

There are complications. One of Trevor's theories is that his mom and Mr. Simonet would both be a lot happier if they were dating each other. Mr. Simonet does not agree. Spacey does a wonderful job of suggesting the pain just beneath the surface of the character; the teacher's life is manageable only because he sticks to his routine. But Trevor plugs away, all but shoving the two adults toward each other. This is, unfortunately, the kind of self-propelling plot device that, once allowed into a movie, takes it over and dictates an obligatory series of events. Since it is self-evident that Trevor is right, we know with a sinking feeling that the screenplay must detour into tentative acceptance, hurt rejection, silly misunderstandings, angry retreats, confessions, tearful reconciliations, and resolutions, all in the usual order.

The movie intercuts between the predictable progress of the romance and the uncertain progress of Trevor's pay-it-forward scheme. We meet various supporting characters who get involved in paying it forward, and the time line is not always clear. The movie opens with one of those off-the-shelf hostage crisis scenes that ends with a criminal crashing into a reporter's car, and a stranger giving the reporter a new Jaguar. He's paying it forward. Then we flash back to "four months earlier" and Trevor's first day of school, but soon we're back to the present again, as the reporter tries to track down the pay-it-forward stories, and the lawyer who gave away the Jaguar tells why.

This leads to another flashback: When the lawyer's daughter had an asthma attack and was ignored in an emergency room, he explains, a gun-waving African-American stabbing victim forced a nurse to give the kid oxygen, and told him to pay it forward. It's an effective cameo, but it's awkward the way the movie cuts between scenes like that, Trevor's own setbacks, and the tentative romance.

With a cleaner story line, the basic idea could have been free to deliver. As it is, we get a better movie than we might have, because the performances are so good: Spacey as a vulnerable and wounded man; Hunt as a woman no less wounded in her own way; and Osment, once again proving himself the equal of adult actors in the complexity and depth of his performance. I believed in them and cared for them. I wish the movie could have gotten out of their way.

Pearl Harbor ★ ½
PG-13, 183 m., 2001

Ben Affleck (Rafe McCawley), Josh Hartnett (Danny Walker), Kate Beckinsale (Evelyn Johnson), Cuba Gooding Jr. (Dorie Miller), William Lee Scott (Billy), Greg Zola (Anthony), Ewen Bremner (Red), Alec Baldwin (Doolittle), James King (Betty), Mako (Admiral Yamamoto). Directed by Michael Bay and produced by Bay and Jerry Bruckheimer. Screenplay by Randall Wallace.

Pearl Harbor is a two-hour movie squeezed into three hours, about how on December 7, 1941, the Japanese staged a surprise attack on an American love triangle. Its centerpiece is forty minutes of redundant special effects, surrounded by a love story of stunning banality. The film has been directed without grace, vision, or originality, and although you may walk out quoting lines of dialogue, it will not be because you admire them.

The filmmakers seem to have aimed the film at an audience that may not have heard of

Pearl Harbor, or perhaps even of World War II. This is the *Our Weekly Reader* version. If you have the slightest knowledge of the events in the film, you will know more than it can tell you. There is no sense of history, strategy, or context; according to this movie, Japan attacked Pearl Harbor because America cut off its oil supply and they were down to an eighteen-month reserve. Would going to war restore the fuel sources? Did they perhaps also have imperialist designs? Movie doesn't say.

So shaky is the film's history that at the end, when Jimmy Doolittle's Tokyo raiders crash-land in China, they're shot at by Japanese patrols with only a murky throwaway explanation about the Sino-Japanese war already under way. I predict some viewers will leave the theater sincerely confused about why there were Japanese in China.

As for the movie's portrait of the Japanese themselves, it is so oblique that Japanese audiences will find little to complain about apart from the fact that they play such a small role in their own raid. There are several scenes where the Japanese high command debates military tactics, but all of their dialogue is strictly expository; they state facts but do not emerge with personalities or passions. Only Admiral Yamamoto (Mako) is seen as an individual, and his dialogue seems to have been singled out with the hindsight of history. Congratulated on a brilliant raid, he demurs, "A brilliant man would find a way not to fight a war." And later, "I fear all we have done is to awaken a sleeping giant."

Do you imagine at any point the Japanese high command engaged in the 1941 Japanese equivalent of exchanging high-fives and shouting "Yes!" while pumping their fists in the air? Not in this movie, where the Japanese seem to have been melancholy even at the time about the regrettable need to play such a negative role in such a positive Hollywood film.

The American side of the story centers on two childhood friends from Tennessee with the standard-issue screenplay names Rafe McCawley (Ben Affleck) and Danny Walker (Josh Hartnett). They enter the Army Air Corps and both fall in love with the same nurse, Evelyn Johnson (Kate Beckinsale)—first Rafe falls for her, and then, after he is reported dead, Danny. Their first date is subtitled "Three Months

Later" and ends with Danny, having apparently read the subtitle, telling Evelyn, "Don't let it be three months before I see you again, OK?" That gets almost as big a laugh as her line to Rafe, "I'm gonna give Danny my whole heart, but I don't think I'll ever look at another sunset without thinking of you."

That kind of bad laugh would have been sidestepped in a more literate screenplay, but our hopes are not high after an early newsreel report that the Germans are bombing "downtown London"—a difficult target, since although there is such a place as "central London," at no time in 2,000 years has London ever had anything described by anybody as a "downtown."

There is not a shred of conviction or chemistry in the love triangle, which results after Rafe returns alive to Hawaii shortly before the raid on Pearl Harbor and is angry at Evelyn for falling in love with Danny, inspiring her timeless line, "I didn't even know until the day you turned up alive—and then all this happened."

Evelyn is a hero in the aftermath of the raid, performing triage by using her lipstick to separate the wounded who should be treated from those left to die. In a pointless stylistic choice, director Michael Bay and cinematographer John Schwartzman shoot some of the hospital scenes in soft focus, some in sharp focus, some blurred. Why? I understand it's to obscure details deemed too gory for the PG-13 rating. (Why should the carnage at Pearl Harbor be toned down to PG-13 in the first place?) In the newsreel sequences, the movies fades in and out of black-and-white with almost amusing haste, while the newsreel announcer sounds not like a period voice but like a Top-40 DJ in an echo chamber.

The most involving material in the film comes at the end, when Jimmy Doolittle (Alec Baldwin) leads his famous raid on Tokyo, flying army bombers off the decks of navy carriers and hoping to crash-land in China. He and his men were heroes, and their story would make a good movie (and indeed has: *Thirty Seconds Over Tokyo*). Another hero in the movie is the African-American cook Dorie Miller (Cuba Gooding Jr.), who because of his race was not allowed to touch a gun in the racist prewar navy, but opens fire during the raid, shoots down two planes, and saves the life of his captain. Nice to see an African-American in the

movie, but the almost total absence of Asians in 1941 Hawaii is inexplicable.

As for the raid itself, a little goes a long way. What is the point, really, of more than half an hour of planes bombing ships, of explosions and fireballs, of roars on the sound track and bodies flying through the air and people running away from fighters that are strafing them? How can it be entertaining or moving when it's simply about the most appalling slaughter? Why do the filmmakers think we want to see this, unrelieved by intelligence, viewpoint, or insight? It was a terrible, terrible day. Three thousand died in all. This is not a movie about them. It is an unremarkable action movie; Pearl Harbor supplies the subject, but not the inspiration. ☞

The Perfect Storm ★ ★ ★ ½
PG-13, 129 m., 2000

George Clooney (Captain Billy Tyne), Mark Wahlberg (Bobby Shatford), Mary Elizabeth Mastrantonio (Linda Greenlaw), John C. Reilly (Murph), William Fichtner (Sully), Karen Allen (Melissa Brown), Allen Payne (Alfred Pierre), Diane Lane (Christina Cotter), John Hawkes (Bugsy), Cherry Jones (Edie Bailey). Directed by Wolfgang Petersen and produced by Paula Weinstein, Petersen, and Gail Katz. Screenplay by Bill Wittliff, based on the book by Sebastian Junger.

The Perfect Storm is a well-crafted example of the film of pure sensation. It is about ships tossed by a violent storm. The film doesn't have complex and involving characters, but they are not needed. It doesn't tell a sophisticated story, and doesn't need to; the main events are known to most of the audience before the movie begins. All depends on the storm. I do not mind admitting I was enthralled.

The movie, based on the best-seller by Sebastian Junger, is mostly about a fishing ship named the *Andrea Gail*, out of Gloucester, Massachusetts, which had the misfortune in 1991 of running into "the middle of the monster" when three great storm systems collided in the Atlantic. We learn about the economic pressures of the swordfishing industry, we meet the crew members and their women, we learn a little of their stories, and then the film is about the ship, the storm, and the people waiting in port for news. A parallel story, about a luxury sailboat in distress, cranks up the suspense even further.

The crew members of the *Andrea Gail* are a job lot of basic movie types. We count Captain Billy Tyne (George Clooney), whose pride has been stung because his catch has fallen behind this season. His crew includes Bobby Shatford (Mark Wahlberg), who is in love with divorced mom Diane Lane; Murph (John C. Reilly), whose seafaring life has led to a friendly but sad separation from his wife and son; Bugsy (John Hawkes), the sort of character who gets overlooked in crowds; Alfred Pierre (Allen Payne), a Jamaican who has ventured into northern waters for the paycheck; and a last-minute addition, Sully (William Fichtner). He and Murph don't like each other. Why not? Jealousy over Murph's wife, the movie says. To provide the plot with some onboard conflict, is my guess.

These characters are not developed in the way that similar seafarers might be developed in a novel by Joseph Conrad or Herman Melville. We learn only their external signs and characteristics; we don't know or much care what makes them tick. That's not a fatal flaw to the film because *The Perfect Storm* is not about the people, but about the storm. When Conrad writes *Lord Jim* or Melville writes *Moby-Dick,* the stories are about the way men's characters interact with the sea and with their shipmates. They are novels about people.

If *The Perfect Storm* had taken that approach, there would be fewer characters and a lot more dialogue; it might be a better film and would certainly be a different one. Its director, Wolfgang Petersen, also made *Das Boot,* the submarine drama, that does develop the deeper human complexities of its characters—but that took so long that the original 210-minute cut was trimmed back to 145 more action-packed minutes for the first U.S. release. At 129 minutes, *The Perfect Storm* delivers the goods but little human insight.

The film's best scenes are more or less without dialogue, except for desperately shouted words. They are about men trapped in a maelstrom of overpowering forces. They respond heroically, because they must, but they are not heroes; their motivation is need. They have

had a bad season, have made one risky last trip, have ventured beyond the familiar Grand Banks fishing grounds to the problematical Flemish Cap. Quentin, the salty old dog who sits at the bar and provides color commentary, gives us the background: "I was last there in '62. Lots of fish. Lots of weather."

They have good luck: a catch of 60,000 pounds of swordfish. Then bad luck: The ice machine breaks down. The catch will spoil unless they get it quickly back to port. There are reports of a gathering storm. Billy lists their choices: "Either we hang out here, or say the hell with it and drive right through." The crew votes to plow right through the storm and collect those paychecks. Of course, they don't understand how big the storm really is, and when another fishing boat skipper (Mary Elizabeth Mastrantonio) tries to tell them, their antenna has blown overboard.

The scenes at sea are intercut with scenes in the bar where most of the Gloucester fishing industry seems to drink; it is conveniently located right at the end of the dock (and Diane Lane conveniently lives right upstairs). This is about right; I do not doubt that the owners, retired sailors, wives, girlfriends, and drinking buddies all stand watch in a saloon during a storm, ordering rounds and eyeing the Weather Channel.

Even before the storm, there are terrific set pieces, as when Murph is yanked overboard by a fishing line, and two men dive in to save him (Sully, his enemy, is the first in the water). But the heart of the film is in the ordeal of two ships caught in the tempest. As the men of the *Andrea Gail* battle wearily against their fate, the skipper attempts to cut loose an anchor. He clings to a swaying beam while holding an acetylene torch; the wonder is that he doesn't burn a hole in himself in the attempt.

Even more exciting is the parallel plot involving a Coast Guard rescue of the sailboat. A passenger (Cherry Jones) pleads with its owner to seek safer waters, but he is a pigheaded millionaire yachtsman with no respect for nature ("This is *my* boat!"). A helicopter rescue is attempted, shown in amazing action footage, and then the tension escalates as the chopper tries to go on to the *Andrea Gail,* a midair refueling is attempted, and eventually men are risking their lives in what seems like a doomed struggle (at one point, a Guardsman who is safe goes back into the sea after a crew mate).

We know intellectually that we're viewing special effects. Tanks and wind machines are involved, and computer graphics and models. This is not important. The impetus of the story drives us forward, and by the end of the film I was wrung out. It's possible to criticize the sketchy characters, but pointless. The movie is about the appalling experience of fighting for your life in a small boat in a big storm. If that is what you want to see, you will see it done here about as well as it can be done.

A Piece of Eden ★ ½

NO MPAA RATING, 112 m., 2000

Marc Grapey (Bob Tredici), Rebecca Harrell (Happy), Robert Breuler (Franco Tredici), Tyne Daly (Aunt Aurelia), Marshall Efron (Andres), Frederic Forrest (Paulo Tredici), Andreas Katsulas (Giuseppe Tredici), Jeff Puckett (Greg Tredici), Tristan Rogers (Victor Hardwick). Directed by John Hancock and produced by Hancock and Ken Kitsch. Screenplay by Dorothy Tristan.

A Piece of Eden is a good-hearted film with many virtues, although riveting entertainment value is not one of them. It's a family comedy that ambles down well-trodden paths toward a foregone conclusion, neither disturbing nor challenging the audience. It was filmed in and around LaPorte, Indiana; the only review I have seen so far comes from a Utah critic, Fawna Jones, who finds it predictable, and describes it quite accurately: "This a movie for those who generally stay away from the theater for fear of being offended and who like their movies to have happy endings."

Going to a movie so you won't be offended is like eating potato chips made with Olestra; you avoid the dangers of the real thing, but your insides fill up with synthetic runny stuff. Watching *A Piece of Eden*, I found myself wanting to be shocked, amazed, or even surprised. The most unexpected thing in the movie is a machine that shakes apple trees to make the apples fall off. That could have prevented a lot of heartbreak in *The Cider House Rules*.

The film opens in New York, where Bob

Tredici (Marc Grapey) runs the struggling Television Publicity Bureau with his secretary, Happy (Rebecca Harrell). She's been late four out of the last five days, and even more ominously, has a psychological block that prevents her from pronouncing the word "publicity" correctly when she answers the phone. (She comes from a family of high-powered analysts, and thinks her block may be approach avoidance.)

Bob gets a call from northeast Indiana, where his family has run a fruit farm since time immemorial. His father, Franco (Robert Breuler), is dying. Bob has an unhappy relationship with the old man but returns home anyway, to learn that the patriarch has rallied enough to spend endless hours in a hospital bed in the living room, making life miserable for everyone with his salt-of-the-earth routine. Franco plans to leave the farm not to Bob but to a relative who has stayed behind in Indiana.

Bob has bright ideas for the farm, including using computers for cost control and starting a petting zoo. But he needs to appear more stable, less like a decadent Manhattanite, and so in desperation he imports Happy to pose as his wife. This leads to scenes that could exist only in a movie, as when they are assigned to bunk down in the barn, and he gets a glimpse of her silhouette through the sheet that hangs from the ceiling just as it did in *It Happened One Night* (1934).

The choices available to the story are limited and obvious. Either Bob will get the farm, or another happy solution will be found, since Fawna Jones is quite correct that this is not a film destined for an unhappy ending. There must also be a near disaster, and there is, when Bob holds an open house for the petting zoo concept and imports a friendly soap opera star (Tristan Rogers) as his celebrity guest. First no members of the public show up. Then they're swamped.

It must be said that the character of the father is a major pain in the netherlands. He is one of those blowhard bearded patriarchs so full of himself and so colorful in unconvincing ways that to have such a person as a parent would be enough to—well, inspire you to flee to New York and open a Television Publicity Bureau. His personality is so insufferable that when he has a change of heart, you don't believe it—you just figure, there goes Dad again, faking it for the evening news.

John Hancock, whose credits include the powerful *Bang the Drum Slowly* and the sweet *Prancer* (a much better family film also set in the same area), does indeed own a fruit farm near LaPorte, and no doubt *A Piece of Eden* flows from his experiences and memories, and those of his wife, the actress Dorothy Tristan, who wrote the screenplay. But the story line runs out of steam about four-fifths of the way through, and the closing scenes lack dramatic interest, dissolving in a haze of landscapes and blue skies and happily-ever-after music.

Pitch Black ★ ★
R, 107 m., 2000

Vin Diesel (Riddick), Radha Mitchell (Fry), Cole Hauser (Johns), Keith David (Imam), Lewis Fitz-Gerald (Paris), Claudia Black (Shazza), Rhiana Griffith (Jack). Directed by David Twohy and produced by Tom Engelman. Screenplay by Twohy and Jim and Ken Wheat.

No other movie opening thrills me more than a vast ship in interstellar space. The modern visual rules for these shots were set by Stanley Kubrick's *2001*, which used a detailed model moving slowly instead of a cheesy model moving fast. Kubrick had the good sense to know that sound does not travel in space, but *Star Wars*, with its deep bass rumbles, demonstrated that it certainly should. And then in the *Alien* and *Star Trek* pictures and in countless others, gigantic space cruisers aimed majestically at the stars, and I felt an inner delight that has its origins in those long-ago days when I devoured pulp space opera by Robert Heinlein and such forgotten masters as Murray Leinster and Eric Frank Russell.

My state of mind is best captured by a pulp mag that was defunct even before I started reading science fiction: *Thrilling Wonder Stories,* without doubt the best title in the history of magazines. I hope for strange and amazing adventures. Sometimes I am gratified. More often I am disappointed. *Pitch Black,* which begins in deep space and ends with a manhunt on a desert planet, falls somewhere in between: clever, done with skill, yet lacking in the cerebral imagination of the best science

fiction. How sad it is that humans travel countless light years away from Earth, only to find themselves inhabiting the same tired generic conventions.

The movie begins during an interstellar mission, with the crew and a dangerous prisoner all in cryo-sleep. The ship collides with a cluster of tiny rock fragments, which penetrate the hull like BBs through cellophane. The captain and several other sleepers are terminally perforated, and Fry (Radha Mitchell) assumes command. The ship crash-lands on a planet that circles somehow within a three-star system, where at least one sun never seems to set, and the surviving crew members have to fight it out with the vicious and cunning prisoner, Riddick (Vin Diesel).

You may remember Diesel from *Saving Private Ryan,* where he was the hard-bitten Private Caparzo. He looks like a mean customer, and he is; he shares no fellow feeling with the other survivors, expresses no responsibility to them, does not consider himself in the same boat, and thinks only of escaping. Oh, and his eyes have a remarkable quality: He can see in the dark. Not a very useful ability on a planet with three suns and no night, right? (Hollow laugh.)

What disappointed me about *Pitch Black,* directed by David Twohy, is that it didn't do more with its alien world and less with its recycled human conflicts. I feel underwhelmed when humans land on another world and are so quickly reduced to jumping out from behind rocks at one another and playing hostage games. *Pitch Black* does have a nice look, all bleached blues and desert sands. And there are some promising story elements, one of which I am about to discuss, so you might want to set this review aside if you plan to see the movie.

The spoiler commences: Yes, night does fall on the planet, every once in a long while when all three suns are in eclipse. I am not sure what complex geometries of space and trajectory are necessary for a planet to exist in a three-star system and somehow manage to maintain any continuity of climate and temperature, but never mind: What is maybe more difficult to accept is that it would develop a life form that appears only in the dark. Since sunlight is the source of heat and energy, Darwinian principles would seem severely challenged by the task of evolving living things that hibernate for twenty-two years between eclipses. How does a thing that lives in the dark evolve in a planet where it is almost always daytime? This is not the kind of question you're supposed to ask about *Pitch Black,* but I'd rather have the answer than any forty-five minutes of this movie.

The story also poses the problem (less challenging from a Darwinian view, to be sure) of whether the Diesel character will cooperate with his species-mates or behave entirely like a selfish gene. Whether this happens or not I leave it to you to discover. By the end of the movie, however, I was wondering if the trip had been necessary; most of this movie's plot could be ported into a Western or a swashbuckler with little alteration. For Twohy, it's a step backward from *The Arrival* (1996), one of the smartest recent science-fiction films—one that really does develop suspense out of challenging ideas of alien conduct (space visitors are secretly warming the Earth to their comfort zone).

My suggestion for his next film: an expedition to the seas beneath the ice of Europe, where volcanic warmth may have allowed life to occur. Consider the physical properties of a life form that evolves under the tiny gravity of such a moon. It could be amorphous, tenuous, and enormous. In sailing a stellar sub through the seas of Io, you might be navigating not toward life, but . . . through it. What would a human crew do in such a situation? Not get into fights and start chasing each other through the sub, I hope.

Place Vendome ★ ★ ★ ½
NO MPAA RATING, 105 m., 2000

Catherine Deneuve (Marianne), Jean-Pierre Bacri (Jean-Pierre), Emmanuelle Seigner (Nathalie), Jacques Dutronc (Battistelli), Bernard Fresson (Vincent Malivert), Francois Berleand (Eric Malivert), Laszlo Szabo (Charlie Rosen), Michael Culkin (De Beers Man). Directed by Nicole Garcia and produced by Christine Gozlan and Alain Sarde. Screenplay by Jacques Fieschi and Garcia.

She is an elegant beauty and a drunk. "The clinic is her second home," they whisper. "She's brought out for special occasions." Her husband owns one of the most famous jewelry shops in the world, on Place Vendome in Paris, across from the Ritz. His secret is that the business is bankrupt. On one of the rare nights when she's at home instead of in rehab, he shows her where he has hidden five superb diamonds. Then he drives his car into the side of a lumber truck and kills himself.

Marianne Malivert, played by Catherine Deneuve, once knew something about the diamond trade herself. She met her husband while making a deal. But "I've forgotten all that," she says. At a business dinner with her husband before his death, she doesn't drink, but eventually she gets up, glides around the table, places a hand on his shoulder, and goes into another room—where he finds her draining leftover wine. "At least start with a new bottle," he says, handing her one. He accepts her alcoholism as a fact of life.

Place Vendome begins as the portrait of a woman who has lost all interest and hope; when she sees her hungover face in a mirror, she recoils in disgust. After her husband's death, a curious thing happens. The name and reputation of the firm is worth something, even if its shelves are bare, and her brother-in-law wants to sell. But she thinks of those five diamonds, stops drinking, and begins to remember her old skills as a jeweler.

That's when the movie edges toward becoming a thriller. Not the kind of thriller with car chases, but a *film noir,* in which shady people appear from out of the past, and Marianne finds herself caught in a net of danger.

One of the pleasures of the movie is how it only gradually reveals the details of relationships. There is a bald man named Jean-Pierre (Jean-Pierre Bacri), for example, who is obsessed with Nathalie (Emmanuelle Seigner), a young woman who works in the store. Marianne knows Nathalie was her husband's mistress. Jean-Pierre is not a bad sort; he wants to help, and soon he is helping Marianne. He has information about Nathalie's associates, especially the handsome, aging, limping Battistelli (Jacques Dutronc), a veteran con man and jewel thief. How strange that Nathalie left Jean-Pierre for Battistelli. How even stranger that Marianne herself was once Battistelli's lover, years ago.

The movie, directed by the French actress Nicole Garcia, knows a lot about diamonds. Anyone who has purchased a wedding ring might be fascinated by the backstage details of the trade. The story takes Marianne's husband to London, for a confrontation with the De Beers cartel, and after his death it takes Marianne to the diamond bourse in Antwerp, which with its long wooden tables looks like a school cafeteria. She unwraps her little paper parcel on one of the tables and diamond buyers cluster around.

Of course the diamonds may be stolen. If they are, their owners will want them back. For that matter, the authorities may be more interested in Battistelli than the diamonds. Marianne is caught in the middle, all the time just one drink away from disaster.

Catherine Deneuve has been a movie star for a long time. She was twenty-one when she starred in *The Umbrellas of Cherbourg* (1964). In 1967, she made the great *Belle de Jour* with Bernard Fresson, who plays her husband in *Place Vendome*. She is one of the world's great beauties, but has usually used her beauty for particular purposes in her roles, instead of simply trading on it. She is not just the blonde, and never the dumb one. Here, at fifty-six, she makes her Marianne look wonderful when she pulls herself together for the business meeting with her husband, and vague and shabby when she drinks. What is best is when she stops drinking and begins to think as a diamond merchant once again; we see not only craft in Marianne's eyes, but cautious joy—she is happy to be competent, to know what she's doing.

This human level is always there beneath the thriller elements. The screenplay takes care to bring the crime story and the personal histories together, so that even the crossed lines of romance work as plot points, not just sentiment. Watching the movie, we see it is not about diamonds, sex, or beauty, but about what a pleasure it is to get up in the morning and know you can do what needs to be done.

Playing by Heart ★ ★ ½
R, 120 m., 1999

Gillian Anderson (Meredith), Ellen Burstyn (Mildred), Sean Connery (Paul), Gena Rowlands (Hannah), Anthony Edwards (Roger), Angelina Jolie (Joan), Jay Mohr (Mark), Ryan Philippe (Keenan), Dennis Quaid (Hugh), Madeleine Stowe (Gracie), Jon Stewart (Trent), Patricia Clarkson (Allison), Nastassja Kinski (Melanie), Alec Mapa (Lana). Directed by Willard Carroll and produced by Meg Liberman, Carroll, and Tom Wilhite. Screenplay by Carroll.

Playing by Heart interweaves the stories of maybe a dozen characters, couples of one sort or another, who try to express how they feel and sometimes succeed. It's like one of those Alan Rudolph films *(Choose Me* or *Welcome to L.A.)* where lonely seekers cruise the city seeking solace. The difference is that Rudolph's characters have tough, wounded personalities, and the characters created here by Willard Carroll are mostly softies—they're in tune with the current trend toward movies that coddle the audience with reassuring sentiments.

Of course, there is some pain along the way. One of the most touching couples consists of a mother (Ellen Burstyn) whose son (Jay Mohr) is dying of AIDS. Their long sickroom conversations contain the stuff of truth. And there is a different kind of truth in the peppy wisecracks of Joan (Angelina Jolie), a club-crawler who meets Keenan (Ryan Philippe), a guy she likes, and can't understand why he goes hot and cold with her. Jolie steals the movie as a woman whose personal style has become so entertaining she can hide behind it.

Other couples include Paul and Hannah (Sean Connery and Gena Rowlands), who are approaching their fortieth wedding anniversary under an unexpected cloud. And Meredith (Gillian Anderson), a theater director who tries dating Trent (Jon Stewart), an architect. And Gracie (Madeleine Stowe), who meets her lover (Anthony Edwards) in hotel rooms, and then comes home to her cold husband, Hugh (Dennis Quaid). And we see Hugh in a different light in a series of deep and deceptive barroom conversations with Patricia Clarkson, Nastassja Kinski, and a drag queen played by Alec Mapa.

All of these people are articulate, and some of them are glib, and although the dialogue sometimes sounds exactly like dialogue, it's often entertaining. I liked the way the drag queen says he's twenty-nine, "and those are real years, not Heather Locklear years." And the way Keenan tells Joan, "What did I do to deserve this?" and means it gratefully, and she observes that's the kind of line that's usually hurled at her by someone on his way out the door.

In a movie with so many characters, there's no time to deeply develop any of them. Some don't really register. Others we enjoy because of their star power. It's a little unlikely that the couple played by Connery and Rowlands would have quite the conversation they have about an affair Connery almost had twenty-five years ago. That's especially true given more urgent circumstances facing them now. But the affection between the two feels real, and there is an invaluable moment when Connery imitates a puppy dog.

As the movie circled from one story to another, I found myself waiting for Angelina Jolie to come round again. With her pouty lips and punk chic look, she's an original; I like the way she's talking to her sister on the phone and when Keenan turns up unexpectedly, she says, "Let me take care of this call" and takes care of it by hanging up. Their relationship is the one that develops the most during the film—the one we care about.

Where it all ends up, the filmmakers have entreated critics not to say. I will obey. There is not a ban on deciding what it all adds up to, however, and I think it amounts to a near miss. It's easy to like the movie because we like the actors in it, and because the movie makes it easy on us and has charming moments. But it feels too much like an exercise. It's yuppie lite—affluent, articulate people who, except for those who are ill, have problems that are almost pleasant. It has been observed that a lot of recent movies about death have gone all soft and gooey at the center. Here's a movie about life that does the same thing.

Play It to the Bone ★ ½
R, 125 m., 2000

Antonio Banderas (Cesar Dominguez), Woody Harrelson (Vince Boudreau), Lolita Davidovich (Grace Pasi), Tom Sizemore (Joe Domino), Lucy Liu (Lia), Robert Wagner (Hank Goody), Richard Masur (Artie), Willie Garson (Cappie Caplan). Directed by Ron Shelton and produced by Stephen Chin. Screenplay by Shelton.

Play It to the Bone ends with a long, gruesome, brutal, bloody prizefight scene, which would be right at home in another movie but is a big miscalculation here, because it is between the two heroes of the story. We like them both. Therefore, we don't want either one to win, and we don't want either one to lose. What we basically want is for them to stop pounding one another. That isn't the way you want your audience to feel during a boxing movie.

The movie stars Antonio Banderas and Woody Harrelson as Cesar and Vince, a couple of has-been welterweights who get an emergency call from Las Vegas: Will they fight on the undercard before tonight's main event with Mike Tyson? Both slots have opened up after one of the scheduled fighters wiped himself out in a car crash and the other overdosed ("drugs are coming out of his ears"). Banderas and Harrelson are buddies and sparring partners who need a fresh start. The deal: They'll split $100,000, and the winner gets a shot at the title.

The movie was written and directed by Ron Shelton, an expert on sports movies; he wrote and directed *Bull Durham, White Men Can't Jump* and *Cobb,* and wrote *Blue Chips.* One of his trademarks is expertise, and yet *Play It to the Bone* isn't an inside job on boxing but an assembly of ancient and familiar prizefight clichés (the corrupt promoter, the dubious contract, the ringside celebrities, the cut that may not stop bleeding, the "I coulda been a contender" scene). Even at that level it doesn't have enough of a boxing story to occupy the running time, and warms up with a prolonged and unnecessary road movie.

The setup: Neither fighter can afford air fare to Vegas. It doesn't occur to them to have the casino prepay their tickets. Instead, they convince Grace (Lolita Davidovich), who is Cesar's girlfriend, to drive them there in her vintage Oldsmobile convertible (all road movies involve classic cars, which drive down back roads with gas stations recycled from *The Grapes of Wrath*). When their credit card is rejected at a pit stop, they pick up Lia (Lucy Liu), a hitchhiker with funds.

The road trip involves many scenes intended to be colorful, including an obligatory fight between the two women. Shelton is good at comic conversation, but here the dialogue doesn't flow and sounds contrived, as when Cesar explains that he was once gay for a year, "but only exactly a year," because he was "trying all sorts of things." Vince, a Jesus freak, is shocked—but only, we sense, because the screenplay tells him he is. Both Cesar's sex life and Vince's spiritual visions are like first-draft ideas that don't flow convincingly from the characters. And what about Grace's motivation for the trip: Her hope of selling the rights to her gizmo inventions to high rollers? Uh, huh.

All leads up to the big fight, during which, as I've said, we want to hide our eyes. Shelton's approach is certainly novel: A match you want to stop before the fighters hit each other any more. It's bad enough that they're fighting, but why, in a silly comedy, did Shelton think he had to outdo *Raging Bull* in brutality? Vince and Cesar hammer each other until it is unlikely either fighter, in the real world, would still be conscious—or alive. It's a hideous spectacle, and we cringe because the movie doesn't know how odd it seems to cut from the bloodshed in the ring to the dialogue of the supporting players, who still think they're in a comedy.

The Pledge ★ ★ ★ ½
R, 124 m., 2001

Jack Nicholson (Detective Jerry Black), Sam Shepard (Eric Pollack), Mickey Rourke (Jim Olstand), Benicio Del Toro (Toby Jay Wadenah), Helen Mirren (Doctor), Robin Wright Penn (Lori), Vanessa Redgrave (Annalise Hansen), Aaron Eckhart (Stan Krolak). Directed by Sean Penn and produced by Michael Fitzgerald, Penn, and Elie Samaha. Screenplay by Jerzy Kromolowski and Mary Olson-Kromolowski, based on the book by Friedrich Durrenmatt.

Sean Penn's *The Pledge* begins as a police story and spirals down into madness. It provides Jack Nicholson with one of his best roles in recent years, as a retired cop who makes a promise and tries to keep it. Like their previous film together as director and actor, *The Crossing Guard* (1995), it isn't a simple revenge story but shows the desire for justice running out of control and becoming dangerous. The story has the elements of a crime thriller (cops, suspects, victims, clues) but finally it's a character study, and in Detective Jerry Black, Nicholson creates a character we follow into the darkness of his compulsion.

As the film opens, Jerry is retiring as a cop—a good cop—in Reno. He's from an earlier generation; you can see that by the way he looks for ashtrays in the offices of colleagues who don't smoke. News comes that the mutilated body of a young girl has been found. Jerry goes on the call (he wants to work out his last day), and eventually finds himself delivering the tragic news to the parents of the little girl.

This scene, staged by Penn on the turkey farm the parents operate, is amazing in its setting (Nicholson wading through thousands of turkey chicks) and its impact (holding a crucifix made by the murdered Ginny, he swears "by his soul's salvation" that he will find the killer). This is the pledge of the movie's title, and eventually it obsesses him.

It appears at first that the killer has been found. Benicio Del Toro plays an Indian, obviously retarded, who was seen running away from the murder scene. Clues seem to link his pickup with the crime. A knife-edged detective (Aaron Eckhart) gets a confession out of him, with Jerry squirming behind the one-way glass and saying the Indian "doesn't understand the question." Then the Indian grabs a gun and shoots himself. Guilty, and dead. Case closed.

Jerry doesn't think so. His years as a cop tell him something is not right. In retirement, he continues to investigate the case, eventually finding that the dead Ginny had made friends with a "giant" she called "the Wizard." Who was this man? Was he the killer? Was he linked with other unsolved killings of young children?

Until this point, *The Pledge* has been a fairly standard, if well-done, police procedural. Now Penn, working from a novel by Friedrich Durrenmatt and screenplay by Jerzy Kromolowski and Mary Olson-Kromolowski, begins the film's descent into Jerry's obsession. He does a strange thing. He buys a gas station and convenience store halfway between two towns where he thinks the "wizard" might have committed crimes. Studying drawings by the dead Ginny, he thinks he knows what kind of vehicle the killer might have used. The store is a trap.

An unexpected thing happens. He meets a mother (Robin Wright Penn) and her young daughter, and they feel an instinctive sympathy which blossoms to his surprise into love. After a couple of divorces, Jerry discovers at last what a happy domestic life can be. We immediately realize that the daughter is a potential victim of the killer, if he is indeed still at large. We assume Jerry realizes this too. But surely he would not use this beautiful little girl as bait?

One problem with Jerry's quest is that he is the only person who believes in it. His former police colleagues think he's gone around the bend; even the chief (Sam Shepard), an old friend, looks sadly at Jerry's unhinged zeal. His gas station trap may be a long shot, or an inspiration, or simply proof he's losing touch with reality. The last third of the movie is where most police stories go on autopilot, with obligatory chases, stalkings, and confrontations. That's when *The Pledge* grows most compelling. Penn and Nicholson take risks with the material and the character, and elevate the movie to another, unanticipated, haunting level.

Sean Penn has been saying for years that he wants to quit acting and be a director. That would be a loss, because he is one of the finest actors alive (consider *Dead Man Walking*). What is clear from the three films he has directed (also including *The Indian Runner* in 1991) is that he has no interest in making ordinary films. He is fascinated by characters under stress. He is bored by the working out of obvious psychological processes.

The character of Jerry here is not merely a good cop, but a retired man, an older man, a man possessed by a fixed idea. He is able at one level to exude charm and stability (one reason the younger woman likes him is that he offers calm and strength after her violent marriage). But we sense deeper, darker currents, and issues he isn't fully aware of himself. By the end of *The Pledge,* the suspense hinges mostly on Jerry, and the solution of the crime is a sideshow. It is here that Nicholson's skill is most needed, and most appreciated: He has to show us a man who has embarked on a terrifying and lonely quest into the unknown places of his mind.

Plunkett and Macleane ★ ½
R, 102 m., 1999

Robert Carlyle (Will Plunkett), Jonny Lee Miller (James Macleane), Alan Cumming (Lord Rochester), Michael Gambon (Lord Chief Justice Gibson), Liv Tyler (Lady Rebecca Gibson), Ken Stott (Chance). Directed by Jake Scott and produced by Tim Bevan, Eric Fellner, and Rupert Harvey. Screenplay by Robert Wade, Neal Purvis, and Charles McKeown, based on an original screenplay by Selwyn Roberts.

Plunkett and Macleane conducts an experiment: Can a movie be constructed entirely out of stylistic excess, without the aid of a story or characters we'd give two farthings for? Answer: Perhaps, but not this time. Here is a film overgrown with so many directorial flourishes that the heroes need machetes to hack their way to within view of the audience. It's not enough to want to make a movie. You have to know why, and let the audience in on your thinking.

The film, set in eighteenth-century London, tells the story of a gentleman named Macleane (Jonny Lee Miller) and an unwashed rogue named Plunkett (Robert Carlyle). Macleane is not entirely a gentleman (the movie opens with him being sentenced for public drunkenness), but at least he knows how to play one, and the accent is right. Plunkett has the better natural manners and charm. When they meet after an unlikely jailbreak, Plunkett suggests that with Macleane's accent and his own criminal expertise, they could make a living stealing from the rich.

When you extract this story from the morass of style through which it wades, it's as simpleminded as an old B Western. The two men lurk in the woods, spring upon the passing carriages of the rich, and relieve them of their wealth. Trouble looms when Macleane is smitten by the beautiful Lady Rebecca Gibson (Liv Tyler), who, wouldn't you know, is the niece of the Lord Chief Justice (Michael Gambon). The pair become known as the Gentlemen Highwaymen, the chief justice is enraged that they have not been captured, and the oily Chance (Ken Stott) is in charge of the chase.

Just as a random hypothesis, let us suppose that one of the pair is captured and sentenced to hang. Take the following multiple-choice quiz. Will he:

a. Hang by the neck until dead.

b. Escape in a daring jailbreak.

c. Receive a pardon on the tearful entreaties of Lady Rebecca.

d. Mount the gallows tree, have the noose slipped around his neck, have the trap door opened, fall to the end of the rope, and hang there for long seconds, before being cut down in a tardy last-moment rescue plan, leaving us in suspense about whether he is dead or alive (unless we have studied the immutable movie genre laws governing such matters).

I will publish the answer at the end of the next millennium or when the sequel to this movie is released, whichever comes first.

Plunkett and Macleane was directed by Jake Scott, son of Ridley Scott, whose own films *(Alien, Blade Runner)* are themselves dripping with dark, gloomy atmosphere, but who knows how to tell a story about interesting characters *(Thelma and Louise)*. The problem with Jake Scott is that he uses background as foreground. There are times early in *Plunkett and Macleane* when there are so many mysterious and opaque objects cluttering the screen that, as we try to peer around them, we wonder if the MPAA warmed up on this movie before obscuring the naughty bits in *Eyes Wide Shut*.

Dialogue and character are always secondary to atmosphere. The highwaymen and their prey are seen through a murk of fog, mist, overgrowth, lantern shadows, bric-a-brac, triglyphs, and metopes; their dialogue has to be barked out between the sudden arrival of more visual astonishments. The sound track is cluttered with a lot of anachronistic music, as if the movie began life as an MTV music video and then had its period violently wrenched back into the past before the contemporary music could be removed. How displaced is the music? The movie is set in 1748, but the song under the credits, if I heard correctly, mentions the Jedi.

If there's one thing that annoys me in a movie (and there are many in this one), it's when the characters escape through a loophole in the cinematic technique. There's a scene where Plunkett and Macleane are trapped inside a carriage, which is riddled with countless bullets, just like a car in a gangster movie. The carriage is surrounded. When it is approached after the fusillade, Plunkett and Macleane have disappeared, and been replaced by a bomb with a burning fuse! How? Is this not physically impossible? We're not even supposed to ask, because we are so very, very entertained by such a clever, clever surprise. My movie history may be shaky, but I believe this sequence was inspired by a Loony Tune.

Note: Readers assure me that a sewer opening beneath the carriage was the means of escape.

Pokémon the First Movie: Mewtwo Strikes Back ★ ★
G, 69 m., 1999

With the voices of: Veronica Taylor, Philip Bartlett, Rachael Lillis, Eric Stuart, Addie Blaustein, and Ikue Otani. Directed by Kunihiko Yuyama and produced by Norman J. Grossfeld, Choji Yoshikawa, Tomoyuki Igarashi, and Takemoto Mori. Screenplay by Takeshi Shudo; adaptation written by Norman J. Grossfeld, Michael Haigney, and John Touhey.

There are times here on the movie beat when I feel like I'm plain in over my head. This is one of those times. My assignment is to review *Pokémon the First Movie: Mewtwo Strikes Back.* I have done research. I have even played a Pokémon card game with a six-year-old Pokémon trainer named Emil. The rules of the game seemed to bear a suspicious resemblance to War. At the end of the game, Emil had all fifty-two cards. I do not know if this is because of his mastery as a trainer, or because he stacked the deck.

The easiest way to understand Pokémon is as a major factor in the U.S.-Japanese balance of trade. It began as a Nintendo Game Boy game, and has since proliferated into spin-offs, clones, ancillary rights, books, videos, TV shows, toys, trading cards, and now this movie. All of this despite the fact that nobody over twelve seems able to explain the Pokémon universe coherently. In the on-line magazine Salon, for example, Cynthia Joyce did an interview with a ten-year-old named Sean Levine, who loves Pokémon. Please study the following exchange:

Cynthia: "Can you explain to me—in simple terms—what the game is about?"

Sean: "Well it's not just a game! It's a whole world. There's TV shows, comic books, little figures, and card game. . . . But my favorite is probably the Game Boy game. And the card game. The goal is to get all 151 types of Pokémon—that's the red and blue version. In the new versions there's 250 types of little creatures. I like collecting the cards—I have the red version and the blue version, so I can get all the Pokémon I need. Some Pokémon cards are actually worth a lot—for example, if you have a first edition Charizard, you can sell it for over 99 bucks."

The interview is longer, but no more helpful. Is there even a game at all, in the sense of Monopoly? Sean cleverly deflects the question into a description of the Pokémon empire, and how much money you can make as a Pokémon tycoon. I used to collect baseball cards, but at least there was a game called baseball, which existed separately from the cards. You don't "play" Pokémon in any sense that involves running around or catching anything or scoring runs or getting dirty. It sounds more like early training for commodities brokers.

Here is the movie. The plot: A villain has found a way to genetically clone one of the Pokémon (Pokemen?), named Mew. His invention is named Mewtwo. He also clones other Pokémon. Each Pokémon has a different kind of power. The hero, Ash Ketcham (so called because he wants to "catch 'em all" and have a complete set of Pokémon), ventures with his friends to the villain's island, where battles take place between lots of different kinds of Pokémon (Pokémi?) and their clones. After an hour of struggle that shakes the very firmament, the Pokémon collapse (they run down instead of dying). There are a lot of speeches about how we now see that fighting is wrong. There will be a sequel, in which no doubt there will be another hour of fighting before the same lesson is learned again.

The animation is bright, colorful, and vibrant. It's eye candy. The story seems very thin, especially compared to such other Japanese anime titles as *My Neighbor Totoro*. The story is idiotic. The individual Pokémon have personalities that make the Teenage Mutant Ninja Turtles look like Billy Crystal. Kids will no doubt love this movie because they can see action involving figures they have collected themselves.

I can't recommend the film or work up much enthusiasm for it because there is no level at which it enriches a young viewer by encouraging thinking or observation. It's just a sound-and-light show linked to the marketing push for Pokémon in general. On the other hand, I may have completely bypassed the point and misinterpreted crucial Pokémon lore. This may disqualify me from ever becoming a Pokémon trainer. I can live with that.

Pola X ★ ★ ★

NO MPAA RATING, 134 m., 2000

Guillaume Depardieu (Pierre), Katerina Golubeva (Isabelle), Catherine Deneuve (Marie), Delphine Chuillot (Lucie), Petruta Catana (Razerka), Mihaella Silaghi (The Child), Laurent Lucas (Thibault), Patachou (Margherite). Directed by Leos Carax and produced by Bruno Pesery. Screenplay by Carax, Lauren Sedofsky, and Jean-Pol Fargeau, based on the novel *Pierre* by Herman Melville.

It takes a raving lunatic to know one. Not that I have ever met Leos Carax, the director of *Pola X*, so that I can say for sure he's as tempestuous and impulsive as the subject of his film, but you aren't described as an "enfant terrible" at the age of thirty-nine without good reason. Certainly Pierre, his hero, is an inspired visionary, a youth inflamed by romantic fantasies, who sees himself as a great artist and is in love with reckless gestures.

The film is a reasonably close adaptation of Herman Melville's 1852 novel *Pierre*. Carax's title is an acronym of the French title, *Pierre, ou les Ambiguities,* and the X refers to the tenth draft of the screenplay. *Pierre* was written following Melville's *Moby-Dick,* and after the classical architecture of its prose, the next novel came as a shock with its lurid fevers.

Melville wrote at white-hot speed, he said, as if in a dream, and for many years *Pierre* was unavailable in an uncensored version (an unexpurgated edition was published in the 1990s). Dealing as it does with Pierre's incestuous obsessions with a mother and a half-sister, it was not what admirers of the great white whale were expecting.

Carax sets his story in present-day France, although with the exception of a few cars, motorcycles, props, and street scenes its period could be the nineteenth century. He tells the story of Pierre (Guillaume Depardieu), a spoiled young aristocrat who has written a trendy best-selling novel and lives in a chateau with his mother, Marie (Catherine Deneuve). They are alarmingly close; they call each other "my brother" and "my sister," he lights two cigarettes and gives her one, he visits her nude in her bath, and so on. Deneuve is able to make scenes like these work because she can float above the carnal, in a realm where sex is a whim rather than a function.

Pierre is engaged to his cousin Lucie (Delphine Chuillot), who lives in a neighboring chalet and is an ethereal blond waif; his mother could no more be jealous of Lucie than if Pierre adopted a cute spaniel. Also on the scene, having recently returned from his labors on the Chicago Stock Exchange, is a dark-browed cousin, Thibault (Laurent Lucas), who in his satanic way resents that Pierre will take Lucie out of his grasp, and also perhaps that Lucie will take Pierre out of his grasp. He refers to them as "the three inseparables," but the other two lean toward separability.

There is a mystery woman (Katerina Golubeva), deep-eyed, long-haired, ragged, and wolflike, who shadows Pierre. The sight of her fills him with deep churnings and obscure dreams. One night as he is roaring through the woods on his motorcycle he surprises her lurking in the gloom, pursues her, and hears her story: "Believe me, Pierre, you are not an only child. I am your sister, Isabelle." In a long, long monologue (it is a stand-alone section in the novel), she tells her story. She is the love child of Pierre's father, was raised in the woods by an old man and woman, speaks simply in a high-pitched voice, is unsocialized and desperate.

Pierre is consumed by a manic need to throw away wealth and happiness, and share Isabelle's poverty and misery. "All my life I have waited for something that would push me beyond this," he says, waving a metaphorical arm to encompass Lucie, Marie, the chateau.

They will live together like brother and sister, he tells Isabelle. The world will think she's his wife. Turned away from fleabag hotels, they reside finally in a vast warehouse occupied by a group of terrorists, who breed their plots while a deathly conductor stands on a catwalk and conducts his orchestra in a mournful symphony for synthesizers, steel drums, and iron bars banged on with hammers.

Feverishly hunched beneath a blanket against the cold, he scribbles out his new novel, which will be great, which will be true, while the sound track itches with the sound of his pen scratching against the paper, like rats sharpening their nails on sandpaper. Meanwhile, he and Isabelle are not living together like most brothers and sisters, and there is a sex scene which would be shockingly graphic if we could quite see it.

Faithful readers will know I have an affection for raving lunatics, and am grateful for films that break free of the dismal bonds of formula to cartwheel into overwrought, passionate excess. This is a weakness, but I am protective of it. *Pola X* may not be successful and its closing passages may drift into the realm of the ludicrous, but "when it's over," as Stephen Holden so accurately wrote after it played in the New York Film Festival, "you'll know you've had an experience."

Guillaume Depardieu, Gérard's hulking blond son, makes a better Pierre than the wan youth I pictured while reading the novel; he projects the sense of self-gratification that motivates Pierre—who is such an egotist that even throwing away his own life is an act of selfishness. Katerina Golubeva will wear on the nerves of some witnesses with her pitiful little-girl voice and her narcissistic way of hiding her face with her hair, but if anyone looks like she was raised in a hovel in the woods, she does. The cool elegance Deneuve brings to the opening scenes makes a useful contrast with the industrial anarchy of the conclusion, with those terrorist musicians pounding joylessly on their anvils. I would rather see one movie like this than a thousand *Bring It Ons*.

Pollock ★ ★ ★ ★
R, 122 m., 2001

Ed Harris (Jackson Pollock), Marcia Gay
Harden (Lee Krasner), Amy Madigan (Peggy
Guggenheim), Jennifer Connelly (Ruth
Klingman), Jeffrey Tambor (Clement Greenberg),
Bud Cort (Howard Putzel), John Heard (Tony
Smith), Val Kilmer (Willem de Kooning).
Directed by Ed Harris and produced by Fred
Berner, Harris, and John Kilik. Screenplay by
Barbara Turner and Susan Emshwiller, based
on the book *Jackson Pollock: An American Saga*
by Steven Naifeh and Gregory White Smith.

Reporter from *Life* magazine: "How do you
know when you're finished with a painting?"

Jackson Pollock: "How do you know when
you're finished making love?"

Jackson Pollock was a great painter. He was
also a miserable man who made everyone
around him miserable a lot of the time. He
was an alcoholic and manic-depressive, and
he died in a drunken car crash that killed an
innocent woman. What Ed Harris is able to
show in *Pollock* is that when he was painting,
he got a reprieve. He was also reasonably happy
during those periods when he stopped drinking.
Then the black cloud would descend again.

Pollock avoids the pitfall of making simplistic one-to-one connections between the artist's
life and his paintings. This is not a movie about
art but about work. It is about the physical
labor of making paintings, and about the additional labor of everyday life, which is a burden for Pollock because of his tortured mind
and hungover body. It is said that it takes more
will for an alcoholic to get out of bed in the
morning than for other people to go through
the day, and there are times when Pollock
simply stops, stuck, and stares into space. He
didn't have de Kooning's luck and find sobriety.

Pollock is often depressed, but *Pollock* is not
depressing. It contains all the hum and buzz of
the postwar New York art world, the vibrant
courage of Pollock's wife, Lee Krasner, the
measured presence of the art critic Clement
Greenberg (who more or less validated abstract
expressionism), and the fun-loving energy of
the millionaire art patron Peggy Guggenheim,
who collected paintings and painters. It was a
time when Pollack traded a painting to pay a

$56 bill at a store, and found himself in *Life*
magazine not long after. Things were on the
move.

This is Ed Harris's movie. He started thinking about it fifteen years ago, after reading a
book about Pollock. He commissioned the
screenplay. He raised the money. He stars in it,
and he directed it. He knew he looked a lot like
Pollock (his father saw the book and thought
the cover photo resembled his son). But his
similarity to Pollock is not just superficial; he
looks a little like Picasso, too, but is unlikely to
find the same affinity. He seems to have made
a deeper connection, to have felt an instinctive
sympathy for this great, unhappy man.

The movie wears its period lightly. It gets
rolling in postwar Greenwich Village. Everybody smokes all the time. Rents are cheap, but
the first time Peggy Guggenheim visits Pollock's studio is almost the last: "I do not climb
up five flights of stairs to nobody home!" Why
did Pollock almost miss his first meeting with
the famous patron? Some damn fool reason.
He had a knack for screwing up, and it's ar-
guable that his career would never have happened if Lee Krasner hadn't poked her head
around his door one day.

Krasner (played by Marcia Gay Harden, evoking enormous sympathy and patience) comes
calling because she wants to see his paintings.
She passes her hand over them as if testing
their temperature. She knows they are good.
She senses that Pollock takes little initiative in
personal matters, and takes charge of their relationship, undressing while Pollock is still
looking for his cigarettes. She goes in with her
eyes open. She knows she's marrying a troubled
man, but stands by him, and is repaid with a
couple of happy years when they get a place in
the country, and he doesn't drink. Then the
troubles all start again—a bottle of beer, a fight,
an upset table at Thanksgiving, and affairs
with hero-worshipping girls like Ruth Klingman
(Jennifer Connelly).

I don't know if Ed Harris knows how to
paint, but I know he knows how to look like
he's painting. There's a virtuoso scene where
he paints a mural for Peggy's townhouse, utterly
confident, fast and sure, in the flow. And others
where we see the famous drip technique (and
see that "anyone" could not do it). His judge
and jury is the critic Clement Greenberg, played

with judicious, plummy certainty by Jeffrey Tambor. He says what he thinks, praising early work and bringing Guggenheim around, then attacking later work even as the world embraces it ("pretentious muddiness").

Pollock is confident, insightful work—one of the best films of the year. Ed Harris is always a good actor but here seems possessed, as if he had a leap of empathy for Pollock. His direction is assured, economical, knows where it's going, and what it wants to do. No fancy visual gimmicks, just the look and feel of this world.

I first saw the movie at the Toronto Film Festival and a day later ran into the painter Julian Schnabel. I mentioned Pollock's suffering. "What happened to Jackson Pollock when he was painting," Schnabel said, "is, he was free." That's what Ed Harris communicates in the film. A man is miserable but he is given a gift. The gift lifts his misery while he employs it. It brings joy to himself and others. It creates space he can hide in, space he can breathe in, space he can escape to. He needs that space, and given his demons, painting is the only way he can find it.   ☞

Pootie Tang ½★
PG-13, 79 m., 2001

Lance Crouther (Pootie Tang), JB Smoove (Trucky), Jennifer Coolidge (Ireenie), Reg E. Cathey (Dirty Dee), Robert Vaughn (Dick Lecter), Wanda Sykes (Biggie Shorty), Chris Rock (Pootie's Father/JB), Cathy Trien (Stacy), David Attel (Frank). Directed by Louis C.K. and produced by Cotty Chubb, David M. Gale, Ali LeRoi, Michael Rotenberg, Dave Becky, and Chris Rock. Screenplay by C.K.

Pootie Tang is not bad so much as inexplicable. You watch in puzzlement: How did this train wreck happen? How was this movie assembled out of such ill-fitting pieces? Who thought it was funny? Who thought it was finished? For that matter, was it finished? Take away the endless opening titles and end credits, and it's about seventy minutes long. The press notes say it comes "from the comedy laboratory of HBO's Emmy Award–winning *Chris Rock Show.*" It's like one of those lab experiments where the room smells like swamp gas and all the mice are dead.

Lance Crouther stars as Pootie Tang, a folk hero who has gained enormous popularity even though nobody can understand a word he says. He crusades against the evil Lecter Corp., which sells cigarettes, booze, drugs, and fast food to kids. Pootie is a regular character on *The Chris Rock Show,* and has a following, but he's more suited to skits than to a feature film—or at least to this feature film, which is disorganized, senseless, and chaotic.

Characters appear and disappear without pattern. Pootie has funny scenes, as when he dodges bullets, and other scenes, as when a woman eats a pie off his face, that seem left in the movie by accident. His secret weapon is his daddy's belt, which he uses against criminals. His daddy (Chris Rock) gave it to him on his deathbed, after being mauled by a gorilla at the steel mill. When the belt is stolen by an evil woman named Ireenie (Jennifer Coolidge), he loses his powers, but is helped by a good woman named Biggie Shorty (Wanda Sykes, who provides more personality than the movie deserves).

Biggie Shorty is a hooker but spends most of her time boogying on street corners and encouraging Pootie Tang. She has a farm in Mississippi she loans Pootie, who, during his recuperation there, is encouraged by the white sheriff to date his daughter. This leads in the direction of a shotgun marriage, until the story thread evaporates and Pootie ends up in bed with Biggie. There is another villain named Dirty Dee (Reg E. Cathey), who is very dirty, and a villain, Dick Lecter, played by Robert Vaughn as if he may have a touch of lockjaw. Bob Costas plays an interviewer on one of those dreadful assignments where the writers thought it was funny simply *that* he was in the movie, instead of giving him anything funny to do.

Material this silly might at least be mindless entertainment for children, but *Pootie Tang* for no good reason includes a lot of language it has no need for. The studios put enormous pressure on the MPAA to award PG-13 ratings to what once would have been R-rated material, and the MPAA obliges. Here is dialogue your MPAA rates PG-13: "You can't hurt a ho with a belt. They like it." Women are routinely described as bitches and slapped around a lot (so are men). I have no problem with street language in movies with a use for the language. But why use it gratuitously in a movie that has no need for it, with a lead character whose TV exposure will attract younger viewers? What's the point?

Anyway, I'm not so much indignant as confused. Audiences will come out scratching their heads. The movie is half-baked, a shabby job of work. There are flashes of good stuff: a music video in the closing titles, some good songs on the sound track, Lance Crouther heroically making Pootie Tang an intriguing character even though the movie gives him no help. This movie is not in a releasable condition.

Price of Glory ★ ★
PG-13, 118 m., 2000

Jimmy Smits (Arturo Ortega), Maria Del Mar (Rita Ortega), Jon Seda (Sonny Ortega), Clifton Collins Jr. (Jimmy Ortega), Ernesto Hernandez (Johnny Ortega), Ron Perlman (Nick Everson), Louis Mandylor (Davey Lane), Sal Lopez (Hector Salmon). Directed Carlos Avila and produced by Moctesuma Esparza, Robert Katz, and Arthur E. Friedman. Screenplay by Phil Berger.

Price of Glory made me feel like I was sitting in McDonald's watching some guy shout at his kids. You read the situation: Here's a man with problems of his own, who is projecting his troubles onto his children—because he thinks he can control them, and he knows he can't control himself. The world has him licked. The situation makes you feel sad and uncomfortable, but it's none of your business. You look away.

Price of Glory gives us two hours of that behavior, and it's a miscalculation so basic that it makes the movie painful when it wants, I guess, to be touching. Jimmy Smits plays Arturo Ortega, a Mexican-American father who was a boxer when he was young, was "brought along too fast" and beaten badly in a fight, and now leads a life obsessed with getting revenge through the lives of his three sons. He brings them up as boxers ("the Fighting Ortegas"), and tries to dominate their lives. But he does such a bad job of masterminding their careers that finally the sons and long-suffering wife see him less as a father than as their cross to bear. Even his rival, a boxing promoter who wants to handle the most promising son, comes

across less as an enemy than as a man with more common sense than Arturo.

Smits is good in this performance—all too good. The movie is earnest and sincere, and an ordeal to watch, because there's no arc to his character, and learning and redemption are too little, too late. He's stuck. He keeps making the same mistakes over and over; he starts as tragic, and ends as a slow study. And he inflicts on his kids (and us) that tiresome strategy of the domineering parent who puts on an act of being reasonable, of "only wanting what's best" for his kids, when clearly his own issues are in charge. He even believes himself when he delivers his sanctimonious and self-serving speeches; the kids turn away, and we pity them.

The other arc in the film is that of a typical boxing movie. It opens with Arturo losing big in an early fight, and then we see him living in New Mexico with his wife, Rita (Maria Del Mar), who sees him clearly, loves him, but puts up with way too much. They have three kids, who are put in the ring at such young ages that we didn't know they made boxing gloves that tiny. (I don't even want to think about kids in the "Peewee Division.") He pushes them, browbeats them; even one kid's victory gets criticized because his style was wrong. We sense here a portrait of all parents who live through young children, pushing them onto the stage, forcing them into competitions they have no taste for, treating them not like kids but like puppets acting out the parents' fantasies.

Flash forward ten years and the kids are young men, but their father has learned nothing. They are Sonny (Jon Seda), Jimmy (Clifton Collins Jr.), and Johnny (Ernesto Hernandez). Sonny is the best boxer, but as the oldest he's the most driven to squirm from under his father's thumb. Jimmy is resentful and rebellious. Johnny has real promise, and as the youngest is most concerned with pleasing his dad. But the family by this point is twisted and distorted by years of Arturo's bullying, as Rita Ortega looks on helplessly.

Like many bullies, Arturo is filled with self-pity, and has a way of creating a family dynamic where guilt suppresses rage. Consider a scene where one of the boys proudly brings home the girlfriend he wants to marry and her parents, for dinner. Arturo behaves like such a jerk that we cringe. A family dinner quite like this could not exist anywhere outside a movie more concerned with making a point than drawing a convincing character.

The story's villain is a professional fight promoter named Nick Everson (Ron Perlman). With his deep-set eyes and burly physique, he's intimidating, and controls the bookings for big fights. I am sure there are people like him all through professional boxing, but what's amazing is that he comes as a surprise to Arturo, who wants to manage his sons himself. Everson has thugs working for him, but he and his men are not vicious, simply hard-boiled. By the end of the film, Everson is looking reasonable compared to Arturo Ortega—even to Arturo himself.

The character scenes are intercut with standard scenes from boxing movies: training, strategy, talking about moves, early fights. None of this stuff is remarkable. What's peculiar is that the film doesn't build toward anything because even as the boxing careers flourish, the character of Arturo drags everything down. At the end there is a victory, and it means nothing—it's ashes, because Arturo has taken out the fun. He just never learns.

The Price of Milk ★ ★
PG-13, 89 m., 2001

Danielle Cormack (Lucinda), Karl Urban (Rob), Willa O'Neill (Drosophilia), Rangi Motu (Auntie), Michael Lawrence (Bernie). Directed by Harry Sinclair and produced by Fiona Copland. Screenplay by Sinclair.

Somewhere in New Zealand, a nation apparently inhabited by less than a dozen people, Lucinda and Rob run a dairy farm. So lonely is Rob that he knows all 175 of his cows by their names—or numbers ("Good morning, 47!"). So carnal is Lucinda that she surprises Rob at strange times and places with sudden, bold invitations to make love. So besotted is Rob that he produces a wedding ring and proposes. So fearful is Lucinda that she seeks advice to be sure that Rob really loves her. So realistic am I that I'm thinking—he'd better, since there is, so far, no other man in the movie.

Lucinda turns to her friend Drosophilia, who advises her to be absolutely sure of Rob's love by setting up a series of tests. In the first Lucinda goes bathing in a vat containing $1,500 worth of milk, spoiling it. Rob is angered, but so fetching is Lucinda's smile and so real her dismay that he plunges in with her, and so fervent are their ecstasies that the milk all but churns into butter right before our eyes.

We are thinking, meanwhile, that whatever else you can say for them, Lucinda, Rob, and Drosophilia are healthy-looking specimens, and look right at place on a farm. No wonder; they are played by Danielle Cormack, Karl Urban, and Willa O'Neill, who have all appeared on TV's *Xena* or *Hercules* (Cormack is the Amazon Ephiny). They were cast in *The Price of Milk* by its writer-director, Harry Sinclair—who, I learn from *Film Journal International*, "started out his project not with a story line, or a face in mind, but a bit of a Russian symphony by early-20th-century composer Anatol Liadov, accidentally heard over the radio while location-scouting. Sinclair was inspired by the music and the place, and themes appeared and fell into line for him."

If true, this would indicate Sinclair was scouting for locations before he knew what his story was about, which may explain the rather awkward tension between the cow farm and what is basically a fairy tale. He adds supernatural elements involving a Maori woman named Auntie (Rangi Motu). One day Lucinda runs straight into Auntie with her car, but Auntie is miraculously untouched, and disappears into the woods.

A few nights later, mysterious hands steal the quilt from Lucinda and Rob's bed, and Lucinda sees it soon after in Auntie's hands. Tracking her down to a cottage in the woods, she sees Auntie sleeping under a pile of dozens of quilts—all stolen for her, we learn, by her nephews (who are golfers, and practice putts between quilt raids). Lucinda demands her quilt back, and is given a series of demands by Auntie that *really* test Rob's love.

There is a place for whimsy and magic realism, and that place may not be on a cow farm in New Zealand. Or perhaps it is, but not with this story. I was never much convinced by the romantic chemistry between Rob and Lucinda, never believed in Drosophilia's jealous scheming, found Auntie tiresome, and was most intrigued by her golfing nephews, small though their roles may be. Imagine a golf movie involving six or seven Maoris on the pro Tour with a magic Auntie. Now there's a movie.

Princess Mononoke ★ ★ ★ ★
PG-13, 133 m., 1999

With the voices of: Claire Danes (San [Princess]), Minnie Driver (Eboshi), Gillian Anderson (Moro the Wolf), Billy Crudup (Ashitaka), Jada Pinkett-Smith (Toki), Billy Bob Thornton (Jigo), John De Mita (Kohroku), John Di Maggio (Gonza). Directed by Hayao Miyazaki and produced by Toshio Suzuki. Screenplay by Miyazaki, English adaptation by Neil Gaiman.

I go to the movies for many reasons. Here is one of them: I want to see wondrous sights not available in the real world, in stories where myth and dreams are set free to play. Animation opens that possibility because it is freed from gravity and the chains of the possible. Realistic films show the physical world; animation shows its essence. Animated films are not copies of "real movies," are not shadows of reality, but create a new existence in their own right. True, a lot of animation is insipid and insulting, even to the children it is made for. But great animation can make the mind sing.

Hayao Miyazaki is a great animator, and his *Princess Mononoke* is a great film. Do not allow conventional thoughts about animation to prevent you from seeing it. It tells an epic story set in medieval Japan at the dawn of the Iron Age, when some men still lived in harmony with nature and others were trying to tame and defeat it. It is not a simplistic tale of good and evil, but the story of how humans, forest animals, and nature gods all fight for their share of the new emerging order. It is one of the most visually inventive films I have ever seen.

The movie opens with a watchtower guard spotting "something wrong in the forest." There is a disturbance of nature, and out of it leaps a remarkable creature, a kind of boar-monster with flesh made of writhing snakes. It attacks villagers, and to the defense comes Ashitaka, the young prince of his isolated people. He is finally able to slay the beast, but his own arm has been wrapped by the snakes and is horribly scarred.

A wise woman is able to explain what has happened. The monster was a boar god, until a bullet buried itself in its flesh and drove it mad. And where did the bullet come from? "It is time," says the woman, "for our last prince to cut his hair and leave us." And so Ashitaka sets off on a long journey to the lands of the west, to find out why nature is out of joint, and whether the curse on his arm can be lifted. He rides Yakkuru, a beast that seems part horse, part antelope, part mountain goat.

There are strange sights and adventures along the way, and we are able to appreciate the quality of Miyazaki's artistry. The drawing in this film is not simplistic, but has some of the same "clear line" complexity used by the Japanese graphic artists of two centuries ago, who inspired such modern work as Hergé's Tintin books. Nature is rendered majestically (Miyazaki's art directors journeyed to ancient forests to make their master drawings) and fancifully (as with the round little forest sprites). There are also brief, mysterious appearances of the spirit of the forest, who by day seems to be a noble beast and at night a glowing light.

Ashitaka eventually arrives in an area prowled by Moro, a wolf god, and sees for the first time the young woman named San. She is also known as Princess Mononoke, but that's more a description than a name; a "mononoke" is the spirit of a beast. San was a human child, raised as a wolf by Moro; she rides bareback on the swift white spirit-wolves, and helps the pack in their battle against the encroachments of Lady Eboshi, a strong ruler whose village is developing ironworking skills and manufactures weapons using gunpowder.

As Lady Eboshi's people gain one kind of knowledge, they lose another, and the day is fading when men, animals, and the forest gods all speak the same language. The lush green forests through which Ashitaka traveled west have been replaced here by a wasteland; trees have been stripped to feed the smelting furnaces, and on their skeletons, yellow-eyed beasts squat ominously. Slaves work the bellows of the forges, and lepers make the weapons.

But all is not black-and-white. The lepers are grateful that Eboshi accepts them. Her people enjoy her protection. Even Jigo, a scheming agent of the emperor, has motives that sometimes make a certain amount of sense.

When a nearby samurai enclave wants to take over the village and its technology, there is a battle with more than one side and more than one motive. This is more like mythical history than action melodrama.

The artistry in *Princess Mononoke* is masterful. The writhing skin of the boar-monster is an extraordinary sight, one that would be impossible to create in any live-action film. The great white wolves are drawn with grace, and not sentimentalized; when they bare their fangs, you can see that they are not friendly comic pals, but animals who can and will kill. The movie does not dwell on violence, which makes some of its moments even more shocking, as when Ashitaka finds that his scarred arm has developed such strength that his arrow decapitates an enemy.

Miyazaki and his collaborators work at Studio Ghibli, and a few years ago Disney bought the studio's entire output for worldwide distribution. (Disney artists consider Miyazaki a source of inspiration.) The contract said Disney could not change a frame—but there was no objection to dubbing into English, because of course all animation is dubbed, into even its source language, and as Miyazaki cheerfully observes, "English has been dubbed into Japanese for years."

This version of *Princess Mononoke* has been well and carefully dubbed with gifted vocal talents, including Billy Crudup as Ashitaka, Claire Danes as San, Minnie Driver as Eboshi, Gillian Anderson as Moro, Billy Bob Thornton as Jigo, and Jada Pinkett-Smith as Toki, a commonsensical working woman in the village.

The drama is underlaid with Miyazaki's deep humanism, which avoids easy moral simplifications. There is a remarkable scene where San and Ashitaka, who have fallen in love, agree that neither can really lead the life of the other, and so they must grant each other freedom and only meet occasionally. You won't find many Hollywood love stories (animated or otherwise) so philosophical. *Princess Monokone* is a great achievement and a wonderful experience, and one of the best films of 1999.

Note: Some of my information comes from an invaluable book, Hayao Miyazaki: Master of Japanese Animation, *by Helen McCarthy, Stone Bridge Press, $18.95.*

Private Confessions ★ ★ ★ ½
NO MPAA RATING, 127 m., 1999

Pernilla August (Anna), Samuel Froler (Henrik), Max von Sydow (Jacob), Thomas Hanzon (Tomas Egerman), Kristina Adolphson (Maria), Anita Bjork (Karin Akerblom), Gunnel Fred (Marta Gardsjo), Sven Lindberg (Bishop Agrell). Directed by Liv Ullmann and produced by Ingrid Dahlberg. Screenplay by Ingmar Bergman.

It is hard to imagine your parents as young people when you are older than they were when they raised you. We understand other adults, but it is so hard to see them clearly; we still regard them through the screens of childhood mystery. In his old age, the thoughts of the Swedish director Ingmar Bergman have turned toward his childhood, and particularly toward the secrets of his parents' marriage.

His father was a Lutheran minister. His films paint his mother as a high-spirited woman who often found her husband distant or tiresome. Both his parents were steeped in religion and theology, which did not prevent them from doing wrong, but equipped them to agonize over it. In four films, one as a director and three where others directed his screenplays, Bergman has returned to the years when he was a child and his parents were in turmoil. *Fanny and Alexander* (1983) was a memory of childhood. Bille August's *The Best Intentions* (1992) was the story of the parents' courtship. *Sunday's Children* (1994), directed by Bergman's son Daniel, was about the boy's uneasy relationship with his father. Now comes *Private Confessions*, the story of his mother's moral struggles. He calls these films fictions, because he imagines things he could not have seen, but there is no doubt they are true to his feelings about his parents. One would not live to eighty-one and tell these stories only to falsify them.

Private Confessions, based on Bergman's 1966 book, has been directed by Liv Ullmann, an actress in many of his best films. The cinematographer is wise old Sven Nykvist, his collaborator for thirty years. The actress playing Anna, his mother, is Pernilla August, who also played Anna in *The Best Intentions*. Uncle Jacob, Anna's spiritual adviser, is Max von Sydow, the tall, spare presence in so many Bergman films from *The Seventh Seal* onward.

The film is divided into five "conversations." An explanation is offered early, by Uncle Jacob. It is often wrongly thought, he tells Anna, that Luther abolished the Catholic sacrament of confession. Not exactly. He replaced it with "private conversations" in which sins and moral questions could be discussed with an adviser. Jacob led young Anna through her confirmation, and they meet again as the film opens in the summer of 1925. She confesses to him that she has been an unfaithful wife. She has cheated on her husband, Henrik, with a younger man, Tomas. Both men are theologians.

Jacob tells her she must break off the relationship, and tell everything to her husband. In the second conversation, set a few weeks later, she follows his advice, and we see that Henrik (Samuel Froler) is a cold man who views adultery less as a matter of passion than as a breach of contract. No wonder, he shouts, that the house contains "chipped glasses, stained cloths, dead plants."

The third conversation takes place before the other two, and involves a rendezvous between Anna and Tomas, which she has arranged in the home of a friend. Here we get insights into the nature of their relationship, and there is the possibility that for a lover, Anna may have selected a man similar to her husband. He feels "gray and inadequate," Tomas tells her the morning after, and keeps repeating, "One must be true." Is it Anna's fate to forever dash her passion against the stony shores of men who think before they feel?

The fourth conversation, which contains the heart of the film, takes place ten years later, when Jacob is dying and wants to know the truth about what happened—about whether Anna followed his advice. She lies to him to spare his feelings. They take communion together, and that sets up the fifth conversation, which takes place before all the others, the day before young Anna's confirmation. In it she confesses to Jacob that she does not feel ready to take communion the next day. One must, of course, be in a state of grace and readiness to take the sacrament, and she does not feel she is. His advice to her at this time is the best he ever gives her.

The film is not about sex or adultery. It is about loneliness and the attempt to defeat it while living within rigid moral guidelines. To understand it completely, we have to remember *The Best Intentions*, which tells the story of Anna and Henrik's courtship, and shows her as warm and generous, he as already crippled by a cold childhood and an inferiority complex. There is just the hint—the barest hint, a whisper only—that the one man in Anna's life who might have given her what she craved was Uncle Jacob.

A film like *Private Confessions* makes most films about romance look like films about plumbing. It is about Bergman's eternal theme, which is that we are all locked in our own boxes of time and space, and most of us never escape them. They have windows but not doors. Anna's problem is not morality but consciousness. To know herself is to accept that no one else will ever truly know her. Her final lie to Jacob accepts this truth, but at least as he dies she can make his own cell a little more peaceful.

Proof of Life ★ ★ ½
R, 135 m., 2000

Meg Ryan (Alice Bowman), Russell Crowe (Terry Thorne), David Morse (Peter Bowman), David Caruso (Dino), Pamela Reed (Janis Bowman), Wolframio Benavides (Honcho). Directed and produced by Taylor Hackford. Screenplay by Tony Gilroy, based on an article "Adventures in the Ransom Trade" by William Prochnau and the book *The Long March to Freedom* by Thomas Hargrove.

Kidnapping is not a rare crime but a lucrative line of business in the Third World, according to *Proof of Life*, a movie that is best when it sticks closest to the tradecraft of a professional K&R man named Terry Thorne. K&R means "kidnap and ransom," we learn, and the specialty has grown along with the crime; somewhere in the world, businessmen are being snatched on an almost daily basis, making lots of work for Terry (Russell Crowe), who masterminds a helicopter snatch of a hostage in the opening sequence and makes his getaway clinging to the landing skips of the chopper.

Cut to Tecala, a fictional Latin American

country where drugs are a major crop and a revolutionary movement has morphed into a professional kidnapping operation. We meet Peter and Alice Bowman (David Morse, Meg Ryan), an American couple going through a bad patch in their marriage, who are living in the country while Peter builds a dam. He thinks the dam will help the locals grow crops. She thinks it's window dressing for the oil company that employs him. They're hardly speaking to each other when she gets word he's been kidnapped.

Enter Terry Thorne, whose job is to negotiate the lowest possible ransom price and rescue the hostage. Exit Terry Thorne, when it's revealed that Bowman's employer didn't pay the premium on his K&R policy. Reenter Terry Thorne, who returns to Tecala because something about Alice Bowman, some quiet unstated appeal with sexual undertones, has brought him back. He will risk his life for free, for the husband of the woman he doesn't know for sure he loves, although he has a strong hunch.

The movie, directed by Taylor Hackford, cuts between Thorne's K&R craft, Alice's guilt and emotional confusion, and the ordeal in the jungle by Peter, played by Morse as a hothead who talks back to the guys carrying the machine guns—not always prudent. Complications enter with Alice's sister-in-law (Pamela Reed); a fellow prisoner of Peter's (Gottfried John), who poses as a crazy missionary; and Thorne's old fighting partner Dino (David Caruso), who is in the country trying to rescue *another* kidnap victim.

The movie's kidnap lore, based on books and articles about professional K&R men, is intriguing. Crowe, as Terry, explains his work to Alice (and to us), and we learn why you never bring in local negotiators (on the take and maybe in on the snatch), why the opening asking price is way high, and how to demand proof the hostage is still alive. Meanwhile Terry and Alice carry on a buried flirtation in which both shyly acknowledge the chemistry between them with a kiss and eloquent body language. A more graphic sex scene was cut from the movie, reportedly because it reflected the real-life liaison between Crowe and Ryan; whether the movie would have been better

with a more overt romance is an interesting question. Obviously Hackford preferred unreleased tension, and building toward his poignant final scene.

I found the movie absorbing in its details and persuasive in its performances, but the overall flight was somehow without lift. I wanted the tension wound tighter. The side relationships, with the sister-in-law and the missionary, were interesting in themselves but put the plot progress on hold. Crowe, Ryan, and Morse are everything the story asks for; her character is doubly interesting because the movie avoids the cliché of the grieving wife and shows a conflicted, sometimes angry woman who had a big fight with the husband just before he was snatched. Crowe's K&R man has a professional code, mostly (we gather) of his own enforcement, that inhibits his romantic feelings. Or is it that he gets off on playing the hero for unavailable women, and then nobly departing before they have the opportunity to choose him if they want to? Morse's role is more down to earth, as a captive who is mistreated but knows he can get away with a lot because he must remain alive to be of value.

I was interested all through the movie—interested, but not riveted. I cared, but not quite enough. I had sympathy with the characters, but in keeping at arm's length from each other they also kept a certain distance from me. Perhaps the screenplay should have been kept simmering until it was reduced a little, and its flavors made stronger.

Pups ★ ★ ★
NO MPAA RATING, 103 m., 1999

Cameron Van Hoy (Stevie), Mischa Barton (Rocky), Burt Reynolds (Daniel Bender), Kurt Loder (Himself), Adam Ferrar (Wheelchair Man), David Allen Graf (Bank Manager), James Gordon (J.P.), Darling Narita (Joy). Directed by Ash and produced by Ash and Daniel M. Berger. Screenplay by Ash.

Pups looks ragged and slammed-together, but that's part of its appeal; the film has a wildness that more care would have killed. It's about a bank robbery and hostage crisis involving a thirteen-year-old and his girlfriend. Why this bank? "It was on the way to school."

The kids, named Stevie and Rocky, are played by Cameron Van Hoy and Mischa Barton in two of the most natural and freed performances I have seen by actors of any age. There is an unhinged quality about Van Hoy's acting; he waves his mother's loaded gun while ordering around the adults he's found in the bank, and although we know his character got his lines by watching TV, his energy level is awesome. He pumps out words and postures, flailing his arms, jazzed by the experience, implying a whole childhood in the way he seizes this power.

Van Hoy is a newcomer. Barton, who plays his girlfriend, has a lot of professional experience, but must never have found a role like this before. You can sense her exhilaration as she behaves the way a thirteen-year-old girl *would* behave—not dampened down by a conventional screenplay. Often they waltz through long takes, working without the net of editing.

The movie is persuasive in the way it shows the steps leading to their absurd decision to rob a bank. Stevie begins by videotaping a fake suicide message, shouting "final warnings" to a mother who, we learn, is out of town on business. Then he finds her loaded gun. His girlfriend, Rocky, comes over, he accidentally fires the gun, they are impressed, and then they head for school—at one point interrupting the trip to lie down in the street. The street scene isn't played for phony suspense; a guy in an SUV drives by and tells them they're jerks.

Stevie has brought along the gun. On an impulse, he walks into a bank and announces a stickup. Rocky tells him he's crazy, but eventually she joins him (what's a girlfriend for?). We meet some of the staff and customers, including an angry guy in a wheelchair (Adam Ferrar) who eggs them on, a bank manager (David Allen Graf) who can't believe this is happening to him, and a customer (Darling Narita) who sneaks puffs on a joint.

Burt Reynolds plays the FBI agent in charge of the force surrounding the bank. It is not a distinguished performance, and one of its peculiarities (the screenplay's fault?) is that instead of using psychological insights in negotiating with the kid, he simply shouts threats,

profanities, and insults over the phone. Maybe Reynolds has been saving up those lines ever since he played the cop with the pint-size sidekick in *Cop and a Half.*

The details of the FBI siege are unconvincing, and an encounter between Rocky and her father rings false, but I think you have to buy the movie's flaws as the price of its anarchic freedom. The stories of the hostages are all loose ends—but then, they would be. *Pups* doesn't make everyone inside the bank into instant friends, but keeps them as strangers who puzzle one another. Orchestrating everything are the two kids, waving their gun and improvising their strategy as they go along.

At one point, having ordered pizzas, the kids think of another demand. "We could be on MTV," Rocky says, thinking of *Real Life.* "You know—like six strangers meet in a bank and are forced to live together." MTV personality Kurt Loder, playing himself, shows up, and his interview with the kids is the heart of the film. He asks them about sex. Stevie says, "I love her—we're gonna get married on the Internet." Loder is from MTV, all right: "You'll be divorced by fifteen and back on the market."

Pups is the second film by Ash, a British director whose *Bang* (1997) starred Darling Narita as an actress who is molested by a cop, handcuffs him, steals his uniform, and spends the day on his motorcycle experiencing how this borrowed identity gives her power and unexpected responsibilities. That movie was shot guerrilla-style for $25,000 and has an eerie power; this one cost a little more, but it was shot in two weeks and has the same feeling that it's running free. Ash's films are unpolished but involving and untamed.

So much depends on the performances. If instead of Van Hoy and Barton the movie had starred safer or more circumspect actors, the energy would have flagged and the flaws of the quick production would have been more of a problem. As it is, *Pups* is a kind of headlong rush toward doom. "The only way to get us out of here is to carry us out in a box," Stevie boasts, using a line he learned from TV. But the FBI won't shoot thirteen-year-olds, will it?

Pushing Tin ★ ★ ★
R, 124 m., 1999

John Cusack (Nick Falzone), Billy Bob
Thornton (Russell Bell), Angelina Jolie (Mary
Bell), Cate Blanchett (Connie Falzone), Jake
Weber (Barry Plotkin), Vicki Lewis (Tina).
Directed by Mike Newell and produced by Art
Linson. Screenplay by Glen and Les Charles,
based on an article by Darcy Frey.

Like an overloaded airplane struggling to lift
off, the characters in *Pushing Tin* leap free of
the runway only to be pulled back down by
the plot. John Cusack and Billy Bob Thornton
play two air-traffic controllers who are prickly
and complex, who take hold of a scene and
shake it awake and make it live, only to be
brought down by a simpering series of happy
endings.

For at least an hour, there is hope that the
movie will amount to something singular. It
takes us into a world we haven't seen much
of—an air-traffic control center. Controllers
peer into their computer screens like kids playing a video game, barking instructions with
such alarming quickness that we wonder how
pilots can understand them. They use cynicism to protect themselves from the terrors of
the job. One guy "has an aluminum shower in
his future." The movie opens with the laconic
observation, "You land a million planes safely,
then you have one little midair, and you never
hear the end of it." This movie is not going to
be shown on airplanes.

Cusack plays Nick Falzone, hotshot con-
troller, on top of his job, happily married to
his sweet wife, Connie (Cate Blanchett, astonishingly transformed from Elizabeth I into a
New Jersey housewife). He works a night shift,
ingests a plateful of grease at the local diner, is
tired but content. Then into his life comes
Russell Bell (Billy Bob Thornton), a cowboy con-
troller from out west, who gets under people's
skins. He rides a hog, needs a shave, schedules
planes so close together that the other controllers hold their breaths. He's married to a
twenty-year-old sex bomb named Mary (Angelina Jolie), who dresses like a lap dancer.

These four characters are genuinely interesting. Russell is an enigma and likes it that
way. He speaks seldom, has tunnel vision when

concentrating on a task, and once stood on a
runway to see what the backwash from a 747
felt like. (The controllers watch him doing
this, in a video that shows him blown away
like a rag doll; in real life, paralysis or death
would probably result.) Thornton, who is emerging as the best specialist in scene-stealing supporting roles since Robert Duvall, is able to
maintain the fascination as long as the screenplay maintains Russell's mystery.

Alas, Hollywood grows restless and unhappy
with characters who don't talk much; that's
why the typical American screenplay is said to
be a third longer than most French screenplays. It's hard to be chatty and still maintain
an air of mystery; the key to Bogart's appeal is
in enigmatic understatement. When Russell
does start speaking (or "sharing") with Nick,
he turns out, alas, to have the mellow insights
of a self-help tape, and at one point actually
advises the younger man to learn to "let go."
This is not what we want to hear from the
same man who, earlier in the movie, when
asked if he has any hobbies, growls, "I used to
bowl, when I was an alcoholic."

The Cusack character is also given a rocky
road by the screenwriters (Glen and Les Charles).
He's a happily married man, but when he sees
the Angelina Jolie character, he melts. She's
weeping in the supermarket over a cart full of
vodka, and he helpfully invites her to a nearby
restaurant. After predictable consequences,
she has a line that would have made her husband proud ("Mr. Falzone, what's the fewest
number of words you can use to get out that
door?"), but instead of following the emotional and sexual consequences to some kind
of bitter end, the movie goes all soft and sentimental.

Cusack does what he does best: incisive intelligence, combined with sincere but sensible
emotion. Blanchett, eccentric in *Oscar and
Lucinda* and regal in *Elizabeth*, is cheery and
normal here, chatting about taking art classes.
Jolie's sexuality is like a bronco that keeps
throwing her; she's too young and vulnerable
to control it. One can imagine a movie that
linked these characters in unforgettable ways,
and this one seems headed for a showdown
before it veers off into platitudes.

At least it spares us an airplane crash. And it
gives us a good scene where Nick, aboard a

461

plane, becomes convinced that Russell is steering them through a thunderstorm. (His behavior here should get him handcuffed by the flight crew and arrested by the FBI, but never mind.) The movie also does an observant job of showing us the atmosphere inside an air-traffic control center, where the job description includes "depression, nervous breakdowns, heart attacks, and hypertension."

The movie is worth seeing for the good stuff. I'm recommending it because of the performances and the details in the air-traffic control center. The director is Mike Newell *(Donnie Brasco, Four Weddings and a Funeral).* His gift in making his characters come alive is so real that it actually underlines the weakness of the ending. We believe we know Russell and Nick—know them so well we can tell, in the last half-hour, when they stop being themselves and start being the puppets of a boring studio ending.

Q

Quills ★ ★ ★ ½
R, 123 m., 2000

Geoffrey Rush (Marquis de Sade), Kate Winslet (Madeleine), Joaquin Phoenix (Coulmier), Michael Caine (Royer-Collard), Billie Whitelaw (Madame LeClerc), Patrick Malahide (Delbene), Amelia Warner (Simone), Jane Menelaus (Renee Pelagie). Directed by Philip Kaufman and produced by Julia Chasman, Peter Kaufman, and Nick Wechsler. Screenplay by Doug Wright, based on his play.

Some are born evil, others choose evil, and some have evil thrust upon them. We are most inclined to forgive the members of the first category. The Marquis de Sade, for example, was hard-wired from birth as one of the most villainous of God's creatures. Although it is impossible to approve of him, it is possible to concede that he did what we are all enjoined to do: Taking the gifts and opportunities at hand, he achieved everything he possibly could. That his achievement is reprehensible does not entirely obscure the fact that his spirit was indomitable and his tenacity courageous. You know you've made your mark when "sadism" is named for you.

Philip Kaufman's *Quills* supplies us with a marquis toned down for popular consumption (you will not discover here that he thought an aristocrat like himself had the right to commit murder in search of pleasure). This marquis stands not so much for sexual license as for freedom of artistic expression, and after he is locked up in an asylum and forbidden to write, he perseveres anyway, using his clothing, his skin, and the walls of his cell as surfaces, and his own blood and excrement in place of ink. A merciful deity would have supplied him with writer's block.

Kaufman's film, based on a play by Doug Wright, mostly takes place after the marquis (Geoffrey Rush) has once again gone too far, after the excesses of his writing and his life have exhausted the license and privilege granted to aristocracy. In 1801, at sixty-one, after twenty-seven years spent in various prisons, he is sealed up in the insane asylum at Charenton. There he finds a sympathetic friend in Father Coulmier (Joaquin Phoenix), a priest who thinks he should continue to write, perhaps to purge himself of his noxious fantasies.

The manuscripts are smuggled out of the asylum by Madeleine (Kate Winslet), and find a covert circulation before Napoleon assigns an administrator named Royer-Collard (Michael Caine) to crack down. The new man's sadistic measures bring out the best in de Sade, who mocks him, taunts him, outsmarts him, and remains indomitable almost to the moment of his death.

Kaufman has confided in interviews that Royer-Collard is inspired to some degree by Kenneth Starr. The type is familiar: the man fascinated by what he has forbidden himself to enjoy, savoring it vicariously through a victim he persecutes enviously. No one is quite so interested in sex as a puritan. The analogy with modern times breaks down, alas, if we seek a correspondence between de Sade and Clinton, whose milder transgressions would have flown quite beneath the marquis's radar.

Quills is not without humor in its telling of the horrendous last years of de Sade's life. There is, for example, the good cheer of Winslet's jolly, buxom laundry maid, who smuggles the manuscripts out of the prison. Father Coulmier is clearly stirred by her, but does not act, and we have the incongruity of the young, handsome man forbidden by religion from pursuing fruits which fall into the hands of the scabrous old letch.

Caine's Royer-Collard, on the other hand, is devoted to the pleasures of the flesh and keeps close watch on his too-young wife, Simone (Amelia Warner), warning, "She is a rare bird and I intend to keep her caged." It is unmistakable that Royer-Collard is attracted to de Sade's sadism, and enjoys practicing it upon the man who gave it a name. If overt sinners are evil, how more contemptible are those who seek the same pleasures under the cover of hypocrisy. De Sade at least acknowledged his tastes.

Geoffrey Rush (the pianist from *Shine*) is a curious choice for de Sade; we might have imagined Willem Dafoe or Christopher Walken in the role, but Kaufman chooses not an actor associated with the bizarre but one associated with madness. De Sade is in the grasp of fixed ideas that sweep all sanity aside; unable to realize his fantasies in the asylum, he creates them through the written word, like a salesman or missionary determined to share his enthusiasm whether or not the world desires it. By the end, the words de Sade writes are indistinguishable, emotionally, from the pain he endures and invites by writing them.

Whether this film will please most audiences is a good question. It is more about the mind than the flesh, and de Sade's struggle is monomania to an excruciating extreme. Yet Kaufman (*The Right Stuff, The Unbearable Lightness of Being*) finds a tone that remains more entertaining than depressing, more absorbing than alarming. It was not much fun to be the marquis, but most of the time in this movie de Sade doesn't know that, and attacks each day with zest and curiosity. Those around him are inspired by a spirit so free, even if his tastes are inexplicable. There is a scene where he dictates a novel through a human chain of other prisoners, who seem more intrigued by his invention than repelled by his images. Audiences may have the same response; we do not share his tastes but we have a certain admiration for his obstinacy.

De Sade has been described as the ultimate extension of the libertarian ideal, but that is lunacy: He goes beyond ideology to madness. Still, he stands as an extreme illustration of the idea that society is best served if everybody behaves according to his own self-interests. And he gets the last laugh: In the face of Father Coulmier's liberal instinct to sympathize and Royer-Collard's conservative attempt to restrain, the marquis remains indomitably himself. It is in his nature. The message of *Quills* is perhaps that we are all expressions of our natures, and to live most successfully we must understand that. Good luck that hardly any of us are dealt such a bad hand as de Sade.

R

The Rage: Carrie 2 ★ ★
R, 104 m., 1999

Emily Bergl (Rachel Lang), Jason London (Jesse Ryan), Dylan Bruno (Mark), J. Smith-Cameron (Barbara Lang), Amy Irving (Sue Snell), Zachery Ty Bryan (Eric), John Doe (Boyd), Gordon Clapp (Mr. Stark). Directed by Katt Shea and produced by Paul Monash. Screenplay by Rafael Moreu.

The Rage: Carrie 2 opens with a woman painting a red stripe at eye-level completely around her living room, while screaming, "You can't have my daughter!" Soon the woman is being carried out of the house in restraints, and her daughter, little Rachel, is being reassured by a cop, who for some reason thinks they should stand outside in the pouring rain instead of inside where it's dry.

Why the rain? For the same reason the movie has all the other props of macabre thrillers, such as blinding flash-frames accompanied by loud whooshes on the sound track. And the snicker-snack noise of two blades clashing, even when there are no blades anywhere around. And, of course, a room filled with hundreds of burning candles. And flashbacks to blood-soaked horrors in the past.

After her mother is shipped off to the asylum, Rachel grows up to become an unpopular teenager (played pretty well, under the circumstances, by Emily Bergl). She's a loner, works at a Fotomat booth, lives with a cruel foster family (even its dog is always trying to run away). One day her best friend Lisa is distraught after a boy seduces and betrays her, and throws herself off the high school roof. Rachel is distraught, and all of the lockers in the high school spring open and start banging.

The wise teacher Mrs. Snell (Amy Irving) has seen this before. Twenty years earlier, she was the friend of Carrie, the jilted girl whose psychic meltdown at a prom killed seventy-three people and burned the high school to the ground. Mrs. Snell tries to counsel Rachel, who gets upset and causes the teacher's paperweight to explode. Soon Mrs. Snell tracks down the secret of Rachel's uncontrollable powers and offers her help.

Rachel is telekinetic, we learn. Well, we knew that. What we didn't know, what indeed has escaped the attention of the ESP industry, is that telekinesis is a genetic trait. Yes, Mrs. Snell tells Rachel: "There's a lab at Princeton working on this. The male is the carrier. It's an inherited recessive trait." Why recessive? If Darwin was right, since telekinesis is so useful, it should be a dominant trait, so that Mayflower guys could move the piano upstairs while relaxing in lawn chairs.

The Rage: Carrie 2 faithfully follows the story arc of Brian De Palma's 1976 thriller. Rachel, like Carrie, is a plain and unpopular girl who is unexpectedly asked out by a popular guy (Jason London). Instead of a prom, the movie leads up to a party after the opening game of the football season. The guy, named Jesse, really does like Rachel, but nevertheless she's set up for heartbreak by cruel girls and heartless football jocks, and responds in a terrifically unrecessive way.

All of this happens like dreamwalking, as if the characters in this movie knew they were doomed to follow the scenario laid down in the first one. Some scenes exist only for contrived distraction, like the utterly pointless one where Rachel's family dog runs into traffic. (Okay, to be fair, it doubles as a Meet Cute, when Jesse takes them to the all-night animal clinic.) There is a scene where Mrs. Snell takes Rachel on a tour of the ruins of the high school that Carrie burnt down, and even she thinks it's curious that the ruins (which are practically still smoldering) haven't been cleared after two decades. Amy Irving intones her dialogue in this scene as if evoking ancient disappointments.

The original *Carrie* worked because it was a skillful teenage drama grafted onto a horror ending. Also, of course, because De Palma and his star, Sissy Spacek, made the story convincing. *The Rage: Carrie 2* is more like a shadow. I can imagine the story conference: "Let's think up some reason why the heroine has exactly the same ability Carrie had, and then let's put her in a story where exactly the same things happen to her, with the same result." People actually get paid for thinking up things like that. Too much, if you ask me.

Random Hearts ★ ★ ½
R, 131 m., 1999

Harrison Ford (Dutch Van Den Broeck),
Kristin Scott Thomas (Kay Chandler), Charles S.
Dutton (Alcee), Bonnie Hunt (Wendy Judd),
Dennis Haysbert (Detective George Beaufort),
Sydney Pollack (Carl Broman), Richard Jenkins
(Truman Trainor), Paul Guilfoyle (Dick
Montoya). Directed by Sydney Pollack and
produced by Pollack and Marykay Powell.
Screenplay by Kurt Luedtke, based on the
novel by Warren Adler.

There are so many good things in *Random Hearts,* but they're side by side instead of one after the other. They exist in the same film, but they don't add up to the result of the film. The film has no result—just an ending, leaving us with all of those fine pieces still waiting to come together. If this were a screenplay and not the final product, you'd see how with one more rewrite, it might all fall into place.

The movie is about two somber, private adults who find out their spouses were having an affair with one another. They find out in an abrupt and final way, when the two cheaters are killed in the crash of a plane they weren't supposed to be on. Curious, how neither of the survivors ever cries at first—not until late in the film, when there are more things to cry about. If you think you're happily married and your spouse dies and is exposed as a cheater, don't you cry anyway? Cry, because you loved them all the same, and now have lost not only your spouse but trust in your memories?

Sydney Pollack's *Random Hearts* is too intent on its agenda to stop and observe that; it is about the living, not the dead. Harrison Ford plays a District of Columbia police sergeant, and Kristin Scott Thomas is a Republican congresswoman from New Hampshire. They meet about forty-five minutes into the film, in a well-written scene in which he wants to find some kind of closure and she doesn't. "What's the last thing you remember about your husband that you *know* was true?" he asks her.

Although the movie is primarily about the relationship between the two survivors, the early scenes have their own fascination. The movie makes it clear to us that the two cheaters are crash victims, but Ford and Thomas walk

through a minefield of available information without making a connection. When Ford finally understands that his wife was not taking the flight for business reasons, he asks, "Are you saying she lied to me?" and we understand how hard this is for him to understand.

How does he feel? Angry? Betrayed? In denial? Ford is an actor able to keep his hand hidden, and he creates interest by not letting us know. He feels *something* strongly, and he wants answers. The congresswoman absorbs the new facts quickly and efficiently: They cheated, they're dead, they're in the past, it's time to move on. Both of these acts are facades, broken by the survivors in a shocking moment when they fall upon each other in unseemly, and therefore convincing, passion.

There are subplots in the movie, but the emotional themes are more intriguing. The subplot involves Ford as an internal affairs investigator who is on the trail of a crooked cop who may have murdered a witness. All good stuff for another movie, but frankly it's just a distraction here. More interesting is her subplot, about the details of a congressional campaign, with Pollack convincing as an adviser who applies spin control to the story of the brave widow. We realize with a certain surprise that she is that rarity in a Hollywood movie, a good-hearted Republican, and later in the film there's amusing pillow talk. "Are you a Democrat?" she asks. "What if I am?" he says. "We talk," she says, "and I give you books to read."

The real interest in the movie involves her emotional discoveries about herself. Ford seems stuck in the fact of betrayal. Thomas seems freed. She reevaluates everything. Does she really want to run for office? What are her values? Startled to be plunged so quickly into a physical affair, she sees herself, the proper congresswoman, eagerly embracing physical abandon with this cop. "Nobody knows who I am anymore," she says. "Nobody knows how easily I can do this."

You hear dialogue like that, and you want more. You don't want the resolution of the cop subplot, even if it is handled with a minimum of cheap violence. You like the fact that the movie doesn't make one of these people good and the other bad, but makes both of them shell-shocked survivors with unexplored potential. You wish you could figure out what Harrison Ford is thinking, but then Ford has made a career out of hiding his thoughts.

Maybe the fundamental problem is the point of view. The interesting character here is the woman, but the movie's star is Harrison Ford, and so the film is told from his point of view, and saddled with the unnecessary crime plot he drags in (a plot with no thematic connection to the rest of the story). How about a movie about a Republican congresswoman who loses her husband and gains a cop who looks just like Harrison Ford? All seen through her eyes. Now there would be a movie.

Ravenous ★ ★ ★
R, 101 m., 1999

Guy Pearce (Boyd), Robert Carlyle (Colqhoun/Ives), David Arquette (Cleaves), Jeremy Davies (Toffler), Jeffrey Jones (Hart), John Spencer (General Slauson), Stephen Spinella (Knox), Neal McDonough (Reich). Directed by Antonia Bird and produced by Adam Fields and David Heyman. Screenplay by Ted Griffin.

I said no food. I didn't say nothing to eat.
—dialogue from *Ravenous*

Of course a vampire is simply a cannibal with good table manners, and *Ravenous* is a darkly atmospheric film about an epidemic of flesh-eating and the fearsome power that it brings. It takes place during the Mexican-American War in an isolated U.S. Army outpost in the Sierra Nevadas, when a half-dead man (Robert Carlyle) staggers into the fort with the story of snowbound travelers, starvation, and worse: "We ate the oxen, then the horses, then a dog, then our belts and shoes . . ."

Eventually one of the party died of starvation, and they ate him. Then they ate others . . . and by now the commander of the fort has heard enough, and determines to send out a party to investigate. All of this is shown in wet, dark colors, with a sound track of chimes and mournful cries, low, ominous, burbling percussion, and far-off female laments. *Ravenous* is the kind of movie where you savor the texture of the filmmaking, even when the story strays into shapeless gore.

The movie stars Guy Pearce, the honest cop

from *L.A. Confidential*, as a man named Boyd who becomes an accidental hero during a battle. Mistaken for dead, he's piled under corpses; blood trickles into his mouth and gives him the strength to capture an enemy outpost. He's decorated, but his commanding officer sees the cowardice beneath his luck, and sends him to a godforsaken outpost where the story takes place.

Fort Spencer is a caretaking operation in a vast wilderness, presided over by Hart (Jeffrey Jones), a genial commanding officer who acts more like a host. The soldiers are all cracking up in one way or another, except for Reich (Neal McDonough), a gung ho warrior. The others include the second in command, Knox (Stephen Spinella), the religious Toffler (Jeremy Davies), Cleaves the cook (David Arquette), and some Indians. From the Indians comes the legend that when you eat another man's flesh, you possess his past and assume his strength, and your hunger becomes insatiable.

The movie has established its cold, ominous tone long before the real story reveals itself. That happens when the characters return to the cave where the travelers are said to have taken shelter. There's a creepy sequence in which Reich and Toffler enter the cave, and then traverse into an inner cave where what they find is not a pretty sight. Then there are surprises and revelations, and unspeakable things happen to some of the characters, or at least we think they do.

The director is a British woman named Antonia Bird; I didn't admire her *Priest*, but she shows she's a real filmmaker. She is wisely more interested in atmosphere than plot, and has an instinct for scenes like the one where a visiting general savors the broth of a bubbling stew. Her shots of meat are all cheerfully off-putting; she revealed at the Sundance premiere that she is a vegetarian, which came as no surprise. She does what is very hard to do: She makes the weather feel genuinely cold, damp, and miserable. So much snow in the movies looks too pretty or too fake, but her locations (in Slovakia) are chilly and ominous.

The film's setup is more fun than its payoff because in a story of this nature we would rather dread what is going to happen than see it. The movie makes much of the strength to be gained by eating human flesh, and there is a final confrontation between two men, both much fortified by their fellows, that feels like one of those superhero battles in a comic book, where neither side can lose.

The screenplay, by Ted Griffin, provides nice small moments of color for the characters (I liked the way Jeffrey Jones's C.O. seemed reasonable in the most appalling ways), and short, spare lines of dialogue that do their work ("He was licking me!"). I also liked the way characters unexpectedly reappeared, and how the movie savors Boyd's inability to get anyone to believe him. And I admired the visceral music, by Michael Nyman and Damon Albarn, which calls attention to itself (common) but deserves to (rare). *Ravenous* is clever in the way it avoids most of the clichés of the vampire movie by using cannibalism, and most of the clichés of the cannibal movie by using vampirism. It serves both dishes with new sauces.

Ready to Rumble ★ ★
PG-13, 100 m., 2000

David Arquette (Gordie Boggs), Oliver Platt (Jimmy King), Scott Caan (Sean Dawkins), Bill Goldberg (Himself), Rose McGowan (Sasha), Diamond Dallas Page (Himself), Joe Pantoliano (Titus Sinclair), Martin Landau (Sal Bandini). Directed by Brian Robbins and produced by Bobby Newmyer and Jeffrey Silver. Screenplay by Steven Brill.

It must be a mixed blessing to be Michael Buffer. He is the man in the tuxedo famous for intoning, "Let's get . . . ready to RUMBLE?" before sporting events and, for all I know, weddings and bingo games. He is rich and famous, yes. But how many times a day/week/month/lifetime do you suppose he has to listen to people shouting Michael Buffer imitations into his ear? And is it discouraging that the excitement is over for him just as it's beginning for everyone else?

These thoughts ran through my mind during *Ready to Rumble*. Buffer appears in the movie and duly performs "Let's get ready to rumble," and so earnestly was I *not* ready to rumble that I wanted the camera to follow him out of the arena instead of staying for a three-cage fight to the death between Jimmy ("The King") King and Diamond Dallas Page.

It's not that I have anything against professional wrestling. I have a newfound respect for it after seeing the documentary *Beyond the Mat*, which establishes without a shadow of a doubt that when you are thrown out of the ring in a scripted fight with a prearranged winner, it nevertheless hurts when you hit the floor. I am in awe of wrestlers—not as athletes, but as masochists. They take a lickin' and keep on kickin'.

The problem with *Ready to Rumble* is that its hero is not a wrestler but an actor, Oliver Platt. Platt is a good comic actor and I have liked him in a lot of movies, but here he is not well used, and occupies a role that would have been better filled by a real wrestler. That is demonstrated every time Diamond Dallas Page is on the screen, playing himself with such ferocity that Platt seems to be playing Jimmy the King in a key heard only by himself.

The plot is easily summarized: *Dumb and Dumber Meet Dumbbell.* David Arquette and Scott Caan are Gordie and Sean, best pals in a Wyoming hamlet where watching the Monday night fights on cable brings the only joy into their lives as sanitation servicemen. By day they suction the contents out of Porta-Potties, and by night they hang out in the parking lot of the convenience store, lecturing callow youths on the glories of wrestling as America's finest sport.

They get tickets to The King's latest title defense, little realizing that the real kingmaker is Titus Sinclair (Joe Pantoliano), this movie's version of Vince McMahon. Titus has declared that The King will go down to Diamond Dallas, and by the end of the fight the loser has been kicked insensible by everyone on the card and banished from wrestling as a hopeless drunk.

When Gordie and Sean's tank truck overturns on the way home, creating a really nasty spill for the fire department to clean up, they take this as a sign that they must leave their town, find The King, and mastermind his comeback. Their plan involves enlisting the once-great, now aging Sal Bandini (Martin Landau) as a trainer. The King is not thrilled: "I don't need a trainer; I need a safe house!" He's right. Landau's scenes demonstrate that as an elderly wrestler he looks no more convincing than he did as a dying millionaire disco dancer in *B.A.P.S.* He's good in serious stuff (hint).

The movie is best when it deals with professional wrestling, and worst (which is most of the time) when it prefers a wheezy prefab plot to the possibilities of its subject. The machinations of a sexpot (Rose McGowan) are tired and predictable, and Platt, who might have done something with decent dialogue, is left on the sidelines while Arquette and Caan shout at each other in a forlorn attempt to reproduce the chemistry of Jim Carrey and Jeff Daniels in *Dumb and Dumber.* I gave that movie only two stars despite the fact that its dead parakeet scene caused me to laugh uncontrollably; now, after sitting through *Ready to Rumble*, with only the occasional grudging "ha!" I know better what a two-star movie looks like.

Recess: School's Out ★ ★ ½
G, 84 m., 2001

With the voices of: James Woods (Dr. Benedict), Andy Lawrence (T. J. Detweiler), Rickey D'Shon Collins (Vince), Jason Davis (Mikey), Ashley Johnson (Gretchen), Courtland Mead (Gus), Pam Segall (Ashley), Dabney Coleman (Principal Prickly), April Winchell (Miss Finster), Robert Goulet (Mikey's Singing Voice). Directed by Chuck Sheetz and produced by Stephen Swofford. Created by Paul Germain and Joe Ansolabehere. Screenplay by Jonathan Greenberg.

The highest school test scores in the world are recorded in Canada, Iceland, and Norway, according to the brilliant but twisted Dr. Benedict, villain of *Recess: School's Out.* And what else do those countries have in common? "It's snowing all the time." Benedict wants to be president, and part of his strategy is to raise U.S. test scores by using a secret green ray to nudge the moon into a different orbit, ending summer—and therefore summer vacation.

It's up to T. J. Detweiler, plucky grammar school kid, to save Earth, and summer vacation, in *Recess: School's Out*, a spin-off of the animated kids' TV program. He gets the responsibility because he's the only kid left behind when all the others board buses and roar off

to summer camp. Meanwhile, Benedict moves his minions and their moon-moving equipment into the Third Street School, "back where it all began."

How so? In the 1960s, we learn, both Benedict and Principal Prickly were idealistic flower children. But then it rained on Benedict's dream, and he turned into the monster he is today. Prickly, on the other hand, simply grew old and lost his youthful enthusiasm in the day-to-day grind. As for Miss Finster, the draconian teacher, it's doubtful she was a child of the 1960s, although she retains some of the lingo (when she gets stuck trying to crawl through a basement window of the school, she cries out, "I'm stuck! Curse these bodacious hips of mine!").

Dr. Benedict, we learn, started out at Third Street School; his career prospered, and he was secretary of education before getting the boot because of his attempts to ban recess. In exile and isolation, his scheme escalated into an attack on the whole summer vacation, and there is a computer simulation of his dream, in which Earth enters a new ice age and the kids presumably all stay inside and study.

Recess is a Disney attempt to reach the same market that Nickelodeon taps with *Rug Rats*, and although it lacks the zany exuberance of *Rugrats in Paris* (2000), it's fast-footed and fun. *Rugrats in Paris* had charms for grown-ups, however, while *Recess: School's Out* seems aimed more directly at grade-schoolers. That makes the 1960s material problematic; do nine-year-olds really care about ancient history? Even if Myra, the fourteen-year-old "singing sensation," performs "Dancin' in the Streets" over the end titles?

The boom in animation has created a lot of voice-over work in Hollywood, and among the voices heard on *Recess* are Dabney Coleman as Principal Prickly, Andy Lawrence as T.J., and Robert Goulet as the singing voice of a character named Mikey (the song is "Green Tambourine," performed in a sequence made by animators who have obviously studied *Yellow Submarine* and the works of Peter Max).

The movie was directed by Chuck Sheetz, who has worked on shows like *King of the Hill* and *The Simpsons*. One of its charms is its defense of recess, which is, we learn, when all the real benefits of primary education take place. I recommend it for kids up to ten or eleven. Parents may find it amusing, but it doesn't have the two-track versatility of *Rugrats in Paris*, which worked for kids on one level and adults on another.

Red Planet ★ ★ ★
PG-13, 116 m., 2000

Val Kilmer (Gallagher), Carrie-Anne Moss (Bowman), Tom Sizemore (Burchenal), Benjamin Bratt (Santen), Simon Baker (Pettengill), Terence Stamp (Chantilas). Directed by Anthony Hoffman and produced by Mark Canton, Bruce Berman, and Jorge Saralegui. Screenplay by Chuck Pfarrer and Jonathan Lemkin.

Red Planet would have been a great 1950s science-fiction film. It embodies the kind of nuts-and-bolts sci-fi championed by John W. Campbell Jr. in his *Astounding* magazine— right down to the notion that a space mission would be staffed by research scientists, and although there would be a woman on board, she would not be the kind of woman depicted in an aluminum brassiere on the covers of his competitors. This is a film where much of the suspense involves the disappearance of algae.

The film has been sneered at in some quarters because it is not the kind of brainless, high-tech computerized effects extravaganza now in favor. I like its emphasis on situation and character. I've always been fascinated by zero-sum plots in which a task has to be finished within the available supplies of time, fuel, and oxygen.

Waiting for the screening to start, I was talking with a dive instructor about the challenge of diving inside glaciers. "Anytime you take away unobstructed access to the surface," he told me, "you're talking technical diving, and that makes you more of an astronaut than a diver." I thought of that during *Red Planet*, which is about four men who have essentially dived down to the surface of Mars, whose air is running out, and who do not have access to the spaceship circling above.

The movie takes place in 2025, when mankind has polluted Earth beyond the point of no return, and is seeking a new planet to colonize. Mars is bombarded with robot space probes carrying various strains of bioengineered algae. The Earth-born organisms seem to thrive, and green pastures spread on Mars. A space mission is launched with a crew of scientists who will investigate a curious thing. The algae seems to have disappeared. Really disappeared. It didn't simply die off, because that would have left withered remains. It seems to have . . . dematerialized.

This discovery takes place after a troubled voyage. The interplanetary ship, commanded by Bowman (Carrie-Anne Moss), has gone through a gamma ray storm, disabling a lot of its equipment. The Mars lander descends to the surface with Gallagher (Val Kilmer), Burchenal (Tom Sizemore), Santen (Benjamin Bratt), Pettengill (Simon Baker), and the scientist-philosopher Chantilas (Terence Stamp). It runs into trouble, too, has to jettison some of its equipment, and then there's a sensational landing scene. The lander is cocooned within huge, tough air bags so it can bounce to a soft landing. But when it bounces off a cliff, the ride gets rocky for the men inside.

Also along is AMEE, a robotic tracker and warrior that has, alas, not been programmed nearly carefully enough with Asimov's Three Laws of Robotics. The men are left with an incomplete landing module, and must depend on a supply station dropped by previous missions. And then . . .

Everything else should come as a surprise. What pleased me, however, was the nature of the situation they find on Mars. The movie's ads seem to suggest bug-eyed monsters of some sort, but the actual story developments are more ingenious and reasonable. John Campbell, who liked semiplausible scientific speculation in his stories, might have enjoyed the way *Red Planet* accounts for the disappearance of the algae. There is a scene—call it the fireworks scene—that in its own way is one of the more memorable encounters I've seen with extraterrestrial life forms.

The acting is serviceable. Most of it consists of functional observations and commands. Terence Stamp is given a brief opportunity to philosophize about the limitations of science, Val Kilmer is convincing as a competent space jockey with a mechanical and scientific background, and Carrie-Anne Moss, whose character Bowman is a nod to Dave Bowman from

2001, is convincing as a no-nonsense pilot. But just like in 1950s sci-fi, the story's strong point isn't psychological depth or complex relationships, but brainy scientists trying to think their way out of a box that grows smaller every minute. To like that kind of story is to like this kind of movie. ☞

The Red Violin ★ ★ ★ ½
NO MPAA RATING, 126 m., 1999

Carlo Cecchi (Nicolo Bussotti), Irene Grazioli (His Wife, Anna), Samuel L. Jackson (Charles Morritz), Sylvia Chang (Xiang Pei), Colm Feore (Auctioneer), Don McKellar (Evan Williams), Greta Scacchi (Victoria Byrd), Jason Flemyng (Frederick Pope), Jean-Luc Bideau (Georges Poussin), Christoph Koncz (Kasper Weiss). Directed by Francois Girard and produced by Niv Fichman. Screenplay by Don McKellar with Girard.

There is a kind of ideal beauty that reduces us all to yearning for perfection. *The Red Violin* is about that yearning. It traces the story of a violin ("the single most perfect acoustical machine I've ever seen," says a restorer) from its maker in seventeenth-century Italy to an auction room in modern Montreal. The violin passes from the rich to the poor, from Italy to Poland to England to China to Canada. It is shot, buried, almost burned, and stolen more than once. It produces music so beautiful that it makes you want to cry.

The film is heedlessly ambitious. In a time of timid projects and easy formulas, it has the kind of sweep and vision we identify with elegant features from decades ago—films that followed a story thread from one character to another, like *Tales of Manhattan* or *La Ronde.* There really is a little something here for everyone: music and culture, politics and passion, crime and intrigue, history and even the backstage intrigue of the auction business. Not many films can encompass a British aristocrat who likes to play the violin while he is having sex, and a Chinese woman who risks her life to protect a violin from the martinets of the Cultural Revolution.

The violin is crafted in Cremona, Italy, in 1681—made by the craftsman Nicolo Bussotti (Carlo Cecchi) for his unborn son. But his wife,

Anna (Irene Grazioli), dies in childbirth after hearing a series of prophecies from a village crone who reads the Tarot deck. The cards provide a structure for flash-forwards to the future adventures of the violin, and at the same time there is a flashback structure, as bidders arrive at the auction house in Montreal and we learn why they desire the instrument.

The film is easy to follow, and yet reveals its secrets slyly. The tale of the violin is a series of stories involving the people who own it over a period of 300 years. Then there is another story, hinted at, slowly revealing itself, involving an expert evaluator of instruments (Samuel L. Jackson). He is the person who proves that this is indeed Bussotti's famous red violin, and solves the mystery of its color. He is also perhaps the person best equipped to appreciate how rare and wonderful the instrument is— but, like many passionate connoisseurs, he lacks the wealth to match his tastes. His plans for the instrument supply a suspenseful ending to a movie that has already given us just about everything else.

The film was directed by the Canadian Francois Girard, and written by him and the actor-director Don McKellar. They also cowrote Girard's brilliant first film, *Thirty-two Short Films About Glenn Gould* (1994), which considered the life and work of the great Canadian pianist in thirty-two separate episodes. *The Red Violin* uses a similar approach, spinning stories and tones out of the central thread.

After the opening sequence involving Bussotti, the violin drifts into the hands of an order of monks, and we rejoin it 100 years later at their orphanage. They dote on a young prodigy named Kasper (Christoph Koncz), who plays with the purity of an angel. The musician Poussin (Jean-Luc Bideau), expert but poor, hears the boy play and adopts him on the spot, despite the doubts of his wife. This sequence develops tenderly, as the old couple grow to love the boy—who sleeps with his violin.

Flash-forward. The violin is in the possession of gypsies (I am not revealing the details of the transfers). It is played by many hands and travels from Poland to England where, in the nineteenth century, it is heard by a rich virtuoso named Frederick Pope (Jason Flemyng), who incorporates it into his concerts and into his lovemaking with his mistress,

Victoria (Greta Scacchi). It is she who fires a bullet at it. The violin next surfaces in a pawn shop in Shanghai where, during the Cultural Revolution, it stands as a symbol of Western decadence. It's defended by a brave musician who points out that Beethoven and Prokofiev were revolutionaries, but is saved only when a music lover (Sylvia Chang) risks her life. Eventually the now-capitalist Chinese government sends it off to Montreal, where it attracts the attention of the Samuel Jackson character.

A brief outline doesn't begin to suggest the intelligence and appeal of the film. The story hook has been used before. *Tales of Manhattan* followed an evening coat from person to person, and *The Yellow Rolls-Royce* followed a car. Max Ophuls's *La Ronde* (1950), Luis Buñuel's *The Phantom of Liberty,* (1974) and Richard Linklater's *Slacker* (1991) all follow chains of characters, entering a scene with one person and exiting it with another. Such structures take advantage of two contradictory qualities of film: It is literal, so that we tend to believe what we see; and it is fluid, not tied down to times and places. All of those titles more or less observe time and place, however; *The Red Violin* follows not a person or a coat, but an idea: the idea that humans in all times and places are powerfully moved, or threatened, by the possibility that with our hands and minds we can create something that is perfect.

Regret to Inform ★ ★ ★
NO MPAA RATING, 72 m., 1999

A documentary directed by Barbara Sonneborn and produced by Kathy Brew, Janet Cole, Megan Jones, Daniel Reeves, Sonneborn, and Todd Wagner. Screenplay by Sonneborn.

On the twentieth anniversary of her first husband's death in Vietnam, Barbara Sonneborn woke up "and I knew I had to go to Vietnam." She was remarried and happy, "and yet Jeff's death and my feelings about the war were still not resolved." Jeff Gurvitz, her high school sweetheart, had been killed in 1968, on her twenty-fourth birthday, eight weeks after arriving in Vietnam. He died while trying to help his radio operator out of a tight spot.

"We had talked about the possibility of Jeff dying," Barbara remembers, in the narration of *Regret to Inform.* "We never talked about the possibility that he would have to kill." After his death, she received a tape recording he had made. It took her twenty years to work up the courage to listen to it. On it, she heard his voice saying he felt like a bystander to his own life—"watching myself do things I never expected or desired to do."

Sonneborn enlists as her translator a woman named Xuan Ngoc Evans, who has memories of her own. One of them is of the day when her five-year-old cousin darted out of a safe place to get a drink of water and was shot dead by a GI. "I remember how his eyes looked," she says. "He had a horrified look in his eye, as much as I did." This woman later worked as a prostitute, dating American soldiers. "I wouldn't have," she says, "if I'd had another choice."

The distinctive thing about Sonneborn's film, which won awards for Best Documentary and Best Cinematography at the 1999 Sundance Festival, is that it remembers the war from both sides, as seen by the women who were touched by it. We meet the widow of a Native American rodeo cowboy, who signed up over her protests because it was his duty. The widow of a man killed by Agent Orange, the defoliant the United States tried to deny was harmful.

And there is the woman who so desperately wanted to deflect her husband's desire to serve that she considered injuring his hand with a hammer. "I wanted to stop him and I thought of smashing his hand, doing it the right way, so it would take six months to heal, time for our baby to be born."

Sonneborn, and her translator and small crew, take the train from one end of Vietnam to another. They talk to Vietnamese war widows. One remembers hiding under a pile of corpses, because to be dead was to be safe. The film makes little distinction between the widows of soldiers who died fighting for the south or the north. All of the memories are painful.

The movie is at pains to remain at the personal level; for women whose husbands fought on opposing sides, the war today is not a political dispute but a huge force that swept away their men, the fathers of their children. Left unsaid is what we see in the background. Vietnam today is independent and communist, the two things we fought to prevent, yet it is not regarded as a dangerous enemy, but a popular tourist destination for Americans—many of them, like Sonneborn, going back looking for answers.

There is one moment in particular that will stay with me a long time. Sonneborn goes to visit the Vietnam War Memorial in Washington, D.C., and talks to a woman who weeps that her husband's name is not included. "My husband should be on the wall," she says. "He left his soul in Vietnam. It took his body seven years to catch up. He went out in the garage and shot himself. He left a note that said, 'I love you sweetheart, but I just can't take the flashbacks anymore.'"

Reindeer Games ★ ½
R, 98 m., 2000

Ben Affleck (Rudy), Charlize Theron (Ashley), Gary Sinise (Gabriel), Clarence Williams III (Merlin), James Frain (Nick), Dennis Farina (Jack Bangs), Isaac Hayes (Zook). Directed by John Frankenheimer and produced by Marty Katz, Bob Weinstein, and Chris Moore. Screenplay by Ehren Kruger.

Reindeer Games is the first all-Talking Killer picture. After the setup, it consists mostly of characters explaining their actions to one another. I wish I'd had a stopwatch to clock how many minutes are spent while one character holds a gun to another character's head and gabs. Charlize Theron and Gary Sinise between them explain so much they reminded me of Gertrude Stein's line about Ezra Pound: "He was a village explainer, excellent if you were a village, but if you were not, not."

Just a nudge, and the movie would fall over into self-parody, and maybe work better. But I fear it is essentially serious, or as serious as such goofiness can be. It opens in prison with cellmates Rudy (Ben Affleck) and Nick (James Frain). Both are about to be set free. Nick has engaged in a steamy correspondence with Ashley (Theron), one of those women who have long-distance romances with convicts. His cell wall is plastered with photos that make her look like a model for cosmetics ads.

But then (I am not giving away as much as it seems, or perhaps even what it seems) Nick is knifed in a prison brawl, and when Rudy walks out of prison and lays eyes on Ashley—well, what would you do? That's what he does. "I'm Nick," Rudy tells her. Soon they make wild and passionate love, which inevitably involves knocking things over and falling out of bed and continuing on the floor. You'd think if people were that much into sex, they'd pay more attention to what they were doing.

Then there's a major reality shift, and perhaps you'd better stop reading if you don't want to know that . . . Ashley's brother Gabriel (Gary Sinise) heads a gang of scummy gunrunners who think Rudy used to work in an Indian casino in upstate Michigan—because, of course, they think Rudy is Nick, and that's what Nick told Ashley about himself. Gabriel and his gang try to squeeze info about the casino's security setup out of Rudy, who says he isn't Nick, and then says he is Nick after all, and then says he isn't, and has so many reasons for each of his answers that Gabriel gets very confused, and keeps deciding to kill him, and deciding not to kill him, and deciding to kill him after all, until both characters seem stuck in a time loop.

There are other surprises, too, a lot of them, each with its explanation, usually accompanied by an explanation of the previous explanation, which now has to be re-explained in light of the new explanation. They all got a lot of 'splainin' to do.

The movie's weakness is mostly in its ludicrous screenplay by Ehren Kruger. The director, John Frankenheimer, is expert at moving the action along and doing what can be done with scenes that hardly anything can be done with. Ben Affleck and Charlize Theron soldier through changes of pace so absurd it takes superb control to keep straight faces. Theron's character looks soft and sweet sometimes, then hard and cruel other times, switching back and forth so often I commend her for not just passing a hand up and down in front of her face: smile, frown, smile, frown.

Perhaps the movie was originally intended to open at Christmas. That would explain the title and the sequence where the casino, which looks like a former Target store, is stuck up by five Santas. But nothing can explain the upbeat final scene, in which, after blood seeps into the Michigan snow, we get a fit of Robin Hood sentimentality. The moment to improve *Reindeer Games* was at the screenplay stage, by choosing another one.

Remember the Titans ★ ★ ★

PG, 113 m., 2000

Denzel Washington (Coach Boone), Will Patton (Coach Yoast), Wood Harris (Big Ju), Ryan Hurst (Bertier), Donald Faison (Petey), Craig Kirkwood (Rev), Ethan Suplee (Lewis Lastik), Kip Pardue (Sunshine). Directed by Boaz Yakin and produced by Jerry Bruckheimer and Chad Oman. Screenplay by Gregory Allen Howard.

Remember the Titans is a parable about racial harmony, yoked to the formula of a sports movie. Victories over racism and victories over opposing teams alternate so quickly that sometimes we're not sure if we're cheering for tolerance or touchdowns. Real life is never this simple, but then that's what the movies are for: to improve on life, and give it the illusion of form and purpose.

Denzel Washington and Will Patton are the stars, two football coaches, one black, one white, whose lives are linked for a season even though neither wants it that way. In 1971, a high school in Alexandria, Virginia, is integrated, and the board brings in Coach Boone (Washington) as the new head coach, replacing Coast Yoast (Patton), who is expected to become his assistant. Yoast understandably does not want to be demoted in the name of affirmative action. Boone doesn't like it either: He lost his own job in North Carolina, and "I can't do that to this man."

But Alexandria's black residents gather on Boone's lawn to cheer for the first black coach at the newly integrated high school, and Boone realizes he has a responsibility. So does Yoast: His white players say they won't play for a black coach, but Yoast doesn't want them to lose college scholarships, so he swallows his pride and agrees to be Boone's assistant, leading the whites back to practice.

All of this is said to be based on life, and no doubt largely is, but life was perhaps harder and more wounding than the film. *Remember the Titans* is not an activist 1970s picture, but more conciliatory in tone. It is more about football than race relations, and it wants us to leave the theater feeling not angry or motivated, but good.

We do. There are true and touching moments in the film, on top of its undeniable entertainment value. I was moved by a scene near the end where an injured white player, who once said he would not play with blacks, now only wants his black "brother" in the hospital room. And there is a delicate series of scenes in which the same white player breaks up with his girlfriend rather than break the bonds he's formed with teammates during an August training camp.

Those training camp scenes of course include the usual identifiable types (the fat kid, the long-haired Californian, the "Rev") who first clash, then bond. It's been seen before, but the director, Boaz Yakin (*Fresh*), brings old situations to new life and carries us along in the current of a skilled popular entertainment. I like the way he shows Boone forcing the blacks and whites to get to know one another.

I admired the way his screenplay, by Gregory Allen Howard, doesn't make Boone noble and Yoast a racist, but shows them both as ambitious and skilled professionals. There are times when Boone treats his players more like marines than high school kids, and Yoast tells him so. And times when Yoast tries to comfort black players that Boone has chewed out, and Boone accuses him of coddling blacks as he would never coddle his fellow whites.

These scenes are tricky, and Washington and Patton find just the right notes to negotiate them. Washington is gifted at delivering big speeches without sounding portentous or seeming to strain. There's an early-morning training run that leads the players to the Gettysburg battlefield, and his remarks there place their experiences in a larger context.

Still, the story sweeps certain obvious questions under the rug.

(1) We see that the whites don't want to play with the blacks, and are afraid of losing their starting positions. But what about the blacks? Weren't they in a black high school last year?

Aren't they losing their team too? Aren't some of them going to be replaced by white starters? The movie shows the whites as resentful and possessive but assumes the black players are grateful for the chance to leave their old school and integrate the other team. Maybe they are, and maybe they aren't. The movie doesn't say.

(2) Since there was certainly an all-black high school in town until this year, there must have been a black coach at that school. What happened to him? Did Coach Boone put him out of work too? That crowd of cheering blacks on Boone's front lawn—have they so quickly forgotten the team and coach they used to cheer?

In the real world such questions would be what the story was all about. But then we would have an entirely different kind of film. *Remember the Titans* has the outer form of a brave statement about the races in America, but the soul of a sports movie in which everything is settled by the obligatory last play in the last seconds of the championship game. Whether the Titans win or lose has nothing to do with the season they have played and what they were trying to prove. But it has everything to do with the movie's sleight of hand, in which we cheer the closing touchdown as if it is a victory over racism.

The movie is heartfelt, yes, and I was moved by it, but it plays safe. On the sound track we hear lyrics like, "I've seen fire and I've seen rain," and, "Ain't no mountain high enough," but not other lyrics that must also have been heard in Alexandria in 1971, such as, "We shall overcome." ☞

The Replacements ★ ★
PG-13, 114 m., 2000

Keanu Reeves (Shane Falco), Gene Hackman (Jimmy McGinty), Brooke Langton (Annabelle Farrell), Orlando Jones (Clifford Franklin), Jon Favreau (Daniel Bateman), Rhys Ifans (Nigel Gruff), Faizon Love (Jamal Jackson), Michael "Bear" Taliferro (Andre Jackson). Directed by Howard Deutch and produced by Dylan Sellers. Screenplay by Vince McKewin.

The Replacements is a slaphappy entertainment painted in broad strokes, two coats thick. It's like a standard sports movie, but with every point made twice or three times—as if we'd never seen one before. And the musical score provides such painstaking instructions about how to feel during every scene, it's like the booklet that tells you how to unpack your computer.

Gene Hackman and Keanu Reeves star, and this is not a distinguished entry in their filmographies. As the movie opens, a football strike is under way, and the crusty old team owner (Jack Warden) has hired Jimmy McGinty (Gene Hackman) to coach the team. Hackman says he'll assemble a pickup team—but only if he can pick the players himself. His first choice is a kid named Shane Falco (Reeves), currently scraping gunk off the sides of boats, but known to McGinty as a promising quarterback.

Perhaps it will help to evoke the mood of the movie if we start with Falco's first scene. He is underwater, working on a boat, when he sees a football on the bottom. He swims down, grabs it, and *discovers it is a trophy—engraved with his own name!* No doubt he tossed it there during a time of despair. This is why they pay screenwriters so well, to think this stuff up. He throws an underwater pass. Just can't keep the kid down.

There is a convention, older than Shakespeare, that drama requires low characters to provide the broth through which the exalted characters swim. In *The Replacements,* Hackman and Reeves are the heroes, and most of the other characters are low comedy, including a Welsh placekicker (Rhys Ifans) who chainsmokes, even while actually on the playing field, and other recruits including a sumo wrestler, a mad dog who attacks anything that is red, and a deaf lineman ("Look at it this way. He'll never be called offsides on an audible").

John Debney's musical score works on this material something like the alternate commentary track on a DVD. It comments on every scene. When Reeves talks, there is sometimes actually a violin beneath him, to lend additional nobility. Hackman gets resolute music. The team has a group of pom-pom cheerleaders who seem to have wandered in from a soft-core film of their own, and there is a scene where their lascivious choreography on the sidelines distracts the San Diego team so severely that our guys pull off a key play. Never before in the history of football movies have the cheerleaders had a larger role than the opposing team.

An even more curious role is given to John Madden and Pat Summerall, playing themselves as play-by-play announcers. It is not *that* hard in the movies to create the illusion that the announcers are actually in a real stadium looking at a real game. But it's too much for *The Replacements*, which stashes them in a booth with a couple of TV monitors and has them stand around awkwardly as if looking at a game. Sometimes they're not even looking in the same direction.

There are of course personal issues to be settled in the movie, and a romance between Falco and cute pom-pommer Annabelle Farrell (Brooke Langton). Also the nasty first-string quarterback from the regular season (Brett Cullen), who fancies Annabelle and hates Falco. And backstage politics involving whether the owner will respect his pledge to let the old coach call the shots.

The movie's approach to labor unions is casual, to say the least. Reeves and all of his teammates are scabs, but *The Replacements* can't be bothered with details like that, and indeed seems to think the regular players are the bad guys. The standard way the media handles such situations is to consider striking players as overpaid and selfish. Of course owners, sponsors, and the media, who dine off the players' brief careers, are more overpaid and more selfish, but that's the way the world turns.

The football footage is at least mostly comprehensible; director Howard Deutch tries to make sense of the plays, instead of opting for shapeless montages of colors and action, as Oliver Stone did in *Any Given Sunday*. But Stone's characters were conceived on a higher level—more complex, smarter, realistic—and his issues were more grown-up, compared to the slam-bam cheerleading that passes for thought here. It goes without saying that everything is settled in the last play in the last seconds of the last game of the season, and if you think *The Replacements* has the nerve to surprise you, you've got the wrong movie.

Requiem for a Dream ★ ★ ★ ½
NO MPAA RATING, 102 m., 2000

Ellen Burstyn (Sara Goldfarb), Jared Leto (Harry Goldfarb), Jennifer Connelly (Marion Silver), Marlon Wayans (Tyrone C. Love), Christopher McDonald (Tappy Tibbons), Louise Lasser (Ada), Keith David (Little John), Sean Gullette (Arnold the Shrink). Directed by Darren Aronofsky and produced by Eric Watson III and Palmer West. Screenplay by Aronofsky, based on the novel by Hubert Selby Jr.

Alcoholics or drug addicts feel wrong when they don't feel right. Eventually they feel very wrong, and *must* feel right, and at that point their lives spiral down into some sort of final chapter—recovery if they're lucky, hopelessness and death if they're not.

What is fascinating about *Requiem for a Dream,* the new film by Darren Aronofsky, is how well he portrays the mental states of his addicts. When they use, a window opens briefly into a world where everything is right. Then it slides shut, and life reduces itself to a search for the money and drugs to open it again. Nothing else is remotely as interesting.

Aronofsky is the director who made the hallucinatory π(1998), about a paranoid genius who seems on the brink of discovering the key to—well, God, or the stock market, or whatever else his tormentors imagine. That movie, made on a tiny budget, was astonishing in the way it suggested its hero's shifting prism of reality. Now, with greater resources, Aronofsky brings a new urgency to the drug movie by trying to reproduce, through his subjective camera, how his characters feel, or want to feel, or fear to feel.

As the movie opens, a housewife is chaining her television to the radiator. It's no use. Her son frees it and wheels it down the street to a pawn shop. This is a regular routine, we gather; anything in his mother's house is a potential source of funds for drug money. The son's girlfriend and best friend are both addicted too. So is the mother: to television and sugar. We recognize the actors, but barely. Sara Goldfarb (Ellen Burstyn) is fat and blowzy in her sloppy housedresses; if you've just seen her in the revived *Exorcist,* her appearance will come as a shock. Her son, Harry (Jared Leto), is gaunt and haunted; so is his girlfriend, Marion (Jennifer Connelly). His pal Tyrone is played by Marlon Wayans, who has lost all the energy and cockiness of his comic persona and is simply trying to survive in a reasonable manner. Tyrone suspects, correctly, that he's in trouble but Harry is in more.

Sara's life passes in modest retirement. She joins the other old ladies out front of their building, where they line up their lawn chairs in the sun. She's addicted to a game show whose host (Christopher McDonald) leads the audience in chanting, "We got a winner!" She's a sweet, naive woman who gets a junk phone call that misleads her into thinking she may be a potential guest on the show. She obsesses about wearing her favorite red dress, and gets diet pills from the doctor to help her lose weight.

She does lose weight, and also her mind. "The pills don't work so good anymore," she complains to the druggist, and then starts doubling up her usage. Her doctor isn't even paying attention when she complains dubiously about hallucinations (the refrigerator has started to threaten her). Meanwhile, Harry talks to Marion about the one big score that would "get us back on track." Tyrone can see that Harry is losing it, but Marion, under Harry's spell, has sex with a shrink (Sean Gullette, star of π) and is eventually selling herself for stag party gang-gropes.

Aronofsky is fascinated by the way in which the camera can be used to suggest how his characters see things. I've just finished a shot-by-shot analysis of Hitchcock's *The Birds* at the Virginia Film Festival; he does the same thing, showing us some things and denying us others so that we are first plunged into a subjective state and then yanked back to objectivity with a splash of cold reality.

Here Aronofsky uses extreme close-ups to show drugs acting on his characters. First we see the pills, or the fix, filling the screen, because that's all the characters can think about. Then the injection, swallowing, or sniffing—because *that* blots out the world. Then the pupils of their eyes dilating. All done with acute exaggeration of sounds.

These sequences are done in fast motion, to show how quickly the drugs take effect—and how disappointingly soon they fade. The in-between times edge toward desperation. Aronofsky cuts between the mother, a prisoner of her apartment and diet pills, and the other three. Early in the film, in a technique I haven't seen before, he uses a split screen in which the space on both sides is available to the other (Sara and Harry each have half the screen, but their movements enter into each other's halves). This is an effective way of showing them alone together. Later, in a virtuoso closing sequence, he cuts between all four major characters as they careen toward their final destinations.

Ellen Burstyn isn't afraid to play Sara Goldfarb flat-out as a collapsing ruin (Aronofsky has mercy on her by giving her some fantasy scenes where she appears on TV and we see that she is actually still a great-looking woman). Connelly, who is so much a sex symbol that she, too, could have disgraced herself in *Charlie's Angels*, has consistently gone for risky projects and this may be her riskiest; the movie is inspired by Hubert Selby Jr.'s lacerating novel, and in her own way Connelly goes as far as Jennifer Jason Leigh did in an equally courageous, quite different, film based on *Last Exit to Brooklyn*, another Selby novel. Leto and Wayans have a road trip together, heading for Florida, that is like a bleaker echo of Joe Buck and Ratso Rizzo's Florida odyssey in *Midnight Cowboy*. Leto's suppurating arm, punished by too many needles, is like a motif for his life.

The movie was given the worthless NC-17 rating by the MPAA; rejecting it, Artisan Entertainment is asking theaters to enforce an adults-only policy. I can think of an exception: Anyone under seventeen who is thinking of experimenting with drugs might want to see this movie, which plays like a travelogue of hell.

Return to Me ★ ★ ★
PG, 115 m., 2000

David Duchovny (Bob Rueland), Minnie Driver (Grace Briggs), Carroll O'Connor (Marty O'Reilly), Robert Loggia (Angelo Pardipillo), Bonnie Hunt (Megan Dayton), James Belushi (Joe Dayton), David Alan Grier (Charlie

Johnson), Joely Richardson (Elizabeth Rueland), Eddie Jones (Emmett McFadden). Directed by Bonnie Hunt and produced by Jennie Lew Tugend. Screenplay by Hunt and Don Lake.

Here's an old-fashioned love story so innocent, so naive, so sweet and sincere that you must leave your cynicism at the door or choose another movie. Bonnie Hunt's *Return to Me* could have been made in 1955, starring Doris Day and James Stewart. It has been made in 2000, starring Minnie Driver and David Duchovny, and I am happy that it has.

Duchovny stars as Bob, a Chicago architect married to Elizabeth (Joely Richardson), who works at the Lincoln Park Zoo. Scenes establishing their happiness are intercut with hospital scenes involving Grace (Driver), who will die of heart disease unless she receives a transplant. To the surprise of nobody in the audience, Elizabeth dies in a tragic accident, and Grace is given her heart.

At the very moment when it starts beating in her chest, Bob, grieving at home, seems to sense it, as heartbeats on the sound track underline the segue. And a year later, Grace and Bob meet in the Old Town family-run restaurant where she works and lives. It is, for both of them, love at first sight, and their romance blossoms until she discovers something that Bob does not know—it is Elizabeth's heart beating in her chest.

Do not fear I have revealed too much of the story, because all of this is essentially setup, easily anticipated. What gives the movie its gentle charm is not the melodramatic story, but the warmth of the performances and the way the movie pokes merrily along, teasing us with rewards and disappointments.

The key element in the success, I think, is the illusion that Bob and Grace are truly in love. Duchovny and Driver (who has a gift for vulnerability) have an unforced chemistry that feels right. It is crucial in a story of this sort that we want the couple to be together— that we care about them. Otherwise we are simply looking at the puppet strings. I did like them, and felt protective toward them, and apprehensive as their inevitable problems approached.

The setting of the film is also old-fashioned, and a little too picturesque for my taste. Many of the scenes play in O'Reilly's Italian restaurant (actually the Twin Anchors), where the Irish and Italian branches of Grace's family offer such contradictory menu choices as chicken vesuvio and corned beef and cabbage. What is strangest about the restaurant is not the menu but the hours: O'Reilly's seems to close early every night so that the old cronies who run the place can sit around the back table, playing poker and holding desultory debates on the relative merits of Frank Sinatra, Dean Martin, and Vic Damone.

These stalwarts include Carroll O'Connor and Robert Loggia as, of course, the Irish and Italian patriarchs, O'Connor's accent a shade too thick. The guys are all busybodies, peering through a back window into the rear garden where many of the key scenes take place, and playing matchmakers for all they're worth. A little trimming of their scenes wouldn't have hurt.

There is, however, a nice unforced feel to the home life of Grace's best friends, Megan and Joe Dayton, played by Hunt and James Belushi with a relaxed domesticity that makes their characters feel real, and not just helpers designed to speed a scene or two. The emphasis on the film is on friends and family, on a much-loved neighborhood woman who moves in a circle of people who want her to be happy.

Watching the film, I became aware that it lacked the gimmicks of many recent romances. It believes in love and fate, stuff like that. Its innocence is crucial to the plot, because much depends on Bob not seeing the scar on Grace's chest while their courtship moves along. In today's sex-happy movies, the secret would have been revealed when they slept together on their second date, but *Return to Me* convincingly lets them move slowly toward intimacy, so that Grace's delayed nudity creates effective tension.

No doubt this film will be disemboweled by cynics among the reviewers. It offers an easy target. It is almost an act of courage, the way it refuses to hedge its bets or cater to irony. It is what it is, without apology or compromise. It made me smile a lot. I have tried to describe it accurately, for the benefit of those who will like it, and those who will not. You know who you are.

Return With Honor ★ ★ ★
NO MPAA RATING, 102 m., 1999

A documentary featuring Lieutenant (jg) Everett Alvarez, Lieutenant Commander Bob Shumaker, Commander Jeremiah (Jerry) Denton, Commander James Stockdale, Lieutenant Colonel Robinson Risner, Lieutenant Commander John McCain, Captain Douglas Peterson, Major Fred Cherry, Lieutenant John McGrath, Seaman Douglas Hegdahl. Directed and produced by Freida Lee Mock and Terry Sanders. Screenplay by Mock, Sanders, and Christine Z. Wiser.

Return With Honor is a documentary about the ordeals of the American prisoners of war in the infamous Hanoi Hilton, a torture facility. We see the faces of these men today, and we even see them in footage shot at the time. We hear their voices, which are level and sane, as military pilots are trained to speak, but which betray depths of emotion.

The war essentially ended for these men when they were captured, and a new chapter began, of personal test. They were so cut off from the world that they learned of the Moon landing only by seeing a Neil Armstrong postage stamp. Their lives were bounded by stone walls and controlled by their captors, who devised methods of torture so refined that "you'd sell your mother down the river in a minute."

And yet the men endured more than it is possible to comprehend. It is interesting that we hear little hate or anger in their voices; as professional soldiers they value a certain stoicism. To be captured was a risk of war. To "return with honor" was their goal, and one defines it: "To be able to say you didn't do anything you'd be ashamed to tell your children." Of course, that did not include napalming civilians and poisoning crops—because in the rules of war mass violence is sanctioned by both sides, and only personal violence, such as torture, is condemned.

The Hanoi Hilton, we learn, has a symbolic history. It was built by the French during the colonial era to hold disobedient Vietnamese subjects, then used by the Viet Cong to hold Americans. Leg clamps were bolted to the beds, and one witness says, "You could look at this place and hear the screams of fifty years." The Viet Cong torturers had refined methods, including a "rope trick" in which prisoners were bound in positions of excruciating pain. Their minds were worked on by morale-crushing video programs showing U.S. antiwar rallies and congressional speeches. "We will win this war on the streets of New York," their captors told them after one show. In a sense they did.

The ingenuity of the prisoners is astonishing. They devised a code of taps to communicate through cell walls, developing friendships with prisoners they had never seen. Put in a propaganda film, Commander Jeremiah Denton blinked out the word "torture" in Morse code with his eyelids. A fellow prisoner held out his middle fingers to send an even more universal code. Lieutenant John McGrath drew on his cell wall with his own blood and pus; after being freed, he drew everything he remembered. Seaman Douglas Hegdahl memorized the names of 268 fellow prisoners.

Return With Honor was directed by Freida Lee Mock and Terry Sanders. Mock's *Maya Lin: A Strong Clear Vision* is a 1994 Oscar-winning documentary about the Vietnam Veteran's Memorial in Washington and the young woman who designed it. After seeing it, two former prisoners told Mock they had a story to be told. This film tells it simply and directly, without spin or flash, with no narration—just the voices of the men themselves, as they talk against a plain background. There is footage of the Hanoi Hilton as it is today (the screams in a way still echoing) and footage of the men at the time, taken by the Viet Cong and showing, for example, Hanoi mobs cursing them during a march through the city.

A few of the faces are familiar. There are short glimpses of Senator John McCain. We see Pete Peterson, who returned to Vietnam in 1997 as our ambassador. And Vice Admiral James Stockdale, Ross Perot's 1992 running mate. No attempt is made to introduce politics into the film: These were brave men who behaved honorably and patriotically, and we are moved by the strength of their spirits. The scenes of their homecoming are enormously affecting.

I saw another Vietnam documentary, *Regret to Inform*, by Barbara Sonneborn, the widow of an American who died in Vietnam. Her film talks with women on both sides about the husbands they lost. It is not really political either, although no one in her film thinks the war was a good idea (it is not much praised in *Return With Honor,* either). The films would make a useful double feature, suggesting that when war places people under unimaginable pain, it is not politics that motivates them—but self-respect, pride, even stubbornness. The message, I think, is that they hope to be able to return with honor to themselves.

Ride With the Devil ★ ★

R, 138 m., 1999

Skeet Ulrich (Jack Bull Chiles), Tobey Maguire (Jake Roedel), Simon Baker-Denny (George Clyde), Jeffrey Wright (Daniel Holt), Jewel (Sue Lee Shelley), Jonathan Rhys Meyers (Pitt Mackerson), James Caviezel (Black John), Thomas Guiry (Riley Crawford), Tom Wilkinson (Orton Brown). Directed by Ang Lee and produced by Ted Hope, Robert F. Colesberry, and James Schamus. Screenplay by Schamus, based on the novel *Woe to Live On* by Daniel Woodrell.

Ride With the Devil is the first Civil War film I can recall that is not told with the benefit of hindsight. It's about characters who don't know the North will win—and sometimes don't much seem to care. It's said that all politics are local; this movie argues that some wars are local too. In Missouri, the only slaveholding state that sided with the Union, it tells the story of a small group of guerrillas with such complex personal motives that it even includes a black man who fights for the South.

The film has been made by Ang Lee, the gifted Taiwan-born, Illinois-educated director *(Sense and Sensibility, The Ice Storm)* who is able to see the Civil War from the outside. Based on a historical novel by Daniel Woodrell, Lee centers his story on Southwest Missouri, where the Missouri Irregulars, known as Bushwhackers, waged a hit-and-run fight against the Union troops, called Jayhawkers. This is basically a local war among neighbors with personal animosities and little interest in the war's ideological underpinnings.

We follow four Bushwhackers in particular: Jake Roedel (Tobey Maguire), Jack Bull Chiles (Skeet Ulrich), George Clyde (Simon Baker-Denny), and the freed black slave Daniel Holt (Jeffrey Wright). The film opens with a farm wedding they attend; later they see the farm burned and its owners murdered by a Jayhawker raid.

Roedel and Chiles want revenge. Clyde, a southerner, believes in Dixie values and traditions, but is complex enough to have freed Holt, once his slave. Holt's motives are the most impenetrable. Why would a former slave fight for the South? He indicates it is out of personal loyalty to Clyde, who freed him and says he "trusts him with my life every day." Also perhaps because of a bond with his comrades. But Holt says little and his eyes often make a silent commentary on what he sees and hears; we wait through the film for a revelation of his deepest feelings.

History, it is said, is written by the victors. The southern side has had its share of historians, too, but before this movie I had not seen a Civil War story about characters whose feelings are local and personal, whose motives were unclear even to themselves, who were essentially young men with guns, forced to fight by the time and place they lived in. To some degree, they are only practicing self-defense. The movie is more interested in their personalities than their adventures—but not so interested that it makes their motives very clear. There is nothing quite so baffling as a character who acts from psychological reasons but possesses little insight into those buried feelings.

The movie is slow and deliberate—too slow. It begins with the enigma of heroes whose cause we do not share, and then has them spend much of their time hunched inside a hideout they have built into a hillside (where it never occurs to them that if they'd fill the chinks between the logs it might be warmer inside). They have long conversations, delivered in language that seems more suited to sermons and editorials than to everyday speech.

Their hideout is on the land of a Missouri family that supports the Confederacy, and soon Chiles is falling in love with Sue Lee (Jewel), a war widow. To give the film credit, it doesn't degenerate into a conventional romance, but plays both Chiles and Sue Lee as desperate in their own ways for an escape from an intolerable situation. There are also grim passages involving wounds, amputations, and desperate armed raids.

The technical and acting credits are first-rate. Frederick Elmes, who also shot *The Ice Storm,* has an uncanny ability to evoke cold and damp. The actors do a good job of being contained by their characters—by not letting modern insights peek through. Jeffrey Wright, who starred in *Basquiat,* is especially intriguing as the freed slave, who keeps his own counsel throughout the movie without sending out signals about what he's doing. Jewel deserves praise for, quite simply, performing her character in a convincing and unmannered way. She is an actress here, not a pop star trying out a new hobby. Ulrich is good, too, although Tobey Maguire's tone—tight, inward, controlled—is beginning to wear on me after this and *The Cider House Rules.* It's time for him to make a dumb teenage comedy (not because I want to see it, but more to clear the cobwebs).

Watching the film, I could see that Ang Lee and his frequent collaborator, the screenwriter James Schamus, were in search of something serious. *Ride With the Devil* does not have conventional rewards or payoffs, does not simplify a complex situation, doesn't punch up the action or the romance simply to entertain. But it is, sad to say, not a very entertaining movie; it's a long slog unless you're fascinated by the undercurrents. It's a film that would inspire useful discussion in a history class, but for ordinary moviegoers, it's slow and forbidding.

The Road to El Dorado ★ ★ ★

PG, 83 m., 2000

With the voices of: Kevin Kline (Tulio), Kenneth Branagh (Miguel), Rosie Perez (Chel), Armand Assante (Tzekel-Kan), Edward James Olmos (The Chief), Jim Cummings (Cortez), Frank Welker (Altivo), Elton John (Narrator). Directed by Eric "Bibo" Bergeron and Don Paul and produced by Bonne Radford and Brooke Breton. Screenplay by Ted Elliott and Terry Rossio.

There is a moment in *The Road to El Dorado* where the two heroes and their profoundly dubious horse are in a rowboat somewhere in the ocean off of Central America. It looks like the end. Then a sea bird appears, circles, and lands on their boat. This is a good omen. Land must be near. Then the bird drops dead. Bad sign. Then a shark leaps out of the sea and snaps up the bird in one gulp. Piling gag on top of gag is the strategy of the film, a bright and zesty animated comedy from DreamWorks.

In the studio's quest to compete with Disney in the feature-length animation sweepstakes, it's a worthy entry. It's not as quirky as *Antz* or as grown-up as *The Prince of Egypt,* but as silly fun it does nicely, and no wonder: Its directors are Disney veterans, and the sound track includes such effective cartoon voices as Kevin Kline, Kenneth Branagh, Armand Assante, Edward James Olmos, and the unsinkable Rosie Perez.

As the movie opens, the heroes, Tulio (Kline) and Miguel (Branagh), are gambling in a waterfront dive in Spain, 1519. They win a map to the treasures of El Dorado, before it's discovered that their dice are loaded and they beat a hasty retreat—pretending to duel with each other to confuse their pursuers. One thing leads to another, and they find themselves on board Cortez's ship as the explorer sails for South America. They're discovered, sentenced to flogging and enslavement, and escape with their horse in a rowboat, which brings us to the bird, the shark, and landfall at a point that corresponds exactly with the treasure map.

The Road to El Dorado doesn't have a hero; it's about supporting characters. In other hands, the story might have centered around Cortez, the explorer, whose ship catches up to Tulio and Miguel in the new land. But this is the story of two pals caught up in events beyond their comprehension, after the roly-poly local chief (voice by Edward James Olmos) mistakes them for gods. The plot then recycles Kipling's *The Man Who Would Be King:* One likes being a god, the other doesn't. Along the way, they get a sidekick of their own, Chel, a local woman. She's voiced by Perez, and looks like her too. She learns their secret—they aren't gods, only men, but likes them anyway, and decides she wants in on their team when the priest (Armand Assante) devises a monster to destroy them.

The movie has songs by Elton John, which may grow on me, but haven't yet, and some funny comedy sequences. The best may be the invention of the game of basketball, with a living ball—a round little creature who contributes his own moves to the game. More comedy comes as the friends realize the game is up, and try to sneak away with some gold of their own.

Freed of a towering central figure like Pocahontas or Tarzan, *The Road to El Dorado* is liberated for goofiness. There are no serious themes lurking about, or uplifting lessons to learn—just a couple of con men in over their heads, their gal pal, and a horse that some of the time is smarter than the other three put together. (Since the horse doesn't speak, it's able to exploit the miming gifts of the animators.) This is not a landmark in the history of feature animation, but it's bright and has good energy and the kinds of witty asides that entertain the adults in the margins of the stuff for the kids.

Road Trip ★ ★
R, 91 m., 2000

Breckin Meyer (Josh), Seann William Scott (E.L.), Amy Smart (Beth), Paulo Costanzo (Rubin), D. J. Qualls (Kyle), Rachel Blanchard (Tiffany), Anthony Rapp (Jacob), Fred Ward (Earl Edwards). Directed by Todd Phillips and produced by Daniel Goldberg and Joe Medjuck. Screenplay by Todd Phillips and Scot Armstrong.

Road Trip is mellow and dirty, which is the wrong combination. It's sweet when it should be raunchy, or vice versa, and the result is a movie that seems uneasy with itself. It wants to be evil, really it does, but every so often its better nature takes over, and it throws sweetness right there in the middle of the dirty stuff and the nudity. We feel unkind, watching it. We'd enjoy the nudity more if it were ribald and cheerful, but it feels obligatory, as if the actresses were instructed to disrobe every five minutes in a movie that's only really interested in sex for commercial reasons.

Nude scenes should be inspired by the libido, not the box office. That's why I object to the phrase "gratuitous nudity." In a movie like this, the only nudity worth having is gratuitous. If it's there for reasons that are clankingly commercial, you feel sorry for the actresses, which is not the point.

The plot is a lamebrained contrivance about a frat boy named Josh (Breckin Meyer), who has been dating Tiffany (Rachel Blanchard of TV's *Clueless*) ever since high school. Now he's a student at Ithaca College, and she has decided she needs room to grow, or concentrate on her major, or something, and she enrolls at the University of Austin, which is not as far from Ithaca as you can get, but might as well be.

Josh and Tiff keep in touch by telephone, but Josh senses her attention waning, and then there's a period when she doesn't answer the phone. Josh meanwhile has been flirting with a campus sexpot named Beth (Amy Smart), and one night she seduces him and they make a video of themselves having sex, perhaps because they have seen the same thing done in *American Pie*, or perhaps because the makers of *Road Trip* are ripping off *American Pie*, which is probably more likely.

Josh has made a sweet video to send to Tiffany, but we get no points for foreseeing the obvious, which is that the wrong video gets mailed to Tiff, and so Josh and his friends, who lack airfare, have to make an emergency road trip to Austin to try to retrieve the video before Tiffany can see it. All of this is complicated by the presence of Jacob (Anthony Rapp), an unpleasant undergraduate whose minor seems to be in stalking.

Josh borrows a car that belongs to his geeky friend Kyle (D. J. Qualls), and takes along his friends Rubin (Paulo Costanzo) and E.L. (Seann William Scott), who is from *American Pie* and thus functions as a cross-cultural trivia bookmark. They have versions of the usual adventures along the way, including an awkward scene where these white boys try to convince the members of an African-American fraternity that they are members. This scene is as uncomfortable as comedy can be, because the humor in it is latently racist, and so the movie lets it remain latent, which means that all the characters, black and white, seem to be standing around self-consciously avoiding tasteless material. (The movie is bereft, unfortunately, of any alternative material.)

Whether Josh gets to the tape before Beth sees it, I will leave for you to determine. And yes, I said "determine" and not "decide," because to be honest with you I was confused. I thought she had seen it, and then it appeared that she had not, all because of a dream sequence that was either (a) incompetently presented, or (b) failed to engage what I fondly think of as my full intelligence.

On the way out of the movie, I met three teenage girls who asked me what I thought of it, and I requested their opinion: Didn't it seem like Beth had seen the video and then that she hadn't? The three girls agreed with me, and said they'd been confused, too, and together we figured out what had happened, which was useful, but not the sort of conversation you should be having. When a movie doesn't have a brain in its head, don't you agree it's kind of unfair to require thought on the part of the audience?

Full disclosure requires me to report that there were several moments in the movie when I did indeed laugh, and that the characters are likable when they are not being required to act dirty for the transient purposes of the screenplay. Those virtues are not enough to redeem the film, but they suggest that the cast should be regarded more as victims than perpetrators.

Romance ★ ★ ★

NO MPAA RATING, 103 m., 1999

Caroline Ducey (Marie), Sagamore Stevenin (Paul), Francois Berleand (Robert), Rocco Siffredi (Paolo). Directed by Catherine Breillat and produced by Jean-Francois Lepetit. Screenplay by Breillat.

There is a fantasy scene in *Romance* where a woman's body is divided by a wall. On one side, from the waist down, she is in a brothel. On the other side, from the waist up, in a delivery room. What is the message of the scene? Don't be too sure you know. I know I don't. It isn't some kind of simplistic message linking childbirth with misuse by men. The woman having the fantasy isn't really against the activities on either side of the wall. Maybe the scene is intended as an illustration of her own confusion about sex.

The woman's name is Marie (Caroline Ducey). She could be the woman Freud was thinking about when he confessed he could not answer the question, "What does a woman want?" Marie asks herself the same question. She wants something, all right. She is unhappy with her boyfriend, Paul, who refuses to sleep with her, and unhappy, too, with the sexual adventures she has. It's like there's a disconnect between her body and her identity. She does things that sometimes make her feel good, but she doesn't feel good because she has done them.

Romance, written and directed by Catherine Breillat, became notorious on the festival circuit because it is an intelligent, radical film by a woman, and at the same time it contains explicit nudity and, as nearly as we can tell, actual sex. It is not arousing or pornographic, because the sex isn't presented in an erotic way; it's more like a documentary of a dogged woman's forced march toward orgasm, a goal she is not sure she values. Marie narrates the film herself, and also seems to be reading pages from her journal; she is baffled by herself, baffled by men, baffled by sex. Even after climax, her hand closes on air.

Of course the film is French. It is said that for the French, wine takes the place of flirting, dining takes the place of seduction, smoking takes the place of foreplay, and talking takes the place of sex. *Romance* is so analytical that you sometimes get the feeling Marie is putting herself through her sexual encounters simply to get material for her journal. These poor guys aren't lovers; they're case studies.

And yet the film has an icy fascination. Perhaps it is a test of how men and women relate to eroticism on the screen. I know few men who like it much (sure proof it is not pornographic). Women defend it in feminist terms, but you have the strangest feeling they're not saying what they really think. At a screening at the Toronto Film Festival, there was some laughter, almost all female, but I couldn't tell if it was nervous, or knowing.

Perhaps the sex content gets in the way, causing our old tapes to play. When we see a stud on the screen (like Rocco Siffredi, in real life an Italian porno actor famous for one very good reason), we go into porno mode and expect to see—well, what we usually see. But *Romance* doesn't have that mode. Marie relates to Paolo (Siffredi's character) as if he is a laboratory specimen. So this is the famous white rat she has heard so much about. Can he bring her pleasure? Is it perhaps a matter of physical endowment?

And what about Robert (Francois Berleand), who offers to tie her up? He is an ordinary man, not handsome, not exciting, but he has all the necessary equipment and skills, and when he makes his offer she agrees, as if he is a guide at Disney World suggesting one more ride she should try before leaving the park. Does she like bondage? She goes back for more. Perhaps it is not the sexual side that pleases her, but the fact that when Robert is arranging his ropes and restraints, at least he is thinking about her.

There is a scene in the movie that looks like rape, but is it? She more or less invites the stranger who mistreats her. She wants—well, she wants to take a chance, and then she finds out she didn't like it. So she's defiant toward the guy, but it's not anger at how he treated her; it's triumph that she feels undefeated. Later, there is a gynecological examination—perhaps the creepiest scene in the movie, as interns line up for their turn.

I did not really enjoy this movie, and yet I recommend it. Why? Because I think it's onto something interesting. Movies buy the whole romantic package, lock, stock, and barrel. People look great, fall in love, and have wonderful sex. Even intelligent characters in smart movies all seem to think more or less the same way while they're in the sack. Erogenous autopilot takes over. Here is a movie about a woman who never stops thinking. That may not be as good for you as it is for her.

Romeo Must Die ★ ½
R, 110 m., 2000

Jet Li (Han Sing), Aaliyah (Trish O'Day), Isaiah Washington (Mac), Delroy Lindo (Isaak O'Day), DMX (Silk), D. B. Woodside (Colin), Anthony Anderson (Maurice), Henry O. (Ch'u Sing). Directed by Andrzej Bartkowiak and produced by Joel Silver and Jim Van Wyck. Screenplay by Mitchell Kapner, Eric Bernt, and John Jarrell.

Shakespeare has been manhandled in countless modern-dress retreads, and I was looking forward to *Romeo Must Die*, billed as a war between Chinese and African-American families, based on *Romeo and Juliet*. After *China Girl* (1987), which sets the story in New York's Little Italy and Chinatown, and *Romeo + Juliet* (1996), which has a war between modern gangsters in a kind of CalMex strip city, why not a martial arts version in Oakland?

Alas, the film borrows one premise from Shakespeare (the children of enemy families fall in love), and buries the rest of the story in a creaky plot and wheezy dialogue. Much is made of the presence of Jet Li, the Hong Kong martial arts star *(Lethal Weapon 4)*, but his scenes are so clearly computer-aided that his moves are about as impressive as Bugs Bunny doing the same things.

Li stars as Han Sing, once a cop, now taking the rap for a crime he didn't commit. He's in a Hong Kong prison as the movie opens. His brother is killed in Oakland after a fight at an African-American dance club, and Sing breaks out of prison to travel to America and avenge his brother. In Oakland, he meets Trish O'Day (Aaliyah, the singer) and they begin to fall in love while she helps him look into the death of his brother.

But what a coincidence! Her father, Isaak (Delroy Lindo), may know more about the death than he should, and soon the two lovers are in the middle of a war between Chinese and black organizations who are involved in a murky plot to buy up the waterfront for a new sports stadium. This real-estate project exists primarily as a clothesline on which to hang elaborate martial arts sequences, including one Jackie Chan–style football game where Jet Li hammers half a dozen black guys and scores a touchdown, all at once.

It is a failing of mine that I persist in bringing logic to movies where it is not wanted. During *Romeo Must Die*, I began to speculate about the methods used to buy up the waterfront. All of the property owners (of clubs, little shops, crab houses, etc.) are asked to sell, and when they refuse, they are variously murdered, torched, blown up, or have their faces stuck into vats of live crabs. Don't you think the press and the local authorities would notice this? Don't you imagine it would take the bloom off a stadium to know that dozens of victims were murdered to clear the land?

Never mind. The audience isn't in the theater for a film about property values, but to watch Jet Li and other martial arts warriors in action. *Romeo Must Die* has a lot of fight scenes, but key moments in them are so obviously special effects that they miss the point. When

Jackie Chan does a stunt, it may look inelegant, but we know he's really doing it. Here Jet Li leaps six feet in the air and rotates clockwise while kicking three guys. It can't be done, we know it can't be done, we know he's not doing it, and so what's the point? In *The Matrix*, there's a reason the guy can fly.

There's a moment in Jackie Chan's *Rumble in the Bronx* when he uses grace and athletic ability to project his entire body through the swinging gate of a grocery cart, and we say, "Yes!" (pumping a fist into the air is optional). Here Jet Li tries the Chan practice of using whatever props come to hand, but the football game looks overrehearsed and a sequence with a fire hose is underwhelming (anybody can knock guys off their feet with a fire hose).

Closing Notes: Many windows are broken in the movie. Many people fall from great heights. There are a lot of rap songs on the sound track, which distract from the action because their lyrics occupy the foreground and replace dialogue. Killers on motorcycles once again forget it is dangerous for them to chase cars at high speed, because if they get thrown off their bikes, it will hurt. The reliable Motorcycle Opaque Helmet Rule is observed (when you can't see the face of a character because the visor is down, chances are—gasp!—it's a woman). No great romantic chemistry is generated between the young lovers, and there is something odd about a martial arts warrior hiding behind a girl's bedroom door so her daddy won't catch him. Delroy Lindo projects competence, calm, and strength in every scene. This movie needs a screenplay.

A Room for Romeo Brass ★ ★ ★
R, 90 m., 2000

Andrew Shim (Romeo Brass), Ben Marshall (Gavin "Knocks" Woolley), Paddy Considine (Morell), Frank Harper (Joseph), James Higgins (Bill), Vicky McClure (Ladine), Bob Hoskins (Steven Laws). Directed by Shane Meadows and produced by George Faber and Charles Pattinson. Screenplay by Paul Fraser and Meadows.

In a small town near Nottingham, two young teenage friends live next door to each other, and get along like all teenage friends do—which is to say, weirdly, with long silences that have no reason, followed by business as usual.

Romeo Brass (Andrew Shim), the pudgy, optimistic son of a black mother and an absent white father, is not the lad to send to the fish and chips shop if you expect to find any chips left in the bag when he gets home. Gavin Woolley (Ben Marshall), nicknamed Knocks, limps from a back disorder, needs surgery, and has a father who would rather watch television than talk to members of his own family. Romeo and Knocks like each other but don't get carried away by it.

This is Ken Loach country, with its working-class characters from the Midlands, but then a little Mike Leigh creeps in. Knocks, whose limp singles him out, is picked on by some school bullies. Romeo, who was sort of the instigator, tries to help him, but then an adult stranger in a van leaps in and breaks it up. This is Morell (Paddy Considine), well named after a mushroom since he flourishes in the shady, damp spaces of his own mind. Coming to visit Romeo and his family, he puzzles them with a dramatic account of his battles between himself and an "unseen entity."

Romeo has a sister named Ladine (Vicky McClure), very attractive, stranded in this backwater, and Morell wants to date her. This is not a simple matter, since Morell is a very peculiar man, unpredictable, erratic, subject to quick shifts of mental weather. At one point Morell actually convinces Romeo to ask his sister out for him, and when Ladine does go on a date, it is more out of boredom and recklessness than any possible interest.

We have by now become familiar with the characters. We kind of understand why, after Knocks comes home from surgery, Romeo doesn't visit him. Embarrassments grow up between kids without any reason. Earlier we understood when Romeo didn't want to stay at home, and Knocks was happy to have him move into his room. Everybody knows everybody's business in this neighborhood; when Romeo's mother berates him for not going to see Knocks, Knocks can hear their argument through the thin walls separating their row houses.

Morell is the character who supplies unpredictability and the possibility of danger. And yet he is not simply a stalker or a psycho or any of the other easily categorizable things he might be in a more ordinary movie. He is different every time we see him, and sometimes surprises himself. He can be dangerous, and then suddenly disarm himself. The performance by Paddy Considine is a work of sullen and unpredictable craft; I was reminded of David Thewlis in Mike Leigh's *Naked*. The film's climax is logical, I suppose, and yet utterly unanticipated—especially in the way it brings in violence through a marginal character.

A Room for Romeo Brass was directed by Shane Meadows, who made *TwentyFourSeven* (1998), the movie where Bob Hoskins started a boxing club for disadvantaged lads who were reduced to fighting in the streets. That film felt like it wanted to be a documentary, and here, too, Meadows seems fascinated by the happenings of everyday life. *Romeo Brass* is a better film, effortless in the way it insinuates itself into these families, touching in the way it shows how fiercely Romeo and Knocks are, despite everything, their own little men.

Rosetta ★ ★ ★ ½
R, 95 m., 2000

Emilie Dequenne (Rosetta), Fabrizio Rongione (Riquet), Anne Yernaux (Mother), Olivier Gourmet (Boss), Bernard Marbaix (Campgrounds Manager), Frederic Bodson (Head of Personnel), Florian Delain (Boss's Son), Christiane Dorval (First Saleswoman), Mireille Bailly (Second Saleswoman). Directed by Luc and Jean-Pierre Dardenne and produced by the Dardennes and Michele and Laurent Petin. Screenplay by the Dardennes.

At night before she goes to sleep, Rosetta has this conversation with herself: "Your name is Rosetta. My name is Rosetta. You found a job. I found a job. You've got a friend. I've got a friend. You have a normal life. I have a normal life. You won't fall in a rut. I won't fall in a rut. Good night. Good night."

This is a young woman determined to find a job at all costs. She is escaping from the world of her alcoholic mother, a tramp who lives in a ramshackle trailer and runs away near the beginning of the story, leaving her daughter to fend for herself. Rosetta sees an abyss yawning beneath her and will go to any length to avoid it.

Her story is told in a film that astonishingly won the Palme d'Or at the 1999 Cannes Film Festival, as well as the Best Actress prize for its star, Emilie Dequenne. The wins were surprising not because this is a bad film (in its uncompromising way it's a very good one), but because films like this—neorealist, without pedigree, downbeat, stylistically straightforward—do not often win at Cannes. *Variety*'s grudgingly positive review categorized it as "an extremely small European art movie from Belgium." Not just European but Belgian.

Rosetta opens with its heroine being fired, unjustly, we think, from a job. She smacks the boss, is chased by the police, returns home to her mother's trailer, and we get glimpses of her life as she sells old clothes for money, and sometimes buries things like a squirrel. She fishes in a filthy nearby stream—for food, not fun. She makes a friend of Riquet (Fabrizio Rongione), a kid about her age who has a job in a portable waffle stand (yes, Belgian waffles in a Belgian art movie). He likes her, is kind to her, and perhaps she likes him.

One vignette follows another. We discover that unlike almost every teenage girl in the world, she can't dance. That she has stomach pains, maybe from an ulcer. One day Riquet falls in the river while trying to retrieve her fishing line, and she waits a strangely long time before helping him to get out. Later she confesses she didn't want him out. If he had drowned, she could have gotten his job. After all, the local waffle king likes her, and she'd have a job already, had it not gone to his idiot son.

What happens next I will leave for you to discover. The film has an odd, subterranean power. It doesn't strive for our sympathy or make any effort to portray Rosetta as colorful, winning, or sympathetic. It's a film of economic determinism, the story of a young woman for whom employment equals happiness. Or so she thinks until she has employment, and is no happier, perhaps because that is something she has simply never learned to be.

Two other films prowled like ghosts in my memory as I watched *Rosetta*. One was Robert Bresson's *Mouchette* (1966), about a poor girl who is cruelly treated by a village. The other was Agnes Varda's *Vagabond* (1986), about a young woman alone on the road, gradually descending from backpacker to homeless person. These characters are Rosetta's spiritual sisters, sharing her proud disdain for society and her desperate need to be seen as part of it. She'll find a job. She'll get a friend. She'll have a normal life. She won't fall in a rut. Good night.

Rugrats in Paris ★ ★ ★
G, 80 m., 2000

With the voices of: Susan Sarandon (Coco La Bouche), John Lithgow (Jean-Claude), Debbie Reynolds (Lulu Pickles), Tim Curry (Sumo Singer), Casey Kasem (Wedding DJ), E. G. Daily (Tommy Pickles), Christine Cavanaugh (Chuckie Finster), Kath Soucie (Phil, Lil, and Betty Deville). Directed by Stig Bergqvist and Paul Demeyer and produced by Arlene Klasky and Gabor Csupo. Screenplay by J. David Stem, David N. Weiss, Jill Gorey, Barbara Herndon, and Kate Boutilier.

Many members of the target audience for *Rugrats in Paris* cannot read, so I am dedicating this review to their parents, especially their moms. I know your secret. You watch *Rugrats* too. It supplies a time in the day when you and the kids can get together in front of the set and both laugh, often for different reasons. You don't make a habit of announcing you're a *Rugrats* fan, but when you get together with other moms and the Rugrats come up, you grin and say you hate to admit it, but you actually *like* the show.

You will like *Rugrats in Paris* too. I liked it. It's better than the 1998 *Rugrats* movie, funnier, weirder, with more stuff for adults to clue into. Or maybe kids also clue into this stuff. Today's real-life rugrats are so hip to the media that a lot of them will even get the *Godfather* satire that opens the movie. (My favorite moment: One of the kids finds a hobbyhorse head in his bed, and another says, "That's what you get for wiping your boogers on Cynthia.")

The original *Rugrats* satirized *2001, Jurassic Park, The Fugitive, Raiders of the Lost Ark,* and Busby Berkeley musicals. This one has fun not only with *The Godfather* but also with *King Kong, Godzilla, Little Indian, Big City, Lady and the Tramp,* and *101 Dalmatians*. It also pokes fun at Euroreptorland, a Japanese-owned theme park in Paris with giant reptiles that look a lot like *The Iron Giant*. (Not many of the kids will know that the artificial wave towering above the park is based on Katsushika Hokusai's famous drawing *The Great Wave* from 1831, but look it up on the Web with them and they'll want the T-shirt).

The plot. As the movie opens, little Chuckie Finster (voice by Christine Cavanaugh) is sad because his dad took him to a wedding where there was a dance all the kids were supposed to dance with their moms, but Chuckie's mom is dead. He thinks his dad ought to get married again. They check out the dating sites on the Web, and one candidate has all the right credentials except that she is not allowed to enter the state of Georgia. Then there's an emergency call from Paris: A raptor is malfunctioning at the theme park, and a friend of the Finsters, a raptor engineer, is summoned to Paris—and mistakenly thinks he was asked to bring along his family and friends.

That's a convenient way for the entire Rugrats crowd to be transported to France, where we meet Coco La Bouche (voice by Susan Sarandon), the witchy theme park executive, whose Japanese boss thinks she should be married and love kids, so she decides to marry Mr. Finster, forcibly if necessary, and adopt Chuckie.

The plot is just the excuse for the goofiness, including a dance line of sumo wrestlers, a thrilling trip to the Princess at the very top of the park, a love affair between a poodle and a mutt, and the Godzilla-style chase through the streets of Paris, with the kids running a giant raptor that scales the Eiffel Tower before finally arriving at Notre Dame Cathedral, where the wedding is in progress.

The graphic style of the movie will be familiar to anyone who watches the TV show. I like it. It's bright and quirky, with the oversized heads of the kids owing a little to Charles Schulz. The dialogue is direct and fundamental, geared to young values: "My dad is marrying a lady who doesn't like me or my wa-wa or any kids." His wa-wa, of course, is his stuffed pet. And there are the usual jokes about poo and pee and farts and stinky didies; as I observed in my *Rugrats* review, kids are fascinated with bodily excretions because they have so recently celebrated their own personal victories over them.

The point is, adults can attend this movie with a fair degree of pleasure. That's not always the case with movies for kids, as no parent needs to be reminded. There may even be some moms who insist that the kids *need* to see this movie. You know who you are.

Rules of Engagement ★ ★ ½
R, 123 m., 2000

Tommy Lee Jones (Colonel Hays Hodges), Samuel L. Jackson (Colonel Terry Childers), Guy Pearce (Major Mark Biggs), Philip Baker Hall (General Hodges), Bruce Greenwood (William Sokal), Blair Underwood (Captain Lee), Anne Archer (Mrs. Mourain), Mark Feuerstein (Captain Tom Chandler), Ben Kingsley (Ambassador Mourain). Directed by William Friedkin and produced by Richard D. Zanuck and Scott Rudin. Screenplay by Stephen Gaghan.

Rules of Engagement works splendidly as a courtroom thriller about military values, as long as you don't expect it to seriously consider those values. It's convincing on the surface, evasive beneath. I found myself involved in the story, and was pleased that for once I couldn't guess how a movie trial was going to turn out. Still, I expected the closing scenes to answer questions and close loopholes, and they evaded the questions and slipped through the loopholes.

The film centers on a relationship forged throughout the adult lifetimes of two marine colonels, Hodges (Tommy Lee Jones) and Childers (Samuel L. Jackson). They fought side by side in Vietnam, where Childers saved Hodges's life by shooting an unarmed POW. That's against the rules of war, but understandable, in this story anyway, under the specific circumstances. Certainly Hodges is not complaining.

Years pass. Hodges, whose wounds make him unfit for action, gets a law degree and becomes a marine lawyer. He also gets a divorce

and becomes a drunk. Childers, much decorated, is a textbook marine who is chosen to lead a rescue mission into Yemen when the U.S. embassy there comes under threat from angry demonstrators.

Exactly what happens at the embassy, and why, becomes the material of a court-martial, after Childers is accused of ordering his men to fire on a crowd of perhaps unarmed civilians, killing eighty-three of them. He convinces his old friend Hodges to represent him in the courtroom drama that occupies the second half of the film. Although the story marches confidently toward a debate about the ethical conduct of war, it trips over a villain who sidetracks the moral focus of the trial.

Remarkable, though, how well Jones, Jackson, and director William Friedkin are able to sustain interest and suspense even while saddled with an infuriating screenplay. Little is done to provide the characters with any lives outside their jobs, and yet I believed in them and cared about the outcome of the trial. If their work had been supported by a more thoughtful screenplay, this film might have really amounted to something.

Some of the lapses can't be discussed without revealing plot secrets. Here's one that can. Hodges makes a fact-finding visit to Yemen, and sees children who were victims of Childers's order to fire (the scene echoes one in *The Third Man*). He returns, drunk and enraged, and accuses Childers of lying to him. Childers punches him. Hodges fights back. They have a bitter brawl—two middle-aged men, gasping for breath—while we try not to wonder how a lame attorney can hold his own with a combat warrior. Finally, with his last strength, Hodges throws a pillow at Childers, and the two bloodied men start laughing. This works fine as an illustration of an ancient movie cliché about a fight between friends, but what does it mean in the movie? That Hodges has forgotten the reason for his anger? That it was not valid?

Much depends, during the trial, on a missing tape that might show what really happened when the crowd was fired on. The tape is destroyed by the national security adviser (Bruce Greenwood), who tells an aide: "I don't want to watch this tape. I don't want to testify about it. I don't want it to exist." How do you get to be the national security adviser if you're dumb enough to say things like that out loud to a witness? And dumb enough, for that matter, to destroy this particular tape in the first place—when it might be more useful to the United States to show it?

Much is made in the movie of the marine esprit de corps, of protecting the lives of the men under your command, of following a warrior code. Yet one puzzling close-up of Childers's eyes during the Vietnam sequence supplies an undertow that influences our view of the character all through the movie: Is he acting as a good marine, or out of rage? This adds usefully to the suspense (movie stars are usually found innocent in courtroom dramas, but this time we can't be sure). But eventually we want more of an answer than we get.

One entire subplot is a missed opportunity. We see the U.S. ambassador (Ben Kingsley) and his wife and son as they're rescued by Childers. Later we hear his testimony in court, and then there's a scene between Hodges and the ambassador's wife (Anne Archer). Everything calls for a courtroom showdown involving either the ambassador or his wife, but there isn't one. Why set it up if you're not going to pay it off?

I ask these questions and yet admit that the movie involved me dramatically. Jones and Jackson work well together, bringing more conviction to many scenes than they really deserve. The fundamental problem with *Rules of Engagement,* I suspect, is that the filmmakers never clearly defined exactly what they believed about the issues they raised. Expert melodrama conceals their uncertainty up to a point, but at the end we have a film that attacks its central issue from all sides, and has a collision in the middle.

Runaway Bride ★ ★

PG, 116 m., 1999

Julia Roberts (Maggie Carpenter), Richard Gere (Ike Graham), Joan Cusack (Peggy), Hector Elizondo (Fisher), Rita Wilson (Ellie), Paul Dooley (Walter), Christopher Meloni (Coach Bob), Jane Morris (Mrs. Pressman), Laurie Metcalf (Mrs. Trout), Jean Schertler (Grandma Julia). Directed by Garry Marshall and produced by Ted Field, Tom Rosenberg, Scott Kroopf, and Robert Cort. Screenplay by Josann McGibbon and Sara Parriott.

Sometimes I embrace contrivance and sometimes it makes me squirmy. Sometimes a movie manipulates me in dumb ways, and I grin and purr. Sometimes I get grumpy. It all has to do with tone. The material may be unlikely, manipulative, and contrived, but sometimes it works and sometimes all you want to do is bark at it.

Consider two films. Garry Marshall's *Pretty Woman* (1990) starred Richard Gere and Julia Roberts as an executive who was shy of emotional commitment and the hooker he finds true love with. Garry Marshall's *Runaway Bride* (1999) stars Julia Roberts and Richard Gere as a woman who gets skittish at the altar and a newspaper columnist who finds true love with her. Same director, same stars, similar Meet Cutes. A hooker and a newspaper columnist are not precisely in the same occupation, but close enough—both enter the lives of strangers, for hire, the difference being that the hooker is invited.

The virtues of *Pretty Woman* do not need repeating. Even its utterly unlikely ending, so contrived it was bizarre, actually worked by the time we steamed up to it. Now here we have the same two actors—actors we like, actors it is good to look at, actors who work easily together—and the same directorial hand at the helm, and they just seem to be going through the motions.

Gere plays Ike Graham, a columnist for *USA Today.* His specialty is banging out last-minute prose off the top of his head (at one point he actually seems to be sitting in a bar and writing in longhand). A drunk tells him about a woman in his hometown named Maggie Carpenter who has left seven or eight guys stranded at the altar. He writes a female-bashing column, prints the woman's name, and is astonished when she writes a snarly letter to the editor. She stranded only three guys, she says, and there are fifteen other inaccuracies; doesn't he check his facts?

How about *USA Today?* Does it check? This guy wouldn't last a day in the real world. But hey, this is a movie, and so we accept the premise that he would quickly journey down to the bucolic movie hamlet where Maggie lives—Hale, Maryland, a village that looks like a postcard, where everybody lives in each other's pockets. I kept waiting for the town to fade to black and white and turn into Pleasantville.

In Hale we meet Maggie's jovial but hard-drinking dad (Paul Dooley), who is a good sport, assuming he has to pay for all the weddings; her best friend, Peggy (Joan Cusack), a hairstylist who reads omens in the flights of geese; and Maggie's Grandma Julia (Jean Schertler), whose theory is that it's not the wedding Maggie is afraid of, but the wedding night. There is also the matter of Maggie's current fiancé, Coach Bob (Christopher Meloni). He's *Runaway Bride*'s equivalent of the guy in a cop picture who has one day to go before retirement.

Back at *USA Today*, Rita Wilson plays Ike's ex-wife, who is now his editor. Hector Elizondo plays her current husband, for the excellent reason that he has appeared in all eleven of Marshall's films and is the director's good-luck charm, or at least that was the theory. Their scenes have no dramatic or comedic importance, leaving us free time to reflect that a movie starring them as the runaway bride and the newspaper columnist instead of Roberts and Gere might have had more zing, if less hair.

It is crashingly obvious to everyone in the theater that Maggie and Ike will eventually find themselves at the altar together, after obligatory preliminary fights, negotiations, and scuffles. We click off the screenplay stops along the way. They have to fight. Suddenly see the other person in a different light. Share confidences. Be involved in a silly misunderstanding. Go to the brink of tragedy. Tell truths. Be saved. And, of course, just as they stand at the brink of False Happiness there has to be a False Crisis, before the Real Crisis and the Real Happiness can be permitted on-screen.

The movie has one great line ("Always a bride, never a bridesmaid"), but even that is sort of inevitable. Movies like this should have an explanatory note at the outset, to help us understand them. Something like, "The following characters all look really great, but don't know anything they haven't learned by watching sitcoms." Having seen Gere and Roberts play much smarter people (even in romantic comedies), it is painful to see them dumbed-

down here. The screenplay is so sluggish, they're like derby winners made to carry extra weight.

Run Lola Run ★ ★ ★
R, 81 m., 1999

Franka Potente (Lola), Moritz Bleibtreu (Manni), Herbert Knaup (Lola's Father), Armin Rohde (Mr. Schuster), Joachim Krol (Tramp), Nina Petri (Mrs. Hanson). Directed by Tom Tykwer and produced by Stefan Arndt. Screenplay by Tykwer.

Run Lola Run is the kind of movie that could play on the big screen in a sports bar. It's an exercise in kinetic energy, a film of nonstop motion and visual invention. A New York critic called it "post-human," and indeed its heroine is like the avatar in a video game—Lara Croft made flesh.

The setup: Lola gets a phone call from her boyfriend, Manni. He left a bag containing 100,000 Deutschmarks on the subway, and a bum made away with it. Manni is expected to deliver the money at noon to a gangster. If he fails, he will probably be killed. His desperate plan: Rob a bank. Lola's desperate plan: Find the 100,000 DMs somehow, somewhere, in twenty minutes. Run, Lola, run!

The director, a young German named Tom Tykwer, throws every trick in the book at us, and then the book, and then himself. The opening credits spring a digital surprise, as a shot of a crowd turns into an aerial point of view and the crowd spells out the name of the movie. Lola sometimes runs so frantically that mere action cannot convey her energy, and the movie switches to animation. There's speed-up, instant replay, black and white, whatever. And the story of Lola's twenty-minute run is told three times, each time with small differences that affect the outcome and the fate of the characters.

Film is ideal for showing alternate and parallel time lines. It's literal; we see Lola running, and so we accept her reality, even though the streets she runs through and the people she meets are altered in each story. The message is that the smallest events can have enormous consequences. A butterfly flaps its wings in Malaysia, causing a hurricane in Trinidad. You know the drill.

Franka Potente, who plays Lola, has a certain offhand appeal. I liked her, though I can't say I got to know her very well, and she was usually out of breath. She runs down sidewalks and the middles of streets, arms pumping, bright red hair flying, stomach tattoo wrinkling in time with her footsteps. She loves Manni and wants to save him from his own stupidity. Occasionally the movie pauses for moments of sharply seen detail, as when her rich father refuses to give her the money, tells her he plans to leave home and marry his mistress, and throws in for good measure: "I'd have never fathered a girl like you. You're a cuckoo's egg."

Manni does his share of running, too, and there are various alternate scenarios involving car crashes, gunshot wounds, and the sly use of that ancient movie situation where guys are carrying a huge sheet of plate glass across the street. Tykwer also adds segments titled "Now and Then," in which he singles out minor characters on the screen and uses just a few startling flash-frames to foresee their entire lifelines.

Run Lola Run is essentially a film about itself, a closed loop of style. Movies about characters on the run usually involve a linear story (*The Fugitive* comes to mind), but this one is basically about running—and about the way that movie action sequences have a life and logic of their own. I would not want to see a sequel to the film, and at eighty-one minutes it isn't a second too short, but what it does, it does cheerfully, with great energy, and very well.

Running Free ★ ½
G, 82 m., 2000

Chase Moore (Young Richard), Jan Decleir (Boss Man), Maria Geelbooi (Nyka), Arie Verveen (Adult Richard), Graham Clarke (Mine Supervisor), Patrick Lyster (Officer). Directed by Sergei Bodrov and produced by Jean-Jacques Annaud. Screenplay by Jeanne Rosenberg, based on a story by Annaud and Rosenberg.

Running Free tells the life story of a horse in its own words. We do not find out much about horses in this process, alas, because the horse thinks and talks exactly like a young boy. The movie is another example, like Disney's *Dinosaur,* of a failure of nerve: Instead of challenging the audience to empathize with real animals, both movies supply them with the minds, vocabularies, and values of humans. What's the point?

As the film opens, the horse, later to be named Lucky, is born in the hold of a ship bound for German Southwest Africa, today's Namibia. It is 1911, and horses are needed to work in the mines. Lucky has to swim ashore while still a nursing colt. He glimpses daylight for the first time, and tells us, "I didn't see anything green in this desert land." Hello? Lucky has never seen anything green at all in his entire life.

But the movie keeps making that same mistake, breaking the logic of the point of view. Adopted by a young orphan stable boy named Richard (Chase Moore), Lucky finds himself in a stable of purebreds ruled by a stallion named Caesar. Lucky wants to make friends with the stallion's daughter, Beauty, but, "I was only the stable boy's horse. I wasn't good enough to play with his daughter." And when Lucky's long-missing mother turns up, Caesar attacks her, apparently in a fit of class prejudice, although you'd think a stallion would be intrigued by a new girl in town, despite her family connections.

Will the mother die from the attack? "I stayed with her all night, praying that she would survive," Lucky tells us. Praying? I wanted the movie to forget the story and explore this breakthrough in horse theology. I am weary of debates about whether our pets will be with us in heaven, and am eager to learn if trainers will be allowed into horse heaven.

The human characters in the movie are one-dimensional cartoons, including a town boss who speaks English with an Afrikaans accent, not likely in a German colony. His son is a little Fauntleroy with a telescope, which he uses to spy on Richard and Lucky. Soon all the Europeans evacuate the town after a bombing raid, which raises the curtain on World War I. The horses are left behind, and Lucky escapes to the mountains, where he finds a hidden lake. Returning to the town, he leads the other horses there, where at last they realize their birthright and Run Free.

Uh-huh. But there is not a twig of living vegetation in their desert hideout, and although I am assured by the movie's press materials that there are wild horses in Namibia to this day, I doubt they could forage for long in the barren wasteland shown in this film. What do they eat?

I ask because it is my responsibility: Of all the film critics reviewing this movie, I will arguably be the only one who has actually visited Swakopmund and Walvis Bay, on the Diamond Coast of the Namib Desert, and even ridden on the very train tracks to the capital, Windhoek, that the movie shows us. I am therefore acutely aware that race relations in the area in 1911 (and more recently) would scarcely have supported the friendship between Richard and Nyka (Maria Geelbooi), who plays the bushman girl who treats Lucky's snakebite. But then a movie that fudges about which side is which in World War I is unlikely to pause for such niceties.

I seem to be developing a rule about talking animals: They can talk if they're cartoons or Muppets, but not if they're real. This movie might have been more persuasive if the boy had told the story of the horse, instead of the horse telling the story of the boy. It's perfectly possible to make a good movie about an animal that does not speak, as Jean-Jacques Annaud, the producer of this film, proved with his 1989 film *The Bear*.

I also recall *The Black Stallion* (1979) and *White Fang* (1991). Since both of those splendid movies were cowritten by Jeanne Rosenberg, the author of *Running Free*, I can only guess that the talking horse was pressed upon her by executives who have no faith in the intelligence of today's audiences. Perhaps *Running Free* would appeal to younger children who really like horses, but see my review of *The Color of Paradise*, a film in release at the same time, for a glimpse of a truly inspired film for family audiences.

Rushmore ★ ★ ½
R, 93 m., 1999

Jason Schwartzman (Max Fischer), Bill Murray (Mr. Blume), Olivia Williams (Miss Cross), Brian Cox (Dr. Guggenheim), Seymour Cassel (Bert Fischer), Mason Gamble (Dirk Calloway), Sara Tanaka (Margaret Yang), Stephen McCole (Magnus Buchan). Directed by Wes Anderson and produced by Barry Mendel and Paul Schiff. Screenplay by Anderson and Owen Wilson.

Max Fischer, the hero of *Rushmore,* is an activity jock, one of those kids too bright and restless to color inside the lines. Although he's a lousy student, that doesn't stop him from organizing a movement to keep Latin on the curriculum of his exclusive prep school. His grades are so bad he's on "sudden death probation," but in his spare time he edits the school magazine and runs the fencing club, the bee-keeping club, the karate team, the French club, and the Max Fischer Players. With his bushy eyebrows and black horn-rims, he looks a little like a young Benjamin Braddock from *The Graduate.*

Max, played by Jason Schwartzman, has a secret. He's in the exclusive Rushmore Academy on a scholarship; his dad is a barber. Always dressed in a tie and snappy blazer (unless in costume for one of his activities), he speaks with an unnerving maturity, and is barely able to conceal his feelings of superiority for the headmaster (Brian Cox) and other adults, who enforce their stuffy rules because they are not, and never were, able to play without a net the way Max can.

Then Max encounters a problem even he cannot outflank. Reading a book in the school library, he finds a quote by Jacques Cousteau written in the margin. The book was recently checked out, he discovers, by Miss Cross (Olivia Williams), a first-grade teacher at Rushmore. She is, he finds, incredibly beautiful, and he falls instantly in love, devising a scheme to attract her attention by running a campaign for a school aquarium. Among the potential donors is a steel tycoon named Blume (Bill Murray). Murray has kids in Rushmore, but hates them. Soon he, too, is in love with Miss Cross.

Up until this point, even a little further, *Rushmore* has a kind of effortless grace. Max Fischer emerges as not just a brainy comic character, but as a kid who could do anything if he weren't always trying to do everything. It's ingenious the way he uses his political and organizing abilities to get his way with people, how he enlists a younger student (Mason Gamble) as his gofer, how he reasons patiently with the headmaster and thinks he can talk Miss Cross into being his girlfriend ("Max, has it ever occurred to you that you're far too young for me?").

Blume is played by Bill Murray with the right note to counter Max's strategies. He is, essentially, a kid himself—immature, vindictive, love-struck, self-centered, physically awkward, but with years more experience in getting his way. (Still, he winds up hiding from life at the bottom of a swimming pool, just like Benjamin.) The movie turns into a strategic duel between Max and Blume, and that could be funny, too, except that it gets a little mean when Max spills the beans to Blume's wife, and it feels too contrived. When plotting replaces stage-setting and character development, the air goes out of the movie.

Rushmore was directed by Wes Anderson and written by Anderson and his college friend, Owen Wilson. It's their second film, after the slight but engaging *Bottle Rocket* (1996). The legend of that film is well known, and suggests that Anderson and Wilson may have a little of Max Fischer in their own personalities—the film may have elements of self-portraiture.

They were friends at the University of Texas who made a short film, pitched it to screenwriter L. M. (Kit) Carson, got his encouragement, took it to the Sundance Film Festival, and cornered famous director James L. Brooks *(As Good As It Gets)*, who liked it enough to help them get financing for a feature from Columbia. I am writing this review during the Sundance festival, where I have met a lot of kids trying to pitch their short films and get production deals, and having a good film is not enough: You also need the relentless chutzpah of a Max Fischer.

Bill Murray has a way of turning up in perfect smaller roles; he stars in his own films, but since *Tootsie,* he has made supporting roles into a sort of parallel career. His Blume admires and hates Max for the same reason: Because he is reminded of himself. There are times when Blume is frustrated in his desire to win Miss Cross for himself, but from an objective viewpoint he can't resist admiring Max's strategy.

Anderson and Wilson are good offbeat filmmakers. They fill the corners of their story with nice touches, like the details of Max's wildly overambitious stage production of *Serpico.* But their film seems torn between conflicting possibilities: It's structured like a comedy, but there are undertows of darker themes, and I almost wish they'd allowed the plot to lead them into those shadows. The Max Fischer they give us is going to grow up into Benjamin Braddock. But there is an unrealized Max who would have become Charles Foster Kane.

S

Save the Last Dance ★ ★ ★
PG-13, 112 m., 2001

Julia Stiles (Sara Johnson), Sean Patrick Thomas (Derek Reynolds), Terry Kinney (Roy), Kerry Washington (Chenille Reynolds), Fredro Starr (Malakai), Vince Green (Snookie), Bianca Lawson (Nikki), Marcello Robinson (Wonk). Directed by Thomas Carter and produced by Robert W. Cort and David Madden. Screenplay by Duane Adler and Cheryl Edwards.

Save the Last Dance begins with standard material but doesn't settle for it. The setup promises clichés, but the development is intelligent, the characters are more complicated than we expect, and the ending doesn't tie everything up in a predictable way. Above all, this is a movie where the characters ask the same questions we do: They're as smart about themselves as we are.

As the film opens, we meet Sara (Julia Stiles), a morose high school girl on a train. Flashbacks fill us in. She was a promising dancer with an audition at Julliard, but her mother was killed in an accident while driving to see her daughter dance. Now there's no money for school; Sara has lost her comfortable suburban existence and is coming to live with her father, Roy (Terry Kinney), a musician who lives in a walk-up flat in a gritty Chicago neighborhood. Roy is not unfriendly, but isn't the parent type.

The students at Sara's high school are mostly African-American, but as we notice this, we notice something else: The movie doesn't fall into ancient clichés about racial tension, the school is not painted as some kind of blackboard jungle, and the students are not electrified by the arrival of—gasp!—a white girl. They have more important things to think about.

Sara is befriended by a girl named Chenille (Kerry Washington), who shows her how easy it is to get your bag stolen if you leave it untended. In class, she notices Derek (Sean Patrick Thomas), whose comments show he's smart. She's taken to a club on Friday night, dances with Derek (who turns out to be Chenille's brother), and starts to like him. Eventu-

ally it becomes a romance, but this is not your basic high school love story, and includes dialogue like, "We spend more time defending our relationship than actually having one."

Derek's best friend is Malakai (Fredro Starr). They've been in trouble together, and Malakai once pulled him out of a situation that could have destroyed his life. Malakai is a petty thief and a gang member; Derek is on a different track (he's just won a scholarship to Georgetown), but loyalty tugs at him when Malakai wants him to come along as backup at a potentially fatal encounter. Derek's choice, and the way the episode ends, may surprise you.

Meanwhile, Derek and Sara dance together—not just at the club, but in a deserted building where he shows her an urban style of dance, and learns of her passion for ballet. All of this is interesting because it is not simply presented as courtship, but as two young people seriously curious about dance. Their romance, when it develops, doesn't show that love is blind, but suggests that it sees very well indeed; the movie doesn't simple-mindedly applaud interracial relationships, and Sara gets bitterly criticized by Derek's sister Chenille: "You come and take one of the few decent men left after drugs, jail, and drive-bys." That overstates the case; there are lots of decent men left, but we understand how she feels.

Do you know who Julia Stiles is? She's one of the most talented of the emerging generation of actresses, although not yet a major star. Born in 1981, acting since she was eleven, she was Ethan Hawke's Ophelia in the modern-dress 2000 version of *Hamlet,* and plays the local teenager who inflames Alec Baldwin in David Mamet's *State and Main* (she was also Freddie Prinze Jr.'s squeeze in the less-than-brilliant *Down to You*). Here she is good in ways that may not be immediately apparent, as when she jockeys for personal space with her bohemian bachelor father, and likes the way she can talk with Derek (ever notice how many teenage lovers in the movies have nothing to say to each other except comments driven directly by the mechanics of the plot?).

Sean Patrick Thomas is good, too, especially in Derek's scenes with Malakai. We see the pull of loyalty struggling with the wisdom of common sense, as Malakai tries to convince him to head into trouble, and Derek fights between his instincts and his intelligence. The movie was directed by Thomas Carter *(Swing Kids, Metro)*, who seems determined to let this be the story of these specific characters and not just an exercise in genre. The movie's awake. It surprises you. You can see Derek and Sara thinking. For them, romance is not the end of the story. Their lives are ahead of them. They're going to college. They have plans. Maybe they'll figure in each other's plans. They'll see. You need a lot of luck if you plan to spend your life with the first person you fall in love with in high school.

Saving Grace ★ ★
R, 93 m., 2000

Brenda Blethyn (Grace), Craig Ferguson (Matthew), Martin Clunes (Dr. Bamford), Tcheky Karyo (Jacques), Jamie Foreman (China MacFarlane), Bill Bailey (Vince), Valerie Edmond (Nicky), Tristan Sturrock (Harvey). Directed by Nigel Cole and produced by Mark Crowdy, Craig Ferguson, and Torsten Leschly. Screenplay by Crowdy and Ferguson.

When Grace's husband falls, jumps, or is pushed out of an airplane and qualifies for his closed-casket funeral, Grace discovers she's been living in a fool's paradise. She occupies a magnificent country home outside a picturesque Cornish village, she dotes on her garden, she heads local committees—and, she discovers, she is bankrupt and owes money she has no possible way of paying.

Her husband was a louse, something everyone in town seems to have known except for Grace (Brenda Blethyn). He was also a ladies' man with a mistress in London, and he spent all the money and borrowed more. Grace is appalled as the movers arrive to carry out the furniture: What is to become of her garden?

The gardener himself suggests the solution. His name is Matthew, played by Craig Ferguson, who also cowrote the movie, and he also works at the vicarage, where he has a few private marijuana plants under cultivation. They're not flourishing in the shade, alas, and he recruits Grace for advice. She suggests moving

them into her greenhouse for better light and food, and, one thing leading to another as in such situations they inevitably do, before long Grace and Matthew are raising dope in wholesale quantities and may make enough money to pay the bills with lots left over.

Saving Grace sets this story in one of those villages that have been a staple of British (and Welsh, Scots, and Irish) comedies since time immemorial: villages in which P. G. Wodehouse novels would be considered realistic, where everyone knows one another, is nice, is an eccentric, plays a role, and winks at those kinds of sins that are harmless and fun. Such villages have had a renaissance in recent years. Think of *Local Hero, Waking Ned Devine, The Snapper, The Full Monty, The Englishman Who Went Up a Hill and Came Down a Mountain, Brassed Off, Circle of Friends, The Van,* and many more.

Do such places exist? I hope so. St. Isaacs, the village in Cornwall that provides the setting for *Saving Grace*, seems like the kind of place you might never want to leave, so friendly are the citizens and charming the aspect. The horrors of modern life have not penetrated here, and Grace only vaguely understands them when she ventures to London on her own to sell her marijuana harvest. For anyone who has ever ventured down Portobello Road in Notting Hill and sniffed the sweet scents on its breezes, there is a good laugh in the sight of middle-aged, respectable Grace trying to find customers. She is wearing a white summer suit—her idea of what is appropriate for a trip to London, but nobody's idea of how a pot dealer should dress.

The London scenes also provide us with a low-level drug dealer named Vince (Bill Bailey), who realizes he is in way over his head, and a higher-level drug dealer named Jacques (Tcheky Karyo), who wants to be menacing and fearful but is disarmed by Grace's naïveté (how do you threaten someone who is oblivious to threats?). When it turns out that Grace has a *lot* of very high-quality marijuana, Vince in particular wants out: "I have to go pick up my daughter from her flute lessons."

The setup of *Saving Grace* is fun, and Blethyn helps by being not just a helpless innocent but a smart woman who depended too much on her husband and now quickly learns to cope.

The London dope scene is also amusing, although more might have been done with Jacques (he sometimes seems at a loss for words). But the film's ending decays into farce that is more or less routine; if it was funny to see one naked old man in *Waking Ned Devine*, how about several naked old ladies this time? We're left with a promising idea for a comedy, which arrives at some laughs but never finds its destination.

Saving Silverman ½★
PG-13, 90 m., 2001

Jason Biggs (Darren Silverman), Steve Zahn (Wayne Le Fessier), Jack Black (J. D. McNugent), Amanda Peet (Judith Snodgrass-Fessbeggler), Amanda Detmer (Sandy Perkus), R. Lee Ermey (Coach), Neil Diamond (Himself). Directed by Dennis Dugan and produced by Neal H. Moritz. Screenplay by Greg DePaul and Hank Nelken.

Saving Silverman is so bad in so many different ways that perhaps you should see it, as an example of the lowest slopes of the bell-shaped curve. This is the kind of movie that gives even its defenders fits of desperation.

Consider my friend James Berardinelli, the best of the Web-based critics. No doubt ten days of oxygen deprivation at the Sundance Film Festival helped inspire his three-star review, in which he reports optimistically, "*Saving Silverman* has its share of pratfalls and slapstick moments, but there's almost no flatulence." Here's a critical rule of thumb: You know you're in trouble when you're reduced to praising a movie for its absence of fart jokes, and have to add "almost."

The movie is a male-bonding comedy in which three friends since grade school, now allegedly in their early twenties but looking in two cases suspiciously weathered for anyone under a hard-living thirty-two, are threatened by a romance. Darren Silverman (Jason Biggs), Wayne Le Fessier (Steve Zahn), and J. D. McNugent (Jack Black) grew up together sharing a common passion for the works of Neil Diamond; their sidewalk band, the Diamonds, performs his songs and then passes the hat.

The band is broken up, alas, when Darren is captured by Judith Snodgrass-Fessbeggler (Amanda Peet), a blonde man-eater who immediately bans his friends and starts transforming him into a broken and tamed possession. "He's my puppet and I'm his puppet master!" she declares, proving that she is unfamiliar with the word *mistress*, which does not come as a surprise. In a movie so desperately in need of laughs, it's a mystery why the filmmakers didn't drag Ms. Snodgrass-Fessbeggler's parents onstage long enough to explain their decision to go with the hyphenated last name.

Wayne and J.D. concoct a desperate scheme to save Darren from marriage. They kidnap Judith, convince Darren she is dead, and arrange for him to meet the original love of his life, Sandy Perkus (Amanda Detmer), who is now studying to be a nun. She hasn't yet taken her vows, especially the one of chastity, and is a major babe in her form-fitting novice's habit.

I was going to write that the funniest character in the movie is the boys' former high school coach (R. Lee Ermey, a former marine drill sergeant). It would be more accurate to say the same character would be funny in another movie, but is stopped cold by this one, even though the screenplay tries (when the boys ask Coach what to do with the kidnapped Judith, he replies, "kill her").

The lads don't idolize Neil Diamond merely in theory, but in the flesh, as well. Yes, Diamond himself appears in the film, kids himself, and sings a couple of songs. As a career decision, this ranks somewhere between being a good sport and professional suicide. Perhaps he should have reflected that the director, Dennis Dugan, has directed two Adam Sandler movies (both, it must be said, better than this).

Saving Silverman is Jason Biggs's fourth appearance in a row in a dumb sex comedy (in descending order of quality, they are *American Pie, Boys and Girls,* and *Loser*). It is time for him to strike out in a new direction; the announcement that he will appear in *American Pie II* does not seem to promise that.

Steve Zahn and Jack Black are, in the right movies, splendid comedy actors; Zahn was wonderful in *Happy, Texas,* and Jack Black stole his scenes in *High Fidelity* and *Jesus' Son.* Here they have approximately the charm of Wilson, the soccer ball. Amanda Peet and Amanda Detmer do no harm, although Peet is too nice to play a woman this mean. Lee Ermey is on a planet of his own. As for Neil Diamond, *Saving*

Silverman is his first appearance in a fiction film since *The Jazz Singer* (1980), and one can only marvel that he waited twenty years to appear in a second film, and found one even worse than his first one.

Say It Isn't So ★
R, 93 m., 2001

Chris Klein (Gilly Noble), Heather Graham (Jo Wingfield), Orlando Jones (Dig McCaffey), Sally Field (Valdine Wingfield), Richard Jenkins (Walter Wingfield), John Rothman (Larry), Jack Plotnick (Leon), Eddie Cibrian (Jack Mitchelson). Directed by James B. Rogers and produced by Bobby Farrelly, Peter Farrelly, and Bradley Thomas. Screenplay by Peter Gaulke and Gerry Swallow.

Comedy characters can't be successfully embarrassed for more than a few seconds at a time. Even then, it's best if they don't know what they've done wrong—if the joke's on them, and they don't get it. The "hair gel" scenes in *There's Something About Mary* are a classic example of embarrassment done right. *Say It Isn't So*, on the other hand, keeps a character embarrassed in scene after scene, until he becomes an ... embarrassment. The movie doesn't understand that embarrassment comes in a sudden painful flush of realization; drag it out, and it's not embarrassment anymore, but public humiliation, which is a different condition, and not funny.

The movie stars Heather Graham and Chris Klein as Jo and Gilly, a hairdresser and a dog-catcher who fall deeply in love and then discover they are brother and sister. Jo flees town to marry a millionaire jerk. Gilly lingers behind in public disgrace until he discovers they are not related after all. But since Jo's family wants her to marry the rich guy, everybody conspires to keep Gilly away. The movie tries for a long-running gag based on the fact that everybody in town mocks Gilly because he slept with his alleged sister. They even write rude remarks in the dust on his truck. This is not funny but merely repetitive.

The movie was produced by the Farrelly brothers, who in *There's Something About Mary* and *Kingpin* showed a finer understanding of the mechanics of comedy than they do here.

Say It Isn't So was directed by James B. Rogers from a screenplay by Peter Gaulke and Gerry Swallow, who show they are students of Farrellyism but not yet graduates. They include obligatory elements like physical handicaps, sexual miscalculations, intestinal difficulties, and weird things done to animals, but few of the gags really work. They know the words but not the music.

Consider a scene in which Chris Klein, as Gilly, punches a cow and his arm becomes lodged in just that portion of the cow's anatomy where both Gilly and the cow would least hope to find it. I can understand intellectually that this could be funny. But to be funny, the character would have to have a great deal invested in *not* appearing like the kind of doofus who would pull such a stunt. Gilly has been established as such a simpleton he has nothing to lose. The cow scene is simply one more cross for him to bear. There is in the movie a legless pilot (Orlando Jones) who prides himself on his heroic aerial abilities. If he had gotten stuck in the cow and been pulled legless down the street—now that would have been funny. Tasteless, yes, and cruel. But not tiresome.

That leads us to another of the movie's miscalculations. Its characters are not smart enough to be properly embarrassed. To be Jo or Gilly is already to be beyond embarrassment, since they wake up already clueless. The genius of *There's Something About Mary* and *Kingpin* was that the characters played by Ben Stiller and Woody Harrelson were smart, clever, played the angles—and still got disgraced. To pick on Gilly and Jo is like shooting fish in a barrel.

Chris Klein's character seems like someone who never gets the joke, who keeps smiling bravely as if everyone can't be laughing at him. We feel sorry for him, which is fatal for a comedy. Better a sharp, edgy character who deserves his comeuppance. Heather Graham's Jo, whose principal character trait is a push-up bra, isn't really engaged by the plot at all, but is blown hither and yon by the winds of fate.

That leaves three characters who are funny a lot of the time: Jo's parents, Valdine and Walter Wingfield (Sally Field and Richard Jenkins), and Dig McCaffey (Orlando Jones), the legless pilot. Valdine is a scheming, money-grubbing con woman who conceals from Gilly the fact that she is not his mother, so that Jo can marry the millionaire. And Walter is her terminally ill husband, communicating through an electronic voice amplifier, who bears a grudge against almost everyone he can see. These characters have the necessary meanness of spirit, and Dig McCaffey is so improbable, as a Jimi Hendrix look-alike, that he gets laughs by sheer incongruity.

On the TV clips, they show the scene where Jo gets so excited while cutting Gilly's hair that she takes a slice out of his ear. Since you have seen this scene, I will use it as an example of comic miscalculation. We see her scissors cutting through the flesh as they amputate an upper slope of his earlobe. This is not funny. It is cringe-inducing. Better to choose an angle where you can't see the actual cut at all, and then have his entire ear spring loose. Go for the laugh with the idea, not the sight, of grievous injury. And instead of giving Gilly an operation to reattach the missing flesh, have him go through the entire movie without an ear (make a subtle joke by having him always present his good ear to the camera). There are sound comic principles at work here, which *Say It Isn't So* doesn't seem to understand.

Note: The end credits include the usual obligatory outtakes from the movie. These are unique in that they are clearly real and authentic, not scripted. They demonstrate what we have suspected: that real outtakes are rarely funny.

Scary Movie ★ ★ ★
R, 85 m., 2000

Carmen Electra (Drew), Dave Sheridan (Doofy), Frank B. Moore (Not Drew's Boyfriend), Keenen Ivory Wayans (Masked Killer), Cheri Oteri (Gail Hailstorm), Regina Hall (Brenda), Mark McConchie (Drew's Dad), Karen Kruper (Drew's Mom), Anna Faris (Cindy), Shawn Wayans (Ray). Directed by Keenen Ivory Wayans and produced by Eric L. Gold and Lee R. Mayes. Screenplay by Shawn Wayans, Marlon Wayans, Buddy Johnson, Phil Beauman, Jason Friedberg, and Aaron Seltzer.

I recently published a book about movies I hated, and people have been asking me which reviews are harder to write—those about great movies or those about terrible ones. The answer is, neither. The most unreviewable movies are those belonging to the spoof genre—movies like *Airplane!* and *The Naked Gun* and all the countless spin-offs and retreads of the same basic idea.

Scary Movie is a film in that tradition: a raucous, satirical attack on slasher movies, teenage horror movies, and *The Matrix*. I saw the movie, I laughed, I took notes, and now I am at a loss to write the review. All of the usual critical categories and strategies collapse in the face of a film like this.

Shall I discuss the plot? There is none, really—only a flimsy clothesline to link some of the gags. The characters? They are all types or targets, not people. The dialogue? You can't review the dialogue in the original movies (like *I Know What You Did Last Summer*) because it is mindlessly functional, serving only to advance the plot. How can you discuss the satire, except to observe it is more mindless? (Some of the dialogue, indeed, seems lifted bodily from the earlier films and rotated slightly in the direction of satire.)

Faced with a dilemma like this, the experienced critic falls back on a reliable ploy. He gives away some of the best jokes and punch lines. He's like a buddy who has just walked out of a movie and tells you the funny stuff before you walk in.

I am tempted. I fight the impulse to tell you that when a character is asked for the name of a favorite scary movie, the answer is "Kazaam." That some of the scenes take place at B.A. Corpse High School. That the teenagers in the movie are played mostly by actors in their late twenties and thirties—and that the movie comments on this. That the movie's virgin has a certificate to prove it. That the invaluable Carmen Electra plays a character not coincidentally named Drew.

The movie takes a shotgun approach to horror and slasher movies, but if it has a single target, that would be Kevin Williamson, screenwriter of *Scream* and coinventor of the self-aware slasher subgenre. There is a sense in which *Scary Movie* is doing the same sort of self-referential humor as *Scream,* since it is not only directed by Keenen Ivory Wayans, cowritten by Shawn and Marlon Wayans (among others), and starring several Wayanses, but makes fun of various Wayans trademarks, especially the obligatory homophobic jokes. (There's a scene involving a closeted jock who can make love to his girlfriend only when she's wearing football shoulder pads.)

The movie also features the wild exaggeration of stereotypical African-American behavior, which is another Wayans specialty. Consider the scene where Regina Hall plays a black woman at *Shakespeare in Love* who shouts, "That ain't no man!" when Gwyneth Paltrow is on the screen, videotapes the movie from her seat, and carries on a cell phone conversation. Funny, though; now that I've written about it, I realize this is not intended to be a satire of African-American behavior, but an attack on the behavior of countless moviegoers, and Wayans has simply used Regina Hall as an example of nontraditional casting. Or maybe not.

The bottom line in reviewing a movie like this is, does it work? Is it funny? Yes, it is. Not funny with the shocking impact of *Airplane!*, which had the advantage of breaking new ground. But also not a tired wheeze like some of the lesser and later Leslie Nielsen films. To get your money's worth, you need to be familiar with the various teenage horror franchises, but if you are, *Scary Movie* delivers the goods.

Note: The original title of Scary Movie *was* Scream If You Know What I Did Last Halloween. *The original title of* Scream *was* Scary Movie. *Still available:* I Still Know What You Did the Summer Before Last.   ☞

The School of Flesh ★ ★ ★
R, 102 m., 1999

Isabelle Huppert (Dominique), Vincent Martinez (Quentin), Vincent Lindon (Chris), Marthe Keller (Madame Thorpe), Francois Berleand (Soukaz), Daniele Dubroux (Dominique's Friend), Bernard Le Coq (Cordier), Roxane Mesquida (Marine). Directed by Benoit Jacquot and produced by Fabienne Vonier. Screenplay by Jacques Fieschi, based on the novel by Yukio Mishima.

We look at French films about love like schoolchildren with our noses pressed against a window. We are so direct about love in North America. We date, we have relationships, we fall in love—as if a natural, unconscious process is taking place. In France, love is more like a discussion, a debate. One has to be right or wrong about it. Not about the other person—about the idea of love itself.

"I don't think you'll go the distance," the older woman says to the younger man in Benoit Jacquot's *The School of Flesh*. Later in the film, he tells her, "One day I decided to live without feelings." The first time she takes him out to dinner, he uses his fingers to pick up the fish on his plate. "Put it down," she says. "Why?" Her face betrays absolutely no expression: "You're with me."

One guesses that in another restaurant, with another woman, he would have used his fork for the fish. He is not without some sophistication; she found him as a bartender in a gay club. Using his fingers was a way of testing her; her response was the answer to an exam question. The exam involved the matter of class differences. They are not concerned that he is working class and she is a professional; what matters is the tug-of-war and who will win as their styles clash.

It's a good question whether romance is involved at all in *The School of Flesh*, which is based on a Japanese novel by Yukio Mishima, who also wrote of class and power. Love is mentioned at various times, but is it a fact or a concept? How much is sex involved, for that matter? The man and woman have sex together, yes, but it doesn't seem as important to them as the battle of wills they engage in. The first time they see each other, they issue a mutual challenge with their eyes. The look they exchange isn't about lust, but power.

That first meeting is in a bar with a primarily gay clientele. Dominique (Isabelle Huppert), who works in the fashion business, sees Quentin (Vincent Martinez) behind the bar. He's a boxer, is twenty years younger, looks tough, has cold eyes—but not colder than Dominique's. Huppert, who is famous for impassivity in her movie roles, has rarely revealed less than here (Stephen Holden wrote that her tears appear "to emanate from a realm somewhere beyond feeling"). Their eyes lock, they size each other up, she leaves and she is back the next night.

She knows from a transvestite in the bar that Quentin is bisexual. Doesn't matter. She is in the grip of the kind of erotomania that must have what it must have. He realizes this and plays with it; there's a scene where he plays a video game in an arcade while she shifts impatiently on her feet, asks that they leave, leaves alone, turns around, comes back—and only then does he acknowledge her. The twist in the movie comes when he starts to become as obsessed with her as she is with him. And when she finds out his secrets—not the ones she thought she knew, but others.

I cannot imagine a Hollywood movie like this. Audiences would be baffled. Imagine two fairly tough stars—a younger guy like Vincent Gallo, say, and an alluring older woman like Susan Sarandon. I can imagine their sex scenes (indeed, I've seen them, between Sarandon and James Spader in *White Palace*). I can imagine conversations in cafés and arguments in bedrooms. What I cannot imagine is the holding back, the restraint, the intellectual side, as the two characters engage in a debate about the proper form of an affair. Ever hear the one about the three guys who see a couple through a window? "What are they doing?" asks the Englishman. "Making love," says the American. "Very badly," says the Frenchman.

Scream 3 ★ ★
R, 116 m., 2000

Neve Campbell (Sidney Prescott), Courteney Cox Arquette (Gale Weathers), David Arquette (Dewey Riley), Parker Posey (Jennifer Jolie), Scott Foley (Roman Bridge), Deon Richmond (Tyson Fox), Patrick Dempsey (Detective Kincaid), Lance Henriksen (John Milton), Liev Schreiber (Cotton Weary), Jenny McCarthy (Sarah Darling), Patrick Warburton (Guard). Directed by Wes Craven and produced by Cathy Konrad, Kevin Williamson, and Marianne Maddalena. Screenplay by Ehren Kruger.

The difference between a trilogy and a sequel, we're told in *Scream 3*, is that sequels go on and on, while a trilogy has a beginning, a middle, and an end: "In a trilogy, nobody's safe. Even the hero can die in the final chapter." So explains one of the movie buffs in the third of this self-aware slasher series in which the characters know all the horror clichés and get trapped in them anyway.

The action this time moves the key surviving actors from the previous *Screams* to Hollywood, where a horror film named *Stab 3* is under way. There is a death, and then another: The killer is slashing the actors in the same order they die in the screenplay. But the third victim may be hard to predict: "There were three different versions of the script," an executive explains, "to keep the ending off the Internet. I don't know which version the killer read." No matter; the fax machine rings, and it's a call from the killer, transmitting revised script pages.

That problem of spoilers on the Net could inspire a slasher movie of its own (serial killer, under delusion he is Freddy Krueger, kills to prove a Web rumor site is wrong). In an attempt to keep Websites from revealing the movie's secrets, Miramax's Dimension division delayed screenings until the last possible moment, and even then banned many Web-based critics from attending (although the lads from Playboy.com were hunkered down happily in the row in front of me).

Anyone who would reveal the identity of the killer in *Scream 3* would in any event be the lowest form of life, since the secret is absolutely unguessable. Why? Because the identity is absolutely arbitrary. It could be anyone in the movie or (this would be a neat twist) none of the above. The characters are so thin they're transparent. They function primarily to scream, split up when they should stick together, go alone into basements and dark rooms, and make ironic references to horror clichés and earlier movies in the series. The director, Wes Craven, covered the self-aware horror genre splendidly in *Wes Craven's New Nightmare* (1994), and this is the lite version.

Some of it is fun. You can play spot-the-cameo with visiting celebs like Roger Corman, Kevin Smith, and Carrie Fisher (she's a studio archivist who explains, "I was up for Princess Leia, but you know who gets it—the one who sleeps with George Lucas"). And you can appreciate the logic behind Parker Posey's reasoning. She plays the actress hired to portray TV journalist Gale Weathers (Courteney Cox Arquette), and tells her, "Everywhere you go, I'm gonna follow you, so if he wants to kill you, you'll be there to be killed, and he won't need to kill me."

Scream 3 is essentially an interlacing of irony and gotcha! scenes. The monster in his (or her) fright mask can be anywhere at any time and jump into the frame at any moment. All we know for sure is that two or three scares will be false. (When will the characters in these movies learn that when victims are being "cut up into fish sticks," it is *not funny* to sneak up behind friends to scare them?)

Neve Campbell is back as the key character, a woman so traumatized she has changed her name, moved to Monterey, and works for a crisis hot line. The camera loves her. She could become a really big star and giggle at clips from this film at her AFI tribute. Also starring are David Arquette as a former deputy, now a would-be security guard who's still in love with Gale Weathers; Scott Foley as the *Stab 3* director; Deon Richmond as a guy who knows all the movie conventions; Liev Schreiber as an ex-con talk show host; Patrick Dempsey as a cop; Lance Henriksen as a demented horror film director with old secrets; and Jenny McCarthy as an actress who does or does not get killed, but certainly wears a dress we will see again in *Playboy*'s annual "Sex in the Cinema" feature. Patrick Warburton, a rising action star, has a funny bit as a "professional celebrity guard" whose clients have "included Julia Roberts and Salman Rushdie."

My own feeling is relief that the series is at last ended. If *Scream* (1996) was like a funny joke, *Scream 2* (1997) was like somebody telling you, "Here's how I heard that joke," and *Scream 3* is like somebody who won't believe you've already heard it. What I will remember from the movie is that everyone uses cell phones constantly, which is convenient for the screenplay, since the characters can be anywhere and still call for help or threaten one another. Remember the 1980 horror movie named *Don't Answer the Phone?* If the *Scream 3* gang had taken that advice, there would have been no movie, just a lot of lonely characters scattered all over California, waiting for calls.

See Spot Run ★ ½
PG, 94 m., 2001

David Arquette (Gordon Smith), Michael Clarke Duncan (Agent Murdoch), Leslie Bibb (Stephanie), Joe Viterelli (Gino Valente), Angus T. Jones (James), Steven R. Schirripa (Arliss Santino), Anthony Anderson (Benny), Paul Sorvino (Sonny Talia). Directed by John Whitesell and produced by Robert Simonds, Tracey Trench, and Andrew Deane. Screenplay by George Gallo, Dan Baron, and Christian Faber, based on a story by Stuart Gibbs, Craig Titley, and Gallo.

See Spot Run is pitched at the same intellectual level as the earlier stories involving Spot, which I found so immensely involving in the first grade. There are a few refinements. The characters this time are named Gordon, Stephanie, and James, instead of Dick and Jane. And I don't recall the *Spot* books describing the hero rolling around in doggy poo, or a gangster getting his testicles bitten off, but times change. The gangster is named Sonny Talia, in a heroic act of restraint by the filmmakers, who could have named him Gino with no trouble at all.

The movie is a fairly desperate PG-rated comedy about a dog that has been highly trained for the FBI's canine corps. After it bites off one of Talia's indispensables, the mob boss (Paul Sorvino) orders a hit on the dog, which is hustled into a version of the witness protection program, only to accidentally end up in the possession of young James (Angus T. Jones) and his baby-sitting neighbor, Gordon (David Arquette), who has a crush on James's mother, Stephanie (Leslie Bibb).

This is all setup for a series of slapstick comedy ventures, in which Gordon is humiliated and besmeared while the dog races about proving it is the most intelligent mammal in the picture. The most excruciating sequence has Gordon shinnying up a gutter pipe, which collapses (as all movie gutter pipes always do), tearing off his underpants and depositing him in one of Spot's large, damp, and voluminous gifts to the ecology. When Gordon is thoroughly smeared with caca, what do you think the odds are that (1) the lawn sprinkler system comes on, and (2) the police arrive and demand an explanation?

Another long sequence involves the destruction of a pet store, as mobsters chase the dog and Gordon gets encased in a large ball of bubble wrap, which is inflated by helium, causing him to . . . oh, never mind. And don't get me started on the scene where he lights the zebra fart.

Movies like this demonstrate that when it comes to stupidity and vulgarity, only the best will do for our children. There seems to be some kind of desperate downward trend in American taste, so that when we see a dog movie like this we think back nostalgically to the *Beethoven* dog pictures, which now represent a cultural high-water mark. Consider that there was a time in our society when children were entertained by the *Lassie* pictures, and you can see that the national taste is rapidly spiraling down to the level of a whoopee cushion.

And yes, of course, there are many jokes in *See Spot Run* involving the passing of gas and the placing of blame. Also a fight with two deaf women. Also an electrified dog collar that is activated by a TV channel changer, causing David Arquette to levitate while sparks fly out of his orifices. And a bus that slides over a cliff. And an FBI agent named "Cassavetes," which must be a masochistic in-joke by the filmmakers to remind themselves of how far they have fallen from their early ideals.

The one actor who emerges more or less unharmed is Michael Clarke Duncan, the gentle giant from *The Green Mile,* who is the dog's FBI handler and plays his scenes with the joy of a man whose stream of consciousness must run like this: *No matter how bad this movie is, at least it's better than working for the City of Chicago Department of Streets and Sanitation. I'm still wading through doggy do, but at least now I'm getting paid a movie star salary for doing it.*

See the Sea and A Summer Dress
★ ★ ★
NO MPAA RATING, 52 m. and 15 m., 1999

Sasha Hails (Sasha), Marina de Van (Tatiana). Directed by Francois Ozon and produced by Oliver Delbosc and Marc Missonnier. Screenplay by Ozon.

Hitchcock believed that suspense came not in action, but in anticipation: not the bomb exploding, but the bomb under the table, waiting to explode. From the first shots of Francois Ozon's *See the Sea,* we sense impending disaster, but we're not sure what form it will take.

There is a simple situation, involving two women and a baby at an isolated beach cottage, and yet the possibilities are many, and we speculate about first one outcome, then another.

Sasha (Sasha Hails), an Englishwoman, is living in a cottage in France with her ten-month-old daughter. Her husband is expected to join them, but seems distant and unreachable. A backpacker knocks at the door. This is Tatiana (Marina de Van), a sullen, expressionless young woman who wants to pitch her tent in the yard. She doesn't ask so much as demand. Sasha's reply is curious: "It's my husband's property. I'd have to ask him." Eventually, maybe because she is lonely or intrigued, Sasha lets Tatiana stay.

What will the outcome be? Ozon creates the atmosphere of hot, drowsy summer moral laxity; we are reminded a little of Laura Dern's erotic boredom in *Smooth Talk.* There is the possibility of sex between the women, reinforced by scenes of casual nudity, but we somehow know that's not the point: Something sinister will happen. And then we're worried about that baby.

Sasha is a loving mother, billing and cooing, but a shockingly irresponsible one. She leaves the infant alone in the bath. Later, she leaves it on the beach while she wanders into a nearby wood, a gay cruising area where one of the anonymous men among the trees supplies what she abruptly indicates she desires. One day Sasha goes into town, and asks Tatiana to baby-sit.

This is not a woman you would choose for a baby-sitter. She is dirty and deliberately ill-mannered, bolting her food and then lifting up her plate to lick it clean. She asks questions in a challenging manner, and her face conceals what she thinks of the answers. We have seen her play a particularly nasty little secret trick on Sasha. In her aimlessness she resembles the heroine of Agnes Varda's *Vagabond,* but that woman was a victim, and Tatiana is not a victim.

The outcome is a surprise, and yet in a way we were waiting for it. The movie is about the waiting. It is fifty-two minutes long, and that's about the right length. Longer, and the plot would have had to add unnecessary details to the spare, clean, ominous style.

On the same program is a fifteen-minute short subject, also by Ozon, named *A Summer Dress,* which is lighter in tone. Apparently filmed on the same beach, it also uses the forest area where men cruise for sex, and also places a heterosexual encounter there, with watching eyes. The film follows a young man, who is perhaps gay, as he goes to the beach for a swim and is boldly invited into the woods by a woman who says she is his age (she looks older). He accompanies her, and what he discovers provides the film's payoff.

Both films are notable for the way they quietly slip into the hidden sexual spaces of their characters. Hollywood movies seem determined these days to present sex as an activity not unrelated to calisthenics. What Ozon knows about sex is like what Hitchcock knows about suspense: not the explosion, but the waiting for the bomb to go off.

Series 7: The Contenders ★ ★ ½
R, 86 m., 2001

Brooke Smith (Dawn), Glenn Fitzgerald (Jeff), Marylouise Burke (Connie), Richard Venture (Franklin), Michael Kaycheck (Tony), Merritt Wever (Lindsay), Angelina Phillips (Doria), Nada Despotovich (Michelle). Directed by Daniel Minahan and produced by Jason Kliot, Katie Roumel, Christine Vachon, and Joana Vicente. Screenplay by Minahan.

Sometimes the most astonishing thing about a movie is hidden right in plain sight. *Series 7: The Contenders* is a satire on reality TV, taking the world of *Survivor* and *Temptation Island* to its logical extension with a TV show where the contestants kill one another. This is not a new idea; the movie is similar to *The Tenth Victim* (1965) and has also been compared to *Death Race 2000, Running Man, EDtv,* and *The Truman Show* in the way it uses actual lives as TV fodder. The classic short story *The Most Dangerous Game* is also lurking somewhere in its history.

No, it's not the idea that people will kill each other for entertainment that makes *Series 7* jolting. What the movie correctly perceives is that somewhere along the line we've lost all sense of shame in our society. It's not what people will do, but what they'll say—what

they eagerly reveal about themselves—that *Series 7* assimilates without even being aware of it. The killing part is the satire, and we expect that to be exaggerated. The dialogue, I suspect, is not intended as satirical at all, but simply reflects the way people think these days. There are still many Americans who choose not to reveal every detail of their private lives the moment a camera is pointed at them, but they don't get on TV much.

Allow me a digression. I was watching *Jerry Springer* the other day, as I often do when I want to investigate the limits of the permissible, and there was a "guest" who was complaining that his girlfriend would not respect his fetish. He likes to vomit during sex. He even had the word for his specialty, but I've forgotten it; "nauseaphilia," no doubt. It was amazing that this guy would reveal his secret on television, but even more astonishing that the girlfriend would also appear, in order to testify how disgusting it was. Anyone so desperate for fame that they will put themselves in a position like that should think, deeply and urgently, about the positive aspects of anonymity.

But what do people say when they meet Springer guests? (1) "Ugh! That was disgusting! You are depraved!" or (2) "I saw you on *Springer.* How do you get on that show?" I suspect the answer is (2).

I make these observations because the characters in *Series 7* have no pride and no shame, and that's more interesting than their willingness to kill one another. The killing is just the gimmick—the satirical hook of the movie—but their willingness to appear on TV and explain the details of their fatal diseases, or allow the cameras to see their filthy hovels, is illuminating. It suggests that fame is the antidote for almost any misfortune.

The movie stars Brooke Smith, that wonderful actress from *Uncle Vanya on 42nd Street,* as Dawn, eight months pregnant, who explains that she must kill people and win the game for the sake of her unborn child. This is a twisted logic with a kind of beauty to it: She kills to defend life. Other contestants include a teenager (Merritt Wever) whose parents drive her to shoot-outs; an ER nurse (Marylouise Burke) whose bloody job and bloody TV role overlap; a father (Michael Kaycheck) with a wife and three kids (he wants to provide for his family);

a guy who lurks in a trailer park (Richard Venture); and a testicular cancer victim (Glenn Fitzgerald), who may be in the game because he wants to die.

The Brooke Smith character is the best drawn and most clearly seen, and as she walks into a convenience store and starts blasting away, we notice the reactions of the bystanders. They understand. They know this is only TV. They are not horrified but intrigued, and they're no doubt wondering, "Am I on now?" The overlap between this behavior and some of the actions during the San Diego school shooting recently are uncanny, and disturbing. The kid who went back into the school with the video camera was interviewed *about how much he had been interviewed.*

Real life has caught up with *Series 7* and overlapped it. The movie was filmed before the first airing of a *Survivor* episode, and must have seemed more radical in the screenplay stage than it does now. We observe that the writer-director, Daniel Minahan, has a good feel for the slick graphics and theme songs of this brand of TV, and knows how the bumpers and the teasers work. But the movie has one joke and tells it too often, for too long. It leaves you with time to think about television, celebrity, and shame. Remind me to tell you sometime about the *other* guests on that *Springer* episode.

Set Me Free ★ ★ ★
NO MPAA RATING, 94 m., 2000

Karine Vanasse (Hanna), Alexandre Merineau (Paul), Pascale Bussieres (The Mother), Miki Manojlovic (The Father), Charlotte Christeler (Laura), Nancy Huston (The Teacher), Monique Mercure (The Grandmother), Anne-Marie Cadieux (The Prostitute). Directed by Lea Pool and produced by Lorraine Richard. Screenplay by Pool.

It is not reassuring when your father tells you, "Books are our only true friends." Where does that leave you—or your mom, or your brother? And yet what he says may be worth hearing. Hanna, the heroine of *Set Me Free*, is a thirteen-year-old growing up in 1963 in Montreal. Her father is distant, disturbed, incapable of supporting his family, and blames everyone but

himself. Her mother is meek and suicidal. It's up to Hanna to find her own way in life, and that's what she does, at the movies.

Art can be a great consolation when you are a lonely teenager. It speaks directly to you. You find the right movie, the right song, the right book, and you are not alone. Books and movies are not our only friends, but they help us find true friends, and tell them apart from the crowd.

One day in the rain, Hanna (Karine Vanasse) sneaks into a theater and sees Jean-Luc Godard's *My Life to Live* (1962), where even the title is significant. It stars Anna Karina as an independent woman in Paris who leaves her husband and works as a prostitute to support herself. She keeps a distance from her clients; cigarettes form a wall between her and the world, and there is a famous shot where, as a man embraces her, she sullenly blows out smoke.

Not the character you would choose as a role model for a thirteen-year-old girl. But Hanna is unhappy and confused. She has just had her first period and does not quite understand it. Her father is cold to her mother, her brother, and herself, but then turns on the charm. There is no money in the household; her father (Miki Manojlovic) calls himself a writer but has published nothing, her mother (Pascale Bussieres) works as a seamstress, and the pawnbroker knows the kids by name. In this confusion, Hanna finds encouragement in the independent woman of the movie, who holds herself aloof, who is self-contained, who lets no man hurt her.

In her life there is some happiness. She idolizes her schoolteacher (Nancy Huston), who looks a little like Anna Karina. She makes a close school friend named Laura, and they share their first kiss together. Does this mean they will grow up to be lesbians? Maybe, but probably not; what it probably means is that they are so young that kissing is a mysterious activity not yet directly wired to sex and gender, and Laura offers tenderness Hanna desperately requires.

In school, like all the students, she is called upon to stand up and give her life details. This leads to her admission that her parents are not married. Religion? "My father is Jewish, my mother is Catholic," she says. And which is she? "Judaism passes the religion through the mother, which would make me Catholic, but Catholicism passes through the father, which would make me Jewish," she says. "Myself, I don't care."

Her father is a refugee from the Holocaust, an intellectual. Their apartment is filled with books. Her mother fell for him the first time she saw him, and got pregnant at sixteen with Paul, her brother. When her father found this out two years later, he decided to care for them, and soon Hanna was born. In a moment of revelation, Hanna's father tells her that he was married in Europe, and that although his wife may have died in the camps, he has no proof, and refuses to think of her as dead. Her mother also confides in Hanna. Despite their troubles, she will never leave her husband: "I need him."

Set Me Free is set in 1963, when the films of the French New Wave would have been influential in French-speaking Quebec. In some of its details, it resembles François Truffaut's *The 400 Blows*, which is about a young boy whose parents are unhappy, and who keeps a shrine to Balzac in his bedroom. Hanna's Balzac is Karina in *My Life to Live*. Leaning against a wall, smoking insolently, not giving a damn, Karina provides not a role model but a strategy. It is not only possible to stand aside from the pain of your life, it can even become a personal style.

The movie gets a little confused toward the end, I think, as its writer and director, Lea Pool, tries to settle things that could have been left unresolved. Hanna's tentative walk on the wild side is awkwardly handled. You walk out not quite satisfied. Later, when the movie settles in your mind, its central theme becomes clear. We grow by choosing those we admire, and pulling ourselves up on the hand they extend. For Hanna, the hands come from her teacher, from her friend, and from the woman in the movie she sees over and over. "I am responsible," says Karina in the movie. "I am responsible," says Hanna to herself. It is her life to live.

Sexy Beast ★ ★ ★ ½
R, 88 m., 2001

Ray Winstone (Gary "Gal" Dove), Ben Kingsley (Don "Malky" Logan), Ian McShane (Teddy Bass), Amanda Redman (Deedee Dove), Cavan Kendall (Aitch), Julianne White (Jackie), Alvaro Monje (Enrique), James Fox (Harry). Directed by Jonathan Glazer and produced by Jeremy Thomas. Screenplay by Louis Mellis and David Scinto.

Who would have guessed that the most savage mad-dog frothing gangster in recent movies would be played by—Ben Kingsley? Ben Kingsley, who was Gandhi, and the accountant in *Schindler's List*, and the publisher in *Betrayal*, and Dr. Watson in *Without a Clue*? Ben Kingsley, whose previous criminal was the financial wizard Meyer Lansky in *Bugsy*? Yes, Ben Kingsley. Or, as his character, Don Logan, says in *Sexy Beast*, "Yes! Yes! Yes! Yes! Yes."

Logan spits the words into the face of a retired London gangster named Dove. He's an inch away, spitting like a drill sergeant, his face red with anger, the veins throbbing on his forehead, his body coiled in rage. Dove (Ray Winstone), whose nickname is "Gal," lives in a villa on the Costa del Sol in Spain with his wife, Deedee (Amanda Redman), also retired, she from the porn business. He has no desire to return to London to assist in "one last job," a bank heist being masterminded by Logan's boss, Teddy (Ian McShane).

But you can't say no to Don Logan. This is what Dove says about him before he arrives in Spain, and when we meet him, we agree. Logan is dangerous not because he is tough, but because he is fearless and mad. You cannot intimidate a man who has no ordinary feelings. Logan is like a pit bull, hard-wired and untrainable. It's in his nature to please his master, and frighten people. He has a disconcerting habit of suddenly barking out absurdities; he has a lopsided flywheel.

Sexy Beast is in a tradition of movies about Cockney villains. It goes on the list with *The Long Good Friday* and *The Limey*. It loves its characters: Dove, the gangster gone soft; Logan, who is driven to impose his will on others; Teddy, who has a cockeyed plan to drill into a safe-deposit vault from the pool of the Turkish bath next to the bank; and Harry (James Fox), who owns the bank and thinks he is Teddy's lover when in fact he is simply the man who owns the bank.

The heist is absurd in its own way, once

Dove gets to London and helps mastermind it. The burglars have total access to the Turkish bath, but it never occurs to them to drain the pool, and so they wear breathing gear while drilling through the walls of the vault next door. The vault predictably fills with water, leading to a wonderful moment when a crook opens a deposit box, finds a container inside, opens it expecting diamonds, and gets a surprise.

The movie opens on an ominous note. While Dove works on his suntan, a boulder bounces down the slope behind his villa, barely misses him, and lands in the pool. In the movie's second act, Don Logan is the boulder. Kingsley's performance has to be seen to be believed. He is angry, seductive, annoyed, wheedling, fed up, ominous, and out of his mind with frustration. I didn't know Kingsley had such notes inside him. Obviously, he can play anyone.

His best scene may be the one when Logan gets on the airplane to fly out of Spain, and the attendant asks him to put out his cigarette. Anyone who lights a cigarette on an airplane these days is asking for it, but Logan is begging for a fight. Notice the improvised lies with which he talks his way out of jail and possibly into a nice check from the airline.

Ray Winstone's work is as strong, but not as flashy. He can play monsters too: He was an abusive father in Gary Oldman's *Nil by Mouth* and Tim Roth's *The War Zone*, and it says something when those two actors cast him as their villain. His Dove is a gangster gone soft, fond of the good life, doting on his wife, able to intimidate civilians but frankly frightened of Logan.

The movie's humor is inseparable from its brutality. The crime boss Teddy (suave and vicious) offers to drive Dove to the airport after the bank job, and that leads to a series of unexpected developments—some jolting, others with deep irony. These are hard men. They could have the Sopranos for dinner, throw up, and have them again. ·   ☞

Shadow Magic ★ ★

PG, 115 m., 2001

Jared Harris (Raymond Wallace), Xia Yu (Liu Jinglun), Xing Yufei (Ling), Liu Peiqi (Master Ren), Lu Liping (Madame Ren), Wang Jingming (Old Liu), Li Yusheng (Lord Tan), Zhang Yukui (Lao Chang). Directed and produced by Ann Hu. Screenplay by Huang Dan, Tang Louyi, Kate Raisz, Bob McAndrew, and Ann Hu.

In Peking in 1902, an Englishman arrives with a hand-cranked projector and a box of the earliest silent movies. Ann Hu's *Shadow Magic* tells the story of how he overcomes tradition to build an audience for the new art form, makes a local disciple, films the people of China, and eventually shows his magic to the empress. It also tells the story of his disciple, a photographer's assistant who is engaged to marry a woman for money but is in love with the daughter of an opera star.

The Englishman, we learn, is based on a real person, although no one seems to have remembered his name (the film calls him Raymond Wallace). The China in the movie may be based on a real China, but it falls too easily into the forms of movie formulas. Watching the movie, I was reminded of a 1922 novel named *Kimono*, by John Paris, that did an extraordinary job of suggesting how *different* Japan seemed to a British visitor in the early years of the century. Surely China was as intimidating, yet the values and customs in this movie seem familiar to a modern Western viewer. The Englishman should be more of a stranger, and China should be more of a strange land.

Consider a scene late in the movie where Wallace (Jared Harris) and his friend Liu Jinglun (Xia Yu), a young photographer, show the new invention to the Dowager Empress. The screening goes well until there is a fire (film combusts easily in *Shadow Magic*, almost on cue), and the foreigner is condemned to death before the empress pardons him, smiling benevolently as she praises the new art form. Is this what would have happened? Surely to be admitted to the presence of the empress a century ago was fraught with more mystery and drama than the movie suggests, and perhaps the empress herself would have been less like good Queen Victoria, cheerfully hailing progress. The movie is more concerned with the story line (premiere-fire-threat-rescue) than with painting the time and place.

The character Liu Jinglun is painted as an ambitious young man who instantly perceives the wonder of the new invention, while almost everyone else (except, of course, the audiences) seems hostile or indifferent. History suggests it was not this way. Movies were eagerly embraced by the curious in all countries, and the opposition by Liu's possessive father seems contrived (he fears a threat to his photography studio). The romantic subplots involving Liu seem composed on autopilot: There is an arranged marriage with a tubby older widow, which must be avoided if he's to fulfill his secret love for the beautiful young Ling (Xing Yufei).

What the movie does achieve is a lively sense of color and energy. As Wallace and Liu photograph local citizens, we're reminded of *The Star Maker,* a 1995 film by Guiseppe Tornatore *(Cinema Paradiso)* about an itinerant photographer who travels the back roads of Sicily, filming people. He pretends to be making Hollywood screen tests, but actually he is recording something much more precious— the faces of those people at that time.

Shadow Magic ends with some of the footage Raymond and Liu have shot, and that suggests a different kind of film that might have been made. Why not, instead of romantic intrigue and family quarrels in a mildly melodramatic plot, make more of an effort to reconstruct what it must have really been like for that nameless Englishman with his equipment? Why not emphasize the barriers of language, race, and custom, and tell us a little more about the intricacies of the earliest cameras and projectors? Why not trust the subject matter instead of shaping it all to fit a formula? I got the feeling all through *Shadow Magic* that the real story was offscreen.

Shadow of the Vampire ★ ★ ★ ½
R, 93 m., 2001

John Malkovich (F. W. Murnau), Willem Dafoe (Max Schreck), Cary Elwes (Fritz Wagner), Eddie Izzard (Gustav von Wangenheim), Udo Kier (Albin Grau), Catherine McCormack (Greta Schroeder), Ronan Vibert (Wolfgang Muller), Ingeborga Dapkunaite (Micheline). Directed by E. Elias Merhige and produced by Nicolas Cage and Jeff Levine. Screenplay by Steven Katz.

The best of all vampire movies is *Nosferatu,* made by F. W. Murnau in Germany in 1922. Its eerie power only increases with age. Watching it, we don't think about screenplays or special effects. We think: This movie believes in vampires. Max Schreck, the mysterious actor who played Court Orlock the vampire, is so persuasive we never think of the actor, only of the creature.

Shadow of the Vampire, a wicked new movie about the making of *Nosferatu,* has an explanation for Schreck's performance: He really was a vampire. This is not a stretch. It is easier for me to believe Schreck was a vampire than that he was an actor. Examine any photograph of him in the role and decide for yourself. Consider the ratlike face, the feral teeth, the bat ears, the sunken eyes, the fingernail claws that seem to have grown in the tomb. Makeup? He makes the word irrelevant.

In *Shadow of the Vampire,* director E. Elias Merhige and his writer, Steven Katz, do two things at the same time. They make a vampire movie of their own, and they tell a backstage story about the measures that a director will take to realize his vision. Murnau is a man obsessed with his legacy; he lectures his crew on the struggle to create art, promising them, "Our poetry, our music, will have a context as certain as the grave." What they have no way of knowing is that some of them will go to the grave themselves in the service of his poetry. He's made a deal with Schreck: Perform in my movie, and you can dine on the blood of the leading lady.

John Malkovich plays Murnau as a theoretician who is utterly uninterested in human lives other than his own. His work justifies everything. Like other silent directors he has a flamboyant presence, stalking his sets with glasses pushed up on his forehead, making pronouncements, issuing orders, self-pitying about the fools he has to work with and the price he has to pay for his art. After we meet key members of the cast and crew in Berlin, the production moves to Czechoslovakia, where Schreck awaits. Murnau explains that the great actor is so dedicated to his craft that he lives in character the clock around, and must never be spoken to except as Count Orlock.

"Willem Dafoe is Max Schreck." I put quotes around that because it's not just a line for a movie ad but the truth: He embodies the Schreck of *Nosferatu* so uncannily that when real scenes from the silent classic are slipped into the frame, we don't notice much difference. But he is not simply Schreck—or not simply Schreck as the vampire. He is also a venomous and long-suffering creature with unruly appetites, and he angers Murnau by prematurely dining on the cinematographer. Murnau shouts in rage that he *needs* the cinematographer, and now will have to go to Berlin and hire another one. He begs Schreck to keep his appetites in check until the final scene. Schreck muses aloud, "I do not think we need . . . the writer . . ." Scenes like this work as inside comedy, but they also have a practical side: The star is hungry, and because he is the star, he can make demands. This would not be the first time a star has eaten a writer alive.

The fragrant Catherine McCormack plays Greta, the actress whose throat Schreck's fangs will plunge into, for real, in the final scene. She, of course, does not understand this, and is a trouper, putting up with Schreck for the sake of art even though he reeks of decay. Concerned about her close-ups, intoxicated by the joy of stardom, she has no suspicions until, during her crucial scene, her eyes stray to the mirror—and Schreck, of course, is not reflected.

The movie does an uncanny job of re-creating the visual feel of Murnau's film. There are shots that look the way moldy basements smell. This material doesn't lend itself to subtlety, and Malkovich and Dafoe chew their lines like characters who know they are always being observed (some directors do more acting on their sets than the actors do). The supporting cast is a curiously, intriguingly, mixed bag: Cary Elwes as Murnau's cinematographer Fritz Wagner (not the one who is eaten), Eddie Izzard as one of the actors, the legendary Udo Kier as the producer.

Vampires for some reason are funny as well as frightening. Maybe that's because the conditions of their lives are so absurd. Some of Anne Rice's vampires have a fairly entertaining time of it, but someone like Schreck, here, seems doomed to spend eternity in psychic and physical horror. There is a nice passage where he submits to a sort of interview from his colleagues, remaining "in character" while answering questions about vampirism. He doesn't make it sound like fun.

"Every horror film seems to become absurd after the passage of years," Pauline Kael wrote in her review of *Nosferatu*, "yet the horror remains." Here Merhige gives us scenes absurd and frightening at the same time, as when Schreck catches a bat that flies into a room, and eats it. Or when Murnau, knowing all that he knows about Schreck, reassures his leading lady: "All you have to do is relax and, as they say, the vampire will do all the work."

Note: Ebert's review of Nosferatu *is at www. suntimes.com/ebert/greatmovies/.*

Shaft ★ ★ ½
R, 98 m., 2000

Samuel L. Jackson (John Shaft), Vanessa Williams (Carmen), Jeffrey Wright (Peoples Hernandez), Christian Bale (Walter Wade), Busta Rhymes (Rasaan), Dan Hedaya (Jack Roselli), Toni Collette (Diane Palmieri), Richard Roundtree (Uncle John), Lee Tergesen (Luger). Directed by John Singleton and produced by Singleton and Scott Rudin. Screenplay by Singleton, Richard Price, and Shane Salerno.

John Singleton's *Shaft* is a blaxploitation film with a modern urban drama trapped inside. Or maybe it's the other way around. On the one hand, we have John Shaft telling a pickup, "It's my duty to please your booty." On the other hand, we have a scene between a rich kid and a drug dealer that's so well written and acted it's chilling.

At the center of the tug-of-war, pulled both ways and enjoying it, is Samuel L. Jackson, as a tough cop who throws his badge back at a judge (literally) and becomes a freelance vigilante. The story's broad outlines are familiar not only from early 1970s black exploitation movies, but also from the early *Dirty Harry* pictures, and when a top cop orders Shaft to get out of his precinct, it's like he's reciting dialogue from the classics.

The movie has the obligatory elements of black exploitation (big cars, drugs, cigars, guns, sleazy nightclubs, gold chains, racism, babes, black leather coats, expensive booze, crooked white cops). But a newer sensibility sneaks in, probably thanks to a screenplay primarily by Richard Price, who wrote *Clockers* and specializes in dialogue that allows the characters some poetry; I like lines like "It's Giuliani time!"

On top of reports that Singleton and Jackson had many disagreements on the set, there were stories that neither of them much liked the Price screenplay, maybe because it nailed the small moments but missed the broader Shaftian strokes. Whatever compromises were made, the result is a movie more interesting than it might have been: not just a retread of the old movie, but Shaft as more complicated than before, and with well-observed supporting characters.

Jackson is at the center of the action, "too black for the uniform, too blue for the brothers," wearing a wicked goatee that looks like it was designed by a comic book artist. He's a cop made angry when a rich man's son (Christian Bale) murders a black youth, gets an easy bail, and skips to Switzerland. As one of the first on the crime scene, Shaft believes that a waitress (Toni Collette) saw more than she admits. Two years pass, the rich kid returns to the country, Shaft nabs him, and then the plot involves his partner (Busta Rhymes), the drug kingpin (Jeffrey Wright), the sexy narcotics cop (Vanessa Williams), the larcenous cop (Dan Hedaya), and his partner Luger (Lee Tergesen). Always look twice at a cop named Luger.

The casting here makes for some interesting echoes. Hedaya, of course, played the crooked cop in The Hurricane, and Christian Bale had the title role in American Psycho. Toni Collette, who was the mother in The Sixth Sense, is a good choice for the waitress; there's always something a little edgy about her. There's another echo in Bale's hairstyle, which evokes uncanny memories of JFK Jr.

One modern thing about the movie is its low sexual quotient. Blaxploitation came along at a time when American movies were sexy, with lots of nudity and bedroom time. Modern action pictures seem prudish by comparison; like Gone in 60 Seconds and Mission: Impossible 2, this one prefers action to sex. Can it be that Hollywood's Friday night specials, which were aimed at teenage boys, have now lowered their sights to include a demographic group so young it thinks girls are creepy?

The most intriguing relationship in the movie is between Bale and Wright, as the rich kid and the drug dealer. There's a scene where Bale comes to Wright, hoping to pay for a hit. Wright is not much into murder for hire, but wants the kid's connections as a way to develop a more affluent clientele for his drugs. The way they talk to each other, the words they choose, the attitudes they strike, the changes they go through, are as subtly menacing as scenes in a film by Lee or Scorsese. The movie doesn't give us stereotypes in these two familiar roles, but closely examined originals.

The John Shaft character is more mainstream, but Jackson has a way of bringing weight to his roles. He always looks like he means it. But there's a disconnect between the realism of the murder case and the fantasy of Shaft's career as an unleashed vigilante who leaves countless dead bodies behind him. Different scenes seem to occupy different levels of reality. Of course the movie ends with a gunfight and a chase scene. That goes without saying.

Is this a good movie? Not exactly; too much of it is on automatic pilot, as it must be, to satisfy the fans of the original Shaft. Is it better than I expected? Yes. There are flashes here of the talent that John Singleton has possessed ever since Boyz N the Hood, and strong acting, and efficient action. Jackson makes a commanding Shaft (and a supporting role by Richard Roundtree, the original Shaft, serves to pass the mantle). The movie is what it is, but more than it needs to be.

Shanghai Noon ★ ★ ★
PG-13, 110 m., 2000

Jackie Chan (Chon Wang), Owen Wilson (Roy O'Bannon), Lucy Liu (Princess Pei Pei), Brandon Merrill (Indian Wife), Roger Yuan (Lo Fong), Xander Berkeley (Van Cleef), Walton Goggins (Wallace), P. Adrien Dorval (Blue). Directed by Tom Dey and produced by Roger Birnbaum, Gary Barber, and Jonathan Glickman. Screenplay by Alfred Gough and Miles Millar.

The best way to criticize a movie, Jean-Luc Godard once said, is to make another movie. In that spirit, Shanghai Noon is the answer to Wild Wild West, although I am not sure these are the kinds of movies Godard had in mind.

Jackie Chan's new action comedy is a wink at Westerns, martial arts, and buddy movies— enriched by a goofy performance by Owen Wilson, who would steal the movie if Chan were not so clever at sharing it with him.

The plot in a paragraph: China, the Forbidden City, 1881. The princess (Lucy Liu) resents her fate and hates her chosen fiancé. Her teacher offers to help her escape to America. She is kidnapped and held for ransom in Nevada. The three best Imperial Guards are selected to rescue her. Jackie Chan goes along as a bag carrier for his uncle, who is their interpreter. In Nevada, Jackie teams up with a train robber named Roy O'Bannon (Wilson), and they rescue the princess with much help from an Indian maiden (Brandon Merrill).

The plot, of course, is only a clothesline for Jackie's martial arts sequences, Wilson's funny verbal riffs, and a lot of low humor. Material like this can be very bad. Here it is sort of wonderful, because of a light touch by director Tom Dey, who finds room both for Chan's effortless charm and for a droll performance by Owen Wilson, who, if this were a musical, would be a Beach Boy.

Wilson has been edging up on us. Most moviegoers don't know who he is. If you see everything, you'll remember him from *Bottle Rocket*, where he was engaging, and *Minus Man*, where he was profoundly disturbing. This movie will make him a star. He is too smart and versatile to be packaged within a narrow range (his career also includes writing credits on *Bottle Rocket* and *Rushmore*), but if he could do only what he does in *Shanghai Noon*, he could support himself with Adam Sandler roles.

His train robber is hard to describe; the character is funny because of his tone, not his dialogue or actions. He's a modern, laid-back, self-centered southern California dude with a Stetson and six-guns. Flirting with a passenger on the train he is robbing, he gets competitive: "I kinda like to do the talking." His comic timing is precise, as in a scene where he and Jackie Chan get into a weird drinking contest while sharing adjacent bathtubs in a bordello, and play a funny and utterly inexplicable word game.

Chan's character is named Chon Wang (say it out loud). As in his 1998 hit *Rush Hour*, he plays a man of limited vocabulary and much action; Chris Tucker in that film and Owen Wilson in this one are motormouths who cover for Chan's shaky English, which is no problem because his martial arts scenes are poetic. He's famous for using the props that come to hand in every fight, and here there is a sequence involving several things we didn't know could be done with evergreen trees.

Lucy Liu, as the princess, is not a damsel in distress, but brave and plucky, and stirred by the plight of her Chinese countrymen, who have been made indentured servants in a Nevada gold town. She doesn't want to return to China, but to stay in America—as a social worker or union organizer, I guess. Not so boldly portrayed is Brandon Merrill's Indian woman, who is married to Jackie in a ceremony that nobody seems to take seriously and that the movie itself has clearly forgotten all about by the time the last shot comes around.

Her pairing with Jackie Chan does, however, create a funny echo of *A Man Called Horse,* and on the way out of the theater I was challenged by my fellow critic Sergio Mims to name all the other movie references. He claimed to have spotted, I think, twenty-four. My mind boggled.

What *Shanghai Noon* proves—and here's how it's a criticism of *Wild Wild West*—is that no matter how much effort is put into production values and special effects, a movie like this finally depends on dialogue and characters. *Wild Wild West,* which came out almost exactly one year earlier, had a top-drawer cast (Will Smith, Kevin Kline, Kenneth Branagh), but what were they given to do? Plow through dim-witted dialogue between ungainly f/x scenes. Here Wilson angles on-screen and starts riffing, and we laugh. And Jackie Chan, who does his own stunts, creates moments of physical comedy so pure it's no wonder he has been compared with Buster Keaton. If you see only one martial arts Western this year (and there is probably an excellent chance of that), this is the one.

Shattered Image ★ ½
NO MPAA RATING, 103 m., 1999

William Baldwin (Brian), Anne Parillaud (Jessie), Graham Greene (Detective), Billy

Wilmott (Lamond), Lisanne Falk (Paula/Laura), Bulle Ogier (Mrs. Ford). Directed by Raul Ruiz and produced by Barbet Schroeder, Lloyd Silverman, and Abby Stone. Screenplay by Duane Poole.

Shattered Image is a film so confoundedly and deliberately difficult to view, I felt like the laboratory mouse that fought its way through the maze and was rewarded with nothing more than a chlorophyll gumball. I sat in the dark, earnestly scribbling notes and trying to make mental connections, until it occurred to me that I was being toyed with. Without giving away the ending, I can say that the plot exists at the level of a child's story that ends, "and then I woke up, and it was all a dream!"

Ah, if that only *did* give away the ending! Raul Ruiz, the director, is fond of stories in which the viewer is kept in the dark about the true nature of the characters' reality. In *Shattered Image* he outdoes himself, with the story of a woman named Jessie (Anne Parillaud, of *La Femme Nikita*) who is either a hit woman who dreams she is a rape victim, or a newlywed who dreams she is a hit woman. Each character wakes up from dreams of the other, and as for Brian (William Baldwin)—who is he, really? Her new husband, or what?

Raul Ruiz is a Chilean-born director who has been involved in nearly eighty films since 1970, has shot in several European languages, and moves into English with *Shattered Image*. His interest in narrative game-playing can be seen to better effect in *Three Lives and Only One Death* (1997), the last film starring Marcello Mastroianni, who plays three roles—or maybe only one—in stories that occupy interlocking time lines.

In that film we quickly understand the underlying principle, and it's absorbing to see the time- and space-shifting that goes on. There are rules, even if they are only dimly understood principles of (take your choice) psychology, hallucination, imagination, or magic. In *Shattered Image* all is arbitrary until the end, and then it gets *really* arbitrary.

Faithful readers will know that I am not hostile to stories that conceal their reality. That was the strategy underlying *Dark City*, my choice as the best film of 1998. But in that film (and in *Three Lives*), the director is the audience's coconspirator, allowing glimpses or guesses of the solution.

Shattered Image, which is set alternately in the Caribbean and the Pacific Northwest, keeps the book of its secrets slammed shut. All is mystery until the "answer," which is singularly unsatisfying. And then there is another problem too. In *Three Lives*, we could always be interested in the actual events as they unfolded. In *Shattered Image*, the events seem more like arbitrary behavior designed to give Jessie something to do when loud noises and other triggers jerk her back and forth between dreams and reality (or reality and dreams, or dreams and dreams).

Apart from the narrative gimmick, the story is not intrinsically interesting. So we're like the mouse, negotiating the maze. There's not much of interest along the way, and when we get to the end and the titles roll up the screen, we have a good idea for a song they could play over the credits: Peggy Lee singing "Is That All There Is?"

She's All That ★ ★ ½
PG-13, 97 m., 1999

Freddie Prinze Jr. (Zack Siler), Rachael Leigh Cook (Laney Boggs), Matthew Lillard (Brock Hudson), Paul Walker (Dean Sampson), Jodi Lyn O'Keefe (Taylor Vaughan), Kevin Pollak (Wayne Boggs), Anna Paquin (Mackenzie Siler), Kieran Culkin (Simon Boggs). Directed by Robert Iscove and produced by Peter Abrams, Robert L. Levy, and Richard Gladstein. Screenplay by R. Lee Fleming Jr.

Sometimes while you're watching a movie, you can sense the presence of a wicked intelligence slipping zingers into a formula plot. I had that feeling all during *She's All That*, which is not based on a blindingly original idea (*Pygmalion* and *My Fair Lady* got there first). It's about how the most popular guy in the senior class makes a bet that he can take a dorky girl and turn her into a prom queen.

There's fun in the plot, but there's more fun around the edges. The movie stars Freddie Prinze Jr. as Zack, who has the third best grade point average in his class, and is also the captain of the soccer team and dates the beautiful class sexpot Taylor (Jodi Lyn O'Keefe). But

Taylor breaks up with him after going to Daytona Beach and meeting Brock Hudson, star of a cable show in which real kids are cast more or less as themselves (MTV's *The Real World* is the model). I only got a quick glimpse, but I think Brock has a tattoo of himself on his right arm.

Taylor is sure she'll be prom queen. Zack's buddies bet him he can't take another girl and make her the queen. He accepts, and chooses Laney (Rachael Leigh Cook), a mousy wallflower who paints down in her basement. In this affluent southern California community, it doesn't help that her dad is "Dr. Pool" (Kevin Pollak), owner of a pool-cleaning service.

Will Laney undergo a startling transformation? What do you think? I wanted to applaud when Zack unleashed the classic line, "Do you always wear those glasses?" Of course, it is an unbreakable rule of this formula that the ugly duckling is a swan in disguise: Rachael Leigh Cook is in fact quite beautiful, as was Audrey Hepburn, you will recall, in *My Fair Lady.* Just once I'd like to see the *Pygmalion* formula applied to a woman who was truly unattractive.

To give the movie credit, it's as bored with the underlying plot as we are. Even the prom queen election is only a backdrop for more interesting material, as *She's All That* explores differences in class and style, and peppers its screenplay with very funny little moments.

Consider, for example, the scene where Zack seeks Laney in the fast-food joint where she works. McDonald's would be too much of a cliché. This is a Middle Eastern franchise: "Would you like to supersize those falafel balls?" Consider a scene that plays in the foreground while Laney's dad is watching *Jeopardy!* in the background and shouting out the answers. (To a question about the printer of the most famous Bible in history, he shouts out "Hewlett-Packard." I couldn't quite catch the question for which his answer is "Lou Rawls" and the correct answer is "the pope.")

Moments like that are almost better than the movie deserves. So is the way the movie treats Taylor, the villainess, who tries to seduce the vain Brock while he's watching himself on TV, and is told to stop getting spit on his chest. And although it's obligatory to have a party scene at which the bad girl humiliates the good girl by pouring something down her dress, I liked the way Taylor told Laney she was "a waste of perfectly good yearbook space."

High school movies never seem that convincing to me, maybe because all the students seem to be in their twenties and don't have zits. Freddie Prinze Jr., I learn, is twenty-three, and Rachael Leigh Cook is twenty. Still, they have a charm in their roles, muted somewhat in Cook's case because the plot requires her to be sullen much of the time. She lurks in the basement painting large dark canvases, and at first Zack doesn't realize he's really falling in love with her.

But of course he is. And although she resists his advances ("What is this, some kind of a dork outreach program?"), nothing can stand in the way of the happy ending. Watching the movie, I was grateful to the director, Robert Iscove, and the writer, Lee Fleming, for taking this weary material and doing what they could with it. There's so little wit in the movies today. Too many characters speak in big, clunky declarative sentences that serve only to push the plot ahead of them, like people trying to shove their cars out of the snow. *She's All That* is not a great movie, but it has its moments.

Shiloh 2: Shiloh Season ★ ★ ★

PG, 96 m., 1999

Michael Moriarty (Ray Preston), Scott Wilson (Judd Travers), Zachary Browne (Marty Preston), Rod Steiger (Doc Wallace), Ann Dowd (Louise Preston), Bonnie Bartlett (Mrs. Wallace), Rachel David (Becky), Joe Pichler (David Howard), Marissa Leigh (Samantha). Directed by Sandy Tung and produced by Dale Rosenbloom and Carl Borack. Screenplay by Rosenbloom, based on novels by Phyllis Reynolds Naylor.

Shiloh 2: Shiloh Season recycles the same characters and, in a way, the same problems as the wonderful original film, but carries the message a little further. The first film was about a boy who is adopted by a dog, loves it, and wants to protect it from its cruel owner—even if that means lying to his parents. This sequel is about how people get to be cruel in the first place, and what you might be able to do to help them.

What's unique about both films, which are

based on novels by Phyllis Reynolds Naylor, is that they're about hard ethical issues that kids can identify with. A boy's dog inspires fierce love and protectiveness, and if he thinks adults (even his parents) might be a threat to the dog, he will instinctively do what he can to protect it. Even lie.

Who is to say he is wrong? Yes, "lying" is wrong—but what if it's the only weapon at your disposal to protect a dog that depends on you? I don't think I'd be pleased if a son of mine betrayed his dog. On the other hand, I don't think I'd let him know that. I'd let him find out in other ways. Sometimes parents and children have to enact these passion plays to learn lessons that are deeper than words.

Shiloh 2 takes place once again in an isolated rural area populated only by the Prestons, their alcoholic neighbor Judd Travers, and the friendly folks at the general store. At one point it occurred to me that the lives of the entire Preston family—father, mother, son, daughters, and dog—were completely dominated by Travers, who is their only visitor and the subject of most of their conversations. But there's a kind of purity to the way the story narrows down to the key players.

Marty Preston (Zachary Browne), now on the edge of adolescence, has been able to buy the dog Shiloh from Travers (Scott Wilson). That pleases his dad and mom (Michael Moriarty and Ann Dowd), and also watchful old Doc Wallace (Rod Steiger), who runs the store with his wife and their granddaughter, who is about Marty's age. But now Travers is drinking heavily, hunting out of season, and trespassing on Preston land. And someone is picking on him—scratching his car, knocking over his mailbox, freeing his remaining dogs.

Who is it? There's a line of dialogue that gives us a good idea, but Travers thinks it's Marty. This leads to several charged confrontations between the hunter and Marty's dad (played by Moriarty with solemn authority). Then there are a couple of emergencies—one serious, one a false alarm—and Shiloh plays a role both times.

Scott Wilson once again brings a humanity to the tricky role of Judd Travers, who is a pathetic being. Yes, he kicks dogs. But he was kicked himself as a child, and is a lonely man, living in poverty. (He claims to support himself by hunting, but his only success during this movie comes when he sits on his front porch and picks off one squirrel.) Doc Wallace knows something about the Travers family, and what he tells Marty leads to the ending, in which a life is redeemed—maybe. (I liked the frankness with which Marty prays, after Travers is injured, that the man get better, "but maybe don't let his legs get good enough to go hunting.")

Families do not often attend "family movies" in theaters, unless they're Disney cartoons or TV spin-offs, but the original *Shiloh* was such a success on video that it justified a sequel. Both films demand to be discussed afterward by parents and their children. Neither is about the kind of dumb, empty-headed stuff that passes for children's entertainment. Kids are not stupid, and they wonder about issues like this. They may also suspect, as the movie observes, that "you have to be taught to be kind."

Shower ★ ★ ★
PG-13, 92 m., 2000

Zhu Xu (Master Liu), Pu Cun Xin (Da Ming), Jiang Wu (Er Ming), He Zheng (He Bing), Zhang Jin Hao (Hu Bei Bei), Lao Lin (Li Ding), Lao Wu (Feng Shun). Directed by Zhang Yang and produced by Peter Loehr. Screenplay by Liu Fen Dou, Zhang Yang, Huo Xin, Diao Yi Nan, and Cai Xiang Jun.

The customers of the bathhouse in *Shower* hardly seem to spend any time anywhere else. The old men are there from morning to night, bathing, soaking, being rubbed, playing cards, and staging fights to the death with their pet crickets (one feeds his champion ant eggs; his opponent accuses him of using "steroids"). Master Liu has run this bathhouse since time immemorial and brushes off his son's suggestions that he retire: "I've done this all of my life and I like doing it!"

The son is Da Ming (Pu Cun Xin), a successful businessman who lives in a distant city, but has returned because of an alarming postcard he received from his retarded brother, Er Ming (Jiang Wu). The postcard seems to indicate that old Liu (Zhu Xu) is dead or dying, but in fact Liu is presiding, as he has for decades, over the closed world of the bathhouse, where steam and ancient customs wall out the changing ways of modern Beijing.

The relationship between Liu and his retarded son is a close one. They're like playmates, racing around the block and staging contests to see who can hold his breath the longest. Er Ming is proud when he's allowed to man the desk by the door, greeting clients, most of whom have presumably known him since he was a child.

But now Er Ming and Da Ming are both grown men, and Da Ming worries about what the future holds for his brother. The city wants to tear down the entire bathhouse district to make way for progress, and then what will happen to Liu, Er Ming, the customers, and the crickets?

Shower, written, directed, and edited by Zhang Yang, is a cozy and good-hearted comedy, not startlingly original but convincing in the way it shows the rhythms of the days and customs of the bathhouse, and how they gradually seduce the harassed and preoccupied visiting brother. Da Ming planned a visit of only a day or two, but in calls to his distant wife, he keeps putting off his return, and the screenplay shows him gradually beginning to care for the family business and its destiny. (A scene where father and son wrestle with plastic sheeting on the roof during a rainstorm is contrived, but effective all the same.)

The best thing in the movie, I think, is the affectionate and yet unsentimental way the father and the retarded son are seen. Yes, Er Ming is slow. But he has good qualities and strong feelings, and has found a niche in life that suits him. He knows all the customers and cares about them; he helps raise the alarm when Mrs. Zhang bursts in looking for her no-good husband.

And look how he rises to the occasion when another customer faces a crisis. This man loves to sing in the shower, and always sings "O Sole Mio." We gather two things about him: He knows only one song, and he can sing only in a shower. There is a crisis when he is pressed into service for a neighborhood talent show, and Er Ming instantly grasps the situation and solves it.

Many recent films from China have emphasized either its exotic past or the unsettled politics of its recent history. But after all, most of its citizens lead ordinary lives and share dreams and fears similar to ours. *Shower* is about everyday people, and although it has some contrived plot devices (including the looming deadline of the city's threat to the bathhouse), it is warm and observant, and its ending is surprisingly true to the material.

Show Me Love ★ ★ ★
NO MPAA RATING, 89 m., 2000

Alexandra Dahlstrom (Elin), Rebecca Liljeberg (Agnes), Erica Carlson (Jessica), Mathias Rust (Johan Hult), Stefan Horberg (Markus), Ralph Carlsson (Father Olof), Maria Hedborg (Mother Karin), Axel Widegren (Little Brother Oskar). Directed by Lukas Moodysson and produced by Lars Jonsson. Screenplay by Moodysson.

This is all I ask of a movie about teenagers: That they be as smart, as confused, as good-hearted, and as insecure as the kids I went to high school with. Such characters are so rare that when you encounter them in a movie like *Show Me Love*, they belong to a different species than the creatures in the weekly Hollywood teenager picture.

Show Me Love is set in Sweden, but could be set in any American small town where kids believe they are desperate outcasts in a cultural backwater. Elin (Alexandra Dahlstrom), one of the girls in the film, pages through a teen magazine and despairs when she finds that raves are "out." Her town is so behind the times that stuff is out before it even gets there. She is bored, bored, bored. She wants to be a model, but is even bored with that.

The movie is also about Agnes (Rebecca Liljeberg), who moved to the town more than a year ago but still has few friends; she's an outsider at school because students whisper she's a lesbian. They have no reason to think that, but they're right. She has a crush on Elin, and locks herself in her room to write her love letters on her computer. One day at a party, a girlfriend bets Elin she won't kiss Agnes, and she does, sending the wrong message to Agnes, who doesn't know about the bet.

This sounds, I know, like the setup for a sexcom, or maybe one of those Swedish romps of long ago (*Therese and Isabelle* comes to mind). What I haven't conveyed is the sweetness, tenderness, and naïveté of all of these scenes, in which both girls are essentially wandering cluelessly through half-understood life choices. What they find at the end of the film is not romance so much as self-knowledge and fortitude, and a disdain for "popularity."

The movie (which outgrossed *Titanic* to become the most successful film in Swedish history) is not a story of heroines and villains. Everyone in it is more or less on the same moral plane. It is not about distant and blockheaded parents (the parents express love and understanding, as best they can, and we sympathize with their attempts to make sense of adolescent despair). It isn't about any of the standard characters (the stupid principal, the class nerd, the social snob) who wander through most Hollywood teenage movies on autopilot. It's about these specific people and their lives.

The movie is funny, gentle, and true. It knows how teenagers can be cruel, and how sharply they can regret it. Early in the film, Agnes's mother throws her a birthday party (she doesn't want one), and it looks like only one guest is going to turn up—her best friend, who is in a wheelchair. Mad at her parents, mad at herself, Agnes lashes out at her friend ("I don't want to be friends with a palsied cripple who listens to the Back Street Boys!") and mocks her gift of perfume. Later, she apologizes. The friend in the wheelchair is not all that deeply upset about the insult, because she has read it, correctly, as more about Agnes than about herself. In most American teenage movies, there's not depth enough for such subtlety: An insult is an insult, without nuance.

The film is refreshing in the way it handles "sex," and I put the word in quotes because there is hardly any sex in the film. While American teenage films cheerfully supply shower scenes, T&A, and four-letter words, this one is released without an MPAA rating, no doubt because its honesty would upset audiences accustomed to a cinema of dirty jokes. Two of the truest moments in the movie occur when the two girls confess they have no sexual experience. The "lesbian" reveals that the kiss on a bet was the first time she has kissed a girl, and Elin, who has a reputation for promiscuity, confides she is a virgin.

Show Me Love is not really about sexuality. It's more about vegetating in a town that makes the girls feel trapped. And it sees that the fault is not in the town, but in the girls: Maybe their boredom is a pose. Maybe all teenagers, in every town, feel like nothing is happening in their lives, and they will never find love or be understood or do thrilling things. Maybe that's just human nature. In its quiet, intelligent, understated way, this film loves teenagers; most teen movies just use them.

Shrek ★ ★ ★ ★
PG, 90 m., 2001

With the voices of: Mike Myers (Shrek), Eddie Murphy (The Donkey), Cameron Diaz (Princess Fiona), John Lithgow (Lord Farquaad). Directed by Andrew Adamson and Vicky Jenson and produced by Aron Warner and John H. Williams. Screenplay by Ted Elliott, Terry Rossio, Joe Stillman, and Roger S. H. Schulman, based on the book by William Steig.

There is a moment in *Shrek* when the despicable Lord Farquaad has the Gingerbread Man tortured by dipping him into milk. This prepares us for another moment when Princess Fiona's singing voice is so piercing it causes jolly little bluebirds to explode; making the best of a bad situation, she fries their eggs. This is not your average family cartoon. *Shrek* is jolly and wicked, filled with sly in-jokes and yet somehow possessing a heart.

The movie has been so long in the making at DreamWorks that the late Chris Farley was originally intended to voice the jolly green ogre in the title role. All that work has paid off: The movie is an astonishing visual delight, with animation techniques that seem lifelike and fantastical, both at once. No animated being has ever moved, breathed, or had its skin crawl quite as convincingly as Shrek, and yet the movie doesn't look like a reprocessed version of the real world; it's all made up, right down to, or up to, Shrek's trumpet-shaped ears.

Shrek's voice is now performed by Mike Myers, with a voice that's an echo of his Fat Bastard (the Scotsman with a molasses brogue in *Austin Powers: The Spy Who Shagged Me*). Shrek is an ogre who lives in a swamp surrounded by "Keep Out" and "Beware the Ogre!" signs. He wants only to be left alone, perhaps because he is not such an ogre after all but merely a lonely creature with an inferiority complex because of his ugliness. He is horrified when the solitude of his swamp is disturbed by a sudden invasion of cartoon creatures, who have been banished from Lord Farquaad's kingdom.

Many of these creatures bear a curious correspondence to Disney characters who are in the public domain: The Three Little Pigs turn up, along with the Three Bears, the Three Blind Mice, Tinkerbell, the Big Bad Wolf, and Pinocchio. Later, when Farquaad seeks a bride, the Magic Mirror gives him three choices: Cinderella, Snow White ("She lives with seven men, but she's not easy"), and Princess Fiona. He chooses the beauty who has not had the title role in a Disney animated feature. No doubt all of this, and a little dig at DisneyWorld, were inspired by feelings DreamWorks partner Jeffrey Katzenberg has nourished since his painful departure from Disney—but the elbow in the ribs is more playful than serious. (Farquaad is said to be inspired by Disney chief Michael Eisner, but I don't see a resemblance, and his short stature corresponds not to the tall Eisner but, well, to the diminutive Katzenberg.)

The plot involves Lord Farquaad's desire to wed the Princess Fiona, and his reluctance to slay the dragon that stands between her and would-be suitors. He hires Shrek to attempt the mission, which Shrek is happy to do, providing the loathsome fairy-tale creatures are banished and his swamp returned to its dismal solitude. On his mission, Shrek is joined by a donkey named The Donkey, whose running commentary, voiced by Eddie Murphy, provides some of the movie's best laughs. (The trick isn't that he talks, Shrek observes; "the trick is to get him to shut up.")

The expedition to the castle of the princess involves a suspension bridge above a flaming abyss, and the castle's interior is piled high with the bones of the dragon's previous contenders. When Shrek and The Donkey get inside, there are exuberant action scenes that whirl madly through interior spaces, and revelations about the dragon no one could have guessed. And all along the way, asides and puns, in-jokes and contemporary references, and countless references to other movies.

Voice-overs for animated movies were once,

except for the annual Disney classic, quickie jobs that actors took if they were out of work. Now they are starring roles with fat paychecks, and the ads for *Shrek* use big letters to trumpet the names of Myers, Murphy, Cameron Diaz (Fiona), and John Lithgow (Farquaad). Their vocal performances are nicely suited to the characters, although Myers's infatuation with his Scottish brogue reportedly had to be toned down. Murphy in particular has emerged as a star of the voice-over genre.

Much will be written about the movie's technical expertise, and indeed every summer seems to bring another breakthrough on the animation front. After the three-dimensional modeling and shading of *Toy Story*, the even more evolved *Toy Story 2*, *A Bug's Life*, and *Antz*, and the amazing effects in *Dinosaur*, *Shrek* unveils creatures who have been designed from the inside out, so that their skin, muscles, and fat move upon their bones instead of seeming like a single unit. They aren't "realistic," but they're curiously real. The artistry of the locations and setting is equally skilled—not lifelike, but beyond lifelike, in a merry, stylized way.

Still, all the craft in the world would not have made *Shrek* work if the story hadn't been fun and the ogre so lovable. Shrek is not handsome but he isn't as ugly as he thinks; he's a guy we want as our friend, and he doesn't frighten us but stirs our sympathy. He's so immensely likable that I suspect he may emerge as an enduring character, populating sequels and spin-offs. One movie cannot contain him.

☞

Signs and Wonders ★ ★ ★
NO MPAA RATING, 104 m., 2001

Stellan Skarsgard (Alec Fenton), Charlotte Rampling (Marjorie), Deborah Kara Unger (Katherine), Dimitris Katalifos (Andreas), Ashley Remy (Siri), Michael Cook (Marcus), Dave Simonds (Kent). Directed by Jonathan Nossiter and produced by Marin Karmitz. Screenplay by James Lasdun and Nossiter.

Signs and Wonders looks through the eyes of a manic-depressive as the world sends him messages and he hurries to answer them. It shows how exhausting it is to be constantly in the grip of exhilaration, insight, conviction, idealism, and excitement—while bombarded all the time with cosmic coincidences. Nobody in the movie calls this man a manic-depressive, but it's as clear as day—or as the bright yellow suit he turns up wearing one morning, convinced it symbolizes his new and improved psyche. As a drama about the ravages of mental illness, the movie works; too bad most of the critics read it only as a romantic soap opera in which the hero is an obsessive sap. They read the signs but miss the diagnosis.

The movie stars Stellan Skarsgard and Charlotte Rampling as Alec and Marjorie, a married American couple living in Athens. ("It doesn't bother to explain away their foreign accents," complains one critic, although 10 percent of all Americans are first-generation and millions have accents.) She works for the embassy; he has a murky job in finance, and is having an office affair with Katherine (Deborah Kara Unger). The affair has been proceeding satisfactorily for months or maybe years, we gather, until one day Alec, beset with guilt, walks out of his house and uses the phone booth across the street to call back home and confess everything to his wife.

This sudden, dramatic confession marks the start of his bipolar illness. He has become seized with the conviction that vast forces are sweeping through him. He can no longer live a lie. Walking his daughter to school, he joins in her game of counting manholes and clocking various signs and portents in the city streets. For her it's a child's game; for him it becomes an obsession.

Marjorie forgives Alec his affair. Some time later, on the ski slopes in another country, he meets Katherine again—coincidentally, he believes. This random, accidental meeting is for Alec a sign that they were meant to be together, and he leaves Marjorie a second time. Then there is a tense, painful conversation with Katherine, after he explains the significance of their meeting, and why it proved they were predestined to be together. "What if I set it up?" she asks, as a woman who would prefer to be loved for herself rather than as the outward sign of cosmic forces.

I don't think we can be sure if Katherine arranged the meeting or not, but Alec decides she did, and that sends him racing back to Marjorie. Having smashed his family once, and then, as she puts it, returned to smash it again, he has run out of goodwill on the home front—and besides, she's in love with another man. Now come the most fascinating passages in Skarsgard's performance, as his mania becomes more evident. He will baby-sit while she goes out with the other man. He deserves to suffer. He will do penance. Yes! Yes! At one point as she shouts at him, he replies: "I want you to be this angry with me! We need this!" About this time the yellow suit turns up.

The movie is maddeningly obscure about details that do not directly involve Alec. We meet Andreas (Dimitris Katalifos), the man Marjorie plans to marry. He is a left-wing journalist, was tortured by the colonels, has an archive of secrets in his flat about right-wing Greek conspiracies, is perhaps a little paranoid. The twice-jilted Katherine, who comes hunting Alec and assumes a false identity, is also deranged; Marjorie is the sane center of the film. By the end, we are not sure exactly how to explain what happens to Andreas, and the movie leaves a lot of other unanswered questions. Perhaps the answer is, the story spins away from Alec, who as his illness progresses can no longer keep all the connections and meanings in order.

Jonathan Nossiter, the director and cowriter, made the 1997 Sundance prize-winner *Sunday*, about a British actress, down on her luck, who meets a man who may be a famous director or may be a homeless derelict. It's a movie about how people can be who we want them to be. *Signs and Wonders* is about a man who knows what he wants from Marjorie and Katherine, but can't get them to play the roles. They can't keep up with his fevered brain, as he connects, disconnects, reconnects. "I am not a frivolous man!" he cries at one point, aware that unless his signs and wonders are real, he is frivolous indeed. I had a friend once who suffered from manic behavior, and he said, "You know what I used to pray for? Boredom."

Simon Magus ★ ★
NO MPAA RATING, 106 m., 2001

Noah Taylor (Simon), Stuart Townsend (Dovid), Sean McGinley (Hase), Embeth Davidtz (Leah), Amanda Ryan (Sarah), Rutger Hauer (Squire),

Ian Holm (Sirius/Boris), Terence Rigby (Bratislav). Directed by Ben Hopkins and produced by Robert Jones. Screenplay by Hopkins.

If there's anything worse than a laborious fable with a moral, it's the laborious fable without the moral. The more I think about *Simon Magus*, the less I'm sure what it's trying to say. It leads us through a mystical tale about Jews, Poles, and an outcast who takes orders from Satan. Both groups would like to build the local railroad station, but the outcast, a mystic, has visions of these very tracks being used to take Jews to the death camps. Does that mean it doesn't matter who builds the station because the trains will still perform their tragic task? In that case, what's the story about except bleak irony?

The movie takes place in nineteenth-century Silesia, bordering Hungary and Austria. Some twenty Orthodox Jews have a small community near a larger gentile town. The new railroad, bypassing the town, has created hard times for everyone. A Jew named Dovid (Stuart Townsend) wants to build a station and some shops, which will help out the woman he loves, a widowed shopkeeper named Leah (Embeth Davidtz). A gentile named Hase (Sean McGinley) also wants to build the station. The land is controlled by the Squire (Rutger Hauer), a dreamy intellectual.

This would be a story about anti-Semitism and real estate were it not for two other characters. Simon (Noah Taylor) is a Jew who is scorned by his own community because of his crazy ways. From time to time, as he makes his way through the gloomy mists of the town and forest, he is approached by Sirius (Ian Holm), who seems to be the devil. When Satan appears in a movie, I always look around for God, but rarely find him; it's usually up to the human characters to defeat the devil. In this case, Simon's visions of the death trains perhaps suggest that God is taking a century off.

The nonsupernatural side of the story involves the good Dovid and the bad Hase (a villain so obvious he lacks only a mustache to twirl). Both want the Squire to make his land available. The Squire, a lonely and bookish man, wants intellectual companionship—someone to read his poems and keep him company around the fire on long winter evenings. Dovid, a Talmudic scholar but not otherwise widely read, takes lessons from Sarah (Amanda Ryan), who is up on poetry. At one point, she and the Squire get into a literature-quoting contest.

Simon Magus creates a sinister subplot in which the evil Hase tries to trick Simon into taking a box with a Christian baby inside and hiding it in the rabbi's house so that a mob can discover it as proof that the Jews plan to eat it. Simon responds with intelligence that surprises us, but what good purpose does it do to resurrect this slander? Most people now alive would never hear of such ancient anti-Semitic calumnies were it not for movies opposing them. Does Ben Hopkins, the writer-director, imagine audiences nodding sagely as they learn that baby-eating was a myth spread by anti-Semites? Isn't it better to allow such lies to disappear into the mists of the past?

In any event, the story is resolved along standard melodramatic lines, and good (you will not be surprised to learn) triumphs. Yet still those death trains approach inexorably through Simon's visions. The papers are filled these days with stories of Polish villagers who rounded up their local Jews and burned them alive. What difference does it make who builds the train station?

Simpatico ★ ½
R, 106 m., 2000

Nick Nolte (Vinnie), Jeff Bridges (Carter), Sharon Stone (Rosie), Catherine Keener (Cecilia), Albert Finney (Simms), Shawn Hatosy (Young Vinnie), Kimberly Williams (Young Rosie), Liam Waite (Young Carter). Directed by Matthew Warchus and produced by Dan Lupovitz, Timm Oberwelland, and Jean-Francois Fonlupt. Screenplay by Warchus and David Nicholls, based on a play by Sam Shepard.

Simpatico is a long slog through perplexities and complexities that disguise what this really is: The kind of B-movie plot that used to clock in at seventy-five minutes on the bottom half of a double bill. It's based on a Sam Shepard play, unseen by me. Since Shepard is a good playwright, we're left with two possibilities: (1) It has been awkwardly adapted, or (2) it should have stayed in Shepard's desk drawer.

The plot involves a kind of exchange of personalities between Carter (Jeff Bridges), a rich Kentucky racehorse breeder, and Vinnie (Nick Nolte), a shabby layabout who has been blackmailing him for years. They were once friends, long ago when they were young, and involved in a scheme to cheat at the track by switching horses. Vinnie has some photos that Carter would not want anyone to see, and that gives him leverage. This time, he interrupts Carter in the middle of negotiations to sell an expensive horse named Simpatico, demanding that he fly to California to get him out of a fix. Seems a supermarket cashier named Cecilia (Catherine Keener) is accusing him of sexual misconduct.

Oh, but it's a lot more complicated than that, and neither Cecilia nor her relationship with Vinnie is quite as described. Two other figures from the past also enter: Rosie (Sharon Stone), now Carter's boozy but colorful wife, and Simms (Albert Finney), once a racing commissioner, now a tracer of bloodlines. Students of *noir* will know that the contemporary story will stir up old ghosts.

Those who are not *noir* lovers won't be in the dark for long, since director Matthew Warchus and his cowriter, David Nicholls, supply flashbacks that incriminate some of the characters (although not, in this day and age, seriously enough to inspire the vast heavings of this leviathan plot). Nolte and Bridges are portrayed as young men by Shawn Hatosy and Liam Waite, a casting decision that adds to the murkiness, since Hatosy, who is supposed to be young Nolte, looks more like young Bridges, and Waite, who is supposed to be young Bridges, looks like nobody else in the movie. This theme is developed further, I suppose, as Nolte and Bridges subtly start to resemble each other.

It happens that I've just revisited a complicated *noir*, Roman Polanski's *Chinatown*, which also involves sexual misconduct in the past and blackmail in the present. One reason it works so well is that the characters seem to drive the plot: Things turn out the way they do because the characters are who they are. The plot of *Simpatico* is like a clockwork mechanism that would tick whether or not anyone cared what time it was.

Simply Irresistible ★ ★ ★
PG-13, 95 m., 1999

Sarah Michelle Gellar (Amanda Shelton), Sean Patrick Flanery (Tom Bartlett), Betty Buckley (Stella), Patricia Clarkson (Lois McNally), Dylan Baker (Jonathan Bendel), Christopher Durang (Gene O'Reilly), Larry Gilliard Jr. (Nolan Traynor). Directed by Mark Tarlov and produced by John Fiedler, Jon Amiel, and Joe Caracciolo Jr. Screenplay by Judith Roberts.

Simply Irresistible begins with one of the more unlikely Meet Cutes in movie history: Sarah Michelle Gellar chases a runaway crab up the trouser leg of the man she is destined to love. She owns one of those restaurants where all the customers know each other, like in a sitcom. I was settling down for a slow ride when somehow the movie caught hold and turned into an enchanting romantic comedy about people who float to the ceiling when they kiss. It's *Like Water for Chocolate* meets *Everyone Says I Love You*.

Gellar plays Amanda Shelton, whose restaurant in New York's SoHo is failing fast. No wonder. She's not such a good cook. Then one day a mysterious stranger appears in her vicinity and brings a magical crab. Yes, a magical crab. And the beady-eyed little crustacean sets itself up in her kitchen and somehow casts a spell. She becomes a great cook. An inspired cook. A cook so good that when the guy with the trousers tastes one of her desserts, he falls in love. "We kissed in a vanilla cloud," he tells his secretary. "This fog—it was warm, and it was wet, and it was like you could see what we were feeling."

The movie is as light as a soufflé, as fleeting as a breath of pumpkin pie on the wind from a widow's window. It is about almost nothing at all, except for a love story, the joy of eating, and a final sequence in a room that looks blessed by Astaire and Rogers.

Sarah Michelle Gellar is the star of TV's *Buffy the Vampire Slayer* and was in the original *I Know What You Did Last Summer*, where she was slashed by the Groton's Fisherman look-alike—a wise career move, freeing her from the sequel so she could make this movie. She plays Amanda Shelton perfectly straight, as a woman who is depressed by how she used to be a bad cook and now she is a great one. (I am reminded of the story about Lawrence Olivier, who moaned after a great performance as Othello, "Yes, but I don't know how I did it!")

Her new love is Sean Patrick Flanery, as Tom Bartlett, the manager of a new gourmet restaurant in the Henri Bendel store. (The second-string romance is between the grandson of Henri Bendel and Tom's secretary. They kiss after eating one of Amanda's eclairs.) Gellar is lovable, but this isn't a movie where the ground shakes, maybe because most of the love scenes take place while the couples are in midair. Nor are there any sex scenes per se. It's all soft, gauzy romance—a Valentine in which the *idea* of great love is disembodied from the old rumpy-pumpy.

When Tom recruits Amanda to cook for the premiere of his new restaurant, the movie generates a scene of simple, pure delight. It's a tough crowd (food critics, sniffy socialites), but after the appetizer, they're weeping with joy. After the entrée, transfixed in ecstatic meditation. Then dessert is served. If there is a heaven, this is its menu.

Simply Irresistible is old-fashioned and obvious, yes, like a featherweight comedy from the 1950s. But that's the charm. I love movies that cut loose from the moorings of the possible, and dance among their fancies. When Woody Allen waltzed with Goldie Hawn on the banks of the Seine and she floated in the air and just stayed up there, my heart danced too. And the closing scenes of *Simply Irresistible* are like that. It's not a great movie. But it's a charmer.

The 6th Day ★ ★ ★
PG-13, 124 m., 2000

Arnold Schwarzenegger (Adam Gibson), Tony Goldwyn (Drucker), Robert Duvall (Dr. Weir), Michael Rapaport (Hank), Sara Wynter (Talia), Wendy Crewson (Natalie Gibson), Rodney Rowland (Wile E. Coyote). Directed by Roger Spottiswoode and produced by Jon Davison, Mike Medavoy, and Arnold Schwarzenegger. Screenplay by Cormac Wibberley and Marianne Wibberley.

On the sixth day, God created man. And man should leave it at that, according to laws that have been passed in *The 6th Day*, Arnold Schwarzenegger's new thriller. In the near future there's a RePet store in every mall that will clone your dead pet for you, but human cloning, although technically possible, has been outlawed.

There is, however, a clandestine market in human clones. Consider the case of Johnny Phoenix, a pro quarterback who's paid $300 million a season but is brain-dead after a game injury. "We have a lifetime contract with a vegetable," one of the team owners moans, before pulling the plug on Johnny's life-support system ("Sorry, Johnny—you're gonna have to take one for the team"). Sad, yes, but whaddaya know: Soon Johnny is back out there quarterbacking again.

All of this is miles away from the life of Adam Gibson (Arnold Schwarzenegger), a helicopter pilot who with his buddy Hank (Michael Rapaport) airlifts rich skiers to the slopes. Adam has a happy home life with his wife, Natalie (Wendy Crewson), and daughter, marred only by the death of their pet dog Oliver. Should Adam have Oliver cloned at RePet? He doesn't think so. He thinks there's something wrong about overturning the fundamental process of life and death.

Adam's friend Hank has fewer scruples, and enjoys life with a computer-generated holographic Perfect Virtual Woman, who greets him after a long day: "I've recorded all your sports programs. Maybe we could watch them together. Or should I just take this dress off right now?" (There is an *SNL* skit there somewhere, about a hard-pressed man taking Viagra to keep up with the insatiable willingness of his Virtual Woman. Perhaps she could be adjusted to say, "Honey, tonight I only feel like a pineapple and pepperoni pizza, a six-pack, and watching you clean your guns.")

Cloning in *The 6th Day* has made great leaps forward since the days of the sheep named Dolly. The cloners don't start with a cloned fertilized egg. Instead, they grow "blanks"—assemblies of protoplasm floating in a nurturing fluid, ready to have the total mind and body information of adults plugged into them. Using a quick eye scan, the cloners can make a "syncording" of the contents of a pet's mind, so it will still recognize its owner and know all the same tricks. And the same thing is done illegally in the movie with humans, by a shadowy corporation run by Drucker (the handsomely reptilian Tony Goldwyn). Robert Duvall is the brilliant scientist for the corporation, but has his doubts.

This process sounds like the Soul Catcher that has been hypothesized by Arthur C. Clarke—the memory chip into which the contents of a human mind might be downloaded. My problem with both processes is that while the resulting clone or chip might know everything I know and remember everything that ever happened to me and think of itself as me, I myself would still be over here in the old container. Immortality for my perfect clone leaves behind what I insist upon considering the real me—something the Goldwyn character has time to reflect on during a melodramatic dying scene.

Such details do not slow the evil corporation, fueled by the genius of Dr. Weir (Robert Duvall) and prodded by the seductive, ruthless Talia (Sara Wynter). They have a scheme to kill and clone Hank, Adam's friend, but by mistake they clone Adam instead, leaving the movie populated by two Arnold Schwarzeneggers who both think they're the real thing. Since that is how most Arnold Schwarzenegger movies feel, this is not as confusing as it sounds.

This much you know from the trailers. What happens next I will not say, although of course it involves meetings both astonished and poignant between the two Adams, whose wife is named Natalie and not Eve only through the superhuman resolve of the screenwriters.

The 6th Day is not in the same league with the great Schwarzenegger films like *Total Recall* and *Terminator 2,* but it's a well-crafted entertainment containing enough ideas to qualify it as science fiction and not just as a futurist thriller. Arnold once again gets mileage out of the contrast between his muscular presence and his everyman persona; at one point, he has dialogue that slyly pairs the two: "My little girl—I don't want to expose her to any graphic violence. She gets enough of that from the media."

Both Drucker and Talia have been cloned many times, causing us to wonder how much they enjoy starting over, and whether any regrets are left behind in the process. We'll never

know: The discarded entities left behind in the cloning process have no way to complain. Instead of living forever through the genes you give to your children, you live forever through reproducing your own genes, which brings evolution to a dead stop, of course. Could you make a syncording of yourself as a child, grow up, clone the kid, and raise yourself as your own child? Speculations like these are inspired by *The 6th Day,* and are part of the fun.

The Sixth Sense ★ ★ ★
PG-13, 106 m., 1999

Bruce Willis (Malcolm Crowe), Haley Joel Osment (Cole Sear), Toni Collette (Lynn Sear), Olivia Williams (Anna Crowe), Trevor Morgan (Tommy Tammisimo), Donnie Wahlberg (Vincent Gray), Peter Tambakis (Darren), Jeffrey Zubernis (Bobby), Bruce Norris (Stanley Cunningham). Directed by M. Night Shyamalan and produced by Frank Marshall, Kathleen Kennedy, and Barry Mendel. Screenplay by Shyamalan.

The Sixth Sense isn't a thriller in the modern sense, but more of a ghost story of the sort that flourished years ago, when ordinary people glimpsed hidden dimensions. It has long been believed that children are better than adults at seeing ghosts; the barriers of skepticism and disbelief are not yet in place. In this film, a small boy solemnly tells his psychologist: "I see dead people. They want me to do things for them." He seems to be correct.

The psychologist is Malcolm Crowe (Bruce Willis), who is shot by an intruder one night in his home—a man who had been his patient years earlier and believes he was wrongly treated. The man then turns the gun on himself. "The next fall," as the subtitles tell us, we see Crowe mended in body but perhaps not in spirit, as he takes on a new case, a boy named Cole Sear (Haley Joel Osment) who exhibits some of the same problems as the patient who shot at him. Maybe this time he can get it right.

The film shows us things adults do not see. When Cole's mother (Toni Collette) leaves the kitchen for just a second and comes back in the room, all of the doors and drawers are open. At school, he tells his teacher, "They used to hang people here." When the teacher wonders how Cole could possibly know things like that, he helpfully tells him, "When you were a boy they called you Stuttering Stanley."

It is Crowe's task to reach this boy and heal him, if healing is indeed what he needs. Perhaps he is calling for help; he knows the Latin for, "From out of the depths I cry unto you, oh Lord!" Crowe doesn't necessarily believe the boy's stories, but Crowe himself is suffering, in part because his wife, once so close, now seems to be drifting into an affair and doesn't seem to hear him when he talks to her. The boy tells him, "Talk to her when she's asleep. That's when she'll hear you."

Using an "as if" approach to therapy, Crowe asks Cole, "What do you think the dead people are trying to tell you?" This is an excellent question, seldom asked in ghost stories, where the heroes are usually so egocentric they think the ghosts have gone to all the trouble of appearing simply so the heroes can see them. Cole has some ideas. Crowe wonders whether the ideas aren't sound even if there aren't really ghosts.

Bruce Willis often finds himself in fantasies and science-fiction films. Perhaps he fits easily into them because he is so down-to-earth. He rarely seems ridiculous, even when everything else on the screen is absurd (see *Armageddon*), because he never overreaches; he usually plays his characters flat and matter-of-fact. Here there is a poignancy in his bewilderment. The film opened with the mayor presenting him with a citation, and that moment precisely marks the beginning of his professional decline. He goes down with a sort of doomed dignity.

Haley Joel Osment, his young costar, is a very good actor in a film where his character possibly has more lines than anyone else. He's in most of the scenes, and he has to *act* in them—this isn't a role for a cute kid who can stand there and look solemn in reaction shots. There are fairly involved dialogue passages between Willis and Osment that require good timing, reactions, and the ability to listen. Osment is more than equal to them. And although the tendency is to notice how good he is, not every adult actor can play heavy dramatic scenes with a kid and not seem to condescend (or, even worse, to be subtly coaching and leading him). Willis can. Those scenes give

the movie its weight and make it as convincing as, under the circumstances, it can possibly be.

I have to admit I was blindsided by the ending. The solution to many of the film's puzzlements is right there in plain view, and the movie hasn't cheated, but the very boldness of the storytelling carried me right past the crucial hints and right through to the end of the film, where everything takes on an intriguing new dimension. The film was written and directed by M. Night Shyamalan, whose previous film, *Wide Awake,* was also about a little boy with a supernatural touch; he mourned his dead grandfather and demanded an explanation from God. I didn't think that one worked. *The Sixth Sense* has a kind of calm, sneaky self-confidence that allows it to take us down a strange path intriguingly.

The Skulls ★
PG-13, 107 m., 2000

Joshua Jackson (Luke McNamara), Paul Walker (Caleb Mandrake), Hill Harper (Will Beckford), Leslie Bibb (Chloe), Christopher McDonald (Martin Lombard), Steve Harris (Detective Sparrow), William Petersen (Ames Levritt), Craig T. Nelson (Litten Mandrake). Directed by Rob Cohen and produced by Neal H. Moritz and John Pogue. Screenplay by Pogue.

I would give a great deal to be able to see *The Skulls* on opening night in New Haven in a movie theater full of Yale students, with gales of laughter rolling at the screen. It isn't a comedy, but that won't stop anyone. *The Skulls* is one of the great howlers, a film that bears comparison, yes, with *The Greek Tycoon* or even *The Scarlet Letter.* It's so ludicrous in so many different ways it achieves a kind of forlorn grandeur. It's in a category by itself.

The movie claims to rip the lid off a secret campus society named the Skulls, which is obviously inspired by the Yale society known as Skull and Bones. The real Skull and Bones has existed for two centuries, and has counted presidents, tycoons, and CIA founders among its alumni. Membership was an honor—until now. After seeing this movie, members are likely to sneak out of the theater through the lavatory windows.

The story: Luke McNamara (Joshua Jackson) attends a university that is never mentioned by name (clues: It is in New Haven and has a lot of big Y's painted on its walls.). He is a townie, rides a bike, lost his father when he was one, is poor, works in the cafeteria. Yet he's tapped for membership in the Skulls because he is a star on the varsity rowing crew.

Luke's best friends are a black student journalist named Will Beckford (Hill Harper) and a rich girl named Chloe (Leslie Bibb). Luke secretly loves Chloe but keeps it a secret because "Chloe's parents own a private jet, and I've never even been in a jet." Another of Luke's friends is Caleb Mandrake (Paul Walker), whose father, Litten (Craig T. Nelson), is a Supreme Court candidate. With soap opera names like Caleb and Litten Mandrake (and Senator Ames Levritt), the film contains an enormous mystery, which is, why doesn't Chloe have a last name? I suggest Worsthorne-Waugh.

Luke is tapped for the Skulls. This involves racing around campus to answer lots of ringing pay phones, after which he and the other new pledges are drugged, pass out, and awaken in coffins, ready to be reborn in their new lives. They go through "revealing ceremonies" inside the Skulls' campus clubhouse, a Gothic monument so filled with vistas and arches and caverns and halls and pools and verandas that Dracula would have something along these lines if he could afford it.

Mel Brooks said it's good to be the king. It's better to be a Skull. Luke and his fellow tappees find $10,000 in their ATM accounts (later they get $100,000 checks). Beautiful women are supplied after an induction ceremony. They all get new sports cars. The Skulls insignia is branded on their wrists with a red-hot iron, but they get shiny new wristwatches to cover the scar. I'm thinking, how secret is a society when hookers are hired for the pledge class? Do they wear those watches in the shower? In this litigious age, is it safe to drug undergraduates into unconsciousness?

Each Skull is given a key to the clubhouse and a rule book. "There's a rule for all possible situations," they're told. I want that book. Rule One: Don't lose the rule book. Will, the journalist, steals Caleb's key and rule book and sneaks inside the clubhouse, and (I am now revealing certain plot secrets) is later found to have hanged himself. But was it really suicide?

Luke thinks Caleb might know, and can ask him, because the Skulls have a bonding ceremony in which new members are assigned soul mates. You are locked in an iron cage with your soul mate and lowered into a pit in the floor, at which time you can ask him anything you want, and he has to answer truthfully, while the other Skulls listen to the words echoing through the crypt.

Many powerful adult men still take the Skulls very seriously. Not only Judge Litten Mandrake but Senator Ames Levritt (William Petersen), who are involved in a power struggle of their own. They put pressure on Luke to end his curiosity about Will's death. The following dialogue occurs, which will have the New Haven audience baying with joy:

"This is your preacceptance to the law school of your choice."

"I haven't even applied yet."

"Imagine that!"

Chloe is enlisted as Luke's sidekick for some Hardy Boys capers, but soon Luke is subjected to a forcible psychiatric examination at the campus health clinic (no laughter here), and bundled off to a mental hospital where, so far-reaching is the influence of the Skulls, he is kept in a zombie state with drugs while the senator and the judge struggle over his future. Oh, and there's a car chase scene. Oh, and a duel, in broad daylight, with all the Skulls watching, in an outdoor pavilion on the Skulls' lawn that includes a marble platform apparently designed specifically for duels.

The real Skull and Bones numbers among its alumni the two George Bushes. Of course, there's no connection between Skull and Bones and the fictional Skulls. Still, the next time George W. has a press conference, a reporter should ask to see under his wristwatch. Only kidding.

SLC Punk! ★ ★ ★
R, 97 m., 1999

Matthew Lillard (Stevo), Michael Goorjian (Bob), Annabeth Gish (Trish), Jennifer Lien (Sandy), Christopher McDonald (Father), Devon Sawa (Sean), Jason Segel (Mike), Summer Phoenix (Brandy). Directed by James Merendino and produced by Sam Maydew and Peter Ward. Screenplay by Merendino.

When people adopt a fearful and aggressive personal style, we forget that somewhere inside, hidden by the punk look, the haircuts, the body piercing, the chains, the tattoos, or the gang regalia, is a person who basically just wants to be loved and understood. Telling the world to go to hell is often the response of people who believe the world has told them to go to hell.

James Merendino's *SLC Punk!* knows that, and the essential sweetness of its hero is what makes the movie more than just an attempt to shock. It's a memory of Salt Lake City in 1985, the high Reagan era, when Stevo and Heroin Bob are, as far as they know, the only two punks in town. They embrace the anarchism embodied in Sex Pistols songs (and there is a hilarious stoned explanation of chaos theory), but the depth of their rebellion can be gauged by the fact that Heroin Bob (Michael Goorjian) has never taken heroin, and has an irrational fear of needles.

Stevo (Matthew Lillard) narrates the film, which is a nostalgic tour of his world, done in much the same tone as Ray Liotta's voice-overs in Scorsese's *GoodFellas*. He explains, he theorizes, he addresses the camera directly, he identifies the various characters and cliques. His approach is anthropological. The Stevo character simultaneously stands inside and outside his world; he keeps an ironic angle on his rebellion, but can't see himself living the life of his father, a former "activist," who now explains, "I didn't sell out. I bought in."

Stevo is stuck in a limbo of parties, music, hanging out, long discussions, recreational mind-altering, and uncertainty. His dad wants him to go to Harvard ("If you want to rebel there, you can do it"). Stevo wants to go to the University of Utah, "and get a 4.0 in Damage." He stays in Salt Lake City and there's a flashback to explain how he got to his current punk state: We see a young Stevo in the basement, playing with Dungeons & Dragons figures, and the future Heroin Bob comes in with a tape, tells him D&D sucks, "listen to this," and leads him out of dweebdom.

Stevo's college career passes, more or less, in the movie's fractured memory style, and Bob's girlfriend Trish (Annabeth Gish) introduces him to Brandy (Summer Phoenix), who asks him, "Wouldn't it be more rebellious if you didn't spend so much time buying blue hair dye and going out to get punky clothes?" There are also details about Stevo's home life (his parents have divorced, his dad having traded in the old wife on a new Porsche), and about the improvisational style of days spent seeing what turns up next.

The film could have taken a lot of cheap shots at the Mormon culture of Salt Lake City, but most of its local details are more in the way of reporting than of satire. Stevo laments, for example, the problems involved in such a basic act as buying a six-pack of beer in a state where only low-alcohol 3.2 beer is sold, and the clerks in the state-owned liquor stores are all cops and phone in tips if you even look like you're thinking of doing anything illegal. There is also a debate with customers in a convenience store about the "curse on the land" and the imminent arrival of Satan. Here we witness something I have long suspected, that the exaggerated fascination with Satan in some religious quarters is the flip side of the heavy metal/Goth/satanic thing. Whether you worship Satan or oppose him, he stars in your fantasies.

Matthew Lillard is an actor easy to dislike, and no wonder, since he often plays supercilious twits. Here his performance dominates the film, and he does a subtle, tricky job of being both an obnoxious punk and a kid in search of his direction in life. He's very good.

In this season of blaming everything on the movies, a film like *SLC Punk!* will no doubt inspire knee-jerk moralists to deplore its depiction of an anarcho-punk lifestyle. But remember: A movie isn't about what it's about, but about how it's about it. What *SLC Punk!* is *really* about is Stevo's ironic distance on his lifestyle—about the way he lives it and analyzes it at the same time. The message isn't "live this way," but "look at the way you live." There's a little something there for all of us.

Sleepy Hollow ★ ★ ★ ½
R, 100 m., 1999

Johnny Depp (Ichabod Crane), Christina Ricci (Katrina Van Tassel), Miranda Richardson (Lady Van Tassel), Michael Gambon (Baltus Van Tassel), Casper Van Dien (Brom Van Brunt), Ian McDiarmid (Dr. Lancaster), Michael Gough (James Hardenbrook), Jeffrey Jones (Steenwyck),

Richard Griffiths (Phillipse). Directed by Tim Burton and produced by Scott Rudin and Adam Schroeder. Screenplay by Andrew Kevin Walker and Kevin Yagher; based on Washington Irving's story "The Legend of Sleepy Hollow."

Tim Burton's *Sleepy Hollow* begins with a story that would not have distinguished one of the lesser Hammer horror films, and elevates it by sheer style and acting into something entertaining and sometimes rather elegant. It is one thing to see a frightened constable being taken for a ride in a carriage by a driver who has lost his head along the way. It is another to see the carriage bouncing down roads that have been modeled on paintings from the Hudson River School. This is the best-looking horror film since Coppola's *Bram Stoker's Dracula*.

It is not, however, titled *Washington Irving's Sleepy Hollow*, perhaps because the story has been altered out of all recognition from the Irving classic. Perhaps not. No power on Earth could persuade me to reread the original and find out. What it depends upon is Burton's gift for bizarre and eccentric special effects, and a superb performance by Johnny Depp, who discards everything we may ever have learned or thought about Ichabod Crane, and starts from scratch.

Depp plays Crane at the "dawn of a new century," he says, as 1799 rolls over to 1800. It is time to discard the barbaric torture of the past, he believes, and bring the legal system up-to-date, with improved methods of investigation and justice. He sees himself as a detective of the new order, and a New York judge, impatient with his constant interruptions, banishes him to the upstate hamlet of Sleepy Hollow, where there has been an outbreak of decapitations. Let him practice forensics there.

As Crane journeys north, the movie casts its visual spell. This is, among other things, an absolutely lovely film, with production design, art direction, and cinematography that create a distinctive place for the imagination. Not a real place—hardly a shot looks realistic, and some look cheerfully contrived—but a place in the mind. I loved the shot where mist extinguishes the torches that have been lighted by the night watch.

Burton's Sleepy Hollow is a dour place, the houses leaning together for support, the shut-

ters slammed against newcomers. There is never a sunny day here. The faces of the village fathers are permanently frozen into disapproval. And the body count is mounting, while the head count stays at zero. The Horseman, it appears, not only decapitates his victims, but takes their skulls with him. "The heads were not found by the bodies?" exclaims Ichabod after his briefing on arrival. "The heads were not found—at all!" says a village elder. Snarls another: "Taken! By the Headless Horseman! Taken—back to hell!"

We meet some of the locals. Old Baltus Van Tassel (Michael Gambon), richest of the burghers. His comely daughter, Katrina (Christina Ricci), and her shapely stepmother, Lady Van Tassel (Miranda Richardson). And other local citizens, including one played by Jeffrey Jones, who always seems to be regarding us dubiously from above, at an oblique angle. The magistrate (Richard Griffiths) seems to know a good deal, at one point whispering to Crane that there are "four graves—but five victims!"

Crane dismisses it all as a case of superstition. He comes equipped with cases full of bizarre instruments of his own invention, including a set of eyepieces that make him look like the optometrist from hell. It becomes clear fairly quickly, however, that Ichabod is stronger on theory than practice, and has not much stomach for disinterring bodies, performing autopsies, or examining wounds. One head was "cut off—and the wound cauterized!" he exclaims, looking a little sick to his stomach. The locals explain that the Horseman's sword was forged in the fires below.

Johnny Depp is an actor able to disappear into characters, never more readily than in one of Burton's films. Together they created Edward Scissorhands and Ed Wood, and now here is an Ichabod Crane who is all posture and carefully learned mannerism, attitude, and fastidiousness. It's as if the Horseman gallops ahead in a traditional horror film, and Depp and Burton gallop right behind him in a satire. There's a lot of gore (the movie deserves its R rating), but it's not *mean* gore, if you know what I mean; it's gore dictated by the sad fate of the Headless Horseman.

The ending is perhaps too traditional. We know that the requirements of the genre absolutely insist on a struggle between Crane and the Horseman, followed by an explanation for his strange rides and harsh justice for those who deserve it. Burton at least does not linger over these episodes, or exploit them; he's too much in love with his moody setup to ruin the fun with final overkill. The most astonishing thing for me about the movie wasn't the Horseman anyway, but the fact that I actually found myself drawn into this old Classics Illustrated material—enthralled by a time and place so well evoked that the Horseman almost seemed natural there.

Note: No power on Earth could drag from me the identity of the unbilled actor who plays the Horseman when he has a head. But you will agree he is the only logical choice.

Small Time Crooks ★ ★ ★
PG, 95 m., 2000

Woody Allen (Ray Winkler), Tracey Ullman (Frenchy), Hugh Grant (David), Michael Rapaport (Denny), Tony Darrow (Tommy), Elaine May (May), Jon Lovitz (Benny), Elaine Stritch (Chi Chi Potter). Directed by Woody Allen and produced by Jean Doumanian.

Small Time Crooks is a flat-out comedy from Woody Allen, enhanced by a couple of plot U-turns that keep us from guessing where the plot is headed. Allen often plays two types of characters, intellectuals and dumbos, and this time he's at the freezing end of the IQ spectrum, as an ex-con and dishwasher with a plan to rob a bank. His wife, Frenchy (Tracey Ullman), is incredulous as he explains his scheme to rent a storefront and tunnel into the bank vault two stores down.

This looks a lot like the master plan in the Italian comedy *Big Deal on Madonna Street*, but in *Small Time Crooks* it's more of a false alarm. Ray and Frenchy open up a cookie store as a front for the heist, the cookies take off big-time, the heist is hopelessly bungled, and then Frenchy's cousin May (Elaine May) blabs to a cop about the tunneling in the basement. This leads indirectly to a franchise operation, and within a year Ray and Frenchy are rich beyond his, if not her, wildest dreams.

The first act of the movie has a lot of fun with Ray and his low-life criminal friends, including Jon Lovitz as a guy who has put his

kids through college by torching buildings, and Michael Rapaport as a tunnel digger who wears his miner's cap backward, baseball cap style, so the light points behind him. If this heist idea had been spun out to feature length, however, it might have grown old and felt like other caper movies. Allen has a twist up his sleeve.

As millionaires, the Winklers put the nouveau in riche. Frenchy lavishes a fortune on their new luxury apartment, where Ray rattles around unhappily (he refuses to look at one abstract painting because it depresses him). At a housewarming, Frenchy offers her guests crudites (pronounced "CRUDE-ites") and adds, "They say I have a flair for decoration. This rug lights up." Ray follows behind miserably: "Show them your collection of leather pigs."

Then David (Hugh Grant) enters their lives. He's a British art expert, suave, a flatterer, and Frenchy wants to hire him to train them in culture. He quickly sees that Frenchy has "outgrown" Ray, and might be ripe for the plucking. He whisks her off on a whirl of gallery shows, opening nights, charity benefits, and chic restaurants, while Ray miserably seeks consolation in the simpler things: Knicks games, junk food, and the comforting company of May.

I've heard Woody Allen accused of making the same movie over and over, which is simply not fair. His recent films include an enchanting musical (*Everyone Says I Love You*), a Felliniesque black-and-white social satire (*Celebrity*), and the goofiness of Sean Penn's second-best jazz guitarist in the world, in *Sweet and Lowdown*. Now comes this straight comedy, with its malaprop dialogue ("I require your agreeance on this") and its sneaky way of edging from an honest bank job to sins like flattery, pride, and embezzlement.

Allen plays a blue-collar version of his basic persona, and has bracketed himself between two of the funniest women in America, Tracey Ullman, who is seen too rarely, and Elaine May, who is hardly seen in movies at all. The supporting cast is written more sharply than is often the case in comedies (where the star gets all the good lines), and there's a lesson lurking somewhere, about how money can't buy you happiness and may even cost you extra by losing it. Dumb as they (allegedly) are, the characters in *Small Time Crooks* are smarter, edgier, and more original than the dreary crowd in so many new comedies. The movie opened on the same day as *Road Trip*. Now there's a choice.

Smiling Fish and Goat on Fire ★ ★ ★
R, 90 m., 2000

Derick Martini (Chris Remi), Steven Martini (Tony Remi), Christa Miller (Kathy), Amy Hathaway (Alison), Bill Henderson (Clive Winter), Rosemarie Addeo (Anna), Heather Jae Marie (Nicole), Nicole Rae (Natalie), Wesley Thompson (Burt Winter). Directed by Kevin Jordan and produced by Derick Martini, Jordan, and Steven Martini. Screenplay by Derick Martini, Jordan, and Steven Martini.

The two brothers who are the heroes of Kevin Jordan's *Smiling Fish and Goat on Fire* are not Native Americans, but their grandmother was half-Indian, and she nicknamed them—Tony is Smiling Fish because he floats in the current, grinning, waiting for the world to drift his way. Chris is Goat on Fire because he wants to get everything exactly right. Chris is an accountant and Tony is an actor, which is the Los Angeles word for unemployed.

In their twenties, they live in the cozy bungalow left them by their parents (whose marriage had an L.A.-style entrance and exit; they met on the Universal tour and died in a traffic accident). Tony and Chris both have girlfriends, but we sense that one relationship is dying and the other looks ominous since the girl cries a lot during sex. And then their lives take a turn for the better with the introduction of two women, a six-year-old girl, a ninety-year-old man, and a chicken named Bob.

Chris (Derick Martini) meets Anna (Rosemarie Addeo), an Italian who works on movies as an animal wrangler. Bob is her chicken. Tony (Steven Martini) meets his postal carrier, Kathy (Christa Miller), who is from Wyoming and has moved to L.A. in hopes that her daughter, Nicole (Heather Jae Marie), will find work as a child actress. Kathy's heart is more or less stolen by Tony when he silences the squeaking wheel on her mail cart with olive oil.

Our hearts, meanwhile, are warmed by the introduction of a character named Clive (Bill Henderson), who is the ninety-year-old uncle of Chris's boss. The boss asks Chris to give Clive a ride to work, and Clive turns out to be a bottomless well of entertainment and wisdom for Chris and Tony, and for us.

He used to work as a sound boom man on African-American movies, Clive says. He met Rebecca, the love of his life, on a Paul Robeson picture. At work, he erects a tent over his cubicle, moves a friendly desk lamp under it, and listens to jazz. The character could steal the movie, but generously shares it with the stories of the brothers and their new loves, and leftover problems with the old loves.

Smiling Fish and Goat on Fire is one of those handmade movies that sneaks into festivals and wins friends. I saw it on the final weekend of the 1999 Toronto Film Festival, where Henderson (who is nowhere near ninety) got a standing ovation. Talking to the filmmakers, I learned that director Jordan and the Martini brothers, who cowrote the screenplay, were longtime friends, that the movie cost $40,000, and that it was shot in the brothers' actual house. (There is an echo here of the Sundance winner *The Brothers McMullen,* also shot in the director's home.)

Many other movies costing $40,000 (and less, and more) have gone to deserved oblivion, but *Smiling Fish and Goat on Fire* has a freshness and charm, a winning way with its not terrifically original material. The movie isn't really about a plot, but about developments in the lives of characters we like. When a standard plot element develops (a possible pregnancy, for example), the movie uses it not for a phony narrative crisis, but for understated human comedy. By not trying too hard, by not pushing for opportunities to manipulate, the movie sneaks up and makes friends.

The brothers Martini are effortlessly likable and convincing in the film, which we feel is close to their personalities if not to the facts of their lives. As for Henderson, I hope casting directors see him here and use him. He has been in a lot of movies (he was the no-nonsense cook in *City Slickers*), but this movie suggests new ways he could be used; it gives him notes we want to hear again. And the way he evokes the lost world of the African-American film industry is like a film within the film; the way

527

he evokes his love for Rebecca, glimpsed only in old photos, is surprisingly moving.

Snatch ★ ★
R, 103 m., 2001

Brad Pitt (One Punch Mickey), Andy Beckwith (Errol), Ewen Bremner (Mullet), Nikki and Teena Collins (Alex and Susi), Sorcha Cusack (Mum O'Neil), Benicio Del Toro (Franky Four Fingers), Sam Douglas (Rosebud), Mike Reid (Doug the Head), Austin Drage (Gypsy Kid), Dennis Farina (Avi). Directed by Guy Ritchie and produced by Matthew Vaughn. Screenplay by Ritchie.

In my review of *Lock, Stock and Two Smoking Barrels,* Guy Ritchie's 1999 film, I wrote: "In a time when movies follow formulas like zombies, it's alive." So what am I to say of *Snatch,* Ritchie's new film, which follows the *Lock, Stock* formula so slavishly it could be like a new arrangement of the same song?

Once again we descend into a London underworld that has less to do with English criminals than with Dick Tracy. Once again the characters have Runyonesque names (Franky Four Fingers, Bullet Tooth Tony, Boris the Blade, Jack the All-Seeing Eye). Once again the plot is complicated to a degree that seems perverse. Once again titles and narration are used to identify characters and underline developments.

There is one addition of considerable wit: In the previous film, some of the accents were impenetrable to non-British audiences, so this time, in the spirit of fair play, Ritchie has added a character played by Brad Pitt, who speaks a Gypsy dialect even the other characters in the movie can't understand. Pitt paradoxically has more success communicating in this mode than some of the others do with languages we allegedly understand. He sounds like a combination of Adam Sandler and Professor Backwards.

Ritchie is a zany, high-energy director. He isn't interested in crime; he's interested in voltage. As an unfolding event, *Snatch* is fun to watch, even if no reasonable person could hope to understand the plot in one viewing. Ritchie is almost winking at us that the plot doesn't matter, that it's a clothesline for his pyrotechnics (if indeed pyrotechnics can employ clotheslines, but don't get me started).

The plot assembles its lowlifes in interlocking stories involving crooked boxing, stolen diamonds, and pigs. After Franky Four Fingers (Benicio Del Toro) steals a diamond in Antwerp and returns to London, a Russian named Boris the Blade (Rade Sherbedgia) and an American gangster named Avi (Dennis Farina) try to separate him from it—not easy, since it is in a case handcuffed to his wrist.

Meanwhile (somehow I don't think "meanwhile" quite says it), a boxer named Gorgeous George is knocked flat, and two shady promoters find themselves in hock to a crime czar. Desperate to find a winner, they recruit the Gypsy played by Pitt, who is a formidable bare-knuckle fighter that London gamblers won't recognize. Also, bodies are fed to pigs. Pitt's character and the Gypsy community where he lives are the most intriguing parts of the movie.

If this summary seems truncated, it's because an accurate description of this movie dialogue might read like the missing chapters from *Finnegans Wake.* Because the actors have cartoon faces, the action is often outrageous, and Ritchie has an aggressive camera style, the movie is not boring, but it doesn't build, and it doesn't arrive anywhere. It's hard to care much about any of the characters, because from moment to moment what happens to them seems controlled by chance. I mentioned the Marx Brothers in my review of *Lock, Stock,* and I thought of them again here, as strangely dressed weirdos occupy an anarchic nightmare.

I don't want Ritchie to "grow." I don't care if he returns to the kind of material that worked for him the first time around. I just want him to get organized, to find the through-line, to figure out why we would want to see the movie for more than its technique. I can't recommend *Snatch,* but I must report that no movie can be all bad that contains the following dialogue:

U.S. Customs Official: "Anything to declare?"

Avi (Dennis Farina): "Yeah. Don't go to England."

Note: I am not so crass as to mention in my review that Guy Ritchie and Madonna recently became man and wife. I save such biographical details for my footnotes, and would overlook them altogether except that it is blindingly clear to me that he should direct, and she should star in, a British remake of Guys and Dolls.

Snow Day ★ ½
PG, 90 m., 2000

Mark Webber (Hal Brandston), Zena Grey (Natalie Brandston), Schuyler Fisk (Lane Leonard), Emmanuelle Chriqui (Claire Bonner), David Paetkau (Chuck Wheeler), Chevy Chase (Tom Brandston), Chris Elliott (Snowplow Man), Jean Smart (Laura Brandston), Pam Grier (Tina). Directed by Chris Koch and produced by Julia Pistor and Albie Hecht. Screenplay by Will McRobb and Chris Viscardi.

Snow Day involves a very, very busy day in the life of an upstate New York teenager named Hal (Mark Webber), who is hopelessly in love with the unavailable school dreamboat, Claire (Emmanuelle Chriqui). He is, he believes, invisible to her, but that changes when a record snowfall forces the schools to close for a day, and gives him an opportunity to demonstrate what a unique and wonderful person he is—potentially, anyway.

The movie surrounds Hal with a large cast of supporting characters—too many probably for a two-hour movie, let alone this one that clocks at ninety minutes including end titles. There's his dad (Chevy Chase), a weatherman who resents having to wear silly costumes; and his mom (Jean Smart), a woman whose career keeps her so busy that she doesn't stop to smell the coffee, or enjoy the snow.

And, let's see, his kid sister, Natalie (Zena Grey), and his best female friend, Lane (Schuyler Fisk), and, of course Snowplow Man (Chris Elliott), whose hated plow clears the streets and thus makes it possible to go to school—not that these kids don't wander all over town on the snow day. In a film top-heavy with plot and character, Snowplow Man should have been the first to go; played by Elliott as a clone of a Texas Chainsaw gang member, he is rumored to have made the snow chains for his tires out of the braces of the kids he's run down.

The arc of the movie is familiar. Hal yearns for Claire and is advised on his campaign by Lane, the loyal gal pal who perhaps represents true love right there under his very nose, were he not too blind, of course, to see it. He has to struggle against a school wiseguy on a high-powered snowmobile, who claims Claire for his own, while his weatherman dad has to wear hula skirts on the air in a fight for ratings with the top-rated local weather jerk. There's also a hated school principal and a square DJ at the ice rink (he likes Al Martino) and the programming executive (Pam Grier) who makes Chevy wear the silly costumes.

One of the inspirations for *Snow Day* is the 1983 classic *A Christmas Story,* also narrated by the hero, also with a kooky dad, also with a dream (a BB gun rather than a girl). But that was a real story, a memory that went somewhere and evoked rich nostalgia. *Snow Day* is an uninspired assembly of characters and story lines that interrupt one another, until the battle against Snowplow Man takes over just when we're hoping he will disappear from the movie and set free the teenage romance trapped inside it.

Acting Observation: Chris Elliott comes from a rich comic heritage (his father is Bob of Bob and Ray), but where his dad treasured droll understatement, Chris froths with overacting. There's a scene toward the end where he's tied to a children-crossing sign and laughs maniacally, like a madman, for absolutely no reason. Why is this funny? He has gone mad? Always was mad? It is funny to hear him laugh? We look curiously at the screen, regarding behavior without purpose.

Observation Two: Chevy Chase has been in what can charitably be called more than his share of bad movies, but at least he knows how to deliver a laugh when he's given one. (When his career-driven wife makes a rare appearance at dinner, he asks his son to "call security.") After the screening of *Snow Day,* I overheard another critic saying she couldn't believe she wished there had been more Chevy Chase, and I knew how she felt.

Third Observation: Through a coincidence in bookings, *Snow Day* and *Holy Smoke,* opened on the same day, and both contain Pam Grier roles that inspire only the thought, what's Pam Grier doing in such a lousy role? A year ago, she was in another lousy teenage movie, *Jawbreaker.* Is this the payoff for her wonderful performance in *Jackie Brown* (1997)? What a thoughtless place is Hollywood, and what talent it must feel free to waste.

Snow Falling on Cedars ★ ★ ★ ½
PG-13, 130 m., 2000

Ethan Hawke (Ishmael Chambers), Youki Kudoh Hatsue Miyamoto, Anne Suzuki (Young Hatsue Imada), Rick Yune (Kazuo Miyamoto), Max Von Sydow (Nels Gudmundsson), James Rebhorn (Alvin Hooks), Sam Shepard (Ishmael's Father), James Cromwell (Judge Fielding), Richard Jenkins (Sheriff Art Moran). Directed by Scott Hicks and produced by Harry J. Ufland, Ron Bass, Kathleen Kennedy, and Frank Marshall. Screenplay by Bass and Hicks, based on the novel by David Guterson.

Snow Falling on Cedars is a rich, many-layered film about a high school romance and a murder trial a decade later. The young lovers are Ishmael Chambers (Ethan Hawke), son of the local newspaper editor in a small Pacific Northwest town, and Hatsue Miyamoto (Youki Kudoh), daughter of Japanese-Americans. They meet at the time of Pearl Harbor, when feeling runs high against local Asians. Ishmael's father (Sam Shepard) runs editorials thundering, "These people are our neighbors," but then the U.S. government seizes their property and trucks them off to internment camps, in a shameful chapter of American history. Ten years later, Ishmael is editor of the paper, covering a murder trial. The defendant is the man Hatsue married in the camp.

Told this way, the story seems like crime and romance, but *Snow Falling on Cedars* reveals itself with the complexity of a novel, holding its themes up to the light so that first one and then another aspect can be seen. The style is crucial to the subject. The story unfolds in flashbacks, overlapping dialogue, half-understood events, flashes of memory, all seen in a variety of visual styles: color, desaturated color, black and white, even a little grainy 16mm. The look and sound of the film are not just easy flashiness, but match the story, which depends on the many different ways that the same events can be seen.

Above all there is a sense of place. Director Scott Hicks and his cinematographer, Robert Richardson, use a wide-screen canvas to envelop the story in trees and snow, rain and lowering skies, wetness and shadows. Rarely has a place been so evoked as part of a narrative. We sense that these people *are* neighbors partly because the forest crowds them together.

In this community the Japanese-Americans work as fishermen and shepherds, farmers and small-business holders, and their teenagers dance to the same pop tunes as everybody else. Yes, the races keep to themselves: Ishmael's mother disapproves of her son's friendship with Hatsue, whose own mother warns her against white boys. But boys with girls in love will fall, as e. e. cummings so simply put it, and Ishmael and Hatsue have a hidey-hole, a green cavern in the roots of a big cedar tree, where they meet to feel happy with one another. He asks her to marry him, and perhaps, if it had not been for the overwhelming fact of the war, this would have been a high school romance with a happy ending.

It is not, and in the early 1950s Ishmael covers a trial at which Kazuo Miyamoto (Rick Yune) is tried for the murder of a local fisherman whose body was found in some nets. He seems to have been bashed with a fish hook. There was bad blood between Kazuo and the victim; they fought a week before the death, and there is old bitterness involving the title to some land that was confiscated during the internment. The courtroom scenes pit a duty-bound prosecutor (James Rebhorn) against a tall, Lincolnesque defense attorney (Max Von Sydow), foreign-born, American to the core.

The movie slowly reveals its connections and motivations, which take on greater importance because the trial may result in all the relationships shifting again. If the husband is guilty, perhaps the teenage lovers can be reunited. Ishmael wants that, but does Hatsue? His resentment at being rejected even colors his coverage of the trial and his thinking about the accused man. We know Hatsue married Kazuo in the camps under pressure from her parents; does she love him? Is he guilty?

The only weakness in the film is its treatment of Kazuo, who is not seen in three dimensions but primarily through Ishmael's eyes. He is the man, after all, who has shared his life with Hatsue, and if they were married in the camps, well, people Ishmael's color put them there. Imagine the same triangle involving Jews and Nazis and see how it feels. We sympathize with Ishmael. Would we sympathize with a Nazi?

Because the movie is centered on Ishmael's point of view, Kazou is the interloper, the thief of love, and now probably a killer as well. From Kazou's point of view, which we can only infer, his society has put him behind barbed wire, discriminated against him, and now is rushing to a prejudiced judgment, while its representative stands ready to snatch away his bride. The movie never really sees him clearly. It places him over there at the defense table, or in long shot, objectively. It doesn't need him as a fully fleshed person, because he functions as a symbol and obstacle.

This may, however, be a weakness the film has to accept in order to get where it is going, because we need fears and confusions to make it more than just a courtroom drama. If we knew Kazou better, we might have a better notion of whether he could kill someone, and that would not help the story. In most movie trials we make fairly good guesses about guilt and innocence, but here there is real doubt, which plays against the bittersweetness of lost love.

And then there is the care given to the opposing attorneys, who are seen as quite particular people, especially Von Sydow, as Nels Gudmundsson, whose hands shake and whose voice sometimes trembles with anger as he defends the principles that drew him to immigrate to this land. The summation to the jury is a set piece in countless movies; rarely have I seen one better acted.

Snow Falling on Cedars is Scott Hicks's first film since *Shine*, the 1996 story of the pianist seized with paralyzing doubts. In both films he sees his stories as a whole, circling to their centers instead of starting at the beginning and trekking through. This film, written by Ron Bass and Hicks from the novel by David Guterson, is unusually satisfying in the way it unfolds. We don't feel the time structure is a gimmick; we learn what we need to know for each scene.

Some of them are of particular power, as when the Japanese-Americans are ordered from their homes by local authorities, told to take no more than will fit in a suitcase, and driven away to the internment "centers." We have seen scenes like this in stories about the Holocaust, and in parables of the future in which America has become a totalitarian state. Not everyone in the audience will have known it actually happened here.

Solomon and Gaenor ★ ★
R, 100 m., 2000

Ioan Gruffudd (Solomon), Nia Roberts (Gaenor), Sue Jones Davies (Gwen), William Thomas (Idris), Mark Lewis Jones (Crad), Maureen Lipman (Rezl), David Horovitch (Isaac), Bethan Ellis Owen (Bronwen), Adam Jenkins (Thomas). Directed by Paul Morrison and produced by Sheryl Crown. Screenplay by Morrison.

In Wales in 1911, it was simply not realistic for a Welsh girl and a Jewish boy to think they could find a happy ending to their love story, unless they were prepared to leave their families and journey elsewhere—to London, say. But since this course is open to them, it is a little difficult to have our hearts broken by the tragedy of *Solomon and Gaenor,* the story of a boy and girl who, essentially, want to have sex more than they want to pay the consequences.

The movie takes place in a coal-mining valley of unrelieved dreariness, which the local chapel seems to mirror in its gray rigidity. Here the sweet-faced Gaenor (Nia Roberts) lives with her family, including a brutish brother. Over the hills in a larger town, a Jewish family, newly immigrated from Russia, runs a pawn shop and clothing business. Here the handsome Solomon (Ioan Gruffudd) works as a door-to-door salesman of dry goods. His family is religious and observant, but Solomon is not, and when his grandfather prays aloud, he asks his father to "stop the old fool's braying."

One day Solomon knocks on doors in the mining village, and when Gaenor opens one of the doors, both of them feel a thrumming of the loins. He makes a red dress for her and gives it as a present, and soon (on their third or fourth meeting after no conversations of consequence) they are in the hayloft.

Their romance is a sweet one; they walk in the fields, and she is entranced by the first boy she has met who speaks poetically and gently. He finds her tender and bewitching—and, of course, available. He lies about himself. His name is Sam Livingstone, he says, posing as a gentile. His father works for the railroads. He meets Gaenor's family for tea (the brother glowering suspiciously), but does not invite her to meet his family because his father is "away."

Sooner or later, as we know and they should, Gaenor will get pregnant. And what will happen then? How the movie handles this is its main contribution to the underlying Romeo and Juliet theme, and so I will not reveal it, except to say that anyone with common sense could have figured out a less tragic ending than Solomon does. I didn't know whether to weep for his fate or his gormlessness.

The technical credits are superb. The valley groans under heavy clouds and snowfall. The houses are dark caves. We can feel the wet and cold underfoot. The treatment of Solomon by Crad (Mark Lewis Jones), the brother, is convincing and not simply routine villainy. The scene in the chapel where Gaenor is denounced by her former fiancé is like a sudden slap in the face.

Ioan Gruffudd and Nia Roberts are convincing in their roles—and moving, up to a point, until we grow impatient with their lack of caution and foresight. Gaenor is not presented as an innocent virgin, but as a woman who perhaps should have been less thrilled by the red dress. Solomon lies to her but never actually says he plans to marry her, and when Gaenor's sister asks, "Has he asked you, then?" she says, "He needs me." It is a reply but not an answer.

I suppose the film intends to be a lament about the way we humans are intolerant of those outside our own group. Both of the families in the film would fiercely oppose a member marrying an outsider, as has been true of most groups in most times. Solomon is more to blame, by concealing his true identity, since he must know that there are few plausible futures for them. Still, it's possible that Gaenor would have slept with him even if she'd known the truth; certainly she has sex with him before knowing the answers to those questions any prudent woman would first want answers to.

The movie's ending wants to inspire tears, but I was dry-eyed, perhaps as a response to its morose labors. It is one thing to be the victim of fate, and it is another thing to go looking for fate and wrestle it to the ground. The genius of *Romeo and Juliet* is that we can understand, step by step, how and why the situation develops. With *Solomon & Gaenor*, it is hard to overlook the folly of the characters. Does it count as a tragedy when the characters get more or less what they were asking for?

Someone Like You ★ ★
PG-13, 97 m., 2001

Ashley Judd (Jane Goodale), Greg Kinnear (Ray), Hugh Jackman (Eddie), Ellen Barkin (Diane), Matthew Coyle (Kooky Staff Member), LeAnna Croom (Rebecca), Hugh Downs (Himself), Marisa Tomei (Liz). Directed by Tony Goldwyn and produced by Lynda Obst. Screenplay by Elizabeth Chandler, based on the novel *Animal Husbandry* by Laura Zigman.

Ashley Judd plays Jane, a woman with a theory, in *Someone Like You*. It is the Old Cow, New Cow theory, and she developed it after reading an article in the science section of the newspaper. According to the article, there is no way to get a bull to service the same cow twice. You can paint the old cow blue or spray it with perfume, but the bull's not fooled: Been there, done that. The theory says that men are like bulls, and that's why they are tirelessly motivated to move on from old conquests to new challenges.

This is not precisely a novel theory, although it has been stated in more appealing forms ("If you can't be with the one you love, love the one you're with"). If the theory is correct, it gets men off the hook for their swinish behavior, since we are hard-wired that way and cannot be blamed for millions of years of tunnel-vision evolution. But is it correct? Even about bulls? On the answer to this question depends Jane's future happiness, as well as ours while we are watching the movie.

In *Someone Like You*, Judd plays Jane Goodale, not the chimp lady but a staffer on a daytime talk show hosted by Ellen Barkin. Also on the staff are Ray (Greg Kinnear) and Eddie (Hugh Jackman). Ray is in a relationship

Eddie is a walking, talking example of the Old Cow, New Cow theory, introducing a new cow to his bedroom every night. Jane likes Ray, and Ray, despite his old cow at home, likes Jane, who is a new cow, and so they have an affair, but then she becomes an old cow and the previous old cow begins to look like a new cow again, and so they break up. Jane has meanwhile given up her apartment because she thought she was going to move in with Ray, and so she becomes Eddie's platonic roommate, clocking the cow traffic.

This is, you will have gathered, a pretty lame premise. The screenplay is based on *Animal Husbandry*, a novel by Laura Zigman, unread by me. As a movie, it knows little about men, women, or television shows, but has studied movie formulas so carefully that we can see each new twist and turn as it creeps ever so slowly into view. Will Ray return to Jane? Will she begin to like Eddie? Can Eddie settle for one cow? What about the identity of Ray's mysterious girlfriend? Students of my Law of Economy of Characters will know that movies are thrifty and have a use for all the characters they introduce, and so the solution to that mystery arrives long, long after we have figured it out.

For a movie about a TV show, this one doesn't know much about television. The whole denouement depends on us believing that this high-rated show would do a telephone interview with an anonymous magazine columnist who has become famous for the Old Cow, New Cow theory, and that Jane (who writes the column anonymously) would then decide to blow her cover, burst onto the set, and deliver an endless monologue about how much wiser she is now than she used to be. The chances of a production assistant standing in front of the star of a TV show and talking for several minutes are approximately zero, especially since, let's face it, she's babbling: Her speech reminded me of something in a barnyard. It's not a cow, although it's often found close to one.

Songcatcher ★ ★ ★
PG-13, 112 m., 2001

Janet McTeer (Dr. Lily Penleric), Emmy Rossum (Deladis Slocumb), Aidan Quinn (Tom Bledsoe), Pat Carroll (Viney Butler), Jane Adams (Elna Penleric), E. Katherine Kerr (Harriet Tolliver), David Patrick Kelly (Earl Gibbons), Greg Cook (Fate Honeycutt), Iris DeMent (Rose Gentry), Stephanie Roth (Alice Kincaid), Mike Harding (Reese Kincaid). Directed by Maggie Greenwald and produced by Richard Miller and Ellen Rigas-Venetis. Screenplay by Greenwald.

Songcatcher tells the story of a woman who goes into the mountains of Appalachia in 1907, and finds the people singing British ballads that are almost unchanged since they arrived two hundred years earlier. It is also a feminist parable transplanted to earlier times, revealing too much consciousness of modern values. I'm more comfortable with the women I find in Willa Cather's novels, who live at about the same time, who strive to be independent and to be taken seriously, and yet are entirely in and of their worlds. The characters in a serious historical story should not know what happens later.

If we accept *Songcatcher* as a contemporary parable in period costumes, however, there is much to enjoy—not least the sound of the songs themselves. "I have never been anywhere where the music is so much a part of life as it is here," says Dr. Lily Penleric (Janet McTeer), the musicologist, who has fled to the mountains in anger after being passed over for an academic appointment she clearly deserves. The people of these North Carolina hills would as soon sing as talk, and indeed there's a scene where Tom Bledsoe (Aidan Quinn) knocks a man down, and the man stands up and starts to sing.

Tom is a suspicious leader of these people, and doubts Dr. Penleric's motives. He thinks she wants to steal his people's songs. He is right, although she calls it collecting, and hauls heavy Edison equipment up the hillside so she can record the songs on wax cylinders and maybe sell them in stores. She considers this preserving their culture. "The only way to preserve our way of life up here," Tom tells her, "is to preserve your way of life—down there."

We meet the people of the settlement: Viney Butler (Pat Carroll), a Ma Joad type; Deladis Slocumb (Emmy Rossum), a young woman with a voice pure and true; Elna Penleric (Jane Adams), the professor's sister, who has come here to start a one-room school; and her fellow teacher and lover Harriet Tolliver (E. Katherine Kerr), who says she will flee if anyone ever discovers she is a lesbian. Then there's David Patrick Kelly as a coal company representative, who wants to strip mine the land. There are so many issues simmering here in the hollow that it's a wonder Jeff Greenfield doesn't materialize and hold a town meeting.

The movie has a good amount of sex for a drama about folk music collecting. The lesbians find a secluded glade in the woods, Dr. Penleric and Tom Bledsoe feel powerful urges, and there's a local philanderer named Reese Kincaid (Mike Harding) who cheats on his wife, Alice (Stephanie Roth). The most startling sex scene involves the musicologist and the mountain man; a piercing scream rents the air, and we see Dr. Penleric running through the woods tearing off her clothes before discovering Tom in a clearing and covering him passionately with kisses. The scream comes from a panther (at first I thought it was the noon whistle), and Lilly has been advised by Viney to flee from such an attack by throwing off her clothes to distract it; as a depiction of Victorian morality making the leap into modern lust, this scene will serve.

I liked the tone of the movie, and its spirit. I liked the lashings of melodrama in the midst of the music collecting. Most of all, I liked the songs, especially one sung by Iris DeMent as a woman who loses her home, and by young Emmy Rossum when she is urged to give the newcomer a sample of her singing voice. *Songcatcher* is perhaps too laden with messages for its own good, but it has many moments of musical beauty, and it's interesting to watch Janet McTeer as she starts with Lily Penleric as a cold, abstract academic, and allows her, little by little, to warm in the sun of these songs.

South ★ ★ ★

NO MPAA RATING, 80 m., 1915 (rereleased 2000)

A documentary featuring Ernest Shackleton, Captain Frank Worsley, Captain Frank Wild, Captain L. Hussey, Lieutenant J. Shenbouse, Frank Hurley, and Tom Crean. Directed by Hurley.

The most astonishing fact about *South* is that it exists at all. This is a documentary filmed in 1915 of Sir Ernest Shackleton's doomed expedition to the South Pole—a venture ending with his ship, *Endurance*, trapped in ice that eventually destroyed it, while he and five men made an 800-mile journey through frigid seas (and then scaled a glacier!) to bring help. That the expedition was filmed and that the film survived the shipwreck is astonishing.

South, which has now been restored, is essentially a home movie shot very far from home. The cinematographer, Frank Hurley, was a crew member whose approach is essentially to point his camera and trust to the subtitles to explain what we see. "Sir Ernest Shackleton, Leader of the Expedition," we read, while Shackleton poses self-consciously for posterity. Another title explains that a sick dog is being given medicine while the others look on enviously, thinking it's being fed. We see the crew member Tom Crean with a litter of puppies born onboard. Later, "Sulky, the black leader dog, trains the pups in harness."

Watching these images, we are absorbed, as we often are with silent film, in a reverie that is a collaboration with the images. We note how surprisingly small the *Endurance* is. How its crew of less than thirty become anonymous figures, bundled beyond recognition in cloth and fur, as they trudge across limitless snow. How the ship seems to be the only thing of human manufacture in the ice world. How later it is joined by another, as Shackleton tests a "motor sledge" which he thought might take the place of dog teams, but which had the unfortunate drawback of needing to be pushed by men or pulled by dogs. (And what dogs! There are breathtaking shots of them pulling a sled through snow powder almost over their heads.)

Some of Hurley's shots speak for themselves. It becomes clear that the worst Antarctic winter ever recorded will prevent the ship from reaching the point where Shackleton wants to drop off men, dogs, and supplies. Hurley and his camera hang from the prow of the *Endurance* as the ship opens up sudden, jagged cracks in the quickly forming ice. We see countless crab seals migrating north, as a title tells us a dismal season is on the way. We see the men building ice pylons to lead back to the ship because, in the storms of the Antarctic night, it is possible to become lost forever just a few yards from safety. And we see an astonishing sight: The *Endurance* photographed in the middle of the polar night with the use of eighteen light-bulbs, which reflect off the ice on every line and mast to make it glitter like a ghost ship.

After the *Endurance* is locked in ice, the men use two-handed logger's saws to try to cut through. When the ship then backs up and tries to ram itself free, Hurley and his camera are positioned on the ice, dangerously close to the front of it, and we imagine them disappearing into a sudden fissure—but the ice holds, eventually breaking the rudder and then caving in the sides of the ship. The dogs are evacuated, skidding nervously to safety down a canvas chute. The camera watches as the *Endurance* tilts and dies, its masts toppling over.

There is, of course, no footage of the 800-mile journey in a small lifeboat that Shackleton completed to bring rescue (not a single man was lost from the expedition). But Hurley does show us the glacier they had to scale on South Georgia Island, in order to reach the inhabited far shore. And an albatross like the one that provided their first meal on land. They encountered "quaint birds and beasts," a subtitle tells us, and "these pictures were obtained with a good deal of time and effort"—an understatement.

There is probably too much natural history toward the end of the film; we see elephant seals while the fate of the stranded crew members hangs in abeyance. Finally all are united and cheered as they return to safety. The *Endurance* did not get anywhere near the South Pole, but the expedition did sail into legend—like Robert Falcon Scott's attempt in 1911–12, where he lost a race to the Pole to the Norwegian Roald Amundsen and died on the return, but far overshadowed the Norwegian's fame. Ironic, that the two most famous British South Pole explorers either failed to begin or died on the way back. (Kevin McCorry, a writer on polar expeditions, quotes Amundsen's laconic commentary, "Never underestimate the British habit of dying. The glory of self-sacrifice, the blessing of failure.")

The overwhelming impression left by *South,* however, is of the bravery of everyone who ventured to the Pole. These men did not have cargo planes to drop supplies, satellites to tell them their position, solar panels for heating and electricity, or even adequate clothing. But they had pluck, and Frank Hurley with his hand-cranked camera recorded them, still to be seen, specks of life and hope in an ice wilderness.

South Park: Bigger, Longer and Uncut ★ ★ ½
R, 80 m., 1999

An animated film with the voices of Trey Parker, Matthew Stone, Isaac Hayes, George Clooney, Minnie Driver, Mike Judge, and Eric Idle. Directed by Trey Parker and produced by Parker and Matt Stone. Screenplay by Parker, Stone, and Pam Brady.

The national debate about violence and obscenity in the movies has arrived in South Park. The "little redneck mountain town," where adult cynicism is found in the mouths of babes, is the setting for vicious social satire in *South Park: Bigger, Longer and Uncut.* The most slashing political commentary of the year is not in the new film by Oliver Stone, David Lynch, or John Sayles, but in an animated musical comedy about obscenity. Wait until you see the bedroom scenes between Satan and Saddam Hussein.

Waves of four-letter words roll out over the audience, which laughs with incredulity: People can't believe what they're hearing. The film has an R rating instead of NC-17 only because it's a cartoon, I suspect; even so, the MPAA has a lot of 'splaining to do. Not since Andrew Dice Clay passed into obscurity have sentences been constructed so completely out of the unspeakable.

I laughed. I did not always feel proud of myself while I was laughing, however. The movie is like a depraved extension of *Kids Say the Darnedest Things,* in which little children repeat what they've heard, and we cringe because we know what the words really mean. No target is too low, no attitude too mean or hurtful, no image too unthinkable. After making *South Park: Bigger, Longer and Uncut,* its creators, Trey Parker and Matt Stone, had better move on. They've taken *South Park* as far as it can go, and beyond.

If you've never seen the original Comedy Central TV show and somehow find yourself in the theater, you'll be jolted by the distance between the images and the content. The animation is deliberately crude, like elements cut out of construction paper. Characters are made of simple arrangements of basic geometrical shapes and solid colors. When they talk, their lips don't move; their entire heads tilt open in synch with the words. The effect is of sophisticated children slamming stuff around on the project table in first grade.

The story: A new R-rated movie has come to town, starring the Canadian stars Terrence and Phillip. It's titled *Asses of Fire.* (That's the mildest vulgarity in the movie, and the most extreme I can print in the paper.) The South Park kids bribe a homeless man to be their "adult guardian," attend the movie, drink in its nonstop, wall-to-wall language, and startle their class at school with streams of four-letter words.

One of their moms, deeply offended, founds the Mothers Against Canada (its acronym no doubt targeted at the cosmetics company). The neighbor to the north is blamed for all of the ills in U.S. society, Terrence and Phillip are arrested and condemned to death, and in retaliation the Canadian Air Force bombs the home of the Baldwin brothers in Hollywood. War is declared, leading to scenes your eyes will register but your mind will not believe, such as a USO show involving Winona Ryder doing unspeakable things with Ping-Pong balls.

The other plot strand begins after little Kenny is killed. (This is not a spoiler; little Kenny is killed in each and every episode of the TV series, always with the line, "Oh, my God! They've killed Kenny!") He goes to hell (we see Hitler and George Burns drifting past) and finds that Saddam Hussein, recently deceased, is having an affair with Satan. Saddam wants sex, Satan wants a meaningful relationship, and they inspire a book titled *Saddam Is from Mars, Satan Is from Venus.*

Key plot point: The deaths of Terrence and Phillip would be the seventh biblical sign of the apocalypse, triggering Armageddon. It's up to the South Park kids to save the world. All of this unfolds against an unending stream of satirical abuse, ethnic stereotyping, sexual vulgarity, and pointed political commentary that alternates common sense with the truly and hurtfully offensive.

I laughed, as I have reported. Sometimes the laughter was liberating, as good laughter

can be, and sometimes it was simply disbelieving: How could they get away with this? This is a season when the movies are hurtling themselves over the precipice of good taste. Every week brings its new surprises. I watch as Austin Powers drinks coffee that contains excrement, and two weeks later I go to *American Pie* and watch a character drink beer that contains the most famous bodily fluid from *There's Something About Mary.* In *Big Daddy,* I see an adult role model instruct a five-year-old on how to trip in-line skaters, urinate in public, and spill the french fries of complete strangers in McDonald's.

Now this—a cartoon, but it goes far beyond anything in any of those live-action movies. All it lacks is a point to its message. What is it saying? That movies have gone too far, or that protests against movies have gone too far? It is a sign of our times that I cannot tell. Perhaps it's simply anarchistic, and feels that if it throws enough shocking material at the wall, some of it will stick. A lot of the movie offended me. Some of it amazed me. It is too long and runs out of steam, but it serves as a signpost for our troubled times. Just for the information it contains about the way we live now, maybe thoughtful and concerned people should see it. After all, everyone else will.

Note: Reading this again, I think it's more of a three-star review. The movie is unsettling, but that's a good thing; my doubts are a tribute to it.

Space Cowboys ★ ★ ★
PG-13, 123 m., 2000

Clint Eastwood (Frank Corvin), Tommy Lee Jones (Hawk Hawkins), Donald Sutherland (Jerry O'Neil), James Garner (Tank Sullivan), Loren Dean (Ethan Glance), Marcia Gay Harden (Sara Holland), James Cromwell (Bob Gerson), William Devane (Eugene Davis). Directed by Clint Eastwood and produced by Andrew Lazar. Screenplay by Ken Kaufman and Howard A. Klausner.

The guys who had the original right stuff get a second chance in *Space Cowboys,* forty-two years after their air force experimental flights in the X-2 rocket plane were replaced by orbiting monkeys and something called "astronauts." When NASA desperately needs expertise that only grizzled veteran Frank Corvin (Clint Eastwood) can offer, he issues an ultimatum: His original team goes into space with him, or else.

"I can't fill up a space shuttle with geriatrics!" moans space program official Bob Gerson (James Cromwell). "The clock's ticking, Bob," says Frank, "and I'm only getting older."

Eastwood has been having fun with his age for years. In *Absolute Power* (1997), accused of being a cat burglar, he tells the cops: "Go down a rope in the middle of the night? If I could do that, I'd be the star of my AARP meetings." The joke is that Eastwood, lean and mean, doesn't seem ready for retirement. And the old air force buddies and rivals he gathers for the space flight aren't old enough for the remake of *Cocoon*. Tommy Lee Jones, like Eastwood, is a plausible action star and will be for years. James Garner and Donald Sutherland are bald and graying here, but don't qualify as codgers. "You sent up John Glenn!" Eastwood barks at the NASA functionary.

Like Eastwood's *Unforgiven*, about veteran Western tough guys, *Space Cowboys* tells a genre story where the heroes have come out of retirement for one last hurrah. As the film opens, a satellite from the former Soviet Union is falling toward Earth, and only an emergency mission can steer it back into orbit. The computer code on board is so ancient only one man can understand it—Eastwood, who wrote it in the first place. "How did American code get on board a Soviet satellite in the middle of the cold war?" Eastwood reasonably asks. The answer is obvious (they stole it), but there's another secret lurking in space that comes as a nasty surprise for the repair crew.

The gathering of the crew takes place in an ancient and obligatory way: The leader (Eastwood) visits each man in the place where life has taken him, and yanks him back into the past. Hawk Hawkins (Tommy Lee Jones) is a stunt pilot. Jerry O'Neil (Donald Sutherland) designs roller coasters. Tank Sullivan (James Garner) is a preacher. They all cave in to Eastwood's call—even though one of them, of course, is an old rival who still bears a grudge.

After the gathering comes a montage in which the men train and prepare—also obligatory in movies like this. Secret schemes are

revealed. Love interest develops between Jones and Marcia Gay Harden, as a space agency functionary. We meet the gum-chewing mission director (William Devane). And there's one of those early scenes where a hero does something daring and tricky in practice, and we know with certainly that he will be required to do it again later in an emergency situation.

Great swatches of *Space Cowboys* are constructed, indeed, out of generic expectations. But the stuff in outer space is unexpected, the surprise waiting out there is genuine, and meanwhile there's the abundance of charm and screen presence from the four veteran actors. There is a reason Eastwood, Garner, Sutherland, and Jones have remained stars for so long, and the movie gives them all characteristic scenes. (Sutherland's ladies' man has a funny moment on the *Jay Leno* show—only a line of dialogue, but it has been well set up and gets a big laugh.)

Space Cowboys lacks the urgency of a movie like *The Right Stuff*—it's too secure within its traditional story structure to make much seem at risk—but with the structure come the traditional pleasures, as well. The actors know where the laughs and thrills are, and respect them. Eastwood as director is as sure-handed as his mentors, Don Siegel and Sergio Leone. We leave the theater with grave doubts that the scene depicted in the final feel-good shot is even remotely possible, but what the hell; it makes us smile.

Spy Kids ★ ★ ★ ½
PG, 90 m., 2001

Antonio Banderas (Gregorio Cortez), Alan Cumming (Fegan Floop), Carla Gugino (Ingrid Cortez), Teri Hatcher (Ms. Gradenko), Angela Lanza (Reporter), Daryl Sabara (Juni Cortez), Tony Shalhoub (Minion), Alexa Vega (Carmen Cortez), Cheech Marin (Uncle Felix). Directed by Robert Rodriguez and produced by Elizabeth Avellan and Rodriguez. Screenplay by Rodriguez.

Spy Kids is giddy with the joy of its invention. It's an exuberant, colorful extravaganza, wall-to-wall with wildly original sets and visual gimmicks, and smart enough to escape the kid's film category and play in the mainstream. You can imagine Robert Rodriguez, the writer and director, grinning as he dreamed up this stuff. And being amazed that his visual-effects team could get it all on film so brilliantly.

The movie begins with Antonio Banderas and Carla Gugino as Gregorio and Ingrid Cortez, spies who were once enemies but then fall in love and get married and have two great kids, Carmen (Alexa Vega) and Juni (Daryl Sabara). They retire from the spy business, but then an evil minion named Minion (Tony Shalhoub) kidnaps the parents, and it's up to the spy kids to rescue them and save the world from the threat of robo-kids and Thumb Monsters.

Minion works for the diabolical Fegan Floop (Alan Cumming), whose job as a kiddie-show host masks his scheme to rule the world. His operation, centered in a fantastical seaside castle, includes workers who are all thumbs, literally: thumbs for heads, arms, and legs. Floop runs a cloning operation to turn out exact robotic copies of the children of powerful people. They look like the originals except for eyes with an eerie glow. Their problem: The brains aren't up to speed. Floop's answer: the Third Brain, which Gregorio Cortez secretly took along with him when he left the spy service.

This sounds, I know, like a plot for eight-year-olds, but Rodriguez charges at the material as if he wants to blow Indiana Jones out of the water, and the movie is just one outrageous invention after another. My feeling is that a "family movie" fails if it doesn't entertain the parents, since they're the ones who have to buy the tickets. Spy Kids is so endlessly imaginative, so high-spirited, so extravagant with its inspirations, so filled with witty dialogue, that the more you like movies, the more you may like this one.

The plot. After the kidnapping, it's up to the kids to rescue their parents, with a little help from their Uncle Felix (Cheech Marin) and guidance from Ms. Gradenko (Teri Hatcher), who claims to be a friend of their mother's from the old spy days. The kids have repaired to a secret "safe house," which is a lot different inside than outside, and they utilize all sorts of spy gimmicks; some they understand, some they don't. What's neat is the way the kids don't

act like kids: They go about their business seriously, and along the way little Juni gains the self-confidence he needs (at school, he was the target of bullies).

Rodriguez has always been in love with special effects (as in his vampire movie From Dusk Till Dawn), and here he combines computer-generated images with brightly colored sets that look like a riot in a paint box. The movie's props range from bubble gum that can be used as a tracking device to the parents' car, which doubles as a submarine. And there's great imagination in a scene where the kids commandeer a combination aircraft-speedboat-submarine with a plump fish design that looks like something Captain Nemo might have dreamed up.

With a movie so enchanting and cheerful, I want to resist sociological observations, but it should be noted that Rodriguez has made a mainstream family film in which most of the heroic roles are assigned to Hispanic characters (at one point, the Banderas character even jokes about all the Latinos on Floop's TV show). It should also be observed that he avoids disturbing violence, that the entire movie is in a cheerful kidding spirit, and that the stunts and skills exhibited by the kids look fun, not scary. The props, even the boat-plane-sub, look like extensions of their toys, not like adult inventions that have been scaled down.

Movies like Spy Kids are so rare. Families are often reduced to attending scatological dumber-and-dumbest movies like See Spot Run—movies that teach vulgarity as a value. Spy Kids is an intelligent, upbeat, happy movie that is not about the comedy of embarrassment, that does not have anybody rolling around in dog poop, that would rather find out what it can accomplish than what it can get away with. It's a treasure.

Startup.com ★ ★ ★
R, 103 m., 2001

A documentary directed by Chris Hegedus and Jehane Noujaim and produced by D. A. Pennebaker.

It seemed like a great idea at the time. They'd build a place on-line where people could go to pay their parking tickets. Startup.com tells the story of two longtime friends who go into business together, create a Website, raise millions, and at one point are worth $12 million—apiece, I think, but it makes no difference, because by the end of their adventure they have lost everything. The movie's story arc is like *Charly* or *Awakenings*, in which the heroes start low, fly high, and crash.

The friends are named Kaleil Isaza Tuzman and Tom Herman. Their idea is so compelling that Tuzman quits a job at Goodman, Sachs to move to the Internet. The story starts in May 1999, when instant Web millionaires were a dime a dozen, and ends in January 2001. The documentary's last shots were filmed only three weeks before it premiered at Sundance, still wet from the lab. As an inside view of the bursting of the Internet bubble, *Startup.com* is definitive. We sense there were lots of stories more or less like this one.

To film this sort of doc, you need access. The movie has it. One codirector, Jehane Noujaim, was Tuzman's Harvard roommate. She's also the cinematographer, and her digital camera has access to startlingly private moments. The other director, Chris Hegedus, has worked on such insider docs as *The War Room*, the story of the Clinton campaign. She coproduced that one with D. A. Pennebaker, the legendary documentarian, who is also the producer this time.

When the film begins, the new company doesn't even have a name. They settle on govWorks.com. Tuzman and Herman make the rounds of venture capitalists, and it's obvious that Tuzman is the expert pitcher, while Herman, more technically oriented, drives his partner crazy by bringing up bright ideas in meetings on the spur of the moment. Tuzman lectures him to stay on message. Dollar signs dance before their eyes. At one point in Boston they're offered $17 million but lose the deal when they can't get their lawyers on the phone.

Meanwhile, of course, there's the problem of actually writing the software. It would seem to me that paying parking tickets over the Internet would involve basic programming skills plus cosmetic packaging, but no, apparently it's rocket science: Eventually govWorks.com has 200 employees working on the site, and still Tuzman despairs that it's not good enough to be released to the public.

Famous figures float in and out of view. The partners smile from the covers of business magazines. Former Atlanta mayor Maynard Jackson turns up as a consultant. Tuzman appears on TV sitting next to President Clinton, who chairs a summit meeting on the Internet. Meanwhile, Tuzman and Herman, under enormous pressure, go through girlfriends and beards. Herman grows his beard and shaves it off so many times that the filmmakers finally photograph him in front of the mirror with a razor, just to explain the continuity errors. And Tuzman's girlfriends complain that he pays them no attention: "Just a call is all I ask," one says. "A simple call saying you're thinking of me, you're busy, but you miss me. That would keep me going for two weeks." She disappears from the film; her replacement also finds Tuzman a moving target.

There are setbacks. The govWorks office is broken into. Files are stolen. But that's not as big a problem as the disappointing software, and then comes the dot.com meltdown that dries up funds just when the site is turning the corner. On the day govWorks was sold to a competitor, we learn, it landed the big New York City contract.

Noujaim's camera catches painfully intimate moments, as the two old friends argue, split, and Herman leaves the company; in an age-old security ritual, he is "escorted from the building" and guards are told not to readmit him. Today, I learn, Tuzman and Herman are back in business together. My guess is, they could make it this time. The Internet is fundamentally sound. The bubble had to burst to correct its crazy overvaluation. Now that sanity has returned, bright guys like Tuzman and Herman can find more opportunities. All they need is another great idea. And better software.

Star Wars Episode I: The Phantom Menace ★ ★ ★ ½
PG, 133 m., 1999

Liam Neeson (Qui-Gon Jinn), Ewan McGregor (Obi-Wan Kenobi), Natalie Portman (Queen Amidala), Jake Lloyd (Anakin Skywalker), Pernilla August (Shmi Skywalker), Frank Oz (Yoda), Ian McDiarmid (Senator Palpatine), Oliver Ford Davies (Sio Bibble), Hugh Quarshie

(Captain Panaka), Ahmed Best (Jar Jar Binks), Samuel L. Jackson (Mace Windu), Ray Park (Darth Maul), Peter Serafinowicz (Voice of Darth Maul), Ralph Brown (Ric Olie), Terence Stamp (Chancellor Valorum). Directed by George Lucas and produced by Rick McCallum. Screenplay by Lucas.

If it were the first *Star Wars* movie, *The Phantom Menace* would be hailed as a visionary breakthrough. But this is the fourth movie in the famous series, and we think we know the territory; many of the early reviews have been blasé, paying lip service to the visuals and wondering why the characters aren't better developed. How quickly do we grow accustomed to wonders. I am reminded of the Asimov story *Nightfall,* about the planet where the stars were visible only once in a thousand years. So awesome was the sight that it drove men mad. We who can see the stars every night glance up casually at the cosmos and then quickly down again, searching for a Dairy Queen.

Star Wars Episode I: The Phantom Menace, to cite its full title, is an astonishing achievement in imaginative filmmaking. If some of the characters are less than compelling, perhaps that's inevitable: This is the first story in the chronology, and has to set up characters who (we already know) will become more interesting with the passage of time. Here we first see Obi-Wan Kenobi, Anakin Skywalker, Yoda, and prototypes of R2D2 and C3PO. Anakin is only a fresh-faced kid in Episode I; in IV, V, and VI he has become Darth Vader.

At the risk of offending devotees of the Force, I will say that the stories in the *Star Wars* movies have always been space operas, and that the importance of the movies comes from their energy, their sense of fun, their colorful inventions, and their state-of-the-art special effects. I do not attend expecting to gain insights into human behavior. Unlike many movies, these are made to be looked at more than listened to, and George Lucas and his collaborators have filled *Phantom Menace* with wonderful visuals.

There are new places here—new *kinds* of places. Consider the underwater cities, floating in their transparent membranes. The Senate chamber, a vast sphere with senators arrayed along the inside walls and speakers floating on pods in the center. And other places: The cityscape with the waterfall that has a dizzying descent through space. And other cities—one city Venetian, with canals, another looking like a hothouse version of imperial Rome, and a third that seems to have grown out of desert sands.

Set against awesome backdrops, the characters in *Phantom Menace* inhabit a plot that is little more complex than the stories I grew up on in science-fiction magazines. The whole series sometimes feels like a cover from *Thrilling Wonder Stories* come to life. The dialogue is pretty flat and straightforward, although seasoned with a little quasi-classical formality, as if the characters had read but not retained *Julius Caesar.* I wish the *Star Wars* characters spoke with more elegance and wit (as Gore Vidal's Greeks and Romans do), but dialogue isn't the point anyway: These movies are about new things to look at.

The plot details (embargoes, blockades) tend to diminish the size of the movie's universe, anyway—to shrink it to the scale of a nineteenth-century trade dispute. The stars themselves are little more than pinpoints on a black curtain, and *Star Wars* has not drawn inspiration from the color photographs being captured by the Hubble telescope. The series is essentially human mythology, set in space but not occupying it. If Kubrick gave us man humbled by the universe, Lucas gives us the universe domesticated by man. His aliens are really just humans in odd skins. Consider Jar Jar Binks, a fully realized, computer-animated alien character whose physical movements seem based on afterthoughts. And Jabba the Hutt (who presides over the Pod race) has always seemed positively Dickensian to me.

Yet within the rules he has established, Lucas tells a good story. The key development in *Phantom* is the first meeting between the Jedi knight Qui-Gon Jinn (Liam Neeson) and the young boy Anakin Skywalker (Jake Lloyd)— who is, the Jedi immediately senses, fated for great things. Qui-Gon meets Anakin in a store where he's seeking replacement parts for his crippled ship. He soon finds himself backing the young slave in a high-speed Pod race—betting his ship itself against the cost of the replacement parts. The race is one of the film's high points, as the entrants rush between high cliff walls in a refinement of a similar race through metal canyons on a spaceship in *Star Wars.*

Why is Qui-Gon so confident that Anakin can win? Because he senses an unusual concentration of the Force—and perhaps because, like John the Baptist, he instinctively recognizes the one whose way he is destined to prepare. The film's shakiness on the psychological level is evident, however, in the scene where young Anakin is told he must leave his mother (Pernilla August) and follow this tall Jedi stranger. Their mutual resignation to the parting seems awfully restrained. I expected a tearful scene of parting between mother and child, but the best we get is when Anakin asks if his mother can come along, and she replies, "Son, my place is here." As a slave?

The discovery and testing of Anakin supplies the film's most important action, but in a sense all the action is equally important, because it provides platforms for special-effects sequences. Sometimes our common sense undermines a sequence (as Jar Jar's people and the good guys fight a 'droid army, it becomes obvious that the 'droids are such bad fighters they should be returned for a refund). But mostly I was happy to drink in the sights on the screen, in the same spirit that I might enjoy *Metropolis, Forbidden Planet, 2001, Dark City,* or *The Matrix.* The difference is that Lucas's visuals are more fanciful and the energy level of his film more cheerful; he doesn't share the prevailing view that the future is a dark and lonely place.

What he does have, in abundance, is exhilaration. There is a sense of discovery in scene after scene of *Phantom Menace,* as he tries out new effects and ideas, and seamlessly integrates real characters and digital ones, real landscapes and imaginary places. We are standing at the threshold of a new age of epic cinema, I think, in which digital techniques mean that budgets will no longer limit the scope of scenes; filmmakers will be able to show us just about anything they can conceive of.

As surely as Anakin Skywalker points the way into the future of *Star Wars,* so does *The Phantom Menace* raise the curtain on this new freedom for filmmakers. And it's a lot of fun. The film has correctly been given the PG rating; it's suitable for younger viewers, and doesn't depend on violence for its effects. As for the bad rap about the characters—hey, I've seen space operas that put their emphasis on human personalities and relationships. They're called *Star Trek* movies. Give me membranous underwater cities and vast, hollow senatorial spheres any day. ☞

State and Main ★ ★ ★
R, 106 m., 2000

Alec Baldwin (Bob Barrenger), Charles Durning (Mayor George Bailey), Philip Seymour Hoffman (Joseph Turner White), William H. Macy (Walt Price), Patti LuPone (Sherry Bailey), Sarah Jessica Parker (Claire Wellesley), David Paymer (Marty Rossen), Rebecca Pidgeon (Ann Black), Clark Gregg (Doug Mackenie), Julia Stiles (Carla Taylor). Directed by David Mamet and produced by Sarah Green. Screenplay by Mamet.

"Marty, we got a new town. Waterford, Vermont." (Pause) "Where is it? That's where it is."

David Mamet has a playful side that's sometimes overlooked, since his plays often favor lowlifes and con men. He delights in using dialogue to provide quick, sideways insights into his characters, and in *State and Main* he's directed his first pure comedy, although of course there was a lot of humor in *Things Change* and his screenplay *Wag the Dog.*

This is a playful movie about a film company that arrives in Waterford, Vermont (explained above), after having to beat a quick retreat out of New Hampshire, allegedly because a town lacked an old mill that could be used as a location, but more directly because Bob Barrenger (Alec Baldwin), the movie's star, has a weakness for junior high school girls.

The lines above are spoken on the phone by Walt Price (William H. Macy), the director of the film within a film. Macy brings along some of the same frustration he used in *Fargo,* as the car salesman trying to conceal fatal evidence, but he's more of a diplomat here, using tact and lies to soothe the townspeople, coddle his temperamental stars, and coax rewrites out of

541

his easily wounded screenwriter (Philip Seymour Hoffman). Of course, he denies that he lies: "It's not a lie. It's a gift for fiction."

Mamet knows, from having directed nine films and written thirty-one, how even the most sensible projects eventually seem to hinge on crucial but utterly absurd details. His characters obsess about "the old mill," and a shot where the camera will be required to enter a firehouse through a window, and whether the heroine will do a topless scene. These details are more important to Walt Price than anything else in his movie, because they are *today's* problems. The long view is quickly abandoned on location.

Mamet populates his film with a large cast of movie pros and townspeople. Charles Durning and Patti LuPone play the town mayor and his wife, who prepare a dinner for the visitors that would shame Martha Stewart. Sarah Jessica Parker plays the actress who unexpectedly refuses to bare her breasts (even though, as the Baldwin character observes, the nation could "draw them from memory"). David Paymer is the harried producer, instructed by the director to find more money even though there is no money to be found.

Hoffman and Rebecca Pidgeon, as the owner of a local bookstore, have a sweet side plot when they suddenly fall in love. She's engaged to be married, but so awestruck by the visiting screenwriter, and so touched when he turns to her for help and advice, that at one point she almost forgets the name of her fiancé (Clark Gregg) while trying to introduce him. Eventually the whole production waits while the writer and his new girl sit on a bench and try to solve screenplay problems. Meanwhile, Julia Stiles uses saucy comic timing in the other major subplot. She's the local teenager who catches the eye of Baldwin's lustful movie star. He'll have to move fast to seduce her before she seduces him.

Visitors from Hollywood are considered heaven-sent by some citizens in the small towns where movies are shot, and the spawn of the devil by others. While the fiancé tries to shake down the production company, the company tries to cover up details involving a scandalous car crash, and meanwhile the cinematographer tries to figure out how his camera can move through a priceless stained-glass

window without breaking it, and the Macy character learns that the old mill and many other buildings were the victims of "a spate of suspicious fires" back in 1960.

With a few adjustments, *State and Main* could be adapted for the stage, where it would play as a farce of the *Noises Off* variety. It's Mamet in a lighthearted mood, playing with dialogue, repeating phrases just because he likes them, and supplying us with a closing line that achieves, I think, a kind of greatness.

Steal This Movie ★ ★ ★
R, 111 m., 2000

Vincent D'Onofrio (Abbie Hoffman), Janeane Garofolo (Anita Hoffman), Jeanne Tripplehorn (Johanna Lawrenson), Kevin Pollak (Gerry Lefcourt), Donal Logue (Stew Albert), Kevin Corrigan (Jerry Rubin), Alan Van Sprang (David Glenn), Troy Garity (Tom Hayden). Directed by Robert Greenwald and produced by Greenwald and Jacobus Rose. Screenplay by Bruce Graham.

Abbie Hoffman inspired some of the zaniest footnotes of the Vietnam War era with improv performances mixing civil disobedience and anarchist street theater. Some of his stunts had a certain brilliance, as when he scattered dollar bills onto the floor of the New York Stock Exchange and the traders dropped scrambling to their knees.

Hoffman was the clown prince of the antiwar movement. While Tom Hayden sawed away seriously at the 1968 Democratic convention, Abbie was announcing plans to drop LSD into the Chicago water supply—a threat Mayor Richard J. Daley took seriously (I remember the Chicago police boats ominously guarding the filtration plant). When Hayden, Hoffman, and their fellow Chicago Seven members were hauled up before Judge Julius Hoffman, surely the last jurist in America who should have been chosen to preside, Hayden and his allies played it straight while Hoffman treated the event like a circus.

Abbie Hoffman's Yippies provided the linguistic link between Hippies and yuppies. *Steal This Movie* provides an untidy and frustrating but never boring look at his life and times. More than anyone else in recent American history, he was able to capture headlines and gain national attention just with the audacity of his imagination. When he announced that he and fellow Yippie Party members would levitate the Pentagon, he drew an enormous crowd—among them Norman Mailer, who confessed that although he doubted Hoffman could do it, he wanted to be there, just in case. Richard Nixon and J. Edgar Hoover didn't get the joke, but then that was the whole point.

The movie traces the trajectory of Hoffman (played by Vincent D'Onofrio) from the early 1960s, when he was a civil rights worker in the South, to the late 1970s, when he had gone underground as "Barry Freed" and was a respected environmental campaigner in upstate New York, fighting to save the St. Lawrence River. Along the way he married Anita Hoffman (Janeane Garofolo), started a family, then fled underground into hiding. His first family, under constant FBI surveillance, was able to meet with him from time to time, but meanwhile, as "Freed," he met and fell in love with Johanna Lawrenson (Jeanne Tripplehorn). That the two women got along fairly well and were able to share Hoffman may indicate their generosity—or maybe just that he was too much for any one woman to deal with.

That was certainly true as it became clear he was suffering from manic depression. His wild antics in the 1960s were matched by deep gloom in the 1970s, and his limitless energy and imagination might have fed from a disorder that was a boost in his earlier life, a crushing burden later (he died a suicide).

Steal This Movie has a title inspired by Hoffman's once famous *Steal This Book,* not a title popular with its publisher. It evokes a time when it was not theft to "rip off" something, because the capitalist pigs, etc., etc. The movie, written by Bruce Graham and directed by Robert Greenwald, has an enormous amount of material to cover, and does it fairly clumsily. Information enters the screen from too many directions. Subtitles treat the material like a documentary. Spoken narration treats it as memory. Actual newsreel footage coexists with reconstructions. This is distracting at first, but the movie smoothes out and finds its rhythm, and the closing passages are quite moving.

One element evoked by the movie is the symbolic role of the American flag during the period—a time which also inspired the hardhat patriotism of "Joe" and the John Prine lyrics:

> *Your flag decal won't get you into heaven anymore.*
> *It's already overcrowded from that dirty little war.*

Abbie Hoffman is seen wearing an American flag shirt and getting in trouble for desecrating it; the movie cuts in footage of Roy Rogers and Dale Evans yodeling while wearing *their* flag shirts. Hoffman insisted that the flag represented all Americans, including those opposed to the war; he resisted efforts of the right to annex it as their exclusive ideological banner.

Vincent D'Onofrio has an interesting task playing the role, since Hoffman seems on autopilot much of the time. He is charismatic and has an instinctive grasp of the dramatic gesture, but can be infuriating on a one-to-one level; the women in his life sometimes wonder whether he really sees and hears them, and can understand what he puts them through. Both Garofolo and Tripplehorn are valuable to the film because they supply the eyes through which we see a man who couldn't clearly see himself.

The late 1960s were thought at the time to be a period of social revolution in America. National Guardsmen were on the campus, demonstrators patrolled the streets, Nixon and Hoover (as shown here) instigated illegal programs to befuddle and discredit their opponents. But the transition from Yippie to yuppie went smoothly for most members of the '60s generation, prosperity soothed the voices of change, and the populace is anesthetized once again. Abbie Hoffman was not a revolutionary but he played one on television. He was prophetic, leading the way for virtual reality: It's not what you are, it's what you say, and whether you say it on TV.

Steam: The Turkish Bath ★ ★
NO MPAA RATING, 96 m., 1999

Alessandro Gassman (Francesco), Francesca d'Aloja (Marta), Halil Ergun (Osman), Serif Sezer (Perran), Mehmet Gunsur (Mehmet),

Basak Koklukaya (Fusun), Alberto Molinari (Paolo), Carlo Cecchi (Oscar), Zozo Toledo (Zozo). Directed by Ferzan Ozpetek and produced by Paolo Buzzi and Ozan Ergun. Screenplay by Stefano Tummolini and Ozpetek.

One of the peculiarities of *Steam: The Turkish Bath* is that it's about the sexual passions of two actors who don't seem very passionate. As the movie opens, they're married. Both are tall, thin, dark, solemn, and secretive. He seems like a well-meaning wimp. She seems like the kind of woman who would close her eyes during sex and fantasize about tomorrow's entries in her Day Timer.

The film opens in Rome, where their marriage seems shaky. They find fault with each other, but in vague terms that don't give us useful insights. Then the man, named Francesco (Alessandro Gassman), flies to Istanbul, where he has been left some property by an aunt.

The building turns out to be a Turkish bath, closed but still fondly remembered in the neighborhood. Francesco makes friends with the family of Osman, the man who used to manage the bath. Osman lives next door with his wife, comely daughter and comelier son. In his home Francesco finds a warmth and cheer that was missing from his sterile existence in Rome, and soon he's languishing in the arms of the son, named Mehmet (Mehmet Gunsur). He extends his stay and begins to renovate the Turkish bath, planning to reopen it.

No one suspects a thing—not even Osman (Halil Ergun), who in the nature of things must have learned a little something about what can go on in the steam. The film is reserved about sex and shy about nudity, employing its greatest passion for travelogue scenes of Istanbul, a city of great beauty and character.

Then Marta (Francesca d'Aloja), Francesco's wife, arrives suddenly from Rome. The story tensions explode at a family dinner, although not quite in the way we expect (what Marta blurts out didn't surprise me, but I was amazed that this cool and well-mannered woman would make such an ugly scene). After moments of truth and revelation, there is a surprise ending that I found particularly unsatisfying.

Afterward, I found myself asking what exactly the point of the movie was. It is not a sex film; it's almost prudish in the reserve of its sex scenes. If it's a coming-out film, so what? Francesco's homosexuality is not a surprise to the audience or even, really, to his wife. If it is about how a man escapes from the fast lane in Rome and discovers the feeling of community in Istanbul—well, good for him.

Perhaps I would have cared more if the leads had been warmer, but both Gassman (son of Vittorio Gassman) and d'Aloja come across as cool and reserved. The Turks are much more fun: Gunsur, as the lover, is friendly and boyish, and Ergun, as the former custodian, is a cheerful man. Serif Sezer, as Ergun's wife and Gunsur's mother, is one of those beauties of a certain age who has lips that make you forget everything else except what it would be like to nibble them.

Stigmata ★ ★
R, 102 m., 1999

Patricia Arquette (Frankie Paige), Gabriel Byrne (Father Andrew Kiernan), Jonathan Pryce (Cardinal Houseman), Nia Long (Donna Chadway), Thomas Kopache (Father Durning), Rade Sherbedgia (Marion Petrocelli), Enrico Colantoni (Father Darius), Dick Latessa (Father Gianni Delmonico). Directed by Rupert Wainwright and produced by Frank Mancuso Jr. Screenplay by Tom Lazarus and Rick Ramage.

Stigmata is possibly the funniest movie ever made about Catholicism—from a theological point of view. Mainstream audiences will view it as a lurid horror movie, an *Exorcist* wannabe, but for students of the teachings of the church, it offers endless goofiness. It confuses the phenomenon of stigmata with satanic possession, thinks stigmata can be transmitted by relics, and portrays the Vatican as a conspiracy against miracles.

The story: In Brazil, a holy priest has come into possession of a lost gospel "told in the words of Jesus himself." In the priest's church is a bleeding statue of the Virgin Mary. The Vatican dispatches a miracle-buster, Father Andrew (Gabriel Byrne), to investigate. "The blood is warm and human," he tells his superiors. He wants to crate up the statue and ship it to the Vatican for investigation, but is prevented. (One pictures a vast Vatican storehouse of screen windows and refrigerator doors bearing miraculous images.)

The old priest has died, and in the marketplace an American tourist buys his rosary and mails it as a souvenir to her daughter, Frankie (Patricia Arquette), who is a hairdresser in Pittsburgh. Soon after receiving the rosary, Frankie begins to exhibit the signs of the stigmata—bleeding wounds on the wrists, head, and ankles, where Christ was pierced on the cross. Father Andrew is again dispatched to investigate, reminding me of Illeana Douglas's priceless advice to her haunted brother-in-law in *Stir of Echoes:* "Find one of those young priests with smoldering good looks to sort of guide you through this."

The priest decides Frankie cannot have the stigmata because she is not a believer: "It happens only to deeply religious people." Psychiatrists quiz her, to no avail ("Is there any stress in your life?" "I cut hair."). But alarming manifestations continue; Frankie bleeds, glass shatters, there are rumbles on the sound track, she has terrifying visions, and at one point she speaks to the priest in a deeply masculine voice, reminding us of nothing so much as Linda Blair in *The Exorcist.*

Now there's the problem. Linda Blair was possessed by an evil spirit. Frankie has been entered by the Holy Spirit. Instead of freaking out in nightclubs and getting blood all over her bathroom, she should be in some sort of religious ecstasy, like Lili Taylor in *Household Saints.* It is not a dark and fearsome thing to be bathed in the blood of the Lamb.

It is also not possible, according to the very best church authorities, to catch the stigmata from a rosary. It is not a germ or a virus. It comes from within. If it didn't, you could cut up Padre Pio's bath towels and start your own blood drive. *Stigmata* does not know, or care, about the theology involved, and thus becomes peculiarly heretical by confusing the effects of being possessed by Jesus and by Beelzebub.

Meanwhile, back at the Vatican, the emotionally constipated Cardinal Houseman (Jonathan Pryce) rigidly opposes any notion that either the statue or Frankie actually bleeds. It's all a conspiracy, we learn, to suppress the gospel written in the actual words of Christ. The film, a storehouse of absurd theology, has the gall to end with one of those "factual" title cards, in which we learn that the "Gospel of St. Thomas," said to be in Christ's words, was denounced by the Vatican in 1945 as a "heresy." That doesn't mean it wouldn't be out in paperback if there was a market for it. It does mean the filmmakers have a shaky understanding of the difference between a heresy and a fake.

Does the film have redeeming moments? A few. Arquette is vulnerable and touching in an impossible role. I liked the idea of placing her character within a working-class world; there's a scene where one of the customers in the beauty shop resists having her hair treated by a woman with bleeding wrists. And Nia Long has fun with the role of Frankie's best friend; when your pal starts bleeding and hallucinating, it's obviously time for her to get out of the house and hit the clubs.

Stigmata has generated outrage in some Catholic circles. I don't know why. It provides a valuable recruiting service by suggesting to the masses that the church is the place to go for real miracles and supernatural manifestations. It is difficult to imagine this story involving a Unitarian. First get them in the door. Then start them on the catechism.

Still Crazy ★ ★ ★
R, 96 m., 1999

Stephen Rea (Tony), Billy Connolly (Hughie), Jimmy Nail (Les), Timothy Spall (Beano), Bill Nighy (Ray), Juliet Aubrey (Karen), Helene Bergstrom (Astrid), Bruce Robinson (Brian). Directed by Brian Gibson and produced by Amanda Marmot. Screenplay by Dick Clement and Ian La Frenais.

Still Crazy is a kinder, gentler version of *This Is Spinal Tap,* telling the story of a 1970s rock band that tries for a reunion twenty years after its last disastrous concert. Two decades have not been kind to the surviving members of Strange Fruit: One is a roofing contractor, one lives in a trailer in his mother's garden and hides from the tax man, one services condom machines in Ibiza, and even the one who held onto his money hasn't held onto enough of it. Two other members are dead.

None of the survivors remember the old days with much affection. There was jealousy, anger, and betrayal among band members, and the drugs and lifestyle didn't help. "God got tired of all that seventies excess," one observes. "That's why he invented the Sex Pistols." The band members have drifted out of touch, and like it that way.

But one day the keyboard man, Tony (Stephen Rea), is recognized in a restaurant by the son of the man who produced the disastrous 1977 concert at which Strange Fruit disintegrated. He suggests a reunion. Tony, who services the condom machines, still believes a little in the dream of rock 'n' roll (he wears Jimmy Hendrix's tooth around his neck). Besides, he needs the money, so he tracks down Karen (Juliet Aubrey), who was the group's secretary and gofer.

Together they go looking for the others, and find them: Ray Simms (Bill Nighy) is a cadaverous poseur living in a Victorian mansion with his bossy Swedish wife (Helena Bergstrom). He keeps his gold records in the crypt. Les Wickes (Jimmy Nail) is a roofer, tracked down by Tony on top of a church. Beano Baggot (Timothy Spall) works in a nursery, lives in a trailer, and fears a jail term from the tax authorities. Hughie (Billy Connolly) is the lead roadie. Brian (Bruce Robinson), the lead guitarist, disappeared long ago and is thought by everyone to be dead.

Not so reluctantly, the Fruit agree to do a "test tour" of Holland as a preliminary to a big seventies revival concert. They need the money. But they are all much decayed since their glory days, and only by not shaving and letting their hair grow rank are they able to conceal how bad they look—by looking worse.

Ray is a particularly dodgy case. Nagged by his wife, who micromanages every moment of his life, he's a recovering addict who is terrified of a fatal lapse back into drugs or booze. He stutters a little, makes profound statements that nobody else can quite understand, and cannot cope with the challenges of an ordinary day. His speech at a wedding reminds me of Rowan Atkinson's inept Mr. Bean.

The filmmakers must have personal experience with neurotic rock stars past their sell-by dates. The director, Brian Gibson, made the Tina Turner biopic *What's Love Got to Do With It,* and the writers are Dick Clement and Ian La Frenais, who wrote *The Commitments,* about an Irish group that would have been a garage band if they'd had a garage. They succeed in making Strange Fruit look and sound like a real band (the music was written and performed by various veterans of Foreigner, Spandau Ballet, Squeeze, and ELO), and there is an authenticity to the backstage desperation, as old wounds are reopened.

There are times when the film edges close to *Spinal Tap* territory, as when young fans are quick to boo the aging and uncertain group. In a way, the spirit of *Spinal Tap* hovers over the entire film, since its deadly aim has forever marked middle-aged rockers as targets of satire. But *Still Crazy* pays attention to the personalities of its heroes, and finds enough humor in reality, as when Ray slams his fiftieth birthday cake against the wall.

Some of the faces, especially Rea and Spall, are familiar from other recent British movies. But it's Bill Nighy who makes the most memorable impression. He conveys fear so well, especially that central kind of fear that forms when you can no longer trust yourself to do the right thing. There is a scene where he unwisely ventured onto some ice that cracks, and the way he handles it is unexpected, and right.

There aren't a lot of plot surprises in *Still Crazy* (the biggest surprise is telegraphed early on), and the ending is more or less as expected—indeed, as decreed by the comeback genre. But the characters are sharply defined and well written, and we come to like them. Twenty years ago they may have seemed like unapproachable rock gods, but now we see them as touching and vulnerable: Once they could do something fairly well, and now they have arrived at the stage in life where they can do it better—if they can do it at all.

Stir of Echoes ★ ★ ★
R, 110 m., 1999

Kevin Bacon (Tom), Kathryn Erbe (Maggie), Illeana Douglas (Lisa), Kevin Dunn (Frank), Conor O'Farrell (Harry), Zachary David Cope (Jake), Eddie Bo Smith Jr. (Neil [Cop]), Lusia Strus (Sheila). Directed by David Koepp and produced by Gavin Polone and Judy Hofflund. Screenplay by Koepp.

Stir of Echoes is a supernatural thriller firmly rooted in a blue-collar Chicago neighborhood, where everyone on the block knows each other—although not as well as they think. Kevin Bacon stars in one of his best performances, as a telephone lineman named Tom Witzky, who plays in a band, wants to break out of the routine of his life, and succeeds all too successfully. "I never wanted to be famous," he tells his wife. "I just never expected to be so ordinary."

But he has an extraordinary gift he doesn't know about: He's a receiver, able to see spirits. This gift is unlocked one boozy night at a beer party, when his sister-in-law Lisa (Illeana Douglas) talks about hypnosis. Tom claims he can't be hypnotized. Lisa tries. She evokes an empty theater and sends Tom drifting toward the screen; he spirals deeply into a trance, and awakens after a terrifying vision of violent but indistinct events in his own house.

The haunting visitations do not go away. They're linked, perhaps, to events on the street, where the neighbors are salt-of-the-earth types who are into buying old houses and fixing them up. Tom's nights are prowled by nightmares, and his lovemaking is interrupted by hallucinations of severed body parts (that will certainly do the trick). He starts calling in sick, and his wife, Maggie (Kathryn Erbe), is worried: Is he getting goofy? After the movies about satanic manifestations in Manhattan skyscrapers, it's nice to see weird things happening to people who hang out in the corner saloon, go to high school football games, and walk down the block to church. In a Manhattan movie, Tom's wife would have sent him to a shrink. In this Chicago version, she tells her sister: "He's used up all his sick days. They're gonna start docking him."

Only his son Jake (Zachary David Cope) understands. Early in the film he asks an unseen presence, "Does it hurt to be dead?" After a vision of a ghostly young woman named Samantha appears to Tom on his living room sofa, Jake reaches out and touches his hand: "Don't be afraid of it, Daddy." We learn that several months ago a mentally retarded girl disappeared in the neighborhood. Her sister baby-sits Jake, who somehow knows the name of the missing girl; Samantha told him.

Then Samantha tells Tom to "dig." So he digs. He digs up the backyard. Then he starts on the cellar. Eventually he brings in a pneumatic drill. This is the movie's weakest section; the writer-director, David Koepp, makes him dig more than is necessary to make the point. The movie's about ghosts, not digging, and I was reminded of Spielberg's *Close Encounters of the Third Kind,* in which Richard Dreyfuss, receiving impulses from aliens, sculpts his mashed potatoes. The director's cut toned down the mashed potatoes, and Koepp might one day consider similar repairs.

Tom's wife, Maggie, meanwhile comes into contact with a Chicago cop (Eddie Bo Smith Jr.) who is also a receiver, and there's an intriguing scene where she stumbles across a meeting of other people who can see supernatural dimensions. I would have liked more of that subplot, which isn't developed, but never mind: Koepp's screenplay dovetails the supernatural stuff with developments among the neighbors which are, wisely, more sad and tragic than sensational.

Kevin Bacon is sometimes able to suggest characters who are being driven mad by themselves. Here he implodes, in a role where that's the right choice; another actor might have reached too far. Kathryn Erbe is not merely worried but also exasperated by her husband, which is the right realistic touch, and Illeana Douglas plays the kind of sister-in-law who takes what you like in your wife and carries it too far. (Asked for advice after nudging these events into motion, she unhelpfully suggests, "Find one of those young priests with smoldering good looks to sort of guide you through this.")

Fred Murphy's photography places these people in the real world, and there is one shot that's a stunner, starting with the lineman up on a pole making a call, and then pulling back and back until we see a vast Chicago River vista and no less than three L trains at the same time. That doesn't have anything to do with ghosts, I know, but it sure is a neat shot.

The Story of Us ★
R, 92 m., 1999

Bruce Willis (Ben Jordan), Michelle Pfeiffer (Katie Jordan), Colleen Rennison (Erin), Jake Sandvig (Josh), Rita Wilson (Rachel), Julie Hagerty (Liza), Paul Reiser (Dave), Tim Matheson (Marty), Red Buttons (Arnie), Jayne Meadows

(Dot), Tom Poston (Harry). Directed by Rob Reiner and produced by Reiner, Jessie Nelson, and Alan Zweibel. Screenplay by Zweibel and Nelson.

Rob Reiner's *The Story of Us* is a sad-sack movie about the misery of a married couple (Bruce Willis and Michelle Pfeiffer) who fight most of the time. Watching it is like taking a long trip in a small car with the Bickersons. I leave it to you to guess whether the movie has a happy ending, but what if it does? A movie like this is about what we endure while we're watching it, not about where it finally arrives.

Meet the Jordans, Ben and Katie. He's a TV comedy writer; she composes crossword puzzles. They have two kids, Erin and Josh. Their marriage is a war zone: "Argument has become the condition for conversation," he observes. They fake happiness for the kids. How did they arrive at such pain? It is hard to say; the movie consists of flashbacks to their fights, but their problems are so generic we can't put a finger on anything.

Gene Siskel used to ask if a movie was as good as a documentary of the same actors having lunch. Watching *The Story of Us*, I imagined a documentary of the marriage of, say, Bruce Willis and Demi Moore. I do not say that to score a cheap point, but because Moore and Willis are spirited and intelligent people who no doubt had interesting fights about real issues, and not insipid fights about sitcom issues.

Example. The movie wants to illustrate poor communication. It shows Pfeiffer at home, where the washing machine is spewing suds all over the room and the kids are fighting. Willis calls her from outside their old apartment building, which is being torn down. He tells her the wrecking ball has just taken out their bedroom. She doesn't pay attention. His feelings are hurt.

The marriage counselor is in: She should shout, "The washer just exploded!" And he should say, "Catch you later!" Another marriage saved. Oh, and if I were her I'd turn off the power to the washing machine.

The movie is filled with lame and contrived "colorful" dialogue. Reiner, who plays a friend of the husband, gives him a long explanation of why appearances deceive. "We do not possess butts," he says, "but merely fleshy parts at the top of our legs." Whoa! Later there is a restaurant scene in which Willis screams angrily in a unsuccessful (indeed, melancholy) attempt to rip off Meg Ryan's famous restaurant orgasm in Reiner's *When Harry Met Sally*. At the end of his tirade, Willis jumps up and tells Reiner what he can "shove up the tops of your legs!"

Doesn't work, because (a) he's too angry to think up or stop for a punch line, (b) the line isn't funny, and (c) the setup wasn't funny either, because the concept isn't funny. Oh, and the scene ends with Reiner doing a double take directly into the camera. How many ways can one scene be mishandled?

Who thought this movie would be entertaining? The same person who thinks we need more dialogue about why guys do the wrong thing with rolls of toilet paper. And who thinks the misery of this film can be repaired by a showboat monologue at the end that's well delivered by Pfeiffer, but reads like an audition scene.

There is a famous short story about an unhappy couple, and about what happens when it comes time to tell their children they're getting a divorce. It is called "Separating," by John Updike. Read it to understand how much *The Story of Us* does not reach for or even guess.

The Straight Story ★ ★ ★ ★
G, 111 m., 1999

Richard Farnsworth (Alvin Straight), Sissy Spacek (Rose), Jane Heitz (Dorothy), James Cada (Danny Riordan), Everett McGill (Tom the Dealer), Jennifer Edwards (Brenda), Barbara E. Robertson (Deer Woman), John Farley (Thorvald), John Lordan (Priest), Harry Dean Stanton (Lyle). Directed by David Lynch and produced by Alain Sarde and Mary Sweeney. Screenplay by Sweeney and John Roach.

The first time I saw *The Straight Story*, I focused on the foreground and liked it. The second time I focused on the background, too, and loved it. The movie isn't just about Alvin Straight's odyssey through the small towns and rural districts of the Midwest, but about the people he finds to listen to and care for him. You'd think it was a fantasy, this kindness of strangers, if the movie weren't based on a true story.

Straight (Richard Farnsworth) is a seventy-three-year-old man from Laurens, Iowa, who learns that his brother is dying, and wants to see him one last time. His eyes are too bad to allow him to drive. He lives with his daughter Rose (Sissy Spacek), who is somewhat retarded and no good behind the wheel. Nor do they have a car. But they have a tractor-style lawn mower, and the moment Alvin's eyes light on it, he knows how he can drive the three hundred miles to Zion, Wisconsin. The first mower konks out, but he gets another one, a John Deere, hitches a little wagon to it, and stubbornly sets off down the road.

Along the way we will learn a lot about Alvin, including a painful secret he has kept ever since the war. He is not a sophisticated man, but when he speaks the words come out like the bricks of a wall built to last. Like Hemingway's dialogue, the screenplay by John Roach and Mary Sweeney finds poetry and truth in the exact choice of the right everyday words. Richard Farnsworth, who was seventy-nine when he made the film, speaks the lines with perfect repose and conviction.

Because the film was directed by David Lynch, who usually deals in the bizarre (Wild at Heart, Twin Peaks), we keep waiting for the other shoe to drop—for Alvin's odyssey to intersect with the Twilight Zone. But it never does. Even when he encounters a potential weirdo, like the distraught woman whose car has killed fourteen deer in one week on the same stretch of highway (". . . and I *have* to take this road!"), she's not a sideshow exhibit and we think, yeah, you can hit a lot of deer on those country roads.

Alvin's journey to his brother is a journey into his past. He remembers when they were young and filled with wonder. He tells a stranger, "I want to sit with him and look up at the stars, like we used to, so long ago." He remembers his courtship and marriage. His army service as a sniper whose aim, one day, was too good. And about years lost to drinking and nastiness. He has emerged from the forge of his imperfections as a better man,

purified, simple, and people along the way seem to sense that.

My favorite, of all of his stops, comes in a small town where he's almost killed when he loses a drive belt and speeds out of control down a hill. He comes to rest where some people in lawn chairs are watching the local firemen practicing putting out a fire.

In the town are twin brothers who squabble all the time, even while charging him by the hour to repair the mower, and a retired John Deere employee named Danny Riordan (James Cada), who lets Alvin camp for a while in his backyard (Alvin won't enter the house, even to use the phone). Danny is a rare man of instinctive sweetness and tact, who sees what the situation requires, and supplies it without display. He embodies all of our own feelings about this lovable old—yes, fool. He gently offers advice, but Alvin is firm: "You're a kind man talking to a stubborn man."

If Riordan and the deer lady and the dueling twins (and a forlorn young girl) are the background I was talking about, so are the locations themselves. The cinematographer, Freddie Francis, who once made the vastness of Utah a backdrop for *The Executioner's Song*, knows how to evoke a landscape without making it too comforting. There are fields of waving corn and grain here, and rivers and woods and little red barns, but on the sound track the wind whispering in the trees plays a sad and lonely song, and we are reminded not of the fields we drive past on our way to picnics, but on our way to funerals, on autumn days when the roads are empty.

The faces in this movie are among its treasures. Farnsworth himself has a face like an old wrinkled billfold that he paid good money for and expects to see him out. There is another old man who sits next to him on a bar stool near the end of the movie, whose face is like the witness to time. And look and listen to the actor who plays the bartender in that same late scene, the one who serves the Miller Lite. I can't find his name in the credits, but he finds the right note: He knows how all good bartenders can seem like a friend bringing a present to a sickroom.

The last notes are also just right. Who will this dying brother be, and what will he say?

Will the screenplay say too much or reach for easy sentimentality? Not at all. Just because you have to see someone doesn't mean you have a lot to gab about. No matter how far you've come.

Note: I later discovered the actor who plays the bartender is Russell Reed.

Stuart Little ★ ★
PG, 92 m., 1999

Geena Davis (Mrs. Little), Hugh Laurie (Mr. Little), Jonathan Lipnicki (George Little). Voices of: Michael J. Fox (Stuart Little), Nathan Lane (Snowbell), Chazz Palminteri (Snowbell), Steve Zahn (Monty), Jim Doughan (Lucky). Directed by Rob Minkoff and produced by Douglas Wick. Screenplay by M. Night Shyamalan and Greg Brooker, based on the book by E. B. White.

Any other consideration about *Stuart Little* must take second place to the fact that it is about a nice family that adopts a mouse. Yes, a mouse, in all dimensions and particulars, albeit a mouse with a cute little sports coat and an earnest way of expressing himself in piping English. Stuart is about two inches long, maybe a little longer. Early in the film Snowbell, the family cat, tries to eat him, but is forced to spit him up, damp but no worse for wear.

I once read the book by E. B. White on which this story is founded. The peculiar thing about the book is that Stuart, in the imagination of the reader, swells until he occupies as much psychic space as any of the other characters. He is a mouse, but his dialogue runs from margin to margin just like the words of the humans, and his needs and fears are as great. Our intelligence tells us Stuart is a mouse, but our imagination makes him into a full-size literary character.

In the book, Stuart works just fine as a character. But movies are an unforgivably literal medium, and the fact is, no live-action movie about Stuart Little can possibly work, *because he is so much smaller than everyone else!*

Stuart is definitely a mouse. He is very, very small. There is something pathetic about a scene where his new parents (Geena Davis and Hugh Laurie) tuck him in at bedtime. It doesn't matter how much they love him or how happy he is to be in this new home; all we can think about is how he hardly needs even the hem of his blanket. All through the movie I kept cringing at the terrible things that could happen to the family's miniature son. It didn't help that a few days earlier I'd seen another movie in which an equally cute and lovable mouse was stamped on by a sadist, and squished.

The movie of course puts Stuart through many adventures, and confronts him with tragic misunderstandings. He is provided with a new wardrobe and a tiny red convertible sportster to race around in, and is chased through Central Park by hungry cats. That sort of thing.

My mind reeled back to the grotesque family "comedy" named *Jack Frost*. That was the film in which a family's father dies and is reincarnated as a snowman. Now that is an amazing thing. If your dad came back as a snowman after being dead for a year, what would you ask him? Perhaps, is there an afterlife? Or, what is heaven like? Or—why a snowman? But no sooner does the snowman in *Jack Frost* appear than it is harnessed to a desperately banal plot about snowball fights at the high school.

Stuart Little is not anywhere near as bad as *Jack Frost* (it is twice as good—two stars instead of one). But it has the same problem: The *fact* of its hero upstages anything the plot can possibly come up with. A two-inch talking humanoid mouse upstages roadsters, cats, little brothers, everything. I tried imagining a movie that would deal seriously and curiously with an intelligent and polite child that looked like a mouse. Such a movie would have to be codirected by Tim Burton and David Lynch.

I am reminded of the old man who finds a frog in the road. "Kiss me," says the frog, "and I will turn into a beautiful princess." The man puts the frog in his pocket. "Didn't you hear my offer?" asks the frog in a muffled voice. "I heard it," the old man says, "but frankly, at my age, I'd rather have a talking frog." My guess is that the makers of *Stuart Little* might not understand the point of this story.

Such a Long Journey ★ ★ ★ ½
NO MPAA RATING, 113 m., 2000

Roshan Seth (Gustad Noble), Soni Razdan (Dilnavaz Noble), Om Puri (Ghulam), Naseeruddin Shah (Major Jimmy Bilimoria), Ranjit Chowdhry (Pavement Artist), Sam Dastor (Dinshawji), Kurush Deboo (Tehmul), Vrajesh Hirjee (Sohrab Noble). Directed by Sturla Gunnarsson and produced by Paul Stephens and Simon MacCorkindale. Screenplay by Sooni Taraporevala, based on the novel by Rohinton Mistry.

India is the closest we can come in today's world to the London of Dickens, with its poverty and wealth side by side, in a society teeming with benevolence and intrigue, eccentrics and thieves, the suspect and the saintly. *Such a Long Journey*, filmed on location in Bombay, is a film so rich in atmosphere it makes Western films look pale and underpopulated. It combines politics, religion, illness, and scheming in the story of one family in upheaval, and is very serious, and always amusing.

The story, set in 1971 at the time of the war between India and Pakistan, is based on the novel of the same name by Rohinton Mistry, an Indian now living in Toronto. I haven't read it, but I have read his latest novel, the magnificent *A Fine Balance*, which has the same ability to see how political issues impact the lives of the ordinary and the obscure. Mistry's novels have the droll irony of Dickens, as when a legless beggar and a beggarmaster turn out to be brothers, and the beggarmaster is so moved that he purchases the beggar a better cart to push himself around on.

Such a Long Journey takes place mostly in and around a large apartment complex, its courtyard, and the street, which the municipal authorities want to widen so that even more choking diesel fumes can cloud the air. We meet the hero, Gustad (Roshan Seth), in the process of defending the old concrete wall that protects his courtyard from the street, and later he strikes a bargain with an itinerant artist (Ranjit Chowdhry), who covers the wall with paintings from every conceivable religious tradition, with the thought that all of the groups represented will join in defending the wall.

A greater struggle is in store for Gustad. A Parsi whose family has fallen on hard times, he works in a bank and is asked by Major Jimmy (Naseeruddin Shah), a friend from long ago, to hide and launder some money. The go-between (Om Puri) implies these are official Indian government funds being secretly transferred to finance the war against Pakistan in Bangladesh. (The movie doesn't require us to know much about modern history in the subcontinent, since the story works entirely in terms of the personal lives of its characters.)

Gustad is a good and earnest man, who has adopted the local idiot as a kind of surrogate son, who is the unofficial mayor of his building, who is always on call to help his neighbors, who dotes on his little daughter, and bursts with pride that his son, Sohrab (Vrajesh Hirjee), has been accepted by the Indian Institute of Technology. Alas, Sohrad doesn't want to go to IIT; he hates engineering and wants to be an artist, and Gustad implores him to reconsider.

Gustad's relationship with his wife has elements of an Indian *Honeymooners*. The kitchen is her turf, where she defiantly spends long hours in consultation with a neighbor woman whom Gustad considers to be a witch (i.e., she has a different set of superstitions than his own). Their marriage is strong when it needs to be, as when their daughter falls ill with malaria.

All of these stories are told against the backdrop of the others who live in the apartment complex, the street vendors outside, and those who are understood to have claims to portions of the courtyard or sidewalk. There is great poverty in India, but because it is so common it's more of a condition of life than a particular shame, and Gustad is on easy terms with the people who live in, as well as on, his street.

Roshan Seth is not a name well known in the West, but his face is familiar; he played Nehru in *Gandhi*, the heroine's father in *Mississippi Masala*, the father again in *My Beautiful Laundrette*, and it is only poetic justice that he starred in the film of Dickens's *Little Dorrit*. In this role (which won him a Canadian Genie as the year's best actor), he plays an everyman, an earnest, worried, funny character always skirting on the edge of disaster, ex-

551

uberantly immersed in his life. The way he masterminds the defense of the precious wall is brilliant, but the way he deals with its fate is even more touching, because it is simply human.

The director, Sturla Gunnarsson, is Icelandic, suggesting the universality of this story; the writer, Sooni Taraporevala, also wrote *Mississippi Masala* and *Salaam Bombay.* Their film is interesting not simply in terms of its plot (the politics, the money), but because of the medium it moves through—the streets of Bombay. It suggests a society that has more poverty than ours, but is not necessarily poorer, because it has a richer texture of daily life. *American Beauty* could not be an Indian story; it would be too hard to imagine Indian city dwellers with that much time to brood and isolate.

Sugar & Spice ★ ★ ★
PG-13, 93 m., 2001

Marley Shelton (Diane Weston), James Marsden (Jack Bartlett), Mena Suvari (Kansas Hill), Marla Sokoloff (Lisa Janusch), Alexandra Holden (Fern Rogers), Rachel Blanchard (Hannah Wold), Sara Marsh (Lucy Whitman), Melissa George (Cleo Miller), Sean Young (Kansas's Mom). Directed by Francine McDougall and produced by Wendy Finerman. Screenplay by Mandy Nelson.

Sugar & Spice puts your average cheerleader movie to shame. It's sassy and satirical, closer in spirit to *But I'm a Cheerleader* than to *Bring It On.* With its shameless pop culture references, wicked satire, and a cheerleader with the hots for Conan O'Brien, it's more proof that not all movie teenagers have to be dumb. (All right, these cheerleaders *are* dumb—but in a smart movie.) I was surprised by the PG-13 rating; the movie is so in tune with its under-seventeen target audience that it's amazing the MPAA didn't slap it with an R.

The movie takes place at Lincoln High School, with a crepe-headed Honest Abe prancing on the sidelines. We meet the A-team of the cheerleader squad, who seem like a cross between Olympic gymnasts and the pom-pom girl who inflamed Kevin Spacey in *American Beauty.* No wonder: Mena Suvari, who

played the pom-pom girl, turns up here as Kansas, a girl whose mom is in prison.

The team leader is Diane (Marley Shelton), a beauty who is stunned when Jack (James Marsden), the captain of the football team, announces at a school assembly that his platform for prom king includes taking her to the prom. They share a wet kiss on stage, and soon Diane is pregnant, which doesn't curtail her cheerleading.

Jack and Diane receive a frosty reception from their parents, but after the movie quotes what for it is scripture ("Papa Don't Preach") they move into a cheap apartment and Jack gets a job at Señor Guacamole. He's fired, there's a financial crisis, and then Diane comes up with an inspiration while watching a heist movie on TV: They can rob a bank!

They do research by watching other crime movies, including *Heat, Point Blank,* and *Reservoir Dogs.* Cleo (Melissa George), the team member with the crush on Conan, makes it more fun by fantasizing Conan's head on the bodies of actors. Hannah (Rachel Blanchard), who has strict churchgoing parents, is allowed to watch only G-rated movies, so she researches *The Apple Dumpling Gang.* Lucy (Sara Marsh), the brains of the outfit, fits it all together. And they rationalize the robbery by saying they can give some of the money to charity: We can buy "one of those starving little kids that Sally Struthers auctions."

The robbery plans include a visit to a local exterminator, who supplies them with guns and insists that his daughter Fern (Alexandra Holden) be allowed to join the cheerleader squad. Fern looks at first like a candidate for one of her dad's poisonous sprays, but cleans up real good. The robbery itself involves disguises: five pregnant Betty dolls and one Richard Nixon. I liked the way a witness, also a cheerleader, sees through the disguises when she observes an "illegal dismount."

The film's narrator is the outsider Lisa (Marla Sokoloff), who has a Bette Midler quality. One of the weirder scenes involves a trip by Kansas to visit her mother (Sean Young) in prison; she needs advice on robbing banks. And the running gag about Conan O'Brien is funny because the passion seems so out of scale with its inspiration. *Sugar & Spice* seems instinctively in sync with its cheerleaders, maybe because it was made by women: director Francine McDougall, writer Mandy Nelson, producer Wendy Finerman. It is not a great high school movie, like *Election,* but it's alive and risky and saucy.

Sugar Town ★ ★ ★
R, 93 m., 1999

Jade Gordon (Gwen), Ally Sheedy (Liz), Larry Klein (Burt), Rosanna Arquette (Eva), John Taylor (Clive), Michael Des Barres (Nick), Martin Kemp (Jonesy), Beverly D'Angelo (Jane), Vincent Berry (Nirvana), Lucinda Jenney (Kate). Directed by Allison Anders and Kurt Voss and produced by Daniel Hassid. Screenplay by Anders and Voss.

Sugar Town knows its characters. It inhabits two overlapping worlds in Los Angeles: The world of people who were famous once, and those who will never be famous but dream of nothing else. "We were all in seminal bands in the seventies and eighties," a middle-aged rock musician observes, sadly and defiantly, at a meeting to discuss forming a new band. The problem with being seminal is that you end up in the shadow of your offspring.

These has-beens have money. Not a lot, in some cases, but enough. The movie slides easily in and out of their homes, comfortable untidy structures in the Hollywood Hills, strong on the "features" Realtors brag about, but looking knocked together out of spare parts of better houses. Their clothes and hair reflect the way they looked when they were famous; their images are made from last year's merchandise.

The movie's insider atmosphere is honestly come by. The codirectors, Allison Anders and Kurt Voss, live in this world themselves, many of the actors are their friends, the houses are where some of these people actually live, and the movie was shot in three weeks. If it were a documentary, it would be a good one.

The problem with being fortyish is that you're still young enough to want to do dangerous things, but too old to ignore the dangers. Drugs are not free from the shadow of rehab. Sex is a need but not a drive; you want it, but it's so much trouble to go out and get it. Always at your back you hear time's winged chariot drawing near. It's bad enough to be asked

to play Christina Ricci's mother, as a former slasher movie queen (Rosanna Arquette) observes, but worse because "*She's* not an ingenue anymore."

The movie cuts between a rich assortment of characters; it's like a low-rent, on-the-fly version of Robert Altman's *The Player* or *Short Cuts.* We meet a production designer (Ally Sheedy) who is so paralyzed by self-help mantras that she has no social life. "Your genital area is completely blocked," says her "openness counselor," offering a massage, which we suspect could unblock it using the most traditional of approaches. Her house is a mess. She hires a housekeeper (Jade Gordon), a showbiz wanna-be we see badgering a drugged-out composer for the "three hit songs" she has paid him to write. When Sheedy finally gets a date (with a music agent), the housekeeper sabotages the date by advising against a sexy black dress and in favor of a painting smock that's "more you," then gets a ride home from the agent and descends directly to openness counseling.

Arquette's former slasher queen lives with an eighties rock hero (John Taylor of Duran Duran). One of his former lovers dumps a kid at his door—his kid, she says—and disappears. The kid (Vincent Berry) hates his name, which is Nirvana. He's about eleven, wears earrings and black eye makeup, and is very angry. "I *said*—call me *nerve!*" he snaps at her. "You want some hot chocolate?" she asks. He softens up considerably when he realizes she is the star of his favorite slasher videos.

Other characters include the pregnant wife (Lucinda Jenney) of a studio musician, her drug-damaged brother-in-law, and the Latino musician who wants to seduce her husband. Jenney's performance is the most touching in the movie, especially in the way she handles the brother-in-law. The rock agent, named Burt (Larry Klein) strikes gold. He discovers a rich widow (Beverly D'Angelo) who will provide backing for an album if she can sleep with a former glam-rock star (Michael Des Barres). Their scene together is the movie's funniest; he painstakingly reproduces his famous image with makeup and clothes, only to have her size up his bare-chested leopard leotard and ask, "Did you pull this out of mothballs just for me?"

One thing you notice in Los Angeles is that everyone seems to be connected to "the business" in one way or another, if only in their plans. Sheedy meets a wheatgrass machine operator at the health food store, who turns out, of course, to have a screenplay and newly taken publicity stills. There's a certain double-reverse poignancy in observing that some of the cast members (Michael Des Barres, John Taylor, Martin Kemp) are indeed rock legends, and some, like Des Barres and Ally Sheedy, are in the midst of actual career comebacks like the others dream of.

The movie is not profound or tightly plotted or a "statement," nor should it be. It captures day-to-day drifting in a city without seasons, where most business meetings are so circular and unfocused it's hard to notice when they stop resulting in deals and simply exist for their own sake. You can make enough money in a brief season of fame that if you are halfway prudent with it, you can live forever like this, making plans and reminding people who you are, or were, or will be.

Summer of Sam ★ ★ ★ ½
R, 136 m., 1999

John Leguizamo (Vinny), Adrien Brody (Ritchie), Mira Sorvino (Dionna), Jennifer Esposito (Ruby), Michael Rispoli (Joey T), Saverio Guerra (Woodstock), Brian Tarantino (Bobby Del Fiore), Al Palagonia (Anthony), Ben Gazzara (Luigi), Bebe Neuwirth (Gloria). Directed by Spike Lee and produced by Lee and Jon Kilik. Screenplay by Lee, Victor Colicchio, and Michael Imperioli.

Spike Lee's *Summer of Sam* is his first film with no major African-American characters, but it has a theme familiar to blacks and other minorities: scapegoating. In the summer of 1977, when New York City is gripped by paranoid fear of the serial killer who calls himself the Son of Sam, the residents of an Italian-American neighborhood in the Bronx are looking for a suspect. Anyone who stands out from the crowd is a candidate.

Lee's best films thrum with a wound-up energy, and *Summer of Sam* vibrates with fear, guilt, and lust. It's not about the killer, but about his victims—not those he murdered, but those whose overheated imaginations bloomed into a lynch mob mentality. There is a sequence near the end of the film that shows a side of human nature as ugly as it is familiar: the fever to find someone to blame, and the need to blame someone who is different.

We see the Son of Sam from time to time in the film, often as a shadowy presence, but his appearances are more like punctuation than drama. The story centers on several characters in a tightly knit neighborhood—one of those neighborhoods so insular that everyone suspects the killer may be someone they know. That's not because they think a killer must live among them, but because it's hard to imagine anyone living anywhere else.

The key characters are two couples. Vinny (John Leguizamo) is a hairdresser with a roving eye, married none too faithfully to Dionna (Mira Sorvino), who is a waitress in her father's restaurant. Ritchie (Adrien Brody) is a local kid who has mysteriously developed a punk haircut and a British accent. He dates the sexy Ruby (Jennifer Esposito), but leads a double life as a dancer in a gay club. The movie doesn't involve them in plot mechanics so much as follow them for human atmosphere; we get to know them and their friends and neighbors, and then watch them change as the pall of murder settles over the city.

Lee is a city kid himself, from Brooklyn, and makes the city's background noise into a sort of parallel sound track. There's the voice of Phil Rizzuto doing play-by-play as Reggie Jackson slams the Yankees into the World Series. The hit songs of the summer, disco and otherwise. The almost sexual quality of gossip; people are turned on by spreading rumors, and feed off each other's excitement. The tone is set by the opening shot of columnist Jimmy Breslin, introducing the film. It was to Breslin that the killer wrote the first of his famous notes to the papers, identifying himself as the monster, and saying he would kill again.

The *Summer of Sam* screenplay, written by Lee with Victor Colicchio and Michael Imperioli, isn't the inside, autobiographical job of a Scorsese film, but more of an analytical outsider's view. We learn things. There is a certain conviction in a scene where the police turn to a local Mafia boss (Ben Gazzara) for help from his troops in finding the killer; he has power in the neighborhood, this is known to everyone, and the cops put it to pragmatic use.

We watch Vinny, the Leguizamo character, as he cheats on his wife, notably with Gloria (Bebe Neuwirth), the sexpot at the beauty salon where he works. We watch as he stumbles on two of Sam's victims and returns home, chastened, believing God spared him, and vowing to start treating his wife better. In this neighborhood, it's personal; if you have a near brush with Sam, it's a sign. And Lee shows us Dionna wearing a blond wig on a date with her husband, because the killer seems to single out brunettes. She does it for safety's sake, but there's a sexual undercurrent: Wearing the wig and risking the wrath of Sam is kind of a turn-on.

The summer of 1977 was at the height of the so-called sexual revolution; Plato's Retreat was famous and AIDS unheard-of, and both of the principal couples are caught up in the fever. Vinny and Dionna experiment at a sex club, and Ritchie gets involved in gay porno films. In a confused way he believes his career as a sex worker is connected to his (mostly imaginary) career as a punk rock star. For him, all forms of show business feel more or less the same.

In the neighborhood, people hang around talking, speculating, killing time, often where the street dead-ends into the water. One of the regulars has a theory that Son of Sam is in fact Reggie Jackson (the killer uses a .44 handgun; Jackson's number is 44). The local priest is also a suspect; after all, he lives alone and can come and go as he wants. And then, slowly, frighteningly, attention becomes focused on Ritchie, the neighborhood kid who has chosen to flaunt his weird lifestyle.

Lee has a wealth of material here, and the film tumbles through it with exuberance. He likes the energy, the street-level culture, the music, the way that when conversation fails, sex can take over the burden of entertainment. And there is a deeper theme, too: the theme of how scapegoats are chosen. What's interesting is not that misfits are singled out as suspects; it's that the ringleaders require validation for their suspicions. At the end of the film, everyone's looking for Vinny. They need him to agree with their choice of victim—to validate their fever. It's as if they know they're wrong, but if Vinny says they're right, then they can't be blamed.

Summer of Sam is like a companion piece to Lee's *Do the Right Thing* (1989). In a different neighborhood, in a different summer, the same process takes place: The neighborhood feels threatened and needs to project its fear on an outsider. It is often lamented that in modern city neighborhoods, people don't get to know their neighbors. That may be a blessing in disguise.

Sunshine ★ ★ ★
R, 180 m., 2000

Ralph Fiennes (Ignatz, Adam, Ivan), Rosemary Harris (Valerie [Older]), Rachel Weisz (Greta), Jennifer Ehle (Valerie [Younger]), Molly Parker (Hannah), Deborah Unger (Carola), William Hurt (Andor Knorr), James Frain (Gustave [Younger]), John Neville (Gustave [Older]). Directed by Istvan Szabo and produced by Robert Lantos, Jonathan Debin, Andras Hamori, and Rainer Koelmel. Screenplay by Szabo and Israel Horovitz.

"One gang was as bad as another," says an old woman at the end of Istvan Szabo's *Sunshine.* In her long lifetime in Hungary she has lived under the emperor, the Nazis, and the Communists. And she watched as the West betrayed the 1956 uprising. She has seen some members of her Jewish family spend the century trying to accommodate themselves to the shifting winds of politics and society, and failing. She has seen other members fight against the prevailing tyrannies, only to find them replaced by new ones.

And she has witnessed the Holocaust bearing down over three generations—not as an aberration, a contagion spread by Hitler, but as the inexorable result of long years of anti-Semitism. We are reminded of the 1999 documentary *Last Days,* also about Holocaust victims in Hungary, which observes that the persecution of the Jews there began fairly late in the war, at a time when Hitler's thinly stretched resources were needed for tasks other than genocide.

But the Nazis had help. "Nice, ordinary Hungarian people did the dirty work," we learn, and there is even the possibility that some members of the Sonnenschein family, which the movie follows over three generations, would have helped had they not been Jewish and therefore ineligible. The movie shows family members determined to think of themselves as good Hungarians. The family name is changed to Sors to make it "more Hungarian," and Adam Sors, in the middle generation, converts to Catholicism, joins an officers' club, and wins a gold medal for fencing in the Olympics.

But assimilation is not the answer, as he learns when he remains too long in Hungary, believing a national hero like himself immune to anti-Semitism. There is a heartbreaking scene in a Nazi death camp where he tells an officer that he is a loyal Hungarian army officer, too—and a gold medalist. "Strip," the officer tells him, and soon his naked body has been crucified and sprayed with water until it forms a grotesque ice sculpture.

Szabo's epic tells the story of one family in one country, but it will do as a millennial record of a century in which one bright political idea after another promised to bring happiness and only enforced misery. The Sonnenschein family fortune is founded on "Sunshine," an invigorating tonic with a secret recipe. The film does not need to underline the symbolism that the formula for the tonic is lost as the century unfolds.

Ralph Fiennes plays the father, son, and grandson, each one rebuffed or repelled by a Hungary in agony. Ignatz Sonnenschein, whose story begins the film (with some flashbacks about his father), is a successful businessman who presides over a comfortable bourgeoisie home and thinks of standing for parliament. His brother Gustave (James Frain, and later John Neville) is disgusted he would support a corrupt regime, and Ignatz speaks hopefully of progressive elements in the regime and the emperor's openness to reform.

After the war, a Communist government gets in briefly, and Gustave joins it. Then the rise of the right ends that chapter, and he is placed under house arrest before fleeing to France. Meanwhile, Fiennes now plays Adam Sors, whose attention is focused on fencing; since the best fencers are in the officers' club, he takes lessons and converts to Catholicism so he can join it too. He doesn't take religion seriously; it's just a ticket you punch in order to fence.

His son Ivan (Fiennes again—uncanny in his ability to suggest the three different personalities) emerges after the war as a police officer under the new Communist regime. Ivan grows close to an idealist named Knorr (William Hurt), who believes in communism and wants to do a good job, and therefore is a threat to the government. This sequence, showing a weary Hungary being betrayed once again by a corrupt regime, is the most effective, because it pounds the message home: The people running the Communist government are more of the nice, ordinary Hungarians who helped with the Holocaust. The point isn't that Hungarians are any worse than anyone else—but that, alas, human nature is much the same everywhere, and more generous with lackeys than heroes.

At three hours Sunshine made some audience members restless when it premiered at the Toronto Film Festival, but this is a movie of substance and thrilling historical sweep, and its three hours allow Szabo to show the family's destiny forming and shifting under pressure. At every moment there is a choice between ethics and expediency; at no moment is the choice clear or easy. Many Holocaust stories (like *Jakob the Liar*) dramatize the tragedy as a simple case of good and evil. And so it was, but that lesson is obvious. The buried message of *Sunshine* is more complex.

It suggests, first, that some Jews were slow to scent the danger because they were seduced into thinking their personal status gave them immunity (so do we all). Second, that those who felt communism was the answer to fascism did not understand how all "isms" distrust democracy and appeal to bullies. Third, that the Holocaust is being mirrored today all over the world, as groups hate and murder each other on the basis of religion, color, and nationality. The Sonnenschein family learned these lessons generation after generation during the century. So did we all. Not that human nature seems to have learned much as a result.

Is there any reason to think fewer people will die in the twenty-first century than died in the twentieth, because they belong to a different tribe?

Superstar ★
PG-13, 82 m., 1999

Molly Shannon (Mary Katherine Gallagher), Will Ferrell (Sky), Elaine Hendrix (Evian), Harland Williams (Slater), Mark McKinney (Father Ritley), Glynis Johns (Grandma), Emmy Laybourne (Helen). Directed by Bruce McCulloch and produced by Lorne Michaels. Screenplay by Steven Wayne Koren.

I wouldn't be surprised to learn that newcomers to the *Saturday Night Live* cast are given two immediate assignments: Find someone you can imitate, and create a goony character. The second assignment has a better payoff. Chevy Chase can no doubt still do a pratfall like Gerald Ford, but who wants him to? But if Martin Short ever resurrects Ed Grimley, I'd buy a ticket. Maybe that's why so many of the *SNL* recurring characters get to star in movie spin-offs. Was *Blues Brothers* the first? How far we have fallen.

Most of the *SNL* goonies are, alas, not as funny as the Brothers, *Wayne's World,* or Ed Grimley—a truth abundantly demonstrated by *Superstar,* a feature-length spin-off based on Molly Shannon's character, Mary Katherine Gallagher. Here is a portrait of a character so sad and hapless, so hard to like, so impossible to empathize with, that watching it feels like an act of unkindness. The film is only eighty-two minutes long, including the generous closing credits, and yet long before it's over it runs out of any reason for existing.

Mary Catherine Gallagher, you may know, is plain and hostile, a homely little bundle of resentment with a supercharged fantasy life. In *Superstar,* she attends a Catholic school and dreams of sharing a wet kiss with Sky Corrigan (Will Ferrell), a football hero. That's all she wants—that, and to become a superstar. She confides these fantasies to a tree. Yes, a tree on the lawn in front of the school, which she French-kisses while whispering lurid scenarios.

I am prepared to concede there could be something funny about French-kissing a tree. To read about it, as you just have, may have inspired a smile. What you do not want to see is a girl actually kissing a tree—licking the bark, rubbing her knee against it, and . . . but I can't go on. The fact destroys the humor. The movie becomes a documentary. We are looking at an actress licking a tree. As Divine demonstrated in his notorious poop scene in *Pink Flamingos,* there are some scenes during which, however willing, we are unable to suspend our disbelief.

There's another problem. Mary Katherine isn't simply an "unpopular" girl—she's creepy and not very nice. She's one of those people who inspires in you the inexplicable desire to be hurtful and cruel. You don't meet people like that very often, but when you meet them, you know who they are. And you want to get away from them before you do something that would undermine your self-image as a nice person.

The plot involves lots of Catholic jokes. A few are funny, including a priceless moment involving twittering nuns, which captures some kind of truth—not about nuns, but about twittering. Others are lame or forced ("Catholic Cheerleaders against VD," Jesus explaining himself as a by-product of REM sleep, Mary Katherine doing a reading from *Sybil* in the confessional). Too bad the Catholic League is so busy attacking good films, like *Dogma,* that it can't spare the time to picket bad ones. I'm not in favor of protesting films on the basis of theology, but to picket them because they're boring could be an act of mercy.

Sweet and Lowdown ★ ★ ★ ½
PG-13, 95 m., 1999

Sean Penn (Emmet Ray), Samantha Morton (Hattie), Uma Thurman (Blanche), Anthony LaPaglia (Al Torrio), Brian Markinson (Bill Shields), Gretchen Mol (Ellie), James Urbaniak (Harry), John Waters (Mr. Hayes). Directed by Woody Allen and produced by Jean Doumanian. Screenplay by Allen.

Emmet Ray is like a man with a very large dog on a leash. The dog is his talent, and it drags him where it wants to go. There are times in *Sweet and Lowdown* when Ray, "the second-best jazz guitarist in the world," seems almost like a bystander as his fingers and his instinct create heavenly jazz. When the music stops he's helpless: He doesn't have a clue when it comes to personal relationships, he has little idea how the world works, and the only way he can recognize true love is by losing it.

Emmet Ray is a fictional character, but so convincing in Woody Allen's *Sweet and Lowdown* that he seems like a real chapter of jazz history we somehow overlooked. Sean Penn, whose performances are master classes in the art of character development, makes him into an exasperating misfit whose sins are all forgiven once he begins to play. With his goofy little mustache and a wardrobe that seems patterned on secondhand guesses about what a gypsy jazzman in Paris might wear, Emmet Ray looks like a square peg lacking even the round hole.

Here is a man who, when we first meet him, is already considered peerless among American jazz guitarists, yet is running a string of hookers as a sideline. Who drinks so much that only sheer good luck spares him, night after night, from getting himself killed. Who is forgiven by his colleagues, most of the time because when he plays there is magic happening right there on the stage.

Here is a man so lonely that he doesn't even know the concept. "Your feelings are locked away so deeply you don't even know where to find them," he's told. He's wounded: "You say that like it's a bad thing." One day on the boardwalk at Atlantic City, he meets the woman who would be the love of his life if he were sufficiently self-aware to understand that. Her name is Hattie (Samantha Morton), and she is a mute, although Emmet is so self-absorbed that it takes him quite a while to realize she never says anything.

Morton plays Hattie like one of the great silent film heroines. Before dialogue, before the Method, before sound, actors were hired because they embodied roles. You could be a carpenter or a secretary one day and be pushed before the camera on the next. Mabel Normand's *The Extra Girl* (1923) tells such a story. Morton is an accomplished British actress, but here she is not used as an actress so much

as a presence, as in the silent days, with eyes that drink in Emmet, a body that yearns toward him, and a heart that's a pool of unconditional love and admiration. Her love is all the more remarkable because she can hear, which allows her not only to understand his music, but to endure his inept and often crude stabs at conversation.

Emmet, of course, is too unhinged to understand what a treasure she is. You don't know what you've got till it's gone. Vain, with an inferiority complex, a pushover for flattery, he is swept away by a society floozy named Blanche (Uma Thurman), who catches him stealing a knickknack at a party. She doesn't care; she's a little fascinated that a man she believes to be a genius would still harbor the instincts of a petty thief. "You have genuine crudeness," she tells him, as if she were saying he had nice eyes.

Sweet and Lowdown is structured by Allen as a docudrama; we hear Allen's own voice explaining passages in Ray's life, and we see jazz experts like Nat Hentoff who comment on aspects of Ray's career. Jazz history often seems constructed out of barroom stories improved upon over the years, and Emmet Ray's life unfolds like lovingly polished anecdotes; there are even alternate endings to some of the legendary episodes.

Looming over everything is Ray's awe of Django Reinhardt, the Spanish gypsy who ruled the Hot Club of Paris from the 1930s to the 1950s; despite having lost fingers in a childhood accident, he played the guitar as nobody has before or since. Again and again, Ray ruefully observes that he is indeed the best—except for that gypsy in France. A moment when he finally encounters Django provides one of the movie's best laughs.

The guitar playing in the movie is actually by Howard Alden. You will want to own the sound track. Alden taught Sean Penn to play the guitar, in lessons so successful that Allen's camera never has to cheat: We hear Emmet Ray and we see Emmet Ray's fingers, and there is never reason to doubt that Penn is actually playing the guitar.

Emmet Ray is the least Woody-like character I can remember at the center of an Allen movie. He embodies Allen's love of jazz, but few of his other famous characteristics, save perhaps for attracting worshipful women. Much has been made in some psychobabble reviews of the fact that Hattie is mute, as if that represents Allen's ideal woman; perhaps it's inevitable that a director whose films have been so autobiographical would attract speculation like that, but Allen's real-life partners, from Louise Lasser through Diane Keaton and Mia Farrow to the Soon-Yi Previn seen in the 1998 documentary *Wild Man Blues,* have all been assertive and verbal. I think Hattie is seen as Emmet's ideal woman, not Woody's, and it's interesting that Allen, who has gradually stopped casting himself as the lead in his films, now seems happy to make the leads into characters other than versions of himself.

I have made Emmet Ray sound like a doofus and a cold emotional monster, and those are elements in his character, but *Sweet and Lowdown* doesn't leave it at that. There is also a sweetness and innocence in the character, and his eyes warm when he's playing. You sense that this is a man who was equipped by life with few of the skills and insights needed for happiness, and that music transports him to a place he otherwise can hardly remember. If Emmet Ray's talent is indeed like a large dog, pulling him around, then I am reminded of a pet cemetery marker in Errol Morris's *Gates of Heaven,* which reads: "I knew love. I knew this dog."

Sweet November ★

PG-13, 114 m., 2001

Keanu Reeves (Nelson Moss), Charlize Theron (Sara Deever), Jason Isaacs (Chaz), Greg Germann (Vince), Liam Aiken (Abner). Directed by Pat O'Connor and produced by Deborah Aal, Erwin Stoff, Steven Reuther, and Elliott Kastner. Screenplay by Kurt Voelker.

Sweet November passes off pathological behavior as romantic bliss. It's about two sick and twisted people playing mind games and calling it love. I don't know who I disliked more intensely—Nelson, the abrupt, insulting ad man played by Keanu Reeves, or Sara, Charlize Theron's narcissistic martyr. Reeves at least has the grace to look intensely uncomfortable during several scenes, including one involving a bag full of goodies, which we will get to later.

The movie is a remake of a 1968 film starring Sandy Dennis and Anthony Newley and, if memory serves, the same bed in a San Francisco bay window. Both films have the same conceit, which only a movie producer could believe: A beautiful girl takes men to her bed for one month at a time, to try to help and improve them. "You live in a box, and I can lift the lid," she explains. Why a month? "It's long enough to be meaningful and short enough to stay out of trouble," Sara says—wrong on both counts.

Read no further if you do not already know that she has another reason for term limits. She's dying. In the original movie the disease was described as "quite rare, but incurable." Here we get another clue, when Nelson opens Sara's medicine cabinet and finds, oh, I dunno, at a rough guess, 598 bottles of pills. The girl is obviously overmedicating. Give her a high colonic, send her to detox, and the movie is over.

Nelson is one of those insulting, conceited, impatient, coffee-drinking, cell phone–using, Jaguar-driving advertising executives that you find in only two places: the movies, and real life. His motto is, speed up and smell the coffee. Sara, on the other hand, acts like she has all the time in the world, even though (sob!) she does not. She sits on the hood of Nelson's car and commits other crimes against the male libido that a woman absolutely cannot get away with unless she looks exactly like Charlize Theron and insists on sleeping with you, and even then she's pushing it.

Nelson gradually learns to accept the gift of herself that she is offering. Actually, he accepts it quickly, the pig, but only gradually appreciates it. So warm, cheerful, perky, plucky, and seductive is Sara that Nelson, and the movie, completely forget for well over an hour that he has an apartment of his own and another girlfriend. By then the inexorable march of the rare but incurable disease is taking its toll, Sara has to go into the hospital, and Nelson finds out the Truth.

Will there be a scene where Sara, with a drip line plugged into every orifice, begs Nelson, "Get me out of here! Take me home!" Do bears eat gooseberries? Will there be a scene where Sara says, "Go away! I don't want you to see me like this!" Do iguanas like papayas? Will there be a scene where Sara's faithful gay friend (Jason Isaacs) bathes and comforts her? Yes, because it is a convention of movies like this that all sexy women have gay friends who materialize on demand to perform nursing and hygiene chores. (Advice to gay friend in next remake: Insist, "Unless I get two good scenes of my own, I've emptied my last bedpan.")

I almost forgot the scene involving the bag full of goodies. Keanu Reeves must have been phoning his agent between every take. The script requires him to climb in through Sara's window with a large bag that contains all of the presents he would ever want to give her, based on all the needs and desires she has ever expressed. I could get cheap laughs by listing the entire inventory of the bag, but that would be unfair. I will mention only one, the dishwashing machine. Logic may lead you to ask, "How can an automatic dishwasher fit inside a bag that Keanu Reeves can sling over his shoulder as he climbs through the window?" I would explain, but I hate it when movie reviews give everything away.

The Swindle ★ ★ ★
NO MPAA RATING, 105 m., 1999

Isabelle Huppert (Betty), Michel Serrault (Victor), Francois Cluzet (Maurice), Jean-Francois Balmer (Monsieur K), Jackie Berroyer (Chatillon), Jean Benguigui (Guadeloupe Gangster), Mony Dalmes (Signora Trotti). Directed by Claude Chabrol and produced by Marin Karmitz. Screenplay by Chabrol.

While their comrades in the French New Wave are either dead (Truffaut, Malle) or work rarely (Godard, Resnais, Rivette), Claude Chabrol and Eric Rohmer soldier on, prolific and creative. Other directors give difficult birth to each new project, but they've created worlds that easily produce new stories—Rohmer the world of minutely observed romance, Chabrol the world of crime and depravity.

The Swindle is Chabrol's fiftieth film, made with the practiced ease of a master. It's typical of his droll confidence that a man sprawls asleep in a chair during a key scene involving death threats and the breaking of fingers—and typical of Chabrol's restraint that he never

cuts to the sleeping man for a quick laugh, but only subtly reveals him on the edges of the screen.

The movie stars Isabelle Huppert and Michel Serrault as Betty and Victor (if those are indeed their real names). She's fortyish, he's seventyish, they're con artists, and it's impossible to say what their personal relationship is: Friends? Lovers? Relatives? Even a hint at the end is left ambiguous. (It's a tribute to the actors, and to Chabrol, that in any given scene they could convincingly have any one of those three relationships.)

The movie starts with a warm-up con game. Betty poses as an available woman in a casino, and reels in a wealthy hardware dealer. She spikes his drink, he passes out in his room, and she and Victor relieve him of some, but not all, of his money—so that when he comes to, he won't remember his wagers well enough to be sure he was robbed.

That caper establishes the working partnership. Then the film ventures into a more complicated con—so complicated we're never quite sure if Betty and Victor are even conning one another. Betty has latched onto a financial courier for a crime syndicate, and has her eyes on the millions of Swiss francs in his locked briefcase. "Swissss! Swissss!" Victor hisses cheerfully, relishing the superiority of Swiss to French francs.

The courier, Maurice (Francois Cluzet), is a polished man about Betty's age, and there's the hint of a romance between them. Or is that only in Victor's jealous eyes? Or is he really jealous? And is Betty planning to steal the money from Maurice and Victor? Or only from Maurice? Or is Victor planning to steal it from Betty? And what about the powerful criminals who consider the money, after all, to be their property?

The plot unfolds as an understated comedy. Serrault, who has made more than 150 films, seems to twinkle as he schemes. Huppert is, of course, famous for her impassivity (see her in *The School of Flesh*), but here she adds a kind of crazy flair, suddenly exaggerating a word or a gesture, as if amusing herself while going through the steps of a confidence charade. The movie adds sneaky little running jokes, like the way Serrault is forever being mistaken for an employee of whatever establishment he's in. Or the way a meal is lovingly ordered (there's great food in almost all of Chabrol's films).

Chabrol has always been an admirer of Hitchcock, and here he displays a Hitchcockian touch from time to time, almost deliberately. Consider the scene where the three principals observe a dance performance at a winter resort: Betty says she is too warm and leaves, followed first by one man and then the other; as they walk down the aisle all eyes are upon them. It's a reminder of how Hitchcock liked to put characters at a public event where escape meant breaking the rules.

By the end of the film we may still be murky about just what Betty and Victor were planning, and about their true relationship. That's part of the fun. Magicians don't reveal their secrets lightly ("The trick is told when the trick is sold"), and neither do con men. The con man this time, of course, is Chabrol, who has conned us into enjoying the entire film without giving away his own secrets.

Swordfish ★ ★ ½
R, 97 m., 2001

John Travolta (Gabriel Shear), Hugh Jackman (Stanley Jobson), Halle Berry (Ginger), Don Cheadle (Agent A. D. Roberts), Vinnie Jones (Marco), Camryn Grimes (Holly Jobson), Sam Shepard (Senator Reisman), Zach Grenier (A. D. Joy). Directed by Dominic Sena and produced by Jonathan D. Krane and Joel Silver. Screenplay by Skip Woods.

Swordfish looks like the result of a nasty explosion down at the Plot Works. It's skillfully mounted and fitfully intriguing, but weaves such a tangled web that at the end I defy anyone in the audience to explain the exact loyalties and motives of the leading characters. There is one person in the movie who is definitely intended to be a hero, but are the villains really villains? Are they even themselves?

The movie stars Hugh Jackman as a brilliant computer hacker named Stanley, who just spent two years in the pen for the crime of hacking a program used by the FBI to snoop on everybody's e-mail. Now he lives in squalor in a house trailer and yearns for the company of his daughter, whose mother inhabits a drunken stupor.

Enter Ginger (Halle Berry), wearing a sexy little red dress, to recruit Stanley as a hacker for a secret project being masterminded by Gabriel Shear (John Travolta). Stanley demurs: He's been forbidden by the courts to touch a computer. She persists, cornering him in a lap-dancery and giving him one minute (at gunpoint) to hack into a government computer. He succeeds, of course, and is offered $10 million to work for Gabriel, who is (a) a patriot protecting us from bad guys, (b) a bad guy, (c) a double agent pretending to be either a patriot or a bad guy, (d) a freelance, (e) Ginger's lover, or (f) Ginger's target. His true identity is even cloudier than that, but I have said enough.

I will, however, discuss the puzzling role of Ginger, the Halle Berry character. She goes through the motions of being the pretty girl who seduces the hero into working for the secret organization. But this is strange, since Stanley shows little interest in her, and Ginger ostensibly belongs to Gabriel. This does not prevent a scene in which Halle Berry bares her breasts to tempt the untemptable Stanley. This scene came as a huge relief because I thought the movies, in their rush to the PG-13 rating, had forgotten about breasts. In the age of computerized sci-fi special effects, beautiful skin finishes a distant second at the box office. Once teenage boys wanted to see Emmanuelle undulating; now they want to see Keanu Reeves levitating.

Swordfish, to be sure, does have great effects. One involves a horrific explosion that seems frozen in time while the camera circles it. It's a great visual moment. Another involves a sequence in which a bus is lifted above the city by a helicopter. There's the obligatory scene in which passengers fall to their deaths out the back of the bus—not exploited as well as in Spielberg's *Jurassic Park 2,* but good enough.

For originality, the best scene is a quieter one. Stanley sits at his computer keyboard and looks at six or eight monitors, hacking away in syncopated rhythm to a song about "50,000 volts of (bleeping)." As he works he talks, his words fitting neatly into the music. The song and the action work nicely together, even if we doubt hackers use their keyboards for percussion.

Dominic Sena directed *Gone in 60 Seconds* last year and is getting better. He can't stop himself from including one absolutely gratuitous car chase, but he takes more time with the plot here, and makes good use of Halle Berry to atone for ignoring Angelina Jolie last summer. He also gets a juicy performance out of Travolta, who opens with a monologue that would have been at home in *Get Shorty*, and plays a character whose dialogue is weirdly persuasive. (He defends his violent actions in hard-boiled realpolitik terms.) I also liked Don Cheadle as an FBI agent who supplies one of the few characters in the movie you can count on to be more or less who he says he is.

I see that I have forgotten to even mention that the movie involves a bank robbery and a hostage crisis. Well, it's that kind of film. The robbery and the crisis weave in and out of the plot like motifs in a symphony; we remember them when they're on-screen, but the movie isn't really about them. It's more about pulling the rug out from under the audience every five minutes or so. There comes a time when you seriously think the characters should wear red or blue shirts to keep from passing to the other team.

T

Taboo ★ ★ ★

NO MPAA RATING, 101 m., 2001

Beat Takeshi (Captain Toshizo Hijikata), Ryuhei Matsuda (Samurai Sozaburo Kano), Shinji Takeda (Lieutenant Soji Okita), Tadanobu Asano (Samurai Hyozo Tashiro), Koji Matoba (Samurai Heibei Sugano), Masa Tommies (Inspecteur Jo Yamazaki), Masato Ibu (Officer Koshitaro Ito), Uno Kanda (Geisha Nishikigi-Dayu). Directed by Nagisa Oshima and produced by Eiko Oshima, Shigehiro Nakagawa, and Kazuo Shimizu. Screenplay by Nagisa Oshima, based on novellas by Ryotaro Shiba.

Nagisa Oshima's *Taboo* tells a story set in the late samurai period, when a youth of unusual beauty is admitted into a training program for warriors, stirring lust among his comrades and even a superior officer. When the film premiered at Cannes in May 2000, the joke was that it would be retitled, "Not to ask, not to tell."

Homosexuality in the military is as old as armies, and was sometimes encouraged as a way of inspiring soldiers to bond; we gather that within the closed world of the Japanese samurai, it was acknowledged as a fact of life. The problem with Sozaburo Kano (Ryuhei Matsuda) is not that he is gay, but that he is so beautiful, so feminine, that he is a distraction and inspires jealousy. He seems fully aware of his appeal, and enhances it with a kind of smoldering passivity that dares the other men to start something.

The movie takes place in Kyoto around 1865, in the last days of traditional samurai. Threatened by new kinds of fighting, new channels of power, and the opening of the country to the West, the men of the Shinsengumi troop adhere all the more rigidly to the samurai code, even enforcing death as a punishment for severe violations. It is strange that a candidate as effeminate as Sozaburo would be one of two finalists chosen after sword-fighting auditions, but then again there is a look in the eye of Captain Hijikata (Beat Takeshi) that hints of hidden agendas.

When Beat Takeshi directs, it is under his real name of Takeshi Kitano. As director and star, he is known for violent macho thrillers, and so his casting here is provocative; imagine John Wayne in *Red River*, with a stirring beneath his chaps every time he looks at Montgomery Clift. Hijikata is not gay, but Sozaburo is beautiful enough to inspire a lonely man to relax his usual standards. A samurai clearly in love with Sozaburo is Tashiro (Tadanobu Asano), a brawny type who feels competitive because both men were recruited at the same time.

Is Sozaburo capable of fighting well enough to carry his weight in the samurai army? He turns out be the best of the young swordsmen, and when a superior orders him to carry out the execution of a disobedient samurai, he beheads the offender without a blink. The thing about Sozaburo, indeed, is that he hardly blinks at anything: Even while another samurai is having sex with him, he hardly seems to notice.

Is this a weakness of the film? Maybe so. Oshima, directing his first film in fourteen years, has found an actor with the physical attributes to play the character, and seems content to leave it at that; his camera regards Sozaburo as an object of beauty but hardly seems to engage him. It's as if the young samurai is a platonic ideal of androgynous perfection, and the movie is not about him but about his effect on the others.

Nagisa Oshima, born in 1932, was a rebel of the Japanese cinema in the 1960s and 1970s, and is most famous for *In the Realm of the Senses* (1976), the story of a love affair that turned into a sadomasochistic obsession, resulting during one sex scene in the hero's loss of that implement he might most require if he hoped to have another one. So great was the crush to attend that film's Cannes premiere that one critic was shoved through a plate-glass window, luckily escaping the hero's fate. Oshima in recent years has become a Japanese TV star, and this film was a surprise to those who assumed he had more or less retired from filmmaking.

Taboo is not an entirely successful film, but it isn't boring. There is a kind of understated humor in the way the senior samurai officers discuss their troublesome young recruit, and a melancholy in the way the samurais follow their code as they are ceasing to be relevant or useful. I am not even sure it was a mistake to have Sozaburo be so passive. If he were a more active, complex character, that would generate a wider range of issues, and he works better within the plot as a catalyst.

I am reminded of a story told by Donald Richie, the great writer on Japanese themes. *In the Realm of the Senses* was based on a true story of a woman who castrated her lover at his request. After serving a prison sentence, she was hired by a Tokyo tavern to appear nightly. At the given hour, she would descend a flight of stairs, walk across the room, and exit. The room would always be jammed, Richie reports. "There she goes!" the customers would say. The character of Sozaburo seems to serve something of the same function in this movie.

The Tailor of Panama ★ ★ ★ ½
R, 109 m., 2001

Pierce Brosnan (Andy Osnard), Geoffrey Rush (Harry Pendel), Jamie Lee Curtis (Louisa Pendel), Brendan Gleeson (Mickie Abraxas), Catherine McCormack (Francesca), Leonor Varela (Marta), Harold Pinter (Uncle Benny), Daniel Radcliffe (Mark Pendel), David Hayman (Luxmore). Directed and produced by John Boorman. Screenplay by Boorman, Andrew Davies, and John Le Carre, based on the novel by Le Carre.

"Welcome to Panama—Casablanca without heroes."

Not that Casablanca had many heroes. The statement is made by Harry Pendel, a tailor in Panama City, to Andy Osnard, a British spy who for his sins has been posted to this diplomatic dead end. The beauty of John Boorman's *The Tailor of Panama* is that the movie has no heroes, either. It's a cynical, droll story about two con men taking advantage of each other and getting away with it because the British and American governments are begging to be lied to. The casting of Pierce Brosnan as Osnard is the perfect touch: Here's a nasty real-world James Bond with no gadgets and no scruples.

The movie is based on the John Le Carre best-seller, showing that when the Cold War ended, its diplomatic gamesmanship continued as farce. In London, we meet Osnard as an amoral cutup in MI6, a gambler and ladies' man with a gift for embarrassing the agency. He's given a chance to redeem himself with the assignment to Panama, where nothing much is happening, although local mischief picks up considerably under his influence.

His strategy: Pick a member of Panama City's British community and use him as a source and conduit for information. He chooses Harry Pendel (Geoffrey Rush), whose firm, Braithwaite and Pendel, claims to be late of London's Saville Row. Actually, as Osnard finds out, there never was a Braithwaite, and Pendel learned to be a tailor while serving a prison term for arson. By threatening to blow Pendel's cover, Osnard gets him to cooperate in a scheme neither one of them quite admits to the other, in which Pendel will supply information which may be dubious, and Osnard will not scrutinize it too suspiciously.

Both men are pragmatists without ideals, although Pendel at least has an inspiration: the safety and security of his American wife (Jamie Lee Curtis) and their two children. That, and his firm, and his farm that is deeply in debt, are all that matter to him. "Where's your patriotism?" Osnard asks him at one point, and he replies: "I had it out in prison—without an anesthetic."

The movie plays as a joy for lovers of well-written, carefully crafted character thrillers. It has a lot of wry, twisted humor. It depends not on chases and killings, but on devious, greedy connivance in a world where everyone is looking out for himself. Its Panama City is still in shock after the Noriega years, and Pendel (who was the dictator's tailor—but then he's the tailor for everyone who can afford him) is well placed to know what's going on. His wife works for the director of the Panama Canal company, and in his tailor shop, which doubles as a club where gentlemen can drop in for a drink or a cigar, he overhears a great deal, although not as much as he tells Osnard he overhears.

He also has genuine contacts with the hidden side of Panama. His shop assistant, the scarred and fierce Marta (Leonor Varela), was a former member of the anti-Noriega underground. And so was his best friend, the shabby, hard-drinking Mickie Abraxas (Brendan Gleeson, from Boorman's *The General*). Both still hold their political ideals, Mickie loudly and defiantly, which inspires Pendel to invent a fictitious radical political movement, which Osnard believes in for reasons of his own.

Osnard, meanwhile, has his eye, and hands, on Francesca (Catherine McCormack), a sexy official in the British embassy, while feeding her boss (David Hayman) his colorful information. Secrets create a vacuum that only more secrets can fill, and soon Osnard is making demands on Pendel, whose wife presumably knows the secrets of the canal company—although not the secrets Pendel invents and passes along.

This round-robin of cynicism and deception takes place against a city of nightclubs and B-girl bars, residential areas and city streets lined with "laundromats" (banks), embassies and the cozy confines of Pendel's shop. Boorman and Le Carre (his executive producer) were wise to shoot the exteriors on location in Panama, where the tropical look makes the overheated schemes seem right at home.

Many thrillers are essentially machines to inject a shock into the audience every few minutes. *The Tailor of Panama* is a real movie, rich and atmospheric, savoring its disreputable characters and their human weaknesses. And there's room for genuine emotion, too, in the way Harry Pendel desperately holds onto the respectability he has conjured out of thin air. And in the way the stubborn, heedless Mickie Abraxas says what he thinks no matter what the risk. The movie is abundant in its gifts, a pleasure for those who like a story to unfold lovingly over a full arc, instead of coming in short, mindless bursts.

The Talented Mr. Ripley ★ ★ ★ ★
R, 140 m., 1999

Matt Damon (Tom Ripley), Gwyneth Paltrow (Marge Sherwood), Jude Law (Dickie Greenleaf), Cate Blanchett (Meredith Logue), Philip Seymour Hoffman (Freddie Miles), Jack Davenport (Peter Smith-Kingsley), James Rebhorn (Herbert Greenleaf), Sergio Rubini (Inspector Roverini), Philip Baker Hall (Alvin MacCarron). Directed by Anthony Minghella and produced by William Horberg and Tom Sternberg. Screenplay by Minghella, based on the novel by Patricia Highsmith.

Villains usually last through only one crime novel, while heroes are good for a whole series. That's a great inconvenience for their authors, because villains are usually more colorful than heroes. Patricia Highsmith's novels about Tom Ripley are the exception, a series of books about a man who is irredeemably bad, and yet charming, intelligent, and thoughtful about the price he pays for his amoral lifestyle.

The Talented Mr. Ripley, her first Ripley novel, published in 1955, shows Ripley in the process of inventing himself and finding his life's work. He was a poor man who wanted to be a rich man, an unknown man who wanted not to be famous but simply to be *someone else*. Some men are envious of other men's cars, or wives, or fortunes. Ripley coveted their identities.

The novel shows him annexing the life and identity of a man named Greenleaf. It was filmed in 1960 by Rene Clement as *Purple Noon*, with Alain Delon as Ripley, and now it has been filmed again by Anthony Minghella *(The English Patient)*, with Matt Damon in the title role. One of the pleasures of the two adaptations is that the plots are sufficiently different that you can watch one without knowing how the other turns out—or even what happens along the way. That despite the fact that they both revolve around Ripley's decision that he can be Greenleaf as well as, or better than, Greenleaf can be himself.

Purple Noon begins with the two men already friends. *The Talented Mr. Ripley*, adapted by Minghella, has a better idea: Ripley is an opportunist who stumbles onto an opening into Greenleaf's life and takes it. He borrows a Princeton blazer to play the piano at a rooftop party in Manhattan, and a rich couple assume he must have known their son Dickie at Princeton. He agrees.

The Greenleafs are concerned about Dickie (Jude Law), who has decamped to the decadence of Europe and shows no sign of coming home. They offer Tom Ripley a deal: They'll finance his own trip to Europe and pay him $1,000 if he returns with their son. Cut to a beach in Italy, where Dickie suns with Marge

Sherwood (Gwyneth Paltrow), and the original deception turns evil.

Remember that Ripley is already impersonating someone—Dickie's old Princeton friend. That works with Dickie ("I've completely forgotten him," he tells Marge), but eventually he wonders if anything Tom tells him is the truth. Ripley, at this point still developing the skills that will carry him through several more adventures, instinctively knows that the best way to lie is to admit to lying, and to tell the truth whenever convenient. When Dickie asks him what his talents are, he replies, "Forging signatures, telling lies, and impersonating almost anyone." Quite true. And then he does a chilling impersonation of Mr. Greenleaf asking him to bring Dickie back to America. "I feel like he's here," Dickie says, as Tom does his father's voice.

By confessing his mission, Tom disarms Dickie, and is soon accepted into his circle, which also includes an epicurean friend named Freddie Miles (Philip Seymour Hoffman). Also moving through Europe at about the same time is a rich girl named Meredith Logue (Cate Blanchett), who believes things about Tom that Dickie must not be allowed to know. But I am growing vague, and must grow vaguer, because the whole point of the movie is to show Tom Ripley learning to use subterfuge, improvisation, and lightning-fast thinking under pressure to become Dickie Greenleaf.

Highsmith wrote *The Talented Mr. Ripley* five years after writing *Strangers on a Train,* which Hitchcock made into a film he sometimes called his favorite. The two stories are similar. *Strangers* is about a man who meets another man and offers to trade crimes with him: I'll kill the person you hate, and you kill the person I hate, and since neither one of us has any connection with our victim or any motive for killing him, we'll never be caught. *Talented* has Dickie blamed for the drowning death of a local woman, and Ripley "trading" that death as a cover-up for another.

Hitchcock's film subtly suggested a homosexual feeling in the instigator, and Tom Ripley also seems to have feelings for Dickie Greenleaf—although narcissism and sexuality are so mixed up in his mind that Ripley almost seems to want to became Greenleaf so

that he can love himself (both Ripley movies have a scene of Ripley dressed in Dickie's clothes and posing in a mirror). This undercurrent is wisely never brought up to the level of conscious action, because so many of Tom Ripley's complicated needs and desires are deeply buried; he finds out what he wants to do by doing it.

Matt Damon is bland and ordinary as Ripley, and then takes on the vivid coloration of others—even a jazz singer. Jude Law makes Dickie almost deserving of his fate, because of the way he adopts new friends and then discards them. Gwyneth Paltrow's role is tricky: Yes, Dickie is her boyfriend, but he's cold and treats her badly, and there are times when she would intuit the dread secret if she weren't so distracted by the way she already resents Dickie.

The movie is as intelligent a thriller as you'll see this year. It is also insidious in the way it leads us to identify with Tom Ripley. He is the protagonist, we see everything through his eyes, and Dickie is not especially lovable; that means we are a coconspirator in situations where it seems inconceivable that his deception will not be discovered. He's a monster, but we want him to get away with it. There is one sequence in the film, involving an apartment, a landlady, the police, and a friend who knows the real Dickie, that depends on such meticulous timing and improvisation that if you made it speedier, you'd have the Marx brothers.

Tango ★ ★ ★ ½
PG-13, 112 m., 1999

Miguel Angel Sola (Mario Suarez), Cecilia Narova (Laura Fuentes), Mia Maestro (Elena Flores), Juan Carlos Copes (Carlos Nebbia), Julio Bocca (Himself), Juan Luis Galiardo (Angelo Larroca). Directed by Carlos Saura and produced by Luis A. Scalella, Carlos Mentasti, and Juan Carlos Codazzi. Screenplay by Saura.

The tango is based on suspicion, sex, and insincerity. It is not a dance for virgins. It is for the wounded and the wary. The opening shots of Carlos Saura's *Tango,* after a slow pan across Buenos Aires, are of a man who has given his life to the dance, and has a bad leg and a walking stick as his reward. This is the weary, graceful Mario (Miguel Angel Sola), who is preparing a new show based on the tango.

At the same time, perhaps Mario also represents Carlos Saura. The movie, one of 1999's Oscar nominees, has many layers: It is a film about the making of a film, and also a film about the making of a stage production. We are never quite sure what is intended as real and what is part of the stage production. That's especially true of some of the dance visuals, which use mirrors, special effects, trick lighting, and silhouettes so that we can't tell if we're looking at the real dancers or their reflections. A special set was constructed to shoot the film in this way, and the photography, by the great three-time Oscar winner Vittorio Storaro, is like a celebration of his gift.

If the film is visually beautiful, it is also ravishing as a musical—which is really what it is, with its passionate music and angry dance sequences. It is said the musical is dead, but it lives here, and Saura of course has made several films where music is crucial to the weave of the story; his credits include *Blood Wedding, Carmen,* and *Flamenco.*

Early in the film, Mario visits a club run by the sinister Angelo Larroca (Juan Luis Galiardo), who asks him a favor: an audition for his girlfriend, Elena (Mia Maestro). Mario can hardly refuse, because Angelo owns 50 percent of the show. Mario watches Elena dance, and realizes she is very good. He begins to fall in love with her, which is dangerous; when he makes a guarded proposal at dinner, she says, "Come off it—you know who I'm living with!"

Yes, he does. So does his estranged wife, Laura (Cecilia Narova), who warns him off the girl. But Mario and Elena draw closer, until finally they are sleeping with each other even though Angelo has threatened to punish cheating with death. What adds an additional element to their romance is Mario's essential sadness; he is like a man who has given up hope of being happy, and at one point he calls himself "A solitary animal—one of those old lions who roam the African savanna."

Of course, there is always the question of how much of this story is real, and how much of it is actually the story of the stage production. Saura allows us to see his cameras at times, suggesting that what we see is being filmed—for this film? Back and forth flow the lines of possibility and reality.

There are several dance sequences of special power. One is an almost vicious duet between Elena and Laura. Another uses dancers as soldiers, and suggests the time in Argentina's history when many people disappeared forever. That time is also evoked by images of startling simplicity: Torture, for example, is suggested by light on a single chair. And there is also a sequence, showing mostly just feet and legs, that suggests the arrival of immigrants to Argentina. You see in *Tango* that there are still things to be discovered about how dancing can be shown on the screen.

Recently, for one reason or another, I've seen a lot of tango. A stage performance in Paris, for example, and the 1997 British movie *The Tango Lesson.* Apart from the larger dimensions of the dance, there is the bottom line of technical skill. The legs of the dancers move so swiftly and so close to one another that only long practice and perfect timing prevents falls—even injuries. With the tango you never get the feeling the dancers have just met. They have a long history together, and not necessarily a happy one; they dance as a challenge, a boast, a taunt, a sexual put-down. It is the one dance where the woman gives as good as she gets, and the sexes are equal.

The romantic stories in *Tango* reflect that kind of dynamic. Mario and his estranged wife talk the way tango dancers dance. The early stages of Mario's seduction of Elena are like an emotional duel. The role of Angelo, the tough guy, is like a stage tango performance when a stranger arrives and tries to take command. It isn't real. It is real. It's all rehearsed, but they really mean it. It's only a show, but it reflects what's going on in the dancers' lives. It's only a dance. Yes, but life is only a dance.

The Tao of Steve ★ ★ ★
PG-13, 90 m., 2000

Donal Logue (Dex), Greer Goodman (Syd), Kimo Wills (Dave), Ayelet Kaznelson (Beth), David Aaron Baker (Rick), Nina Jaroslaw

(Maggie), John Hines (Ed), Selby Craig (Chris), Craig D. Lafayette (Matt). Directed by Jenniphr Goodman and produced by Anthony Bregman. Screenplay by Duncan North with Greer Goodman and Jenniphr Goodman.

"Men and women both want to have sex, but women want to have sex fifteen minutes after us, so if you hold out for twenty, she'll be chasing you for five."

This is the wisdom of Dex, the hero of *The Tao of Steve*, who seems to get a lot of sex, considering he is a fat, thirty-two-year-old grade school teacher who shares the rent with three roommates, wears only a bathrobe whenever he possibly can, and has a dog that can intercept whipped cream sprayed directly from the can.

Dex (Donal Logue) lives in Santa Fe, where at his college reunion he makes love with an old girlfriend in the stacks of the library, then returns her glowing to her husband. Other old girlfriends gossip behind his back: "I can't believe how much weight he's gained." And they confront him about it. "You were Elvis!" one says accusingly. "Yeah," he says. "Well, now I'm fat Elvis."

But Dex has no trouble getting girls, and is happy to offer advice to his friends, in long talks spiked with references to Thomas Aquinas and Steve McQueen. He likes the name "Steve." To him, it represents all that is cool in life—the smooth, the lithe, the brave. He rattles off names: "Steve McQueen, Steve McGarrett, Steve Austin." (The least cool name, in case you were wondering, is Stu.) Playing pool and drinking beers, he explains his seductive techniques to guys who are thinner but hornier. There are three rules:

1. Eliminate your desire ("Women can smell an agenda").
2. Be excellent in their presence (even if it's only at throwing a Frisbee).
3. Withdraw (this is illustrated by the twenty-minute strategy).

Like many Don Juans, including Don Juan himself, Dex spends more time talking about sex than experiencing it. Then he's blindsided by Syd (Greer Goodman), who is in town as a set designer for the Sante Fe Opera, and catches his eye and tugs at his heart. He likes her. He likes her so much he desires her, which is against the rules. He desires her so much he

allows her to sense his desire, which leads to the shattering revelation that they have *already* had sex—years ago, in college—and she remembers it but he doesn't, which is not being cool like Steve.

The Tao of Steve is an easygoing but bright comedy that focuses on Donal Logue's effortless charm (he won the Best Actor Award at Sundance). It creates the feeling of settling in comfortably with old friends, and no wonder: Greer Goodman is not only the costar but cowrote the screenplay with her sister, Jenniphr Goodman, who is the director. It contains the insight, common to all stories about theories of love, that these theories never work out in practice, and eventually Dex is just as needy as some poor jerk who doesn't have the benefit of his deep wisdom.

One of the things I like about the movie is the wit of its dialogue, the way sentences and conversations coil with confidence up to a conclusion that is totally unexpected. It's the same sort of verbal humor I'm enjoying right now in the novel I'm reading, *A Heartbreaking Work of Staggering Genius* by Dave Eggers. So much dialogue, in print and on the screen, is machined to serve the plot. You don't often get the impression the people are really talking. Logue and the other actors here have the kind of back-and-forth timing of friends who have been kidding around for a long time, who know each other's timing, who have created entertaining personas for themselves.

Of course, all stories like this eventually come down to *commitment*, a word that strikes a chill into the heart of any man who lives in a bathrobe and feeds his dog out of the whipped cream can. Dex has his theories about it ("Don Giovanni slept with 1,000 women because he was afraid he wouldn't be loved by one"), but in practice, as Syd helps him to understand, you sooner or later have to make your choice, or you end up counting flowers on the wall.

Note: If there is one suspicion I have about the film, it's that Donal Logue is not as fat as the character he plays. At Sundance, he didn't exactly look underfed, but he didn't have that tire around his middle, and my best guess is that's padding. That may help to explain why he refuses to take off his shirt in the movie. If it isn't, that may also explain it. ☞

Tarzan ★ ★ ★

G, 88 m., 1999

With the voices of: Brian Blessed (Clayton), Glenn Close (Kala), Minnie Driver (Jane), Tony Goldwyn (Tarzan), Nigel Hawthorne (Professor Porter), Lance Henriksen (Kerchak), Wayne Knight (Tantor), Alex D. Linz (Young Tarzan), Rosie O'Donnell (Terk). Directed by Kevin Lima and Chris Buck and produced by Bonnie Arnold. Screenplay by Tab Murphy, Bob Tzudiker, and Noni White, based on the story "Tarzan of the Apes" by Edgar Rice Burroughs.

Something deep within the Tarzan myth speaks to us, and Disney's new animated *Tarzan* captures it. Maybe it's the notion that we can all inhabit this planet together, man and beast, and get along. The surface of the movie is adventure, comedy, and movement—there are sequences here as exciting as the ballroom scene in *Beauty and the Beast*—but underneath is something of substance. The most durable movie character in history emerges this time as a man who asks the question, "Why are you threatened by anyone different than you?"

This is not the confident Tarzan of so many Edgar Rice Burroughs novels and Johnny Weissmuller movies, discovering cities of gold. It is a Tarzan who knows from the day he compares his hand with the hand of Kala, the ape who has adopted him, that he is different. A Tarzan who is still different even after he meets other humans—because his experience is not the same. The movie doesn't insist on this thread of meaning, but it gives the movie weight. Like all the best Disney animated films, this one is about something other than cute characters and cheerful songs. It speaks even to the youngest members of the audience, who, like Tarzan, must have days when they feel surrounded by tall, rumbling, autocratic bipeds.

The movie is also a lot of fun. It has scenes that move through space with a freedom undreamed of in older animated films, and unreachable by any live-action process. Disney uses a process called Deep Canvas, a computer-assisted animation tool that handles the details during swoops through three dimensions. There's a sequence where Tarzan helps Jane escape from a band of monkeys, and as they hurtle through the treetops and loop-the-loop on byways of vines, it's like a roller-coaster ride.

The origin of Tarzan is one of the great masterstrokes of twentieth-century fiction. Burroughs, who never visited Africa, imagined it in much the same way that a child might, peering into a picture book of gorillas and elephants. The opening sequence of *Tarzan* encapsulates the story of how the young British baby and his parents were shipwrecked on the coast of Africa, built a treehouse, and lived in it. In the film, the infant is discovered by the curious gorilla Kala, after Sabor the leopard has killed his parents (offscreen, mercifully, although of course almost all Disney movies are about orphans in one way or another). She names the baby Tarzan, and brings it home to the family, where her mate, Kerchak, growls, "He can stay—but that doesn't make him my son!"

The look of the African forest is one of the great beauties of the film. There is such a depth to some scenes, and a feeling of great space in shots like the one where a waterfall tumbles off a mountain wall, while tiny birds make their way through the sky. Against this primeval wilderness, the Disney animators strike a sort of compromise with the laws of the jungle. Some animals (the leopard, for example) are true to their natures and are predators. Others, like the humanoid apes, are sentimentalized; Kala, voiced by Glenn Close, sounds like a suburban mom, and Terk, the wacky sidekick, sounds like—well, Rosie O'Donnell.

The leader of the pack, Kerchak (Lance Henrikson), is rumbling and distant, but there's an elephant who talks like a twelve-stepper ("I've had it with you and your emotional constipation"). Oddly, the animals have normal English dialogue when they are heard by one another, but are reduced to soft gutturals in the presence of outside humans. (Tarzan, who has been chatting with Kala for years, is reduced to talking in little coos after Jane turns up, and we are denied what would no doubt have been an invaluable scene in which Kala tells him the facts of life.)

Jane is voiced by Minnie Driver, as a peppy British girl with lots of moxie. She's come with her father, the walrus-faced Professor Porter (Nigel Hawthorne), to study the gorillas; their guide is Clayton (Brian Blessed), with the graying sideburns of Stewart Granger and the sneers of a Victorian villain. The human plot, as you can guess, includes Clayton's nefarious plans for the gorillas and Tarzan's defense of them. The more interesting plot involves the tug-of-war after Tarzan and Jane fall in love ("I'm in a tree with a man who talks with gorillas!"). Will he return to London with her, or will she stay in the jungle? Burroughs had one answer; Disney has another.

There are, of course, no Africans in this movie. (The opening song promises us a paradise unspoiled by man.) This may be just as well. The Tarzan myth doesn't take place in Africa so much as in a kind of archetypal wilderness occupied only by its own characters. Burroughs used some Africans in his books, but that was after Tarzan got involved in politics (fighting the Germans in South West Africa, for example). At the stage of the story where this film is set, the presence of any additional characters would be disastrous, because they would bring in the real world, and this story has to close out reality to work at all. (*The Lion King*, of course, didn't even have room for Tarzan.)

Tarzan, like *The Hunchback of Notre Dame,* represents another attempt by Disney to push the envelope of animation. Taking a page from the Japanese, where animation is an accepted art form for serious films, *Tarzan* isn't a kiddie cartoon but a movie that works on one level for children (who will like the "Trashin' the Camp" production number), and another for adults (who may stir at scenes like the one where the gorillas reveal themselves to their visitors). The Disney animators also borrow a technique that has been useful to the Japanese, of exaggerating the size of eyes and mouths to make emotions clearer.

I saw *Tarzan* once, and went to see it again. This kind of bright, colorful, hyperkinetic animation is a visual exhilaration. Animation cuts loose from what we can actually see, and shows us what we might ideally see. Like *Mulan* and *A Bug's Life,* this is a film where grownups do not need to be accompanied by a nonadult guardian.

The Taste of Others ★ ★ ★
NO MPAA RATING, 112 m., 2001

Jean-Pierre Bacri (Castella), Anne Alvaro (Clara), Christiane Millet (Angelique), Brigitte Catillon (Beatrice), Alain Chabat (Deschamps), Agnes Jaoui (Manie), Gérard Lanvin (Moreno), Anne Le Ny (Valerie). Directed by Agnes Jaoui and produced by Christian Berard and Charles Gassot. Screenplay by Jaoui and Jean-Pierre Bacri.

Finding out somebody has bad taste is like discovering he needs dental work. Things were fine until he opened his mouth. Of course, your good taste might be my bad taste, and vice versa. For example, I know there are people who don't go to foreign films, and I am patient with them, as I would be with a child: With luck, they may evolve into more interesting beings. And then they could think about the lessons of *The Taste of Others.*

This is a film about a busy industrialist named Castella (Jean-Pierre Bacri) who is blindsided by love and idealism. As the movie opens his life is affluent but uninspiring. He is surrounded by material comforts, all of them dictated by his wife, an interior decorator. She is the kind of woman who, when she says something loving and affectionate, he has to look up to see if she's talking to him or the dog.

Castella signs up for English lessons, but is impatient at the work required; he gets stuck on the pronunciation of "the." He asks the teacher if she doesn't have a "fun" way to learn English. She doesn't, so he fires her. That night, his wife drags him kicking and screaming to a local dramatic production, and he falls in love with the leading actress. This is, of course, the very same woman who was the English teacher, but at first he doesn't realize that, because now she is surrounded by the aura of Art.

He pursues the actress, named Clara (Anne Alvaro). She is fortyish, attractive but not beautiful, a member of the artsy-fartsy set in their provincial town. She, of course, is not attracted to Castella, who has crass tastes and materialistic values and has led the life of money rather than the life of the mind. But he persists. He sends her flowers. He turns up everywhere. When she doesn't like his dorky mustache, he shaves it off. The movie doesn't present this simply as a romantic infatuation, but goes the additional step: It sees that Castella is in love not only with Clara, but with what she represents: the life of the arts, of the theater, of ideas, of questioning things, of developing your own taste. We are reminded of Jack Nicholson in *As Good as It Gets,* when he tells Helen Hunt, "I love you because you make me want to be a better man."

Meanwhile, things are shaky on the home front. Castella sees a painting he likes, brings it home, and hangs it on the wall. Whether it's a good painting is beside the point: It is *his* painting. When his wife rejects it in horror, he says very quietly, "Angelique . . . I like this picture," and those are words she should listen to very carefully if she values their marriage.

There's a parallel relationship in the movie between Castella's bodyguard, Moreno (Gérard Lanvin), and the barmaid Manie (played by Agnes Jaoui, the film's director). Manie sells hashish as a sideline, and Moreno disapproves. This, too, is a matter of taste: Anyone who sells drugs is telling you something about themselves that you don't want to know more about. The difference is, you can stop selling drugs, but you may never be able to tell a good painting from a bad one, or know why the decor of a living room should not hurt the eyes. Castella continues his lonely quest, uneasily joining Clara and her bohemian friends in the café they frequent after performances of the play, and eventually—well, people evolve, and taste involves not only judging superficial things, but being able to see beneath them.

One of the delights of *The Taste of Others* is that it is so smart and wears its intelligence lightly. Films about taste are not often made by Hollywood, perhaps because it would so severely limit the box office to require the audience to have any. *The Taste of Others* will be all but impenetrable to anyone unable to appreciate what's going on under the dialogue, under the action, down there at the level where we instinctively make judgments based on taste, style, and judgment. It's not, of course, that there's a right or wrong about taste. It's more that your taste defines the kinds of people who want to share it with you. Here's a test: If, as your taste evolves over a lifetime, you find that it attracts more interesting friends, you're on the right track.

Teaching Mrs. Tingle ★ ½
PG-13, 94 m., 1999

Helen Mirren (Mrs. Tingle), Katie Holmes (Leigh Ann Watson), Jeffrey Tambor (Coach Wenchell), Barry Watson (Luke Churner), Marisa Coughlan (Jo Lynn Jordan), Liz Stauber (Trudie Tucker), Michael McKean (Principal Potter), Molly Ringwald (Miss Banks), Vivica A. Fox (Mrs. Gold). Directed by Kevin Williamson and produced by Cathy Konrad. Screenplay by Williamson.

Helen Mirren is a very good actress. All too good for *Teaching Mrs. Tingle,* where she creates a character so hateful and venomous that the same energy, more usefully directed, could have generated a great Lady Macbeth. She is correct to believe that comic characters are best when played straight. They depend on the situation to make them funny. There is nothing funny about the situation in *Teaching Mrs. Tingle.*

The movie resembles *Election* in its attempt to deal with the dog-eat-dog world of ambitious high school students, where grade points can make an enormous difference. But it lacks that movie's sly observations about human nature, and bludgeons the audience with broad, crude, creepy developments. Here is a movie that leaves us without anyone to like very much, and no one to care about. It was written and directed by Kevin Williamson, whose screenplays for the *Scream* pictures depend on comic slasher situations for their appeal; here, required to create more believable characters, he finds the wrong ones for this kind of story.

Katie Holmes stars as Leigh Ann Watson, an honor student only a few percentage points shy of becoming class valedictorian. Much depends on the grade she gets in history, a class that Mrs. Tingle (Mirren) rules with an iron fist and cruel sarcasm. She seems to take an almost erotic delight in humiliating her students in public, and singles out Leigh Ann for special ridicule, maybe just because she's smart and pretty.

Also in the picture: Jo Lynn Jordan (Marisa Coughlan), Leigh Ann's best friend; their classmate and friend Luke Churner (Barry Watson), who combines the better qualities of slobs and oafs; and Trudie Tucker (Liz Stauber), who is

Leigh Ann's bitter rival for valedictorian. Oh, and there's Michael McKean as the high school principal; Mrs. Tingle knows he's in AA and threatens to blackmail him for secret drinking. And Coach Wenchell (Jeffrey Tambor), whose relationship with Mrs. Tingle is reflected in his nickname, Spanky (in this case it is best spelled Spankee).

Leigh Ann turns in a history project in the form of a journal that might have been kept by a pilgrim woman; it's leather-bound, with meticulous calligraphy and decorations, and would make the judges of the History Book Club weep with gratitude. Mrs. Tingle scornfully mocks it after only glancing at the front page. Later, she pounces on the three friends in the gym. Luke has stolen a copy of Mrs. Tingle's final exam and stuffs it into Leigh Ann's backpack, where Mrs. Tingle finds it. Now Leigh Ann faces expulsion.

All of this serves as setup to the heart of the movie, which is spent with Mrs. Tingle tied to her bed while the three students desperately try to figure out what to do next. If this were a serious hostage or kidnapping movie, some of the resulting material might seem appropriate. Mirren approaches Mrs. Tingle like a prisoner of war in a serious film, playing mind games with her captors. There are scenes that are intended as farce (unexpected arrivals and phone calls), but they're flat and lifeless. We have no sympathy for Mrs. Tingle, but at least she has life, while the three students are simply constructions—walking, talking containers for the plot.

Is it possible that some high school students hate their teachers so much that they'll play along with *Teaching Mrs. Tingle*? I doubt it, because Mrs. Tingle isn't hateful in an entertaining way. She belongs in one of those anguished South American movies about political prisoners and their captors facing ethical dilemmas. And the kids belong in *Scream 3*.

Tea with Mussolini ★ ★ ½
PG, 117 m., 1999

Cher (Elsa), Judi Dench (Arabella), Joan Plowright (Mary), Maggie Smith (Lady Hester), Lily Tomlin (Georgie), Baird Wallace (Luca), Charlie Lucas (Luca [child]), Massimo Ghini (Paolo). Directed by Franco Zeffirelli and produced by Riccardo Tozzi, Giovannella Zannoni, and Clive Parsons. Screenplay by John Mortimer and Zeffirelli, based on Zeffirelli's autobiography.

How accurate *Tea with Mussolini* is I cannot say, but it is based on the autobiography of the film director Franco Zeffirelli, who directed it, so we can be sure it is true to what he remembers, or wants to remember. The film tells of a boy named Luca, born out of wedlock to a clothing manufacturer in Florence. His mother is dead, his father's wife visits him at school to hiss that he is a bastard, and his best friend is an old expatriate Brit named Mary (Joan Plowright), who has been hired to turn him into a perfect English gentleman.

As the film opens in the early 1930s, we are told, the Italians and the British have a mutual love affair. We see it reflected in the daily lives of a gaggle of eccentric British ladies of more than a certain age, who gather in Doney's Tea Rooms and the galleries of the Uffizi to gossip—about each other, mostly. After Luca's father orders Mary to return him to the orphanage, she finds she cares for him too much, and takes him instead to live with her at the Pensione Shelley. And thus young Luca is plunged into the intrigues and artistic passions of the "Scorpioni," which is the nickname for the ladies with their stinging wit.

These ladies are played by a cast as eclectic as it is engaging. The grand dame of the Scorpioni is Lady Hester (Maggie Smith), the widow of the former British ambassador. The artistic soul of the group is Arabella (Judi Dench), who informs young Luca, "I have warmed both hands before the fires of Michelangelo and Botticelli." The most visible eccentric, in a congregation of flamboyance, is Georgie (Lily Tomlin), an archaeologist who works among the ruins in pants and overalls that match her cheerfully lesbian inclinations. Mary seems almost average in this company, a sweet lady who supports herself by typing florid Italian into sensible English.

And then there is Elsa Morganthal (Cher), an outlandish American who swoops in and out of Florence like a summer squall. She's an art collector, whose purchases are financed by a rich and absent husband (who is "too cheap to slip a poor girl a little Picasso"). Resembling

Peggy Guggenheim, who made her headquarters in Venice, Elsa is loud, flamboyant, and unwise enough to fall in love with her chauffeur, a cad with patent-leather hair who sells fake art to her, steals her money, and when the time comes, betrays her to the fascists.

The character of Luca is a little overwhelmed by all of these outsize personalities, and indeed the movie might actually have been better without him. Yes, Luca is supposed to be Zeffirelli, and the director is telling his own story—but he seems to inhabit it mostly as an observer. The two actors engaged to play Luca aren't given much to say, and although as a young man Luca joins the Resistance, that activity consists mostly of lurking behind trees and appearing when he is required by the plot. Zeffirelli may look out through Luca's eyes, but not into a mirror.

The ladies supply quite enough entertainment all on their own. Lady Hester charges off to Rome for tea with Mussolini, who assures her that she and her British friends have nothing to worry about, and then poses for photos that will be useful propaganda (ambassador's wife has tea with dictator, finds him a nice chap). Soon, however, the brownshirts are breaking the windows of the tearoom, and the ladies are put under custody and shipped off to a beautiful mountaintop village.

The movie is heavier with events than with plot. Things are always happening, but it's hard to see the connections, and the material involving Elsa's love affair, Lady Hester's draft-dodging male relative, and Arabella's dog all coexists uneasily. (The draft dodger hides from the fascists by dressing in drag, only to finally snap, run into the street, cry out "I'm a man!" strip off his dress, and join the Resistance.) Elsa, the Cher character, meanwhile ignores the dangers for a Jew in Italy, and makes unwise statements such as, "Musso? I think his butt's too big to push around the dance floor."

I enjoyed the movie in a certain way, as a kind of sub–Merchant-Ivory combination of eccentric ladies and enchanting scenery. I liked the performances of the women (including Cher; people keep forgetting what a good actress she can be). I wanted to see more of Tomlin's bracingly frank archaeologist (why do movie lesbians have to recite so much dialogue that keys off their sexuality?). But the movie

seemed the stuff of anecdote, not drama, and as the alleged protagonist, Luca/Franco is too young much of the time to play more than a bystander's role. Zeffirelli, of course, grew up to direct better movies *(Romeo and Juliet,* the Burton-Taylor *Taming of the Shrew,* the Mel Gibson *Hamlet)* and opera, and to speak flawless English.

10 Things I Hate About You ★ ★ ½
PG-13, 94 m., 1999

Heath Ledger (Patrick Verona), Julia Stiles (Katarina Stratford), Joseph Gordon-Levitt (Cameron James), Larisa Oleynik (Bianca Stratford), David Krumholtz (Michael Eckman), Larry Miller (Mr. Stratford), Andrew Keegan (Joey Donner), Susan May Pratt (Mandella), Gabrielle Union (Chastity), Allison Janney (Counselor), Daryl "Chill" Mitchell (English Teacher). Directed by Gil Junger and produced by Andrew Lazar. Screenplay by Karen McCullah Lutz and Kirsten Smith.

I'm trying to remember the last movie I saw that didn't end with a high school prom. *Ravenous,* maybe. Even the *next* film I've seen, *Never Been Kissed,* ends with a prom. The high school romance genre has become so popular that it's running out of new ideas, and has taken to recycling classic literature.

My colleague James Berardinelli made a list recently: *Clueless* was based on *Emma, She's All That* was inspired by *Pygmalion,* and *Cruel Intentions* was recycled from *Les Liaisons Dangereuses* (prompting Stanley Kauffmann to observe that it was better back in the days when high school students were allowed to take over the city government for a day, instead of remaking French novels). To this list we might also add the update of *Great Expectations,* Cinderella's true story in *Ever After,* and *William Shakespeare's Romeo and Juliet,* which was anything but. There's even *Rage: Carrie 2*—a retread of *Carrie,* a work that ranks in my opinion right up there with the best of Austen, Shaw, and Shakespeare.

10 Things I Hate About You is inspired, in a sortuva kinduva way, by Shakespeare's *The Taming of the Shrew,* in the same sense that *Starship Troopers* was inspired by *Titus Andronicus.* It doesn't remake Shakespeare so much as evoke him as a talisman by setting its story at Padua High School, naming its characters Stratford and Verona, making one of the heroines a shrew, etc. There is even a scene where the shrew is assigned to rewrite a Shakespeare sonnet.

And yet . . . gee, the movie is charming, even despite its exhausted wheeze of an ancient recycled plot idea (boy takes bribe to ask girl to prom, then discovers that he really likes her—but then she finds out about the bribe and hates him). I haven't seen that idea in almost two months, since *She's All That* (boy makes bet he can turn plain wallflower into prom queen and does, but falls in love with her, after which she discovers, etc., etc.).

The story this time involves two Seattle sisters. Bianca Stratford (Larisa Oleynik) is popular and wears a lot of red dresses. Her shrewish older sister Katarina (Julia Stiles) is unpopular, never dates, and is the class brain. (When the English teacher asks his class for reactions to a Hemingway novel, she snaps, "Hemingway was an alcoholic who hung around Picasso hoping to nail his leftovers.")

Two guys want to take Bianca to the prom. One is shy and likable. The other is a blowhard. But Bianca's father (Larry Miller) has forbidden her to date until her older sister Katarina starts going out. So a plot is hatched to convince Patrick (Heath Ledger), the school outlaw, to ask her to the prom. He takes a $300 bribe, but then realizes that Kat is actually quite lovely, etc., and really falls in love with her, after which, etc.

I think we simply have to dump the entire plot and appreciate the performances and some of the jolliest scenes. I liked, to begin with, the spirit of the high school teachers. Allison Janney is the sex-mad counselor, and Daryl "Chill" Mitchell is the English teacher who performs Shakespeare's sonnets as if they were rap lyrics. (I've got news for you: They work pretty well as rap, and I expect the album any day.)

I also liked the sweet, tentative feeling between Ledger and Stiles. He has a scene that brings the whole movie to an enjoyable halt. Trying to win her heart, he waits until she's on the athletic field, and then sings "I Love You Baby" over the P.A. system, having bribed the marching band to accompany him. Those scenes are worth the price of admission—almost. But then other scenes are a drag.

All teenage movies have at least one boring and endless party scene, in which everyone is wildly dressed, drunk, and relentlessly colorful (in *Never Been Kissed,* some of the kids come as the Village People). These scenes inevitably involve (a) a fight, (b) barfing, and (c) a tearful romantic breakup In Front of Everybody. That scene was tedious, and so was a scene where the would-be lovers throw paint balloons at each other. I know there has to be a scene of carefree, colorful frolic, but as I watched them rubbing paint in each other's hair I began to yearn for that old standby, the obligatory Tilt-a-Whirl ride.

I liked the movie's spirit, and the actors, and some of the scenes. The music, much of it by a band named Letters to Cleo, is subtle and inventive while still cheerful. The movie almost but not quite achieves liftoff against the gravitational pull of the tired story formula. Sometimes it's a mistake to have acting this charming; the characters become so engaging and spontaneous we notice how they're trapped in the plot.

The Terrorist ★ ★ ★ ½
NO MPAA RATING, 95 m., 2000

Ayesha Dharkar (Malli), Parmeshwaran (Vasu), Vishnu Vardhan (Thyagu), Bhanu Prakash (Perumal), Vinshwa (Lotus). Directed by Santosh Sivan and produced by Jit Joshi and A. Sreekar Prasad. Screenplay by Sivan, Ravi Deshpande, and Vijay Deveshwar. In Tamil with English subtitles.

She is nineteen years old and a soldier in a revolutionary movement. Her brother has died for the cause, and she has killed for it. A volunteer is needed for a suicide mission. She steps forward, fiercely and silently, and is accepted. She will become a "thinking bomb," and after she places a garland of flowers around a politician's neck, she will blow them both to pieces.

The Terrorist does not name its time or place, or the politician, but it seems broadly inspired by the 1991 assassination of India's Rajiv Gandhi. It is not a political film, but a personal one. If you have ever wondered what kind of person volunteers to become a human bomb, and what they think about in the days before their death, this film wonders too.

And its director, Santosh Sivan, does something filmmakers find almost impossible. It follows this young woman without identifying with her mission. We do not want her to succeed. Films are such a first-person medium—they identify so strongly with their protagonists—that they generate sympathy even for evil: Did we want Hannibal Lecter to escape? Of course we did. And at the end of *The Day of the Jackal* (1973) we instinctively wanted the assassin to succeed, simply because we had been following him for two hours. Of course we think murder is wrong, but fiction tends to argue for its heroes. Consider *Crime and Punishment.*

In *The Terrorist,* we do not want the young girl, named Malli, to succeed. That's despite the way the movie paints her loyalty to her cause, and the possibility that her cause is right. The movie is quiet and persuasive as it shows Malli learning more about her life in what may be her last days than she ever knew before.

Played by Ayesha Dharkar, a young actress with expressive eyes and a beauty that is innate, not cosmetic, Malli doesn't talk much, and we sense that she has deep wounds; her brother's death in the same cause suggests a painful background. After she volunteers for the mission, she is passed along an underground network of conspirators to the farm where she will spend her final days. One of her guides is a boy of thirteen or fourteen named Lotus (Vinshwa), who leads her down the center of a shallow river and shows her where to step to avoid land mines and booby traps. He has guided many others this way, he says; they have all later been killed. When a truck blows up, he weeps: "There will be blood everywhere." No more than a child, he is traumatized by his life.

Also on the journey she meets a young soldier who is mortally wounded. In a scene of great delicacy, she cradles him on the forest floor, and he whispers that he has never been so close to a woman in his life. Nor, we sense, has she ever been so close to a man. Just as Sivan makes a movie that does not identify with its violent mission, so he creates a love scene that is not about sex, but communication, surcease, healing.

Eventually Malli arrives at a farm and is given a room of her own. We meet the farmer Vasu (Parmeshwaran) and his helper. These are characters to remind us of the gentle humor of the great Indian novelist R. K. Narayan. Their philosophy and religion is a part of their lives, and the farmer tells Malli: "A flower is the earth smiling." He always sets an extra place at dinner for his wife, who is in a coma and has not stirred for seven years. Malli sees the woman in the room next to her own, staring sightlessly at nothing.

Malli's terrorist contact and his sidekick rehearse her carefully, and select clothing that will conceal the bomb strapped around her middle. They are narrow functionaries, telling her that news of her action will go out to all the world. It is unclear if the farmer knows of her mission (I think he doesn't). He argues for life, not in words so much as in how he conducts his own life.

Malli says little in the film. Sometimes the sound track uses the sound of quiet breathing, which places us inside her head. She regards herself in the mirror, and we intuit what she's thinking. Conversations she has with the farmer put her action in a new light, with new consequences. All leads up to an ending that is the right ending for this film, although few members of the audience will anticipate it.

There is no shortage of those prepared to sacrifice their lives to kill others and advance their cause. If we disagree with them, they are fanatics. If we agree, they are heroes. At least they are personally involved and prepared to pay with their lives, which in a sense is more ethical than killing by remote control at long distance and calling it "modern warfare."

But what do they think? How do they feel? I've often wondered what goes through the mind of a condemned prisoner, who knows the exact hour of his death. How much stranger it must seem to be your own willing executioner: to die voluntarily because an idea is bigger than yourself. In my mind, the self is the biggest of all ideas; without it, there are no ideas. Does Malli arrive at this conclusion?

That's the Way I Like It ★ ★ ★
PG-13, 95 m., 1999

Adrian Pang (Ah Hock), Madeline Tan (Ah Mei), Pierre Png (Richard), Anna Belle Francis (Julie), Steven Lim (Boon), Westley Wong (Bobby), Caleb Goh (Leslie/Ah Bend). Directed by Glen Goei and produced by Goei, Jeffrey Chiang, and Tan Chih Chong. Screenplay by Goei.

That's the Way I Like It is a lighthearted disco kung-fu musical—a Singapore retread of *Saturday Night Fever* crossed with a little Bruce Lee. It's not a satire, but another pass through the same material, right down to the Galaxy 2000 Disco, the ear-boxing at the dinner table, and the famous white suit. John Travolta must be smiling.

Singapore, 1977. Adrian Pang plays Ah Hock, a guy who works in a supermarket, dreams of owning a new Triumph motorcycle, and has been many times to see *Forever Fever*, which is the Singapore title for the Travolta film. When a local disco announces a dance contest with a prize big enough to buy the Triumph, he signs up for dance lessons at the Bonnie and Clyde Dance Studio.

Meanwhile, at home, Ah Hock gets no respect. In the original movie, the family doted on the older brother, who was a priest. In this film, it's the younger brother, who is studying to be a doctor. Ah Hock is seen as the family goof-up, and in a scene that will resonate for lovers of the Travolta film, his father slaps him alongside the head, and Ah Hock bursts out in Singapore English: "Why you have to hit my hair?" True to the tradition of the Hollywood movie, the other brother makes a stunning announcement at the dinner table; Travolta's brother revealed he was leaving the priesthood, while Ah Hock's brother has changed his name from Ah Bend to Leslie, and further revelations follow.

Saturday Night Fever has Travolta abandoning his sweet neighborhood girlfriend in order to choose a lovelier girl as his contest partner. Same thing here; good, loyal Ah Mei (Madeline Tan) gets replaced by slinky Julie (Anna Belle Francis), angering her own boyfriend, a rat. The contest of course ends with Ah Hock doing a solo, the disco ball painting the room in light as the sound track reprises familiar songs (the movie has a lot of the same music, covered by Singapore soundalikes).

Two imaginary advisers inspire Ah Hock on his way to the big contest: Bruce Lee, whose motto from *Enter the Dragon* ("Don't think—feel") becomes his credo, and John Travolta himself, who appears in fantasy sequences and gives him advice about life. (Well, not really Travolta, but a look-alike seen in shadow and profile, like Humphrey Bogart in *Play It Again, Sam*.) Inspired, Ah Hock finds a locally tailored knock-off of Travolta's famous white suit.

Adrian Pang makes a likable hero, not without humor about his own predicaments, filled with passion and energy as he battles with his boss at the supermarket, and conquers a last-minute trap set by the bad guy. *Saturday Night Fever* this movie isn't, but it's not supposed to be: It's a funny homage, a nod to the way some movies are universal in their appeal. I said Travolta must be smiling. Gene Siskel, who bought the original white disco suit at a charity auction and treasured it as much as Ah Hock cherishes his, must be grinning too.

The Theory of Flight ★ ★ ½
R, 100 m., 1999

Helena Bonham Carter (Jane), Kenneth Branagh (Richard), Gemma Jones (Anne), Holly Aird (Julie). Directed by Peter Greengrass and produced by Ruth Caleb, Anant Singh, Helena Spring, and David Thompson. Screenplay by Richard Hawkins.

Godard said that the best way to criticize a movie is to make another movie. That has already been done in the case of *The Theory of Flight*, a British film about a young woman in a wheelchair who desperately desires to have sex. The movie that eclipses this one is *Dance Me to My Song*, an Australian film that played in 1998 at the Cannes Film Festival and silenced the audience with its stark courage. (It still lacks American distribution.)

The Theory of Flight stars Helena Bonham Carter as Jane, the young woman in the chair, who suffers from ALS and uses a voice synthesizer to help her communicate. It is a good performance—but just that, a performance. What is astonishing about *Dance Me to My Song* is that it was written by a young woman named Heather Rose, who has cerebral palsy, lives in a chair, communicates with a machine—and actually plays Julia, the heroine of her movie.

To compare Jane and Julia is not fair, since neither film could have known about the other and both are good-hearted. But I will do it anyway. Jane, the Bonham-Carter character, has had bad luck with her helpers, until she draws the quirky Richard (Kenneth Branagh), an artist who has been assigned to her after being sentenced to community service for having caused a lot of trouble when he jumped off a building with homemade wings.

Compare that idealized situation with the plight of Julia, in the Australian movie. Her disease is so advanced she can barely move, and she has been assigned a series of empty-headed and cruel companions who steal her money and let her lie in her own messes while they chatter on the phone.

Jane wants sex, and informs Richard by playing a little speech that she has programmed into her synthesizer. "Help me lose my virginity," she says. "I know realistically I'll never get the whole deal. But that doesn't mean I shouldn't get as much as I can."

For Julia it is not that easy (not that it is easy for Jane). She is a virtual captive of her apartment, has no way to meet other people, and in an astonishing sequence takes things into her own hands. Using her battery-powered chair, she escapes from her house and onto the sidewalk, where she accosts a young man and begins, in her own way, to seduce him. Consider that Heather Rose plays all of these scenes herself, without doubles, and is cruelly handicapped in speech and movement, and you will begin to guess how powerful it all becomes.

Both young women are frank in their speech. They like four-letter words, which growl out of their synthesizers like Stephen Hawking on a bad day. Both of their targets are at first disbelieving, then reluctant. And so on. Enough of the plots.

Recently I have been getting a lot of flak from readers who object to my review of *Patch Adams*, the Robin Williams film. How can I dislike this film, they ask, when its message is so heartwarming? The movie argues that doctors must care more for their patients, they in-

form me, and that laughter is the best medicine. Some of the letters are from people whose loved ones are critically ill, and have either endured impersonal medical treatment, or benefited from doctors and nurses who do care.

I agree with these correspondents that laughter is the best medicine. I agree that the personal touch is invaluable in the healing professions. But they have confused the message with the movie. Who could disagree with the sentiments in *Patch Adams*? And what do they have to do with the film's shameless and manipulative cynicism? I write back: "Remember, it's not what the movie is about—it's *how* it's about it!"

I wish I could rent a theater and show these good people a double feature of *The Theory of Flight* and *Dance Me to My Song*. Here are two movies that are essentially about the same thing. The British film uses big stars and cutes everything up (much of the plot involves whether Branagh can build a flying machine, and whether he and the young woman can overcome their personal versions of fear of flying). The Australian film is an act of the will by a cerebral palsy sufferer whose own achievement is even greater than her heroine's. (As anyone in Hollywood can tell you, it is a lot easier to get someone to sleep with you than to get a screenplay produced.)

The Theory of Flight is actually fairly enjoyable. At least it doesn't drown its message in syrup and cornball sentiment like *Patch Adams*. It has a lot of refreshing humor. But then, when you see the real thing, when you see *Dance Me to My Song*, you're struck by the difference. Two movies. Same story. Same objective. Similar characters. Similar situation. One is an entertainment. The other is a thunderbolt.

The Thin Red Line ★ ★ ★
R, 170 m., 1999

Sean Penn (First Sergeant Welsh), Adrien Brody (Corporal Fife), Nick Nolte (Lieutenant Colonel Tall), Jim Caviezel (Private Witt), John Cusack (Captain Gaff), George Clooney (Captain Bosche), Ben Chaplin (Private Bell), Woody Harrelson (Sergeant Keck), Elias Koteas (Captain Staros), John Travolta (Brigadier General Quintard). Directed by

Terrence Malick and produced by Robert Michael Geisler, John Roberdeau, and Grant Hill. Screenplay by Malick, based on the novel by James Jones.

The actors in *The Thin Red Line* are making one movie, and the director is making another. This leads to an almost hallucinatory sense of displacement, as the actors struggle for realism, and the movie's point of view hovers above them like a high school kid all filled with big questions. My guess is that any veteran of the actual battle of Guadalcanal would describe this movie with an eight-letter word much beloved in the army.

The movie's schizophrenia keeps it from greatness (this film has no firm idea of what it is about), but doesn't make it bad. It is, in fact, sort of fascinating: a film in the act of becoming, a field trial, an experiment in which a dreamy poet meditates on stark reality. It's like horror seen through the detachment of drugs or dementia. The sound track allows us to hear the thoughts of the characters, but there is no conviction that these characters would have these thoughts. They all seem to be musing in the same voice, the voice of a man who is older, more educated, more poetic and less worldly than any of these characters seem likely to be. The voice of the director.

Terrence Malick is the director of two of the best films I have ever seen, *Badlands* (1973) and *Days of Heaven* (1978). *The Thin Red Line* feels like an extension of the second film, in which a narrator muses on the underlying tragedy that is sometimes shown on the screen, sometimes implied. Both films are founded on a transcendental sense that all natural things share their underlying reality in the mind of God. The film opens with a question: "Why does nature contend with itself?" It shows a crocodile, a killing machine. Later, as men prove more deadly than crocodiles, it shows a bird, its wing shattered by gunfire, pulling itself along the ground. In a way the film is not about war at all, but simply about the way in which all living beings are founded on the necessity of killing one another (and eating one another, either literally or figuratively).

The film opens with an idyll on a Pacific island. Two soldiers have gone AWOL and live blissfully with tribal people who exist in a pre-lapsarian state, eating the fruit that falls from the trees and the fish that leap from the seas, and smiling contentedly at the bounty of Eden. This is, the movie implies, a society that reflects man's best nature. But reality interrupts when the two soldiers are captured and returned to their army company for the assault on a crucial hill on Guadalcanal.

During the battle scenes, there will be flashbacks to the island idyll—and other flashbacks as a solider remembers his love for his wife. Against these simple pleasures is stacked the ideology of war, as expressed by a colonel (Nick Nolte) who read Homer at West Point ("in Greek") and is intoxicated to be in battle at last after having studied it so long. The plot of the second act of the film involves the taking of a well-defended hill, and the colonel prefers that it be attacked in a frontal assault; a captain (Elias Koteas) resists this plan as suicidal, and is right from a strategic point of view but wrong when viewed through the colonel's blood lust: "You are not gonna take your men around in the jungle to avoid a goddamn fight."

The soldiers are not well developed as individual characters. Covered in grime and blood, they look much alike, and we strain to hear their names, barked out mostly in one syllable (Welsh, Fife, Tall, Witt, Gaff, Bosche, Bell, Keck, Staros). Sometimes during an action we are not sure who we are watching, and have to piece it together afterward. I am sure battle is like that, but I'm not sure that was Malick's point: I think he was just not much interested in the destinies and personalities of individual characters.

It was not this way in the novel by James Jones, which inspired the screenplay. Jones drew his characters sharply, and indicated the ways in which each acted according to his ability and personality; his novel could have been filmed by Spielberg in the style of *Saving Private Ryan*. Malick's movie sees it more as a crapshoot. For defying his superior officers, the captain is offered first a court-martial, later a Silver Star, and then a Purple Heart. It is all the same. He is also transferred stateside by the colonel, and instead of insisting on staying with his men, he confesses he is rather happy to be going. This is not a movie of conventional war clichés.

The battle scenes themselves are masterful in creating a sense of the geography of a particular hill, the way it is defended by Japanese bunkers, the ways in which the American soldiers attempt to take it. The camera crouches low in the grass, and as Malick focuses on locusts or blades of grass, we are reminded that a battle like this must have taken place with the soldiers' eyes inches from the ground. The Japanese throughout are totally depersonalized (in one crucial scene, their language is not even translated with subtitles); they aren't seen as enemies, so much as necessary antagonists—an expression of nature's compulsion to "contend with itself." (One wonders what murky philosophical voice-over questions were floating above the Japanese soldiers in *The Thin Red Line*. Were they also dreaming about nature, immortality, humanity, and death?)

Actors like Sean Penn, John Cusack, Jim Caviezel, and Ben Chaplin find the perfect tone for scenes of a few seconds or a minute, and then are dropped before a rhythm can be established. We get the sense that we are rejoining characters in the middle of interrupted actions. Koteas and Nolte come the closest to creating rounded performances, and Woody Harrelson has a good death scene; actors like John Travolta and George Clooney are on screen so briefly they don't have time to seem like anything other than guest stars.

The central intelligence in the film doesn't belong to any of the characters, or even to their voice-over philosophies. It belongs to Malick, whose ideas about war are heartfelt but not profound; the questions he asks are inescapable, but one wonders if soldiers in combat ever ask them (one guesses they ask themselves what they should do next, and how in the hell they can keep themselves from being shot). It's as if the film, long in preproduction, drifted away from the Jones novel (which was based on Jones's personal combat experience) and into a meditation not so much on war, as on film. Aren't most of the voice-over observations really not about war, but about war films? About their materials and rationales, about why one would make them, and what one would hope to say?

Any film that can inspire thoughts like these is worth seeing. But the audience has to finish the work: Malick isn't sure where he's going or what he's saying. That may be a good thing. If a question has no answer, it is not useful to be supplied with one. Still, one leaves the theater bemused by what seems to be a universal law: While most war films are "antiwar," they are always antiwar from the point of view of the winning side. They say, "War is hell, and we won." Shouldn't antiwar films be told from the point of view of the losers? War was hell, and they lost.

The Third Miracle ★ ★ ★
R, 119 m., 2000

Ed Harris (Father Frank Shore), Anne Heche (Roxanne), Armin Mueller-Stahl (Archbishop Werner), Barbara Sukowa (Helen O'Regan), Ken James (Father Paul Panak), James Gallanders (Brother Gregory), Caterina Scorsone (Maria Witkowski), Michael Rispoli (John Leone). Directed by Agnieszka Holland and produced by Fred Fuchs, Steven Haft, and Elie Samaha. Screenplay by John Romano and Richard Vetere, based on the novel by Vetere.

Here is a rarity, a film about religion that is neither pious nor sensational, simply curious. No satanic possessions, no angelic choirs, no evil spirits, no lovers joined beyond the grave. Just a man doing his job. The man is Father Frank Shore, and he is a postulator—a priest assigned to investigate the possibility that someone was a saint. If he is convinced, he goes before a church tribunal and argues the case against another priest whose job is popularly known as "the devil's advocate."

Ed Harris plays Frank Shore as a man with many doubts of his own. After deflating one popular candidate for sainthood, he became known as "the miracle killer," and in his dark moments he broods that he "destroyed the faith of an entire community." Now perhaps he will have to do it again. It is 1979, in a devout Chicago ethnic community, and a statue weeps blood every November. That is the month of the death of a woman named Helen O'Regan (Barbara Sukowa), who is credited with healing young Maria Witkowski, dying of lupus.

Was Helen indeed a saint? Is the statue weeping real blood? What blood type? Father Shore is far from an ideal priest. We first see him working in a soup kitchen, having left more mainstream duties in a crisis of faith. Maybe he doesn't believe in much of anything anymore—except that the case of Helen O'Regan deserves a clear and unprejudiced investigation.

Many a saint has made it onto holy cards with somewhat dubious credentials (Did Patrick really drive the snakes from Ireland? Did Christopher really carry Jesus on his shoulders?). But in recent centuries the church has become rigorous in recognizing miracles and canonizing saints—so rigorous that the American church has produced only three saints. In an age when many churches scorn science and ask members to simply believe, the Catholic Church retains the rather brave notion that religion really exists in the physical world, that miracles really happen and can be logically investigated.

The Third Miracle, directed by Agnieszka Holland, has been written by John Romano and Richard Vetere, and based on Vetere's novel. It has no scenes of Arnold Schwarzenegger trying to prevent Satan from impregnating a virgin with the Antichrist. Instead, it is about church politics, and about a priest who doubts himself more than his faith.

His life only grows more complicated when he meets Roxanne O'Regan (Anne Heche), the daughter of the dead candidate for sainthood. There is a delicate scene at her mother's grave, where she and the priest have joined over a bottle of vodka to celebrate Helen's birthday. Their dialogue does that dance two people perform when they seem to be talking objectively but are really flirting. Finally Roxanne asks Frank if he believes all the church stuff. He asks her why she wants to know. "Because I can tell you like this," she says, on exactly the right note of teasing and invitation.

Ah, but the infallible church is made of fallible men. Frank can harbor doubts and lusts and nevertheless think his job is worth doing. Up against him is the fleshy, contemptuous Archbishop Werner (Armin Mueller-Stahl), the devil's advocate, who thinks three saints are quite enough for America. And then there is the problem of Maria Witkowski (Caterina Scorsone), who may have been cured of lupus but now is on life support after drug abuse and prostitution. "God wasted a miracle!" her mother cries.

Agnieszka Holland is a director whose films embody a grave intelligence; her credits include *Europa, Europa,* about a Jewish boy who conceals his religion to survive the Holocaust; *The Secret Garden,* based on the classic about a girl adrift in a house full of family secrets; and *Washington Square,* Henry James's novel about an heiress who is courted for her money. She pays close attention to the emotional weather of her characters, and is helped here by Ed Harris, whose priest talks as if he has finally decided to say something he's been thinking about for a long time, and Anne Heche, whose Roxanne approaches sexuality like a loaded gun.

In *The Third Miracle* Holland is not much interested in getting us to believe in miracles, or in whether Father Frank is true to his vow of chastity. She is concerned more with the way institutions interact with the emotions of their members. People *need* to believe in miracles, which is why, paradoxically, they resent those who investigate them. Believers aren't interested in proof one way or the other: They want validation. The fact that the church has refused to recognize the appearances of the Virgin at Medjugorje has done nothing to discourage the crowds of faithful tourists. There is a temptation (literally) for the church to go along with popular fancy and endorse the enthusiasms of the faithful. But to applaud bogus saints would be an insult to the real ones.

As Father Shore and Archbishop Werner face each other across a table in a board room, they are like antagonists in any global corporation. They would like to introduce a miraculous new product, but must be sure it will not damage the stock of the company. By seeing the church as an earthly institution and its priests as men doing their best to remain logical in the face of popular ecstasy, *The Third Miracle* puts Hollywood's pop spirituality to shame.

Thirteen ★ ★ ★ ½
NO MPAA RATING, 87 m., 2000

Wilhamenia Dickens (Nina), Lillian Folley (Lillian), Don Semmens (Artist), Michael Aytes (Michael), Michael Jeffrey (Social Worker), Dawn Tinsley (Social Worker), David Scales

(Lillian's Male Friend), Doug Washington (Nina's Uncle). Directed and produced by David D. Williams. Screenplay by Williams.

Summon if you will the sound of a voice telling a favorite story. The details are well known to the other listeners, but not to you. The story is about a young girl much loved and worried about. It has been rehearsed in other tellings, and shaped by memory so that it reflects the girl's personality as much as the events. The tone of that story is the tone of *Thirteen*.

The person telling the story is Lillian (Lillian Folley). The story is about her thirteen-year-old daughter, Nina (Wilhamenia Dickens). Nina is just at that age when talkative kids turn into brooding and unpredictable teenagers. One day Nina disappears from home, and there is a search for her. Neighbors, friends, and the police get involved, and then Nina turns up again.

The movie tells this story in a documentary style. It is fiction, but the actors are basically playing themselves. It was written, produced, directed, photographed, and edited by David D. Williams, a Virginia filmmaker, and the actors are his neighbors. Lillian is an old friend. Watching this movie is not like being confronted with the determination of a plot. It is like sitting in a rocking chair on the porch while Lillian tells the story once again, and everybody smiles, even Nina.

The film is not angry, experimental, or confrontational, and no more fits in the underground or "indie" categories as in the mainstream. That's because it exists in no tradition. It is unique, the expression of particular voices, a deep understanding of the characters, and an interest in who they are.

I saw *Thirteen* for the first time in 1998 at the Virginia Film Festival in Charlottesville. In 1999, I invited it to my first Overlooked Film Festival in Urbana, Illinois. In the spring of that year, David Williams won the Someone to Watch Award at the Independent Spirit Awards in Santa Monica, California—given by other independent filmmakers to a new voice they wanted to recognize. Every time I have seen the film with an audience, it has created its spell. We are freed of contrivance, and allowed into lives.

From Virginia I wrote:
Nina is not a talkative girl. She keeps to herself. One senses that her imagination is so populated that outsiders are not needed. One also senses that at some point in her life she put up a wall. Not one of those unscalable walls of mental illness, but a temporary wall, like you find around construction sites.

Nina and Lillian live within the rhythms of an extended African-American family, where telephone calls form a network to keep everyone updated on everyone else, right down to distant cousins and the relatives of ex-spouses. Neighbors and relatives are in and out of the house all day, and in times of emergency they turn up unbidden to see how they can help.

For Lillian, Nina is a fascinating case study. She observes her, speculates about her, reports on her activities. When Nina disappears there is a search—but *Thirteen* doesn't traffic in the false alarms of conventional cinema. We know all along where Nina has gone. And the manner of her return supplies the trigger that all moviegoers know: That moment when you stir and say to yourself that this is going to be a good film.

The movie contains a lot of humor, quiet and understated. Nina wants to buy a car. She is thirteen and cannot drive, but Lillian accepts her ambition as Nina works at every job she can find to make money. She's blunt and direct with her employers, isn't shy to apply for grown-up jobs, asks for a higher salary, studies car magazines. Boys aren't in the picture yet. She is a freestanding, self-contained original. There is no attempt to ingratiate her with the audience.

In real life, Wilhamenia came to Lillian as a foster child, and was later adopted. They do live together in the house we see. But the characters in the movie are not quite the same as the actors, and the director is the third collaborator, using them to reflect larger truths about relationships.

All of this provides an incomplete picture of the film, I know, but it doesn't reduce easily to description. David D. Williams earlier made a documentary about Lillian, a neighbor, and then began this film, which is fiction based on the facts of the two women's personalities. It's not exactly improvised, he said, there was an outline, but no written dialogue, and many of the moments occur spontaneously.

The result is one of the truest films I've seen about the ebb and flow of a real relationship. Not one pumped up by a plot and a crisis and resolution, but one in which time flows and small changes accumulate. It's not a question of coming to the conclusion, but of starting a new chapter. *Thirteen* focused my attention the way the films of Robert Bresson do, challenging me to look into Nina and guess what she was thinking, and what deeper feelings were manifesting themselves in her comings and goings and her dream of a car.

Thirteen Days ★ ★ ★
PG-13, 135 m., 2001

Kevin Costner (Kenny O'Donnell), Bruce Greenwood (John F. Kennedy), Steven Culp (Robert Kennedy), Dylan Baker (Robert McNamara), Henry Strozier (Dean Rusk), Kevin Conway (General Curtis LeMay), Len Cariou (Dean Acheson). Directed by Roger Donaldson and produced by Marc Abraham, Peter O. Almond, Armyan Bernstein, Kevin Costner, and Kevin O'Donnell. Screenplay by David Self, based on a book by Ernest R. May and Philip D. Zelikow.

The 1962 Cuban missile crisis was the closest we've come to a world nuclear war. Khrushchev installed Russian missiles in Cuba, ninety miles from Florida and within striking distance of 80 million Americans. Kennedy told him to remove them, or else. As Russian ships with more missiles moved toward Cuba, a U.S. Navy blockade was set up to stop them. The world waited.

At the University of Illinois, I remember classes being suspended or ignored as we crowded around TV sets and the ships drew closer in the Atlantic. There was a real possibility that nuclear bombs might fall in the next hour. And then Walter Cronkite had the good news: The Russians had turned back. Secretary of State Dean Rusk famously said, "We went eyeball to eyeball, and I think the other fellow just blinked."

The most controversial assertion of Roger Donaldson's *Thirteen Days,* an intelligent new political thriller, is that the guys who blinked were not only the Russians, but also America's own military commanders—who backed down not from Soviet ships but from the White House. The Joint Chiefs of Staff and Air Force general Curtis LeMay are portrayed as rabid hawks itching for a fight. It's up to presidential adviser Kenny O'Donnell (Kevin Costner) and Secretary of Defense Robert McNamara (Dylan Baker) to face down the top brass, who are portrayed as boys eager to play with nuclear toys. "This is a setup," O'Donnell warns President Kennedy (Bruce Greenwood). If fighting breaks out at a low level, say with Castro shooting at an American spy plane, "the chiefs will force us to start shooting."

This version of events, the viewer should be aware, may owe more to the mechanics of screenwriting than to the annals of history. In a movie where the enemy (Khrushchev) is never seen, living and breathing antagonists are a convenience on the screen, and when McNamara and a trigger-happy admiral get into a shouting match it's possible to forget they're both supposed to be good guys. Yet the cold war mentality did engender military paranoia, generals like LeMay were eager to blast the commies, and Kennedy was seen by his detractors as a little soft. "Kennedy's father was one of the architects of Munich," grumbles Dean Acheson, Truman's secretary of state and an architect of the cold war. "Let's hope appeasement doesn't run in the family."

My own feeling is that serious students of the missile crisis will not go to this movie for additional scholarship, and that for the general public it will play, like Oliver Stone's *JFK,* as a parable: Things might not have happened exactly like this, but it sure did feel like they did. I am not even much bothered by the decision to tell the story through the eyes of Kenneth O'Donnell, who according to Kennedy scholars can barely be heard on White House tapes made during the crisis, and doesn't figure significantly in most histories of the event. He functions in the movie as a useful fly on the wall, a man free to be where the president isn't and think thoughts the president can't. (Full disclosure: O'Donnell's son Kevin, the Earthlink millionaire, is an investor in the company of *Thirteen Days* producer Armyan Bernstein.)

Costner plays O'Donnell as a White House

jack of all trades, a close adviser whose office adjoins the Oval Office. He has deep roots with the Kennedys. He was Bobby's roommate at Harvard and Jack's campaign manager, he is an utterly loyal confidant, and in the movie he helps save civilization by sometimes taking matters into his own hands. When the Joint Chiefs are itching for an excuse to fight, he urges one pilot to "look through this thing to the other side"—code for asking him to lie to his superiors rather than trigger a war.

The movie's taut, flat style is appropriate for a story that is more about facts and speculation than about action. Kennedy and his advisers study high-altitude photos and intelligence reports, and wonder if Khrushchev's word can be trusted. Everything depends on what they decide. The movie shows men in unknotted ties and shirtsleeves, grasping coffee cups or whiskey glasses and trying to sound rational while they are at some level terrified. What the Kennedy team realizes, and hopes the other side realizes, is that the real danger is that someone will strike first out of fear of striking second.

The movie cuts to military scenes—air bases, ships at sea—but only for information, not for scenes that will settle the plot. In the White House, operatives like O'Donnell make quiet calls to their families, aware they may be saying good-bye forever, that the "evacuation plans" are meaningless except as morale boosters. As Kennedy, Bruce Greenwood is vaguely a look-alike and sound-alike, but like Anthony Hopkins in *Nixon,* he gradually takes on the persona of the character, and we believe him. Steven Culp makes a good Bobby Kennedy, sharp-edged and protective of his brother, and Dylan Baker's resemblance to McNamara is uncanny.

I call the movie a thriller, even though the outcome is known, because it plays like one. We may know that the world doesn't end, but the players in this drama don't, and it is easy to identify with them. They have so much more power than knowledge, and their hunches and guesses may be more useful than war game theories. Certainly past experience is not a guide, because no war will have started or ended like this one.

Donaldson and Costner have worked together before, on *No Way Out* (1987), about a

staff member of the secretary of defense. That one was a more traditional thriller, with sex and murders; this time they find almost equal suspense in what's essentially a deadly chess game. In the long run, national defense consists of not blowing everything up in the name of national defense. Suppose nobody had blinked in 1962 and missiles had been fired. Today we would be missing most of the people of Cuba, Russia, and the U.S. Eastern Seaboard, and there'd be a lot of poison in the air. That would be our victory. Yes, Khrushchev was reckless to put the missiles in Cuba, and Kennedy was right to want them out. But it's a good thing somebody blinked.

The 13th Warrior ★ ½
R, 103 m., 1999

Antonio Banderas (Ahmed Ibn Fahdlan), Diane Venora (Queen Weilew), Dennis Storhoi (Herger [Joyous]), Vladimir Kulich (Buliwyf), Omar Sharif (Melchisidek), Anders T. Andersen (Wigliff [King's Son]), Richard Bremmer (Skeld [Superstitious]), Tony Curran (Weath [Musician]). Directed by John McTiernan and produced by McTiernan, Michael Crichton, and Ned Dowd. Screenplay by William Wisher and Warren Lewis, based on *Eaters of the Dead* by Crichton.

Released more than a year after it was completed, *The 13th Warrior* shows every sign of a production run amok. With a budget said to be over $100 million, it displays a lot of cash on the screen, but little thought. To extract the story from the endless scenes of action and carnage is more effort than it's worth. The film seems to have been conceived from the special effects on down. Instead of beginning with a good story and then adding f/x as needed, it apparently began with f/x and then the story was shoehorned into the pauses in the action.

It could have been different. This could, indeed, have been a fascinating tale. Based on *Eaters of the Dead,* a 1974 novel by Michael Crichton, the story combines two intriguing sources. One is the real-life adventure of Ahmed Ibn Fahdlan, an Arab poet who traveled north to the Viking lands in the tenth century. The other is the Old English epic poem *Beowulf.* At some point early in the production, it was apparently determined that endless scenes of longhaired Vikings in sword fights would be more interesting than the telling of these stories.

Antonio Banderas, perhaps hoping for another swashbuckling success like *The Mask of Zorro*, stars as Ahmed, a poet who has the misfortune to fall in love with the wife of a powerful friend of the Sultan. Threatened with dire consequences, Ahmed joins a veteran courtier (Omar Sharif in a cameo) in traveling north as an ambassador to the Vikings, where he is seen as a curiosity and a challenge. The Norsemen cheerfully insult him, confident he doesn't understand them, but a montage shows him learning the language and startling them with his reply. Soon he's called upon to recite a poem at a funeral, a scene that develops inadvertently into a hilarious version of history's first poetry slam.

Times are not good for the Vikings. A mysterious tribe of enemies who believe they possess the spirits of bears presents a flesh-eating threat. They have returned, as I recall, from ancient times. Thirteen warriors must be chosen to fight the evil. Ahmed is, of course, destined to be the thirteenth. He's a poet, not a fighter, but quickly learns to wield a scimitar.

And that's about it, except for miles and miles of carnage. (It's a little unsettling to sit through nonstop slaughter and then witness a pious conclusion that celebrates "a useful servant of God.") The movie's director of record is John McTiernan *(Die Hard, The Last Action Hero)*, although after an earlier version of the film performed badly in sneak previews, new scenes were reportedly shot under the direction of Michael Crichton. It's all to no avail: *The 13th Warrior* is another example of f/x run wild, lumbering from one expensive set-piece to the next without taking the time to tell a story that might make us care.

This Is My Father ★ ★ ★
R, 120 m., 1999

Aidan Quinn (Kieran O'Day), Moya Farrelly (Fiona Flynn), James Caan (Kieran Johnson), Gina Moxley (Mary Flynn), Colm Meaney (Seamus), Moira Deady (Mrs. Kearney), Stephen Rea (Father Quinn), John Cusack (Eddie Sharp, the Pilot), Brendan Gleeson (Officer Jim). Directed by Paul Quinn and produced by Nicolas Clermont and Philip King.

On my first trip to Ireland, in 1967, I was taken to a party after the pubs closed. There were bottles of whiskey and Guinness stout, someone had a concertina, and there was a singsong. In the bedroom, a couple was making out. Eventually they emerged to join the party, and I noticed that, to my young eyes, they were "old"—in their forties.

On the way home, I asked my friend McHugh about that, and he explained that they had been engaged for fifteen years, that they were putting off marriage until the man made more money, and until "family matters" got sorted out. Necking at parties was undoubtedly the extent of their sex lives, since intercourse before marriage was a mortal sin. I said I thought it was sad that two middle-aged people, who had loved each other since they were young, had put their lives on hold. "Welcome to Ireland," he said.

It is not like that anymore in Ireland, where some of the old customs have died with startling speed. But that is the Ireland remembered in *This Is My Father*, a film about lives ruled by guilt, fear, prejudice, and dour family pride. For every cheerful Irish comedy about free spirits with quick wits, there is a story like this one, about characters sitting in dark rooms, ruminating on old grudges and fresh resentments, and using the rules of the church, when convenient, as justification for their own spites and dreads.

The movie is said to be based on a true family story and has been made by Chicago's Quinn brothers. Aidan Quinn stars as an orphaned tenant farmer who falls in love with the daughter of the woman who owns the land he works. Paul Quinn directs. Declan Quinn, the cinematographer, is known for such work as *Leaving Las Vegas*. It is so much a family project that there is even a role for a friend, John Cusack, who drops in out of the sky in a small plane, lands on the beach, and figures in a scene as charming as it is irrelevant.

The heart of the story involves Kieran O'Day (Aidan Quinn) and Fiona Flynn (Moya Farrelly), who fall passionately in love in 1939. He is an orphan, being raised by a tenant couple named the Maneys (Donal Donnelly and Maria McDermottroe) on land owned by Fiona's mother, Mary (Gina Moxley). The mother has fierce pride, not improved by a drinking problem, and looks down on her neighbors. Of course she opposes a liaison between her daughter and a tenant.

This story is told in flashback. In the present day, we meet a sad, tired high school teacher (James Caan) whose mother is dying and whose life is going nowhere. He determines to go back to Ireland and search for his roots. In the village where his mother came from, he finds an old gypsy woman (Moira Deady) who remembers with perfect clarity everything that happened in 1939, and triggers the flashbacks. The modern story is almost not essential (we forget Caan in the midst of the flashback), but it does trigger a happy ending in which much is explained.

The key element in the romance between Kieran and Fiona, and the one that reminded me of my first visit to Ireland, is the way their sex lives are ruled by others, whose own real motives are masked under the cover of church law. Mrs. Flynn is spiteful, mean, and bitter, or she would find a way for her daughter to be happy. Kieran's love is all the more poignant because he sincerely believes himself to be an occasion of sin for Fiona, and castigates himself for endangering her immortal soul.

Fiona's mother pays lip service to the church, but her real motives are fueled by class prejudice and social climbing, and there is a cruel moment when she accuses Kieran of molesting her daughter. She also threatens the Maneys, who have raised him, with the loss of their land and livelihood. One scene which rings true to life is the way the village policemen, negotiating a tricky path between the laws of this world and the next, give Kieran broad hints about their plans for eventually arresting him—should he still be in the vicinity, of course. Sensibly, he is not, but the cost of his freedom is his happiness, and that price is underlined by a message which the Caan character discovers, and delivers several decades too late.

I believe *This Is My Father* is indeed based on true family stories (or legends, which are the same thing), because it insists on details that are more important to the narrator than to the listener. The entire construction of the Caan character, for example, is explained no doubt by a relative's visit back to the old country. The story might have been simpler, sadder, and sweeter if it had taken place entirely in 1939—but like all stories, it belongs to the teller, not the subject.

Thomas and the Magic Railroad ★
G, 79 m., 2000

Alec Baldwin (Mr. Conductor), Peter Fonda (Burnett Stone), Mara Wilson (Lily), Russell Means (Billy Twofeathers), Didi Conn (Stacy), Michael E. Rodgers (Junior), Cody McMains (Patch), Edward Glen (Voice of Thomas). Directed by Britt Allcroft and produced by Allcroft and Phil Fehrle. Screenplay by Allcroft.

Very early in *Thomas and the Magic Railroad*, Thomas the Tank Engine and another locomotive are having a conversation. Their eyes roll and we hear their voices—but their mouths do not move. No, not at all. This is such an odd effect that I could think of little else during their conversation. In an era when animated dinosaurs roam the earth, ships climb 200-foot walls of water, and Eddie Murphy can play five people in the same scene, is it too much to ask a tank engine to move its lips while speaking?

I think not. Either their mouths should move or their eyes should not roll. Take your pick. I felt like a grinch as I arrived at this conclusion, for Thomas was a cute tank engine and he steamed through a fanciful model countryside that was, as these things go, nice to look at. I was still filled with goodwill toward Thomas and his movie. That was before I met Burnett Stone.

He is the character played by Peter Fonda, and he spends much of his time in a cave deep within Muffle Mountain with Lady, a tank engine he has been trying to repair for years, but without luck: "I've never been able to bring her to life," he complains. "To make her steam." Fonda is so depressed by this failure that he mopes through the entire role, stoop-shouldered, eyes downcast, step faltering, voice sad, as if he had taken the screenplay too literally ("Burnett is depressed because he cannot get Lady to run") and did not realize that, hey, this is a kiddie movie!

Other actors are likewise adrift in the film. A few years ago Alec Baldwin was delivering the electrifying monologue in *Glengarry Glen*

Ross. Now he is Mr. Conductor, about twelve inches tall, materializing in a cloud of sparkle dust in a geranium basket. I do not blame him for taking a role in a children's movie, not even a role twelve inches high. I do question his judgment in getting into this one.

Thomas and the Magic Railroad is an inept assembly of ill-matched plot points, meandering through a production that has attractive art direction (despite the immobile mouths). Many of the frames would make cheerful stills. Thomas and his fellow trains, even Evil Diesel, have a jolly energy to them, and I like the landscapes and trees and hamlets.

But what a lugubrious plot! What endless trips back and forth between the Isle of Sodor and the full-sized town of Shining Time! What inexplicable characters, such as Billy Twofeathers (Russell Means), who appear and disappear senselessly. What a slow, wordy, earnest enterprise this is, when it should be quick and sprightly.

That *Thomas and the Magic Railroad* made it into theaters at all is something of a mystery. This is a production with "straight to video" written all over it. Kids who like the Thomas books might—*might*—kinda like it. Especially younger kids. Real younger kids. Otherwise, no. Perhaps the success of the Harry Potter books has inspired hope that Thomas, also a British children's icon, will do some business. Not a chance. And in an age when even the cheapest Saturday morning cartoons find a way to make the lips move, what, oh what, was the reasoning behind Thomas's painted-on grin?   ☞

The Thomas Crown Affair ★ ★ ½
R, 114 m., 1999

Pierce Brosnan (Thomas Crown), Rene Russo (Catherine Banning), Denis Leary (Michael McCann), Ben Gazzara (Andrew Wallace), Frankie Faison (Paretti), Fritz Weaver (John Reynolds), Charles Keating (Golchan), Mark Margolis (Knutzhorn), Faye Dunaway (Psychiatrist). Directed by John McTiernan and produced by Pierce Brosnan and Beau St. Clair. Screenplay by Leslie Dixon and Kurt Wimmer, based on a story by Alan R. Trustman.

The Thomas Crown Affair uses a $100 million art theft as foreplay between two people who, unfortunately, are both more interested in the theft than in each other. Pierce Brosnan stars in the title role, as a man who has everything money can buy, and has moved on to what money can't buy—a $100 million Monet, which he steals in broad daylight from the Metropolitan Museum of Art. Then he becomes interested in something money might be able to buy: an insurance investigator named Catherine Banning (Rene Russo).

His theft has been so clever it might never be possible for her to prove he took the painting. So he more or less *tells* her he was the thief, a conclusion she has arrived at on her own. Her problem is that without the painting or any other evidence, she doesn't have a case. For that matter, she's not a cop and isn't interested in a conviction so much as in saving her company from having to write a $100 million check.

The movie is a retread of Norman Jewison's 1968 film, which starred Steve McQueen as a bank robber opposite Faye Dunaway, and had a lot of split-screen photography that quickly wore out its welcome. This movie has a superior caper but less chemistry. The way Thomas Crown gets the painting out of the Met, and what happens to it subsequently, is really very cleverly devised. But while McQueen and Dunaway seemed barely able to keep their hands off of one another, Brosnan and Russo play elegant mind games that sometimes seem almost designed to postpone the rumpy-pumpy.

The movie has been directed by John McTiernan *(Die Hard, The Hunt for Red October)* with less steam and more suavity than his usual credits; it's the kind of sophisticated caper that Cary Grant used to walk through without getting his suit wrinkled. The caper and investigation are the backdrops for an elaborate seduction in which Crown essentially asks the woman's permission to steal the painting. He seems to think he deserves points for having masterminded the theft as a challenge rather than a job: If a man doesn't need $100 million, I gather, he isn't as much to blame for stealing it.

Teasing Banning with hints and scraps of clues, he flies her off to his villa in the Caribbean, takes her on a glider flight, buys her dinners, and gives her presents, including a painting she makes the mistake of admiring. He also suggests that the life of an insurance investigator is not nearly as interesting as the life of his mistress—which may be true, but is undermined somewhat by her suspicion that he already has a mistress and is just stringing her along.

The movie has a low-key, luxurious feeling to it. It's languorous and comfortable. Brosnan and Russo seem to massage their words before saying them. But it all feels like an exercise. We don't sense that they're really important to one another: The game is more important for both of them than the prize. Faye Dunaway, who has a role here as Crown's (unnecessary) psychiatrist, had more electricity in 1968 and still does than Rene Russo, who was exciting opposite Clint Eastwood in *In the Line of Fire*, but now matches Brosnan's dreamy detachment. There's much more tension between Sean Connery and Catherine Zeta-Jones in the somewhat similar *Entrapment*.

I dunno. It's not a bad movie. It might be fun to see on an airplane or to rent on video. But despite the cleverness of the caper and the beauty of the lush locations, the wit in the dialogue and the neat twists and turns, it never seems to risk anything. There's something odd about a caper romance where you never believe anyone is really ever going to go to jail or bed.

Three Kings ★ ★ ★ ★
R, 115 m., 1999

George Clooney (Sergeant Major Archie Gates), Mark Wahlberg (Sergeant Troy Barlow), Ice Cube (Chief), Spike Jonze (Conrad Vig), Nora Dunn (Adriana Cruz), Mykelti Williamson (Colonel Horn), Jamie Kennedy (Walter), Cliff Curtis (Amir). Directed by David O. Russell and produced by Charles Roven, Paul Junger Witt, and Edward L. McDonnell. Screenplay by Russell, based on a story by John Ridley.

Three Kings is some kind of weird masterpiece, a screw-loose war picture that sends action and humor crashing head-on into one another and spinning off into political anger. It has the freedom and recklessness of Oliver Stone or Robert Altman in their mad-dog days, and a visual style that hungers for impact. A lot of movies show bodies being hit by bullets. This one sends the camera inside to show a bullet cavity filling up with bile.

David O. Russell, who wrote and directed, announces his arrival as a major player. Like the best films of Scorsese, Stone, Altman, and Tarantino, this one sings with the exhiliration of pure filmmaking, and embodies ideas in its action and characters. Most movies doze in a haze of calculation and formula; *Three Kings* is awake and hyper.

The movie takes place at the end of the Gulf War of 1991 ("Operation Desert Storm," according to the Pentagon publicists). The first words set the tone: "Are we shooting?" The truce is so new that soldiers are not sure, and a guy waving a white flag gets his head shot off in a misunderstanding. Shame. Three U.S. soldiers find an Iraqi with a piece of paper stuck where the sun don't shine. An officer issues a rubber glove and tells a private to pull it out. The guy wants two gloves, but he'll do it with one, he's told: "That's how the chain of command works."

The map shows the location of gold bullion looted from Kuwait by Saddam's troops and buried in secret bunkers. ("Bullion? Is that a little cube you put in hot water?") The three soldiers are Sergeant Troy Barlow (Mark Wahlberg), Chief Elgin (Ice Cube), and Private Conrad Vig (Spike Jonze). They attract the attention of Sergeant Major Archie Gates (George Clooney), a Special Forces veteran who decides on the spot to lead them on an unauthorized mission to steal the treasure. This involves dumping the cable news reporter he's been assigned to escort. She's Adriana Cruz, played by Nora Dunn as a Christiane Amanpour clone so driven by journalistic zeal that she is heedless of her own safety or anything else but a story. The gold, of course, would be a story.

The movie unreels with breakneck energy; it's one of those experiences like *Natural Born Killers*, where death and violence are a drumbeat in the background of every plot point. Russell's screenplay illustrates the difference between a great action picture and the others: The action grows out of the story, instead of the story being about the action. The Clooney character commandeers a Humvee and leads his men on a loony ride through the desert, where their target practice with footballs somehow reminded me of the water-skiing sequence in *Apocalypse Now*.

A political undercurrent bubbles all through the film. A truce has been declared, and Saddam's men have stopped shooting at Americans and fallen back to the secondary assignment of taming unhappy Iraqis who were expecting him to be overthrown. ("Bush told the people to rise up against Saddam. They thought they'd have our support. They didn't. Now they're being slaughtered.") Strange, the irony in Iraqis killing Iraqis while American gold thieves benefit from the confusion.

Most Hollywood movies stereotype their Arab characters. *Three Kings* is startling in the way it shows how the world is shrinking and cultures are mixing and sharing values. Clooney and his men see a woman shot dead by Saddam's men, and later meet her husband and children. Is this man a tearful anonymous desert simpleton, grateful to his brave saviors? Not at all. "I'm a B-school graduate from Bowling Green," he tells them. "Your planes blew up all my cafés."

It's a small world, made smaller by the culture of war. The TV journalist stands calmly in the middle of danger, accepted by both sides because they think it's natural they should be on television. When the Mark Wahlberg character is captured and locked in a room, he finds it filled with the loot of war, including a lot of cell phones. When he tries to call his wife in America to give her the coordinates of his position, he has to deal with obtuse telephone operators.

Three Kings has plot structure as traditional as anything in *Gunga Din* or an *Indiana Jones* picture, and links it to a fierce political viewpoint, intelligent characters, and sudden bursts of comedy. It renews clichés. We've seen the wounded buddy who has to be dragged along through the action. But we haven't seen one with a lung wound, and a valve hammered into his chest to relieve the built-up air pressure. We've seen desert warfare before, but usually it looks scenic. Russell's cameraman, Newton Thomas Sigel, uses a grainy, bleached style that makes the movie look like it was left out in a sandstorm.

Like many natural action stars, Clooney can do what needs to be done with absolute conviction; we believe him as a leader. Wahlberg and Ice Cube seem caught up in the action, Wahlberg as a natural target, the Cube as a National Guardsman who believes he stands inside a ring of Jesus' grace. Spike Jonze, himself a director *(Being John Malkovich)*, is the obligatory hillbilly, needed for the ethnic mix we always get in war movies. It's interesting how Nora Dunn's cable journalist isn't turned into a cheap parody of Amanpour, but focuses on the obsessiveness that possesses any good war correspondent.

This is David O. Russell's third picture, after *Spanking the Monkey* (liked by many, unseen by me) and the inventive, unhinged comedy *Flirting With Disaster* (1997). Like that one, *Three Kings* bounces lots of distinct characters against one another and isn't afraid to punctuate the laughs with moments of true observation and emotion. This is his first movie with a studio budget, and it shows not only enthusiasm, but the control to aim that enthusiasm where he wants it to go. *Three Kings* is one of the best movies of 1999, even if I kept wondering why it wasn't named *Four Kings*.

Three Seasons ★ ★ ★
PG-13, 113 m., 1999

Don Duong (Hai [Cyclo Driver]), Nguyen Ngoc Hiep (Kien An), Tran Manh Cuong (Teacher Dao), Harvey Keitel (James Hager), Zoe Bui (Lan), Nguyen Huu Duoc (Woody [Peddler]), Minh Ngoc (Truck Driver), Hoang Phat Trieu (Huy). Directed by Tony Bui and produced by Jason Kliot, Joana Vicente, and Tony Bui. Screenplay by Tony Bui, based on a story by Tony Bui and Timothy Linh Bui.

We require Asia to be ancient, traditional, and mysterious. It fills a need. We don't want to know that Hong Kong is a trade capital and Japan is an economic giant. We're looking for Shangri-La, for the sentimental fantasies of generations of Western writers who fell for the romantic idea of the East—and centuries of Eastern writers who did too.

Three Seasons, filmed in Ho Chi Minh City by Tony Bui, a twenty-six-year-old American born in Vietnam, allows us to enjoy fantasies which, in America, would be politically incorrect. Like the best-selling *Memoirs of a Geisha,* it romanticizes prostitution, makes poverty picturesque, transforms hardship into fable. We do not approve of small boys working as street peddlers, of young women organized to sell flowers for a cult, of hookers servicing rich businessmen and snubbing their own people. But because *Three Seasons* is so languorously beautiful, because it has the sentiment of a Chaplin film, because exotic customs and settings are so seductive, we change the rules. What is wrong in Chicago becomes colorful, even enchanting, in the former Saigon.

I say all this as a disclaimer, because I'm certainly not above the pleasures of a film like *Three Seasons.* Taken as reporting, it shows deplorable conditions. Taken as a fable, it's enchanting. Art often offers us such bargains; it is better to attend *La Bohème* than to freeze in a garret. No wonder *Three Seasons* won everything in sight at Sundance: Grand Jury Prize, Audience Award, and Best Cinematography.

The movie takes place in a modern Vietnam that, at first, looks like the past. Beautiful young women in tiny flat-bottomed boats paddle in shallow waters among flower pads. As they pick white lotus blossoms, they sing. The scene is overshadowed by a dark temple that looks abandoned. "It is the Teacher's house," one of the new girls is told. "He has not left it for years. None of us have ever seen him."

The newcomer, named Kien An (Nguyen Ngoc Hiep), is trucked with the others into the city to sell their flowers. We meet some of the others who live there. Woody (Nguyen Huu Duoc) is a boy of nine or ten who sells gum and cigarettes from a box that hangs from a strap around his neck. Hai (Don Duong) drives a cyclo (a bicycle rickshaw) and hangs out with his buddies near the luxury hotels, where the towels must be perfumed because "everyone we drive from there has a fresh smell." Lan (Zoe Bui) is a prostitute who works the big hotels; she runs from a shop, leaps into Hai's cyclo, and asks him to step on it.

Then there's James Hager (Harvey Keitel), the mysterious American who has spent weeks sitting in an aluminum chair on a sidewalk, smoking and staring into space. His story is more modern. He left a daughter behind in Vietnam, and has come back to find her, and "maybe make some kind of peace with this place." (Keitel is the film's executive producer, once again lending his presence to a director's first film; no actor has put himself more on the line in support of young filmmakers.)

The interlocking stories of these characters remind us not only of Chaplinesque sentimentality, but also of the poor street people of Italian neorealist films like *Bicycle Thief* and *Shoeshine,* and of the languorous beauty of recent Asian films like *The Scent of Green Papaya* and *Raise the Red Lantern.* Lisa Rinzler's cinematography makes the city and surrounding countryside look poor but breathtakingly beautiful, and even sad shots, like the little peddler standing in the rain, have a kind of poetic grace.

Of the stories, the one I responded to most deeply involved the hooker and the cyclo driver, who loves and respects her. One day she says her dream is to spend the whole night in an air-conditioned room. He asks her price ($50), wins that much in a race for cyclo drivers, and treats her to her dream. She is grateful, but resists his further advances: She somehow feels she is not entitled to ordinary human emotion.

There are touching, somewhat contrived, revelations involving the unseen Teacher, whose teaching seems far in the past. The song of the new young girl reminds him of the songs of the floating market in his childhood, "the only time I was pure and whole." And she discovers his secrets. The outcome of the story involving the American G.I. is less effective, because we've seen such material before.

Three Seasons is extravagantly beautiful, especially in scenes where artifice is permitted, as when an unlikely shower of spring blossoms floats down from the sky. It's a remarkably ambitious work by the twenty-six-year-old Bui, who financed it on a shoestring but makes it look expensive. It arrives billed as the first American fiction film shot entirely in postwar Vietnam; although Bui acknowledges his script had to win government approval, he was allowed to portray prostitution and poverty—perhaps because the city is seen not in a documentary way, but through the lens of fable. The result may not reflect the Vietnam of reality, but it's as close to life as most romantic melodramas, which is probably the point. And it's a lot more interesting.

3,000 Miles to Graceland ★ ½
R, 125 m., 2001

Kurt Russell (Michael), Kevin Costner (Murphy), Courteney Cox (Cybil Waingrow), David Kaye (Jesse [Her Son]), Christian Slater (Hanson), Bokeem Woodbine (Franklin), Kevin Pollak (Marshall Damitry), David Arquette (Gus), Jon Lovitz (Jay Peterson), Ice-T (Hamilton). Directed by Demian Lichtenstein and produced by Elie Samaha, Lichtenstein, Richard Spero, Eric Manes, and Andrew Stevens. Screenplay by Richard Recco and Lichtenstein.

Here's a movie without an ounce of human kindness, a sour and mean-spirited enterprise so desperate to please it tries to be a yukky comedy and a hard-boiled action picture at the same time. It's about a gang that robs a casino while masquerading as Elvis impersonators. I was nostalgic for the recent *Sugar and Spice*, in which cheerleaders rob a bank while masquerading as five pregnant Betty dolls (plus one Richard Nixon).

The movie has a heavy-duty cast, with top billing shared by Kurt Russell and Kevin Costner. Russell once played Elvis, very well, on TV, and hits some of the right verbal notes here. Costner, the leader of the gang, chain-smokes and looks mean. His fellow criminals include Christian Slater, David Arquette, and Bokeem Woodbine, who is the black guy and therefore the first to die, following an ancient cliché this movie lacks the wit to rewrite.

The casino robbery involves a gory bloodbath, all gratuitous, all intercut with an Elvis revue on one of the show stages. Not intercut a little, but a lot, complete with dancing girls, until we see so much of the revue we prefer it to the shooting. (Looks like dozens of patrons are killed, but the movie of course forgets this carnage the minute it's over.) The gang makes off with the loot, there is the inevitable squabble over how to divvy it up, and then the movie's most intriguing and inexplicable relationship develops.

This is between Kurt Russell and Courteney Cox, who plays the mom of a bright young kid (David Kaye), and is stranded in the Last Chance Motel, one of those movie sets from a *Road Runner* cartoon. Cox's character is intriguing because we never understand her motivation, and inexplicable because she doesn't, either. She really does like Russell, I guess, and that explains why they're in the sack so quickly, but then the kid, who is about eight, creeps into the bedroom and steals Russell's wallet. The movie never questions the wisdom of showing the kid in the room while his mother is in bed with a stranger. One imagines that the filmmakers were so tickled by the plot point that the moral questions just didn't occur to them.

At a point later in the movie, the Cox character drives off in a car containing most of Russell's loot, while leaving her son behind with him. Would a mother do this? Some would, but most movies wouldn't consider them heroines. There is an "explanation" for her behavior, based on the fact that Russell, a bank robber she has known for about ten minutes, is obviously a good guy and likes the boy—but, come on.

The plot is standard double-reverse, post–*Reservoir Dogs* irony, done with a lot of style and a minimum of thought. It's about behavior patterns, not personalities. Everybody is defined by what they do. Or what they drive: As the film opens, Russell is in a 1957 red Cadillac, and Costner drives a Continental convertible of similar vintage, perhaps because they want to look like Elvis impersonators, more likely because all characters in movies like this drive 1950s cars because modern ones are too small and wimpy.

The cast stays top-drawer right down to the supporting roles. Kevin Pollak turns up as a federal marshal, Jon Lovitz is a money launderer, Ice-T is hired muscle. You guess they all liked the script. But the Russell and Costner characters are so burdened by the baggage of their roles that sometimes they just seem weary, and the energy mostly comes from Courteney Cox—and from the kid, who seems to be smarter than anyone else in the film, and about as experienced.

I will give *3,000 Miles to Graceland* credit for one thing, a terrific trailer. When a bad movie produces a great trailer, it's usually evidence that the raw materials were there for a good movie. I can imagine a blood-soaked caper movie involving Elvis disguises, a lonely tramp, and her bright-eyed son, but it isn't this one.

Three to Tango ★
PG-13, 98 m., 1999

Matthew Perry (Oscar Novak), Neve Campbell (Amy Post), Dylan McDermott (Charles Newman), Oliver Platt (Peter Steinberg), Cylk Cozart (Kevin Cartwright), John C. McGinley (Strauss), Bob Balaban (Decker), Deborah Rush (Lenore). Directed by Damon Santostefano and produced by Bobby Newmyer, Jeffrey Silver, and Bettina Sofia Viviano. Screenplay by Rodney Vaccaro and Aline Brosh McKenna.

Neve Campbell is amazingly cute. I have admired her in other movies, but now, in *Three to Tango*, which gave me nothing else to think about, I was free to observe her intently. She has wide, intelligent eyes, kissable lips, and a face both sweet and carnal, like Doris Day's. I support her decision to never wear any garment that comes within a foot of her neck.

In *Three to Tango* she is mired in a plot of such stupidity that there is only one thing to do, and that is to look at her. In her more erotic moments she twinkles with enjoyment at her own naughtiness; consider a scene where she slithers in a bubble bath and describes a lesbian flirtation with her Brazilian roommate in college. She's having as much fun with this dialogue as we are.

She's telling the story to a character named Oscar (Matthew Perry), who she thinks is gay. It's all a misunderstanding. Oscar and his business partner Peter (Oliver Platt), who *is* gay, are architects who desperately need a $90 million commission from a rich Chicago builder (Dylan McDermott). The builder is a married man and the Neve Campbell character, named Amy, is his mistress. He assigns Oscar to "keep an eye" on Amy, assuming that Oscar is safe because he's gay.

Why does everyone think Oscar is gay? Because this is an Idiot Plot, in which no one ever says what obviously must be said to clear up the confusion. That's because they want that commission. We see a model for their $90 million project, which resembles Chicago's Lincoln Park Conservatory in the eighth month of its pregnancy.

Of course, Oscar and Amy fall in love. And what a Meet Cute they have! On their first evening together, they go out, their taxi explodes (yes, explodes), and they run in the rain and wade in the mud and find a restaurant where they eat tuna melts that make them sick, and they run outside and hurl. This is the Meet Cute as Meet Puke. And on the same date she manages to cause Oscar incredible pain with a sharp door handle to his netherlands. No movie like this is complete without male pattern bruising.

Only about a week after first being considered gay, Oscar is named Gay Man of the Year. It's like they're waiting outside the closet with his trophy. He can't decline the honor because he wants the commission. But then, at the awards banquet, a door in the back opens and Amy walks in. (This is the old Dramatic Late-Arriving Person Who Means Everything to the Speaker Ploy.) Looking into her wide, intelligent eyes, cunningly placed eighteen inches above her wide, intelligent breasts, Oscar blurts out the truth: "I am not gay!" Then we hear the Slowly Gathering Ovation (one brave man stands up and starts to clap slowly, others follow, applause builds to crescendo).

I was wondering how easily the Gay Man of the Year could get a standing ovation for announcing at the awards banquet that he was not gay, but my question was answered in the end credits. Although skyline shots and one early scene create the impression that the movie was made in Chicago, it was actually shot in Toronto. Those Canadians are just so doggone supportive.

This review would not be complete without mention of a scene where Oscar grows distraught and runs through the streets of Chinatown. As he approaches the camera, several Peking ducks, or maybe they are only chickens, are thrown at him from offscreen. Why? Why, indeed. Why, oh why.

Time and Tide ★ ★ ★
R, 113 m., 2001

Nicholas Tse (Tyler), Wu Bai (Jack), Anthony Wong (Uncle Ji), Couto Remotigue (Miguel), Candy Lo (Ah Hui), Cathy Chui (Ah Jo). Directed and produced by Tsui Hark. Screenplay by Koan Hui and Hark.

I denounced *The Mummy Returns* for abandoning its characters and using its plot "only as a clothesline for special effects and action sequences." Now I recommend *Time and Tide,* which does exactly the same thing. But there is a difference. While both films rely on nonstop, wall-to-wall action, *Time and Tide* does a better job, and plugs its action and stunt sequences into the real world with everyday props, instead of relying on computers to generate vast and meaningless armies of special-effects creatures.

It's one thing to create an Egyptian-canine-sand warrior on your computer, multiply it by 1,000, and send the results into battle. It's another thing to show a man rappelling down the sides of the interior courtyard of a high-rise apartment building, with the camera following him in a vertiginous descent. In *The Mummy Returns,* you're thinking of the effects. In *Time and Tide,* you're thinking you've never seen anything like *that* before.

Time and Tide is by Tsui Hark, a master of the martial arts action genre, returning to his Hong Kong roots after a series of Hollywood-financed coproductions starring Jean-Claude Van Damme. To describe its plot would be futile. No sane moviegoer should expect to understand most of what happens from a narrative point of view, beyond the broadest outlines of who is more or less good, and who is more or less bad. In general terms, the hero, Tyler (Nicholas Tse), is trapped in a war between two drug cartels, while simultaneously tracking a lesbian policewoman named Ah Jo (Cathy Chui), who was made pregnant by Tyler during an evening neither one can quite remember. The situation is further complicated by Tyler's friendship with the older mercenary Jack (Wu Bai), who has returned from adventures in South America and has also impregnated a young woman.

That gives us two roughly parallel action strands, populated by characters who look confusingly similar at many moments because we get only glimpses of them surrounded by frenetic action. Does Tsui Hark know this? Yes, and I don't think it bothers him. This is the man whose command of his genre helped make Jet Li into a star, and whose range also encompassed the legendary fantasy *A Chinese Ghost Story.*

Time and Tide is essentially a hyperactive showcase for Tsui Hark's ability to pile one unbelievably complex action sequence on top of another. Characters slip down the sides of parking garages on fire hoses, they crash through plate-glass windows, they roll out of range of sprays of machine-gun fire, they are pulled down staircases by ankle chains, they engage in chases involving every conceivable mode of transportation, and there is a sequence near the end where Tyler assists Ah Jo in giving birth while she uses his gun to fire over his head at their attacking enemies.

Who is Tsui Hark (pronounced "Choy Huck")? After more than sixty features he is the Asian equivalent of Roger Corman, I learn from a *New York Times* profile by Dave Kehr. He was born in Vietnam in 1951 when it was under French rule, immigrated to Hong Kong at fifteen, later studied at Southern Methodist University in Dallas, and edited a newspaper in New York's Chinatown. "From the beginning," Kehr observed, "Mr. Tsui was always willing to go a little bit further than his colleagues." He was "an instinctive postmodernist for whom style was its own justification. [He] created a cinema meant to appeal to the eye, ear, and skin far more than to the brain."

Certainly my eyes, ears, and skin were more involved than my brain as I watched *Time and Tide,* and that explains why I liked it more than *The Mummy Returns,* even though both films could be described as mindless action adventures. With *The Mummy Returns* I was repeatedly reminded that one extravagant visual sequence after another was being tied together with the merest of plot threads, which even the actors treated in a semi-ironic fashion. With *Time and Tide,* the plot might be as tenuous, but the actors treated it with ferocious seriousness (whatever it was), and the presence of flesh-and-blood actors and stunt people created an urgency lacking in the obviously fabricated *Mummy* effects.

After that childbirth-and-gunfire sequence near the end, there's one in which the newborn infant, in a small wooden box, is thrown through the air to save its life. As matters of taste go, is that more defensible than the scene in *Freddy Got Fingered* where Tom Green whirls the newborn infant around his head by its umbilical cord, saving its life? Yes, I would say, it is (the modern film critic is forced into these philosophical choices). It is defensible because there is a difference between thinking, "This is the grossest moment I have ever seen in a movie," and, "Gee, I hope the kid survives!"

Time Code ★ ★ ★
R, 93 m., 2000

Stellan Skarsgard (Alex Green), Saffron Burrows (Emma), Salma Hayek (Rose), Jeanne Tripplehorn (Lauren Hathaway), Glenne Headly (Therapist), Holly Hunter (Executive), Danny Huston (Randy), Kyle MacLachlan (Bunny Drysdale). Directed by Mike Figgis and produced by Figgis and Annie Stewart. Screenplay by Figgis.

I remember the gleam in Mike Figgis's eyes when he talked of filming *Leaving Las Vegas* in cheaper, faster 16mm instead of the standard 35mm. "We didn't have to get a permit from the city or rope off the streets," he said. "We just jumped out of the car, set up the camera, and started shooting." Yes, and made the best film of 1995. Now he's directed a production where they didn't even have to set up the camera.

Time Code was shot entirely with digital cameras, handheld, in real time. The screen is split into four segments, and each one is a single take about ninety-three minutes long. The stories are interrelated, and sometimes the characters in separate quadrants cross paths and are seen by more than one camera. This is not as confusing as it sounds, because Figgis increases the volume of the dialogue for the picture he wants us to focus on, and dials down on the other three.

What is the purpose of the experiment? Above all, to show it can be done. With *Leav-ing Las Vegas,* the camera strategy came second to the story, and was simply the best way to get it on the screen. In *Time Code,* the story is upstaged by the method, sometimes more, sometimes less, and a viewer not interested in the method is likely to be underwhelmed.

What Figgis demonstrates is that a theatrical film can be made with inexpensive, lightweight digital cameras, and that the picture quality is easily strong enough to transfer to 35mm. He also experiments with the notion of filming in real time, which has long fascinated directors. Hitchcock orchestrated *Rope* (1948) so that it appeared to be all one shot, and Godard famously said that the truth came at twenty-four frames per second, and every cut was a lie.

Apart from proving it can be done, however, what is the purpose of Figgis's experiment? The first films ever made were shot in one take. Just about everybody agrees that the introduction of editing was an improvement. To paraphrase Wilde's Lady Bracknell: To make a film in one unbroken shot may be regarded as a misfortune; to make it in four looks like carelessness. Figgis has put style and technique in the foreground, and it upstages the performances in what is, after all, a perfunctory story.

When I go to an experimental film, I am in one mind-set. When I go to a mainstream feature, I am in another. If the film works, it carries me along with it. I lose track of the extraneous and am absorbed by the story. Anything that breaks this concentration is risky, and Figgis, with a four-way screen, breaks it deliberately. The film never happens to us. We are always conscious of watching it. The style isn't as annoying as it might sound, but it does no favors to the story.

Cinema semiologists speak of the "disjoined signifier," and by that they refer to the separation of the viewer from the signified—in this case, from the story. So there I've done it. Used the words "semiologists" and "disjoined signifier" in a review. My students will be proud of me. Most readers will have bailed out. My defense is that *Time Code* is not likely to attract anyone who doesn't know what semiology is—or, if it attracts them, will not satisfy them.

The story involves interlocking adulteries,

told in four parallel stories that begin at 3 P.M. on November 19, 1999, on Sunset Boulevard in or near Book Soup and the office building on the corner. We meet a limousine lesbian, Lauren (Jeanne Tripplehorn), a cokehead who is in love with Rose (Salma Hayek) and eavesdrops on her with a paging device as she has quick and meaningless sex with an alcoholic film executive (Stellan Skarsgard). Other characters include the executive's wife (Saffron Burrows), an ad executive (Holly Hunter), a shrink (Glenne Headly), and others in and around the entertainment industry. There is pointed satire during a "creative meeting" (an oxymoron), and at the end passion bursts out. The action is interrupted by no less than three earthquakes, which must have required fancy timing in coordinating the cameras and actors.

There may be a story buried here somewhere, and even splendid performances. We could try to extract them on a second or third viewing, but why use a style that obscures them? If *Time Code* demonstrates that four unbroken stories can be told at the same time, it also demonstrates that the experiment need not be repeated.

Still, I recommend the film. Mike Figgis is a man who lives and breathes the cinema (see his 1999 film *The Loss of Sexual Innocence* for an altogether more breathtaking and, yes, daring experiment in storytelling). While most filmmakers are content to plod their dreary way from one foregone conclusion to another, Figgis is out there on the edge, joyously pulling off cockamamie stunts like this one. I'm glad I saw the film. It challenged me. The actors were the coproducers and joined in the spirit of the enterprise, testing their own limits. *Time Code* has a place in the history of the movies. But now I want to see Figgis cut back to one camera (digital if he must), resume editing, and conduct experiments that are more likely to arouse my sense of awe than my sense of timing.

A Time for Drunken Horses ★ ★ ★
NO MPAA RATING, 80 m., 2000

Ayoub Ahmadi (Ayoub), Ameneh Ekhtiar-Dini (Ameneh), Mehdi Ekhtiar-Dini (Madi), Rojin Younessi (Rojin). Directed and produced by Bahman Ghobadi. Screenplay by Ghobadi.

A Time for Drunken Horses supplies faces to go with news stories about the Kurdish peoples of Iran, Iraq, and Turkey, people whose land to this day is protected against Saddam's air force by a no-fly zone enforced by the United States. Why Saddam or anyone else would feel threatened by these isolated and desperately poor people is an enigma, but the movie is not about politics. It is about survival.

In dialogue over some of the opening scenes, we meet three young Iranian Kurdish children: Ameneh, a teenage girl; Ayoub, her brother, who is about twelve; and Madi, their fifteen-year-old brother, a dwarf whose fiercely observant face surmounts a tiny and twisted body. They live with their father, who, Ameneh matter-of-factly reports, works as a smuggler, taking goods by mule into Iraq, where they fetch a better price.

The children work every day in a nearby town. They are child labor, put to work wrapping glasses for export, or staggering under heavy loads they carry around the marketplace. Their hand-to-mouth existence undercuts easy Western theories about child labor; they work to eat, and will be dead if they don't.

We see them in the back of a truck bringing them back to their village, and there is a shot that emotionally charges the whole film. Ayoub and Ameneh sit close together, both helping to hold little Madi. Ayoub caresses the hair of the little creature, and Ameneh gently kisses him. They love their crippled brother, who never speaks throughout the film, who must have regular injections of medicine, who needs an operation, who will probably die within the year even if he gets the operation.

The truck is stopped by guards and impounded. The three siblings struggle together through the snow, separated now from their father. Their existence is more desperate than ever. They become involved with mule trains that smuggle truck tires over the mountains to Iraq. The high mountain passes are so cold that the mules are given water laced with alcohol to keep them going—thus the title. Ameneh agrees to marry into a Kurdish family from across the mountains if they will pay for Madi's operation. What happens then I will not reveal.

The movie is brief, spare, and heartbreaking. It won the Camera d'Or, for best first film, at

Cannes 2000. Some find it boring, but I suspect they are lacking in empathy (one Internet critic magnanimously concedes that the movie "might have contained some appeal" if "my life were pathetic enough"). *A Time for Drunken Horses* has the same kind of conviction as movies like *The Bicycle Thief, Salaam Bombay,* and *Pixote*—movies that look unblinkingly at desperate lives on the margin.

The larger message is perhaps in code. The Iranian cinema, agreed to be one of the most creative in the world today, often makes films about children so that politics seem beside the point, even if they are not. First-time filmmaker Bahman Ghobadi, who wrote and directed this film, may or may not have intended to do anything but tell his simple story, but the buried message argues for the rights of ethnic minorities in Iran, and everywhere.

His visual style is documentary. There is little doubt that most of what we see is actually happening, or does happen much as it is represented here. The sight of the mules with two big truck tires lashed to their backs has an intrinsically believable quality.

As for the children, Madi (Mehdi Ekhtiar-Dini) is obviously sadly malformed; there is a touching shot of his eyes peering out apprehensively from beneath the big hood of his coat as he rides in a mule's saddlebag. Ameneh is played by Ameneh Ekhtiar-Dini, who has the same last name as Madi, and is probably his sister; I learn from the notes that in general "the villagers play themselves." I have read about the Kurds being bombed, about the no-fly zone. All merely words, until I saw this movie. Now I will think of little Madi peering out to see what luck he can expect today.

Time Regained ★ ★ ★ ½
NO MPAA RATING, 165 m., 2000

Catherine Deneuve (Odette de Crecy), Emmanuelle Béart (Gilberte), Vincent Perez (Morel), John Malkovich (Charlus), Pascal Greggory (Saint-Loup), Marie-France Pisier (Madame Verdurin), Christian Vadim (Bloch), Arielle Dombasle (Madame de Farcy), Marcello Mazzarella (The Narrator), Chiara Mastroianni (Albertine). Directed Raul Ruiz and produced by Paulo Branco. Screenplay by Gilles Taurand and Ruiz, based on the book by Marcel Proust.

There are times when memory is simply a tool, supplying needed information, and others when it is like a ghostly time machine, summoning the experiences of our past so sharply that we gasp with loss and regret. Marcel Proust's *Remembrance of Things Past* is a work of memory, fed by the legend of the dying novelist in his cork-lined room, tended by the faithful maid Celeste, revisiting the scenes of his past. The memories of his narrator are awakened by the taste and aroma of a madeleine, a kind of pastry he loved as a child; in middle age its taste opens the floodgates of memory.

His novel does not tell a story so much as circle the materials; our lives are not plotted, but happen to us. We are the slate upon which others write our story, and at the end we possess the book but are mystified by those who wrote it. Who were our parents, really, and those we loved? More than any other novelist, Proust gave his life to the examination of it, and "Proustian" evokes a reverie in which the past is more vivid than the insubstantial present. His novel is considered by many the greatest of the twentieth century—considered by more, perhaps, than have actually read it, because its great length makes it one of those works often begun and rarely finished.

Today I sit down to write a review of *Time Regained,* the new film by Raul Ruiz, based on the last volume of Proust's novel but informed by all of them. I type my words in a study lounge of the Illini Union at the University of Illinois in Urbana. In a chair over there by the wall I was sitting on the day in 1963 when the news came that John F. Kennedy had been shot. Last night I attended my high school reunion, where in the faces of middle-aged men I saw grinning boys, and we called the women by their maiden names.

Afterward I parked my car near the corner of Washington and Maple, and walked in the midnight moonlight down the sidewalks of my youth, retracing my paper route—even today I know which houses took the *Courier.* The houses were all the same. I remembered who lived in them. I remembered the names of the dogs that used to greet me, and my own dog Blackie who came along, and an evergreen that brushed the sidewalk. I saw my parents on the porch in metal rocking chairs,

595

smoking cigarettes in the dark, talking softly. Where my car was parked there was a light green 1954 Ford—mine. Those memories are what Proust's novel is about. Not his memories, mine. We have the same memories. Only the names and the places are different. We still bow in wonder toward the first loves of our adolescence. We do not miss them, do not wish ourselves to recapture them, do not regret the present but the past. The point is that they are gone, and soon all will be gone. Memories, their objects, ourselves.

I walk out of the Illini Union and down Green Street, past the Co-Ed theater, which is gone, where my father took me to get Cleo Moore's autograph, and past the Capital, which is gone, where I drank beer with Larry Woiwode before he became a novelist, and past the Turk's Head, which is gone, where Simon told me who Samuel Johnson was, and the Book Nook downstairs, which is gone, where I bought *Boswell's Life of Johnson*. All gone.

The movie opens with an old man in bed (Marcello Mazzarella), being brought tea by his maid. He looks through photographs, which trigger memories, as the furniture in the room rearranges itself for other times. The movie circles the memories. We meet the women who once so captivated him. Here is Gilberte (Emmanuelle Béart). He did not love her so much as learn from her that he could love. Here is her mother, Odette (Catherine Deneuve). And Albertine (Chiara Mastroianni), another, more troublesome, love; in life, Mastroianni is Deneuve's daughter, and the resemblance suggests Albertine's subterranean connection with Odette . . . and her mother. What does it mean? The photographs evoke but do not explain.

Here is Gilberte's eventual husband, Robert de Saint-Loup (Pascal Greggory). He is composed, intact, as a younger man, but then he goes into the trench warfare of World War I, and when he returns he is crazed by his memories, and talks while shoveling food into his mouth like an animal who wants to eat before larger animals steal his kill. And here is Baron de Charlus (John Malkovich), who plays the role of the slightly elevated, bemused observer—a man like the man we all have in our lives, who seems to stand outside and have a wider view. In my high school that was David

Ogden Stiers. Yes, the actor who played Winchester on *M*A*S*H*. He has never attended a reunion, but is discussed every ten years by the rest of us, who recall in wonder that he always talked like that. He came to Urbana from Peoria. Where did he learn to talk like Winchester? Tall, confident, and twinkling, he would ask, "And what have we here?"

Time Regained does not tell a story and you will be disappointed if you go looking for one. It does not contain anything like all of *Remembrance of Things Past*, because the novel is too vast to be contained in a film. It is not about memories but memory. Yours, mine, Proust's. Memory makes us human. Without it, we would live trapped inside the moving dot of time as it slides through our lives. But to remember the past is to experience its loss. Never again will Blackie come with me on my paper route. The *Courier* is not published anymore. The cigarettes killed my parents. High school reunions really take it out of you.

Titan A.E. ★ ★ ★ ½
PG, 92 m., 2000

With the voices of: Matt Damon (Cale), Bill Pullman (Korso), John Leguizamo (Gune), Nathan Lane (Preed), Janeane Garofalo (Stith), Drew Barrymore (Akima), Ron Perlman (Professor Sam Tucker), Alex D. Linz (Young Cale). Directed by Don Bluth and Gary Goldman and produced by David Kirschner, Goldman, and Bluth. Screenplay by Ben Edlund, John August, and Joss Whedon, based on a story by Hans Bauer and Randall McCormick.

Here's the animated space adventure I've been hoping for—a film that uses the freedom of animation to visualize the strangeness of the universe in ways live action cannot duplicate, and then joins its vision to a rousing story. Don Bluth and Gary Goldman's *Titan A.E.* creates the kinds of feelings I had as a teenager, paging eagerly through Asimov and Heinlein. There are moments when it even stirs a little awe.

The movie is pure slam-bam space opera. Its stills could be transferred intact to the covers of old issues of *Amazing Stories*. Yet it has the largeness of spirit that good SF can generate:

It isn't just action and warfare, but also a play of ideas. Some of its galactic visuals are beautiful in the same way photos by the Hubble Space Telescope are beautiful: They show a careless hand casting colors and energy across unimaginable expanses of space, using stars and planets as its paintbox.

As the film opens, in A.D. 3028, Earth has been destroyed by the evil race of Drej, who fear the intelligence of humans. Survivors flee on spaceships, one of them the gigantic *Titan,* which carries crucial information on board. That ship was designed by the hero's father, who apparently disappears along with the *Titan.*

When we first meet Cale (voice by Matt Damon), he's a "colony bum," working in a space dump floating between the stars, where conditions are harsh ("I wish they'd kill my food before they give it to me"). He's bitter and indifferent because he believes he has been abandoned by his father. Yet he holds the key to the future of Earth and mankind in the palm of his hand—literally, in the form of a genetically coded map that reveals the hiding place of *Titan.* Soon he's on a mission to find *Titan,* with partners including a beautiful girl named Akima (Drew Barrymore), who treasures Earth's heritage and collects artifacts of its past, like baseballs. The captain of their expedition is the grave, responsible Korso (Bill Pullman); Gune (John Leguizamo) is the navigator.

The main story involves their journey to find *Titan* before the Drej can capture or destroy it. This quest involves high and low comedy, an exciting chase scene, and then one of the most involving hunt sequences I've seen in any movie, animated or not—a cat-and-mouse game played out in the Ice Rings of Tigrin. These are massive structures of interstellar ice, which form a ring like a miniature galaxy. They offer some protection from the sensing devices of the Drej, but can tear a spaceship to pieces with their huge, jagged masses.

The Ice Rings sequence is a perfect example of what animation can do and live action cannot. The vast, frozen shards of ice are clear and ominous, with a convincing presence, and the sound track does a masterful job of adding a dimension. We know sound does not travel in space, but do not care, because the groanings and creakings of the ancient ice masses are like cries of despair, and somewhere within the frozen maze lies *Titan* with its precious cargo.

The movie is rambunctious in its action scenes, which owe more than a little to *Star Wars* (just as *Star Wars* owes more than a little to old pulp SF and Saturday serials). But it's not simpleminded. I liked a scene where the heroes are trying to sneak past a hostile and suspicious guard. They've constructed counterfeit uniforms. The guard leads them on, pretends to be fooled, and then laughs in their faces, telling them their uniforms are obviously constructed from bedspreads. "An intelligent guard!" says one of the good guys. "Didn't see that one coming."

The movie adds small details that evoke the wonder of the universe. At one point in the journey, the ship is followed by space sprites—energy beings that follow space vessels and mean good luck, as dolphins do at sea. We get a sense of space not merely as a fearsome void, but as a place big enough to include even whimsy. And *Star Wars* is evoked again with the tradition that the human heroes have cartoonish sidekicks. Preed (voice by Nathan Lane) is a first mate who seems to have a genetic similarity to Jar Jar Binks in *The Phantom Menace.* Stith (Janeane Garofalo) is the weapons master who looks like an extremely callipygian kangaroo. The evil Drej are seen as crackling white-blue force fields, seemingly at one with their ships.

One test for any movie is when you forget it's a movie and simply surf along on the narrative. That can happen as easily with animation as live action, and it happens here.

I argue for animation because I believe it provides an additional dimension for film art; it frees filmmakers from the anchor of realism that's built into every live-action film, and allows them to visualize their imaginations. Animation need not be limited to family films and cheerful fantasies. The Japanese have known that for years, and *Titan A.E.* owes as large a debt to Japanese anime as to *Star Wars.*

The movie works as adventure, as the *Star Wars* pictures do (and as live-action SF films like *Starship Troopers* do not). It tells a story cleverly designed to explain more or less reasonably why Cale, in the words of the ancient SF cliché, "has the future of Earth in his hands!" There is a sense of wonder here.

597

Titus ★ ★ ★ ½
R, 165 m., 2000

Anthony Hopkins (Titus), Jessica Lange (Tamora), Alan Cumming (Saturninus), Harry Lennix (Aaron), Jonathan Rhys Meyers (Chiron), Angus Macfadyen (Lucius), Matthew Rhys (Demetrius), Colm Feore (Marcus), James Frain (Bassianus), Laura Fraser (Lavinia). Directed by Julie Taymor and produced by Jody Patton, Conchita Airoldi, and Taymor. Screenplay by Taymor, adapted from William Shakespeare's *Titus Andronicus*.

So bloodthirsty is Shakespeare's *Titus Andronicus* that critics like Harold Bloom believe it must be a parody—perhaps Shakespeare's attempt to settle the hash of Christopher Marlowe, whose plays were soaked in violence. Other readers, like the sainted Mark Van Doren, dismiss it out of hand. Inhuman and unfeeling, he called it, and "no tragedy at all if pity and terror are essential to the tragic experience." Certainly most agree it is the least of Shakespeare's tragedies, as well as the first.

But consider young Shakespeare near the beginning of his career, trying to upstage the star dramatists and attract attention to himself. Imagine him sitting down to write the equivalent of today's horror films. Just as Kevin Williamson's screenplays for *Scream* and *I Know What You Did Last Summer* use special effects and wild coincidence to mow down their casts, so does *Titus Andronicus* heap up the gore, and then wink to show the playwright is in on the joke.

Titus as *Scream 1593*? Bloom cites the scene where Titus is promised the return of his sons if he will send Saturninus his hand—only to find the hand returned with only the heads of his sons. Grief-stricken, Titus assigns tasks. He, with his remaining hand, will carry one of the heads. He asks his brother to take the other. That leaves the severed hand. At this point in the play his daughter, Lavinia, has no hands (or tongue) after being raped and mutilated by the emperor's sons, and so he instructs her, "Bear thou my hand, sweet wench, between thy teeth." Bloom invites scholars to read that line aloud without smiling, and says Shakespeare knew the play "was a howler, and ex-

pected the more discerning to wallow in it self-consciously."

That is exactly what Julie Taymor has done, in a brilliant and absurd film of *Titus Andronicus* that goes over the top, doubles back, and goes over the top again. The film is imperfect, but how can you make a perfect film of a play that flaunts its flaws so joyfully? Some critics have sniffed at its excesses and visual inventions—many of them the same dour enforcers who didn't like the biblical surprise in *Magnolia*. I have had enough good taste and restraint for a lifetime, and love it when a director has the courage to go for broke. God forbid we should ever get a devout and tasteful production of *Titus Andronicus*.

It cannot be a coincidence that the title role is played by Anthony Hopkins. Not when by Act 5 he is serving Tamora (Jessica Lange) meat pies made out of her sons, and smacking his lips in precisely the same way that Hannibal Lecter drooled over fava beans. *Titus Andronicus* was no doubt Lecter's favorite Shakespeare play, opening as it does with Titus returning to Rome with the corpses of twenty-one of his sons and their four surviving brothers, and pausing in his victory speech only long enough to condemn the eldest son of Tamora, vanquished queen of the Goths, to be hacked limb from limb and the pieces thrown on a fire.

Titus is not the hero of the film because it has no hero. He is as vicious as the others, and when he notes that "Rome is a wilderness of tigers," he should have included himself. Hopkins plays him, like Hannibal Lecter, as a man pitiable, intelligent, and depraved, as he strides through a revenge story so gory that there seems a good chance no one will be left alive at the end.

Some of the contrivance is outrageous. Consider the scene where a hole in the forest floor gradually fills up with corpses, as Aaron the Moor (Harry Lennix), the play's grand schemer, unfolds a devious plan to defeat both Titus and Saturninus and seduce Tamora. This hole, of course, would be convenient on the stage, where it could be represented by a trap door, but in the woods, as Saturninus (Alan Cumming) apprehensively peers over the side, it takes on all the credibility of an Abbott and

Costello setup. Or consider the scene late in the play where Titus breaks the neck of his own long-suffering daughter, as if losing her tongue and arms were not bad luck enough, and then pities the fates that made him do it.

Taymor is the director of the Broadway musical *The Lion King*, which is one of the most exhilarating experiences I have ever had in a theater. In her first film she again shows a command of costumes and staging, ritual and procession, archetypes and comic relief. She makes it clear in her opening shot (a modern boy waging a food fight with his plastic action figures) that she sees the connection between *Titus Andronicus* and the modern culture of violence in children's entertainment. *Titus* would make a video game, with the tattooed Tamora as Lara Croft.

Taymor's period is basically a fanciful version of ancient Rome, but in the mix she includes modern cars and tanks, loud speakers and popemobiles, newspapers and radio speeches. Like Richard Loncraine and Ian McKellen's *Richard III* (1995), she sees the possibilities in fascist trappings as Saturninus seizes control of Rome and marries Tamora. There's a jazzy wedding orgy, crypto-Nazi costuming, and a scene staged in front of a vast modern structure made of arches, a reminder of the joke that fascist architecture looked like Mussolini ordered it over the phone.

She lavishes great energy on staging and photography. Like the makers of a cartoon, Taymor and her cinematographer, Luciano Tovoli, sometimes move the camera in time with music or sound effects; as the picture swoops or pulls away, so does Elliot Goldenthal's score. There are scenes of rigid choreography, as in the entry into Rome, where Titus's army marches like the little green soldiers in *Toy Story*. And other scenes where the movements are so voluptuous we are reminded of *Fellini Satyricon*.

Mark Van Doren was correct. There is no lesson to be learned from *Titus Andronicus*. It is a tragedy without a hero, without values, without a point, and therefore as modern as a horror exploitation film or a video game. It is not a catharsis, but a killing gallery where the characters speak in poetry. Freed of pious meaning, the actors bury themselves in technique

and the opportunity of stylized melodrama. Anyone who doesn't enjoy this film for what it is must explain: How could it be other? This is the film Shakespeare's play deserves, and perhaps even a little more.

Tomcats no stars
R, 92 m., 2001

Jerry O'Connell (Michael Delaney), Shannon Elizabeth (Natalie), Jake Busey (Kyle Brenner), Jaime Pressly (Tricia), Horatio Sanz (Steve), Shelby Stockton (Mistaken Bride), Heather Ankeny (New Girl), Joseph D. Reitman (Dave), David Ogden Stiers (Surgeon), Bill Maher (Carlos). Directed by Gregory Poirier and produced by Alan Riche, Tony Ludwig, and Paul Kurta. Screenplay by Poirier.

The men in *Tomcats* are surrounded by beautiful women, but they hate and fear them. That alone is enough to sink the film, since no reasonable person in the audience can understand why these guys are so weirdly twisted. But then the film humiliates the women, and we wince when it wants us to laugh. Here is a comedy positioned outside the normal range of human response.

The movie belongs to an old and tired movie tradition, in which guys are terrified that wedding bells may be breaking up that old gang of theirs (like *The Brothers*, an African-American version of the theme, but gentler and nicer). There is always one guy who is already (unhappily) married, one who is threatened with marriage, one who claims he will never marry, and then the hero, who wants to marry off the unmarriageable one to win a bet. This plot is engraved on a plaque in the men's room of the Old Writer's Retirement Home.

The twist this time: The guys all agree to pay into a mutual fund. The last one still single collects all the money. The fund quickly grows to nearly $500,000, so their fund must have bought hot tech stocks. (In the sequel, those same stocks—oh, never mind.)

The guy who vows never to marry is Kyle (Jake Busey). He likes to take his dates golfing and run over them with the cart. They bounce right up and keep smiling. The guy who wants to collect the money is Michael (Jerry O'Connell). He comes into a valuable piece of information: Kyle met one perfect woman, cruelly dumped her, and has always wondered if he made a mistake. Michael tracks down the woman, who is Natalie (Shannon Elizabeth), and enlists her in his scheme. She'll seduce and marry Kyle and get her revenge—oh, and she wants half the money too.

The complication, which is so obvious it nearly precedes the setup, is that Michael and Natalie fall for each other. This despite the fact that by going along with his plan she reveals herself as a shameless vixen. The movie then runs through an assembly line of routine situations, including bad jokes about S & M and a proctologist who suspects his wife is a lesbian, before arriving at a sequence of astonishing bad taste.

Read no further if through reckless wrongheadedness you plan to see this movie. What happens is that Kyle develops testicular cancer and has to have surgery to remove one of his testicle teammates. During recovery he develops a nostalgia for the missing sphere, and sends Michael on a mission to the hospital's Medical Waste Storage room to steal back the treasure.

Alas, through a series of mishaps, it bounces around the hospital like the quarry in a handball game before ending up on the cafeteria plate of the surgeon who has just removed it, and now eats it, with relish. The surgeon is played by that accomplished actor David Ogden Stiers, my high school classmate, who also does Shakespeare and probably finds it easier.

The movie has other distasteful scenes, including a bachelor party where the star performer starts with Ping-Pong balls and works up to footballs. If the details are gross, the movie's overall tone is even more offensive. All sex comedies have scenes in which characters are embarrassed, but I can't remember one in which women are so consistently and venomously humiliated, as if they were some kind of hateful plague. The guys in the movie don't even seem to enjoy sex, except as a way of keeping score.

Tomcats was written and directed by Gregory Poirier, who also wrote *See Spot Run* and thus pulls off the neat trick, within one month, of placing two titles on my list of the worst movies of the year. There is a bright spot. He used up all his doggy-do-do ideas in the first picture.

Too Much Sleep ★ ★ ★
NO MPAA RATING, 86 m., 2001

Marc Palmieri (Jack), Pasquale Gaeta (Eddie), Philip Galinsky (Andrew), Nicol Zanzarella (Kate), Judy Sabo Podinker (Judy), Peggy Lord Chilton (Mrs. Bruner). Directed by David Maquiling and produced by Jason Kliot and Joana Vicente. Screenplay by Maquiling.

David Maquiling's *Too Much Sleep* is rich and droll, and yet slight—a film of modest virtues, content to be small, achieving what it intends. It tells the story of a twenty-four-year-old security guard who is separated from his gun through a scam while riding the bus. He can't go to the cops because the gun wasn't registered. So he spends the next few days trying to track down the gun himself.

This summary, however, completely fails to reflect the tone of the movie, which is a coming-of-age comedy about how there are a lot of seriously weird people in the world. Jack (Mark Palmieri) enlists the help of a deli owner named Eddie (Pasquale Gaeta), a know-it-all who has a theory about everything and is an endless source of advice fascinating primarily to himself. Eddie has connections with the cops, and comes up with a list of locals whose M.O. fits the scam on the bus, and Jack wanders from one suspect to another in a kind of disbelieving daze. During this process he comes of age to the extent possible in a few days—at the end of the movie, he is a little older and a little wiser, but not much.

Jack sleeps too much and rarely seems quite awake. He sleeps too much because he has nothing interesting to do. He still lives at home, in a bedroom filled with his possessions from high school, and during the long nights on the job he listens to self-help tapes about starting his own business (he should begin, he learns, "by choosing a name"). He lives in a bland, boring suburb, or so he thinks, but during his odyssey in search of the gun he discovers that it is populated by strange and wonderful people, easily as eccentric as anyone in a De Niro crime movie or an Australian comedy.

These people talk a lot. I especially enjoyed

Mrs. Bruner (Peggy Lord Chilton), the mother of a guy Jack urgently wants to question. She chatters away about her son and her late husband, in a conversation where sunny memories suddenly turn cloudy, and her timing and daffy energy is so infectious the whole audience is chuckling, partly in disbelief. (This is her first movie credit; where did she come from? She's like the sister of the Swoozie Kurtz character in *True Stories*.)

I also liked Pasquale Gaeta as Eddie. Guys like this are fun because they are obviously con men, but verbal, entertaining, and ingratiating. Watch the way Eddie shamelessly flatters Mrs. Bruner and makes up facts about her son (whom he has never seen) while Jack is upstairs plundering the kid's room. Eddie is a natural, but why did he take on this job of being Jack's adviser and sidekick in the search for the gun? He hardly knows Jack, has to have their mutual connection described in detail, calls him by the wrong name, and yet is like a father to him.

I think Eddie gets involved in Jack's search because it's in his nature to stick his nose in. To make other people's business his own. To play the role of wise guy. To show how he has the inside info. This is, amazingly, only his second movie; where does David Maquiling, the writer-director, find these engaging naturals?

And who, for that matter, is Maquiling? I learn that he's a Filipino-American who based this seemingly all-American story on a legend from his native land, and that the Eddie character represents a shaman in the original version. Yes, but every culture has shamans, and *Too Much Sleep* has been so Americanized it seems like a road movie (all on city streets) that makes itself up as it goes along. Maquiling loves the specifics of dialogue. He has an ear for word choices, for how people pause for a second after uttering outrageous lies, and for the way the suburbs (his suburbs, at least) are not homogenized flatlands but breed people who go slightly mad in intriguing ways.

When I recommend a movie like this, there are always people who go to see it and challenge me: "What was *that* about?" Sometimes they send me their ticket stubs and demand a refund. They're not used to films this specific and unsprung. Others will cherish it as a treasure. Depends on what you're looking for. *Too*

Much Sleep doesn't shake you by the throat with its desire to entertain. It doesn't *want* you to roll in the aisles. It would rather you smiled than laughed out loud. It is enormously amused by the way people invent themselves as characters, and allows itself to be entertained by their preposterous sublimity.

Topsy-Turvy ★ ★ ★ ★
R, 160 m., 2000

Allan Corduner (Arthur Sullivan), Jim Broadbent (William Schwenck Gilbert), Lesley Manville (Lucy Gilbert ["Kitty"]), Ron Cook (Richard D'Oyly Carte), Timothy Spall (Richard Temple), Wendy Nottingham (Helen Lenoir), Kevin McKidd (Durward Lely), Martin Savage (George Grossmith), Shirley Henderson (Leonora Braham), Alison Steadman (Madame Leon). Directed by Mike Leigh and produced by Simon Channing-Williams. Screenplay by Leigh.

Mike Leigh's *Topsy-Turvy* is the work of a man helplessly in love with the theater. In a gloriously entertaining period piece, he tells the story of the genesis, preparation, and presentation of a comic opera—Gilbert and Sullivan's *The Mikado*—celebrating all the dreaming and hard work, personality conflict and team spirit, inspiration and mundane detail of every theatrical presentation, however inspired or inept. Every production is completely different, and they are all exactly like this.

As the movie opens, Arthur Sullivan and William Schwenck Gilbert rule the London stage. Their comic operettas, produced by the famed impresario Richard D'Oyly Carte, have even paid for the construction of the Savoy Theater—where, alas, their latest collaboration, *Princess Ida,* has flopped so badly that even Gilbert's dentist tells him it went on too long.

Sullivan, the composer, has had enough. Newly knighted by the queen, he decides it is time to compose serious operas: "This work with Gilbert is quite simply killing me." He flees to Paris and a bordello, where D'Oyly Carte tracks him down and learns that there may never be another collaboration between Gilbert (Jim Broadbent) and Sullivan (Allan Corduner). When Sullivan returns to London, he has a meeting with Gilbert, tense and studiously polite, and rejects Gilbert's latest scenario, which is as silly as all of the others: "Oh, Gilbert! You and your world of Topsy-Turvy-dom!"

The two men are quite different. Sullivan is a womanizer and dandy, Gilbert a businessman with an eagle eye for theatrical detail. One day in the middle of the impasse, his wife, Kitty (Lesley Manville), drags him to London's newly opened Japan exhibition, where he observes a Kabuki performance, sips green tea, and buys a sword that his butler nails up over the door. Not long after, as he paces his study, the sword falls down, and inspiration strikes: Gilbert races to his desk to begin writing *The Mikado.*

The world of Gilbert and Sullivan is one of whimsical goofiness, presented with rigorous attention to detail. The fun is in the tension between absurd contrivance and meticulous delivery; consider the song "I Am the Very Model of a Modern Major-General" from *The Pirates of Penzance,* which is delivered with the discipline of a metronome, but at breakneck pace. The form itself is a poke in the eye for Victorian values: The plots and songs uphold the conventional while making it seem clearly mad.

Mike Leigh might seem to be the last of modern British directors to be attracted to the world of the Savoy operas. His films, which do not begin with finished screenplays but are "devised" by the director in collaboration with his actors, have always been about modern Britain—often about inarticulate, alienated, shy, hostile types, who are as psychologically awkward in his comedies as in his hard-edged work. His credits include *Life Is Sweet, Naked,* and *Secrets and Lies,* and nothing remotely in the same cosmos as Gilbert and Sullivan.

But think again. Leigh has worked as much in the theater as for film, and his films depend more than most on the theatrical disciplines of improvisation and rehearsal. In London his productions have often been in vest-pocket theaters where even details like printing the tickets and hiring the stagehands may not have escaped his attention. He is a man of the theater in every atom of his being, and that is why there is a direct connection between his work and Gilbert and Sullivan.

The earlier reaches of *Topsy-Turvy* resemble in broad outline other films about theater: a flop, a crisis, a vow to never work again, a sudden inspiration, a new start. All well done, but the film begins to glow when the decision is made to go ahead with *The Mikado.* This is not merely a film that goes backstage, but also one that goes into accounting ledgers, hiring practices, costume design, personnel problems, casting decisions, sex lives, and the endless detail work of rehearsal: Hours of work are needed to manufacture and perfect even a silly throwaway moment, so that it is thrown away with style and wit, instead of merely being misplaced.

My favorite scene is one in which Gilbert rehearses his actors in line readings. The actor George Grossmith (Martin Savage) expresses insufficient alarm, and Gilbert reminds him that his character is under sentence of death, "by something lingering. By either boiling oil or melted lead. Kindly bear that in mind." There is also much travail over the correct pronunciation of "corroborative."

Many of the cast members are veterans of earlier Leigh films, including the pear-shaped, pouty-lipped Timothy Spall, whose character blinks back tears as his big song seems doomed in dress rehearsal. Jim Broadbent makes a precise Gilbert, bluff and incisive, and Allan Corduner's Sullivan is a study in the partner who cannot admit that his greatness lies always in collaboration. Leigh's construction is canny as he follows big musical numbers like "Three Little Maids" from rehearsal through opening night, and the costumes and sets faithfully recreate the classic D'Oyly Carte Co. productions.

Not everyone is familiar with Gilbert and Sullivan. Do they need to be to enjoy *Topsy-Turvy*? No more, I suspect, than one needs to know all about Shakespeare to enjoy *Shakespeare in Love*—although with both films, the more you do know, the more you enjoy. The two films have been compared because both are British, both are about theatrical geniuses, both deal with theatrical lore. The difference is that *Shakespeare in Love* centers on a love story, and *Topsy-Turvy* is about love of the theater. Romantic love ages and matures. Love of the theater, it reminds us, is somehow always adolescent—heedless, passionate, guilty.

Toy Story 2 ★ ★ ★ ½
G, 85 m., 1999

Tom Hanks (Woody), Tim Allen (Buzz Lightyear), Don Rickles (Mr. Potato Head), Jim Varney (Slinky Dog), Wallace Shawn (Rex), John Ratzenberger (Hamm), Annie Potts (Bo Peep), Joan Cusack (Jessie the Cowgirl), R. Lee Ermey (Sergeant), Kelsey Grammer (Prospector), Jodi Benson (Barbie), Estelle Harris (Mrs. Potato Head), Wayne Knight (Toy Collector), Laurie Metcalf (Mrs. Davis), John Morris (Andy), David Ogden Stiers (Bullseye). Directed by John Lasseter and produced by Helene Plotkin and Karen Robert Jackson. Screenplay by Andrew Stanton, Rita Hsiao, Doug Chamberlain, and Chris Webb.

I forgot something about toys a long time ago, and *Toy Story 2* reminded me. It involves the love, pity, and guilt that a child feels for a favorite toy. A doll or an action figure (or a Pokémon) is *yours* in the same way a pet is. It depends on you. It misses you. It can't do anything by itself. It needs you and is troubled when you're not there.

Toy Story 2 knows this, and for smaller viewers that knowledge may be the most important thing about it—more important than the story or the skill of the animation. This is a movie about what you hope your toys do when you're not around—and what you fear. They have lives of their own, but you are the sun in the sky of their universe, and when you treat them badly their feelings are wounded.

The story begins with Andy, the little boy who owns the *Toy Story* toys, going off to camp. Woody, the cowboy, is in bad shape with a torn arm, and gets left behind. This is crushing to Woody, but worse is to come, when he gets scooped up by Big Al the toy collector, repaired, mended, and repainted—and scheduled for sale to a toy museum in Japan.

At first this adventure is kind of fun for Woody, who finds out for the first time that he is part of a set of toys, the Roundup Gang, that also includes a cowgirl named Jessie, a horse named Bullseye, and a prospector named Stinky Pete. Woody is blown away to discover he even starred in a black-and-white TV puppet show in the fifties, and begins to think that since Andy might eventually abandon him, he might enjoy retiring as the star attraction in a toy museum.

Meanwhile, Buzz Lightyear and the other toys return from camp, discover what has happened, and lead a dangerous cross-town mission to rescue Woody. And we begin to get insights into the private lives of toys. Stinky Pete, for example, is bitter because no kid ever bought him, and he's still in his original box. Jessie is spunky and liberated, but this cowgirl does get the blues; she sings the winsome "When She Loved Me" about her former owner Emily, who tossed her under the bed and forgot her. "You never forget kids, but they forget you," Buzz sighs, but he argues for the position that it is better to be loved for the length of a childhood than admired forever behind glass in a museum.

The movie once again features the enchanting three-dimensional feel of computer-generated animation by Pixar, and has been directed by John Lasseter, the creator of the 1995 *Toy Story.* The tale of this film is almost as thrilling as Woody's fate: It was originally intended as a lowly direct-to-video release, but then the early scenes played so well that Pixar retrenched and started over again with a theatrical feature. In other words, this isn't a made-for-video that they decided to put into theaters, but a version intended from the first to be theatrical. That's important, because it means more detail and complexity went into the animation.

The stars of the voice track certainly seem to remember how they once identified with toys. Many of the actors from the first movie are back again, including Tom Hanks as Woody, Tim Allen as Buzz, Don Rickles as Mr. Potato Head, and Jim Varney as Slinky Dog. The key newcomer is Joan Cusack as Jessie the cowgirl, and she brings new life to the cast by confronting the others with a female character who's a little less domestic than Mrs. Potato Head.

Hanks is responsible for what's probably the movie's high point; he sings "You've Got a Friend in Me," and seems to speak for all toys everywhere. His Woody has, indeed, grown into quite a philosopher. His thoughts about life, love, and belonging to someone are kind of profound. The screenplay by Andrew Stanton, Rita Hsiao, Doug Chamberlain, and Chris Webb isn't just a series of adventures (although

603

there are plenty of those), but a kind of inside job in which we discover that all toys think the way every kid knows his toys think.

Traffic ★ ★ ★ ★
R, 147 m., 2001

Michael Douglas (Robert Wakefield), Don Cheadle (Montel Gordon), Benicio Del Toro (Javier Rodriguez), Luis Guzman (Ray Castro), Erika Christensen (Caroline Wakefield), Dennis Quaid (Arnie Metzger), Catherine Zeta-Jones (Helena Ayala), Steven Bauer (Carlos Ayala), Albert Finney (Chief of Staff), James Brolin (General Ralph Landry), Jacob Vargas (Manolo Sanchez), Tomas Milian (General Arturo Salazar), Miguel Ferrer (Eduardo Ruiz). Directed by Steven Soderbergh and produced by Edward Zwick, Marshall Herskovitz, and Laura Bickford. Screenplay by Stephen Gaghan.

Our laws against illegal drugs function as a price support system for the criminal drug industry. They do not stop drugs. Despite billions of dollars spent and a toll of death, addiction, crime, corruption, and lives wasted in prison, it is possible today for anyone who wants drugs to get them. "For someone my age," says a high school student in the new film *Traffic*, "it's a lot easier to get drugs than it is to get alcohol."

Who supports the drug law enforcement industry? A good many honest and sincere people, to be sure. Also politicians who may know drug laws are futile, but don't have the nerve to appear soft on the issue. And corrupt lawmen, who find drugs a lucrative source of bribes, kickbacks, and payoffs. And the drug cartels themselves, since the laws make their business so profitable. If the decriminalization of drugs were ever seriously considered in this country, the opponents would include not only high-minded public servants, but the kingpins of the illegal drug industry.

These are the conclusions I draw from *Traffic*, Steven Soderbergh's new film, which traces the drug traffic in North America from the bottom to the top of the supply chain. They may not be your conclusions. Draw your own. Soderbergh himself does not favor legalizing drugs, but believes addiction is a public health problem, not a crime. Certainly drugs breed crime—addicts steal because they must—and a more rational policy would result in a lower crime rate and a safer society.

The movie tells several parallel stories, which sometimes link but usually do not. We meet two Mexican drug enforcement cops. Two San Diego DEA agents. A midlevel wholesaler who imports drugs from Mexico. A high-level drug millionaire who seems to be a respectable businessman. A federal judge who is appointed the U.S. drug czar. And his teenage daughter, who becomes addicted to cocaine and nearly destroys her life. We also meet a Mexican general who has made it his goal to destroy a drug cartel—but not for the reasons he claims. And we see how cooperation between Mexican and American authorities is compromised because key people on both sides may be corrupt, and betray secrets.

The movie is inspired by a five-part *Masterpiece Theater* series named *Traffik*, which ran ten years ago and traced the movement of heroin from the poppy fields of Turkey to the streets of Europe. The story in North America is much the same, which is why adapting this material was so depressingly easy. At every level, the illegal drug business is about making money. If there is anything more lucrative than an addictive substance that is legal, like alcohol or tobacco, it is one that is illegal, like drugs—because the suppliers aren't taxed or regulated and have no overhead for advertising, packaging, insurance, employee benefits, or quality control. Drugs are produced by subsistence-level peasants and move through a distribution chain of street sellers; costs to the end user are kept low to encourage addiction.

Soderbergh's film uses a levelheaded approach. It watches, it observes, it does not do much editorializing. The hopelessness of anti-drug measures is brought home through practical scenarios, not speeches and messages—except for a few. One of the most heartfelt comes from a black man who observes that at any given moment in America, 100,000 white people are driving through black neighborhoods looking for drugs, and a dealer who can make $200 in two hours is hardly motivated to seek other employment.

The key performance in the movie is by Michael Douglas, as Robert Wakefield, an Ohio judge tapped by the White House as the nation's new drug czar. He holds all the usual opinions, mouths all the standard platitudes, shares all the naive assumptions—including his belief that he can destroy one of the Mexican cartels by cooperating with the Mexican authorities. This is true in theory, but in practice his information simply provides an advantage for one cartel over the other.

Wakefield is a good man. His daughter, Caroline (Erika Christensen), is an honor student. One night at a party with other teenagers, she tries cocaine and likes it, very much. We see how easily the drug is available to her, how quickly she gets hooked, how swiftly she falls through the safety nets of family and society. This is the social cost of addiction, and the rationale for passing laws against drugs— but we see that it happens *despite* the laws, and that without a profit motive drugs might not be so easily available in her circle.

In Mexico, we meet two hardworking cops in the drug wars, played by Benicio Del Toro and Jacob Vargas, who intercept a big drug shipment but then are themselves intercepted by troops commanded by an army general (Tomas Milian), who is sort of the J. Edgar Hoover of Mexican drug enforcement. In California, we meet a middleman (Miguel Ferrer) who imports and distributes drugs, and two federal agents (Don Cheadle and Luis Guzman) who are on his trail. And we meet the top executive for this operation, a respectable millionaire (Steven Bauer) and his socialite wife (Catherine Zeta-Jones), who has no idea where her money comes from.

Soderbergh's story, from a screenplay by Stephen Gaghan, cuts between these characters so smoothly that even a fairly complex scenario remains clear and charged with tension. Like Martin Scorsese's *GoodFellas, Traffic* is fascinating at one level simply because it shows how things work—how the drugs are marketed, how the laws are sidestepped. The problem is like a punching bag. You can hammer it all day and still it hangs there, impassive, unchanged.

The movie is powerful precisely because it doesn't preach. It is so restrained that at one moment—the judge's final speech—I wanted one more sentence, making a point, but the movie lets us supply that thought for ourselves. And the facts make their own argument: This war is not winnable on the present terms, and takes a greater toll in human lives than the drugs themselves. The drug war costs $19 billion a year, but scenes near the end of the film suggest that more addicts are helped by two free programs, Alcoholics Anonymous and Narcotics Anonymous, than by all the drug troops put together.

Trekkies ★ ★ ★
PG, 86 m., 1999

A documentary directed by Roger Nygard and produced by Keith Border. Narrated by Denise Crosby and featuring LeVar Burton, Frank D'Amico, John de Lancie, James Doohan, Michael Dorn, Jonathan Frakes, DeForest Kelly, Walter Koenig, Kate Mulgrew, Anne Murphy, Nichelle Nichols, Leonard Nimoy, William Shatner, Brent Spiner, and George Takei.

When Barbara Adams of Little Rock, Arkansas, was called to serve as a Whitewater juror, she arrived dressed appropriately, in her opinion. She was in a lieutenant commander's uniform as commanding officer of the USS *Artemis,* the Little Rock unit of the Federation Alliance. In other words, she was a *Star Trek* fan.

When the judge demurred at her costume and she made national news, she refused to back down: "If the president himself were on trial," she said, "I would still wear the uniform. I am an officer in the Federation universe twenty-four hours a day." Plus, she was setting a good example: "I don't want my officers to ever be ashamed to wear their uniforms."

As Adams is making these statements in *Trekkies,* a new documentary, I was looking closely for any sign of a smile. She was dead serious. *Star Trek* is her life. Old soldiers get their dress uniforms out of mothballs to prove the point that "formal wear" can mean either a tuxedo or a military uniform. And Lieutenant Commander Adams honors her uniform in the same spirit.

Not everyone in *Trekkies* is as serious about the long-running series of TV programs and movies. But most of them are as obsessed. Consider Denis Bourguinon, a dentist in Orlando whose Star Base Dental is an office completely designed around a *Star Trek* motif. Even

605

his aides and hygienists are in uniform. One says she held out for a year before putting on the outfit. What convinced her? "He told me I had to."

Then there is the Canadian man who has designed a motorized life-support chair like one seen in the series, and drives around town in it, only his head visible above what looks like a steam cabinet. Or the father-and-son team whose pickup looks like a lunar lander and might someday be able to "shoot a 1,000-foot beam." And consider the *Star Trek* auction where someone bid $40 for a half-filled water glass used by a cast member with a virus. The lucky bidder drank the rest of the water so he could have the virus too.

I've been vaguely aware of the further shores of *Star Trek* fandom through my mail and contact with audiences at screenings. And I've sensed a certain tone of awe about it in the voices of many cast members I've interviewed, from Leonard Nimoy and William Shatner on down, or up. It's not so much a hobby, more a way of life. "Somewhere in the world," Denise (Tasha Yar) Crosby, the film's narrator, informs us, "there is a *Star Trek* event every weekend." We meet Richard Arnold, a *Star Trek* consultant, who has visited 360 of them.

Trekkies and Trekkers evolved out of the older and broader-based science-fiction fandom, which began with mimeographed magazines in the 1940s and went on to sponsor gigantic WorldCons and influence the tone and jargon of the Web (many Web pages are mutated fanzines). Fandom began the tradition of dressing in the costumes of science-fiction characters, and *Star Trek* fandom is intensely involved in that side of things—to such a degree that the dentist and his wife cheerfully hint that many different species play roles in their fantasy lives.

To some degree, dressing up and role-playing in a *Star Trek* context may be a cover for cross-dressing impulses in general. To a much larger degree, it is probably just good fun. I was going to say "good, clean fun," but was reminded of an attractive black woman in the movie who, as Mistress Janeway, pens popular S&M fantasies with a *Star Trek* theme, in which aliens do things to one another that humans can hardly hope to appreciate.

Sinclair Lewis, who I believe invented the term "boosterism," would appreciate a uniquely American strain in Trekdom, which feels compelled, like so many popular movements, to cloak its fun in do-gooderism. Trekkies talk at length about how the world would be a saner and more peaceful place if the *Star Trek* philosophy ruled our lives. No doubt it would be a lot more entertaining, too, especially during root canals.

The Trial ★ ★ ★
NO MPAA RATING, 118 m., 1963 (rereleased 2000)

Anthony Perkins (Joseph K), Jeanne Moreau (Miss Burstner), Orson Welles (Advocate), Madeline Robinson (Mrs. Brubach), Elsa Martinelli (Hilda), Suzanne Flon (Miss Pittl), Akim Tamiroff (Bloch), Romy Schneider (Leni). Directed by Orson Welles and produced by Alexander Salkind. Screenplay by Welles, based on the novel by Franz Kafka.

I was once involved in a project to convince Orson Welles to record a commentary track for *Citizen Kane*. Seemed like a good idea, but not to the great one, who rumbled that he had made a great many films other than *Kane* and was tired of talking about it.

One he might have talked about was *The Trial* (1963), his version of the Kafka story about a man accused of—something, he knows not what. It starred Anthony Perkins in his squirmy post-*Psycho* mode, it had a baroque visual style, and it was one of the few times, after *Kane*, when Welles was able to get his vision onto the screen intact. For years the negative of the film was thought to be lost, but then it was rediscovered and restored.

The world of the movie is like a nightmare, with its hero popping from one surrealistic situation to another. Water towers open into file rooms, a woman does laundry while through the door a trial is under way, and huge trunks are dragged across empty landscapes and then back again. The black-and-white photography shows Welles's love of shadows, extreme camera angles, and spectacular sets. He shot it mostly inside the Gare d'Orsay in Paris, which, after it closed as a train station and before it was reborn as a museum, offered vast spaces;

the office where Perkins's character works consists of rows of desks and typists extending almost to infinity, like a similar scene in the silent film *The Crowd*.

Franz Kafka published his novel in Prague in 1925; it reflected his own paranoia, but it was prophetic, foreseeing Stalin's Gulag and Hitler's Holocaust, in which innocent people wake up one morning to discover they are guilty of being themselves. It is a tribute to his vision that the word "Kafkaesque" has, like "catch-22," moved beyond the work to describe things we all see in the world.

Anthony Perkins is a good choice to play Joseph K, the bureaucrat who awakens to find strange men in his room, men who treat him as a suspect and yet give him no information. Perkins could turn in an instant from ingratiating smarminess to anger, from supplication to indignation, his voice barking out ultimatums and then suddenly going high-pitched and stuttery. And watch his body language as he goes into his confiding mode, hitching closer to other characters, buddy-style, looking forward to neat secrets.

The film follows his attempts to discover what he is charged with, and how he can defend himself. Every Freudian slip is used against him (he refers to a "pornograph player," and a man in a black suit carefully notes that down). He finds himself in a courtroom where the audience is cued by secret signs from the judge. He petitions the court's official portrait painter, who claims he can fix cases and obtain a "provisional acquittal." And in the longest sequence, he visits the cavernous home of the Advocate, played by Welles as an ominous sybarite who spends much of his time in bed, smoking cigars and being tended by his mistress (Romy Schneider).

The Advocate has obscure powers in matters such as Joseph K is charged with, whatever they are. He has had a pathetic little man living in his maid's room for a long time, hoping for news on his case, kissing the Advocate's hand, falling to his knees. He would like Joseph to behave in the same way. The Advocate's home reaches out in all directions, like a loft, factory, and junk shop, illuminated by hundreds of guttering candles, decorated by portraits of judges, littered with so many bales of old legal papers that one shot looks like the closing scene in *Citizen Kane*. But neither here nor elsewhere can Joseph come to grips with his dilemma.

Perkins was one of those actors everyone thought was gay. He kept his sexuality private, and used his nervous style of speech and movement to suggest inner disconnects. From an article by Edward Guthmann in the *San Francisco Chronicle*, I learn that Welles confided to his friend Henry Jaglom that he knew Perkins was a homosexual, "and used that quality in Perkins to suggest another texture in Joseph K, a fear of exposure."

"The whole homosexuality thing—using Perkins that way—was incredible for that time," Jaglom told Guthmann. "It was intentional on Orson's part: He had these three gorgeous women (Jeanne Moreau, Romy Schneider, Elsa Martinelli) trying to seduce this guy, who was completely repressed and incapable of responding." That provides an additional key to the film, which could be interpreted as a nightmare in which women make demands Joseph is uninterested in meeting, while bureaucrats in black coats follow him everywhere with obscure threats of legal disaster.

But there is also another way of looking at *The Trial*, and that is to see it as autobiographical. After *Citizen Kane* (1941) and *The Magnificent Ambersons* (1942, a masterpiece with its ending hacked to pieces by the studio), Welles seldom found the freedom to make films when and how he desired. His life became a wandering from one place to another. Beautiful women rotated through his beds. He was reduced to a supplicant who begged financing from wealthy but maddening men. He was never able to find out exactly what crime he had committed that made him "unbankable" in Hollywood. Because Welles plays the Advocate, there is a tendency to think the character is inspired by him, but I can think of another suspect: Alexander Salkind, producer of *The Trial* and much later of the *Superman* movies, who like the Advocate, liked people to beg for money and power which, in fact, he did not always have.

Seen in this restored version (available on video from Milestone), *The Trial* is above all a visual achievement, an exuberant use of camera placement and movement and inventive lighting. Study the scene where the screaming girls chase Joseph K up the stairs to the painter's studio and peer at him through the slats of the walls, and you will see what Richard Lester saw before he filmed the screaming girls in *A Hard Day's Night* and had them peer at the Beatles through the slats of a railway luggage car.

The ending is problematical. Mushroom clouds are not Kafkaesque because they represent a final conclusion, and in Kafka's world nothing ever concludes. But then comes another ending: the voice of Orson Welles, speaking the end credits, placing his own claim on every frame of the film, and we wonder, is this his way of telling us *The Trial* is more than ordinarily personal? He was a man who made the greatest film ever made, and was never forgiven for it.

Trick ★ ★
R, 90 m., 1999

Christian Campbell (Gabriel), John Paul Pitoc (Mark), Tori Spelling (Katherine), Steve Hayes (Perry), Brad Beyer (Rich), Lorri Bagley (Judy), Kevin Chamberlin (Perry's Ex), Clinton Leupp (Miss Coco Peru). Directed by Jim Fall and produced by Eric d'Arbeloff, Fall, and Ross Katz. Screenplay by Jason Schafer.

There's an e-mail making the rounds that urges gay moviegoers to "support" gay-themed films by being sure to attend on the crucial opening weekend. It cites a similar effort to encourage blacks to support black films from the outset. I myself have urged readers to support various films that might be overlooked, but it's all a futile enterprise: No one in the history of the movies has purchased a ticket to "support" a film. People go only because they really want to.

Besides, what message would it send to "support" a gay film like *Trick*? The message, I suppose, would be that gays should have romantic comedies just as dim and dumb as the straight versions—although I cannot offhand remember many recent straight films this witless. The movie imposes a Doris Day story line on material that wants to be more sexual; it's about a character whose quasi-virginity is preserved through an improbable series of mishaps and coincidences.

The Doris Day character this time is Gabriel (Christian Campbell, Neve's brother), an office worker who dreams of writing musical comedies, even though he admits to his best pal Katherine (Tori Spelling) that his kind of song is dead. He's right. She sings an audition piece to deadening effect, and in the dark I scribbled: "She's singing the *whole song!*" The movie confuses a comic moment with a musical number.

Disconsolate, Gabriel drifts into a gay bar, where his groin thrums at the sight of Mark (John Paul Pitoc), a go-go boy whose nickname is not "Beer Can" because of his drinking habits. Of course Mark would forever be out of reach of the shy Gabriel—or so he thinks, until they run into each other on the subway, make eye contact, and end up trying to find a place where they can be alone together.

This is where the Doris Day plot difficulties kick in. Spelling won't vacate Gabe's apartment because she has to print 500 copies of her résumé, and later his macho roommate and ditzy girlfriend claim the turf for their own. Gabe and Mark drift through the night to drag clubs and diners, increasingly discouraged. Why, oh why, is there no place where they can have sex?

There's a problem with the character of Mark, played by Pitoc with an occasional sour look, as if he's unsure whether to smolder or leave. He follows Gabe around faithfully, but never really seems to *want* to sleep with him: He's like a man waiting to collect an overdue car payment. Gabe, meanwhile, actually brags to people that his new friend is a go-go boy; he's like a deejay on a date with a porn actress.

Another problem is that the director, Jim Fall, treats too many of the supporting actors as if he owes them favors. It's as if he promised them big scenes if they worked cheap. We get full-length renditions in piano bars, Spelling's protracted audition, and so on. It's as if the screenplay wants to keep moving but the camera can't drag itself away from whatever it's watching.

Would this same movie be entertaining with heterosexual characters? In today's world, it would hardly be thinkable. The premise is so hackneyed that any characters in this plot would come across as dopes. I guess the Mark character would be the boy in the straight version, which makes his sullen passivity all the stranger: It's like he's allowing himself to be dragged around by a partner much keener on the whole idea than he is.

Trippin' ★ ★ ½
R, 92 m., 1999

Deon Richmond (Gregory Reed), Donald Adeosun Faison (June), Maia Campbell (Cinny Hawkins), Guy Torry (Fish), Aloma Wright (Louis Reed), Harold Sylvester (Willie Reed), Cleavon McClendon (Jamal), Bill Henderson (Gramps), Michael Warren (Shapik). Directed by David Hubbard (as David Raynr) and produced by Marc Abraham and Caitlin Scanlon. Screenplay by Gary Hardwick.

To judge by a lot of the movies I've been seeing, the most pressing issue of our time (indeed, the *only* issue in most movies about teenagers) is who to take to the senior prom. Faithful readers will know that this question has been raised in at least six movies already this year, and I'm not even counting the one about who Carrie II will kill at the prom.

Trippin' transports this issue to the African-American community, in a high-spirited comedy about a likable senior named Gregory Reed (Deon Richmond), who puts off everything until the last possible moment. When he approaches his parents with a request for "funds to finance my senior prom activities," they laugh at him: He hasn't even sent in his college applications yet, his dad points out. First things first.

Gregory's problem is that he lives in a world of daydreams. The movie opens with one—an island fantasy, shot in the style of a music video, with Gregory basking in the admiration of a brace of Hawaiian Tropics girls. A friend of his, who wears leg braces, inspires a daydream in which he becomes the Terminator crossed with RoboCop. And a visit to an army recruiting office triggers a fantasy in which Gregory receives the Medal of Honor—plus, the president tells him, "unreleased CDs from Tupac and Notorious B.I.G."

Gregory has fallen in love with Cinny Hawkins (the beautiful Maia Campbell), and would like to ask her to the prom—but lacks the funds and the courage. His friends advise him to impress her with his bright future, so he lies and says he's been given a full scholarship to UCLA. There's a sweet scene where they wander through a dock area, dreaming of the voyages they could take—on the sea and in life.

There seems to be, alas, a requirement that almost every movie about black teenagers include drugs somewhere in the plot. *Trippin'* supplies a no-good drug dealer who at one point has Gregory's friend hanging upside down from a crane, and the scenes involving this villain don't really seem necessary. I guess the crime stuff is there to provide the plot with prefab suspense, but it might have been more fun to develop Cinny's character more fully, since there's a lot more to her than simply beauty.

Trippin' does have some amiable scenes involving Gregory's family, including his strict dad (Harold Sylvester), his sympathetic mother (Aloma Wright), and Gramps (Bill Henderson), who has no truck with attempts to improve his nutrition, and bangs on the table while demanding pork sausage. And there's a no-nonsense teacher (Michael Warren) who tries to jolt Gregory out of his mind-trips and into some kind of organized approach to the rest of his life.

The movie is sweet, but predictable, and we get about three more daydreams than we really require. Deon Richmond and Maia Campbell both possess radiant smiles, which is important in a movie where a character's appearance supplies at least half of the character development. Whether Richmond and Campbell will someday be getting the kind of roles that go to Denzel Washington and Halle Berry is impossible to predict, but on the basis of their work here, it's not implausible.

Did I like the movie? Not enough to recommend it, except to someone who really wants to see another senior prom cliffhanger. Still, there are so many grim and gritty urban violence movies that it's good to see nice African-American kids in a comedy, even if it's so lacking in imagination that it finds it necessary to hang them upside down.

Trixie ★ ★
R, 115 m., 2000

Emily Watson (Trixie Zurbo), Dermot Mulroney (Dex Lang), Nick Nolte (Senator Drummond Avery), Nathan Lane (Kirk Stans), Brittany

Murphy (Ruby Pearli), Lesley Ann Warren (Dawn Sloane), Will Patton (Red Rafferty), Stephen Lang (Jacob Slotnick), Mark Acheson (Vince Deflore). Directed by Alan Rudolph and produced by Robert Altman. Screenplay by Rudolph, based on a story by Rudolph and John Binder.

Trixie has all the trappings and suits of woe of a comedy, but then it changes horses of a different color and turns into a thriller in the middle of the stream. That razes our expectations. It's not a success, but it's a closed mist, and kind of fun in its own ways and means.

I should warn you, however, that if you are not amused by cheerfully mangled language, you may think too much Trixie is not a treat. The movie stars Emily Watson as Trixie Zurbo, an undercover detective for a casino, who consistently and without flail commits a malappropriation every time she opens her mouth.

She gets her man "by hook or by ladder," she declares, and tells one bad guy he's a "Jekyll of all trades." Her sister is having a baby, "but I don't know if I'm gonna be an uncle or an aunt yet." She often finds herself "between a rock and the deep blue sea."

Trixie is hired on the overnight shift of the casino, which is located in a mountain area next to a scenic lake. She makes a pal of a lounge act (Nathan Lane). And she falls afoul of some local cheeseballs who are involved in the shade of influence peddling and real estate wheeler-stealing. That happens because Dex Lang (Dermot Mulroney) draws designs on her body. He works for a con man named Red Rafferty (Will Patton). Dex sneaks Trixie onto Red's boat for a little quality dock time, and they're on board when Red turns up with the crooked state senator Drummond Avery (Nick Nolte) and the senator's maintenance squeeze, Dawn Sloane (Lesley Ann Warren).

The plot is standard for anyone who has read Ross MacDonald, or seen any movie involving gambling, real estate, and hook-or-by-crooked politicians. I guess the director, Alan Rudolph, intended *Trixie* as a *film noir* satire, but he's famous for the loose flywheels on his plots, and this one spins off in separated directions. First, the movie starts goofy and then gets more straight, which is perplexing. Second, Trixie as a character exists in a whirl of her own. Her typical shot involves looking into the camera and intonating lines like, "Either fish or get off the pot!"

Rudolph's characters exist at an angle from the reel world; when he works in a genre, he likes to avoid the genre's conventions, which sort of defeats its own purpose. With most genre movies, we know what's going to happen next but don't care. With Rudolph, we care what's going to happen next but don't know.

Nick Nolte fits easily into the Rudolph universe, and almost visibly expands with the freedom the director gives him. This is his third recent Rudolph film, after the unsuccessful *Breakfast of Champions* (1998) and the wonderful *Afterglow* (1997), in which Nolte, as a fix-it man, gave one of his best performances opposite the Oscar-nominated Julie Christie.

Nolte brings a poker-faced charm to dialogue other actors might find unsayable. At one point his senator orders everyone to "stop clowning around"—because "as a child my dad took me to the circus and a clown killed him." This line is delivered so offhandedly that it could be true, could be intended to be funny, could be a train of thought jumping the tracks, or could even be intended to intimidate by its sheer goofiness.

Emily Watson is a newcomer to Rudolph's films, but seems like a member of his repeatatory company. She is gifted at many diffident tones, but as Trixie, curiously, the character she reminds us of is the innocent in the totally different film *Breaking the Waves*. She has the same kind of wide-eyed innocence, the same straight-ahead approach to the world, the same heedlessness for danger. As Trixie puts it, she's able to "grab the bull by the tail and look him in the eye."

Does the movie work? Not on the whole. But individual scenes have a great comic zest. I like the way the confusion develops on board the boat. Later there is a nice scene where the senator is publicly humiliated at a private club when his privates get too much publicity. This is not the sort of movie you make it your business to see in a theater. But if you're ever surfing cable TV and come across it, you'll linger, unless you're entirely out of your rocker.

610

True Crime ★ ★ ★
R, 127 m., 1999

Clint Eastwood (Steve Everett), Isaiah Washington (Frank Beachum), Denis Leary (Bob Findley), Lisa Gay Hamilton (Frank's Wife), James Woods (Alan Mann), Diane Venora (Barbara). Directed by Clint Eastwood and produced by Eastwood, Richard D. Zanuck, and Lili Fini Zanuck. Screenplay by Larry Gross, Paul Brickman, and Stephen Schiff, based on the novel by Andrew Klavan.

Clint Eastwood's *True Crime* follows the rhythm of a newspaperman's day. For those who cover breaking news, many days are about the same. When they begin, time seems to stretch out generously toward the deadline. There's leisure for coffee and phone calls, jokes and arguments. Then a blip appears on the radar screen: an assignment. Seemingly a simple assignment. Then the assignment reveals itself as more complicated. The reporter makes some calls.

If there's anything to the story at all, a moment arrives when it becomes, to the reporter, the most important story in the world. His mind shapes the form it should take. He badgers sources for the missing pieces. The deadline approaches, his attention focuses, the finish line is the only thing visible, and then facts, story, deadline, and satisfaction come all at the same time. A deadline reporter's day, in other words, is a lot like sex.

Eastwood uses this rhythm to make *True Crime* into a wickedly effective thriller. He plays Steve Everett, a reporter for the *Oakland Tribune*. Steve used to work out east, but got fired for "screwing the owner's underage daughter." The movie's Web page says he worked for the *New York Times*, but this detail has been dropped from the movie, no doubt when the information about the owner's daughter was added. Now he's having an affair with the wife of Findlay, his city editor (Denis Leary).

Everett's personal life is a mess. His wife, Barbara (Diane Venora), knew he cheated when she married him, but thought it was only with her. Now they have a young daughter, but Everett seems too busy to be a good dad (there's a scene where he pushes her stroller through the zoo at a dead run). Everett's also a little shaky; he was a drunk until two months ago, when he graduated to recovering alcoholic.

He's assigned to write a routine story about the last hours of a man on death row: Frank Beachum (Isaiah Washington), convicted of the shooting death of a pregnant clerk in a convenience store. Both the city editor and the editor-in-chief (James Woods) know Everett is a hotshot with a habit of turning routine stories into federal cases, and they warn him against trying to save Beachum at the eleventh hour. But it's in Everett's blood to sniff out the story behind the story. He becomes convinced the wrong man is going to be executed. "When my nose tells me something stinks—I gotta have faith in it," he tells Beachum.

This is Eastwood's twenty-first film as a director, and experience has given him patience. He knows that even in a deadline story like this, not all scenes have to have the same breakneck pace. He doesn't direct like a child of MTV, for whom every moment has to vibrate to the same beat. Eastwood knows about story arc, and as a jazz fan he also knows about improvising a little before returning to the main theme.

True Crime has a nice rhythm to it, intercutting the character's problems at home, his interviews with the prisoner, his lunch with a witness, his unsettling encounter with the grandmother of another witness. And then, as the midnight hour of execution draws closer, Eastwood tightens the noose of inexorably mounting tension. There are scenes involving an obnoxious prison chaplain, and a basically gentle warden, and the mechanical details of execution. Cuts to the governor who can stay the execution. Tests of the telephone hot lines. Battles with his editors. Last-minute revelations. Like a good pitcher, he gives the movie a nice slow curve, and a fast break.

Many recent thrillers are so concerned with technology that the human characters are almost in the way. We get gun battles and car chases that we don't care about, because we don't know the people firing the guns or driving the cars. I liked the way Eastwood and his writers (Larry Gross, Paul Brickman, and Stephen Schiff) lovingly added the small details. For example, the relationships that both the reporter and the condemned man have with their daughters. And a problem when the prisoner's little girl can't find the right color crayon for her drawing of green pastures.

In England twenty-five years ago, traditional beer was being pushed off the market by a pasteurized product that had been pumped full of carbonation (in other words, by American beer). A man named Richard Boston started the Real Beer Campaign. Maybe it's time for a movement in favor of real movies. Movies with tempo and character details and style, instead of actionfests with Attention Deficit Disorder. Clint Eastwood could be honorary chairman.

The Trumpet of the Swan ★ ½
G, 75 m., 2001

With the voices of: Dee Baker (Louie), Jason Alexander (Father), Mary Steenburgen (Mother), Reese Witherspoon (Serena), Seth Green (Boyd), Carol Burnett (Mrs. Hammerbotham), Joe Mantegna (Monty), Sam Gifaldi (Sam). An animated film directed by Richard Rich and produced by Lin Oliver. Screenplay by Judy Rothman Rofé, based on the novel by E. B. White.

The Trumpet of the Swan is an innocuous family feature that's too little, too late in the fast-moving world of feature animation. I would have found it slow going anyway, but seeing it not long after the triumph of *Shrek* made it seem even tamer and more flat. Maybe younger children will enjoy it at home on video, but older family members will find it thin.

The story is adapted from a 1970 E. B. White fable about a swan named Louie who is born without a voice. While his sisters, Ella and Billie, are trumpeter swans with magnificent calls, Louie paddles around in disconsolate silence. His father, desperate, raids a music store in Billings, Montana, and steals a trumpet, which Louie learns to play.

The young cygnet is a quick study. Encouraged by a local boy named Sam (voice by Sam Gifaldi), Louie enrolls in the local (human) school and learns to communicate by using a blackboard he straps around his neck. But his father's theft of the trumpet weighs upon him, and eventually he flies to Boston and appears in jazz clubs to raise cash to pay for the instrument.

There's more, involving his romance with the feathery Serena (voice by Reese Witherspoon), who in despair over Louie's absence waddles to the altar with the dastardly Boyd (Seth Green). Much is made of the buildup to the Serena-Boyd vows, but once they are interrupted by Louie's last-minute arrival, there are no further wedding scenes, leading thoughtful viewers to wonder whether Serena's nestful of eggs represents a little premarital featherdusting. It wouldn't be the first time a bird fell for a trumpet player.

Tumbleweeds ★ ★ ★
PG-13, 100 m., 1999

Janet McTeer (Mary Jo Walker), Kimberly J. Brown (Ava Walker), Jay O. Sanders (Dan), Gavin O'Connor (Jack Ranson), Michael J. Pollard (Mr. Cummings), Laurel Holloman (Laurie Pendleton), Lois Smith (Ginger). Directed by Gavin O'Connor and produced by Gregory O'Connor. Screenplay by Gavin O'Connor and Angela Shelton.

American movies have a deep faith that if you hit the road and point west, at the end of the journey you will find—well, whatever you're looking for. Romance, fame, truth, understanding, all dreamed of as you look out over the sea. Those who go west are often poor, or unlucky in love, or have been roughly treated by life. Those who go east, on the other hand, are usually smart, aggressive, and ambitious. Has there ever been a movie in which a couple of losers from the Dust Bowl, down on their luck, head east and arrive in triumph at Coney Island?

We also have a faith in the wisdom of youth, and in the ability of parents to be redeemed by children. (We have an equal faith in the ability of children to be redeemed by parents, but fewer adults than teenagers buy movie tickets, so fewer of those movies are made.) *Tumbleweeds*, like *Anywhere But Here*, which opened only a month earlier, is about a troubled mother and her wise daughter, who share a road journey to California while both deal with the mother's immaturity and untidy sex life.

Is there a rule that we must prefer one of these films to the other? I don't know why there should be. I liked them about equally well, and certainly *Tumbleweeds*, which premiered in January 1999 at Sundance, cannot be blamed because its distributor couldn't get it into theaters before its twin.

Tumbleweeds is a little grittier than *Anywhere But Here*; it lacks the gloss of the other film and is positioned a notch or two lower on the socioeconomic ladder. In *Anywhere*, the mother pins her hopes on romance with an orthodondist, while in *Tumbleweeds* it is a truck driver who looks like the Marlboro Man. Both movies make much of the daughters' school opportunities, reminding us that America is a classless society where the speedometer is set back to zero for every generation. Ava (Kimberly J. Brown) may find herself spending the night with her mother, Mary Jo (Janet McTeer), in a borrowed camper, but she is auditioning to play Juliet, and no child is wholly disadvantaged who has access to Shakespeare.

Mary Jo is a woman who depends on the kindness of strange men. She has a mental Rolodex of guys who once thrummed to her charms, and pilots an old car around the Southwest looking them up. Her memory improves on reality; a man recalled as a leading car dealer turns out to run a used parts lot. But the friendly Marlborian truck driver (played by Gavin O'Connor, the director and cowriter) seems at first to be promising. He fixes a leaking hose in her radiator, later finds himself in the same pool hall where she stops for a drink, and soon Mary Jo and Ava are moving in.

By now they are in San Diego, where Mary Jo seeks employment. One of her interviewers is Michael J. Pollard, who examines her résumé and observes that either she likes to move around a lot or she's a wanted woman. She gets a job as a phone slave at a guard company (she calls you when your alarm goes off). But then the Marlboro Man gets angry when she doesn't order what he recommends at a restaurant. "I know where this is going," she says, having much experience of men who believe their kind suggestions should be understood as orders.

Will they move towns again? Resume the quest for the right man, the right home, the right school for Ava? Ava thinks not. As played by Brown, she is a thoughtful, appealing young woman who knows her mother all too well. McTeer makes Mary Jo into a woman who has two basic problems: A fatal attraction to the wrong men, and an inability to stay put long enough to work herself up the job ladder.

There is a right man around. He is Dan (Jay O. Sanders), a coworker who lost his own wife and tells Ava about that in one of the movie's best scenes. Will they get together? Would that be the right thing for either one of them? Movies like *Tumbleweeds* exist in the details, not the outcome. Even a happy ending, we suspect, would be temporary. We don't mind, since the characters have been intriguing to know and easy to care about.

Turn It Up ★ ½
R, 83 m., 2000

Pras Michel (Diamond), Ja Rule (Gage), Tamala Jones (Nia), Vondie Curtis-Hall (Diamond's Father), Jason Stratham (Mr. B.), John Ralston (Mr. White). Directed by Robert Adetuyi and produced by Madonna and Guy Oseary. Screenplay by Ray "Cory" Daniels, Chris Hudson, Kelly Hilaire, and Adetuyi, based on *Ghetto Supastar,* the book and album by Prakazrel "Pras" Michel.

Turn It Up tells the story of a moral weakling who compromises his way through bloodbaths and drug deals while whining about his values. It's one of those movies where the more the characters demand respect, the less they deserve it. What's pathetic is that the movie halfway wants its hero to serve as a role model, but neither the hero nor the movie is prepared to walk the walk.

The rap singer Pras, of the Fugees, stars as Diamond, who dreams of becoming a superstar and spends hours in the studio, fine-tuning his tracks with small help from his cokehead mixer. Diamond's best friend is Gage (the rap singer Ja Rule), who finances the studio time by working as a runner for the drug dealer Mr. B (Jason Stratham). Diamond helps on deliveries, including one in the opening scene that leads to a shoot-out with a Chinese gang.

Dead bodies litter the screen, but there is not one word in the rest of the movie about whether Diamond and Gage are wanted by the police for questioning in the matter of perhaps a dozen deaths. By the end of the film, the two of them have killed, oh, I dunno, maybe six or eight other guys, but when we see the words "One Year Later" on-screen at the end, it is not to show Pras in prison but simply to share some sad nostalgia with him.

The movie is very seriously confused in its objectives, as if two or three story approaches are fighting for time on the same screen. Gage is an uncomplicated character—a sniveling weakling with a big gun who murders in cold blood. Diamond is more of a puzzle. He is loyal to Gage, and yet demurs at some of his buddy's activities ("She's pregnant," he protests, when Gage wants to kill a cleaning woman who witnessed one of their massacres). He seems to accept Gage's lowlife atrocities as the price of getting his studio time paid for and not having to actually work for a living.

The stuff involving Gage, Mr. B, and the significantly named music executive Mr. White is standard drug-rap-ghetto-crime thriller material. But when Diamond's mother dies and his homeless, long-missing father (Vondie Curtis-Hall) turns up, another movie tries to get started. The father explains he abandoned his wife and son because he put his music first, and that was the start of his downfall. Now he sees his son doing the same thing. What he doesn't know is that Diamond has a pregnant girlfriend (Tamala Jones), and won't even give her his cell phone number because that's the first step on the long slide to enslavement by a woman.

Diamond's father listens to his demo tracks and abruptly drops a loud and clear message of music criticism into the movie: "Your music is too processed. You grew up on digitized music—you think that keyboard sample sounds like a real piano." Then his dad takes him to the American Conservatory of Music and plays classical music for him on a grand piano that apparently stands ready in a large empty space for the convenience of such visitors, and later tries to talk Diamond out of going along with Gage on a dangerous drug run.

Well, Diamond doesn't much want to go anyway. He keeps talking about how Gage should chill, and how he wants to get out of the drug and gun lifestyle, and how he loves his woman and wants to be a father to his unborn child, but he never really makes any of those hard decisions. It never occurs to him that he is living off of Gage's drug-soaked earnings—that his studio sessions are paid for by the exploitation of the very people he thinks his songs are about. He can't act on his qualms, I guess, because the movie needs him for the action scenes. *Turn It Up* says one thing and does another; Diamond frets and whines, while the movie lays on gunfire, torture, and bloodshed (the scene where Mr. B offers to run Gage's face through a meat slicer is memorable).

My guess is that Vondie Curtis-Hall had substantial input on his scenes, which have a different tone and sounder values than the rest of the movie. His advice to his son is good, and his performance is the best thing in the movie. But *Turn It Up* doesn't deserve it. Here is a film that goes out of its way to portray all the bad guys as white or Chinese, and doesn't have the nerve to point out that the heroes' worst enemies are themselves.

20 Dates ½★

R, 88 m., 1999

Myles Berkowitz (Himself), Richard Arlook (His Agent), Tia Carrere (Herself), Elisabeth Wagner (Elisabeth), Robert McKee (Himself). Directed by Myles Berkowitz and produced by Elie Samaha, Jason Villard, and Mark McGarry. Screenplay by Berkowitz.

20 Dates tells the story of Myles Berkowitz, a man who wants to make a film and to fall in love. These areas are his "two greatest failures, professional and personal," so he decides to make a film about going out on twenty dates. By the end of the film he has won the love of the lovely Elisabeth—maybe—but his professional life is obviously still a failure.

The film has the obnoxious tone of a boring home movie narrated by a guy shouting in your ear. We learn how he gets a $60,000 investment from a man named Elie Samaha and uses it to hire a cameraman and a soundman to follow him around on his dates. Elie is never seen on film, but is taped with an (allegedly) hidden recorder while he threatens Berkowitz, complains about the quality of the footage, and insists on sex, stars—and a scene with Tia Carrere.

Elie has a point. Even though $60,000 is a low budget, you can't exactly see the money up there on the screen. I've seen features shot for half as much that were more impressive.

What's worse is that Berkowitz loses our trust early in the film and never regains it. I don't know how much of this film is real, if any of it is. Some scenes are admittedly staged, and others feel that way.

Even though Berkowitz presumably displays himself in his best light, I couldn't find a moment when he said anything of charm or interest to one of his dates. He's surprised when one woman is offended to learn she's being photographed with a hidden camera, and when another one delivers an (unseen) hand wound that requires twenty stitches. The movie's best dialogue is: "I could have sworn that Karen and I had fallen in love. And now, it's never to be, because I couldn't ever get close to her—at least not closer than ninety feet, which was specified in the restraining order."

One of his dates, Stephanie, is a Hollywood wardrobe mistress. He asks her for free costumes for his movie (if it's a documentary, why does it need costumes?). She leaves for the rest room, "and I never saw her again." Distraught, he consults Robert McKee, a writing teacher, and McKee gives him theories about screen romance, which are irrelevant, of course, to an allegedly true-life documentary.

And what about Elie? He sounds unpleasant, vulgar, and tasteless (although no more so than many Hollywood producers). But why are we shown the outside of the county jail during his last conversation? Is he inside? What for? He promises to supply Tia Carrere, who indeed turns up in the film, describing Elie as a "very good friend." She may want to change her number.

There's a 1996 film available on video named *Me and My Matchmaker*, by Mark Wexler, about a filmmaker who consults a matchmaker and goes on dates, which he films himself. It is incomparably more entertaining, funny, professional, absorbing, honest, revealing, surprising, and convincing than *20 Dates*. It works wonderfully to demonstrate just how incompetent and annoying *20 Dates* really is.

28 Days ★ ★ ★
PG-13, 103 m., 2000

Sandra Bullock (Gwen Cummings), Viggo Mortensen (Eddie Boone), Dominic West (Jasper), Elizabeth Perkins (Lily), Azura Skye (Andrea), Steve Buscemi (Cornell), Alan Tudyk (Gerhardt), Michael O'Malley (Oliver), Reni Santoni (Daniel). Directed by Betty Thomas and produced by Jenno Topping. Screenplay by Susannah Grant.

Every drunk considers himself a special case, unique, an exception to the rules. Odd, since for the practicing alcoholic, daily life is mostly unchanging, an attempt to negotiate daily responsibilities while drinking enough but not too much. When this attempt fails, as it often does, it results in events that the drunk thinks make him colorful. True variety comes only with sobriety. Plus, now he can remember it.

This is the lesson learned by Gwen Cummings, the character played by Sandra Bullock in *28 Days*. As the story opens, her life is either wild and crazy, or confused and sad, depending on where you stand. She parties all night with her boyfriend Jasper (Dominic West). After the clubs, the drinks, the designer drugs, they commence what may turn out to be sex, if they can stay awake long enough. Then a candle starts a fire, which they extinguish with champagne. What a ball.

In the morning, Gwen's day begins with a pass at the refrigerator so smooth and practiced she hardly seems to even open it while extracting a cold beer. Gwen is an accident waiting to happen—to herself, or innocent bystanders. Her victim is her sister Lily (Elizabeth Perkins). "Gwen, you make it impossible to love you," Lily says when she arrives late at the church for Lily's wedding. At the reception, Gwen delivers an insulting toast, knocks over the cake while dancing, steals a limousine to go buy another cake, and crashes it into a house. Not a good day.

Cut to Serenity Glen, where Gwen has been sentenced to twenty-eight days of rehab in lieu of jail time. The PA system makes a running commentary out of *M*A*S*H*-style announcements. The patients do a lot of peppy group singing (too much, if you ask me). "I don't have a health problem," Gwen protests. "I play Ultimate Frisbee twice a week." The patients include the usual cuckoo's nest of colorful characters, although they're a little more plausible than in most inmate populations. We meet Daniel (Reni Santoni), a doctor who pumped his own stomach to control his drinking, and wound up giving himself an emergency tracheotomy. Gerhardt (Alan Tudyk), prissy and critical, a dancer and coke addict. And Andrea (Azura Skye), Gwen's teenage roommate.

Gwen's counselor is Cornell, played by Steve Buscemi, who inspires a grin when we see him in a movie, because he's usually good for strange scenes and dialogue. Not this time; he plays the role straight, revealing toughness and a certain weary experience, as if all of Gwen's cherished kookiness is for him a very, very old joke. There's a nice scene where she says exactly the wrong things to him before discovering he's her counselor.

Another fellow patient is Eddie Boone (Viggo Mortensen), a baseball pitcher with a substance abuse problem. Of course they begin a tentative, unstated courtship. Of course Jasper, on weekend visits, misunderstands ("Where are all the celebrities?" he asks on his first arrival, looking around for Elizabeth Taylor). Of course there is a fight. This subplot is predictable, but made perceptive because Gwen and Eddie illustrate the lifeboat mentality in which sailors on the ship of rehab have only each other to cling to.

The movie was written by Susannah Grant, who also wrote Julia Roberts's hit film *Erin Brockovich*. I differed with *Erin* for the same reason I like *28 Days*: The tone of the central character. I found that Roberts, enormously likable though she is, upstaged the material in *Erin Brockovich* by unwise costume choices and scenes that were too obviously intended as showcases. Bullock brings a kind of ground-level vulnerability to *28 Days* that doesn't make her into a victim but simply into one more suitable case for treatment. Bullock, like Roberts, is likable, but in *28 Days* at least that's not the point.

Note: 28 Days *is rated* PG-13 *and might be effective as a cautionary tale for teenagers.*

The 24-Hour Woman ★ ★ ★
R, 95 m., 1999

Rosie Perez (Grace Santos), Marianne Jean-Baptiste (Madeline Labelle), Patti LuPone (Joan Marshall), Karen Duffy (Margo Lynn), Diego Serrano (Eddie Diaz), Wendell Pierce (Roy Labelle), Melissa Leo (Dr. Suzanne Pincus). Directed by Nancy Savoca and produced by Richard Guay, Larry Meistrich, and Peter Newman. Screenplay by Savoca and Guay.

The look in Grace's eyes is hard to describe as she watches her daughter, Daisy, take her first steps, and no wonder: She's seeing it on video. She missed her daughter's first birthday and the first steps because she was arrested trying to jump over a subway turnstile with a birthday present. And she yelled at the cop because she was so frustrated after a crazy day at work and then the struggle to find the toy, one of those overnight sensations that inspires buying panics at Toys-R-Us.

Grace, played at top speed by Rosie Perez, is a TV producer just finishing her first year as a working mom. She's at the end of her rope. First came the surprise news that she was pregnant. Then her husband, the host of the show, announced her pregnancy on TV. Then the executive producer (Patti LuPone) found out she's expected to deliver in November: "During sweeps!" Then the show made her pregnancy a ratings-winner on cable, and it got picked up by a network. Meanwhile Grace has been running herself ragged, trying to keep up.

Her mom smiles at Grace's faith that she can be a mother and hold a full-time job: "I remember when you were born. I was gonna write my novel while you slept." But Grace tries to juggle both lives, although hiring a nanny is an alarming experience: "So far all we've met are Nazi nurses and emotionally disturbed women with no skills." To balance her experience, there's the case of her new assistant, Madeline (Marianne Jean-Baptiste), who is returning to the workforce after taking time out for a family, and whose husband (Wendell Pierce) is playing househusband, not without grumbles.

The 24-Hour Woman is a message picture wrapped inside a screwball comedy, with a touch of satire aimed at TV talk shows. It doesn't all work, but it happens so fast we don't get stuck in the awkward parts. Rosie Perez's Grace is the engine that pulls the story with so much energy she seems to vibrate. Some will see her character as exaggerated.

Not me. She's half-Brooklynite and half–TV producer, and from what I've seen of both species, hyperactivity is built in.

The only person on the show more driven than Grace is the Patti LuPone character, who has true tunnel vision and cares only about ratings and programming gimmicks (one of her segment titles: "Romancing the Stone: How to Kick-Start Your Man's Love Machine"). The message of the movie is that new mothers who want to work are pretty much on their own. They get more lip service than real help from their husbands, and fellow females at work are running too hard to pause for sisterhood. "Take your baby and go home," Joan shouts at her at one point. "I got a show to do here."

The movie's not an idealized *Ms.* magazine vision of a working mom breast-feeding between conference calls. Its message is more Darwinian: Motherhood releases powerful drives in a woman, which are good for her children but bad for her career. No matter how hard Grace tries, she can't get rid of the guilt when she's not with her baby. And the other people in her life, who do not share these mother's instincts, simply do not care as much, or at all.

The movie was directed and cowritten by Nancy Savoca, who in three earlier films also considered social institutions through a woman's eyes. Her *True Love* (1989) was about a bride who suddenly understood that she was being sacrificed on the altar of her family's expectations. Her *Dogfight* (1991) was about a woman who discovers she has been asked out on a date as part of a contest—four guys on their way to Vietnam are trying to see who can pick up the homeliest girl. And *Household Saints* (1993) was about a grandmother who was a devout Catholic, a mother and a husband who had drifted into secular ways, and a granddaughter who literally wanted to be a saint. Behavior that would have seemed admirable to the grandmother seemed like insanity to the mother.

Now comes *The 24-Hour Woman,* which one imagines contains some of Savoca's own experiences. Her casting of Rosie Perez is a good one, because Perez is the most grounded of actors; you can't find the slightest hint of theory or conceit in her performances, which seem founded on total identification with the character. She isn't a "working woman" or a "Puerto Rican yuppie" but simply Grace Santos, with her marriage, her kid, and her job. She doesn't have time for abstractions. This isn't the kind of movie that would make a working woman think twice about having a child. It would make her think twice about having a job. And if that's reactionary, then tough luck: What's a mom going to do when little Lily starts crying and only one person can comfort her?

Twice Upon a Yesterday ★ ½
R, 92 m., 1999

Lena Headey (Sylvia Weld), Douglas Henshall (Victor Bukowski), Penelope Cruz (Louise), Gustavo Salmeron (Rafael), Mark Strong (Dave Summers), Eusebio Lazaro (Don Miguel), Charlotte Coleman (Alison Hayes), Elizabeth McGovern (Diane). Directed by Maria Ripoll and produced by Juan Gordon. Screenplay by Rafa Russo.

Twice Upon a Yesterday has the kind of title that promises you'll hate the movie, and in this case the movie doesn't disappoint. It's a tedious contrivance about a messy drunk who is given a second chance in life, only to discover that life has a grudge against him both times. The story gives us a London actor named Victor (Douglas Henshall), who breaks up with his girlfriend, Sylvia (Lena Headey), telling her he loves someone else. Then his new love wears thin and he discovers he loves Sylvia after all—too late, because she's moved on with her life.

Enter a fairy godmother–type figure, a barmaid played by Elizabeth McGovern, who steers him toward a couple of trash collectors who are meant to remind us of Don Quixote and Sancho Panza. They show him, in a trash bin, all of the parts of his life he has thrown away, and give him another chance—reeling the thread of time backward so that he can retrieve his fatal mistake with Sylvia.

But hold on a second. Movies like this are always blinded by their concern for the hero and *his* all-important second chance. What about Sylvia? Breaking up with Victor was the best thing that's ever happened to her, we feel—after having spent more time with him than we really want to, even if it is his movie. When he says, "I don't know where I am in time," how can we be sure he's confused by the plot machinations and not merely sloshed?

Victor is a bore who's smashed most of the time, and if the great wheels of the universe revolve to give him a second chance, is there no hope for the Sylvias? Are women simply a plot convenience for the hero? I ask even though the film was directed by a woman, Maria Ripoll. She should have known better.

Movies come in cycles, governed by some occult law of synchronicity, and recently there have been several movies about alternatives in time, with the characters trying first one and then another set of decisions. Divergent time lines figured in *Groundhog Day,* with Bill Murray living the same day until he got it right. Gwyneth Paltrow, in *Sliding Doors,* was snared in alternate time lines, romance, and adultery. The new German film *Run Lola Run* plays the same twenty minutes three different ways. And now here's poor Victor, stumbling into the past to try to repair the wreckage of his life.

Much depends, in these films, on whether we care for the hero. If we like him, we wish him well. Victor is not likable. There is, however, a character we like quite a lot: Louise (Penelope Cruz), who mysteriously replaces McGovern as the barmaid, and whom Victor falls in love with. I must not reveal too much about the plot—including exactly when, and why, this romance takes place—but trust me, if we wanted Victor to find happiness, it would be a lot easier to forgive him for finding it again and again.

Twin Falls Idaho ★ ★ ★ ★

R, 105 m., 1999

Mark Polish (Blake Falls), Michael Polish (Francis Falls), Michele Hicks (Penny), Lesley Ann Warren (Francine), Patrick Bauchau (Miles), Jon Gries (Jay), Garrett Morris (Jesus), William Katt (Surgeon). Directed by Michael Polish and produced by Marshall Persinger, Rena Ronson, and Steven J. Wolfe. Screenplay by Mark Polish and Michael Polish.

In a hotel like this, we feel, anything could happen. There is a certain kind of fleabag, with a barren lobby and a strange elevator operator, which has developed in the movies as a mythic backdrop for private eyes, addicts, crooks on the lam, would-be novelists—anyone who needs to hide out on a budget.

Twin Falls Idaho opens with a hooker being dropped off in front the Hotel Idaho and knocking on a room door, which is opened a crack to reveal a sad and solemn face. The room is occupied, we learn, by the Falls brothers, Blake and Francis, who are joined at the hip and share one leg. It is their birthday, and Francis has ordered her as a gift for his brother—and therefore possibly for himself, we speculate, our minds working out how many genitals might accompany three legs.

The hooker, whose name is Penny (Michele Hicks), flees when she understands the situation. She has to return because she has forgotten her purse, and this time she gets drawn into the world of Blake and Francis (played by identical twins Mark and Michael Polish). They aren't angry at her for leaving, just as they didn't seem much aroused by her arrival. Sex, we guess, may be something they have little experience of; this birthday present may have been more of a gesture, an act of defiance. Where did the twins come from? What is their story?

Penny has walked in on a scene making it clear that Francis is sick. She knows a doctor who will make a house call, she tells them, unless he wants his wife to find out about her. Miles (the urbane and yet somehow ominous actor Patrick Bauchau) arrives, and we learn that Francis has a weak heart. Blake's heart is keeping them both alive, but that may not last for long, and then they will both die—or Francis will, leaving Blake with a loneliness so profound, after the life they have led, that he can scarcely imagine it. (He tells Penny he has never been alone, except for the moment before he goes to sleep and the first moment after he wakes up.)

Twin Falls Idaho was written by the Polish brothers and directed by Michael. It is one of those films not much interested in plot but fascinated by what it is like to be somebody, or two somebodies. The movie doesn't depend on special effects to create a shared body (except for one shot that's not especially convincing), and instead uses the performances. Mark and Michael Polish seem constantly to be confiding in one another, and indeed when you spend your life within inches of another person's ear, you learn to murmur. We can imagine their lifetime of isolation from the normal things people do, and there is a heartbreaking dream shot toward the end of the film, just showing two boys riding bicycles.

Soon it is Halloween, and Penny (who is a prostitute by desperation, not through career choice) takes the brothers to a costume party. This could, of course, be the occasion for bad jokes, but it inspires her empathy: "Show some compassion. This is the one night of the entire year when they're both normal." Gradually we get glimpses of where they came from. We meet their enigmatic mother (Lesley Ann Warren). We hear a little of their story. We learn that they may have checked into the hotel to die. Hicks is gentle, tender, and sad with them, setting the film's tone (although there is also room for irony and even some laughter).

I have a special feeling for movies that want to forget about plot and conflict, and spend their time instead in regarding particular lives. Like π or *Happiness*, this film is a meditation on the situation of its characters. There's no payoff, no answer, no solution, no resolution, because how can there be? You are who you are, and life either goes on or it doesn't. The key bond in the film seems to be between the brothers, but then we realize their bond is given, not chosen, and so doesn't mean as much as the bond between the two of them and Penny. Her business is to minister to the lonely and the needy, and these two boys make her feel so helpless that her own solitude is exposed. In its quiet, dark, claustrophobic way, this is one of the best films of 1999.

Two Family House ★ ★ ★ ½
R, 104 m., 2000

Michael Rispoli (Buddy Visalo), Kelly Macdonald (Mary O'Neary), Katherine Narducci (Estelle Visalo), Kevin Conway (Jim O'Neary), Matt Servitto (Chipmunk), Michele Santopietro (Laura), Louis Guss (Donato), Rosemary DeAngelis (Marie). Directed by Raymond De Felitta and produced by Anne Harrison and Alan Klingenstein. Screenplay by De Felitta.

There really was an Uncle Buddy, and he really did finally open his own bar on Staten Island, and sing on Saturday nights to the customers. *Two Family House* vibrates with the energy of his presence. You can sense that real things are at risk, that Buddy really did finally break out of the jail of his life, that everyone in the old neighborhood thought he was insane, that only now can we look back and see that Buddy was a kind of hero.

As the movie opens, Buddy Visalo (Michael Rispoli) is in the navy and sings in a talent show. He's an Italian-American crooner, and Arthur Godfrey hears him and offers him an audition. But his fiancée, Estelle, won't let him go. She finds the idea "embarrassing," she says. Eventually Godfrey hires Julius LaRosa as his crooner, and it eats away inside Buddy that the job might have been his.

Estelle is played by Katherine Narducci, who like Rispoli is familiar from *The Sopranos*. Estelle is the kind of woman who grows taller by standing on the back of her husband's dreams. Buddy wants to open his own bar. "Serving drinks to a lot of bums?" Estelle sneers. "You want to turn me into a barmaid?" She wants them to stay back "where we belong, not making fools of ourselves, not having everybody laugh behind our backs." She would gladly send Buddy out into the world to a soul-crushing job for the rest of his life rather than let him take a chance.

Now this is where the story gets interesting, and begins to accumulate the elements of family legend. Buddy buys a two-family house, planning to turn the downstairs into Buddy's Bar and rent the upstairs for income. He discovers he already has upstairs tenants: an Irish-American boozer named Jim O'Neary (Kevin Conway) and his considerably younger wife, named Mary (Kelly Macdonald), who is pregnant. There is an added detail: Her baby will be half-black. Who the father is we are not sure. Why the father is not Jim we can figure out just by looking at him: He is one of those drunks who give alcoholics a bad name.

Now all the pieces are in place for a story that must have been heard many times in many versions by Raymond De Felitta, Buddy's nephew, who wrote and directed this film. To some members of the family, Buddy was no doubt a lunatic loser. To others, who perhaps kept their opinions to themselves at family gatherings, he was a nice guy who was trying to do the right thing.

What with one thing and another, Buddy

619

breaks loose from Estelle and decides to help this Mary O'Neary and her baby. Angelo, the guy who runs the bar down the street, thinks he's crazy: "You see that guy," he asks his regulars. "He threw his whole life away." But the narrator of the film, whose identity is revealed at the end, sees it differently: "It remains an undisputed fact that every man has one moment of total selflessness in his life."

What makes *Two Family House* such a touching and effective film is that every one of Buddy's decisions is made as a direct response to the situation in front of him. He is not particularly fond of African-Americans (indeed, knows almost none). He does not approve of adultery. At one point, after they have a fight, he evicts Mary, only to find her another place to live. He is no bleeding-heart liberal, but he confesses to her: "I thought it was kinda brave, keeping the kid." He helps her out because he is touched by her situation, and can see she is a good person. One night when he turns up late at her place, she thinks he's after sex, but "No, that ain't why—I just want to talk with someone."

I can imagine this movie as an uplifting parable, but it wouldn't be as convincing and it wouldn't have the moment-to-moment fascination of Buddy's journey. The movie's ideas and values are completely contained in its action. Nobody makes any big speeches. Buddy just does what a decent guy would do.

Michael Rispoli gets one of the roles of a lifetime. Buddy's the kind of guy we all know, who is unwilling to accept the hand that life (or his wife) had dealt him. His victory may be small in the great scheme of things, but it is satisfying. When everyone told him he was throwing his life away, did he dream that someday his nephew would make this movie, in which he comes across as, well, kind of a hero?

Two Family House opened in Chicago on the same day as *Pay It Forward*, which is a feel-good valentine for the audience. *Pay It Forward* is quite happy to have big speeches, little speeches, and earnest expressions of belief about its message, which is that if we do a good turn and someone "pays it forward" instead of paying it back, what a wonderful world this would be. *Two Family House* is about a guy doing someone a good turn when she

needs it. It doesn't need the uplifting apparatus of *Pay It Forward*. It may not be as commercial, but I suspect it may strike deeper in the hearts of its viewers.

200 Cigarettes ½ ★
R, 97 m., 1999

Ben Affleck (Bartender), Casey Affleck (Tom), Janeane Garofalo (Ellie), Courtney Love (Lucy), Gaby Hoffmann (Stephie), Kate Hudson (Cindy), Martha Plimpton (Monica), Paul Rudd (Kevin), Guillermo Diaz (Dave), Brian McCardie (Eric), Christina Ricci (Val), Jay Mohr (Jack), Angela Featherstone (Caitlyn). Directed by Risa Bramon Garcia and produced by Betsy Beers, David Gale, and Van Toffler. Screenplay by Shana Larsen.

All those cigarettes, and nobody knows how to smoke. Everybody in *200 Cigarettes* smokes nearly all the time, but none of them show any style or flair with their cigarettes. And the cinematographer doesn't know how to light smoke so it looks great.

He should have studied *Out of the Past* (1947), the greatest cigarette-smoking movie of all time. The trick, as demonstrated by Jacques Tourneur and his cameraman, Nicholas Musuraca, is to throw a lot of light into the empty space where the characters are going to exhale. When they do, they produce great white clouds of smoke, which express their moods, their personalities, and their energy levels. There were guns in *Out of the Past*, but the real hostility came when Robert Mitchum and Kirk Douglas smoked at each other.

The cast of *200 Cigarettes* reads like a roll call of hot talent. They're the kinds of young stars who are on lots of magazine covers and have Web pages devoted to them, and so they know they will live forever and are immune to the diseases of smoking. I wish them well. But if they must smoke in the movies, can't they at least be great smokers, like my mother was? When she was smoking you always knew exactly how she felt because of the way she used her cigarette and her hands and the smoke itself as a prop to help her express herself. She should have been good; she learned from Bette Davis movies.

The stars of *200 Cigarettes*, on the other

hand, belong to the suck-and-blow school of smokeology. They inhale, not too deeply, and exhale, not too convincingly, and they squint in their close-ups while smoke curls up from below the screen. Their smoke emerges as small, pale, noxious gray clouds. When Robert Mitchum exhaled at a guy, the guy ducked out of the way.

I suppose there will be someone who counts the cigarettes in *200 Cigarettes* to see if there are actually 200. That will at least be something to do during the movie, which is a lame and labored conceit about an assortment of would-be colorful characters on their way to a New Year's Eve party in 1981. Onto the pyre of this dreadful film are thrown the talents of such as Ben Affleck, Casey Affleck, Janeane Garofalo, Courtney Love, Gaby Hoffmann, Kate Hudson, Martha Plimpton, Paul Rudd, Guillermo Diaz, Brian McCardie, Jay Mohr, Christina Ricci, Angela Featherstone, and others equally unlucky.

Ricci and Love have the kinds of self-contained personalities that hew out living space for their characters no matter where they find themselves, but the others are pretty much lost. The witless screenplay provides its characters with aimless dialogue and meaningless confrontations, and they are dressed not like people who might have been alive in 1981, but like people going to a costume party where 1981 is the theme. (There is not a single reason, by the way, why the plot requires the film to be set in 1981 or any other year.)

Seeing a film like this helps you to realize that actors are empty vessels waiting to be filled with characters and dialogue. As people, they are no doubt much smarter and funnier than the cretins in this film. I am reminded of Gene Siskel's bottom-line test for a film: "Is this movie more entertaining than a documentary of the same people having lunch?" Here they are contained by small ideas and arch dialogue, and lack the juice of life. Maybe another 200 cigarettes would have helped; coughing would be better than some of this dialogue.

Two Women ★ ★ ★ ½
NO MPAA RATING, 96 m., 2000

Niki Karimi (Fereshteh), Marila Zare'i (Roya), Mohammad Reza Forutan (The Stalker). Directed by Tahmineh Milani. Screenplay by Milani.

She is a brilliant student who seems to be leading her own life in the Tehran of the early 1980s. Then the madness of men reaches out and swats her down. Her story is told in *Two Women,* an angry and heartbreaking film, made in Iran by a woman, about a patriarchal society that puts cruel limits on the freedom of women to lead independent lives.

Fereshteh is from a provincial town, and it is to her father's credit that he allows her to attend university, since he believes her proper place is at home, married, giving him grandchildren. In Tehran she excels in a "man's" field, sciences, and loves the heady freedom of books, classrooms, campus life, and her friends.

Perhaps it is her very air of freedom that attracts the strange young man on the motorbike, who begins to stalk her. Fereshteh's spirit has not been broken, and that both attracts and appalls him. He is an erotomaniac able to think of nothing but this woman. He makes advances bordering on assault. He sees her frequently with a young man, her cousin, and thinks it is her boyfriend. One day, after she has rejected his advances, the man on the motorbike speeds up and throws acid at the cousin.

There is a court case, but it is almost beside the point. She has disgraced her family. How? By being involved in a scandal that calls attention to her status as an independent woman. There is almost the thought that it must have been her own fault, to so inflame a man that he would make an acid attack. Fereshteh's father pulls her out of school, makes her return to their small town, and forces an arranged marriage with a man in his forties who is no worse than most of the men of his age and class in the town—which is to say, a man totally incapable of understanding her needs and rights.

Two Women deals in the details of daily life in postrevolutionary Iran: in the unspoken ways that a woman's duties, her clothing, her behavior, who she speaks to, what she says, all express her servitude in a male-dominated society. Her husband is a pathetic creature whose self-esteem seems to depend largely on his ability to limit and control her. When she behaves with any independence, he feels like a cowboy who has been thrown by his horse: His duty, obviously, is to beat and train her until she becomes a docile beast.

The movie expresses powerful currents in Iranian society. It was directed by Tahmineh Milani, whose films have made her a symbol of hope among feminists in Iran—although, really, why would one need to be a feminist to believe women should be as free as men? Her film steps carefully. It makes no overt or specific criticisms of Iranian laws or politics; it focuses on Fereshteh's life and plight, and we are left to draw our own larger conclusions.

I met Milani and her husband, Mohammed, an architect, at the Calcutta Film Festival in November 1999, and was struck by how hopeful she seemed about the currents of change in her homeland, which until a generation ago was one of the more progressive societies in the Middle East. And indeed, recent election results show an overwhelming sentiment for modernizing Iran once again, and moderating the stern rule of the fundamentalist clerics.

At every film festival I attend, I hear that the new Iranian cinema is the most exciting in the world. Films like this are evidence of it. So is a new Iranian children's film named *The Color of Paradise*, about a small blind boy, very bright, who is taken out of school and apprenticed to a blind carpenter—because the boy's father, a widower, feels a blind son will be a liability in the marriage market. These films tell very specific human stories, but their buried message is clear: They swim through the waters of a rigid patriarchy that fears change and distrusts women. The extra beat of anger, throbbing beneath the surface, gives them a transforming energy.

U

U-571 ★ ★
PG-13, 115 m., 2000

Matthew McConaughey (Tyler), Bill Paxton (Dahlgren), Harvey Keitel (Chief), Jon Bon Jovi (Emmett), David Keith (Coonan), Thomas Kretschmann (Wassner), Jake Weber (Hirsch), Jack Noseworthy (Wentz). Directed by Jonathan Mostow and produced by Dino De Laurentiis and Martha De Laurentiis. Screenplay by Mostow, Sam Montgomery, and David Ayer.

U-571 is a clever windup toy of a movie, almost a trailer for a video game. Compared to *Das Boot* or *The Hunt for Red October,* it's thin soup. The characters are perfunctory, the action is recycled straight out of standard submarine formulas, and there is one shot where a man is supposed to be drowning and you can just about see he's standing on the bottom of the studio water tank.

To some degree movies like this always work, at least on a dumb action level. The German destroyer is overhead dropping depth charges, and the crew waits in hushed suspense while the underwater explosions grow nearer. We're all sweating along with them. But hold on a minute. We saw the Nazis rolling the depth charges overboard, and they were evenly spaced. As the first ones explode at a distance, there are several seconds between each one. Then they get closer. And when the charges are right on top of the sub, they explode one right after another, like a string of firecrackers—dozens of them, as leaks spring and water gushes in and lights blink and the surround sound rocks the theater.

At a moment like this, I shouldn't be thinking about the special effects. But I am. They call attention to themselves. They say the filmmakers have made a conscious decision to abandon plausibility and put on a show for the kids. And make no mistake: This is a movie for action-oriented kids. *Das Boot* and *The Hunt for Red October* were about military professionals whose personalities were crucial to the plot. The story of *U-571* is the flimsiest excuse for a fabricated action payoff. Submarine

service veterans in the audience are going to be laughing their heads off.

Matthew McConaughey stars as Tyler, an ambitious young man who thinks he's ready for his first command. Not so fast, says Captain Dahlgren (Bill Paxton). He didn't recommend his second-in-command because he thinks he's not ready yet: not prepared, for example, to sacrifice the lives of some men to save others, or the mission. This info is imparted at one of those obligatory movie dance parties at which all the navy guys look handsome in white dress uniform, just before they get an emergency call back to the boat.

The mission: A German U-boat is disabled in the mid-Atlantic. On board is the secret Enigma machine, used to cipher messages. The unbreakable Enigma code allows the Nazis to control the shipping lanes. The mission of Dahlgren, Tyler, and their men: Disguise their U.S. sub as a Nazi vessel, get to the other sub before the German rescuers can, impersonate Germans, capture the sub with a boarding party, grab Enigma, and sink the sub so the rescuers won't suspect what happened.

"But we're not marine fighting men," protests one of the sailors. "Neither is the other crew," says a marine on board, who has conveyed these instructions. "And I'll train your men." Uh-huh. In less than a week? There are no scenes of training, and I'm not sure what happened to the marine.

The details of the confrontation with the Nazi sub I will not reveal. Of course it goes without saying that Tyler gets a chance to take command and see if he has what it takes to sacrifice lives in order to save his men and his mission, etc. If you remember the vivid personalities of the sub crews in *Das Boot* and *Red October,* you're going to be keenly aware that no one in this movie seems like much of an individual. When they do have dialogue, it's functional, spare, and aimed at the plot. Even Harvey Keitel, as the Chief, is reduced to barking out declarative sentences.

The crew members seem awfully young, awfully green, awfully fearful, and so headstrong they border on mutiny. There's a scene where the (disguised) U.S. sub is checked out by a German reconnaissance plane, and a young sailor on the bridge panics. He's sure the plane is going to strafe them, and orders the man on the deck machine gun to fire at it. His superior officer orders the gunner to stand fast. The kid screams "Fire! Fire!" As the plane comes closer, the officer and the kid are both shouting their orders at the gunner. Without actually consulting navy regulations, my best guess is, that kid should be court-martialed.

You can enjoy *U-571* as a big, dumb war movie without a brain in its head. But that doesn't stop it from looking cheesy. Producers Dino and Martha De Laurentiis and director Jonathan Mostow *(Breakdown)* have counted on fast action to distract from the plausibility of most of the scenes at sea (especially shots of the raft boarding party). Inside the sub, they have the usual clichés: The sub dives to beyond its rated depth, metal plates creak, and bolt heads fire loose under the pressure.

U-571 can't be blamed for one story element that's standard in all sub movies: The subs can be hammered, battered, shelled, depth-bombed, and squeezed by pressure, and have leaks, fires, shattered gauges, ruptures, broken air hoses, weak batteries, and inoperable diesel engines—but in the heat of action, everything more or less somehow works. Better than the screenplay, anyway.

In case you're wondering, the German sub on display at the Museum of Science and Industry in Chicago is *U-505*, and it was boarded and captured not by submariners, but by sailors from the USS *Pillsbury,* part of the escort group of the carrier USS *Guadalcanal.* No Enigma machine was involved. That was in 1944. An Enigma machine was obtained on May 9, 1941, when HMS *Bulldog* captured *U-110.* On August 23, 1941, *U-570* was captured by HMS planes and ships, without Enigma. This fictional movie about a fictional U.S. submarine mission is followed by a mention in the end credits of those actual British missions. Oh, the British deciphered the Enigma code too. Come to think of it, they pretty much did everything in real life that the Americans do in this movie.

Unbreakable ★ ★ ★
PG-13, 107 m., 2000

Bruce Willis (David Dunne), Samuel L. Jackson (Elijah Price), Robin Wright (Megan Dunne), Spencer Treat Clark (Jeremy Dunne), John Patrick Amedori (Hostage Boy), Joe Perillo (Jenkins), Sean Oliver (Police Officer), Jose L. Rodriguez (Truck Driver). Directed by M. Night Shyamalan and produced by Barry Mendel, Sam Mercer, and Shyamalan. Screenplay by Shyamalan.

At the center of *Unbreakable* is a simple question: "How many days of your life have you been sick?" David Dunne, a security guard played by Bruce Willis, doesn't know the answer. He is barely speaking to his wife, Megan (Robin Wright), but like all men he figures she remembers his life better than he does. She tells him she can't remember him ever being sick, not even a day. They have this conversation shortly after he has been in a train wreck that killed everybody else on board, but left him without a scratch. Now isn't that strange.

The question originally came to him in an unsigned note. He finds the man who sent it. This is Elijah Price (Samuel L. Jackson), who runs a high-end comic-book store with a priceless stock of first editions. Elijah has been sick a lot of days in his life. He even had broken bones when he emerged from the womb. He has spent a long time looking for an unbreakable man, and his logic is plain: "If there is someone like me in the world, shouldn't there be someone at the other end of the spectrum?"

Unbreakable, the new film by M. Night Shyamalan, is in its own way as quietly intriguing as his *The Sixth Sense.* It doesn't involve special effects and stunts, much of it is puzzling and introspective, and most of the action takes place during conversations. If the earlier film seemed mysteriously low-key until an ending that came like an electric jolt, this one is more fascinating along the way, although the ending is not quite satisfactory. In both films Shyamalan trusts the audience to pay attention and makes use of Bruce Willis's everyman quality, so that we get drawn into the character instead of being distracted by the surface.

The Jackson character is not an everyman.

Far from it. He is quietly menacing, formidably intelligent, and uses a facade of sophistication and knowledge to conceal anger that runs deep: He is enraged that his bones break, that his body betrays him, that he was injured so often in grade school that the kids called him "Mr. Glass." Why does he want to find his opposite, an unbreakable man? The question lurks beneath every scene.

This story could have been simplified into a—well, into the plot of one of Elijah Price's old comic books. Shyamalan does a more interesting thing. He tells it with observant everyday realism; he's like Stephen King, dealing in the supernatural and yet alert to the same human details as mainstream writers. How interesting, for example, that the Robin Wright character is not simply one more bystander wife in a thriller, but a real woman in a marriage that seems to have run out of love. How interesting that when her husband is spared in a crash that kills everyone else, she bravely decides this may be their opportunity to try one last time to save the marriage. How interesting that David Dunne's relationship with his son is so strong, and that the boy is taken along for crucial scenes like the first meeting of David and Elijah.

In *Psycho*, Hitchcock made us think the story was about the Janet Leigh character, and then killed her off a third of the way into the film. No one gets killed early in *Unbreakable*, but Shyamalan is skilled at misdirection: He involves us in the private life of the comic dealer, in the job and marriage problems of the security guard, in stories of wives and mothers. The true subject of the film is well guarded, although always in plain view, and until the end we don't know what to hope for, or fear. In that way it's like *The Sixth Sense*.

There is a theory in Hollywood these days that audiences have shorter attention spans and must be distracted by nonstop comic-book action. Ironic that a movie about a student of comic-book universes would require attention and patience on the part of the audience. Moviegoers grateful for the slow unfolding of *The Sixth Sense* will like this one too.

The actors give performances you would expect in serious dramas. Jackson is not afraid to play a man it is hard to like—a bitter man, whose intelligence only adds irony to anger.

Willis, so often the centerpiece of brainless action movies, reminds us again that he can be a subtle actor, as muted and mysterious as actors we expect that sort of thing from—John Malkovich or William Hurt, for example. If this movie were about nothing else, it would be a full portrait of a man in crisis at work and at home.

I mentioned the ending. I was not quite sold on it. It seemed a little arbitrary, as if Shyamalan plucked it out of the air and tried to make it fit. To be sure, there are hints along the way about the direction the story may take, and maybe this movie, like *The Sixth Sense,* will play even better the second time— once you know where it's going. Even if the ending doesn't entirely succeed, it doesn't cheat, and it comes at the end of an uncommonly absorbing movie. ☞

Up at the Villa ★ ★ ★
PG-13, 115 m., 2000

Kristin Scott Thomas (Mary Panton), Sean Penn (Rowley Flint), Anne Bancroft (Princess San Ferdinando), James Fox (Sir Edgar Swift), Jeremy Davies (Karl Richter), Derek Jacobi ("Lucky" Leadbetter), Massimo Ghini (Beppino Leopardi), Dudley Sutton (Harold Atkinson). Directed by Philip Haas and produced by Geoff Stier. Screenplay by Belinda Haas from the novella by W. Somerset Maugham.

Does anyone read Somerset Maugham anymore? From the 1920s to the 1950s he was the most respected "popular" novelist in the world, or the most popular "respected" novelist (the praise was always tempered with quotation marks). He traveled the world to the haunts of British expatriates; his stories, whether set in Singapore or Italy, often dealt with the choice between prudent and passionate romance. He knew his characters; he had a deep knowledge of shallow people.

Philip Haas's *Up at the Villa* is based on Maugham's novella about a group of British expats in Florence, enjoying their last days of mannered sloth before the outbreak of World War II. It is not the same story that Franco Zeffirelli told in his 1999 movie *Tea With Mussolini,* but his characters and these characters would have known each other by name.

The villa of the title is occupied by a temporary guest, Mary Panton (Kristin Scott Thomas), a pretty widow in her mid-thirties. Her husband drank up and gambled away their money and himself. Now she depends on the kindness of friends. An old friend named Sir Edgar Swift (James Fox) has just journeyed over from Cannes to propose marriage to her. He is tall, slender, will not see sixty again, and has manners that make you want to sit very still. Soon he will be named governor of Bengal; Mary would become the first lady of British society in Calcutta. Mary's adviser on this possibility is the Principessa San Ferdinando (Anne Bancroft), who has a town house, thanks to a rich Italian husband, now dead, "so ugly he frightened the horses."

Sir Edgar's is an attractive offer to Mary. She asks time to think it over. She doesn't love Sir Edgar—but what, asks the princess, does love have to do with it? In a frank heart-to-heart, the princess explains that she married for security and took lovers for entertainment, although sex, she sighs, supplies you in old age with neither the fond memories nor the security of wealth. Once, says the princess (Bancroft delivering this confidence at the end of a virtuoso monologue as they walk in the garden), she made love recklessly for a single night with a risky young man, just for the fun of it.

At the princess's table in a restaurant that night, Mary is seated next to a brash, rich American named Rowley Flint (Sean Penn). He is married, separated, bold. He wants to spend the night with her. She likes him, but says no. He responds insolently, she slaps him and dumps him, and on the way home picks up a pathetic little unshaven violinist she saw in the restaurant. He is Karl Richter (Jeremy Davies), an Austrian refugee from Hitler. She takes pity on him and brings him into her bed, where, inspired by the princess's story, she gives him such a night to remember that she is still wearing her pearls in the morning.

Now the plot develops surprises. A hint or two: Mary turns to Rowley to help her out of a fix. The local Fascist Party chief (Massimo Ghini) threatens legal action against Rowley. Mary is prepared to betray a confidence of the princess to help Rowley. And then Sir Edgar returns for his answer. "I have some things I must tell you," she says, and the camera moves outside on the lawn and we see them through a window as they talk. In my notes I wrote: "She's got a lot of 'splaining to do."

This whole movie is about manners. There is sex and violence, but the movie is not about giving in to them; it's about carrying on as if they didn't exist—as if the part of you that was involved was a distant relation who will not be asked back again very soon. Kristin Scott Thomas is smashing, as Mary Panton would say. She is a woman with no financial means, who must decide between loveless security and insecure love. She has to jump fast; she will be thrown out of the villa and declared an enemy alien any day now. Yet . . . Mary has character. The whole movie leads up to, and savors, exactly what she tells Sir Edgar, and exactly what he tells her, and then, after they both think about what they have been told, what they tell each other. It is an exquisite verbal minuet; modern psychobabble would shred their conversational elegance like a madman with a machete.

It is not necessary to have manners to appreciate them, but you must at least understand why other people would want to have them. That is the case with the wild card in the cast, "Lucky" Leadbetter (Derek Jacobi), an old queen with his hair and beard dyed ginger. He looks so uncannily like the satanic dancing man in the nightclub scene in *La Dolce Vita* that I'll bet Jacobi showed the movie to his barber. "Lucky" is not essential to the story but knows all the characters and where, and why, the skeletons are buried, and he will make all of this into a story someday. Like Maugham.

Urban Legends: Final Cut ★ ★
R, 94 m., 2000

Jennifer Morrison (Amy Mayfield), Matthew Davis (Travis/Trevor), Hart Bochner (Professor Solomon), Loretta Devine (Reese), Joseph Lawrence (Graham), Anson Mount (Toby), Eva Mendes (Vanessa), Jessica Cauffiel (Sandra), Marco Hofschneider (Simon), Anthony Anderson (Stan), Michael Bacall (Dirk). Directed by John Ottman and produced by Neal H. Moritz, Gina Matthews, and Richard Luke Rothschild. Screenplay by Paul Harris Boardman and Scott Derrickson.

Amy: *The winner is basically guaranteed a chance at directing in Hollywood.*

Trevor: *Do you think that somebody would kill for that?*

You betcha. *Urban Legends: Final Cut* takes place at a film school where the best senior thesis film wins the Hitchcock Prize—a $15,000 stipend and a shot at the big time. As students start dropping like flies, it becomes clear that a mad slasher is on the loose, and eventually a kid figures out they were all involved in making the same film. Amy (Jennifer Morrison) screens the film, which is lousy, and then notices a splice before the end credits. "Did somebody change the credits on Travis's film?" his brother Trevor (Matthew Davis) asks. "No," she says portentously. "Somebody changed the film on Travis's credits."

Find out who stole the film and you'll have your killer, in a thriller that (like *Scream 3*) is about the making of a movie. The movie is set at the Orson Welles Film Center of Alpine University, so named although no mountains are ever seen (it was shot at Trent University in Peterborough, Ontario).

Some of these students should repeat freshman year. "You stole my (bleeping) genre!" shouts Toby, before walking off of Amy's film, blissfully unaware that although almost anything can be stolen from another movie, its genre is in the public domain. Toby (Anson Mount) was going to be the director of photography. He's replaced by Simon (Marco Hofschneider), who is also none too canny in the ways of the film world. He walks onto a set just as the first assistant says, "Speed!" This is usually the word before "Action!" but Simon interrupts with a loud, "Excuse me!" Talking when the camera is rolling is usually reserved for the actors, something you want your D.P. to know.

Amy's idea for a film: A serial killer commits a series of crimes based on urban legends. This is what happened in the original *Urban Legend* (1998), but in *Final Cut* there aren't many urban legend killings because the filmmakers are killed instead. An exception: One girl wakes up in an ice-filled bathtub with her kidney missing, leading to a great line from the 911 operator. "I just woke up in an ice-filled bathtub!" the victim gasps. "Don't tell me—your kidney's gone," says the operator.

The film was directed by John Ottman, who also coedited and wrote the music. He has a good command of the genre, and carefully inserts the It's Only a Dream scene, the It's Only a Bird scene, the It's Only a Movie scene, and the Talking Killer scene. The killer has to talk a lot, because he needs to explain motives and rationales that are none too evident until he spells them out. This leads to an inventive comic riff on the basic Tarantinesque Mexican-standoff scene, in which there are more guns than are really practical.

Urban Legends: Final Cut has slick production credits and performances that are quite adequate given the (narrow) opportunities of the genre. It makes the fatal mistake, however, of believing there is still life in the wheezy serial-killer-on-campus formula, and spends way too much time playing horror sequences straight when laughs might have been more bearable. I don't know if you're tired of terrified girls racing through shadowy basements pursued by masked slashers while the sound track pulses with variations on the *Halloween* theme, but I am. Real tired. This time the killer wears a fencing mask, and at the end no one even thinks to say, "Touche!"

V

Varsity Blues ★ ★
R, 100 m., 1999

James Van Der Beek (Mox), Jon Voight (Coach Kilmer), Paul Walker (Lance Harbor), Ron Lester (Billy Bob), Scott Caan (Tweeder), Richard Lineback (Joe Harbor), Tiffany C. Love (Collette Harbor), Amy Smart (Julie Harbor). Directed by Brian Robbins and produced by Tova Laiter, Mike Tollin, and Robbins. Screenplay by W. Peter Iliff.

Varsity Blues is not your average sports movie. It brings an outsider viewpoint to the material, which involves a Texas high school quarterback who would rather win an academic scholarship than play football. The character, named Mox and played by James Van Der Beek of TV's *Dawson's Creek*, is a good kid—so good that at one point he asks himself why he's always being so good—and although the movie contains *Animal House*–style gross-outs, it doesn't applaud them.

The central struggle is between Mox and Coach Kilmer (Jon Voight, in another of a group of striking recent performances). Kilmer is a close-cropped martinet who addresses pep rallies with a vaguely Hitlerian salute, and has won two state titles and twenty-two district championships in thirty years. Now he wants the twenty-third, at any cost.

The movie takes place in a west Texas town not unlike the setting of *The Last Picture Show*, although the kids get away with even more these days. (When one steals a squad car and drives around town with his buddies and their girlfriends, all naked, that merely inspires some "boys will be boys" talk at the local diner.) Some plot elements are hard to believe (could a high school teacher get away with stripping at a nearby topless club?), but others, including the way players are injected with painkillers before a big game, feel truthful.

The movie was directed by Brian Robbins, who made the high-spirited *Good Burger* (1997), and here again we see the impulses of a satirist winking from behind the constraints of a genre. I enjoyed, for example, the subplot involving Mox's kid brother, the religion-obsessed Kyle, who makes his first entrance with a crucifix strapped to his back and by the end of the film has founded a cult with his playmates. Maybe his spirituality is inherited; their father asks Mox, "Did you pray for more playing time?"

The arc of the movie involves one football season, during which Coach Kilmer will or will not win his twenty-third title. Of course it ends with a Big Game and a Big Play, with seconds on the clock, but this is a movie that doesn't buy into all the tenets of our national sports religion; the subtext is that winning *isn't* everything.

One of Mox's friends is the enormous Billy Bob (Ron Lester), whose breakfast consists of pancakes chased down with syrup swigged straight from the bottle. Without revealing what happens to him, I will express my gratitude to Robbins and his writer, W. Peter Iliff, for not marching lockstep down the well-traveled road of inevitable developments. I also enjoyed the relationship between Mox and Lance (Paul Walker), the starting quarterback; instead of making Lance into the obligatory jerk, the movie pays more attention. To the standard role of the town sexpot, Tiffany C. Love brings a certain poignancy; she always goes for the starting quarterback, but she's not a slut so much as a realist.

All of this sounds as if *Varsity Blues* is a good movie, and parts of it are, but the parts never quite come together. Scenes work, but they don't pile up and build momentum. Van Der Beek is convincing and likable, Voight's performance has a kind of doomed grandeur, and the characters are seen with quirky humor. (When Billy Bob gets knocked cold during a game, for example, and the trainer asks him how many fingers he's holding up, Mox explains, "With Billy Bob, you gotta go true or false. Billy Bob, is he holding up fingers? Yes or no?") The movie doesn't quite get over the top, but you sense that Brian Robbins has the right instincts, and is ready to break loose for a touchdown.

The Velocity of Gary ★ ★
R, 100 m., 1999

Thomas Jane (Gary), Vincent D'Onofrio (Valentino), Salma Hayek (Mary Carmen),

Olivia d'Abo (Veronica), Chad Lindberg (Kid Joey). Directed by Dan Ireland and produced by Dan Lupovitz. Screenplay by James Still.

The Velocity of Gary proves once again that it's less interesting to see unconventional people express traditional values than to see conventional people express untraditional values.

Movies about the sexual underground seem compelled to show their rebels bonding together into symbolic families; their characters may seen bizarre, but at heart they express profoundly conservative social values. I'm more intrigued by films like *Happiness* and *In the Company of Men*. It's more fun to see conventional characters break the rules than for outlaws to follow them.

The Velocity of Gary (subtitled *Not His Real Name*) chronicles the world of Times Square male hustlers, porno stars, drag queens, and doughnut shop waitresses. All of these people are, of course, touchingly good-hearted, smiling through bad times. Vincent D'Onofrio stars, as Valentino, a well-known porn actor whose worsening illness (never named) causes his two lovers to join in making them all a home. The lovers are the hustler Gary (Thomas Jane) and the waitress Mary Carmen (Salma Hayek), and also in the picture is the deaf drag queen Kid Joey (Chad Lindberg), who mimes to the songs of Patsy Cline—not easy when you can't hear them.

All of these characters are engaging in a conventional sort of way, although their behavior seems generated less by their lives than by the demands of the screenplay. Consider an early scene where Gary, bare to the waist, soaks himself at a fire hydrant and then stalks off into the city. Hydrants can be refreshing on a hot day, and this makes a great shot, but would a homeless man lightly contemplate hours in wet jeans and squelchy shoes? No matter; soon he's rescued Kid Joey from gay-bashers, carrying the Kid off in his arms like John Wayne with Natalie Wood in *The Searchers*.

The director is Dan Ireland, who also worked with D'Onofrio in *The Whole Wide World*, the 1997 film about pulp writer Robert E. Howard. That one, about a man who sat in his room in Texas and wrote about Conan the Barbarian, was quietly, sadly gripping. In *The Velocity of Gary*, there is never quite the feeling that these people occupy a real world; their colorful exteriors are like costumes, and inside are simply actors following instructions.

Vertical Limit ★ ★ ★
PG-13, 126 m., 2000

Chris O'Donnell (Peter Garrett), Bill Paxton (Elliot Vaughn), Robin Tunney (Annie Garrett), Nicholas Lea (Tom McLaren), Scott Glenn (Montgomery Wick), Izabella Scorupco (Monique Aubertine), Temuera Morrison (Major Rasul), Stuart Wilson (Royce Garrett), Augie Davis (Aziz), Roshan Seth (Colonel Amir Salim). Directed by Martin Campbell and produced by Lloyd Phillips, Robert King, and Campbell. Screenplay by King and Terry Hayes.

Somebody, I think it was me, was observing the other day that Hollywood never really stopped making B pictures; they simply gave them $100 million budgets and marketed them as A pictures. *Vertical Limit* is an example: It's made from obvious formulas and pulp-novel conflicts, but strongly acted and well crafted. The movie may be compared with *The Perfect Storm*, another adventure about humans challenging the implacable forces of nature. One difference is that *Storm* portrays the egos and misjudgments of its characters honestly, and makes them pay for their mistakes, while *Vertical Limit* chugs happily toward one of those endings where everyone gets exactly what they deserve, in one way or another, except for a few expendable supporting characters.

It's a danger signal whenever a movie brings nitroglycerine into the plot. Nitro has appeared in good films like *The Wages of Fear* and *Sorcerer*, but even there it exhibits its most peculiar quality, which is that it invariably detonates precisely in synch with the requirements of the plot.

Vertical Limit introduces nitro into a situation where three climbers are trapped in an ice cave near the top of K-2. They are a venal millionaire ("This is a life statement for me"), an experienced guide, and the hero's sister. The hero gathers a group of six volunteers on a possibly suicidal rescue mission. They bring along nitro, and although I know that explosives are used from time to time on mountains to jar loose avalanches, the movie never explains how an uncontrollable nitro explosion has the potential to help the trapped victims more than harm them. The one scene where nitro is used as intended does nothing to answer the question.

The rest of the time, the nitro is necessary to endanger the rescue party, to provide suspense, to shock us with unintended explosions, and to dispose of minor characters so there won't be anything but speaking parts left for the climax. The nitro serves as evidence that *Vertical Limit* is not so much a sincere movie about the dangers and codes of mountain climbing as a thriller with lots of snow. At that, however, it is pretty good, and I can recommend the movie as a B adventure while wondering what kind of an A movie might have been made from similar material.

Chris O'Donnell stars as Peter Garrett, a *National Geographic* photographer. He and his sister Annie (Robin Tunney) are shown with their father in the opening title sequence, which ends with Peter cutting a rope that sends his father falling to his death but spares himself and Annie. Otherwise three lives might have, or would have, been lost. Peter and Annie disagree about this, although the legendary toeless mountaineer Montgomery Wick (Scott Glenn) tells Peter he did the right thing, and it follows as the night follows day that someone in the movie will reprise that final decision sooner or later.

Annie, a famous climber, is trapped on the mountain with the millionaire Elliot Vaughn (Bill Paxton) and Tom McLaren (Nicholas Lea), an ace guide. Vaughn owns an airline, and his dream is to stand on the summit of K-2 at the moment one of his inaugural flights zooms overhead. This involves an ascent in risky climbing weather, and a crucial error when McLaren thinks they should turn back and is overruled by the headstrong Vaughn.

Mountain climbing always inspires the same nightmare for me: I am falling from a great height, and cursing myself all the way down for being stupid enough to have climbed all the way up there voluntarily. I've seen climbing documentaries in which climbers do amazing things, although none quite so amazing as some of the stunts in *Vertical Limit*. The blend of stunt work and effects is seamless,

and there's real suspense as they edge out of tight spots, even if occasionally we want to shout advice at the screen. (In one scene, a climber is hanging by an arm over the edge of a cliff, and another climber walks up to the edge, which is at a fearsome angle, while untethered. In another, a climber anchors her ice-ax *way* too close to the edge.)

One effective sequence shows the six rescuers being landed at 22,000 feet by a risky helicopter drop. Others show the suddenness with which things can go wrong. There are the absolute deadlines imposed by the reality of the mountain (after climbers dehydrate, they die). And strong performances, particularly by Glenn as the hard-bitten climber with a private agenda. *Vertical Limit* delivers with efficiency and craft, and there are times, when the characters are dangling over a drop of a mile, when we don't even mind how it's manipulating us.

The Virgin Suicides ★ ★ ★ ½
R, 97 m., 2000

James Woods (Mr. Lisbon), Kathleen Turner (Mrs. Lisbon), Kirsten Dunst (Lux Lisbon), Josh Harnett (Trip Fontaine), Hanna Hall (Cecilia Lisbon), Chelsea Swain (Bonnie Lisbon), A. J. Cook (Mary Lisbon), Leslie Hayman (Therese Lisbon), Danny DeVito (Dr. Horniker). Directed by Sofia Coppola and produced by Francis Ford Coppola, Julie Costanzo, Dan Halsted, and Chris Hanley. Screenplay by Sofia Coppola, based on the novel by Jeffrey Eugenides.

It is not important how the Lisbon sisters looked. What is important is how the teenage boys in the neighborhood thought they looked. There is a time in the adolescent season of every boy when a particular girl seems to have materialized in his dreams with backlighting from heaven. Sofia Coppola's *The Virgin Suicides* is narrated by an adult who speaks for "we"—for all the boys in a Michigan suburban neighborhood twenty-five years ago, who loved and lusted after the Lisbon girls. We know from the title and the opening words that the girls killed themselves. Most of the reviews have focused on the girls. They miss the other subject—the gawky, insecure yearning of the boys.

The movie is as much about those guys, "we," as about the Lisbon girls. About how Trip Fontaine (Josh Harnett), the leader of the pack, loses his baby fat and shoots up into a junior stud who is blindsided by sex and beauty, and dazzled by Lux Lisbon (Kirsten Dunst), who of the perfect Lisbon girls is the most perfect. In every class there is one couple that has sex while the others are still talking about it, and Trip and Lux make love on the night of the big dance. But that is not the point. The point is that she wakes up the next morning, alone, in the middle of the football field. And the point is that Trip, as the adult narrator, remembers not only that "she was the still point of the turning world then" and "most people never taste that kind of love" but also, "I liked her a lot. But out there on the football field, it was different."

Yes, it was. It was the end of adolescence and the beginning of a lifetime of compromises, disenchantments, and real things. First sex is ideal only in legend. In life it attaches plumbing, fluids, gropings, fumblings, and pain to what was only an hour ago a platonic ideal. Trip left Lux not because he was a pig, but because he was a boy, and broken with grief at the loss of his—their—dream. And when the Lisbon girls kill themselves, do not blame their deaths on their weird parents. Mourn for the passing of everyone you knew and everyone you were in the last summer before sex. Mourn for the idealism of inexperience.

The Virgin Suicides provides perfunctory reasons why the Lisbon girls might have been unhappy. Their mother (Kathleen Turner) is a hysteric so rattled by her daughters' blooming sexuality that she adds cloth to their prom dresses until they appear in "four identical sacks." Their father (James Woods) is the well-meaning but emasculated high school math teacher who ends up chatting about photosynthesis with his plants. These parents look gruesome to us. All parents look gruesome to kids, and all of their attempts at discipline seem unreasonable. The teenage years of the Lisbon girls are no better or worse than most teenage years. This is not the story of daughters driven to their deaths.

The story it most reminds me of, indeed, is *Picnic at Hanging Rock* (1975), about a party of young girls, not unlike the Lisbon sisters in appearance and sexual experience, who go for a school outing one day and disappear into the wilderness, never to be seen again. Were they captured? Killed in a fall? Trapped somehow? Bitten by snakes? Simply lost in the maze of nature? What happened to them is not the point. Their disappearance is the point. One moment they were smiling and bowing in their white dresses in the sun, and the next they were gone forever. The lack of any explanation is the whole point: For those left behind, they are preserved forever in the perfection they possessed when they were last seen.

The Virgin Suicides is Sofia Coppola's first film, based on the much-discussed novel by Jeffrey Eugenides. She has the courage to play it in a minor key. She doesn't hammer home ideas and interpretations. She is content with the air of mystery and loss that hangs in the air like bitter poignancy. Tolstoy said all happy families are the same. Yes, but he should have added, there are hardly any happy families.

To live in a family group with walls around it is unnatural for a species that evolved in tribes and villages. What would work itself out in the give-and-take of a community gets grotesque when allowed to fester in the hothouse of a single-family home. A mild-mannered teacher and a strong-willed woman turn into a paralyzed captive and a harridan. Their daughters see themselves as captives of these parents, who hysterically project their own failure upon the children. The worship the girls receive from the neighborhood boys confuses them: If they are perfect, why are they seen as such flawed and dangerous creatures? And then the reality of sex, too young, peels back the innocent idealism and reveals its secret engine, which is animal and brutal, lustful and contemptuous.

In a way, the Lisbon girls and the neighborhood boys never existed, except in their own adolescent imaginations. They were imaginary creatures, waiting for the dream to end through death or adulthood. "Cecilia was the first to go," the narrator tells us right at the beginning. We see her talking to a psychiatrist after she tries to slash her wrists. "You're not even old enough to know how hard life gets," he tells her. "Obviously, doctor," she says, "you've never been a thirteen-year-old girl." No, but his profession and every adult life is to some degree a search for the happiness she does not even know she has.

Virus ★
R, 96 m., 1999

Jamie Lee Curtis (Kit Foster), William Baldwin (Steve Baker), Donald Sutherland (Captain Everton), Joanna Pacula (Nadia), Marshall Bell (J. W. Woods Jr.), Julio Oscar Mechoso (Squeaky), Sherman Augustus (Richie), Cliff Curtis (Hiko). Directed by John Bruno and produced by Gale Anne Hurd. Written by Chuck Pfarrer and Dennis Feldman, based on the Dark Horse Comic Book Series *Virus* by Chuck Pfarrer.

Ever notice how movies come in twos? It's as if the same idea descends upon several Hollywood producers at once, perhaps because someone who hates movies is sticking pins in his dolls. *Virus* is more or less the same movie as *Deep Rising*, which opened a year earlier. Both begin with small boats in the Pacific. Both boats come upon giant floating ships that are seemingly deserted. Both giant ships are inhabited by a vicious monster. Both movies send the heroes racing around the ship trying to destroy the monster. Both movies also have lots of knee-deep water, fierce storms, Spielbergian visible flashlight beams cutting through the gloom, and red digital readouts.

Deep Rising was one of the worst movies of 1998. *Virus* is easily worse. It didn't help that the print I saw was so underlit that often I could see hardly anything on the screen. Was that because the movie was filmed that way, or because the projector bulb was dimmed to extend its life span? I don't know and in a way I don't care, because to see this movie more clearly would not be to like it better.

Virus opens with berserk tugboat captain Donald Sutherland and his crew towing a barge through a typhoon. The barge is sinking and the crew, led by Jamie Lee Curtis and William Baldwin, want to cut it loose. But the barge represents the skipper's net worth, and he'd rather go to the bottom with it. This sequence is necessary to set up the skipper's avarice.

In the eye of the storm, the tug comes upon a drifting Russian satellite communications ship. In the movie's opening credits, we have already seen what happened to the ship: A drifting space cloud enveloped the *Mir* space station and sent a bolt of energy down to the ship's satellite dish, and apparently the energy included a virus that takes over the onboard computers and represents a vast, if never clearly defined, threat to life on Earth.

Sutherland wants to claim the ship for salvage. The crew board it and soon are fighting the virus. "The ship's steering itself!" one character cries. The chilling answer: "Ships don't steer themselves." Uh, oh. The methods of the virus are strange. It creates robots, and uses them to grab crew members and turn them into strange creatures that are half-man, half–Radio Shack. It's up to Curtis, Baldwin, and their crewmates to outsmart the virus, which seems none too bright and spends most of its time clomping around and issuing threatening statements with a basso profundo voice synthesizer.

The movie's special effects are not exactly slick, and the creature itself is a distinct letdown. It looks like a very tall humanoid figure hammered together out of crushed auto parts, with several headlights for its eyes. It crunches through steel bulkheads and crushes all barriers to its progress, but is this an efficient way for a virus to behave? It could be cruising the Internet instead of doing a Robocop number.

The last half-hour of the movie is almost unseeable. In dark dimness, various human and other figures race around in a lot of water and flashlight beams, and there is much screaming. Occasionally an eye, a limb, or a bloody face emerges from the gloom. Many instructions are shouted. If you can explain to me the exact function of that rocket tube that turns up at the end, I will be sincerely grateful. If you can explain how anyone could survive that function, I will be amazed. The last shot is an homage to *The African Queen,* a movie I earnestly recommend instead of this one.

The Visit ★ ★ ★
R, 107 m., 2001

Hill Harper (Alex Waters), Obba Babatunde (Tony Waters), Rae Dawn Chong (Felicia McDonald), Billy Dee Williams (Henry Waters), Marla Gibbs (Lois Waters), Phylicia Rashad (Dr. Coles), Talia Shire (Marilyn Coffey), David

Clennon (Bill Brenner). Directed and produced by Jordan Walker-Pearlman. Screenplay by Walker-Pearlman, based on the play by Kosmond Russell.

The Visit tells the story of a thirty-two-year-old prison inmate, up for parole, dying of AIDS, trying to come to terms with his past. In a series of prison visits with his parents, his brother, a prison psychiatrist, and a woman who was his childhood friend, he moves slowly from anger to acceptance—he becomes a better person.

This outline sounds perhaps too pious to be absorbing, and the final scenes lay on the message a little thick. But *The Visit* contains some effective performances, not least from Hill Harper as Alex, the hero. I remembered him from *Loving Jezebel* and from a supporting role in *He Got Game*, but wasn't prepared for the depth here; this performance announcing Harper is to be taken seriously. Another surprise comes from Billy Dee Williams; we think of him as a traditional leading man, but here he is as a proud, angry, unyielding father—an authority figure who takes it as a personal affront that his son has gone wrong.

But has he gone wrong? Alex is doing twenty-five years for a rape he says he didn't commit. His mother (Marla Gibbs) believes him. His father remembers that Alex stole from them, lied to them, was a junkie and a thief, and thinks him capable of anything. Alex's brother Tony (Obba Babatunde), well dressed, successful, mirrors the father's attitudes; it diminishes them to have a prisoner in the family.

The movie doesn't crank up the volume with violence and jailhouse clichés, but focuses on this person and his possibilities for change. The key law enforcement officials are not sadistic guards or authoritarian wardens, but people who listen. Phylicia Rashad plays the psychiatrist, trying to lead him past denial into acceptance, and there are several scenes involving a parole board that are driven by insight, not the requirements of the drama. The board members, led by Talia Shire, discuss his case, express their doubts, get mad at one another, seem real.

Rae Dawn Chong plays Felicia, the old friend, who has her own demons; a former addict and a prostitute, she killed an abusive father, but now has her life together and visits Alex at the urging of Tony (it's perceptive of the movie to notice how reluctant family members often recruit volunteers to do their emotional heavylifting). Her story and other conversations trigger flashbacks and fantasies, in a story that has enormous empathy for this man at the end of a lost life. (The screenplay by director Jordan Walker-Pearlman is from a play by Kosmond Russell, based on his relationship with a brother in prison.)

Watching the movie, I was reminded of a powerful moment in *The Shawshank Redemption*, when the Morgan Freeman character, paroled as an old man, is asked if he has reformed. He says such words have no meaning. He is no longer the same person who committed the crime. He would give anything, he says, to grab that young punk he once was and shake some sense into him. *The Visit* is about the same process—the fact that the prisoner we see is not the same person who was convicted. If, that is, he is lucky enough to grow and change. The last act of *The Visit* hurries that process too much, but the journey is worth taking.

W

Waking the Dead ★ ★ ½
R, 105 m., 2000

Billy Crudup (Fielding Pierce), Jennifer Connelly (Sarah Williams), Janet McTeer (Caroline Pierce), Molly Parker (Juliet Beck), Sandra Oh (Kim), Hal Holbrook (Isaac Green), Lawrence Dane (Governor Kinosis), Paul Hipp (Danny Pierce). Directed by Keith Gordon and produced by Gordon, Stuart Kleinman, and Linda Reisman. Screenplay by Gordon and Robert Dillon, based on the novel by Scott Spencer.

There is a mystery in *Waking the Dead,* and at the end we are supplied with its answer, but I have seen the movie twice and do not know for sure what the answer is. There are two possibilities. Either would do. If it were a thriller or a ghost story, it wouldn't much matter, but the film has serious romantic and political themes, and in one way or another we really need to know, or it's all been a meaningless game.

The film begins in 1982, with a young politician named Fielding Pierce (Billy Crudup) who learns on the news that his friend Sarah Williams (Jennifer Connelly) has been killed by a car bomb attack in Minneapolis. She was working with a group of political activists opposed to U.S. actions in Chile. Fielding screams out in anguish, and we flash back to his first meeting with Sarah, in 1972, when she was his brother's secretary. The brother publishes a magazine very like *Rolling Stone.* Fielding is in the Coast Guard to avoid service in Vietnam. Sarah is self-confident, outspoken, political.

The film, based on the novel by Scott Spencer, is a tug-of-war between Fielding's desire to work within the system and Sarah's conviction that it's rotten to the core. As they grow closer romantically, they grow further apart politically, until finally their love is like a sacrifice thrown on the bonfire of their ambitions. There comes a time at a fund-raising benefit when Sarah tells off a fat-cat who has written a column supporting the military junta in Chile. That is not good for Fielding's career.

The film does a lot of flashing back and forth between 1972, when Fielding's life is simple and idealistic, and 1982, when he is in the hands of Chicago political fixers. Hal Holbrook is assigned once again to the Hal Holbrook Role, which he has won so often it should be retired: He has to sit in the shadows of a boardroom or a private club, smoke a cigar, drink a brandy, and pull strings behind the scenes. He is the go-between for Fielding and Governor Kinosis (Lawrence Dane), who offers Fielding a shot at a safe congressional seat.

Fielding wants it. Sarah sees it as the selling of his soul. As the two of them ride the L together, Jennifer Connelly has a strong and bitter scene in which she explains exactly what he is doing and why it is wrong. They're drifting apart, and Fielding resents the presence in her life of a gimlet-eyed radical priest. We see her meeting with Chilean refugees. She leaves for Chile to bring some more out. Then she dies in the car bombing.

Or does she? The film toys with us, and with Fielding, who begins to imagine he sees Sarah here and there—on the street, in a crowd. There is one almost subliminal shot in which her face flashes on a TV screen, just as he turns away. Did he see it? Or was it in his imagination? Or did he not see it? And in that case, since we saw it, was it the first shot of the next story on the news, or a subtle hint that this movie has something in common with *Ghost?*

To speculate would be to give away the ending—which I can't do anyway, since I'm not sure of it. What I do know is that *Waking the Dead* has a good heart and some fine performances, but is too muddled at the story level to involve us emotionally. It's a sweet film. The relationship between Sarah and Fielding is a little deeper and more affectionate than we expect in plot-driven melodramas.

There are fuzzy spots; we never find out anything specific about Sarah's political activism, we never see the Chicago pols actually trying to influence Fielding in an inappropriate way, and we never know exactly what role the Catholic Church plays, except to lend its cinematic images and locations. I was amused when another critic pointed out that, to save money perhaps, the moviemakers show Fielding savoring his political victory all alone by himself.

Oscar nominee Janet McTeer plays Fielding's sister, in the kind of role every actress hopes she can escape from by getting an Oscar nomination. Paul Hipp plays his Jann Wennerish brother, who falls in love with a Korean hooker (Sandra Oh) he meets in a massage parlor, and tries to convince Fielding to pull strings so she can get her green card. This entire subplot should have been excised swiftly and mercilessly. And at the end, we are left with—what? When we invest emotional capital, we deserve a payoff.

A Walk on the Moon ★ ★
R, 106 m., 1999

Diane Lane (Pearl Kantrowitz), Viggo Mortensen (Walker Jerome), Liev Schreiber (Marty Kantrowitz), Anna Paquin (Alison Kantrowitz), Tovah Feldshuh (Lilian Kantrowitz), Bobby Boriello (Daniel Kantrowitz). Directed by Tony Goldwyn and produced by Dustin Hoffman, Goldwyn, Jay Cohen, Neil Koenigsberg, Lee Gottsegen, and Murray Schisgal. Screenplay by Pamela Gray.

"Sometimes I just wish I was a whole other person," says Pearl Kantrowitz, who is the subject, if not precisely the heroine, of *A Walk on the Moon*. It is the summer of 1969, and Pearl and her husband, Marty, have taken a bungalow in a Catskills resort. Pearl spends the week with their teenage daughter, their younger son, and her mother-in-law. Marty drives up from the city on the weekends.

The summer of 1969 is, of course, the summer of Woodstock, which is being held nearby. And Pearl (Diane Lane), who was married at a very early age to the only man she ever slept with, feels trapped in the stodgy domesticity of the resort—where wives and families are aired while the man labors in town. She doesn't know it, but she's ripe for the Blouse Man (Viggo Mortensen).

The Blouse Man drives a truck from resort to resort. It opens out into a retail store, offering marked-down prices on blouses and accessories. Funny, but he doesn't look like a Blouse Man: With his long hair and chiseled features, he looks more like a cross between a hippie

and the hero on the cover of a paperback romance. He senses quickly that Pearl is shopping for more than blouses, and offers her a free tie-dyed T-shirt and his phone number. The T-shirt is crucial, symbolizing a time when women of Pearl's age were in the throes of the Sexual Revolution. Soon Pearl is using the phone number. "I wonder," she asks the Blouse Man, "if you had plans for watching the moon walk?"

A Walk on the Moon is one small step for the Blouse Man, a giant leap for Pearl Kantrowitz. In the arms of the Blouse Man, she experiences sexual passion and a taste of freedom, and soon they're skinny-dipping just like the hippies at Woodstock. The festival indeed exudes a siren call, and Pearl, like a teenage girl slipping out of the house for a concert, finally sneaks off to attend it with the Blouse Man. Marty (Liev Schreiber), meanwhile, is stuck in the Woodstock traffic jam. And their daughter, Alison (Anna Paquin), who has gotten her period and her first boyfriend more or less simultaneously, is at Woodstock, too—where she sees her mother.

The movie is a memory of a time and place now largely gone (these days Pearl and Marty would be more likely to take the family to Disney World or Hawaii). It evokes the heady feelings of 1969, when rock was mistaken for revolution. To be near Woodstock and in heat with a long-haired god, but not be able to go there, is a Dantean punishment. But the movie also has thoughts about the nature of freedom and responsibility. "Do you think you're the only one whose dreams didn't come true?" asks Marty, whose early marriage meant he became a TV repairman instead of a college graduate.

Watching the gathering clouds over the marriage, Pearl's mother-in-law, Lilian (Tovah Feldshuh), sees all and understands much. If Pearl is not an entirely sympathetic character, Lilian Kantrowitz is a saint. She calls her son to warn him of trouble, she watches silently as Pearl defiantly leaves the house, and perhaps she understands Pearl's fear of being trapped in a life lived as an accessory to a man.

So the underlying strength of the story is there. Unfortunately, the casting and some of the romantic scenes sabotage it. Liev Schreiber is a good actor and I have admired him in many movies, but put him beside Viggo Mortensen and the Blouse Man wins; you can hardly blame Pearl for surrendering. (I am reminded of a TV news interview about that movie where Demi Moore was offered $1 million to sleep with Robert Redford. "Would you sleep with Robert Redford for a million dollars?" a woman in a mall was asked. She replied: "I'd sleep with him for 50 cents.")

The movie's problem is that it loads the casting in a way that tilts the movie in the direction of a Harlequin romance. Mortensen looks like one of those long-haired, bare-chested, muscular buccaneers on the covers of the paperbacks; all he needs is a Gothic tower behind him, with one light in a window. The movie exhibits almost unseemly haste in speeding Pearl and the Blouse Man toward love-making, and then lingers over their sex scenes as if they were an end in themselves, and not a transgression in a larger story. As Pearl and the Blouse Man cavort naked under a waterfall, the movie forgets its ethical questions and becomes soft-core lust.

Then, alas, there is the reckoning. We know sooner or later there will be anger and recrimination, self-revelation and confession, acceptance and resolve, wasp attacks and rescues. We've enjoyed those sex scenes, and now, like Pearl, we have to pay. Somewhere in the midst of the dramaturgy is a fine performance by Anna Paquin (from *The Piano*) as a teenage girl struggling with new ideas and raging hormones. Everytime I saw her character on screen, I thought: There's the real story.

The War Zone ★ ★ ★ ★

NO MPAA RATING, 99 m., 2000

Ray Winstone (Dad), Tilda Swinton (Mum), Lara Belmont (Jessie), Freddie Cunliffe (Tom), Colin J. Farrell (Nick), Aisling O'Sullivan (Carol), Kate Ashfield (Lucy). Directed by Tim Roth and produced by Sarah Radclyffe and Dixie Linder. Screenplay by Alexander Stuart, based on his novel *The War Zone*.

It must have been something like this in medieval times, families living in isolation, cut off from neighbors, forced indoors by the weather, their animal and sexual functions not always shielded from view. Tim Roth's *The War Zone*, brilliant and heartbreaking, takes place in the present but is timeless; most particularly it is cut off from the fix-it culture of psychobabble, which defines all the politically correct ways to consider incest. The movie is not about incest as an issue, but about incest as a blow to the heart and the soul—a real event, here, now, in a family that seems close and happy. Not a topic on a talk show.

The movie takes place in winter in Devon, which is wet and gray, the sky squeezing joy out of the day. The family has moved from London "to make a fresh start," the mother says. They live in a comfortable cottage, warm and sheltered, life centering around the big kitchen table. Mom (Tilda Swinton) is very pregnant. Dad (Ray Winstone) is bluff and cheery, extroverted, a good guy. Tom (Freddie Cunliffe) is a fifteen-year-old, silent and sad because he misses his friends in London. Jessie (Lara Belmont) is eighteen years old, ripe with beauty. This looks like a cheerful story.

Roth tells it obliquely, sensitive to the ways families keep secrets even from themselves. Early in the film the mother's time comes and the whole family rushes to the hospital; there's a car crash, but a happy ending, as they gather in the maternity ward with the newcomer, all of them cut and bruised, but survivors. Back at home, there is a comfort with the physical side of life. Mom nurses her child in kitchen scenes like renaissance paintings. Tom is comfortable with his sister's casual nudity while they have a heart-to-heart talk. Mum helps wash her men at the kitchen sink, Jessie dries her brother's hair in the laundry room, the family seems comfortable with one another.

Then Tom glimpses a disturbing part of a moment between his father and his sister. He challenges Jessie. She says nothing happened. Something did happen, and more will happen, including a scene of graphic hurtfulness. But this isn't a case of Tom discovering incest in his family and blowing the whistle. It's much more complicated. How does he feel about his sister and about her relationship with her new boyfriend, Nick? What about his father's eerie split personality, able to deny his behavior and see Tom's interference as an assault on their happy family? What about the mother's willingness not to know? What about his sister's denial? Does it spring from shame, fear, or a desire to shield Tom and her mother from the knowledge?

And what about a curious episode when Jessie and Tom visit London, and Jessie almost seems to have set up Tom to sleep with one of her friends—as what? Consolation? A bribe? Revenge? The movie's refusal to declare exactly what the London episode means is admirable, because this is not a zero-sum accounting of good and evil, but a messy, elusive, painfully complex tragedy in which no one is driven by just one motive.

When Tom is accused of destroying the family and having a filthy mind, there is a sense in which he accepts this analysis. One critic of the film wrote that a "teenaged boy (from the big city, no less) would surely be more savvy—no matter how distraught—about the workings and potential resolutions of such a situation." Only in textbooks. When you're fifteen, what you learn in social studies and from talk shows is a lot different from how you confront your own family.

Incest is not unfamiliar as a subject for movies, but most incest stories are about characters simplified into monsters and victims. We know intellectually that most child abusers were abused children, but few films pause to reflect how that lifelong hurt reflects itself in real situations. The father here is both better and worse because of his own probably traumatic childhood. He must long ago have often promised himself that he would be different than his own father, that he would be a good dad—loving, kind, warm, cheerful—and so he is, all except for when he is not. When he's accused of evil, he explodes in anger—the anger of the father he is now and also the anger of the child he once was. For a moment his son is, in a sense, the abuser, making Dad feel guilty and shameful just as his own father must have, and tearing down all his efforts to be better, to be different.

Unsurprisingly, *The War Zone* affects viewers much more powerfully than a simple morality tale might. It is not simply about the evil of incest, but about its dynamic, about the way it plays upon guilt and shame and addresses old and secret wounds. The critic James Berardinelli says that when he saw the movie at the

Toronto Film Festival, a viewer ran from the theater saying he couldn't take it anymore, and went looking to pull a fire alarm. Tim Roth was standing near the exit and intercepted him, becoming confessor for an emotional outpouring that the movie had inspired.

Roth is one of the best actors now working, and with this movie he reveals himself as a director of surprising gifts. I cannot imagine *The War Zone* being better directed by anyone else, even though Ingmar Bergman and Ken Loach come to mind. Roth and his actors, and Stuart's screenplay, understand these people and their situation down to the final nuance, and are willing to let silence, timing, and visuals reveal what dialogue would cheapen. Not many movies bring you to a dead halt of sorrow and empathy. This one does.

The Watcher ★ ★
R, 93 m., 2000

James Spader (Campbell), Marisa Tomei (Polly), Keanu Reeves (Griffin), Robert Cicchini (Mitch), Scott A. Martin (FBI Agent), Jenny McShane (Diana), Chris Ellis (Hollis), Joe Monaco (Policeman). Directed by Joe Charbanic and produced by Chris Eberts, Elliott Lewitt, and Jeff Rice. Screenplay by Darcy Meyers, David Elliot, and Clay Ayers.

The Watcher is about still another serial killer whose existence centers around staging elaborate scenarios for the cops. If these weirdos would just become screenwriters in the first place, think of the lives that could be saved. Keanu Reeves stars as Griffin, a murderer who follows an FBI agent named Campbell (James Spader) from Los Angeles to Chicago, complaining about the cold weather but explaining he had to move because "things didn't work out with your successor." Killing just wasn't the same without Campbell to bug.

According to a theory floated by Campbell's therapist (Marisa Tomei), the killer and the agent may need each other, or are they brothers neither one ever had. Freud would cringe. Griffin is indeed forever seeking Campbell's reaction; what the agent thinks is more important to him than what his victims think. Griffin spends relatively little time killing his victims, but must spend days preparing presentations for Campbell.

He sets puzzles, issues challenges, sends him FedEx packages with photos of the next victims, devises elaborate booby traps, and recklessly follows the agent (who does not know what he looks like) right onto elevators. Finally he sets up a face-to-face meeting in a cemetery. The psychology here is a little shaky. Although some serial killers may have issues with the law, most of them focus, I think, on their victims and not on some kind of surrogate authority figure.

The movie's structure is simple: Killer issues challenge, agent rises to bait, desperate citywide search leads to still more frustration. *The Watcher* devotes an inordinate amount of its running time to Chicago police cars with sirens screaming as they hurtle down streets and over bridges, never turning a corner without almost spinning out. There are also a lot of helicopters involved. At one point the killer is pinpointed "twenty miles north of the city," a map shows Lincolnwood, and the cops converge at first on the Wrigley Building, before relocating to an abandoned warehouse. I know you're not supposed to fret about local geography in a movie where a city is a backdrop and not a map, but aren't there a *lot* of people who know the Wrigley Building is not twenty miles north of the city? Maybe the helicopter pilots are disoriented; in the chase that opens the movie, they come whirling into town from Lake Michigan, which makes for a nice opening shot while not answering the puzzle of how many miles from shore they are usually stationed.

The actors cannot be faulted. They bring more to the story than it really deserves. Spader has his hands on an intriguing character; Agent Campbell's tragic history (shown in flashbacks) has led to migraines so bad that he injects himself with pain medication straight into the stomach muscle. Painkillers have made him start losing his way and forgetting stuff, he complains to Tomei, and a Chicago cop calls him "Captain Barbiturate," observing, "If his pupils don't dilate, we don't need him." Migraines literally cripple their victims, but Campbell has one of those considerate cases that never strike when he is saving lives or pursuing fugitives.

Spader's quiet exchanges with Tomei are effective, too, even if we know her character was put on earth to get into big trouble. Reeves, as the killer, has the fairly thankless task of saying only what the movie needs him to say; he's limited by the fact that his killer has no real dimension or personality apart from his function as a plot device. The final confrontation is an example: Is he more interested in revenge, or in demonstrating the ingenuities of his booby-trapped scenario? It goes without saying, I guess, that the scene features hundreds of candles. Just once in a pervert killer movie, I wish they'd show a scene where he's pushing a cart through the Hallmark store, actually buying all those candles ("Do you have any that are unscented and aren't shaped, like, uh, little Hummel figures?").

Way of the Gun ★ ★ ½
R, 120 m., 2000

James Caan (Joe Sarno), Benicio Del Toro (Longbaugh), Ryan Phillippe (Parker), Juliette Lewis (Robin), Taye Diggs (Jeffers), Nicky Katt (Obecks), Scott Wilson (Mr. Chidduck). Directed by Christopher McQuarrie and produced by Kenneth Kokin. Screenplay by McQuarrie.

Way of the Gun is a wildly ambitious, heedlessly overplotted post-Tarantino bloodfest—the kind of movie that needs its own doggie bag. There's a good story buried somewhere in this melee, surrounded by such maddening excess that you want to take some home and feed it to undernourished stray movies.

The film is the directorial debut of Christopher McQuarrie, who won an Oscar for his screenplay for *The Usual Suspects.* He is a born director, and now what he needs to meet is a born editor. There are scenes here so fine, so unexpected, so filled with observation and nuance, that you can hardly believe the notes he's hitting. And then he'll cycle back for another round of *Wild Bunch* gunplay—not realizing that for Sam Peckinpah the shoot-out was the climax, not the punctuation.

Both of these McQuarrie films have loop-the-loop plots, unexpected reversals and revelations, and closing lines that call everything else into question—although not, I hasten to add, in the same way. Can this one really be only 120 minutes long? It has enough plot for a series. I'd love to see the prequel, in which these characters twist themselves into narrative pretzels just *setting up* all the stuff that pays off here.

Benicio Del Toro and Ryan Phillippe star as Mr. Longbaugh and Mr. Parker (the "mister" is a reminder of *Reservoir Dogs*). Having exhausted all their chances at normal lives (we doubt they tried very hard), they tell us in the narration that they "stepped off the path and went looking for the fortune we knew was ours." At a sperm bank, they overhear a conversation about a millionaire whose seed is being brought to term by a surrogate mother, who is always kept under armed guard. Their idea: Kidnap the mother and collect ransom.

The notion of kidnapping a (very) pregnant woman would provide complications enough for some directors, but not for McQuarrie, who hurtles into a labyrinth involving crisscrossing loyalties among the millionaire's current bodyguards, his shady employers, his long-time enforcers, the enforcer's old pal, and a gynecologist whose involvement in the case is more (and less) than professional.

The pregnant woman is played by Juliette Lewis, who is the movie's center of sanity. She is the only one who talks sense and understands more or less why everyone is doing everything—occasionally, so thick is the going, she'll simply explain things to the other cast members on a need-to-know basis. Mr. Longbaugh and Mr. Parker drive her into Mexico, the bodyguards (Taye Diggs and Nicky Katt) follow—and so does grizzled old Joe Sarno (James Caan), the suicidal but competent enforcer who is relied upon by the shady millionaire (Scott Wilson). It is a measure of McQuarrie's skill that the millionaire's wife plays a full and essential role in the movie while uttering a total of perhaps nine words.

Much of the movie consists of cat-and-mouse games, car chases, and shoot-outs. McQuarrie scatters fresh moments among the wearying routine of gunfire; shots of guys dashing into the frame with machine guns have become tiresome, but I liked the way Phillippe vaulted into a dry fountain that contained a nasty surprise. And the way the car chase slowed down to an elusive and tricky creep (I didn't believe it, but I liked it).

James Caan is very good here as the professional gunman who has seen it all. He's supposed to be on the same side as the bodyguards, but distrusts them, and tells one: "The only thing you can assume about a broken-down old man is that he is a survivor." McQuarrie gives Caan clipped lines of wisdom, and he has a wonderful scene with Del Toro in which he explains his functions and his plans. He and Wilson have another nice scene—two old associates who trust each other only up to a point. Jeffers, the Taye Diggs bodyguard, meanwhile maintains cool competence while everything nevertheless goes wrong, and is only one of several characters who reveal an unexpected connection.

Up to a point, a twisting plot is entertaining. We enjoy being fooled and surprised. But we have to halfway believe these things could really happen—in a movie, anyway. McQuarrie reaches that point and sails past it like a ski jumper. We get worn down. At first you're surprised when you get the rug pulled out from under you. Eventually, if you're a quick study, you stop stepping on it.

As a video, viewed at less than full attention, *Way of the Gun* could nicely fill the gaps of a slow Saturday night. It's when you focus on it that you lose patience. McQuarrie pulls, pummels, and pushes us, makes his characters jump through hoops, and at the end produces carloads of "bag men" who have no other function than to pop up and be shot at (all other available targets have already been killed). Enough, already.

The Wedding Planner ★ ★
PG-13, 100 m., 2001

Jennifer Lopez (Mary Fiore), Matthew McConaughey (Steve Edison), Bridgette Wilson-Sampras (Fran Donelly), Justin Chambers (Massimo), Alex Rocco (Mary's Father), Erik Hyler (Dancer), Huntley Ritter (Tom). Directed by Adam Shankman and produced by Peter Abrams, Deborah Del Prete, Jennifer Gibgot, Robert L. Levy, and Gigi Pritzker. Screenplay by Pamela Falk and Michael Ellis.

Jennifer Lopez looks soulfully into the eyes of Matthew McConaughey, but is he looking back? One of the many problems of *The Wedding Planner* is that we can't tell and don't much care. When a plot depends on two people falling in love when they absolutely should not, we have to be able to believe at some level that they have been swept up by a destiny beyond their control. McConaughey seems less inflamed by his sudden new romance than resigned to it.

Lopez stars in the title role as Mary Fiore—yes, a wedding planner. With her walkie-talkie headset, cell phone, clipboard, spotters, and video crews, she's mission control as her clients walk down the aisle. Racing to an appointment, she meets Dr. Steve Edison (McConaughey) in one of the most absurd Meet Cutes in many a moon. Her Gucci heel gets stuck in a manhole cover, a garbage Dumpster rolls down a hill toward her, and Steve hurls her out of the way and, of course, lands on top of her; it's love at first full-body contact.

That night they have a perfect date, watching movies in the park. Mary has always been the wedding planner, never the bride (uh-huh—this is as convincing as Julia Roberts's old flame choosing another bride in *My Best Friend's Wedding*). Now she walks on air, until her current client, the millionairess Fran Donelly (Bridgette Wilson-Sampras), introduces Mary to the man Fran will marry, who is, of course, Dr. Steve Edison.

If Steve is engaged, why did he mislead Mary with that night of movies and soul talk? Because he is a dishonest louse, or, as the movie explains it, because he had no idea he would be thunderstruck by love. Since he is in love with Mary, the only sensible thing to do is call off his wedding to Fran and buy a season ticket to movies in the park. But the movie cannot abide common sense, and recycles decades of clichés about the wrong people getting married and the right ones making stupid decisions.

There are times when the movie's contrivance is agonizing. Consider all the plot mechanics involving Mary's Italian-American father (Alex Rocco) and his schemes to marry her off to Massimo, her childhood playmate from the old country (Calvin Klein model Justin Chambers, sounding as Italian as most people named Chambers). Consider how Mary spends her free time (on a Scrabble team) and how she accepts a proposal of marriage by spelling "OK" with Scrabble tiles when "Yes" would be more appropriate plus get her more points.

And consider a "comic" sequence so awkward and absurd it not only brings the movie to a halt but threatens to reverse its flow. While Mary and Steve wander in a sculpture garden, they accidentally knock over a statue, and the statue's male hardware gets broken off. Mary has some superglue in her purse, and they try to glue the frank and beans back in place, but alas, the broken part becomes stuck to Dr. Steve's palm. If he had gone through the rest of the movie like that it might have added some interest, but no: Mary also has some solvent in her purse. When you have seen Jennifer Lopez ungluing marble genitals from the hand of the man she loves, you have more or less seen everything.

A plot like this is so hopeless that only acting can redeem it. Lopez pulls her share of the load, looking genuinely smitten by this guy, and convincingly crushed when his secret is revealed. But McConaughey is not the right actor for this material. He seems stolid and workmanlike, when what you need is a guy with naughtier eyes: Ben Affleck, Steve Martin, William H. Macy, Alec Baldwin, Matt Dillon.

Bridgette Wilson-Sampras is, however, correctly cast as Fran, the rich bride-to-be. She's an Anna Nicole Smith type who gets the joke and avoids all the usual clichés involving the woman who gets left at the altar, perhaps because she realizes, as we do, that getting dumped by Dr. Steve is far from the worst thing that could happen to her. We sense midway in the movie that Mary and Fran could have more interesting conversations with each other than either one will have with Dr. Steve, and no matter which one marries him, we sense a future, five to eight years from now, after the divorce, when the two girls meet by chance at a spa (I see them at the Golden Door, perhaps, or Rancho La Puerta) and share a good laugh about the doc.

Western ★ ★

NO MPAA RATING, 121 m., 1999

Sergi Lopez (Paco), Sacha Bourdo (Nino), Elisabeth Vitali (Marinette), Marie Matheron (Nathalie), Basile Sieouka (Baptiste), Jean-Louis Dupont (Policeman), Olivier Herveet (Hospital Doctor). Directed by Manuel Poirier and produced by Maurice Bernart. Screenplay by Poirier and Jean Francois Goyet.

Western is a road movie about a friendship between two men and their search for the love of the right woman. The roads they travel are in western France, in the district of Brittany, which looks rough and dour but, on the evidence of this film, has the kindest and most accommodating women in the world.

The Meet Cute between the men occurs when Paco (Sergi Lopez), a shoe salesman from Spain, gives a lift to Nino (Sacha Bourdo), a Russian who lived in Italy before moving to France. Nino tricks Paco and steals his car, and when the stranded Paco sees him on the street the next day, he chases him and beats him so badly Nino lands in the hospital. Paco visits him there, says he is sorry to have hit him so hard, and the men become friends. Since Paco has lost his job along with his car, they hit the road.

Road movies are the oldest genre known to man, and the most flexible, since anything can happen on the road and there's always a fresh supply of characters. Paco, who has always been a ladies' man, in fact has already found a woman: Marinette (Elisabeth Vitali), who befriended him after his car was stolen and even let him sleep overnight on her sofa bed. Soon they've kissed and think they may be in love, but Marinette wants a thirty-day cooling-off period, so the two men hitch around Brittany, depending on the kindness of strangers.

If Paco has always had luck with women, Nino has had none. He's a short, unprepossessing man with a defeatist attitude, and one day Paco stands next to him at the roadside, points to a nearby village, and says, "I'm sure that in that town, there has to be a woman for you." "Really?" "Yes, there is a minimum of one woman in every town in France for you."

This belief leads them to conduct a phony door-to-door survey as a ruse for finding the right woman for Nino, and along the way they make a new friend, Baptiste (Basile Sieouka), an African from Senegal in a wheelchair. He teaches them the "bonjour" game, in which they get points every time a stranger returns their greeting. "Go back where you came from!" one man snarls at Baptiste, who laughs uproariously; all three of these men are strangers in a foreign land.

The emotional center of the story comes when Paco meets a woman named Nathalie (Marie Matheron), who invites them home for dinner, likes the way Nino cooks chicken, and unexpectedly goes for Nino rather than Paco. This woman's lifestyle seems unlikely (she is a male daydream of an earth mother), but she provides the excuse for the film's ending—which is intended as joyous, but seemed too pat and complacent to me.

Western, directed and cowritten by Manuel Poirier, won the Grand Jury Prize, or second place, in 1997 at Cannes; that's the same prize *Life Is Beautiful* won in 1998. Set in France, it absorbed a certain offhand flair. The same material, filmed in America, might seem thin and contrived; the adventures are arbitrary, the cuteness of the men grows wearing, and when Nino has an accident with a chainsaw, we can see contrivance shading off into desperation.

The movie is slow-going. Paco and Nino are the kinds of open-faced proletarian heroes found more often in fables than in life. Their luck as homeless men in finding a ready supply of trusting and hospitable women is uncanny, even unbelievable. The movie insists on their charm, instead of letting us find it for ourselves. And although the leading actresses are sunny and vital, they are fantasy women, not real ones (who would be smarter and warier).

One of the women in the film collects children fathered by an assortment of men who capture her fancy and then drift away, apparently with her blessings. The movie smiles on this practice, instead of wondering how she found so many men so indifferent to their own children. By the end of the film she has given birth to her own orphanage, and could hire the family out as a package to the casting director for *Oliver Twist*. The jury at Cannes loved this, but I squirmed, and speculated that the subtitles and the European cachet gives the film immunity. In English, with American actors, this story would be unbearable.

Whatever It Takes ★ ½
PG-13, 92 m., 2000

Shane West (Ryan Woodman), Jodi Lyn O'Keefe (Ashley Grant), Marla Sokoloff (Maggie Carter), James Franco (Chris Campbell), Julia Sweeney (Ryan's Mom). Directed by David Hubbard and produced by Paul Schiff. Screenplay by Mark Schwahn, loosely based on Edmund Rostand's play *Cyrano de Bergerac.*

Whatever It Takes is still another movie arguing that the American teenager's IQ level hovers in the low 90s. It involves teenagers who have never existed, doing things no teenager has ever done, for reasons no teenager would understand. Of course, it's aimed at the teenage market. Maybe it's intended as escapism.

The screenplay is "loosely based on *Cyrano de Bergerac,*" according to the credits. My guess is, it's based on the Cliff's Notes for *Cyrano,* studied only long enough to rip off the scene where Cyrano hides in the bushes and whispers lines for his friend to repeat to the beautiful Roxanne.

Cyrano in this version is the wonderfully named Ryan Woodman (Shane West), whose house is next door to Maggie (Marla Sokoloff). So close, indeed, that the balconies of their bedrooms almost touch, and they are in constant communication, although "only good friends." Ryan has a crush on Ashley (Jodi Lyn O'Keefe), the school sexpot. His best pal Chris (James Franco) warns him Ashley is beyond his grasp, but Ryan can dream.

If you know *Cyrano,* or have seen such splendid adaptations as Fred Schepisi's *Roxanne* (1987) with Steve Martin and Daryl Hannah, you can guess the key scene. Ryan talks Chris into going out with Maggie and then hides behind the scenery of a school play while prompting him with lines he knows Maggie will fall for. With Maggie neutralized, Ryan goes out with Ashley—who is a conceited, arrogant snob, of course, and will get her comeuppance in one of those cruel scenes reserved for stuck-up high school sexpots.

The film contains a funny scene, but it doesn't involve any of the leads. It's by Ryan's mom (Julia Sweeney), also the school nurse, who lectures the student body on safe sex, using a six-foot male reproductive organ as a visual aid. She is not Mrs. Woodman for nothing. As a responsible reporter I will also note that the film contains a nude shower scene, which observes all of the rules about nudity almost but not quite being shown.

And, let's see, there is a scene where Ashley gets drunk and throws up on her date, and a scene set in an old folks' home that makes use of enough flatulence to score a brief concerto. And a scene ripped off from *It's a Wonderful Life,* as the high school gym floor opens up during a dance to dunk the students in the swimming pool beneath. Forget about the situation inspired by *Cyrano:* Is there *anything* in this movie that isn't borrowed?

What Lies Beneath ★ ★
PG-13, 130 m., 2000

Michelle Pfeiffer (Claire Spencer), Harrison Ford (Norman Spencer), Katharine Towne (Caitlin Spencer), Miranda Otto (Mary Feur), James Remar (Warren Feur), Victoria Bidewell (Beatrice), Diana Scarwid (Jody), Joe Morton (Psychiatrist), Dennison Samaroo (Ph.D. Student No. 1). Directed by Robert Zemeckis and produced by Steve Starkey, Zemeckis, and Jack Rapke. Screenplay by Clark Gregg, based on the story by Sarah Kernochan and Gregg.

What Lies Beneath opens with an hour or so of standard thriller scare tactics, done effectively, and then plops into a morass of absurdity. Lacking a smarter screenplay, it milks the genuine skills of its actors and director for more than it deserves, and then runs off the rails in an ending more laughable than scary. Along the way, yes, there are some good moments.

Michelle Pfeiffer stars as Claire Spencer, the happily married wife of Dr. Norman Spencer (Harrison Ford), a scientist. They're renovating his old family house on the shores of a lake. A house that, when she is home alone, seems haunted—with doors that open by themselves, picture frames that keep falling over, a tub that fills itself, a dog that barks at invisible menaces, and a neighbor who has possibly murdered his wife.

Gruff, no-nonsense Dr. Spencer, of course, dismisses his wife's fears, and sends her to a psychiatrist. All of her early scenes are reasonable enough, even if the doors open themselves two or three times more than necessary. It's when we start to learn the motivation for the manifestations that we grow first restless, finally incredulous.

There's a bag of tricks that skillful horror directors use, and they're employed here by Robert Zemeckis *(Back to the Future, Forrest Gump)*, who has always wanted, he says, to make a suspense film—"perhaps the kind of film Hitchcock would have done in his day," according to one of his coproducers, Jack Rapke. Hitchcock would not, however, have done this film in his day or any other day, because Hitchcock would have insisted on rewrites to remove the supernatural and explain the action in terms of human psychology, however abnormal.

Zemeckis does quote Hitchcock; there's a scene where Pfeiffer spies on a neighbor with binoculars, and is shocked to see the neighbor spying back, and we are reminded of *Rear Window.* He also uses such dependable devices as harmless people who suddenly enter the frame and startle the heroine. And mirrors that suddenly reveal figures reflected in them. And shots where we are looking at a character in front of windows, and the camera slowly pans, causing us to expect a face to appear in the window.

All of these devices are used with journeyman thoroughness in *What Lies Beneath,* but they are only devices, and we know it. Late in the film, when the heroine walks close to the hand of a character who is assumed to be dead, the audience laughs, because it knows—or thinks it knows—that in a horror film no one is ever really dead on the first try. Such devices at least involve the physical world and the laws of nature as we understand them. What's happening in the supernatural scenes I leave you to decide; I think some of them are supposed to be real, others hallucinations, others seen in different ways by different characters.

Michelle Pfeiffer is very good in the movie; she is convincing and sympathetic, and avoids the most common problem for actors in horror films—she doesn't overreact. Her character remains self-contained and resourceful, and the sessions with the psychiatrist (Joe Morton) are masterpieces of people behaving reasonably in the face of Forces Beyond Their Comprehension. Harrison Ford is the most reliable of actors, capable of many things, here

required to be Harrison Ford. The Law of Economy of Character Development requires that his husband be other than he seems, since he isn't needed as his wife's confidant and sidekick (Diana Scarwid's character fills that slot). As for the possibly wife-killing neighbor, I can forgive that red herring almost anything because it pays off in a flawless sight gag at a party.

I've tried to play fair and not give away plot elements. That's more than the ads have done. The trailer of this movie thoroughly demolishes the surprises; if you've seen the trailer, you know what the movie is about, and all of the suspense of the first hour is superfluous for you, including major character revelations. Don't directors get annoyed when they create suspense and the marketing sabotages their efforts?

The modern studio approach to trailers is copied from those marketing people who stand in the aisles of supermarkets, offering you a bite of sausage on a toothpick. When you taste it, you know everything there is to be known about the sausage except what it would be like to eat all of it. Same with the trailer for *What Lies Beneath.* I like the approach where you can smell the sausage but not taste it. You desire it just as much, but the actual experience is still ahead of you. Trailers that give us a smell and not a taste, that's what we need. ☞

What Planet Are You From? ★
R, 100 m., 2000

Garry Shandling (Harold Anderson), Annette Bening (Susan Hart), Greg Kinnear (Perry Gordon), Ben Kingsley (Graydon), Linda Fiorentino (Helen Gordon), John Goodman (Roland Jones), Caroline Aaron (Nadine Jones), Judy Greer (Rebecca). Directed by Mike Nichols and produced by Nichols, Garry Shandling, and Neil Machlis. Screenplay by Shandling, Michael Leeson, Ed Solomon, and Peter Tolan.

Here is the most uncomfortable movie of the new year, an exercise in feel-good smut. *What Planet Are You From?* starts out as a dirty comedy, but then abandons the comedy, followed by the dirt, and by the end is actually trying to be poignant. For that to work, we'd have to like the hero, and Garry Shandling makes that difficult. He begrudges every emotion, as if there's no more where that came from. That worked on TV's *Larry Sanders Show*—it's why his character was funny—but here he can't make the movie's U-turn into sentimentality.

He plays an alien from a distant planet, where the inhabitants have no emotions and no genitals. Possibly this goes hand in hand. He is outfitted with human reproductive equipment, given the name Harold Anderson, and sent to Earth to impregnate a human woman so that his race can conquer our planet. When Harold becomes aroused, a loud whirling noise emanates from his pants.

If I were a comedy writer I would deal with that alarming noise. I would assume that the other characters in the movie would find it extremely disturbing. I put it to my female readers: If you were on a date with a guy and every time he looked dreamy-eyed it sounded like an operating garbage disposal was secreted somewhere on his person, wouldn't you be thinking of ways to say you just wanted to be friends?

The lame joke in *What Planet Are You From?* is that women hear the noise, find it curious and ask about it, and Harold makes feeble attempts to explain it away, and of course the more aroused he becomes the louder it hums, and when his ardor cools the volume drops. You understand. If you find this even slightly funny, you'd better see this movie, since the device is never likely to be employed again.

On Earth, Harold gets a job in a bank with the lecherous Perry (Greg Kinnear), and soon he is romancing a woman named Susan (Annette Bening) and contemplating the possibility of sex with Perry's wife, Helen (Linda Fiorentino). Fiorentino, of course, starred in the most unforgettable sexual put-down in recent movie history (in *The Last Seduction*, where she calls the bluff of a barroom braggart). There is a scene here with the same setup: She's sitting next to Harold in a bar, there is a humming from the nether regions of his wardrobe, etc., and I was wondering, is it too much to ask that the movie provide a hilarious homage? It was. Think of the lost possibilities.

Harold and Susan fly off to Vegas, get married, and have a honeymoon that consists of days of uninterrupted sex ("I had so many orgasms," she says, "that some are still stacked up and waiting to land"). Then she discovers Harold's only interest in her is as a breeder. She is crushed and angry, and the movie turns to cheap emotion during her pregnancy and inevitable live childbirth scene, after which Harold finds to his amazement that he may have emotions after all.

The film was directed by Mike Nichols, whose uneven career makes you wonder. Half of his films are good to great (his previous credit is *Primary Colors*) and the other half you're at a loss to account for. What went into the theory that *What Planet Are You From?* was filmable? Even if the screenplay by Garry Shandling and three other writers seemed promising on the page, why star Shandling in it? Why not an actor who projects joy of performance—why not Kinnear, for example?

Shandling's shtick is unavailability. His public persona is of a man unwilling to be in public. Words squeeze embarrassed from his lips as if he feels guilty to be talking. *Larry Sanders* used this presence brilliantly. But it depends on its limitations. If you're making a movie about a man who has a strange noise coming from his pants, you should cast an actor who looks different when it isn't.

What's Cooking? ★ ★ ★ ½
PG-13, 106 m., 2000

Alfre Woodard (Audrey Williams), Dennis Haysbert (Ronald Williams), Ann Weldon (Grace Williams), Mercedes Ruehl (Elizabeth Avila), Victor Rivers (Javier Avila), Douglas Spain (Anthony Avila), A. Martinez (Daniel), Lainie Kazan (Ruth Seeling), Maury Chaykin (Herb Seeling), Kyra Sedgwick (Rachel Seeling), Julianna Margulies (Carla), Estelle Harris (Aunt Bea), Joan Chen (Trinh Nguyen), Will Yun Lee (Jimmy Nguyen), Kristy Wu (Jenny Nguyen), Jimmy Pham (Gary Nguyen), Brennan Louie (Joey Nguyen), Kieu Chinh (Grandma Nguyen). Directed by Gurinder Chadha and produced by Jeffrey Taylor. Screenplay by Paul Mayeda Berges and Chadha.

Thanksgiving is not a religious or patriotic holiday, and it's not hooked to any ethnic or national group: It's a national celebration of the fact that we have survived for another year, we eat turkey to observe that fact, and may, if we choose, thank the deity of our choice. We exchange no presents and send few cards. It's on a Thursday, a day not associated with any belief system. And it nods gratefully to American Indians, who have good reason to feel less than thrilled about the Fourth of July and Columbus Day.

What's Cooking? celebrates the holiday by telling interlocking stories about four American families, which are African-American, Jewish, Latino, and Vietnamese. They all serve turkey in one way or another, surrounded by traditional dishes from their groups; some are tired of turkey and try to disguise it, while an Americanized Vietnamese girl sees the chili paste going on and complains, "Why do you want to make the turkey taste like everything else we eat?"

These families have been brought together by the filmmaker Gurinder Chadha, an Indian woman of Punjabi ancestry and Kenyan roots, who grew up in London and is now married to Paul Mayeda Berges, a half-Japanese American. Doesn't it make you want to grin? She directed; they cowrote. All four of the stories involve the generation gap, as older family members cling to tradition and younger ones rebel. But because the stories are so skillfully threaded together, the movie doesn't feel like an exercise: Each of the stories stands on its own.

Generation gaps, of course, go down through more than one generation. Dennis Haysbert and Alfre Woodard play the parents of a college student who would rather be a radical than a professional, but another source of tension at the table is the presence of his mother, who casts a practiced eye over her daughter-in-law's menu, and is shocked that it lacks macaroni and cheese, an obligatory item at every traditional African-American feast.

The Vietnamese family runs a video store. Grandma Nguyen (Kieu Chinh) is of course less assimilated than her family, but in the kitchen her eye misses nothing and her strong opinions are enforced almost telepathically. There's trouble because a younger sister has found a gun in her brother's room. Joan Chen plays the mother, a peacemaker in a family with a father who rules too sternly.

The Latino Thanksgiving starts uneasily when the kids are at the supermarket and run into their dad (Victor Rivers), who is separated from their mom (Mercedes Ruehl). They invite him to dinner without asking her; on the other hand, she hasn't told them she has invited her new boyfriend, a teacher.

The Jewish couple (Lainie Kazan and Maury Chaykin) greet their daughter (Kyra Sedgwick), her lover (Julianna Margulies), and Aunt Bea (Estelle Harris), one of those women who asks such tactless questions that you can't believe she's doing it by accident. The parents accept their daughter's lesbianism, but are at a loss to explain it (should they have sent her to that kibbutz?).

During this long day secrets will be revealed, hearts will be bared, old grudges settled, new ones started, pregnancies announced, forgiveness granted, and turkeys carved. And the melting pot will simmer a little, for example when a Latino girl brings home her Asian boyfriend (her brother tries to make him feel at home with a hearty conversation about Jackie Chan and Bruce Lee). If the Asian boy feels awkward at his girlfriend's table, he reflects that she is not welcome at all in his family's home. Or is she?

All that I've said reflects the design of the film. I've hardly even started to suggest the texture and pleasure. There are so many characters, so vividly drawn, with such humor and life, that a synopsis is impossible. What's strange is the spell the movie weaves. By its end, there is actually a sort of tingle of pleasure in seeing how this Thanksgiving ends, and how its stories are resolved. In recent years most Thanksgiving movies have been about families at war. Here are four families that have, in one way or another, started peace talks.

What's the Worst That Can Happen? ★
PG-13, 95 m., 2001

Martin Lawrence (Kevin Caffery), Danny DeVito (Max Fairbanks), John Leguizamo (Berger), Glenne Headly (Gloria), Carmen Ejogo (Amber Belhaven), Bernie Mac (Uncle Jack), Larry Miller (Earl Radburn), Nora Dunn (Lutetia Fairbanks). Directed by Sam Weisman and produced by Lawrence Turman, David Hoberman, Ashok Amritraj, and Wendy Dytman. Screenplay by

645

Matthew Chapman, based on the novel by Donald E. Westlake.

What's the Worst That Can Happen? has too many characters, not enough plot, and a disconnect between the two stars' acting styles. Danny DeVito plays a crooked millionaire, Martin Lawrence plays a smart thief, and they seem to be in different pictures. DeVito as always is taut, sharp, perfectly timed. Lawrence could play in the same key (and does, in an early scene during an art auction), but at other times he bursts into body language that's intended as funny but plays more like the early symptoms of St. Vitus's dance.

There is an old comedy tradition in which the onlookers freeze while the star does his zany stuff. From Groucho Marx to Eddie Murphy to Robin Williams to Jim Carrey, there are scenes where the star does his shtick and the others wait for it to end, like extras in an opera. That only works in a movie that is about the star's shtick. *What's the Worst That Can Happen?* creates a world that plays by one set of comic rules (in which people pretend they're serious) and then Lawrence goes into mime and jive and odd wavings of his arms and verbal riffs, and maybe the people on the set were laughing but the audience doesn't, much.

The plot involves Lawrence as a clever thief named Kevin Caffery, who frequents auctions to find out what's worth stealing. At an art auction, he meets Amber Belhaven (Carmen Ejogo), who is in tears because she has to sell the painting her father left her; she needs money for the hotel bill. She has good reason to be in tears. The painting, described as a fine example of the Hudson River School, goes for $3,000; some members of the audience will be thinking that's at least $30,000 less than it's probably worth.

If Kevin is supplied with one love interest, Max Fairbanks (DeVito) has several, including his society wife (Nora Dunn), his adoring secretary (Glenne Headly), and Miss September. (When she disappears, Max's assistant, Earl (Larry Miller), observes there are "eleven more months where she came from.") Kevin also has a criminal sidekick named Berger (John Leguizamo), and then there is his get-

away driver Uncle Jack (Bernie Mac), and a Boston cop (William Fichtner) who is played for some reason as a flamboyant dandy. If I tell you there are several other characters with significant roles, you will guess that much of the movie is taken up with entrances and exits.

The plot involves Kevin's attempt to burgle Max's luxurious shore estate, which is supposed to be empty but in fact contains Max and Miss September. After the cops are called, Max steals from Kevin a ring given him by Amber Belhaven, and most of the rest of the movie involves Kevin's determination to get it back, intercut with Max's troubles with judges, lawyers, and accountants.

The jokes and the plots are freely and all too sloppily adapted from a Dortmunder novel by Donald E. Westlake, who once told me he only really liked one of the movies made from his books *(The Grifters)*, and probably won't raise the count to two after this one. A comedy needs a strong narrative engine to pull the plot through to the end, and firm directorial discipline to keep the actors from trying to act funny instead of simply being funny. At some point, when a movie like this doesn't work, it stops being a comedy and becomes a documentary about actors trying to make the material work. When you have so many characters played by so many recognizable actors in a movie that runs only ninety-five minutes, you guess that at some point they just cut their losses and gave up.

Note: Again this summer, movies are jumping through hoops to get the PG-13 rating and the under-17 demographic. That's why the battle scenes were toned down and blurred in Pearl Harbor, *and no doubt it's why this movie steals one of the most famous closing lines in comedy history, and emasculates it. The* Front Page *ended with "The son of a bitch stole my watch!" This one ends with "Stop my lawyer! He stole my watch!" Not quite the same, you will agree.*

What Women Want ★ ★ ★
PG-13, 110 m., 2000

Mel Gibson (Nick Marshall), Helen Hunt (Darcy Maguire), Marisa Tomei (Lola), Lauren Holly (Gigi), Mark Feuerstein (Morgan), Alan Alda (Dan Wanamaker), Valerie Perrine (Margo),

Delta Burke (Eve). Directed by Nancy Meyers and produced by Susan Cartsonis, Bruce Davey, Gina Matthews, Nancy Meyers, and Matt Williams. Screenplay by Josh Goldsmith, Cathy Yuspa, and Diane Drake.

What women want is very simple: a man willing to listen when they're speaking to him. They also want a lot of other things, but that will do for starters. This we learn from *What Women Want,* a comedy about a man who is jolted by electricity and develops the ability to read women's minds.

You would assume that this ability would make him the world's greatest lover, since he would know precisely what to do and when to do it, and indeed the movie's hero does triumph in that area, although not without early discouragements. (Extreme detumescence can result when a man discovers that during the throes of passion his lover is asking herself, "Is Britney Spears on *Leno* tonight?")

Mel Gibson stars as Nick Marshall, an ad executive who thinks he's next in line for a top job at his Chicago agency. But his boss (Alan Alda) passes him over for Darcy Maguire (Helen Hunt), a hot steal from another agency. Nick declares war, at about the same time he develops the ability to read women's minds. His knack of stealing Darcy's best ideas is a dirty trick, but he's ambitious and shameless.

He is also a man who needs to listen to women more. We learn he was raised in Vegas as the pampered child of a showgirl, and has been doted on by admiring females ever since— including, recently, the sexy Lola (Marisa Tomei), who works in the coffee store he patronizes. At work, two assistants (Valerie Perrine and Delta Burke) approve categorically of everything he does, but mind reading reveals they never think about this. Many of the other women in the office, he is horrified to learn, pretend to like him but don't.

Because he feels chastened, and because he wants to win a valuable account, Nick starts a crash program to research being a woman. This leads him to experiment with lip gloss, eye shadow, pantyhose, and exfoliation, in scenes positioned somewhere between *Tootsie* and Arnold Schwarzenegger's *Junior.* Amazingly, given the opportunities, Gibson, king of the tush scenes, keeps his netherlands out of view during these adventures.

It's clear that Nick and Darcy will sooner or later fall in love, I suppose, and that's a cinematic first: Although Mel Gibson has been voted the World's Sexiest Man in one of those meaningless magazine-cover polls, this is his first romantic comedy. He and Hunt are not a match made in heaven, but that's one of the appeals as they edge closer together. Less appealing is the way he dumps poor Lola (Tomei), who really deserves better.

The movie, directed by Nancy Meyers, doesn't flow so much as leap from one good scene to another over the crevices of flat scenes in between. The movie is considerably slowed down by the unnecessary character of a suicidal file clerk, who does nothing of any interest until late in the movie, when Nick befriends her in a scene that serves no purpose except to delay us on our way to the happy climax which can be seen signaling eagerly from the next reel.

If the movie is imperfect, it's not boring and is often very funny, as in a solo dance that Nick does in his apartment to Sinatra singing "I Won't Dance." This is, we imagine, the way the Tom Cruise character in *Risky Business* might have ended some of his evenings if he had grown up to be Nick Marshall. I also liked the way Gibson handled the sex scene, where his look of joy and complete self-satisfaction at the end is equaled only by Jack Nicholson's famous Triumph T-shirt moment in *Five Easy Pieces.*

Note: The look and feel of the movie is just right. The set for the ad agency's office is inviting and seems lived in. Inspired by Chicago's nineteenth-century Monadnock Building, it looks plausible as an ad agency headquarters and allows sight lines that are important to the action. Great work by production designer Jon Hutman, art directors Gae Buckley and Tony Fanning, and set decorator Rosemary Brandenburg, and if you wonder why I list their names, you'll know when you see their work.

When Brendan Met Trudy ★ ★ ★

NO MPAA RATING, 95 m., 2001

Peter McDonald (Brendan), Flora Montgomery (Trudy), Marie Mullen (Mother), Pauline McLynn

(Nuala), Don Wycherley (Niall), Maynard Eziashi (Edgar), Eileen Walsh (Siobhan), Barry Cassin (Headmaster). Directed by Kieron J. Walsh and produced by Lynda Myles. Screenplay by Roddy Doyle.

Roddy Doyle has written an original screenplay, and now we know his secret. He wrote the novels that became the rollicking Irish comedies *The Commitments, The Snapper,* and *The Van,* and now here's *When Brendan Met Trudy.* If the title reminds you of *When Harry Met Sally,* that's because half the scenes in the movie are likely to remind you of other movies. Roddy Doyle's secret is, he's a movie fan. The kind of movie fan so fanatic that he creates a hero named Brendan who not only has a poster of Godard's *Breathless* in his office, but another one in his flat.

Brendan, played by Peter McDonald, is a sissy. He runs like a girl, with his arms held out rigidly at his sides, and he sings in the church choir, and he's so shy that when the choir members go into the pub for a pint after practice, he stands by himself at the bar. And there he's standing one night, a sitting duck, when Trudy accosts him. She's the kind of girl who can insult you, pick you up, get you to buy her a drink, keep you at arm's length, and tell you to sod off, simultaneously and charmingly.

Flora Montgomery is the actress. She's got one of those round, regular faces, pretty but frank, like your best friend's sister—the kind of girl you agree would make a great catch for some lucky bloke, but not, you add in an unspoken footnote, for yourself. Trudy doesn't leave Brendan with the free time for such sophistry, however, and soon he is in love with her and proving that he may run like a sissy but he makes love like that Jack Nicholson character with the "Triumph!" T-shirt.

All the same, Brendan has his misgivings. Trudy sneaks out at night, wearing a ski mask. And the TV news reports that young men have been castrated in Dublin by a mysterious masked predator. Could it be Trudy? One night she attempts to add a little spice to their sex by wearing her mask, and he is so terrified that she has to talk him down by confessing she is not a phantom castrator, but merely a thief.

This news comes as a shock to honest Brendan, a schoolteacher whose students openly mock him and whose only escape is going to the movies. Soon Trudy is going to the movies with him, and soon he is going on midnight raids with her, and the Doyle screenplay, directed by Kieron J. Walsh, casts many of their adventures in the form of classic movie scenes, sometimes even with the same dialogue. This is possible because when Brendan finds himself facedown in the gutter, his first thought is not to climb to his feet, but to imagine himself as William Holden in *Sunset Boulevard.*

The more movie references you recognize (from *Once Upon a Time in the West* to *The Producers*), the more you're likely to enjoy *When Brendan Met Trudy,* but the movie works whether you identify the scenes or not. It has that unwound Roddy Doyle humor; the laughs don't hit you over the head, but tickle you behind the knee. And there is, as usual, Doyle's great pleasure in kidding the Irish. At one point Brendan and Trudy visit a miniature Irish landscape, which includes an "Irish Famine Village," and it is so real, they agree "you can almost see them starving." The effect these miniature famine victims have upon Brendan's sex life, and how he deals with it, is making me smile again right now.

Where the Heart Is ★ ★ ½
PG-13, 121 m., 2000

Natalie Portman (Novalee Nation), Ashley Judd (Lexie Coop), James Frain (Forney), Stockard Channing (Sister Husband), Joan Cusack (Ruth Meyers), Jim Beaver (Clawhammer), Rodger Boyce (Harry the Policeman), Dylan Bruno (Willy Jack Pickens), Keith David (Moses Whitecotton), Sally Field (Mama Lil), Richard Jones (Mr. Sprock). Directed by Matt Williams and produced by Susan Cartsonis. Screenplay by Lowell Ganz and Babaloo Mandel, based on the novel by Billie Letts.

Remember that game in school where the teacher would write the first sentence of a story and then pass it around the class? Everybody would write a sentence, but the paper was folded so you could read only the last sentence before yours. *Where the Heart Is* has a screenplay like that, zigging and zagging and wildly careening from one melodramatic development to the next. What halfway holds it together are the performances, which are convincing and deserve a story with a touch more sanity.

The movie is based on a popular novel by Billie Letts, about a seventeen-year-old unwed mother named Novalee Nation (Natalie Portman), who is abandoned by her no-good boyfriend in a Wal-Mart in Sequoia, Oklahoma, and lives secretly in the store until she gives birth to her child, little Americus. The baby is delivered by the town's substitute librarian, Forney (James Frain), who has been following her, moonstruck, and breaks through the store's plate-glass window as she goes into labor. She finds a home locally with Sister Husband (Stockard Channing) and her partner, Mr. Sprock (Richard Jones).

Novalee is lucky to have landed in a town populated exclusively by character actors. Everyone in Sequoia, and indeed everyone in her life, is a salt-of-the-earth, good ol' eccentric, and that surely includes her new best friend Lexie Coop (Ashley Judd) who is always going and getting herself pregnant. When Novalee names her new baby Americus, Lexie is impressed. She names her kids after snacks: Praline, Baby Ruth . . .

The people in the movie are lovable and sympathetic, and if they live in a world of folksy fantasy, at least it looks like a good place to live. For example, Novalee makes a friend of Moses Whitecotton (Keith David), a photographer in the Wal-Mart, and soon she's exhibiting talent as a gifted photographer. But the characters have to negotiate the plot like runners through a minefield, as one weird and improbable situation after another comes up. At one point Novalee is about to be sucked up into the funnel cloud of a tornado, and clings upside down to the steps of the storm shelter with the fingertips of one hand while snatching little Americus as the child is about to be blown past her. Uh-huh.

There are times when you wonder, how self-aware *are* these people? Sister Husband is wonderfully played by Channing, who brings humanity and warmth to the character, but what's with her blessing before meals: ". . . and we ask forgiveness, Lord, for the fornication

that Mr. Sprock and I have committed again this morning right here on this very kitchen table." Does she know that's funny? Or is she being sincere?

God has to forgive a lot of fornicating in this movie. Lexie, the Judd character, is forever taking up with the wrong man. She seems to be the town nurse, but has an imperfect understanding of birth control, not to mention abysmal taste in men (until at last she meets Ernie the Exterminator). Novalee's own unorthodox delivery gets on the TV news and attracts the attention of devout folks from as far away as Midnight, Mississippi, who travel to Sequoia, kidnap Americus, and abandon the infant in the crib of the local nativity scene. (The symbolism of this act is elusive; it could as easily be sacrilegious as disapproving.)

Novalee's first boyfriend, the father of her child, is the no-good would-be country singer Willy Jack Pickens (Dylan Bruno). After he abandons her, he's arrested while in the company of a fourteen-year-old hitchhiking thief, and is sent off to prison. When Novalee has the "Wal-Mart baby" and becomes a TV star, that fetches her lying mother, Mama Lil (Sally Field) from New Orleans. Meanwhile, the story follows later developments in Willy Jack's case, as he signs with a hard-boiled talent agent (Joan Cusack).

By now I'm ducking down in my seat to keep out of the line of fire of the plot. This movie is so heavy on incident, contrivance, coincidence, improbability, sudden reversals, and dizzying flash-forwards (sometimes years at a time) that it seems a wonder the characters don't crash into each other in the confusion. Melodramatic elements are slapped on top of one another like a hurry-up plasterboarding job. The happy ending is so laboriously obvious that it's a little amazing, really, how Natalie Portman manages to find sweetness in it, for Novalee and for us.

Portman is quite an actress. I've been an admirer since her early work in *Beautiful Girls*. Here she's the calm eye of the storm, mightily aided by Ashley Judd, who brings a plausibility to Lexie that the character surely needs. James Frain, as the lonely librarian with a secret in his family, has to undergo a remarkable personality change, from skitterish neurotic to stable nice guy, but the movie is so busy he finds time to sneak off and do that. There is a core of truth to these three and their story, and real humanity in Channing's work as Sister Husband, but it would all mean a lot more if the screenplay had dialed down its manic inventions. And every time I looked at Portman or Judd, I was aware that whatever else Sequoia, Oklahoma, may lack, it obviously has makeup and hair facilities to rival Beverly Hills.

Where the Money Is ★ ★ ★
PG-13, 89 m., 2000

Paul Newman (Henry), Linda Fiorentino (Carol), Dermot Mulroney (Wayne), Susan Barnes (Mrs. Foster), Anne Pitoniak (Mrs. Tetlow), Bruce MacVittie (Karl), Irma St. Paul (Mrs. Galer), Michel Perron (Guard). Directed by Marek Kanievska and produced by Ridley Scott, Charles Weinstock, Chris Zarpas, and Christopher Dorr. Screenplay by E. Max Frye, Topper Lilien, and Carroll Cartwright.

Where the Money Is has a preposterous plot, but it's not about a plot; it's about acting. It's about how Paul Newman at seventy-five is still cool, sleek, and utterly self-confident, and about how Linda Fiorentino's low, calm voice sneaks in under his cover and challenges him in places he is glad to be reminded of. Watching these two working together is like watching a couple of thoroughbreds going around a track. You know they'll end up back where they started and you don't even have any money on the race, but look at that form.

Fiorentino plays a discontented nurse in a small town, married to the same guy (Dermot Mulroney) since high school. "We were king and queen of the prom, so it sort of made sense to get married," she tells Newman. "When did it stop making sense?" he asks. Newman can say a line like that to a woman and convince her it *never* made sense, even if she didn't know it until he asked the question.

I have given away a plot point by revealing that he speaks. In the opening scenes of the movie, he appears to be an old man paralyzed by a stroke. He can't move his body, he can't talk, he doesn't even look at anything. It's all an act: He's a veteran bank robber who has studied yoga in order to fake stroke symp-

toms, so he can be moved from prison to the retirement home, which he figures will be easier to escape from. Actually, it's not such a big point to reveal, since (a) we somehow intuit that Paul Newman wouldn't be starring in the movie if he didn't move or speak for ninety minutes, and (b) all the TV commercials and review clips show him moving and speaking.

The old crook, named Henry, is a good actor, and fools everybody except Carol, the nurse played by Fiorentino. She notices subtle clues, and tries to coax him out of his shell with a lap dance (she is dressed at the time, but in a nurse's uniform, which is always interesting). He resists. This is good yoga. She abandons sex for more direct methods, and he's forced to admit that he can indeed walk and talk. By later that night he's even dancing in the local tavern with Carol and her husband, Wayne.

Carol realizes that Henry is her ticket out of town. Either he still has a lot of money stashed away from all those bank jobs, or he can help her steal some more. Wayne finds this thinking seriously flawed, but eventually the three of them end up as partners in an armored car heist. The heist is as to the movie as Sinatra's cigarette and drink are to his song: superfluous, but it gives him something to do with his hands.

Newman you know all about. At his age he has such sex appeal that when the husband gets jealous, we believe it. He has that shucks, ma'am grin, and then you see in his eyes the look of a man who is still driving racing cars, and can find an opening at 160 mph. He counsels Wayne about an encounter with some dangerous men: "Be cool to these guys, right? Look them in the eye—but not like you're gonna remember their faces."

Fiorentino is a special case, an actress who in the wrong movie *(What Planet Are You From?)* seems clueless, and in the right one *(After Hours, The Last Seduction)* can make every scene be about what she's thinking she'd rather be doing. She is best employed playing a character who is the smartest person in the movie, which is the case this time.

As for the bank robber and his stroke: A lot of reviews are going to pair this movie with *Diamonds,* another 2000 movie involving a great movie star and a stroke. That one starred Kirk Douglas, who really did have a stroke, and has made a remarkable comeback. But the strokes in the two plots aren't the connection—after all, one is real and one is fake, and that's a big difference. The comparison should be between two aging but gifted stars looking for worthy projects.

Diamonds has a plot as dumb as a box of tofu. *Where the Money Is* has a plot marginally smarter, dialogue considerably smarter, and better opportunities for the human qualities of the actors to escape from the requirements of the story. After you see this movie, you want to see Paul Newman in another one. After you see *Diamonds,* you don't want to see another movie for a long time.

The Whole Nine Yards ★ ★ ★
R, 99 m., 2000

Bruce Willis (Jimmy Tudeski), Matthew Perry (Oz Oseransky), Rosanna Arquette (Sophie), Michael Clarke Duncan (Frankie Figs), Natasha Henstridge (Cynthi), Amanda Peet (Jill), Kevin Pollak (Yanni Gogolack), Harland Williams (Buffalo Steve). Directed by Jonathan Lynn and produced by David Willis and Allan Kaufman. Screenplay by Mitchell Kapner.

A subtle but unmistakable aura of jolliness sneaks from the screen during *The Whole Nine Yards,* and eventually we suspect that the actors are barely suppressing giggles. This is the kind of standard material everyone could do in lockstep, but you sense inner smiles, and you suspect the actors are enjoying themselves. George C. Scott said that a key element in any role was "the joy of performance"—the feeling that the actor is having a good time. This cast seems vastly amused.

Of course, I have no way of knowing if that was really the case. The actors may have hated one another and spent their evenings having anonymous pizzas delivered to each other's hotel rooms. All I can report is my subjective feeling. I know this is not the greatest comedy of all time, or even of the first seven weeks of the century, but I was entertained beyond all expectation.

One of the reasons for that is a perfect performance by Amanda Peet. I say it is perfect because it exactly matches what is required,

and then adds a level of heedless glee. I do not write as a longtime fan: Amanda Peet has been in seventeen previous movies without inspiring any cartwheels, but this time, as an ambitious young woman named Jill who would like to kill people for a living, she is so disarmingly, infectiously funny that finally all she has to do is smile to get a laugh.

Jill's role model is Jimmy Tudeski (Bruce Willis), a professional hit man known as Jimmy the Tulip. As the film opens, he has moved in next door to a Montreal dentist named Oz Oseransky (Matthew Perry), whose French-Canadian wife, Sophie (Rosanna Arquette), smokes cigarettes and wishes he were dead. So insufferable is this woman that Jill, who is Oz's office receptionist, volunteers, "You'd be doing the world a favor if you just had her whacked."

Everybody is having everybody whacked in *The Whole Nine Yards.* Jimmy the Tulip is being sought by Yanni Gogolak (Kevin Pollak), a Chicago gangster, who wants him whacked. Sophie wants Oz to go to Chicago and rat on the Tulip so they can collect the finder's fee. Oz does not much want to do this, but flies to Chicago and is taken under the muscular arms of Yanni's henchman Frankie Figs (Michael Clarke Duncan, the big guy from *The Green Mile*), and ushered into the Gogolak presence. Every actor in the movie has at least one juicy scene, and Pollak has fun with his, combining an impenetrable accent with key words that are spat out like hot oysters.

There is more to the plot, all of which you will have to discover for yourself. What I can describe is the amusement the actors exude. Bruce Willis has played countless hit men. This one simply has to stand there and suggest the potential for painful action. "It's not important how many people I kill," he explains to Perry; "what's important is how I get along with the people who are still alive." Willis glows as absurdities revolve around him. One of those absurdities is Matthew Perry's dentist, who is always running into things, like glass doors and Michael Clarke Duncan. He falls in love with the Tulip's wife, Cynthia (Natasha Henstridge), who is being held captive by Gogolak—but there I go with the plot again.

I think you have to be observant during this

film. There are some moments that are likely to be funny no matter what, but others depend on a certain momentum that gets going if you tune in to the underlying good humor. Here is a cast full of actors required to be silly while keeping a straight face, and somehow they have developed a faith that the screenplay is funny, and, of course, their belief makes it funny, and there you are.

And it would be worth renting the video just to study Amanda Peet's face and listen to her voice during her early encounters with the Tulip. She makes it all look so easy we forget that what she accomplishes is just about impossible: She is funny because of her personality without resorting to a "funny personality." They don't teach that in acting school.

The Widow of St. Pierre ★ ★ ★ ★
R, 112 m., 2001

Juliette Binoche (Madame La), Daniel Auteuil (Le Capitaine), Emir Kusturica (Neel Auguste), Michel Duchaussoy (Le Gouverneur), Philippe Magnan (President Venot), Christian Charmetant (Commissaire de la Marine), Philippe Du Janerand (Chef Douanier), Reynald Bouchard (Louis Olliver). Directed by Patrice Leconte and produced by Frederic Brillion and Gilles Legrand. Screenplay by Claude Faraldo.

A man gets drunk and commits a senseless murder. He is condemned to death by guillotine. But in the 1850s on a small French fishing island off the coast of Newfoundland, there is no guillotine, and no executioner. The guillotine can be shipped from France. But the island will have to find its own executioner, because superstitious ship's captains refuse to allow one on board.

Time passes, and a strange and touching thing happens. The murderer repents of his crime, and becomes a useful member of the community. He saves a woman's life. He works in a garden started by the wife of the captain of the local military. The judge who condemned him frets, "His popularity is a nuisance." An islander observes, "We committed a murderous brute and we're going to top a benefactor."

The Widow of St. Pierre is a beautiful and haunting film that tells this story, and then tells another subterranean story, about the seasons of a marriage. Le Capitaine (Daniel Auteuil) and his wife, referred to by everyone as Madame La (Juliette Binoche), are not only in love but in deep sympathy with each other. He understands her slightest emotional clues. "Madame La only likes desperate cases," someone says, and indeed she seems stirred by the plight of the prisoner. Stirred and . . . something else. The film is too intelligent and subtle to make obvious what the woman herself hardly suspects, but if we watch and listen closely we realize she is stirred in a sensual way by the prospect of a prisoner who has been condemned to die. Le Capitaine understands this and, because his wife is admirable and he loves her, he sympathizes with it.

The movie becomes not simply a drama about capital punishment, but a story about human psychology. Some audience members may not connect directly with the buried levels of obsession and attraction, but they'll sense them—sense something that makes the movie deeper and sadder than the plot alone can account for. Juliette Binoche, that wonderful actress, is the carrier of this subtlety, and the whole film resides in her face. Sad that most of those who saw her in *Chocolat* will never see, in this film, how much more she is capable of.

The Widow of St. Pierre is a title that carries extra weight. The French called a guillotine a "widow," and by the end of the film it has created two widows. And it has made a sympathetic character of the murderer, named Neel and played by the dark, burly Yugoslavian director Emir Kusturica. It accomplishes this not by soppy liberal piety, but by leading us to the same sort of empathy the islanders feel. Neel and a friend got drunk and murdered a man for no reason, and can hardly remember it. The friend is dead. Neel is prepared to die, but it becomes clear that death would redress nothing and solve nothing—and that Neel has changed so fundamentally that a different man would be going to the guillotine.

The director is Patrice Leconte, whose films unfailingly move me, and often (but not this time) make me smile. He is obsessed with obsession. He first fascinated me with *Monsieur Hire* (1989), based on a Simenon story about a little man who begins to spy on a beautiful woman whose window faces his. She knows he is looking, and plays her own game, until everything goes wrong. Then there was *The Hairdresser's Husband* (1990), about a man obsessed with hair and the women who cut it. Then *Ridicule* (1996), about a provincial landowner in the reign of Louis XVI, who wants to promote a drainage scheme at court and finds the king will favor only those who make him laugh. Then *The Girl on the Bridge* (1999), about a knife-thrower who recruits suicidal girls as targets for his act—because what do they have to lose?

The Widow of St. Pierre is unlike these others in tone. It is darker, angrier. And yet Leconte loves the humor of paradox, and some of it slips through, as in a scene where Madame La supplies Neel with a boat and advises him to escape to Newfoundland. He escapes, but returns, because he doesn't want to get anyone into trouble. When the guillotine finally arrives, he helps bring it ashore, because he doesn't want to cause work for others on his account. He impregnates a local girl and is allowed to marry, and the islanders develop an affection for him and begin to see the judge as an alien troublemaker from a France they believe "doesn't care about our cod island."

Now watch closely during the scene where Neel marries his pregnant bride. Madame La hides it well during the ceremony, but is distraught. "It's all right; I'm here," Le Capitaine tells her. What's all right? I think she loves Neel. It's not that she wants to be his lover; in the 1850s such a thought would probably not occur. It's that she is happy for him, and is marrying him and having his child vicariously. And Le Capitaine knows that, and loves her the more for it.

The movie is not even primarily about Neel, his crime, his sentence, and the difficulty of bringing about his death. That is the subplot. It is really about the captain and his wife. About two people with good hearts who live in an innocent, less self-aware time, and how the morality of the case and their deeper feelings about Neel all get mixed up together. Eventually Le Capitaine takes a stand, and everyone thinks it is based on politics and ethics, but if we have been paying attention we know better. It is based on his love for his wife, and the ethics are an afterthought.

Wild Wild West ★
PG-13, 107 m., 1999

Will Smith (James T. West), Kevin Kline (Artemus Gordon), Kenneth Branagh (Dr. Arliss Loveless), Salma Hayek (Rita Escobar), Ted Levine (McGrath), Frederique Van Der Wal (Amazonia), Musetta Vander (Munitia), Sofia Eng (Miss Lippenreider), M. Emmet Walsh (Coleman). Directed by Barry Sonnenfeld and produced by Sonnenfeld and Jon Peters. Screenplay by S. S. Wilson, Brent Maddock, Jeffrey Price, and Peter S. Seaman, based on a story by Jim Thomas and John Thomas.

Wild Wild West is a comedy dead zone. You stare in disbelief as scenes flop and die. The movie is all concept and no content; the elaborate special effects are like watching money burn on the screen. You know something has gone wrong when a story is about two heroes in the Old West, and the last shot is of a mechanical spider riding off into the sunset.

Will Smith and Kevin Kline costar, as special federal agents who are assigned by President U. S. Grant to investigate the disappearance of lots of top scientists. They stumble over a plot to assassinate Grant by a megalomaniac who wants to give half the country back to Britain and Spain, and keep the rest in the hands of the villain. Salma Hayek teams up with them, as a woman who says her father was one of the kidnapped geniuses. The bad guy (Kenneth Branagh) is a mad inventor who makes giant steam-powered iron tarantulas and spiders, which are not very practical in Monument Valley, but who cares?

Certainly not anyone in the movie. Smith and Kline have so little chemistry they seem to be acting in front of rear-projections of each other. They go through the motions, but there's no eye contact. Imagine Bill Clinton and Kenneth Starr as partners in a celebrity golf tournament.

The Kline character is said to be a master of disguise, and first appears in drag as a dance hall girl, wearing a false plastic bosom so persuasive that when a siren turns up later in the movie, her décolletage looks unconvincing by comparison. That doesn't stop Smith from giving her cleavage a few jolly thumps, and then telling a white lynch mob he was simply following the example of his African ancestors, who communicated by pounding on drums—and bosoms, I guess. (In a movie where almost nothing is funny, the race references are painfully lame.)

One of the running gags is about how the Kline character can invent almost anything, right on the spot. He rigs a rail car so that it can shoot people into the air, have them fall through openings that appear in the roof, and land in a chair. The rig works in opposition to the first law of motion, but never mind: In a movie where anything can happen, does it matter that anything does?

Kenneth Branagh's character has no body from the waist down, but operates from a clever wheelchair and, later, with mechanical legs. He has weird facial hair and lots of bizarre plans, and an evil general on his payroll has a weird miniature ear trumpet permanently screwed into the side of his face. His gigantic artificial war machines look like they were recycled from *Star Wars,* right down to their command cockpits.

There are moments when all artifice fails and you realize you are regarding desperate actors, trapped on the screen, fully aware they've been left hanging out to dry. Consider an early scene where Will Smith and a sexy girl are embracing in a water tank when the evil General McGrath rides into town. Smith is made to look at McGrath out of a knothole, while continuing to make automatic midair smooching movements with his lips—as if he doesn't realize he's not still kissing the woman. Uh-huh.

Wild Wild West is so bad it violates not one but two rules from *Ebert's Bigger Little Movie Glossary.* By casting M. Emmet Walsh as the train engineer, it invalidates the Stanton-Walsh Rule, which states that no movie starring Harry Dean Stanton or M. Emmet Walsh can be altogether bad. And by featuring Kevin Kline without facial hair, it violates the Kevin Kline Mustache Principle, which observes that Kline wears a mustache in comedies but is clean-shaven in serious roles. Of course, Kline can always appeal on the grounds that although he is clean-shaven in his principal role here, he sports facial hair in three other roles he plays in the movie—or perhaps he could use the defense that *Wild Wild West* is not a comedy.

William Shakespeare's A Midsummer Night's Dream ★ ★ ★
PG-13, 115 m., 1999

Kevin Kline (Nick Bottom), Michelle Pfeiffer (Titania), Rupert Everett (Oberon), Stanley Tucci (Puck [Robin]), Calista Flockhart (Helena), Anna Friel (Hermia), Christian Bale (Demetrius), Dominic West (Lysander), David Strathairn (Theseus), Sophie Marceau (Hippolyta). Directed by Michael Hoffman and produced by Leslie Urdang and Hoffman. Screenplay by Hoffman, based on the play by William Shakespeare.

"Reason and love keep little company together nowadays."

So says Bottom in Shakespeare's *A Midsummer Night's Dream,* and he could be describing the play he occupies. It is an enchanted folly, suggesting that romance is a matter of chance, since love is blind; at the right moment we are likely to fall in love with the first person our eyes light upon. Much of the play's fun comes during a long night in the forest, where a mischief-maker anoints the eyes of sleeping lovers with magic potions that cause them to adore the first person they see upon awakening.

This causes all sorts of confusions, not least when Titania, the Fairy Queen herself, falls in love with a weaver who has grown donkey's ears. The weaver is Bottom (Kevin Kline), and he and the mischievous Puck (Stanley Tucci) are the most important characters in the play, although it also involves dukes, kings, queens, and high-born lovers. Bottom has a good heart and bumbles through, and Puck (also called Robin Goodfellow) spreads misunderstanding wherever he goes. The young lovers are pawns in a magic show: When they can't see the one they love, they love the one they see.

Michael Hoffman's new film of *William Shakespeare's A Midsummer Night's Dream* (who else's?) is updated to the nineteenth century, set in Italy, and furnished with bicycles and operatic interludes. But it is founded on Shakespeare's language and is faithful, by and large, to the original play. Harold Bloom complains in his wise best-seller *Shakespeare: The Invention of the Human* that the play's romantic capers have been twisted by modern adaptations into "the notion that sexual violence and bestiality are at the center of this humane and wise drama." He might approve of this version, which is gentle and lighthearted, and portrays Bottom not as a lustful animal but as a nice enough fellow who has had the misfortune to wake up with donkey's ears—"amiably innocent, and not very bawdy," as Bloom describes him.

Kevin Kline is, of course, the embodiment of amiability, as he bashfully parries the passionate advances of Titania (Michelle Pfeiffer). Her eyes have been anointed with magical ointment at the behest of her husband, Oberon, (Rupert Everett), who hopes to steal away the young boy they both dote on. When she opens them to regard Bottom, she is besotted with love and inspired to some of Shakespeare's most lyrical poetry:

I'll give thee fairies to attend on thee;
And they shall fetch thee jewels from
the deep,
And sing, while thou on pressed flowers
dost sleep.

Meanwhile, more magical potions, distributed carelessly by Puck, have hopelessly confused the relationships among four young people who were introduced at the beginning of the play. They are Helena (Calista Flockhart), Hermia (Anna Friel), Demetrius (Christian Bale), and Lysander (Dominic West). Now follow this closely. Hermia has been promised by her father to Demetrius, but she loves Lysander. Demetrius was Helena's lover, but now claims to prefers Hermia. Hermia is offered three cruel choices by the duke, Theseus (David Strathairn): marry according to her father's wishes, go into a convent, or die. Desperate, she flees to a nearby wood with Lysander, her true love. Helena, who loves Demetrius, tips him off to follow them; maybe if he sees his intended in the arms of another man, he will return to Helena's arms.

The wood grows crowded. Also turning up at the same moonlit rendezvous are Bottom and his friends, workmen from the village who plan to rehearse a play to be performed at the wedding of Theseus and *his* intended, Queen Hippolyta (Sophie Marceau). And flickering about the glen are Oberon, Titania, Puck, and assorted fairies. Only the most determined typecasting helps us tell them apart: As many times as I've been through this play in one form or another, I can't always distinguish the four young lovers, who seem interchangeable. They function mostly to be meddled with by Puck's potions.

Hoffman, whose wonderful *Restoration* recreated a time of fire and plague, here conducts with a playful touch. There are small gems of stagecraft for all of the actors, including Snout, the village tinker, who plays a wall in the performance for the duke, and makes a circle with his thumb and finger to represent a chink in it. It's wonderful to behold Pfeiffer's infatuation with the donkey-eared Bottom, whom she winds in her arms as "doth the woodbine the sweet honeysuckle gently twist"; her love is so real, we almost believe it. Kline's Bottom tactfully humors her mad infatuation, good-natured and accepting. And Tucci's Puck suggests sometimes that he has a darker side, but is not so much malicious as incompetent.

Midsummer Night's Dream is another entry in Shakespeare's recent renaissance on film. Consider *Much Ado About Nothing*, Ian McKellen's *Richard III*, Al Pacino's documentary *Looking for Richard*, Laurence Fishburne as *Othello*, Branagh's *Hamlet*, Helena Bonham Carter in *Twelfth Night*, Baz Luhrmann's modern street version of *Romeo and Juliet*, the Lear-inspired *A Thousand Acres*, the remake of *Taming of the Shrew* as *10 Things I Hate About You*, and the bard's celebration in *Shakespeare in Love*, *Hamlet* with Ethan Hawke, Branagh's *Love's Labour's Lost*, Mekhi Phifer as Othello in the modern urban drama *O*, and Anthony Hopkins in *Titus*, based on the rarely staged Titus Andronicus ("All Rome's a wilderness of tigers").

Why is Shakespeare so popular with filmmakers when he contains so few car chases and explosions? Because he is the measuring stick by which actors and directors test themselves. His insights into human nature are so true that he has, as Bloom argues in his book, actually created our modern idea of the human personality. Before Hamlet asked, "To be, or not to be?" dramatic characters just were. Ever since, they have known and questioned themselves. Even in a comedy like *Midsummer*, there are quick flashes of brilliance that help us see ourselves. "What fools these mortals be," indeed.

Windhorse ★ ★
NO MPAA RATING, 97 m., 1999

Dadon (Dolkar), Name Withheld (Pema), Jampa Kelsang (Dorjee), Richard Chang (Duan-ping), Lu Yu (Mr. Du), Tenzin Pema (Young Dolkar), Deepak Tserin (Young Dorjee), Pasang Dolma (Young Pema). Directed and produced by Paul Wagner. Screenplay by Julia Elliot, Thupten Tsering, and Wagner.

Windhorse is a well-meaning but clunky film about a Tibetan family's life under Chinese occupation. Its heart is in the right place, and there's intrinsic interest in a film that was daringly shot partly on location in Tibet itself. But anyone interested enough in the cause of Tibet to attend the film is probably going to consider the story a simplistic melodrama.

The prologue begins in 1979, when children playing in the streets become witnesses to the killing of a relative by Chinese soldiers. We jump forward to 1998, and meet the children as grown-ups. Dolkar (Dadon) sings in a karaoke bar and dates a Chinese broadcast official named Duan-ping (Richard Chang). Her brother Dorjee (Jampa Kelsang), who hates the Chinese, spends most of his time drinking and playing pool. Their cousin Pema (played by a Tibetan actress whose name has been withheld) has become a nun.

Duan-ping, more of a dupe than a villain, realizes he can curry favor with his superiors by recruiting Dolkar to sing on the local TV station, which carries mostly propaganda. She rehearses songs in praise of Chairman Mao, and invites her boyfriend home for tea; her grandmother spits in it in the kitchen before coming in to serve.

Meanwhile, Pema's nunnery is ill-treated by Chinese officials, who forbid anyone to possess a picture of the Dalai Lama—or even think of him. One day in the market she grows so filled with emotion that she shouts anti-Chinese slogans and is arrested. Eventually she is delivered by the Chinese to the home of her cousins so badly beaten her life is in danger.

Under these circumstances, can Dolkar still go ahead with the TV show? Will Dorjee sober up and play a role? What will happen to Pema? These are all the matters of melodrama, and it's at this level that the movie chooses to work; change the name and the costumes, and it's as simplistic as any other propaganda film. Perhaps on video, in the right hands, in Tibet, it will play as a powerful statement. But judged for its film qualities rather than its politics, it's routine. The qualities that recommend it are the authentic locations and the conviction of the actors, who deserved a more challenging screenplay.

Note: The film's value as politics is underlined by a controversy at the 1998 Hawaii International Film Festival, where the Chinese protested its inclusion in competition for the main prize. Director Paul Wagner at first withdrew the film from the festival, then decided to allow it to show out of competition, on the reasonable grounds that he would rather have it seen than make a point.

Wing Commander ★
PG-13, 100 m., 1999

Freddie Prinze Jr. (Blair), Saffron Burrows (Deveraux), Matthew Lillard (Maniac), Tcheky Karyo (Paladin), Jurgen Prochnow (Gerald), David Suchet (Sansky), Ginny Holder (Rosie Forbes), David Warner (Tolwyn). Directed by Chris Roberts and produced by Todd Moyer. Screenplay by Roberts.

Jurgen Prochnow, who played the submarine captain in *Das Boot,* is one of the stars of *Wing Commander,* and no wonder: This is a sub movie exported to deep space, complete with the obligatory warning about the onboard oxygen running low. "Torpedoes incoming!" a watch officer shouts. "Brace yourself!" It's 500 years in the future. If the weapons developed by the race of evil Kilrathi only inspire you to "brace yourself," we might reasonably ask what the Kilrathi have been doing with their time.

Other marine notes: "Hard to port!" is a command at one point. Reasonable at sea, but in space, where a ship is not sailing on a horizontal surface, not so useful. "Quiet! There's a destroyer!" someone shouts, and then everyone on board holds their breath, as there are subtle sonar "pings" on the sound track, and we hear the rumble of a giant vessel overhead. Or underhead. Wherever. "In space," as *Alien* reminded us, "no one can hear you scream." There is an excellent reason for that: Vacuums do not conduct sound waves, not even those caused by giant destroyers.

Such logic is, of course, irrelevant to *Wing Commander*, a movie based on a video game and looking like one a lot of the time, as dashing pilots fly around blowing up enemy targets. Our side kills about a zillion Kilrathi for every one of our guys that buys it, but when heroes die, of course, they die in the order laid down by ancient movie clichés. The moment I saw that one of the pilots was an attractive black woman (Ginny Holder), I knew she'd go down, or up, in flames.

The plot involves war between the humans and the Kilrathi, who have refused all offers of peace and wish only to be targets in the crosshairs of video computer screens. Indeed, according to a Web page, they hope to "destroy the universe," which seems self-defeating. The Kilrathi are ugly turtleoid creatures with goatees, who talk like voice synthesizers cranked way down, heavy on the bass.

Against them stand the noble earthlings, although the film's hero, Blair (Freddie Prinze Jr.) is suspect in some circles because he is a half-breed. Yes, his mother was a Pilgrim. Who were the Pilgrims? Humans who were the original space voyagers and developed a gene useful for instinctively navigating in "space-time itself." (Just about all navigation is done in space-time itself, but never mind.) Pilgrims went too far and dared too much, so timid later men resented them—but if you need someone to skip across a Gravity Hole, a Pilgrim is your man.

There are actors on board capable of splendid performances. The commander of the fleet is played by David Warner, who brings utter believability to, alas, banal dialogue. Two of the other officers, played by Tcheky Karyo and Prochnow, are also fine; I'd like to see them in a real navy movie. Prinze shows again an easy grace and instant likability. Matthew Lillard, as a hotshot pilot named Maniac, gets into a daredevil competition with the Holder character, and I enjoyed their energy. And the perfectly named Saffron Burrows has a pleasing presence as the head of the pilot squadron, although having recently seen her in a real movie (Mike Figgis's *The Loss of Sexual Innocence*, at Sundance), I assume she took this role to pay the utility bills.

These actors, alas, are at the service of a submoronic script and special effects that look like a video game writ large. *Wing Commander* arrived at the end of a week that began with the death of the creator of *2001: A Space Odyssey*. Close the pod bay door, Hal. And turn off the lights.

The Winslow Boy ★ ★ ★ ½
G, 110 m., 1999

Nigel Hawthorne (Arthur Winslow), Jeremy Northam (Sir Robert Morton), Rebecca Pidgeon (Catherine Winslow), Gemma Jones (Grace Winslow), Guy Edwards (Ronnie Winslow), Matthew Pidgeon (Dickie Winslow), Colin Stinton (Desmond Curry), Aden Gillett (John Watherstone). Directed by David Mamet and produced by Sarah Green. Screenplay by Mamet, based on the play by Terence Rattigan.

The Winslow Boy, based on a play set in 1912, is said to be a strange choice for David Mamet, whose work usually involves lowlifes and con men, gamblers and thieves. Not really. This film, like many of his stories, is about whether an offscreen crime really took place. And it employs his knack for using the crime as a surface distraction while his real subject takes form at a buried level. *The Winslow Boy* seems to be about a young boy accused of theft. It is actually about a father prepared to ruin his family to prove that the boy's word (and by extension his own word) can be trusted. And about a woman who conducts two courtships in plain view while a third, the real one, takes place entirely between the lines.

The movie is based on a 1940s play by Terence Rattigan, inspired by a true story. It involves the Winslow family of South Kensington, London—the father a retired bank official, wife pleased with their life, adult daughter a suffragette, older son at Oxford, younger son a cadet at the Royal Naval Academy. One day the young cadet, named Ronnie, is found standing terrified in the garden. He has been expelled from school for stealing a five-shilling postal order.

In a scene that establishes the moral foundation for the entire story, his father, Arthur, calls him into the study after dinner and demands the truth, adding, "A lie between us cannot be hidden." Did he steal the money? "No, father, I didn't." The father is played by Nigel Hawthorne (*The Madness of King George*), who is stern, firm, and on the brink of old age. He believes his son and calls in the family solicitor to mount a defense. Soon one of the most famous attorneys in London has been hired: Sir Robert Morton (Jeremy Northam), who led the defense of Oscar Wilde. The father devotes his family's large but finite resources to the expensive legal battle, which eventually leads to the older son being brought home from Oxford, servants being dismissed, and possessions being sold. Arthur's wife, Grace (Gemma Jones), protests that justice is not worth the price being paid, but Arthur persists in his unwavering obsession.

The court case inspires newspaper headlines, popular songs, public demonstrations, and debates in Parliament. It proceeds on the surface level of the film. Underneath, hidden in a murk of emotional contradictions, is the buried life of the suffragette daughter, Catherine (Rebecca Pidgeon). She is engaged to the respectable, bloodless John Watherstone (Aden Gillett). She has known for years that Desmond, the family solicitor (Colin Stinton), is in love with her. As the case gains notoriety, John's ardor cools: He fears the name Winslow is becoming a laughingstock. And as John fades, Desmond's hopes grow. But the only interesting tension between Catherine and a man involves her disapproval of the great Sir Robert Morton, who rejects her feelings about women's equality and indeed disagrees with more or less every idea she possesses.

It is an interesting law of romance that a truly strong woman will choose a strong man who disagrees with her over a weak one who goes along. Strength demands intelligence, intelligence demands stimulation, and weakness is boring. It is better to find a partner you can contend with for a lifetime than one who accommodates you because he doesn't really care. That is the psychological principle on which Mamet's hidden story is founded, and it all leads up to the famous closing line of Rattigan's play, "How little you know about men." A line innocuous in itself, but electrifying in context.

In a lesser film, we would be required to get involved in the defense of young Ronnie Winslow, and there would be a big courtroom scene and artificial suspense and an obligatory payoff. Mamet doesn't make films on automatic pilot, and Rattigan's play is not about who is right, but about how important it is to be right. There is a wonderful audacity in the way that the outcome of the case happens offscreen and is announced in an indirect manner. The real drama isn't about poor little Ronnie, but about the passions he has unleashed in his household—between his parents, and between his sister and her suitors, declared and undeclared.

A story like this, when done badly, is about plot. When done well, it is about character. All of the characters are well-bred, and brought up in a time when reticence was valued above all. Today's audiences have been raised in a climate of emotional promiscuity; confession and self-humiliation are leaking from the daytime talk shows into our personal styles. But there's no fun and no class in simply blurting out everything one feels. Mamet's characters are interesting precisely because of the reserve and detachment they bring to passion. Sixty seconds of wondering if someone is about to kiss you is more entertaining than sixty minutes of kissing. By understanding that, Mamet is able to deliver a G-rated film that is largely about adult sexuality.

That brings us to the key performances by Jeremy Northam and Rebecca Pidgeon, as Sir Robert and the suffragette. Pidgeon's performance has been criticized in some circles (no doubt the fact that she is Mrs. Mamet was a warning flag). She is said to be too reticent, too mannered, too cold. Those adjectives describe her performance, but miss the point. What her critics seem to desire is a willingness to roll over and play friendly puppy to Sir Robert. But Pidgeon's character, Catherine, is not a people-pleaser; she is scarcely interested in knowing you unless you are clever enough to clear the hurdle of her defenses. Her public personality is a performance game, and Sir Robert knows it—because his is too. That's why their conversations are so erotic. Spill the beans, and the conversation is history. Speak in code, with wit and challenge, and the process of decryption is like foreplay.

With a Friend Like Harry ★ ★ ★
R, 117 m., 2001

Laurent Lucas (Michel), Sergi Lopez (Harry), Mathilde Seigner (Claire), Sophie Guillemin (Plum), Laurie Caminata (Sarah), Lorena Caminata (Iris), Victoire de Koster (Jeane). Directed by Dominik Moll and produced by Michel Saint-Jean. Screenplay by Gilles Marchand and Moll.

Michel uses the rest room of a highway oasis to splash some water on his face. He is addressed by a man who smiles too long and stands too close, and pauses as if expecting Michel to say something. Michel doesn't know what to say. The stranger introduces himself as Harry—an old school friend. Michel doesn't remember him, but Harry's memory is perfect. He remembers the girl they both dated, and quotes a poem Michel wrote for the school magazine.

When people make a closer study of us than we make of ourselves, we grow uneasy. They seem too needy. We want them to get a life. But Harry (Sergi Lopez) has an ingratiating way, and soon has inspired a dinner invitation. Michel (Laurent Lucas) and his wife, Claire (Mathilde Seigner), are on their way to their summer cottage with their noisy daughters. Harry and his girlfriend, Plum (Sophie Guillemin), come along.

We don't like this Harry. He sticks like glue. He insinuates. He makes offers and insists on them. He doesn't respect the distance strangers should keep from one another. He doesn't think of himself as a stranger. It's not wholesome. You can't put your finger on specific transgressions, but his whole style is a violation. He starts conversations Michel has no wish to join. "How do you like Plum?" Harry asks. "She's not brainy like Claire, but she has an animal intelligence that I like. Know what I mean?" Michel doesn't want to know what he means.

With a Friend Like Harry, directed by Dominik Moll, works like a thriller, but we can't put our finger on exactly why we think so. Maybe it's only about an obnoxious pest. Yet Harry is admittedly helpful: Michel and Claire's old car has no air conditioning, and Harry presents them with a brand-new, bright red SUV. No obligation. He wants to. What are friends for?

Harry is a nickname for Satan. Is this Harry the devil? By using the name, the movie nudges us toward the possibility. On the other hand, maybe he's simply a pushy guy named Harry. Maybe the locus of evil is located elsewhere in the movie. Maybe Harry brings out the worst in people.

Movies like this are more intriguing than thrillers where the heroes and villains wear name tags. We know there's danger and possibly violence coming at some point, but we don't know why, or how, or even who will initiate it. Meanwhile, everyday horrors build up the tension. Michel and Claire's family cabin is rude and unfinished, almost a shack. "It needs a lot of work." Yes—but upstairs there is a brand-new bathroom with shocking pink tile. This is the gift of Michel's parents, who wanted to "surprise" them.

What do you do when someone surprises you with a gift that you consider a vulgar eyesore, and you're stuck with it? Are the people who give such gifts really so insensitive? Are their gifts acts of veiled hostility? A new SUV is at least something you want. A shocking pink bathroom is the wrong idea in a rustic country cabin. It might . . . well, it might almost be a gift to be rid of people who insist on such annoyances.

Sergi Lopez, who plays Harry, last appeared in *An Affair of Love*, the insidious French film about the couple who meet through the classifieds and spend one afternoon a week in a hotel room doing something that apparently no one else in the world wants to do, except for them. We never find out what it is. In that movie, before the situation grew complicated, his face bore the contentment of a man whose imaginary pockets are full.

Here he turns up the dial. He's bursting with confidences, reassurances, compliments, generosity. We realize with a shock that the most frightening outcome of the movie would be if it contained no surprises, no revelations,

659

no quirky twist at the end. What would really be terrifying is if Harry is exactly as he seems, and the plot provides no escape for Michel and Claire, and they're stuck with their new friend. *With a Friend Like Harry*, you don't need enemies.

Woman on Top ★ ★ ½
R, 93 m., 2000

Penelope Cruz (Isabella Oliveira), Murilo Benicio (Toninho Oliveira), Harold Perrineau Jr. (Monica Jones), Mark Feuerstein (Cliff Lloyd), John DeLancie (Alex Reeves). Directed by Fina Torres and produced by Alan Poul. Screenplay by Vera Blasi.

Woman on Top is like one of those lightweight 1950s Universal romances, depending for its charm on the appeal of the actors, and supplying them with a story lighter than air. Even now, the formula seduces us for an hour or so before the movie sinks under the weight of its dim-wittedness. These characters in this story need to be smarter. And yet two of the leads, Penelope Cruz and Harold Perrineau Jr., are wonderful, and emerge untouched from the wreckage.

Cruz plays Isabella, a woman from the enchanted Brazilian state of Bahia, who is an artist with food (the character owes something to Tita, the heroine of *Like Water for Chocolate*). When she cooks, aromas waft from her pot and under the noses of men, and it is love at first bite. She falls for the macho hunk Toninho (Murilo Benicio), marries him, slaves in his restaurant, and is happy. There is one technicality. She was born with motion sickness. It doesn't affect her if she's in control. In a car, she must drive. She prefers the stairs to the elevator. And in bed, she has to be on top.

This drives Toninho crazy, and she catches him with another woman. "I'm a man!" he cries. "I have to be on top *sometimes!*" But in a rage she flies off to San Francisco and moves in with her best friend, Monica Jones, who is a transvestite played by Perrineau in a performance both funny and endearing. "Monica Jones" doesn't sound like the name of someone who grew up in Salvador, the capital of Bahia, but then this is one of those multinational movies where the ethnic flavor is suggested by speaking English with an accent.

Isabella's cooking soon wins her a show on local TV, with Monica as her sidekick, and Cruz is bewitching as she demonstrates how to inhale the soul of the pepper, and how to teach your fingers to salt without thinking. Cruz is bewitching all through the movie, but her beauty and charm have to pull a heavy train of clichés and inevitable developments—as when the national network execs want her to "look less ethnic," use Tabasco instead of real peppers, wear a low-cut dress, work under brighter lights, and "lose the freak" (Monica). Her American quasi-boyfriend (Mark Feuerstein) loves her cooking but sides with the suits, and what happens next will be predictable for all but those seeing their first motion picture.

Cruz is a Spanish star who was recently electrifying in Pedro Almodovar's *All About My Mother* and was indescribably sexy and funny in *Jamon, Jamon* (1992), which translates as "Ham, Ham" and which you should put at the top of the list of films you really should have seen. *Woman on Top* wants to combine the sexual freedom of Almodovar with the magical realism of *Like Water for Chocolate*, but succeeds in doing for its sources what the TV execs want to do to Isabella: going for the broad and dull commercial approach instead of the wicked inside curve.

And yet Cruz herself is lovable and charismatic, and we can just about believe it when she walks down the street with a dish she has cooked, and hundreds of men follow her like sheep. Perrineau is lovable, too; he plays Monica not as a stereotyped drag queen but as a character who would be believed by most of the audience as a woman if it were not for his entrance and the tip-offs in the dialogue. The performance is all the more impressive since Perrineau (the narrator of HBO's *Oz* and the man killed by the bear in *The Edge*) is not a professional transvestite but is simply playing a role—so well, he's invaluable in every scene he's in, and steals his share.

But the story is a slow slog toward the obvious. The evil TV execs are out of the Recycled Character Department. The Brazilian husband is a convenience, not a necessity. The

American boyfriend is a dope. And the movie plays its story so very safely that it sidesteps all the comic and romantic possibilities in the Monica character. She's more like a mascot, when in a smarter movie she would have been the wild card. This is the kind of movie you sort of like, and yet even while you're liking it, you're thinking how much better these characters and this situation could have been with a little more imagination and daring. Starting with Isabella and Monica, what did they have to lose?

Wonder Boys ★ ★ ★ ★
R, 112 m., 2000

Michael Douglas (Grady Tripp), Tobey Maguire (James Leer), Frances McDormand (Sara Gaskell), Robert Downey Jr. (Terry Crabtree), Katie Holmes (Hannah Green), Richard Thomas (Walter Gaskell), Rip Torn (Q). Directed by Curtis Hanson and produced by Scott Rudin and Hanson. Screenplay by Steve Kloves, based upon the novel by Michael Chabon.

My father was an electrician at the University of Illinois. He never taught me a thing about electricity. "Every time I walk through the English building," he said, "I see the professors in their offices with their feet up on the desk, reading books and smoking their pipes. Now that's the life for you."

I thought I would be an English professor. Then I got into this game. Sometimes I am overwhelmed with a sense of loss: I remember myself walking across the snowy campus at dusk, a book bag thrown over my shoulder, on the way to the seminar room to drink coffee and talk about Cather or Faulkner. And I remember the endless weekends, driving around town in somebody's oversize American car, following rumors of parties. And the emotional and romantic confusion that played out at those parties, where everyone was too smart and too high and filled with themselves.

Wonder Boys is the most accurate movie about campus life I can remember. It is accurate, not because it captures intellectual debate or campus politics, but because it knows two things: (1) students come and go but the faculty actually lives there, and (2) many faculty members stay stuck in graduate student mode for decades. Michael Douglas plays a character like that. It is his best performance in years, muted, gentle, and wondering. He is a boy wonder long past his sell-by date, a fifty-ish English professor named Grady Tripp who wrote a good novel seven years ago and now, everyone believes, has writer's block.

Wonder Boys follows him around a Pittsburgh campus in winter during a literary festival, as characters drift in and out of focus on his emotional viewfinder. His wife (we never see her) has just left him. His boss is Walter Gaskell (Richard Thomas), the head of the English department. Walter's wife, Sara (Frances McDormand), is the chancellor. Grady is having an affair with Sara. His New York editor, Crabtree (Robert Downey Jr.), is in town for the festival, and wonders where the new manuscript is. The famous writer "Q" (Rip Torn) is a visiting speaker. Two of Grady's students occupy his attention: James Leer (Tobey Maguire), who has written a novel and is moody and difficult and a pathological liar; and Hannah Green (Katie Holmes), who rents a room in Grady's house and would probably share his bed, although it has not come to that.

Because Grady is tired, depressed, and continuously stoned on pot, these characters all have more or less equal importance. That is, when he's looking at them they represent problems, and when they're absent, he can forget about them.

The movie is an unsprung screwball comedy, slowed down to real-life speed. Mishaps trip over one another in their eagerness to mess with Grady's mind. One thing leads to another. He goes to a party at the Gaskells' house and Sara tells him she is pregnant. He steps outside for a reefer, sees James standing in the dark with a gun, invites him in, and sneaks him upstairs to show him a secret closet where Walter Gaskell keeps his treasure (the suit Marilyn Monroe wore on her wedding day). Then the Gaskells' blind dog bites him and James shoots the dog dead.

At a certain velocity, this would be wacky. One of the wise decisions of *Wonder Boys* is to avoid that velocity. Grady plods around town in a pink bathrobe, trying to repair damage, tell the truth, give good advice, be a decent

661

man, and keep his life from falling apart. The brilliance of the movie can be seen in its details: (1) Hannah is brought onstage as an obvious love interest, but is a decoy; (2) Crabtree picks up a transvestite on the airplane, but dumps him for James, who is not exactly straight or gay (neither is Crabtree); (3) when the transvestite needs a ride, Grady says, "I'm your man" but their drive results not in sex but in truth-telling; and (4) Sara is not hysterical about being pregnant and is understanding, actually, about Grady's chaotic lifestyle.

So all the obvious payoffs are short-circuited. No mechanical sex scenes. No amazing revelation that the transvestite is not a woman (everyone in the movie clocks him instantly). No emotional show-offs. And the sex in the movie, gay and straight, is handled sanely, as a calming pastime after long and nutty evenings. (Notice how comfortable the Downey character is with his weaknesses of the flesh.)

Let me give one more example of how the movie uses observation instead of wheezy clichés. When Q, the writer, is giving his speech, he pontificates about piloting the boat of inspiration to the shore of achievement. James utters a loud, high-pitched giggle. In a lesser movie James would have continued, making some kind of angry and rebellious statement. Not in *Wonder Boys*, where James thinks Q is ludicrous, laughs rudely once, and then shuts up.

And listen to the dialogue. Grady has been working on his second novel so long it now runs well over 2,000 single-spaced pages. Hannah suggests tactfully that by including the "genealogies of everyone's horses, and their dental records," Grady's work "reads as if you didn't make any choices." The right line in a movie that does make choices. She also wonders if the book would have more shape if he hadn't been stoned when he wrote it. Yes, his brilliant first book was written on reefer, but then a lot of first novels are written long before they're actually put down on paper.

Wonder Boys is the first movie by Curtis Hanson since his *L.A. Confidential.* In a very different way, it is as accomplished. The screenplay by Steve Kloves, based on a novel by Michael Chabon, is European in its preference for character over plot. This is a funny and touching story that contains dead dogs, Monroe memorabilia, a stolen car,

sex, adultery, pregnancy, guns, dope, and cops, but it is not about any of those things. It is about people, and especially about trying to be a good teacher.

Could one weekend on a real campus possibly contain all of these events? Easily, given the tendency of writers to make themselves deliberately colorful. Grady knows exactly what he's doing. Of Hannah he observes: "She was a junkie for the printed word. Lucky for me, I manufactured her drug of choice." 🖝

Wonderland ★ ★ ★
R, 108 m., 2000

Gina McKee (Nadia), Molly Parker (Molly), Shirley Henderson (Debbie), John Simm (Eddie), Ian Hart (Dan), Kika Markham (Eileen), Jack Shepherd (Bill), Enzo Cilenti (Darren). Directed by Michael Winterbottom and produced by Michele Camarda and Andrew Eaton. Screenplay by Laurence Coriat.

Michael Winterbottom's *Wonderland* tells the story of three sisters in south London, each lonely in her own way, and of their husbands, parents, blind dates, neighbors, and children, all lonely too, during four rainy days in November. You seek in this movie for someone who is doing it right, who has found happiness, and all you come up with is the grown son who ran away from it all. Does that mean these people are unusual? Not at all. Most people are not terrifically happy most of the time. That's why, according to this movie, they invented booze, professional sports, television, hairdressing, and sex.

I saw the film at about the same time I took a fresh look at *Nashville* (1975), Robert Altman's film of interlocking lives. Altman has often ventured into these constructions, where you find out gradually how the characters are related; think also of his *Short Cuts* and *The Player,* and of two Paul Thomas Anderson films influenced by him, *Boogie Nights* and *Magnolia.* While most plots march from the beginning to the end of a film, these kinds of films move in circles, suggesting that life is not a story but a process. They're more true to life. Reality isn't a march toward a happy ending, but a long series of small and hopeful sideways moves toward dimly sensed goals.

Why do I feel touched by *Wonderland* and other films like it? Because these films are about themselves and not about me. The real subject of most conventional films, especially the summer special-effects pictures, is me—how they make me feel, how they shock me, how they scare me, how I feel during the chase scenes. There is nothing to be discovered about human nature in them. A movie like *Wonderland*, on the other hand, is about them—about people I am not and will never be, but who are all around me in the city, and share this time and society. F/X pictures come out of the screen at me. Movies like *Wonderland* invite me into the screen with them. I am curious. I begin to care.

The sisters in *Wonderland* are Nadia (Gina McKee), Molly (Molly Parker), and Debbie (Shirley Henderson). Nadia works in a Soho café and answers singles ads. Molly is pregnant, and living with Eddie (John Simm), who sells small appliances, has very low self-esteem, and painfully rehearses how he will tell her he has quit his job. Debbie is a hairdresser, who has a young son by Dan (Ian Hart).

We also meet their parents: Eileen, their mother (Kika Markham), critical of everyone and everything, who steals out in the night to poison the neighbor's dog; and Bill (Jack Shepherd), who turns up hopefully at his daughters' places to help out, who is trapped in a loveless marriage, who does indeed find one moment of happiness. That comes when he locks himself out of the house and is invited in by a neighbor, the Caribbean woman across the street; they dance, sweetly, and it is clear there could be more, but he ducks out—he's broken, and doesn't have the nerve.

Dan has custody of his son for a weekend, long enough to give him object lessons in rage. He grows terrifyingly angry in traffic, takes the kid to a soccer game, which plays as violent mayhem, and eventually passes out at home, drunk. The boy is resourceful, riffles his dad's pants pockets for money, and disappears to a nearby funfair (it is Guy Hawkes's Day, celebrated in England with fireworks and the ritual burning of the traitor who tried to blow up Westminster). That leads to a panicked search for the missing boy, and a reunion at police headquarters; Dan is not a bad man, just a frustrated one, untidy with his emotions.

Life is made of moments like these. Eddie quits his job without telling Molly, who doesn't see how they'll make ends meet with her pregnant. We know what she doesn't: That he hates his work, is terrified of social situations, tries painfully to rehearse how he will break the news to her, and flees rather than face her. Nadia has sex with a man she meets through the singles ads. He is very eager to have her leave his apartment once they've finished. Riding home, on the upper deck of a red London bus, she is surrounded by couples, and weeps. Franklyn (David Fahm), the son of the woman across the street, sits for hours in his room; his mom tells him he bottles everything up, and is like a total stranger. Later he and Nadia unexpectedly have a conversation that reveals much about their loneliness.

A movie like this is an act of attention. Winterbottom and screenwriter Laurence Coriat go out into their city and attend to how people live and how they feel. Like Studs Terkel in his books, they are listeners to ordinary lives. We watch not because we are "entertained" but because we begin as curious, end as sympathetic. The movie has no big point to make. If it did, it would be dishonest to itself.

The Wood ★ ★ ★
R, 106 m., 1999

Sean Nelson (Young Mike), Trent Cameron (Young Roland), Duane Finley (Young Slim), Malinda Williams (Young Alicia), Taye Diggs (Roland), Omar Epps (Mike), Richard T. Jones (Slim), Elayn Taylor (Roland's Mother), De'Aundre Bonds (Young Stacey), Sanaa Lathan (Alicia), Lisa Raye (The Bride), Tamala Jones (Tanya). Directed by Rick Famuyiwa and produced by Albert Berger, Ron Yerxa, and David Gale. Screenplay by Famuyiwa.

The Wood is a sweet, lighthearted comedy about three friends who stick together from high school until a wedding day. Nothing unusual about that, but these are African-American characters, and Hollywood seems incapable of imagining young black men who are not into violence, drugs, and trouble. The black middle class, millions of Americans, is generally invisible to moviemakers, who retail negative images of life in the hood—often for the entertainment of suburban kids, white and black, whose own lives are completely different.

The movie's title provides a clue: the wood, not the hood. Apart from the obvious pun, it applies to Inglewood, California, where three friends meet in high school, date, have some narrow escapes from trouble, and come of age. The film opens on the wedding day of Roland (Taye Diggs), and we meet his best friends Slim (Richard T. Jones) and Mike (Omar Epps), who narrates directly to the camera.

The wedding cake has arrived, but Roland is missing, and his buddies track him down to the house of a former girlfriend. He's terrified of marriage, and as his friends try to give him courage and make him presentable (he's been drinking), we get flashbacks to their younger days.

The flashback scenes, set in the eighties, are the real heart of the movie. As young men, the characters are played by Sean Nelson (Mike), Trent Cameron (Roland), and Duane Finley (Slim). And they're black teenagers like we rarely see in the movies: not angry, not alienated, not inarticulate, not packing guns, not into trouble—but sharing values, hopes, and fears typical of any adolescent. Most black teenagers are like this, although you wouldn't guess it from the movies. They have a lot in common with the heroes of *American Pie,* although they're not nearly as sexually sophisticated. (That's accurate, I think. Few porno stars have as much self-assurance as the kids in *American Pie.* Amazing, that the *Pie* raunch-fest and this, much more innocent coming-of-age movie, have the same R rating.)

We join the three friends in various rites of passage. We see Mike getting a crush on a girl. Working up the nerve to ask her to dance. Not knowing what to say. Being encouraged by the girl's friendship—and, yes, her sympathy. Getting in a playground fight with her brother. The girl Mike likes is Alicia (played as a teenager by the warm, supportive Malinda Williams), and there's a funny sequence that is a lot more accurate about early sexual experiences, I think, than *American Pie* will ever know.

There's another sequence that powerfully shows how close kids can come to getting in real trouble. The three friends are in a convenience store when it is stuck up—by someone they know but do not like. They do not sup-

port him, but are more or less forced to join him and a buddy in a car, which is soon stopped by the cops. A bust at that point would have forever altered their lives, giving them rap sheets as accomplices to armed robbery. Lives can be destroyed by being in the wrong place at the wrong time.

Although the adult stars top-line the movie, the flashback structure feels piled on top of the real story. The writer-director, a USC film school graduate named Rick Famuyiwa, would have been wise to dump the 1990s stuff altogether and stick with the kids in the eighties, although that would have cost him the marquee value of Diggs and Epps. The movie feels a little uncertain, as if it's moving from present to past under the demands of a screenplay rather than because it really feels that way. But the growing-up stuff is kind of wonderful.

The World Is Not Enough ★ ★ ★ ½
PG-13, 128 m., 1999

Pierce Brosnan (James Bond), Sophie Marceau (Elektra), Robert Carlyle (Renard), Denise Richards (Christmas Jones), Robbie Coltrane (Valentin Zukovsky), Judi Dench (M), Desmond Llewelyn (Q), John Cleese (R), Maria Grazia Cucinotta (Cigar Girl). Directed by Michael Apted and produced by Michael G. Wilson and Barbara Broccoli. Screenplay by Neal Purvis, Robert Wade, and Bruce Feirstein.

If *The World Is Not Enough* is a splendid comic thriller, exciting and graceful, endlessly inventive, because it is also the nineteenth James Bond movie, it comes with so much history that one reviews it like wine, comparing it to earlier famous vintages; I guess that's part of the fun. This is a good one.

Instead of summarizing the plot, let's tick off the Bond trademarks and see how they measure up:

1. Bond himself. Pierce Brosnan. The best except for Sean Connery. He knows that even the most outrageous double entendres are pronounced with a straight face. He is proud that a generation has grown up knowing the term "double entendre" only because of Bond movies.

2. Regulars. There's real poignancy this time, because Q, the inventor of all of Bond's giz-

mos, is retiring. Desmond Llewelyn has played the character in almost every Bond film since *From Russia With Love* in 1963 (notable exception: *Live and Let Die* in 1973, when the producers dropped Q after an insane decision that the series needed fewer gimmicks). Llewelyn is now eighty-five, and after demonstrating a few nice touches on his latest inventions, he sinks from sight in an appropriate and, darn it, touching way.

3. Guest stars. Who could replace Q? John Cleese, of course. "Does this make you . . . R?" asks Bond, after Cleese demonstrates a BMW speedster with titanium armor "and six cup holders."

4. M16. Judi Dench is back for the third time as Bond's boss M, with the same regal self-confidence she displayed as Queens Elizabeth *(Shakespeare in Love)* and Victoria *(Mrs. Brown)*. She does not condescend to the role, but plays it fiercely, creating an intelligence chief who actually seems focused and serious, even in the uproar of a Bond plot.

5. Sex bombs. Usually two major ones, a good girl who seems bad, and a bad girl who seems good. Both first-rate this time. Sophie Marceau plays Elektra King, daughter of a tycoon behind an oil pipeline linking the old Soviet oil fields to Europe. Denise Richards plays Christmas Jones, a nuclear scientist whose knowledge can save or doom the world. I will not reveal who is bad/good or good/bad.

6. Chase sequences. Lots of them. By powerboat on the Thames (and across dry land, and back on the Thames), and then into a hot-air balloon. By skis down a mountain, pursued by hang-gliding, bomb-throwing parasailers whose devices convert into snowmobiles. By land, in the BMW. Under the sea, as Bond breaks into a submarine and later pursues a villain by popping outside the sub and then in again.

7. Megalomaniac villains. There is a terrific early appearance of the archterrorist Renard (Robert Carlyle). His oversized skull rises from the floor in a hologram, and then takes on flesh. M explains that a bullet in his brain is gradually robbing him of his senses, but that "he'll grow stronger every day until he dies." Bond walks around the hologram, and reaches inside Renard's head to trace the path of the bullet. Another villain is played by Robbie Coltrane, who gets mileage out of always seeming like he'd really prefer to be a nice guy.

8. Locations. Not simply the oil fields of Azerbaijan, but Frank Gehry's new art museum in Bilbao, Spain, which figures in a nifty opening sequence, and the Millennium Dome on the banks of the Thames, which becomes a landing pad after a balloon explodes. Also a Hindu holy place with flames that never die.

9. Weird ways to die. How about vivisection by helicopter-borne rotary tree-trimming blades? Or garroting in an antique torture chair?

10. Sensational escapes. There is nothing like a Bond picture to make you believe a man can safely bungee-jump from a tall building, after tying one end of a window shade cord to his belt and the other end to an unconscious body.

All of these elements are assembled by director Michael Apted and writers Neal Purvis, Robert Wade, and Bruce Feirstein into a Bond picture that for once doesn't seem like set pieces uneasily glued together, but proceeds in a more or less logical way to explain what the problem and solution might be. Bond's one-liners seem more part of his character this time, not wisecrack inserts, and Carlyle's villain emerges as more three-dimensional and motivated, less of a caricature, than the evil-doers in some of the Bond films.

My favorite moment? A small one, almost a throwaway. The movie answers one question I've had for a long time: How do the bad guys always manage to find all their equipment spontaneously, on remote locations where they could not have planned ahead? After the snow chase sequence, a villain complains morosely that the parasails were rented, and "were supposed to be returned."

X

Xiu Xiu: The Sent-Down Girl ★ ★ ★
R, 99 m., 1999

Lu Lu (Wen Xiu), Lopsang (Lao Jin), Gao Jie (Mother), Li Qianqian (Sister), Lu Yue (Father), Qiao Qian (Chen Li), Gao Qiang (Peddler), Qin Wenyuan (Motorcycle Man). Directed by Joan Chen and produced by Chen and Alice Chan. Screenplay by Chen and Yan Geling, based on Yan Geling's novella "Tian Yu."

May you live in interesting times.
　　　　—Chinese curse, perhaps apocryphal

In a time of movies about sex and silly teenagers, here is a film that arrives with a jolt of hard reality, about a fifteen-year-old Chinese girl who was not lucky enough to be born into the consumer paradise of *American Pie*. To those who find savage satire in *South Park: Bigger, Longer and Uncut* (I am among them), here is a story about people who would weep with joy to have the problems *South Park* attacks.

Joan Chen's *Xiu Xiu: The Sent-Down Girl* is set in 1975, when the madness of the Cultural Revolution was still destroying the lives of millions of Chinese. A plague of fanaticism was upon the land. Wen Xiu (the title is her nickname) lives in the provincial city of Chengdu, goes to school, has a boyfriend, wears blouses sewn by her father, a tailor. Then she is selected to be "sent down" to a remote rural area, where as a city girl she can have her revolutionary values renewed by living with the proletariat. Countless others were also exiled from home, family, and friends by such directives.

The girl (Lu Lu) is sent to the high steppes near Tibet to live in the tent of a horse herder named Lao Jin (Lopsang). A wide river snakes through the territory, hardly seeming to flow. Lao Jin's tent, patched and leaky to the cold winds, is considered a safe haven because it is known in the district that he was castrated by "enemy soldiers" (their nationality unclear). Xiu Xiu is not a brave, independent heroine, a woman warrior; she is a kid, homesick and frightened, and not very sophisticated about her situation.

Life with Lao Jin is painted by Chen as essentially a lonely exile in a far place, where the man does most of the work and Xiu Xiu behaves much as a teenager might if she were sent to the farm for the summer. She is modest, undresses behind curtains, treats Lao Jin in an almost condescending fashion, does not see how much he cares for her, and about her. On the day when she has been away for six months, she puts on her nice sweater and a scarf, expecting officials to come and return her to her home.

They do not come. She has essentially been forgotten. (The ostensible purpose of her exile was to train horses for a women's cavalry that does not exist.) "Every place is the same," Lao Jin reassures her, a philosophy that is no consolation. One day a passing stranger tells her that there are ways a pretty girl can buy her way home. And soon, after an abrupt transition, she is having sex with him—and then with a series of men who all promise they can get her sent back to Chengdu, although why would they bother, when it is so pleasant to have her convenient to their needs?

Xiu Xiu is based on a screenplay and novel by Yan Geling, who teaches at Columbia College Chicago. It was shot on location in China, even in the forbidden zone near Tibet, by Chen, the Chinese-born actress from *Tai Pan, The Last Emperor,* and *Heaven and Earth.* Born in 1961, she was making her first movies at about the time this story is set. The film was made without the approval of the Chinese government, and since most of the scenes are set in remote isolation, there was no one to see— and, indeed, there are no overt political statements in the film, although it functions as a cry of regret and rage.

Other films have been set in this same period: *The Blue Kite; Farewell, My Concubine; To Live.* They were about the madness in the cities, where friends and neighbors denounced each other to save their own lives. This one is about evil on a larger scale (bureaucracies destroying lives because of policies no one seems responsible for) and a smaller one (the unspeakable cruelty of the man who rapes Xiu Xiu after giving her false hopes). Those other films were Chinese productions, although given limited release in China because of their politics (the Chinese government was, however, happy to earn foreign exchange by having them shown overseas). *Xiu Xiu* will not be seen in China, nor is Chen welcome to return there; it is the kind of film which in a simple parable indicts an entire nation and its sainted leader, Mao.

Because Lao Jin is an inarticulate peasant and Xiu Xiu is a naive and immature girl, there is little dialogue between them. This is not a movie about opposites attracting, but about two fellow prisoners who scarcely speak the same language. We are invited to interpret their looks, their silences, and their feelings—especially Lao Jin's passive sadness as Xiu Xiu is violated. The resolution of their stories, when it comes, is almost inevitable. During the film, a cadre of displaced young "revolutionaries" look at a propaganda film in which shiny-faced workers sing patriotic songs. I have a fantasy in which the characters in half a dozen American teenage sex comedies wander into the wrong room at the multiplex and see *Xiu Xiu.*

X-Men ★ ★ ½
PG-13, 96 m., 2000

Hugh Jackman (Logan/Wolverine), Patrick Stewart (Xavier), Ian McKellen (Magneto), Famke Janssen (Dr. Jean Grey), James Marsden (Cyclops), Halle Berry (Storm), Anna Paquin (Rogue), Tyler Mane (Sabretooth), Rebecca Romijn-Stamos (Mystique), Ray Park (Toad). Directed by Bryan Singer and produced by Lauren Shuler Donner and Ralph Winter. Screenplay by David Hayter, based on a story by Tom DeSanto and Singer.

The origin story is crucial to all superhero epics, from the gods of ancient Greece right down to Superman's parents. Next in importance is an explanation of superpowers: what they are, how they work. That's reasonable when there is one superhero, like Superman or the Crow, but in *X-Men,* with eight major characters and more in supporting roles, the movie gets top-heavy. At the halfway mark, it had just about finished introducing the characters.

That matches my experience of the *X-Men* comic books. The characters spent an inordinate amount of time accounting for themselves. Action spills across full pages as the heroes *splatt* and *kerrruuunch* each other, but

the dialogue balloons are like little advertisements for themselves, as they describe their powers, limitations, and motivations.

Since the Marvel Comics empire hopes *X-Men* is the first entry in a franchise, it's understandable that the setups would play an important role in the first film. If only there were more to the payoff. The events that end the movie are sort of anticlimactic, and the special effects, while energetic, are not as persuasive as they might be (at one point an airplane clearly looks like a model, bouncing as it lands on water).

X-Men is at least not a manic editing frenzy for atrophied attention spans. It's restrained and introspective for a superhero epic, and fans of the comic books may like that. Graphic novels (as they sometimes deserve to be called) take themselves as seriously as the ones without pictures, and you can tell that here when the opening scene shows Jews being forced into death camps in Poland in 1944. One could argue that the Holocaust is not appropriate subject matter for an action movie based on a comic book, but having talked to some *X-Men* fans I believe that in their minds the story is as deep and portentous as, say, *Sophie's Choice.*

The Holocaust scene introduces Magneto (Ian McKellen) as a child; his mental powers twist iron gates out of shape. The narrator informs us that "evolution takes thousands and thousands of years," which is putting it mildly, and that we live in an age of great evolutionary leaps forward. Some of the X-Men develop paranormal powers that cannot be accounted for by the strictly physical mutations that form the basis of Darwinian theory; I get restless when real science is evoked in the name of pseudoscience, but hey, that's just me.

Magneto's opponent in *X-Men* is Xavier (Patrick Stewart), another mutant of the same generation. They aren't enemies so much as ideological opposites. Magneto, having seen the Holocaust, has a deep pessimism about human nature. Xavier, who runs a school for mutants in Westchester County, where it doubtless seems no stranger than the other private schools, hopes these new powers can be used for good. Bruce Davison plays the McCarthy-like senator who waves a list of "known mutants" during a congressional hearing and wants them all registered—no doubt for dire purposes. Magneto wants to counter by using a device that can convert world leaders to mutants. (The world leaders are conveniently meeting on an island near Ellis Island, so the Statue of Liberty can be a prop.)

How a machine could create a desired mutation within a generation is not much explored by the movie, which also eludes the question of why you would want to invest your enemies with your powers. No matter; Xavier, who can read minds, leads his good mutants in a battle to foil Magneto, and that's the plot, or most of it.

X-Men is arguably heavy on mutants; they have a way of coming onstage, doing their tricks, and disappearing. The leads are Wolverine (Hugh Jackman), whose fists sprout deadly blades; Cyclops (James Marsden), who wears a wraparound visor to control and aim his laserlike eyes; the prosaically named Dr. Jean Grey (Famke Janssen), who can move objects with her mind; Storm (Halle Berry in a platinum wig), who can control the weather; and Rogue (Anna Paquin), a teenager who is new to this stuff. I can't help wondering how a guy whose knuckles turn into switchblades gets to be the top-ranking superhero. If Storm can control, say, a tropical storm, she's obviously the most powerful, even if her feats here are limited to local climate control.

Magneto's team is not as colorful as the good guys, and includes Mystique (Rebecca Romijn-Stamos), who in the Japanese *anime* tradition can change her shape (as her costume tries to keep up), and Toad (Ray Park), who has a tongue that can whip out to great distances. Why is it that Xavier's team has impressive skills, while Magneto's team has specialties that would prove invaluable to a stripper?

I started out liking this movie, while waiting for something really interesting to happen. When nothing did, I still didn't dislike it; I assume the X-Men will further develop their personalities if there is a sequel, and maybe find time to get involved in a story. No doubt fans of the comics will understand subtle allusions and fine points of behavior; they should linger in the lobby after each screening to answer questions.

Y

The Yards ★ ★ ★
R, 115 m., 2000

Mark Wahlberg (Leo Handler), Joaquin Phoenix (Willie Gutierrez), Charlize Theron (Erica Stoltz), James Caan (Frank Olchin), Ellen Burstyn (Val Handler), Faye Dunaway (Kitty Olchin), Andrew Davoli (Raymond Price), Steve Lawrence (Arthur Mydanick), Tony Musante (Seymour Korman), Victor Argo (Paul Lazarides), Tomas Milian (Manuel Sequiera). Directed by James Gray and produced by Nick Wechsler, Paul Webster, and Kerry Orent. Screenplay by Gray and Matt Reeves.

There is a sad, tender quality in *The Yards* I couldn't put my finger on, until I learned that the director's father inspired one of the characters. The movie is set around the yards where the New York mass transit trains are made up and repaired. It is about a kid who gets out of jail, wants to do right, and gets in trouble again. And about his uncle, who works on both sides of the law. This uncle is not an evil man. When he breaks the law, it's because in his business those who do not break the law don't remain in business. The system was corrupt when he found it and will be corrupt when he leaves it. He has to make a living for his family.

It's that ambiguity that makes the film interesting. Most crime movies have a simplistic good vs. evil moral structure. When *The Godfather* came along, with its shades of morality within a shifting situation, it exposed most mob pictures as fairy tales. *The Yards* resembles *The Godfather* in the way it goes inside the structure of corruption, and shows how judges and elected officials work at arm's length with people they know are breaking the law. But it also resembles *Mean Streets,* the film about two childhood friends who get in over their heads.

Early in the film, Frank explains his business: "If it's on a train or a subway, we make it or we fix it." This process involves bribes, kickbacks, and theft. But Frank is a reasonable and measured man who operates within a system that everyone tacitly accepts, even the police. There's a way things are done, everybody gets taken care of, everybody's happy. I was intrigued by how the writer-director, James Gray, makes Frank not a villain but a hardworking guy who breaks the law, yes, but isn't a bad guy in the usual movie sense.

Then I learned that Frank was somewhat inspired by Gray's own father, who was involved in the same racketeering scandal that led to the 1986 suicide of Queens borough president Donald Manes, who stabbed himself when it was revealed he had taken payoffs. When your father is supposed to be the bad guy, you don't always see it that way. It gets complicated.

Complications are what *The Yards* is about. As the movie opens, Leo (Mark Wahlberg) has been released from prison, where he took the rap for his buddies on an auto theft charge. He was a stand-up guy, and is welcomed home at a party including his best friend Willie (Joaquin Phoenix). Leo's dad is dead. His mother, Val (Ellen Burstyn), has a sister, Kitty (Faye Dunaway), whose second husband is Uncle Frank. By her first marriage she has a daughter, Erica (Charlize Theron), who is dating Willie. So everyone is connected.

Leo goes to Uncle Frank looking for a job as a machinist. But that takes an apprenticeship, and Leo needs money; his mother has a heart condition. He seeks out Willie, who runs a crew for Frank, applying muscle in the yards. On his first night with Willie, everything goes wrong. A yardmaster is killed, and Leo beats up a cop. The cop fingers Leo, the only person he saw. "I didn't kill anyone," Leo tells Uncle Frank. "Then who did?" Leo shrugs in a way that lets Frank understand.

The movie is about how all of these relatives and friends deal with the tightening vise of the law. If Leo keeps quiet, he goes up for murder. If he talks, everyone goes down. Is Uncle Frank guilty? Yes, guilty of having a man like Willie on his payroll and using him for illegal purposes. But not guilty of murder. And there are shadings all around; a district police commander, offered a bribe to keep the cop from testifying, observes the cop was known for being free with his nightstick—a euphemism, we sense, for things left unsaid.

Mark Wahlberg, as Leo, doesn't pop out as

the "hero" of this film, but plays the character as withdrawn and sad. His mother is dying. His early promise died in prison. He doesn't have a higher education. There is a poignancy in the performance we don't often see in movies about organized crime; he isn't reckless or headstrong, but simply unlucky, and required to make desperate moral decisions.

The cast occupies the same uncertain terrain. Willie is played by Phoenix as a man who has to betray Leo or go down himself. He can't keep his mind on Erica when his world is coming down around him. Frank is in a painful dilemma: Leo is his wife's nephew, not some punk who can be taken care of. When family members gather, vast silences lurk outside their conversations because there is so much they know and cannot say.

The Yards is not exhilarating like some crime movies, or vibrant with energy like others. It exists in a morose middle ground, chosen by Gray, deliberately or not, because this is how his own memories feel. When indictments come down in political scandals, the defendants often say they were only trying to operate within the system. So they were. Their other choice was to find a new line of work. The system endures. If you don't take the payoff, someone else will. Fairly nice people can live in this shadowland. Sometimes things go wrong.

Yi Yi ★ ★ ★ ½
NO MPAA RATING, 173 m., 2001

Nien-Jen Wu (N.J.), Issey Ogata (Mr. Ota), Elaine Jin (Min-Min), Kelly Lee (Ting-Ting), Jonathan Chang (Yang-Yang), Yupang Chang (Fatty), Chen Xisheng (A-Di), Ke Suyun (Sherry Chang-Breitner), Adrian Lin (Lili), Tang Ruyun (Grandma), Michael Tao (Da-Da), Xiao Shushen (Xiao Yan), Xu Shuyuan (Lili's Mother), Zeng Xinyi (Yun-Yun). Directed by Edward Yang and produced by Kawai Shinya and Tsukeda Naoko. Screenplay by Yang.

"Daddy, I can't see what you see and you can't see what I see. How can we know more than half the truth?"

So asks little Yang-Yang, the eight-year-old boy in *Yi Yi,* a movie in which nobody knows more than half the truth, or is happy more

than half the time. The movie is a portrait of three generations of a Taiwanese family, affluent and successful, but haunted by lost opportunities and doubts about the purpose of life. Only rarely is a film this observant and tender about the ups and downs of daily existence; I am reminded of *Terms of Endearment.*

The hero of the film is N.J., an electronics executive with a wife, a mother-in-law, an adolescent daughter, an eight-year-old son, and a life so busy that he is rushing through middle age without paying much attention to his happiness. He's stunned one day when he sees a woman in an elevator: "Is it really you?" It is. It is Sherry, his first love, the girl he might have married thirty years ago. Now she lives in Chicago with her husband, Rodney, an insurance executive, but she follows him fiercely to demand, "Why didn't you come that day? I waited and waited. I never got over it."

Why didn't he come? Why did he marry this woman instead of that one? It is a question raised in the first scene of the movie, at another wedding, where a hysterical woman apologizes to the mother of the groom: "It should have been me marrying your son today!" Perhaps, but as a character observes near the end of the film, if he had done things differently, everything might have turned out about the same.

The family lives in a luxury high-rise. We gradually get to know its members and even the neighbors (one couple fights all the time). The mother-in-law has a stroke, goes into a coma, and the family takes turns reading and talking to her. One day N.J. (Nien-Jen Wu) comes home to find his wife, Min-Min (Elaine Jin), weeping: "I have nothing to say to Mother. I tell her the same things every day. I have so little. How can it be so little? I live a blank. If I ended up like her one day . . ." Yes, but one day, if we live long enough, we all do. Talking to someone in a coma, N.J. observes, is like praying: You're not sure the other party can hear, and not sure you're sincere.

Little Yang-Yang (Jonathan Chang) is too young for such thoughts, and adopts a more positive approach. He takes a photo of the back of his father's head, since the father can't see it and therefore has no way of being sure it is there. And he takes photos of the mosquitoes on the landing outside the apartment, sneaking out of school to collect the prints at the photo shop (his teacher ridicules his "avant-garde art").

Meanwhile, N.J. is visited by memories of Sherry. Should he have married her? One of his few confidants and friends is a Japanese businessman, Mr. Ota (Issey Ogata); it is a measure of the worlds they live in that their conversations must be conducted in English, the only language they have in common. They sing in a karaoke bar, and then Mr. Ota quiets the room by playing sad classical music on the piano. Late one night, returning to a darkened office, N.J. telephones Sherry (Ke Suyun). She wonders if they should start all over with each other.

N.J.'s teenage daughter, Ting-Ting (Kelly Lee), is also considering cheating, with Fatty (Yupang Chang), her best friend's boyfriend. They actually check into a love hotel, but "it's not right," he says. That's the thing about life: You think about transgressions, but a tidal pull pushes you back toward what you know is right.

The point of *Yi Yi* is not to force people into romantic decisions. Many mainstream American films are impatient; in them, people meet, they feel desire, they act on it. If you step back a little from a movie like *3,000 Miles to Graceland,* you realize it is about stupid, self-ish, violent monsters; the movie likes them and thinks it is a comedy. Our films have little time for thought, and our characters are often too superficial for their decisions to have any meaning—they're just plot points.

But the people in *Yi Yi* live considered lives. They feel committed to their families. Their vague romantic yearnings are more like background noise than calls to action. There are some scenes of adultery in the movie, involving characters I have not yet mentioned, but they come across as shabby and sad.

The movie is about the currents of life. But it's not solemn in a Bergmanesque way. N.J. and his family live in a riot of everyday activity; the grandmother in a coma is balanced by Yang-Yang dropping a water balloon on pre-cisely the wrong person. Some scenes edge toward slapstick. Others show characters through the cold, hard windows of modern skyscrapers, bathed in icy fluorescence, their business devoid of any juice or heart.

There was a time when a film from Taiwan would have seemed foreign and unfamiliar—when Taiwan had a completely different culture from ours. The characters in *Yi Yi* live in a world that would be much the same in Toronto, London, Bombay, Sydney; in their economic class, in their jobs, culture is estab-lished by corporations, real estate, fast food, and the media, not by tradition. N.J. and Yang-Yang eat at McDonald's, and other characters meet in a Taipei restaurant named New York Bagels. Maybe the movie is not simply about knowing half of the truth, but about knowing the wrong half of the truth.

Note: Yi Yi *is unrated; it is appropriate for mature audiences. It was named best film of the year by the National Society of Film Critics.*

You Can Count on Me ★ ★ ★ ★
R, 109 m., 2000

Laura Linney (Sammy Prescott), Mark Ruffalo (Terry Prescott), Rory Culkin (Rudy), Matthew Broderick (Brian), Jon Tenney (Bob), J. Smith-Cameron (Mabel), Ken Lonergan (Priest). Directed by Ken Lonergan and produced by Barbara De Fina, John Hart, Larry Meistrich, and Jeff Sharp. Screenplay by Lonergan.

Sammy is a divorced mom, has an eight-year-old son, works as a loan officer at the bank, is making ends meet, dates a guy named Bob who doesn't excite her, and hates her new boss. Terry is her easy-come, easy-go brother, one of those charmers that drive you nuts be-cause you love them but you can't count on them. *You Can Count on Me,* a film of great, tender truth, begins as they meet again after one of Terry's long, unexplained silences.

As the film opens, Terry (Mark Ruffalo) has left behind a girlfriend and come to visit Sammy (Laura Linney) in the little town of Scottsville, New York. She glows with happi-ness to see him; they raised each other after their parents died in an accident. Gradually her joy fades as she realizes he hasn't come home to stay, but just wants to borrow money. It's the same old story.

We meet Rudy (Rory Culkin), Sammy's son, a good kid, close to his mother, suspi-cious of Terry at first, then growing crazy about him—because Rory aches for his absent father, and Terry does dadlike stuff, like taking him to a pool hall. Sammy is bitter about her ex-husband, won't talk to her son about him, has closed that chapter.

At the bank, the new manager is Brian (Matthew Broderick). He's one of those infuriating midlevel executives who has been promoted beyond his competence. The bank, like many other corporations, mistakes his tactlessness for tough managerial skills. Brian has no empathy and takes cover behind the regulations. "Is there anyone else who can pick your son up after school?" he asks Sammy, who gives up her lunch hour so she can slip out every afternoon and meet Rudy. It goes without saying that Brian's regard for the rules does not extend to himself, which is why he is willing to have an affair with Sammy even though he has a pregnant wife at home.

Sammy's personal life is limited. In a small town, there are few available men. Bob (Jon Tenney) is a nice enough guy, but forgets to call her for weeks at a time, and seems reluctant to commit—not that she thinks she wants to marry him anyway. One of the truest scenes in the movie comes when Sammy calls him one day to arrange a meeting for sex. Kind of like calling the plumber.

The situation in Scottsville is static when Terry comes to town. Because he's unpredictable and irresponsible, but good-hearted in his half-baked way, he acts as a catalyst. Yes, he forgets to meet Rudy after school. Yes, he ignores his commitments. Yes, it is irresponsible for him to take that eight-year-old kid to a pool hall. But when he lifts Rudy up to the table and Rudy takes a shot and sinks the ball, *this is what the kid needs!* He needs a guy in his life to take the place of the absent father he is so curious about.

Of course, Terry knows Rudy Sr., the exhusband. They probably went to school together. He takes matters into his own hands and drives the kid to the house of his father, the louse, in a well-written scene where what happens is kind of inevitable.

The characters in *You Can Count on Me* have been freed from the formulas of fiction and set loose to live lives where they screw up, learn from their mistakes, and bumble hopefully into the future. Ken Lonergan, the writer-director, is willing to leave things open. He shows possibilities without immediately sealing them with decisions. Laura Linney and Mark Ruffalo are open actors who give the impression of spontaneous notions; they are not programmed. We like them. We share their frustration. We despair of Terry even while we see he means well.

I admire the way Linney shows Sammy struggling with issues of right and wrong. Yes, she sleeps with the married bank manager— and with Bob. She doesn't feel right about it. She goes to her priest, played by Lonergan, the filmmaker. "What is the church's official position on fornication and adultery?" she asks, although she should have a good working knowledge of the answer. "Well," says the priest, wanting to be helpful, aware of situational ethics, "it's a sin . . ."

Yes. But after seeing the film I want you to ponder three possibilities. (1) The priest is quietly attracted to Sammy himself, although he would probably never act on his feelings. (2) Sammy's reason for sleeping with Brian, the bank manager, may have originated in passion, but includes a healthy component of office politics. (3) She may be coming around to the notion that Bob is not entirely unacceptable as a mate.

I call these possibilities because the movie does not seal them, or even take a position on them. They're serious matters, but the movie can be funny about them. Not funny like a comedy, but funny like at the office when some jerk makes enemies, and his enemies pounce. Then there are quiet little sarcastic asides around the watercooler, where you share your joy at the downfall of an ass. Such moments can be so enormously rewarding.

Beyond and beneath that is the rich human story of *You Can Count on Me.* I love the way Lonergan shows his characters in flow, pressed this way and that by emotional tides and practical considerations. This is not a movie about people solving things. This is a movie about people living day to day with their plans, fears, and desires. It's rare to get a good movie about the touchy adult relationship of a sister and brother. Rarer still for the director to be more fascinated by the process than the outcome. This is one of the best movies of the year.

The Best Films of 2000

It was not a great year for the movies. The year's best films absorbed us with their stories and narratives, instead of electrifying us with their stylistic invention as *Being John Malkovich, Magnolia,* and *Three Kings* did last year. The only title in my top ten with that kind of bold invention is *Requiem for a Dream,* although *Traffic* did a skillful job of juggling parallel stories, and *George Washington* was a triumph of style in a more muted key.

And yet, as stories, what pleasure they gave! "I almost hugged myself" during *Almost Famous,* I wrote, and a friend told me he was looking forward to seeing it again even before it was over. *Wonder Boys* was the kind of character study that evokes another person's life so observantly we know our way around in it—and so, in a comedy, was *High Fidelity.* Two of the year's best films, *You Can Count on Me* and *George Washington,* evoked the feelings of the characters instead of just marching them past the stations of the plot; they didn't force closure on stories that by their nature could not be closed.

Special effects were central to the power of *The Cell* and *Crouching Tiger, Hidden Dragon*—but how astonishing to learn the treetop and rooftop scenes in *Tiger* were *not* done with computers but with human beings suspended from lifelines! Effects also helped evoke the drug-addicted worlds in *Requiem for a Dream,* with its subjective close-ups of how it feels when the dose hits. And in *Pollock,* Ed Harris learned to paint (or at least look like he could paint) like Jackson Pollock, in a film suggesting it was easier to paint Pollock's paintings than live his life.

The Best Films of 2000
1. *Almost Famous*

Huckleberry Finn as fifteen-year-old rock critic, in one of the best coming-of-age movies ever made. Writer-director Cameron Crowe based the film on his own experiences when he was fifteen, convinced a *Rolling Stone* editor he was an adult, and was assigned to accompany the Allman Brothers on a road trip.

In the film, Patrick Fugit is perfectly cast as the young, bright, earnest kid who talks himself

into a magazine assignment and goes on the road with a band named Stillwater. One performance after another is given with uncanny accuracy: Billy Crudup as the rock-god lead guitarist, not as fearsome as he looks; Kate Hudson as the groupie Penny Lane, who adores the Crudup character but takes sympathy on the kid; Frances McDormand as the hero's mother, trusting him on this first step into adulthood but laying down the law about drugs and lecturing Crudup over the phone in a classic scene; and Jason Lee, as the lead singer, who wants better billing on the T-shirts.

2. *Wonder Boys*

Another film about a writer—this one a fifty-ish college professor played by Michael Douglas, who wrote one very good novel and has been working on a second for much too long. We follow him through a winter weekend on a chilly campus in Pittsburgh, as his life comes crashing down. He drinks too much, is stoned on pot, wanders forlornly in a shabby bathrobe, is facing the end of his affair with the chancellor (Frances McDormand), is hiding from his editor (Robert Downey Jr.) who has been promised the long-delayed manuscript, and deals uncertainly with two of his best students. *Wonder Boys* is the first movie by Curtis Hanson since *L.A. Confidential.* It's as surefooted, but more tender about its characters, more sympathetic to the way their dreams elude them. At its center is Michael Douglas's best performance.

3. *You Can Count On Me*

Laura Linney plays Sammy, a single mom, in a film filled with Oscar-caliber performances. She has an eight-year-old son, is a bank loan officer, is doing okay financially, is dating a guy who doesn't excite her, and hates her new boss. Then her brother Terry (Mark Ruffalo) shows up in town. He's a charmer who drives her nuts because she loves him but can't trust him.

You Can Count on Me, a film of great tender truth, begins as they meet again after one of Terry's long, unexplained silences. The movie, written and directed by Ken Lonergan, avoids

673

soppy payoffs and looks at these people with an affectionate but level gaze; one of the joys of the film is the way it avoids steering the plot into neat resolutions, but shows its characters dealing with life in all its baffling contradictions.

4. *Traffic*

Steven Soderbergh's film has the courage and ambition to survey the drug problem in America in all of its frustrating facets. Interlocking stories involve the chain of sale and use: two honest Tijuana cops, a Mexican army general, a middle-man importer, a wealthy and respectable American businessman who is secretly a drug lord, two undercover San Diego drug agents, an Ohio judge who is appointed the nation's new drug czar, and his daughter, who becomes addicted to cocaine.

Each story stands on its own, and it's surprising, considering how much ground the story covers, how strongly the characters emerge— especially Benicio Del Toro as a Mexican cop and Michael Douglas as a parent faced with drugs in his own family. The movie sees addiction as a public health problem, not a crime, and many audience members may be led to the conclusion that the nation's drug laws function mostly as a price-support system for the drug industry.

5. *George Washington*

The most stylistically entrancing of the year's films drifts through summer days that seem aimless until a terrifying event interrupts the calm. The movie takes place in a rusty industrial cityscape of abandoned factories and rail yards, where the heroes, children around the age of twelve, play and kill time, and engage in desultory conversations. We meet some of their family members, and when an accident happens we see how it becomes a dread secret. The power of the movie is not in the plot but in the mood, which has an uncanny resonance with *Days of Heaven,* even though the two films are otherwise quite different. It allows us to join the rhythm, slowness, and heat of summer days, and knows how conversations can hang hauntingly in the air.

6. *The Cell*

A thriller that combines psychology with psychic abilities, a serial killer with a police procedural, and stark landscapes and sterile laboratories with an astonishingly imagined mindscape. Jennifer Lopez stars as a social worker who's involved in a project to share the thoughts of a little boy locked in a coma—she hopes to coax him out—when the FBI enlists her in an urgent attempt to enter the mind of a serial killer and discover the location of his latest victim before a fatal deadline. Tarsem, the director, is a visual virtuoso who juggles his story lines effortlessly; it's dazzling, the way he blends so many notes, styles, and genres into a film so original.

7. *High Fidelity*

The movies don't often focus on the everyday lives of young working people, but here is a comedy with charm and heart about the owner of a Chicago used vinyl store (John Cusack), his two opinionated employees, and the women in (and mostly out) of his life. Directed by Stephen Frears, the movie is a comedy of attitude: It studies the strategies used by the characters to combine relative poverty with the conviction of being one of the chosen. Cusack, always a fine actor, surpasses himself here as a man who morosely compiles lists of ex-girlfriends and hopefully sallies forth to make the same mistakes again.

8. *Pollock*

A triumph for Ed Harris, who in his directing debut has made one of the best biopics about an artist; this is a film that contains understanding about the art world and how it juggles greed and inspiration while trying to accommodate the impossible personalities of many artists. Harris stars in a powerful, nuanced performance as Jackson Pollock, an important abstract expressionist who found professional success and personal misery. Marcia Gay Harden costars as his painter wife, Lee Krasner, who knows what she's getting into when she courts the alcoholic, depressive painter, and stands beside him as long as she can take it.

9. *Crouching Tiger, Hidden Dragon*

Ang Lee grew up on Taiwan reading martial arts novels, and the images in his memory were an influence on this film, he says. Poetic and more thoughtful than most works in the genre, it also contains some of the most exhilarating action sequences ever filmed. Viewing a rooftop chase and a heart-stopping fight by two characters clinging to swinging treetops, I assumed it was computer animation of some sort, and was astonished when Lee told me those were real actors up there, hanging from cranes on invisible wires. For once the action wasn't the point in the martial arts movie: It was the canvas for a story of myth and obsession, beautifully told.

10. *Requiem for a Dream*

Most drug movies focus on the world of addicts rather than the inner space they retreat to when they're using. Darren Aronofsky's movie is intensely subjective, using extreme close-ups to show drug reactions, dilating pupils, etc., and then using speeded-up action and sound to recreate the delusional worlds of his characters. At the heart of the film is a great, brave performance by Ellen Burstyn, as a housewife who gets hooked on diet pills and hallucinates that she is destined to appear on TV. Jared Leto plays her son and Jennifer Connelly his girlfriend; addicted to heroin, they undergo a sickening descent to self-destruction.

Special Jury Prize

At many film festivals, the Special Jury Prize is awarded to a film that didn't quite win first place. This year I'm choosing ten titles, listed alphabetically, for such an award. Any of these titles could easily qualify for the top ten list.

Before Night Falls is painter Julian Schnabel's second film, after *Basquiat* (1996), to show an artist driven to homelessness and despair by the inner demons of his art. It tells the story of the Cuban poet and novelist Reinaldo Arenas, who ran away from home to join Castro's rebels but was later imprisoned and persecuted for his homosexuality and his work. Javier Bardem plays him as whimsical, petulant, bighearted, and brave.

Best in Show was the funniest movie of the year, a mockumentary by Christopher Guest about a dog show, its dogs and their owners, the officials, and a hilarious broadcast team. Fred Willard steals scenes as the color commentator, hilariously inappropriate and misinformed, and the movie exploits one of the basic formulas of comedy, the attempt to give form and shape to that which is not formable and shapable—a dog, for example.

Chuck and Buck. Miguel Arteta's film is about childhood friends who meet again after many years. Chuck (Chris Weitz) incautiously invites Buck (Mike White) to visit him sometime in L.A., and Buck turns up with the persistence of a stalker, insinuating himself into Chuck's life while remaining totally oblivious to hints and snubs.

The Contender. In a year when party politics played a larger role than ever before, this was a political thriller about a Democratic president (Jeff Bridges) who wants to fill a vice-presidential vacancy by appointing a woman senator (Joan Allen). A Republican committee head (Gary Oldman) objects, and William Petersen plays a Democratic governor whose own bid for the post leads into murky waters. Written and directed by Rod Lurie, whose October film served as a curtain-raiser for an autumn of partisan debate.

Dancer in the Dark. "Some reasonable people will admire this film," I wrote, "and others will despise it. An excellent case can be made for both positions." Lars von Trier, the Danish architect of the Dogma movement, starred the pop singer Bjork as a Washington State punch-press operator going blind. The plot was as deliberately melodramatic and manipulative as an early silent movie, and then von Trier pulled the rug out from under his dark images with unexpected musical numbers. Audiences had to figure out for themselves if they liked it, and why.

Jesus' Son. Billy Crudup had a good year, with this film and *Almost Famous* demonstrating his ability to disappear into a role. How could the cocky guitar god of the rock movie also be the mournful drifter from Iowa in this one? Samantha Morton costars, as his fellow druggie, and the movie follows Crudup through a derailed relationship and into rehab, a job in an emergency room (Jack Black from *High Fidelity* is hilarious as an orderly), and into a strange romance with Holly Hunter and a stint as the editor of a newsletter at an old folks' home. Why is he the son of God? Aren't we all?

Rosetta. Winner of the Palme d'Or at the 1999 Cannes Film Festival, this is a film centering on a virtuoso performance. Emilie Dequenne (who won as best actress) plays the title character, a poor young woman from the wrong side of the tracks, whose sights are set firmly on finding a better job. Beneath her yawns a chasm of homelessness and poverty, and somehow her desperation seems to create problems, not solutions. The performance is deadpan, inward, containing painful secrets, and impossible to forget.

Shadow of the Vampire. Willem Dafoe gives one of the most astonishing performances of 2000, based on one of the most astonishing performances of 1922, Max Schreck's title role in F. W. Murnau's *Nosferatu.* E. Elias Merhige's *Shadow* is a movie about the filming of the silent classic, which all but founded the vampire genre. His twist: Schreck really *was* a vampire. John Malkovich plays Murnau, Catherine McCormack plays Schreck's costar (guess what happens to her), and Dafoe quite simply embodies Schreck and his performance. Avoiding the pitfall of irony, it plays the material straight, which is truly scary.

The Terrorist. Santosh Sivan's film from India is simple and deep, the story of a few days in the life of a teenage girl revolutionary (Ayesha Dharkar) who volunteers to become a human bomb in an assassination attempt. What goes through her mind during the few days of training before the crucial moment? She is sent to a farm for a waiting period, and the farmer, who may not know of her mission, introduces her to his wife, who has been immobile in a coma for years. In its direct, subtle way, the film generates enormous power.

Titus was the Roman gladiator film to see in 2000, not the bloated *Gladiator* with its see-through special effects. Julie Taymor, director of *The Lion King* on Broadway, wrote and directed this version of Shakespeare's tragedy, bridging ancient and modern times and creating a visually brilliant frame for Anthony Hopkins's title performance.

Special Recognition
Every seven years, director Michael Apted revisits the same group of British citizens to ask them how they're getting on. This project, which began as the documentary *7 Up,* is now up to *42 Up* and is a stirring use of film as a time machine. We have seen these people as children, teenagers, young students, newlyweds, and now into early middle age. We see that for many of them, the child was indeed father to the man, while for others (especially the troubled Neal), life holds great surprises. Seven years ago we feared

for his future. Now he has had an amazing turn of fortune. Few films offer such a provoking insight into the nature of time and personality.

Documents from Life
The average moviegoer doesn't often attend a documentary, maybe because it's too much like going back to school. A shame, since a good documentary can generate drama and tension that fiction films can only envy. The year's five best docs were:

Dark Days, about the people who build their homes in the eternal darkness of the railroad tunnels beneath Manhattan; *The Eyes of Tammy Faye,* about the rise and fall and rise and fall and rise of TV's weep 'n' pray queen; *The Filth and the Fury,* about the strange birth and chaotic death of the Sex Pistols, pioneers of punk rock; *Paradise Lost 2,* continuing the story of three young men from West Memphis, Arkansas, who seem to have been framed for a murder while a more likely suspect all but turns himself in on-screen; and *South,* also known in an expanded version as *Endurance,* with its actual footage from Ernest Shackleton's doomed 1915 expedition to the South Pole.

Honorable Mention
Billy Bob Thornton's *All the Pretty Horses,* with Matt Damon and Henry Thomas as young cowboys seeking their dreams on the Mexican prairie; Frederic Fonteyne's *An Affair of Love,* with its erotic secret behind closed doors; John Swanbeck's *The Big Kahuna,* with Kevin Spacey and Danny DeVito debating life, death, and sales; the high-pressure sales tactics in *Boiler Room;* Peter Lord and Nick Park's *Chicken Run,* with birds desperately trying to avoid becoming pot pies; *Chocolat,* Lasse Hallstrom's enchanting fable about a woman who trusts generosity and shames the prudes; *The Claim,* Michael Winterbottom's sad story of a man who creates his own world but cannot fill it with his own family; Lodge Kerrigan's *Claire Dolan* and its great performance by Katrin Cartlidge as a hooker trapped by her own life; and Majid Majidi's *The Color of Paradise,* from Iran, about a blind boy who is a hindrance to his father's remarriage plans.

Also Gregory Hoblit's *Frequency,* with its touching communication between a father and a son over the decades; Patrice Leconte's *The*

Girl on the Bridge, as a knife thrower offers a would-be suicide a job; Karyn Kusama's *Girlfight,* with Michelle Rodriguez's blazing performance as a young woman who would rather fight than anything; *Joe Gould's Secret,* by Stanley Tucci, who starred Ian Holm in the story of a character who claimed to be writing an oral history of New York, and has an oblique influence on the New Yorker writer telling his story.

Also Bruno Dumont's *L'Humanite,* the hypnotic story of a drab policeman and a monstrous crime; Robert Redford's *The Legend of Bagger Vance,* about golf and eternity; *Legend of Drunken Master,* one of Jackie Chan's most amazing performances; Scott Elliott's *A Map of the World,* with Sigourney Weaver's brilliant work as a stubborn farm woman; Wolfgang Petersen's *The Perfect Storm* and its awesome special effects; Nicole Garcia's *Place Vendome* with Catherine Deneuve as an alcoholic who pulls it together and reenters the diamond trade; Phil Kaufman's *Quills,* with Geoffrey Rush as a dying but indomitable Marquis de Sade.

And Scott Hicks's *Snow Falling on Cedars,* the softly, beautifully told story of a murder trial that hinges on racism; Sturla Gunnarsson's *Such a Long Journey,* based on the Rohinton Mistry novel about everyday life in Bombay; Sam Raimi's *The Gift,* with Cate Blanchett's perfectly modulated work as a psychic whose gift mires her in a redneck murder case; *Thirteen,* David D. Williams's lovely story of a teenage girl who disappears, reappears, and grows up a little; Roger Donaldson's *Thirteen Days,* with Kevin Costner in the riveting story of the Cuban missile crisis; *Time Regained,* Raul Ruiz's inventive treatment of Proust; the animated *Titan AE* by Don Bluth and Gary Goldman, with its spellbinding cat-and-mouse chase through intergalactic ice rings; Raymond De Felitta's *Two Family House,* with Michael Rispoli as a man who can't help doing the right thing; Tahmineh Milani's *Two Women,* from Iran, about a woman who disgraces her family because a madman attacks her; Sofia Coppola's *The Virgin Suicides,* a sad and gentle meditation on doom; and the jolly *What's Cooking* by Gurinder Chadha, which cuts between African-American, Jewish, Vietnamese, and Latino families in Los Angeles on Thanksgiving.

And I also valued *Aimee & Jaguar, American Psycho, Cast Away, Croupier, Dr. T and the Women, East Is East, Ghost Dog, Hamlet, House of Mirth, Human Resources, Kadosh, La Ciudad, Meet the Parents, Me Myself I, Mifune, My Dog Skip, Nurse Betty, Pola X, Return to Me, Small Time Crooks, Space Cowboys, State and Main, Tao of Steve, Tigerland, Time Code, Time for Drunken Horses,* and *Unbreakable.*

Interviews

Nicolas Cage

Los Angeles, California, December 22, 2000—Nicolas Cage is not the first actor you'd think of to play a family man. He made his reputation on the edge, playing characters hanging precariously to life, sanity, sobriety. He won an Oscar for *Leaving Las Vegas,* playing a man whose head seems ready to explode. And remember him in the Cannes winner *Wild at Heart,* as the mad dog looking for a "rockin' good time." Earlier in 2000, he starred in *Gone in 60 Seconds* as a man trying to steal fifty cars in one night.

But here's Cage in *The Family Man,* a tire salesman, happily married, changing diapers and awakened in the morning by the big wet tongue of the family dog. To be sure, he doesn't start out as a family man; he's a high-powered corporate type until a strange metaphysical event lets him find out what life would have been like if he'd married his sweetheart instead of getting on that plane to London.

"I'm playing normal," Cage mused. "I like to play eccentric characters because there's something fun about them; it gives me a chance to transform. But Jack Campbell in *The Family Man* is closer to my true self."

He says it, and you believe it, but if he jumped onto the table the next moment and sang "Hound Dog," you'd believe that too.

In *The Family Man,* he costars with Tea Leoni as a man who finds out what life would have been like with a wife and family. The plot is uncannily similar to *Me Myself I,* a Rachel Griffiths movie from earlier in 2000 which I liked better—partly because I was seeing the story for the first time, partly because it ended more satisfactorily. But I liked Cage a lot in *The Family Man,* all the more because he was easier to see than in *Gone in 60 Seconds,* where he and the plot were moving targets.

We were talking after a screening of *The Family Man.* He liked the normal role, he said, but liked being a daredevil actor too. He was happy in the days he played the crazy guy in *Wild at Heart* or *Vampire's Kiss* or *Raising Arizona,* but it was getting to be time for him to add some more strings to his bow.

"The change happened right after *Trapped in Paradise* (1994), a movie which I wasn't very happy with; I didn't think I was doing my best work. After that I went into *Kiss of Death* with Barbet Schroeder directing, and I felt like I got out of the goofball comedy roles. It gave me a chance to play a character. And I went from there into *Leaving Las Vegas,* so something shifted at that time. It seemed like I got better control or access to my abilities."

There was another crucial role in there, I said, in *Guarding Tess* (1994), playing a Secret Service man assigned to guard the widow of a president (Shirley MacLaine), and that was a normal role, too—in a great movie.

That's the one that got away, I said. I thought it would be a hit.

"I think if I'd made it today it would have had a better shot," Cage said. "It had a lot to do with the growth of my work or my ability to get work. But at the time I wasn't in the position I'm in now, and the marketing didn't make anyone say, hey, you gotta see this movie."

Your career got big-time a year later, with *Leaving Las Vegas.*

"Right. I never want to get calcified into one type of movie. *Gone in 60 Seconds* is the type of movie you go to in order not to think about anything. It's like putting on a certain kind of music where you're not concentrating. I go there, I get the popcorn, I get my mind off my problems. *Leaving Las Vegas* is the type of movie that is closer to me in terms of my soul, where I wanna examine questions about life that perturb or excite me; I wanna dig a little deeper. I feel fortunate to be able to do both.

"With the larger commercial films, because they cost so much money, producers and studios are hesitant to take a chance on eccentric or unusual or exciting breakthrough material. It's the independents that will do it. And then what happens, in a case like *Pulp Fiction,* is that the movie is a big hit and then the studios start copying it. But they don't wanna be the first to do it. So as an actor if I really wanna keep sharp I have to make smaller movies that challenge me."

He took a chance like that in *8MM* (1999), the Joel Schumacher film where he played a private investigator venturing into the world of snuff films. It had to be recut to avoid an NC-17 rating, and then was widely attacked for its raw subject matter.

"I thought it was about the question why do people enjoy human suffering," Cage said, "and that's my biggest concern in life. I wanted to examine that."

He didn't think he was taking a chance with another 1999 film, Martin Scorsese's *Bringing Out the Dead*—Scorsese is one of the greatest of directors—but the movie inexplicably failed to do business. Cage played a paramedic in the Hells' Kitchen neighborhood of New York, in a role with overtones of Christ.

"One of the issues with having a career that has different areas, like mine," Cage said, "is that sometimes people can be confused. If a movie is promoted as an action adventure, which you can certainly do with a paramedic film, it can make people expect to pay their $8 to see something like *Gone in 60 Seconds*. Instead, they got an in-depth character analysis tone poem by Martin Scorsese. So they felt cheated. Maybe there was confusion there. I'm still trying to sort that out. I thought Marty's work on that was incredible."

And now comes *The Family Man*, which has a nice, cozy PG-13 rating and Cage, as we observed, changing diapers.

"I was experimenting just being me and seeing if that would be interesting to watch," Cage said. "This is my most extreme character. Just a normal guy."

Sean Connery

December 20, 2000—Ten things I learned while talking with Sean Connery:

1. In his new movie, *Finding Forrester*, Connery plays a reclusive writer who is drawn out of hibernation by a bright black kid. The veteran actor, who just turned seventy, read a first draft of the script and not only committed to the project but agreed to coproduce it. That despite the fact that the screenwriter, Mike Rich, had never made a movie sale before; he wrote it while working as a newsman for a Portland, Oregon, radio station.

2. It's basically a two-character movie involving a great novelist and a teenager named Jamal who hides his academic ability by pretending to be more interested in basketball. Connery's costar, sixteen-year-old Rob Brown, had never acted in a movie before, and this was a big role in basically a two-person story. "I did a test and it was obvious that the boy was really something and his instincts were all right. It's pretty rare, you know, to get that. In terms of learning, he was wide open, and he's very smart; straight A's in his subjects and everything; he's still in school. He's only turned sixteen. And listens, works, works. He never disappointed me any way along the line."

3. "We did it all step-by-step in an old-fashioned, professional way—get the jokes right and the characters right, and you get as much humor and what have you—and rehearsed for two weeks in Canada, and then finished dead on time."

4. On the character of Forrester: "I went for the mix of J. D. Salinger and William Burroughs as I imagined them. *Finding Forrester* as a title really means you do find Forrester, and he finds himself in a way, and the real key to it is the boy."

5. "I like going mostly on instinct in choosing roles. I choose what I would like to see, and 50 or 60 percent of the time I'm satisfied with how it goes. *Red October* is one thing and *Robin and Marian* is another. *Finding Forrester* is very compact, intense—an emotional movie. It's about friendship. *The Man Who Would Be King* is the only other film I've done that touched on the subject of friendship. Friendship is not first in the queue of movie commodities and has to be firmly dealt with to get the real message across. Forrester and Jamal are two most unlikely people to end up across the table typing together. But everybody who's seen it has been emotionally caught by the story."

6. "I think my most overlooked picture was *Family Business* (1989). I've never been able to work out why it had absolutely no curiosity value. I don't know anybody who went to see it. I know the mistake of the film, but I liked the idea. The character I played, the father of Dustin (Hoffman), the grandfather of Matthew Broderick, dies in a hospital and of course I had the solution, but it was too late: He should have come to his own funeral, explaining he wasn't dead because he had switched cars. That would have solved it. But I still don't understand why

there wasn't any measure of curiosity about that picture."

7. "With James Bond, people are sure there's gonna be a bit of sex, a bit of fun, a bit of action, a bit of drama, and it's gonna be a bit of a joyride. My personal choice is *From Russia With Love* because that's got all the glamour and the locations and the twists and the humor and rather good storytelling, and places like Istanbul. The Bond pictures will continue on, I suppose."

8. The key to the whole Bond series came from Terence Young, who directed *Dr. No* and *From Russia With Love,* the first two, as well as *Thunderball,* and added the consistent note of droll humor.

9. At seventy Connery is still considered one of the sexiest men alive, and recently played a romantic lead opposite Catherine Zeta-Jones. What's the secret of still playing in that league, I ask, and he grins: "Have good hairpieces. But also one of the things is that I started quite early going without hairpieces, in *Robin and Marian* and in films like that, and although Robin was mentally twelve, the sense of playing that kind of hero changed all the boundaries and limitations. As for baldness, they're all shaving their heads now. My wife says in the Japanese warrior movies, they shave the head out of a gesture of respect for age."

10. *Finding Forrester* is now playing in a few big markets: "It's not a teenager's movie—but it might be, you know. And there must be quite a sea of black audiences who'd be interested in seeing somebody who is a rather marvelous character like that boy."

Morgan Freeman

April 10, 2001—Morgan Freeman was tired. He said he hadn't been able to sleep all night. It was the end of the afternoon, and he was relaxed and unwound and in a stream-of-consciousness mood. We sat in a Chicago hotel room with a coffee pot. I had come to talk about his new thriller, *Along Came a Spider,* but the conversation poked into this corner and that, and took us to places I might not have asked about. Listen to him as he speaks:

"Have you ever been in jail? I have. I was a kid. I was in the air force and I'd gone with a friend of mine to Los Angeles. When we left the base, he left his Class-A pass sitting on the table.

We were hitchhiking because he was out of money. I had a little money but I didn't want to take the bus and leave him. The police stopped us on the freeway. He asked both of us for ID and I had mine and my friend didn't have his. The cop said, 'Well, we're gonna have to call the shore patrol because we don't know if you're AWOL.' He told me, 'You got money—you take a bus.' I said, 'I'm with him.' So I went to jail for four days.

"You have to go out and dig ditches for them; pick and shovel. It's not my kind of work. I am not doing this. I have a reputation for being kind of cocky. I told the guard I had to go to the infirmary. When I was twelve years old I fell off a tree and I cut my foot something awful. The tendon was cut and the toe of my left foot drew up, and I had this awful corn. So they saw that and sent me back to my cell. I called the sergeant and said, 'Do you need help? Because I can type.' So these guys come back all sweaty and dusty, handling pick axes, and I'm sittin' up drinking coffee and typing. Charmed life."

So you can use that jail time when you play Nelson Mandela?

"Oh, absolutely. Yet, if you ask, what kind of research do you do for your roles? I say I don't do research; it's on the page. But in reality you're always doing research. You're always studying people."

The Mandela picture, which will film next year, has the potential to be great, he said. He and producer Anant Singh and director Shekhar Kapur agreed that it would focus on Mandela himself, not on South African history. That means a lot of scenes in prison.

"I've been in three prisons. One was Kingston Prison in Toronto and one was in Mansfield, Ohio, where we did *Shawshank Redemption.* Prison is full of people with very strange societal needs, and that's scary. When we were doing *Brubaker* we were in a prison for the criminally insane. They said, 'Don't talk to the inmates.' Well, what do you do if a guy accused of butchering his family comes up and speaks to you? You don't refuse to talk to him. Richard Pryor tells a joke about how he's in prison with this guy who killed everybody in his family. He says, 'Why did you kill 'em all?' And the guy says, 'They was home.'"

In *Along Came a Spider,* you're back again as the forensic psychologist Dr. Alex Cross.

"As franchises go, he's one of the better ones. He's almost magical in his abilities. He's very like Sherlock Holmes. One of my joys was Jeremy Brett doing Sherlock Holmes. I'm drawn to that sort of cerebral detective. So if I'm going to have opportunities like this and I'm going to succumb, this is the best one."

The movie is filled with loopholes, some of which are closed, and others I'm not so sure about. Are you confident that if we study this movie carefully enough, all of our questions are answered?

"No, I'm not at all. Because when script changes are being made for whatever reason—studio, director, what have you—it creates problems in the fabric of the grand structure. You've got a series of pieces that hold together. You know it's a circle. But the little spokes that should tie it all together don't always exist.

"We had two or three phone calls in the movie—you didn't see them, because they cut them out. The kidnapper realizes there's been a major change in his situation and he calls Alex and asks a question, 'Where's Jezzy?' And Alex says, 'Something's wrong, isn't there?' And the two of them become this other entity in the structure of the maze."

The kidnapper and the detective are trying to figure out the third side of the triangle together. Would it have been better with those calls in there?

"I think so. If we could have gotten it structured the way I wanted to structure it. Because at the beginning, the kidnapper is looking for a playmate, you know. This is not a game, but Cross understands his need. Then they realize the game has more than two players."

I write this Movie Answer Man column where people send me questions. Somebody observed that you almost always play a loner, a self-contained person. You rarely, if ever, play a family man with a wife and kids. Although in *Nurse Betty,* as it turned out, you were a family man.

"Well, I have a kid anyway. But I'm smiling at that question, because there is a really deep part of me that's like that, you know—single and alone. The character in *Lean on Me* had a wife and kids. You just never saw them. *Driving Miss Daisy*—in the end you just saw his granddaughter. I shouldn't actually come off very well as a father figure. I can, because it's only acting, but my kids all grew up on the periphery of my life. The mothers had control of them, and I was always gone one way or another . . ."

I want to ask you about Neil LaBute's *Nurse Betty.* Certain movies, as time goes by, enlarge themselves in the mind while others evaporate. *Nurse Betty* had mixed success. Some of the reviews seemed unreasonably hostile toward it. I liked it, but now I find it continuing to grow and expand in my memory.

"Might turn out to be like *Shawshank,* you know. Have you ever met Neil LaBute? I'm like everybody else who works with him—I'm totally in love. He's got this really strange mindset that is so much fun. I mean, he has a total sense of humor. It may not always be apparent, but even in *In the Company of Men,* it was there; it had to do with a man's take on what other men do."

The role in *Nurse Betty* was a departure from your usual roles: He was complicated, tender, but mean.

"It was a departure. Aside from *Street Smart* [his first major role, for which he got a 1988 Oscar nomination as a vicious pimp], I really haven't had much of an occasion to do anything with that kind of approach. It's much more dramatic playing an evil guy. Playing a good guy is like room tone. The other kind of role provides all of the fireworks, the drama, you know. I watch *Spider* and I think I could have upped the ante a little bit more, maybe."

You're lucky that after *Street Smart* you didn't get typecast.

"It's not luck. I really had to work at that. People saw that movie, and it was like I must have really come off the street. People say I don't like to repeat roles. 'No,' I say, 'I don't like to do the same character in different venues.' They say, 'I wrote this with you in mind.' Oh, yeah? Which me?"

William Friedkin

September 26, 2000—For twenty-seven years he defended his original cut of *The Exorcist,* says William Friedkin, who directed the timeless horror classic. For all of those years, William Peter Blatty, who wrote the original novel and screenplay and produced the film, argued for a longer version.

"I finally heard something in his voice a year ago that made me want to go back and look at it again," said Friedkin. "It wasn't easy for me to say to him after twenty-seven years: 'You know what? I think I was wrong.'"

Friedkin's new version, eleven minutes longer than the 1973 original, opened to reviews that generally agreed the film still holds the power to shock and entertain. But some critics, myself included, questioned a revised ending.

And I also suggested that the new version might have less to do with art than with marketing. That was why Friedkin called me Friday, and why he was mad.

I wrote: "While these scenes may have various rationales in the minds of Friedkin and Blatty, they have one obvious rationale in the thinking at the studio: They provide an excuse for the theatrical rerelease, and will help sell the video, even to those who already own the earlier version."

I could hear the anger in his voice.

"You can say you don't like this version, and that's fine," Friedkin told me. "But to call it a marketing ploy is way off base. We had to take them to the wall to release this version. The studio (Warner Bros.) was never in favor of it. They wanted it to open in two theaters in New York and Los Angeles. We had to fight them to even think about it. They hate us because we forced them to do this by exercising a load of muscle, and if it turns out to be successful, it has nothing to do with them."

According to Friedkin, the current command at Warner Bros. has no stake in the film "because they weren't around when it was made." When the original version was rereleased in England a year ago and grossed $13 million in a month, he said, the studio was unhappy because "it outgrossed their own new picture, *Lethal Weapon 4*, and that made them look bad."

It has been known for years that Friedkin and Blatty disagreed about the final cut of the film. Friedkin showed studio executives a cut that was about 140 minutes long. The studio wanted it trimmed to two hours, fearing the longer running time would turn off audiences. Friedkin trimmed it and liked his trims, feeling the 120-minute version was tauter.

"When the picture came out," he recalled, "Bill was vitriolic. He was harsh. He would denounce the picture. Then, over the years, our relationship mellowed into friendly banter. Bill has been begging me for years to go back and examine the footage that we cut. A year ago, we looked at it together, and I told him, 'I think you're right. But even if you're not, I'll do it for you anyway, because it's your right.'"

Now, says Friedkin of the new 131-minute version, "I think this is better."

Dubious "director's cuts" have become notorious in recent years for justifying new video releases. After talking to Friedkin, I believe I was wrong to suggest that was the case this time.

But what about the ending? "It's like a guest who keeps talking after the party is over," I told him.

The original ending is a somber, quiet note. In the revised ending, a surviving priest makes small talk with a detective (Lee J. Cobb), who likes to imagine weird movie casts and suggests *Wuthering Heights* with Jackie Gleason and Lucille Ball. In my review, I called this new ending "catastrophic."

"I originally thought it should just cut off at the end," Friedkin said. "Blatty always thought we should show normal life resuming. Now I prefer this ending. I love seeing Lee J. Cobb. It reminds me how great he was to work with. Does the new ending have anything to do with the movie? No. It's an aesthetic consideration. I'm a changed guy. I had a much harder edge in those days. I don't have that edge now.

"Have you ever heard the story of how the French painter Bonnard, when he was an old man, went into the Louvre with a paintbrush and started touching up his paintings? They threw him out. 'But they're my paintings!' he said. He saw them differently now. I feel the same way. Given the chance, I'd go back and redo everything I've done."

Ed Harris

February 15, 2001—Ed Harris's journey to an Oscar nomination started fifteen years ago, when his dad, Robert, was working at the bookstore of the Art Institute of Chicago. "He was walking down the aisle," Harris said, "and he saw this face staring out at him from a book cover. It looked somewhat similar to me, so he sent it to me for my birthday in 1986, and he even said maybe there was a film in there somewhere."

The book was *To a Violent Grave*, by Jeffrey Potter, and the face on the cover was of Jackson Pollock, the brilliant abstract expressionist artist, who suffered from alcoholism and manic depression. There was, it turned out, a film in there—and in another book, *Jackson Pollock: An American Saga* by Steven Naifeh and Gregory White Smith. The film is *Pollock*. Ed Harris directed it and plays Pollock, and it is one of the best films of the year. It won a Best Actor nomination for Harris, and a Supporting Actress nomination for Marcia Gay Harden, who plays Pollock's wife, the painter Lee Krasner. (She won the Oscar.)

Harris found some points of connection between himself and Pollock, he said, "but they're kinda tricky to talk about because they're very personal." One of them was the way Pollock's career took precedence over his personal life.

"When I first began acting," he said, "that was it. That's all I was concerned about and I wanted to be the best I could be. Pollock wanted to be the best painter he could be. I was a very isolated individual during that time. I was just working. I didn't have tons of friends. I became paralyzed in the company of strangers. And I had a little bit of a problem here and there with substance abuse, so a lot of the territory was not unfamiliar to me. Having a family, your priorities change a bit."

He read the books and brooded on them, visited Pollock's paintings, and even started to paint a little himself.

"I didn't take any art lessons. I began to experiment, fool around. I had some paint and brushes and sticks around, started seeing the effects of different gestures and began to work on bigger surfaces. I got to the place where I felt confident enough to try to paint something, not a Pollock, but something in his style that worked for me. I got an inkling of what it would be like to live your life as a painter. I'd go to bed and think about it and couldn't wait to get up to the studio the next day and try to make it work."

What he discovered in the process was that Pollock's famous "drip technique" was difficult and challenging and not something "anyone could do," although that was an accusation in Pollock's lifetime.

"His work became about the act of painting. You can see the focus and the concentration. There's one thing I really learned; this was not a haphazard endeavor on this guy's part. Every gesture had an intention behind it. I mean, it really did; this was not like an accident going on here."

We were talking one day last week in Chicago. He was visiting his parents, staying at their house in Evanston, and no doubt wondering if on Tuesday he or his film would win Oscar nominations.

"It would be great for the film if it got a couple of nominations," he said, "but I'm not counting on it. Plus, Pollock's a tough guy to give it to. A lot of people find him intolerable. Most of the time the academy's kinda voting for performances they can root for."

Best Picture isn't for people who get drunk and kill themselves?

"I guess the exception would be *Leaving Las Vegas*."

He grinned. Harris at fifty is compact, quiet, focused, one of the best actors of his generation. He has had two Oscar nominations, for *The Truman Show* and *Apollo 13*, and has played roles as different as a doubting priest in *The Third Miracle*, Watergate figure E. Howard Hunt in *Nixon*, a slick-talking salesman in *Glengarry Glen Ross*, an aquanaut in *The Abyss*, and John Glenn in *The Right Stuff*, the movie that brought him early stardom in 1983. He's married to the actress Amy Madigan, also from Chicago; her father is the retired political commentator John Madigan.

It's interesting, I said, that both Pollock and you married people who are acclaimed in the same art. Pollock's wife, Lee Krasner, was herself a famous artist.

"When I met Amy we were doing a play. There's a bond there. You know what each other's doing, you know what you're going through. It's important to be able to share that. But it's not something you always talk about. Pollock and Krasner didn't really discuss painting in formalistic terms."

And it's the same with you and Amy?

"We're getting along a little better than they were. But you talk more about it on the outside, you know. It's difficult to speak about the kind of intricacies or the secret places you go or the kind of magic of what you do—hopefully, if there is any. You talk about what happened on the set that day. Or if you're doing theater then you start penetrating the written word, especially if you're working together, and get deeper and deeper into the text. That can get pretty exciting."

When you were interviewed on the Actors' Studio TV program, I said, you said Phil Kaufman, the director of *The Right Stuff*, talked to you about drinking getting in the way of the work. Maybe that's a talk Kaufman should have had with Jackson Pollock.

"Yeah, no kidding. Well, back in those days, I was partying pretty heavy. Not during filming. I'd be in good shape during the day but I think he knew I was maybe staying out a little late on a couple of nights and he just said, watch it, man, because it can get you, you know.

"Ultimately I realized, yeah, it's catching up to me. Other than a very few instances, it never affected my work, but it affects how you go through life. I mean, it's a great thing to use to escape what you feel. After you've worked a long hard day and you wanna have a beer and you end up four hours later having had as many as you could drink in that time. That's a problem."

In the film, Harris charts Pollock's relationship with booze and pills. The artist has long periods when he's sober and productive, and then, just when things seem to be going well, he picks up a beer.

"There was this whole cyclical thing to Pollock," Harris said. "He'd go off the deep end. When he was sober a few years toward the end, he created most of the things he's known for. But then he didn't want to keep doing what he was doing, and the celebrity thing kicked in, and when he got the recognition and approval I think he realized it was relatively meaningless. I think that was really frightening to him—so, yeah, it's time to drink again. I think at the end of his life he was really just in unbearable pain, emotionally."

Mick Jagger

Park City, Utah, January 25, 2001—Mick Jagger is taller than you'd think, thin as a rail, dressed in clothes that were never new and only briefly fashionable. There is a studious unconcern about appearance, as if, having been Mick Jagger all these many years, he can wear whatever he bloody well pleases.

He is at the Sundance Film Festival as a producer. He and Lorne Michaels have produced

and Michael Apted has directed *Enigma*, a Sundance entry about the British codebreakers at the top-secret Bletchley Park facility, who cracked the German naval code when it had 150 million million million possible solutions, and then cracked it again after it was improved to 4,000 million billion solutions.

He wanted to get into film production, he said, because "I got rather bored with people trying to involve me in their projects and then the projects would fall to pieces. I thought well, wait a minute, if I'm interested in this, I should start doing the things that I'm interested in, and not the things other people want me to do."

In the movie business it helps get a project financed if a big name like Jagger's is "attached" to it. Better to attach himself to his own project and eliminate the middle men.

Enigma is based on a best-selling novel by Robert Harris, a riveting read, long unfilmed because it's not exactly cinematic to show a lot of mathematicians sitting in a room drinking coffee, smoking cigarettes, thinking hard, and writing on yellow pads.

"It's very hard to do a movie about intellectual activity," Jagger mused. We were sitting in an upstairs room of a bar named Gamekeepers, drinking mineral water. "It's even hard to do a movie about painters. What are they doing? Painting. This could have been a movie about guys sitting in rooms with pencils.

"Fortunately, in the real-life Bletchley Park, they invented a way of decoding the Nazi signals using a kind of mechanical computer. They built these things called bombs where you put instructions in and the machines would click away. The man with a pencil would make a calculated guess what the code was, and then the bomb would go through the permutations and say yes or no."

Enigma is, however, luckily about more than computers. It is also about romance and betrayal. The film stars Dougray Scott as Tom Jericho, the brilliant mathematician who has returned after a nervous breakdown, Saffron Burrows as the beautiful war worker who caused the breakdown and then went missing, and Kate Winslet as the plucky operative in the radio reception room, who transcribes the German signals and helps Tom solve the mystery of the code and the missing woman. Jeremy Northam is the British intelligence operative who wonders if all three are spies.

"It's not just about code-breaking," Jagger said, "but about love, and it's got some underlying moral questions also about how many lives can be lost for the greater good."

Hearing Jagger say things like that is tricky because you have the rock 'n' roll persona in your mind, and the person sitting across from you speaks in a well-educated British drawl, like someone on an upmarket talk show. I mentioned that I'd seen the Rolling Stones at the Double Door in Chicago, in a warm-up performance the night before the Stones's most recent tour kicked off at the United Center.

"That was a nice night," he said. "That was one of those nights when it all goes nicely." He seemed to be describing another person in another life.

Enigma's director, Michael Apted, "is an old friend," Jagger said. "I knew him from years ago. He's a well-known English documentary filmmaker as well as a feature filmmaker. We had meetings with him and he seemed right for the job, and then he got this offer to do the last Bond movie, so we had a hiatus of a year while he did the Bond movie and so we had to keep the whole thing waiting."

The screenplay is by Tom Stoppard, famed playwright and screenwriter *(Shakespeare in Love)*, and a formidable force when crossed.

"Tom's an old friend of mine," said Jagger, who has excellent taste in old friends, "and since this is an intellectually challenging story, I thought he would suit it. But everyone else was kind of afraid of Tom, intellectually. He's not a mean person, but he's not a person that you can make mistakes with. If you go in and say, 'Scene 38B is not really working,' you'd better know why it's not working. Everyone was afraid to do that. So that was my job. To say what I would say to any writer, because if it's not working, it's not working."

You had the personal authority to say things to Stoppard that other people were afraid to say.

"I'd tell him in a nice way, and I'd still get the intellectual gob reply back, you know. He would say things like, 'So you want the Woman's Own approach.'"

A lot of people would be hesitant to tell Mick Jagger something he might not want to hear, I said. I think it's amusing that there's somebody who doesn't want to hear what *you* have to say.

"These sort of alliances make for interesting results."

Have you had any fun at Sundance?

"No, I came here last night, and I went to a party where Macy Gray was supposed to be singing. She wasn't there. I had a few drinks and left. That was my Sundance experience."

Will you see any movies?

"I have to go back to Los Angeles tomorrow. I do go to Cannes quite often for a couple of days, to see what movies are around. And I was at Venice this year. It was fun."

Jagger said his company has two other projects in the works, one by Martin Scorsese called *The Long Play*, about two guys who grow in the music business over thirty years, and the other based on the poet Dylan Thomas's life and marriage.

He hasn't starred in many movies, but people still talk about his androgynous druggie rock star, playing host to a gangster on the run, in Nicolas Roeg's *Performance* (1970).

"I saw it on television not long ago," Jagger said. "What I found interesting was the social observations that were being made and the use of documentary-style footage. It was really quite ahead of its time. It's a good movie; I think it holds up."

He had another dramatic role in 1970, *Ned Kelly*, about the famous Australian outlaw. I asked if he's read Peter Carey's new novel about Kelly.

"People have told me it's fantastic."

So maybe your company would return to Ned Kelly for another picture?

"I think I've done my Ned Kelly years."

Ang Lee

December 19, 2000—I had this amazing conversation with Ang Lee, the director of *Crouching Tiger, Hidden Dragon*. It started when I mentioned the "computer work" used in a scene where two swordfighters are clinging to the tops of swaying trees.

"No computers," said Lee.

"The people were really up there?" I asked.

"Actually doing it."

"In the trees?"

"Yes. The scene doesn't have the usual horror movie slickness because the people we are photographing are real. They're actually up there. Everything you see is real except the wires, which we digitally removed."

"You had them hanging from safety wires?"

"Yes."

"On cranes?"

"Yes. It was sort of dangerous. From construction cranes. Scary."

"I would have bet it was done with a computer."

"No. The softest things are the hardest things to do on a computer. Making the leaves bend, showing the clouds, wind, water . . ."

"How about when they're dancing over the rooftops?" I asked, referring to an early chase scene where the actors run up the sides of walls and seem to float from one rooftop to another.

"It's real. They're actually doing it. There is no virtual reality, as they call it; I don't have that kind of money."

I was still struggling to get my bearings. "So . . . you used stunt people, right?"

"Some. Most of those scenes the actors did themselves."

"Themselves?" I'm thinking of Chou Yun Fat and Michelle Yeoh, big worldwide stars, breaking their necks or other valuable parts.

"Most of the time. If you see face front, it's them. Even side, most of the time, it's them. I like to really see them, although the stunt men could do it better. The emotional effect is different when you see their faces. See, computers look like computers. We're not there yet. The kind of technique I used in this film doesn't match the Hollywood standard of slickness. Hollywood is more technically astonishing but they don't necessarily capture the human feelings. Our movie is less perfect but more human."

I think he's being too hard on himself. *Crouching Tiger* is the most impressive martial arts movie I have ever seen. Not because of the stunts, although they are startling, but because of the overall effect. Ang Lee told me his film was influenced not so much by other martial arts movies as by the books he read when he was young, books that emphasized myth and romance as much as action.

"The author whose book I started with, Wang Du Lu, is really writing Greek tragedy. And, similar to my taste, he has a strong woman, and a contemptible woman. And he is focused on the values of the characters. They are warriors, and also role models. They have simple moral codes about personal transcendence. How do you perfect yourself into a higher state? When you're enlightened, you're more focused. I think that's the element that this genre has gradually lost over the years, with the emphasis on action. I can't tell you how many people, especially who grew up as I did reading those books, come and tell me this is what martial arts film should be."

For Ang Lee, the film comes as a departure from what he's done before—but then all of his films seem like departures. Born forty-six years ago in Taiwan, educated at the University of Illinois at Urbana, living in New York, he moves effortlessly from genre to genre. Look at his titles. After the early hits *The Wedding Banquet* (1993) and *Eat Drink Man Woman* (1994), which spanned his Chinese and American backgrounds, he adapted Jane Austen's *Sense and Sensibility* (1995), which won an Academy nomination as one of the year's best films and won an Oscar for Emma Thompson's screenplay. Then came the completely different *The Ice Storm* (1997), about angst-ridden suburbanites, and the Civil War–era adventure *Ride With the Devil* (1999).

"You stand in the middle of two different cultures," I said.

"I have to connect with the material emotionally, on a gut level. From genre to genre for me is like an actor playing a different part. I get scared and have a lot to learn, but a few weeks into the production I feel at ease. I don't feel alienated. And then just because I go back to the Chinese culture with this film doesn't mean I know what to do. Every movie, I'm taking a chance."

Spike Lee

October 3, 2000—Spike Lee hears that his new film, *Bamboozled,* is the center of a storm of controversy.

"I don't think it's even started yet, really," he says. "But I don't think I would call it a controversy; I would say it was a loud discussion."

Very loud. His movie, a bitter satire of the way African-American images are marketed in the media, uses images that are deliberately offensive. Will audiences take them in the spirit Lee intended?

Lee knows something about controversy

over charged images. When his great *Do the Right Thing* opened in 1989, he recalls, the writer Joe Klein predicted the film would incite blacks to riot. Instead, it was hailed as an important contribution to black-white dialogues.

Bamboozled is also filled with troubling images, although this time both blacks and whites seem to share feelings of uncertainty as they watch the screen.

In the film, Damon Wayans plays a Harvard-educated black cable executive who is badgered by his boss because he creates shows that are "too white." Fed up, Wayans creates *Mantan— The New Millennium Minstrel Show.* He expects to be fired, but the show turns into a surprise hit. It stars two homeless black street dancers (Savion Glover and Tommy Davidson) wearing exaggerated blackface in a *Hee-Haw* type format set in a watermelon patch on a southern plantation.

Some who have seen the film believe the images fly over the top of satire and are themselves offensive.

"We knew going in that this film would generate responses like this," Lee told me during a Chicago visit last week. "There's a range of images that can make you angry. It makes me angry. It makes me sad. It makes me try to understand how do these images come about in the first place, and what are their effects. But you don't have to put on blackface in the twenty-first century to be a part of the minstrel act. It's the new millennium and it's the same old stuff."

Minstrel shows didn't star only white actors. Many blacks put on the typical minstrel blackface to take advantage of their popularity. The formula was always the same: Jokes based on the stupidity and laziness of the black characters, performed for the entertainment of mostly white audiences.

What minstrel act do you see going on right now? I asked him.

"A lot of music videos. I would definitely say that they've evolved into a minstrel show. And a lot of shows on television."

Any particular videos or shows?

Lee sighed. "I don't think it does any good to say Spike Lee doesn't like this artist or that show. But as far as the music videos go—those gangsta-rap videos, they talk about 'my hos' and 'my bitches' and that's a twenty-first-century form of the minstrel show.

"I'm not saying those types of films and TV shows should not be made. I just think that shouldn't be the only thing. We need to expand, stretch out. It's kind of sad. Why do we always have to be relegated to the ghetto of sitcoms? I'm gonna try to do an episodic television show that's a drama. There's so much more that can be explored. Hopefully somebody who's courageous at one of these networks will take a chance and move in that direction."

The summer of 2000, he said, was a summer of enormous success for black-themed comedy films. He cited *Scary Movie,* Martin Lawrence in *Big Momma's House,* Eddie Murphy in *Nutty Professor II: The Klumps,* and his own *Original Kings of Comedy,* which will be his highest-grossing film.

"It's like they're treating this as a big awakening in Hollywood," Lee said. "I don't see it like that because all the films are comedies. When you do comedy, for the most part it's very safe. I'm happy for everybody involved. I'm elated with the success of *Original Kings of Comedy,* but when films like *Beloved* and *Rosewood,* films like that, that type of subject matter, when those films get people to come out, then that's the day for true celebration. We're not there yet. Studios are very reluctant to make those types of films."

Lee said the idea for *Bamboozled* started with his first visits to the movies, "and watching the little TV my parents would let me watch." He was aware that black characters were often marginalized or made into caricatures: "It's from a lifetime of accumulating images."

The end titles of the film play over a montage of African-American collectibles—coin banks, Mammy dolls, Uncle Toms, pickaninnies. I wondered if all audience members would read these racially charged images in the spirit Lee intended.

"You cannot underestimate the intelligence of the audience," he said. "The audiences are smarter than that; they are intelligent and they will know exactly what it is up on the screen and why."

I've talked to some people, black and white, who found the images offensive no matter what you were saying about them, I said.

"I understand that perfectly. My grandmother would say exactly the same thing: 'Spike, why you bringing back this stuff? We're trying to move ahead.' I'm not of the belief that we've evolved and put all that behind us, and don't need to dredge up all that stuff. There are Jewish people who say they don't want to see images from Auschwitz. Other people say that stuff needs to be seen, that the world must never forget what happened in Poland and Germany. I think this is the same thing, and we need to confront it."

Kasi Lemmons

March 1, 2001—When I ran into Kasi Lemmons on the opening night of this year's Sundance Film Festival, I almost wanted to wince. That was because I was going to see her new film, *The Caveman's Valentine,* the next day. "And there is no way," I told her, trying to make a joke out of it, "that it can be as good as your last film, because nobody can make the best film of the year twice in four years."

"I just hope you enjoy it," she said, and to my relief, I did. *The Caveman's Valentine* isn't a great film like her 1997 debut, *Eve's Bayou,* but it's a good one. It's a thriller about a homeless man (Samuel L. Jackson) who finds himself investigating a murder that may have been committed by a famous photographer. It meets the requirements of the crime genre, but it also has qualities indicating it was made by a real filmmaker—sharp social observation, quirky wit, supporting characters from left field.

For Lemmons, the film is an important step, bringing her into the mainstream after a first film that was so astonishingly good. *Eve's Bayou* was a success—it was the top-grossing independent film of its year—but Hollywood measures success by a different scale, and *Caveman* will open on many more screens than *Bayou* ever dreamed of.

In the movie, Jackson plays a once-brilliant pianist, a student at Julliard, who now lives in a cave in a New York park and wanders the streets under layers of coats, his dreadlocks obscuring his fierce gaze. When a frozen body is found outside his cave, the police (including his daughter) consider it an accident, but he suspects murder. His first suspect is an enemy he believes lives at the top of the Chrysler Building and attacks him with mysterious rays. Later, when he begins to zero in on a rich photographer, nobody listens.

For Lemmons, *Caveman* is the second time

Jackson has been instrumental in her career. By agreeing to star in *Eve's Bayou,* at less than his usual salary, he made that low-budget film possible. This time, involved in preproduction on the caveman story, he suggested Lemmons as the director.

"So now you're a director, period?" I asked.

"A writer-filmmaker," she said; she's working on a big novel.

She had a lot of success as an actress, most famously as Clarice's roommate at the FBI academy in *The Silence of the Lambs,* also in *Candyman, School Daze, Vampire's Kiss,* and *Gridlock'd,* directed by her husband, Vondie Curtis-Hall. But from her first days at NYU film school, she said, she had her sights set on directing. One of her first short films, *Fall From Grace,* was about the homeless in New York.

"I would use a long-lens camera. I'd tell them I was going to film them and ask if they minded. I'd make them lunch and then I'd step back and wait. And through the lens of the camera you could see a lot of these people were mentally ill and were involved in some very dynamic inner struggles, that you couldn't get inside. The point I was trying to make was that we should take a closer look at the human beings around us.

"In New York City you kinda have a tunnel vision and you try not to see too much. I wanted to ask, what's on that person's mind? Who is that person? Where did they come from? How did they get on the street? Do they have a family? And so when I read *Caveman,* it was an opportunity for me to get inside of one of those people."

"One of the best things about the film," I said, "is the way you find to present the caveman. He is clearly mentally ill, yes, but he makes a certain kind of sense. You didn't make him into some kind of a sideshow where we're distracted by his bizarre behavior."

"We discussed where to pitch him," Lemmons said. "Samuel had a great grasp of the character. He really knows what he's doing. But when you've got a performance like that you do have to look at the whole picture once you've edited it together, and kind of refine it. It doesn't work if you've got a man who's screaming for the whole picture. Lots of times we would try various levels. He could give us a range of behavior. But he was always convincing. You know, when he was in the full makeup and the wig and everything, I couldn't find Sam Jackson the actor. The voice doesn't sound like him. He morphed into that character."

On my way out I said I'd been in a big discussion earlier that day, when I said her first name rhymed with "Casey" and a friend said it rhymed with "Cazzie."

"Casey," she said. "Somehow the other pronunciation got around, but I do all I can to stomp it out. My name is Karen, but when I was a kid nobody ever called me Karen, they called me Kati or Kasi. And Katy was K-A-T-I and Kasi was K-A-S-I, and that's the story."

Errol Morris

Park City, Utah, January 29, 2001—There is a tall curtain at one end of the room, and from time to time Errol Morris peeks out from behind it like the Wizard of Oz. All of the seats are taken in the House of Docs for his demonstration of his latest interviewing device—Megatron, Son of Interrotron. Technicians scurry about, wearing ski parkas instead of white lab coats, but nevertheless looking like the minions of a James Bond villain about to demonstrate a device that will (cackle) gain control of mankind.

In the audience, other famous documentarians have gathered like scientists about to see their sacred theories overthrown. I see Freida Lee Mock, who won the Oscar for *Maya Lin;* George Nierenberg, who made *Say Amen, Somebody;* Kate Davis, who is here with *Southern Comfort;* Anne Makepeace, of *Baby, It's You;* and Mark Lewis, of *Cane Toads* and *The Natural History of the Chicken* fame. Reid Rosefelt, Morris's publicist, presides like a Vatican protocol chief.

I grab a reserved seat in the front row. It is not reserved for me, but I do not stand on ceremony. I would want to be up front for Einstein too. "It is time to begin," says Rosefelt, and from the loudspeakers we hear Errol Morris's disembodied voice: "Yes, I think so too."

Rosefelt sits in a straight chair in front of the curtain. He looks into what appears to be a TelePrompTer. On a screen high and to the right, we see the face of Errol Morris. Another screen, to the left, is split into four segments, all showing different views of Morris.

"When Reid is looking into the camera in front of him, he is looking straight into my eyes," says the voice of Morris. "And I am looking straight into his."

I am ready for him to start swinging a gold watch on its chain while Rosefelt goes into a trance and promises never to send out another press release. Instead, Morris explains the theory of the Megatron, a revolutionary improvement on the Interrotron.

But let's back up a second. Morris is perhaps the most famous and successful documentary maker in America. He will soon relaunch his television program *First Person* on the Independent Film Channel. An earlier incarnation on Bravo was described by *Time* as one of the year's ten best TV shows.

Morris's credits include *Gates of Heaven,* a pet cemetery documentary that I have listed as one of the ten best films of all time, as well as *The Thin Blue Line,* which freed an innocent man from Death Row in Texas; *A Brief History of Time,* starring physicist Stephen Hawking; *Fast, Cheap and Out of Control,* which was about intelligent robots, lion tamers, topiary gardeners, and naked mole rats; and *Mr. Death,* the story of a Holocaust denier whose dream is to invent more humane execution devices. Morris's TV show has featured films on Temple Granding, a woman recognized as the world's leading designer of cattle-handling systems even though she is autistic, and a parrot that was an eyewitness to a murder (but can its testimony be believed?).

On many of these films, Morris used the Interrotron, his own invention. "I like the name," he explains, "because it combines the words 'interview' and 'terror.'" It also reminds him of alien devices in 1950s science-fiction movies. Instead of sitting face-to-face with his interview subjects, he has them look into a TV camera. They see Morris's face reflected on a screen. Morris looks into another camera and sees the subject. One is somehow not surprised to learn that two-way mirrors are involved.

Morris likes this approach because (a) "This way the subject is looking straight into the eyes of the audience, instead of off to the side of the camera," (b) "I can maintain unbroken eye contact," (c) "People will say things to a TV camera they won't say to a human being," and (d) "Sometimes if I just pause and wait, people feel compelled to say something because the Interrotron is waiting, and so they speak even if they don't mean to."

Reason (d) is buttressed by Morris's Twenty-Minute Rule. This is his theory that if you let people talk for twenty minutes without interrupting them, they will start spilling the beans whether they want to or not.

How does the Megatron differ from the Interrotron? It can use twenty cameras instead of one. The split screen behind Rosefelt was showing the views from four of them. This capability doesn't change the eye-to-eye interview experience, but does allow Morris a greater selection of different kinds of shots when he is editing.

Morris had his technicians turn the camera from Rosefelt to the audience for questions. He could see his interrogators, and they could see him—a spectral black-and-white presence inside the camera. He said he had toyed with marketing the Megatron, but for now prefers to keep it proprietary. To be sure, there didn't seem to be an enormous demand; Mock, Davis, and Makepeace were not jostling for a look behind the curtain, and Lewis and Nierenberg had adjourned to the House of Docs Cafe for coffee and oatmeal muffins. So for the foreseeable future, Morris may have the Megatron all to himself.

He likes it that way. "I am toying with the idea," he said, "of an Interrobot, which I could send to your house while I stay in the studio."

Joel Schumacher

Toronto, Canada, October 1, 2000—Joel Schumacher is not exactly singing *Amazing Grace,* but from the way he talks, he once was lost and now he's found, was blind but now he sees.

Here is the man who directed *Batman and Robin* and *Batman Forever,* with their combined production and marketing budgets of maybe $250 million, and he has made a $10 million movie in twenty-eight days and he says, "This film afforded me one of the purest experiences you can possibly have as a filmmaker."

The movie is named *Tigerland* and it stars a cast of unknowns in the story of draftees in the last stages of advanced infantry training before Vietnam. After basic training, they're promoted to Fort Polk's "Tigerland," a training ground that duplicates the reality and dangers of Vietnam.

The army has headaches with this group of the trainees, however, because of the troublesome Bozz, who is relentless in resisting authority.

Bozz is a focus for the fears and resentments in his group, and the officers seem in danger of losing control of these young men.

Schumacher shot the movie in 16mm, abandoning the demanding 35mm cameras and their crews of acolytes, leaving behind the elaborate lights and support mechanisms of big-budget movies, filming fast and close to the action. It was a declaration of independence after his toil in the service of blockbusters.

"My goal in life since I was a kid was to be a director in order to tell good stories," he told me one day at the Toronto Film Festival. "The goal was not to protect a Hollywood career. I felt I had to back away from the summer blockbuster world because the box office was starting to become more important than the movie. It was scaring me. I felt like I'd lost myself."

Schumacher is a sunny man with a quick smile; nothing about him suggests that most of his projects have involved versions of death—notably in *Flatliners* (1990), a drama about cocky medical students who try to investigate the afterlife experience by actually dying, and then trusting their friends to resuscitate them with a tale to tell.

"Some of my earlier films (*St. Elmo's Fire, Dying Young, The Lost Boys, Cousins*) were small-budget pictures with actors who were relative unknowns at the time," he said. "I'm back to that with *Tigerland.* This feels comfortable to me. Working with unknowns in a risky project is exciting."

How unknown? His lead, a twenty-four-year-old actor from Dublin named Colin Farrell, missed the audition. "His plane was late. I thought he wasn't coming. I was leaving the hotel when he showed up and just filled the room. He was very funny, smart, a great heart and soul, a dirty mouth, interesting."

Schumacher had to catch a plane, but asked Farrell to send him something. Farrell, who was also here at the Toronto Film Festival, picks up the story: "We got a camcorder and borrowed someone's apartment, and my sister ran the camera and read the part of the two girls in the bar from offscreen, and I did my best West Texas and sent it off to Joel."

He got the job. That's not how actors are auditioned for a Batman movie.

"What happens with success," Schumacher

said, "is, you start to protect the success by repeating the success. That led me down a road that wasn't comfortable for me. I'm not complaining. I was overpaid to do those jobs. It's fun to make *Batman.*

"But the way those pictures are made! I don't know how we do it. You get there in the morning, you have a little rehearsal, and everybody goes to hair and makeup—which on a Batman movie could take four or five hours. Then you've got to film a scene that all our careers and the future of all the toy licensing, Wal-Mart, Kmart, fast food franchises, the Warner Bros. studio stores, and Hasbro Toys are all hinging on. And you gotta get that done before lunch."

Working with special effects, he said, creates a weird kind of distancing effect between the director, the actors, and the material.

"You're sitting looking at a video monitor on a huge sound stage with the cast far, far away from you, and hundreds of extras, and you're shouting directions into a microphone or bullhorn. And even when you're close to the actors, they have so much armor and makeup around them that you're constantly trying to get some humanity out of it.

"And then there's the blue screen, which a lot of the time is the way special effects are done. The actor is alone and there behind him is a big screen, which eventually I'm going to put computer graphics on—people attacking, space ships—and I'm shouting, 'Look up, look right, look left, here they come on that side, now they're gonna get you!' You're back to being four years old going, 'Bang bang, you're dead!' That's not an exciting way to direct."

Still, he said, he understands why movies are made that way.

"The more money you spend to make a movie, the more fair it is for the people who give you the money to expect more asses on the seats. The more asses they expect, the more you have to go toward vanilla, because vanilla is the biggest-selling flavor, even if Rocky Road and Cherry Garcia are more interesting."

On *Tigerland,* he said, he could "smell the truth" when he read Ross Klaven's original screenplay.

"He lived it. He went through boot camp and training and Vietnam and came back. He became a novelist and this is his first screenplay. There really was a Bozz. This is a story that hasn't

been told. It isn't about the war; it's about the war at home. The war within people."

Bozz is frank about his own motivation, which is not to get killed. He finds all the loopholes and gets other guys out of the war, helping them manipulate the rules. His captain despairs, because he can see that Bozz would be a great leader if he were not such a lousy soldier. As it is, he does a brilliant job of leading his fellow trainees in the wrong direction.

"You're this kid," Schumacher said. "You're nineteen, which is the average age of the soldier who went and died in Vietnam. You're drafted. You have no choice. You know that your family, your school, your girlfriend, your country are all torn apart by this war, and no one agrees on anything. And you're told, don't think. Just do. Just kill."

Were you in the war?

Schumacher smiled ironically. "I lived through it, most of it in a drug haze, but that was one of the wars at home too. I was, I guess, another kind of a casualty through it, but I survived, as Ross Klaven did."

Schumacher, a longtime recovering addict, has always been frank about his onetime drug usage (indeed, he makes it into Liz Smith's new autobiography as a purveyor of emergency overdose advice). As he talked about freeing himself from the box-office blockbuster syndrome, it was like he had moved on to a new kind of recovery.

Steven Soderbergh

January 2, 2001—It is universally agreed that a Steven Soderbergh film will win an Oscar nomination as one of the best pictures of the year. But which one? *Traffic,* with Michael Douglas and Catherine Zeta-Jones, a year-end release that examines the illegal drug trade in North America? Or *Erin Brockovich,* the March release starring Julia Roberts as a maverick legal crusader?

Or both? "That would be nice," Soderbergh says. "If they invite me, I'm going."

The thirty-seven-year-old director is on a roll, after those two big hits and the solid critical success of the thrillers *Out of Sight* (1998), with George Clooney and Jennifer Lopez, and *The Limey* (1999), with Terence Stamp as a cockney looking for revenge.

Soderbergh was the poster boy for the independent film movement after his 1989 Sundance and Cannes hit *sex, lies, and videotape*, but then his career meandered; the wonderful coming-of-age film *King of the Hill* (1993) was surrounded by the flops *Kafka* (1991), *Underneath* (1995), and the 1996 *Schizopolis*, which was hardly even released. Dark days—and then four home runs in a row.

"I think *Out of Sight* sort of galvanized me," Soderbergh mused. We were talking in Los Angeles after the early screenings of *Traffic.* "It's an important film from a personal standpoint because I was in danger of marginalizing myself by some of the choices I was making. I was aware while I was making *Out of Sight* that if it were not viewed as a creative success I was really gonna be in trouble. There was a lot of self-imposed pressure. Luckily it turned out well, and even though it didn't make money, it was viewed as a creative success. And that made people think of me a little differently; I wasn't just art-house boy anymore."

Now comes *Traffic*, which has made dozens of year-end best film lists. It tells parallel stories about the North American drug traffic, from the cocaine cartels of Mexico to the corridors of Washington. Key players include Benicio Del Toro as an honest Mexican cop, Catherine Zeta-Jones as the wife of a drug kingpin, Don Cheadle as a San Diego DEA agent, Michael Douglas as the Ohio judge who is tapped as the U.S. drug czar, and Erika Christensen as his teenage daughter, who gets hooked on cocaine.

The movie is cagey in its approach: It doesn't preach. "One of the interesting things about your film," I told Soderbergh, "is that you can't walk out and say exactly what your message is."

"That was our goal."

RE: When I walked out of the theater, I had drawn my own conclusion.

SS: Which is . . .

RE: The laws against drugs are simply operating as a price support system.

SS: You're technically correct. The problem is, decriminalization is not gonna happen. To legalize drugs would be in violation of every international trade agreement we currently have. If the United States legalizes, what happens to Canada and Mexico? This country would turn into a huge pharmaceutical house. So then you say, we'll just get everybody to legalize at the same time. What are the odds of that happen-

ing? One thing most people can agree on is that locking up drug addicts is not a good idea. We're not locking up alcoholics, so why are we locking up drug addicts?

RE: You'd look at the compulsory sentences and the huge prison population, and . . .

SS: My solution would be to approach this as a health care issue, not a criminal issue. In the film, Michael Douglas is in charge of enacting policies that he doesn't want to see his daughter be the victim of. We just had two presidential candidates who apparently have both had exposure to some sort of drugs, and they wouldn't talk about their personal experiences, and they didn't say anything about what their policies would be. You couldn't get a peep out of them.

RE: It's too politically fraught, I suppose.

SS: We've put ourselves in that position by demonizing drugs instead of looking at them realistically as one of many things you're exposed to in life that can derail you. We've made them evil; we've turned it into a big moral issue. We need to back up a little and look at it with a clearer vision. We say this is the worst possible thing you can ever do, when we oughta be saying, "Hey, we need to be more compassionate about people who have a problem with this." But then you're attacked for being soft on drugs.

RE: I liked the way you told the story through separate strands: Mexico, San Diego, Ohio, Washington.

SS: It was crucial that each of the stories have its own distinct look, so you knew where you were all the time. I tried to come up with visual schemes that reflected the way I felt when I was in those various locations. The Mexico stuff is very bleached and has this sort of tobacco patina. The East Coast is very cool. San Diego has a blossomy feeling to the light; very idyllic, to contrast with the rot underneath. I pushed those looks to more of an extreme, since I was the cinematographer.

RE: It must have been hard to organize all this material.

SS: It was, by a factor of ten, the most difficult development experience I've ever been through. [Screenwriter] Steve Gaghan is a bright, talented guy, and I don't know who else could have done it. We went into production with a screenplay that was 165 pages long because I decided, let's just shoot it. I'll figure it out in the editing room, because I can't tell what's gonna rise to the surface.

RE: You have big stars and yet everybody is a supporting actor in this movie, in a sense. Any problems with that?

SS: Not that I was aware of. I was lucky to get people like Michael and Catherine, because of their understanding of their place within the film. It was a combination of their intuition and our conversations and then showing up on the set with the camera on my shoulder, and not a lot of lights, if any, and sensing that a naturalistic performance will fit here.

RE: Michael and Catherine had a lot of personal publicity over their romance while the film was being made. Do you, as the director, just kind of ignore that?

SS: Yes. I mean, I'm not the one who is being chased by the video cameras the moment I step into sight, like Catherine was. It was hard on them and it's a distraction, but it wasn't at as intense a level as it got to be later with the wedding and everything.

RE: Your career, the last four films in particular, has gone terrifically well. How does that affect your ability to look at projects?

SS: The good news is, perhaps that I get a look at interesting material sooner, and that instead of five layers between me and the performers that I'm trying to reach, there are now two. But I'm not really interested in money, accumulating power, courting acclaim. The reason I get up in the morning is to go to work.

Liv Ullmann

February 11, 2001—Many great artists are flawed. Few have been more courageous in their examinations of conscience than Ingmar Bergman. Now in his early eighties, he lives on Faro, a Baltic island where he has long retreated between movies. He directed his last feature film, *Fanny and Alexander,* a memory of childhood, in 1983. Since then he has written a series of screenplays to be directed by those close to him. In these, he seems to be trying to evaluate his life and asking loved ones to forgive him his trespasses.

Best Intentions (1992), directed by Bille August, was about his parents' courtship. *Sunday's Children* (1994), directed by his son Daniel, was about how Bergman's clergyman father created a household where public piety was joined with private anguish. *Private Confessions* (1996), directed by his longtime actress and onetime lover Liv Ullmann, was about his mother's moral struggles.

Now comes what is probably the final chapter of this moral autobiography, *Faithless,* also directed by Ullmann, which tells the story of an old man who hires an actress to help him re-create scenes from his life that puzzle and shame him. Since some of those scenes may intersect Ullmann's own experiences with him, there is a sense of risk.

With the exception of a handful of comedies, Bergman's whole career has been about big questions and elusive answers. At first he looked outside, in moral fables like *The Seventh Seal, Wild Strawberries,* and *The Virgin Spring,* but then came his *Silence of God* trilogy in the 1960s *(Through a Glass Darkly, Winter Light, The Silence)* and, in 1966, the great *Persona,* in which an artist (Ullmann) simply stopped speaking altogether. Ever since he has been on an inward journey.

Faithless, which premiered at Cannes in May 2000, stars Erland Josephson as an elderly director named . . . Bergman. We remember Josephson as the star of Bergman's *Scenes from a Marriage* (1974), about a crisis of marriage and adultery seen in midstream. Now the actor plays a man looking back and trying to make sense of his moral untidiness. Through art and imagination, he evokes the ghost of a woman named Marianne (Lena Endre), whom he once loved. He asks her to help him re-create their past, and as she does, flashbacks show her cheating on her husband with a character named David, who is "Bergman" as a young man.

Wheels within wheels. The old man wants to see her adultery through her own eyes. Did he lead her into sin? Did he lie to her? Did he lie to himself?

One afternoon I sat with Liv Ullmann on a balcony overlooking the sea at Cannes, and talked about the movie. I had met her before in other incarnations. She was a Hollywood star in the 1970s *(Lost Horizon, 40 Carats,* Oscar nominations for *The Emigrants* and *Face to Face).* I visited the set of *Face to Face* in Stockholm and saw her as part of Bergman's tightly knit group of collaborators; even the tea lady had been with him for thirty years.

Now here she was at sixty, with a film that

was perhaps as autobiographical for her as for Bergman. In the hurly-burly of Cannes, where greed, buzz, and celebrity are the currencies, she was a little like a ghost at the feast, a reminder of the years before commerce replaced art.

RE: When I saw this film I was reminded of the sacrament of confession.

LU: I'm sure that's what Ingmar wanted, although he would never say those words. But I would say those words. This time we are living in doesn't have many values. It's easy to do short little steps in other directions, because who cares?

RE: Today's movies are serious about unimportant things, and ironic about important things.

LU: This is not the first film Ingmar has made about values, about loving and losing and passion. Every film he has made has been about that, in different ways. I think it is brave of a filmmaker to be able to do that again and again. Maybe he's telling it for the last time. Maybe he sees this story as his life, and he's told it, and it's over. If he writes something again maybe it will be about endless love . . .

RE: He is asking for absolution?

LU: He cannot forgive himself. I told him two years ago: "You have to forgive yourself for whatever betrayal you have committed." "I cannot forgive myself," he said. That's why I made a scene where he appears with himself as a young man, and forgives that young man, even if he can't forgive himself as an old one.

RE: Is Marianne, the actress the old man hires, actually his daughter from that affair, now grown up?

LU: I've never thought of that. But you know, why not? Because a writer doesn't know everything he's creating. The best stories are when the listeners are putting in their own stories. To me, that little child is Ingmar, and whatever happened to him when he was a little child. To me, Marianne is not the daughter. To me, she's that part within him that is more feminine; that part within him that wants to be stroked when he's tired.

RE: Your lives have been intertwined since *Persona,* and that's been the most important fact in your artistic life.

LU: In some ways maybe not just my artistic life but my whole life, because I've known him as long as anyone except my sister. We worked so closely together and then we were friends so

much longer; we did two films when we loved and now this and then we have a daughter together and we are still friends. You lose and you love and then lose again and this has been a relationship where we never lost.

RE: I remember when I visited Stockholm he had his little cell in the studio. He had an army cot and a table and chair and a bar of chocolate and an apple. And we sat there and he said he was watching the television the night before, and they were interviewing Antonioni. He said he couldn't take his eyes off Antonioni's face. He said the most important subject of the cinema is the human face. As I watched your film I thought of that.

LU: If you use really brilliant actors, if they know they can trust you, they will open up their faces. Like this incredible scene where Lena Endre is sitting in the window and saying she's leaving the child. The first take was very good, professional. But then I said, "Okay, now you do it for yourself." And then it was incredible.

RE: Does it make it more intimate for you that you know from the inside what it is to be an actor?

LU: A lot of actors are scared of the camera. I can allow them to know that the camera loves them, if they are true. That makes me a good director for actors because I know what not to say to them.

RE: Bergman has seen the film?

LU: I talked to Ingmar when he had just seen the finished film. For two years, since he handed me the screenplay, we hadn't talked about it. He never saw anything, he was never part of it. He left it to me. Now there was one thing he asked me to take out. It's in the end. She says goodnight and she's gone and he's lonely. He goes to the window and he looks out, and what I showed out there was him walking on the beach. I don't even want to say why I had it there.

Ingmar said, "I beg of you, take that away. Please take that away." I said, "Ingmar, you mustn't because it is so much the film. It's done with love." He said, "You have to understand, it looks like I will commit suicide." "No, no," I said, "it's not going to look like that—I swear." He begged. I took it away and put an empty island in the same place.

Today I called him, and he said, "I've seen it again. You're right. Put it back again." And I will. It means something.

When he was sixty years old he celebrated his birthday on that island, on that beach. And my daughter was there; she was five years old. And they went down to exactly that same place and he said to her, "When you are sixty what will you do then?" She said, "I'll have a big party and my mother will be there. She'll be really old and stupid and gawky, but it's gonna be great." And he looked at her and said, "And what about me? Will I not be there?" And the five-year-old looked up at him and she said, "Well, you know, I'll leave the party and I'll walk down to the beach and there on the waves you will come dancing towards me."

I wanted him on the beach because of everything he's done in life, and because he was brave to write this film at a time when nobody wants it. They want entertainment. I think it is great to work with a writer who dares to dance on the waves.

Essays

Rethinking the Ratings

September 21, 2000—Is it necessary to subject our children to unrelenting violence and kinetic mindlessness in the name of entertainment, and to market R-rated movies and the equivalent video games to younger consumers? Most reasonable people would say it is not. At the other end of the market, it is also wrong to abandon the concept of films intended for adults only.

A movement is growing to rethink the ratings system. Congressional hearings are under way. In a blow to Jack Valenti's stonewall defense of the MPAA ratings, the Directors Guild of America has called for an overhaul of the movie ratings. Sooner or later, Hollywood's chickens had to come home to roost.

The movie industry created its Code and Ratings Administration in the late 1960s to head off local censorship. That worked, but the original vision faded, the adult category collapsed, and the R category became polluted with material not suitable for those under seventeen, at the same time that theaters in general stopped enforcing its guidelines anyway.

The open secret was that Hollywood counted on under-seventeen dollars for its R-rated special-effects and horror movies. At the same time, it carelessly abandoned the concept of adult films. "Adults only" used to be the only ratings category; in recent years it's the only one missing. Adult choices have faded while twelve-year-olds sample a buffet of entertainment options. Today the nation is in the curious position of (1) retailing unsuitable content to kids, while (2) having no workable category for adult material.

We have arrived at this condition through an erosion of the ratings system. Movies that would have been NC-17, like *Scary Movie,* are now R. Movies that would have been R, like *Coyote Ugly,* are PG-13. The MPAA consults its guidelines and pounds its gavel. What is needed is an approach that is guided less by mysteriously flexible guidelines, and more by the overall suitability of a film for various age groups—a commonsense informational approach for parents. It could resemble the excellent Website www.screenit.com. Visit that site and you will see how comparatively useless the MPAA ratings are.

Consider. *Coyote Ugly,* which glorifies girls who dance on top of bars to sell more drinks, gets a PG-13 because there is technically no nudity. But *Almost Famous,* which shows a bright teenage boy successfully negotiating the minefield of a rock tour and forming a value system with the support of his mother, gets an R because of brief and insignificant nudity and language, and drug use presented as a cautionary lesson. If you were to see the two movies side by side you might be as mystified as I am why the MPAA thinks one is appropriate for thirteen-year-olds, while the other is questionable for seventeen-year-olds. But of course the MPAA cannot have values; it can only count beans, or nipples, or four-letter words.

The R category is ready to burst from the questionable material crammed into it. At the same time, the younger teenage market is served with movies that are R in their hearts but PG-13 to the MPAA bean-counters. How do you make an R into a PG-13? Keep the same story and values, but eliminate the nudity and language. Violent action is okay. You can kill people as long as you keep your clothes on and watch the F-word.

The R category is under such pressure to stretch because the adults-only category is missing in action. As the Directors Guild observes: "The NC-17 rating ... has been an abject failure: Many films that should not be seen by minors are re-cut so that they receive a 'hard' R rating." The DGA calls for a new "simple, clean and detailed rating," a "code of conduct governing the marketing of movies intended for mature audiences," and "zero tolerance" in the enforcement of ratings.

This is common sense. The NC-17 rating is useless, because with rare exceptions no studio will release an NC-17 film. Why not? Because some media outlets will not accept the ads, because some theater leases forbid such movies from being shown, and also because of greed.

Jack Valenti and his employers have no enthusiasm for any rating that would require them to deny admission to a single customer. The R rating is so porous that almost anyone who really wants to see an R movie can do so. The DGA's call for "zero tolerance" is no doubt chilling for Valenti and his bosses.

The DGA wants movement in two areas—more protection for children through strictly enforced ratings, and more freedom for adults through a rehabilitation of NC-17. It is time, the DGA says, for a simpler, more useful code. It seems to me five categories are required:

G: Suitable for all.
PG-13: Some content may not be appropriate
    for younger children.
    R: No one under 17 without parent or
      guardian.
    A: Adults only.
    X: Pornography.

While R should be more strictly observed, the PG-13 category should be graded more realistically. Worthwhile movies often contain some "language," and may contain sexuality. Teenagers have heard the words. They have seen breasts. They had when I was thirteen, and they certainly have today. A movie like *Almost Famous* should not be rated R because of its mild (and edifying) treatment of sex, drugs, and rock 'n' roll. It applies *values* to its content. It shows a kid in the real world, trying to do the right thing.

The R and A categories should be enforced with "zero tolerance." The X is not an issue since porno is not in theaters, but it must exist *simply to establish* that an A movie is not an X movie. How to define the difference between A and X? The porn industry knows what a porn film is, and so do its customers: An X film presents sexual behavior graphically. It is based on the "money shot." A-rated movies might suggest sexual activity, but could not depict it in gynecological detail.

Such a ratings system would have to come with acknowledgements that the studios and exhibitors are sincerely prepared to release A-rated movies and enforce the R rating. As the DGA's statement points out, the current impasse means that directors' visions are compromised, while at the same time "adult-oriented movies are seen by the very groups for which they are not intended." It's time for a change.

"I Had a Dream . . ."

March 29, 2001—The voice from the television set was measured and familiar, the cadence one that has been engraved on my memory.

"I have a dream . . ." the voice said. I glanced up, and saw Martin Luther King delivering his most famous speech, given at the Lincoln Memorial during the March on Washington.

It was a camera angle I hadn't seen before. And, oddly, he wasn't flanked by other civil rights leaders, but was standing all by himself. As his words continued, the camera's point of view circled to look out over his head and down the Mall, which was completely empty.

CGI, I thought. Computer-generated imagery. Then the tag line came on. It was a commercial for Alcatel, a company involved in communications networks and cell phones. An Alcatel newspaper ad with the same image spells out the message: "Before you can inspire . . . you must first connect." Via Alcatel, of course.

I was filled with anger and sadness.

Not this speech, I thought. Not this moment in American history.

Ads have exploited almost every image worth quoting in our society. United Airlines has made it impossible for anyone to ever again hear Gershwin's "Rhapsody in Blue" without thinking about airplanes. Fred Astaire, the most graceful dancer in movie history, was seen dancing with a DustBuster. Such ads are pathetic, yes, but I suppose the copyright owners have a legal right to license them, and if the estates have no regard for the reputation of Gershwin or Astaire, well, that's greed for you.

But surely there are a few moments too sacred, too special, to be bought and sold. I would have thought Dr. King's "I have a dream" speech was one of them.

It shines like a beacon in our history. It belongs to all of us. It does not belong to Alcatel, which should not have had the temerity and insensitivity to use it in an ad. And in a way, it doesn't belong to the King estate, either. The estate should consider itself the protector of this speech, not its retailer.

Perhaps, I thought, the speech was somehow in the public domain, and Alcatel had ripped it off to sell its networks and cell phones.

I called the Martin Luther King Center in Atlanta, and spoke with Robert Vickers, its public relations spokesman.

"I am afraid you will have to fax me your questions in writing," he said.

"I have only one question," I said. "Did the King Center license the Alcatel TV commercial?"

"Yes," he said. "It was licensed by the King estate's intellectual properties management."

"Have you had a lot of calls about the ad?" I asked.

"Yes," he said, "comments both ways."

I started to ask how much the speech sold for, but he told me about the fax again. I didn't much feel like sending the fax. I knew the price. Thirty pieces of silver.

On Julia Roberts

Date tk, 2001—"A major beauty with a fierce energy," I wrote when I first saw her, in *Mystic Pizza* (1988). That didn't require deep thought. What I didn't guess is that we would see so much of the beauty and so little of the power. Julia Roberts has the spine and presence to play ferocious characters, but is usually assigned to portray charming pluck or winsome sensuality. Here is an actress who should be ripping the clothes off her contemporaries, like Johnny Depp, Matt Dillon, and Keanu Reeves. But her relationships are more often with middle-aged men who buy her with money or win her with dazzling Older Guy Charisma. She has never been in love with John Cusack, but she's fallen for Sam Shepard, Ed Harris, Woody Allen, Nick Nolte, Richard Gere (twice), Patrick Bergin, and even John Malkovich as Jeckyl and Hyde, for chrissakes. She finally takes on Brad Pitt in *The Mexican*. About time.

Hollywood doesn't know what to make of her. She's too tall, too sunny, too generous, too challenging. How do you write a movie about a force of nature? You tame it with comedy or twist it with thrills. You explain how bashful Hugh Grant has to be persuaded that, yes, it's okay for him to sleep with a movie star. And how Woody Allen's daughter overheard things at the shrink's that allowed Woody to reflect her innermost thoughts. And why her old boyfriend invites her to a wedding with his child bride. In *Erin Brockovich* they assign Aaron Eckhard as a biker boyfriend. He's a powerful actor but he's reduced to a nutless cipher by the screenplay's manifest indifference to him (Hollywood doesn't want its sweetheart smeared with Harley grease).

Observing the chemistry between Roberts and Denzel Washington, some critics attacked *The Pelican Brief* because they never snoggle—but the movie opened with her lover, Sam Shepard, being blown to pieces, which would make a quick new romance rather tactless.

Her best movie is *Pretty Woman*. Her second-best is the one no one went to see, maybe because they couldn't remember the title: Lasse Hallstrom's *Something to Talk About* (1995), where she was the daughter of the millionaire horseman Robert Duvall and wife of the philandering Dennis Quaid. It was a role that gave her something to do, and surrounded her with characters who had agendas of their own and didn't exist entirely to react to her. And in *Everyone Says I Love You* Woody Allen had fun making a point of the strategies older guys use to win her in the movies.

So far it has been a star career, with the natural gifts and the talent in the foreground, and the early fierce energy in reserve. When she takes a chance, as she did in *Mary Reilly,* she gets shot down (how dare she play Dr. Jeckyl's Edinburgh housemaid, etc.). The danger is that she will continue to make box-office hits and never make a timeless film. She should call Scorsese and offer to work for free. Julia Roberts has made twenty-five films and only *Pretty Woman* is likely to be widely known in fifty years. She has *America's Sweethearts* coming up. It's not about Mary Pickford, but it made me think of her, the greatest female star of *her* time. You can see a whole lot of silent films before you feel the need to see one of hers.

Monument and Movie Make Inappropriate Gestures

May 29, 2001—I am looking at an artist's rendering for the World War II Memorial, which Congress and President Bush have decided with unseemly haste should deface the Mall. It looks like a big tacky mausoleum from a nineteenth-century cemetery. Anyone of ordinary taste can see that it is boilerplate, utterly lacking the bold artistic vision which made the Vietnam Memorial one of the nation's holy places.

To plonk it down on the Mall between the Lincoln Memorial and the Washington Monument, spoiling the vista, is a spectacularly bad idea. But Congress last week voted to bypass the usual regulatory process and rush into construction, and Bush signed the law on Memorial Day. Veterans of the war are dying every day, supporters of the memorial argued, and it is important that before they're all gone they be recognized with this monstrosity.

There is some kind of awful symmetry in the fact that the wrong memorial is approved over the same weekend when *Pearl Harbor* opened in the nation's movie theaters. As the memorial is to the Mall, the movie is to Pearl Harbor—a garish, expensive, tasteless exercise appealing to the lowest common denominator.

The memorial dishonors the veterans by inflicting a banal design on a sacred place. And the movie dishonors the deaths at Pearl Harbor by making them the backdrop for Hollywood clichés. Its pilots play games of chicken, treating historic airplanes like models in a video game. It forgets that Asians lived in Hawaii at the time of the war. It softens the history lesson with a love triangle of staggering idiocy. It informs us that hundreds of sailors are trapped alive beneath the sea, and then never mentions them again as lovers quarrel.

Our government has rushed to aid both enterprises. The movie's world premiere was held on the deck of an aircraft carrier. The World War II Memorial is being imposed by Congress over the protests of architects, urban planners, and many of the veterans themselves. "We could have memorialized World War II in a place that would not have defaced the National Mall, which is a historic symbol of our nation's democracy," World War II veteran George Peabody told the AP. "I will never feel good about this."

Imagine a world in which good taste played a role equal with political expediency. In that world, the navy would have asked to preview *Pearl Harbor,* would have found it appalling, and would have quietly refused the use of its aircraft carrier. And in that world, Congress and the president would have taken one look at the proposed memorial and seen that it was gaudy and inappropriate for the Mall.

That those who fought World War II should be honored, there can be no question. They saved modern civilization. It is as simple as that. Every living person owes them gratitude. They deserve to be honored (1) with a striking and powerful memorial, and (2) with a location for the memorial that will not stir resentment and disappointment in future generations.

As long as the World War II Memorial stands, it will always be described as an eyesore and a blot on the Mall. That is not the right way to honor the veterans. Long after the politicians who hurried it through have disappeared from the scene, their haste and bad taste will be discussed in classrooms and textbooks, and by ordinary citizens who walk out onto the Mall and see with their own eyes and their own common sense what Congress and Bush could not figure out: This is the wrong memorial in the wrong place.

As for *Pearl Harbor,* at least it isn't playing on the Mall.

Fake Critic, Fake Quotes

June 6, 2001—Everybody in the movie world, except for certain executives at Columbia Pictures, is chortling today over *Newsweek*'s exposé of how the studio created a fake movie critic who praised its movies in ads.

According to the nonexistent David Manning of the *Ridgefield* (Conn.) *Press,* Rob Schneider's *The Animal* is "another winner" and Heath Ledger of *A Knight's Tale* is "this year's hottest new star!" The quotes were apparently written by someone in the studio's ad department.

Many critics see this as a shocking development. I am encouraged. If David Manning had not been unmasked as a fiction, he could have been a powerful weapon against the quote whore system now popular in Hollywood.

Here is how the system works. Entertainment "journalists" are flown to Los Angeles at studio expense. They are lodged at a nice hotel (usually the Four Seasons). They are taken to a premiere of a movie and allowed interviews with the stars. And they get a per diem payment, which David Poland, a Web-based industry analyst, pegs at $200.

For this largess they are not exactly expected to praise *every* picture they see. But if they dislike too many of them, they'll be off the freebie junket list. Since the TV stations and newspapers that employ them expect lots of celebrity interviews, this could cost them their jobs. (When I attend a junket, my employers pay my expenses.)

How do you qualify as a quote whore? You give good quote. Freebie junketeers sometimes scribble down words of praise and pass them to publicists right there at the junket. In one case documented by *Variety*, a publicist wrote up several "sample" quotes and asked the junketeers to sign up for the ones they liked.

If the fictitious David Manning had not been unmasked, he could have made it easier for hardworking junketeers by prostituting himself on their behalf. He could have supplied the glowing quotes, and they could have returned home intact with their celebrity interviews.

Of course, the system only works in the first place because many moviegoers believe that anything in quotes in an ad must be the truth.

Just this weekend, the ads for *What's the Worst That Could Happen* had quotes saying, "A supercool comedy!" and "Martin Lawrence is the man! Danny DeVito is terrific!" The curious thing about these quotes is that they were not attributed to *anybody*. They were just . . . quotes.

The wise moviegoer looks for quotes attributed to critics he knows and trusts (even trusting them to be wrong is good enough). Or, before committing nine bucks and two hours of life, the moviegoer might even read the actual full-length review as it appeared in print. Now there's an idea.

In Memoriam

Richard Farnsworth

Richard Farnsworth, who basked in glory last April as the oldest man ever nominated for an Academy Award, died of a self-inflicted gunshot wound on Friday, October 6, 2000, at his ranch in Lincoln, New Mexico. He was eighty.

His fiancée, Jewel Van Valin, revealed a secret Farnsworth had kept all through the Oscar hoopla: He had been diagnosed several years ago with terminal cancer.

"I was in the other room and I heard the shot," she told the Associated Press. "He was in incredible pain today. He was going downhill."

Farnsworth was nominated for his strong and true performance as the hero of David Lynch's *The Straight Story*, based on the life of an Iowa man named Alvin Straight, who wanted to visit a dying brother who lived 300 miles away in Wisconsin. Straight's eyes were not good enough to drive a car, so he drove a lawn tractor all the way there.

"He was very ill in that movie," Van Valin said, "but phenomenally he made it through. He didn't want the world to know he was sick."

When Farnsworth was offered the role, he initially turned it down because, he told me, he feared a bad hip might give him trouble. But Lynch assured him he'd make a special silicone seat on the tractor. "So I said, okay. I'm so glad I did. I'd hate to have got out there and not be able to finish it."

I talked to Farnsworth in September 1999 at the Telluride Film Festival, where *The Straight Story* had just premiered to a standing ovation. Using a cane and accompanied by Van Valin, he made his way down the street to the Floradora Saloon for a buffalo burger, his single daily martini, and some thoughts about acting in old age.

"I've almost been out of this business for fifteen years," he said. "Just ranching. The last film I did was pretty rowdy. It was called *The Getaway*. I come in at the last. But I didn't have to use any four-letter words. I've never had to curse in a movie and I'm not about to start in now."

Farnsworth thought of himself as a cowboy and a rancher, and spent most of his time on his spread in Lincoln, a town of 150 that bills itself "The Capital of Billy the Kid Country." Its bank is famous because of the luminaries who stuck it up, and Pat Garrett once owned the hotel. Farnsworth liked Stetson hats and cowboy boots, and Miss Van Valin always dressed like a schoolmarm in an old Western.

Farnsworth was a walking treasure of movie lore, one of the oldest active actors in Hollywood. He started in movies as a stuntman, he told me: "I roped and rodeoed, and in 1937 Paramount put an ad in the paper that they wanted 200 riders for *Marco Polo*. It was $7 a day to ride, and the wrangling was about $12 a day. I'd been working at a barn for $5 a week. I worked on the movie for five weeks and made enough money to buy a car, and that's it. I stayed and did *Gunga Din* the next year. That got me started. I did *A Day at the Races* with the Marx Brothers. I was a steeplechase rider."

He did stunt work for the great director John Ford, "but never as an actor, because he'd get a little bit hostile with actors. I couldn't stand somebody shouting." On the Ford pictures he became "as close as you can get" to Henry Fonda, and it was Henry's daughter, Jane, who remembered the old cowhand when they were casting her movie *Comes a Horseman*, in 1978. That got him his first Oscar nomination, as Best Supporting Actor.

"They wanted an old guy that could rope and ride," he recalled. "I'd done that plenty as a stuntman. But when they called me over and showed me the script, God, there was so much in it that I didn't think I could handle. Alan Pakula, who was directing it, said, 'You'll have ten weeks to shoot it. We don't shoot these in one day, you know. You might go for days and not even work.' So I took the script and practiced. It seemed to go pretty good. I went back and I read a few lines with Jane Fonda, and Pakula says, 'You do it just like that. You got the job.'"

In 1982, at sixty-two, he got his first starring role, in *The Grey Fox*, as a stagecoach robber who gets out of jail after thirty-three years, finds stagecoaches have disappeared, and adjusts to modern times by robbing trains.

Farnsworth was a man who prided himself on his horsemanship and his daily work routine. When he arrived at the Oscars, he was in pain which again he blamed on the "bad hip," but said he was going in for replacement surgery right after the awards. He lost the Oscar to Kevin Spacey *(American Beauty)* but, "I feel well to have been nominated. I might not get a chance again."

In *The Straight Story,* Farnsworth's performance drew praise all over the world, especially for the quiet, no-nonsense way he expressed his deep feelings about his dying brother. He tells a priest who takes him in for the night: "I want to make peace. I want to sit with him. Look up at the stars. Like we used to do so long ago."

Stanley Kramer

At a time when Hollywood was timid, Stanley Kramer was brave. They said he made "message movies," as if that was a fault, but his messages broke down barriers, and he made some pretty good films along the way.

Kramer died on Monday, February 19, 2001, at eighty-seven. He had been inactive for more than twenty years, but even when Hollywood had no more work for him, he kept his oar in, moving to Seattle and turning out a newspaper column, until old age slowed him down.

As a producer, in a postwar era when producers were hands-on and strong ones had as much creative input as directors, he championed realistic social dramas like the prizefighting movie *Champion* (1949), with Kirk Douglas; *Home of the Brave* (1949), about a black soldier on patrol with a white unit in the segregated army; *The Men* (1950), Marlon Brando's screen debut, as a paralyzed veteran; *High Noon* (1952), with its one good man standing against intimidation; and *The Wild One* (1954), with Brando again, unforgettable as the leader of a motorcycle gang.

As a director, Kramer's *The Defiant Ones* (1958) starred Tony Curtis and Sidney Poitier as escaped convicts, white and black, chained together; *On the Beach* (1959) was a powerful story of the survivors of nuclear war; *Inherit the Wind* (1960) paired Spencer Tracy and Fredric March in the story of a famous courtroom battle between Darwinism and fundamentalism; *Judgment at Nuremberg* (1961) dealt with war crimes against

Jews; *Ship of Fools* (1965) was about a shipload of Jewish refugees denied safe harbor; and *Guess Who's Coming to Dinner* (1967), probably his most famous film, paired Tracy and Katharine Hepburn as parents told by their daughter (Katharine Houghton) that she plans to marry a black man (Poitier). Along the way he also made *It's a Mad Mad Mad Mad World* (1963), a comedy with a fervent cult following.

Later in Kramer's career the messages began to date; he was savaged by critics for *R.P.M.* (1970), about the student revolution (they couldn't see Ann-Margret as a left-wing graduate student).

Kramer loved to talk, to debate, to stay in the fray. I remember a night in 1968 when he was in Chicago to talk to students about *Guess Who's Coming to Dinner* and ended up in O'Rourke's Pub in Old Town with a pitcher of beer and an eager audience.

He'd been on a speaking tour ("Stanford, Michigan, you name it") and was shell-shocked, he said.

"The college kids have been poisoned by that Kael woman before I get there. Pauline Kael. The one who wrote 9,000 words about *Bonnie and Clyde* in *The New Yorker* when ninety would have been enough. She goes around giving speeches about all the phonies in Hollywood and then I arrive in town. A big, fat sitting duck."

He sipped his half-and-half and found it good.

"You know what's the matter with the approach these college kids take to movies?" he said. "They operate on the fetish system. If a director is an official hero, he can do no wrong. Hitchcock. Howard Hawks. The kids worship them; they memorize every foot of film. Hitchcock is good, sure. But sometimes he makes clinkers too. You'd think so. But not the college kids."

Kramer was not an auteur hero, and knew it. *Guess Who's Coming* was being attacked, he said, "on the grounds that it's too perfect. Poitier is rich and famous and practically ready to win the Nobel Prize. And Tracy and Hepburn are progressive, enlightened, liberal parents with lots of cash. And Katharine Houghton is an ideal young woman.

"Hell, we deliberately made the situation perfect, and for only one reason: If you take away all the other motives for not getting married, then you leave only one question. Will Tracy forbid the marriage because Poitier's a

Negro? That is the only issue, and we deliberately removed all other obstacles to focus on it."

He leaned forward. "Think about that," he said. "Here you have an interracial marriage, and audiences are practically throwing rice. But then the critics come along and say I chickened out by making Poitier a perfect Negro. He should have been a mailman instead of a famous doctor, according to them. But they're wrong. They're dead wrong. Because if Poitier had been a mailman, the girl's family would have disapproved of him because he was a mailman, not because he was a Negro. Don't you see?"

Sure, one of his listeners said. But couldn't you solve that by making the girl's father a mailman too?

"That would have been another movie," Kramer said. "We made this one. For one thing, the roles we made were perfectly suited to Tracy and Hepburn, and a great many people are going to be pleased that those two got together for one more film before Tracy died. They had something on the screen no other couple ever matched."

That was Stanley Kramer: defending the movie on ideological grounds, but in touch, too, with star power. As much as anyone else, he was responsible for launching the careers of Douglas, Brando, and Poitier. He found them early and knew what he'd found. Maybe he sent a lot of messages in his films, but he didn't sell out; is it more noble to make mindless special-effects pictures like the ones Hollywood now favors?

I talked with him for the last time in 1979, at the USA Film Festival in Dallas. He was there with his last film, *The Runner Stumbles*, with Dick Van Dyke and Kathleen Quinlan as a priest and a nun who fall in love. Not a great film, but an earnest one, in which the characters spend more time on their moral qualms than their romance. He was more concerned with debating the issues than exploiting the situation, and that was the thread that ran through his long and honorable career.

Jack Lemmon

Jack Lemmon was great, and he was beloved. Usually a movie star is one or the other. Lemmon, who died June 27, 2001, at seventy-six, was one of the screen's most irrepressible young men, one of its most irascible old men, and, in between, its indispensable everyman.

Few Hollywood deaths have been more widely mourned; one was the passing in 2000 of Lemmon's longtime acting partner Walter Matthau. Together, they played the Odd Couple, the Grumpy Old Men, and the Front Page reporters. Apart, they played just about everything else.

Lemmon got eight Oscar nominations and won twice, as Best Supporting Actor at the dawn of his career in *Mister Roberts* (1955), where he played a conniving navy ensign, and as Best Actor in *Save the Tiger* (1973), as a troubled executive. His other Best Actor nominations suggest his remarkable range: He was the cross-dressing musician in *Some Like It Hot* (1959), the harried young executive in *The Apartment* (1960), the alcoholic in free-fall in *Days of Wine and Roses* (1962), the stubbornly honest nuclear worker in *The China Syndrome* (1979), the dying father in *Tribute* (1980), and the father determined to find a son who has disappeared in *Missing* (1982).

Intense and garrulous as a young man, he liked to describe how his first directors tried to get him to dial down his energy for the intimacy of the movie camera. He had a lifelong working relationship with the director Billy Wilder; together they made seven films, including *Some Like It Hot*, which was named in an American Film Institute poll as the greatest comedy of all time.

"I'd do a take," Lemmon recalled, "and Billy would say it was great, great—but could I give him just a little less? Take two. Also great. But just a little less. Take three. Fabulous. But . . . a little less. After about nine takes, I said, 'Whaddya want, for chrissakes? Nothing?' And Billy raised up his eyes to heaven and said, 'Please God, yes.'"

Lemmon won his first Oscar for his third film, in 1955, and fifty-four years later won an Emmy for his last work, the made-for-TV adaptation of the best-seller *Tuesdays With Morrie*. In that one he played a dying professor who meets for regular talks about life with one of his students. Looking at the body of work, I am awestruck by the range and depth of his performances. He is the very definition of the complete actor: a man who can range across the spectrum of possible roles, who can play slapstick *(The Great Race)*, light comedy *(Irma La Douce, The Fortune Cookie)*, farce *(Buddy, Buddy)*, slices of life *(Mass Appeal)*, naturalistic realism

(*Short Cuts*), political drama (*JFK*), serious drama (*A Life in the Theater, The Entertainer*), and pure tragedy (his character in *Glengarry Glen Ross* is his version of *Death of a Salesman*).

Who else was so able to find himself at home in completely different characters and genres? And yet Lemmon was never a prima donna, and was known in the business as a rock-solid professional who turned up on time, did his job without anguish, and was unselfish with other actors and supportive of younger ones. He joked that acting had made him a master of one thing in life: "Crossword puzzles. I sit in my trailer between shots and fill out one goddamned book of them after another."

Lemmon's dedication to his craft became especially apparent in later years, when both he and Matthau faced health problems. In a 1994 interview, Matthau remembered the filming of their big hit *Grumpy Old Men*, which involved ice-fishing scenes in Minnesota.

"I didn't want to go to Minnesota in the middle of January," Matthau told me, "so I said to Lemmon, 'Listen, Lemmon, maybe we can do this in Hawaii or Florida because one of us is not coming back if we go to Minnesota.' Because in Minnesota, it gets so cold that the body wishes to retain the heat; otherwise you die. In order to retain the heat, the coronary arteries are immediately constricted for retention of heat, and as soon as you restrict the coronary arteries, you're subject to a heart attack, you're subject to a stroke, you're subject to double pneumonia. I got all of them. Lemmon, nothing happened to him at all. Just once. I stopped the shooting and I went over to the producer and I said, 'Better get him to a hospital; something's wrong with him.' His tongue, it was so cold, it was forty below zero without the windchill factor, his tongue had stuck to his gums. That's how cold it was."

There was also a long-running gag between them about the time in Utah when Lemmon choked on a horehound drop and Matthau claimed to have saved his life with the Heimlich maneuver—a story Lemmon liked to say was true, except for the candy, the choking, and the maneuver.

When I think of Jack Lemmon, the first image that comes to mind is from Wilder's *Some Like It Hot*, in that upper berth in the sleeping car, as Marilyn Monroe says, "If there's ever anything I can do for you . . ." and he answers, "I can think of a million things." At the time, of course, he is disguised in women's clothes as "Daphne," to elude Chicago gangsters who are chasing him. Writing about the movie, Pauline Kael said Lemmon was "demonically funny—he really begins to think he's sexy in those women's clothes." At the end of the movie, Lemmon sets up a line by Joe E. Brown that has been called the greatest closing line in movie history. Brown is a millionaire who has fallen in love with "Daphne" and wants to get married. Lemmon takes off his wig and says, "You don't understand, Osgood. I'm a man." Brown replies: "Well, nobody's perfect."

Unlike most actors, Lemmon never had a dry spell. But starting with *Some Like It Hot* in 1959 he had an extraordinary run—one of the hottest streaks any actor has ever had, with three nominations in four years. In 1960 came Wilder's *The Apartment*, with Lemmon as the lowly clerk whose apartment becomes a hot-sheet hotel for Fred MacMurray. In 1962 came two amazing films: Blake Edwards's *Days of Wine and Roses* and Wilder's *Irma La Douce*.

The thread that runs through all his performances is a kind of unstated, omnipresent honesty. You always feel that the Jack Lemmon character—whoever he is, whatever he is—is sincere. Even in farce, you feel he really believes it's important how the absurd plot turns out. He's one of those rare actors who can be in a ridiculous scene and never seem to catch on that it's ridiculous. Kael is right about *Some Like It Hot*; his drag performance works because *he* thinks he looks great.

There's another quality about Lemmon that's harder to define. If you look at his performances at the ends of the spectrum—the comedies and tragedies—you always sense the potential for the opposite tone. There's something a little sad and sympathetic beneath even his cockiest comic characters, and always the possibility that his tragic figures will find something to smile about.

Lemmon was never better than in James Foley's *Glengarry Glen Ross*, based on the David Mamet play, where he plays a character named Shelley (The Machine) Levene—one of Mamet's team of hopeless real-estate salesmen. Shelley was once a great salesman. Now he is out of luck, desperately needs money, and is hiding personal problems. He goes out in the rain to pay a house call on a prospect who does not want to buy any real estate. The prospect knows it, we know it, and Shelley knows it. But he keeps on trying, against all odds, to *will* this man to buy this property.

Watch the body language and listen to the dialogue, as Lemmon shows us a man at the end of his rope, trying to fake self-confidence. It is great work, but not simply because Shelley is sad and pathetic. No, Lemmon reaches deeper to make it so good: He realizes that Shelley actually believes in the dream he is selling, believes the client—a jerk—might actually enjoy living in this real-estate development. That's why the scene is so good—not because the Lemmon character has given up all hope and abandoned all values, but because he hasn't.

Lemmon had been fighting cancer in recent years, and died of complications of the disease at the University of Southern California's Norris Cancer Center. At his bedside were his wife, the actress Felicia Farr, their daughter, Courtney, and his son, Chris (by first wife Cynthia Stone).

I interviewed Mr. Lemmon in 1992, when he was given a lifetime achievement award by the Chicago International Film Festival. Our discussion ranged far and wide over many great films and performances, and finally, with a big smile, he joked: "Roger, you might as well just get down on your knees right now, and thank God you're in the presence of one of the greatest actors you'll ever see."

It was the simple truth.

Anthony Quinn
A man needs a little madness, or else he never dares cut the rope and be free.
—Anthony Quinn in *Zorba the Greek*

Anthony Quinn practiced a fine madness, and in a life spanning eighty-six years he won two Academy Awards, was nominated for two more, fathered thirteen children by six women, and married three times—once when he was eighty-two and she was thirty-five. And in every Greek restaurant in the world for the past thrity-seven years there comes a time every night when someone gets up and thinks he can dance like Zorba the Greek.

Quinn died at 9:29 A.M. Sunday, June 3, 2001, in a Boston hospital. His friend Vincent "Buddy" Cianci, mayor of Providence, Rhode Island,

said the cause was respiratory failure. "He was larger than life," Cianci told the AP, but the phrase would have appeared in every obituary whether Cianci said it or not.

Long before he portrayed Zorba in 1964, Quinn was an exuberant manifestation of the life force. Born in 1915 in Chihuahua, Mexico, he was a quarter Irish, a quarter Mexican, and, he said, half Aztec Indian on his mother's side. His father met his mother while a member of Pancho Villa's revolutionary army.

He had a way with ethnic roles that made him convincing, not only as the screen's most famous Greek, but also as an Italian strongman in Fellini's *La Strada* (1954), a Cuban fisherman in *The Old Man and the Sea* (made for TV in 1990), a Libyan guerrilla leader in *Lion of the Desert* (1981), a working-class Mexican machoman in *The Children of Sanchez* (1978), and an Arab sheik in *Lawrence of Arabia* (1962).

Quinn won his Oscars for *Viva Zapata!* (1952), where he was the brother of the famous rebel Emiliano Zapata, and for *Lust for Life* (1956), as the painter Paul Gauguin, who befriends Vincent van Gogh. He was nominated for two Oscars as Best Actor, for *Wild Is the Wind* (1957) and *Zorba the Greek* (1964).

His long career began in 1933 when Mae West, who had an eye for strapping young men, gave him a role in one of her stage productions. He played Mafia dons several times, the pope (in *The Shoes of the Fisherman*), and billionaire Aristotle Onassis *(The Greek Tycoon).*

His last role was one of his best. In *A Walk in the Clouds* (1995), he plays the patriarch of an old Mexican-California wine-growing family. A young soldier (Keanu Reeves) happens on the vineyard and falls in love with Quinn's granddaughter; there is family opposition to this outsider, but the old man sees that he is good, takes him on a walk to explain the mystique of the grape, and in a line perhaps only Quinn could have made convincing, tells him, "You are an orphan no longer."

Quinn was the stuff of legend in Hollywood, and also enlivened the movie communities of Italy, France, Mexico, and Spain. He wed into Hollywood royalty, marrying Katherine DeMille, the daughter of the director Cecil B. DeMille. After that marriage ended in divorce, he married Iolanda Addolori, whom he met when she was the wardrobe mistress on Fellini's *La Strada*.

That marriage ended in 1997 in a scandalous divorce splashed over the covers of the supermarket tabloids, and he married Kathy Benvin, thirty-five, who presented him with his thirteenth child. His last years were spent in Providence, where he had many friends and reveled in his late fatherhood. The AP reported that, unlike many actors who mismanage their salaries, he was a canny investor who died with an estate worth "hundreds of millions."

As an actor Quinn often played broad and simple roles, complaining that Hollywood could see him only as a gangster or an ethnic type. Occasionally he broke out of typecasting (Stanley Kramer had him play a left-wing college professor in *R.P.M.* in 1969), and he was capable of great subtlety (as in *A Walk in the Clouds*—and listen to the delicacy with which, as Onassis, he explains the financial details of their marriage to Jacqueline Kennedy in *The Greek Tycoon*).

But it was as a joyous, exuberant, macho life force that Anthony Quinn will be best remembered. He dared to cut the rope and be free.

Jason Robards

Jason Robards, who was the greatest interpreter of the works of America's greatest playwright, died Tuesday, December 26, 2000, at seventy-eight. Death came at 2:45 P.M. at Bridgeport (Connecticut) Hospital, after a long struggle with cancer.

Moviegoers who saw him play Tom Cruise's dying father in *Magnolia* (1999) were witnessing his last and one of his bravest performances; he knew he was ill while making the film, and found great urgency and poignancy in the role.

Robards appeared in some fifty-four films, and won Academy Awards back-to-back for two of them, *All the President's Men* (1976), where he played *Washington Post* editor Benjamin Bradlee, and *Julia* (1977), where he played left-wing crime writer Dashiell Hammett. Robards was presented with the National Medal of Arts in 1997 by President Clinton.

His heart was in the theater, and it was the work of the playwright Eugene O'Neill that lured him onto the stage. Born in Chicago in 1922, he was the son of one of the best-known American actors of the first half of the last century, Jason Robards Sr., whose career ended in the 1950s just as his son's was beginning. As a young man the junior Robards had little interest in the theater, served in the navy for seven years, and then, while reading the works of O'Neill, decided he might want to try his hand at acting.

In 1953, he began a historic alliance with the director Jose Quintero, who helped bring about a revival of interest in the half-forgotten O'Neill. Quintero cast him in several plays, and in May 1956, they collaborated on O'Neill's *The Iceman Cometh* at the Circle in the Square in New York, with Robards playing Hickey, the salesman who appeared in a bar for his annual "periodical" drunk. It was one of the key events in American theater.

Robards also appeared on Broadway in O'Neill's *A Long Day's Journey Into Night*, which was made into a 1962 film by Sidney Lumet, costarring Katharine Hepburn. With its 174-minute running time it gave a good idea of Robards's ability to span the dramatic arc in O'Neill's epic dramas.

Another of his many triumphs with O'Neill was in *A Moon for the Misbegotten*, which he opened in on Broadway in 1973 opposite Colleen Dewhurst. Later they brought it to the Academy Playhouse in Lake Forest, Illinois, for a run where I was able to see firsthand how the screen could never completely reflect the depth of his power as an actor.

Robards, never conventionally handsome, was suited for the craggy, crusty, independently minded characters he often played. His film career was uneven because, at some level, he didn't take the movies seriously—he preferred to be on the stage, he said, where no director could say "cut!" Some of his films he made for the money. But you could assemble a season of good offbeat movies from his work, many of them made with iconoclastic directors attracted to Robards's own risk taking.

Those titles would include *A Thousand Clowns* (1965), based on the Herb Gardner play about a misfit TV writer who becomes the guardian of a young nephew; Roger Corman's *The St. Valentine's Day Massacre* (1967), as Al Capone; Sergio Leone's *Once Upon a Time in the West* (1968); Sam Peckinpah's *The Ballad of Cable Hogue* (1970), with Robards issuing ultimatums to God to give him water in the middle of the desert; Dalton Trumbo's *Johnny Got His Gun* (1971); Peckinpah's *Pat Garrett and Billy the Kid* (1973); L. Q. Jones's strange sci-fi fantasy *A Boy and His Dog* (1975); Jonathan Demme's *Melvin and Howard* (1980), as Howard Hughes; Ron Howard's *Parenthood* (1989), as Steve Martin's father; Howard's *The Paper* (1994); and Paul Thomas Anderson's *Magnolia* (1999).

In 1972, Robards, then a heavy drinker, was in a car accident that did severe damage to his face, and even after plastic surgery left him with a scar on his lip which only added to his character. He quit drinking in 1974, he said. He was married four times, once to Lauren Bacall, whose first husband, Humphrey Bogart, many said he resembled. For the last thirty years he was married to Lois Robards, and they lived in Fairfield, Connecticut. He had six children.

Film Festivals

Toronto Film Festival
Toronto: A Film Lover's Film Festival

Toronto, Canada, September 6, 2000—I missed the first Toronto Film Festival. So did a lot of other people. I've attended every one since. The second was like a gathering of conspirators who raced from theater to theater on the rumors of screenings. But the festival has grown so steadily that its twenty-fifth anniversary event can safely be called the most important film festival in North America, and one of the top handful in the world.

The searchlights at Toronto scan the skies outside the big evening galas, which Hollywood studios often use to premiere their big fall releases (Oscar winners *American Beauty* and *Boys Don't Cry* were premiered last September). But the galas are the icing on a very considerable cake. Toronto has depth as well as glitter, and there will be surveys of independent and foreign films, documentaries, revivals, cult films, and experimental videos to go along with the big features.

The statistics are startling. By the festival's count, 329 films will play and 178 will be having either their world or North American premieres. The press contingent is expected to top 900 this year. The stars and directors attending will include Robert Altman, Kenneth Branagh, Al Pacino, Robin Wright-Penn, Faye Dunaway, Stephen Frears, Stellan Skarsgard, Cuba Gooding Jr., Robert Duvall, Ang Lee, David Mamet, Joel Schumacher, Sarah Jessica Parker, Liv Ullmann, Claude Chabrol, Gwyneth Paltrow, and John Malkovich, who will be being himself.

Toronto is unique in that it is not only important, but audience-friendly; not every festival (starting with Cannes) can make that statement. Screenings are open to the general public, and many film lovers plan their vacation around the screenings; I've talked before screenings with moviegoers actually planning to squeeze in fifty or sixty films.

I've seem some of the entries already, at Cannes, and will look forward to seeing how they play for Toronto's more movie-minded, less commercially oriented, audiences. The festival doesn't have an official jury, but it does hand out a lot of prizes, including the Peoples' Choice Award, which is voted on by the moviegoers themselves. My guess is that Paul Cox's wonderful, heartbreaking *Innocence,* which was my favorite film at Cannes, has a good chance at that prize; it just won the People's Choice mention at Montreal, plus the top prize of that festival, Toronto's fierce competitor. It is a love story about older people that younger people seem to love.

Among the high-profile films for the weekend are two Hollywood premieres, Rod Lurie's *The Contender,* with Joan Allen and Jeff Bridges, and Cameron Crowe's *Almost Famous,* with Kate Hudson, Frances McDormand, and Philip Seymour Hoffman. Playing on Friday night is David Mamet's *State and Main,* a comedy about a film being made in a small New England town; it stars Sarah Jessica Parker, Philip Seymour Hoffman (again), and Rebecca Pidgeon in what is said to be vintage Mamet crossed with screwball comedy.

Arriving on Sunday is Ang Lee's *Crouching Tiger, Hidden Dragon,* starring Chow Yun-Fat and Michelle Yeoh and representing the gifted director's first venture into the martial arts genre after such credits as *The Ice Storm.* Also playing Sunday is a movie buff's special treat, *Shadow of the Vampire,* a macabre thriller about the making of F. W. Murnau's famous silent classic *Nosferatu,* which more or less invented the vampire genre. Willem Dafoe and Malkovich star.

Toronto is twenty-five, and so is the career of British director Stephen Frears, who will be honored with a special tribute and a retrospective of such titles as *My Beautiful Laundrette, The Grifters,* and this year's wonderful *High Fidelity.* Another British director, Kenneth Branagh, will close the festival with his *How to Kill Your Neighbor's Dog,* about an L.A. playwright. It stars Lynn Redgrave. In between comes the great Robert Altman, with *Dr. T and the Women,* starring Richard Gere in a scathing comedy about a womanizing Dallas gynecologist.

But all of these are just the titles I've heard

about now, before the festival has opened. The best moments in Toronto are when you walk into a film you haven't heard much, or anything, about, and it gives you a great experience. I felt that way in recent years about *Elizabeth, Boys Don't Cry, Down in the Delta, Mansfield Park,* and *Smiling Fish and Goat on Fire.*

That last title, by the way, was touted by the Dude, somewhat legendary film rep Jeff Dowd, who has an uncanny eye for sleepers, and this year faxes me he is putting his "considerable weight" behind *The Truth About Tully,* with Anson Mount and Julianne Nicholson, described as "one summer that forever changes a distant father and his two sons." I told him I would come to see it if he promised not to use the line, "After that summer, nothing would ever be the same" even once in my hearing.

Festival Opens with Three Magical Films

September 8, 2000—It was the opening weekend of the twenty-fifth anniversary Toronto Film Festival. The summer was over, and it was safe for the good movies to open again. Summer is the season devoted to the mindless feeding of our base desires for low entertainment. Autumn is when we get new three-ring binders and iron our chinos and go back to school. Something ineffable in the first cool day of September makes us think deeper thoughts, and nurture our better natures. This passes, but for a time we feel virtuous and want to go to movies that will reveal the secrets of life.

Three movies in that category played here Friday, one at its world premiere. Well, actually, more like 100 movies opened, but I have just arrived and the festival is mostly ahead of me. These are the three I have seen. Each is magical in its own way.

They were *Almost Famous,* Cameron Crowe's semiautobiographical memory of being a fifteen-year-old rock critic for *Rolling Stone* magazine. And *Innocence,* Paul Cox's film about two people who fell in love when they were young and discover, decades later, that they have never fallen out of love. And *Faithless,* Liv Ullmann's harrowing film about divorce and infidelity, based on a screenplay by Ingmar Bergman.

Almost Famous is the kind of movie you savor, realizing how good it is and how surefooted and true. It tells the story of a fifteen-year-old

kid from San Diego named William Miller (Patrick Fugit), very earnest, very serious, carefully raised by a mother (Frances McDormand) who is both New Age and old-fashioned. He lives and breathes rock and roll. And through a series of misunderstandings and lucky breaks, he finds himself assigned by *Rolling Stone* magazine to cover the road tour of Stillwater, invariably referred to as "a mid-level rock band." He bonds with the lead guitarist (Billy Crudup) and with a groupie (Kate Hudson) who defines herself as a "Band Aide," but is a sweet and good spirit. She cares about William, who is about her age but infinitely less experienced in the strange turns of the world.

Cameron Crowe was himself a teenage *Rolling Stone* correspondent, and the film is autobiographical. It is also funny, profound, and very observant about human nature; it never cheapens the story, never goes for the obvious ways of exploiting the material, but is about a young man finding himself and his talent. Crowe also made *Say Anything* (1989), one of the best movies ever made about teenagers, and here he shows he still remembers exactly what it is like to be a kid, and smart, and in over your head, but trusting yourself.

Paul Cox's *Innocence,* from Australia, came here straight after winning the audience prize and sharing the top jury prize at the Montreal festival. I think it has the potential to break out into a great popular hit. It's a love story about teenagers who pledge themselves to each other, are parted by circumstances and wrong turns, and meet again fifty years down the road. Charles Tingwell plays a widower; he reaches out to his former love, played by Julia Blake, who has long resided in a dead marriage and now finds that their romance still burns with the hot flame of youth.

What must she do about this? Must she be conventional and respectable and resigned, or must she listen to her heart? What is crucial about this film is that it's not an exercise in Hallmarkian sentiment, but a realistic and uncompromised look at people who are smart and experienced—young, but not foolish, at heart. It's a tough sell, since romances involving seniors are not commercial, but everyone who sees this movie loves it, and the word of mouth is passionate.

Faithless is the other side of the coin, stirring

the ashes of love. Liv Ullmann directed it from an Ingmar Bergman screenplay, and it is about "Bergman" (Erland Josephson), an elderly movie director who hires an actress (Lena Endre) to work with him on a screenplay. He will ask her questions, she will answer, he will think out loud, and then there are flashbacks to the scenes he evokes. In a sense, she may not be there at all; he may be talking to his own memories. He feels guilt and confusion: What really did happen in those romances and betrayals, and what really was meant by it all?

Bergman (the real Bergman), at eighty-two, has much to remember. He is one of the greatest of all directors, but his romantic life has been a minefield. He has been married five times, and although he never married Ullmann, he did have a daughter (the novelist Linn Ullmann) by her. In her middle age, Ullmann has become a gifted director, and by collaborating on this material she and Bergman have engaged in the kind of truth-seeking the movies (and life) rarely allow.

* * *

Now I plunge into the maelstrom. The press screening of every evening's gala presentation is at 8:30 A.M., and then the screenings march toward midnight in a dozen venues, while stars and directors crowd the hotel lobbies and there are parties on top of parties. I was invited to a midnight spaghetti supper tonight and had to say, no, when I start eating spaghetti at midnight I get behind and never catch up. The critic at this festival is like a long-distance runner, stopping only to grab an Evian (and a Toronto bran muffin) between milestones.

But on Thursday night there was a calm before the storm. I was on the back porch of Club Lucky with Dusty and Joan Cohl. I met them twenty-five years ago at Cannes, where Dusty in his cowboy hat ruled the terrace of the Carlton Hotel and announced that he and Bill Marshall and Hank van der Kolk would start a festival in Toronto. I have come every year since the second, and seen Toronto grow into the most important film event in North America.

Dusty was wearing a tie. I think I also saw him wearing a tie at his daughter's wedding. Usually it is a T-shirt. He had been honored earlier at an anniversary party before the opening night film, and now he held court with old friends. But at 11 P.M. he stood to attention and announced it was time for Joan and him to go to the opening night party—4,000 people down by the lakefront. We made plans to meet at a screening the next morning. He's a role model at this festival: You heedlessly launch yourself into a week of films, as if life is a festival, and there might be something great starting in ten minutes.

Ghosts of Festivals Past Haunt Toronto

September 11, 2000—The ghosts of good films and old friends haunt the streets of Toronto this year. I am in a nostalgic mood, inspired by the twenty-fifth anniversary of the festival.

I hurry between press screenings in the fourteen venues of the Varsity, but on my way into the building I pass the Backstage, where in earlier years frigid gusts of air-conditioning blew through the room while we braced our knees to keep from sliding out of the slanted seats. The facade of the University Theater, where once there were tributes to Beatty, Scorsese, and Duvall, now stands stripped of its body, the skeleton of the projection booth poised eerily in the sky.

George Christie, the *Hollywood Reporter* columnist, holds an annual luncheon for longtimers and visiting stars and directors at the Four Seasons. I run into Margaret Gardner, the legendary London publicist who brought her clients and their films to Toronto when it was not a must-stop on the festival circuit. I remember Renee Furst, the New York publicist who campaigned for foreign films as if they were religions, and who worked her last Toronto festival knowing she had months to live. I say hi to director Norman Jewison and his wife, Dixie. They held the Sunday festival picnic on their farm when all the guests could fit into a couple of buses, and we marched into the woods to observe the maple sap dripping from the trees.

I see former directors of the festival—Dusty Cohl, Wayne Clarkson, Helga Stephenson, and the current boss, Piers Handling, serene as he governs the maelstrom. I hear that Bill Marshall, who cofounded the festival with Dusty and Hank van der Kolk, is in the hospital.

Garth Drabinsky, facing troubles in the Cineplex Odeon lawsuits, sits next to me at the luncheon. He sighs as he mentions "the current situation" in passing. He is saluted in Christie's toast because in George's mind the primary identity of everyone in the room is as "a member of our annual luncheon family" and our real lives are obscure diversions.

Walking into the Uptown on Sunday morning, I have a sudden flash of Jay Scott, the late film critic of the *Toronto Globe and Mail,* ahead of me on the stairs, wearing the sleeveless T-shirt of an unknown punk band, his shoulder bag jammed with press releases and tapes. He always moved as if he was on his way to a great film only he could rescue from oblivion. He put a paragraph into every sentence. Thinking of Jay, I remember David Overby, who searched the distant corners of world cinema for discoveries, programmed them into the festival, and defended them while chain-smoking the Gauloises that killed him.

At the anniversary dinner in honor of Stephen Frears on Saturday night, I see connections in the way people are grouped. Here is John Cusack, a foot taller than you expect, grinning in the corner with Cameron Crowe. In 1989, Crowe directed him in *Say Anything,* one of the best movies ever made about teenagers, and the film that launched Cusack's career. Now Crowe is here with *Almost Famous,* a film that seems to be unanimously loved. And here is Patrick Fugit, the star of *Almost Famous,* also taller than you expect. Does he look at Cusack and muse?

Here is Donald Westlake, the mystery writer, who adapted his novel *The Grifters* into a screenplay for Frears. It also starred Cusack. Westlake is attending the dinner, he says, because "I've been involved in twenty-three movies since 1966, and Stephen Frears is the only one of those directors I would walk across the street to speak to."

Jeff Bridges is clowning with Jeff Dowd. Dowd is the Dude, a producer's rep and publicist who works as a buccaneer for films he loves. He started with the Coen brothers' *Blood Simple,* and they immortalized him in *The Big Lebowski.* Bridges played Lebowski in the movie. Now the Dude pulls out a joint—just as a prop, he says, for a photo with Bridges.

I stay for the cocktail hour but not for the dinner, because I must see *The Trouble With Tully* at 10 P.M. It is the Dude's cause this year. As we lope down Bloor Street, we talk about *George Washington,* one of this year's really special films. There is a line in the movie, one character saying to another: "Is that the Bible or

Shakespeare?" He assumes if it sounds poetic and inspiring it must come from one of the two holy books.

Our conversations always drift far from where they start. I inform the Dude that Shakespeare's name is hidden in the 46th Psalm of the King James Version. "There is a theory that he did a little rewriting and touching up on the psalms," I say.

"I can absolutely understand that," the Dude says. "A lot of artists, they'll make a commercial between gigs, pick up a little change."

I am thinking about how effortlessly the Dude personifies the Dude. We wait for the light to change so we can cross the street. He sighs.

"I ran into Huey Lewis, man," he says. "Huey plays Gwyneth Paltrow's father in *Duets.* I'm exactly the same age as Huey is, but I'm not ready to start thinking about Gwyneth Paltrow as my daughter yet."

I know, Dude. I know. And so we beat on, boats against the current, borne back ceaselessly into the past.

Early Favorites Emerge at Toronto Festival

September 11, 2000—Notes after emerging from early screenings at the Toronto Film Festival:

Rod Lurie's *The Contender,* which premiered here over the weekend, is the most boldly partisan big-star film in decades. Starring Joan Allen, Jeff Bridges, and Gary Oldman in the story of congressional hearings marred by sexual scandal, it's up-front and even defiant with its liberal, pro–Democratic Party politics.

Allen stars as a senator who is nominated for vice president after the incumbent dies in office. Oldman plays the hostile Republican head of the House Judiciary Committee, who gets evidence seeming to prove the senator participated in a drunken gang-bang in college. Bridges is the president who must decide whether to withdraw the nomination, and Christian Slater is the Democratic congressman who might trade his vote for power. In the wings is a Democratic governor (William Petersen) who desperately wants to be vice president.

The plot depends on the Allen character's flat refusal to confirm, deny, or even discuss her sex life, which she considers her own business. "Is the plot a veiled reference to Monicagate?" I asked Bridges. "Veiled?" he said. "I don't think it's so veiled."

Lurie, a former film critic for *Los Angeles* magazine and the son of political cartoonist Ranan Lurie, grew up in a political household and told me he has always wondered why movies don't take sides more often. His film is not a fictional version of President Clinton's troubles, he said, but an ideological protest against the invasion of privacy. The tactics of Kenneth Starr seem to hover behind the plot to discredit the nominee, and Oldman's character is a sanctimonious infighter who relishes power and hates the president. "When I wrote that character I had Arlen Specter and Henry Hyde in mind," says Lurie.

The film was produced independently because "studios were shy about a movie this upfront about politics" and wanted to replace Joan Allen, the Steppenwolf founder who won an Oscar nomination as Patricia Nixon in Oliver Stone's *Nixon*. "But I wrote the movie for her," Lurie said. "I think she's the best actress in the world, and the only actress for this role." After the film was completed it so impressed Steven Spielberg and Jeffrey Katzenberg at DreamWorks that it became that studio's first pickup of an outside production.

Allen was being talked about at Toronto as a sure thing for another Oscar nomination. There's a scene in the film where she tells Congress what she believes in. "In the editing room, I was sitting with Steven Spielberg and he suggested we have a little music swell up under her speech," Lurie said. "I said the music would indicate we supported what she was saying. Steven said, 'What's wrong with that? We do.'" The music is in.

Every festival has a small, heartfelt film that slips in without big publicity and starts stealing hearts. I've seen two so far at Toronto this year. *The Truth About Tully*, directed by first-timer Hilary Birmingham, is set on a hard-pressed Nebraska farm, where two grown sons help their widowed father work the land. While financial troubles and old secrets bedevil their dad (Bob Burrus), Tully (Anson Mount) dates a local stripper (Catherine Kellner) so jealous she shoots up the hood of his aging Cadillac. Earl (Glenn Fitzgerald) makes friends with Ella, a freckle-faced neighbor (Julianne Nicholson)

who wants to be a vet. She also wants to be Tully's wife, but only if he grows up.

That outline makes the story seem like a simple slice of life, but there are depths and shadows in the film, and a powerful performance by Burrus, as a father who still loves the wife who betrayed him. What is interesting is the way Ella's healthy, centered personality sort of eats away at the family's angst and gloom. The movie seems to have an unusual emotional impact on audiences; there were tears and brave smiles after it was over.

George Washington is the other early discovery at this year's festival. Written and directed by David Gordon Green, a Texas filmmaker who has previously worked only on shorts and documentaries, it's the story of poor teenagers, mostly black, some white, living in an industrial area so blasted and forlorn it looks like a landscape of purgatory.

We meet Buddy, a thirteen-year-old, his heart broken because Nasia, the film's twelve-year-old narrator, has stopped being his girlfriend. She wants "someone more mature," and chooses George, who is no catch: He's a little retarded, and wears a football helmet because of a soft skull.

The film has an uncanny ease in its sometimes improvised scenes. Characters seem relaxed after long knowledge of one another, and events are not driven by the plot but take place with the haphazard suddenness of life. The prevailing mood is one of sadness, isolation, bafflement, but there are flashes of humor based on how very peculiar and contrary we humans can be. Watching the film, I saw it as a tightwire act, and wondered how Green was spinning such an involving story out of such apparently slight and offhand materials. In its mastery of style, the film plays notes it seems to be inventing.

Two comedies have been big audience-pleasers, but need not be discussed much now because they open soon. David Mamet's *State and Main* is about a film crew occupying a small New England town and changing it (and themselves) in strange and wonderful ways; it's his first pure comedy. Christopher Guest's *Best of Show* is a hilarious mocumentary (by the director of *Waiting for Guffman*) about the Mayflower Dog Show. Worth the admission simply for Fred Willard's performance as a broadcast color commentator who strikes notes of vulgar stupidity with unerring precision.

What One Critic Looks for in a Movie

September 12, 2000—I walk out of the Uptown and there's a TV crew on the sidewalk, and although they are no doubt hoping for Parker Posey, they ask me a question anyway: "What do you look for in a festival film?" I say I'm not really looking for anything in particular, blah, blah, but for some reason the question reverberates all during the day.

What *do* I look for?

1. I look for a film that is trying to find a new way to use old materials—that wants to reshape the world into the form of the filmmaker's dream.

Consider *George Washington,* a film I wrote about the other day. It is original in every atom of its being. The director, David Gordon Green, moves beyond conventional narrative, and yet still wants to use the materials of a story. There are characters and locations and dialogue, and nothing is intended to be confusing, and there are no frenzies of the camera. It is about poor people, many of them children, in a kind of rusted urban wasteland, where death comes as an accident and stays as a shameful secret.

2. I look for a film that is about the textures of particular people, and that cares about who they really are, instead of plugging actors into ready-made templates.

Consider *Keep the River on Your Right: A Modern Cannibal Tale.* This is a documentary I saw at the end of a very, very long day, and I even dozed off once—but I was interested even while I slept, if you know what I mean. It is about the life of an eighty-year-old gay Jewish man named Tobias Schneebaum, whose age and sexuality and Jewishness are all part of the story. Ostensibly, it is about his adventures over half a century as a popular anthropologist who walked into the rain forests of Peru and New Guinea and lived with the tribes he found there, becoming accepted as a brother and lover, and in one case going along on a raid that led to cannibalism. Yes, he ate human flesh.

In tapes of old talk shows promoting his books, he tells Mike Douglas or Charlie Rose what the flesh tasted like, and that bisexuality is common in primitive societies. In new footage,

the documentary retraces his steps and he meets a former lover in New Guinea and returns to the ancient ruins of Peru. But as he talks during this footage, we realize that the movie isn't about his travels and isn't about cannibalism, and isn't even about how he walked all alone into the jungle in tennis shoes and depended for his survival on the kindness of strangers. It is about the wisdom and acceptance that comes with age. Tobias Schneebaum has manifestly become a contented man, whose memories assure him he did not lead an empty life.

3. I look for movies that use genres as the canvas, not the purpose.

Consider Ang Lee's *Crouching Tiger, Hidden Dragon* and E. Elias Merhige's *Shadow of the Vampire.* Both deal with genres—martial arts and vampire movies. Both say the same thing: Our imaginations are ruled by archetypes, but we have free will and need not follow the rules. Lee's film is about a young girl who is destined for marriage and a predictable life, and who finds a destiny that is wildly romantic and daring. Merhige's film is not about how vampires suck the blood of their victims, but about how movies suck the blood of their makers; it is based on the filming of Murnau's great silent film *Nosferatu,* which created the vampire genre, and today seems uncannily real—as if it were about the real vampire who inspired all the other ones.

4. I look for movies that contain wisdom about life. Not a "message" so much as a demonstration of what works and what doesn't work for people.

Consider Ed Harris's *Pollock* and Stephen Daldry's *Billy Elliott.* The first is about an artist who cannot drink, but does, and makes his life a torture for himself and those who love him. The second is about a working-class boy in a British mining town who decides he wants to be a ballet dancer, and after a rocky patch finds that his rough-edged dad and brother will support him.

The lesson, I think, is that if art is not fun and does not give you pleasure, if there is no joy in its creation, it is not worth doing. Pollock created paintings that sell for millions of dollars, but why would anyone who knows about their making want to look at one? No matter how good you think a Pollock painting is, you must always wonder what he could have accomplished if he had been blessed with joy. That lesson is explained in *Billy Elliott,* in a remarkable scene where the young boy, who thinks he has failed his audition, tries to tell the judges how happy he feels when he dances.

Pollock's marriage is a hell for Lee Krasner, his wife, who believes in his talent but despairs of his suffering. He lies, insults, alienates, cheats, and then suffers through agonies of remorse, knowing that alcohol triggers his demons and drinking anyway—maybe because he wants to hurt himself and (unforgivably) others. Billy Elliott's rough-edged father and brother know nothing about ballet, but when the father sees that dancing makes his son joyous, he supports him, and then the boy's art brings joy to his family.

5. *I look for a movie that makes me ask, "What the hell was* that *about?"—as long as I ask with a smile.*

Consider Roy Andersson's *Songs from the Second Floor.* It is utterly, bafflingly mysterious. It comes from another planet, which happens to be located on our own. It is about the sad and bewildered citizens of a gloomy, doomy city who blunder their way through one embarrassing and inexplicable event after another. If Buñuel and Tati and Beckett and Buster Keaton and Werner Herzog had collaborated on a film, it would not look like this, but it would want to.

Low-Cost Formats Give Filmmakers New Freedom

September 14, 2000— Spike Lee's new film was shot on digital video. Joel Schumacher's new film was shot on 16mm. The formats probably made the films possible. Video is not film and 16mm is not 35mm, but the artistic imagination is the same, and the lower-priced formats allow spontaneity and speed that you can't get when you're dragging a 35mm camera and all of its lights and acolytes everywhere you go.

Lee's film is *Bamboozled,* a heartfelt, anguished comedy (if that is the word) about negative images of blacks in American popular culture. Schumacher's film is *Tigerland,* about a free spirit who all but brings an infantry basic training program to a halt. Both were made for a whole lot less than Lee spent on *Malcolm X* or Schumacher on *Batman Forever.*

I saw the Schumacher film here at Toronto

and ran into him in the hotel lobby, and he went into a description of his filming experience that translates as "free at last!" He shot for twenty-eight days, for less than $10 million, and got every shot he wanted, he said, and made the film exactly the way he saw it. No rewrites, no interference, no calls for A-list stars, because the less expensive medium got the suits off his back.

Lee I'll be talking to next week, about a lot more than the format, since his film is so confrontational to audiences black or white. I saw it recently (not in the festival), and I know, without having to ask him, that video made the film possible. The material is too problematical to be financed in the ordinary 35mm way.

In the last couple of years I've argued against video *projection* and in favor of film in theaters. Light through celluloid remains for me the medium of choice when I go to the movies. But *filming* on video or 16mm is another matter. I've seen a lot of great-looking bad films, and 35mm didn't save them. But when a film is engaged and original and working, no one is likely to think much about the medium.

You can tell, though, when you're looking at video. The medium has advocates who claim it is as good as film, but that is an ideological claim, not a factual one. There is something problematical about the definition of images in video. There's a lack of richness in the image quality; you get the feeling that's all there is and there isn't any more. A lack of vividness in the bright colors. Shadows that don't go all the way to black. A strange reluctance in fast camera movements, as if the image is hurrying to keep up with the camera. In the case of 16mm, the definition and the quickness are there, but the richness we see in 35mm will look a little diluted.

Good filmmakers can work around these limitations. They know how to light, how to art direct, how to process, how to move the camera to sidestep the limitations. Look at *Tigerland.* The movie is compelling and alive; it's down in the mud with draftees in basic training, and it's in the face of drill sergeants shouting at their victims. The shots aren't possible only because of 16mm (Spielberg was in lots of mud in *Saving Private Ryan*), but the story itself, one senses, was possible only because Schumacher cut loose from the studio albatross and shot fast and free in 16.

"In any picture, if you don't have something in the can by noon, you're in big trouble," he was telling me. "You get there early in the morning, you're fooling with the lights, you're working with the camera moves, and then it's lunchtime. With 16, you go right to work. You can move the camera quickly. You can handhold. You can think of something and do it and see if it works. It was a wonderful feeling."

If Schumacher got a freedom of movement, Lee obviously got a freedom of theme. *Bamboozled* is as personal and political and quixotic a film as he's made, and although he attacks racist images of blacks in the movie, he does it by using them, lots of them, and many people will be offended (it's the Ted and Whoopi at the Friars' Club syndrome). Video was like his shortcut around the people who would have been shy about financing this material.

At a festival like Toronto, there's a class system in formats: 35mm is best, video is a means to an end (16mm is fading away). But sometimes a small, experimental film will be in 35, because it needs to be.

Look at David Gordon Green's *George Washington,* as good-looking as any film in the festival. I assume it had such a small budget that the decision to shoot in 35mm wide screen represented a significant portion of the available money. Video would have made it easier, but robbed it of its quality; the images evoke the same voluptuous sense of place as Terrence Malick's *Days of Heaven.* Schumacher's goal was to catch the quick and spontaneous exchanges of anger, humor, and power; he didn't need the look, but the flexibility. Spike Lee wanted to express passionate ideas in a controversial way, and his medium gave him the freedom to say them.

Spike Lee shot his film on miniDV on a Sony DX1000 camera that retailed at around $4,000. Sitting in the audience, looking at the movies, are young directors who know they can make a movie with as little as $3,000 in hardware: $1,500 for the digital video camera, $1,500 for the computer, give or take a few accessories and software programs. That's freedom. What's interesting is to see the big guys, the Lees and Schumachers, embracing it with the same joy as the kids.

Festival Films Deliver Healthy Dose of Disbelief

September 15, 2000—I was on Pamela Wallin's TV show, sitting between the director Norman Jewison and the critic Brian D. Johnson, and Johnson said: "You know how they always talk about the suspension of disbelief? There are days when I would simply settle *for* disbelief."

"I'm stealing that," I told him. "It'll be in print by tomorrow."

Disbelief. Yes. You see something in a movie and you cannot believe your eyes. Usually you can't believe how good it is, how smart or original. Sometimes you can't believe how bad it is. If it is bad enough to inspire disbelief, at least it is not boring.

We're not talking here only about ecstatic disbelief—the kind inspired, say, by Darren Aronofsky's π, when the hero drills a hole in his skull, or in Spike Jonze's *Being John Malkovich,* when Malkovich enters a roomful of himself, or in Ang Lee's *Crouching Tiger, Hidden Dragon,* when characters leap free of gravity.

We're also talking of more everyday human forms of disbelief. I was watching George Tillman Jr.'s *Men of Honor,* for example. It stars Cuba Gooding Jr. as Carl Brashear, the first African-American diver in the U.S. Navy, and shows how he overcame racism to become a diver and then kept diving even after having his leg amputated. Brashear is a genuine hero, and I felt disbelief at the way his battle never seemed to be over—he overcame one obstacle only to be faced with another. How does a man like that keep hope?

And what about Reinaldo Arenas, the hero of Julian Schnabel's *Before Night Falls.* At the age of sixteen Arenas ran away from home to join the Cuban rebels in the hills, but within a few years Castro's revolution had made him a prisoner and an outcast, a man who was jailed and beaten for the sins of being an artist and a homosexual, who wrote his books while homeless, who once literally tried to float away to Florida on an inner tube. Who was born into illiteracy and illegitimacy, ate dirt as a child to still his hunger, and wrote ten novels and many books of poetry. How does a man like *that* keep hope?

And what about Darren Aronofsky's *Requiem for a Dream*? Among its interlocking stories, drawn from Hubert Selby Jr.'s *Last Exit to Brook-*

lyn, is one starring Ellen Burstyn as a lonely widow who watches the game shows and starts taking diet pills and takes more and more of them until the people on TV are talking to her. (Neil LaBute's *Nurse Betty* has a more benign form of this behavior.) I watch Burstyn implode, mentally and physically, and I think I have never seen madness portrayed this heartbreakingly before. How does a woman like that open her eyes every day?

Then there is Andrucha Waddington's *Me, You, Them,* starring Regina Case ("the Oprah of Brazil") as Darlene, a poor peasant woman from a backward area, who begins with one child, has two more, and is pregnant with a fourth—while succeeding, in a macho society, in arranging things so that she lives under the same roof with three men who all consider themselves in one way or another her husband. The movie is often very funny, but it's not a comedy; we are asked to consider the ways in which a woman who is fully aware of her power can free herself of the rules of her society. We watch in . . . disbelief.

Later on the day I saw *Me, You, Them,* I saw Terence Davies's *House of Mirth,* based on the Edith Wharton novel about a woman who begins with good prospects in high society and ends in despair. Gillian Anderson's Lily Bart moves among the idle and languorous rich of New York in the early 1900s; she and the man she really loves (Eric Stoltz) agree that her business is to find a rich man and seek employment (for that is what it is) as his wife. But she has problems with scruples and timing: By the point when she is willing to make an unpleasant choice of partner, it is too late. All through the movie I thought of Darlene in *Me, You, Them,* who would have had every man in the movie happily contributing to her upkeep. Can a woman allow the silly codes of stupid people to destroy her life? It happens all the time. The disbelief in *House of Mirth* is Lily's, as it gradually occurs to her what hypocrites she lives among; the aristocrats of Wharton's New York are vermin compared to the poor people in Waddington's Brazil.

And then what about Bozz (Colin Farrell), the hero of Joel Schumacher's *Tigerland,* who finds himself in advanced basic training for Vietnam in 1971. Bozz is infected by a basic disregard for authority, a contempt for stupidity,

and a desire not to lose his life in the war. He is like a virus in the army's system; he doesn't set about to sabotage the training regime, but because he is not broken, because he will not become a cog, he nearly brings it to a halt. We see him subjected to insults, beatings, and punishments, and he comes up winking. We can't believe he gets away with it, but he does, because there is something in all of us, even a drill sergeant, that admires a person who will not cave in.

All of those kinds of disbelief came this year at the end of a long summer during which I could believe almost everything in most of the movies I saw—all too easily, and without much joy. "Why did you like *The Cell* so much?" people ask me while we wait for a movie to begin. I thought it was visionary, original, reaching for the incredible. That's what I try to tell them. Mostly they listen in disbelief.

The Awards

September 18, 2000—Films set in imperial China, the American South, and Iceland won the most important awards here Sunday, as the twenty-fifth Toronto Film Festival came to a close. The festival has no jury and is officially noncompetitive, yet managed to honor more than a dozen films at its closing brunch. There were lots of ties.

The most important prize is probably the Volkswagen Discovery Award, voted on by some 775 critics at the festival. It was shared this year by *George Washington,* by David Gordon Green, a bittersweet tale of life and death in a rusting cityscape; and Baltasar Kormakur's *101 Reykjavik,* starring Victoria Abril in a comedy where her character marries a man while carrying on an affair with his mother. The title refers to the address of the only tree in the Icelandic capital.

Ang Lee's *Crouching Tiger, Hidden Dragon* won the Benson and Hedges People's Choice Award, voted on by festival patrons and calculated according to a weighted system that does not penalize smaller films. *Crouching Tiger* is nevertheless a gloriously big epic, starring the Hong Kong action stars Yun-Fat Chow and Michelle Yeoh in a visionary adventure where the characters seem set free from the force of gravity.

The Dish, Rob Sitch's delightful comedy from Australia, placed second in the People's Choice balloting. It's set in the hamlet of Parkes, Australia, which is atwitter in 1969 when its giant radio telescope is recruited to relay the first TV signals from the Moon. There was a tie for third place between Paul Cox's *Innocence,* also from Australia, about two people in their late sixties who renew a teenage love affair, and Stephen Daldry's *Billy Elliot,* about a working-class boy from a British mining town, who wants to be a ballet dancer.

The VW Discovery awards produced not only a tie for first place, but another tie for second, involving Marziyeh Meshkini's *The Day I Became a Woman,* about an Iranian woman imprisoned by her own family, and *The Iron Ladies,* by Yongyooth Thongkonthun, about a Thai volleyball team made up of transvestites and transsexuals.

The Fipresci Award is given every year by a jury selected by the international film critics' federation. Its award went to another Thai film, the crime drama *Bangkok Dangerous,* by twin brothers Oxide and Danny Pang.

The City TV award for the best first Canadian feature went to Philippe Falardeau's *La Moitie Gauche du Frigo* ("the left-hand side of the fridge"), a film about two friends who decide to make a documentary as one of them searches for a job; the film takes over their lives. The City of Toronto Award for best Canadian feature went to Gary Burns's *Waydowntown,* about a group of friends who bet a month's salary on who can stay inside the longest; the film takes place inside the maze of Calgary office buildings, malls, and pedestrian walkways. The National Film Board of Canada's John Spotton award for best short film went to Michele Cournoyer's *Le Chapeau.*

Some of the winning films do not have dis-

tribution, and the festival recognition could be invaluable. *The Dish* and *George Washington* are in that category—the first with broad popular appeal, the second destined for lots of best ten lists. For Paul Cox's *Innocence,* festivals have been a lifeblood. It played out of competition at Cannes ("too sentimental," a festival insider sniffed), but generated enthusiastic reviews and word of mouth, and then went on last month to win both the Peoples' Choice Award and the jury prize at Montreal. Toronto adds more momentum to the kind of film that people discover for themselves.

As for *George Washington,* it has the same kinds of evocative qualities as Terrence Malick's great *Days of Heaven* (1978)—it uses lush photography and a wondering, nostalgic narration to tell a sad story that is half-understood but deeply felt. At a time when most movies snuggle into safe genres and fear to challenge audiences, this one is a bold stylistic achievement.

Ang Lee's *Crouching Tiger, Hidden Dragon* will get wide distribution, and is likely to open up the martial arts genre to new audiences; it has the physical exuberance common to all action pictures, but also a poetry and lyrical visual beauty that transcends its origins.

The Dish raises interesting questions. It's made by the same producer-director team who made *The Castle,* a hilarious comedy that Miramax inexplicably shelved after a halfhearted release effort. Audiences loved it; now here is another quirky Australian comedy they love. Will it find its audience? I ran into director Rob Sitch and producer Michael Hirsch on the last day of the festival. They were in talks with distributors, they said. "Miramax?" No comment.

Hawaii Film Festival
Moving *Maryam* Showcased at Hawaii Film Festival

Honolulu, Hawaii, November 7, 2000—It must not have been easy to be an Iranian-American teenager in 1979, going to high school while your neighbors were tying yellow ribbons 'round their old oak trees. Especially since some of your neighbors were too dim to figure out that the Iranians in America were mostly pro-Shah and not supporters of the hostage-

takers. "Iranians go home," the mobs shouted, waving their flags while contradicting the American ideal.

Maryam, an extraordinary film playing here at the twentieth Hawaii International Film Festival, tells the story of an Iranian-American family in New Jersey, balanced precariously between the values of their former land and their new one.

It's seen mostly through the eyes of their

sixteen-year-old daughter, Maryam (Mariam Parris), who likes to be called Mary. She's a good student, wise and centered, with a good sense of humor, which she needs. Her father (Shaun Toub) is a local doctor; her mother (Shohreh Aghdashloo) is a housewife. It is a convention in movies about immigrant families to show the parents as strict, forbidding monsters, but actually Mary's parents are reasonable and loving, even if her dad has firm rules against serious dating, lipstick, stuff like that.

A cousin named Ali (David Ackert) arrives from Iran to study physics at the local university. Within the last year, he has become an observant Muslim and an admirer of the Ayatollah Khomeini. Mary's parents are not so religious, and prospered under the Shah. Ali moves into a spare bedroom, bringing the tensions of Iran to New Jersey just at the time when hostages are taken at the American embassy and anti-Iran sentiment in the United States becomes a fever. Fictional scenes are underlined by TV news footage from the time.

The movie could have been a shrill political statement, but is not. The writer-director, Ramin Serry, wants to observe, to empathize. Mary has a shy romance with a boyfriend. She's active as a newscaster on the school's closed-circuit TV station. The blond bimbos who hang out in the rest room, smoking, make crude remarks about her Iranian background, which she deflects with intelligence and irony. But then the Shah flies to New York seeking treatment for his cancer, and Ali is seized with revolutionary fervor.

More details should await my review. I left the theater admiring the movie not only for its ideas (it urges us to see people, not labels), but also for its artistry: In a time when most movie teenagers are bubble-headed pawns in sex comedies, here is a teenager with brains and courage, who doesn't simply rebel against her parents but wants to understand them, and who doesn't collapse into weeping victimhood but depends on her mind and values. *Maryam* is powerful, important, and very moving.

* * *

I've seen several other good films here at the Hawaii festival, which stands at the crossroads of the Pacific and specializes in films from the nations surrounding the ocean.

One of the best was *Anak,* by Rory Quintos, from the Philippines, which centers on a wonder-ful performance by Vilma Santos. She plays a "domestic helper," one of thousands who leave their families in the Philippines every year to work as household servants for rich families in places like Hong Kong. She took the job to make money, leaving her three children with her husband. Returning on leave with money and presents, she finds they have changed, especially the older daughter, who has fallen in with a bad crowd.

Glimpses of her life in Hong Kong are brief, but telling, especially when her husband dies and she is unable to attend his funeral because her employers, going on vacation, want her to watch their flat—and hide her passport while locking her in. Returning home, she's a whirlwind of cheerful chatter, but we see how that's an act, how inside she hurts and is heartbroken. Gradually the film reveals her true feelings.

Another good film is from China: *Breaking the Silence* stars the leading Chinese actress, Gong Li, as a single mother with her son, who is hard of hearing. She has to deal with the bureaucracy and hard economic times of the new China. Hearing aids are expensive. Schools do not want to admit hearing-impaired students. She, too, finds a job as a housecleaner, and discovers that her boss thinks of her as a sexual convenience. The director, Sun Zhou, said after the screening that some scenes had been cut by Chinese authorities, no doubt because they seemed critical of the new China's social welfare policies. What is left gets the point across, and is strong and memorable.

Final Fantasy Challenges Action Genre

November 30, 2000—Consider the eyes of Aki in *Final Fantasy.* They are from a movie. Is it live action, or animated?

A graphic arts expert might correctly vote that the eyes were created by a computer, but for most filmgoers, they're as real as any other eyes in the movies. They belong to a heroine named Aki, who is the star of a new kind of movie that premieres in July 2001.

The movie, *Final Fantasy,* has already stirred more curiosity and anticipation than any other release set for next year. It's based on the nine generations of the best-selling "Final Fantasy" video game, currently on the Sony PlayStation platform. More than 30 million copies have been sold. Now comes the movie, a big-canvas science-fiction fantasy, budgeted at more than $100 million, set in the year 2065 and involving locations, sights, and action that would be impossible in a real-world action movie.

It's being made here entirely inside computers by 200 digital artists from twenty-two countries, mostly the United States and Japan, headquartered in a skyscraper in downtown Honolulu. If their work is successful, you'll think you're looking at real human beings having adventures in the real world. Not a *plausible* real world, to be sure, but a world that doesn't look like any animation you've ever seen. It's more like the realistic worlds of high-end graphic novels. Aki and the others will not be human in the sense that you expect to run into them at Wal-Mart, but real in the sense that their faces, their skin, their motions do not seem animated but like idealized versions of real people.

"The life is in the eyes," says Andy Jones, who is the animation director for the film. "We want to make them look like they're thinking for themselves."

To do that, the animation team has developed sophisticated software that has, for example, 100 different on-screen slides controlling the elements in Aki's face. On the movie's Website (www.finalfantasy.com), you can see a demo of how they create wrinkles and skin texture. They photograph human actors in motion and use them as guides for realistic action. The characters move through locales that look like futuristic sci-fi landscapes, and yet have the kind of texture, weight, and detail you would expect in a real, if visionary, world.

The peculiar effect of *Final Fantasy* is hard to explain or anticipate, which is why I was impressed by the impact of two trailers for the movie, which were shown here during a panel discussion at the Hawaii Film Festival. On the big screen with surround sound, they up the stakes in the action-blockbuster genre. You can get a hint of that impact at the Website; the big-screen impact is much more decisive.

The movie is being produced by Chris Lee, a Hawaii native and former head of production at Columbia, where his credits included *As Good As It Gets* and *Jerry Maguire*. He has teamed on the project with Hironobu Sakaguchi, head of Square, the producer of the video game. Honolulu was chosen as headquarters for the four-year

effort because it is in the United States and yet livable for Japanese-speakers.

What sort of software does the team use? "We all start with the same basic software," says Jones. "It's what you do with it." The elaborate controls for the facial expressions of the leading characters, for example, were perfected in-house, and are much more ambitious than anything previously tried in animation.

"The computer helps us out," Lee says, "but essentially it still comes down to an artist creating artwork." Brief shots of several scenes in the trailers suggest that the artists have located themselves in a world resembling the future Earth, but freed themselves to toy with gravity. The same freedom is expressed in *Crouching Tiger, Hidden Dragon,* Ang Lee's martial arts movie where the human characters leap from one treetop to another to do battle.

If the movie is as impressive as the trailer suggests, *Final Fantasy* may decisively change the way action epics look in the future. Most current big-canvas blockbusters try to combine live action and computer-generated images seamlessly. But you can see or sense the seams, Lee says: "In a movie like *The Haunting,* there's a disconnect between reality and CGI. Here, the characters and the world all inhabit the same reality."

If *Final Fantasy* is successful, it will challenge the reign of action stars like Arnold Schwarzenegger and directors like George Lucas, who make films that place human actors in special-effects settings. If Jabba the Hut can be created by a computer, Lucas may find himself asking, why not Luke Skywalker? Could a producer like Chris Lee simply license Schwarzenegger's name, appearance, and voice, and create a digital version of him in an animated adventure?

Maybe, but Lee has little enthusiasm for digital copies of real people: "It would be *easier* to duplicate Humphrey Bogart than to come up with someone new," he says, "but the challenge is in creating new characters." He might have added (but did not) that once you create them you own them, and they don't have agents.

One thing they've discovered in creating new digital actors, Jones said, is that scientific theory is right, and perfectly symmetrical faces are perceived as attractive. Look at the faces on the Website head shots and you'll see they're all perfectly balanced, left matching right, although my guess is the villains will go slightly askew in the finished movie.

As for the voices, *Final Fantasy* has hired the voice-over talents of Ming-Na, the voice of Disney's Mulan, as Aki, and other characters are being voiced by Alec Baldwin, James Woods, Donald Sutherland, Ving Rhames, and Steve Buscemi. Could a computer synthesize voices too? "Yes," says Lee, "but they'd all sound like the lady who gives you the correct time of day."

Sundance Film Festival
Sundance Report No.1

Park City, Utah, January 17, 2001—Sundance has become the nation's most important film festival through an unbeatable combination: inconvenient location, lousy weather, overcrowded screening facilities, municipal hostility, and a ten-day lineup of films that in some cases will never be heard of again.

That's one way to look at it, and there are dark days when I plow through blizzards while late to a screening, find what looks like a legal parking space, and have my car towed by freelance buccaneers working on a commission system.

But there are other times that are magical. Like (from last year) racing into the library for my last possible chance to see *Girlfight.* Seeing Ethan Hawke's *Hamlet* in the little Egyptian Theater on Main Street. Watching incredible documentaries like *On the Ropes.* Hearing Bernard Rose extol the low-budget digital filmmaking of *ivansxtc.* Running into Johnny Rotten after the Sex Pistols documentary *The Filth and the Fury.* Meeting the Buddhist monk who directed *The Cup,* the first film from Bhutan. Or discovering a sleeper like *Panic,* with William H. Macy as a hit man steered through a midlife crisis by the younger but wiser Neve Campbell. Witnessing passionate debates on the future of digital filmmaking. And running into Val Kilmer, Kevin Spacey, Jodie Foster, Danny DeVito, and, yes, Tammy Faye Bakker.

All in all, I'd hate to miss Sundance. It would be the perfect festival, if only it were held in Santa Barbara.

This year's festival begins Thursday night with the premiere in Salt Lake City of Christine Lahti's *My First Mister,* about a love affair between a disturbed seventeen-year-old (Leelee Sobieski) and her boss at a clothing store (Albert Brooks). Then the festival moves up the hill to Park City, for its opening night on Friday of *Caveman's Valentine,* the much-discussed film starring Samuel L. Jackson as a Manhattan street person, directed by Kasi Lemmons (whose *Eve's Bayou* was the best film of 1997).

Sundance's focus is on the independent film movement, and it was here that the movement and the festival were put on the map in 1989 with the premiere of Steven Soderbergh's *sex, lies and videotape.* Since then indies have become an energizing force in the American film industry, with new faces like Quentin Tarantino *(Pulp Fiction),* Spike Lee *(Do the Right Thing),* Paul Thomas Anderson *(Boogie Nights),* Antonia Bird *(Safe),* Spike Jonze *(Being John Malkovich),* Kimberly Peirce *(Boys Don't Cry),* Todd Solondz *(Happiness),* and Neil LaBute *(In the Company of Men).*

This year's festival includes premieres of new movies of leading indie directors like Tom DeCillo, whose *Double Whammy* stars Denis Leary and Steve Buscemi in a story of homicide cops; Lea Pool's *Lost and Delirious,* with hot newcomer Piper Perabo in a story of self-discovery; Michael Apted, whose *Enigma* stars Kate Winslet in a Tom Stoppard screenplay about breaking the Nazi code; veteran indie Bobby Roth's *Jack the Dog,* about a compulsive womanizer; and Peter Care's *The Dangerous Lives of Alter Boys,* with Jodie Foster as a nun who disapproves of Kieran Culkin and his friends.

Also, Allison Anders's *Things Behind the Sun,* with Kim Dickens as a young rock musician; Gary Oldman and Skeet Ulrich as dim drifters in David Seltzer's *Nobody's Baby;* indie heroines Lili Taylor and Courtney Love in Bob Gosse's *Julie Johnson* (Lili is a Houston housewife with a secret passion for theoretical physics); Lee Davis's *3 A.M.,* with Danny Glover, Pam Grier, and Sarita Choudhury in a story of New York cabbies; and Michael Rymer's *Perfume,* of which perhaps all you have to know is that it stars Jeff Goldblum and is illustrated by a photo of eight nude fashion models.

That's just a sampling of the major premieres. There are also foreign films, documentaries, sidebars, revivals, experiments, workshops, and of course the refusenik satellite festivals like Slamdance and Nodance.

What's the single screening I'm most looking forward to? That would be Richard Linklater's *Waking Life,* an animated film by the director of *Slacker, Before Sunrise,* and *Dazed and Confused.* The movie was made by Linklater with two Austin, Texas, computer animation wizards, Bob Sabiston and Tommy Pallotta, who use their new software, named RotoShop, to convert live-action digital footage into stylized animation. The breakthrough here is that they did it at home, on relatively inexpensive Macintosh G4s. ("By contrast," writes *Wired* mag, "Pixar *(Toy Story)* this year bought 250 Silicon Graphics workstations, which typically run up to $30,000 a pop.")

Waking Life may be good, may be bad (with Linklater, I'm betting on good). But it will certainly showcase this year's most important breakthrough. By showing how high-quality, good-looking, full-motion animation can be put into the hands of the Garage Studios, it will be for Sundance 2001 what the breakthrough of digital video was a few years ago. I think it's called putting the means of production into the hands of the workers.

Opening Night

January 19, 2001—Mugging by postcard is the white-collar crime of choice at the Sundance Film Festival. Filmmakers fly to Utah with suitcases filled with postcards advertising their films, which they hand out to anybody who looks vaguely promising. I have nineteen in my pocket right now.

The official First Postcard of the 2001 festival was presented to me ten seconds after I arrived at the press office, by Jonathan Hyman and Andy Berman, the producer and director of *Bit Players.*

"When is it playing?" I asked.

"In the Short Film Program," they said.

"I don't get to see a lot of the short films," I said.

"But it's in the *first* Short Film Program," they said.

"Thanks for the card," I said. I walked ten steps in the direction of the theater and was stopped by Agnieszka Wostowicz-Vosloo of Poland, who gave me a postcard for her film, *Pate.*

"It's in the Short Film Program," she said. "But it's in the *first* Short Film Program."

I may go. I'll know half the people there.

* * *

The opening night film is held every year in Salt Lake City, in the cavernous Abravanel Hall. This year it was the odd and affecting *My First Mister,* the feature-length directorial debut of the actress Christine Lahti. Leelee Sobieski stars as a pierced seventeen-year-old Goth, a loner angry at the world, whose life is changed when she meets Albert Brooks, as a forty-nine-year-old loner who wears suspenders and manages a clothing store. Their relationship doesn't proceed beyond hugging, nor should it, because it is not about sex but about finding someone who will listen.

* * *

The lobby of the hall was jammed with film crews from all the entertainment channels, plus CNN, MTV, Fox, and the local stations. This is the only American film festival covered on the national news, which is amazing if you remember, as I do, the years when it was contained in the downtown Egyptian Theater, a shopping center triplex, and meeting rooms at the Holiday Inn.

"What does this festival really mean?" I was asked by CNN. I supplied an answer that was a little longer than a sound bite and a little shorter than an inaugural address, ending with the words ". . . entry point for new filmmakers."

"That's the crux of it!" said my interviewer. "Could you repeat just that?"

"It's an entry point for new filmmakers," I said.

"Great!"

* * *

My first sighting of the Dude was immediately after the screening of *My First Mister.*

Faithful readers will know that the Dude, aka Jeff Dowd, is to film festivals what a tout is to race tracks, with the difference that the Dude usually backs winning ponies, even if they are not his own. He had an early bet on *The Blair Witch Project.* Dowd is a "producer's rep," which means he shepherds films and their makers through the minefields of Sundance, Toronto, and Cannes.

This year he was shepherding Sergio Castilla, the Chilean director of *Te Amo* (Made in Chile), Castilla's actor son Adrian, plus two attractive young women, Victoria Villanueve, a producer from Argentina, and Janneke Boeck, a producer from Germany ("but we are roommates in New York").

"Look at that line," he said, spotting 2,000 people lined up for the opening night party. "Forget it. We'll go back later." He had heard of the Dead Goat, a bluegrass saloon that was down the street, down an alley and downstairs, which is pretty far down for Salt Lake City, and we all went there for Dead Goat Burgers.

"You gotta see this," the Dude told me, giving me a postcard for *Scratch*. "It's about hip-hop DJs. The buzz is terrific."

"Is that the buzz you're hearing or the buzz you're starting?" I asked.

"Both," said the Dude serenely.

* * *

Now we all drive up the hill to Park City, which for the next nine days will be the epicenter of the independent film community and, it must be said, an entry point for new filmmakers. This year 894 features, 342 documentaries, 515 foreign films, and 2,020 shorts were submitted to the festival, whose dazed selectors emerged with 120 films, plus the shorts of Hyman, Berman, and Wostowicz-Vosloo.

"There's a lot of buzz about *Donnie Darko*," three young women told me as I entered my hotel lobby.

"Are you connected with it?"

"Uh-huh."

"I don't think it's buzz if it's your own film you're talking about," I said. "I think it has to be someone else's film. But give me a postcard?"

Sex at Sundance

January 22, 2001—I've seen nine movies so far at this year's Sundance festival, and can report with absolute certainty that there is no trend, unless it is that South American filmmakers are more relaxed around sex than North Americans. But then, we already knew that.

"When I was growing up in Chile," the director Sergio Castilla said before the screening of his *Te Amo* (Made in Chile), "there were never any films about young people. So I wanted to make one."

He has, and judging by the result, the young people's films he had in mind were the ones starring Sylvia Kristel as a sexy tutor who seduced her teenage students. *Te Amo* (Made in Chile)

stars Castilla's son, Adrian, as a sixteen-year-old born in Chile, raised in New York, and back home again after a divorce. His mother is always absent, and his care has been entrusted to a twenty-five-year-old nanny who has been sexually abusing him for years.

The difference between *Te Amo* and, say, *My Tutor* is that Castilla is a serious and gifted filmmaker who has made a tender, thoughtful coming-of-age film; I was reminded of Louis Malle's tightrope act in the equally controversial *Murmur of the Heart*. The young hero is part of a crowd of two boys and two girls who find an abandoned house and make it their headquarters for a summer during which they discover themselves.

Subtitled films have a hard time at the xenophobic U.S. box office, but *Te Amo* is easier going because about half of the dialogue is in English. Audiences may be attracted by the promise of sex, but they will discover that for Castillo, sex is not the destination of a movie but part of a larger purpose. He asks: Can the fragility of the sixteen-year-old's teenage crush on his first girlfriend survive his experiences with the nanny?

Consider too the charming *Me, You, Them*, by the Brazilian filmmaker Andrucha Waddington, which made its way here via the Cannes and Toronto festivals. The film features Regina Case, a Brazilian TV star, as Dolores, a young woman from a backward province who is abandoned, pregnant, at the altar. Deprived of a husband, Dolores eventually finds herself supplied with no less than three—at the same time, and living peacefully together under the same roof.

The film is said to be based on a real-life case of polygamy, and also has echoes of the Brazilian classic *Dona Flor and Her Two Husbands*. It does not sensationalize its story in any way, but simply shows that for someone like Dolores, who is an earth mother without even trying, one thing leads to another. The film is sly and funny in the way it shows the three husbands, macho products of a patriarchal society, becoming stablemates.

The most unexpected sex scene so far at Sundance is no doubt in *The Caveman's Valentine*, the new film by Kasi Lemmons, whose *Eve's Bayou* was the best film of 1997. Once again she works with Samuel L. Jackson, this time playing a homeless man, probably schizophrenic, who lives in a cave in a New York park. When a frozen body is found in a tree near his cave, the Caveman finds himself drawn into the investigation (his daughter is a cop).

The police think they've solved the crime. The Caveman thinks not. A fearsome sight in his filthy clothes, his face hidden behind a curtain of dreadlocks, he was once a brilliant musician—and after he cleans up in order to visit the studio of a famous artist who is a suspect, he attracts the attention of the artist's chic sister (Ann Magnuson), who . . . well, it wasn't what the Caveman was expecting. It's intriguing how Jackson finds the right line for the character, who is convincingly homeless and mentally ill, and yet accessible and sympathetic.

Two wonderful comedies in three years have come from the Australian team of director Rob Sitch and producer Michael Hirsh. They made the hilarious *The Castle* in 1999, a story of a family home six inches from a jumbo jet runway; I'm convinced Miramax forfeited a *Full Monty*-scale hit by sitting on its hands after buying the film. I've seen it with three audiences that found it uproarious.

Now comes *The Dish*, which *will* get proper distribution—it's being released by Warner Bros.—and takes place mostly on July 20, 1969—the day the first live television signals were beamed from the Moon. The backwater Australian town of Parkes is aflutter because the world's largest radio telescope is located there, and will relay the historic signals to an audience of 600 million. At least, that's the plan before everything starts to go wrong, in an inspired human comedy that somehow makes radio astronomy and slapstick fit together. Sam Neill stars, as the man who tried to hold things together when the Australians "lost" the astronauts.

Richard Kelly's *Donnie Darko* stars Jake Gyllenhaal as a suburban teenager whose mental disturbance may have opened a wormhole in the space-time fabric. It's an odd, haunting combination of science fiction and coming-of-age, accurate in its view of adolescents, touching in the human qualities of Donnie's parents (Mary McDonnell is especially warm), and with a plot so labyrinthine that explaining it has become this year's version of the "Usual Suspects" game. The movie has the potential to be a breakthrough hit among adventurous teenagers.

Tom DiCillo's *Double Whammy* stars Denis Leary, Elizabeth Hurley, and Steve Buscemi in a New York cop story reminiscent of *Pulp Fiction* and *Bound*. Tortured by a bad back, Leary screws up two high-profile situations in a row before meeting chiropractor Hurley, who straightens out more than his back.

DeMane Davis and Khari Streeter were here a few years ago with a remarkable, unheralded sleeper named *Black & White & Red All Over,* and are back this year with *Lift,* starring Kerry Washington as a skilled shoplifter who seems to be stealing as a way of healing childhood wounds. Lonette McKee plays the distant mother she tries to reach with expensive gifts, and the film uses an interesting visual style to contrast the booster's everyday life with the elevated plane she seems to float in when she's stealing.

Having seen *Scratch,* by Doug Pray, I know as much as I am ever going to need to know about the use of turntables as musical instruments. The film goes to the beginnings of the hip-hop, DJ, and MC scene, even interviewing the inventor of the technique of manipulating short vinyl passages to create new works of art. We meet Q-bert, the Filipino-American who is perhaps the best of the recent turntablists, and follow another artist into a basement storeroom of hundreds of thousands of old vinyl records—it's like the closing shot of *Citizen Kane,* for real. The film never quite allows us to hear a performance all the way through, but that's poetic justice, since sampling a performance is the essence of turntabalism.

A Mysterious Beauty

January 22, 2001—You can't take food or drinks into the Eccles Theater here at the Sundance Film Festival, so you stand in the lobby, gobbling sandwiches from the little refreshment stand. I had my mouth full of roast beef on French bread with some kind of horseradish cream sauce when a beautiful woman smiled at me.

Yes, beautiful. She was tall, with a mane of raven hair, wide-set intelligent eyes, and a smile that made me curse the evil chefs of Utah for stuffing my mouth with horseradish cream at just such a moment when I would desire to appear most charming and composed.

"You wrote such a nice thing about me once," she said. "You wrote that I was the most beautiful woman in the movies since Daphne Zuniga."

At least, that is what I *thought* she said. This article will reveal that in fact I have no idea what she actually said, perhaps because the horse-radish cream was sloshing too near the delicate mechanisms of my inner ear.

I swallowed with an eagerness that would have alarmed Dr. Heimlich, and told her I was sure that I always wrote the absolute truth. I looked at her and I said to myself, "If this is not in fact Daphne Zuniga herself, then I do not have the slightest idea who she is, and since she has just informed me that she is *not* Daphne Zuniga, I don't have a clue who I'm talking to."

"Are you in this film?" I asked, stalling for time.

"No, I'm just here for fun," she said. "I'm not in any films in the festival this year."

My mind was racing. This was a nightmare. You can't go into print to describe a woman as the most beautiful woman in the movies since Daphne Zuniga and then forget her name. Nor can you smile and say, "I'm terribly sorry, woman-so-beautiful-I-singled-you-out-in-print, but what was your name again?"

Was the real Daphne Zuniga that tall? I asked myself. I had always sort of pictured her as a little shorter. On the other hand, she first inspired my admiration with her wonderful work in Rob Reiner's *The Sure Thing*, one of the best young love movies I have ever seen, and her costar there was John Cusack, who is a lot taller than people think he is, which may account for her being tall and yet seeming shorter next to the misleading Cusack.

"Is that one of those digital cameras?" she asked.

"Yes," I said. "I'm shooting for the paper."

"I was in Roddy McDowall's last film," she said. "He took pictures of everyone in all of his pictures. What an honor to be in one of Roddy's books, right there with Bette Davis."

"Let me take a photo of you," I said, thinking, Kenny Turan of the *L.A. Times* just went inside. I'll show the photo to him. He knows all the stars.

The beautiful woman was a natural model. I took several shots, and each time she gave me personality, poise, humor. Her eyes twinkled. She was a good sport. She smiled from the inside. Then the festival started ringing the bell that meant it was time to go into the screening.

Suddenly inspiration struck. "Give me your e-mail address," I said, "and I'll e-mail you a copy of the photo!"

"Great," she said, and wrote it down, and I stuffed it into my pocket. She said she hoped I saw some great movies, and then we plunged into the mob and were swept into the theater.

I grabbed a seat, stuffed my sub-zero Eddie Bauer goose down parka underneath it, and pulled out the piece of paper. It held an e-mail address and a name: Daphne Zuniga.

Piper Perabo and Human Consciousness

January 22, 2001—Your day fits together like this: You attend a speech by one of the most brilliant brain scientists in the world, who explains how the mind processes emotion and feeling, and how the movies exploit that capacity. Then you go to see *Lost and Delirious*, a film starring three beautiful young women in a story involving lesbianism at a boarding school.

You find Lea Pool's *Lost and Delirious* to be one of the most carefully crafted, most *professional* films you've seen at this year's Sundance Film Festival. But that isn't why you like it so much. You're absorbed from beginning to end because the characters are enormously interesting and likable. And because they are gorgeous. And because you could hear a pin drop in the 1,400-seat Eccles Theater during the sex scenes, which are not explicit but are erotic.

You have taken as your credo this statement by the critic Robert Warshow: "A man goes to the movies. The critic must be honest enough to admit that he is that man." I am honest enough. I am that man. I, personally, was stirred, involved, and absorbed by *Lost and Delirious*. It was a *movie*, not a statement, an exercise, a stylistic breakthrough or anything else but a superbly told story, with grace and grand romantic gestures.

My mind, I had been assured only hours earlier by Antonio Damasio, head of the brain lab at the University of Iowa and author of the current best-seller *The Feeling of What Happens*, is so good at processing incoming information that when it sees a smile it takes only milliseconds to ready my facial muscles to smile back. Damasio, a neurobiologist, was the first in the "big thinkers" series launched by Robert Redford to bring nonfilm speakers to Sundance.

My mind is constantly in the process of telling

me a story based on everything that happens to me, Damasio said, and this story becomes my autobiography. A movie invites me to give over my mind to its story, and it can also add to my life story. But of course my reaction will be influenced by all that has happened to me before I see the movie. I am the man. I bring myself to the movie.

I enjoyed *Lost and Delirious* not simply because it was about beautiful women (Piper Perabo, Jessica Pare, Mischa Barton). Piper Perabo was in *Coyote Ugly,* and I did not enjoy that so much. But here the three women play characters who engaged my sympathy. They are roommates in an all-female boarding school, an expensive one and a very good one. Perabo is Paula, a free spirit, a heedless romantic. Pare is Tori, the woman Paula is having an affair with, and Barton is Mary, their uncertain new roommate.

These characters are not depicted as neurotic, twisted, stupid, or clichéd. They are alive and free to be themselves. The crisis in the story comes when Tori makes a conscious decision to break off the love affair, and Paula responds with hurt, anger, and rebellion (she actually challenges Tori's new boyfriend to a duel). Mary is the witness and narrator.

The engine driving the film is romanticism; the characters believe the great speeches by Shakespeare, and try to act in the same heroic way. Paula is such a romantic she even denies that she and Tori are lesbians: They are individuals who share a great love, she passionately explains to Mary, and their love transcends sexual roles and is not defined by them. They are like Antony and Cleopatra.

Okay. So the rest of my review can await the movie's opening. This article is about the mind and the emotions, about how we personally see a movie and it interacts with our autobiography. I found myself sympathetic to the attitudes in *Lost and Delirious,* I liked the way the characters thought and interacted, and how they shaped and tested their values. I felt great attention for Paula; Perabo makes her into a lost soul, but a great one, willing to live by her principles. Her bold acting-out (in class, in the dining hall, and at a dance on parents' day) makes her an enormously attractive rebel. She is the Jack Nicholson of seventeen-year-old boarding school girls.

Coming out of the theater, I ran into a crowd of young men, a few years older than the characters in the movie. They did not like it. As they explained their reaction to me, I sensed irony in every word they used. They held themselves apart from the movie. They were wise to what it was trying to do. They were proof against its appeal. They were shielded from its sincerity and romanticism. The characters were over the top. They had logical problems with the plot.

Well, that's how it works. The mind is wired to the emotions and to the inner autobiography, and life has armed them with irony. But my God, I thought, if they are in their early twenties and already so guarded against grand romantic gestures, what can they do in life except make money? Where will their dreams sneak in? When two girls stand desperately in the moonlit woods and share an oath based on the vows of Lady Macbeth, where are these young men's minds? Can't they conceive that idealistic young women might cast their own crisis in the terms of a tragic heroine?

And apart from anything else, didn't they respond as healthy young men to the sight of those beautiful young women? Couldn't they even like the movie for its erotic content? Sexual appreciation is a valid response in the movies—one of the oldest and most sincere. A man goes to the movies. I am that man. I would rather be lost and delirious than found and secure.

Something to Say About Sex

January 24, 2001—Here is the most fundamental rule of film criticism: A movie is not about what it is about, but about how it is about it. The subject does not and cannot make a movie good or bad. Only the style, the approach, the method, the craftsmanship, the purpose, and the message can make a movie good or bad.

"Will the American public accept the sex scenes in this movie?" I was asked by a French TV crew after the screening of Patrice Chereau's *Intimacy.*

"Why not?" I said. "The American public spends billions of dollars on pornography, and the sex scenes here are not pornographic." Yet they do involve full frontal nudity. So the movie will be released either unrated or with the dreaded NC-17, and will not play in most American cities—or states, for that matter.

The whole matter will be interpreted in terms of the movie's sexual content. And yet—here is the crucial point—will anything useful be said about the style, approach, purpose, and message of the sex?

Intimacy, a film in English by a French director, stars Mark Rylance and Kerry Fox as a man and woman in their late thirties who meet for anonymous sex on Wednesdays. Eventually he grows curious about her, follows her, and discovers she is an actress with a husband (Timothy Spall) and young son. She teaches drama classes, and is appearing in *The Glass Menagerie* in a small London pub venue (the door from the main bar helpfully says, "Toilets and Theater").

This is not a review, and so I won't go into detail about the plot. I want to talk about the sex. My inspiration is a conversation I had with Kristina Nordstrom, who runs the Women Filmmakers Symposium in Los Angeles. We found ourselves eating sandwiches on the steps of the Eccles Center between screenings.

"Of course, no woman would be attracted to sex like that," she said.

"Why not?"

"The sex in the movie all involves the bottom of the ninth inning. A woman would be turned off by a man who doesn't spend time being tender and sweet, and showing that he cares for her. There's no foreplay. She walks in, they rip off each other's clothes, and a few seconds later they're in a frenzy. Any woman would know that this movie was directed by a man."

I knew after seeing *Intimacy* that I had problems with it, including the way the lover approaches the husband, and the way the husband reacts. I also had admiration for it, especially the nonsexual aspects of the performances by Rylance (from *Angels and Insects*) and Fox (from *Shallow Grave*). The movie is based on stories by Hanif Kureishi, a London writer.

What Nordstrom said helped the movie click into focus: Yes, the sex is wrong. It will be described as frank, fearless, bold, and risk taking, etc. There will be a controversy over whether the film should get the NC-17 rating or go out unrated. But all of this will miss the point. The movie is not about sex. It is about *how* it is about sex.

Consider *An Affair of Love,* a French film by Frederic Fonteyne released in 2000. It was about a man and a woman who meet once a week to do something, we don't know what, behind closed doors. They met through personal ads.

Apparently their mutual interest is so rare that they are surprised to find a partner who shares it. We never find out what it is, and we never see what happens behind the closed doors.

Both *Intimacy* and *An Affair of Love* deal with what happens when the anonymity breaks down; when the man and woman become individuals to each other and grow curious about more than the sessions they share. *An Affair of Love* handles this in a poignant way: Shyness and fear set in. *Intimacy* handles it with the man tracking the woman, meeting her husband, and insolently dropping transparent hints about what the woman does on Wednesdays. The film is in sympathy with this behavior, which is the social equivalent of the man's sexual style. The husband is set up as a clueless dupe, and the typecasting of Timothy Spall makes it impossible for him to be anything else.

Ninety-nine percent of the sex in movies is useless as information, as inspiration, as provocation. It is simply behavior recorded on film. Occasionally a film comes along that has something to say about sex. We may agree or not. It is our job as moviegoers to make up our own minds. The sad thing is, our society makes that difficult by marginalizing the most useful of such films. Our society is saturated with sex, but it is juvenile, denatured, and thoughtless. We love swimsuit issues and music videos with lots of T&A. We allow pornography so long as it is kept in its ghetto. But when a film comes along that wants to *say* something about sex, we cower and flee. And the MPAA and the movie industry make sure it is marginalized.

"Will the American public accept the sex scenes in this movie?"

That isn't the problem, I should have said. The American public will not *see* the sex scenes in this movie. And even seeing them is only the first step. Then you have to think about them. Even if you disapprove, as Nordstrom does, the film has served a purpose. Even this article *about* it has been more useful than all the millions of words and pictures devoted to the lives of Anna Nicole Smith, Pamela Anderson, and the other founts of American sexual inspiration.

Waking Life

January 24, 2001—One day at Sundance, three wonderful films:

Richard Linklater's *Waking Life* is a technical

breakthrough and an amazing film, both in the same package. It charts the odyssey of a hero seeking the truth about dreams and reality, and uses an artistic approach that takes live-action footage and transforms it into breathtaking animation.

There was a standing ovation after the Tuesday night premiere here, from a savvy audience that had already been briefed about the film's technical side by articles in *Wired* and *Res* magazines. What they were perhaps not ready for was how good the film was, entirely apart from its animation wizardry.

Linklater is the Austin-based filmmaker who is fascinated by big questions and answers. His *Before Sunrise* had Julie Delpy and Ethan Hawke as two strangers who meet on a train and wander around Vienna, Austria, for a long night of philosophy and flirtation. His first film, *Slacker,* jumped from one set of characters to another, never doubling back as it eavesdropped on conversations all over Austin.

Now here is *Waking Life,* with Wiley Wiggins (or his animated avatar) arriving in town and finding himself launched, through bizarre events, into a series of conversations with people who speak profoundly but engagingly on life, death, free will, existentialism, dreams, and the nature of reality (Hawke and Delpy even turn up to continue their conversation).

All the scenes were shot live-action and then transformed into shimmering, magical, seductive animation. Tommy Pallotta and Bob Sabiston, two Austin computer animation wizards who have made films of their own, led a team of sixty artists, each one assigned to a different character, as they used Sabiston's RotoShop software to transform reality into graphic artistry.

It was not lost on the Sundance audience, which contained many indie filmmakers with more ideas than money, that this gorgeous film was made with handheld digital cameras, and the animation was done on Macintosh computers, not expensive workstations. *Waking Life* points the way for independents to play in the same league as major Hollywood animators.

* * *

Todd Field's *In the Bedroom* is a deep, moving, perfectly observed, heartbreaking film, one of the great accomplishments unveiled at this year's festival. As it opens, we meet a couple in love (Marisa Tomei and Nick Stahl). She is a mother of two, in the process of divorcing her abusive husband. He is a college student, headed for graduate school. His parents (Sissy Spacek and Tom Wilkinson) are worried about the age difference and the effect on their son's college plans, although in their understated Maine way they like her as a person.

Events happen which challenge the parents in painful and fundamental ways. Field and his cowriter, Robert Festinger, do not force these events into a conventional plot, but wait, listen, and exercise enormous empathy. And Wilkinson and Spacek are transcendent in the way they humanize two difficult, stubborn, angry people. Tomei, too, gets her best serious role, with its moments of tenderness and truth, and foreboding.

Todd Field, at thirty-six an accomplished actor *(Eyes Wide Shut, Twister, Radio Days),* here shows he is a real director—not someone who felt like making a film, but one with a genuine gift and a clear vision about the story he wants to tell and the way he wants to tell it.

* * *

Tony Bui's *Three Seasons* swept the 1999 Sundance festival, winning the Grand Jury Prize, the audience award, and the cinematography award. It told three interlinked stories about Vietnam, and was the first American-produced feature shot in that country since the war.

Now his brother, Timothy Linh Bui, is here with *Green Dragon,* a story set in the relocation camp at Camp Pendleton, California, where thousands of displaced Vietnamese were temporarily housed in Quonset huts until "sponsors" could be found to help them relocate in America. Strands of several stories are followed, involving the pain of separation, homesickness, political tensions, and a feeling of betrayal by Vietnamese who trusted American promises.

Don Duong stars as a Vietnamese who helps run the camp with the American officer in charge (Patrick Swayze); Forest Whitaker has an affecting role as a cook who enlists a little boy in helping him paint a mural of a dragon. The movie continues the chronicle that the Buis are creating about Vietnamese-Americans.

Hedwig, Etc.

January 26, 2001—A jilted transsexual, a city priest, a rock musician, a man with no memory, a Jewish anti-Semite, and a headless chicken.

Six movies ranging from good to great. After two more days at the Sundance Film Festival, I review my notes.

Hedwig and the Angry Inch looks likely to be one of the commercial hits launched at Sundance this year. It's a weird and lovable musical about an East German who has a sex change operation to pose as an American GI's bride. The operation is botched, the marriage ends in divorce, and Hedwig and her band tour an American restaurant chain where they sometimes have to sing from behind the salad bar.

John Cameron Mitchell, an engaging, androgynous actor who becomes electrified when he sings, stars as Hedwig, and also directed. He collaborated on the original New York and Los Angeles stage play with composer/musician Stephen Trask and many other members of the movie's cast, including Miriam Shor, who plays Hedwig's second husband. The plot hinges on the devastation Hedwig feels when she befriends a young man (Michael Pitt) who later steals all her songs and becomes a rock star.

The plot is like *Rocky Horror* meets *Beyond the Valley of the Dolls,* with elements of *Cabaret* and Fassbinder. The music is terrific. Despite its gender confusion and frankness about sex, the movie has a certain innocence, and Hedwig is like an opera heroine who keeps on singing as her life collapses around her. The movie has generated a lot of excitement here, and rolls out nationally from New Line.

* * *

At the other end of every conceivable scale is Eugene Martin's contemplative, profound *Diary of a City Priest.* David Morse stars in a quiet, absorbing performance as a hardworking inner-city priest who does his best to meet the spiritual and physical demands of his job, but is drowning in more problems than he can solve. The hungry come to his door, the despairing to his confessional, and when well-meaning suburbanites give him an "almost new" car, his first thought is: How long will this last in my neighborhood?

Martin said before the screening that his hero is Robert Bresson, the introspective French filmmaker whose *Diary of a Country Priest* this film obliquely resembles. Watching it, I was aware of how rarely we see true spirituality in practice. We get a lot of "religious" films that are basically

sectarian propaganda, but hardly ever a movie that seriously considers the struggle of a man trying to lead a good and useful life—a man quietly trying to be a saint.

* * *

A different kind of spiritual struggle takes place in Henry Bean's *The Believer,* which has stirred enormous controversy here. Ryan Gosling stars, in one of the best performances of the festival, as a virulent anti-Semite, very bright, who is adopted by an American fascist group—and then even they grow wary of his extremism.

Flashbacks tell the hidden story: This young man was born and raised Jewish, and engaged in protracted and articulate arguments with his teachers in religion classes. His basic argument is with God, whom he feels is an egotistical bully. His anti-Semitism is partly self-hatred, partly madness, partly just the stubbornness of a bright kid who cannot stand to lose an argument.

No one quarrels with the power or artistry of the film, but *The Believer* inspired many conversations about its content; the protagonist is articulate and unrelenting as he speaks against Jews, and because he is Jewish himself (unlike, say, Ed Norton's character in *American X*), some feared the film could do more harm than good.

* * *

Memento has been a buzz-champ since the early days of Sundance; I caught up with it and found out why. Directed by Christopher Nolan, it stars Guy Pearce *(L.A. Confidential)* as a man determined to avenge the murder of his wife. The twist: He has had short-term memory loss ever since the murder and can hold thoughts for only a few minutes. So he resorts to memos, maps, even tattoos on his body, to help him keep track of his progress. Carrie-Anne Moss plays a woman who wants to help him (he sometimes thinks), and Joe Pantoliano is either for him or against him, depending on which memo he reads. This is a movie so deviously constructed it makes *The Usual Suspects* look like Hitchcock. Imagine *Groundhog Day* recycling ten times an hour.

* * *

Kim Dickens gives a brave and strong performance in Allison Anders's *Things Behind the Sun,* starring as a self-destructive rock musician who after being raped in early adolescence has spiraled into booze and bad sex. Gabriel Mann plays a rock journalist who arrives to interview her; his secret is that the rapist was his brother. Don Cheadle is her manager, protector, and sad sometime lover; he cares for her, hopelessly. There's raw honesty here, bared nerves, and resolution that is not soppy or sappy but elevates to a kind of poetry of reconciliation.

* * *

Mark Lewis is the *Cane Toads* man. If you saw that weird and hilarious documentary, about how Australia was infested by toads whose skin turned out to be hallucinogenic, you know that *The Natural History of the Chicken* is no ordinary chicken movie. Lewis finds a woman in West Palm Beach who coddles her rare chicken like a member of the family, others who know their chickens by name, and one family that dreams of paying off the farm after their chicken continues to live and thrive after having its head cut off. There are also the property owners whose lives become impossible after a neighbor starts raising 100 roosters. "I hate to sound ethnocentric," says one tight-lipped neighbor, "but you know you're a redneck if you're raising roosters for cockfighting."

The Winners

January 29, 2001—*The Believer*, a controversial film about a Jewish anti-Semite, won the Grand Jury Prize as best dramatic film at the twentieth Sundance Film Festival here Saturday night. *Southern Comfort*, about an extended family of transsexuals in rural Georgia, won the Grand Jury Prize for documentaries.

The selection of *The Believer* was a surprising and not particularly popular choice; louder applause greeted the Audience Award winner for most popular feature, *Hedwig and the Angry Inch*, a transvestite rock musical, and the audience also cheered prizes for *Memento* and *In the Bedroom*.

On the other hand, *The Believer* is the kind of film that inspires admiration, opposition, and debate more than cheers. The film, written and directed by Henry Bean, stars Ryan Gosling in a powerful performance as a young Jewish skinhead who grew up in angry debates with his religion teachers, and became convinced God is an egotistical bully. Concealing his Jewish identity, he commits hate crimes and muggings,

and is an articulate spokesman for anti-Semitic beliefs at meetings of a fascist organization— whose leaders are embarrassed by his fervor, believing anti-Semitism is passé.

Bean said after the ceremony that his film is based on the true story of a Jewish anti-Semite from two decades ago, "and is also inspired by my own love and hate for my religion."

Two films with gay themes were double winners. John Cameron Mitchell's *Hedwig and the Angry Inch*, which he starred in and directed, won not only the Audience Award but also the jury prize for best direction. And *Scout's Honor*, directed by Tom Shepard, shared the Audience Award for documentaries and the Playboy Foundation's Freedom of Expression Award. It deals with a fight joined by two heterosexuals, one twelve, the other seventy, against the anti-gay policies of the Boy Scouts. The Audience Award for docs was a tie; also honored was *Dogtown and Z-Boys*, directed by Stacy Peralta, about a tightly knit group of young skateboarders in Santa Monica, and Peralta become another double winner by taking home the Directing Award in the doc category.

The Audience Award for world cinema went to *The Road Home*, by the Chinese director Zhang Yimou. It stars Zhang Ziyi, from the current hit *Crouching Tiger, Hidden Dragon*, who prepares to return her father's coffin to his native village.

A special jury prize went to Tom Wilkinson and Sissy Spacek for their acting in *In the Bedroom*, the story of a marriage tested by tragedy. In the doc section, a special jury prize went to *Children Underground*, by Edet Belzberg, about homeless small children living in a Bucharest subway station.

The Excellence in Cinematography award went, in the doc section, to legendary filmmaker Albert Maysles, for *Lalee's Kin: The Legacy of Cotton*, and in the feature section to Giles Nuttgens, for his work in *The Deep End*, which stars Tilda Swinton as a mother whose attempts to protect her child involve her in danger. The Maysles film is about a Mississippi Delta family struggling out of poverty.

The Waldo Salt Screenwriting Award was given to Christopher Nolan for *Memento*; he also directed it.

A special jury award went to *Coffin Joe*, a

documentary about "the most banned man in Brazil," horror filmmaker Jose Mojica Marins. The sixty-five-year-old filmmaker was present to accept, sporting his trademark long fingernails.

The award for *Southern Comfort* led to a dramatic grouping onstage, when director Kate Davis was joined by Lola Cola, a male-to-female transsexual whose partner, a female-to-male transsexual named Robert Eads, died after being refused surgery for ovarian cancer. Also onstage were Maxwell Anderson and Cori Anderson, another transsexual couple.

Some partygoers at the postawards bash expressed surprise that *The Believer* won, since it falls far outside the politically correct spectrum on anti-Semitism. It is not an anti-Semitic film, but its hero voices his opinions more or less unchallenged, and his personal fate is not necessarily a reply to those views. Bean said ambiguity, confusion, contradiction, and paradox are at the heart of his film.

Two of the winners have been snapped up by major indie distributors. *In the Bedroom* has been purchased by Miramax, and *The Deep End* by Fox Searchlight—although after that deal was signed, Miramax honcho Harvey Weinstein reportedly called with his own bid, and was said to be trying to obtain the rights from Fox.

Waking Life, the sensational animated film by Richard Linklater which combines philosophical ideas with magical images, was not eligible because it played outside the competition.

Sundance audiences headed home Sunday after a festival that was generally agreed to be the best in recent years. They were not looking forward to next year, when the Winter Olympics come to Park City. Sundance will be held a week earlier, but many rooms are already booked by Olympic advance forces, and it's said many festival events may be moved to Salt Lake City, thirty miles down the hill.

Final Wrap-Up

January 29, 2001—This was an especially satisfying Sundance Film Festival. Day after day, clicking off three to four screenings, I became heartened by the good health of independent films. Of course, thanks to the dumbed-down distribution system and bookers with blinders, some of the films I liked most may never play in some cities (or states). But at least they exist, and thank God for cable and video stores.

I was blindsided by the Grand Jury Prize for *The Believer,* the film about the Jewish anti-Semite; I didn't see it coming. I'm not sure what writer-director Henry Bean's message was (and his postaward comments about his "love and hate for my religion" were little help), and I was surprised that the jury passed over the majestic depth and confidence of Todd Field's *In the Bedroom*—or, if they wanted to go for "edgier" work, Christopher Nolan's *Memento.*

Edgy was the favorite buzzword at Sundance this year. It seemed to refer to a visual style that called attention to itself, but some of the films that ventured closest to the edge were masterful in their control. *In the Bedroom* is an example: Tom Wilkinson and Sissy Spacek, who got special jury awards for their acting, were as good as actors can be, showing us a marriage that works and then breaks down after a tragedy, and how a wounded silence grows between two people who loved each other.

Memento deserved its screenwriting award for Nolan, whose story is the most daring exercise in concentric circles since *Usual Suspects.* Guy Pearce stars as a man who tries to avenge the murder of his wife even though he suffers from short-term memory loss, and can remember things for only a few minutes at a time. The last line is classic: "Now, where was I?"

Kate Davis's winning documentary *Southern Comfort* focuses on two rural Georgia couples that both consist of male-to-female and female-to-male transsexuals. You'd expect such a doc to be set in San Francisco, not in the land of pickup trucks, mobile homes, outdoor barbecues, rifles, Marlboros, and beer in long-necked bottles. Robert Eads, once named Barbara, is the hero of the piece: a chain-smoking, bearded transsexual who dies of ovarian cancer after no doctor in the area will agree to treatment ("my other patients would be embarrassed").

No more challenging and delightful film was shown than *Waking Life,* by Richard Linklater, about the odyssey of a hero seeking for the meaning of life and dreams. Its metaphysical and scientific discussions hold up as ideas *and* entertainment, and the animation underlines the content and makes it sparkle. The film is exuberant with its own skill. Linklater had another film in the festival, *Tape,* a three-hander with Ethan Hawke, Robert Sean Leonard, and Uma Thurman locked in a motel room and rehashing a ten-year-old trauma. It was like an indie digital homage to Fassbinder's *Bitter Tears of Petra von Kant.*

Tilda Swinton creates a masterful performance in *The Deep End,* as a mother who wants to protect her seventeen-year-old son from a thirty-year-old predator, and finds herself concealing a murder, warding off a blackmail attempt, and dealing with a family health crisis. The most fascinating thread in the film involves the way one of two blackmailers develops sympathy for her plight.

Allison Anders's *Things Behind the Sun* lingers in my memory. Kim Dickens gives a courageous performance as a rock singer who drinks and seeks sexual trouble because of a childhood rape. One of the most beautiful things about the film is the way her wound is healed by a visit to the house where the rape took place—where the Latino woman who now lives there instinctively senses that she needs a friend, and is one.

Lili Taylor plays a stubborn housewife who turns her life completely around in Bob Gosse's *Julie Johnson.* She throws out her domineering husband, signs up for night school classes, discovers a flair for higher math, and is amazed when she and her best friend (Courtney Love) become lovers. But the film isn't simply intellectual rags to riches; there's a third act that explores the deeper implications of the woman's need to change and the limitations of her friend.

Piper Perabo is another actress who was electrifying here, in Lea Pool's *Lost and Delirious.* This was one of the most purely absorbing and entertaining films of the festival, the story of three boarding school girls, with Perabo as a heroine in love with grand, passionate gestures. Her energy and exuberance lifted the film into the realm of courageous, heedless romance.

Why do so many Korean films explore the far reaches of sex and violence? I heard on CNN today that sex is being taught for the first time in South Korean secondary schools. Judging by films like Ki Duk Kim's *The Isle,* they don't have much to learn. This is a film with sideways connections to *Woman in the Dunes,* the Japanese classic. It's about a mute woman who runs a sort of floating motel; small fishing huts stand on barges that float in a lake, and she and her boat are the only connection to shore. She develops a passion for one of the fishermen, a shady character, and their relationship escalates into sadomasochism so unexpected and extreme that even a hardened Sundance audience was, yes, shocked.

Cannes Film Festival
Jean-Luc Godard Returns to Cannes Film Festival

Cannes, France, May 10, 2001—Forty-one years after his *Breathless* swept in the French New Wave and helped herald the modern era of filmmaking, Jean-Luc Godard is back at the Cannes Film Festival this year with a new film. The onetime "enfant terrible" is seventy-one now, and the 1960s film generation that marched under his banner is old and gray, but his very presence inspires a certain trembling in the air as the fifty-forth Cannes festival opens. The giants are back in town.

Last year's festival was generally thought to be below par. This year's is anticipated with intense excitement by the moviegoers gathering on the French Riviera. Of course, until we see the movies we won't know for sure, but on the basis of track records, preview screenings, and buzz, important films are about to be seen.

One of the key events of the festival will be among the first: the unveiling of the restored and expanded director's cut of Francis Ford Coppola's *Apocalypse Now.* I was at Cannes for the film's world premiere in 1979, and that was one of the greatest moviegoing experiences of my life. We did not suspect then that *Apocalypse Now* was not the beginning of something but the end—that wildly ambitious epic films would become rare as Hollywood skewed toward no-brainer, block-booked, multiplex Friday-night specials. *Apocalypse Now Redux* includes scenes shot but not used in the original cut, including a visit to a French plantation in Vietnam and an encounter with *Playboy* playmates.

The festival's opening night film is traditionally French, but this year tradition falls, and Australian director Baz Luhrmann will be here with *Moulin Rouge,* starring Nicole Kidman and Ewan McGregor. Maybe the French loophole is that it's set in Paris, in 1902. It's like a combination of a nineteenth-century opera, a 1950s Hollywood musical, and a 2001 music video, all drenched in lush colors with exuberant melodrama and wall-to-wall music. I'll write more tomorrow.

The directors whose films are in the Official Selection may not be familiar to casual moviegoers, but serious cineasts vibrate just from the list of names: not only Godard, but the veterans Shohei Imamura, Manoel de Oliveira, Jacques Rivette, Nanni Moretti, Ermanno Olmi, and Raoul Ruiz. Leading world filmmakers like Hirokazu Kore-Eda from Japan, Mohsen Makhmalbaf from Iran, Alexander Sokurov from Russia, and Hsiao-hsien Hou from Taiwan. And cutting-edge Americans like Sean Penn, David Lynch, Wayne Wang, and the Coen brothers (plus Coppola's son Roman, whose *CQ* is in the competition only three years after his daughter Sofia's *The Virgin Suicides* played here). Also honored by being selected: *Shrek,* the much-anticipated new animated feature from DreamWorks.

Some 3,000 critics and reporters will make their morning pilgrimages to the Palais des Cinema for the early press screening, and double back for the second official selection in the afternoon. In the evening, black-tie audiences will promenade up the famous red-carpeted stairs while breathless French fashion commentators review the gowns. And somehow for ten days we will all forget that *The Mummy Returns* grossed $70.1 million in its opening weekend, and will line up eagerly to see the latest work by directors like de Oliveira, who is ninety-three and hardly ever finds that he needs to use special effects.

It wouldn't be Cannes without rumors, and the hottest is that Quentin Tarantino, whose *Pulp Fiction* won the Golden Palm in 1994, will unveil the surprise premiere of a Western he filmed secretly in Mexico this year. That's the possibility being floated by the Web's well-connected Harry Knowles. Is it possible for Tarantino to make a film in secret? I say no. I hope yes.

In addition to the Official Selection, there are major sidebar programs at Cannes, including the Critics' Week, the Director's Fortnight, and Un Certain Regard; only in France would it

be a compliment to hold a film in "a certain regard." The most eagerly awaited selection here is *Storytelling,* by Todd Solondz, whose *Happiness* was a sensation here three years ago. Jennifer Jason Leigh and Alan Cumming are presenting *The Anniversary Party,* which they cowrote and codirected and costar in, along with Gwyneth Paltrow, Kevin Kline, Jennifer Beals, Jane Adams, and Phoebe Cates, in a story that rips the lid off Beverly Hills and slams it down on the characters. The U.S. indie director Hal Hartley, another Cannes favorite, is here with *No Such Thing,* starring Sarah Polley as a journalist who meets an Icelandic monster, and likes it. Growling, fearsome, beloved Abel Ferrara has the opening night film in Un Certain Regard, *R-Xmas,* of which next to nothing is known—not even its cast.

Among the Yank movies in the Director's Fortnight: Scott McGehee and David Siegel's *The Deep End,* a thriller starring Tilda Swinton as a mother protecting her son (I loved it at Sundance); Ethan Hawke's *Chelsea Walls,* set in New York's fabled, seedy Chelsea Hotel and starring his wife, Uma Thurman; and Arliss Howard's *Big Bad Love,* starring his wife, Debra Winger, with Cannes regular Rosanna Arquette.

How many of these will I see? All of them, I hope. I'll be filing more or less daily reports from France—the only place on Earth where you wait longer for the check than you wait for the meal.

Moulin Rouge

May 10, 2001—"With money like this, think what could be done with the Chicago Film Festival!" declared a Cannes Film Festival visitor on Wednesday night. I think the visitor was me. I was not referring to the cost of the Cannes festival, but to the cost of the party after the opening night premiere of *Moulin Rouge.* There has never been a Cannes party like it—and take it from me, I've seen plenty, including the bash on Roman Polanski's pirate ship.

Nicole Kidman reigned like the queen of cinema over a celebration inside a series of vast circus tents that suggested the Moulin Rouge nightclub in Paris. With authentically worn floorboards, lush velvet walls, revolving stages, and disco balls, this was an extravaganza to awe the most decadent festivalgoer. Chefs in toques labored over freshly made omelets and crepes, waiters circled with champagne, and when the cancan girls bounced onto the center stage, even Rupert Murdoch, lord of all media, stood on his chair for a better look.

Murdoch owns 20th Century–Fox, which produced the movie and paid for this largess. To have your film open the Cannes festival is an honor so unimaginably grand that normally only French films are considered adequate. *Moulin Rouge* tells a story set entirely in Paris in 1900—but every foot of the film was shot in Murdoch's native Australia, and both Kidman, the star, and Baz Luhrmann, the director, are Aussies. This is like Canada winning the Olympics.

"We have been working on this party for months!" Christian Garcon Funnily Enough shouted in my ear. He advised me to grab a table in the center performance area, although there would be action everywhere else too. "I am from Los Angeles," he said, "although I am a Frenchman, funnily enough. My company plans parties like this." And what is your name? I shouted. "Christian Garcon Funnily Enough," he shouted back, handing me a card that read "Christian Garcon." Ask a friend who speaks French to explain this paragraph, which contains a joke, funnily enough.

The movie struck just the right note to kick off this fifty-fourth festival. The postscreening buzz, confirmed by most of the Thursday morning reviews, was that *Moulin Rouge* hit a home run. The hyperkinetic musical tells the story of a doomed romance between a Parisian dance-hall girl (Kidman) and a starving writer (Ewan McGregor), who must compete for her charms with a rich and venal duke (Richard Roxburgh). John Leguizamo, using artificial braces to look shorter, plays the dwarfish artist Toulouse Lautrec, and Jim Broadbent is Zidler, the impresario who knows the dancer's sad secret.

The movie is a tour of a century of style. It has the luridly melodramatic plot of a nineteenth-century opera, the lush color and art direction of a 1950s Hollywood musical, and the frenetic energy of a brand-new music video. On Thursday morning, I motored out to the Hotel du Cap d'Antibes, the expensively inconvenient home of the biggest stars at the festival, to interview the principals. They were arrayed in a series of cabanas staggering down a hillside toward the sea, and as I marched from one to another I learned:

From Baz Luhrmann, director of the film: "We develop a new cinematic language every ten years, and today, when every kid has a digital camera and is familiar with the conventions of naturalism, it is time to return to the grander styles of the cinema's past."

From Ewan McGregor, who plays the starving writer: It was important that, in the middle of the whirlwind, his character and Kidman's remain focused on the truth of their relationship.

From John Leguizamo, who plays Toulouse Lautrec: "I walked on artificial legs that were fitted to my knees, to make me four feet, eleven inches tall, exactly his height. Because Toulouse was born to first cousins, there were a lot of things wrong with him. His tongue was very thick, and he had a high-pitched lisp. His legs were very short. He was, however, unusually well endowed, which is why his nickname was The Tripod."

An interview with Nicole Kidman was scheduled for after lunch. At the hotel's Eden Roc Restaurant, where Miramax's Harvey Weinstein was table-hopping, there was much talk about whether "Middle America" would go for the movie. Also some gloom.

"Do they know what a musical is?" asked one studio rep.

"Do they know where Paris is?" asked another.

"Do they know what Paris is?" asked a third.

My answer to all three questions: They will not have found out from the movies you have been making for them.

After lunch, a seance with the tall and regal Nicole Kidman. "What a party that was," she said. "We partied all night."

You look fresh and relaxed, I said.

"I am an actress."

Soon I was back at my beloved Hotel Splendid. For the price of lunch at the du Cap one can stay for a week at the Splendid, breakfast included. The hotel, alas, is not in a serene location, but located directly across the street from the beach with the giant party tents. On the stairs I ran into Ken Turan, film critic of the *Los Angeles Times*.

"Grumble, grumble," he said.

Are you grumbling?

"Do you know how late that Moulin Rouge

party lasted last night?" he asked. "I'll tell you. It lasted until 4 A.M."

You were there until the end?

"I never left my room."

It was loud, we agreed, but not as loud as three years ago, when an Austin Powers billboard was erected directly beneath our windows, and broadcast the cackles of a sneering villain twenty-four hours a day. It takes men of steel to cover the festival. You can't just sit around on your tripod.

Apocalypse Now

May 11, 2001—They were giants who walked the earth in those days. To see *Apocalypse Now* once again is to measure how ambition has faltered in these latter days of Hollywood. This is a big, confident, exuberant, passionate movie, a reminder that movies need not merely confirm our petty tastes and pander to our most immediate desires, but can make our imaginations sing.

Francis Ford Coppola's epic about Vietnam, the 1979 grand prize winner at Cannes, returned here Friday in a restored version with fifty-three additional minutes of footage. Even its "director's cut" makes no small claims: Instead of the five or ten additional minutes a lesser film might offer, this one adds half the running time of an ordinary movie. The visual and sound restoration, masterminded by Walter Murch, the Oscar-winning sound designer of the 1979 version, is breathtaking. During the helicopter assault on a village, when a mad colonel (Robert Duvall) blasts Wagner from loudspeakers, the effect is the same as it was in 1979—literally spine-tingling.

It is appropriate that Coppola bring *Apocalypse Now Redux*, as it is now called, back here to Cannes in this lengthened version. It was here twenty-two years ago that he stirred up controversy and possibly cost himself a solo Palm d'Or (his film had to share the grand prize with Volker Schlondorff's minor *The Tin Drum*). Coppola described the film as a "work in progress," and famously called the Cannes premiere an "out-of-town tryout," inspiring Andrew Sarris's immortal question, "Where's town?" He also unwisely shared his doubts about the ending of the film, cueing a herd of film critics to wonder if the ending worked, without knowing what he actually meant by "the ending." (He was referring to decisions about the closing

titles; they thought he meant the entire Marlon Brando sequence.)

The movie was shot on location in the Philippines under unimaginably difficult conditions; the filming has been documented in George Hickenlooper and Fax Bahr's *Hearts of Darkness: A Filmmaker's Apocalypse,* a harrowing record of how close Coppola and his team came to physical and emotional collapse.

Many scenes were shot that didn't make the original 150-minute version. In *Redux,* there are three major restorations and a few minor ones. The most important new scene is an extended visit by the hero, Captain Willard (Martin Sheen), to a French plantation remaining from the days when Vietnam was French Indochina. The plantation is guarded by a private army and occupied by the remnants of the families that have owned it for generations. The dinner-table conversation includes a lot of background on Vietnam's history, from the colonial point of view, and then there's a sexual interlude involving Willard and the widow of one of the French.

Two other scenes are briefer. One involves more Marlon Brando dialogue during the last act of the movie. The other involves a second encounter with the *Playboy* bunnies who are touring Vietnam to boost troop morale. In a famous scene in the original film, their USO show turns into a riot and they have to be airlifted away from rampaging troops. (GIs clinging to the helicopter's skids provide an eerie echo of newsreel shots of the evacuation of the U.S. Embassy in Saigon.) In the new scenes, the bunnies' helicopter is grounded in the jungle, having run out of gas, and Willard and his boat crew encounter them during their long upriver journey to seek the mysterious Colonel Kurtz (Marlon Brando). Trading petrol for favors, they engage in dalliance inside a helicopter being pelted with rain (the scene was shot during a monsoon). An ironic point is made when a member of Willard's crew, infatuated with a centerfold, is more interested in the woman reproducing her exact magazine pose than in relating to her as an actual person.

We are, of course, fascinated to see this new footage, but I am not sure its addition is an improvement to the original *Apocalypse Now.* Maybe that's because I'm so familiar with the great film in its original form. My feeling is that the additional fifty-three minutes delays the movement of the film's central story arc; that we are distracted, especially by the plantation scene, from the inexorable upriver progress toward Kurtz. As for the second *Playboy* scene, it simply doesn't work dramatically. It feels like a scene where Coppola never got the footage or performances he wanted, or never defined what function the scene was supposed to play.

The Brando footage, on the other hand, only deepens a great performance. When the film was originally released, some critics sniped at the way Coppola shot Brando in such deep shadow, but it seemed right to me. The movie is based on Joseph Conrad's *Heart of Darkness,* about a journey into the Congo to seek a Mr. Kurtz who has established his own kingdom in the jungle, and Brando's looming, half-seen presence strikes an eerie chord: He has the presence to make the journey seem important.

Another performance at the end of the movie also grows after twenty-two years. That's Dennis Hopper's drugged freelance photographer, who has become part of Kurtz's compound, and sings his praises in hallucinatory free-association. In 1979, this character inspired distracting echoes of Hopper's pothead motorcyclist in *Easy Rider;* now it can be seen more clearly as right for this movie.

Apocalypse Now was never intended as a realistic Vietnam picture (like Oliver Stone's *Platoon*), but as an allegory, in which the American nation advanced into the Vietnam quagmire and found an opponent who was more determined and had more to win or lose than we did. Brando tells a story about children who are inoculated by Americans and then have their inoculated limbs hacked off by the Viet Cong; he calls that cruelty "brilliant," because it shows how deep the Viet Cong's determination runs, and how implacable it is.

Apocalypse Now Redux will open in American theaters in August, twenty-two years to the day from its original theatrical premiere. It is one of the few movies that must be seen by anyone who takes the cinema seriously. The new footage will be of intense interest to those who love the film. I hope, however, that on the home video version the original cut is preserved as the "real" film, since the additional fifty-three minutes essentially create a new film with less tension and focus. The nice thing about DVDs is that we can have it both ways.

Speaking English

May 14, 2001—The woman hopes to slip illegally into Afghanistan from Iran to save her sister's life. She is helped along the way by a sympathetic doctor. The film is by one of the great Iranian directors. You are already imagining the subtitles at the bottom of the screen, but no: The woman has been living in Canada, speaks English, and narrates the journey into a tape recorder. And the doctor is a black American; they speak English together.

There was a time when English was limited to films from English-speaking countries, but no more. At this year's Cannes Film Festival, more than ever, English is the international language. "Accent is on English," says the headline in the Cannes edition of the *Hollywood Reporter.* It is one of six daily trade journals published here in English; another is in French, and one is bilingual.

The *Reporter* article notes a trend toward English-language coproductions even from non-English countries. In Germany last year, 23 percent of all movies were filmed in English. In France, 13 percent. The film I described above is the searing, heartbreaking *Qandahar,* by Mohsen Makhmalbaf, a leader of the Iranian cinema, which has taken world festivals and markets by storm. It's a French-Iranian coproduction, but most of the dialogue is in English.

That isn't just a ploy to crack the American market, which is so provincial that foreign films of any description are avoided. It's a play for the world market, for audiences not only in England, Canada, and Australia, but also in markets including Scandinavia, Germany, Holland, France, Hong Kong, India and South Africa, where English is spoken by most educated filmgoers.

Is something being lost in the translation? Is it reasonable that a film set in Iran and Afghanistan should be in English? Soon after seeing *Qandahar,* I was debating this point with Gerson and Uma da Cunha, from Bombay. She is a producer, casting director, and subtitler; he is a poet, actor, and political activist. They said I was wrong to think of English as the possession of English-speaking countries.

"It is quite plausible that an Afghan, raised in Canada, would try to return home on a family mission, and that she would find an African-American along the way," Gerson de Cunha said. In the movie, the black American is presented as an idealist who originally went to Afghanistan to join in the war against the Russians; now he is disillusioned with both sides, especially with the fearsome fundamentalist Taliban regime, and tries merely to help people he comes into contact with.

English was once seen as a colonial language, Gerson told me, but has now escaped the possession of the former colonial powers and is making its own way around the world. "Without English," he said, "there would be no way for the intelligentsia in India to communicate with one another. It is the major reason India has been so successful in Internet technology."

We were speaking, of course, in English. I also unthinkingly used English yesterday in discussing films with Michel Simon, the leading French critic, and Anant Singh, the leading distributor from South Africa, and with every single retail, restaurant, or hotel clerk I encountered. I can read French subtitles and newspapers, but have no confidence in speaking it.

"The people you are speaking to do not think that way," Uma told me, because they use English the same way you do. The da Cunhas told me of a meeting they had just come from, where the Germans and Italians had only English as a common language.

Then again, at a dinner for the Independent Film Channel, I found myself talking with Catherine Verret, vice chairman of Unifrance, the French film giant, and she switched into French. Funny, I thought: She doesn't realize she's no longer speaking English, which has been our common language for twenty-five years. "English?" I gently prompted her. "Mais non!" she said, and continued in French. The scary thing was, I could even understand what she was saying, which translated as: "It is time for you to speak French!" I couldn't agree with her more.

Vanity Fair

May 14, 2001—The Mercedes taxi whirs through the night along the old beach road to Antibes, past the sleeping villages and sudden flashes of light from bars and bouillabaisse joints, and deposits us at the Hotel du Cap d'Antibes. We are attending the *Vanity Fair* party at the Cannes Film Festival. We walk down a cool marble staircase and emerge on a high, wide deck over-

looking the sea. Luxury yachts are anchored a few hundred yards offshore. Across the bay the lights of Cannes beckon.

"You almost got crushed this afternoon," says Hugh Hefner, who is the first person I see. He introduces me to Stephanie, one of his seven dates. While taking a photo at his birthday party earlier in the day, I'd been caught in a human wave of paparazzi.

"Everybody in the back started to push," I say.

"If they'd pushed any harder, it would have been sodomy," he observes.

We see Liv Ullmann, who is Madame la President of the Cannes jury this year. We discuss theories about *Faithless*, her film based on a screenplay by Ingmar Bergman. I say my original theory was insane, but after a second viewing I understand the film better. She thinks my first theory might have something going for it.

My wife, Chaz, and I make our way through the gathering. It is not a throng. There is space for guests to mingle on the broad expanse. Here is Bob Shaye, president of New Line Pictures. He has invested $170 million in *Lord of the Rings*, which will come out at Christmas. "Everyone thinks we've bet the company," he says, "but after selling the international rights, the video, and the aftermarkets, we're 85 percent covered. What kills me is the cost of sequels. *Rush Hour* cost us $32 million. It's a hit, so we make a sequel. The sequel costs $92 million."

Jackie Chan materializes. He seems like the happiest man on Earth. I extend my hand at the exact moment that he performs a dramatic bow, and my thumb pokes him in the eye. He staggers back shouting, "Aie! Aie! Aie!" and cartwheeling his arms, just like in his movies. "Is not serious wound," he says. "I have just finish new movie." I ask what it is called. *Rush Hour 2*, he smiles.

Here is Kirk Kerkorian, who buys and sells movie studios and Las Vegas casinos. He is eighty-five, the father of a two-year-old. We talk about the rating system. He is youthful, alert, witty. We drift over to Helga Stephenson, former director of the Toronto Film Festival, and Catherine Verret of Unifrance Films. "Kirk Kerkorian is incredibly sexy," they whisper, checking him out. Helga says she has a friend who has the hots for him: "I said, 'Yeah, sure, he's a billionaire.' My friend says, 'Trust me, honey, it isn't the money.'"

Here is a richer man than Kerkorian: Paul Allen, the Microsoft billionaire. He is a movie nut. We talk about the classic movie palace he renovated and operates in Seattle. "Once a year we show something in Cinerama," he says. "We found the projectors in South America and refurbished them. We have the three big screens, everything." I think of the Mel Brooks line: "It's good to be the king."

Jean-Claude Van Damme drifts by in dark glasses. Barry Diller is with his wife, Diane von Furstenberg. Here is the actor Ethan Hawke. He directed *Chelsea Walls*, playing in the Director's Fortnight. I admire him because you can't catch him making easy choices for quick money.

"You are thirty-one and have been acting for sixteen years, and have never killed anyone in a movie," I say. "That's quite an achievement."

"Well, of course, I killed two people in *Hamlet*," he says, "but how was I supposed to know it was Polonius in the closet?"

Waiters circulate with silver trays groaning with hors d'oeuvres. There are four bars. Here is Graydon Carter of *Vanity Fair*, whose party on Oscar night is the most coveted ticket in town. Now he is conquering Cannes. What he offers the guests at his parties is—the other guests. Jugglers circulate, passing out glowing plastic balls, which you can use to illuminate the steps down to the pool.

Lawrence Bender materializes. He is the legendary producer who made his fame with Quentin Tarantino's *Pulp Fiction*. Tomorrow he will be honored as producer of the year at a ceremony presided over by Gilles Jacob, the president of the Cannes festival. He is worried about his speech. I advise him: "Say that you speak little French, and so you decided to quote Groucho Marx when he was honored in 1972 by the festival."

"What did Groucho say?"

"He bowed to Gilles Jacob and said, 'Voulez-vous couchez avec moi?'"

"Which means . . ."

"'Will you sleep with me?' What about the rumor that Tarantino has made a film in secret and will premiere it at the festival?" This has been reported by Harry Knowles on his Ain't It Cool Website, and has everyone in a lather.

"Fat chance," he says. "Assuming Quentin could make a film in secret, how would he do the secret postproduction? Where would he find the secret labs and sound-mixing studios?"

Joel and Ethan Coen are standing in the shadow of a pillar. Their film *The Man Who Wasn't There* will premiere tomorrow. The press screening is at 8:30 A.M. "I don't know if I like the idea of the critics seeing the film that early in the morning," says Joel. I tell him the sun is shining, the birds are singing, the dew is still on the tables in the cafés. "Yeah, and it's already 1 A.M.," he says, looking at me as if I should be in bed.

Here is Jack Valenti. He calls everybody by name. "Roger," he says, "what are we going to do about this bill being introduced by Joe Lieberman and Hillary Clinton, which would make it against the law to advertise R-rated movies to people under seventeen?"

I agree it is among the more harebrained pieces of legislation ever conceived.

"The Super Bowl has 87 percent viewers over seventeen," he says. "If we advertise a movie on the Super Bowl and the other 13 percent see the ad, do we go to jail? The only show we'll be able to advertise on is Jim Lehrer."

"There's always C-SPAN," I say.

"I'm gonna use that," Valenti chuckles.

"The insanity," I said, "is that they are applying legal penalties based on a voluntary rating system that has no standing in the law."

"Exactly. The irony is, if we didn't rate the movies, they wouldn't *have* the R rating to enforce their law."

"Now you're talking," I said.

Reviews at Midpoint

May 14, 2001—The best film at Cannes so far this year was made in 1979. That's the melancholy conclusion of *Variety* and the *Hollywood Reporter*, the daily trade journals printed at the festival—and I didn't have to read the papers to figure that out.

At midpoint in the fifty-fourth Cannes there are a few good films in the official competition and a lot of disappointments. No film, in or out of the competition, has emerged as a sensational discovery, the way past festivals produced *Pulp Fiction, The Piano*—or *Apocalypse Now*.

The opening night film, Baz Luhrmann's

Moulin Rouge, collected some revisionist sneers after its mostly glowing original reviews, but at least it represents the same kind of exuberance and passion that Francis Ford Coppola brought to his Vietnam epic in 1979. It's a wildly artificial showbiz extravaganza, with operatic emotions and lush visuals shot on boldly artificial sets, and you can feel the love that went into it.

There is passion of a more somber tone in *Qandahar,* by the forty-four-year-old Iranian director Mohsen Makhmalbaf, whose twenty-year-old daughter, Samira, won the jury prize here last year with *Blackboards.* His film tells the story of Nafas (Niloufar Pazira), an Afghan who has long lived in Canada, and now tries to sneak back into Afghanistan from Iran, to convince her sister not to commit suicide.

Afghanistan cowers beneath the cruel Taliban regime, which makes the journey hazardous; no woman can be seen by a man not in her family, so Nafas pays a man to let her pose as his third wife and ride into Afghanistan on his cart. The land has seen an epidemic of amputations because of land mines; the sister lost both of her legs, and there is a harrowing scene where men with one leg race across the desert on crutches to compete for artificial limbs dropped by a UN helicopter.

Another favorite in the festival's first half was *No Man's Land,* by Danis Tanovic of Bosnia, who tells a rich, comic parable of his region's troubles in the story of a patrol trapped between two sides in the Bosnian-Serbian war. The situation centers around a man who has fallen on a land mine and cannot be moved without being killed. Building on irony and paradox, Tanovic has made a modern *Catch-22.*

I also enjoyed the weird, mad intensity of *The Pianist,* a film by Michael Haneke of Austria, starring Isabelle Huppert as a virginal music professor who explodes into a sadomasochistic relationship with one of her students. Having lived for years under the thumb of her domineering mother and nurtured her feelings in secret, she gives herself over with abandon to the young man, who is not quite ready for her willingness, or her needs.

The Anniversary Party, an American film codirected by Jennifer Jason Leigh and Alan Cumming, played in the sidebar Un Certain Regard section and shamed many entries in the Official Selection. The story of a long night of truth-telling and marital meltdown among rich friends and neighbors in Beverly Hills, it contains surprisingly powerful performances by such as Jennifer Beals, John C. Reilly, Kevin Kline, Phoebe Cates, and the directors.

Among other high-profile American entries, *Shrek,* the delightful animated feature from DreamWorks, generated great enthusiasm from audiences, who were surprised at the way it layers its story with elements of satire.

But *The Man Who Wasn't There,* the new film from the Coen brothers, got a more mixed reception. It's a black-and-white *film noir* in the 1940s style, starring Billy Bob Thornton as a barber who attempts to get rich quick with a dry-cleaning scheme by blackmailing the boss of his wife (Frances McDormand). "A ninety-minute film that plays for two hours," Michel Simon, the influential French critic, sniffed to me after the screening. Yes, but I want to see it again, because I almost always find that a Coen brothers film cannot be appreciated in a single viewing.

Todd Solondz, whose *Happiness* stirred up Cannes three years ago, is back with *Storytelling,* another excursion into the psyches of sad, lonely, twisted people. Many of my colleagues decided Solondz has made one too many trips to the well, but I want to see it again, because in the arid wasteland of schlock Friday openings, most movies don't go to the well at all. One viewing was probably enough, however, for *Chelsea Walls,* by Ethan Hawke, telling interlocking stories in New York's fabled Chelsea Hotel and never generating much interest in or between them.

Another disappointment was *Distance,* by the gifted young Japanese director Hirokazu Kore-Eda, whose *Maborosi* and *After Life* are wonderful films. Here he tells the story of a group of survivors and relatives of a cult that attempted to poison Tokyo's drinking water; they gather for a morose pilgrimage, in a story so unfocused, mumbling, and low-key it's difficult to identify the characters and impossible to care about them.

Perhaps the most roundly disliked of the official entries so far is *Roberto Succo,* by Cedric Kahn of France, who follows the adventures of an Italian serial killer as he murders his way through the French countryside. The film links one violent episode with another but develops no tension, no psychological depth, no point of view; it's a series of ugly, brutal crimes by a repulsive killer, who finds a series of extraordinarily stupid women to ride along with him. The cops in the movie look like college students who rented their uniforms.

The best may still be to come. Playing tomorrow is Sean Penn's *The Pledge*, with one of Jack Nicholson's best performances. It was greeted with indifference by a lot of American critics when it opened at year's end. I admired it then, admire it more now, expect the Europeans to hail it. And there are new works in the week ahead by some of the giants: Olmi, David Lynch, Godard, Rivette, Moretti, Imamura. The best may still be ahead.

Doug the Recycler

May 16, 2001—Faithful readers will recall that when the home video revolution was new, I interviewed a man at Cannes who sold movies by the pound. His motto: "Back up your car and I'll load up the trunk."

His formula was to advertise in *Variety* for "finished movies," buy them for peanuts, give them new titles and commission dramatic artwork for the covers. He confessed that the movies inside had nothing to do with the titles or the artwork.

"Don't the customers complain?" I asked.

"They get the movie they *think* they're buying, *plus* the one I sell them," he explained. "Two for the price of one!"

It is now the twenty-first century, and home video consumers are no longer taken in by bait-and-switch tactics. Meet Doug Schwab. He makes real movies with real stars at rock-bottom prices, and distributes them direct to video. When he was fifteen he went to work in the first video store in New Orleans. Now he is thirty-seven and did $12 million last year. There are producers here with names you would recognize who didn't do $12 million last year.

I met Doug because he was sitting at the next table at La Pizza, down by the old yacht harbor. For as long as anyone can remember, it has been run by Adrien Passigli, the Danny DeVito of pizza. He makes the best pizza in Cannes. I know because a local guy sitting on the other side told me so. You always meet the people who are sitting at the next table in France, because they are closer than the people who are

sitting at your table in America. If you can't find your napkin, just wipe your mouth on the next guy's elbow.

"We have a great new tactic," Doug was telling me. "We take the formula of a classic movie and remake it as an urban picture. For example, remember *The Apartment*, with Jack Lemmon? Terrific picture. We remade it as *The Crib*. This young guy in the music business has all these older executives who want a place to take their ladies. You remember the story. Now we're making *Keeping It Real*, which is a remake of *It Happened One Night*, starring the rap singer Kurupt."

Doug used to be a buyer for Blockbuster. Then he met Tanya York, a nineteen-year-old Jamaican who had made her own movie and was trying to sell it to Blockbuster. It was called *Return to Frogtown*. She was trying so hard to sell it, Doug said, that "she pulled at my heartstrings." He decided she had a winning formula with direct-to-video cheapies, and went into business with her. "The company is called York-Maverick Ltd.," he said. "She's president of York and I'm president of Maverick. She didn't want to work for me, and vice versa."

The Y-M catalog now numbers about 400 titles, Schwab said. "A lot of them star rap singers. It's a funny thing. The music stars all want to be in movies, and the movie stars all want to be in music. We have Brian Hooks in *Nothing to Lose*. It cost less than $500,000, and is No. 4 on the direct-to-video charts."

The key to his success, he said, is the artwork on the cover of his videos. "We give good art," he explained. "You walk into Best Buy, you see fifty copies of *Gladiator* and four copies of our new DVD. So the art has to sell it. You take *Out Kold*, our new title starring Ice T, Tiny Lister Jr., and Kool Mo Dee. You look at the artwork on that box, you'll think it's a theatrical film that'll be nominated for awards."

Schwab says he uses young directors. "We like them to have one movie under their belt, so they know how to work with a small budget." I said he sounded like the Roger Corman of his time. Corman was the legendary 1960s exploitation producer who gave breaks to young directors like Francis Coppola and Martin Scorsese. "I would be honored to be compared to Corman," Schwab said. "Our films may not stand up to his, but in sheer volume we're getting closer."

Big Bad Distributors

May 17, 2001—"Shoot the distributors." That was Alan Cumming's helpful suggestion as eight American directors debated the sorry state of independent film distribution here Wednesday, at the annual American Directors Panel at the Variety Pavilion. The big studios monopolize thousands of multiplex screens with movies aimed at teenage boys, and more inventive films for adults get shoved aside.

Also suggested: Establish chains of indie boutique theaters that would use digital projection to show movies beamed down by satellite. But the cost of film and prints is a minor part of overhead, director Wayne Wang argued, when compared to the costs of marketing and advertising. The panelists were depressed about gridlock at the box office, where the lowest common denominator rules, and more challenging movies are brushed aside by distributors who care more about volume than quality.

I've been emceeing this panel for ten years or so, and never sensed such sadness on the part of directors who have made good films and now find it difficult to get them to American audiences.

"We were helped because we shot with a cast of close friends, and their names will help get us bookings," said Jennifer Jason Leigh, who cowrote and codirected *The Anniversary Party* with Cumming. Being able to advertise Gwyneth Paltrow will mean a lot.

But David Siegel and Scott McGehee, cowriters and codirectors of *The Deep End*, said an obsession with the star system can be inhibiting to directors. Their thriller, about a mother who attempts to protect her son by hiding a corpse, stars Tilda Swinton in a powerful performance. They wanted the British actress from the first, they said, but had to facedown studios who offered shortlists of established stars and wouldn't finance the script without them. "We finally raised the money from among friends and acquaintances," Siegel said. (On the other hand, their use of the Croatian-American star Goran Visnjic, who replaced George Clooney on *E.R.*, won't hurt the box office.)

Wang, whose *The Center of the Earth* is about a Vegas weekend between a dot-com millionaire and a stripper, said shooting on digital video saved him time and money. *The Anniversary Party* was also shot on video, but panelists agreed video had a different look than film and the savings weren't significant compared to ad and marketing costs. Hostility to digital in the audience was loud: One audience member asked the panelists to make a vow to stick to film, and another kept repeating, "Read McLuhan!" after arguing that video and film had different effects on the human brain.

Interesting, that a panel of eight "American" directors included four born overseas. Wang was born in Hong Kong, Cumming is from Scotland, Amos Kollek *(Queenie in Love)* was born in Israel, and Michel Gondry *(Human Nature)* in France. The other member of the panel was Arliss Howard, whose *Big Bad Love* stars his wife, Debra Winger.

Also in Cannes, legendary French director Jean-Luc Godard screened his touching *Eulogy for Love*, predicted it would not be seen in America except in "a few small theaters," attacked mainstream Hollywood cinema as pointless, said Steven Spielberg was "not a very good director," and offered to provide a shot-by-shot deconstruction of one of Spielberg's films. That would make a fascinating DVD commentary track!

Also on Wednesday, American maverick David Lynch unreeled his strange new *noir* dreamfantasy, *Mulholland Drive*, and told me the French backing of the film made it possible, since American studios insisted (here we go again) on a shortlist of stars and meddled with screenplays.

Reverand Jesse Jackson, in town to open the festival's Agora sidebar program of films from Africa and by black filmmakers, called for more black-oriented films at Cannes. Agora itself is helping to improve the situation, with twelve features this year from such countries as the United States, Egypt, England, Guinea, Burkina Faso, Mali, Tunisia, and the Ivory Coast. The chances of these films opening soon in a U.S. theater near you? Near zero.

On the other hand, as long as American audiences sleepwalk into the films with the loudest and most expensive ad campaigns, can you blame distributors for devoting every screen in sight to *The Mummy Returns*? They clean up in the short run by catering to teenagers, but make their multiplexes into no-go zones for adult filmgoers by ignoring their tastes. Why can't the U.S. movie distribution system offer more selection and variety?

To nobody's amazement, the panel ended without a solution. There are a lot of good films here at Cannes, but the shame is, in many cases, you have to come to Cannes to see them.

More Cannes

May 17, 2001—The old men still have the right stuff. Jean-Luc Godard at seventy and Jacques Rivette at seventy-three, two founders of the French New Wave, have returned in triumph to Cannes with their new films—for Rivette, the first in ten years. And three younger rebels also scored, as the festival bounced back from its early doldrums. Sean Penn's *The Pledge* and David Lynch's *Mulholland Drive* were cheered, and the Italian director Nanni Moretti is a front-runner for a major prize after the premiere of his *The Son's Room*.

The surprise among these films was *Va Savoir* (roughly *Who Knows?*), by Rivette, whose films tend to be long and brittle. This one clocked at 150 minutes, but was a supple delight, a farce played in low key with romance and flirtation in an Italian theater troupe visiting Paris. The leading lady, now living with her director, encounters her former lover; the director sparks love from the daughter of a book collector; the former lover's current lover is seduced by the half-brother of the daughter, and around and around.

One expects Rivette to be a little austere, but here a smile plays at the corners of his mouth; romantic triangles grow into quadrangles, and everything is finally settled on the stage of the Pirandello play the troupe is producing. Developments look gloomy, even tragic, and then the sun comes out in a series of coincidences; you'd never expect Rivette to remind you of the benevolent Eric Rohmer, most hopeful of French directors, but here he actually does.

Godard, whose *Breathless, My Life to Live, Masculine-Feminine,* and *Weekend* were banner carriers of the New Wave in the 1960s, grew obscure in a series of experimental recent video productions, but came to Cannes this year with *Eloge de L'Amour,* which many loved and everyone at least understood. It was like the old days, as critics pushed, shoved, and elbowed their way into the screening.

Godard begins with the story of three couples (young, adult, old) and then spins off into flashbacks and conversations involving his usual preoccupations: America, politics, mass communication, capitalism as the enemy of spontaneity. The characters spice their conversation with so many references we seem to be in Godard's Familiar Quotations; he uses black-and-white, saturated color, intertitles, double and triple exposure, dyes, stop-motion, speed-up, and slow-down, in a movie that finally seems to ask: Has it been worthwhile for him to spend his life making movies that are largely ignored by audiences who prefer Steven Spielberg?

At one point you can feel his pain as he has a character say, "Mrs. Schindler was never paid; she's living in poverty in Argentina." Even if true, it's irrelevant, since Mrs. Schindler, after all, was not a source of the Spielberg film, and Spielberg gave away most of his profits to fund the Holocaust Memory Project. But if the charge is unfair, Godard's angst is real, and the movie feels like a bittersweet summation of one of the key careers in modern cinema.

Nanni Moretti's *The Son's Room,* which could win the Palme d'Or, seems destined for commercial success because it tells a deeply touching story in a bright, perceptive way; one is reminded of *Kramer vs. Kramer* or *Ordinary People.* The movie stars Moretti as a therapist, happily married with two teenage children, whose life is shaken by an unexpected tragedy. Many of Moretti's earlier films, such as *Caro Diario* and *April,* have placed him resolutely in the foreground; here he steps back into a family unit and tells a story of surprising power. Hardened critics were snuffling.

David Lynch's *Mulholland Drive* surprised me by how much I enjoyed it, since I am not one of his habitual fans. It's a Los Angeles dream sequence in the style of a *film noir,* involving two newcomers—sunny blonde Naomi Watts and intriguing brunette Laura Elena Harring—in a story where one Hitchcockian situation segues into another with nightmare logic. Does the film lose its way at the end, as the characters seem to cut loose from their identities, or is that just the restlessness before waking? This one I look forward to seeing again.

I reviewed Sean Penn's *The Pledge* when it opened in January. It has only grown in stature with more familiarity. Jack Nicholson gives one of his best performances as a good cop, retired, who becomes obsessed with a case, is surprised by late love, and lets these two commitments become tragically entangled.

And then for pure fun, after all of this art high and low, there's *Tears of the Black Tiger,* a lurid and exuberant Western from Thailand. It's playing in the marketplace, where crowds line up early to grab seats. The movie has audacious fun with blatantly artificial sets and effects, wildly overdone color and sound schemes, and a plot that shames mere melodrama. Miramax has picked it up for U.S. distribution.

AMFAR Benefit

May 18, 2001—Harvey Weinstein promised to dance in a thong if the AMFAR charity auction raised $2 million here Thursday night. The rich and the famous, who wined and dined in a big tent with Dame Elizabeth Taylor, wisely stopped just short of that milestone.

The AMFAR dinner, which raises money for the American Foundation for AIDS Research, is a star-spangled fixture of the Cannes festival. The tone of this year's evening was set by chairman and auctioneer Weinstein, the Miramax chief, who said he'd start the ball rolling by pledging $100,000.

He also donated 500 tickets to *The Producers,* the hottest show on Broadway, and they were hammered down for either $167,000 or $200,000; the tumult was so great it was hard to be sure.

Other hot items on the auction block: breakfast with Elizabeth Hurley ($12,000); Shirley Bassey sings "Goldfinger" just for you ($100,000, paid by Elizabeth Taylor); Mick Jagger's personal Fender Squier Stratocaster guitar (certified in person by Jerry Hall, $52,000); and a walk-on part for a child in *Spy Kids 2* ($26,000).

Buses and limos carted some 500 guests up to the little hill town above Cannes where Chef Roger Verge, his white mustache bristling with excitement, welcomed them to his famous Moulins du Mougin inn. The guests mingled in the garden, where models dressed in white feathers posed as living statues inside glass boxes.

I wandered into a debate involving the singer-songwriter Lisa Nunez, the artist Maggie Wachsberger, and the producer Jacqueline DeLaurentiis, who voiced their strong suspicion that some of the models were transvestites. Later who should I meet but Freddie Galfas, whose agency booked the models. "Genuine," he said. "One hundred percent women. You can take it from me."

It was a little awe inspiring standing in the garden with half a dozen stunningly beautiful women towering a foot above everyone else. The supermodel Adriana Karembeu was regal in white. Naomi Campbell was slinky in an outfit that prudently concealed her navel (a few years ago, Weinstein and arms dealer Adnan Khashoggi got into a bidding war for her navel ring, even though she insisted it was not for sale). Tallest of the models was the elegant Michelle Norkett, from Des Plaines, Illinois. She is pals with famous artist Peter Beard, who insisted that I photograph him kissing her foot. People are not stuck up at AMFAR.

Reporter's Notebook

May 21, 2001—Pages from a Cannes diary:

Euzhan Palcy strikes me as proof that great directors can come from anywhere—but they must know they are directors and trust that they are great. As a ten-year-old schoolgirl on the Caribbean island of Martinique, she made her own movies at night in her room, casting shadow-plays on the wall. By the age of seventeen, she had produced short documentaries for the local TV station and recorded albums of songs and stories for children.

She went to high school in Paris, returned to French-speaking Martinique, made an hour-long documentary for local television, won a scholarship to the Sorbonne, and returned home to direct *Sugar Cane Alley* (1984), the story of a poor child growing up in a shack by the cane fields who is befriended by adults who notice his intelligence, and who wins a scholarship that will free him from a life of manual labor.

Talking with Palcy one afternoon in the South African Pavilion at Cannes, I remembered that I rated *Sugar Cane Alley* four stars—and there were four more stars in 1989 for her *A Dry White Season,* which won Marlon Brando an Oscar nomination for his performance as a crusty liberal lawyer in the time of apartheid.

In the pavilion, Palcy had just been given the Sojourner Truth Award, the annual prize of Agora, the organization that presents films from Africa during the festival. But why, I asked her, have I seen no features from her since 1989? You missed them, she says: *Simeon* (1992) was a musical fairy tale set in Martinique. Then she made a documentary about the Martinique poet and philosopher Aime Cesaire, and in 1999 directed *Ruby Bridges,* a film about a six-year-old girl in a newly desegregated school, for *The Wonderful World of Disney.* She has just finished *The Killing Yard,* starring Alan Alda and Morris Chestnut, about the 1971 Attica prison uprising; it will play on Showtime in September.

"I could have worked more," she said. "After all, I have my bills to pay. But I will not make a film just to be making a film. If my heart is not in it, my head will not follow." She despairs, she said, of a Hollywood mentality that only wants to repeat proven formulas, starring a small group of A-list stars.

As for Cannes? "I came to do business and talk to people," she said. "In 1984, I submitted *Sugar Cane Alley,* and the festival told me it was not for them. I later discovered that they never even viewed it. I submitted it to Venice, and it won the Silver Lion, plus the best actress prize, and then won the Cesar, the national French award for best first film. When I made *A Dry White Season,* of course, they wanted it because of Brando. But I had no time for them."

* * *

The cash-only Hotel du Cap d'Antibes, the most expensive hotel in France, has perpetrated a new outrage.

This year, no evening drinks are being served in its famous lobby bar because the bar became too crowded and noisy. Even though one must theoretically be a hotel guest (or with a guest) to drink there, the bar mysteriously filled with hundreds of gate-crashers, many of them quite plausibly hookers.

The new policy was explained to me by Anant Singh, the South African producer.

"Now all evening drinking is down the hill at the hotel's Eden Roc," he said. "You pay admission to get in. It costs 1,000 francs ($200). For that, they give you three tickets, each good for a drink. You feel like someone at a school dance."

What about the hookers? Just as many as ever. They don't accept tickets.

Awards

May 21, 2001—The jury stunned but did not displease a black-tie audience here Sunday night, with the awards for the fifty-fourth Cannes Film Festival. It's not that the winners were unpopular, but that they were unexpected. Everyone predicted Nanni Moretti's *The Son's Room,* the story of an Italian family devastated by the death of a son, would win something— but not the Palme d'Or, or top prize. Everyone expected French legend Isabelle Huppert to win as best actress for her searing performance in *The Piano Teacher,* and she did—but not that the film would also win for best actor and take home the special jury prize.

There were hints of dissent on the jury when its president, Liv Ullmann, referred to passion and "even anger" in their discussions. I heard rumors that Billy Bob Thornton, the star of the Coen brothers' *The Man Who Wasn't There,* was asked to fly back for the ceremonies, and then waved off. It was whispered that the unexpected best actor award to Benoit Magimel for *The Piano Teacher* might show the influence of Mathieu Kassovitz, the fiery young French actor-director on the jury.

The director's award was shared equally by two Americans, David Lynch and Joel Coen, both former winners of the Palme d'Or (Coen for *Barton Fink* in 1991, Lynch for *Wild at Heart* in 1990). Lynch won for *Mulholland Drive,* a nightmarish *noir* about Hollywood crime and sex; Coen, working as always with his writer-producer brother Ethan, won with *The Man Who Wasn't There,* with Thornton as a barber whose cheating wife (Frances McDormand) inspires him to attempt a deadly scam.

The best screenplay award went to Danis Tanovic of Bosnia for *No Man's Land,* a darkly ironic film that takes place between Bosnian and Serbian lines in 1993 when soldiers from both sides are trapped together in a trench with an apparently dead man who has fallen on a land mine. He turns out to be alive after all; if he moves, they all die.

In a festival with many strong entries from Asia, there was only one prize for that part of the world, a technical award to famed sound engineer Tuu Duu-Chih, who worked on Hsiao-Hsien Hou's *Millennium Mambo,* about a disco girl trapped in a spiral of drugs and degradation. The Camera d'Or winner, for the best first film, was *Atanarjuat,* by Zacharias Kunuk, an Inuit film made in the Arctic Circle.

Festival president Gilles Jacob strongly advises the jury that the awards should be passed around. The three top prizes for *The Piano Teacher* raised eyebrows in a competition where the French giants Jean-Luc Godard and Jacques Rivette were passed over despite the success of their films. It was also surprising that two of the festival's best-received films, *Qandahar* by Iran's Mohsen Makhmalbaf, about a woman trying to sneak into Afghanistan to save her sister, and *The Officer's Ward* by France's Francois Dupeyron, about a man horribly scarred in World War I, went home empty-handed.

The Palme d'Or winner, Moretti's *The Son's Room*, is a tender, moving film that seems destined for popular success. He stars, as a father whose son's death ends a long period of serenity for his family, and generates painful guilt and second thoughts. *The Piano Teacher* stars Huppert as a virginal fortyish piano teacher whose young student (Magimel) boldly tries to seduce her and is overwhelmed by the passionate sadomasochistic volcano he uncovers.

Unlike the Academy Awards, which last for hours and hours and are punctuated by countless commercials, the Cannes award ceremony lasts about thirty minutes. The jury files onstage and sits to the right. The emcee (this year Charlotte Rampling) takes a podium to the left. There is no opening monologue. Famous presenters (this year including Hollywood stars Jodie Foster, Nick Nolte, Melanie Griffith, and Antonio Banderas) introduce each category, The emcee asks the jury president (Liv Ullmann) for the winner, and she announces it. Winners usually actually say something in their acceptance speeches, instead of reading a laundry list of thanks. Then the lights go out, and everybody watches a movie.

Questions for the Movie Answer Man

Accents

Q. I recently saw the movie *Quills* with Geoffrey Rush and noticed something that has bothered me with other films. Why do films set in France, like 1998's *Les Miserables,* have the actors speak in a British accent? Obviously, these characters would have spoken French so there would be no need for them to use a British accent. I understand that some of these actors are British or Australian but in *Les Miserables* and *Quills* American actors like Uma Thurman and Joaquin Phoenix use British accents. I think its kind of dumb to try and be so accurate with sets and costumes from a certain period in history but to so blatantly mess up the language by trying to make France more British.
—Jacob DeSomery, Marlboro, Massachusetts

A. It makes no logical sense at all, but it is an ancient Hollywood tradition that in English-language pictures Americans use an American accent and foreigners use British accents. There are exceptions, and sometimes French characters will have French accents, etc., but the rule is still often observed. In *Hannibal,* on the other hand, the Italians have Italian accents, perhaps because they are played by Italian actors who have shaky British accents.

A.I.

Q. Why do I not see Stanley Kubrick's name anywhere in the ad for Steven Spielberg's upcoming film *A.I. Artificial Intelligence*? Didn't Kubrick already write the screenplay for the movie, and was only waiting for technology to improve before he made it? I've heard rumors of Kubrick sending Spielberg pages and pages of story ideas for *A.I.,* so shouldn't he be given at least some credit for the film?
—Ken Berglund, Long Beach, California

A. Kubrick did not write the screenplay, although he worked long and hard in preparing the picture. The screen credits will be for a Spielberg screenplay, based on a screen story by Ian Watson and a story by Brian Aldiss. To emphasize Kubrick's name would be an unseemly use of his reputation, although it is likely Spielberg will reference him in some way, perhaps in a dedication. You are correct that Kubrick and Spielberg had long talks about the movie, and that Kubrick shelved it because he felt it needed special effects that were not available when he began preparing the project.

Q. Ain't It Cool News reports on a labyrinth of Web pages apparently connected to the upcoming Spielberg flick, *A.I. The Blair Witch Project* began the phenomena of pre-release Web strategies, but they have nothing on the multiple sites and stories that *A.I.* has brought to life. What do you make of a Web story which exists at such an extensive level?
—Dave Jaycock, Victoria, British Columbia

A. This is an intriguing publicity stunt. Ain't It Cool, Corona Coming Attractions, and many other popular fan sites have reported that in the movie's on-line trailer, the closing credits draw attention to Jeanine Salla. A Web search for her name leads to a labyrinth of sites from the twenty-second century, touching on aspects of artificial intelligence. Clues lead to phone numbers leading to other pages. Both AICN and Corona have links to the sites; the Yahoo Club "Cloudmaker" discusses them.

Q. You and your readers have complained that many trailers spoil the movie by telling too much of the story. Ad guys sometimes don't have respect for the film or for the viewers. This year, however, I am amazed by the advertising genius behind the *A.I.* campaign. The trailers are vague and mysterious, especially the early Internet ones. The Websites, phone numbers, and e-mails that you can access if you follow clues from the trailers are brilliant. They actually tease you and make you thirst for more.
—Jeff Hollander, Nevada City, California

A. My idea of a great campaign. Evoke the spirit of the movie instead of cannibalizing the good parts.

Q. I have noticed a shift in the marketing of the movie *A.I.* What started out as a media blitz promoting the movie as almost *E.T. II*— another loving, touching, sci-fi Spielberg masterpiece—now seems to play up the film as dark and portentious, with Spielberg now quick to point out that this was a Stanley Kubrick project that he picked up and finished off. What's your take on this?

—Don Money, Andover, Massachusetts

A. I think the revised approach is more accurate. This is not a children's movie and indeed contains many dark and disturbing images; it is closer to *A Clockwork Orange* than *E.T.*, although it has elements reminding me of both.

Q. There's a debate going on about the ending of *A.I.* (Spoiler Warning!). The question is whether the beings that David and Teddy encounter 2,000 years later are mechas or aliens, like out of Spielberg's *Close Encounters of the Third Kind*. My immediate reaction was that they were advanced mechas, and that the CE3K imagery was just Spielberg playing with our expectations of what aliens look like. There are plenty of clues in the film that they're mechas, and almost nothing that I saw suggests aliens, but I'm surprised by how many people thought they were aliens. So, who's right?

—Greg Dean Schmitz, Upcomingmovies.com

A. They're mechas, although they look uncannily like the aliens at the end of *Close Encounters*. Indeed, Tony Wang of Calgary, Alberta, writes: "Why would Spielberg make the mechas at the end so similar to the aliens in *Close Encounters* as to cause most of us to miss the point at the end of the movie about machines? Very few people I know who saw the movie did not conclude that they were aliens." Spielberg adds another red herring by having them fabricate a familiar environment for his little hero David, to make it easier to study him. This is one of *A.I.*'s many homages to Stanley Kubrick, reminding us that the *2001* astronaut, named Dave, ended up in a bedroom and bath

apparently fabricated by aliens to make him feel comfortable.

Almost Famous

Q. I recently saw *Almost Famous* for the third time. I was wondering what Penny Lane was carrying in the tackle box in the first half of the film.

—Michael Ladowski, South Holland, Illinois

A. Cameron Crowe, the writer-director of the film, replies: "It's a fashion statement. It's a radical idea for a purse, dreamed up by a girl with a lot of style and a lot of makeup. Thanks for noticing it."

Amores Perros

Q. Everybody in Mexico is talking about the Oscar nomination for *Amores Perros*, which is the first production from this country in thirty-three years to be selected for that award. However, knowing the Academy and the hype machine behind *Crouching Tiger, Hidden Dragon,* I know its chances of winning are very slim. I was just wondering, how come *Crouching Tiger, Hidden Dragon* is nominated for Best Picture and Best Foreign Film; isn't that a bit of an unfair advantage?

—Patricio Lopez, Monterrey, Mexico

A. It may be a disadvantage, splitting the vote.

Q. In the Mexican Oscar nominee *Amores Perros* there's a disclaimer that "no animals were harmed in the making of this movie." I don't buy that for a minute. Are we supposed to believe that these dogs are just "acting" in the fight pit? Can dogs really be trained to just pretend, to such an extent?

—David Avalos, Chicago, Illinois

A. The film includes violent scenes in which fighting dogs are apparently maimed and killed. The American Humane Association has issued a statement saying it did not monitor the Mexican production, and the disclaimer "is unauthorized by AHA." However, the AHA's detailed review of the film describes a video submitted by the filmmakers which shows how the fight scenes were filmed. Trained security dogs "that played aggressively with one another" were used; their mouths were muzzled invisibly to prevent harm; makeup was used for blood, and tranquilizers were used to make the dogs appear dead. The AHA concludes: "There is no program of humane oversight for film in Mexico. Therefore, AHA appreciates the voluntary efforts of the Mexican trainers and handlers who have demonstrated a deep concern for the welfare of the animals in their care during the production. However, although the dogs were unharmed, tranquilization is not allowed under the AHA Guidelines. AHA believes that tranquilization of an animal is a risk that we do not recommend for the purposes of filmmaking. Also, AHA's Guidelines are not utilized in Mexico. For these reasons, AHA has rated the film 'Questionable.'"

Anime

Q. In a recent Answer Man response, you said, "I hope 'anime' isn't one of those terms like Kleenex that becomes generic. If it's Japanese it's anime, and if it's not Japanese, it's not." Actually, "anime" was originally the French word for "cartoon." The Japanese took the word because they liked it, and it eventually spread throughout Japanese culture. But in reality, anime and animation are interchangeable words, and if ownership of the word goes to anyone, it goes to the French. Weird, huh?

—Jonathan Cotleur, North Ridgeville, Ohio

A. I will grant the origin of the word to the French. But I do believe "anime" correctly refers, in English if not in French, to Japanese animation and no other.

Apostrophes

Q. On your TV show, Richard Roeper referred to *Bridget Jones-ses Diary*. I had been taught to form the possessive by adding an apostrophe, so that it sounds like *Bridget Jones' Diary*, without the added syllable. They may spell it " 's" but it should be spoken as though it was spelled correctly, or "s." Please blame my high school English grammar teacher, Mrs. Emily Midgette, deceased.

—Robert McKenzie, Nathalie, Virginia

A. The first rule in Strunk and White's *The Elements of Style* reads: "Form the possessive singular of nouns by adding 's." So "Jones's"

is the correct spelling. But how to pronounce it? I turned to an expert, Kaylie Jones, whose novel was made into the wonderful movie *A Soldier's Daughter Never Cries*. She responds: "The teacher was a little too exclusive with her grammar rules. Both are acceptable, although I prefer Jones' for speed and look. But the *New Yorker*, for example, prefers Jones's, and lists, in fact, *Bridget Jones's Diary* as the title. For pronunciation, definitely Jonzez. The other sounds absurd. So you and Roeper were right."

Autographs

Q. As a birthday present I received my mother-in-law's autograph collection which was compiled by a relative of hers in a silver store located in the Mexico City airport during the 1940s and 1950s. It includes names such as Errol Flynn, Orson Welles, Ann Miller, Paulette Godard, Joe Louis, Joe DiMaggio, and Cantinflas. Whenever I show it to anybody they claim it must be worth quite a bit. Is there a market for such a thing, or just sentimental value?

—Gerardo Valero, Mexico City, Mexico

A. Various kinds of DiMaggio signatures go for between $50 and $200. Ann Miller is closer to $10. Might be interesting to try selling the whole collection as one item on eBay.

Ben Hur

Q. I was recently watching the wonderful new DVD of *Ben Hur* and during the chariot race it looks as if a man is actually killed when run over by a chariot. It happens at the 24:00 minute mark of side B. According to the IMDB the only injury during the long filming of the race was a stuntman's cut chin. Are my eyes fooling me?

—J. S. McLain, Asbury Park, New Jersey

A. Richard Roeper, whose forthcoming book *Hollywood Urban Legends* deals with such matters, replies: "There is no evidence that anybody was killed during the making of the 1959 version of *Ben Hur*, but the rumor has been around for decades. It's definitely an urban legend. However, there is a general consensus that a stuntman was killed during the filming of the 1926 *Ben Hur*."

Beyond the Mat

Q. *Beyond the Mat* took a "behind the scenes" look at the world of professional wrestling. But watching it on DVD, I may have spotted two sections which suggest it may not be a real documentary. There is a section where a "former third-grade teacher" is described as moving away from teaching and on to wrestling. In the "Special Features" section of the DVD, the theatrical trailer shows the same person being asked "You gave up Wall Street for this?" to which he replies "Wall Street wasn't fun, wrestling is." It seems as if different versions were shot. Secondly, the section depicting Mick Foley's losing match to "The Rock" shows him seemingly receiving medical attention for a gash on the right side on the top of his head, and his family reacting to it. But on DVD, using pause and zoom, you can clearly see, when he is preparing for the match, someone rigging a prosthetic to his head in this exact spot and in a very brief frame you can see it is a fake gash of some kind. I don't know if this is a fake documentary, but odd things seem to be going on with this film.
—Steven Diaz, Venice, California

A. Barry Blaustein, the film's director, replies: "Believe me, *Beyond the Mat* is a 'genuine documentary.' Regarding the first question: Matt Hyson, the wrestler your reader asked about, was a third-grade teacher. He left teaching and went to work on Wall Street while pursing his dream to be a professional wrestler. As you may know, trailers are often done before the final cut of the film. When the trailer was edited, my cut of the film had mentioned both his previous professions. For the sake of timing and pacing, I chose just to mention Matt's teaching background in the final edit. Sorry for the confusion.

"I can also assure you the gash on Mick Foley's head is very real and not some kind of prosthetic. After all his years in the ring, the skin on Mick's forehead, like that of many wrestlers, is very tender and can bleed quite easily. The salve being tended to Mick's forehead was to take care of head injuries Mick had received in a previous match."

Black-and-White

Q. Bored on a Thursday evening, I decided to watch Van Sant's *Psycho* remake with the color turned off—and what an improvement! The film was far better. I turned on the color a few times throughout, and found it to look rather cheap. But when the black and white was on, the film—unnecessary as it was— was easily watchable.
—Leigh Emshey, Innisfail, Alberta

A. I've done that with films too, especially films that *want* to be b&w, like *Fargo*. Color often provides distracting emotional cues.

Blow

Q. The penultimate frame of *Blow* tells us that George Jung's daughter has never come to visit him in prison. Yet the credits list "Kristina Jung" in the cast, playing the part of "Clerk." She won't visit her father in jail, but has no qualms in appearing in a movie about him? What's up with that?
—Craig Avitabile, Milton, Massachusetts

A. A New Line rep says, yes, it is George Jung's daughter. She played a clerk but the scene was cut out. They decided to credit her anyway.

Bowdlerization

Q. I have run across a Website that edits movies for you. You send them a movie and they edit it to a "PG" equivalent—even movies like *Saving Private Ryan* and *Schindler's List*, using a computerized system that edits almost seamlessly. They are trying to convince movie studios to market different versions of movies—for example, PG or PG-13 versions of R-rated movies. What do you think of this idea? Personally I think it is an interesting idea, and as long as people have a choice to view whichever version they want I don't see a problem.
—Erik Goodwyn, Elizabethtown, Kentucky

A. Much the same reasoning was used by a man named Thomas Bowdler (1754–1825), who edited Shakespeare to take out all the parts that might offend, and has been immortalized in the word "bowdlerization." Good movies are works of art, not links of sausage. A PG-rated version of *Saving Private*

Ryan would not be *Saving Private Ryan* at all. My source indicates that before Bowdler gave his name to the process, edited versions of Shakespeare were known as "castrated." Of course, that is a word Bowdler would have frowned upon.

Q. I read about this Utah company called cleanflicks.com. You send in your film, which contains "questionable" material. They edit anything they find obscene. Language, nudity, drinking, smoking, etc. Of course this is done at a fee. What I find odd is, since the films are deemed obscene by their standards, why is it okay for them to view them in the editing process?
—D. R. Smith Jr., Bellfower, California

A. Apparently because the more dirty movies you see, the more morally superior you become to those you are protecting. I am planning to send them *See Spot Run*.

Q. I was musing over your indignation about objectionable scenes or language being removed from movies for viewers who request such. At a restaurant, am I obliged to eat everything served, even items which disagree with me? Or can I skip the clam chowder? If I may discriminate in those areas, why should I not have the option of selecting a movie in which the f-word has been excised eighty-three times? Will my understanding of the "art" somehow be diminished if I deprive myself of the whole experience?
—W. D. Grissom, Cabot, Arkansas

A. You don't have to order the chowder, but you can't go into the kitchen and remove spices from the chef's recipe. My theory is, either see the movie the director made, or don't. If you think as movies as a pastime, this may not seem important. If you think of them as an art, it is.

Cast Away

Q. Doesn't the Wilson character in the *Cast Away* picture strike you as the Mother of All Product Placements?
—David Garcia, San Antonio, Texas

A. No. Wilson is not named for the sporting goods company but for Tom Hanks's wife, Rita Wilson.

Q. In the movie *Cast Away*, Tom Hanks leaves on his assignment overseas before the plane crashes. When he says good-bye to Helen Hunt on the tarmac, they trade Christmas presents in his Jeep. He walks away and returns with a gold-wrapped box, which they are supposed to open together on New Year's Eve. The plane crashes, four years later he returns from the island, and she gives him his Jeep back. There was no mention of the little gold box or a possible engagement ring that might have been in the box. Was that scene filmed or edited out, and if it was filmed, might we see it on a future CD?
—Dom Najolia, Chicago, Illinois

A. If it did indeed contain an engagement ring, you'd suppose they'd both remember it. But a 20th Century–Fox rep says such a scene was never written in the script to begin with, so it was not filmed and edited, nor will it be on the DVD version.

Cell Phones

Q. I recently went to see *Crouching Tiger, Hidden Dragon* and was only able to enjoy about half of the movie because the cell phone of the guy sitting behind me rang loudly, and he proceeded to have a ten-minute conversation right there in the theater. At times like this I believe insensitivity in our society has become boundless.
—James Culver, Spokane, Washington

A. It has. So he will understand if you "spill" your soda over your shoulder into his lap. My friend Anant Singh, a leading exhibitor in South Africa, has installed electronic devices that block cell phones in his theaters. Why don't our theaters do the same?

Q. Re your item about cell phones in theaters: The Canadian government has recently announced plans to research legalizing signal jamming technology to block cellular phone signals in restaurants, theatres, libraries, or other locations. It's a shame when what's essentially a simple case of etiquette has to be enforced. Have the times become desperate enough to justify the extreme measures?
—Leigh Emshey, Vancouver, British Columbia

A. Yes. Cell phones make slaves of their

owners, who are powerless to avoid annoying innocent bystanders.

The Cell

Q. There is a ton of stuff on da 'net, especially on Ain't It Cool News, about how you've gone nuts for loving *The Cell,* such an "amoral, empty, detestable" film that it seems to be fashionable to hate. This is especially disturbing because *The Cell* is absolutely wonderful, the kind of visual storytelling that Hollywood *never* puts out, and a lot of film lovers seem bent on squelching further attempts at such creativity. Why are people refusing to look at *The Cell* like they look at other movies? Why oh why is there so much hate for this movie—and for those who love this movie?

—Sean Molloy, San Francisco, California

A. Great movies always inspire the most passion. When a movie really gets to you, you either go with it, or switch on the defense mechanisms. If you don't go with it, the more it gets to you, the angrier you become.

Q. In your review of *The Cell* you described the outfits worn by Jennifer Lopez and others while voyaging into the minds of patients as "virtual reality gear." I think the opposite was the case. The outfits were probably worn by the characters to completely desensitize them from the external world so that the therapy could not be interrupted. That's probably also why they were suspended in midair. During the therapy sessions the characters did not move their bodies at all. If they were wearing virtual reality gear their bodies, conceivably, would have been mimicking their movements.

—Jordan Potasky, Toronto, Ontario

A. You are quite right. Tarsem, the film's director, replies: "I'm afraid your reader hit it on the nose. In essence, the suits were to aid in the transition while going into someone's mind. Lacking an 'outer skin' (due to the suits) created an undisturbed journey. I incorporated the suspension to assist in a feeling of weightlessness."

Q. First off, let me helpfully inform you that you are insane for thinking *The Cell* is one of the best movies of the year. But I must

ask you, what was that cartoon that Jennifer Lopez was watching on television when she was trying to sleep? It looked really neat, and I'd like to see the whole thing.

—Kevin Fischer, Minneapolis, Minnesota

A. If you can name five movies so far this year that were more creative and original than *The Cell,* be my guest. A New Line spokesman says Lopez was watching the Japanese anime, *Fantastic Planet.*

Q. Re your query about how the serial killer got hooks on his back in *The Cell:* He could go to any body-modification shop to get piercings and have just about anything hanging from just about anywhere, no questions asked. Ask someone what a "Prince Albert" is.

—Barbara Ann White, Baltimore, Maryland

A. I did. I wish I hadn't.

Censorship

Q. I've noticed that some scenes in certain movies are being deleted or edited for video. *Beetlejuice* and *Basic Instinct* are two examples. In *Basic Instinct,* the infamous interrogation scene was blurred in the crucial area, and in *Beetlejuice,* my favorite line in the whole movie, "Nice (bleeping) model!" was deleted. Is there some kind of marking on the packaging alerting the consumer that the movie is an edited version?

—Roger J. Rialmo, Chicago, Illinois

A. Certain video chains silently edit some films to conform to their ideas of what is proper. Because they do not want to lose sales, they are not frank about this practice. If you get an edited film from a video store, my advice would be to stop patronizing that store.

Q. I rented *The Whole Nine Yards* the other day, and couldn't help but notice that some of Amanda Peet's nudity had been covered up by a conveniently placed railing. How long is the entertainment industry going to allow video stores to dictate what is acceptable? When I rent a video, I want to see exactly what the producers and director wanted me to see, not some CEO's version of morality!

—Kevin Ryan, Berwyn, Illinois

A. The silent bowdlerization of videos is a sneaky practice. When you rent a video that has been censored, inform the store manager that he has lost your business.

Q. Someone asked the Answer Man about a staircase railing in front of Amanda Peet's naked parts in *The Whole Nine Yards,* and you told him the movie had probably been bowdlerized. Actually, that railing was in the theatrical version too. That's just the way the movie was shot. Blaming the poor fellow's video store manager was mean.
—Binky Melnik, New York

A. But not as mean as telling the poor reader he only *thought* he saw the naughty bits.

Q. I recently rented *On the Edge* again, with Bruce Dern and Pam Grier, and found Grier's part had been completely deleted. Not just the sex and nudity scenes, but every reference to her character—in my opinion, a worthy plot point in Dern's development. Was this motivated by worries about interracial relationships? That would have disturbing implications.
—Steve Testori, Albuquerque, New Mexico

A. More likely, once they took out all the sex and nudity involving Grier, what was left made no sense and also had to go. I hope you demanded your money back and told the store they had lost your business.

Q. *Picnic at Hanging Rock* has always been one of my favorite films. I was astounded to discover that Blockbuster Video has tagged the DVD as an "adults only" rental due to its nonrating by the MPAA. Tell me something. Do the people who work at Blockbuster watch their own movies before deciding who can and can't check them out?
—Joe Schwind, Frederick, Maryland

A. *Picnic at Hanging Rock,* one of the titles in my series of Great Movies reviews, is far from an "adults only" movie. Blockbuster slaps the same "Youth-Restricted Viewing" sticker on any movie that is not rated, whether it's a wet T-shirt documentary or a children's film from Czechoslovakia. It's their way to score points as a family store without making the slightest effort to actu-

ally evaluate the films in question. More hypocrisy: It will not carry NC-17 movies, but it will carry the unrated "director's cuts" of R-rated movies—which sometimes must, by definition, be the NC-17 versions.

Q. Steve Ramos, a film critic for the *City-Beat* alternative weekly in Cincinnati, has been banned from the Esquire Theater for exposing the theater's decision to cut a scene out of Wayne Wang's *The Center of the World.* He's not allowed to even buy tickets at the theater, which has also removed *CityBeat* distribution racks, and canceled all advertising in the alternative weekly. Your comment?
—Greg Nelson, Chicago, Illinois

A. Gary Goldman, president of the company that owns the theater, has followed a wrong decision with a foolish one. It was illegal for his company to alter the film, and Ramos was doing his job by reporting it. Now the theater, which specializes in art films, is sending a message to its customers that it is provincial and small-minded, and has no respect for the films it shows or for the maturity of its customers. The film was released under an adults-only policy by Artisan; adults do not need to be protected by self-appointed censors.

Q. On the 4th of July, American Movie Classics ran a special called *Grilling with the Godfather.* All day long they played *The Godfather* and *The Godfather: Part II* along with a documentary special. While watching the films I noticed something. Each film has its share of graphic violence which was left almost intact. But all the swearing, nudity, and the sex scene between Sonny and his girl were censored and cut heavily. Why is it that sex, nudity, and swear words are viewed as more obscene than someone getting a bullet right between the eyes or a guy being shot right in the eye? Why bother showing *The Godfather* if it can't be enjoyed the way Coppola meant it to be?
—Woodrow Williams, Bolingbrook, Illinois

A. It seems especially imprudent of AMC since so many people know those movies virtually by heart. How many complaints would they have received for showing them uncut? My guess: Fewer than for censoring them.

Chocolat

Q. There is an uncanny resemblance between *Chocolat* and *Mary Poppins*. Both are set in conservative communities. The heroines have supernatural auras, and apply unconventional philosophies of sweetness— one with a "spoonful of sugar," the other with chocolate to better the community. Both carry carpetbags big enough to hold a warehouse. Both leading men are musically inclined jacks-of-all-trades. Both antagonists become more open-minded human beings. Both comic reliefs like hot drinks. There were many original films in the past few years, but it is rare that these are celebrated by the Academy. Is this the same fear of the unfamiliar manifested in *Chocolat*?

—Gabriel Noel

A. I knew that formula seemed familiar! Here's a letter from George Iacono of Northfield, Illinois: "I had this nagging feeling while watching *Chocolat,* and then it hit me: it was *Footloose* all over again! Freethinker breezes into stodgy, uptight town and dares to try to turn the folks on to a happier lifestyle, much to the chagrin of a curmudgeonly pillar of the community."

Citizen Kane

Q. Last semester my Journalism 101 class watched *Citizen Kane*. The professor asked for a show of hands of those who didn't like it. The majority of over 100 students raised their hands! I have peers who would rather watch junk movies like *Road Trip* or *Armageddon* before they would watch *2001: A Space Odyssey*! Why do people my age have an aversion to great movies made before they were born?

—Al Miller, Ames, Iowa

A. Everyone is a freshman at one point. A few grow out of it. Any journ student who doesn't love to watch *Citizen Kane* should switch majors.

Clueless

Q. I read on the Internet Movie Database that Britain's Plain English Campaign, "which hands out an annual Foot in Mouth award honoring the celebrity who makes the most baffling verbal statement during the previous year," picked Alicia Silverstone as this year's winner. She won for this comment about her movie *Clueless:* "I think that *Clueless* was very deep. I think it was deep in the way that it was very light. I think lightness has to come from a very deep place if it's true lightness." According to the article, John Lister, spokesman for the campaign, told the BBC: "That quote left us all scratching our heads." What do you think?

—Susan Lake, Urbana, Illinois

A. Silverstone's comment is perfectly clear anyone but a dunderheaded Plain Englishman, and deserves a space somewhere between "less is more" and "the incredible lightness of being." Her words describe the multilayered magic of Emma, the Jane Austen novel on which the movie is based. The British should be grateful for her efforts; she brings poetry and wit to a celebrity comment, and is not simply adding to the oversupply of dumb movie star quotes. John Lister should try Listerine for his scalp condition.

The Contender

Q. I was on an airplane recently and the in-flight movie was *The Contender*. I'd already seen it, and noticed that the dedication by director Rod Lurie after "The End" in the theatrical version—"For our daughters"—was missing in the airline version. I can't imagine it was trimmed for content or for time, so I can only guess that it was cut because Lurie thought better of it. What led to this decision?

—Tim Carvell, San Francisco, California

A. Rod Lurie replies: "For some reason all films on airlines have to be under two hours long. Trims were necessary. In order not to hurt the story line of the film, the reprise— which lasts a full minute—got cut from the end. I suppose that the 'For our daughters' dedication got lost in the mix as well. This saddens me because that dedication represented not only why I made this film but also why Joan Allen, Jeff Bridges, and Sam Elliott— all of whom have daughters—agreed to be in it. But at least we were able to maintain the integrity of the movie."

Q. Gary Oldman, who plays the GOP congressman in *The Contender,* is attacking his own movie. Mr. Showbiz quotes *Premiere* magazine, where "Oldman and his manager, Douglas Urbanski, accuse DreamWorks honchos Steven Spielberg, David Geffen, and Jeffrey Katzenberg—all Democrats—of turning the political drama upside down to make it mesh with their pro–Al Gore agendas." According to this report, Oldman says when DreamWorks bought the film rights, the company forced director-writer Rod Lurie to turn *The Contender* into an unbalanced, Democrat-friendly tale. Urbanski alleges the film is a "piece of propaganda" on par with that produced by Nazi propagandist Joseph Goebbels. What's your take?

—Susan Lake, Urbana, Illinois

A. Goebbels? Urbanski should take two aspirins and go to bed. Oldman's charges are perplexing because as one of the film's executive producers he read the script and played the character and must have known what the politics were. I referred his attack to Rod Lurie, the writer-director of *The Contender,* who replies: "There is just no truth to this. The most telling thing about the *Premiere* piece is that not one specific cut is cited as evidence. There were several cuts made to the film, but they were not initiated by DreamWorks. Indeed, those cuts were made with the intention of making Shelly Runyon [Oldman's character] look less sinister as opposed to more sinister. One was another scene of collusion with Christian Slater's character. One scene put back into the film is when Shelly has that profound and sad moment with his wife. Having worked for *Premiere* now and then, I can assure you that the writer was trying to help create a story rather than report on one."

Q. I just read your review of *The Contender* with Jeff Bridges and Joan Allen. My wife and I had to laugh when we saw the trailer, because we just *knew* Gary Oldman's character was going to be an evil, mean, and nasty Republican. As it turns out, we were right! *Random Hearts* is the only film I can recall where a Republican politician was treated as a sympathetic character in a Hollywood film. Can you think of any others?

—Marc Giller, Tampa, Florida

A. But the movie does have positive Republican portrayals—the Allen character's father, played by Philip Baker Hall, and Democratic sleazeballs—the characters played by Christian Slater and William Petersen. Still, you have a point about Hollywood political movies in general. This is not a conspiracy but a reflection of the tendency for liberals to be drawn to the arts while conservatives channel their energies elsewhere. There are of course exceptions. Bruce Willis and Arnold Schwarzenegger have the clout to make a pro-GOP movie if they wanted to. So does The Rock. That one I'd love to see.

Q. In *The Contender* the vice-president dies and the president has to decide whom to appoint as his successor. Forgive me if I am in error, but in America, isn't the successor to the vice-presidency the secretary of state?

—Michael Mandy, Antioch, California

A. No. The twenty-fifth amendment provides: "Whenever there is a vacancy in the office of the Vice President, the President shall nominate a Vice President who shall take office upon confirmation by a majority vote of both Houses of Congress."

Credits

Q. Why are directors credited twice at the beginning of many films—once when the credits start with "A film by [stick director's name here]" and again at the end of the opening credits "directed by [director's name again]?"

—Mark Gill, Petal, Mississippi

A. For an answer, the AM turned to Kevin Smith, director of several films which were directed by Kevin Smith, as well as proprietor of www.psycomic.com, a Kevin Smith Website. He replies:

"It's because directors are completely insecure. Why else would you need to remind the audience of something you just told them mere minutes ago? There are alternate theories as well. For starters, it's a marketing hook. If you can throw up 'A Quentin Tarantino Film' on a poster or commercial spot, more people are going to attend, since *Pulp Fiction* had many fans, and Quentin's name stands for quality on a picture. Along those lines, there are certain films that just feel like their director. 'A Spike Lee Joint.' 'A Martin Scorsese Picture.' These are directors who've been making films for many years, and have earned that title cred, in addition to the normal 'Directed by' credit, if that's their thing.

"What bugs me about the 'A Film by . . .' credit at the start of most flicks is that it's used by people who haven't been making films forever—so their possessory credit is neither marketable nor earned. That's when the 'A Film by . . .' nonsense is more egocentric than anything else. It's also highly insulting to everyone else who made the picture—the cast and crew—from leading lady to lowest P.A. on the totem pole, because it insinuates that the director made that film all by his or her lonesome, and no one else helped. That's just a lie, because filmmaking is one of the most collaborative art forms there is. One cat hogging all the credit is as exclusionary as a restricted country club.

"For the record, I've never taken that possessory credit. I'm satisfied with the credits I deserve—written and directed by . . .—because that's all I ever do on the films I've made. Write and direct them. Without the hundreds of other names you've seen on the credits of *Clerks, Mallrats, Chasing Amy,* and *Dogma,* I never would've been able to make those films. And I'll be damned if I'd ever rob all those craftsmen and -women of their due by declaring that they were all 'Films by Me.'

"Besides, I feel it's always healthy to spread the blame around, in case the flick tanks."

Crouching Tiger, Hidden Dragon

Q. I just saw *Crouching Tiger, Hidden Dragon* and loved the movie but didn't really understand the ending. Can you help?

—Rick Klimovitz, Southampton, Pennsylvania

A. Reid Rosefelt, publicist for the movie, tells me: "Director Ang Lee and cowriter/producer James Schamus are often asked to explain the ending of *Crouching Tiger, Hidden Dragon,* and they have always resisted doing so, as they prefer to let the audience discover it for themselves. Part of the answer can be found in the story Lo Chang Chen tells Jen Zhang Ziyi in the desert: 'We have a legend. Anyone who dares to jump from the mountain, God will grant his wish. Long ago, a young man's parents were ill, so he jumped. He didn't die. He floated away, far away, never to return. He knew his wish had come true. If you believe, it will happen. The elders say, a faithful heart makes wishes come true.'"

Q. I recently imported the *Crouching Tiger, Hidden Dragon* DVD, with both English subtitles and an English dubbed track. I watched the movie in its original Mandarin, with the English subtitles. The sentences on the screen seemed simple and brief. Later, I watched the movie again with the English dub. To my surprise, the dubbed dialogue was vastly different from the subtitles: more poetic, complete, and powerful.

—Scott Gillan, Manhattan, Kansas

A. The AM consulted both James Shamus, who wrote the movie, and Sony Pictures vice president Michael Schlesinger. They disagree about the desirability of dubbing, but agree about subtitles.

Schamus: "First of all, I'm thrilled with his response to the dub—the folks at Sony and we worked long and hard on it, and the results are stupendous. It's probably the best dub into English of any film I know of, certainly of any film from Asia in my lifetime. By comparison, it is more verbally fleshed out than the subtitles, which I am also proud of: Ang Lee and I wrote and rewrote them, as on all our films. Technical restraints limit the number of characters that can be printed, as well as the amount of time subtitles can stay on-screen, and if one wishes people to both read and see one's film those constraints are reasonable. In any case, modern DVD technology is going to change the way we relate to foreign films, giving us the chance to both hear the true grain of the actors' voices and languages, as well as, with the flick of a remote control, enjoying the picture without subtitles."

Schlesinger: "The writer is correct. Dubbed dialogue sometimes needs to be 'padded' to match the length of the spoken sentence, while subtitles need to be short so they can be read before the actor finishes the line. For comparison, the writer should check out the DVD of *Princess Mononoke,* which contains two sets of subtitles: one a literal translation of the Japanese dialogue, the other a more 'fluid' translation. They're subtly but intriguingly different from each other . . . and considerably more different than the wretched English dubbing. And in answer to his final question: no, dubbing is never preferable to subtitling, even on a *Godzilla* movie. One of an actor's most important tools is his/her voice: take that away, and you lose the heart of the performance."

Dancer in the Dark

Q. I walked out of *Dancer in the Dark* last night, not because it was awful. I found it compelling and difficult but because my wife had fled the theater ten minutes before during the scene in which Selma and Bill struggle over her money, unable to bear the suffering any more. My initial response was to stay and watch this troubling, fascinating film to the end, but I realized that I was more worried about my wife than I was about the characters. So I left, silently apologizing to Bjork and Lars Van Trier. 1. Did I do the right thing? 2. Does this mean she gets to pick the next movie, even if it's directed by Nora Ephron and features a talking cat?
—Colin Meeder, Frankfurt, Germany

A. 1. Yes; always stand by your wife. 2. No; she owes you one.

Q. Wassup with Bjork's dead-bird dress at the Oscars?
—Susan Lake, Urbana, Illinois

A. Style does not consist of letting a haute couture stylist supply you with a free gown in return for promotional considerations. Style consists of wit, imagination, and the courage to be yourself. Bjork is a silly lovable goose, and her dress was a perfect choice.

Disney's The Kid

Q. Regarding *Disney's The Kid:* The Answer Man reported that the Chaplin estate got nasty over the use of the title "The Kid," so Disney altered it. I wonder if this is really true, because (1) *The Kid* is from 1921 and clearly in the public domain; and (2) You can't copyright a title in any event. Presumably, Disney has lawyers who know this stuff.
—Jeff Joseph

A. My source was Ray Pride, film critic for *New City* in Chicago, who responds: "Yes, but Chaplin did sometimes perform that sweet little trick of adding musical scores later and presenting the result as a new, freshly copyrightable artifact. In the late 1970s when I was programming at Northwestern, the Chaplin estate was formidable at repackaging and protecting the work—not that I know that's the case with *The Kid*. The noncopyrightability of a title is true, too, but there is the MPAA registry to contend with—the gentleman's club among the major studios that banks all the potential titles they can think of, then horse-trade them when necessary. (As in Columbia browbeating Miramax over *Scream*, as if anyone remembered their *Screamers* of a couple years earlier.)"

Dogma

Q. While watching the DVD of *Dogma*, I noticed that in the scene where Linda Fiorentino's character is trying to convince Jay and Silent Bob to accompany her to New Jersey, Jay says, "I feel like she's Ben Kenobi, I'm Han Solo, you're Chewy, and we're in that (bleeped)-up bar!" Aren't Jay and Silent Bob inspired by C3P0 and R2D2? One is tall, slender, and speaks at great and annoying lengths while the other is short, fat, and hardly utters a word.
—Roy Chang, New York, New York

A. Kevin Smith replies: "From as far back as *Mallrats* people have been asking me this question, and I have to admit it's an interesting theory. However, I'd be lying if I said the similarities were intentional. While Jay and Silent Bob may suggest the world's most famous droids, it's purely coincidence. However, if my embracing of your theory makes you rush out and see *Jay and Silent Bob Strike Back* when it hits theaters nationwide August 24th, then may I take this opportunity to say that there has never been a more astute observation of my work."

Driven

Q. In your review of *Driven*, you wrote, "Whether they admit it or not, fans go to auto races to see crashes." I usually enjoy reading your reviews, but that's because your statements usually exhibit some rational thinking process. This one did not.

—Ron Hickman, San Jose, California

A. I should have written "many" fans. But what do you think would happen to attendance if racing was made into a safe sport? Current speeds and equipment make it a deadly profession for the drivers. The fans seem able to live with that.

Dubbin' in the Rain

Q. My aunt in Minneapolis, Dolores DeFore, has a question for you. She is a big fan of *Singin' in the Rain* and recently saw the rereleased version at a local theater. But she was aghast to read in a local paper that Debbie Reynolds didn't do her own singing in the movie. If not, why not, since she has a great voice?

—Mary Houlihan, Chicago, Illinois

A. Debbie Reynolds has a great voice but was not a seasoned pro when, at nineteen, she got a lead in the greatest of all musicals. She had her work cut out for her with non-stop dancing lessons to keep up with the gifted hoofers Gene Kelly and Donald O'Connor. Some but not all of her songs in the movie were dubbed. According to Tim Dirks of the Greatest Films Website (www.filmsite.org), her singing voice was dubbed by Betty Noyes in "Would You?" and "You Are My Lucky Star." And here's a twist. Remember the big scene at the end where Lina Lamont (Jean Hagen) has a speaking voice so raspy that Kathy Selden (Reynolds) stands behind the curtain and dubs it live? Dirks says: "Debbie's speaking voice as Kathy—when impersonating Lina Lamont's lines—was dubbed by Jean Hagen herself!"

Q. I just finished watching *Fellini's 8½* with my wife, and she made the interesting observation that certain lines of dialogue in the film were clearly spoken in English and over-dubbed in Italian, while other lines remained in English. Also, the dubbing in general was terrible—it often seemed as though the actors were actually speaking entirely different dialogue from that on the soundtrack. Is there any rational explanation that you know of for these anomalies?

—Sam Lustig, Los Angeles, California

A. All Italian movies from that period were filmed with the actors speaking their own languages, whatever they were, and then dubbed later, even into the same language. Lex Barker spoke English and was dubbed into English; Marcello Mastroianni spoke Italian and was dubbed into Italian; Anita Ekberg spoke Swedish and was dubbed into Italian.

DVDs

Q. With DVDs making up at least half of the total stock of rental stores, it's clear that DVDs are taking over. But I have to ask: What's the projected market life cycle of DVDs? How long before they're replaced by the next great media technology?

—David Barnes, Menlo Park, California

A. Michael Schlesinger, vice president of Sony Pictures, replies: No one can say with any certainty. After all, in 1980, did anyone seriously believe that the LP would become virtually obsolete in barely five years? All I can offer is an educated guess, which is yes, DVD probably will be around for quite a spell. The industry, realizing how it screwed up by positioning the laser disc as a high-end item, has gone all out to make DVD the medium of choice for Everyone. If it were to abruptly introduce another format anytime soon, I sincerely believe consumers would rise up in revolt."

Q. I have a wide-screen video projection system and I have been told there are differences in picture quality on DVDs that have wide screen as well as standard aspect ratios. What should I look for?

—Emerson Thorne, Chicago, Illinois

A. My video guru, Fred Thomas of Mills Custom Audio and Video in Oak Park, tells me: "Standard DVDs with the picture in the 1.33:1 ratio are not affected. But when you shop for letterbox or wide-screen versions, you should look for the words 1.85:1 or 2.35:1 anamorphic wide screen, or enhanced for wide-screen TVs. This information is generally in small print on the back of the DVD jacket. Anamorphic or enhanced versions yield between 25 to 35 percent more resolution than standard wide screen, thus producing higher-quality pictures on your wide-screen system."

Q. I have a bone to pick with the Criterion Collection video label. I recently rented their DVD of *The Seven Samurai*, and seeing this incredible film was one of the defining experiences of my movie-watching life. Naturally I had an appetite for other Kurosawa films, and decided my next rental would be *Yojimbo*. The DVD mentioned it was filmed in "Toho-vision." The notes listed it as being in the "original" 2.35:1 aspect ratio, which was how the movie was presented. But during the opening credits, the lead actor's name was displayed in block letters as TOSHIRO MIFUN. The missing "E" represents quite a bit of the image that was cut off. This leads me to believe that Criterion is deceiving us by not presenting the complete image, yet calling it the "original" Tohovision. Are my suspicions correct?
—Cameron J. Ladd, Los Altos, California

A. Being able to see a film in its original aspect ratio has become one of the selling points of DVD, and Criterion is traditionally fanatic on this score. I asked Peter Becker, president of the Criterion Collection, for his response, and he says: "The cropping you see seems far more pronounced during the title sequence than it is throughout the rest of the film. The element Toho furnished us for *Yojimbo* included the English language title sequence, in which the film titles are outside of the safe action area. This has the effect of emphasizing a very slight cropping at the edges of the screen (overscanning) which is inherent in all standard television sets. We have since developed a much clearer line of communication with the technical experts at Toho and do not expect this problem to recur in the future."

The Exorcist

Q. I could not agree more with your review of *The Exorcist* rerelease, I think it is a blatant example of ego and greed trampling over fine art. The additions add *nothing* to the film and disrupt the momentum. William Friedkin would have done better to stand by his original cut of the film rather than mysteriously change his view shortly after releasing a DVD version that has him defending, on the sound

track, every cut he has now restored of the "lost footage." He was right about every point he made and now suddenly takes it all back. I feel cheated.
—Kevin Ullery, Chicago, Illinois

A. Friedkin told me he made these changes to respect the wishes of author/producer William Peter Blatty. He insisted they had nothing to do with another DVD release, and said: "I don't even know if they're going to bring this out of DVD." I was in San Francisco over the weekend and discussed this issue with the director Werner Herzog, who told me: "Three months after I finish a film, I destroy all the unused material. A carpenter does not sit on his shavings."

The Fast and the Furious

Q. Why do guys like action and fast movement in movies? What's with blowing things up real good and flipping cars?
—Troylene Ladner, Jersey City, New Jersey

A. We are hard-wired that way at birth, but can overcome our low tastes and become admirers of fine movies, simply by taking a vow never to attend a movie with a trailer featuring that guy who always intones, "In a world—where . . ."

Q. In *The Fast and the Furious*, I think the best thing about the movie was that there were no computer-generated images (except for the opening credits). The movie was exciting because the car chases were real. That Charger really went end-over-end at the end of the movie. Compare that to *Driven*, where the car chases and crashes were less real than a video game at my local arcade. Even if *Driven* hadn't been such an abysmal movie in every other way, the CGIs still would have ruined it.
—Greg Berry, San Francisco, California

A. It would be a shame if the art and craft of stunt driving were replaced by computers. There is a certain undefinable reality to the real thing that we sense, rather than see.

Film Critics

Q. I go to you for insightful commentary and enlightening criticism about films. Who amongst your peers do you go to?
—Fred Duong, Garland, Texas

A. The most valuable film critic in America is Stanley Kauffmann of the *New Republic.* I appreciate many of my colleagues for their wit, intelligence, insight, and language, but Kauffmann is the one I turn to with the thought that, if we disagree, I may very well be wrong.

Freddy Got Fingered

Q. Your review of *Freddy Got Fingered* fits with the majority opinion that it is a disgusting gross-out with no redeeming qualities. But I can't get around A. O. Scott's positive review for the *New York Times,* where he states that parts of the film were "rigorous and chaotic, idiotic and brilliant," and might end up in the Museum of Modern Art. How can two well-established critics have such vastly different opinions?

—Alexander Parker, Oberlin, Ohio

A. In my review, I wrote: "Many years ago, when Surrealism was new, Luis Buñuel and Salvador Dali made *Un Chien Andalou,* a film so shocking that Buñuel filled his pockets with stones to throw at the audience if it attacked him. Green, whose film is in the Surrealist tradition, may want to consider the same tactic. The day may come when *Freddy Got Fingered* is seen as a milestone of neo-Surrealism."

I meant that seriously. The film fails in its attempt to be funny and entertaining, but it is certain to become a cult item, and Scott's review is defensible. He may have been moved by its sheer brazen boldness. He was not alone among major critics; *Freddy* was also praised by Jay Carr of the *Boston Globe,* Chris Hewitt of the *St. Paul Pioneer-Press,* and John Zebrowski of the *Seattle Times.* On the other hand, James Berardinelli, the respected Web-based critic, wrote, "I have gotten better entertainment value from a colonoscopy." That review no doubt inspired Tom Green to slap his forehead and exclaim, "The colonoscopy! I forgot to put in the colonoscopy!"

The Gift

Q. Why in *The Gift* did Cate Blanchett's character read Zener cards instead of Tarot cards? Zener cards are used solely for the purpose of testing psychic ability. (See Bill

Murray in the beginning of *Ghostbusters.*) So the climatic scene is silly (Oh no, not three pairs of squiggly lines in a row!). Did they think Tarot cards were clichés?

—Dara Jade, Montreal, Quebec

A. Many psychics believe cards are simply a device to free their intuitions, and have no power of their own. My guess is that the Blanchett character was at one time or another tested for psychic ability, and was given the Zener cards to keep.

Gladiator

Q. I've been reading lately that *Gladiator* may be the top contender for Best Picture this year. Two questions: (1) Are these prognosticators mad? (2) In your opinion, what was the last truly mediocre movie to take home the Best Picture Oscar?

—Dan Conley, Chicago, Illinois

A. Oscar talk about *Gladiator* has grown since it got five Golden Globe nominations. Enthusiasm for the movie baffles me. Its special effects are muddy and substandard, and its story combines elements of 1950s Hollywood gladiator epics with staging by the World Wrestling Federation. Among the mediocre Best Picture winners are *The Sound of Music, Around the World in 80 Days,* and *The Greatest Show on Earth.*

Q. My award for the most amazing nomination this year: *Gladiator* for best special effects. Wow. One of the worst looking films I've ever seen. And somehow, they *didn't* nominate *Crouching Tiger.* Guess since the effects weren't computer generated, they don't count. When I first saw *Gladiator,* I thought it was so-so as a movie. But as time has passed, I've grown to actively dislike it. I have a feeling that the people who like it never saw *Ben Hur* or *Spartacus* in 70mm on the big screen, and think, somehow, that it's a good film. It's not.

—Jeff Joseph, Sabucat Productions,
Lancaster, California

A. You are not alone. Marlin deTardo of Cleveland writes: "As I understand it, that nomination would have been made by people who work in the effects field—shouldn't they at least know better?" And Jon Bougher of Weare, New Hampshire, writes: "The shots of the Coliseum were nothing less than cartoonish. *The Cell*'s marvelous visual effects were passed over to make room for *Gladiator*. Even though the Academy is full of politics, the visual-effects category is usually the one that gets it right."

Yes, but not this year. The nomination does not speak well for the expertise of the nominating group in that branch of the Academy.

Q. I'm dumbfounded by *Gladiator* winning the Oscar. I caught this amazing glitch in the first ten minutes. The scene: The Germanic hordes, lumbering out of the winter woods to challenge the Roman legions, chanting a war song. The problem: The song isn't German or even European. It's African. It's a war chant lifted directly from the 1964 classic, *Zulu*. And I mean lifted directly, with the same voices, the exact words.

—John Markey, San Antonio, Texas

A. Al Goldstein of Novato, California, also wrote the AM accusing the movie of a "direct rip-off." I consulted Professor Nate Kohn of the University of Georgia, who was the producer of *Zulu Dawn* (1979). He responds: "Ridley Scott certainly did not lift the *Zulu* sound track. He probably accidentally approximated it. I looked at the first ten minutes of *Gladiator,* and there are remarkable similarities to both *Zulu* and *Zulu Dawn,* though more to *Zulu Dawn.* The warrior chant in both Zulu films, designed to spread fear among the enemy, is 'Uzu,' which I believe is Zulu for 'kill.' The German hordes are indeed chanting a similar word, although to me it sounded more like 'ooooo'—no 'z' in there. But the way the chant is heard, disembodied and sudden, sounding as if it is echoing off the hills of Zululand, is indeed very similar to the Zulu films. Also, the disembodied voice echoing out of the bush in *Gladiator* mirrors directly a scene in *Zulu Dawn* when an offscreen Zulu warrior yells the obvious question at the invading imperial army: 'Why do you come to the land of the Zulu?' Add to that the camera set-ups, the framing, the hand-to-hand combat, and you have a sequence that looks and sounds a lot like the Battle of Isandhlwana in *Zulu Dawn.* More than anything, the resemblance comes from the nature of the chant's echo—it does sound exactly

like the African echo. Interestingly, both Ridley Scott and *Zulu Dawn* director Douglas Hickox I believe once worked at the same company making television commercials in London. There is a great similarity of style. Either that, or there is really only one way to shoot large armies with shields and spears going at each other. Another reason *Gladiator* is more like *Zulu Dawn* is that on *Zulu* director Cy Endfield only had 100 Zulu extras, so he couldn't compose the panoramic warrior scenes in the way we could on *Zulu Dawn* with 6,000 extras."

Godard and Spielberg

Q. At a Cannes press conference for his *Elegy of Love,* the French director Jean-Luc Godard was critical of Steven Spielberg and lashed out at *Schindler's List,* saying, "To reconstruct Auschwitz the way he did, as an artist, an author, he did not have the right to do that, and it's my duty to point a finger at him." Can you shed any light on why Godard feels such contempt? Is he saying that some people "own" culture and others don't?

—Danny Stuyck, Houston, Texas

A. It is valid for Godard to criticize the film if he doesn't like it, but to say Spielberg had no right to make it is arrogant and ignorant. In Godard's new film, a character says that Mrs. Schindler "was never paid, and lives in poverty in Argentina." This neatly, perhaps maliciously, ignores the fact that Spielberg devoted his film's profits to setting up the Shoah Memorial Project, which has videotaped the memories of some 50,000 Holocaust survivors. Godard should be ashamed of himself.

The Grinch

Q. I just took my family to see *The Grinch*. I was a little hesitant after your review. I sat next to my four-year-old. It was so neat watching his eyes light up and hearing his giggling. I think he helped me let go and fall into the magic of the fantasy. I think to enjoy this movie you have stop being an adult. Let the kid in you come out and just enjoy the fantasy. Let yourself feel the magic.

—Kevin Egan, Colorado Springs, Colorado

A. With *Rugrats in Paris,* I had no trouble

letting the kid come out. The success of *The Grinch* has surprised me and the majority of the nation's film critics, who hated it. I'm glad you enjoyed it, but I still see it as a dreary and scary downer.

As Angela Brotchie of Nanaimo, British Columbia, writes: "The little boy I care for went to see *The Grinch* with his mother today and came back saying, 'That wasn't the Grinch, he was scary.' Shouldn't a movie about the Grinch be aimed more at children and not be coated with creepy colors, odd and grotesque creatures, and rated PG? I'm twenty and still watch and enjoy the original Grinch cartoon. I'm pretty sure that when audiences rushed to see the new Grinch, they were expecting the same charm the original had. How disappointing."

Q. I caught up with *The Grinch* recently, and while I wasn't all that moved by it, there was one scene which made me laugh hysterically. When we looked outside the window of a Who-Christmas party, we saw all the adults putting their car keys into a fishbowl. The first thing that popped into my mind was a seventies key party à la *The Ice Storm.* Please tell me that Ron Howard decided to inject some subversive swinging reference into a children's film.
—Devon Gallegos, Los Angeles, California

A. A studio rep responds: "Unfortunately, Ron Howard is busy in preproduction for his new film and is unavailable for comment. However, during a press junket a similar question was overheard in regard to the keys in the bowl. The unofficial response was that Mr. Howard said it was put in to promote responsible driving."

Hannibal

Q. Is it just me, or do the advertisements and trailers for *Hannibal* make him a sound an awful lot like that other twenty-first century killing machine: HAL 9000, in *2001*?
—Dave Huhta, San Diego, California

A. You're on target. In the commentary track for the Criterion DVD of *Silence of the Lambs,* Anthony Hopkins says he told director Jonathan Demme and writer Ted Tally in 1989 that he thought he might play Dr. Lecter

a little like Hal 9000, an extremely intelligent machine.

Q. In *Silence of the Lambs,* Lecter was able to unlock his handcuffs with a mere pen component, which he managed to steal with *both* hands cuffed and behind his back, but in *Hannibal,* with only *one* hand cuffed and an entire kitchen to take utensils from, he's forced to chop off his hand. Go figure.
—Jess Chia, Richmond, British Columbia

A. I was disappointed he did not save it for a snack.

Q. A dentist friend suggests that instead of going to such lengths to restrain Hannibal Lecter, they should have simply removed all his teeth. Your opinion?
—Adrian Chiles, BBC Radio, Birmingham, England

A. Those dentists have the same solution for everything.

Q. I just saw *Hannibal.* I noticed that actor-director Spike Jonze *(Being John Malkovich)* was credited as playing Donnie Barber, a redneck who supplies Lecter with the pancreas and thymus for his famous meal with Clarice Starling and Paul Krendler. Jonze is not seen in the film. Was his part edited out, or was it a hoax?
—William Shaw, Kalamazoo, Michigan

A. An MGM rep says the scene involved was talked about but never shot. However, Jonze is listed in the movie's entry at the Internet Movie Database, which perhaps got it from preproduction credits.

Hot-Air Balloon Rule

Q. In your review of *The Mummy Returns,* you point out that you once wrote "no good movie features a hot-air balloon." What about *Before Night Falls,* whose hot-air-balloon scene rips off Tarkovsky's *The Mirror*?
—Mathew Wilder, Los Angeles, California

A. Sarah Masiulewicz of Chicago and John Walkerstein of Baltimore mention *The Wizard of Oz,* and Jeff Dentzer of Cleveland reminds me of Ray Harryhausen's *Mysterious Island.* My Glossary Rule states "good movies *rarely* contain a hot-air balloon," but perhaps it is time to retire this rule.

Hoop Dreams Update

Q. What is the update on the two athletes in *Hoop Dreams*? Did they finish college?

—Libby Johnston, Pittsburgh, Pennsylvania

A. The update is nothing but good news. Chicagoan John Iltis, who was instrumental in marketing the film, replies:

"William Gates was a gang intervention counselor in Oak Park, Illinois, and recently completed his degree from Marquette University where he played basketball for four years. William and his wife Catherine have three children, and he is currently working in northern Illinois for CEDA, an organization that helps people make the transition from welfare to work. When Mrs. Gates finishes college and gets her degree, William plans to return to Marquette University to attend law school.

"Arthur Agee has formed the Arthur Agee Role Model Foundation, which helps inner-city young people strive for a higher education. According to Steve James, the director of *Hoop Dreams,* Arthur has a budding acting career. James cast Arthur in a supporting role in the TNT movie *Passing Glory,* and Arthur has also secured supporting roles in two upcoming films, *Shall We Dance?* and *The Fixer.* Arthur played basketball at a junior college and then played for two years at Arkansas State. He has not yet graduated."

Interviews

Q. The Internet Movie Database quotes you as saying, "I am utterly bored by celebrity interviews. Most celebrities are devoid of interest." Did you really say that, and if so, what do the celebrities think?

—Murray Leeder, Calgary, Alberta

A. I think they're more bored than I am. Interviews involving access, insight, and personality are one thing. But mostly what we get these days are three-minute charades monitored by paranoid publicists, with the celebs repeating the same sound bites over and over. I'll never forget long, free-associating interviews I had with stars like Lee Marvin, John Wayne, Woody Allen, Shirley MacLaine, and Robert Mitchum, who said what they thought, didn't give a damn about image, and worked without a net—or a publicist.

Intimacy

Q. I noticed in your article about *Intimacy* you belittled Anna Nicole Smith and Pamela Anderson as useless "founts of sexual inspiration." I wonder, does this make all the words and pictures about Marilyn Monroe useless as well?

—Nicholas Norcia, Glenmoore, Pennsylvania

A. I never used the word "useless."

Key Largo and Politics

Q. A friend tells me that in the 1940s movie *Key Largo,* Edward G. Robinson makes a speech to Bogart that is timely right now. Here's how he quotes it: "Let me tell you about Florida politicians. I make them. I make them out of whole cloth just like a tailor makes a suit. I get their name in the newspaper, I get them some publicity, and get them on the ballot. Then after the election we count the votes, and if they don't turn out right, we recount them and recount them again until they do." Is this on the level?

—Margo Howard, Boston, Massachusetts

A. Your friend's approximation, which has been forwarded widely on the Web and was quoted December 10 in the *New York Times,* is a shameless rewrite tailored to fit the news. The words "Florida," "recount," and "politician" do not appear in the correct quote.

Tim Dirks, whose Website (www.filmsite.org) is an invaluable repository of movie descriptions and dialogue, tells me that Robinson (a gangster) is speaking to a roomful of characters (including Bogart), while trying to intimidate and ridicule the local deputy. Robinson says:

"You hick! I'll be back pulling strings to get guys elected mayor and governor before you ever get a ten-buck raise. Yeah, how many of those guys in office owe everything to me. I made them. Yeah, I made 'em, just like a—like a tailor makes a suit of clothes. I take a nobody, see? Teach him what to say. Get his name in the papers, and pay for his campaign expenses. Dish out a lotta groceries and coal. Get my boys to bring the voters out. And then count the votes over and over again 'til they added up right and he was elected. Yeah —then what happens? Did he remember when the going got tough, when the heat was on? No, he didn't wanna. All he wanted was to save his own dirty neck . . . Yeah, 'Public Enemy' he calls me. Me, who gave him his 'Public' all wrapped up with a fancy bow on it."

Kings of Comedy

Q. I want to know why the *Kings of Comedy* is not at the theaters downtown? Is that bias or what? What's the explanation for not showing it? To me that's discrimination. I hear its sales are pretty good.

—Daphne White, Chicago, Illinois

A. Spike Lee's concert film starring four stand-up comics is an enormous hit, passing the $50 million mark. In its original release it was booked on less than 900 screens, in predominantly black areas, allegedly because Paramount thought white audiences were unfamiliar with the comedians. The studio says it always planned to widen the release as word of mouth spread. My guess: The studio was caught flat-footed by the movie's popularity. It shouldn't have been. Black comedians are "crossing over" to white audiences all the time now, because of their success on cable.

A Knight's Tale

Q. I saw *A Knight's Tale* over the weekend and must admit that my incredulous laughter after the medieval crowd does a rendition of Queen's "We Will Rock You" turned into embarrassed enjoyment by the end of the project. Much as *Congo* could be taken as a guilty little pleasure, this film seemed to enjoy just how preposterous it was. I get angry when a film like *Gladiator* takes a flamethrower to history, because it wants to act like an epic. *A Knight's Tale* makes no claims to being anything other than a fun movie. Should I seek help for enjoying this lighthearted romp?

—Roy Roychoudhury, Brentwood, California

A. Not at all. It does what it does quite nicely. Strange coincidence, that *A Knight's Tale, Shrek,* and *Moulin Rouge,* released within two weeks of each other, would all use modern songs in stories set decades or centuries ago.

Laughter

Q. I have noticed a lot of laughter during serious movies. During *Cast Away* audience members were constantly laughing during Hank's seclusion on the island, often when he was talking to his friend Wilson. I get the feeling that audience members do not know how to react to a certain scene and they instead react with laughter.

—Daniel Lowe, Edmonds, Washington

A. You may be right. Inappropriate laughter usually means (1) something in the movie makes the audience feel uncomfortable; (2) in an age of irony, the sincere has become amusing, or (3) you are at the Brew and View.

Q. I recently saw the rerelease of *The Exorcist.* I am only seventeen years old, but, unlike my generation, I respect great filmmaking. I was sickened to hear people my own age actually laughing throughout the whole film. I don't find any part of the film to be funny. I've seen it six times and I think it is the most frightening and disturbing film of all time. Is *The Exorcist* outdated for my generation, or are the majority of us just too stupid to understand the concept of a great film?

—Chris Weltsch, Creshill, Illinois

A. Yours is one of dozens of messages I've received from people enraged that young viewers laughed through *The Exorcist.* My guess is that many of them were not accompanied by parents or guardians; so much for the R rating. Maybe that rating exists not to protect kids who hardly seem to have been disturbed but to protect adults from the reactions of some kids?

Here are other reports:

"The most disturbing thing had nothing to do with the movie, but rather the audience's reaction to it. They were laughing! Have we become so desensitized that we find this material laughable, while formulaic bloodbaths such as *Urban Legends* are taken seriously?"

—Nick Clark, Grapevine, Texas

"I was shocked when the audience laughed at every scene involving the possessed Linda Blair. It ruined the tone of the film for me."

—Weston Currie, Burbank, California

"The audience broke out into hysterics. It was kind of like watching *The Rocky Horror Picture Show*. I could tell that half of the audience was feeling the same way I was, shocked at the weird irreverence, so not *everyone* was laughing. If audiences today are watching *The Exorcist* for its humor value, I'm just gonna give up."

—Sean Molloy, San Francisco, California

My own opinion? We have entered an ironic age when television and movies have trained young audiences to laugh at whatever frightens, mystifies, or puzzles them. Maybe that's why surveys show many teenagers get most of their political news from comedy shows.

Leaf and Joaquin Phoenix

Q. Are Leaf Phoenix of *Space Camp* and *Parenthood* and Joaquin Phoenix of *Gladiator* and *Far from Paradise* the same person? They look and sound exactly the same. If not, then are they brothers?

—Veronica Cruz, Burke, Virginia

A. They are the same person.

The Legend of Bagger Vance

Q. In your review of *The Legend of Bagger Vance*, you ask of Bagger, "Is he a real person or a spirit? You tell me." The book is loosely based on the Hindu scripture the Bhagavad Gita. The main character in the Gita is Arjuna—just as Damon's character is R. Junuh. The name "Bagger Vance" comes from the Hindu word "bhagavan," which means God manifesting himself as a person. So Will Smith is God! In the Gita, Arjuna eventually realizes that his friend and charioteer is actually Krishna himself.

—Dennis Andersen, Newman Lake, Washington

A. My theological consultant Father Andrew Greeley agrees: "The Will Smith character is clearly God. Who would have guessed She would appear as a caddy?"

Logos

Q. Must every production and distribution company involved in a film play its corporate logo sequence at the start of a movie? At a recent screening of *Bridget Jones's Diary*

I counted no less than five such sequences. Each time I thought the film might be starting it turned out to be yet another logo sequence. On a related note, am I alone in thinking that the quality of these logo sequences has deteriorated over the years? Compare today's long, boring, computer-generated sequences with the classics of the past, such as the roaring lion of MGM, the thrilling music of 20th Century–Fox, and, best of all, Rank's man-with-a-gong. These were instantly recognizable and acted as a cue to the moviegoer to settle back and relax, as the film was about to start.

—Alun C. Evans, Seattle, Washington

A. International coproductions mean lots of different companies put money into movies, and they all want to tack on their own titles. I agree with you that the classic titles are the best. Amazing, that Miramax paid a reported million dollars for its logo, which is that tacky computer-generated skyline. My favorite among the new ones: The leaping tiger for Mandalay Entertainment.

Loser

Q. Homage alert! Did you notice the striking similarities between Amy Heckerling's *Loser* and Billy Wilder's *The Apartment*? The skeletal plots are identical: Nerdy guy has a crush on a woman who likes him but who, in turn, has a crush on an authority figure who's taking advantage of her. Beyond that, there are several scenes in *Loser* that echo Wilder's film:

(1) In *The Apartment*, Shirley MacLaine stands up Jack Lemmon at a performance of *The Music Man*. In *Loser*, Jason Biggs is stood up at a concert.

(2) In *The Apartment*, a good doctor pumps Shirley MacLaine's stomach and gives a warning to Lemmon, who pretends to be her boyfriend. In *Loser*, a good doctor pumps Mena Suvari's stomach and gives a warning to Biggs, who pretends to be Suvari's boyfriend.

(3) In *The Apartment*, Lemmon's unsavory superiors party at his place and he has to clean up afterward. In *Loser*, Biggs's unsavory roommates party at his place and he has to clean up afterward.

(4) In *The Apartment*, MacLaine stays at

Lemmon's place to recuperate and he offers to cook for her. In *Loser,* Suvari stays at Biggs's place and he offers to cook for her.

(5) At the end of *The Apartment,* Fred MacMurry complains to MacLaine how Lemmon "threw that big, fat promotion in my face." At the end of *Loser,* Greg Kinnear complains how Biggs threw a big A grade back in his face.

(6) Both films end with the heroine finally wising up and rushing back to the hero's apartment/animal hospital quarters for a happy ending. Are you as shocked/impressed as I am?

—Joe Baltake, film critic,
Sacramento (California) Bee

A. As a wise man once said: In literature, it's plagiarism; in cinema, it's homage.

Memento

Q. Your *Memento* argument may not fill up to the top. You cited two problems: (1) how does Lenny remember he can't make new memories? and (2) the backwards chronology is merely stylistic. My replies: Lenny doesn't "remember" he can't remember. The shorthand of his tattoos and notes fills in some blanks and clears some cobwebs, but he can never fully grasp reality. As for the backwards chronology, it *builds* to the shattering conclusion that Lenny has achieved the ultimate con by scamming himself into a perpetual revenge cycle. The structure of *Memento* enabled the film to climax with Lenny's fall from grace. The people behind *Memento* knew what they were doing. Then again, I may not recall the film or your review of it accurately. Where was I?

—Eric Shapiro, Los Angeles, California

A. The Answer Man has been flooded on this subject. Many readers have mentioned Leonard's tattoo, "Remember Sammy Jankis," about a man whose short-term memory problems led him to kill his wife with too many insulin injections. Others have pointed out that when we see Sammy in the hospital and a nurse walks in front of him, there is a split-second shot afterward in which Sammy has been replaced by Leonard. On Chicago's Mancow Mueller radio show, Joe Pantoliano, costar of the movie, flatly stated (Spoiler Warning!) that there was no Sammy Jankis, that Sammy was an attempt by Leonard's memory to displace guilt, and that Leonard killed his wife. Discussing this with Mancow, I asked, "but can you prove that from the movie?" No, he said, he couldn't. There are two kinds of plot explanations: (1) those you assemble and take to the movie, where they seem to fit, and (2) those you find in the movie and remove from it. Only the second is critically valid. I believe the Leonard/Sammy connection is likely, but not provable. We are in for a new round of the *Pulp Fiction–Usual Suspects–Sixth Sense* phenomenon, in which people endlessly analyze a movie. I continue to believe the purpose of *Memento* is not to give us a puzzle to solve, but to provide us with the experience of Leonard's dilemma.

Movie Critics

Q. I imagine that as a critic you don't have to pay for most of the movies you see. I don't hold it against you, but when you review a film, do you take into account that you might have felt different about it if you'd had to pay for it?

—Joshua Alpern, Ann Arbor, Michigan

A. I pay for it with two hours of my life. Also, have you looked at the cost of parking?

Q. I noticed that the TV commercial for *Blow* says "the critics are unanimous." The only thing you can count on from film critics is that they are never unanimous.

—Herb Sasman, Santa Fe, New Mexico

A. When I hear critics are "unanimous," I turn to rottentomatoes.com, which measures critical response on its Tomatometer. Among major critics, 47 percent approved of *Blow* and 53 percent did not.

Q. The Answer Man ran an item about how the ads for *Blow* claimed the critics "unanimously" praised it even though about half of them disliked it. I have to ask: *has* there ever been a movie which critics supported unanimously?

—Brad Randall, Plano, Texas

A. Rottentomatoes.com has been monitoring the nation's major movie critics since August 1998. Since then, ten films have scored

100 percent on its Tomatometer. They are, in diminishing order of number of reviews, *Toy Story 2, Chicken Run, A Hard Day's Night, The Truman Show, Life Is Beautiful, The Taste of Others, Sense and Sensibility, L.A. Confidential, The Winslow Boy,* and *The Girl on the Bridge.*

Q. I read the Answer Man item about ten films that got unanimous praise from the Tomatometer at rottentomatoes.com, which tracks the opinions of major critics. Were there any movies that got unanimous *dis*approval?
—Bin Lee, Irvine, California

A. Stephen Wang, chief technical officer of Rotten Tomatoes, replies: "The Top Ten Rotten movies, in order of increasing Tomatometer, are *3 Strikes,* the only movie with unanimous disapproval, followed by *Lost Souls, Chill Factor, The Mod Squad, The Avengers, Bless the Child, Battlefield Earth, Down to You, Urban Legends: Final Cut,* and *Jawbreaker.* To give you an idea of the range, *Jawbreaker,* statistically the best film on this list, scored 3 percent favorable."

Q. I couldn't help but laugh at the recent incident involving "David Manning," the fake critic invented by Sony. Did they actually think they could get away with it? It makes me wonder how many of these other "Quote Whores" actually exist. Do these executives actually think the moviegoing public is that dumb?
—Bill Treadway Jr., Astoria, New York

A. Yes, and they're right. Quotes in ads sell tickets, even if the quotes are from critics no one has any reason to trust. Here's my question in the aftermath of the Manning scandal: Has anyone ever actually seen Jeff Craig of *Sixty Second Previews* at a movie? For that matter, does anyone know what *Sixty Second Previews* is? I ask in all sincerity.

Q. In the aftermath of the scandal about Sony's fake critic David Manning, the Answer Man asked, "Has anyone ever actually seen Jeff Craig of *Sixty Second Previews* at a movie? For that matter, does anyone know what *Sixty Second Previews* is? I ask in all sincerity."
I once worked for a radio station that aired *Sixty Second Previews,* a daily modular pro-

gram one minute in length. Jeff Craig is the host of the thing, but since the program comes on CD a month at a time, he apparently hasn't actually seen most of the movies—thus "previews," not "reviews." Still, his gushing about an upcoming movie he hasn't yet seen ends up being used as blurbs in movie ads.
—Ron Breeding, Little Rock, Arkansas

A. In a magazine profile, Craig said he has employees who attend some of the movies for him, since he's too busy to see all of them himself. Strange, since real critics actually see the movies they review, and even find time to write whole long reviews about them, instead of action-packed blurbs.

MPAA Ratings

Q. Everyone is up in arms over *Hannibal* getting an R instead of an NC-17. What about the PG-rated *See Spot Run,* the most disgusting excuse for a "family" movie I've ever seen? You've no idea the sensation I got when I took my four- and eight-year-old kids to a movie that tried to get laughs from a man's testicles getting bitten off by a dog, and David Arquette trying to make a Chaplin-type ballet out of falling into doggy-doo. Where are the censors when you really need them?
—Steve Bailey, Jacksonville Beach, Florida

A. I wish they were more liberal in permitting adult content for adults, and more conservative in permitting it for children.

Q. After seeing *Hannibal*'s extremely graphic violence, I wonder how the people who decide film ratings have an ounce of credibility left. When the film *Clerks* came out, it almost got an NC-17 rating due to language. Now we have a movie like *Hannibal* with gory scenes that remind me of *Day of the Dead* and *Dawn of the Dead.* How in the world can they give *Hannibal* an R rating and not look like a bunch of monkeys?
—Kayvan Koie, Plainfield, Indiana

A. The R rating for *Hannibal* has inspired amazement even from those who liked the movie. Indie filmmakers have long claimed that movies from major studios, backed by strong producers, are given a pass in the ratings. Was that the case this time? As Richard

Redwolf of San Antonio, Texas, writes: "*Hannibal* and *Billy Elliott*, two movies I loved, received the same rating. I didn't realize a man eating his own brain and a story about a young boy and his ballet shoes were so much alike."

Q. Wouldn't Senator Joe Lieberman's proposed legislation making it a crime to advertise R-rated movies to those under seventeen mean that the MPAA would have to become an official regulatory body, necessitating congressional oversight, appointments, funding, and public access to proceedings?
—Dave Harbinson, Atlanta, Georgia

A. Yes, among countless other obvious and undesirable complications. This legislation, cosponsored by Senator Hillary Clinton, is so idiotic it deserves comparison with the *Star Wars* missile shield.

The Mummy Returns

Q. Your review of *The Mummy Returns* was harsh on what is, was, and always will be a popcorn movie—a fun jaunt through Indiana Jones territory. It was meant to open the summer with a bang, and has achieved that. In a movie where they have resurrected an ancient mummy and there are magic powers abounding, does it really matter if Rick O'Connell can run 1,000 miles an hour, or that one of two armies can emerge unscathed from battle? So why take issue with "unbelievable" ideas and scenes? I review movies for a Website, and gave *The Mummy Returns* a mostly glowing review, as a popcorn movie. It won't go on my list next to *Fight Club*, *The Usual Suspects*, or *Run Lola Run*, but it is still good fun.
—J. Scott, Oakville, Ontario

A. There are good popcorn movies *(The Mummy)* and bad ones *(The Mummy Returns)*. Critics should not give movies a pass via the popcorn loophole, but be as rigorous with popcorn movies as any other kind. *The Mummy Returns* cheats on story and character and condescends to its audience with mindless special effects that are not engendered by anything we can care about.

Q. You wrote about the character outrunning the sunrise in *The Mummy Returns*.

There is another problem. The filmmakers had the shadow "disappear" from the wrong way, by having the sun rise from behind Rick and Alex. You can prove this to yourself in a home science project by using a flashlight, an object (a pillow or binder), your arm, and the wall. (1) Place the light source in one hand and hold it about a foot to your side. (2) Have your other arm about two feet away from the light source, and have the light source point directly at your other arm to the point where you can see the light cast upon it. Now, place your object in the direct path of the light source, so as to block the light. Here's where third-grade science class kicks in. Watch your "wall" arm, as you raise the light source above the object. You will notice that the shadow "fades away" in the opposite direction than what is depicted in *The Mummy Returns*.
—Joel Mahler, Livermore, California

A. How many arms did you need to perform this experiment? I needed three.

Names

Q. In a recent Answer Man column, you said some of the character names in *Unbreakable* were changed because they "couldn't get clearance" on them. What the heck does that mean? I'm sure it doesn't mean what it sounds like—that you have to get permission from some centralized Name Clearinghouse to call a character "Billy," or whatever. So what *does* it mean?
—E. Snider, Provo, Utah

A. Michael Schlesinger of Sony Pictures, my favorite Hollywood executive, tells me: "This has been common practice for decades. Studios always clear character names to avoid potential lawsuits from real people with the same name who feel they might be defamed somehow. A classic example of this is *A Day at the Races*. Groucho's character was originally named Quackenbush, but a real doctor by that name let MGM know he'd just love to sue the studio if they used his name for a, well, quack. So it was changed to Hackenbush. Current examples of this include *Seinfeld*; the show was sued by a guy named Costanza who claimed to be the inspiration for Jason Alexander's character; the case was thrown out just last week."

Q. I liked your Great Movies review of *Shane*. But there was one missing (and key) element: Shane's name. In Yiddish, spelled schoen, it means "beautiful" or "pretty," as in the old Andrews Sisters song "Bei Mir Bist Du Schoen." Shane has no first name. Just that. It fits.

—Name Withheld Because I Work Across the Street, Chicago, Illinois

A. I'd consider this a coincidence, except that the movie does portray Shane as a pretty boy in a store-bought shirt, and contrasts him with the hard-boiled toughs played by Jack Palance and Ben Johnson. The song lyrics include:

Bei mir bist du schoen, again I'll explain
It means you're the fairest in the land

Q. I read your positive review of *Unbreakable*, proceeded to see this fantastic movie twice in three days, and then reread your review. This time, I noticed that you listed the character names of the wife and child as "Megan" and "Jeremy." In the movie, their names were "Audrey" and "Joseph." I then read two more on-line reviews of the movie, and to my surprise, I found the exact same error with the names. My question is: How did you all make the same mistake?

—Michael A. Weinstein, State College, Pennsylvania

A. You are correct. The Internet Movie Database also has it wrong, probably because the names were Megan and Jeremy in the original script and publicity materials. A spokesperson for the studio explains: "It was a clearance problem. We couldn't get clearance on the original names." I don't always write down the names of all the characters in movies, trusting to the studio press materials and sources like imdb.com.

Nicolas Cage

Q. If everyone in the United States sent Nicolas Cage a dollar do you think he would stop being in movies? It's not that he's bad—he's quite adequate—he's just plain in too many of them. Do you think it would work?

—Ray Broms

A. I like Cage as an actor. But your plan interests me. I suggest that everyone in the United States send me a dollar, and I will stop reviewing his movies.

Not in My Town

Q. Having relocated to Madison, Wisconsin, from New York City a little over a year ago I knew I would have to wait along with the rest of the country for movies to open. The problem is that the waits have gotten longer and longer. Here are a few films that are not showing here yet, although they have been reviewed in national publications and the stars have made their rounds on the talk shows: *Crouching Tiger, Hidden Dragon, The House of Mirth, Quills, Before Night Falls, State and Main, O Brother, Where Art Thou?* Meanwhile, here is what's still sucking up good theater space in my new hometown: *Charlie's Angels, Remember the Titans, Little Nicky, Men of Honor, Bedazzled,* and *Unbreakable*! Please feel some pity for me and help me understand what the studio thinking is behind all this.

—Richard Thomas, Madison, Wisconsin

A. Most of America faces the same dilemma, and is waiting for the same movies. Many movies open early on a few screens for Oscar consideration, but don't go wide until the holiday blockbusters begin to fade toward the end of January. The theory is that they generate buzz in the meantime. The most amazing fact in your letter is that *Bedazzled* is still playing in Madison. Maybe the studio forgot to ask for it back.

Q. I've noticed an increasing trend that the films you are most enthusiastic about *(You Can Count on Me, A Time for Drunken Horses, Billy Elliot)* are only playing in big cities. The worst films are on 3,000-plus screens (*Little Nicky, Charlie's Angels,* etc.). I realize theatrical exhibition is a commercial business, but with the multiplex owners filing bankruptcy you'd think they might try reserving one screen per multiplex for a film that's not targeted at the teenage demographic. *Billy Elliot* finally opened here this weekend and I was encouraged to see the theater was about 75 percent full. Since all the studios care about is the money, wouldn't it be in their best interest to force the theater chains to book some of their smaller boutique films in order to expand the theatrical marketplace?

—Ed Slota, Providence, Rhode Island

A. Who cares about the films one way or the other? The theater owners are preoccupied with the concession stand, which is where they make most of their money, since the studios keep up to 90 percent of the ticket price. If only fans of good films spent as much at the candy counter as fans of bad films do, there would be no problem. Here is my new review of *A Time for Drunken Horses*—"A great Iranian popcorn movie!"

Nutty Professor II: The Klumps

Q. I was truly astonished by your review of *Nutty Professor II: The Klumps.* Just which of the following did you find "hilarious"? Anal rape? Projectile defecation? Public flatulence? The elderly being sexual? Impotence? Uncontrollable erections? And add blatant sexism and racism to that list. I agree wholeheartedly that Murphy is a genius and Rick Baker's special effects were absolutely astonishing. That makes this truly disgusting travesty all the more tragic. But what is most amazing of all is that the MPAA gave this a PG-13. After all the things you have said about them in the past how could you let them off the hook?

—Mike Kerrigan, Redondo Beach, California

A. It is not *what* it is about, but *how* it is about it. Your list misrepresents the movie by ignoring its tone. "Projectile defecation" sounds horrible—but it was done by a hamster, and is the sort of thing kids love. Nothing remotely offensive about it. Anal rape? By a hamster? Come on! Flatulence? We joked about it all though grade school. Uncontrollable erections? Boys have that problem at a certain age, and everyone knows it, and it is often the source of classroom embarrassment. A movie like this helps them see it's part of life. Impotence? That's been a subject of humor since Shakespeare, and before. Sexism? Racism? Only to a member of the Politically Incorrect Police Force.

O Brother, Where Art Thou?

Q. Recently I saw *O Brother, Where Art Thou?* In the opening credits it says that it's based on Homer's *Odyssey.* Not knowing much about *The Odyssey,* I was wondering if a better understanding of the story would help *O Brother* make more sense. I obviously noticed that the hero's name was Ulysses, the mayor's name was Homer, and I knew that John Goodman's character represented a cyclops, but are there more connections that would help me understand the movie better?

—George Coutretsis, Long Grove, Illinois

A. Even though you haven't read *The Odyssey,* you were able to identify the major parallels. That may be explained by the fact that the Coens say they haven't read *The Odyssey,* either. I suspect they get private amusement out of red herrings, like saying *Fargo* was based on a true story when it wasn't.

Orson Welles

Q. In my most recent viewing of Orson Welles's *Touch of Evil,* I was struck for the first time by how much the ending—as Marlene Dietrich walks away with the sound of the piano overlapping—reminded me of the ending of *The Third Man,* as Valli walks away with the sound of the zither overlapping. And in each case, walking away from the grave/body of the Orson Welles character. Am I imagining this, or is it possible that Welles did the *Evil* ending as a sort of sly reference or homage to *The Third Man*?

—Tom Simoneaux, Charlotte, North Carolina

A. For a verdict, I turned to Jonathan Rosenbaum, film critic of the *Chicago Reader,* a leading authority on Welles. He tells me: "There's no definitive way of answering this question, but my personal opinion is that it's a little far-fetched. Valli at the end of *The Third Man* walks directly past Joseph Cotten, cutting him dead, and is walking in the general direction of the camera. Dietrich walks away from the camera, and turns around briefly just to say 'Adios.' I can't imagine that Welles would consciously do an homage of this sort in any of his pictures, because the whole direction in his work is to do something different every time—which is precisely what made him so unbankable. Whenever Peter Bogdanovich or someone else would suggest to him that one moment in a film of his evoked another moment in another film he was associated with, he would invariably wince at the thought. The echoes of *The Third Man* in Welles's *Mr. Arkadin* are another matter, because *Arkadin* grew directly out of the Harry Lime radio shows— making this less an homage than a matter of leaving behind some of the traces of its origins."

Q. I understand that Alfonso Arau's remake of Orson Welles's *The Magnificent Ambersons,* based on Welles's original script, will premiere this summer at the Munich film festival.

—Lee Gordon, Irvine, California

A. This I look forward to seeing. I never saw the point of Gus Van Sant's shot-by-shot remake of *Psycho,* but here we have a classic film whose ending was butchered by the studio against Welles's wishes. So a remake of the complete screenplay is a fascinating experiment.

Oscars

Q. Must the Academy Award for Best Supporting Actor be awarded to a human being? I ask because I thought the most impressive character in *Cast Away* was Wilson, the volleyball.

—Clay Cerny, Chicago, Illinois

A. In this category, it's a horse race between Wilson and the refrigerator in *Requiem for a Dream.*

Q. Why doesn't the Academy of Motion Picture Arts and Sciences allow the studios to buy ad time during the Oscar telecast? The Super Bowl is packed with movie ads. The Oscars are usually the second- or third-highest-rated special of the year. What could be better for business than promoting your upcoming releases to a captive audience of movie fans?

—Ed Slota, Providence, Rhode Island

A. Bruce Davis, executive director of the Academy, replies: "We suspect that 'Ed Slota' is an alias for one of the studio marketing heads. There's no question that our large annual audience, heavy with movie lovers, is a group the studios would love to dangle their newest movies in front of. And they would be happy to pay us north of $2 million a minute for the privilege. The Academy governors prefer however that the Academy Awards broadcast focuses attention on the art, rather than the business, of motion pictures, and they're afraid that if the evening is steadily punctuated with sales pitches for new releases, that distinction may become a little blurry. Yes, they're quite aware that by the next morning Oscar will have been enlisted as a point man in a whole new regiment of marketing campaigns, but for the Awards night itself, we like to draw a sharp, clear line between our show content and the ads that make it possible."

Q. Is the Academy required to nominate a Miramax film for Best Picture annually? Give me a break! They passed on *Almost* and *You Can Count on Me* to appease Harvey Weinstein with *Chocolat?*

—David Spillers, Tulsa, Oklahoma

A. Miramax cannot be faulted for campaigning enthusiastically for its pictures. The voters can, however, be criticized for voting for the best campaigns instead of the best pictures. Nominations for films like *Gladiator* and *Chocolat* indicate the Academy membership is surprisingly unsophisticated.

Q. Where does the Academy get the figure of one billion people watching the telecast worldwide? I was in London on Oscar night, and despite hours of effort could not find a TV showing it. If the Oscar telecast was essentially unavailable in London, the foreign city most likely to have a large viewership, how can there possibly be one billion viewers worldwide?

—Michael C. Kingsley, Plantation, Florida

A. Bruce Davis, executive director of the Motion Picture Academy, replies: "What time was Mr. Kingsley looking for the Oscars in London? BSkyB carries them live, which means that they begin at 1:30 A.M. Sky then carries an edited ninety-minute version at a more humane time the next morning. You need a dish to receive the broadcast, but lots of people see it. The 'billion' figure for the world audience is not one the Academy disseminates, although I won't say an enthusiastic producer of the broadcast hasn't used it in interviews on occasion. An audience that size would require that one out of every six men, women, and infants on the planet were watching the Oscars. Since we don't come close to that ratio in the United States, it seems unlikely that we roll it up in Swaziland or mainland China. The odd thing is that nobody can really say what the world numbers are for a television event are, because Nielsen-type ratings services don't exist in most territories outside the United States."

Q. Re the theory that the Oscars have "nearly a billion viewers." Last year Nielsen estimated 80 million U.S. viewers, which is about 29 percent of Americans. According to Boxofficeguru.com, U.S. movies top out around 60 percent in terms of international box office. If we assume that the composition of the Oscar audience is similar to the worldwide box office, that's 200 million viewers, which even by standards of Hollywood Hype falls short of "nearly a billion."
—Matthew Butterick, San Francisco, California

A. Now let's go to work on those McDonald's numbers.

Pearl Harbor

Q. In your review of *Pearl Harbor* you mention the pointless use of soft focus and blurred imagery during the hospital sequences. I believe it's the same reason why the "action" sequences are rather bloodless, and that is to secure the summer, family-friendly, PG-13 rating. To take an important historic event of such horror, and tone it down to a mere action set piece is sad. This is War Lite.
—Tim Cooper, Anchorage, Alaska

A. I understand you are correct, and the distracting and irrational soft focus was inserted to get the PG-13 rating. Forty minutes of the air raid were okay for PG-13, but God forbid we should see the results. Will no one save us from the flywheels at the MPAA Ratings Board? Will Hollywood ever again accord adult filmmakers as much respect as teenagers?

Q. Re *Pearl Harbor.* The lines you quote from the Japanese admiral Yamamoto are accurate. He was not sympathetic to the militarists like Tojo (he once pulled Tojo's chair out from under him!) and was opposed to war with the United States. He had studied in California, liked America, and feared her industrial might.
—Steve Thompson, Alexandria, Virginia

A. I wrote that his lines had been "rewritten" but should have said "singled out."

Q. Doris Miller, the African-American cook who shot down two planes and saved the captain's life, was not honored "posthumously" as you say in your review but was given the Navy Cross on May 27, 1942, on the deck of the carrier *Enterprise,* personally presented by Admiral Chester Nimitz.
—Malcolm Kelly, *National Post,* Toronto, Ontario

A. I unwisely relied on the movie's official press notes, which state: "A controversial figure, Miller posthumously received the Navy Cross . . ." Since historical accuracy is not the movie's strong point, I was foolish not to double-check.

Q. Why does mainstream Hollywood persist in its stereotypical, racist depiction of history in films such as *Pearl Harbor*? The beautiful shot of Japanese planes flying low over white kids playing baseball is symptomatic. Hawaii has a multiracial population, but you'd never know it from the film.
—Vernon Miller, Woodland Park, Colorado

A. My best guess: The filmmakers never gave that a moment's thought. Either that, or they made a conscious decision to leave out Asians.

Q. *Pearl Harbor* grossed over $70 million on Memorial Day weekend. Can you comment on the following quote: "It's the nicest way to address the critics," said Chuck Viane, Disney's head of distribution. "You do it with grosses."
—Sean Spyres, Springfield, Missouri

A. Here is another interesting quote, from an interview David Mamet gave to Richard Covington of Salon.com:
"I like mass entertainment. I've written mass entertainment. But it's the opposite of art because the job of mass entertainment is to cajole, seduce, and flatter consumers—to let them know that what they thought was right is right, and that their tastes and their immediate gratification are of the utmost concern of the purveyor. The job of the

artist, on the other hand, is to say, wait a second, to the contrary, everything that we have thought is wrong. Let's reexamine it."

Phone Numbers

Q. I was watching the movie *The Insider* and noticed that Al Pacino's character has the *exact same* phone number as Kevin Spacey's in *American Beauty*—555-0199. Is this an actual phone number, or is it a number that screenwriters are required to put in, or a fantastic one in a trillion chance? Or did one copy the other?

—Ryan Vlastelica, Hong Kong, China

A. Coincidence, helped by the fact that almost all phone numbers in movies begin with the nonexistent exchange "555."

Q. Regarding Ryan Vlastelica's question about two identical movie phone numbers: The range of phone numbers reserved for fictional use has been reduced from 555-XXXX (10,000 numbers) to just 555-01XX (100 numbers). A repeated number is only a 1-in-100 coincidence, and really more likely than that because writers will like some numbers more than others.

—Mark Brader, Toronto, Ontario

A. Quite true. All movie phone numbers must fall between 555-0100 and 555-0199.

Pollock

Q. Ed Harris is the movies' greatest chameleon. In *Pollock* he looks and acts just like Jackson Pollock. In *The Right Stuff* he looks and acts just like John Glenn. In *Glengarry Glen Ross* he's a hassled, paranoid salesman. The list goes on and on. How does he do it, beyond just raw talent? Does he just have one of those personas upon which anything can be projected? If he doesn't win the Academy Award for *Pollock,* then there truly is no justice in this world.

—Alvin Epstein, Santa Monica, California

A. He's an actor. That's his job, and he's superb at it. To be fair, he does look a lot like John Glenn and Jackson Pollock; his father Robert, seeing a book about Pollock, thought for a second it was Harris on the cover, and sent it to his son, planting the original idea for the film.

Popcorn

Q. Theaters make most of their profits on concessions, correct? Why are they always understaffed, with long lines? Selling just two bags of popcorn would pay for a new employee for an hour.

—John Daleiden, Phoenix, Arizona

A. My film critic friend Jim Emerson of Seattle once managed theaters. He replies: "It's a matter of economics. Theaters want to have as few people as possible on the payroll. While the feature is running, exhibitors don't want to pay for unproductive downtime. There are usually ten minutes of trailers and advertising, giving customers extra time to get their goodies before the feature begins."

Presidential Movie-Watching

Q. President Clinton was well known as a fan of the cinema. What about President Bush?

—Dirk Neely, Los Angeles, California

A. White House spokesman Scott Stanzel says the president saw the following movies at the White House between January 20 and April 9: *13 Days, Varian's War,* and *61*.* The first is about JFK's Cuban missile crisis; the second stars William Hurt as a man who helped refugees escape Nazi Germany; the third is a biopic about Mickey Mantle, Roger Maris, and the asterisk next to Maris's sixty-one home runs.

Q. I read a news article claiming that all of the films President Bush shows on *Air Force One* have been bowdlerized to remove graphic violence and sex. I find it profoundly disturbing that someone who was elected to defend our rights routinely watches censored versions of films that destroy the artistic visions of their creators.

—Dirk Neely, Los Angeles, California

A. It's sad that our president doesn't want to share the same experience as other American moviegoers, if only to inform himself.

Prison Movies

Q. The movie *The Green Mile* used the tag line, "Not all prisoners are bad; not all guards are good." This got me to thinking. When was the last time a prison movie depicted the guards as good? I'm not referring to a single good-hearted guard subverting an evil system, but a genuinely sympathetic portrayal of prison guards in general. I checked out the Internet Movie Database, which had five pages of movies with the keyword "prison." Of the titles I recognized, all portrayed the guards as corrupt, sadistic, racist, etc. This seems to be especially true since the 1960s, but even in older films the guards seem to have been portrayed as an evil, menacing force.

—Edgar Burke, Johnson City, Tennessee

A. Of course *Shawshank Redemption,* from the same author and director as *The Green Mile,* also has some sympathetic guards. Otherwise, the only movie I can think of with good jailers is *Quills,* where Joaquin Phoenix plays the Marquis de Sade's sympathetic warden. He is soon replaced by a sadist, of course, although perhaps de Sade considered that an improvement.

The Producers

Q. With the enormous critical and financial success of *The Producers* on Broadway, and since the movie is your all-time favorite comedy, I am curious to know how you like the stage version.

—Richard Motroni, Redwood City, California

A. I saw the Broadway-bound production in Chicago and loved it. It would be unethical for me to comment on the New York production, however, since Mel Brooks sold me 100 percent of the rights.

Product Placement

Q. In *House on Haunted Hill* there is a scene where a character is fooling around with some video hardware. Near him are some video boxes. On the Blockbuster version of this video, they have superimposed the Blockbuster logo onto the boxes! The reason it caught my eye was the visual effect looked superimposed—these didn't look like Blockbuster videos just sitting there. They've taken the liberty of forcing product placement into the film. I was wondering if the studio knew about this, and what their opinion was.

—Chris Bushnell, San Francisco, California

A. Oh, yeah, the studio knew, all right, although director William Malone was none too happy. He replies: "The studio made a deal with Blockbuster prior to the theatrical release of the film. An optical effect was indeed utilized in placing the Blockbuster logo onto the videocassettes, and this effect appears in all versions of the film. It's part of the commercialism in film today."

Note: After the above appeared, the AM received further clarification from Pamela Godfrey, vice president for worldwide publicity at Warner Bros. She wrote: "In response, firstly we do not make 'Blockbuster' versions of videos; all copies are identical. Secondly, we screened a VHS copy in our office and noted that videos with the Blockbuster logo did appear in the film and would have been part of the scene when shot. Product placement is commonplace to most contemporary movies and is a creative decision between production designers and producers."

Quotes

Q. The other night I saw an advertisement for the Sally Field–directed beauty pageant movie *Beautiful.* The ad said Rosie O'Donnell called it funny. Is this movie so bad it can't even find praise from obscure venues like "Wake Up Winnipeg!"—and has to take quotes from talk shows where the actors appear to plug the film and the host therefore gives clearly biased praise?

—Matt Rogina, Chicago, Illinois

A. Yes.

Q. I read an ad for *Little Nicky* that said, "Don't miss the film Roger Ebert calls 'Adam Sandler's best movie so far!'" Huh? I thought you gave it 2.5 stars and a thumbs-down.

—Susan Lake, Urbana, Illinois

A. I did. But they quoted me accurately. Of course, it would have been even more accurate to say: "Thumbs down for Adam Sandler's best movie so far!"

Q. You have been victimized by the movie ads again. Whose quote do I see on an ad for *See Spot Run* but yours, calling the film "a series of slapstick comedy adventures." Allow me to recall a Dennis Miller rant, where he mentioned he could say, "I'd rather be in a gas chamber than watch this movie again," and the studios would shorten it to 'A gas!'"

—Adam J. Hakari, Barron, Wisconsin

A. I originally wrote: "a series of slapstick comedy ventures [not "adventures"] in which Gordon is humiliated and besmeared while the dog races about proving it is the most intelligent mammal in the picture." Here's another quote they could have used: "Movies like this demonstrate that only the best will do for our children." Or, in my full version, "Movies like this demonstrate that when it comes to stupidity and vulgarity, only the best will do for our children."

Q. The back of the DVD release of *Your Friends & Neighbors* reads, "One of the most talked about comedies of the season. . . . If you enjoy passion, lust, sexuality, and light-hearted humor, this is your circle of friends." This is about as accurate as saying that *Psycho* was a feel-good movie about a guy who loved birds.

—Carl Miller, Duke University, Durham, North Carolina

A. Both blurbs and trailers often reflect the movie the studio wishes the director had made, rather than the movie he made.

Q. I have just seen a TV ad for *Atlantis,* and I think I have witnessed history. Among the critics' blurbs was "Adventure." Just that one word: "Adventure." I recorded the spot on TV and studied it. There are actually three one-word reviews: "Awesome" (Stephen Type Too Small to Read), "Action" (Katie O'Grady of KPTV, Portland), and "Adventure" (Gary Schrendel of KGTV, San Diego). This development has huge implications that I can just barely grasp. If the size of a single atom of film criticism—the unit which you can't make smaller without a huge explosion—is now one single word, what chance does a critic have?

—Andy Ihnatko, Westwood, Massachusetts

A. In my own review, I use the phrase "animated adventure," but that's probably too inside baseball for the average viewer.

Q. When I noticed an ad with lots of rave quotes for *Scary Movie 2,* I couldn't help but look closer. Most are the usual bits of hyperbole from people you've never heard of, but then I saw one attributed to Jack Matthews of *Newsday*—a reputable critic. His quote reads, in full: "It's inspired by *The Exorcist, American Pie, Raging Bull, Hannibal, Charlie's Angels, Mission: Impossible, What Lies Beneath, House on Haunted Hill,* CBS's *Survivor,* NBC's *The Weakest Link,* and Firestone's collapsible tires." At no point does he actually offer any opinion about the actual film; all the quote does is list many of the subjects that are so ineptly parodied. Could this be the wave of the future for movie ad quotes? Are studios so desperate for name quotes in the post–David Manning era that they are now using strictly informational sentences, hoping people don't realize the difference between fact and opinion?

—Peter Sobczynski, Liberty Newspapers, Chicago

A. The movie was released by a branch of Miramax, which recently asked me if they could use a quote from my negative review of *The Closet.* The quote was: "Turns the tables on *La Cage aux Folles.*" And so it does, but not at the same level of achievement.

Rain in the Movies

Q. In nearly every film made, in at least one scene, there is evidence it has rained recently. What do you think of this apparent rain fascination?

—Dan Mouritsen, Logan, Utah

A. There is a lot of recent rain, especially in night scenes, because the wet streets reflect light and are incomparably more photogenic.

Red Eyes

Q. The trick to making bad movies more interesting is red eyes. Imagine that for a brief moment a character's eyes become supernaturally red. You'd be surprised how often this helps explain things. In *Volcano* there is this little boy who spends the second half of the film walking through the city as it crumbles around him, threatening to crush him at any moment. At the end of the film the boy is reunited with his mom and there is a big hug. Right then I imagined the little boy's eyes flickering red, suggesting he is the satanic figure who caused the volcano to erupt in the first place. Interesting, huh?

—Brad Smissen, Anaheim, California

A. I'm trying it right now on Wilson, the volleyball from *Cast Away*.

Red Planet

Q. I just read your review of *Red Planet*. What are Isaac Asimov's Three Laws of Robotics?

—Carol Antonow, Grand Rapids, Michigan

A. Good Dr. Asimov postulated that if mankind ever created a race of robots, we would have to protect ourselves by programming them with three crucial laws. They are: "1. A robot may not injure a human being, or, through inaction, allow a human being to come to harm. 2. A robot must obey the orders given it by human beings except where such orders would conflict with the First Law. 3. A robot must protect its own existence as long as such protection does not conflict with the First or Second Law." Asimov then wrote the book *I, Robot*, which consists of stories in which robots or their masters find and exploit loopholes.

Remember the Titans

Q. I'm someone who lived through the real story of *Remember the Titans*. I was a teacher at T.C. Williams from 1967 to 1972, and was the football PA announcer. To answer the questions posed at the end of your review:

There were actually three high schools in Alexandria before 1971. G.W. was the downtown school and had a 50/50 racial split, T.C. Williams had a 70/30 white/black ratio, and Hammond was pretty much all white. Herman Boone was actually the head coach at T.C. for two years before the schools merged. Yoast was the coach at Hammond. The G.W. coach was ready for retirement and did so. So while the decision to give Boone the head job was gutsy it wasn't that big a deal. The black players at T.C. weren't upset about the decision because they knew Boone knew them pretty well. The movie makes Alexandria look like Redneckville. It wasn't, although the coaching fraternity was a "Good Ole Boy Network." I cannot remember one racial incident or fight in the halls either before or

after the three schools merged. I think Boone's job with the team helped make that happen. I watched the movie on Friday night with a friend who had been a junior at T.C. in 1972. We both agreed that what happened in Alexandria in 1971 wasn't that big a deal, but we loved the movie and in retrospect think that it was a hoot being a part of history.

—Don Kubie, Westport, Connecticut

A. In other words, T.C. Williams was already integrated, and Boone was already its coach, when mostly white Hammond was merged with it, and Boone simply kept his job rather than taking Yoast's job? And there were no racial incidents or fights? I guess that wouldn't have made as good a movie.

Requiem for a Dream

Q. I recently read a review of Darren Aronofsky's *Requiem for a Dream* in which the reviewer encouraged teenagers to ignore the film's NC-17 rating and do everything they could to see this film. As a sixteen-year-old I wonder if you think this is the right thing for teens my age. Is this another bad job of the MPAA giving harsh ratings to films teenagers should see, like *Almost Famous*?

—Ryan Vooris, Herkimer, New York

A. The movie has not been rated NC-17 or anything else. But Artisan, the distributor of *Requiem for a Dream*, has announced a policy of strict enforcement of an adults-only policy. This is an indirect endorsement of the A rating I have long suggested. The policy has caused some theater chains to ask Artisan to share the burden of hiring the necessary security guards—or hall monitors, so to speak—a tacit admission that ratings are not much enforced at present.

Q. Isn't the film *Requiem for Dream* based on Hubert Selby Jr.'s novel of the same name, and not on his other novel *Last Exit to Brooklyn*? Your review and others cited *Last Exit*, but I think that's wrong.

—William Swenson, Minneapolis, Minnesota

A. You are correct. Although *Last Exit* was inexplicably linked to the movie in some reference material, the director, Darren Aronofsky, tells the AM: "*Requiem for a Dream* is based on the 1978 novel of the same name by

Hubert Selby Jr. Selby's first novel was *Last Exit to Brooklyn* which was turned into a movie in 1989 by Uli Edel and has a knockout performance from Jennifer Jason Leigh. Thundermouth Press has just reissued a paperback of *Requiem for a Dream* that has a new intro by yours truly. It's a great book, a work of poetry, and I recommend it."

Q. In *Requiem for a Dream,* I noticed a recurring scene where Jared Leto's character walks out on a pier trying to reach Jennifer Connelly, who is standing at the edge looking out toward the water. It struck me instantly that this scene is identical to one of the last shots of *Dark City,* in which Jennifer Connelly stands on a pier in the exact same spot of the frame while Rufus Sewell approaches her. The scenes are so similar it seems impossible that this was done unintentionally.
—John Kane, Richmond, Virginia

A. Director Darren Aronofsky responds: "The pier scene comes from a personal moment in my own life. When I was a teenager, I once met a girl I had a crush on out at that Coney Island pier. When I was writing the script, before I cast Jennifer, I decided to draw on this personal moment. Unfortunately, I had missed *Dark City* and had no idea there was a similar image in Alex Proyas's film. When we got to the pier Jennifer told me how strange it was that both films used this image. At that point, it was too late to change things. So I went for it. Since the shoot I've watched *Dark City* and was amazed that not only did we use a similar shot but we used the same actor. I guess I fed off of some ether that Alex created and presented to the universe. So I owe him thanks as I owe so many filmmakers who continue to influence me consciously and unconsciously."

Q. Having missed it in the theater I was excited to rent *Requiem for a Dream* on video. However, Blockbuster only carries the "edited version" of the film without giving the customer any choice. Is this a policy? This makes it seem as though all the fighting Darren Aronofsky did to keep his original, uncut vision was in vain once the movie hit the video shelves.
—Jeremy Sigel, Rockville, Maryland

A. Some chains want to protect you from yourself. They ban unrated and NC-17 films, but don't put their money where their mouths are by refusing to carry such films altogether. Instead, they offer edited versions which distort the director's original vision. The chains should be honest enough to ban the films outright, instead of taking business from stores that respect the original versions.

Here is director Darren Aronofsky's reply: "When I first showed the film to Artisan we agreed that no matter what happened we would release the cut as is. Unfortunately, the MPAA gave us the ill-fated NC-17 rating. Since Artisan agreed to release the film as is, I agreed to deliver an R-rated edited version for the video output deals that demand an R film. Companies like Blockbuster will not release NC-17 or unrated films and since this is a huge market for a distributor they have tremendous leverage. Artisan, in their kindness, agreed to clearly mark the film as the 'edited version.' I would of course encourage all film fans to buy or rent my 'director's cut.' Unfortunately, it is impossible to get the 'unrated director's cut' at Blockbuster or Hollywood because of their policies. You will need to go to other outlets to get the proper cut. By the way, the 'unrated director's cut' DVD has all of the extra features, missing scenes, behind the scenes, etc., while the 'edited version' has none of them. Another reason to seek out the director's cut."

Sam Taylor

Q. In your review of *Down to Earth,* you make a reference to the old Hollywood joke about the credits in *The Taming of the Shrew* (1929), which supposedly read "screenplay by William Shakespeare, with additional dialogue by Sam Taylor." I've seen the recut 1966 version of the film, and there is no such credit. Is this pure myth, or are there variant prints floating around out there with this credit?
—Michael Harrison, Santa Fe, New Mexico

A. I've heard the story countless times, and double-checked the credit on the Internet. I'm sure you're right about the version you saw, but for an overall verdict I turned to Tim Dirks, whose www.filmsite.org is a trove of accurate info about movies. He tells me controversy rages: "The legend is debunked on the Internet Movie Database by James Moffat of Melbourne, Australia, who says the credit line is 'pure myth.' But The IMDB's listing for the film prints the credit information. Leonard Maltin's *Movie and Video Guide* says, 'This is the film with the infamous credit, "By William Shakespeare, with additional dialogue by Sam Taylor."' And Baz Lurhmann, director of *Romeo + Juliet*, confirms the credit in an interview at www.middleenglish.org."

Scary Movie

Q. About *Scary Movie*. I would say "uncivilized" is the only word to do it justice. I was curious to see it after the mention you made in reply to a reader's query on Sunday. So I went. The thought of any child seeing that movie makes me want to track down each of the filmmakers and somehow call them to account for the damage they are doing. With garbage like this, I am in favor of outright censorship. A society that puts up with *Scary Movie* (and I suppose there may be even worse) is a society without the will to defend itself. Anyway, my point was to ask, since the rating system is an obvious failure, if you have ever thought of devising a rating system of your own, to guide parents wondering whether a movie is suitable for their children. I am sure parents would be grateful. I note that you did mention the coarse nature of the film—but wouldn't a "don't let your kids watch this" be more effective?

—Nick Hamilton, Chicago, Illinois

A. I do sometimes warn parents when I think a PG-13 movie is not for the kids, but now I see that since parents completely disregard the R rating, a warning is sometimes appropriate there too. The amazing thing is that this movie did untold millions in business and lots of parents took their kids. I got other letters from shell-shocked parents. The MPAA's greedy refusal to allow a workable adult rating means the R rating has been stretched beyond all reason and now encompasses material which is clearly for "adults only," including the genital gags in *Scary Movie*.

Second Second Assistant Director

Q. I have often read the ending credits and wondered exactly what each person's job is. At the end of *The Perfect Storm*, I saw credits for "Assistant Director," "Second Assistant Director," and "Second Second Assistant Director." Now I just gotta ask. Exactly what does a "Second Second Assistant Director" do?

—Alan Altman, New Fairfield, Connecticut

A. I referred your query to the writer-director Kevin Smith *(Clerks, Chasing Amy, Dogma)*, who replies:

"The term 'Second Second AD' is really a smoke screen. This term is employed in movies as a polite way of saying 'Third AD.' If you say 'Third AD' really fast, many times, you might notice how easy it would be to say 'Turd AD.' According to lore on the set, that's why AD's opted for 'Second Second' as opposed to simply 'Third'—because people on set never missed an opportunity to refer to them as 'the Turd.'

"The actual job of the Third AD, or Second Second, is to carry out the Second AD's wishes. The job of the Second AD is to carry out the Assistant Director's wishes. The job of the Assistant Director is to make the Director's life miserable by constantly reminding him or her that we're running behind schedule. In essence, the entire AD team is on set solely to enrage the director (well, that and to direct background action of extras, bring the actors to and from their trailers, and have the talent sign out after the shooting day is completed). An interesting side note—it's the job of the AD to utter those immortal words 'Stand by for picture,' and 'Roll sound,' and in the case of some extremely lazy directors, 'Action.'"

Sexy Beast

Q. I just saw Jonathan Glazer's *Sexy Beast*, which I really admired, and after writing my review decided to read what others have said about it. I was heartened by the largely positive response Glazer's film has elicited, but disappointed that most critics felt compelled to express surprise and, in some cases, utter shock that Glazer is actually a graduate of (gasp!) music videos and television commercials. TV ads and music videos have been the primary source of new filmmakers for more than twenty years now—arguably, beginning with Ridley Scott, who made his first feature, *The Duellists,* in 1977—yet there are film writers who behave as if this is some kind of newfangled, and undesirable, trend. Why can't we finally accept commercials and videos as just other training grounds for filmmakers?

—Joe Baltake, film critic,
Sacramento (California) Bee

A. You make an excellent point, and indeed some of the most visually alive new films, like Tarsem's *The Cell,* Baz Luhrmann's *Moulin Rouge,* and Spike Jonze's *Being John Malkovich,* are from directors with short-form experience. *Sexy Beast* is one of the summer's real discoveries, and is likely to get an Oscar nomination for Ben Kingsley.

Shrek

Q. Was the ogre in the title role in *Shrek* inspired in some way by Max Schreck, the German actor who starred in *Nosferatu*?

—Susan Lake, Urbana, Illinois

A. He was not, according to DreamWorks founder Jeffrey Katzenberg, who masterminded the film. The screenwriters were not familiar with the silent classic.

Q. In a recent Movie Answer Man column you stated that the title *Shrek* is not a reference to Max Schreck since the screenwriters of the recent animated film were not familiar with Murnau's masterpiece *Nosferatu.* How can this be? How can someone get to the point where they are making megabudget movies that actually get produced and yet be so ignorant of film?

—Gil Jawetz, Brooklyn, New York

A. You pose an excellent question.

Q. If the moral of *Shrek* is to not judge others (or yourself) based on superficialities such as physical appearance, how can we reconcile this message with the disparaging remarks about the king's height? Green stinky ogres shouldn't be subjected to ridicule, but it is acceptable to make jokes at the expense of short people? Maybe instead of worrying about going bald, I should dye my head green.

—Nick Smith, Erie, Pennsylvania

A. Good idea, Stinky!

Special Effects

Q. In your review of Jackie Chan's latest American release, *The Legend of the Drunken Master,* you praised his athletic skills but wrote that computerized special effects have made them sort of obsolete: "When you see bodies whirling in air in *The Matrix,* you don't think about computers, you simply accept them. But what Chan does, he is more or less, one way or another, actually doing."

I disagree with your remarks about computers. In *The Matrix,* yes, I accepted the fight scenes—I thought they were very cool because the style was completely new—but I couldn't *help* thinking of computers. There was nothing even remotely "real" about those fight scenes. The "whirling bodies" defied gravity in a fascinating but totally artificial way. And now we have *Charlie's Angels* (unfortunately), which employs the exact same animation techniques in its fight scenes. When I watch Chan in action, I feel awe and exhilaration; when I see Drew Barrymore jump in the air, kick a bad guy in the face five times, do a backflip, and land lightly on her feet, I feel nothing but ennui.

—Brad Miller, Dallas, Texas

A. But do most audiences know the difference, or care? Clint Eastwood risked his life by literally hanging suspended from a single rope thousands of feet in the air in *The Eiger Sanction,* and slipped into a sneak preview where he overheard someone asking, "I wonder how he did that?" Computers have, I think, devalued the special skills and grace of someone like Jackie Chan.

Stadium Seating

Q. I am finding it hard to adjust to the stadium seating arrangement of the new generation megaplexes. Don't get me wrong, most of the theaters are beautiful, the seats comfortable, and the sound excellent (if sometimes too loud). What I don't like is having to sit so close to the screen. I am used to that seventies rule that said the best way to view a film is to sit at a distance proportionate to one and one half the width of the screen. I can't do that in these tiny "screening rooms." What do you think?

—Lou Rosenberger, Bethlehem, Pennsylvania

A. Stadium seating seems like a good thing but may be a mixed blessing. Apart from patrons stumbling down the stairs (which is a real problem), there is the psychological argument that a movie plays better when we look up at it, not down at it or straight at it. The solution is not to raise the seats for better sight lines, but to raise the screens while gently raking the floor—just like in the classic movie palaces. According to some vision specialists, the ideal place to sit in a movie theater is twice as far back as the screen is wide. Most stadium seating makes that impossible. On the other hand, two of Chicago's best-known film critics always sit in the front row, so go figure.

Star Ratings

Q. Hello from Iran. I am very happy that these new foreign movies such as *A Time for Drunken Horses* are there for you to see. I am a movie critic myself. I usually go through your writings, such as *Nutty Professor 2,* which I saw today and didn't like. I noticed that you gave it three stars. Why should Eddie Murphy and Janet Jackson in a very empty movie with no feeling other than crude jokes on people (no funny jokes, no real interesting subjects, and yes, there was good makeup), get three stars, the same as *Drunken Horses*?

—Sara Sedighi Millikin, Tehran

A. Star ratings are a kind of convenient shorthand for readers, but should always be seen as relative, not absolute. They are awarded with a generic spin: *Nutty Professor* was a three-star comedy, *A Time for Drunken Horses* was a three-star serious drama, and on an absolute scale *Horses* was indeed deeper, more affecting, and more important than *Nutty.*

Star Wars Episode I: The Phantom Menace Rewrite

Q. Is it legal for someone to rewrite a script and improve it after the movie is out? Or is it even ethical? One guy did such for *Star Wars Episode 1: The Phantom Menace.*

—Richard Sol, Los Angeles, California

A. There are at least three "corrected" versions, either revising or all but eliminating the character of Jar Jar Binks. One is a rewritten screenplay. Another is a reedited version of the video of the film, shorter and with some scenes rearranged. Of course this is against the law, but George Lucas seems to be taking it pretty well, perhaps because this kind of fan activity is a compliment, and enhances interest in the film. There's detailed coverage at www.zap2it.com.

Strong Language

Q. Why do filmmakers insist on "strong language"? I realize some films such as *Goodfellas* or *Full Metal Jacket* gain a level of realism necessary to the subject, but most films use extraordinary amounts of unnecessary language. Take *Magnolia,* for example—a film everyone should see for what it says about people, but poisoned by every character but one possessing a serious vocabulary problem. What gives? Is *Streetcar Named Desire* any less powerful because it was written in a time less free than this one? Would the classics of *film noir* be grittier with fouler language? David Mamet's *The Spanish Prisoner* did not need the same language as his other works to be just as good and more enjoyable to sit through. I am not asking for Disney films but for more thoughtful, literate, and yes, civil writing.

—David Walters, Dallas, Texas

A. I referred your query to the director Allison Anders, whose powerful new film *Things Behind the Sun* contains a certain amount of "language." She replies:

"While admittedly among the guilty as a filmmaker who uses a lot of f-words, I also often wish we could return to the days when the restraints of the industry forced us filmmakers to economize on language, violence, and nudity. If we're going for naturalism in our characters (I tend to make films about rock musicians or gang members!) we use the freedom allotted us by the ratings system to go for the real and the natural, for how these people would truly talk. This is a freedom I don't think we filmmakers would want to lose, but, like you, I wonder sometimes if we wouldn't make our work more powerful by having to curb the strong language and reach for more literate solutions in our dialogue. Having gone through a reedit due to an undesirable rating from the MPAA, I found the scene, after much of the nudity was cut, was made far more intense by playing most of it on the actresses' face. Artists hate to admit it, but boundaries are just as important as freedom to the success of one's work and restraint forces us to come up with new solutions which often surprise us."

Swordfish

Q. John Travolta says in *Swordfish* that the front companies set up by the government had $400 million in the bank in the mid-eighties, and "fifteen years later," it has grown to $9.5 billion. That's 24 percent interest compounded annually. Aren't these flaws distracting when they appear in an otherwise completely plausible movie?

—Bennett Haselton, Seattle, Washington

A. You're saying *Swordfish* is an otherwise completely plausible movie? Would that include the scene of the bus full of hostages dangling from the helicopter? In a movie like this, 24 percent is a modest return.

Q. I just wanted to point out that in your review for *Swordfish*, you quoted a song as "50,000 Volts of (bleeping)." The word in the song is not the f-word, it is "funk."

—Chris Frazier, Seattle, Washington

A. I hate it when these singers don't enunciate clearly.

Q. You stated in your review of *Swordfish* that Dominic Sena is getting better as a director. Let's not forget his first film was the small, powerful Brad Pitt film *Kalifornia* (1993). I eagerly awaited his follow-up for seven years. The follow-up I got was the pointless *Gone in 60 Seconds*.

—Josh Korkowski, Minneapolis, Minnesota

A. My oversight. *Kalifornia* was on my list of the best films of 1993. It was an amazingly good debut.

The Tao of Steve

Q. You observed that Donal Logue did not remove his shirt in *The Tao of Steve*, and said

you suspected he was not as fat as the character he played. Logue's apparent weight was a combination of both padding and some extra weight he gained for the *Tao* film. This information came from Logue when he was at the Seattle Film Festival this spring. Donal said he quickly lost the extra weight as he went from filming *The Tao of Steve* to *The Patriot*.

—Patrick Ryan, Bainbridge Island, Washington

A. Since movies love it when fat guys take off their shirts, I knew something was up.

Thalberg Award

Q. Dino De Laurentiis is set to receive the Thalberg Award this year because of the "consistently high quality" of his work. Is this the same high quality work that includes *King Kong, King Kong Lives, Mandingo, Dune, Conan the Destroyer,* and *Diabolik* (a film that was even shown on *Mystery Science Theater*)? Did the Academy run out of producers to honor?

—James Livingston, Boston, Massachusetts

A. To be fair, De Laurentiis's long career also includes work by Fellini, de Sica, and Bergman and American productions like *Ragtime, The Dead Zone,* and, although I didn't much like it, *Hannibal*. De Laurentiis is a legend with a career spanning sixty years. Perhaps the problematical word in the citation is "consistently."

One consistently distinguished producer of high quality work who deserves Academy recognition: Ed Pressman.

Thomas and the Magic Railroad

Q. In your review of *Thomas and the Magic Railroad,* you wrote: "In an age when even the cheapest Saturday morning cartoons find a way to make the lips move, what, oh, what, was the reasoning behind Thomas's painted-on grin?" That's easy: It's because that's the way it has always been for years and years of the TV show *Shining Time Station* and the many videotapes, and young children eat it up. My seven- and three-year-old sons have loved watching both the show and the tapes since they turned one year old, and they wouldn't expect the movie to be any other way. Obviously, the movie is intended for the legions of Thomas fans. Although I have not yet seen it, nothing in your review indicates that those young children will be disappointed (which you do imply in your next-to-last paragraph). I'm sure I won't like it any more than I like the tapes and TV show, but the movie obviously isn't intended for me or any other adults.

—Evan H. Zucker, San Diego, California

A. I confess I have never watched *Shining Time Station* and did not know that the lips don't move on TV. But they should! If you have eyes and they move, and you can talk, then your lips should move too. Low budget shortcuts are one thing on TV. Now that Thomas is a movie star, he should have been given a break.

Thumbs Up

Q. The new Sandra Bullock movie *Miss Congeniality* contains eight thumbs-up gestures. This is a record for the number of thumbs in a single film. I have a theory that since the creation of the Ebert and Siskel program, Hollywood has strategically placed "thumbs-up" gestures in movies not only to subconsciously suggest to audiences they're watching a "thumbs-up" film, but also to suck up to a certain influential movie critic who has trademarked this particular digital communiqué. Sound nutty? Here's just a partial listing of thumbs-up gesturing in recent movies:

French Stewart in *Love Stinks,* Famke Janssen in *House on Haunted Hill,* Jessica Pare in *Stardom,* John Travolta and Lisa Kudrow in *Lucky Numbers,* Jesus Christ in *Dogma,* Minnie Driver in *Beautiful,* Damon Wayans in *Bamboozled,* Robin Williams in *Father's Day,* Kathleen Quinlan in *Breakdown,* Rowan Atkinson in *Bean,* Angelina Jolie and John Cusack in *Pushing Tin,* Craig Ferguson in *Big Tease,* Jenna Elfman in *Keeping the Faith,* Stephen Baldwin in *Flintstones in Viva Rock Vegas* (plus a thumbs-up billboard cutout over the end credits), Joaquin Phoenix in *Gladiator,* Lupe Ontiveros in *Buck and Chuck,* Richard Dreyfuss in *The Crew,* Eddie Murphy in *The Klumps,* Ginger the Chicken in *Chicken Run,* Bruce Willis and Spencer Breslin in *Disney's The Kid,* Tim Meadows (five times) in *The Ladies Man,* plus Will Farrell in *The*

Ladies Man, an unidentified army officer in *The Puppet Masters,* and Mark Fuerstein in *Woman on Top.* Want further proof? Check out the one-sheet for the movie *Bye, Bye, Love* where a thumbs-up has obviously been inserted into a photo of the main cast. (You can tell it's inserted, because the hand seems too large for the people and it doesn't really seem to belong to anyone in the picture.) Is my theory sound, or have I been watching too many Shannon Tweed cable epics co-starring Andrew Stevens?

—Dann Gire, *The Daily Herald,*
Arlington Heights, Illinois

A. I have subjected your valuable data to a penetrating statistical analysis. You name twenty-three movies. I did not review five of them. Of the eighteen remaining, I gave ten thumbs-down and eight thumbs-up. Of course, the thumb gesture in *Gladiator* may not count, because thumbs-up in Roman times meant what thumbs-down means today. In response to your second question, Shannon Tweed and Andrew Stevens have costarred in five movies, including the intriguing *Body Chemistry 4: Full Exposure.* Anyone who knows they have costarred in more than three is watching too many.

Ticket Prices

Q. Why is it that all movie admission prices are the same even though each movie costs a different amount to produce? If one movie costs $10 million to produce and another costs $50 million to produce, shouldn't the admission price reflect this? I believe I should not have to pay the same amount to see an art film as a big production film.

—Becky Wilson, Mission, Kansas

A. Would you spend $40 to see *See Spot Run*? Seriously: Instead of being concerned with unit costs, like the car industry, the movie industry corrects for budgets by the anticipated size of the audience. No studio is likely to spend $100 million on a film it doesn't expect to gross much more than that. As for the theaters themselves, they make most of their money at the refreshment stand.

Q. Why is a film's success determined by the dollar amount of the box-office take, instead of total number of tickets sold? Ticket prices today are higher than ten years ago. Therefore today's films don't have to sell nearly as many tickets to reach the $100 million mark. It would be interesting to compare the number of tickets sold for a 1965 hit like *Thunderball* with a modern hit like *Titanic,* on a level playing field.

—Jerome Ritchey, Champaign, Illinois

A. Such comparisons are deliberately overlooked when companies tout new box-office records, because the real reason for such publicity is to create a herd mentality among moviegoers who assume that popularity equals quality. It is shameful, however, that the news media solemnly parrot the numbers without pointing out your obvious point.

Q. I read in David Poland's Web column: "American Multi-Cinema is test-marketing a monthly movie pass in Omaha and Oklahoma City, allowing the holder to see a movie a day every day of the month for just $17.50 in Omaha and $14.50 in Oklahoma City." How do you think they can do this, and do you think it will work?

—Susan Lake, Urbana, Illinois

A. Poland adds that the chain plans to pay the studios their usual share of each admission. How does this make economic sense? It's a brilliant demonstration of the bottom line of movie exhibition: Theaters make most of their money at the refreshment stand. Since most heavy moviegoers presumably already go on weekends, this will bring them out during the slower nights of the week, and AMC will turn a profit from the popcorn and candy.

Titles

Q. There is a trend in Hollywood to come up with the blandest title possible. I understand that *Rocket Boys* was the original title for *October Sky,* and *Dancing About Architecture* became *Playing by Heart* (worse yet, it could have been *If They Only Knew*). Bonnie Hunt's recent comedy was titled an uninspiring *Return to Me.* Don't studios realize that audiences are attracted to exciting titles that reflect the nature of the movie? Even simple titles like *The Abyss* and *L.A. Confidential* are

not going to be confused with other movies, unlike the titles *Extreme Measures* or *Maximum Risk*—who is going to remember what those were about? Huh? What is going on here?

—Corey Whaley, Edmond, Oklahoma

A. Couldn't agree with you more. I'm especially confused by the Basic Fatal Syndrome: *Basic Instinct, Fatal Attraction, Fatal Instinct, Fatal Beauty,* etc. Here, on the other hand, are titles no one could confuse: *Being John Malkovich, Shakespeare in Love, Mighty Peking Man, Mission to Mars, Space Cowboys, Perfect Storm.* The most wrongheaded name-change I can think of was when they took the wonderful *Cops Tips Waitress $2 Million* and changed it to *It Could Happen to You.* Changing *Rocket Boys* to *October Sky* was almost as dumb. And the forgettable new title *Bring It On* was originally called *Cheer Fever* (although *Cheerleader Fever* would have been better still). By the way, *The Abyss* almost had its title changed because market research showed many people did not know what an abyss was.

Q. I want to hear someone agree with me that rereleasing *Raiders of the Lost Ark* as *Indiana Jones and the Raiders of the Lost Ark* is really, really stupid. I saw the actual video box on a shelf. Is this now the new, official title of this film? What I mean to say is, will this film now be filed under "I" instead of "R"? If you ask me, *Raiders* deserves to be set apart from the other films in the series.

—Joel Tallent, Brooklyn, New York

A. It's stupid, but not as stupid as rereleasing *The Exorcist* with the formerly perfect ending now followed by a conversation about a version of *Wuthering Heights* starring Jackie Gleason and Lucille Ball. I am not making this up.

Q. Bruce Willis likes to make movies with numbers in the titles. His first movie role was *The First Deadly Sin* (1980), in which he was uncredited. He was in *Loaded Weapon 1, Die Hard 2, Look Who's Talking Too, Die Hard 3, Four Rooms, The Fifth Element, The Sixth Sense, The Whole Nine Yards,* and *Twelve Monkeys.*

—Scott Honea, Corsicana, Texas

A. I think you should also give him the benefit of the doubt on *Last Man Standing.*

Toronto Locations

Q. I saw a piece on TV about an upcoming movie named *Angel Eyes.* It stars Jennifer Lopez as a uniformed Chicago police officer. I am a Chicago police sergeant, and I have been pushing a beat car for twenty-two years. I am also an actor and a film location safety supervisor. I have worked part-time on almost every major film production made in this town since 1985. What really made me mad was that this Chicago movie was being shot in Toronto! While the Canadian and Toronto governments have subsidized their movie industry, Mayor Daley wants to tax it out of existence. There is a 6 percent head tax on equipment rental and a head tax on employees. There are no good studio facilities in Chicago; we work in converted rust belt factories. We need to build a studio in Chicago and have the incentives to do work here.

—Name withheld, Chicago, Illinois

A. The other side of this coin is the amusing reluctance of studios to admit their films are shot in Toronto. They send a unit to Chicago for a quick shot of the skyline, and then frame every Toronto shot to block out landmarks like the CN Tower. Why not just set the movie in Toronto? Why is Chicago seen as so desirable that movies lie about it? One theory: In TV ads, that gruff announcer's voice saying he's a Chicago cop! has a certain ring that he's a Toronto cop! somehow lacks.

Trailers and Commercials

Q. Having seen the trailer for *What Lies Beneath,* I already knew some of the big surprises. What amazed me when I went to see the movie was how long it took to get to them. If the studio is determined to reveal the surprises before you go into the theater, it doesn't seem fair to make you wait an hour.

—Kelly MacNamara, Chicago, Illinois

A. I've always assumed the heathens in the marketing department were responsible for the spoilers. Reading David Poland's column on the Web, I find I'm living in a fool's paradise. He quotes *What Lies Beneath* director Robert Zemeckis:

"We know from studying the marketing of movies, people really want to know exactly every thing that they are going to see before they go see the movie. It's just one of those things. To me, being a movie lover and film student and a film scholar and a director, I don't . . . I relate it to McDonald's. The reason McDonald's is a tremendous success is that you don't have any surprises. You know exactly what it is going to taste like. Everybody knows the menu. So it's not like you go to McDonald's and think, 'I wonder what I feel like eating today?'"

That's why, I guess, so many trailers reveal the secrets of their movies. But we deserve a break today.

Q. In the trailer for *Highlander: Endgame,* the villain is cut in two, is called a sorcerer, suspends a sword in midair, and views people on a magic floating crystal ball. The heroes are seen jumping through a "Poltergeist-style swirling vortex." None of these scenes are in the movie. The villain isn't a sorcerer, just a guy good at cutting off heads and hissing like the emperor in *Star Wars.* I've since found out from the *Highlander* Internet newsgroup that the scenes I mentioned were shot just for the *Highlander: Endgame* trailer and were never going to be in the movie. Not even scenes that were later cut but scenes that were never going to be used. How different can a trailer be from the film before it is just lying?

—Ian Boothby, Vancouver, British Columbia

A. This trailer seems different enough. I haven't seen *Highlander: Endgame,* since I was in Thailand when it opened, and would have been prepared to go even farther to avoid it, if necessary. I note on the Rotten Tomatoes Website that it scored 11 out of 100 on the Tomatometer, with three positive reviews and twenty-seven negative. Quite possibly anybody who has seen *Highlander: Endgame* is grateful that the trailer doesn't remind them of the movie.

Q. While at the movies tonight I saw a trailer for *Cast Away,* which revealed the ending of the movie. The next time you run into the marketing geniuses who decide these things, could you please do me a very big favor and beat them senseless with a large two-by-four?

—Ed Slota, Providence, Rhode Island

A. Louisa Aikin of Scottsdale is also annoyed: "The trailer gives away one of the big plot points—whether or not Tom Hanks's character manages to get home." And Aaron Widera of Long Beach writes: "Why would I or anybody who has seen the *Cast Away* trailer now playing in theaters and available on the Internet, pay to see a movie that I've already seen? I now know every important plot point, *including* the ending. Is this trailer-as-spoiler trend ever going to end?"

Jeffrey Godsick, executive vice president for publicity and promotions for 20th Century–Fox, responds to the Answer Man: "*Cast Away* is not a film about a man's attempts to escape from a remote island. Instead, it explores his physical and psychological journey during his stay on the island, as well as the unexpected emotional challenges he faces upon his return."

Having seen the movie, I disagree with Godsick. The Hanks character spends most of the movie uncertain about his future, and so should the audience. But many studios now frequently tell the entire story, including the ending, in their trailers.

Q. I am surprised that you were critical of Robert Zemeckis for giving away the plot to *Cast Away* in the trailer for the movie. While I share your disgust at this marketing tactic, Zemeckis is not doing anything different than what Shakespeare did at the beginning of *Romeo and Juliet*. I guess that it proves that audiences haven't changed in 400 years.
—Hugh Kearney, Clearwater, Florida

A. Shakespeare made you buy a ticket and enter the theater, where his introduction was part of the play. He didn't reveal the ending in his handbills.

Q. The original trailer for *Series 7* was most disturbing. It seemed to be a serious movie about people killing each other as a game. Then I saw a different trailer. The tone had changed. Perhaps because I'd read about the movie being a dark comedy about the "survival"-type shows on TV, I knew more of what it was about. It's interesting that the new trailer came out just after the recent high school shootings. It's also interesting because one of the stars has been on TV talking about

how this movie is *not* for children but only for adults. But the ads are clearly aimed at kids.
—Carol Iwata, Chicago, Illinois

A. No matter how grim or challenging the subject matter of a movie, the ads and trailers often try to present it as a jolly good time. Often the filmmakers cannot be blamed; the studio makes ads representing the movie they wish had been made, rather than the movie that was actually made.

Q. I just saw the movie *Along Came a Spider* and wonder if the trailer was intended for a different film. In the preview there was one scene showing the little girl running from a helicopter into her parents' arms. A second had a police officer looking down and saying to Morgan Freeman, "You had better take a look at this." As I recall, neither shot made it into the finished product. Was there postproduction tampering?
—Terry Dow, Winnipeg, Ontario

A. Rich Heimlich of Cherry Hill, New Jersey, has a similar complaint: "In the trailer for *Bridget Jones's Diary* we're shown a clip of Bridget answering the phone in a sexy way and then saying, 'Oh hello, Dad' but in the movie it becomes, 'Oh hello, Mom.' Why?"

Trailers are often edited from rough early cuts of movies, and use shots that may be absent in the final version. And the editors of trailers feel free to take anything from anywhere in the film and edit it together in any way without any regard for the film's actual plot.

Q. I was watching an ad for a Taco Bell tie-in with *Tomb Raider*, during which several scenes from the movie were flashed, among them the scene where Lara Croft is leaped on by the giant robot. I noticed that the pistols that were supposed to be in her hands had been digitally erased from this scene, so it just looked like she was waving her clenched fists at the robot. Were the guns taken out to make the scene appear less violent?
—James Culver, Spokane, Washington

A. Obviously. One problem with the digital revolution is that films become infinitely malleable. There is no longer a definitive image, but only a continuing process of fine-tuning for different audiences. In this case, the ad was changed from a fair fight to a one-sided assault, with the woman not as warrior but as victim.

Q. I noticed something about the commercials for *Baby Boy*. The Jody character used to say, "I love you girl; you got my son and you probably gonna be my wife"—which is what he says in the movie. But recently the ads were changed to omit the "probably." I can imagine why they changed it but I'm not sure it's ethical.

—Geeha Leem, Berkeley, California

A. Completely unethical, since the word "probably" is the key to the sentence, and an insight into Jody's character.

2001: A Space Odyssey

Q. On the first day of the new millennium, as a fan of *2001: A Space Odyssey,* I was led to your Website in search of a review. I noticed a slight technical error. You write about the scene when a bone is thrown into the air by prehistoric man and is transformed into a "space shuttle." In reality the space shuttle is a nuclear bomb orbital platform, according to *The Making of Kubrick's 2001,* edited by Jerome Agel.

—C. Mathew Curtz, San Diego, California

A. You are correct. Of course a space shuttle and a bomb platform might look very much the same. If you have to read the book to find out what it is, then on the basis of the film's interior evidence it could be either, or neither. I should have said "space platform," which would have covered me.

Q. Now that 2001 is upon us, I am waiting with great anticipation for the theatrical re-release of *2001: A Space Odyssey.* I understand that Stanley Kubrick edited out about twenty minutes of the film a week after its world premiere. It is almost certain that those deleted scenes still exist. Is there any word that Warner Bros. may include any part of those deleted scenes in the film's rerelease? It would seem like a good marketing ploy. It is not likely that Kubrick still has the legal authority to keep those scenes out of the film from beyond the grave.

—Richard Moyer, Beaverton, Oregon

A. I saw the original longer cut of *2001* at a screening the night before its world premiere. Kubrick (who refused to fly) edited the film right up until the last moment; the press breathlessly followed his progress as he edited on board the QE2 from Southampton to New York and then in a special railroad car as it made its way to Los Angeles. He complained he was still not finished but the studio had a deadline to meet and showed the longer version, which got generally negative reviews, although not from me. Then Kubrick made the trims for the theatrical release. The missing scenes essentially duplicate material still in the film, such as a shot of the pod leaving the ship. Kubrick's final cut is, I think, the best one, and, yes, his estate has the legal power to keep the missing scenes out of the film.

Tyrene Manson and *On the Ropes*

Q. Do you have an update on the fate of Tyrene Manson, the star of the documentary *On the Ropes*? Her Golden Gloves career was ended when she was jailed on dubious drug charges, although her parole board allowed her to attend the Oscars last March when the movie was nominated as Best Documentary.

—Susan Lake, Urbana, Illinois

A. Tyrene Manson is another victim of shabby criminal courts and draconian drug laws. A tiny amount of cocaine was found in a house she shared with other adults, including an uncle who had a drug conviction. There was no evidence she had ever used or sold drugs. After a legal defense that seems (in the film) laughable, she was separated from her two nieces and imprisoned. Her case has been followed by Diane Mellon of Park City, Utah, who informs me:

"Tyrene was denied parole in the fall of 2000, and on Thanksgiving Day she married George Walton, another fighter featured in the film. The ceremony was at the Leviticus Church of God in Christ, where she has a work-release job, and the ceremony was officiated over by Pastor Pullings. Pastor was always there for her, and assisted her during her trial as well as the time she has been incarcerated. He is just fifty years old, and suffered a heart attack two days after the wedding. We are all praying for his full recovery.

Tyrene will not come before the parole board again until the fall of 2001. She is still in a halfway house two nights a week."

Unbreakable

Q. I just read your review of *Unbreakable.* I'm afraid you didn't get the whole point of the movie. This film is not a "serious drama" as you state in your review. The entire movie is tongue in cheek. It's sly and witty, with lots of laughs for those who get the joke. The joke is that the entire movie is a comic book about a new superhero, in which the hero discovers his powers. The very name of the Bruce Willis character, David Dunn, is in the classic comic-book tradition of Peter Parker, Clark Kent, and Lois Lane. Similarly, Mr. Glass is in the tradition of The Joker, The Riddler, Pruneface, etc. The Bruce Willis character goes out in the rain wearing a hooded poncho reminiscent of Batman's hood and cape. I think the movie is a victim of bad marketing. The previews should have shown some of the lighter scenes to give the audience more appropriate expectations.

—Jared Laskin, Los Angeles, California

A. I agree it's a comic-book story, but not that it's funny, except to an in-group. I think the filmmakers would agree: It works as drama, that's the thing. The marketers must have known what they were doing, since it opened with a sensational $50 million week.

Q. During the movie *Unbreakable* I noticed that there were several periods after the train wreck scene that had subtle sounds of a train chugging. Was this intended or was this just an isolated problem with the sound?

—Mathew Berg, Oak Park, Illinois

A. Director M. Night Shyamalan says you are not hearing things. Throughout *Unbreakable* there are various noises put into the background of the sound track to heighten the drama and atmosphere. One of the noises used is the sound of a train.

Videotapes

Q. Why are videocassette movies getting physically lighter? The tapes in my collection that are seven to ten years old are definitely heavier than the feature tapes of the last few years. Is cheaper tape being used? Has technology changed? Is the quality reduced? Will the newer tapes have a shorter (or longer) shelf life?

—John Tirpak, Fairfax, Virginia

A. I went for an opinion to Michael Schlesinger, vice president of Sony Classics, who replies:

"There are several answers. One obvious reason is that lighter plastic is being used for the shells. (That is also true of audiocassettes.) For another, thinner tape is being used; it was originally developed for longer-length cassettes, but companies are using it right down the line. Look in the window of a new T-120; compared to one made years ago, it will look like there's less tape, though in fact there isn't. (The same is true of film; the newer Mylar stocks are far thinner than the old Polyesters.) I don't believe audio and video quality are affected in any way, though of course more care should be exercised when scanning or shuttling. As for prerecorded tapes, if a movie is under ninety minutes long, it will be recorded on a T-90; one that runs 100 minutes would be on a T-105, and so on. Less tape equals less weight."

Villains

Q. I watched *The Perfect Storm* last night and did not like it. But I noticed something interesting. Though the antagonist in the story is the storm, a lesser evil is the boat owner played by Michael Ironside. Clooney and crew return to sea for economic reasons, and Ironside's character personifies the ugly side of capitalism. In films where the enemy is nature (*Jaws, Towering Inferno, Titanic,* etc.), there is often a subplot involving some greedy corporation or officials who worsen the situation by "putting profits before human life." *The Grinch* takes a negative viewpoint toward the commercialization of Christmas, and yet you can't walk into a mall without stepping on a Grinch product. I would suggest that these anticapitalist clichés have become so standard that Hollywood filmmakers plug them in without even thinking about how contradictory they are to their own motives.

—Mike Spearns, St. John's, Newfoundland

A. Consider also the evil billionaire mountain climber in *Vertical Limit;* Nicolas Cage as a selfish executive at the beginning of *The Family Man;* Tom Hanks learning that company profits are not the most important thing in *Cast Away;* and the evil upper-class society twits in *House of Mirth.* It is easier for a camel to pass through the eye of a needle than for a rich man to be the hero in a movie.

What Lies Beneath

Q. I recently saw *What Lies Beneath* with my lovely, forearm-bruising girlfriend, and we are debating over the final fade to black. She saw a simple fade from the graveyard to black, nothing more. However, I am convinced there is a faint, flashed image of the ghost that spends most of the film popping in and out of reflections in a similar manner.

—Matt Thiesen, Maple Grove, Minnesota

A. According to a DreamWorks spokesperson, there is indeed a latent image of the ghost hidden in the snow at the very end of the film.

Wide-Screen Ratios

Q. I have been buying nothing but widescreen DVDs, whenever possible. Wide screen allows you to see the movie as it was intended to be seen, while pan and scan robs you of the director's visual composition. But I've noticed a peculiar thing: In *Network,* for example, there is a scene in which Faye Dunaway and William Holden enter a room with a bed and she begins stripping. In the theatrical release, her nipples show clearly as she is about to get into bed. Ditto in the pan-and-scan version, but not in the wide-screen version! I recently bought *Ghost Story* (1981). In it there is a scene where Alice Krige is standing nude before a glass door. When Craig Wasson enters the room, she turns. In the pan-and-scan version, her pubic area may be seen; in the wide-screen version, the picture is cut off below the navel. I am not a dirty old man, but I despise censorship. Please tell me this is not a trend in wide screen; that anything near the edge of the frame that may be objectionable will just be clipped.

—Jim Cameron, Soddy-Daisy, Tennessee

A. There is an innocent explanation, and it has to do with framing, Many movies are shot with more headroom and footroom on the frame than is ever intended to be seen in

the theater. A wide-screen plate in the projector gate defines the area intended to be framed and shown. When the wide-screen movie is transferred to a pan-and-scan video, areas may be revealed that the director never intended to be seen. If you indeed saw nudity in the theatrical version of *Network,* that was probably because the projectionist in that theater had the film incorrectly framed.

Q. Recently, I saw *The Patriot* at Chicago's Water Tower theater. When the film began, the audience noticed that the picture was off the screen. It extended about one foot off the top and bottom and approximately three feet off of each side onto the curtains and the walls. I mentioned this to the manager at the start of the film, hoping to have it corrected. I was told by her, "We know. The film they sent us was too large for our screen. There is nothing that can be done about it." I mentioned that I have been in theaters with much smaller screens than this one and not had a problem. I also noted that we shouldn't be expected to pay $8.50 for a movie when we are being denied a portion of the picture. She just shrugged it off.

—Jason Steele, Chicago, Illinois

A. A movie can be configured to show on any size screen. All it takes is a projectionist who knows what he's doing. The movie does not have a "size," but a format, and the projector must be adjusted to frame the film in that format. *The Patriot* was filmed in the ratio of 2.35 to 1, true wide screen, but movies in that format have been shown in every theater countless times.

Wonder Boys

Q. I rented *Wonder Boys.* When I put the cassette in, a message came up that said the film was "formatted to fit my screen." So I thought, "Okay, no letterbox." But then, at the end of the message, it said the film was "Edited for Content." What does this mean, exactly? Are the thought police watering down what I can watch?

—Matt Jaycox, Chicago, Illinois

A. Michael Mustizer of Waterbury, Connecticut, also wondered, "what has been edited either out or in?" The answer: Only one name. Martin Blythe, vice president for publicity of Paramount Home Video, tells me: "In the movie, the Toby McGuire character includes Alan Ladd in a list of suicides. The character is incorrect about this, and out of respect for his family, we deleted his name from the home video and DVD releases."

Wrecked Rectals

Q. There is an unfortunate typo in your Great Movie review of *Jaws,* when you cite this dialogue: "I pulled a tooth the size of a shot glass out of the rectal of a boat out there, and it was the tooth of a Great White." I believe it was not a "rectal" but a "wrecked hull."

—Peter T. West, Media Officer, National Science Foundation's Office of Polar Programs, Arlington, Virginia

A. The North Pole is melting and this you're worried about? That's a mistake but not a typo. I thought I heard "rectal" and double-checked with Tim Dirk's invaluable Greatest Films of All Time site (www.film-site.org). He also heard Richard Dreyfuss say "rectal." I asked Dirk for his response. He writes: "Here's the quoted line from the revised final draft screenplay, found on the Web: 'I just pulled a shark tooth the size of a shot glass out of the hull of a wrecked boat out there.' In playing the laser disc version myself, I heard 'the rectal of a boat.' Since the final screenplay version does use the words 'hull of a wrecked boat,' I'm assuming that Richard Dreyfuss just reversed the words. However, 'wrecked hull' sure sounds like 'rectal,' doesn't it, especially in Dreyfuss's rapid-fire mouth?"

I've just listened to the DVD again. It sure sounds like Dreyfuss says "rectal"—but I concede he meant "wrecked hull."

Appendix: Questions That Will Not Die

The Answer Man has a special folder for the Questions That Will Not Die. These questions are like urban legends. While the general population faithfully repeats the story about the blind date who stole the kidney, the Answer Man is asked yet once again if there is not a ghost in *Three Men and a Baby.* This section is dedicated to answering Questions That Will Not Die and no others. Clip and save. Please.

Boom Mikes

Q. I recently attended a screening of the film *Boiler Room,* and was horrified at how many times the boom mike fell into the picture from the top and, at one point, from the right. It ruined what I felt was a fairly solid film. I was told afterward that the boom mike plunge was the fault of the projectionist. However, it would seem to me that a good director wouldn't permit the boom to be shown in any part of the final print. Who's to blame?

—Andrew Magary, New York, New York

A. You were told correctly. When you see a boom mike in a movie, 99 percent of the time the fault is not with the director or cinematographer, but with the projectionist, who has

framed the movie incorrectly. If you could see the entire surface area of every frame in every film, you'd see a lot of boom mikes. But you're never supposed to.

Frogs from the Sky

Q. (Spoiler Warning!) In the recent movie *Magnolia,* the ending scene showed frogs pouring from the sky. Why was this happening?

—Janet Brown, Hermosa Beach, California

A. Well, frogs *do* sometimes just rain from the sky. Stranger things have happened. But the movie contains a clue by providing several references to Exodus 8:2, which says: "Let my people go, that they may serve me. And if thou refuse to let them go, behold I will smite all thy borders with frogs, and the river shall swarm with frogs, which shall go up and come into thine house, and into thy bedchamber, and upon thy bed, and into the house of thy servants, and upon thy people, and into thine ovens, and into thy kneading-troughs, and the frogs shall come up both upon thee, and upon thy people, and upon all thy servants." Then God and Moses have a conversation about the frogs and how to get rid of them.

The Ghost of the Wizard

Q. My friends say you can see a dead man hanging in a tree in *The Wizard of Oz*. I have looked for it but can't find it. Can you help me?
—Joseph Rogers, Evanston, Illinois

A. I've written several times that there is no hanged man in a tree. How likely is it that MGM could shoot a Judy Garland musical on a sound stage with a crew of hundreds, and not notice the body? Again I am indebted to the Internet Movie Database: "At the beginning of the 'We're Off to See the Wizard' sequence, there is a disturbance in the trees off to the right. This was rumored to be one of the crew hanging himself, but is in fact an animal handler recapturing an escaped animal."

Marisa Tomei's Oscar

Q. I heard Rex Reed say on a talk show that Marisa Tomei didn't really win the Oscar—that Jack Palance got confused and read her name instead of Vanessa Redgrave's. Is this true?
—Greg Nelson, Chicago, Illinois

A. When Joseph Gonzales of Waco, Texas, asked this question, the Answer Man replied: "The accountants for Price Waterhouse, who have memorized the name of every winner, are poised backstage ready to race out and make an on-the-spot correction should anyone mistakenly (or deliberately!) announce the wrong winner—which would be hard to do, since the presenter is reading from a card that has only one name written on it."

But that was not good enough for Chicago's James Berg, who wrote: "Reed explained that a 'stoned' or 'drunk' Palance read the last name on the Teleprompter and did not properly open the envelope." So the Answer Man turned to Bruce Davis, executive director of the Academy, who issued an official statement: "The legend of Marisa Tomei's 'mistaken Oscar' has appeared in various forms over the years and in that short time has achieved the status of urban myth. There is no more truth to this version than to any of the others we've heard. If such a scenario were ever to occur, the Price Waterhouse people backstage would simply step out onstage and point out the error. They are not shy." Not only is the rumor untrue, it is unfair to Marisa Tomei, and Rex Reed owes her an apology.

The Real Columbia Lady

Q. Many have remarked on the Columbia Logo Lady's striking resemblance to Annette Bening. Did my eyes play a trick when the logo came up before *What Planet Are You From?* or was she changed to actually *be* Annette Bening? Let me cast my vote solidly in favor of studios that allow filmmakers to play with the logo in such a manner; it's often the most creative moment in the film.
—Steven P. Senski, Plover, Wisconsin

A. A Columbia spokesman replies: "Nothing was done to change the logo. It is not Annette Bening and has never been Annette Bening and we get this question constantly." (The Answer Man nevertheless not unreasonably wonders: If it isn't Annette Bening, why did Columbia make it look so much like her?)

Three Men and a Baby

Q. It recently came to my attention that there is a ghost in *Three Men and a Baby*. If you start the tape at 1:01:13 the camera pans across a window behind Ted Danson and Celeste Holm, who are walking into a room, and at a spot by the window curtains, the rifle that was presumably used in the killing of a young boy may be clearly seen, with the barrel pointing down. At 1:02:53, they move back, passing the window again, and where the gun was forty seconds earlier, there is a young boy standing whose feet do not appear to be touching the floor. The figure of both the gun and the boy are very clear and unmistakable. I was told that a boy was killed in the very room where the filming took place, and that no one has an explanation for the apparitions that appear in the background of this scene.
—Jim Cameron, Soddy-Daisy, Tennessee

A. And Amy Akpan of Eager, Arizona, writes: "I was just wondering, in the movie *Three Men and a Baby,* if the boy in the background of one of the scenes is really a ghost?" And Daniel Lutz of Orangeburg, North Carolina, writes: "A friend of mine told me about something called 'The Ghost of *Three Men and a Baby*.'" And Patrick McManus of Yardley, Pennsylvania, writes, "there is a part where the mother comes over to see the baby and while walking past the window there is a kid behind the curtain . . ." No, there is no ghost in *Three Men and a Baby*.

The Internet Movie Database explains: "When Jack's mother comes to visit Mary, you can see in the background what appears to be a little boy standing in a doorway. There is a rumor that this is the ghost of a little boy who died in the apartment in which the film was shot. This rumor is false, as the interiors were all shot on a sound stage in a movie studio. The 'ghost' is actually a cardboard cutout of Jack wearing a tuxedo. This prop appears later in the film, when Mary's mother comes to collect her."

Ebert's Little Movie Glossary

These are contributions to my glossary project. Hundreds of entries were collected in *Ebert's Bigger Little Movie Glossary,* published in 1999. Contributions are always welcome.

* * *

Beverly Hills $9,021,000. None of the main characters in a "chick flick" are ever poor. In fact, they are usually quite wealthy.

—Todd Burfeind, Chino Hills, California

"The Center of the World" vs. "Freddy Got Fingered" Syndrome. The worse a movie is, the more forgiving the MPAA will be when rating it.

—Ed Pegg Jr., Champaign, Illinois

Cuisinartless Rule. Whenever a movie character puts food or drink into a blender, they will proceed to cover the blender carelessly, so that the contents explode in their face when the blender is turned on.

—Cynthia Langston, Stamford, Connecticut

Dance of the Unwashed Masses. In any movie about rigid societies, the "little people" will have an opportunity to break out folk instruments and engage in a party at which we learn that the simple pleasures are still the best. Often juxtaposed against an upper-class party at which no one seems to be enjoying themselves. See *Titanic, Chocolat.*

—Josh Powers, Washington, D.C.

Dapper Demon Rule. Satan is always impeccably dressed in the movies, with suits, silk ties, expensive shoes. He never wears jeans and T-shirts. Sandals, shorts, and a tank top would better fit the heat of the underworld.

—Steven Dalli, Los Angeles, California

Dead Man Sleeping. When a dead man's eyes are closed in the movies, the lids are shut with one hand, never two, and both at once, never one and then the other.

—R.E.

Eavesdropping Stall Device. Whenever two characters discuss a third one in a rest room, the third character inevitably happens to be in one of the stalls, and emerges after the first two have left.

—R.E.

Excedrin Toothache #1. Characters in movies never drink water when taking aspirin. They just throw a handful into their mouths and grind away.

—Rob Smentek, Haddon Heights, New Jersey

.45-Caliber Pick-Up. Almost all movie poker games involve a threat of immediate violence, even when the players are friends.

—Ian Waldron-Mantgani, Liverpool, England

Fountain of Youth. Whenever a childless male is forced to change a diaper for the first time and the infant is a male, the infant will inevitably and energetically urinate on him. Seen most recently in *Family Man.*

—Ed Slota, Providence, Rhode Island

Get Your Kicks Off Route 66. When characters in movies need to drive to the coast, no matter how big a rush they're in, they always take picturesque back roads that lead to encounters in wayside taverns with humorous or ominous locals. Often these roads also lead to the Grand Canyon. See *Nurse Betty,* etc.

—Michael Miner, Chicago, Illinois

Grandstand Play. In any scene where a father arrives at a sporting event to watch his son play, the game must be in progress and, just before the next play, the son must look up into the stands, see his father, and share a wave. Nothing of importance ever happens in the game until the father arrives.

—Mark Oristano, Dallas Cowboys Radio Network

Harmless Arrangements. Enraged wives who throw flower vases at their husbands will invariably miss, often hitting a closing door.

—Gerardo Valero, Mexico City, Mexico

Identified UFOs. If Unidentified Flying Objects land in the countryside, they are peaceful, but if they land in the city, they are dangerous.
—Steven Dalli, Los Angeles, California

I'm the King of the T&A World! All feature films directed by James Cameron since 1984 have names that begin either with the letter A or with the letter T: *Terminator, Terminator II, Titanic, True Lies, Aliens, Abyss.*
—Juha Terho, Helsinki, Finland

The L-Shaped Groom. In bed scenes, the top sheet is invariably adjusted in an "L" shape, so that it covers only the man's groin area, yet extends above the woman's breasts.
—Mac VerStandig, Washington, D.C.

Obligatory Trailer Scratch. In a movie trailer for a flat-out comedy (Adam Sandler, teenage gross-out, etc.), there will inevitably be a moment when the trailer shows a change in the plot; it is accompanied by the sound of record being scratched off its groove.
—Bradley Richman, New York, New York

Phantom Phantom Rule. In any case where a movie crew member or unauthorized person accidentally appears in the background of a shot, a legend will develop to explain the appearance—usually involving suicide, a shotgun, and the spirit of the deceased haunting the set. Examples: The folklore surrounding *The Wizard of Oz* and *Three Men and a Baby.*
—Colin M. Chisholm, Chicago, Illinois

The Rule of III. Any movie character with a "III" at the end of his name is a stuck-up snob.
—R.E.

Slam, Bam, Thank You, Continuity Man! Movies almost never show people locking their cars, even in tough neighborhoods. Cars are only locked so that later they cannot be unlocked quickly in an emergency.
—Edwin Jahiel, Urbana, Illinois

SLOW-MO-OH-NO: A character Realizes that a fellow protagonist is in immediate danger before the Endangered does. If the Realizer is then shown in slow motion running toward the Endangered screaming "NOOOOOOO!" the Endangered is a goner.
—Mike Spearns, St. John's, Newfoundland

Strafing Panic Syndrome. When an airplane strafes humans on the ground, the targets invariably run away from the plane. Logic suggests they would have a better chance of not being hit if they ran toward it, since that would shorten the time they are in range. See *Pearl Harbor,* etc.
—R.E.

There's No Business Like Monkey Business. Just as any film can be improved by the addition of Rosie Perez, any film can be improved by the presence of a monkey, chimp, gibbon, ape, etc. Examples: the monkey funeral in *Sunset Boulevard,* the martini-drinking gorilla in *Congo,* the Nazi monkey in *Raiders of the Lost Ark.* The rule is invalidated if the film also features a former cast member of TV's *Taxi.*
—Peter Sobczynski, Chicago, Illinois

Upper Shelf Rule. All women who work in bookstores are first seen poised on the rungs of ladders.
—R.E.

Vivaldi Coefficient. The probability that Vivaldi's *Four Seasons* will be used in a scene requiring classical music is inversely proportional to the movie's quality, and approaches 100 percent in buddy-cop movies where the villain is giving a lavish dinner party.
—Josh Powers, Washington, D.C.

Zero Zero Sept Rule. James Bond's complete knowledge of the language of countries he visits is proven when he utters no more than one or two short sentences, typically while ordering dinner.
—Gerardo Valero, Mexico City, Mexico

Reviews Appearing in All Editions of the *Movie Home Companion, Video Companion,* or *Movie Yearbook*

A

About Last Night . . . , 1986, R, ★★★★   1998
Above the Law, 1988, R, ★★★   1995
Above the Rim, 1994, R, ★★★   1995
Absence of Malice, 1981, PG, ★★★   1998
Absolute Power, 1997, R, ★★★½   1998
Accidental Tourist, The,
   1988, PG, ★★★★   1998
Accompanist, The, 1994, PG, ★★★½   1998
Accused, The, 1988, R, ★★★   1998
Ace Ventura: Pet Detective,
   1994, PG-13, ★   1998
Ace Ventura: When Nature Calls,
   1995, PG-13, ★½   1998
Addams Family, The, 1991, PG-13, ★★   1997
Addams Family Values,
   1993, PG-13, ★★★   1998
Addicted to Love, 1997, R, ★★   1998
Addiction, The, 1995, NR, ★★½   1997
Adjuster, The, 1992, R, ★★★   1998
Adventures of Baron Munchausen, The,
   1989, PG, ★★★   1998
Adventures of Ford Fairlane, The,
   1990, R, ★   1992
Adventures of Huck Finn, The,
   1993, PG, ★★★   1998
Adventures of Priscilla, Queen of the
   Desert, The, 1994, R, ★★½   1998
Adventures of Rocky & Bullwinkle,
   The, 2000, PG, ★★★   2002
Adventures of Sebastian Cole, The,
   1999, R, ★★★   2002
Affair of Love, An, 2000, R, ★★★½   2002
Affliction, 1999, R, ★★★★   2002
Afterglow, 1998, R, ★★★   2001
After Hours, 1985, R, ★★★★   1998
After Life, 1999, NR, ★★★★   2002
After the Rehearsal, 1984, R, ★★★★   1998
Against All Odds, 1984, R, ★★★   1998
Age of Innocence, The,
   1993, PG, ★★★★   1998
Agnes Browne, 2000, R, ★★½   2002
Agnes of God, 1985, PG-13, ★   1989
A.I. Artificial Intelligence,
   2001, PG-13, ★★★   2002
Aimee & Jaguar, 2000, NR, ★★★   2002
Air Bud, 1997, PG, ★★★   2000

Air Bud 2: Golden Receiver, 1998, G, ★½   2001
Air Force One, 1997, R, ★★½   2000
Airplane!, 1980, PG, ★★★   1998
Airport, 1970, G, ★★   1996
Airport 1975, 1974, PG, ★★½   1996
Aladdin, 1992, G, ★★★   1998
Alan Smithee Film Burn Hollywood
   Burn, An, 1998, R, no stars   2001
Alaska, 1996, PG, ★★★   1999
Albino Alligator, 1997, R, ★★   2000
Alex in Wonderland, 1971, R, ★★★★   1998
Alice, 1990, PG-13, ★★★   1998
Alice Doesn't Live Here Anymore,
   1974, PG, ★★★★   1998
Alien Nation, 1988, R, ★★   1994
Alien Resurrection, 1997, R, ★½   2000
Aliens, 1986, R, ★★★½   1998
Alien³, 1992, R, ★½   1997
Alive, 1993, R, ★★½   1997
All About My Mother, 1999, R, ★★★½   2002
All Dogs Go to Heaven, 1989, G, ★★★   1998
Allegro Non Tropo, 1977, NR, ★★★½   1995
Alligator, 1980, R, ★   1990
All Night Long, 1981, R, ★★   1986
All of Me, 1984, PG, ★★★½   1998
All the Little Animals, 1999, R, ★★★   2002
. . . All the Marbles, 1981, R, ★★   1986
All the President's Men,
   1976, PG, ★★★½   1998
All the Pretty Horses,
   2000, PG-13, ★★★½   2002
All the Right Moves, 1983, R, ★★★   1998
All the Vermeers in New York,
   1992, NR, ★★★   1998
Almost an Angel, 1990, PG, ★★½   1995
Almost Famous, 2000, R, ★★★★   2002
Along Came a Spider, 2001, R, ★★   2002
Altered States, 1980, R, ★★★½   1998
Always, 1989, PG, ★★   1997
Amadeus, 1984, PG, ★★★★   1998
Amarcord, 1974, R, ★★★★   1998
Amateur, 1995, R, ★★½   1996
Amati Girls, The, 2001, PG, ★   2002
American Beauty, 1999, R, ★★★★   2002
American Buffalo, 1996, R, ★★½   1999
American Dream, 1992, NR, ★★★★   1998

Beyond the Valley of the Dolls, 1970, NC-17, Stars N/A — 1997

Bicentennial Man, 1999, PG, ★★ — 2002

Big, 1988, PG, ★★★ — 1998

Big Bang, The, 1990, R, ★★★ — 1995

Big Brawl, The, 1980, R, ★¹/₂ — 1986

Big Business, 1988, PG, ★★ — 1993

Big Chill, The, 1983, R, ★★¹/₂ — 1998

Big Daddy, 1999, PG-13, ★¹/₂ — 2002

Big Easy, The, 1987, R, ★★★★ — 1998

Big Eden, 2001, PG-13, ★★ — 2002

Big Foot, 1971, PG, ¹/₂★ — 1990

Big Hit, The, 1998, R, ★ — 2001

Big Kahuna, The, 2000, R, ★★★¹/₂ — 2002

Big Lebowski, The, 1998, R, ★★★ — 2001

Big Momma's House, 2000, PG-13, ★★ — 2002

Big One, The, 1998, PG-13, ★★★ — 2001

Big Red One, The, 1980, PG, ★★★ — 1996

Big Squeeze, The, 1996, R, ★ — 1999

Big Tease, The, 2000, R, ★★ — 2002

Big Town, The, 1987, R, ★★★¹/₂ — 1998

Bill & Ted's Bogus Journey, 1991, PG-13, ★★★ — 1998

Billy Bathgate, 1991, R, ★★ — 1993

Billy Elliot, 2000, R, ★★★ — 2002

Billy Jack, 1971, PG, ★★¹/₂ — 1993

Billy's Hollywood Screen Kiss, 1998, R, ★★ — 2001

Bird, 1988, R, ★★★¹/₂ — 1998

Birdcage, The, 1995, R, ★★★ — 1999

Bird on a Wire, 1990, PG-13, ★★¹/₂ — 1993

Birdy, 1985, R, ★★★★ — 1998

Bitter Moon, 1994, R, ★★★ — 1998

Black and White, 2000, R, ★★★ — 2002

Black Cauldron, The, 1985, PG, ★★★¹/₂ — 1987

Black Marble, The, 1980, PG, ★★★¹/₂ — 1998

Black Rain (Japan), 1990, NR, ★★★¹/₂ — 1998

Black Rain (Michael Douglas), 1989, R, ★★ — 1993

Black Robe, 1991, R, ★★¹/₂ — 1994

Black Stallion, The, 1980, G, ★★★★ — 1998

Black Stallion Returns, The, 1983, PG, ★★¹/₂ — 1986

Black Widow, 1987, R, ★★¹/₂ — 1991

Blade, 1998, R, ★★★ — 2001

Blade Runner, 1982, R, ★★★ — 1998

Blade Runner: The Director's Cut, 1992, R, ★★★ — 1997

Blair Witch Project, The, 1999, R, ★★★★ — 2002

Blame It on Rio, 1984, R, ★ — 1987

Blast From the Past, 1999, PG-13, ★★★ — 2002

Blaze, 1989, R, ★★★¹/₂ — 1998

Blind Date, 1987, PG-13, ★★¹/₂ — 1988

Blink, 1994, R, ★★★¹/₂ — 1998

Bliss, 1997, R, ★★★¹/₂ — 1998

Blood and Wine, 1997, R, ★★★¹/₂ — 1998

Blood Guts Bullets and Octane, 1999, NR, ★★¹/₂ — 2002

Blood Simple, 1985, R, ★★★★ — 1998

Blood Simple: 2000 Director's Cut, 2000, R, ★★★★ — 2002

Blow, 2001, R, ★★¹/₂ — 2002

Blown Away, 1994, R, ★★ — 1996

Blow Out, 1981, R, ★★★★ — 1998

Blue, 1994, R, ★★★¹/₂ — 1998

Blue Chips, 1994, PG-13, ★★★ — 1998

Blue Collar, 1978, R, ★★★★ — 1998

Blue Kite, The, 1994, NR, ★★★★ — 1998

Blue Lagoon, The, 1980, R, ¹/₂★ — 1991

Blues Brothers, The, 1980, R, ★★★ — 1998

Blues Brothers 2000, 1998, PG-13, ★★ — 2001

Blue Sky, 1994, PG-13, ★★★ — 1998

Blue Steel, 1990, R, ★★★ — 1998

Blue Streak, 1999, PG-13, ★★★ — 2002

Blue Velvet, 1986, R, ★ — 1998

Blume in Love, 1973, R, ★★★★ — 1998

Blush, 1996, NR, ★★¹/₂ — 1999

Bob Roberts, 1992, R, ★★★ — 1998

Bodies, Rest and Motion, 1993, R, ★★ — 1994

Body Double, 1984, R, ★★★¹/₂ — 1998

Bodyguard, The, 1992, R, ★★★ — 1998

Body of Evidence, 1993, R, ¹/₂★ — 1994

Body Shots, 1999, R, ★★ — 2002

Body Snatchers, 1994, R, ★★★★ — 1998

Bogus, 1996, PG, ★★★ — 1999

Boiler Room, 2000, R, ★★★¹/₂ — 2002

Bolero, 1984, NR, ¹/₂★ — 1993

Bone Collector, The, 1999, R, ★★ — 2002

Bonfire of the Vanities, The, 1990, R, ★★¹/₂ — 1998

Boogie Nights, 1997, R, ★★★★ — 2000

Book of Shadows: Blair Witch 2, 2000, R, ★★ — 2002

Boomerang, 1992, R, ★★★ — 1998

Boost, The, 1988, R, ★★★¹/₂ — 1998

Bootmen, 2000, R, ★¹/₂ — 2002

Booty Call, 1997, R, ★★★ — 1998

Bopha!, 1993, PG-13, ★★★¹/₂ — 1998

Born on the Fourth of July, 1989, R, ★★★★ — 1998

Born Yesterday, 1993, PG, ★ — 1994

Borrowers, The, 1998, PG, ★★★ — 2001

Bostonians, The, 1984, PG, ★★★ — 1998

795

C

Crocodile Dundee in Los Angeles,
   2001, PG, ★★   2002
Cronos, 1994, NR, ★★★   1998
Crooklyn, 1994, PG-13, ★★★½   1998
Crossing Delancey, 1988, PG, ★★½   1995
Crossing Guard, The, 1995, R, ★★½   1997
Cross My Heart, 1987, R, ★★½   1989
Crossover Dreams, 1985, PG-13, ★★★   1995
Crossroads, 1985, R, ★★★½   1998
Crouching Tiger, Hidden Dragon,
   2000, PG-13, ★★★★   2002
Croupier, 2000, NR, ★★★   2002
Crow, The, 1994, R, ★★★½   1998
Crucible, The, 1996, PG-13, ★★   1999
Cruel Intentions, 1999, R, ★★★   2002
Cruise, The, 1998, NR, ★★★   2001
Crumb, 1995, R, ★★★★   1997
Crusoe, 1989, PG-13, ★★★½   1995
Cry-Baby, 1990, PG-13, ★★★   1998
Cry Freedom, 1987, PG, ★★½   1997
Crying Game, The, 1992, R, ★★★★   1998
Cry in the Dark, A, 1988, PG-13, ★★★   1998
Cup, The, 2000, G, ★★★   2002
Curdled, 1996, R, ★★   1999
Cure, The, 1995, PG-13, ★★½   1996
Curly Sue, 1991, PG, ★★★   1998
Curse of the Pink Panther, 1983, PG, ★½   1986
Cutthroat Island, 1995, PG-13, ★★★   1998
Cutting Edge, The, 1992, PG, ★★½   1994
CyberWorld 3D, 2000, NR, ★★★   2002
Cyborg, 1989, R, ★   1992
Cyrano de Bergerac, 1990, PG, ★★★½   1998

D

Dad, 1989, PG, ★★   1993
Daddy Nostalgia, 1991, PG, ★★★½   1998
Dadetown, 1996, NR, ★★   1998
Damage, 1993, R, ★★★★   1998
Dancer in the Dark, 2000, R, ★★★½   2002
Dances With Wolves,
   1990, PG-13, ★★★★   1998
Dance With a Stranger, 1985, R, ★★★★   1998
Dance With Me, 1998, PG, ★★★   2001
Dancing at Lughnasa, 1998, PG, ★★½   2001
Dangerous Beauty, 1998, R, ★★★½   2001
Dangerous Ground, 1997, R, ★★   1998
Dangerous Liaisons, 1988, R, ★★★   1998
Dangerous Minds, 1995, R, ★½   1997
Daniel, 1983, R, ★★½   1987
Dante's Peak, 1997, PG-13, ★★½   1998
Dark City, 1998, R, ★★★★   2001
Dark Crystal, The, 1982, PG, ★★½   1991

Dark Days, 2000, NR, ★★★½   2002
Dark Eyes, 1987, NR, ★★★½   1998
Dark Half, The, 1993, R, ★★   1994
Dark Obsession, 1991, NC-17, ★★★   1998
D.A.R.Y.L., 1985, PG, ★★★   1998
Date with an Angel, 1987, PG, ★   1989
Daughters of the Dust, 1992, NR, ★★★   1998
Dave, 1993, PG-13, ★★★½   1998
Dawn of the Dead, 1979, R, ★★★★   1998
Day After Trinity, The,
   1980, NR, ★★★★   1998
Day for Night, 1974, PG, ★★★★   1998
Day I Became a Woman, The,
   2001, NR, ★★★½   2002
Daylight, 1996, PG-13, ★★   1999
Day of the Dead, 1985, R, ★½   1992
Day of the Jackal, The, 1973, PG, ★★★★   1998
Days of Heaven, 1978, PG, ★★★★   1998
Days of Thunder, 1990, PG-13, ★★★   1998
Daytrippers, The, 1997, NR, ★★   2000
Dazed and Confused, 1993, R, ★★★   1998
D.C. Cab, 1983, R, ★★   1986
Dead, The, 1987, PG, ★★★   1998
Dead Again, 1991, R, ★★★★   1998
Dead Calm, 1989, R, ★★★   1998
Dead Man Walking, 1995, R, ★★★★   1999
Dead of Winter, 1987, PG-13, ★★½   1993
Dead Poets Society, 1989, PG, ★★   1998
Dead Pool, The, 1988, R, ★★★½   1998
Dead Presidents, 1995, R, ★★½   1998
Dead Ringers, 1988, R, ★★½   1993
Dead Zone, The, 1983, R, ★★★½   1998
Dear America: Letters Home from
   Vietnam, 1988, PG-13, ★★★★   1998
Dear God, 1996, PG, ★   1999
Death and the Maiden, 1995, R, ★★★   1998
Death in Venice, 1971, PG, ★★½   1994
Deathtrap, 1982, R, ★★★   1998
Death Wish, 1974, R, ★★★   1998
Death Wish 3, 1985, R, ★   1993
Death Wish II, 1982, R, no stars   1993
Deceived, 1991, PG-13, ★★   1993
Deceiver, 1998, R, ★★   2001
Deconstructing Harry, 1997, R, ★★★½   2000
Deep Blue Sea, 1999, R, ★★★   2002
Deep Cover, 1992, R, ★★★½   1998
Deep Crimson, 1998, NR, ★★★½   2001
Deep End of the Ocean, The,
   1999, PG-13, ★½   2002
Deep Impact, 1998, PG-13, ★★½   2001
Deep Rising, 1998, R, ★½   2001
Deer Hunter, The, 1978, R, ★★★★   1998

Drive, He Said, 1971, R, ★★★   1998
Drive Me Crazy, 1999, PG-13, ★★½   2002
Driven, 2001, PG-13, ★★½   2002
Driving Miss Daisy, 1989, PG, ★★★★   1998
Drop Dead Gorgeous, 1999, PG-13, ★★   2002
Drop Zone, 1994, R, ★★½   1997
Drowning by Numbers, 1991, NR, ★★   1995
Drowning Mona, 2000, PG-13, ★★   2002
Dr. Seuss' How the Grinch Stole
   Christmas, 2000, PG, ★★   2002
Dr. Strangelove, 1964, PG, ★★★★   1997
Dr. T and the Women, 2000, R, ★★★   2002
Drugstore Cowboy, 1989, R, ★★★★   1998
Dry White Season, A, 1989, R, ★★★★   1998
D3: The Mighty Ducks, 1996, PG, ★   1999
Dudley Do-Right, 1999, PG, ★★½   2002
Duets, 2000, R, ★★½   2002
Dumb and Dumber, 1994, PG-13, ★★   1998
Dune, 1984, PG-13, ★   1988
Dungeons & Dragons,
   2000, PG-13, ★½   2002
Dutch, 1991, PG-13, ★½   1993
Dying Young, 1991, R, ★★   1994

E

Earth, 1999, NR, ★★★   2002
Earth Girls Are Easy, 1989, PG, ★★★   1998
East Is East, 2000, R, ★★★   2002
East-West, 2000, PG-13, ★★½   2002
Easy Money, 1983, R, ★★½   1994
Easy Rider, 1969, R, ★★★★   1997
Eating Raoul, 1983, R, ★★   1995
Eddie, 1996, PG-13, ★½   1999
Eddie and the Cruisers, 1983, PG, ★★   1987
Edge, The, 1997, R, ★★★   2000
Edge of 17, 1999, NR, ★★   2002
Edge of the World, The, 2000, NR, ★★★   2002
Ed's Next Move, 1996, R, ★★★   1999
EDtv, 1999, PG-13, ★★½   2002
Educating Rita, 1983, PG, ★★   1995
Education of Little Tree, The,
   1998, PG, ★★★   2001
Edward Scissorhands, 1990, PG-13, ★★   1997
Ed Wood, 1994, R, ★★★½   1998
Eel, The, 1998, NR, ★★★   2001
Efficiency Expert, The, 1992, PG, ★★★   1998
8½ Women, 2000, R, ★★★   2002
Eighth Day, The, 1997, NR, ★★★   2000
8 Heads in a Duffel Bag, 1997, R, ★★   2000
Eight Men Out, 1988, PG, ★★   1993
8MM, 1999, R, ★★★   2002
Eight Seconds, 1994, PG-13, ★★   1995

84 Charing Cross Road, 1987, PG, ★★   1993
84 Charlie Mopic, 1989, R, ★★★   1998
Election, 1999, R, ★★★½   2002
Electric Dreams, 1984, PG, ★★★½   1989
Electric Horseman, The, 1979, PG, ★★★   1998
Eleni, 1985, PG, ★★★   1987
Elephant Man, The, 1980, PG, ★★   1995
Elizabeth, 1998, R, ★★★½   2001
El Mariachi, 1993, R, ★★★   1998
El Norte, 1983, R, ★★★★   1998
Emerald Forest, The, 1985, R, ★★   1988
Emma, 1996, PG, ★★★   1999
Emmanuelle, 1975, X, ★★★   1998
Emperor's New Groove, The,
   2000, G, ★★★   2002
Emperor's Shadow, The, 1999, NR, ★★★   2002
Empire of the Sun, 1987, PG, ★★½   1995
Empire Strikes Back, The,
   1980, PG, ★★★★   1998
Empire Strikes Back, The (reissue),
   1997, PG, ★★★★   2000
Encounter in the Third Dimension,
   1999, NR, ★★   2002
Endless Love, 1981, R, ★★   1991
End of Days, 1999, R, ★★   2002
End of the Affair, The, 1999, R, ★★½   2002
End of Violence, The, 1997, R, ★★   2000
Endurance, 1999, G, ★★★   2002
Enemies, a Love Story, 1989, R, ★★★½   1998
Enemy at the Gates, 2001, R, ★★★   2002
Enemy Mine, 1985, PG-13, ★★½   1988
Enemy of the State, 1998, R, ★★★   2001
Englishman Who Went Up a Hill But
   Came Down a Mountain, The,
   1995, PG, ★★★   1998
English Patient, The, 1996, R, ★★★★   1999
Entrapment, 1999, PG-13, ★★★   2002
Eraser, 1995, R, ★★★   1999
Erin Brockovich, 2000, R, ★★   2002
Escape from L.A., 1996, R, ★★★½   1999
Escape from New York, 1981, R, ★★½   1988
E.T.—The Extra-Terrestrial,
   1982, PG, ★★★★   1998
Eureka, 1984, R, ★★★   1986
Evening Star, The, 1996, PG-13, ★½   1999
Event Horizon, 1997, R, ★★   2000
Ever After, 1998, PG-13, ★★★   2001
Everlasting Piece, An, 2000, R, ★★★   2002
Everybody's All-American, 1988, R, ★★   1993
Everyone Says I Love You,
   1997, R, ★★★★   1998
Eve's Bayou, 1997, R, ★★★★   2000

Final Fantasy, 2001, PG-13, ★★★½ — 2002
Finding Forrester, 2000, PG-13, ★★★ — 2002
Fire, 1997, NR, ★★★ — 2000
Firefox, 1982, PG, ★★★½ — 1998
Fire in the Sky, 1993, PG-13, ★★½ — 1994
Firestarter, 1984, R, ★★ — 1987
Fireworks, 1998, NR, ★★★ — 2001
Firm, The, 1993, R, ★★★ — 1998
First Blood, 1982, R, ★★★ — 1998
Firstborn, 1984, PG, ★★ — 1987
First Deadly Sin, The, 1980, R, ★★★ — 1986
First Knight, 1995, PG-13, ★★ — 1997
First Wives Club, The, 1996, PG, ★★ — 1999
Fish Called Wanda, A, 1988, R, ★★★★ — 1998
Fisher King, The, 1991, R, ★★ — 1994
Fitzcarraldo, 1982, PG, ★★★★ — 1998
Five Easy Pieces, 1970, R, ★★★★ — 1998
Five Heartbeats, The, 1991, R, ★★★ — 1998
Five Senses, The, 2000, R, ★★★ — 2002
Flamingo Kid, The, 1984, PG-13, ★★★½ — 1998
Flashback, 1990, R, ★★★ — 1998
Flashdance, 1983, R, ★½ — 1994
Flash Gordon, 1980, PG, ★★½ — 1988
Flash of Green, A, 1985, NR, ★★★ — 1987
Flatliners, 1990, R, ★★★ — 1998
Flawless, 1999, R, ★★★ — 2002
Fled, 1996, R, ★★ — 1999
Flesh and Bone, 1993, R, ★★ — 1995
Fletch, 1985, PG, ★★½ — 1995
Fletch Lives, 1989, PG, ★½ — 1995
Flintstones, The, 1994, PG, ★★½ — 1997
Flintstones in Viva Rock Vegas, The, 2000, PG, ½★ — 2002
Flipper, 1995, PG, ★★ — 1999
Flirt, 1996, NR, ★★ — 1999
Flirting, 1992, NR, ★★★★ — 1998
Flower of My Secret, The, 1996, R, ★½ — 1999
Flubber, 1997, PG, ★ — 2000
Fly Away Home, 1996, PG, ★★★½ — 1999
Fog, The, 1980, R, ★★ — 1988
Follow Me Home, 1998, NR, ★★★ — 2001
Fool for Love, 1985, R, ★★★ — 1998
Fools Rush In, 1997, PG-13, ★★★ — 1998
Footloose, 1984, PG, ★½ — 1995
Forces of Nature, 1999, PG-13, ★ — 2002
Forever Young, 1992, PG, ★★½ — 1994
Forget Paris, 1995, PG-13, ★★★½ — 1998
For Keeps, 1988, PG-13, ★★★ — 1998
For Love of the Game, 1999, PG-13, ★½ — 2002
For Love or Money, 1993, PG, ★★ — 1995
Formula, The, 1980, R, ★★ — 1987
For Queen and Country, 1989, R, ★★ — 1992

Forrest Gump, 1994, PG-13, ★★★★ — 1998
For Richer or Poorer, 1997, PG-13, ★★ — 2000
For Roseanna, 1997, PG-13, ★★★ — 2000
Fort Apache, the Bronx, 1981, R, ★★ — 1987
For the Boys, 1991, R, ★★ — 1993
48 HRS, 1982, R, ★★★½ — 1998
42 Up, 2000, NR, ★★★★ — 2002
For Your Eyes Only, 1981, PG, ★★ — 1998
Four Days in September, 1998, R, ★★ — 2001
Four Friends, 1981, R, ★★★★ — 1998
4 Little Girls, 1997, NR, ★★★★ — 2000
Four Rooms, 1995, R, ★★ — 1998
1492: Conquest of Paradise, 1992, PG-13, ★★★ — 1996
Fourth Protocol, The, 1987, R, ★★★½ — 1998
Fourth War, The, 1990, R, ★★★ — 1998
Four Weddings and a Funeral, 1994, R, ★★★½ — 1998
Fox and the Hound, The, 1981, G, ★★★ — 1998
Foxes, 1980, R, ★★★ — 1998
Frances, 1983, R, ★★★½ — 1998
Frankie and Johnny, 1991, R, ★★½ — 1995
Frankie Starlight, 1995, R, ★★★½ — 1998
Frantic, 1988, R, ★★★ — 1998
Fraternity Vacation, 1985, R, ★ — 1990
Freddy Got Fingered, 2001, R, no stars — 2002
Freeway, 1997, R, ★★★½ — 1998
Free Willy, 1993, PG, ★★★½ — 1998
Free Willy 3: The Rescue, 1997, PG, ★★★ — 2000
French Kiss, 1995, PG-13, ★★ — 1997
French Lieutenant's Woman, The, 1981, R, ★★★½ — 1998
Frenzy, 1972, R, ★★★★ — 1998
Frequency, 2000, PG-13, ★★★½ — 2002
Fresh, 1994, R, ★★★★ — 1998
Freshman, The, 1990, PG, ★★★½ — 1998
Friday the 13th, Part II, 1981, R, ½★ — 1993
Fried Green Tomatoes, 1992, PG-13, ★★★ — 1998
Friends & Lovers, 1999, NR, ½★ — 2002
Friends of Eddie Coyle, The, 1973, R, ★★★★ — 1998
Frighteners, The, 1996, R, ★ — 1999
Fright Night, 1985, R, ★★★ — 1996
Fringe Dwellers, The, 1987, PG-13, ★★★½ — 1996
Frogs for Snakes, 1999, R, no stars, — 2002
From Dusk Till Dawn, 1996, R, ★★★ — 1999
From the Journals of Jean Seberg, 1996, NR, ★★★½ — 1999
Frozen Assets, 1992, PG-13, no stars — 1994
Fugitive, The, 1993, PG-13, ★★★★ — 1998

Goonies, The, 1985, PG, ★★★	1998
Gordy, 1995, G, ★★	1996
Gorillas in the Mist, 1988, PG-13, ★★★	1998
Gorky Park, 1983, R, ★★★½	1998
Gossip, 2000, R, ★★	2002
Gotcha!, 1985, PG-13, ★★	1986
Governess, The, 1998, R, ★★★	2001
Goya in Bordeaux, 2000, R, ★★	2002
Grace of My Heart, 1996, R, ★★½	1999
Graduate, The, 1997, PG, ★★★	1998
Grand Canyon, 1992, R, ★★★★	1998
Grass, 2000, R, ★★	2002
Gravesend, 1997, R, ★★	2000
Grease, 1998, PG, ★★★	2001
Great Balls of Fire, 1989, PG-13, ★★	1994
Great Expectations, 1998, R, ★★★	2001
Great Gatsby, The, 1974, PG, ★★½	1998
Great Mouse Detective, The, 1986, G, ★★★	1996
Great Muppet Caper, The, 1981, G, ★★	1994
Great Santini, The, 1980, PG, ★★★★	1998
Greedy, 1994, PG-13, ★★	1995
Green Card, 1991, PG-13, ★★★	1998
Green Mile, The, 1999, R, ★★★½	2002
Green Room, The, 1978, PG, ★★★	1998
Gregory's Girl, 1982, PG, ★★★	1998
Gremlins, 1984, PG, ★★★	1998
Gremlins II, 1990, PG-13, ★★½	1995
Grey Fox, The, 1983, PG, ★★★½	1998
Greystoke, 1984, PG, ★★★	1998
Gridlock'd, 1997, R, ★★★	1998
Grifters, The, 1991, R, ★★★★	1998
Groove, 2000, R, ★★	2002
Gross Anatomy, 1989, PG-13, ★★★	1998
Grosse Pointe Blank, 1997, R, ★★½	1998
Groundhog Day, 1993, PG, ★★★	1998
Grumpier Old Men, 1995, PG-13, ★★	1997
Grumpy Old Men, 1993, PG-13, ★★	1997
Guantanamera, 1997, NR, ★★★	2000
Guardian, The, 1990, R, ★	1992
Guarding Tess, 1994, PG-13, ★★★½	1998
Guelwaar, 1994, NR, ★★★★	1998
Guilty as Sin, 1993, R, ★★★	1996
Guilty by Suspicion, 1991, PG-13, ★★★½	1998
Guimba the Tyrant, 1996, NR, ★★★	1999
Guinevere, 1999, R, ★★★½	2002
Gunmen, 1994, R, ★½	1995

H

Habit, 1997, NR, ★★★	1998
Hackers, 1995, PG-13, ★★★	1998
Hair, 1979, R, ★★★★	1998

Hairspray, 1988, PG, ★★★	1998
Half Moon Street, 1986, R, ★★★	1998
Halloween, 1978, R, ★★★★	1998
Halloween: H2O, 1998, R, ★★	2001
Halloween III, 1982, R, ★½	1993
Halloween II, 1981, R, ★★	1993
Hamlet, 1990, PG, ★★★½	1998
Hamlet, 1997, PG-13, ★★★★	1998
Hamlet, 2000, R, ★★★	2002
Handmaid's Tale, The, 1990, R, ★★	1995
Hanging Garden, The, 1998, R, ★★★	2001
Hanging Up, 2000, PG-13, ★★	2002
Hangin' With the Homeboys, 1991, R, ★★★	1998
Hannah and Her Sisters, 1985, PG-13, ★★★★	1998
Hannibal, 2001, R, ★★½	2002
Hans Christian Andersen's Thumbelina, 1994, G, ★★	1995
Happiness, 1998, NR, ★★★★	2001
Happy Gilmore, 1996, PG-13, ★½	1999
Happy, Texas, 1999, PG-13, ★★★	2002
Hard Choices, 1986, NR, ★★★½	1998
Hardcore, 1979, R, ★★★★	1998
Hard Eight, 1997, R, ★★★½	1998
Hardly Working, 1981, R, no stars	1986
Hard Rain, 1998, R, ★	2001
Hard Way, The, 1991, R, ★★★½	1998
Harlan County, U.S.A., 1976, PG, ★★★★	1998
Harlem Nights, 1989, R, ★★	1993
Harmonists, The, 1999, R, ★★★	2002
Harold and Maude, 1971, PG, ★½	1991
Harriet the Spy, 1996, PG, ★★	1999
Harry & Son, 1984, PG, ★	1986
Harry and the Hendersons, 1987, PG, ★★	1993
Harry and Tonto, 1974, PG, ★★★★	1998
Hate (La Haine), 1995, NR, ★★★	1999
Haunting, The, 1999, PG-13, ★★★	2002
Havana, 1990, R, ★★★	1998
Hav Plenty, 1998, R, ★½	2001
Head Over Heels, 2001, PG-13, ★½	2002
Hear My Song, 1992, R, ★★★½	1998
Hearse, The, 1980, PG, ½★	1986
Heart Beat, 1980, R, ★★½	1991
Heartbreakers, 1985, R, ★★★½	1998
Heartbreakers, 2001, PG-13, ★★★	2002
Heartbreak Hotel, 1988, PG-13, ★	1994
Heartbreak Kid, The, 1972, PG, ★★★½	1998
Heartbreak Ridge, 1986, R, ★★★	1998
Heartburn, 1986, R, ★★	1993
Heartland, 1981, PG, ★★★★	1998

Look Who's Talking Now, 1993, PG-13, ★ — 1995
Loose Cannons, 1990, R, ★ — 1992
Lord of Illusions, 1995, R, ★★★ — 1998
Lords of Discipline, 1983, R, ★★ — 1991
Lorenzo's Oil, 1993, PG-13, ★★★★ — 1998
Loser, 2000, PG-13, ★★ — 2002
Losing Isaiah, 1995, R, ★★½ — 1997
Loss of Sexual Innonence, The,
 1999, R, ★★★½ — 2002
Lost & Found, 1999, PG-13, ★ — 2002
Lost Angels, 1989, R, ★★½ — 1992
Lost Boys, The, 1987, R, ★★½ — 1993
Lost Highway, 1997, R, ★★ — 1998
Lost in America, 1985, R, ★★★★ — 1998
Lost in Space, 1998, PG-13, ★½ — 2001
Lost in Yonkers, 1993, PG, ★★★ — 1998
Lost Souls, 2000, R, ★★ — 2002
Lost World: Jurassic Park, The,
 1997, PG-13, ★★ — 1998
Louie Bluie, 1985, NR, ★★★½ — 1996
Love Affair, 1994, PG-13, ★★★ — 1998
Love Always, 1997, R, ½★ — 2000
Love & Basketball, 2000, PG-13, ★★★ — 2002
Love and Death on Long Island,
 1998, PG-13, ★★★½ — 2001
Love and Human Remains,
 1995, NR, ★★½ — 1997
Love and Other Catastrophes,
 1997, R, ★★ — 2000
Love & Sex, 2000, NR, ★★ — 2002
Love Field, 1993, PG-13, ★★½ — 1997
Love Is the Devil, 1998, NR, ★★★½ — 2001
love jones, 1997, R, ★★★ — 1998
Love Letters, 1984, R, ★★★½ — 1998
Lover, The, 1992, R, ★★ — 1996
Lovers of the Artic Circle, 1999, R, ★★★ — 2002
Lovers on the Bridge, The,
 1999, R, ★★★ — 2002
Love's Labour's Lost, 2000, PG, ★★½ — 2002
Love Serenade, 1997, R, ★★★ — 2000
Lovesick, 1983, PG, ★★★ — 1989
Love Story, 1970, PG, ★★★★ — 1998
Love Streams, 1984, PG-13, ★★★★ — 1998
Love! Valour! Compassion!,
 1997, R, ★★★ — 1998
Love Walked In, 1998, R, ★★ — 2001
Loving Jezebel, 2000, R, ★★½ — 2002
Low Down, The, 2001, NR, ★★★ — 2002
Lucas, 1985, PG-13, ★★★★ — 1998
Lucie Aubrac, 1999, R, ★★½ — 2002
Lucky Numbers, 2000, R, ★★ — 2002
Lumiere & Company, 1996, NR, ★★★ — 1999

Lust in the Dust, 1985, R, ★★ — 1990
Luzhin Defence, The, 2001, PG-13, ★★½ — 2002

M

Maborosi, 1997, NR, ★★★★ — 1998
Mac, 1993, R, ★★★½ — 1998
Macbeth, 1972, R, ★★★★ — 1998
Madadayo, 2000, NR, ★★★ — 2002
Madame Bovary, 1991, NR, ★★★ — 1998
Madame Butterfly, 1996, NR, ★★★ — 1999
Madame Sousatzka, 1988, PG-13, ★★★★ — 1998
Mad City, 1997, PG-13, ★★½ — 2000
Mad Dog and Glory, 1993, R, ★★★½ — 1998
Mad Dog Time, 1996, R, no stars — 1999
Made in America, 1993, PG-13, ★★★ — 1998
Madeline, 1998, PG, ★★★ — 2001
Mad Love, 1995, PG-13, ★★★ — 1998
Mad Max Beyond Thunderdome,
 1985, R, ★★★★ — 1998
Madness of King George, The,
 1995, NR, ★★★★ — 1998
Mafia!, 1998, PG-13, ★★ — 2001
Magnolia, 2000, R, ★★★★ — 2002
Major Payne, 1995, PG-13, ★★★ — 1998
Making Love, 1982, R, ★★ — 1988
Making Mr. Right, 1987, PG-13, ★★★½ — 1998
Malcolm X, 1992, PG-13, ★★★★ — 1998
Malena, 2000, R, ★★ — 2002
Malice, 1993, R, ★★ — 1995
Mambo Kings, The, 1992, R, ★★★½ — 1998
Manchurian Candidate, The,
 1962, PG-13, ★★★★ — 1997
Mandela, 1997, NR, ★★★ — 2000
Manhattan, 1979, R, ★★★½ — 1998
Manhattan Murder Mystery,
 1993, PG, ★★★ — 1998
Manhattan Project, The,
 1986, PG-13, ★★★★ — 1998
Man in the Iron Mask, The,
 1998, PG-13, ★★½ — 2001
Man in the Moon, The,
 1991, PG-13, ★★★★ — 1998
Mannequin, 1987, PG, ½★ — 1990
Manny and Lo, 1996, R, ★★★½ — 1999
Man of Iron, 1980, NR, ★★★★ — 1998
Man of the Century, 1999, R, ★★★ — 2002
Manon of the Spring, 1987, PG, ★★★★ — 1998
Man on the Moon, 1999, R, ★★★½ — 2002
Mansfield Park, 1999, PG-13, ★★★★ — 2002
Man Who Cried, The, 2001, R, ★★★ — 2002
Man Who Knew Too Little, The,
 1997, PG, ★ — 2000

Mighty Quinn, The, 1989, R, ★★★★	1998
Milagro Beanfield War, The, 1988, R, ★★½	1993
Miles From Home, 1988, R, ★★★	1998
Milk Money, 1994, PG-13, ★	1996
Miller's Crossing, 1990, R, ★★★	1998
Mimic, 1997, R, ★★★½	2000
Minus Man, The, 1999, R, ★★★	2002
Miracle Mile, 1989, R, ★★★	1998
Miracle on 34th Street, 1994, PG, ★★★	1998
Mirror Has Two Faces, The, 1996, PG-13, ★★★	1999
Misery, 1990, R, ★★★	1998
Mishima, 1985, R, ★★★★	1998
Miss Congeniality, 2000, PG-13, ★★	2002
Miss Firecracker, 1989, PG, ★★★½	1998
Missing, 1982, R, ★★★	1998
Mission, The, 1986, PG, ★★½	1993
Mission Impossible, 1996, PG-13, ★★★	1999
Mission Impossible 2, 2000, PG-13, ★★★	2002
Mission to Mars, 2000, PG-13, ★★½	2002
Mississippi Burning, 1988, R, ★★★★	1998
Mississippi Masala, 1992, R, ★★★½	1998
Miss Julie, 2000, R, ★★★	2002
Mister Johnson, 1991, PG-13, ★★★	1998
Mo' Better Blues, 1990, R, ★★★	1998
Moderns, The, 1988, NR, ★★★	1998
Mod Squad, The, 1999, R, ★★	2002
Mommie Dearest, 1981, PG, ★	1998
Mona Lisa, 1986, R, ★★★★	1998
Money Pit, The, 1986, PG-13, ★	1991
Money Talks, 1997, R, ★★★	2000
Money Train, 1995, R, ★½	1997
Mon Homme, 1998, NR, ★★	2001
Monkeybone, 2001, PG-13, ★½	2002
Monkey Trouble, 1994, PG, ★★★	1998
Monsieur Hire, 1990, PG-13, ★★★★	1998
Monsignor, 1982, R, ★	1987
Month by the Lake, A, 1995, PG, ★★★½	1998
Monty Python's Meaning of Life, 1983, R, ★★½	1995
Monument Ave., 1998, NR, ★★★	2001
Moonlighting, 1982, PG, ★★★★	1998
Moon Over Parador, 1988, PG-13, ★★	1993
Moonstruck, 1987, PG, ★★★★	1998
Morning After, The, 1986, R, ★★★	1996
Mortal Thoughts, 1991, R, ★★★	1998
Moscow on the Hudson, 1984, R, ★★★★	1998
Mosquito Coast, The, 1986, PG, ★★	1993
Motel Hell, 1980, R, ★★★	1996

Mother, 1997, PG-13, ★★★½	1998
Mother and the Whore, The, 1999, NR, ★★★★	2002
Mother Night, 1996, R, ★★½	1999
Mother's Day, 1980, R, no stars	1991
Moulin Rouge, 2001, PG-13, ★★★½	2002
Mountains of the Moon, 1990, R, ★★★½	1998
Mouse Hunt, 1997, PG, ★★	2000
Mr. and Mrs. Bridge, 1991, PG-13, ★★★★	1998
Mr. Baseball, 1992, PG-13, ★★★	1998
Mr. Death: The Rise and Fall of Fred A. Leuchter Jr., 2000, PG-13, ★★★★	2002
Mr. Destiny, 1990, PG-13, ★★	1992
Mr. Holland's Opus, 1996, PG, ★★★½	1999
Mr. Jealousy, 1998, R, ★★½	2001
Mr. Jones, 1993, R, ★★★	1998
Mr. Magoo, 1997, PG, ½★	2000
Mr. Mom, 1983, PG, ★★	1987
Mr. Nice Guy, 1998, PG-13, ★★★	2001
Mr. Saturday Night, 1992, R, ★★★	1995
Mrs. Brown, 1997, PG, ★★★½	2000
Mrs. Dalloway, 1998, PG-13, ★★★½	2001
Mrs. Doubtfire, 1993, PG-13, ★★½	1998
Mrs. Parker and the Vicious Circle, 1994, R, ★★★½	1998
Mrs. Winterbourne, 1996, PG-13, ★★½	1999
Mr. Wonderful, 1993, PG-13, ★½	1995
Much Ado About Nothing, 1993, PG-13, ★★★	1998
Mulan, 1998, G, ★★★½	2001
Mulholland Falls, 1996, R, ★★★½	1999
Multiplicity, 1996, PG-13, ★★½	1999
Mumford, 1999, R, ★★★½	2002
Mummy, The, 1999, PG-13, ★★★	2002
Mummy Returns, The, 2001, PG-13, ★★	2002
Muppet Christmas Carol, The, 1992, G, ★★★	1998
Muppet Movie, The, 1979, G, ★★★½	1998
Muppets from Space, 1999, G, ★★	2002
Muppets Take Manhattan, The, 1984, G, ★★★	1998
Muppet Treasure Island, 1996, G, ★★½	1999
Murder at 1600, 1997, R, ★★½	1998
Murder in the First, 1995, R, ★★	1996
Murder on the Orient Express, 1974, PG, ★★★	1998
Muriel's Wedding, 1995, R, ★★★½	1998
Murphy's Romance, 1985, PG-13, ★★★	1998
Muse, The, 1999, PG-13, ★★★	2002
Music Box, 1990, PG-13, ★★	1993

Music Lovers, The, 1971, R, ★★   1993
Music of Chance, The, 1993, NR, ★★★   1998
Music of the Heart, 1999, PG, ★★★   2002
My Beautiful Laundrette, 1986, R, ★★★   1998
My Best Fiend, 2000, NR, ★★★   2002
My Best Friend's Wedding,
   1997, PG-13, ★★★   1998
My Bodyguard, 1980, PG, ★★★½   1998
My Brilliant Career, 1980, NR, ★★★½   1998
My Cousin Vinny, 1992, R, ★★½   1998
My Dinner with André,
   1981, NR, ★★★★   1998
My Dog Skip, 2000, PG, ★★★   2002
My Fair Lady, 1964, G, ★★★★   1997
My Family, 1995, R, ★★★★   1998
My Father's Glory, 1991, G, ★★★★   1998
My Father the Hero, 1994, PG, ★★   1995
My Favorite Martian, 1999, PG, ★★   2002
My Favorite Season, 1995, NR, ★★★   1999
My Favorite Year, 1982, PG, ★★★½   1998
My Fellow Americans, 1996, PG-13, ★★½   1999
My Giant, 1998, PG, ★★   2001
My Girl, 1991, PG, ★★★½   1998
My Girl 2, 1994, PG, ★★   1995
My Heroes Have Always Been Cowboys,
   1991, PG, ★★   1992
My Left Foot, 1989, R, ★★★★   1998
My Life, 1993, PG-13, ★★½   1995
My Life So Far, 1999, PG-13, ★★★   2002
My Mother's Castle, 1991, PG, ★★★★   1998
My Name Is Joe, 1999, R, ★★★½   2002
My Own Private Idaho, 1991, R, ★★★½   1998
My Son the Fanatic, 1999, R, ★★★½   2002
My Stepmother Is an Alien,
   1988, PG-13, ★★   1993
Mystery, Alaska, 1999, R, ★★½   2002
Mystery Men, 1999, PG-13, ★★   2002
Mystery Science Theater 3000:
   The Movie, 1996, PG-13, ★★★   1999
Mystery Train, 1990, R, ★★★½   1998
Mystic Pizza, 1988, R, ★★★½   1998
Myth of Fingerprints, The, 1997, R, ★½   2000
My Tutor, 1983, R, ★★★   1986

N

Nadine, 1987, PG, ★★½   1993
Naked, 1994, NR, ★★★★   1998
Naked Gun, The, 1988, PG-13, ★★★½   1998
Naked Gun 33⅓: The Final Insult,
   1994, PG-13, ★★★   1998
Naked Gun 2½: The Smell of Fear,
   The, 1991, PG-13, ★★★   1998

Naked in New York, 1994, R, ★★★   1998
Naked Lunch, 1992, R, ★★½   1994
Name of the Rose, The, 1986, R, ★★½   1995
Narrow Margin, 1990, R, ★½   1992
Nashville, 1975, R, ★★★★   1998
Nasty Girl, The, 1991, PG-13, ★★½   1993
National Lampoon's Animal House,
   1978, R, ★★★★   1998
National Lampoon's Christmas
   Vacation, 1989, PG-13, ★★   1995
National Lampoon's Loaded Weapon I,
   1993, PG-13, ★   1994
Natural, The, 1984, PG, ★★   1995
Natural Born Killers, 1994, R, ★★★★   1998
Navy Seals, 1990, R, ★½   1992
Necessary Roughness,
   1991, PG-13, ★★★   1996
Needful Things, 1993, R, ★½   1995
Negotiator, The, 1998, R, ★★★½   2001
Neighbors, 1981, R, ★★★   1996
Nell, 1994, PG-13, ★★★   1998
Nelly and Monsieur Arnaud,
   1996, NR, ★★★½   1999
Nenette et Boni, 1997, NR, ★★★   2000
Net, The, 1995, PG-13, ★★★   1998
Network, 1976, R, ★★★★   1998
Never Been Kissed, 1999, PG-13, ★★★   2002
Neverending Story, The,
   1984, PG, ★★★   1998
Never Say Never Again,
   1983, PG, ★★★½   1998
New Age, The, 1994, R, ★★★½   1998
New Jack City, 1991, R, ★★★½   1998
New Jersey Drive, 1995, R, ★★★   1998
Newsies, 1992, PG, ★½   1993
Newton Boys, The, 1998, PG-13, ★★   2001
New York, New York, 1977, PG, ★★★   1998
New York Stories, 1989, PG   1998
   Life Lessons, ★★★½
   Life Without Zoe, ★½
   Oedipus Wrecks, ★★
Next Best Thing, The, 2000, PG-13, ★   2002
Niagara, Niagara, 1998, R, ★★★   2001
Nick and Jane, 1997, R, ½★   2000
Nico and Dani, 2001, NR, ★★★   2002
Nico Icon, 1996, NR, ★★★   1999
Night and the City, 1992, R, ★★   1994
Night at the Roxbury, A, 1998, PG-13, ★   2001
Night Falls on Manhattan,
   1997, R, ★★★   2000
Nightmare on Elm Street 3, A: Dream
   Warriors, 1987, R, ★½   1990

Pulp Fiction, 1994, R, ★★★★ — 1998

Pumping Iron II: The Women,
1985, NR, ★★★¹/₂ — 1988

Punchline, 1988, R, ★★ — 1992

Pups, 1999, NR, ★★★ — 2002

Purple Hearts, 1984, R, ¹/₂★ — 1987

Purple Noon, 1960, PG-13, ★★★ — 1999

Purple Rose of Cairo, The,
1985, PG, ★★★★ — 1998

Pushing Tin, 1999, R, ★★★ — 2002

Pyromaniac's Love Story, A,
1995, PG, ★★ — 1996

Q

Q, 1982, R, ★★¹/₂ — 1993

Q&A, 1990, R, ★★★¹/₂ — 1998

Queen Margot, 1994, R, ★★ — 1997

Queen of Hearts, 1989, NR, ★★★¹/₂ — 1998

Queens Logic, 1991, R, ★★¹/₂ — 1994

Quest for Camelot, 1998, G, ★★ — 2001

Quest for Fire, 1982, R, ★★★¹/₂ — 1998

Quick and the Dead, The, 1995, R, ★★ — 1996

Quick Change, 1990, R, ★★★ — 1995

Quicksilver, 1985, PG, ★★ — 1987

Quigley Down Under,
1990, PG-13, ★★¹/₂ — 1994

Quills, 2000, R, ★★★¹/₂ — 2002

Quiz Show, 1994, PG-13, ★★★¹/₂ — 1998

R

Race the Sun, 1996, PG, ★¹/₂ — 1999

Racing with the Moon, 1984, PG, ★★★¹/₂ — 1998

Radio Days, 1987, PG, ★★★★ — 1998

Radio Flyer, 1992, PG-13, ★¹/₂ — 1994

Rage: Carrie 2, The, 1999, R, ★★ — 2002

Rage in Harlem, A, 1991, R, ★★★ — 1998

Raggedy Man, 1981, PG, ★★★¹/₂ — 1995

Raging Bull, 1980, R, ★★★★ — 1998

Ragtime, 1981, PG, ★★★¹/₂ — 1998

Raiders of the Lost Ark,
1981, PG, ★★★★ — 1998

Rainbow, The, 1989, R, ★★★ — 1998

Raining Stones, 1994, NR, ★★★¹/₂ — 1998

Rainmaker, The, 1997, PG-13, ★★★ — 2000

Rain Man, 1988, R, ★★★¹/₂ — 1998

Raise the Red Lantern, 1992, PG, ★★★★ — 1998

Raise the Titanic, 1980, PG, ★★¹/₂ — 1986

Raising Arizona, 1987, PG-13, ★¹/₂ — 1995

Rambling Rose, 1991, R, ★★★ — 1998

Rambo: First Blood Part II,
1985, R, ★★★ — 1996

Ran, 1985, R, ★★★★ — 1998

Random Hearts, 1999, R, ★★¹/₂ — 2002

Ransom, 1996, R, ★★★ — 1999

Rapa Nui, 1994, R, ★★ — 1997

Rapture, The, 1991, R, ★★★★ — 1998

Ravenous, 1999, R, ★★★ — 2002

Razor's Edge, The, 1984, PG-13, ★★¹/₂ — 1988

Reach the Rock, 1998, R, ★ — 2001

Ready to Rumble, 2000, PG-13, ★★ — 2002

Ready to Wear, 1994, R, ★★¹/₂ — 1997

Real Blonde, The, 1998, R, ★★★ — 2001

Real Genius, 1985, PG-13, ★★★¹/₂ — 1998

Reality Bites, 1994, PG-13, ★★ — 1995

Real McCoy, The, 1993, PG-13, ★★ — 1995

Re-Animator, 1985, NR, ★★★ — 1998

Recess: School's Out, 2001, G, ★★¹/₂ — 2002

Red, 1994, R, ★★★★ — 1998

Red Corner, 1997, R, ★★ — 2000

Red Heat, 1988, R, ★★★ — 1998

Red Planet, 2000, PG-13, ★★★ — 2002

Red Rock West, 1994, R, ★★★¹/₂ — 1998

Reds, 1981, PG, ★★★¹/₂ — 1998

Red Sonja, 1985, PG-13, ★¹/₂ — 1987

Red Violin, The, 1999, NR, ★★★¹/₂ — 2002

Ref, The, 1994, R, ★★★ — 1998

Regarding Henry, 1991, PG-13, ★★ — 1994

Regret to Inform, 1999, NR, ★★★ — 2002

Reindeer Games, 2000, R, ★¹/₂ — 2002

Relic, The, 1997, R, ★★★ — 1998

Remains of the Day, 1993, PG, ★★★¹/₂ — 1998

Remember the Titans, 2000, PG, ★★★ — 2002

Renaissance Man, 1994, PG-13, ★¹/₂ — 1995

Rendevous in Paris, 1996, NR, ★★★¹/₂ — 1999

Replacement Killers, The,
1998, R, ★★★ — 2001

Replacements, The, 2000, PG-13, ★★ — 2002

Repo Man, 1984, R, ★★★ — 1998

Requiem for a Dream,
2000, NR, ★★★¹/₂ — 2002

Rescuers Down Under, The,
1990, G, ★★★ — 1998

Reservoir Dogs, 1992, R, ★★¹/₂ — 1998

Restoration, 1996, R, ★★★¹/₂ — 1999

Return of the Jedi (Special Edition),
1997, PG, ★★★★ — 1998

Return of the Living Dead,
1985, R, ★★★ — 1987

Return of the Secaucus Seven,
1981, NR, ★★★ — 1998

Return to Me, 2000, PG, ★★★ — 2002

Return to Oz, 1985, PG, ★★ — 1987

Return to Paradise, 1998, R, ★★★¹/₂ — 2001

Return With Honor, 1999, NR, ★★★ — 2002

S

She's All That, 1999, PG-13, ★★½ — 2002
She's Having a Baby, 1988, PG-13, ★★ — 1993
She's Out of Control, 1989, PG, no stars — 1992
She's So Lovely, 1997, R, ★★★ — 2000
She's the One, 1996, R, ★★ — 1999
Shiloh, 1997, PG, ★★★½ — 2000
Shiloh 2: Shiloh Season, 1999, PG, ★★★ — 2002
Shine, 1996, PG-13, ★★★★ — 1999
Shining Through, 1992, R, ★★ — 1994
Shirley Valentine, 1989, R, ★ — 1993
Shoah, 1986, NR, ★★★★ — 1998
Shock to the System, A, 1990, R, ★★★ — 1996
Shooting Party, The, 1985, NR, ★★★ — 1987
Shootist, The, 1976, PG, ★★★½ — 1998
Shoot the Moon, 1982, R, ★★★½ — 1998
Shoot to Kill, 1988, R, ★★★ — 1996
Short Cuts, 1993, R, ★★★★ — 1998
Shower, 2000, PG-13, ★★★ — 2002
Showgirls, 1995, NC-17, ★★½ — 1997
Show Me Love, 2000, NR, ★★★ — 2002
Shrek, 2001, PG, ★★★★ — 2002
Shy People, 1988, R, ★★★★ — 1998
Sick: The Life & Death of Bob Flanagan,
   Supermasochist, 1997, NR, ★★★½ — 2000
Sid & Nancy, 1986, R, ★★★★ — 1998
Sidewalk Stories, 1989, R, ★★★½ — 1998
Siege, The, 1998, R, ★★½ — 2001
Signs and Wonders, 2001, NR, ★★★ — 2002
Silence of the Lambs, The,
   1991, R, ★★★½ — 1998
Silent Movie, 1976, PG, ★★★★ — 1998
Silent Running, 1972, G, ★★★★ — 1998
Silkwood, 1983, R, ★★★★ — 1998
Silverado, 1985, PG-13, ★★★½ — 1998
Simon Birch, 1998, PG, ★★★ — 2001
Simon Magus, 2001, NR, ★★ — 2002
Simpatico, 2000, R, ★½ — 2002
Simple Men, 1992, R, ★★ — 1995
Simple Plan, A, 1998, R, ★★★★ — 2001
Simple Wish, A, 1997, PG, ★½ — 2000
Simply Irresistible, 1999, PG-13, ★★★ — 2002
Sing, 1989, PG-13, ★★★ — 1996
Singin' in the Rain, 1952, G, ★★★★ — 1997
Singles, 1992, PG-13, ★★★ — 1998
Single White Female, 1992, R, ★★★ — 1996
Sirens, 1994, R, ★★★½ — 1998
Sister Act, 1992, PG, ★★½ — 1996
Sister Act 2: Back in the Habit,
   1993, PG, ★★ — 1995
Sisters, 1973, R, ★★★ — 1998
Six Days, Seven Nights,
   1998, PG-13, ★★½ — 2001

Sixteen Candles, 1984, PG, ★★★ — 1998
6th Day, The, 2000, PG-13, ★★★ — 2002
Sixth Man, The, 1997, PG-13, ★½ — 2000
Sixth Sense, The, 1999, PG-13, ★★★ — 2002
Skin Deep, 1989, R, ★★★ — 1998
Skulls, The, 2000, PG-13, ★ — 2002
Slacker, 1991, R, ★★★ — 1998
Slam, 1998, R, ★★½ — 2001
SlamNation, 1998, NR, ★★★ — 2001
Slappy and the Stinkers, 1998, PG, ★★ — 2001
Slaves of New York, 1989, R, ½★ — 1993
SLC Punk!, 1999, R, ★★★ — 2002
Sleeper, 1973, PG, ★★★½ — 1998
Sleeping with the Enemy, 1991, R, ★½ — 1994
Sleepless in Seattle, 1993, PG, ★★★ — 1998
Sleepy Hollow, 1999, R, ★★★½ — 2002
Sleuth, 1972, PG, ★★★★ — 1998
Sliding Doors, 1998, PG-13, ★★ — 2001
Sling Blade, 1996, R, ★★★½ — 1999
Slugger's Wife, The, 1985, PG-13, ★★ — 1986
Slums of Beverly Hills, 1998, R, ★★★ — 2001
Small Change, 1976, PG, ★★★★ — 1998
Small Soldiers, 1998, PG-13, ★★½ — 2001
Small Time Crooks, 2000, PG, ★★★ — 2002
Smash Palace, 1982, R, ★★★★ — 1998
Smiling Fish and Goat on Fire,
   2000, R, ★★★ — 2002
Smilla's Sense of Snow, 1997, R, ★★★ — 1998
Smoke, 1995, R, ★★★ — 1998
Smoke Signals, 1998, PG-13, ★★★ — 2001
Smokey and the Bandit II, 1980, PG, ★ — 1986
Smooth Talk, 1986, PG-13, ★★★½ — 1998
Snake Eyes, 1998, R, ★ — 2001
Snapper, The, 1993, R, ★★★½ — 1998
Snatch, 2001, R, ★★ — 2002
Sneakers, 1992, PG-13, ★★½ — 1994
Sniper, 1993, R, ★★★ — 1996
Snow Day, 2000, PG, ★½ — 2002
Snow Falling on Cedars,
   2000, PG-13, ★★★½ — 2002
Soapdish, 1991, PG-13, ★★★½ — 1998
So I Married an Axe Murderer,
   1993, PG-13, ★★½ — 1995
Soldier of Orange, 1980, PG, ★★★½ — 1986
Soldier's Daughter Never Cries, A,
   1998, R, ★★★½ — 2001
Soldier's Story, A, 1984, PG, ★★½ — 1993
Solomon and Gaenor, 2000, R, ★★ — 2002
Some Kind of Wonderful,
   1987, PG-13, ★★★ — 1998
Some Mother's Son, 1996, R, ★★★ — 1999
Someone Like You, 2001, PG-13, ★★ — 2002

T

This Is My Life, 1992, PG-13, ★★★	1996
This Is Spinal Tap, 1984, R, ★★★★	1998
Thomas and the Magic Railroad, 2000, G, ★	2002
Thomas Crown Affair, The, 1999, R, ★★½	2002
Thousand Acres, A, 1997, R, ★★	2000
Three Kings, 1999, R, ★★★★	2002
Three Lives and Only One Death, 1997, NR, ★★★	2000
Three Men and a Baby, 1987, PG, ★★★	1998
Three Men and a Little Lady, 1990, PG, ★★	1994
Three Musketeers, The, 1993, PG, ★★	1995
3 Ninjas Kick Back, 1994, PG, ★★½	1995
Three of Hearts, 1993, R, ★★★	1996
Three Seasons, 1999, PG-13, ★★★	2002
Threesome, 1994, R, ★★★	1996
3,000 Miles to Graceland, 2001, R, ★½	2002
Three to Tango, 1999, PG-13, ★	2002
3 Women, 1977, PG, ★★★★	1998
Throw Momma from the Train, 1987, PG-13, ★★	1993
Thunderheart, 1992, R, ★★★½	1998
THX 1138, 1971, PG, ★★★	1998
Ticket to Heaven, 1981, R, ★★★½	1998
Tie Me Up! Tie Me Down!, 1990, NR, ★★	1993
Tiger's Tale, A, 1988, R, ★★	1989
Tightrope, 1984, R, ★★★½	1998
'Til There Was You, 1997, PG-13, ½★	1998
Tim Burton's Nightmare Before Christmas, 1993, PG, ★★★½	1998
Time and Tide, 2001, R, ★★★	2002
Time Bandits, 1981, PG, ★★★	1998
Time Code, 2000, R, ★★★	2002
Timecop, 1994, R, ★★	1997
Time for Drunken Horses, A, 2000, NR, ★★★	2002
Time of Destiny, A, 1988, PG-13, ★★★½	1998
Time Regained, 2000, NR, ★★★½	2002
Times of Harvey Milk, The, 1985, NR, ★★★½	1997
Tin Cup, 1996, R, ★★★	1999
Tin Drum, The, 1980, R, ★★	1988
Tin Men, 1987, R, ★★★	1998
Titan A.E., 2000, PG, ★★★½	2002
Titanic, 1997, PG-13, ★★★★	2000
Titus, 2000, R, ★★★½	2002
To Be or Not To Be, 1983, R, ★★★	1998
To Die For, 1995, R, ★★★½	1998
To Gillian on Her 37th Birthday, 1996, PG-13, ★★	1999
Tokyo Story, 1953, G, ★★★★	1997
To Live, 1994, NR, ★★★½	1998
To Live and Die in L.A., 1985, R, ★★★★	1998
Tom and Viv, 1995, PG-13, ★★½	1996
Tomcats, 2001, R, no stars	2002
Tommy, 1975, PG, ★★★	1998
Tomorrow Never Dies, 1997, PG-13, ★★★	2000
Too Beautiful for You, 1990, R, ★★★½	1998
Too Much Sleep, 2001, NR, ★★★	2002
Tootsie, 1982, PG, ★★★★	1998
Topaz, 1970, PG, ★★★½	1998
Top Gun, 1986, PG, ★★½	1998
Top Secret!, 1984, R, ★★★½	1998
Topsy-Turvy, 2000, R, ★★★★	2002
Torch Song Trilogy, 1988, R, ★★★½	1998
To Sleep With Anger, 1990, PG, ★★½	1993
Total Recall, 1990, R, ★★★½	1998
Toto le Heros, 1992, NR, ★★½	1994
Touch, 1997, R, ★★½	2000
Tough Enough, 1983, PG, ★★★	1986
Tough Guys Don't Dance, 1987, R, ★★½	1993
To Wong Foo, Thanks for Everything! Julie Newmar, 1995, PG-13, ★★½	1997
Toys, 1992, PG-13, ★★½	1994
Toy Story, 1995, G, ★★★½	1998
Toy Story 2, 1999, G, ★★★½	2002
Track 29, 1988, R, ★★★	1996
Trading Places, 1983, R, ★★★½	1998
Traffic, 2001, R, ★★★★	2002
Trainspotting, 1996, R, ★★★	1998
Traveller, 1997, R, ★★★	2000
Trees Lounge, 1996, R, ★★★½	1999
Trekkies, 1999, PG, ★★★	2002
Trespass, 1992, R, ★★½	1994
Trial, The, 1994, NR, ★★½	1996
Trial, The, 2000, NR, ★★★★	2002
Trial and Error, 1997, PG-13, ★★★	1998
Tribute, 1981, PG, ★★★	1996
Trick, 1999, R, ★★	2002
Trippin', 1999, R, ★★½	2002
Trip to Bountiful, The, 1985, PG, ★★★½	1998
Trixie, 2000, R, ★★	2002
Tron, 1982, PG, ★★★★	1998
Troop Beverly Hills, 1989, PG, ★★	1994
Trouble in Mind, 1985, R, ★★★★	1998
Troublesome Creek: A Midwestern, 1997, NR, ★★★	2000
True Believer, 1989, R, ★★★	1996

Varsity Blues, 1999, R, ★★ 2002
Velocity of Gary, The, 1999, R, ★★ 2002
Velvet Goldmine, 1998, R, ★★ 2001
Verdict, The, 1982, R, ★★★★ 1998
Vertical Limit, 2000, PG-13, ★★★ 2002
Very Bad Things, 1998, R, ★ 2001
Very Brady Sequel, A, 1996, PG-13, ★★¹/₂ 1999
Vice Versa, 1988, PG, ★★★¹/₂ 1998
Victor/Victoria, 1982, R, ★★★ 1998
Videodrome, 1983, R, ★¹/₂ 1988
Vincent, 1989, NR, ★★★★ 1998
Vincent & Theo, 1990, PG-13, ★★★¹/₂ 1998
Violets Are Blue, 1986, PG-13, ★★★ 1987
Virgin Suicides, The, 2000, R, ★★★¹/₂ 2002
Virtuosity, 1995, R, ★★★ 1998
Virus, 1999, R, ★ 2002
Vision Quest, 1985, R, ★★★¹/₂ 1998
Visions of Eight, 1973, NR, ★★★ 1998
Visions of Light: The Art of
  Cinematography, 1993, NR, ★★★¹/₂ 1998
Visit, The, 2001, R, ★★★ 2002
Visitors, The, 1996, R, ★★ 1999
Vixen, 1969, X, ★★★ 1996
Volcano, 1997, PG-13, ★¹/₂ 1998

W

Waco: The Rules of Engagement,
  1997, NR, ★★★¹/₂ 2000
Wages of Fear, The, 1953, NR, ★★★★ 1997
Wag the Dog, 1998, R, ★★★★ 2001
Waiting for Guffman, 1997, R, ★★★ 1998
Waiting to Exhale, 1995, R, ★★★ 1998
Waking Ned Devine, 1998, PG, ★★★ 2001
Waking the Dead, 2000, R, ★★¹/₂ 2002
Walkabout, 1971, PG, ★★★★ 1998
Walk in the Clouds, A,
  1995, PG-13, ★★★★ 1998
Walk on the Moon, A, 1999, R, ★★ 2002
Wall Street, 1987, R, ★★★¹/₂ 1998
WarGames, 1983, PG, ★★★★ 1998
War of the Roses, The, 1989, R, ★★★ 1998
War Party, 1989, R, ★ 1991
Warriors of Virtue, 1997, PG, ★★ 2000
War Room, The, 1994, NR, ★★★¹/₂ 1998
War Zone, The, 2000, NR, ★★★★ 2002
Washington Square, 1997, PG, ★★★ 2000
Watcher, The, 2000, R, ★★ 2002
Watcher in the Woods, The,
  1981, PG, ★★ 1986
Waterboy, The, 1998, PG-13, ★ 2001
Waterdance, The, 1992, R, ★★★¹/₂ 1998
Waterworld, 1995, PG-13, ★★¹/₂ 1997

Wayne's World, 1992, PG-13, ★★★ 1998
Wayne's World 2, 1993, PG-13, ★★★ 1998
Way of the Gun, 2000, R, ★★¹/₂ 2002
Weavers: Wasn't That a Time!, The,
  1982, PG, ★★★★ 1998
Wedding, A, 1978, PG, ★★★¹/₂ 1998
Wedding Banquet, The, 1993, NR, ★★★ 1998
Wedding Planner, The, 2001, PG-13, ★★ 2002
Wedding Singer, The, 1998, PG-13, ★ 2001
Weeds, 1987, R, ★★★ 1996
Weekend at Bernie's, 1989, PG-13, ★ 1992
Week's Vacation, A, 1980, NR, ★★★¹/₂ 1998
Weird Science, 1985, PG-13, ★★★¹/₂ 1998
Welcome Home, 1989, R, ★★ 1992
Welcome Home, Roxy Carmichael,
  1990, PG-13, ★★ 1993
Welcome to Sarajevo, 1998, R, ★★ 2001
We're No Angels, 1990, PG-13, ★★★ 1998
Wes Craven's New Nightmare,
  1994, R, ★★★ 1998
Western, 1999, NR, ★★ 2002
Wetherby, 1985, R, ★★★★ 1998
We Think the World of You,
  1989, PG, ★★★ 1996
Whales of August, The, 1987, NR, ★★★ 1998
What Dreams May Come,
  1998, PG-13, ★★★¹/₂ 2001
Whatever, 1998, R, ★★★ 2001
Whatever It Takes, 2000, PG-13, ★¹/₂ 2002
What Lies Beneath, 2000, PG-13, ★★ 2002
What Planet Are You From?, 2000, R, ★ 2002
What's Cooking?, 2000, PG-13, ★★★¹/₂ 2002
What's Eating Gilbert Grape?,
  1994, PG-13, ★★★★ 1998
What's Love Got to Do With It,
  1993, R, ★★★¹/₂ 1998
What's the Worst That Can Happen?,
  2001, PG-13, ★ 2002
What Women Want, 2000, PG-13, ★★★ 2002
When a Man Loves a Woman,
  1994, R, ★★★★ 1998
When Brendan Met Trudy,
  2001, NR, ★★★ 2002
When Harry Met Sally . . . ,
  1989, R, ★★★ 1998
When the Cat's Away, 1997, R, ★★★ 2000
When We Were Kings, 1997, PG, ★★★ 2000
Where Angels Fear to Tread,
  1992, PG, ★★ 1994
Where the Boys Are, 1984, R, ¹/₂★ 1987
Where the Buffalo Roam, 1980, R, ★★ 1991
Where the Day Takes You, 1992, R, ★★★ 1996

Wyatt Earp, 1994, PG-13, ★★   1995

X, Y, Z

Xanadu, 1980, PG, ★★   1988

X Files: Fight the Future, The,
1998, PG-13, ★★★   2001

Xiu Xiu: The Sent-Down Girl,
1999, R, ★★★   2002

X-Men, 2000, PG-13, ★★½   2002

Yards, The, 2000, R, ★★★   2002

Year of Living Dangerously, The,
1983, PG, ★★★★   1998

Year of the Gun, 1991, R, ★★★   1996

Year of the Horse, 1997, R, ★   2000

Year of the Quiet Sun, 1986, PG, ★★★★   1987

Yentl, 1983, PG, ★★★½   1998

Yi Yi, 2001, NR, ★★★½   2002

You Can Count on Me, 2000, R, ★★★★   2002

Youngblood, 1985, PG-13, ★★   1987

Young Doctors in Love, 1982, R, ★★   1991

Young Einstein, 1989, PG, ★   1992

Young Frankenstein, 1974, PG, ★★★★   1998

Young Poisoner's Handbook, The,
1996, NR, ★★★½   1999

Young Sherlock Holmes,
1985, PG-13, ★★★   1998

Your Friends and Neighbors,
1998, R, ★★★★   2001

You've Got Mail, 1998, PG, ★★★   2001

Zabriskie Point, 1970, R, ★★   1991

Zelig, 1983, PG, ★★★   1998

Zentropa, 1992, R, ★★★   1996

Zero Effect, 1998, R, ★★★½   2001

Zorro, the Gay Blade, 1981, PG, ★★   1991

Note: The right-hand column is the year in which the review last appeared in *Roger Ebert's Movie Home Companion, Roger Ebert's Video Companion* or *Roger Ebert's Movie Yearbook.*

Index

A

Aaliyah: *Romeo Must Die*, 484

Aaron, Caroline: *Anywhere But Here*, 33; *What Planet Are You From?*, 643

Abecassis, Yael: *Kadosh*, 303

Abraham, Adam: dir., *Man of the Century*, 357

Abraham, F. Murray: *Finding Forrester*, 217

Abrahams, Jon: *Meet the Parents*, 364; *Outside Providence*, 429

Acheson, Mark: *Trixie*, 609

Ackland, Joss: *Passion of Mind*, 434

Adams, Jane: *Anniversary Party, The*, 28; *Mumford*, 390; *Songcatcher*, 533

Adams, Joey Lauren: *Beautiful*, 50; *Big Daddy*, 63

Adamson, Andrew: dir., *Shrek*, 515

Aday, Meat Loaf: *Crazy in Alabama*, 135; *Fight Club*, 211

Addeo, Rosemarie: *Smiling Fish and Goat on Fire*, 527

Addy, Mark: *Down to Earth*, 163; *Flintstones in Viva Rock Vegas, The*, 220; *Knight's Tale, A*, 310

Adelstein, Paul: *Bedazzled*, 53

Adetuyi, Robert: dir., *Turn It Up*, 613

Adolphson, Kristina: *Private Confessions*, 457

Adventures of Rocky & Bullwinkle, The, 1

Adventures of Sebastian Cole, The, 2

Affair of Love, An, 3

Affleck, Ben: *Boiler Room*, 77; *Bounce*, 81; *Dogma*, 159; *Forces of Nature*, 221; *Pearl Harbor*, 439; *Reindeer Games*, 473; *200 Cigarettes*, 620

Affleck, Casey: *Desert Blue*, 150; *Drowning Mona*, 170; *200 Cigarettes*, 620

Affliction, 4

After Life, 5

Agnes Browne, 6

Ahmadi, Ayoub: *Time for Drunken Horses, A*, 594

A.I. Artificial Intelligence, 7

Aiken, Liam: *I Dreamed of Africa*, 281; *Sweet November*, 559

Aimee & Jaguar, 8

Aird, Holly: *Theory of Flight, The*, 576

Aitken, Isabella: *Big Tease, The*, 67

Akhtar, Fatemeh Cheragh: *Day I Became a Woman, The*, 146

Akinnuoye-Agbaje, Adewale: *Mummy Returns, The*, 392

Alba, Jessica: *Idle Hands*, 280

Alcais, Aurelia: *Autumn Tale*, 40

Alcais, Yves: *Autumn Tale*, 40

Alda, Alan: *What Women Want*, 646

Ales, John: *Nutty Professor II: The Klumps*, 413

Alexander, Jane: *Cider House Rules, The*, 119

Alexander, Jason: *Adventures of Rocky & Bullwinkle, The*, 1; *Trumpet of the Swan, The*, 612

Alexi-Malle, Adam: *Bowfinger*, 82

Algar, James: dir., *Fantasia 2000*, 206

Alice, Mary: *Catfish in Black Bean Sauce*, 104

All About My Mother, 9

Allaux, Berangere: *Inside/Out*, 283

Allcroft, Britt: dir., *Thomas and the Magic Railroad*, 585

Allegre, Ginette: *L'Humanite*, 328

Allen, Joan: *Contender, The*, 127

Allen, Karen: *Perfect Storm, The*, 440

Allen, Kevin: *Big Tease, The*, 67; dir., *Big Tease, The*, 67

Allen, Mark S.: *Blood Guts Bullets and Octane*, 72

Allen, Tim: *Galaxy Quest*, 229; *Toy Story 2*, 603

Allen, Woody: *Company Man*, 126; *Small Time Crooks*, 526; dir., *Small Time Crooks*, 526; *Sweet and Lowdown*, 557

Alley, Kirstie: *Drop Dead Gorgeous*, 169

Allred, Corbin: *Anywhere But Here*, 33; *Diamonds*, 153

All the Little Animals, 11

All the Pretty Horses, 12

Almani, Mariam Palvin: *Circle, The*, 120

Almela, Laura: *Amores Perros*, 22

Almereyda, Michael: dir., *Hamlet*, 257

Almodovar, Pedro: dir., *All About My Mother*, 9

Almost Famous, 13

Along Came a Spider, 14

Altman, Robert: dir., *Cookie's Fortune*, 129; *Dr. T and the Women*, 172

Alvarez, Lt. (jg) Everett: *Return With Honor*, 479

Alvaro, Anne: *Taste of Others, The*, 570

Alwi, Syed: *Anna and the King*, 27

Amado, Chisco: *Nico and Dani*, 407

Amati Girls, The, 16

Amedori, John Patrick: *Unbreakable*, 624

American Beauty, 17

American Movie, 18

American Pie, 19

American Psycho, 20

Amiel, Jon: dir., *Entrapment*, 194

Among Giants, 21

Amoni, Toni: *Ninth Gate, The*, 408

Amores Perros, 22

Analyze This, 23

Anders, Allison: dir., *Sugar Town*, 553

Andersen, Anders T.: *13th Warrior, The*, 583

Anderson, Anthony: *Big Momma's House*, 66; *Kingdom Come*, 307; *Me, Myself & Irene*, 366; *Romeo Must Die*, 484; *See Spot Run*, 501

Anderson, Gillian: *House of Mirth, The*, 274; *Playing by Heart*, 445; *Princess Mononoke*, 456

Anderson, Miles: *King Is Alive, The*, 308

Anderson, Paul Thomas: dir., *Magnolia*, 355

Anderson, Stanley: *Arlington Road*, 34

Anderson, Wes: dir., *Rushmore*, 492

Andrei, Damir: *Caveman's Valentine, The*, 105

Angarano, Michael: *Almost Famous*, 13; *Music of the Heart*, 395

I

J